HARRY L. RINKER

THE OFFICIAL®
PRICE GUIDE TO

COLLECTIBLES

HARRY L. RINKER

COLLECTIBLES

Third Edition

HOUSE OF COLLECTIBLES

THE BALLANTINE PUBLISHING GROUP • NEW YORK

House of Collectibles and the HC colophon are trademarks of Random House, Inc.

Published by: House of Collectibles
The Ballantine Publishing Group
201 East 50th Street
New York, New York 10022

Distributed by The Ballantine Publishing Group, a division of Random House, Inc., New York, and simultaneously in Canada by Random House of Canada Limited, Toronto.

www.randomhouse.com/BB/

Manufactured in the United States of America

ISSN: 1094–3862

ISBN: 0–676–60158–8

Third Edition: September 1999

10 9 8 7 6 5 4 3 2 1

RINKER ENTERPRISES, INC.

HARRY L. RINKER
President

DENA C. GEORGE	DANA G. MORYKAN	KATHY WILLIAMSON
Associate Editor	Senior Editor	Associate Editor

NANCY BUTT	VIRGINIA REINBOLD	RICHARD SCHMELTZLE
Librarian	Controller	Support Staff

ABOUT THE AUTHOR — HARRY L. RINKER

Harry L. Rinker is one of the most forthright, honest, and "tell-it-like-it-is" reporters in the antiques and collectibles field today. He is the King of Collectibles, the last of the great antiques and collectibles generalists.

Rinker is president of Rinker Enterprises, Inc., a firm specializing in providing consulting, editorial, educational, photographic, research, and writing services in the antiques and collectibles field. He also directs the Institute for the Study of Antiques & Collectibles, serving as the principal instructor for its seminars and conferences.

Rinker is a prolific antiques and collectibles writer. Other House of Collectibles titles by Rinker include *The Official Price Guide to Flea Market Treasures, Fifth Edition, Dinnerware of the 20TH Century: The Top 500 Patterns, Silverware of the 20TH Century: The Top 250 Patterns,* and *Stemware of the 20TH Century: The Top 200 Patterns.* Rinker is also the author of *Hopalong Cassidy: King of the Cowboy Merchandisers* and co-author with Dana G. Morykan of *Garage Sale Manual & Price Guide* and with Norman Martinus of *Warman's Paper.*

Rinker on Collectibles, a weekly syndicated column, appears in trade and daily newspapers from coast to coast. Often highly opinionated and controversial, it is one of the most widely read columns in the antiques and collectibles trade.

Rinker is a frequent television and radio guest. He often refers to himself as the "national cheerleader for collectibles and collecting." His television credits include *Oprah, NBC—Today Show, ABC—Good Morning America, Home Matters,* and *MPT Wall Street Week With Louis Rukeyser. Whatcha Got,* a ninety-second antiques and collectibles daily feature, can be heard on the Internet at WWW.Kaleden.com. Rinker also does weekly call-in radio shows for KFGO (Fargo, ND), KLTF (Little Falls, MN), KROC (Rochester, MN), WGEE (Green Bay, WI), WNPV (Lansdale, PA), and WSAU (Wausau, WI).

Each year Rinker lectures and/or makes personal appearances in over a dozen cities across the United States, often sponsored by the Antiques and Collectibles Dealers Association, trade publications, and antiques mall or show promoters. In 1996 Rinker and James Tucker co-founded the National Association of Collectors.

Rinker is a dedicated accumulator, a collector of collections. He is continually adding new items to over 250 different collections. Among collectibles collectors, he is best known for his collections of Hopalong Cassidy memorabilia and jigsaw puzzles, the latter exceeding 5,000 examples.

"One great thing about spending time with Harry is that you come away with some great 'Harry' stories. People who have met him trade these stories like bubble gum cards. Each person tries to have the most outrageous story to tell. I brought back some good ones."

Connie Swaim, Editor, Eastern Edition, *AntiqueWeek*

"He was brash, he was iconoclastic, he was funny, and above all, he was thought provoking."

Cheryl York-Cail, *Unravel the Gavel*

"Not many people in this business can put their names above the titles. Rinker is one, not just because of his bold manner and talent for promotion, but also because of his proven know-how."

David Christenson, *The Old Times*

ABBREVIATIONS

3-D = 3-dimensional
4to = 8 x 10"
8vo = 5 x 7"
12mo = 3 x 5"
ADS = autograph document signed
adv = advertising or advertisement
ALS = autograph letter signed
AOG = all over gold
AP = album page signed
approx = approximately
AQS = autograph quotation signed
C = century
c = circa
cov = cover
CS = card signed
d = depth or diameter
dec = decorated or decoration
dj = dust jacket
dwt = penny weight
DS = document signed
ed = edition
emb = embossed
ext = exterior
FDC = first day cover
FH = flat handle
folio = 12 x 16"
ftd = footed
gal = gallon
ground = background
h = height
HH = hollow handle
hp = hand painted
illus = illustrated, illustration, or illustrator
imp = impressed
int = interior
j = jewels
K = karat
l = length
lb = pound

litho = lithograph or lithographed
LS = letter signed
mfg = manufactured, manufacturer, or manufacturing
MIB = mint in box
MIP = mint in package
mkd = marked
MOC = mint on card
NM = near mint
NMIB = near mint in box
NMOC = near mint on card
NOS = new old stock
orig = original
oz = ounce
pat = patent
pc = piece
pcs = pcs
pkg = package or packaging
pp = pages
pr = pair
PS = photograph signed
pt = pint
qt = quart
rect = rectangular
sgd = signed
SP = silver plated
sq = square
SS = sterling silver
ST = stainless
TLS = typed letter signed
unmkd = unmarked
unpg = unpaginated
unsgd = unsigned
Vol = Volume
vol = volumes
w = width
wg = white gold
yg = yellow gold
# = number

CONTENTS

INTRODUCTION

Welcome to the third edition of the *Harry L. Rinker The Official Price Guide to Collectibles*. In three short years, it has become The Force for those seeking the latest pricing information and trends for objects made after 1920. This starship is now located at the very heart of the collectibles universe.

The antiques and collectibles market is experiencing boom times as the 1990s end. Record prices within the antiques sector continue a trend making the best largely unaffordable to the average collector. The market as a whole remains trendy. Collectibles are where the action is. If you have any doubts, check out auction and direct sales on the Internet.

Collectibles pricing is in a constant state of flux. If you fail to keep up with these price shifts annually, you are at a decided disadvantage.

How does *Harry L. Rinker The Official Price Guide to Collectibles* differ from other general antiques and collectibles price guides? First, it focuses on the heart of today's antiques, collectibles, and desirables market—the period between 1920 and the present. Between 80% and 85% of all the material found at auctions, flea markets, antiques malls, shops, and shows dates from this period. Further, today's collectors are primarily 20th-century collectors.

Each year the percentage of individuals collecting 18th- and 19th-century material compared to the whole grows less and less. While there will always be collectors for this early material, they will need deep pockets. Pre-1920 antiques are expensive. Most post-1920 antiques, collectibles, and desirables are both affordable and readily available.

Second, it is comprehensive. This book is filled with the things with which your parents, you, and your children lived and played. Nothing is missing. You will find furniture, decorative accessories, and giftware along with the traditional character and personality items, ceramics, glass, and toys. It is a complete document of the 20th-century American lifestyle.

Third, because *Harry L. Rinker The Official Price Guide to Collectibles* is an annual publication, it is capable of responding more quickly to market changes and developments. It contains over one hundred categories not found in its only competitor. Categories are constantly being restructured and reorganized so that they accurately reflect how things are collected in today's antiques and collectibles market.

I will never be accused of complacency because of what this book contains—no same-old, same-old here. Every category is put to the test. If it no longer has collect-ing validity, it is dropped or merged into a general category. Dozens of new categories appear for the first time, another indication of how rapidly the collectibles market changes.

Fourth, over the years I have developed a reputation in the trade for being extremely opinionated and outspoken. I call 'em like I see 'em. I am not a member of the "if you can't say something nice, don't say anything at all" school.

As a reporter, my job is to present the facts and to interpret them. You will not find any artificial price propping in this book. If prices within a category are being manipulated or highly speculative, I spell it out. Whether you agree or not is not the issue. Unlike the good news price guides, *Harry L. Rinker The Official Price Guide to Collectibles* is designed to make you think.

ANTIQUES, COLLECTIBLES, & DESIRABLES

Harry L. Rinker The Official Price Guide to Collectibles contains antiques, collectibles, and desirables. This being the case, why doesn't this book have a different title? The answer is twofold. When most individuals think of things made in the 20th century, they think of collectibles. People do not like to admit that objects associated with their childhood have become antiques. Further, not everyone, especially manufacturers of contemporary collectors' editions and giftware, separates collectibles and desirables into two different categories. They prefer them lumped together.

What is an antique, a collectible, and a desirable? An antique is anything made before 1945. A collectible is something made between 1945 and the early 1970s. Antiques and collectibles have a stable secondary resale market. A desirable is something made after the mid-1970s. Desirables have a speculative secondary resale market.

As each year passes, the number of people who disagree with my definition of an antique lessens. The year 1945 is an important dividing line. Life in America in 1938 was very different from life in America in 1948. The immediate post-World War II period witnessed the arrival of the suburbs, transfer of wartime technology, e.g., injection molding, into domestic production, television, women in the work force, a global view, and, most importantly, the Baby Boomers.

Today, there are three generations of adult collectors who grew up in the post-1945 time period—those whose childhood (by my definition the period between ages 7 and 14) occurred between 1945 and 1960, between 1960 and the mid-1970s, and between the mid-1970s and the late 1980s. Half of today's population was born after 1960. All they know about John F. Kennedy is what they read in history books. They cannot answer the question: Where were you when you heard JFK was shot?

I used to define a collectible as something made between 1945 and 1962. I have now extended the end date to the early 1970s. The reason is Rinker's Thirty-Year Rule: "For the first thirty years of anything's life, all its value is speculative." It takes thirty years to establish a viable secondary resale market. Some early 1970s objects, especially in vintage clothing, costume jewelry, and movie, music, and television memorabilia, have achieved a stable secondary market. The number is only going to increase.

Will there come a time when I have to move the antique date forward? The answer is yes. I strongly suspect that by 2010, material from the 1950s will definitely be considered antique. However, 2010 is ten years in the future. In the interim, a collectible remains an object made between 1945 and the early 1970s.

America is a nation of collectors. There are more collectors than non-collectors. However, not everyone collects antiques and collectibles. Many individuals collect contemporary objects ranging from Hallmark ornaments to collectors' edition whiskey bottles. These are the desirables. It is as important to report on the market value of desirables as it is antiques and collectibles.

I do not care what someone collects. All I care about is that they collect. The joy of collecting comes from the act of collecting. I resent those who make value judgments relative to what is and is not worth collecting. I know Avon collectors who are far more caring, willing to share, and knowledgeable of the history and importance of their objects than wealthy collectors whose homes are filled with Colonial period furniture and accessories. There is no room for snobbery in today's collecting community. You will find none in this book.

Manufacturers of desirables market them as collectibles. They are not collectibles as I define the term. Desirables have not stood the test of time. Some undoubtedly will become collectibles and even eventually antiques. However, the vast majority will not. Their final resting place is more likely to be a landfill than a china cabinet or shelf.

Harry L. Rinker The Official Price Guide to Collectibles reports on objects in play, i.e., things that are currently being bought and sold actively in the secondary market. Desirables are as much in play as antiques and collectibles. Hence, they belong in this book.

ORGANIZATION

Categories: Objects are listed alphabetically by category beginning with Abingdon Pottery and ending with Zsolnay pottery. In the past decade, dozens of collectible subcategories, e.g., Barbie and Star Wars, have evolved as full-blown, independent collecting categories. This book's categories clearly illustrate the manner in which objects are being collected in the late 1990s.

If you have trouble locating an object, check the index. Collectibles are multifaceted, i.e., they can be assigned to more than one category. A 1949 C&O Railroad calendar picturing Chessie and her kittens playing with a toy train would be equally at home in the Advertising Character, Calendar, Cat, Illustrator, Railroad, or Toy Train categories. Such objects have been extensively cross-referenced. Do not give up after checking your first and second classification choices. Most post-1920 objects cross over into six or more collecting categories.

Category Introduction: An object has many values. Financial is only one of them. The pleasure of owning an object and the nostalgic feelings it evokes are others.

It is a proven fact that the more that is known about an object, the more its value increases. It is for this reason that the histories found in this book are more substantial than those found in other general price guides. Every object has multiple stories attached to it—who made it, when it was made, how it was made, how it was used, why it was saved, etc. The histories answer many of these questions.

Occasionally one or two additional pieces of information—collecting tips and/or market trends—are included with the history. You will not find these insider tips in other general price guides. Of all the information found in this book, these may prove to be the most valuable of all.

References: In many cases, you will find the information you seek in this book. What happens when you do not? Where do you turn next? The answer is the references listed in this book.

Each reference listing contains the name of the author, complete title, edition if appropriate, publisher, and publishing date of the book. This information will enable you to purchase the book, locate it at a library, or have the location of a copy searched through interlibrary loan.

Two principal criteria—availability and quality of information, descriptions, and pricing—were used to select the books that are listed. Almost every book listed is still in print. An occasional exception was made for a seminal work in the category.

Unfortunately, the antiques and collectibles field is plagued with price guides that are nothing more than poorly done point-and-shoot priced picture books or whose prices in no way reflect true market values. They are not listed as references in this book even though they are in print.

Accuracy of information is one of the main hallmarks of this book. Nothing is gained by referencing a source that does not adhere to these same high standards. *Harry L. Rinker The Official Price Guide to Collectibles* is designed to earn your trust. Carefully selecting the references is only one example of that commitment.

David J. Maloney, Jr.'s *Maloney's Antiques & Collectibles Resource Directory, 4th Edition* (Antique Trader Books/Krause Publications), is the most important reference book, next to this one of course, in the field. Buy it. I wear out a copy a year. If you use it properly, so will you.

Periodicals and Newsletters: A list of general antiques and collectibles trade periodicals with full addresses and telephone numbers is part of this book's front matter. The periodicals and newsletters listed within a category relate specifically to that category. They are the first place to turn when looking for further information about that category.

Collectors' Clubs: Collectors' clubs play a vital role in the collecting field. They put collectors in touch with one another. Their newsletters contain information simply not found elsewhere. Their annual conventions allow for an exchange of information and objects. Their membership lists are often a who's who within the category.

Trying to keep track of the correct mailing address for a collectors' club is a full-time job. A club's address changes when its officers change. In some clubs, this occurs annually. The address provided has been checked and double-checked. Hopefully, it is current.

A few individuals and manufacturers have created collectors' clubs as sales fronts. With a few exceptions, e.g., Royal Doulton, these are not listed. The vast majority of clubs listed have an elected board of directors and operate as non-profit organizations.

Reproduction Alert: Reproductions (an exact copy of a period piece), copycats (a stylistic reproduction), fantasy items (in a shape or form that did not exist during the initial period of manufacture or licensing), and fakes (deliberately meant to deceive) are becoming a major problem within the antiques and collectibles field. It would require a book more than double the size of this one to list all the objects that fall within these categories.

Reproduction alerts have been placed throughout the book to serve more as a reminder that problems exist than to document every problem that exists. Do not assume that when no reproduction alert appears, the category is free of the problem. Assume every category has a problem. Make any object you are purchasing prove to you that it is right.

The *Antique & Collectors Reproduction News* (PO Box 12130, Des Moines, IA 50312, annual subscription $32) is a publication devoted to tracking current reproductions, copycats, fantasy items, and fakes. Consider subscribing.

Listings: The object descriptions and value listings are the heart and soul of this book. Listings contain the details necessary to specifically identify an object. Unlike some price guides whose listings are confined to one line, this guide sets no limit other than to provide the amount of information needed to do the job right. While this approach results in fewer listings, it raises the accuracy and comprehension level significantly. Better to be safe than sorry.

Each category's listings are only a sampling of the items found in that category. Great care has been taken to select those objects that are commonly found in the marketplace. A few high-end objects are included to show the price range within a category. However, no price guide has value if the listed objects cannot be found or are priced so high few can afford them.

If you do not find the specific object you are seeking, look for comparable objects similar in description to the one that you own. A general price guide's role is to get you into the ballpark and up to the plate. Great care has been taken in each category to provide listings that represent a broad range of items within a collecting category. Ideally, when looking for a comparable, you should find two or more objects that fit the bill.

The listing format is quick and easy to use. It was selected following a survey of general price guide users. Surprisingly, it allows for more listings per page than an indented system.

Auction Price Boxes: While the values provided in this price guide come from a wide variety of sources, people continually ask, "What does it sell for at auction?" A partial answer to this question is found in the Auction Prices boxes scattered throughout this book.

The assumption is that the highest values are achieved at auction. This is not always the case. Dealers purchase a large percentage of objects sold at auction. This is why all auction prices are carefully evaluated and adjusted when necessary before being used in the general listings of this price guide.

The auction boxes are also designed to introduce you to auction houses with which you may not be familiar. There are hundreds of great regional and specialized auction houses conducting catalog sales throughout the United States. I am pleased to help you make their acquaintance.

Index: The index is a road map that shows you the most direct route to the information you are seeking. Take a moment and study it. Like any road map, the more you use it the more proficient you will become.

When researching your object, always start with the broadest general category. If this proves unsuccessful, try specific forms of the object and/or its manufacturer. Remember, because of their multifaceted nature, 20th-century collectibles are at home in multiple categories. Perseverance pays.

Illustrations: Great care has been taken in selecting the illustrations that appear in this book. They are not just fill. Illustrations indicate the type of object or objects commonly found in the category. They come from a variety of sources—auction houses, authors, field photography, and mail and trade catalogs.

This book provides caption information directly beside or beneath the illustration. You do not have to hunt for it in the text listings as you do in some other guides.

The Rinker Enterprises staff works hard to change the illustrations that appear in each edition. This is why you should retain and not discard previous editions of this book. *Harry L. Rinker The Official Price Guide to Collectibles* saved in series becomes a valuable identification and priced picture book to collectibles.

PRICE NOTES

The values in this book are based on an object being in very good to fine condition. This means that the object is complete and shows no visible signs of aging and wear when held at arm's length. If the value is based on a condition other than very good or fine, the precise condition is included in the descriptive listing.

Prices are designed to reflect the prices that sellers at an antiques mall or collectibles show would ask for their merchandise. When an object is collected nationally, it is possible to determine a national price consensus. Most of the objects in this book fall into that category. There are very few 20th-century collectibles whose values are regionally driven. Even racing collectibles, once collected primarily in the South, have gone national.

There are no fixed prices in the antiques and collectibles market. Value is fluid, not absolute. Price is very much of the time and moment. Change the circumstances, change the price. *Harry L. Rinker The Official Price Guide to Collectibles* is a price guide. That is all it is—a guide. It should be used to confirm, not set prices.

Must the original box or packaging accompany an object for it to be considered complete? While some would argue that the answer is yes, especially for post-1980s material, this book is based on the assumption that the box and object are two separate entities. If the price given includes the box, the presence of the box is noted in the description.

Prices represent the best judgment of the Rinker Enterprises staff after carefully reviewing all the available price source information related to the collecting category. It is not required that an object actually be sold during the past year to be listed in this book. If this policy was followed, users would have a distorted view of the market. Sales of common objects are rarely documented. A book based solely on reported prices would be far too oriented toward the middle and high ends of the market.

Instead, each category's listings have been carefully selected to reflect those objects within the category that are currently available in the antiques and collectibles market. Commonly found objects comprise the bulk of the listings. A few hard-to-find and scarce examples are included. These show the category's breadth and price range.

PRICE SOURCES

The values found in this book come from a wide variety of sources—auctions, dealers, direct sale catalogs and lists, field research, the Internet, private individuals, and trade periodicals. All prices are carefully reviewed and adjusted to reflect fair market retail value.

Several criteria are used in deciding what sources to track. All sections of the country must be represented. This is a national, not a regional, price guide. The sources must be reliable. Listings must be specific. Prices must be consistent, not only within the source but when compared to other national price sources. There must be a constant flow of information from the sources. Auctions held by collectors' clubs at their annual conventions are the one exception.

ADVISORS

While not creating a formal Board of Advisors for this third edition, I did request information from experts for a few categories. When the listings in a category are exclusively from this information, I have included their name and address in an "Advisor" heading at the bottom of the category introduction.

However, do not assume for one moment that I lacked or failed to seek advice from hundreds of antiques mall managers, appraisers, auctioneers, authors, dealers, private collectors, show promoters, and others during the preparation of this book. During the twenty-plus years in which I have been actively involved in the antiques and collectibles field, I have established a network of individuals upon whom I can call whenever a question arises. In many cases, my contacts within a collecting category are several individuals strong.

AMERICANA VERSUS INTERNATIONALISM

Americana, defined as things typical of America, is an obsolete term. It should be dropped from our collecting vocabulary.

First, the entire world is rapidly becoming Americanized. American movies, music, and television play as major a role outside as they do inside America. Burger King, Foot Locker, McDonald's, and Toys 'R Us have gone global. Barbie has a far higher worldwide recognition factor than any human personality.

Second, foreign collectors are not content to only collect objects produced and licensed in their countries. America is the great mother lode of 20th-century collectibles. When African, European, Far Eastern, or South American collectors want Star Wars memorabilia, they come to America to buy. The role played by foreign buyers in the antiques and collectibles market continues to increase.

Third, thanks to the Internet, most individuals need only turn on their computers to sell and buy collectibles anywhere in the world. The Internet is not limited by international boundaries. It is turning us into world citizens no matter what our personal preferences.

Finally, many "American" goods are manufactured offshore or contain parts that were made abroad. Defining something as being distinctly American is no longer easy. We live in an age when new designs can be copied within days of their appearance. Foreign manufacturers are quick to make products that look like the American form.

Let's delete "Americana" and send it to the trash bin.

A BUYER'S GUIDE, NOT A SELLER'S GUIDE

Harry L. Rinker The Official Price Guide to Collectibles is a buyer's guide. Values reflect what someone should expect to pay for an object he wishes to purchase.

This book is not a seller's guide. Do not be mistaken and assume that it is. If you have an object listed in this book and wish to sell it, expect to receive 30% to 40% of the price listed if the object is commonly found and 50% to 60% if the object is harder to find. Do not assume that a collector will pay more. In the 1990s antiques and collectibles market, collectors expect to pay what a dealer would pay for merchandise when buying privately.

Also, there is no guarantee that you will do better at auction. First, you will pay a commission for selling your goods. Second, dealers buy the vast majority of antiques and collectibles sold at auction. They certainly are not going to resell them for what they paid for them.

The method most likely to result in your selling objects for the values found in this book is to become an antiques dealer. This is not as easy as it sounds. Selling antiques and collectibles is hard work.

There is no one best way to sell antiques and collectibles. Much depends on how much time, effort, and money you wish to expend.

In the final analysis, a good price is one for which the buyer and seller are equally happy. Make as many of your transactions as possible win-win deals. Keep your focus on the object, not the buying and selling process.

COMMENTS INVITED

Every effort has been made to make this price guide useful and accurate. Your comments and suggestions, both positive and negative, are needed to make the next edition even better. Send them to: Rinker Enterprises, Inc., 5093 Vera Cruz Road, Emmaus, PA 18049.

ACKNOWLEDGMENTS

Many annual price guides look surprisingly similar from year to year. In fact, when their illustrations and price listings are compared, the similarity becomes all too apparent. In some cases only a few prices are changed.

No one will ever make this accusation about *Harry L. Rinker The Official Price Guide to Collectibles.* I, the Rinker Enterprises staff, and House of Collectibles have too much pride in this product to allow this to happen. We want you to feel the purchase price of this book is a bargain when compared to the wealth of new, up-to-date information that it contains.

This book is a team effort, as are all Rinker Enterprises' books. I captain the starship *Rinker Enterprises.* As with any captain, my responsibilities are primarily administrative and

promotional. My personal appearances have increased by more than 50% this past year. I am engaged in a significant expansion of my media presence in the areas of commercial radio and the Internet. I receive requests daily for consultation on topics ranging from the value of objects to developments within the field. These opportunities are wonderful. They allow me to uncover trends that sit-at-home price guide writers miss.

The *Rinker Enterprises'* bridge crew uses this information when deciding what categories of collectibles will appear in this title. The crew has served on the bridge since this starship was launched. Their position is secure as long as they wish to remain. Each enjoys my full confidence. Each deserves as much credit as me for the quality of this book.

The entire Rinker Enterprises staff worked on the preparation of this book. Kathy Williamson researched and compiled the bulk of the listings. Dena George was responsible for the acquisition and scanning of images. Nancy Butt updated the references and other information appearing in the category introductions. Dana Morykan provided overall supervision and final layout for this project.

Virginia Reinbold continues to serve admirably as our financial officer. The physical plane that makes up our starship runs smoothly thanks to Richard "Cap" Schmeltzle.

Bertelsmann AG's acquisition of Random house resulted in several changes to the House of Collectibles' staff in New York. We now have the pleasure of working with Susan Randol (executive editor), Laura Paczosa (editing), Cindy Berman (managing editorial contact), Autumn Daughettee (assistant to Susan), and Geoff MacDonald (publicity). Alex Klapwald continues to guide us through the production process. Thanks to this new House of Collectibles crew for its strong support.

Thanks also to the hundreds of auctioneers, auction houses, collectors, dealers, trade publications' staffs, and others associated with the antiques and collectibles field who answered "yes" to our requests for help. I have done my best to thank each of you personally. My apologies to anyone I may have missed.

Finally, all our thanks to you, the purchaser and user of this title. It would not exist without you. I pledge my efforts and those of the Rinker Enterprises staff to ensuring that this and future editions of *Harry L. Rinker The Official Price Guide to Collectibles* continue to earn your support and loyalty.

Rinker Enterprises, Inc.   Harry L. Rinker
5093 Vera Cruz Road   Author
Emmaus, PA 18049   June 1999

STATE OF THE MARKET

The boom times for antiques, collectibles, and desirables continue. In fact, they are too good. There is evidence that the bull market of the early to mid-1980s has returned. Fueled in part by unrealistic prices bid on Internet auctions and a return of high-end record prices achieved by New York and other auction houses, more and more sellers are beginning to assume that there is no limit to the price for which they can sell an object.

The recession of the late 1980s and early 1990s proved otherwise. There is a price point at which every object will no longer sell. Lessons are often lost over time. Any individual who has been involved with collecting for less than ten years has no memories of the disastrous market collapse of 1987-89. They know only good times, nothing about the bad. Looking back is as important as looking forward.

The current boom is primarily investor driven. Antiques and collectibles have become commodities and are traded like wheat futures and pork bellies. The interior decorator, a major player in the early to mid-1980s boom market, remains in the background.

Investing in antiques and collectibles requires far different skills than buying them for personal enjoyment. Investing in antiques and collectibles is high risk, far riskier than investing in the stock market. The market remains extremely trendy. Liquidation, especially when forced, is difficult and costly. Living with one's mistakes is embarrassing and humiliating.

Collectibles from the 1950s continue to slip, especially commonly found and middle range material. Even objects from the early Sixties is cooling somewhat. The hot collecting period of the moment is the mid-1960s to the mid-1970s. Hot categories include advertising, clothing, movie and television collectibles, music, and toys. Pieces that speak period, i.e., there is no question what decade they are from, remain the most desirable.

The death knell has sounded for Beanie Babies. Many established sellers are abandoning ship. Current examples sell at recommended retail. The market continues to collapse for middle and low-end retired Beanie Babies. Revisions to Beanie Babies price guides no longer occur annually. Magazines such as *Beans* have fallen on hard times. McDonald's third Beanie Baby promotion did not turn out to be a charm.

Alas, the demise of Beanie Babies does not mean the desirables market is free from speculation. There is no cure for speculative fever. Longaberger baskets and Hallmark ornaments remain inflicted with this disease.

Thanks to George Lucas and his movie *Star Wars:* Episode 1 *The Phantom Menace,* the toy collecting community received a much needed shot in the arm. Kudos to Lucas for carefully controlling the manufacture and distribution of all new *Star Wars* licensed products so that store shelves remained full for weeks after the toys' introduction. Toy scalpers wept. Lucas found the key to immunizing licensed products against speculative fever. The availability of the full range of *Star Wars* toys on the Internet at sites such as **www.eToys.com** and **www.Amazon.com** also helped keep the scalpers in check.

The Internet's role within the collecting community continues to grew exponentially. Reality is that the Internet has probably realized less than ten percent of its potential growth in the collecting sector. Many trade periodicals are receiving complaints from readers that far too much is being written about the Internet. Tune in. Do not tune out. Read and reread as much as possible about the Internet.

The Internet will not replace traditional sale venues such as auctions, antiques malls, antiques shops, antiques shows, flea markets, and trade periodicals. It is a new addition to the sales mix. Those who think it is "the" answer and rely on it exclusively are making a major mistake. The Internet is "an" answer, just one of many.

Rivals of all types continue to test eBay's "King of the Hill" status in the area of online auctions. Amazon.com appears in the strongest competitive position. AuctionUniverse is fizzling. Sotheby's announced it will spend $25 million to create an Internet auction site. Christie's remains mired at the race's starting gate. Check out eHammer, a very promising middle- to high-end Internet auction environment. Also keep an eye open for specialized Internet auctions, such as **www.potteryauction.com** and **www.justglass.com**. These offer a viable alternative for the serious collector who does not want to waste time sorting through the myriad of listings, many for the most commonly found objects, on large sites such as eBay.

Life is rosy at the moment for Internet auctions. But, there is a storm brewing. The Federal sales tax exemption will expire in less than two years. States with licensed auctioneer laws are considering moving against individuals who operate within the state and are auctioning material on the Internet without meeting the state's licensing requirements. Auctions are the largest source of Internet fraud complaints. Everyone from consumer advocates to state attorneys general are taking a closer look at the problem.

Auctions are only one method of selling on the Internet. Antiques mall sites such as **www.antiqnet.com**, **www.collectoronline.com**, **www.kaleden.com**, and **www.tias.com** are well established. Antique Networking and Kaleden have developed programs for antiques malls that enable them to list their dealers and consigned merchandise on the Internet. Several individuals are exploring the opportunities of creating Internet listing storefronts within antiques malls. *AntiqueWeek* and other periodicals continue to seek ways to effectively use the Internet for classified advertisements.

The need remains for a global search engine that will effectively scan all antiques and collectibles Internet sites. **Www.rubylane.com** is making strides in this area. The global search engine on **www.collect.com** leaves much to be desired.

The Internet is rich with antiques, collectibles, and desirables research information. Most of it is still free. Internet access to the Kovels' price guide data is available for a fee. I found it easier to take their book off the shelf and look up the information I needed than wade through the numerous search requests and wait for the data uploads to occur.

Watch for major advances in the amount and quality of audio and video antiques and collectibles information available on the Internet. Those with real audio can listen to **Whatcha Got,** my weekly antiques and collectibles call-in show, every Saturday between 10:00 and 11:00 AM Central Time by tuning to **www.fargoweb.com/kfgo**. A daily ninety second short form version of **Whatcha Got** can be found on **www.kaleden.com**.

In last year's State-of-the-Market report, I drew attention to consolidation occurring within the publishing sector, especially by Krause Publications and Landmark Specialty Publications. I also noted that "Internet antiques and collectibles sites, antiques malls, and antiques shows offer ripe opportunities." Consolidation reached fever pitch in 1999. One is reminded of the cartoon of a larger fish devouring a smaller fish only to be devoured itself by a large fish who is in the process of being devoured by an even larger fish.

The "King of the Hill" competition between Krause Publications and Landmark Specialty Publications ended abruptly in June 1999 when Krause Publications swallowed Landmark Specialty Publications whole. RIP to the periodical *Toy Trader* and the Antique Trader Books imprint. These may not be the only casualties.

Prior to being consumed by Krause Publications, Landmark Specialty Publications' Regional Antique Publications acquired *Antique & Collectables* (El Cajon, CA), *Antique Gazette* (Nashville, TN), *Antique Journal* (San Francisco, CA), *Antique Review* (Worthington, OH), and *Cotton & Quail Antique Trail* (Monticello, FL). Regional Antique Publications also launched two new publications, *Antique Journal for the Northwest* and *Antique Journal's Auction Times for the West,* and served as publisher of three newsletters for the Antiques & Collectibles Associations.

In the auction sector, Butterfield & Butterfield (San Francisco) acquired Dunning's, a Chicago/Elgin based auction company, as a means of gaining access to the Midwest and Plains states. Butterfield & Butterfield closed the Elgin operation in favor of concentrating its Chicago efforts on a new auction gallery downtown. While in the process of establishing more than ten regional offices to feed Chicago

and San Francisco, Butterfield & Butterfield entered into a partnership with Amazon.com to broadcast its auctions live on the Internet. Just as Butterfield & Butterfield was about to issue an IPO, eBay bought it and froze out Amazon.com. Amazon.com countered by forming a partnership with Kruse International, a leading auction company of antique and classic automobiles. Within a week of the two firms announcing this partnership, eBay bought Kruse International. Once again Amazon.com found itself on the outside looking in. Do not be surprised if Amazon.com does something spectacular to break out of its bridesmaid role.

Consolidation continues within the antiques mall sector. AntiqueLand USA, headquartered in Austin, Texas, has acquired half a dozen antiques malls in the Southwest. Additional acquisitions are planned. AntiqueLand is headed by a group of individuals with corporate America business expertise and little knowledge of the collecting sector. In a somewhat different twist, Crown America, a shopping mall developer and operator, has opened corporately owned and operated antiques malls in three of its mall sites.

While the ownership and management of several antiques shows changed during the past year, no consolidation occurred. DMG (the Daily Mirror Group) owns one of the largest English antiques shows. They are just one of several English companies looking at the American antiques and collectibles marketplace. International ownership and partnersips will most likely occur within the next decade.

Jim and Yvonne Tucker, founders of the Antiques and Collectibles Dealers Association and the National Association of Collectors (of which I am a co-founder), created two additional professional organizations, the Antiques & Collectibles Show Promoters Association and the National Association of Antiques Malls, and combined all four organizations under the banner of the Antiques and Collectibles Associations (PO Box 2782, Huntersville, NC 28070).

In early March 1999 the Antiques and Collectibles Associations held a national three-day antiques and collectibles convention in Las Vegas. More than 350 individuals from all segments of the field attended. The convention included the first ever antiques and collectibles trade show. The convention drew broad based support, although there were conspicuous absences, e.g., Krause Publications.

We will be millenniumed to death over the next eighteen months. Ignore it. It will pass. The American Bicentennial did. Save your money. This book will never contain a millennium collectibles category in my or your lifetime.

The Rinker Enterprises databases and educational seminars that I hoped would be available on the Internet still remain in the development stage. They will make it eventually, but I cannot provide a firm date. The primary reason is that I have chosen several more creative projects for my participation on the Internet. You can learn about them by visiting my web site at **www.rinker.com**. If you do not have a computer, check with your grandchildren. They most likely have one and know how to use it.

ANTIQUES & COLLECTIBLES PERIODICALS

Rinker Enterprises receives the following general and regional periodicals. Periodicals covering a specific collecting category are listed in the introductory material for that category.

NATIONAL MAGAZINES

*Antique Trader's Collector
    Magazine & Price Guide*
PO Box 1050
Dubuque, IA 52004-1050
(800) 334-7165
web: traderpr@mwci.net

Antiques & Collecting Magazine
1006 South Michigan Avenue
Chicago, IL 60605
(800) 762-7576
fax: (312) 939-0053
e-mail: lightnerpb@aol.com

Collectors' Eye
Woodside Avenue, Suite 300
Northport, NY 11768
(516) 261-4100
fax: (516) 261-9684
web: www.collectorseye.com

Collectors' Showcase
7134 South Yale Avenue
Suite 720
Tulsa, OK 74136
(888) 622-3446
web: centralcirculation@webzone.com

Collectibles, Flea Market Finds
Goodman Media Group, Inc
1700 Broadway
New York, NY 10019
(800) 955-3870

NATIONAL NEWSPAPERS

The Antique Trader Weekly
PO Box 1050
Dubuque, IA 52004-1050
(800) 334-7165
fax: (800) 531-0880
web: www.collect.com/antique trader
e-mail: traderpubs@aol.com

*Antique Week (Central and
    Eastern Editions)*
27 North Jefferson Street
PO Box 90
Knightstown, IN 46148
(800) 876-5133
fax: (800) 695-8153
web: www.antiqueweek.com
e-mail: antiquewk@aol.com

Antiques and the Arts Weekly
The Bee Publishing Company
PO Box 5503
Newtown, CT 06470-5503
(203) 426-8036
fax: (203) 426-1394
web: www.thebee.com
e-mail: editor@thebee.com

Collectors News
506 Second Street
PO Box 156
Grundy Center, IA 50638
(800) 352-8039
fax: (319) 824-3414
web: collectors-news.com
e-mail: collectors@collectors-news.com

Maine Antique Digest
911 Main Street
PO Box 1429
Waldoboro, ME 04572
(207) 832-4888
fax: (207) 832-7341
web: www.maineantiquedigest.com
e-mail: mad@maine.com

Warman's Today's Collector
Krause Publications
700 East State Street
Iola, WI 54990
(800) 258-0929
fax: (715) 445-4087
web: www.krause.com
e-mail: todays_collector@krause.com

REGIONAL NEWSPAPERS

New England

The Fine Arts Trader
PO Box 1273
Randolph, MA 02368
(800) 332-5055
fax: (781) 961-9044
web: www.fineartstrader.com

MassBay Antiques
254 Second Avenue
Needham, MA 02494
(800) 982-4023
e-mail: mbantiques@cnc.com

New England Antiques Journal
4 Church Street
PO Box 120
Ware, MA 01082
(800) 432-3505
fax: (413) 967-6009
e-mail: visit@antiquesjournal.com

*New Hampshire Antiques
    Monthly*
PO Box 546
Farmington, NH 03835-0546
(603) 755-4568

Treasure Chest
One Richmond Square
Suite 215E
Providence, RI 02906
(800) 557-9662
fax: (401) 272-9422

Unravel the Gavel
14 Hurricane Road, #1
Belmont, NH 03220
(603) 524-4281
fax: (603) 528-3565
web: www.the-forum.com/gavel
e-mail: gavel96@worldpath.net

Middle Atlantic States

Antiques & Auction News
Route 230 West
PO Box 500
Mount Joy, PA 17552
(717) 653-4300
fax: (717) 653-6165

Antiques Tattler (Adamstown)
PO Box 457
Adamstown, PA 19501

New York City's Antique News
PO Box 2054
New York, NY 10159-5054
(212) 725-0344
fax: (212) 532-7294

New York-Pennsylvania Collector
PO Box C
Fishers, NY 14453
(800) 836-1868
fax: (716) 924-7734
e-mail: wolfepub@frontiernet.net

*Northeast Journal of Antiques &
    Art*
364 Warren Street
PO Box 635
Hudson, NY 12534
(518) 828-1616
(800) 836-4069
fax: (518) 828-9437

Renninger's Antique Guide
2 Cypress Place
PO Box 495
Lafayette Hill, PA 19444
(610) 828-4614
fax: (610) 834-1599
web: www.renningers.com

South

Antique Finder Magazine
PO Box 16433
Panama City, FL 32406-6433
(850) 236-0543
fax: (850) 914-9007

Antique Gazette
6949 Charlotte Pike
Suite 106
Nashville, TN 37209
(800) 660-6143
fax: (615) 352-0941

The Antique Shoppe
PO Box 2175
Keystone Heights, FL 32656
(352) 475-1679
fax: (352) 475-5326
web: www.antiquenet.com/
   antiqueshoppe
e-mail: EDSOPER@aol.com

*The Antique Shoppe of the
   Carolinas*
PO Box 640
Lancaster, SC 29721
(800) 210-7253 or
(803) 210-7253
fax: (803) 283-8969

Carolina Antique News
PO Box 241114
Charlotte, NC 28224
(704) 553-2865
fax: (704) 643-3960
e-mail: publishr@concentric.net

Cotton & Quail Antique Trail
205 East Washington Street
PO Box 326
Monticello, FL 32345
(800) 757-7755
fax: (850) 997-3090

MidAtlantic Antiques Magazine
Henderson Newspapers, Inc.
304 South Chestnut Street
PO Box 908
Henderson, NC 27536
(252) 492-4001
fax: (252) 430-0125

*The Old News Is Good News
   Antiques Gazette*
41429 West I-55 Service Road
PO Box 305
Hammond, LA 70404
(504) 429-0575
fax: (504) 429-0576
e mail: gazette@i–55.com

Second Hand Dealer News
18609 Shady Hills Road
Spring Hill, FL 34610
(813) 856-9477

*Southeastern Antiquing and
   Collecting Magazine*
PO Box 510
Acworth, GA 30301-0510
(770) 974-6495 or
(888) 388-7827
web: www.go-star.com
e-mail: antiquing@go-star.com

Southern Antiques
PO Drawer 1107
Decatur, GA 30031
(404) 289-0054
fax: (404) 286-9727
web: www.kaleden.com

The Vintage Times
PO Box 7567
Macon, GA 31209
(888) 757-4755
web: www.mylink.met\~antiques
e-mail: antiques@mylink.net

Midwest

The American Antiquities Journal
126 East High Street
Springfield, OH 45502
(937) 322-6281
fax: (937) 322-0294
web: www.americanantiquities.com
e-mail: MAIL@americanantiquities.com

*The Antique Collector and
   Auction Guide*
Weekly Section of *Farm and
   Dairy*
185-205 East State Street
Box 38
Salem, OH 44460
(330) 337-3419
fax: (330) 337-9550
web: farmanddairy.com

Antique Review
12 East Stafford Street
PO Box 538
Worthington, OH 43085
(614) 885-9757
fax: (614) 885-9762

Auction Action News
1404½ East Green Bay Street
Shawano, WI 54166
(715) 524-3076
fax: (800) 580-4568
e-mail: auction@auctionaction
   news.com

Auction World
101 12th Street South
Box 227
Benson, MN 56215
(800) 750-0166
fax: (320) 843-3246
web: www.finfolink.morris.mn.us/
   ~jfield
e-mail: mfield@infolink.morris.mn.us

The Collector
204 South Walnut Street
PO Box 148
Heyworth, IL 61745-0148
(309) 473-2466
fax: (309) 473-3610

Collectors Journal
1800 West D Street
PO Box 601
Vinton, IA 52349-0601
(800) 472-4006
fax: (319) 474-3117
e-mail: antiquescj@aol.com

Discover Mid-America
400 Grand, Suite B
Kansas City, MO 64106
(800) 899-9730
fax: (816) 474-1427
web: discoverypub.com/kc
e-mail: discoverypub@aol.com

Great Lakes Trader
132 South Putnam Street
Williamston, MI 48895
(800) 785-6367
fax: (517) 655-5380
web: GLTrader@aol.com

*Indiana Antique Buyer's News,
   Inc*
PO Box 213
Silver Lake, IN 46982
(219) 893-4200 or
(888) 834-2263
fax: (219) 893-4251
e-mail: iabn@hoosierlink.net

Ohio Collectors' Magazine
PO Box 1522
Piqua, OH 45356
(937) 773-6063

The Old Times
63 Birch Avenue South
PO Box 340
Maple Lake, MN 55358
(800) 539-1810
fax: (320) 963-6499
web: www.theoldtimes.com
e mail: oldtimes@lkdllink.net

Yesteryear
PO Box 2
Princeton, WI 54968
(920) 787-4808
fax: (920) 787-7381

Southwest

The Antique Traveler
109 East Broad Street
PO Box 656
Mineola, TX 75773
(903) 569-2487
fax: (903) 569-9080

*Antiques & Collectibles Traveler's
   Guide*
PO Box 8851
Apache Junction, AZ 85278
Phone/fax: (602) 596-2935

Arizona Antique News
PO Box 26536
Phoenix, AZ 85068
(602) 943-9137

Auction Weekly
PO Box 61104
Phoenix, AZ 85082
(602) 994-4512
fax: (800) 525-1407
web: www.auctionadvisory.com

The Country Register, Inc
PO Box 84345
Phoenix, AZ 85071
(602) 942-8950
fax: (602) 866-3136
web: www.countryregister.com

West Coast

Antique & Collectables
500 Fensler, Suite 205
PO Box 12589
El Cajon, CA 92022
(619) 593-2930
fax: (619) 447-7187

*Antique Journal for California
   and Nevada*
2329 Santa Clara Avenue
Suite 207
Alameda, CA 94501
(800) 791-8592
fax: (510) 523-5262
e-mail: antiquesjrl@aol.com

*Antique Journal For the
   Northwest*
3439 North East Sandy Blvd
Suite 275
Portland, OR 97232
(888) 845-3200 or
(503) 284-6009
fax: (503) 284-6043

Antiques Plus
PO Box 5467
Salem, OR 97304
(503) 391-7618

Collector
436 West 4th Street, Suite 222
Pomona, CA 91766
(909) 620-9014
fax: (909) 622-8152
web: www.collectorsconference.com
e-mail: Icollect@aol.com

Old Stuff
VBM Printers, Inc.
336 North Davis
PO Box 1084
McMinnville, OR 97128
(503) 434-5386
fax: (503) 435-0990
web: www.vbmpublishing.com
e-mail: bnm@pnn.com

The Oregon Vintage Times
856 Lincoln #2
Eugene, OR 97401
(541) 484-0049
web: www.efn.org/~venus/antique/
   antique.html
e-mail: venus@efn.org

West Coast Peddler
PO Box 5134
Whittier, CA 90607
(562) 698-1718
fax: (562) 698-1500
web: www.westcoastpeddler.com
e-mail: antiques@westcoastpeddler.com

INTERNATIONAL NEWSPAPERS

Australia

*Carter's Homes, Antiques &
   Collectables*
Carter's Promotions Pty. Ltd.
Locked Bag 3
Terrey Hills, NSW 2084
Australia
(02) 9450 0011
fax: (02) 945-2532
web: www.carters.com.au
e-mail: michelle@carters.com.au

Canada

Antique Showcase
Trajan Publishing Corp
103 Lakeshore Road, Suite 202
St. Catherines, Ontario
Canada L2N 2T6
(905) 646-7744
fax: (905) 646-0995
e-mail: office@trajan.com

Antiques and Collectibles Trader
PO Box 38095
550 Eglinton Avenue West
Toronto, Ontario
Canada M5N 3A8
(416) 410-7620
fax: (416) 784-9796

The Upper Canadian
PO Box 653
Smiths Falls, Ontario
Canada K7A 4T6
(613) 283-1168
fax: (613) 283-1345
e-mail: uppercanadian@recorder.ca

England

Antiques Trade Gazette
Circulation Department
17 Whitcomb Street
London WC2H 7PL
England
(0171) 930 4957
fax: (0171) 930 6391
web: www.atg-online.com
e-mail: info@atg-online.com

Antiques & Art Independent
PO Box 1945
ComelyBank
Edinburgh, EH4 1AB
07000 765 263
fax: 07000 268 408
e-mail: antiquesnews@hotmail.com

Finland

Keräilyn Maailma
Vuorikatu 22 B 65
00100 Helsinki
(09) 170090

France

France Antiquités
Château de Boisrigaud
634900 Usson
(04) 73-71-00-04
e-mail: France.Antiquites@wanadoo.fr

La Vie du Collectionneur
B. P. 77
77302 Fontainbleau Cedex
(01) 60-71-55-55

Germany

Antiquitäten Zeitung
Nymphenburger Str. 84
D-80636 München
(089) 12 69 90-0

Sammler Journal
Journal-Verlag Schwend GmbH
Schmollerstrasse 31
D-74523 Schwäbisch Hall
(0791) 404-500
e-mail: info.sj@t-online.de

Sammler Markt
Der Heisse Draht
   Verlagsgesellschaft mbH
Drostestr. 14-16
D-30161 Hannover
(0511) 390 91-0
e-mail: www.dhd.de/sammlermarkt/

Spielzeug Antik
Verlag Christian Gärtner
Ubierring 4
D-50678 Köln
(0221) 3199316

Tin Toy Magazin
Verlag, Redaktion, Anzeigen,
   Vertrieb
Mannheimer Str. 5
D-68309 Mannheim
(0621) 739687

Trödler & Sammeln
Gemi Verlags GmbH
Pfaffenhofener Strasse 3
D-85293 Reichertshausen
(08441) 4022-0
web: www.vpm.de/troedler

AUCTION HOUSES

The following companies generously supply Rinker Enterprises, Inc., with copies of their auction/sales lists, press releases, catalogs and illustrations, and prices realized. In addition, the auction houses in **bold** typeface graciously provide Rinker Enterprises, Inc. with photographs, digital images, and/or permission to scan images from their catalogs.

Action Toys
PO Box 102
Holtsville, NY 11742
(516) 563-9113
fax: (516) 563-9182

Sanford Alderfer Auction Co., Inc.
501 Fairgrounds Road
Hatfield, PA 19440
(215) 393-3000
fax: (215) 368-9055
web: www.alderfercompany.com
e-mail: auction@alderfercompany.com

American Social History and Social Movements
4025 Saline Street
Pittsburgh, PA 15217
(412) 421-5230
fax: (412) 421-0903

Apple Tree Auction Center
1616 West Church Street
Newark, OH 43015
(740) 344-4282
fax: (740) 344-3673
web: www.appletreeauction.com

Arthur Auctioneering
563 Reed Road
Hughesville, PA 17737
(800) ARTHUR-3

Auction Team Köln
– Breker –
Postfach 50 11 19
D-50971 Köln
Germany
Tel: 0221/38 70 49f
fax: 0221/37 48 78
Jane Herz, International Rep USA
(941) 925-0385
fax: (941) 925-0487

Aumann Auctions, Inc.
20114 Illinois Route 16
Nokomis, IL 62075
(888) AUCTN-4U
fax: (217) 563-2111
e-mail: aumannauct@ccipost.net

Bill Bertoia Auctions
1881 Spring Road
Vineland, NJ 08361
(609) 692-1881
fax: (609) 692-8697
web: bba.ccc.nj.net
e-mail: bba@ccnj.net

Butterfield & Butterfield
220 San Bruno Avenue
San Francisco, CA 94103
(415) 861-7500
fax: (415) 861-8951
web: www.butterfields.com
e-mail: info@butterfields.com

Butterfield & Dunning
441 West Huron Street
Chicago, IL 60610
(312) 377-7500
fax: (312) 377-7501
web: www.butterfields.com
e-mail: info@butterfields.com

Cards From Grandma's Trunk
The Millards
PO Box 404
Northport, MI 49670
(616) 386-5351

Cerebro
PO Box 327
East Prospect, PA 17317
(800) 69-LABEL
fax: (717) 252-3685
web: www.cerebro.com
e-mail: cerebro@cerebro.com

Christie's East
219 East 67th Street
New York, NY 10021
(212) 606-0400
fax: (212) 452-2063
web: www.christies.com

Christie's Inc.
502 Park Avenue
New York, NY 10022
(212) 546-1000
fax: (212) 980-8163
web: www.christies.com

Christmas Morning
1806 Royal Lane
Dallas, TX 75229-3126
(972) 506-8362
fax: (972) 506-7821

Cobb's Doll Auctions
1909 Harrison Road
Johnstown, OH 43031-9539
(740) 964-0444
fax: (740) 927-7701

Collectors Auction Services
RR 2, Box 431 Oakwood Road
Oil City, PA 16301
(814) 677-6070
fax: (814) 677-6166
web: www.caswel.com
e-mail: manderton@mail.usachoice.net

Collector's Sales and Service
PO Box 4037
Middletown, RI 02842
(401) 849-5012
fax: (401) 846-6156
web: www.antiquechina.com
e-mail: collectors@antiquechina.com

Copake Auction, Inc.
226 Route 7A, PO Box H
Copake, NY 12516
(518) 329-1142
fax: (518) 329-3369
web: www.usi-ny.com/copakeauction
e-mail: copakeauction@netstep.net

Robert Coup
PO Box 348
Leola, PA 17540
(717) 656-7780
fax: (717) 656-8233
e-mail: polbandwgn@aol.com

Dawson's
128 American Road
Morris Plains, NJ 07950
(973) 984-6900
fax: (973) 984-6956
web: www.dawsonsauction.com
e-mail: dawson1@idt.net

William Doyle Galleries
175 East 87th Street
New York, NY 10128
(212) 427-2730
fax: (212) 369-0892
web: www.doylegalleries.com
e-mail: info@doylegalleries.com

Dunbar's Gallery
76 Haven Street
Milford, MA 01757
(508) 634-8697
fax: (508) 634-8698
e-mail: Dunbar2bid@aol.com

Early American History Auctions, Inc.
7911 Herschel Avenue
Suite 205
La Jolla, CA 92037
(619) 459-4159
fax: (619) 459-4373
web: www.earlyamerican.com
e-mail: auctions@earlyamerican.com

Early Auction Co.
Roger and Steve Early
123 Main Street
Milford, OH 45150
(513) 831-4833
fax: (513) 831-1441

Ken Farmer Auctions & Estates,
  LLC
105A Harrison Street
Radford, VA 24141
(540) 639-0939
fax: (540) 639-1759
web: www.kenfarmer.com
e-mail: auction@usit.net

Fink's Off The Wall Auction
108 East 7th Street
Lansdale, PA 19446
(215) 855-9732
fax: (215) 855-6325
web: www.finksauctions.com
e-mail: lansbeer@finksauctions.com

Flomaton Antique Auction
277 Old Highway 31
Flomaton, AL 36441
(334) 296-3059

Frank's Antiques & Auctions
Box 516
2405 North Kings Road
Hilliard, FL 32046
(904) 845-2870
fax: (904) 845-4000
e-mail: franksauct@aol.com

Freeman\Fine Arts of
  Philadelphia, Inc.
1808 Chestnut Street
Philadelphia, PA 19103
(215) 563-9275
fax: (215) 563-8236
werb: www.auctions-on-line.com/
  Freeman

Chuck Furjanic, Inc.
PO Box 165892
Irving, TX 75016
(800) 882-4825
fax: (972) 257-1785
e-mail: furjanic@onramp.net

Garth's Auction, Inc.
2690 Stratford Road
PO Box 369
Delaware, OH 43015
(740) 362-4771
fax: (740) 363-0164
web: www.garths.com

Glass-Works Auctions
PO Box 180
East Greenville, PA 18041
(215) 679-5849
fax: (215) 679-3068
web: www.glswrk–auction.com
e-mail: glswrk@enter.net

Greenberg Shows and Auctions
7566 Main Street
Sykesville, MD 21784
(410) 795-7447
fax: (410) 549-2553
e-mail: auction@greenbergshows.com

Green Valley Auctions, Inc.
Route 2, Box 434-A
Mount Crawford, VA 22841
(540) 434-4260
fax: (540) 434-4532
web: www.greenvalleyauctions.com
e-mail: gvai@shentel.net

Marc Grobman
94 Paterson Road
Fanwood, NJ 07023-1056
(908) 322-4176
e-mail: mgrobman@worldnet.att.net

GVL Enterprises
21764 Congress Hall Lane
Saratoga, CA 95070
(408) 872-1006
fax: (408) 872-1007
e-mail: jlally@kpcb.com

Gypsyfoot Enterprises, Inc.
PO Box 5833
Helena, MT 59604
(406) 449-8076
fax: (406) 443-8514
e-mail: Gypsyfoot@aol.com

Hake's Americana and
  Collectibles
PO Box 1444
York, PA 17405-1444
(717) 848-1333
fax: (717) 852-0344
e-mail: hake@hakes.com

Gene Harris Antique Auction
  Center, Inc.
PO Box 476
203 South 18th Avenue
Marshalltown, IA 50158
(515) 752-0600
fax: (515) 753-0226
web: www.marshallnet.com/ghaac
e-mail: ghaac@marshallnet.com

Norman C. Heckler & Co.
Bradford Corner Road
Woodstock Valley, CT 06282
(860) 974-1634
fax: (860) 974-2003

Horst Auction Center
50 Durlach Road
Ephrata, PA 17522
(717) 859-1331
fax: (717) 738-2132

Michael Ivankovich Antiques,
  Inc.
PO Box 2458
Doylestown, PA 18901
(215) 345-6094
fax: (215) 345-6692
web: www.wnutting.com
e-mail: wnutting@comcat.com

Jackson's Auctioneers &
  Appraisers
2229 Lincoln Street
Cedar Falls, IA 50613
(319) 277-2256
fax: (319) 277-1252
web: jacksonsauction.com

S. H. Jemik
PO Box 753
Bowie, MD 20715
(301) 262-1864
fax: (410) 721-6494
e-mail: Shjemik@aol.com

James D. Julia, Inc.
PO Box 830
Route 201, Skowhegan Road
Fairfield, ME 04937
(207) 453-7125
fax: (207) 453-2502
web: www.juliaauctions.com
e-mail: jjulia@juliaauctions.com

Gary Kirsner Auctions
PO Box 8807
Coral Springs, FL 33075
(954) 344-9856
fax: (954) 344-4421

Charles E. Kirtley
PO Box 2273
Elizabeth City, NC 27906
(252) 335-1262
fax: (252) 335-4441
e-mail: ckirtley@coastalnet.com

Kruse, International
PO Box 190
5540 County Road 11-A
Auburn, IN 46706
(800) 968-4444
fax: (219) 925-5467

Henry Kurtz, Ltd.
163 Amsterdam Avenue
Suite 136
New York, NY 10023
(212) 642-5904
fax: (212) 874-6018

Lang's Sporting Collectables,
  Inc.
14 Fishermans Lane
Raymond, ME 04071
(207) 655-4265
fax: (207) 655-4265

Leland's
36 East 22nd Street, 7th Floor
New York, NY 10010
(212) 545-0800
fax: (212) 545-0713

Los Angeles Modern Auctions
PO Box 462006
Los Angeles, CA 90046
(213) 845-9456
fax: (213) 845-9601
web: www.lamodern.com
e-mail: peter@lamodern.com

Howard Lowery
3812 West Magnolia Boulevard
Burbank, CA 91505
(818) 972-9080
fax: (818) 972-3910

Majolica Auctions
Michael G Strawser
200 North Main
PO Box 332
Wolcottville, IN 46795
(219) 854-2859
fax: (219) 854-3979

Manion's International Auction
  House, Inc.
PO Box 12214
Kansas City, KS 66112
(913) 299-6692
fax: (913) 299-6792
web: www.manions.com
e-mail: collecting@manions.com

Ted Maurer, Auctioneer
1003 Brookwood Drive
Pottstown, PA 19464
(610) 323-1573
web: www.maurerail.com

Mechantiques
26 Barton Hill
East Hampton, CT 06424
(860) 267-8682
fax: (860) 267-1120
web: www.Mechantiques.com
e-mail: mroenigk@aol.com

Gary Metz's Muddy River Trading Co.
PO Box 1430
251 Wildwood Road
Salem, VA 24153
(540) 387-5070
fax: (540) 387-3233

Wm Morford
RD 2
Cazenovia, NY 13035
(315) 662-7625
fax: (315) 662-3570
e-mail: morf2bid@aol.com

Ray Morykan Auctions
1368 Spring Valley Road
Bethlehem, PA 18015
(610) 838-6634

New England Absentee Auctions Inc.
16 Sixth Street
Stamford, CT 06905
(203) 975-9055
fax: (203) 323-6407
e-mail: NEAAuction@aol.com

New England Auction Gallery
PO Box 2273
West Peabody, MA 01960
(978) 535-3140
fax: (978) 535-7522
web: www.old-toys.com
e-mail: dlkrim@star.net

Norton Auctioneers
Pearl At Monroe
Coldwater, MI 49036-1967
(517) 279-9063
fax: (517) 279-9191
web: www.nortonauctioneers.com
e-mail: nortonsold@cbpu.com

Nostalgia Publications, Inc.
21 South Lake Drive
Hackensack, NJ 07601
(201) 488-4536

Ingrid O'Neil
PO Box 60310
Colorado Springs, CO 80960
(719) 473-1538
fax: (719) 477-0768
e-mail: memorabilia@ioneil.com

Richard Opfer Auctioneers, Inc.
1919 Greenspring Drive
Timonium, MD 21093
(410) 252-5035
fax: (410) 252-5863

Ron Oser Enterprises
PO Box 101
Huntingdon Valley, PA 19006
(215) 947-6575
fax: (215) 938-7348
web: members.aol.com/RonOserEnt
e-mail: RonOserEnt@aol.com

Pacific Book Auction Galleries
133 Kearney Street, 4th Floor
San Francisco, CA 94108
(415) 989-2665
fax: (415) 989-1664
web: www.nbn.com/pba

Past Tyme Pleasures
101 First Street, Suite 404
Los Altos, CA 94022
(510) 484-4488
fax: (510) 484-2551

Pettigrew Auction Co.
1645 South Tejon Street
Colorado Springs, CO 80906
(719) 633-7963
fax: (719(633-5035

Phillips New York
406 East 79th Street
New York, NY 10021
(212) 570-4830
fax: (212) 570-2207
web: www.phillips-auctions.com

Postcards International
2321 Whitney Avenue, Suite 102
PO Box 185398
Hamden, CT 06518
(203) 248-6621
fax: (203) 248-6628
web: www.vintagepostcards.com
e-mail: quality@vintagepostcards.com

Poster Mail Auction Co.
PO Box 133
40189 Patrick Street
Waterford, VA 20197
(703) 684-3656
fax: (540) 882-4765

Provenance
PO Box 3487
Wallington, NJ 07057
(973) 779-8785
fax: (212) 741-8756

David Rago Auctions, Inc.
333 North Main Street
Lambertville, NJ 08530
(609) 397-9374
fax: (609) 397-9377
web: www.ragoarts.com

Lloyd Ralston Gallery
109 Glover Avenue
Norwalk, CT 06850
(203) 845-0033
fax: (203) 845-0366

Red Baron's Antiques
6450 Roswell Road
Atlanta, GA 30328
(404) 252-3770
fax: (404) 257-0268
e-mail: rbaron@onramp.net

Remmey Galleries
30 Maple Street
Summit, NJ 07901
(908) 273-5055
fax: (908) 273-0171
web: www.remmeygalleries.com

L. H. Selman Ltd.
123 Locust Street
Santa Cruz, CA 95060
(800) 538-0766
fax: (831) 427-0111
web: paperweight.com
e-mail: selman@paperweight.com

Skinner, Inc.
Boston Gallery
The Heritage On The Garden
63 Park Plaza
Boston, MA 02116
(617) 350-5400
fax: (617) 350-5429
web: www.skinnerinc.com

Sloan's Washington DC Gallery
4920 Wyaconda Road
North Bethesda, MD 20852
(800) 649-5066
fax: (301) 468-9182
web: www.sloansauction.com

Smith & Jones, Inc. Auctions
12 Clark Lane
Sudbury, MA 01776
(978) 443-5517
fax: (978) 443-2796
web: smithandjonesauctions.com
e-mail: smthjnes@gis.net

R. M. Smythe & Co., Inc.
26 Broadway, Suite 271
New York, NY 10004-1701
(800) 622-1880
fax: (212) 908-4047
web: www.rm-smythe.com

SoldUSA, Inc.
6407 Idlewild Road
Building 2, Suite 207
Charlotte, NC 28212
(877) SoldUSA
fax: (704) 364-2322
web: www.soldusa.com

Sotheby's London
34-35 New Bond Street
London W1A 2AA
0 (171) 293-5000
fax: 0 (171) 293-5074

Sotheby's New York
1334 York Avenue
New York, NY 10021
(212) 606-7000
web: www.sothebys.com

Stanton's Auctioneers
144 South Main Street
PO Box 146
Vermontville, MI 49096
(517) 726-0181
fax: (517) 726-0060

Steffen's Historical Militaria
PO Box 280
Newport, KY 41072
(606) 431-4499
fax: (606) 431-3113

Streamwood, Inc.
Chris R. Jensen
PO Box 1841
Easley, SC 29641-1841
(864) 859-2915
fax: (800) 453-0398
web: www.streamwood.net
e-mail: cjensen@streamwood.net

Susanin's
Gallery 228, Merchandise Mart
Chicago, IL 60654
(312) 832-9800
fax: (312) 832-9311
web: www.theauction.com

Swann Galleries, Inc.
104 East 25th Street
New York, NY 10010
(212) 254-4710
fax: (212) 979-1017

Theriault's
PO Box 151
Annapolis, MD 21404
fax: (410) 224-2515

'Tiques Auction
RR 1, Box 49B
Old Bridge, NJ 08857
(732) 721-0221
fax: (732) 721-0127
web: www.tiques.com
e-mail: tiquesauc@aol.com

Tool Shop Auctions
Tony Murland
78 High Street
Needham Market
Suffolk, 1P6 8AW England
Tel: (01449) 722992
fax: (01449) 722683
web: www.toolshop.demon.co.uk
e-mail: tony@toolshop.demon.co.uk

Toy Scouts, Inc.
137 Casterton Avenue
Akron, OH 44303
(330) 836-0668
fax: (330) 869-8668
e-mail: toyscout@akron.infi.net

Tradewinds Auctions
PO Box 249
24 Magnolia Avenue
Manchester-by-the-Sea, MA
    01944
(978) 768-3327
fax: (978) 526-3088

Victorian Images
PO Box 284
Marlton, NJ 08053
(609) 953-7711
fax: (609) 953-7768
web: www.tradecards.com/vi
e-mail: rmascieri@aol.com

Tom Witte's Antiques
PO Box 399
Front Street West
Mattawan, MI 49071-0399
(616) 668-4161
fax: (616) 668-5363

York Town Auction Inc.
1625 Haviland Road
York, PA 17404
(717) 751-0211
fax: (717) 767-7729
e-mail: yorktownauction@cyberia.com

CATALOG SALES

Robert F. Batchelder
1 West Butler Avenue
Ambler, PA 19002
(215) 643-1430

Wayland Bunnell
199 Tarrytown Road
Manchester, NH 03103
(603) 668-5466
e-mail: wtarrytown@aol.com

J.M. Cohen, Rare Books
2 Karin Court
New Paltz, NY 12561
(914) 883-9720
fax: (914) 883-9142
web: www.kiwiclub.org/jmcrb/
e-mail: jmcrb@ulster.net

The Doctor's Bag
397 Prospect Street
Northampton, MA 01060
(413) 584-1440

Joel Markowitz
Box 10
Old Bethpage, NY 11804
(516) 249-9405
web: www.sheetmusiccenter.com
e-mail: smctr@sheetmusiccenter.com

Charles F. Miller
708 Westover Drive
Lancaster, PA 17601
(717) 285-2255
fax: (717) 285-2255

Harold R. Nestler
13 Pennington Avenue
Waldwick, NJ 07463
(201) 444-7413

Cordelia and Tom Platt
2805 East Oakland Park
    Boulevard #380
Fort Lauderdale, FL 33306
(954) 564-2002
fax: (954) 564-2002
web: www.ctplatt.com
e-mail ctplatt@ctplatt.com

Ken Prag
PO Box 14817
San Francisco, CA 94114
(415) 586-9386
e-mail: Kprag@planeteria.net

Ken Schneringer
271 Sabrina Ct.
Woodstock, GA 30188
(770) 926-9383
web: old-paper.com
e-mail: trademan68@aol.com

Bill Smith
56 Locust Street
Douglas, MA 01516
(508) 476-2015

Toy Soldiers Etcetera
732 Aspen Lane
Lebanon, PA 17042-9073
(717) 228-2361
fax: (717) 228-2362

    If you are an auctioneer, auction company, or antiques and collectibles dealer and would like your name and address to appear on this list in subsequent editions, you can achieve this by sending copies of your auction lists, dealer sales lists, press releases, catalogs and illustrations, prices realized, and/or photographs or digital images to: **Rinker Enterprises, Inc., 5093 Vera Cruz Road, Emmaus, PA 18049.**

ABINGDON POTTERY

The Abingdon Sanitary Manufacturing Company began manufacturing bathroom fixtures in 1908 in Abingdon, Illinois. The company's art pottery line was introduced in 1938 and eventually consisted of over 1,000 shapes and forms decorated in nearly 150 different colors. In 1945 the company changed its name to Abingdon Potteries, Inc. The art pottery line remained in production until 1950, when fire destroyed the art pottery kiln. After the fire, the company focused once again on plumbing fixtures. Eventually, Abingdon Potteries became Briggs Manufacturing Company, a firm noted for its sanitary fixtures.

Reference: Joe Paradis, *Abingdon Pottery Artware: 1934–1950*, Schiffer Publishing, 1997.

Collectors' Club: Abingdon Pottery Club, 210 Knox Hwy 5, Abingdon, IL 61410.

Ashtray, black, round, #317	$20.00
Bookends, pr, colt, #363, 6" h	375.00
Bookends, pr, seagulls, #305	150.00
Bowl, light blue, ribbed sides, #658, 10" l	20.00
Bowl, Regency, #536, 9" l	15.00
Cache Pot, white floral design, #559, 5½" h	20.00
Candle Holders, pr, Fern Leaf, #427, 5½" h	45.00
Console Bowl, Scroll, #478, 11½" l	25.00
Console Set, Classic, #125 bowl and two #126 candlesticks, price for set	100.00
Cookie Jar, baby finial, #561, 11" h	600.00
Cookie Jar, plaid, #697D, 8½" h	100.00
Cookie Jar, rocking horse shape, #602D, 10½" h	300.00
Cookie Jar, Three Bears, #696D, 8¾" h	250.00
Double Cornucopia, #482, 11" l	25.00
Figure, peacock, #416, 7" h	60.00
Figure, swan, white, #661, 3¾" h	50.00
Figure, swordfish, yellow, #657, 4½" h	55.00
Flowerpot, Egg & Dart, #347	15.00
Jar, figural pelican, #609, 6½" h	150.00
Leaf Dish, Traveler's Palm, #530	40.00
Pitcher, Fern Leaf, green, #430, 8" h	130.00
Planter, emb gazelle, yellow, #704, 4¾" h	45.00
Planter, figural daffodil blossom, #668D, 5¼" h	75.00
Planter, figural donkey, blue, #669, 7½" h	65.00
Planter, figural ram, yellow, #671, 4" h	30.00
Salt and Pepper Shakers, pr, Daisy pattern, #680, 4" h	15.00
String Holder, Chinaman's head, #702D, 5½" h	175.00
Vase, blue, #141, 5" h	30.00
Vase, Delta shape, turquoise, #108, 8" h	40.00
Vase, emb anchor, blue, #632, 7½" h	45.00
Vase, emb horse head, blue, #659, 8½" h	45.00
Vase, emb iris, #628D, 8" h	60.00
Vase, Geranium, #389, 7" h	50.00
Vase, Grecian, #553, 13" h	55.00
Vase, green, #174, 7" h	50.00
Vase, Rhythm, green, #380, 7¾" h	60.00
Vase, star shape, #463, 7½" h	25.00
Vase, Tassel, white, #537, 9" h	65.00
Vase, Tulip, green, #320, 4" h	75.00
Wall Mask, male, white, #376M, 7½" h	200.00
Wall Pocket, apron, #699D, 6" h	100.00
Wall Pocket, butterfly shape, #601D, 8½" h	110.00
Wall Pocket, Fern Leaf Tri, green, #435	125.00
Wall Pocket, match box, white, cherries design, #675D	90.00

ACTION FIGURES

Early action figures depicted popular television western heroes from the 1950s and were produced by Hartland. Louis Marx also included action figures in several of its playsets from the late 1950s.

Hassenfield Bros. triggered the modern action figure craze with its introduction of G.I. Joe in 1964. The following year Gilbert produced James Bond 007, The Man From U.N.C.L.E., and Honey West figures. Bonanza and Captain Action figures arrived in 1966.

In 1972 Mego introduced the first six superheroes in a series of thirty-four. Mego also established the link between action figures and the movies with its issue of Planet of the Apes and Star Trek: The Motion Picture figures.

The success of the Star Wars figures set introduced by Kenner in 1977 prompted other toy companies to follow suit, resulting in a flooded market. However, unlike many collecting categories, scarcity does not necessarily equate to high value.

References: John Bonavita, *Mego Action Figure Toys With Values*, Schiffer Publishing, 1996; Tom Heaton, *The Encyclopedia of Marx Action Figures*, Krause Publications, 1999; John Marshall, *Action Figures of the 1960s*, Schiffer Publishing, 1998; John Marshall, *Action Figures of the 1980s, Schiffer Publishing, 1998;* Stuart W. Wells III and Jim Main, *The Official Price Guide to Action Figures, Second Edition,* House of Collectibles, 1999.

Periodicals: *Lee's Action Figure News & Toy Review,* 556 Monroe Turnpike, Monroe, CT 06468; *Tomart's Action Figure Digest,* Tomart Publications, 3300 Encrete Ln, Dayton, OH 45439.

Collectors' Club: Classic Action Figure Collector's Club, PO Box 2095, Halesite, NY 11743.

Note: All figures are complete and in mint condition in original packaging. For additional listings see G.I. Joe, Star Trek, and Star Wars.

Batman Animated Series, Anti-Freeze Batman	$10.00
Batman Animated Series, Bruce Wayne	20.00
Batman Animated Series, Clayface	20.00
Batman Animated Series, Joker	30.00
Batman Animated Series, Killer Crock	15.00
Batman Animated Series, Knight Star Batman	10.00
Batman Animated Series, Lightning Strike Batman	10.00
Batman Animated Series, Mr Freeze	25.00
Batman Animated Series, Phantasm	35.00
Batman Animated Series, Pogo Stick Joker	10.00
Batman Animated Series, Poison Ivy	20.00
Batman Animated Series, Robin	25.00
Batman Animated Series, Robin/Dick Grayson	10.00
Batman Animated Series, Scarecrow	20.00
Bend N Flex, Aquaman	100.00
Bend N Flex, Batman	125.00
Bend N Flex, Captain America	175.00
Bend N Flex, Robin	125.00
Bend N Flex, Shazam	100.00
Bend N Flex, Spiderman	150.00
Bend N Flex, Superman	125.00
Bend N Flex, Tarzan	75.00
Best of the West, Captain Maddox, Marx	170.00
Best of the West, Chief Cherokee, tan body, brown accessories, Marx	200.00

Coppers and Gangsters, Dick Tracy, Playmates, 1990, $5.00.

Best of the West, Jamie West, Marx **75.00**
Best of the West, Janice West, Marx **75.00**
Best of the West, Johnny West, Marx **130.00**
Black Hole, Captain Dan Holland, 12" **50.00**
Captain Action, Aqualad, 12" **350.00**
Captain Action, Aquaman, 12" **195.00**
Captain Action, Batman, 12" **195.00**
Captain Action, Buck Rogers, 12" **250.00**
Captain Action, Captain Action, 12" **175.00**
Captain Action, Captain America, 12" **195.00**
Captain Action, Flash Gordon, 12" **195.00**
Captain Action, Lone Ranger, red, 12" **195.00**
Captain Action, Phantom, 12" **195.00**
Captain Action, Robin, 12" **350.00**
Captain Action, Spider-Man, 12" **395.00**
Captain Action, Superboy, 12" **295.00**
Captain Action, Superman, 12" **250.00**
Captain Action, Tonto, 12" **195.00**
DC Heroes, Batman, 5", Series I, 1990 . . . . **10.00**
DC Heroes, Superman, 5", Series I, 1990 . . . . **20.00**
Dick Tracy, Breathless, 14", Applause **30.00**
Fantastic 4, Blastaar **5.00**
Fantastic 4, Firelord **10.00**
Fantastic 4, Glactus **20.00**
Fantastic 4, Human Torch **10.00**
George Washington, 8", Mego/Kresge **40.00**
History of Batman, Batman, 12", error logo, FAO
    Schwartz **250.00**
History of Superman, Superman, 12", FAO Schwartz **150.00**
Inspector Gadget, 12", Galoob **150.00**
Lone Ranger, Butch Cavendish, 10", Gabriel **40.00**
Lone Ranger, Crooked Gambler, 10", Gabriel **25.00**
Lone Ranger, Gun Runners, 10", Gabriel **25.00**
Lone Ranger, Little Bear Indian Boy, 10", Gabriel **60.00**
Lone Ranger, Lone Ranger, 10", Gabriel **60.00**
Lone Ranger, Mysterious Prospector and Mule, 10",
    Gabriel **60.00**
Lone Ranger, Red Sleeves Apache Indian, 10", Gabriel **60.00**
Lone Ranger, Scout, 10", Gabriel **60.00**
Lone Ranger, Tonto, 10", Gabriel **60.00**
Lord of the Rings, Gollum, Knickerbocker **250.00**

Marvel Heroes, Daredevil #1, Series I, Toy Biz, 1990 . . . . . . **20.00**
Marvel Heroes, Deathlock, Series I, Toy Biz, 1990 . . . . **5.00**
Marvel Heroes, Green Goblin, Series I, Toy Biz, 1990 . . . . . **10.00**
Marvel Heroes, Hulk, Series I, Toy Biz, 1990 . . . . **10.00**
Marvel Heroes, Invisible Woman #1, Series I, Toy Biz,
    1990 . . . . **60.00**
Marvel Heroes, Silver Surfer #1, Series I, Toy Biz, 1990 . . . . **10.00**
Marvel Special Collectors Edition, Mary Jane, 12" **60.00**
Marvel Special Collectors Edition, Rogue, 12" **25.00**
Marvel Special Collectors Edition, Scarlet Spider/Spider-
    man, 12" **50.00**
Marvel Special Collectors Edition, Spiderman, 12" **45.00**
Marvel Special Collectors Edition, Storm, 12" **25.00**
Marvel Special Collectors Edition, Wolverine, 12" **35.00**
New Batman Adventures, Joker, 12" **45.00**
New Batman Adventures, Nightwing, 12" **35.00**
Nightmare Before Christmas, Behemoth, 6" **40.00**
Nightmare Before Christmas, Jack, 12" **150.00**
Nightmare Before Christmas, Sally, 6" **60.00**
Nightmare Before Christmas, Santa, 12" **75.00**
Pocket Heroes, Aquaman, white card **200.00**
Pocket Heroes, Green Goblin, white card **200.00**
Pocket Heroes, Hulk, white card **100.00**
Pocket Heroes, Superman, white card **100.00**
Power Rangers, Billy, Blue Ranger, 18", 1993 . . . . **10.00**
Power Rangers, Jason, Red Ranger, 18", 1993 . . . . **10.00**
Power Rangers, Kimberly, Pink Ranger, 18", 1993 . . . . . . **10.00**
Power Rangers, Trini, Yellow Ranger, 18", 1993 . . . . **10.00**
Power Rangers, Zach, Black Ranger, 18", 1993 . . . . **10.00**
Princess of Power, Catra **40.00**
Princess of Power, Clawdeen **35.00**
Princess of Power, Flutterina **60.00**
Princess of Power, Frosta **40.00**
Princess of Power, Glimmer **40.00**
Princess of Power, Mermista **60.00**
Princess of Power, Peekablue **60.00**
Princess of Power, Sweetbee **50.00**
Robin Hood, Robin Hood, 8", Mego **250.00**
Robin Hood, Will Scarlett, 8", Mego **275.00**
Rookies, Mike, 8" **50.00**
Rookies, Terry, 8" **50.00**
Secret Wars, Baron Zemo, Mattel **20.00**
Secret Wars, Captain America, Mattel **20.00**
Secret Wars, Constrictor, Mattel **50.00**
Secret Wars, Daredevil, Mattel **20.00**
Secret Wars, Falcon, Mattel **30.00**
Secret Wars, Freedom Fighter, Mattel **20.00**
Secret Wars, Hobgoblin, Mattel **50.00**
Secret Wars, Iceman, Mattel **65.00**
Secret Wars, Iron Man, Mattel **20.00**
Secret Wars, Kang, Mattel **10.00**
Secret Wars, Wolverine, gray claws, Mattel **35.00**
Six Million Dollar Man, Maskatron **140.00**
Superheroes, Aquaman, 8", Mego **175.00**
Superheroes, Batman, 12", Mego **65.00**
Superheroes, Captain America, 8", Mego **275.00**
Superheroes, Captain America, 12", Mego **150.00**
Superheroes, Conan, 8", Mego **400.00**
Superheroes, Falcon, 8", Mego **150.00**
Superheroes, Green Arrow, 8", Mego **350.00**
Superheroes, Green Goblin, 8", Mego **300.00**
Superheroes, Hulk, 8", Mego **65.00**
Superheroes, Human Torch, 8", Mego **100.00**
Superheroes, Ironman, Mego **195.00**

Superheroes, Lizard, 8", Mego 225.00
Superheroes, Mangler, Comic Heroes, Mego 350.00
Superheroes, Mr Fantastic, 8", Mego 75.00
Superheroes, Mr Mxyzptlk, 8", Mego 115.00
Superheroes, Mr Mxyzptlk, Smirk, 8", Mego 125.00
Superheroes, Penguin, 8", Mego 135.00
Superheroes, Riddler, 8", Mego 350.00
Superheroes, Riddler, Fist Fighter, Mego 250.00
Superheroes, Robin Fist Fighter, 8", Mego 275.00
Superheroes, Shazam, 8", Mego 160.00
Superheroes, Spider-Man, 8", Mego 125.00
Superheroes, Spider-Man, fly away action, 12", Mego . . . 95.00
Superheroes, Superman, 8", Mego 125.00
Superheroes, Superman, 12", Mego 150.00
Superheroes, Tarzan, 8", Mego 125.00
Superheroes, Wonder Woman, 8", Mego 450.00
Super Knights, Black Knight, 8", Mego 350.00
Super Powers, Brainiac, Kenner 20.00
Super Powers, Cyclatron, Kenner 40.00
Super Powers, Desaad, Kenner. 20.00
Super Powers, El Captain Ray, Kenner 195.00
Super Powers, Firestorm, Kenner 40.00
Super Powers, Flash, Kenner 10.00
Super Powers, Green Arrow, Kenner. 40.00
Super Powers, Hawkman, Kenner 40.00
Super Powers, Joker, Kenner 25.00
Super Powers, Kalibak, Kenner. 20.00
Super Powers, Lex Luther, Kenner 10.00
Super Powers, Mantis, Kenner 25.00
Super Powers, Martian Headhunter, Kenner 40.00
Super Powers, Mr Miracle, Kenner 60.00
Super Powers, Orion, Kenner. 25.00
Super Powers, Parademon, Kenner 20.00
Super Powers, Samurai, Kenner 65.00
Super Powers, Steppenwolf, Kenner 50.00
Super Powers, Tyr, Kenner 40.00
Talking Heroes, Venom, 5". 10.00
Total Justice, Green Lantern, 1996 . . . . 10.00
Universal Monster, Frankenstein, 8", Mego 90.00
Voltron, Doom Commander 15.00
Voltron, Princess Allura 15.00
WCW, Lex Luger, 5", Galoob, 1990 . . . . 20.00
WCW, Ron Simmons, 5", Galoob, 1990. . . . . 20.00
WCW, Sting, blue tights, 5", Galoob, 1990. . . . . 20.00
WWF, Adrian Adonis, 10", LHN. 20.00
WWF, Blue Referee, 10", LHN. 40.00
WWF, Bobby Heenan, 10", LHN 30.00
WWF, Brutus Beefcake, 5", Hasbro, 1990. . . . . 15.00
WWF, Fred Classie Blassie, 10", LHN. 25.00
WWF, Hulk Hogan, 5", Hasbro, 1990 . . . . 20.00
WWF, Hulk Hogan #2, 5", Hasbro, 1991 . . . . 20.00
WWF, Johnny V, 10", LHN. 30.00
WWF, Mean Gene, 10", LHN. 30.00
WWF, Million Dollar Man, green, 5", Hasbro, 1991 . . . . . 18.00
WWF, Mr Fujic, 10", LHN. 25.00
WWF, Roddy Piper, 10", LHN 25.00
WWF, Rowdy Piper, 5", Hasbro, 1991 . . . . 15.00
WWF, Superfly Jim Snuka, 5", Hasbro, 1991. . . . . 12.00
WWF, Ted Dibiase, 10", LHN 40.00
WWF, Vince McMahon, 10", LHN 40.00
X-Men, Cyclops 10.00
X-Men, Gladiator, Phoenix Series. 5.00
X-Men, Phoenix, Phoenix Series 15.00
X-Men, Wolverine #3 . . . . 20.00

ADVERTISING

Advertising premiums such as calendars and thermometers arrived on the scene by the 1880s. Diecut point-of-purchase displays, wall clocks, and signs were eagerly displayed. The advertising character was developed in the early 1900s. By the 1950s the star endorser was firmly established. Advertising became a big business as specialized firms, many headquartered in New York City, developed to meet manufacturers' needs. Today television programs frequently command well over one hundred thousand dollars a minute for commercial air time.

Many factors affect the price of an advertising collectible—the product and its manufacturer, the objects or persons used in the advertisement, the period and aesthetics of design, the designer and/or illustrator, and the form the advertisement takes. Almost every advertising item is sought by a specialized collector in one or more collectibles areas.

References: Michael Bruner, *Advertising Clocks,* Schiffer Publishing, 1995; Michael Bruner, *Encyclopedia of Porcelain Enamel Advertising, 2nd Edition,* Schiffer Publishing, 1999; Michael Bruner, *More Porcelain Enamel Advertising,* Schiffer Publishing, 1997; Douglas Congdon-Martin, *America For Sale: A Collector's Guide to Antique Advertising,* Schiffer Publishing, 1991; Douglas Congdon-Martin, *Tobacco Tins,* Schiffer Publishing, 1992; Fred Dodge, *Antique Tins* (1995, 1999 value update), *Book II* (1998), *Book III* (1999), Collector Books.

Ted Hake, *Hake's Guide to Advertising Collectibles,* Wallace-Homestead, Krause Publications, 1992; Sharon and Bob Huxford, *Huxford's Collectible Advertising, Third Edition* (1997), *Fourth Edition* (1998), Collector Books; Jim and Vivian Karsnitz, *Oyster Cans,* Schiffer Publishing, 1993; Ray Klug, *Antique Advertising Encyclopedia,* Schiffer Publishing, 1997; *Letter Openers: Advertising & Figural,* L-W Book Sales, 1996; Linda McPherson, *Modern Collectible Tins,* Collector Books, 1998; Robert Reed, *Paper Advertising Collectibles: Treasures from Almanacs to Window Signs,* Antique Trader Books, 1998; B. J. Summers, *Value Guide to Advertising Memorabilia, Second Edition,* Collector Books, 1999; David Zimmerman, *The Encyclopedia of Advertising Tins, Vol. I* (1994) and *Vol. II* (1998), Collector Books.

Periodicals: *Paper Collectors' Marketplace* (PCM), PO Box 128, Scandinavia, WI 54977; *The Paper & Advertising Collector* (PAC), PO Box 500, Mount Joy, PA 17552.

Collectors' Clubs: Advertising Cup and Mug Collectors of America, PO Box 680, Solon, IA 52333; Antique Advertising Assoc of America, PO Box 1121, Morton Grove, IL 60053; The Ephemera Society of America, PO Box 95, Cazenovia, NY 13035; Inner Seal Club (Nabisco), 4585 Saron Dr, Lexington, KY 40515; Porcelain Advertising Collectors Club, PO Box 381, Marshfield Hills, MA 02051; Tin Container Collectors Assoc, PO Box 440101, Aurora, CO 80044.

REPRODUCTION ALERT

Ashtray, Champion Ford, ceramic, spark plug in center,
    3¹/₂" h, 5" d **$130.00**
Ashtray, Fisk Glider, rubber tire with glass insert, 6¹/₂" d. . . . **200.00**
Ashtray, Smith's General Store, Birdseye, IN, tin **5.00**
Baseball Bat, Bonnie Laddie Shoes, wood, 34" l **30.00**
Bill Clamp, Star Brand Shoes, metal, calendar insert **35.00**

Bill Clip, Chandlers Shoes 30.00
Bill Clip, Syracuse Stadium Shoe 35.00
Blotter, Converse Athletic Shoes, man holding sneaker,
    5³⁄₄ x 3¹⁄₄" 10.00
Blotter, Dixon "Best" Colored Pencils, artist at easel, 3¹⁄₄
    x 6" 8.00
Blotter, Goodrich Sport Shoes, 5³⁄₄ x 3¹⁄₂" 5.00
Blotter, Morton's Salt, "When It Rains It Pours," salt can-
    ister, 6¹⁄₄ x 3¹⁄₄" 5.00
Blotter, Northwestern Mutual Life Insurance, red and
    white, 1940 calendar, 9¹⁄₄ x 4" 10.00
Blotter, Sundial Shoes, Bonnie Laddie, "Tops Them All,"
    blue, 6 x 3" 10.00
Booklet, Jell-O, Genesee Pure Food Company, Leroy,
    NY, multicolor cover, ©1920, 14 pgs 20.00
Booklet, Quaker Oats, "Travels of a Rolled Oat," 1933
    Chicago World's Fair souvenir, black and white,
    recipes, 12 pgs 20.00
Box, Magnolia Brand Condensed Milk, wood, black let-
    tering, 7 x 19 x 13" 30.00
Brochure, Cushman Scooter Company, Truckster, multi-
    color, 1955, 24 pgs, 6 x 3³⁄₈" 5.00
Brochure, Metropolitan Life Insurance, The Metropolitan
    Mother Goose, color illus, 1920s 25.00
Coloring Set, Bird's Eye, coloring book and crayons, orig
    General Foods premium mailer 25.00
Cookbook, Poll Parrot Shoes, 1937 . . . . 5.00
Dictionary, Red Goose Shoes, Webster's, 1926 . . . . 5.00
Dispenser, Viking Snuff, dark blue ground, white letter-
    ing, red trim, "Guaranteed Fresh," 1950s, 15" h 100.00
Dispenser, Workmate Chewing Tobacco, yellow ground,
    green lettering and wintergreen leaves, 1950s, 15" h 65.00
Display, APW Toilet Paper, diecut cardboard, girl sitting
    on oversized roll of toilet paper, 1920s, 4 pcs 1,100.00
Display, Beacon Blankets, diecut litho cardboard, multi-
    colored, elderly man in cannonball bed pulling up
    blanket, "B-r-r-rrr!, Beacon Blankets Make Warm
    Friends," 41" h, 40" w 150.00

Ashtray, Ing-Rich 50th Anniversary, porcelain, 6" d, $66.00. Photo courtesy Collectors Auction Services.

Display, Ferry's Seeds, wood box, paper label, metal rack, with newer seed packets, 18" h, 30" w, 12" d, $330.00. Photo courtesy Collectors Auction Services.

Display, Elgin Watch, turquoise and pink futuristic 1950s
    vanity with 2 mirrors and moving watch mount, 1950s
    woman in ivory gown with pink sequins spins to
    admire herself in mirror as watchband passes through
    ring, c1955, 19 x 15 x 10" 675.00
Display, Flower Seeds, diecut cardboard, standup, pur-
    ple, white, green, and black, "The Loveliest Garden
    can be yours easily-economically with these Flower
    Seeds 10¢, Plan Your Garden Now!," complete with
    seed packets, 41" h, 24" w 150.00
Display, Hotpoint Toast-overs, diecut cardboard, easel
    back, Happy Hotpoint character, c1925, 9¹⁄₄ x 13¹⁄₄" 100.00
Display, Ide Shirts, cardboard, standup, well-dressed
    man snapping on cufflink, green ground, "New Ideas
    in Ide Shirts, Pre-Shrunk Collars," 1930s, 17" h, 14" w 75.00
Display, Marlin Double Edge Blades, cardboard wall
    hanger, holds 20 pkgs, 13¹⁄₂ x 9" 50.00
Display, Mohawk Carpet, Indian boy standing on tree
    stump beating drum, "Carpet Craftsmanship from the
    Looms of Mohawk," c1948, 23" h 300.00
Display, Slinky, wholesome 1950s youngster holding
    Slinky, electric motor lifts and lowers one hand creat-
    ing "walking" effect, with period Slinky in orig box,
    c1956, 16¹⁄₂ x 16¹⁄₂ x 7¹⁄₂" 950.00
Display, Swing's Coffee, black man seated atop Swing's
    Coffee box pours cup of coffee from white and red
    enamel coffeepot into enamel mustache cup, man
    moves lips, raises eyebrows, rolls eyes, and "drinks"
    coffee, coffee disappears into tube in cup, reappears
    in coffeepot, c1925, 29 x 17¹⁄₂ x 15¹⁄₂" 2,500.00
Display, Tinkertoy, electrified revolving Tinkertoy paddle
    wheel, c1940, 19 x 19 x 5¹⁄₂" 550.00
Display, Wyler Watch, rotating clock with round brass
    finish face with red plastic chapters, obverse fitted
    with 2 display racks for Wyler Incaflex watches,
    c1940, 20" h 150.00
Doll, Cream of Wheat, cloth, 1920, 18" h 150.00
Doll, Kellogg's, cloth, Little Red Riding Hood, 13¹⁄₂" h 40.00
Doll Patterns, Kellogg's Snap, Crackle and Pop, unused,
    c1948 . . . . 175.00
Door Push, Copenhagen Tobacco, porcelain, "Made
    From High Grade Tobacco, Best Chew Ever Made,"
    Art Deco design, red, white, yellow, and black,
    13¹⁄₄" h, 3³⁄₄" w 300.00

Door Push, Gorton's Fish, porcelain, "Eat Gorton's Codfish in Cans, Ready to Use," black lettering, yellow ground, 6 x 3½" **575.00**

Door Push, Sunbeam Bread, porcelain, dark blue ground, red and white lettering, "Reach for Sunbeam Bread," 2¾" h, 26½" w **100.00**

Fan, Putnam Fadeless Dyes, General Israel Putnam on horseback escaping British Dragoons, 6½ x 8½" **25.00**

Fan, Weatherbird Shoes, 1925 June-Sept calendar on reverse **20.00**

Fan, Worcester Salt, Worcester Salt Company, NY, cardboard, wood stick, black and white, 12 ½" h, 9½" w **35.00**

Flour Sack, Sleepy Eye Flour, cloth, Indian head, red and black lettering, 36" h, 16" w **225.00**

Fruit Crate Label, apples, Blewett Pass, auto on mountain road, 1940s **1.00**

Fruit Crate Label, apples, Mountain Goat, white mountain goat standing on cliff, snow-capped mountains and forest in background **2.00**

Fruit Crate Label, apricots, Brentwood Acres, 3 apricots on branch, blue ground . . . . **.25**

Fruit Crate Label, lemons, Cutter, cutter ship in choppy seas, orange and gold sky, Oxnard, dated 1937 . . . . **3.00**

Fruit Crate Label, oranges, Redlands Choice, shiny blue draped cloth behind large orange and blossoms, Redlands, 1938 . . . . **8.00**

Fruit Crate Label, tomatoes, Bungalow, large tomato, bungalow and grounds, Washington, 1920s, lug size **1.50**

Globe, Red Goose Shoes, metal, 6" d, 9" h **125.00**

Label, brooms, Skysweep, single prop biplane, dated 1931 . . . . **.50**

Letter Opener, Lincoln, Nebraska Telephone & Telegraph Silver Anniversary, logo on handle **75.00**

Magic Book, Weatherbird Bag of Tricks, 1932 . . . . **20.00**

Memo Book, Weatherbird Shoes, "Big Boy," 3 x 5" **10.00**

Menu, Hotel Astor, NY, watercolor city scenes, 1945 . . . . **7.50**

Menu, Mickey Mantle's Holiday Inn, c1950 . . . . **75.00**

Menu Cover, Chapell's Ice Cream, celluloid, ice cream float and sundae, 4 menu pages inside, 1926, 5 x 7¼" . . . **385.00**

Mirror, Arnold's Bakery, 25th Anniversary, black and white, 1923 . . . . **65.00**

Mirror, Maccabees Insurance, green, black, red, and white, 1920s **50.00**

Mirror, Revelation Tooth Powder, blue and gray, 1920s **25.00**

Paperweight, Crane Company 50th Anniversary, bronzed metal, 1930 . . . . **10.00**

Paperweight, Fageol Safety Coach, cast lead, 1920s bus replica, inscription both sides **20.00**

Paperweight, National Cash Registers, cast iron, painted, figural register **65.00**

Pinback Button, Big Chief White Bread, red, white, and blue, 1930s **20.00**

Pinback Button, Pilgrim Bread and Cakes, blue, white, and orange, 1920–30 . . . . **15.00**

Pinback Button, "Ride The Green Lane Of Safety In A New 1939 Hudson," green, blue, black, and white **15.00**

Pocketknife, Purina, plastic red and white checkerboard handles with black lettering, 2 steel blades, Kutmaster, 1950s, 3" l **25.00**

Poster, Granger Tobacco, sea captain, 1931, 30 x 42" **65.00**

Poster, Hill Brothers Fur Company, price list on back, 1928 . . . . **20.00**

Poster, International Stock Food, litho paper, cattle yard, multicolor, wood frame, 21" h, 27" w **175.00**

Box, Space Whistling Rocket, fireworks, $20.00. Photo courtesy Frank's Antiques & Auctions.

Poster, Ivory Soap, paper, linen back, "Ivory Soap. It Floats," white lettering, black ground, 17" h, 56½" w **45.00**

Poster, Lifebuoy Soap, cardboard, "Send for this Baseball Book," 1942, 13 x 17" **50.00**

Poster, Lux Soap, cardboard, Ann Sheridan, "My Beauty Care," 14 x 11" **30.00**

Poster, Poll Parrot Shoes, cardboard, boy performing circus tricks, 11 x 17" **20.00**

Poster, Rinso Soap, cardboard, Amos 'n' Andy, "Shop Early, Friday is Amos 'n' Andy Night," 1944, 11 x 14" **125.00**

Poster, Royal Baking Powder, product illus, 1920s, 25 x 20" **35.00**

Poster, Swan Soap, cardboard, George Burns and Gracie Allen, 11 x 14" **50.00**

Pull Toy, Red Goose Shoes, fish shape, 7" l **50.00**

Punch-Out Book, Red Goose Shoes, Chimpanzee Shoe, St. Louis Zoo, 10½ x 10" **25.00**

Ruler, Peters Weatherbird Shoes, 6" **10.00**

Ruler, Red Goose Shoes, folding, 2' **15.00**

Shelf Strip, Red Spot Coffee, tin, red lettering on yellow ground, 20 x 2¾" **30.00**

Shoe Horn, A. S. Beck Shoes, metal, 1940s **5.00**

Sign, ACME Quality Paint and Varnishes, diecut porcelain, 2 sided, blue, red, white, and yellow, 26" h, 27½" w **100.00**

Sign, Allen's Foot Ease, diecut cardboard, young girl wearing hat and dress, feet rotate to simulate walking, 6" h, 3½" w **10.00**

Sign, BVD Union Suits, litho tin, man wearing union suit, black ground, "We Sell Loose Fitting Union Suits," 1920s, 13" h, 9" w **225.00**

Sign, Chief Paints, painted tin, 2 sided, Indian chief wearing headdress, 12" h, 28" w **135.00**

Sign, DuPont Paints and Varnishes, "Brilliant Mfg. Co. Phila. PA," porcelain, flange, black and red lettering, yellow ground, black border, 16" h, 16" w **100.00**

Sign, Fry's Breakfast Cocoa, J. S. Fry & Sons, Ltd., Bristol & London, porcelain, cocoa package, 21" h, 14" w **135.00**

Sign, Hart Brand Canned Foods, litho tin over cardboard, product images, 9 x 13" **925.00**

Sign, Ken-L Ration Dog Food, diecut tin, dog's head, 24 x 17". **200.00**

Sign, Kern's Bread, metal flange, "Take Home Kern's Bread," yellow and white swirled ground, c1960 . . . . **85.00**

Sign, Knox Gelatine, Charles B. Knox Co., Johnstown, NY, diecut litho cardboard, 4 sided, cow head flanked by 2 young chefs holding molded gelatin desserts, 16" h, 15" w, 9½" d **2,250.00**

Sign, Lambertville "Snag Proof" Rubber Boots & Shoes, painted metal, 2 large boots, small Charlie McCarthy figure, 4 small cartoon figures, framed, 15" h, 19½" w . . . **775.00**

Sign, Lenox Soap, porcelain, black lettering, ivory ground, 6" h, 10" w **100.00**

Sign, Lictonic, emb tin, painted, yellow oval with horse holding box, "Saves Feed, Saves Money, Improves Stock, Prevents Disease," 9" h, 20" w **300.00**

Sign, Maxwell House Coffee, cardboard, 1920s coffee tin and inverted cup logo, yellow and white checkerboard background, 9 x 13 . . . . **350.00**

Sign, Morton's Salt, porcelain, rect, red and white lettering, black and white ground, red and white border, "We Sell Morton's Salt, Blocks-Barrels-Bags-Packages, The Best Grades For Every Purpose, Osage Flour & Feed Co.," 17½" h, 47½" w **250.00**

Sign, New Ice Refrigerator, emb tin, red, yellow, and black ground, red and white lettering, family racing to refrigerator, "Scientific Refrigeration at low cost," 20½" h, 30" w **30.00**

Sign, Old Dutch Cleanser, tin over cardboard, woman scouring pot and cleanser canister **500.00**

Sign, Old Reliable Coffee, heavy paper, man smoking pipe and product image, 33½ x 16" **50.00**

Sign, Old Reliable Coffee, waxboard, black lettering on yellow ground, 10 x 12" **25.00**

Sign, Oxydol Soap, diecut cardboard, 2 sided, Mammy holding soap box, 10 x 9" **250.00**

Sign, Park Pollard Co Lay or Bust Feeds, HD Beach Co., emb tin, chickens, c1920 . . . . **1,000.00**

Sign, Pear's Soap, diecut cardboard, granny wearing bonnet scrubbing young boy, "You Dirty Boy," 17½" h, 14½" w **200.00**

Sign, Phoenix Assurance Company, porcelain, phoenix rising from flames, blue, black, red, and white, 12" h, 18" w **200.00**

Sign, Pioneer Hog Feed, tin, center circle with hog's head, "Feed Your Hogs Buttermilk For More Pork," yellow, blue, red, white, and black, 19½" h, 14" w **375.00**

Sign, Poll Parrot Shoes, cardboard, easel back, girl holding bouquet, 11 x 14" **10.00**

Sign, Poll Parrot Shoes, cardboard, easel back, white lettering on green ground, 6" h, 3½" w **10.00**

Sign, Purina, "Fresh Eggs For Sale," paper, red and white checkerboard bottom, 1947, 26 x 19" **75.00**

Sign, Purity Butter Pretzels, diecut cardboard, easel back, boy holding huge pretzel, 1920s, 22 x 13". **135.00**

Sign, Weight Watchers, porcelain, from old scale, black and white, silhouette of shapely woman flanked by fat woman and thin woman, "She Did Not Care" below fat and thin women, "She Watched Her Weight" below shapely woman, 9½" h, 8½" w **400.00**

Sign, Weyerhauser Balsam-Wool Blanket, porcelain, navy, turquoise, white, and orange, snow-capped cottage scene, "It Tucks In!," Veribrite Signs, 1930s, 23" h, 36" w **315.00**

Sign, Kellogg's Corn Flakes, diecut cardboard, 2-pc, c1948, 40" h, 35" w, $105.00. Photo courtesy Collectors Auction Services.

Snowdome, Skelly-Hood Tubeless Tires, glass dome with tire and billboard, red plastic base with white lettering, 4 x 3 x 3". **150.00**

Spinner, Skiles Electric Bread, celluloid, hand shaped, 2½ x 1¼" **180.00**

Store Card, Allen-A Hosiery, cardboard, standup, beautiful woman wearing red gown displaying stocking-clad legs, c1930s, 12" h, 8" w **70.00**

Store Card, Cyclone Twister Cigars, cardboard, word "Cyclone" in twister above windswept ground, 16" h, 12" w **150.00**

Store Card, Ide Shirts, cardboard, blue ground, man with shirt draped over arm, "Eyed With Admiration, Shirts of Unusual Character," 1930s, 12" h, 9" w **55.00**

Thermometer, Clown Cigarettes, litho paper dial, black, yellow, and white, 9" d **65.00**

Thermometer, Doan's Pills, diecut wood, man holding aching back, black and white, 21" h, 5" w **275.00**

Thermometer, Hills Bros. Coffee, porcelain, old man in yellow nightgown drinking cup of coffee, white lettering, red ground, white border, "Patent No. 11324265, Beach Coshocton, O.," 21" h, 8½" w **550.00**

Thermometer, Jordan's Ready-To-Eat Meats, wood, enamel paint, yellow ground, black trim, stamped red lettering, c1930, 15" h **50.00**

Thermometer, Mail Pouch Tobacco, metal, dark blue ground, white lettering, "Chew Mail Pouch Tobacco, Treat Yourself to the Best," 39" h, 8½" w **100.00**

Thermometer, McKesson's Aspirin, porcelain, product box and bottle, 27" h, 7" w **350.00**

Thermometer, Sauer's Flavoring, C. F. Sauer Co, Richmond, VA, wood, painted, product image, 24" h, 6½" w **275.00**

Thermometer, Stephenson Union Suits, porcelain, red, white, and black, 1 man wearing suit, other holding shirt, 39" h **950.00**

Tin, Campfire Marshmallows, campfire scene. **35.00**

Tin, Countess Cookies, Bond Bakers, boys playing various sports around sides, 8" h **45.00**

Thermometer/Barometer, Blue Gillette Blades, porcelain on wood, 27¹/₂" h, 6¹/₄" w, $1,925.00. Photo courtesy Collectors Auction Services.

Tin, Forest & Stream Tobacco, fisherman, pocket size **75.00**

Tin, Golden Pheasant Condoms, pheasant on branch, 2¹/₈ x 1⁵/₈ x ¹/₄" **125.00**

Tin, Hoadley Blood Orange Pellets, square, red ground, black and orange lettering, c1930, 5" w, 8¹/₂" h **50.00**

Tin, Jackie Coogan Salted Nut Meats, man on elephant, black and white label, 7¹/₂" h, 6³/₄" d **30.00**

Tin, King Cole Coffee, king, key open type **20.00**

Tin, Len Wright's Chocolate Biscuits, paper label with Art Deco motif **30.00**

Tin, Luzianne Coffee, black mammy, red ground **50.00**

Tin, Mexene Chili Powder, devil stirring cauldron, 30 oz. **75.00**

Tin, Miners and Puddlers Smoking Tobacco, red ground, red, black, and ivory lettering, 3 miners at center, bail handle, c1930, 6³/₄" h **75.00**

Tin, Old Reliable Typewriter, typewriter ribbon, beavers chewing trees **25.00**

Tin, Peerless Maid Confections, square, yellow ground, red and white candy cane striped corners, multicolor candies on 2 sides, lady with parasol other 2 sides, c1940, 5 lbs, 4¹/₂" sq, 10¹/₄" h **45.00**

Tin, Planter's Cashews, Mr. Peanut, 4 oz, 1944 . . . . **40.00**

Tin, Pure Honey, "William Garwood Jr., Batavia NY. Copyright 1923" and "Al Root Company" at top, tin, red ground, apiary vignette, bail handle, 5 lb, 6" h, 5" w **40.00**

Tin, Southern Rose Shortening, red rose, bail handle **15.00**

Tin, Sphinx Condoms, litho tin, hinged lid, 1939, 1⁵/₈ x 2¹/₄ x ¹/₄" **250.00**

Tin, Sunshine Biscuit, Capitol building and cherry blossoms **75.00**

Tin, Texide Water Cured Prophylactics, litho tin, natives harvesting latex from rubber trees, 1930s, 1¹/₂ x 2 x ¹/₄" **40.00**

Tin, Times Square Smoking Mixture, United Cigar Stores, vertical pocket tin, nighttime Times Square, NY scene, 4³/₈ x 3 x ⁷/₈" **400.00**

Tin, Tropical Brand Crystalized Ginger, black and white, shield with palm tree and alligator **20.00**

Tin, Veteran Coffee, gold, black and white, keywind, 1 lb, 3¹/₂ x 5" **75.00**

Tin, Watkins Baking Powder, woman holding cupcakes, red and yellow, trial size, 1³/₄ x 2¹/₂" **70.00**

Tin, Wishbone Coffee, green and white, 4 lb size, 7¹/₂ x 7¹/₂" **175.00**

Tin, Wizard of Oz Peanut Butter, bail handle, 2 lb **50.00**

Tin, Yankee Doodle Dandy Candy, drum shape, children parading around sides, cloth strap, 1920s, 8 oz, 5⁵/₈" d, 2³/₈" h **50.00**

Tin, Yorkshire Farm Peanut Butter, litho tin, children holding ribbons, bail handle, 3¹/₄ x 3³/₄" **850.00**

Toy Glider, Red Goose Shoes, goose shape, 9" l **10.00**

Trolley Card, Beech-Nut Tomato Catsup, Beechnut Packing Co., Canojohave, NY, USA, cardboard, seated man reaching for catsup bottle, "Excuse me for reaching," multicolored, white ground, 11¹/₂" h, 21" w . . . **100.00**

Trolley Card, Scott's Emulsion, cardboard, multicolored, boy and girl shooting marbles, c1924, 11" h, 24" w **185.00**

Trolley Card, Smith Brothers Cough Drops, cardboard, caricature men, one with cane wearing underwear and brown hat, other fully dressed wearing bowler, "...and it's just as silly to ever be without," 2 cough drop boxes, framed, 17¹/₂" h, 28" w **200.00**

Vase, Diamond Cleaners, red and black Scotty dogs, 1920–30, 5" h **200.00**

Watch Fob, Poll Parrot Shoes, "Solid Leather Shoes" **50.00**

Watch Fob, Right Food Co., "It pays to feed hogs...," diecut pig, gold wash **65.00**

Welcome Mat, Red Goose Shoes, rubber, red ground, "Welcome Red Goose" **75.00**

Whistle, Dairy Queen, cone, plastic. **10.00**

Whistle, Endicott Johnson Shoes **20.00**

Whistle, Finck's "Detroit Special Overalls," cardboard, 2-sided **95.00**

Whistle, Haines Shoes, plastic, orange and black, "Blow And Talk Of Haines The Shoe Wizard, Shoes For All," late 1940s **20.00**

Whistle, Hurd Shoes **15.00**

Whistle, IGA Oats and Cream Cereal, wooden, 1¹/₂" **15.00**

Whistle, Melorol Ice Cream, cardboard with metal bird **10.00**

Whistle, Oscar Meyer, plastic, Weiner Mobile **10.00**

Whistle, Peters Weatherbird Shoes **20.00**

Whistle, Red Goose Shoes, tin, 2¹/₄". **45.00**

Whistle, Silver Eagle Turkeys, "Clean as a Whistle" **15.00**

Whistle, Zig Zag Food Confection, metal, bird **35.00**

Window Decal, King Edward Cigars, red shield, 8¹/₂ x 7" **20.00**

Window Sign, Sunbeam Bread, paper, bread loaf shape, 24 x 10" **40.00**

Trolley Card, Heinz Rice Flakes, cardboard, 21 x 11", $100.00. Photo courtesy Frank's Antiques & Auctions.

Tin, Royal Baking Powder, paper label, red ground, 4" h, 2³/₈" d, 6 oz, $25.00. Photo courtesy Ray Morykan Auctions.

ADVERTISING CHARACTERS

Many companies created advertising characters as a means of guaranteeing product recognition by the buying public. Consumers are more apt to purchase an item with which they are familiar and advertising characters were a surefire method of developing familiarity.

The early development of advertising characters also enabled immigrants who could not read to identify products by the colorful figures found on the packaging.

Trademarks and advertising characters are found on product labels, in magazines, as premiums, and on other types of advertising. Character subjects may be based on a real person such as Nancy Green, the original "Aunt Jemima." However, more often than not, they are comical figures, often derived from popular contemporary cartoons. Other advertising characters were designed especially to promote a specific product, like Mr. Peanut and the Campbell Kids.

References: Patsy Clevenger, *The Collector's World of M&M's,* Schiffer Publishing, 1998; Pamela Duvall Curran and George W. Curran, *Collectible California Raisins,* Schiffer Publishing, 1998; Warren Dotz, *Advertising Character Collectibles,* Collector Books, 1993, 1997 value update; Joan Stryker Grubaugh, *A Collector's Guide to the Gerber Baby,* published by author, 1996; Ted Hake, *Hake's Guide to Advertising Collectibles,* Wallace-Homestead, Krause Publications, 1992; Mary Jane Lamphier, *Zany Characters of the Ad World,* Collector Books, 1995; Myra Yellin Outwater, *Advertising Dolls,* Schiffer Publishing, 1997; Robert Reed, *Bears & Dolls in Advertising,* Antique Trader Books, 1998; David and Micki Young, *Campbell's Soup Collectibles from A to Z,* Krause Publications, 1998.

Collectors' Clubs: Campbell Soup Collectors Club, 414 County Lane Ct, Wauconda, IL 60084; Sorry Charlie...No Fan Club For You, 7812 NW Hampton Rd, Kansas City, MO 64152.

Note: See also Planter's Peanuts.

REPRODUCTION ALERT

California Raisins, fan club watch set, digital watch and
   3 interchangeable vinyl watch bands, 1987, MOC **$18.00**
Campbell Kids, Campbell's Soup, trolley adv, multicolor,
   soup can and girl, dark green ground, "Campbell's
   Condensed Soups, 10¢," framed, 13" h, 23" w 75.00
Charlie Tuna, Star-Kist, clock, brass, windup, "Sorry
   Charlie" sign hanging from fish hook beside Charlie,
   1969, 6" h. 50.00
Chico, Santa Fe Railway, figure, painted composition,
   base inscription "Santa Fe All the Way," 1970s, 5¹/₂" h 175.00
Dino Dinosaur, Sinclair Oil, ashtray, silvered metal, fig-
   ural Dino in center, 1950s, 7¹/₄" l 45.00
Dutch Boy, Dutch Boy Paint, figure, papier-mâché, hold-
   ing orig 2-sided cardboard sign, 15" h figure 450.00
Dutch Boy, Dutch Boy Paint, match holder, emb diecut
   litho tin, Dutch Boy holding paintbrush, 6³/₄" h, 3¹/₂" w . . **1,000.00**
Elsie the Cow, Borden's, button, Elsie head and "Elsie
   Says" on front, Borden's advertising on reverse,
   brown, yellow, and white, 1¹/₂" d 50.00
Elsie the Cow, Borden's, matchbooks, image of Elsie's
   head on cover, set of 10 books in orig milk carton
   container, ©1957 . . . . 35.00

AUCTION PRICES – COFFEE TINS

Wm. Morford, Absentee Auction, December 5, 1998. Prices include a 10% buyer's premium.

American Mills Samson Brand, J.S. Silvers & Bro.,
   Cranbury, NJ, litho tin, small top, man prying
   open lion's mouth with hands, 1 lb, 5¹/₂ x 4³/₄" . . . **$688.00**
Blue Bonnet, Springfield Grocer Co., Springfield,
   Mo., litho tin, key wind lid, woman wearing blue
   bonnet, 1 lb, 4 x 5" 298.00
Christy's Brand, litho tin, plantation workers in
   fields, 1 lb, 6 x 4¹/₄" 385.00
Coffee House, Bacon, Stickney & Co., Albany, NY,
   litho tin, 1834 men dining at Coffee House, 1 lb,
   4 x 5" 231.00
Elizabeth Park Brand, Vogel Bros., Hartford, CT,
   litho tin, key wind, garden scene, 1 lb, 4 x 5" 798.00
Happy Hour Brand, Campbell Holton & Co.,
   Bloomington, IL, litho tin, steaming cup of cof-
   fee, 6 x 4" 253.00
Honor Brand, cardboard, tin top and bottom,
   George Washington, 6 x 4⁵/₈ x 3¹/₈" 220.00
Mammy's Favorite Brand, C.D. Kenny Co., Buffalo,
   NY, litho tin, black woman serving coffee, 4 lbs,
   10⁵/₈ x 6" 468.00
Old Andy Brand, cardboard, paper label, President
   Andrew Jackson, 1 lb, 3⁵/₈ x 5¹/₄" 231.00
Old Mansion, C.W. Antrim, Richmond, VA,
   unopened key wind with key on top, mansion
   scene, 1 lb, 3¹/₂ x 5" 220.00
Old Master, Blodgett Beckley Co., Toledo, paper
   label, bearded man, 1 lb, 6 x 4" 99.00
Phillips, Phillips Inc., Massachusetts and
   Connecticut, litho tin, key wind, farm scene,
   1 lb, 4 x 5" 330.00
Quality Inn, Sorver McEvoy Co., Phila., litho tin,
   key wind, horse–drawn carriage in front
   of inn, 1 lb, 4 x 5¹/₈" 209.00
Rose of Kansas Brand, litho tin, pry–lid, sunflower,
   3³/₄ x 5¹/₄" 1,018.00
Senate Brand, Newell & Truesdell Co., Binghamton,
   NY, litho tin, Capitol building, 1 lb, 6 x 4" 303.00
Sunshine, Mogar Coffee Co., Inc., Brooklyn, key
   wind, king drinking coffee, 1 lb, 4 x 5" 220.00
Tropical Brand, litho tin, palm trees and native, 1 lb,
   3¹/₂ x 5" 253.00

Happy Oil Drop, Esso, lighter, plastic and brass, French, 2½" h, 1" w, $82.00. Photo courtesy Collectors Auction Services.

AKRO AGATE

The Akro Agate Company was founded in Ohio in 1911 primarily to manufacture agate marbles. In 1914 the firm opened a large factory in Clarksburg, West Virginia.

Increasing competition in the marble industry in the 1930s prompted Akro Agate to expand. In 1936, following a major fire at the Westite factory, Akro Agate purchased many of Westite's molds. Akro Agate now boasted a large line of children's dishes, floral wares, and household accessories. The company also produced specialty glass containers for cosmetic firms, including the Mexicali cigarette jar (originally filled with Pick Wick bath salts) and a special line made for the Jean Vivaudou Company, Inc.

The Clarksburg Glass Company bought the factory in 1951.

Akro Agate glass has survived the test of time because of its durability. Most pieces are marked "Made in USA" and often include a mold number. Some pieces have a small crow in the mark. Early pieces of Akro made from Westite molds may be unmarked but were produced only in typical Akro colors and color combinations.

Reference: Gene Florence, *The Collectors Encyclopedia of Akro Agate Glassware, Revised Edition,* Collector Books, 1975, 1992 value update, out of print.

Collectors' Club: Akro Agate Collector's Club, 10 Bailey St, Clarksburg, WV 26301.

Note: See Children's Dishes and Marbles for additional listings.

REPRODUCTION ALERT: Reproduction pieces are unmarked.

Chiquita, creamer, cobalt blue **$9.00**
Chiquita, cup and saucer, transparent cobalt blue **17.50**
Concentric Ring, cup, opaque green **5.00**
Concentric Ring, teapot, open, blue, 2⅞" h **15.00**
Graduated Dart, flowerpot, orange and white marble-
   ized **17.50**
Graduated Dart, jardiniere, closed handle, bell shaped,
   green and white marbleized **35.00**
Interior Panel, creamer, opaque blue, large **42.50**
Interior Panel, cup and saucer, opaque pink **25.00**
Interior Panel, plate, child's, opaque green **7.00**
Interior Panel, teapot, open, opaque pink **10.00**
J Pressman, creamer and sugar, cobalt **12.00**
J Pressman, demitasse cup, green **10.00**
J Pressman, demitasse cup, pink **25.00**
J Pressman, plate, child's, fired-on green **5.00**
J Pressman, red cup and yellow saucer, child's **5.00**
J Pressman, soup bowl, child's, fired-on red **5.00**
Lily Planter, oxblood and lemonade marbleized, #657,
   5¼" **10.00**
Octagonal, closed handle, plate, child's, green **5.00**
Octagonal, closed handle, saucer, child's, beige **4.00**
Octagonal, closed handle, set, child's, plates and cups,
   green, 17 pcs **150.00**
Octagonal, closed handle, set, child's, plates and teapot,
   blue, 17 pcs **150.00**
Octagonal, closed handle, tumbler, child's, green **12.00**
Stacked Disc, tumbler, child's, opaque beige **12.00**
Stacked Disc, water pitcher, child's, opaque green **10.00**
Stippled Band, cup, child's, green **20.00**
Stippled Band, cup and saucer, cobalt blue **35.00**

Elsie the Cow, Borden's, salt and pepper shakers, pr, figural Elsie heads, ceramic, 1950s, 1½" h **50.00**
Esso Fat Man, bank, plastic, figural, 5" h **110.00**
Exxon Tiger, water pitcher, clear glass, orange, black, and white tiger head, black lettering "Put A Tiger In Your Tank" in 8 different languages, Anchor Hocking, late 1960s, 9½" h **30.00**
Froggy, Buster Brown Shoes, mask, paper, "Froggy The Gremlin," ©1946, McConnell **35.00**
Happy Oil Drop, Esso, drinking glass, "Happy Motoring Club" and frosted repeating Happy images around sides, 1960s, 4" h **15.00**
Johnny, Philip Morris, pinback button, Johnny shouting "Vote for Philip Morris," red and black on white ground, 1¼" d **30.00**
Jolly Green Giant, Minnesota Valley Canning Company, kite, Giant on white ground, c1970 . . . . **35.00**
Lennie Lennox, Lennox Furnace Co, bank, ceramic, figural Lennie, c1950, 7¼" h **150.00**
Mr Bibidendum, Michelin Tires, ashtray, plastic, black and white figural Michelin man, 4¾" h, 5" w **110.00**
Nipper, sign, porcelain, oval, dog staring into music box speaker, "His Master's Voice," black ground, gold border, 18½" h, 26" w **500.00**
Poppin' Fresh, Pillsbury, doll, cloth, stuffed, white with red, white, and blue accents, 1970s, 12" h **25.00**
Reddy Kilowatt, bank, hard vinyl, figural Reddy, 1950s, 5" h **750.00**
Reddy Kilowatt, lighter, "Let Reddy Do It," chromed metal, Zippo, c1960, 1½" h **60.00**
Reddy Kilowatt, pinback button, Reddy holding "Safety First" sign, red and green on white ground, 1¼" d **30.00**
Snap, Crackle, and Pop, Kellogg's, cloth doll images, c1948, set of 3 . . . . **175.00**
Speedy Alka-Seltzer, bank, soft vinyl, figural Speedy, c1960, 5¾" h **150.00**
Speedy Alka-Seltzer, sign, diecut cardboard, winking Speedy image, 1960s, 5 x 11" **80.00**
Willie Penguin, Kool Cigarettes, sign, diecut cardboard standup, Willie playing trumpet above cigarette pack, 9¼ x 12⅝" **125.00**

ALADDIN LAMPS

Victor Samuel Johnson founded the Western Lighting Company in Kansas City, Missouri, in 1907. In 1908 the company became the Mantle Lamp Company of America. In 1909, Johnson introduced the Aladdin lamp. Although the company has diversified and become as well known for its lunch boxes and vacuum bottles as its lamps, Aladdin lamps are still being manufactured today.

References: J. W. Courter, *Aladdin Collectors Manual & Price Guide #18: Kerosene Mantle Lamps,* published by author, 1998; J. W. Courter, *Aladdin Electric Lamps: Collectors Manual & Price Guide #3,* published by author, 1997; J. W. Courter, *Aladdin: The Magic Name in Lamps, Revised Edition,* published by author, 1997.

Collectors' Club: Aladdin Knights of the Mystic Light, 3935 Kelley Rd, Kevil, KY 42053.

REPRODUCTION ALERT: Tall Lincoln Drape, Short Lincoln Drape, glass and paper shades.

Note: All kerosene lamps priced with complete burners.

Model 4, table, satin brass	**$300.00**
Model 12, style 1253, floor, Verde Antique, 1930–32	**175.00**
Model 21C, style B-400, caboose, aluminum font	**50.00**
Model A, style 100, table, Venetian, white, 1932–33	**100.00**
Model B, hanging, flat steel frame, parchment shade	**200.00**
Model B, style 104, table, Colonial, clear, 1933	**100.00**
Model B, style B-80, table, Beehive, clear, 1937–38	**100.00**
Model B, style B-86, table, Quilt, green moonstone, 1937	**300.00**
Model B, style B-95, table, Queen, white moonstone, oxidized bronze base, 1937–39	**375.00**
Model B, style B-100, table, Corinthian, clear, 1935–36	**80.00**
Model B, style B-120, table, Majestic, white moonstone, 1935–36	**375.00**
Model B, style B-130, table, Orientale, ivory, 1935–36	**50.00**
Model B, style B-425, floor, ivory lacquer	**200.00**
Model C, hanging, aluminum hanger and font, white paper shade	**50.00**

Alacite Table Lamps, electric, illuminated base, fluted Whip-O-Lite shade, alacite scrolled finial, c1938, 23" h, price for pair, $287.50. Photo courtesy Jackson's Auctioneers & Appraisers.

ALUMINUM WARE

The mass production of hand-wrought aluminum decorative accessories is indebted to the inventiveness of Charles M. Hall and Paul T. Heroult. Hall of the United States and Heroult in France, working independently, simultaneously discovered an inexpensive electrolytic reduction process in 1886. Soon after, the price of aluminum dropped from $545 per pound to 57¢ per pound.

Aluminum ware's popularity thrived throughout the lean Depression years and into the first years of World War II, when aluminum shortages caused many factories to close. Some resumed production after the war; however, most pieces no longer originated with the artistic craftsman—the Machine Age had arrived. By the late 1960s, decorative aluminum was no longer in fashion.

References: Dannie Woodard and Billie Wood, *Hammered Aluminum: Hand-Wrought Collectibles,* published by authors, 1983, 1990 value update; Dannie A. Woodard, *Hammered Aluminum Hand-Wrought Collectibles, Book Two,* Aluminum Collectors' Books, 1993.

Newsletter: *The Continental Report,* 5128 Schultz Bridge Rd, Zionsville, PA 18092.

Collectors' Clubs: Hammered Aluminum Collectors Assoc, PO Box 1346, Weatherford, TX 76086; Wendell August Collectors Guild, PO Box 107, Grove City, PA 16127.

Arthur Armour, casserole	**$180.00**
Arthur Armour, magazine rack, dogwood	**10.00**
Arthur Armour, tray, butterfly, small size	**25.00**
Arthur Armour, tray, round, wild horses	**125.00**
Continental, candelabrum, 3-light, #833	**125.00**
Continental, cocktail shaker, mum	**45.00**
Continental, coffee service, includes coffee urn, sugar, creamer, and tray	**200.00**
Continental, ice bucket, mum, bud finial on lid, #705	**75.00**
Continental, tray, cut corners, mum, large size	**35.00**
Continental, tray, paisley, #1003, large size	**45.00**
Continental, tray, round, handles, pansies, large size	**55.00**
Continental, tumbler, mum, ftd	**35.00**

Admiration Products Co., tray, Florette pattern, 17" d, $20.00.

Everlast, ashtray, berry sprig 20.00
Everlast, butler's tray and stand 110.00
Everlast, candle holders, pr, Bali bamboo, each with
    3-ftd stand and 2 candle cups 225.00
Everlast, coasters, daisies, set 35.00
Everlast, ice bucket, Bali bamboo 50.00
Everlast, patio cart, some accessories missing 750.00
Everlast, silent butler, oval, scalloped edges, rose 30.00
Everlast, tray, tab handles, daisy 35.00
Everlast, wine cooler with stand 250.00
Hand Forged, silent butler, roses 20.00
Laird Forge, plate, #444, 11¼" d 20.00
Rodney Kent, basket, handled, ruby red dish 35.00
Rodney Kent, bread tray, handles 35.00
Rodney Kent, napkin holder 25.00
Rodney Kent, silent butler, flower, ribbon handle 50.00
Wendell August, cigarette box, pine 150.00
Wendell August, double server, apple blossom, la
    Mirada inserts 350.00
Wendell August, smoking stand, pine 150.00
World, candelabra 60.00
World, creamer and sugar 15.00

Cookie Jar, Liberty Bell, 9¾" h 250.00
Cookie Jar, locomotive, #200, 7½" h 150.00
Cookie Jar, majorette, 11¼" h 450.00
Cookie Jar, pig in a poke, 12½" h 200.00
Cookie Jar, pup on pot, 11½" h, blue pot 80.00
Cookie Jar, rooster, 11" h 80.00
Cookie Jar, spool of thread, thimble finial, 10¾" h 200.00
Cookie Jar, strawberry 120.00
Cookie Jar, treasure chest, brown, 8¾" h 175.00
Cookie Jar, wrapped box, 9½" h 165.00
Cookie Jar, yarn doll, yellow yarn, 12" h 175.00
Cookie Jar, Yogi Bear, 10" h 475.00
Planter, bear and beehive, 5½" h 20.00
Planter, cat and fishbowl, 5¾" h 25.00
Planter, Davy Crockett at tree stump, 5" h 50.00
Planter, Dutch girl between tulip blossoms, 7½" h 20.00
Planter, man with pushcart, 5⅞" h 15.00
Planter, rooster and corn cob, 6¼" h 15.00
Planter, tugboat, 9½" l 25.00
Salt and Pepper Shakers, pr, bears wearing bibs 15.00
Salt and Pepper Shakers, pr, cat in basket, 3¾" h 14.00
Salt and Pepper Shakers, pr, seated cow, 3" h 16.00

AMERICAN BISQUE

The American Bisque Company, founded in Williamstown, West Virginia in 1919, was originally established for the manufacture of china head dolls. The company soon began producing novelties such as cookie jars, ashtrays, serving dishes, and ceramic giftware.

B. E. Allen, founder of the Sterling China Company, invested heavily in the company and eventually purchased the remaining stock. In 1982 the company operated briefly under the name American China Company. The plant ceased operations in 1983.

American Bisque items have various markings. The trademark "Sequoia Ware" is often found on items sold in gift shops. The Berkeley trademark was used on pieces sold through chain stores. The most common mark found consists of three stacked baby blocks with the letters A, B, and C.

Reference: Mary Jane Giacomini, *American Bisque*, Schiffer Publishing, 1994.

Bank, Casper, 8½" h $500.00
Bank, pig wearing diaper, 9" h 275.00
Bank, Popeye, blue and white, 7" h 475.00
Cookie Jar, Animal Crackers, 8½" h 70.00
Cookie Jar, baby elephant, 13¼" h 225.00
Cookie Jar, bear, wearing bib, 11¼" h 175.00
Cookie Jar, bell, "Ring for Cookies," bell in lid, 10" h 75.00
Cookie Jar, butter churn, 10" h 40.00
Cookie Jar, cat, hands in pockets, mkd "U.S.A.," 11½" h 160.00
Cookie Jar, chef, 12" h 150.00
Cookie Jar, chick, yellow, 12¼" h 60.00
Cookie Jar, clown, 11" h 160.00
Cookie Jar, coffeepot, 9½" h 85.00
Cookie Jar, cow/lamb turnabout 175.00
Cookie Jar, Dutch boy, mkd "U.S.A.," 12½" h 75.00
Cookie Jar, grandma, gold trim, 12¾" h 300.00
Cookie Jar, hot chocolate mug, 9¼" h 200.00
Cookie Jar, ice cream maker, 9¾" h 475.00
Cookie Jar, kittens on ball of yarn, 9½" h 130.00
Cookie Jar, lantern, 13" h 275.00

AMERICAN INDIAN

Post-1920 American Indian, a.k.a. Native American, objects divide into two basic groups: (1) objects made for use within the tribe and (2) objects made for the tourist trade. Tribal pieces are subdivided into ceremonial and utilitarian objects. Tourist items subdivide into pre-1940 objects which are highly desirable and post-1945 objects which have only modest collector interest at the moment.

As with all American Indian material, it is extremely important to identify the tribe of the maker. Identification with a specific maker, especially if featured in a museum collection or major reference book, also is a value added factor.

Individuals, from school teachers to missionaries, who worked on Indian reservations often received handmade artifacts as gifts. Carefully check the authenticity of such an attribution before paying a premium price for an object.

References: Lar Hothem, *North American Indian Artifacts, 6th Edition*, Krause Publications, 1998; Marian Rodee, *Weaving of the Southwest*, Schiffer Publishing, 1987.

Periodicals: *American Indian Art Magazine*, 7314 E Osborn Dr, Scottsdale, AZ 85251; *The Indian Trader*, PO Box 1421, Gallup, NM 87305.

REPRODUCTION ALERT: Watch out for American Indian jewelry imported from the Philippines. Several villages changed their names to correspond to the names of Native American tribes, e.g., Zuni. The Filipinos have plenty of company in the faking of American Indian crafts. Brazilians, Nigerians, and Pakistanis weave copies of Apache, Navajo, and Pima baskets. Mexicans weave imitation Navajo blankets. Chinese carve animal fetishes. Thai workers also make imitation jewelry. The Filipinos are branching out. Their latest fakes include Hopi kachina dolls.

Bag, beaded in variety of colors on buckskin, in foliate
    motif, with word "souvenir" on front panel, star with
    3-leaf pattern on reverse, fringe around edge, hide
    cloth lined handle, 9 x 7" $70.00

Pottery Jar, Hopi, polychrome, orange and black slip stylized bird device, sgd "Fawn" with penciled purchase date "9.74," 12" h, $460.00. Photo courtesy Skinner, Inc., Boston, MA.

Basket, Apache, burden basket, indented base, tall flaring sides, center row of connecting diamonds, with leather and tin cone suspensions, 9½" h, 14¼" d **145.00**

Basket, Hopi, polychrome, coiled, flat base, flaring sides with terraced connecting diamonds in black, red, and yellow on natural, small handle each side, 3½" h, 6¼" d **85.00**

Basket, Navajo, wedding basekt, polychrome, coiled, woven in typical materials and designs, 3" h, 12½" d **80.00**

Basket, Southeast, oblong, woven, polychrome plaiting of glossy natural and dark brown river cane, 4" h, 9¼" l **115.00**

Basket, Thompson River, child's imbricated burden basket, typical form, 2 cloth handles, 5½" h, 7" d **285.00**

Blouse, Navajo, dance, sewn on green velvet with tack dec on chest, back and arms, pink and white trim below and around collar and cuffs, 19" l **150.00**

Bowl, painted black foliate motif on tan ground, Santo Domingo Pottery, 4½ x 7½". **80.00**

Bowl, polychrome paint with geometric design on tan slip, "Ginny Garcia" on side, Zia Pottery, 3¾ x 8½" **35.00**

Bowl, shallow form, painted black and brown int, with circle enclosing 2 zigzag lines flanked by half circle, on creamy orange slip, Hopi Pottery, 2¼ x 7" **35.00**

Bracelet, Navajo, inlaid crushed coral and turquoise with center bird design, reversible panel, sides with hook motif, stamped inside "CJ," 7 x 2¼" **60.00**

Bracelet, silver and turquoise, open work band, 2 blue turquoise stones with bent wire, teardrop and leaf dec, 7 x 3¼". **45.00**

Drum, circular wood frame with stretched hide at each end and hide lacing joining together, 9¾ x 8½" **60.00**

Gloves, pr, beaded on hide with floral motif on cuff, 13½" l **140.00**

Hair Roach, natural brown deer hair sewn on cloth base, length of base 12½" l with stand **240.00**

Jar, typical form, black geometric design on brown ground, B Soto Casas Grande, 5½ x 7". **35.00**

Kachina Doll, possibly Poli, polychrome torso and face with overhanging large, brown tablita, polychrome kilt and sash with feather adornment, repair to articulated arms, missing toes, mid 20th C, 11" h **450.00**

Lithograph, Robert Redbird, male and female Indians in village scene, sgd lower right, matted, framed and under glass, 12 x 18". **35.00**

Moccasins, pr, child's, made of Woodland beaded tanned hide, red cloth vamp with flower design in blues, pink, yellow and red, red cloth trim around 2-button cuff, 6½" l **160.00**

Necklace, red coral bead, 30 strands, 30" l **60.00**

Necklace, silver and turquoise, single strand of round beads interspersed with tubular beads, large teardrop pendant with leaf relief and turquoise stone drop, 24" l **45.00**

Seed Jar, typical form, black and brown paint on white ground, rosette on each side, flanked by geometric fine line design, Acoma Pottery, 5 x 5" **70.00**

Vase, cylindrical form, black and brown paint on creamy orange slip with geometric designs, Hopi Pottery, 6½ x 3¼" **55.00**

Vase, wedding, polished black finish, Sammy Narrajo Santa Clara Pottery, sgd on bottom, 7 x 6½" **45.00**

Weaving, Navajo, black, red and brown on ivory, overall pattern of connecting diamonds, 53 x 26" **30.00**

Weaving, Navajo, black, red and ivory, overall squash blossom design and terraced border at each end, 86 x 58" **60.00**

Weaving, Navajo, gold, black, green and white on brown ground, with 5 Yei figures holding feather staffs, 34 x 40" **90.00**

Weaving, Navajo, red, black, brown and ivory, with serrated "X" pattern, 64 x 39½" **150.00**

ANCHOR HOCKING

The Hocking Glass Company was founded in Lancaster, Ohio in 1905. Although the company originally produced handmade items, by the 1920s the firm was manufacturing a wide variety of wares including chimneys and lantern globes, tableware, tumblers, and novelties. Hocking introduced its first line of pressed glass dinnerware in 1928. Molded etched tableware was released shortly thereafter.

Following the acquisition of several glass houses in the 1920s, Hocking began producing new glass containers. In 1937 Hocking merged with the Anchor Cap and Closure Corporation, resulting in a name change in 1939 to Anchor Hocking Glass Corporation. In 1969 the company became Anchor Hocking Corporation.

References: Gene Florence, *Anchor Hocking's Fire-King & More*, Collector Books, 1998; Philip Hopper, *Royal Ruby, Schiffer Publishing, 1998*.

Note: See Depression Glass and Fire-King for additional listings.

Ashtray, Early American Prescut, #818-G, 7¾" d **$3.00**
Berry Bowl, Bubble, crystal, 4" d **4.00**
Bowl, Mayfair, pink, 10" d **30.00**
Bread and Butter Plate, Bubble, light blue, 6¾" d **3.00**
Cake Plate, Early American Prescut, ftd, #706, 13½" **18.00**
Cake Plate, Mayfair, pink, handled, 12" d **50.00**
Cocktail, Mayfair, pink, 3 oz **115.00**
Creamer, Bubble, light blue **35.00**
Creamer, Mayfair, pink **30.00**
Cup and Ringed Saucer, Mayfair, pink **50.00**
Cup and Saucer, Mayfair, blue **75.00**
Deep Bowl, Mayfair, pink, 12" d **60.00**
Dessert Bowl, Early American Prescut, #765, 5⅜" d **2.50**
Dinner Plate, Bubble, forest green, 9⅜" d **25.00**

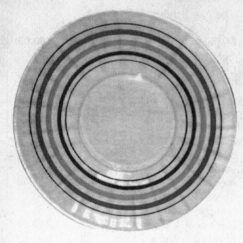

Plate, Panelled Ring-Ding, crystal with black, red, yellow, green, and black stripe, 6¹/₄" d, $2.50.

Dinner Plate, Panelled Ring-Ding.	12.00
Grill Plate, Bubble, light blue, 9³/₈" d	20.00
Pitcher, Mayfair, pink, 80 oz, 8¹/₂" h	105.00
Plate, Mayfair, pink, 5³/₄" d	14.00
Platter, Bubble, oval, light blue, 12" l	16.00
Platter, Mayfair, pink, 12" l	30.00
Platter, Panelled Ring-Ding	18.00
Relish Tray, oval, #778, 8¹/₂" d	5.00
Sherbet, Mayfair, pink, 3" d	17.00
Sugar, Bubble, forest green	12.00
Sugar, Mayfair, pink.	30.00
Tidbit Tray, Bubble, 2 tier, royal ruby	38.00
Tumbler, Early American Prescut, #731, 10 oz	4.00
Vegetable, Mayfair, blue, oval	70.00

ANIMAL COLLECTIBLES

The hobby of collecting objects depicting one's favorite animal has thrived for years. The more common species have enjoyed long lives of popularity. Cats, dogs, cows, horses, and pigs are examples of animals whose collectibility is well established. Their markets are so stable, in fact, that they merit separate listings of their own.

The desirability of other animals changes with the times. Many remain fashionable for only a limited period of time, or their popularity cycles, often due to marketing crazes linked to advertising.

References: Lee Garmon and Dick Spencer, *Glass Animals of the Depression Era,* Collector Books, 1993, out of print; Everett Grist, *Covered Animal Dishes,* Collector Books, 1988, 1996 value update.

Newsletter: *The Glass Animal Bulletin,* PO Box 143, North Liberty, IA 52317.

Collectors' Club: The Frog Pond, PO Box 193, Beech Grove, IN 46107.

Note: See Beswick, Breyer Horses, Cat Collectibles, Cow Collectibles, Dog Collectibles, Elephant Collectibles, Figural Planters & Vases, Figurines, Grindley Pottery, Horse Collectibles, Pig Collectibles, Royal Doulton, and other manufacturer categories for additional listings.

Bear, bank, metal, 4¹/₂" h	$20.00
Bear, figure, ceramic, tumbling, Shawnee	65.00

Camel, ashtray, Whimtray, Wade Ceramics	20.00
Chicken, salt and pepper shakers, pr, gold paint on yellow ground, Grindley Pottery, 3³/₈" h and 3³/₄" h	10.00
Deer, figure, ceramic, pink, gold dec, Grindley Pottery, 6¹/₂" h	15.00
Dragon, nutcracker, brass	50.00
Elephant, ashtray, Occupied Japan	15.00
Elephant, cheese cutting board, elephant shape, cherry hardwood, 8 x 13"	85.00
Fish, salt and pepper shakers, pr, gold paint on green ground, Grindley Pottery, paper label, 2¹/₄" h	15.00
Flamingo, demitasse cup and saucer, 2 birds	20.00
Flamingo, television lamp, Lane, 14"	150.00
Fox, figure, ceramic, blue, yellow, and black on white ground, Grindley Pottery, paper label, 3⁷/₈ x 5"	15.00
Frog, match holder, cast iron, 2 pcs, match striker under mouth, Pointer Stoves and Ranges adv	225.00
Hedgehog, dish, cov, mkd "Wade/Porcelain/Made in England," 2¹/₄ x 4"	30.00
Hippo, cookie jar, Brush Pottery.	350.00
Lion, bank, cast iron, still, gold enamel paint, red painted details to eyes and mouth, 5" l	48.00
Lion, pin dish, cov, white milk glass, 4³/₄ x 3¹/₂"	10.00
Monkee, holding branch at left side, bottle opener, black body, tan chest and face markings, brown branch, John Wright Co, 2¹/₂" h	130.00
Owl, creamer, milk glass	25.00
Owl, thermometer, plaster body, 6" h	75.00
Ox, planter, pulling covered wagon, Occupied Japan, 2¹/₂ x 5³/₄"	12.00
Penguin, salt and pepper shakers, pr, gold paint on blue ground, Grindley Pottery, paper label, 3⁵/₈" h	20.00
Rabbit, candy container, papier-mâché, Germany	55.00
Rabbit, door knocker, old paint	125.00
Rabbit, windup, plastic, with spring motor, 9" l	30.00
Ringneck Pheasant, figure, crystal, hollow base, K R Haley Glassware Co, 11¹/₂" h	20.00
Sheep, cast iron, still, gold toned enamel painted finish, coin slot at base of neck, some age patina, 5¹/₂" l	48.00
Skunk, bank, earthenware, Napco, Japan, paper label, 6¹/₂" h	6.00

Lion, produce label, Lion Brand Selected Vegetables, ©1925, 9" h, 7" w, $4.00.

Squirrel, figure, ceramic, gold paint on teal ground,
Grindley Pottery, paper label on tail, 3¼" h **15.00**

Squirrel, figure, Red Rose Tea premium **5.00**

Squirrel, windup, tin body, fur tail, nut in mouth, jumping action, mkd "Made in Occupied Japan," 5" h **70.00**

Swan, planter, mkd "Frankoma/228," 5¾ x 7½" **25.00**

Trout, bottle opener, cast iron, red, orange, and green
body, Wilton Products, 5" l **80.00**

Turtle, cookie jar, upside down turtle, California
Originals. **50.00**

Turtle, doorstop, painted green, 8" l **85.00**

Whale, paperweight, brass, 2¼ x 3¼", paper label **8.00**

Zebra, figure, ceramic, gold stripes, Grindley Pottery,
5¾" h **25.00**

ANIMATION ART

To understand animation art, one must understand its terminology. The vocabulary involving animation cels is very specific. The difference between a master, key production, printed or publication, production, and studio background can mean thousands of dollars in value.

A "cel" is an animation drawing on celluloid. One second of film requires over twenty animation cels. Multiply the length of a cartoon in minutes times sixty times twenty-four in order to approximate the number of cels used in a single cartoon strip. The vast quantities of individual cels produced are mind-boggling. While Walt Disney animation cels are indisputably the most sought after, the real bargains in the field exist elsewhere. Avoid limited edition serigraphs. A serigraph is a color print made by the silk-screen process. Although it appears to be an animation cel, it is not.

References: Jeff Lotman, *Animation Art: The Early Years, 1911–1954,* Schiffer Publishing, 1995; Jeff Lotman, *Animation Art: The Later Years, 1954–1993,* Schiffer Publishing, 1996.

Periodicals: *Animated Life,* PO Box 2182, Uniontown, PA 15401; *Animation Magazine,* 28024 Dorothy Dr, Ste 300, Agoura Hills, CA 91301; *In Toon,* PO Box 487, White Plains, NY 10603.

Collectors' Club: Animation Art Guild, Ltd, 330 W 45th St, Ste 9D, New York, NY 10036.

Gouache on Celluloid, *101 Dalmatians,* Walt Disney
Studio, 1961, 5½ x 11½" cel of 3 of Pongo's and
Perdita's pups, cel trimmed to 12½ x 29", framed **$1,265.00**

Gouache on Celluloid, Bugs Bunny's Busting Out All
Over, Warner Bros. Studio, 1980, 6¼ x 6" full figure
cel of Bugs Bunny from animated TV show, Chuck
Jones production number "CJ-53" on bottom edge,
untrimmed, matted **350.00**

Gouache on Celluloid, Foghorn Leghorn, Warner Bros.
Studio, 1983, 7 x 7½" (including signature) cel from
animated film, signed by Friz Freleng, with Warner
Bros. copyright and seal, untrimmed, framed **630.00**

Gouache on Celluloid, The Jetsons, Hanna-Barbera
Studio, 1962, 3 x 6¼" cel of George at controls of
family's flying car as 1¼ x 1" cel of Elroy in space bubble blasts off for school, from original animated TV
show, cels trimmed to 6¼ x 8½", framed **860.00**

Gouache on Celluloid, *The Jungle Book,* Walt Disney
Studio, 1967, 6 x 4½" cel of Baloo holding Mowgli,
cel trimmed to 12 x 16", framed **1,100.00**

Gouache on Celluloid, Yogi Bear and Boo Boo, Hanna-
Barbera Studio, c1960, 7½ x 9½" hand-inked full figure cels set over portion of background overlay cel
and paper backing, prepared by studio for promotional and publicity purposes, cels trimmed to 8 x 10",
matted, cel paint professionally restored **550.00**

Gouache on Celluloid with Tempera Background Sheet,
George of the Jungle, Jay Ward Studio, 1967, 9 x 11¾"
hand-inked cel of George, Ursula, and Shep, over
tropical scene, untrimmed, framed **975.00**

Pencil on Animation Sheet, *Fantasia,* Walt Disney
Studio, 1940, Hyacinth Hippo prepares for "Dance of
the Hours," blue and black pencil, 8¼ x 10½", framed. . **1,150.00**

Pencil on Animation Sheet, *Orphan's Picnic,* Walt
Disney Studio, 1936, Donald Duck throwing tantrum,
red and black pencil, 3¼ x 4½", matted **400.00**

Pencil on Animation Sheet, The Flintstones, Hanna-
Barbera Studio, c1960, 6 x 10" original model sheet
drawing from early prime time animated TV show,
features 4 full figure poses of Fred Flintstone, light
creasing, few small margin spots, small edge tear,
matted **485.00**

Watercolor and India Ink on Heavyweight Paper,
Pinocchio, Walt Disney Studio, 1940, heartbroken
Geppetto carries Pinocchio from sea following escape
from Monstro the Whale, signed by artist Gustaf
Tenggren, 10½ x 14", framed **39,000.00**

APPLIANCES

The turn of the century saw the popularity of electric kitchen appliances increase to the point where most metropolitan households sported at least one of these modern conveniences. By the 1920s, innovations and improvements were occurring at a rapid pace. The variations designed for small appliances were limitless.

Some "firsts" in electrical appliances include:

1882 Patent for electric iron (H. W. Seeley [Hotpoint])
1903 Detachable cord (G. E. Iron)
1905 Toaster (Westinghouse Toaster Stove)
1909 Travel iron (G. E.)
1911 Electric frying pan (Westinghouse)
1912 Electric waffle iron (Westinghouse)
1917 Table Stove (Armstrong)
1918 Toaster/Percolator (Armstrong "Perc-O-Toaster")
1920 Heat indicator on waffle iron (Armstrong)
1920 Flip-flop toasters (all manufacturers)
1920 Mixer on permanent base (Hobart Kitchen Aid)
1920 Electric egg cooker (Hankscraft)
1923 Portable mixer (Air-O-Mix "Whip-All")
1924 Automatic iron (Westinghouse)
1924 Home malt mixer (Hamilton Beach #1)
1926 Automatic pop-up toaster (Toastmaster #1h-A-A)
1926 Steam iron (Eldec)
1937 Home coffee mill (Hobart Kitchen Aid)
1937 Automatic coffee maker (Farberware "Coffee Robot")
1937 Conveyance device toaster ("Toast-O-Lator")

References: E. Townsend Artman, *Toasters*, Schiffer Publishing, 1996; Helen Greguire, *Collector's Guide to Toasters & Accessories,* Collector Books, 1997; *Toasters and Small Kitchen Appliances: A Price Guide,* L-W Book Sales, 1995.

Collectors' Clubs: Electric Breakfast Club, PO Box 306, White Mills, PA 18473; Old Appliance Club, PO Box 65, Ventura, CA 93002; Upper Crust: The Toaster Collectors Assoc, PO Box 529, Temecula, CA 92593.

Note: For additional listings see Fans, Electric and Porcelier Porcelain.

Blender, Osterizer, chrome, beehive shaped base, 1940s. . . . **$30.00**
Blender, Sears, Roebuck & Co, white enameled body **30.00**
Blender, Waring, enameled body, Bakelite lid, early
   1950s. **20.00**
Broiler, Mirro Corp, aluminum, 1950s **25.00**
Broiler, Regal Co, aluminum, stylized handles, 1950s. **30.00**
Coffeepot, Coffeemaster, Sunbeam, chrome, 2 tier **35.00**
Coffeepot, Flavo Matic, West Bend, silo shaped, gold
   colored aluminum, 1950s **40.00**
Coffeepot, Forman Family, urn shaped, chrominum on
   brass. **20.00**
Coffeepot, Royal Family Housewares, Bakelite handles
   and knobs. **25.00**
Coffeepot, Superfast, Farberware, egg shaped, patented
   1958–73. . . . . **15.00**
Food Cooker, Nesco Electric Casserole, National Enamel
   & Stamping Co, Inc, Milwaukee, WI, cream colored
   body, green enamel lid, high/low control, 3-prong
   plug, early 1930s, 9" d. **25.00**
Fry Pan, Sunbeam, "Controlled Heat Automatic Frypan,
   1930. . . . . **15.00**
Hot Plate, Buffet Queen, chrome, Bakelite handles,
   2 burners, 1940s **20.00**
Hot Plate, Signature, Montgomery Ward, white, chrome
   top, 1940s. **20.00**
Hot Plate, Westinghouse, Mansfield, OH, round top,
   green porcelain metal top surrounding element, hol-
   low legs, no control, 7½" d top, 1920s. **25.00**
Iron, Landers, Frary, and Clark, Universal, 1924–38 . . . . **20.00**

Iron, Steam-O-Matic, cast aluminum, 1930s. **20.00**
Malt Mixer, Machine Craft, Los Angeles, CA, Model B,
   18¾" h **60.00**
Mixer, Dormey, Dormeyer, hand held **15.00**
Mixer, Mixmaster, Sunbeam, pink, 1950s **100.00**
Mixer, Sunbeam Jr, yellow enamel body, hand held,
   1950s **35.00**
Roaster, Dominion Electric Co, chrome, attached cord **35.00**
Roaster, Sunbeam, Bakelite handles, 1952 . . . . **40.00**
Sandwich Grill, Victorian Sandwich Grill, Berstead Mfg
   Co, Fostoria, OH and Oaksville, Ontario, Canada,
   rect, nickel body, permanent plates, flared legs,
   curved mounts, black turned handles, 1920s, 10" l **20.00**
Toaster, General Mills, Minneapolis, MN, Cat #GM5A,
   2-slice pop-up chrome body, black Bakelite base,
   white dec sides, AC/DC, red, knob, light and dark
   control, early 1940s. **20.00**
Toaster, Toastwell, chrome, loaf shaped, 1940s. **50.00**
Toaster, Westinghouse, chrome, brown mottled Bakelite
   base, 1936–46 . . . . **50.00**
Waffle Iron, Hotpoint, General Electric, chrome, black
   wooden handles and knobs, round, 1930s **45.00**
Waffle Iron, Manning Bowman & Co, chrome, white
   Bakelite handles, 1924 . . . . **50.00**
Waffle Iron, Westinghouse, chrome, black Bakelite han-
   dles with incised leaf design, 1950s **40.00**
Waffle Iron/Grill, Dominion, Dominion Electric Co,
   brown Bakelite handles, sq **40.00**
Washing Machine, Bendix & Philco Bendix, Duomatic,
   27" cabinet, 1959–1967 . . . . **50.00**
Washing Machine, General Electric, early V12 perforat-
   ed basket models, 1961–1964 . . . . **25.00**
Washing Machine, Kenmore, Lady Kenmore, pink,
   turquoise, 1962–1964 . . . . **50.00**
Washing Machine, Maytag, combination washer/dryer,
   Models 340W, 440C, 1958–1965. . . . . **250.00**
Water Pot, Hurri-Hot Electri-Cup, Dormeyer, chrome
   body, automatic, 1950s **12.00**

ART POTTERY

Art pottery production was at an all-time high during the late 19th and early 20th centuries. At this time over one hundred companies and artisans were producing individually designed and often decorated pottery which served both utilitarian and aesthetic purposes. Artists often moved from company to company, some forming their own firms.

Condition, quality of design, beauty in glazes, and maker are the keys in buying art pottery. This category covers companies not found elsewhere in the guide.

References: Susan and Al Bagdade, *Warman's American Pottery and Porcelain,* Wallace-Homestead, Krause Publications, 1994; Paul Evans, *Art Pottery of the United States, Second Edition,* Feingold & Lewis Publishing, 1987; Ralph and Terry Kovel, *Kovels' American Art Pottery: Collector's Guide to Makers, Marks and Factory Histories,* Crown Publishers, 1993; David Rago, *American Art Pottery,* Knickerbocker Press, 1997; Dick Sigafoose, *American Art Pottery: A Collection of Pottery, Tiles and Memorabilia, 1800–1950,* Collector Books, 1997.

Newsletter: *Pottery Lovers Newsletter,* 4969 Hudson Dr, Stow, OH 44224.

Electric Beater, metal and glass, mkd "Chicago Electric Mfg. Co., Type AV, Made in U.S.A.," 3-cup capacity, $30.00.

Collectors' Club: American Art Pottery Assoc, PO Box 834, Westport, MA 02790.

Additional Listings: See California Faience, Clewell, Cowan, Fulper, Marblehead, Moorcroft, Newcomb, Niloak, North Dakota School of Mines, Potteries: Regional, Rookwood, Roseville, Teco, Van Briggle, Weller, and Zane.

American Art Clay Co., pair of Art Deco busts of a woman, 1 glossy ivory glaze, 1 turquoise glaze, stamped mark, 7" h **$275.00**

Ashby Guild, vase, cylindrical, ruby red aventurine glaze, oval stamp, 8¼" h, 4" w **500.00**

Batchelder, vase, bulging shoulder, narrow neck, clear to opaque olive green glaze, 8¼" h **200.00**

Batchelder, vase, flared shape, closed rim, mottled cobalt glossy glaze, brown ground, 5¾" h **275.00**

Bybee, creamer, cov, blue-green glaze, 5" h **20.00**

Bybee, vase, "Seldon Bybee" mark, dark red, 7" h **35.00**

Chelsea Keramic Art Works, dish, round, glossy speckled brown glaze over glossy blue ground, stamped "Chelsea Keramic Works/Robertson and Sons," 4¼" d **50.00**

Chelsea Keramic Art Works, vase, iridescent Sang-de Boeuf glaze, die stamped "CKAW," 6" h, 3½" w **1,450.00**

Dalpayrat, pitcher, spherical, matte green and red mottled glaze, stamped "Dalpayrat/23," 3" h, 3" d **325.00**

Delphin Massier, vase, corseted, painted with thistles in polychrome, sgd in ink, 7" h, 5¼" w **450.00**

Hampshire, vase, ovoid, emb with broad leaves, feathered blue and white matte glaze, imp "Hampshire Pottery," 7" h, 4" w **650.00**

Jugtown, bowl, Chinese blue glaze, Jugtown Ware stamp, 4" h, 7¼" d **550.00**

Jugtown, vase, ovoid, metallic gunmetal and Chinese blue glaze, imp "Jugtown Ware," 6" h, 5" w **450.00**

Jugtown, vase, pear shaped, mottled red and Chinese blue glaze, 5½" h, 4" d **1,600.00**

Jugtown, vessel, semi-ovoid, incised band near rim, red and turquoise Chinese blue glaze, Jugtown Ware stamp, 5½" h, 6½" d **2,750.00**

Merrimac, vase, tooled and applied dogwood blossoms and leaves, leathery matte green glaze, imp mark, hairline crack, 7½" h, 4¼" w **2,500.00**

Merrimac, vessel, tooled and applied underwater plants, matte green glaze, unmkd, artist sgd "EB," 8" h, 4¾" w . . **3,500.00**

North State, vase, corseted, 2 wrap-around handles, mottled dark red matte glaze, unmkd, 10¼" h, 7" w **600.00**

Norweta, vase, bulbous, white and blue crystalline glaze, stamped "Norweta," 10" h, 6¼" w **1,750.00**

Overbeck, figure, southern man in pink coat and light blue pants holding hat, mkd, 4¼" h **225.00**

Overbeck, tumbler, set of 4, band of green stylized grasshoppers, light yellow ground, 4" h **1,500.00**

Overbeck, vessel, excised with 3 panels of stylized birds in dusty pink against mauve ground, incised "OBK/FM," 5½" h, 5" w **3,000.00**

Paul Revere, trivet, goose on hill medallion, dark blue ground, impressed mark, 1924, 5½" d **600.00**

Paul Revere, vase, bulbous swirls, Robin's Egg blue semi-matte glaze, ink mkd "P.R.P./11-20," 1920, 8¾" h, 7¼" w **450.00**

Paul Revere, vase, ovoid, band of green trees on satin blue-gray ground, imp circular mark, small glaze bubble on body, 1924, 6¼ x 3½" **1,425.00**

Children's Dishes, plate, mug, and saucer, mkd "SEG/7-22/L...,"
price for set, $1,210.00. Photo courtesy Smith & Jones, Inc. Auctions.

Paul Revere, vase, tapering, closed-in rim, mottled flowing medium green microcrystalline glaze, ink mark and paper label, 7½" h, 7" w **375.00**

Pewabic, bowl, matte green glaze, high relief repeating leaves, imp "Pewabic" under maple leaves, 6¼" h, 2¾" d **1,550.00**

Pewabic, low bowl, emb with lily pads forming ring handles, flowing matte green glaze, imp "Pewabic," 2½" h, 8½" w **3,250.00**

Pewabic, vase, blue metallic glaze, pink and gold accents, 4" h **775.00**

Pisgah Forest, cameo vase, dec by Walter Stephen, white pioneering scene, dead matte gray ground, raised mark, 1953, 5½ x 3½" **250.00**

Pisgah Forest, vase, bulbous, celadon and caramel crystalline glaze, partially obscured mark, 8" h, 5¾" w **825.00**

Poxon, low bowl and flower frog, semi-matte brown, mauve, and green speckled glaze, imp "Poxon/Los Angeles," 3" h, 7½" w bowl **125.00**

Rekston, vase, bulbous, dec with slip-painted daffodils on glossy brown ground, stamp mark, 7¼" h, 5" w **175.00**

Saturday Evening Girls, bookends, pr, night scenes with owls, ink marked "S.E.G./11-21," flat chip on bottom of one, 1921, 4 x 5" **1,425.00**

School of Cleveland, William Sinz, bust of lady, ivory glaze, incised "W. Sinz," 7" h, 3½" w **300.00**

Vance Avon, vase, tapering, incised stylized trees in landscape in green and brown on amber ground, incised "Tollic/157," 11¼" h, 4½" d **1,700.00**

Volkmar/Durant Kilns, centerpiece bowl, wide rim tapering to base, crackled Persian glazes, turquoise int, blue ext, incised "Durant/1928," 6½" h, 13½" d **750.00**

Volkmar/Durant Kilns, vase, ovoid, ftd, thick mottled brown and yellow glaze, incised "Volkmar/1949," 9¼ x 5" **650.00**

Volkmar/Durant Kilns, vase, spherical, ftd, matte mottled green and yellow glaze, incised "Volkmar/1931," 6½ x 6" **550.00**

Walrath, centerpiece flower frog, figural nude, sheer matte green glaze with clay showing through, incised "Walrath," 8½" h, 6" w **750.00**

Walrath, paperweight, scarab, matte French blue glaze, incised "Walrath Pottery," 2¼" h, 3½" l **650.00**

Wannopee, pedestal, emb vinescroll dec, buttressed corners, majolica green glaze, imp mark, 5½" h, 6½" sq **55.00**

Wheatley, chamberstick, emb leaves, scroll handle, leathery matte green glaze, chip and flake to bobeche, unmkd, 4" h, 6" d **450.00**

Wheatley, jardiniere, 4 buttressed handles, leathery matte green glaze, 7" h, 7¾" w **3,000.00**

Wheatley, tile, emb lion, organic matte brown glaze, 7¾" sq **250.00**

Zark, vessel, emb with buttressed feet and stylized bows, matte blue and green glaze, inicsed "Ozark," 4½" h, 3¼" d **775.00**

ASHTRAYS

Ashtrays can be found made from every material and in any form imaginable. A popular subcategory with collectors is advertising ashtrays. Others include figural ashtrays or those produced by a particular manufacturer. It is still possible to amass an extensive collection on a limited budget. As more people quit smoking, look for ashtrays to steadily rise in price.

Reference: Nancy Wanvig, *Collector's Guide to Ashtrays,* Collector Books, 1997, out of print.

Advertising, Bud Light, ceramic, cream, dark blue letters outlined in red, 5¼" d **$5.00**

Advertising, Corning Glass Center, glass, blue name, center logo, 3½" sq **5.00**

Advertising, Disneyland, ceramic, pink and blue Magic Kingdom and Tinker Bell on white ground, 5" d **15.00**

Advertising, Hershey's, glass, center brown logo, 4" d **10.00**

Advertising, Jim Beam Bourbon Whiskey, metal, center bottle illus on white ground, name on red rim, 4½" d **5.00**

Advertising, Mack Trucks, ST, applied rest with bulldog figure in center, 6" d **20.00**

Advertising, Rock Island, glass, clear, red and white decal with "Rock Island The Road of Planned Progress...Geared to the Nation's Future," 4½ x 5 x 1¾" **20.00**

Art Deco, jadite, translucent pale green, gold enamel trim, triangular shape, 5" w **20.00**

Advertising, Fatima Turkish Cigarettes, ceramic, 3" h, 4" w, $175.00. Photo courtesy Collectors Auction Services.

Boot, glass, cobalt blue, 1 rest, 3¾" h **12.00**

Commemorative, "1776 Bicentennial 1976" above flag, eagle, and bell illus, "200 Years of Progress" below, 5⅜" d **8.00**

Cowboy, pot metal, copper finish, Japan, 5" l **20.00**

Elephant, bronze, white, sand casting, 6¼" l **55.00**

Fish, Chase Chrome, 6¼" l **20.00**

Indian Head, ceramic, red, white, blue, brown, and black, Japan, 3¾" w **5.00**

Pail, glass, 2½" h. **5.00**

Shoe, high style, brass, 1 rest, 4⅞" l **20.00**

Souvenir, Theodore Roosevelt National Park, ceramic, center with grazing buffalo on white ground, 5¼" d **5.00**

Western Hat, ceramic, yellow, Catalina Pottery, 6½" l **40.00**

World's Fair, aluminum, "Raytheon Souvenir-Bristol Industrial Exhibition," 1953 . . . . **15.00**

AUTO & DRAG RACING

The earliest automobile racing occurred in Europe at the end of the 19th century. By 1910, the sport was popular in America as well. The Indianapolis 500, first held in 1911, has been run every year except for a brief interruption caused by World War II. Collectors search for both Formula 1 and NASCAR items, with pre-1945 materials the most desirable.

References: Mark Allen Baker, *Auto Racing: Memorabilia and Price Guide,* Krause Publications, 1996; James Beckett and Eddie Kelley (eds.), *Beckett Racing Price Guide and Alphabetical Checklist, Number 2,* Beckett Publications, 1997; David Fetherston, *Hot Rod Memorabilia & Collectibles,* Motorbooks International, 1996; Jack MacKenzie, *Indy 500 Buyer's Guide,* published by author, 1996.

Periodical: *TRACE Magazine,* PO Box 716, Kannapolis, NC 28082.

Newsletter: *Quarter Milestones,* 53 Milligan Ln, Johnson City, TN 37601.

Collectors' Clubs: Auto Racing Memories, PO Box 12226, St Petersburg, FL 33733; National Indy 500 Collectors Club, 10505 N Delaware St, Indianapolis, IN 46280.

REPRODUCTION ALERT

Catalog, 501 Fiat and Winners 1925 Autodrome, illus, color lithos, photogravures **$175.00**

Coloring Book, Hot Rod, #1313, with soap box racer cut-out, color illus, 16 black and white pp, Abbott Publishing Co, WI, c1950, 11 x 12¾". **10.00**

Courtesy Card, Indianapolis Motor Speedway, May 30, 1951. . . . . **55.00**

Display, Fossil Watch Co, 3 joined replica motor oil cans, inscribed "Racer's Choice," small black and white checkered racing flag symbol, 1944, 3½ x 7 x 9¼" h **40.00**

Flag, cloth, black and white checkered pattern with "Speedway Souvenir" and race car in center oval, wood pole, c1950s, 17 x 17", price for pair **60.00**

Game, Crazy Car Race, Steven Mfg, 1972 . . . . **20.00**

Game, Flip It: Auto Race and Transcontinental Tour, De Luxe Game Corp, c1920s, 11⅜ x 9⅜ x 1" **45.00**

Paperweight, Indianapolis Motor Speedway "500 Mile Race, May 30, 1931," plaster cast, 3" h, 7¹/₂" l, $235.00. Photo courtesy Collectors Auction Services.

Postcard, Indy Speedway, early track image with trees in
infield, full-length aerial view, postmarked 1935 . . . . **10.00**
Poster, "12 Hours of Sebring," paper, Mar 22 and 23,
1963, 28¹/₂" h **275.00**
Program, 12th Annual Talladega 500-Alabama Inter-
national Motor Speedway, sgd by Buddy Baker, Cale
Yarborough, Darrell Waltrip, Benny Parsons, Bobby
Allison, David Pearson and James Hylton, 1980 . . . . **75.00**
Program, Indianapolis Motor Speedway Corp, 37th 500
Mile Race, May 30, 1953, paper, 105 pp, 8¹/₂ x 11" **65.00**
Ticket, Corona Road Race, May 30, 1953, price for pair **50.00**
Ticket, Indianapolis Speedway, 19th International 500
Mile Sweepstakes, Saturday, May 30, 1931 . . . . **75.00**
Trading Card, Winston Drag Racing 24K Gold, John
Force, Action Packed, common card. **12.00**
Tumbler, Indy souvenir, frosted, red racing car center,
1960s, 5¹/₈" h **10.00**

AUTOGRAPHS

Early autograph collectors focused on signature only, often discarding the document from which it was cut. Today's collectors know that the context of the letter or document can significantly increase the autograph's value.

Standard abbreviations denoting type and size include:

ADS   Autograph Document Signed
ALS   Autograph Letter Signed
AP   Album Page Signed
AQS   Autograph Quotation Signed
CS   Card Signed
DS   Document Signed
FDC   First Day Cover
LS   Letter Signed
PS   Photograph Signed
TLS   Typed Letter Signed

References: Mark Allen Baker, *The Standard Guide to Collecting Autographs, Krause Publications, 1999;* Kevin Martin, *Signautres of the Stars: A Guide for Autograph Collectors, Dealers, and Enthusiasts,* Antique Trader Books, 1998; George Sanders, Helen

Sanders, and Ralph Roberts, *The Sanders Price Guide to Autographs, 4th Edition,* Alexander Books, 1997; George Sanders, Helen Sanders and Ralph Roberts, *The Sanders Price Guide to Sports Autographs, 2nd Edition,* Alexander Books, 1997.

Periodicals: *Autograph Collector,* 510-A S Corona Mall, Corona, CA 91719; *Autograph Times,* 1125 Baseline Rd, #2-153-M, Mesa, AZ 85210.

Newsletters: *Autograph Research,* 862 Thomas Ave, San Diego, CA 92109; *Autographs & Memorabilia,* PO Box 224, Coffeyville, KS 67337.

Collectors' Clubs: The Manuscript Society, 350 N Niagara St, Burbank, CA 91505; Universal Autograph Collectors Club, PO Box 6181, Washington, DC 20044.

REPRODUCTION ALERT: Forgeries abound. Signatures of many political figures, movie stars, and sports heroes are machine or secretary signed rather than by the individuals themselves. Photographic reproduction can also produce a signature resembling an original. Check all signatures using a good magnifying glass or microscope.

Abbott, Bud and Lou Costello, AP, ink signatures on light
blue page, 3 x 2" **$550.00**
Astor, John Jacob, CS, 3 x 2" **195.00**
Backus, Jim, PS, black and white, 8 x 10". **50.00**
Benchley, Peter, typescript sgd, titled "Jaws-Chapter
One," contains first 3 paragraphs on white paper, blue
ink signature, 8 x 10". **65.00**
Blatty, William Peter, orig sketch of female face with
word "Boo!" in balloon coming from her mouth, on
7 x 10" white board. **150.00**
Carmichael, Hoagy, PS, black and white, casual pose,
8 x 10" **250.00**
Crichton, Michael, postcard sgd, color scene from
Jurassic Park, 7 x 5" **60.00**
Davis, Angela, CS, 5 x 3". **75.00**
Davis, Bette, program, American Film Institute Life
Achievement Award Dinner, A Salute to Bette Davis,
Mar 1, 1977, black ink signature on lavender page
oposite early black and white photo, 11 x 11" **150.00**
Dewey, Thomas E, TLS, 1939. . . . . **60.00**
Diddley, Bo, PS, color, dated 1997, 8 x 10" **95.00**
Duke, Charlie, Ed Mitchell, and Harrison Schmidt, astro-
nauts, FDC **125.00**
Duke, David, CS, black ink signature, 5 x 3" **50.00**
Edwards, Ralph, PS, sepia, 8 x 10". **45.00**
Eisenhower, Julie Nixon and David, PS, black and white,
dated 1991, 8 x 10". **75.00**
Fortas, Abe, ALS, official Supreme Court card, "Dear
Judge Bornstein-Thank you for your most welcome
letter. I'm very grateful-Abe Fortas," dated Oct 14,
1968, 6 x 4¹/₂". **250.00**
Garcia, Jerry, album sgd, *Go to Heaven* **350.00**
Garland, Judy, DS, bank check, filled in and sgd, Jan 22,
1965, check included in black mat to right of close-up
color photo, random glittering stars and music notes,
black metallic plate with name in gold letters beneath
photo, under glass, black frame, 28 x 16". **950.00**
Ginsburg, Allen, orig sketch of bedraggled flower with
"4AM my flower's wilted," on 4 x 6" yellow card **250.00**
Grey, Zane, check sgd, 1931 . . . . **200.00**

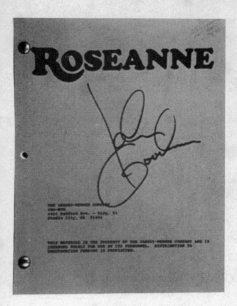

John Goodman, script from Roseanne show #701, Sep 14, 1993, 11" h, 8½" w, $198.00. Photo courtesy Collectors Auction Services.

AUTOMOBILES

The Antique Automobile Club of America instituted a policy whereby any motor vehicle (car, bus, motorcycle, etc.) manufactured prior to 1930 be classified as "antique." The Classic Car Club of America expanded the list, focusing on luxury models made between 1925 and 1948. The Milestone Car Society developed a similar list for cars produced between 1948 and 1964.

Some states, such as Pennsylvania, have devised a dual registration system for classifying older cars—antique and classic. Depending upon their intended use, models from the 1960s and 1970s, especially convertibles and limited production models, fall into the "classic" designation.

References: Robert H. Balderson, *The Official Price Guide to Collector Cars, Eighth Edition,* House of Collectibles, 1996; James T. Lenzke and Ken Buttolph (eds.), *1999 Standard Guide to Cars & Prices: Prices For Collector Vehicles 1901–1990, Eleventh Edition,* Krause Publications, 1998.

Periodicals: *Car Collector & Car Classics,* 8601 Dunwoody Pl, Ste 144, Atlanta, GA 30350; *Hemmings Motor News,* PO Box 100, Rt 9W, Bennington, VT 05201; *Old Cars Price Guide,* 700 E State St, Iola, WI 54990.

Collectors' Clubs: Antique Automobile Club of America, 501 W Governor Rd, PO Box 417, Hershey, PA 17033; Classic Car Club of America, 2300 E Devon Ave, Ste 126, Des Plaines, IL 60018; Milestone Car Society, PO Box 24612, Indianapolis, IN 46224; Veteran Motor Car Club of America, PO Box 360788, Strongsville, OH 44136.

Note: Prices are for cars in good condition.

Austin-Healey, 1959, Sprite, roadster, 4 cyl	$5,000.00
Buick, 1933, Model 50, sedan, 8 cyl	4,100.00
Buick, 1939, Roadmaster, sedan, 8 cyl	6,000.00
Buick, 1953, Super, hardtop, 8 cyl	6,000.00
Buick, 1959, Le Sabre, hardtop, 4 door, 8 cyl	2,000.00
Buick, 1965, Wildcat, convertible, 8 cyl	3,200.00
Cadillac, 1962, Park Avenue, short sedan, V 8 cyl	5,000.00
Cadillac, 1967, Fleetwood, sedan, V 8 cyl	6,000.00
Cadillac, 1969, Fleetwood, limousine, V 8 cyl	3,000.00
Chevrolet, 1959, Biscayne, sedan, 8 cyl	2,000.00
Chevrolet, 1960, Bel Air, coupe, hardtop, V 8 cyl	3,600.00
Chevrolet, 1962, Fleetside, pickup, long box	7,500.00
Chevrolet, 1964, Chevelle, station wagon, 4 door, 8 cyl	2,000.00
Chevrolet, 1969, Corvair, coupe, 6 cyl	2,000.00
Chevrolet, 1973, El Camino, pickup	4,200.00
Chevrolet, 1974, Caprice Classic, convertible, V 8 cyl	5,000.00
Chrysler, 1937, Royal, sedan, 6 cyl	3,200.00
Chrysler, 1949, New Yorker, sedan, V 8 cyl	3,000.00
Chrysler, 1953, Windsor, sedan, V 8 cyl	3,000.00
Chrysler, 1959, Saratoga, sedan, V 8 cyl	2,000.00
Chrysler, 1963, Imperial, convertible, V 8 cyl	6,800.00
Crosley, 1950, station wagon, 4 cyl	1,300.00
Dodge, 1947, Model D24, sedan, 6 cyl	2,500.00
Dodge, 1947, Series WD-15, pickup, ¾ ton	1,250.00
Dodge, 1959, Custom Royal, sedan, 4 door, V 8 cyl	2,500.00
Dodge, 1964, Dart 170, sedan, 2 or 4 door, 6 cyl	2,000.00
Dodge, 1970, Polara 500, convertible, V 8 cyl	5,000.00
Ford, 1950, Custom, sedan, 2 door, V 8 cyl	2,200.00
Ford, 1953, Customline, sedan, 2 door, V 8 cyl	1,700.00

Gypsy Rose Lee, program, "Biography," Denver Playtime/ Artists' Repertory Theatre, blue ink signature, 1948	195.00
Hearst, Patricia, TLS, plain white stationery, 7 x 9"	350.00
Herman, Woody, PS, sepia, 5 x 7"	75.00
Holmes, Oliver Wendell, CS, dated 1928, 5 x 3"	350.00
Karloff, Boris, partly printed DS, sgd in blue ballpoint, 1965, 8 x 14"	425.00
Kelly, Walt, ADS, bank check, green ink signature, 1956	325.00
Kiss, PS, Gene Simmons, Paul Stanley, Peter Criss, and Ace Frehley, full color, in costume, 8 x 10"	250.00
LaBelle, Patti, PS, black and white glossy, 8 x 10"	60.00
Little Richard, PS, black and white, blue felt tip pen signature, 8 x 10"	95.00
Mailer, Norman, TLS, dated Dec 15, 1955, 3 paragraphs, full signature, 8 x 10"	145.00
Mead, Margaret, newsphoto, article sgd under image	55.00
Meredith, James H, FDC, 1974	75.00
Miller, Glenn, TLS, Glenn Miller Orchestra stationery, green ink signature, orig envelope, dated Jul 24, 1939, 8½ x 11"	650.00
Nutting, Wallace, LS, personal stationery, imprinted vignette of one of his works on upper center of first page, orig holograph envelope, 1941, 2 pp	275.00
Pershing, John J, TLS, thank-you note, hotel stationery	145.00
Price, Vincent, CS, orig profile sketch	150.00
Ringling, John, ticket, top imprinted "Ringling Bros and Barnum & Bailey combined show/Pass...Season 1924," black ink signature on bottom, 4 x 2½"	550.00
Roosevelt, Eleanor, TLS, *Woman's Home Companion* stationery, thank-you note, 8 x 10"	135.00
Rubic, Enro, FDC, 1983	50.00
Sagan, Carl, FDC, 1975	95.00
Stewart, Rod, program, Rod Stewart-Labor Day '84 RKO Radio Concert Series, signature across face, opens to 16 x 20" poster	95.00
Thaxter, Cilia, AQS, 30-line poem, plain paper, 5 x 7"	60.00
Vaughn, Stevie Ray, PS, full color, "Soul to Soul" above blue felt tip pen signature, 8 x 10"	550.00
Wendelin, Rudolph, orig ink sketch of Smokey the Bear with "Be Extra Careful with Fire, Prevent Forest Wildfires, 1973" on 4 x 8" white paper, sgd with both names on lower white blank area	125.00

Ford, 1956, Country Squire, station wagon, V 8 cyl **4,000.00**
Ford, 1960, Galaxie, town sedan, V 8 cyl supercharged . . . **2,500.00**
Ford, 1966, Thunderbird, hardtop, V 8 cyl **5,000.00**
Ford, 1967, Fairlane, sedan, V 8 cyl. **1,800.00**
Ford, 1971, LTD, convertible, V 8 cyl **3,500.00**
General Motors, 1955 pickup, ¾ ton, 6 cyl **3,000.00**
Hudson, 1933, Essex-Terraplane Series, mail delivery
  van **6,000.00**
Hudson, 1955, Hornet, sedan, V 8 cyl. **1,400.00**
International Harvester, 1964, Scout Series, pickup,
  2-wheel drive **1,100.00**
Lincoln, 1955, Custom, sedan, 8 cyl **5,000.00**
Lincoln, 1965, Continental, sedan, 4 door, V 8 cyl. **6,000.00**
Mercury, 1968, Cougar XR7 GTE 428, coupe, V 8 cyl **5,000.00**
Oldsmobile, 1963, Jetfire, coupe, V 8 cyl **5,000.00**
Oldsmobile, 1973, Custom Cruiser, station wagon, V 8
  cyl **2,000.00**
Plymouth, 1957, Plaza, coupe, V 8 cyl **3,000.00**
Plymouth, 1964, Barracuda, coupe, V 8 cyl 273 . . . . **3,000.00**
Pontiac, 1939, Deluxe 8, touring sedan, 8 cyl **4,200.00**
Pontiac, 1968, Catalina, hardtop, 2 door, V 8 cyl **2,400.00**
Pontiac, 1969, Bonneville, station wagon, V 8 cyl **1,750.00**
Pontiac, 1970, Tempest, sedan, 6 cyl. **2,000.00**
Pontiac, 1973, Ventura, coupe, 6 cyl **1,750.00**
Studebaker, 1963, Lark Regal, station wagon, V 8 cyl. **3,000.00**
Triumph, Spitfire 1500, roadster, I-4 engine **3,500.00**
Volkswagen, 1953, Micro Bus, station wagon, 4 cyl. **4,000.00**
Volkswagen, 1974, Thing **4,000.00**

AUTOMOBILIA

Automobilia can be broken down into three major collecting categories—parts used for restoring cars, advertising and promotional items relating to a specific make or model of car, and decorative
accessories in the shape of or with an image of an automobile.
Numerous subcategories also exist. Spark plugs and license plates
are two examples of automobilia with reference books, collectors
clubs, and periodicals dealing specifically with these fields.

References: David K. Bausch, *The Official Price Guide to
Automobilia,* House of Collectibles, 1996; Steve Butler,
Promotionals 1934–1983: Dealership Vehicles in Miniature, L-W
Book Sales, 1997; Lee Dunbar, *Automobilia,* Schiffer Publishing,
1998; David Fetherson, *Hot Rod Memorabilia and Collectibles,*
Motorbooks International, 1996; Ron Kowalke and Ken Buttolph,
Car Memorabilia Price Guide, 2nd Edition, Krause Publications,
1998; Jim and Nancy Schaut, *American Automobilia: An
Illustrated History and Price Guide,* Wallace-Homestead, Krause
Publications, 1994.

Periodicals: *Hemmings Motor News,* PO Box 100, Rt 9W,
Bennington, VT 05201; *Mobilia,* PO Box 575, Middlebury, VT
05753; *PL8S: The License Plate Collector's Magazine,* PO Box 222,
East Texas, PA 18046.

Collectors' Clubs: Automobile License Plate Collectors Assoc, Inc,
PO Box 77, Horner, WV 26372; Automobile Objects D'Art Club,
252 N 7th St, Allentown, PA 18102; Hubcap Collectors Club, PO
Box 54, Buckley, MI 49620; Spark Plug Collectors of America,
4262 County Rd 121, Fulton, MO 65251.

**Pocketknife, Ford, blue and cream colored plastic grips, 3" l
closed size, $138.00.** Photo courtesy Collectors Auction Services.

Brake Light, chromed housing, steel bumper bracket,
  clear and red lenses at top, green lens above emb
  "SLO," Ace, 10" w **$20.00**
Brochure, "See America First...In America's Stand-Out
  Car," color and black and white illus, 1941 . . . . **25.00**
Can, Frigidtest Antifreeze, tin, qt, full contents, 5½" h,
  4" d **85.00**
Can, Guardian Imperial Oil, tin, "Parafield Oils Limited
  Ottawa Canada," qt, 6½" h, 4" d, missing top **40.00**
Can, Sunoco Sunfleet Oil, tin, police car, cement truck,
  bulldozer, tractor and 2 trucks around bottom, Sun Oil
  Co, Philadelphia, PA, qt, full contents, 5½" h, 4" d **45.00**
Case, Gargoyle Cylinder Lubricant, metal, 2 porcelain
  adv signs on front, "1054" on metal slug plate, 19" h,
  5" d **400.00**
Cigarette Case, Oldsmobile Dealer Jamboree, alu-
  minum, hard molded plastic divided inserts, applied
  3" l brass plate on lid with "White Sulphur Springs,
  West Virginia Oldsmobile Dealer Jamboree March 31
  April 1, 1941," 5 x 3 x 2". **40.00**
Display, AC Spark Plug, tin, repaired spark plugs in
  boxes, 10" h, 11" d **165.00**
Display, Bosch Battery, countertop, chalkware, 25" h,
  7½" w **600.00**
Display, Buss Auto Fuses, metal, 7½" h, 8½" w **140.00**
Gearshift Knob, figural dice, hard rubber, black with red
  dots, threaded brass insert in base, 1930s, 1¼" sq **25.00**
Globe, Mobil Premium Gas, plastic, 13½" d **200.00**
Globe, National Premium, 1 pc, glass, painted lettering,
  19" h, 22" w **165.00**
Globe, Red Crown, milk glass, 1 pc, metal base, 16½" d **210.00**
Horn, Beep-Beep Car Horn, painted, red and black
  enamel, colorful decal depicting alien and spaceship
  center, complete with horn button, wiring and mount-
  ing accessories, Jubilee, 6 x 5¾ x 3", MIB. **25.00**
Key Ring, metal, Texaco, for men's room, 6¼" h, 3½" w **130.00**
License Plate, Arkansas, Land of Opportunity or Natural
  State **2.00**
License Plate, District of Columbia, inaugural, 1957 . . . . . . **150.00**
License Plate Attachment, Pembroke Air Park, Inc, paint-
  ed metal, reflective lettering, 6" h, 11" w **60.00**
Lighter, figural Buick car, metal, lighter opens when
  hood ornament pulled, Occupied Japan, 1¾" h **150.00**
Patch, Automobile Association of America, cloth,
  woven, red on white, Official Timer Midget Racing **15.00**
Salt and Pepper Shakers, pr, Mobilgas, plastic, decal
  reads "Basha's Service Station Main St. Westminster,
  Mass. Tel. Tr. 4-9977," 2⅝" h **90.00**
Sign, Atlantic, porcelain, 1 sided, 9" h, 13" w **45.00**
Sign, Michelin Tires, tin, 28½" h, 24" w **70.00**

Sign, Mobil Premium, porcelain, rounded edges, 12" h,
13½" w **10.00**
Sign, Pure-Pep, porcelain, "I.R. 48-712" at bottom,
12" h, 10" w **75.00**
Spark Plug, Champion Gas Engine Special, #34, ½" **15.00**
Spark Plug, Everfire, porcelain, repaired **65.00**
Spark Plug, Rex, mica, large plug, 18mm **18.00**
Tireflator, Eco, metal and glass, restored, 16½" h, 9" w **425.00**
Toy, station wagon, lightweight layered wood, plastic
windows, back door and side door opens, Buddy L
decal on doors, wood and metal wheels, Buddy L,
6" h, 19½" l **185.00**

AUTUMN LEAF

Autumn Leaf dinnerware was manufactured by Hall China
Company and issued as a premium by the Jewel Tea Company. The
pattern was originally produced between 1933 and 1978. Many
other companies produced matching kitchen accessories.

References: C. L. Miller, *The Jewel Tea Company: Its History and
Products,* Schiffer Publishing, 1994; Margaret and Kenn Whitmyer,
The Collector's Encyclopedia of Hall China, Second Edition,
Collector Books, 1994, 1997 value update.

Collectors' Club: National Autumn Leaf Collectors Club, 62200 E
236 Rd, Wyandotte, OK 74370.

Note: Pieces are in good condition with only minor wear to gold
trim unless noted otherwise

DINNERWARE

Baker, French, 4½" **$65.00**
Ball Jug **45.00**
Ball Tilt Pitcher **48.00**
Berry Bowl **8.00**
Bowl, 6¼" d **25.00**
Butter Dish, 1 lb **500.00**
Cake Server **550.00**
Candy Dish, metal base **500.00**
Casserole, round, 2 qt **25.00**
Cereal Bowl **14.50**
Coffeepot, drip **275.00**
Coffeepot, electric **400.00**
Cookie Jar, rayed **250.00**
Cookie Jar, Zeisel **150.00**
Creamer, J-Sunshine **40.00**
Creamer and Sugar, rayed **75.00**
Cream Soup **40.00**
Cup, conic **75.00**
Cup and Saucer **12.50**
Cup and Saucer, St Denis **56.00**
Custard Cup **9.50**
Dinner Plate **18.50**
Drip Jar, rayed **25.00**
Flat Soup **25.00**
Fondue Set **200.00**
Goblet, ftd, 10½ oz **60.00**
Gravy Boat **28.50**
Grease Bowl, cov **25.00**
Marmalade Liner **38.00**
Mayonnaise, cov, with underplate **50.00**

Mug, Irish **30.00**
Mustard, 3 pc **85.00**
Pepper Shaker **20.00**
Pickle Dish, Ruffled-D **35.00**
Pitcher, ice lip, Douglas **475.00**
Plate, 6" d **5.50**
Plate, 7" d **8.50**
Plate, 9" d **12.50**
Platter, oval, 13½" l **40.00**
Salad Bowl **20.00**
Salt and Pepper Shakers, pr **25.00**
Sugar Lid **25.00**
Teapot, Aladdin **75.00**
Teapot, rayed **55.00**
Tidbit, 2 tier **75.00**
Utility Jug **25.00**
Vegetable, divided, oval **175.00**
Warmer, oval **175.00**

MATCHING ACCESSORIES

Bread Box, tin **$150.00**
Candlesticks, pr **75.00**
Canister, tea, tin, copper lid, 4" h **35.00**
Clock, battery operated **250.00**
Clock, electric **695.00**
Coaster **10.00**
Dish Towel, cotton **40.00**
Flatware, 6 pc, ST **140.00**
Flour Sifter, tin **350.00**
Mixer Cover, plastic **45.00**
Placemat, plastic **40.00**
Skillet, 9½" d **90.00**
Thermos **325.00**
Tray, glass and wood **200.00**
Tumbler, flat, frosted, 4¾" h **36.00**
Tumbler, flat, frosted, 5½" h **23.00**
Vase **200.00**

Cake Plate, $22.00. Photo courtesy Ray Morykan Auctions.

AVIATION COLLECTIBLES

Most collections relating to the field of aviation focus on one of four categories—commercial airlines, dirigibles, famous aviators, or generic images of aircraft.

Early American airlines depended on government subsidies for carrying mail. By 1930, five international and thirty-eight domestic airlines were operating in the United States. A typical passenger load was ten. After World War II, four-engine planes with a capacity of 100 or more passengers were introduced.

The jet age was launched in the 1950s. In 1955 Capitol Airlines used British-made turboprop airliners in domestic service. In 1958 National Airlines began domestic jet passenger service. The giant Boeing 747 went into operation in 1970 as part of the Pan American fleet.

Reference: Richard R. Wallin, *Commercial Aviation Collectibles: An Illustrated Price Guide,* Wallace-Homestead, 1990, out of print.

Periodical: *Airliner,* PO Box 521238, Miami, FL 33125.

Collectors' Clubs: Aeronautica and Air Label Collectors Club, PO Box 1239, Elgin, IL 60121; CAL/NX211 (Charles Lindbergh), 913 Wylde Oak Dr, Oshkosh, WI 54904; World Airline Historical Society, 13739 Picarsa Dr, Jacksonville, FL 32225.

Baggage Tag, TWA, plastic, red, white "TWA Press," reverse with pocket for inserting identification, attached strap, 1960s. **$20.00**
Bank, Goodyear blimp, porcelain, pedestal base, 8½" l. **50.00**
Cap, souvenir, aviator style skull cap, "We Saw The Graf Zep" on sides **125.00**
Comic Book, Aviation Cadets, Street & Smith, 1943 . . . . **12.00**
Game, Flight Captain, E S Lowe, 1972 . . . . **20.00**
Game, International Airport, Magic Wand, 1975. . . . . **12.00**
Game, Jet Race Game, Built-Rite, 1960s **15.00**
Handkerchief, Pan American Airways, 12" sq **15.00**
Knife and Spoon, United Air Lines, star logo on end of handles, International Silver Co **20.00**
Letter Opener/Pen Knife, North Central Airways, white metal letter opener attached to gilt pen knife shaped handle with pearl-like insert panel, blade mkd "Colonial, Prov., R.I.". **20.00**
Magazine, *Sky Lines,* Aug 1933, 8½ x 11½". **15.00**
Manual, Jeppesen Airway Manual, brown leatherette cov, metal binder rings, ©1967 . . . . **20.00**
Paperweight, Goodyear-Zeppelin Corp, zeppelin hangar replica, "Goodyear Zeppelin" on sides, simulated side windows, 1930s **80.00**
Plate, Western Airlines, white porcelain, gold rim, gold and blue logo on side, bottom mkd "Western Airlines ABCO Tableware 0447-30850 Japan," 5½" d, price for set of 5 . . . . **20.00**
Playing Cards, Delta Air Lines, San Francisco on back. **10.00**
Poster, TWA to Las Vegas, 1953 . . . . **20.00**
Salt and Pepper Shakers, pr, TWA, plastic, tan, 1950s, 1 x 1¼" h. **15.00**
Scarf, Trans-Canada Airlines, blue, gray, green, black, red, and yellow on pink ground, color printed early airplanes around edge with large DC-8 in center, "TCA DC-8 Jetliner Service," 29" sq **20.00**
Schedule, Piedmont Airlines, color, flight schedule by Fairchild F27 Pacemaker aircraft, logo on front, 1958 . . . . . **20.00**

Desk Lighter, chrome, lighter pops up when propeller is turned, mkd "Made in U.S.A. Flint," 3¾" h, 5" wingspan, 6" l, $165.00. Photo courtesy Collectors Auction Services.

Sheet Music, *Lindy, Lindy,* black, white, and orange cov, Gilbert and Abel Baer, ©1927 . . . . **20.00**
Travel Bag, Pan Am, white vinyl, blue trim, loop handles, logo on each side, orig tag, 13 x 13", 1960s **25.00**
Tray, American Airlines, SP, emb American Airlines eagle flying to right, "AA" in center, orig box mkd "The Captain's Flagship American Airlines, Inc," 6" d **45.00**
Tumbler, American Air Lines, gold stylized Golden Falcon symbol, mkd "Made in Japan," 1940s, price for set of 12 . . . . **85.00**
Uniform, flight crew, blue sports coat with bullion stripes at cuffs, gilt buttons, c1961 . . . . **10.00**
Wings, pilot's, Transcontinental and Western Air Inc, 2 sided, gold toned bronze wing with Indian head facing left in center, 1930–50 . . . . **75.00**

AVON

David H. McConnell founded the California Perfume Company in 1886. Saleswomen used a door-to-door approach for selling their wares. The first product was "Little Dot," a set of five perfumes. Following the acquisition of a new factory in Suffern, New York, in 1895, the company underwent several name changes. The trade name Avon, adopted in 1929, was derived from the similarity the Suffern landscape shared with that of Avon, England.

Reference: Bud Hastin, *Bud Hastin's Avon & C.P.C. Collector's Encyclopedia, 15th Edition,* Collector Books, 1998.

Newsletter: *Avon Times,* PO Box 9868, Kansas City, MO 64134.

Collectors' Club: National Assoc of Avon Collectors, Inc, PO Box 7006, Kansas City, MO 64113.

Avonshire Blue Soap Dish and Soap, wedgwood blue and white over clear glass **$8.00**
Before and After, cologne and hair lotion set, 1953–54 . . . . . **35.00**
Cameo Brush and Comb, plastic, Rapture **3.00**
Country Kitchen Trivet, ceramic, 1980–82, 7½" l **6.00**

Cardinal, red glass, Bird of Paradise Cologne, 2 fl. oz., #32859, 4" h, 4½" l, $7.50.

Country Talc Shaker, gray and blue speckled metal can
  with shaker top, Charisma Talc, 1977–79, 3 oz 3.00
Enchanted Frog Sachet, cream colored milk glass with
  plastic lid, Occur!, 1973–76, 1.25 oz 5.00
Fire Fighter's Stein, ceramic, gold bell lid and trim, 1989,
  9" h 45.00
Four Wheel Drive Decanter, black glass, after shave,
  1987, 3 oz 8.00
Gold Cadillac Decanter, gold paint over clear glass,
  Wild Country After Shave,1969–73, 6 oz 10.00
Gone Fishing Decanter, blue glass boat, white plastic
  fisherman with yellow rod, Tai Winds, 1973–74, 5 oz 10.00
Honey Bear Baby, yellow painted glass, blue plastic
  bear on lid, 1974–76, 4 oz 4.00
Quail Decanter, brown glass, gold cap, Deep Woods
  After Shave, 1973–75, 5.5 oz 9.00
Remember When School Desk Decanter, black glass
  with light brown plastic seat front and desk top, red
  apple for cap, Cotillion Cologne, 1972–74, 4 oz 8.00
Silver Fawn Decanter, clear glass with silver coating,
  Charisma Cologne, 1978–79, .5 oz 3.00
Snail Perfume, clear glass, gold cap, Brocade, 1968–69,
  .25 oz 12.00
Super Cycle Decanter, gray glass, Sports Rally Bracing
  Lotion, 1971–72, 4 oz 9.00
Teatime Powder Sachet, frosted white with gold cap,
  Sonnet, 1974–75, 1.25 oz 7.00
Viking Discoverer Decanter, blue-green glass, red and
  white metal sail, Everest, 1977–79, 4 oz 10.00

BANKS

The earliest still banks were made from wood, pottery, gourds, and later, cast iron. Lithographed tin banks advertising various products and services reached their height in popularity between 1930 and 1955. The majority of these banks were miniature replicas of the products' packaging.

Ceramic figural banks were popular novelties during the 1960s and 1970s. The most recent variation of still banks are molded vinyl banks resembling favorite cartoon and movie characters.

References: Don Duer, *Penny Banks Around the World,* Schiffer Publishing, 1997; Beverly and Jim Mangus, *Collector's Guide to Banks,* Collector Books, 1998; Andy and Susan Moore, *Penny Bank Book: Collecting Still Banks,* Schiffer Publishing, 1984, 1997 value update; Tom and Loretta Stoddard, *Ceramic Coin Banks,* Collector Books, 1997; Vickie Stulb, *Modern Banks,* L-W Book Sales, 1997.

Newsletters: *Glass Bank Collector,* PO Box 155, Poland, NY 13431; *Heuser's Quarterly Collectible Diecast Newsletter,* 508 Clapson Rd, PO Box 300, West Winfield, NY 13491.

Collectors' Club: Still Bank Collectors Club of America, 4175 Millersville Rd, Indianapolis, IN 46205.

Note: All banks listed are still banks unless noted otherwise.

Baseball Mitt, holding ball, painted plaster, 1970s, 9½" h **$50.00**
Bugs Bunny, leaning against tree stump, metal, c1947, 5" h **90.00**
Fisherman, figural, bobbing head, painted composition,
  1960s, 7" h 45.00
Lassie, painted plaster, 1950s, 16½" h 85.00
Lone Ranger Strong Box, textured leatherette over brass,
  Lone Ranger on rearing Silver on front, Sun Life
  Insurance Co emblem on back, ©1938, 3½" h 120.00
Magic Mountain, figural character, painted composition,
  orange body with pink dots, 1960s, 6½" h 50.00
McGovern/Shriver, cardboard canister with tin top and
  bottom, "Small Change for Big Changes, 1972, 5" h,
  3" d 15.00
Nash Car, 1953–54 promotional, cast metal, 7½" l 75.00
Orphan Annie and Sandy, seated figures, ceramic,
  glossy, ©1982, 6½" h 20.00
Poll Parrot Shoes, metal and cardboard cylinder, 1½" h,
  1⅝" d 35.00
Porky Pig, painted composition, early 1940s, 6⅜" h 100.00
Radio, clear glass, figural radio, emb knobs and "Radio
  Bank" on front and back, 1930s, 4" l, 3" h 40.00
Rex Water Heaters, figural water heater, litho tin, 1930s,
  7½" h, 3" d 60.00
Robot Coin Sorting Bank, hard plastic, 1970s, 6" h 50.00
Rocket, "Dimes Space Bank," white plastic with blue
  space capsule and red base, early 1960s, 4¾" h 20.00
Schmoo, dark blue plastic, 7" h 75.00
Shell Motor Oil, figural shell symbol, hard plastic,
  1950s, 4" h 125.00
Strato Bank, cast metal, mechanical, rocket launches
  coins into moon, aqua colored, 1950s, 8" l, 3½" h 60.00
Truck, EZE-Orange, orange and white body, rubber tires,
  1950s, 7" l 60.00
TV Bank, hard plastic, 1960s, 5" h, MIP 15.00
Veedol Oil, oil can, litho tin, 1950s, 2¾" h, 2⅛" d 40.00

Phillips 66, clear glass, emb "Phill-Up with Phillips 66, See What You Save," 4¾" h, $150.00. Photo courtesy Collectors Auction Services.

BARBER SHOP, BEAUTY SHOP & SHAVING

The neighborhood barber shop was an important social and cultural institution in the first half of the 20th century. Men and boys gathered to gossip, exchange business news, and check current fashions. With the emergence of *unisex* shops in the 1960s, the number of barber shops dropped by half in the United States. Today, most men and women patronize the same shops for services ranging from haircuts to perms to coloring.

References: Ronald S. Barlow, *The Vanishing American Barber Shop,* Windmill Publishing, 1993; Lester Dequaine, *Razor Blade Banks,* published by author, 1998; Roy Ritchie and Ron Stewart, *Standard Guide to Razors, Second Edition,* Collector Books, 1998; Jim Sargent, *Sargent's American Premium Guide to Pocket Knives & Razors…, 4th Edition,* Books Americana, Krause Publications, 1995.

Collectors' Clubs: National Shaving Mug Collectors' Assoc, 320 S Glenwood St, Allentown, PA 18104; Safety Razor Collectors Guild, PO Box 885, Crescent City, CA 95531.

Ashtray, glass, round, red, white, and blue striped rim, "Porcelain Enameled Signs, Barber Poles, William Marvy Co. St. Paul 2, Minn." adv, 5" d **$80.00**

Barber Bottles, clear glass, fired-on labels, Lotion, Water, and Shampoo, Lan Lay, Inc, screw-on lids, set of 3 . . . . **50.00**

Barber Chair, child's, porcelain with cushion back and seat, wooden horse mounted in front, Koken, 45" h **2,200.00**

Burma Shave Road Signs, 2-sided, "Burma-Shave/The/ Sign/Of A/Perfect/Shave" on front, "Burma-Shave" on back, white lettering on red ground, each sign 17" h, 40" w, set of 6 . . . . **1,000.00**

Calendar, B Stuebeur's Sons Decorated Shaving Cups, paper with archival backing, metal band across top, calendar missing, 18¾" h, 12½" w **65.00**

Clock, Realistic Hair Beauty, round metal case with tin face and scrolled wire dec, 18" h, 15" w **20.00**

Comb Sales Rack, diecut cardboard display holder, "Gay Clip Combs," includes 6 plastic combs in various colors, each with metal clip, 9" h, 11" w **15.00**

Globe, "Massage, Barber, Bobbing," red and white painted metal frame, milk glass lenses, 15" d lens, 19½" h, 18" w **600.00**

Globe, metal frame with 2 glass lenses, "Beauty Shoppe" and profile of woman's head, 15" d **750.00**

Jar, cylindrical, frosted glass with "Antiseptic" and Red Cross symbol in red, chrome lid, 10" h, 3¾" d **60.00**

Jar, cylindrical with domed glass lid, Sanek Neck Strips, clear glass, decal label, aluminum lid, "©Kimberly Co. Mfrs. Neemar, Wis.," 9½" h, 5" d **150.00**

Razor, Gem Safety Razor, gold plated, white handle, plastic case, 1940s, 5⅛" l **12.00**

Razor Sterilizer, chrome, "Sterilizer Corp. of America, Brooklyn, NY," 9½" h, 7" w **175.00**

Shaving Mug, gilded Masonic emblem, 4" h **95.00**

Sign, "Beauty Shoppe" and profile of woman's head, porcelain, 12" h, 24" w **375.00**

Sign, Gillette, porcelain 2-sided flange, pictures safety razor and pkg of Gillette Blue Blades, 19½" h, 21½" w . . **3,350.00**

Sign, Jervis Antiseptic Hair Tonic, diecut cardboard standup, man kissing woman, c1970s, 27½" h **40.00**

BARBIE

The first Barbie fashion dolls, patented by Mattel in 1958, arrived on toy store shelves in 1959. By 1960, Barbie was a marketing success. The development of Barbie's boyfriend, Ken, began in 1960. Many other friends followed. Clothing, vehicles, doll houses, and other accessories became an integral part of the line.

From September 1961 through July 1972 Mattel published a Barbie magazine. At its peak, the Barbie Fan Club was the second largest girls' organization, next to the Girl Scouts, in the nation.

Barbie sales are approaching the 100 million mark. Annual sales exceed five million units. Barbie is one of the most successful dolls in history.

References: Fashion and Accessories: Joe Blitman, *Barbie Doll and Her Mod, Mod, Mod, Mod World of Fashion,* Hobby House Press, 1996; Joe Blitman, *Francie and Her Mod, Mod, Mod, Mod World of Fashion,* Hobby House Press, 1996; Sarah Sink Eames, *Barbie Doll Fashion, Vol. I: 1959–1967* (1990, 1998 value update), *Vol II: 1968–1974* (1997), Collector Books; Rebecca Ann Rupp, *Treasury of Barbie Doll Accessories: 1961–1995,* Hobby House Press, 1996.

General: Scott Arend, Karla Holzerland and Trina Kent, *Skipper: Barbie's Little Sister,* Collector Books, 1998; J. Michael Augustyniak, *The Barbie Doll Boom,* Collector Books, 1996; J. Michael Augustyniak, *Collector's Encyclopedia of Barbie Doll Exclusives and More,* Collector Books, 1997; Sibyl DeWein and Joan Ashabraner, *The Collectors Encyclopedia of Barbie Dolls and Collectibles,* Collector Books, 1977, 1996 value update; Robert Gardner, *Fashion Dolls Exclusively International: ID and Price Guide to World-Wide Fashion Dolls,* Hobby House Press, 1997; A. Glenn Mandeville, *Doll Fashion Anthology and Price Guide, 5th Revised Edition,* Hobby House Press, 1996; Marcie Melillo, *The Ultimate Barbie Doll Book,* Krause Publications, 1996; Lorraine Mieszala, *Collector's Guide to Barbie Doll Paper Dolls,* Collector Books, 1997.

Patrick C. Olds and Myrazona R. Olds, *The Barbie Doll Years: 1959–1996, Third Edition,* Collector Books, 1999; Margo Rana, *Barbie Doll Exclusively for Timeless Creations: 1986–1996, Book III,* Hobby House Press, 1997; Margo Rana, *Barbie Exclusives, Book II,* Collector Books, 1996; Margo Rana, *Collector's Guide to Barbie Exclusives: Identification and Values,* Collector Books, 1995; Jane Sarasohn-Kahn, *Contemporary Barbie: Barbie Dolls 1980 and Beyond, 1998 Edition,* Antique Trader Books, 1997; Beth Summers, *A Decade of Barbie Dolls and Collectibles, 1981–1991,* Collector Books, 1996; Kitturah B. Westenhouser, *The Story of Barbie, Second Edition,* Collector Books, 1999.

Periodicals: *Barbie Bazaar,* 5617 6th Ave, Kenosha, WI 53140; *Miller's Barbie Collector,* PO Box 8722, Spokane, WA 99203.

Collectors' Club: Barbie Doll Collectors Club International, PO Box 586, White Plains, NY 10603.

ACCESSORIES

Carrying Case, Barbie Goes Travelin', vinyl, multicolored car and plane illus, black handle, ©1965, 3 x 10 x 15½" **$30.00**
Diary, One Year Diary, vinyl, glossy, ©Mattel 1961, 1 x 4 x 5½" **30.00**
Game, Barbie's Little Sister Skipper, Mattel, 1964 . . . . **75.00**
Hangers, plastic, white, "For Barbie, Francie, Skipper And Skooter Doll Clothes And All Doll Cases and Trunks For These Dolls," Standard Plastic Products, ©Mattel 1965, 5½ x 6" sealed package, MIP **30.00**
High Stepper Horse, Mattel, 1994 . . . . **30.00**
Magazine, *Mattel Barbie Magazine,* Jan-Feb 1969, 22 pp **15.00**
Ornament, Hallmark, 1994, MIB **75.00**
Thermos, litho metal, red plastic cup, full color illus, black ground, ©Mattel 1962, 8½" h **35.00**

CLOTHING

Barbie and Midge Fashion Outfit, #2084, blouse, cloth, plain, with red vinyl clutch purse, ©1961 Mattel, MIP **$30.00**
Barbie and Midge Fashion Outfit, #2084, sheath skirt, with black plastic cradle-style telephone, ©1962 Mattel, MIP **30.00**
Barbie and Midge Fashion Outfit, #2084, skirt, cloth, plain, gathered, with red plastic open-toe pump shoes, ©1962 Mattel, MIP **35.00**
Barbie and Midge Fashion Outfit, playsuit, scoop neck, floral pattern, wide red vinyl belt, golden bracelet, ©1962 Mattel, MIP **35.00**

Rollerblade Snack Stand, #7243, ©1991, $25.00.

Barbie Fashion Outfit, #912, Cotton Casual, navy blue and white striped sunback dress, yellow/orange accent fabric bows on bodice, with white plastic open-toe pump shoes and fashion catalogue, ©1958 Mattel, MIP **85.00**
Barbie Fashion Outfit, #986, Sheath Sensation, red fabric dress, whtie straw hat with red ribbon hatband, with white plastic open-toe pump shoes, white fabric gloves and fashion catalogue, ©1958 Mattel, MIP **85.00**
Campus Sweetheart, #1616 . . . . **500.00**
Garden Tea Party, #1606, 1964, MIP **125.00**
Ken Fashion Outfit, hooded sweatshirt, orange, white drawstring at neck, hand warmer sleeve pocket at waist, ©1961 Mattel, MIP **35.00**
Picnic Set, #967, 1959–61 . . . . **200.00**

DOLLS, BARBIE

Angel Face Barbie, #5640, 1982 . . . . **$10.00**
Barbie Swirl Ponytail, #850, ash and lemon blonde, 1964 . . . . **300.00**
Barbie Twist & Turn, #1160, 1966 . . . . **175.00**
Barbie with Growin' Pretty Hair, #1144, 1970 . . . . **150.00**
Bubblecut Barbie Sidepart, #850, 1962 . . . . **400.00**
Day-to-Night Barbie, #7945, 1984 . . . . **10.00**
Dramatic New Living Barbie, #1116, 1969 . . . . **125.00**
Dream Bride Barbie, #1623, 1991 . . . . **10.00**
Fashion Jeans Barbie, #5315, 1981 . . . . **15.00**
Gold Medal Olympic Barbie Skier, #7264, 1974 . . . . **40.00**
Hawaiian Barbie, #7470, 1975 . . . . **35.00**
Icelandic Barbie, #9844, Dolls of the World series, 1990 . . . . **50.00**
Kissing Barbie, #2597, 1978 . . . . **25.00**
Magic Curl Barbie, #3856, 1981 . . . . **10.00**
Romantic Bride Barbie, #5848, 1991 . . . . **15.00**
Sun Lovin' Malibu Barbie, #1067, 1978 . . . . **5.00**
Supersize Barbie, #9828, 1976 . . . . **75.00**
Talking Barbie Spanish, #8348, 1967 . . . . **450.00**
Tropical Barbie, #1017, 1985 . . . . **5.00**
Twirley Curls Barbie, #3379, 1982 . . . . **5.00**
Wal-Mart Frills and Fantasy, #1374, 1988 . . . . **15.00**
Western Stampin' Barbie, #10293, 1993 . . . . **8.00**
Woolworth's Sweet Lavender, #2522, 1992 . . . . **15.00**

DOLLS, BARBIE'S FRIENDS

Beach Blast Miko, #3244, 1988 . . . . $5.00
Busy Talking Steffie, #1186, 1971 . . . . 125.00
California Ken, #4441, 1987 . . . . 8.00
Francie Twist & Turn, #1170, 1965 . . . . 150.00
Free Moving Cara, #7283, 1974 . . . . 30.00
Free Moving Ken, #7280, 1974 . . . . 15.00
Free Moving PJ, #7281, 1974 . . . . 30.00
Gold Medal Olympic PJ Gymnast, #7263, 1974 . . . . 30.00
Growing Up Skipper, #7259, 1974 . . . . 40.00
Ken, #1020, bendable leg, 1965 . . . . 150.00
Midge, #3216, Cool Times series, 1988 . . . . 25.00
Midge, #9360, Barbie and the All Stars series, 1989 . . . . 15.00
New Good Lookin' Ken, #1124, 1969 . . . . 60.00
Rocker Dana, #1196, 1985 . . . . 10.00
Sensations Bopsy, #4967, 1987 . . . . 12.00
Skipper Pose 'N Play, 1973 . . . . 40.00
Skooter, #1040, 1965 . . . . 50.00
Sun Lovin' Malibu Christie, #7745, 1978 . . . . 5.00
Wet 'n Wild Kira, #4120, 1989 . . . . 5.00
Yellowstone Kelley, #7808, 1973 . . . . 175.00

PLAYSETS

Barbie Loves McDonald's Restaurant, #5559, 1983 . . . . $100.00
Fashion Stage, #1148, 1971 . . . . 75.00
Pizza Party Skipper's Pizza Shop 10.00
Skipper Deluxe Dream House 275.00
Step 'n Style Boutique, #2769, 1989 . . . . 35.00
Western Round Up, #5018, 1981 . . . . 25.00

VEHICLES

Allen's Roadster $125.00
Around Town Scooter 20.00
Baywatch Rescue Boat 15.00
Hot Wheels Barbie Camaro, First Edition, MIB 65.00
Jaguar XJS 50.00
Travelin' Trailer/Off-Road Vehicle and Horse Trailer 75.00
United Airlines Barbie Friend Ship 185.00

BARWARE

During the late 1960s and early 1970s it became fashionable for homeowners to convert basements into family rec rooms, often equipped with bars. Most were well stocked with both utilitarian items (shot glasses and ice crushers) and decorative accessories. Objects with advertising are usually more valuable than their generic counterparts.

References: Mark Pickvet, *The Encyclopedia of Shot Glasses,* Glass Press, 1998; Stephen Visakay, *Vintage Bar Ware,* Collector Books, 1997.

Collectors' Club: International Swizzle Stick Collectors Assoc, PO Box 1117, Bellingham, WA 98227.

Note: See also Breweriana, Cocktail Shakers, and Whiskey Bottles.

Bottle Stopper, kissing couple, wood, carved, hp, press
    lever in back, they turn and kiss each other $35.00
Coaster, Ye Tavern Brew, Lafayetter Brewery, Lafayetter,
    IN, red, yellow, and black, 3" d 6.00

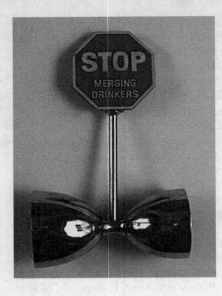

Drink Measure, "Stop, Merging Drinkers," chrome and plastic, $3.00.

Cocktail Shaker, aluminum, Bakelite base and top, 8
    matching aluminum goblets and tray, West Bend
    Aluminum Co, c1933 . . . . 75.00
Ice Bucket, aluminum, green ceramic liner, 1960s 10.00
Ice Bucket, plastic inlay, Servemaster, 1950–60s, 7" h 8.00
Lamp, hanging, plastic shade with stained glass designs,
    Anheuser Busch logo, globe shaped clear glass bulb
    cover inside, 22" d 40.00
Liquor Set, liquor bottle and 2 shot glasses, crock style
    bottle with crossed bones at neck, skull stopper, emb
    "Name Your Poison" across face of bottle, 2 matching
    brown glaze skull shot glasses, "Hand painted
    Tilso—Japan" paper label, 1950s 25.00
Martini Set, 4 pc, gold and black dec, brass wire rack,
    1970s 35.00
Martini Set, glass, pitcher and glasses, pheasants dec,
    brass stirrer 20.00
Swizzle Stick, glass, cobat blue 1.50
Vodka Dispenser, M*A*S*H 4077th Vodka Dispensing
    System, clear glass IV bottle, with stand and roses,
    orig box 20.00

BASEBALL CARDS

Baseball cards were originally issued by tobacco companies in the late 19th century. The first big producers of gum cards were Goudey Gum Company of Boston (1933–41) and Gum, Inc. (1939). After World War II, Gum, Inc.'s successor, Bowman, was the leading manufacturer. Topps, Inc. of Brooklyn, New York, followed. Topps bought Bowman in 1956 and monopolized the field until 1981 when Fleer of Philadelphia and Donruss of Memphis challenged the market.

References: James Beckett, *The Official 2000 Price Guide to Baseball Cards, 19th Edition,* House of Collectibles, 1999; James Beckett and Theo Chen (eds.), *Beckett Baseball Price Guide, Number 20,* Beckett Publications, 1998; Allan Kaye and Michael McKeever, *Baseball Card Price Guide, 1997,* Avon Books, 1996; Bob Lemke (ed.), *1999 Standard Catalog of Baseball Cards, 8th Edition,* Krause Publications, 1998; Sports Collectors Digest, *1999 Baseball Card Price Guide, 13th Edition,* Krause Publications, 1999.

Periodicals: *Beckett Baseball Card Monthly,* 15850 Dallas Pkwy, Dallas, TX 75248; *Card Trade,* 700 E State St, Iola, WI 54990; *Tuff Stuff,* PO Box 569, Dubuque, IA 52004.

Bazooka, 1960, #4, Hank Aaron, Panel 2 . . . . **$50.00**
Bazooka, 1961, common player **3.50**
Bazooka, 1963, #17, Don Drysdale, Panel 6 . . . . **15.00**
Bazooka, 1967, #4, Richie Allen, Panel 2 . . . . **3.00**
Bazooka, 1971, #9, Bobby Murcer **2.50**
Bowman, 1948, #36, Stan Musial **200.00**
Bowman, 1949, #36, Pee Wee Reese **45.00**
Bowman, 1949, #65, Enos Slaughter **16.50**
Bowman, 1950, #251, Les Moss **4.50**
Bowman, 1951, #165, Ted Williams **175.00**
Bowman, 1952, #52, Phil Rizzuto **35.00**
Bowman, 1953, common player (1-112) **7.00**
Bowman, 1954, #177, Whitey Ford **25.00**
Bowman, 1955, common player (1-96) **2.00**
Bowman, 1989, #12, Billy Ripken . . . . **.02**
Bowman, 1995, #114, Mike Bovee . . . . **.10**
Burger King Phillies, complete set (23) **2.00**
Burger King Yankees, complete set (23) **2.50**
Donruss, 1981, #2, Rollie Fingers . . . . **.75**
Donruss, 1982, #29, Sparky Anderson . . . . **.10**
Donruss, 1983, #1, Fernando Valenzuela . . . . **.20**
Donruss, 1983, #43, Mickey Mantle puzzle card, Hall of
   Fame Heroes . . . . **.05**
Donruss, 1983, #152, Keith Hernandez . . . . **.20**
Donruss, 1984, #49, Lance Parrish . . . . **.40**
Donruss, 1985, #172, Wade Boggs **2.00**
Donruss, 1986, common player . . . . **.10**
Donruss, 1986, complete set (660) **80.00**
Donruss, 1987, #2, Roger Clemens . . . . **.50**
Donruss, 1987, #154, Willie Randolph . . . . **.10**
Donruss, 1990, complete set (12), Grand Slammers series **2.00**
Donruss, 1991, common player, Previews series **15.00**
Donruss, 1992, complete set (784) **15.00**
Fleer, 1923, #47, Babe Ruth **240.00**
Fleer, 1950, #47, Cy Young **2.00**
Fleer, 1959, complete set (80), Ted Williams series **525.00**
Fleer, 1962, #4, Brooks Robinson **20.00**
Fleer, 1981, complete set (660) **50.00**
Fleer, 1983, #463, Nolan Ryan **2.00**

Topps, 1976, #104, Cincinnati Reds checklist, $.75. Photo courtesy Ray Morykan Auctions.

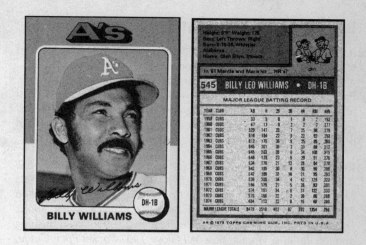

Topps, 1975, #545, Billy Lee Williams, $3.00. Photo courtesy Ray Morykan Auctions.

Fleer, 1987, common player . . . . **.05**
Fleer, 1987, complete set (44), Game Winners series **5.00**
Fleer, 1987, complete set (44), Hottest Stars series **4.00**
Fleer, 1987, complete set (132), Star Stickers series **15.00**
Fleer, 1988, #276, Jose Canseco . . . . **.50**
Hostess, 1978, complete singles (150) **50.00**
Hostess, 1979, #30, Greg Luzinski, Panel 10 . . . . **.25**
Hostess Twinkies, 1977, complete set (150) **65.00**
Kahn's Wieners, 1967, complete set (48) **300.00**
Kahn's Wieners, 1968, #30, Chico Ruiz **5.00**
Kellogg's, 1973, #25, Willie Stargell **1.00**
Kellogg's, 1976, common player **40.00**
Kellogg's, 1976, complete set (57) **18.00**
Kellogg's, 1978, #3, Mike Schmidt **1.00**
Leaf, 1948, #1, Joe DiMaggio **525.00**
Leaf, 1960, common player (73-145) **5.00**
Leaf, 1986, #260, Pete Rose . . . . **.40**
Leaf, 1987, #4, Darryl Strawberry . . . . **.15**
Leaf, 1988, complete set (264) **5.00**
O-Pee-Chee, 1966, #1, Willie Mays **60.00**
O-Pee-Chee, 1967, #45, Roger Maris **16.00**
O-Pee-Chee, 1968, #170, Jim Fregosi **70.00**
O-Pee-Chee, 1978, complete set **50.00**
Pinnacle, complete set, Mickey Mantle series **15.00**
Pinnacle, complete set, Philadelphia Phillies Photocards
   series **10.00**
Pinnacle, complete set, Rookies series **7.00**
Score, 1988, common player . . . . **.05**
Score, 1988, complete set (660) **15.00**
Topps, 1952, common player (1-80) **14.00**
Topps, 1953, #27, Roy Campanella **52.00**
Topps, 1954, complete set (250) **2,000.00**
Topps, 1955, #2, Ted Williams **100.00**
Topps, 1956, #230, Chico Carrasquel **4.00**
Topps, 1958, #187, Sandy Koufax **55.00**
Topps, 1960, common player (1-440) **1.00**
Topps, 1961, #228, Yankees Team **10.00**
Topps, 1977, #120, Rod Carew **2.00**
Topps, 1978, complete set (726) **80.00**
Upper Deck, 1989, complete set (800) **125.00**
Upper Deck, 1990, #4, Curt Young . . . . **.05**
Upper Deck, 1991, complete low series (1-700) **15.00**
Wheaties, 1937, common player, series 9 . . . . **12.00**

BASEBALL MEMORABILIA

Baseball traces its beginnings to the mid-19th century. By the turn of the century it had become America's national pastime.

The superstar has always been the key element in the game. Baseball greats were popular visitors at banquets, parades, and more recently at baseball autograph shows. Autographed items, especially those used in an actual game, command premium prices. The bigger the star, the bigger the price tag.

References: Mark Allen Baker, *Sports Collectors Digest Baseball Autograph Handbook, Second Edition,* Krause Publications, 1991; Mark Baker, *Team Baseballs: The Complete Guide to Autographed Team Baseballs,* Krause Publications, 1992; David Bushing, *Sports Equipment Price Guide,* Krause Publications, 1995; David Bushing and Joe Phillips, *Vintage Baseball Glove 1997 Pocket Price Guide, Vol. 1, No. 5,* published by authors, 1997; Douglas Congdon-Martin and John Kashmanian, *Baseball Treasures: Memorabilia From the National Pastime,* Schiffer Publishing, 1993; Kevin Keating and Mike Kolleth, *The Negro League Autograph Guide,* Antique Trader Books, 1998; Mark Larson, *Sports Collectors Digest Complete Guide to Baseball Memorabilia, Third Edition,* Krause Publications, 1996; Mark Larson, Rick Hines, and Dave Platta (eds.), *Mickey Mantle Memorabilia,* Krause Publications, 1993; Tuff Stuff (eds.), *Baseball Memorabilia Price Guide,* Antique Trader Books, 1998; Jim Warren II, *Tuff Stuff's Complete Guide to Starting Lineup: A Pictorial History of Kenner Starting Lineup Figures,* Antique Trader Books, 1997.

Periodicals: *Baseball Hobby News,* 4540 Kearny Villa Rd, San Diego, CA 92123; *Sports Collectors Digest,* 700 E State St, Iola, WI 54990; *Tuff Stuff,* PO Box 569, Dubuque, IA 52004.

Collectors' Clubs: Society for American Baseball Research, PO Box 93183, Cleveland, OH 44101; The Glove Collector, 14057 Rolling Hills Ln, Dallas, TX 54240.

Note: See Hartland Figures for additional listings.

Ashtray, porcelain, white, colorful baseball, bat and top
    hat logo with blue "New York Yankees" in center
    inside gold ring, 8" sq **$20.00**
Autograph, Ted Williams, PS, color printed drawing,
    blue signature, 8 x 10" **25.00**
Bat, Louisville Slugger, P27, Robin Young, sgd, unused,
    1984 . . . . **350.00**
Bobbing Head, ceramic, Cincinnati Reds, full decals,
    green base with white bottom, 7³/₄" h **25.00**
Book, *Baseball and Softball Rules Book,* Draper-Maynard
    Co Athletics, 29 pp, 1936 . . . . **30.00**
Bottle Cap, Coca-Cola, Tug McGraw, New York Mets,
    1967–68 . . . . **1.00**
Desk Set, baseball and card, on oak base, sgd by Don
    Mattingly, Rawlings, 1984 . . . . **20.00**
Doll, Jackie Robinson, composition, fully jointed, paint-
    ed molded hair and facial features, incomplete,
    Allied-Brand Doll Mfg Co, c1950, 13" h **180.00**
Folder, "Salute To The Champions Night," Yankee
    Stadium, Saturday Sep 25, 1954, 9 x 12" **65.00**
Game, All-Pro Baseball, Ideal, 1967 . . . . **40.00**
Game, Brett Ball Ninth Inning Game, 1981 . . . . **30.00**
Game, Electric Baseball, Electric Game Co, 1940s **60.00**
Glove, leather, dark gray, worn, 1920s **100.00**

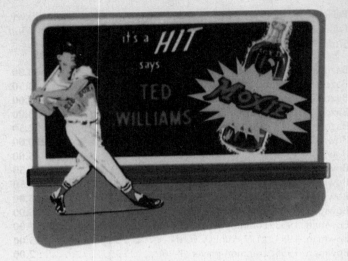

Sign, "It's a HIT says Ted Williams," Moxie adv, diecut cardboard, easel back, orig mailer, c1950s, 11 x 13¹/₂", **$1,925.00.** Photo courtesy Wm. Morford.

Glove, Ted Williams Signature model, #16156, Sears **25.00**
Handbook, Baseball's 100th Anniversary, Esso premium,
    52 pp, statistics, bluetone photos, and records, 1939,
    5¹/₂ x 8¹/₂" **20.00**
Magazine, *Sports Illustrated,* Stan Musial cov, Jul 1952 . . . . . . **35.00**
Paperback Book, *Mickey Mantle/The Indispensable
    Yankee,* first edition, May 1961, 4¹/₄ x 7" **20.00**
Patch, uniform, San Francisco Giants All-Star Game, 1984 . . . **30.00**
Pennant, felt, blue, "New York Yankees" with Uncle Sam,
    1950–60s, 28" l **20.00**
Pin, gilt, color enamel KC Royals logo in center, "Second
    World Series" at top, "Royals" at bottom, with plastic
    snap case, 1 x 1¹/₄" **40.00**
Pinback Button, Vernon Gomez of the New York
    Yankees, litho tin, ³/₄" d **20.00**
Poster, Let's Go Mets, *Sports Illustrated,* 1969 . . . . **35.00**
Program, 1964 Yankees-Cardinals World Series, 68 pp,
    8¹/₂ x 11¹/₄" **40.00**
Shirt, wool, light gray button-down front, maroon satin-
    like "Cardinals" sewn across front, black and red pip-
    ing trim, "80" sewn on back, Coane, Philadelphia, PA,
    1940s **35.00**

BASKETBALL CARDS

Muriad cigarettes issued the first true basketball trading cards in 1911. In 1933 Goudey issued the first basketball cards found in gum packs. The era of modern hoop basketball trading cards dates from 1948 when Bowman created the first set devoted exclusively to the sport. By the 1950s Topps, Exhibit Supply Company, Kellogg's, Wheaties, and other food manufacturers joined with Bowman in creating basketball trading cards. Collectors regard the 1957–58 Topps set as the second true modern basketball set.

Today basketball trading card sets are issued by a wide variety of manufacturers. Collectors also must contend with draft card series, special rookie cards, insert or chase cards and super premium card sets. Keeping up with contemporary issues is time consuming and expensive. As a result, many collectors focus only on pre-1990 issued cards.

References: James Beckett, *The Official 2000 Price Guide to Basketball Cards, 9th Edition,* House of Collectibles, 1999; Sports Collectors Digest, *1999 Standard Catalog of Basketball Cards, 2nd Edition,* Krause Publications, 1998; Tuff Stuff (eds.), *Tuff Stuff's Complete Basketball Card Price Guide & Checklist,* Antique Trader Books, 1998.

Periodicals: *Beckett Basketball Card Magazine,* 15850 Dallas Pkwy, Dallas, TX 75248; *Sports Cards,* 700 E State St, Iola, WI 54990.

Fleer, 1973, #18, "The Shots," Free Throw	$.35
Fleer, 1988–89, #43, Dennis Rodman	5.00
Fleer, 1990–91, complete set (198)	3.00
Fleer, 1991–92, complete set (400)	5.00
Fleer, 1992–93, #299, Scottie Pippen	.05
Fleer, 1993–94, #3, Patrick Ewing, All Stars series	1.50
Globetrotters Cocoa Puffs 28, 1971–72, #23, Meadowlark Lemon	1.00
Globetrotters Cocoa Puffs 28, 1971–72, #28, Freddy "Curly" Neal	1.50
Globetrotters Cocoa Puffs 28, 1971–72, complete set (28)	20.00
Hoops, 1989–90, complete set (352)	14.00
Hoops, 1990–91, complete set (440)	7.00
Hoops, 1992–93, #337, Larry Bird, Tournament of the Americas	.05
Hoops, 1992–93, complete set (3), More Magic Moments series	32.00
Hoops, 1994–95, complete set (450)	3.00
SkyBox, 1990–91, complete set (423)	10.00
SkyBox, 1991–92, complete set (659)	25.00
Topps, 1957–58, common card (1–80)	20.00
Topps, 1969–70, #1, Wilt Chamberlain	20.00
Topps, 1970–71, common card (1–110)	1.00
Topps, 1970–71, complete set (175)	450.00
Topps, 1972–73, #215, Billy Cunningham	1.00
Topps, 1974–75, #1, Kareem Abdul-Jabbar	3.50
Topps, 1974–75, complete set (264)	150.00
Topps, 1981–82, #41, Darrell Griffith	.15
Ultra, 1993–94, #145, Charles Barkley	.05
Upper Deck, 1991–92, #45, Magic Johnson	.10
Upper Deck, 1991–92, complete set (10), Jerry West Heroes series	4.50
Upper Deck, 1991–92, complete set (500)	10.00
Upper Deck, 1992–93, complete set (10), Larry Bird series	4.50
Wonder Bread, Globetrotters, 1974, complete set (6)	20.00

BASKETBALL MEMORABILIA

The first basketball game was played on a regulation 94 x 50' court in 1891. James Naismith, physical director of the Y.M.C.A. College, Springfield, Massachusetts, originated the game. Early basketball collectibles relate to high school and college teams.

Professional basketball was played prior to World War II. However, it was not until 1949 and the founding of the United States National Basketball Association that the sport achieved national status. Competing leagues, franchise changes, and Olympic teams compete for collector loyalty.

Reference: Roderick Malloy, *Malloy's Sports Collectibles Value Guide,* Attic Books, Wallace-Homestead, Krause Publications, 1993.

Sticker Book, A Golden Book #2398, ©1992 USA Basketball, $4.00.

Coin, NCAA Illinois Final Four, 1989	$50.00
Figure, Karl Malone, Kenner Starting Lineup, 1988	200.00
Game, Basketball Card Game, Built-Rite, 1940s	25.00
Magazine, *Basketball Sport Stars,* Wilt Chamberlain, 1973	12.00
Magazine, *Basketball Weekly,* NCAA All-Americans, Mar 1968	8.00
Media Guide, Celtics, 1980–81	30.00
Media Guide, New York Nets, 1970–71	8.00
Ornament, Magic Johnson, Hoop Stars Keepsake Ornament, Hallmark, MIB	20.00
Poster, Billy Cunningham, *Sports Illustrated,* 1968–71	15.00
Sticker, Pete Maravich, Topps, 1971–72	8.00
Ticket Stub, NBA All-Star Game, Los Angeles, 1972	8.00
Ticket Stub, NCAA Division 1 Final Four, Kansas City, 1954	20.00
Valentine's Cards, Michael Jordan, 32 cards and envelopes, MIB	20.00

BAUER POTTERY

John Bauer founded the Paducah Pottery in Paducah, Kentucky, in 1885. John Andrew Bauer assumed leadership of the pottery in 1898 following the death of John Bauer. In 1909 the pottery moved its operations to Los Angeles, California.

The company's award winning artware line was introduced in 1913. Molded stoneware vases were marketed shortly thereafter.

In 1931 Bauer Pottery began production of its most popular line—Ring ware. Decorated in brightly colored glazes, it included over a hundred different shapes and sizes in table and kitchen lines. Ring ware proved to be Bauer's most popular and profitable pattern. Other successful lines include Monterey (1936–45), La Linda (1939–59), and Brusche Contempo and Monterey Moderne (1948–61). Increasing competition at home and abroad and a bitter strike in 1961 forced Bauer to close its doors in 1962.

References: Jack Chipman, *Collector's Encyclopedia of Bauer Pottery,* Collector Books, 1997; Mitch Tuchman, *Bauer: Classic American Pottery,* Chronicle Books, 1995.

Newsletter: *Bauer Quarterly,* PO Box 2524, Berkeley, CA 94702.

Brusche Contempo, gravy, pink speck	$20.00
Brusche Contempo, tea set, teapot and four #46 mugs, spice green	50.00
Brusche Contempo, vegetable, indigo brown, 7½" d	20.00
Gloss Pastel Kitchenware, batter bowl, yellow	80.00
Gloss Pastel Kitchenware, cookie jar	75.00
Gloss Pastel Kitchenware, custard, gray	18.00
Gloss Pastel Kitchenware, jug, 1 qt.	35.00
Gloss Pastel Kitchenware, teapot, Aladdin, 8 cup	125.00
La Linda, ball jug, ice lip, gray	100.00
La Linda, bread and butter plate, pink, 6" d	6.00
La Linda, carafe, chartreuse, wood handle	25.00
La Linda, creamer, turquoise	20.00
La Linda, cup and saucer, dark brown	20.00
La Linda, custard, ivory	15.00
La Linda, dinner plate, chartreuse	18.00
La Linda, dinner plate, ivory	15.00
La Linda, fruit dish, yellow	12.00
La Linda, ramekin, burgundy	8.00
La Linda, salt shaker, tall, turquoise	15.00
La Linda, teapot, 8 cup, olive green	35.00
La Linda, tumbler, dark brown, 8 oz	15.00
La Linda, vegetable bowl, pink, 9½" d	25.00
Monterey Moderne, bread and butter plate, burgundy, 6" d	10.00
Monterey Moderne, butter dish, ivory	50.00
Monterey Moderne, chop plate, burgundy, 13" d	45.00
Monterey Moderne, coffee server, orange-red, wood handle, 8 cup	40.00
Monterey Moderne, cup, green	15.00
Monterey Moderne, gravy boat, burgundy	40.00
Monterey Moderne, luncheon plate, 9½" d, blue	12.00
Monterey Moderne, nesting bowls, orange-red, set of 3, 7", 8", and 9" d	125.00
Monterey Moderne, pitcher, 2 qt, green	45.00
Monterey Moderne, platter, yellow, 17" l	45.00
Monterey Moderne, sauce boat, burgundy	45.00
Monterey Moderne, soup bowl, burgundy, 7" d	30.00
Monterey Moderne, vegetable, divided, blue	45.00
Ring, batter bowl, burgundy, 1 qt.	100.00
Ring, butter dish, cov, orange-red.	150.00
Ring, canister, 6"	75.00
Ring, canister, 6¾"	125.00
Ring, casserole, individual, 5½" d	50.00
Ring, casserole, orig holder, orange, 7" d	130.00
Ring, chop plate, orange-red, 17" d	225.00
Ring, cup and saucer, after dinner	50.00
Ring, dinner plate, white, 10" d	20.00
Ring, eggcup, turquoise	85.00
Ring, jug, 1 qt.	50.00
Ring, mixing bowl, olive green, 1 qt.	25.00
Ring, mustard	150.00
Ring, nesting bowls, set of 3, 6", 7", and 8", 9" d	115.00
Ring, nappy, #5, black	65.00
Ring, pickle dish	20.00
Ring, platter, oval, 9" l	25.00
Ring, punch bowl, 14" d	250.00
Ring, relish, 3 part, 10½" d	40.00
Ring, soufflé dish	150.00
Ring, sugar shaker, jade green	295.00
Ring, tumbler, delph blue, metal handle, 6 oz	30.00
Ring, vegetable, divided, oval	70.00

BEANIE BABIES

The market is flooded with Beanie Baby price guides. Consider carefully how accurately they reflect the secondary retail market. A few years from now, their only value will be the ability to look nostalgically back on the craze and think "if I had only sold then."

These values are highly conservative and far more realistic than those found in many Beanie Baby price guides. They reflect the market. They **DO NOT** prop the market. With a few exceptions, e.g., the very first Beanie Babies, most are selling at one-half to one-third of book—the more recent the example, the greater the discount. The Beanie Baby market collapse is at hand. A year from now, sellers will thank their lucky stars if they can get these prices.

All items are priced each. Beanie Babies without tags have little or no value. New Tag = hang tag with star; Old Tag = hang tag without star; R = retired; D = discontinued.

References: Sharon Brecka, *Bean Family Pocket Guide,* Antique Trader Books, 1999; Les and Sue Fox, *The Beanie Baby Handbook,* West Highland Publishing, 1997; Peggy Gallagher, *The Beanie Baby Phenomenon, Volume 1: Retired,* published by author, 1997; Rosie Wells, *Rosie's Price Guide for Ty's Beanie Babies,* Rosie Wells Enterprises, 1997.

Periodicals: *Beans! Magazine,* PO Box 569, Dubuque, IA 52004; *Mary Beth's Beanie World Monthly,* PO Box 500, Missouri City, TX 77459.

Ally the Alligator, new tag, R 10/1/97	$15.00
Ants the Anteater, new tag	5.00
Batty the Bat, new tag	5.00
Bernie the St Bernard, new tag	5.00
Blackie the Bear, new tag	5.00
Blackie the Bear, old tag	25.00
Blizzard the Snow Tiger, new tag, R 5/1/98	8.00
Bronty the Brontosaurus, old tag, R 6/1/96	300.00
Brownie the Bear, old tag, R 7/1/93	600.00
Bubbles the Fish, new tag, R 5/11/97	25.00
Bucky the Beaver, old tag, R 5/11/97	45.00
Caw the Crow, old tag, R 6/1/96	300.00
Chilly the Polar Bear, old tag, R 12/31/94	750.00
Chocolate the Moose, old tag	50.00
Chops the Lamb, new tag, R 1/1/97	25.00
Congo the Gorilla, new tag	5.00
Coral the Fish, old tag, R 1/1/97	60.00
Curly the Bear, new tag	5.00
Daisy the Cow, old tag	30.00
Derby the Horse, white dot on forehead, new tag	5.00
Digger the Crab, orange, old tag, R 7/1/95	325.00
Digger the Crab, red, old tag, R 5/11/97	50.00
Doby the Doberman, new tag	5.00
Doodle the Rooster, new tag, R 7/1/97	18.00
Ears the Bunny, old tag, R 5/1/98	30.00
Fetch the Golden Retriever, new tag	5.00
Flash the Dolphin, old tag, R 5/11/97	50.00
Flip the Cat, old tag, R 10/1/97	35.00
Floppity the Bunny, lavender, new tag, R 5/1/98	8.00
Flutter the Butterfly, old tag, R 6/1/96	300.00
Freckles the Leopard, new tag	5.00
Garcia the Bear, tie-dyed, new tag, R 10/1/97	75.00
Gobbles the Turkey, new tag	5.00
Gracie the Swan, new tag, R 5/1/98	8.00
Grunt the Razorback, old tag, R 5/11/97	75.00

Glory the Bear, new tag, $5.00.

Happy the Hippo, lavender, old tag, R 5/1/98	45.00
Hippity the Bunny, mint green, new tag, R 5/1/98	8.00
Hoot the Owl, old tag, R 10/1/97	40.00
Hoppity the Bunny, pink, new tag, R 5/1/98	8.00
Iggy the Iguana, new tag	5.00
Inch the Worm, felt antennae, old tag, D 6/1/96	80.00
Inky the Octopus, tan, with mouth, old tag, D 7/1/95	300.00
Jobber the Parrot, new tag	5.00
Jolly the Walrus, new tag, R 5/1/98	8.00
Kiwi the Toucan, old tag, R 12/31/96	75.00
Kuku the Cockatoo, new tag	5.00
Lefty the Donkey, new tag, R 12/31/96	100.00
Legs the Frog, old tag, R 10/1/97	50.00
Liberty the Bear, new tag, R 12/31/96	100.00
Lizzy the Lizard, tie-dyed, old tag, R 1/1/95	350.00
Lucky the Ladybug, 7 glued-on dots, old tag, D 12/31/96	125.00
Lucky the Ladybug, 11 printed spots, new tag, R 5/1/98	8.00
Lucky the Ladybug, 21 printed spots, D	100.00
Manny the Manatee, new tag, R 5/11/97	30.00
McDonald's Teenie Beanie Babies, 1997, R 4/97	5.00
Mel the Koala, new tag	5.00
Nanook the Husky, new tag	5.00
Nip the Cat, white face and belly, old tag, R 7/1/95	225.00
Nuts the Squirrel, new tag	5.00
Patti the Platypus, magenta, old tag, R 7/1/96	275.00
Peace the Tie-Dyed Bear, new tag	20.00
Peanut the Elephant, light blue, old tag, R 5/1/98	125.00
Peking the Panda, old tag, R 1/1/95	700.00
Pinchers the Lobster, old tag, R 5/1/98	40.00
Pouch the Kangaroo, new tag	5.00
Pounce the Cat, new tag	5.00
Prance the Cat, new tag	5.00
Puffer the Puffin, new tag	5.00
Punchers the Lobster, old tag, D 7/1/93	1,250.00
Quackers the Duck, with wings, old tag, R 5/1/98	30.00
Radar the Bat, old tag, R 5/11/97	100.00
Rainbow the Chameleon, new tag	5.00
Righty the Elephant, new tag, R 1/1/97	100.00
Ringo the Raccoon, old tag	30.00
Rocket the Bluejay, new tag	5.00
Rover the Dog, new tag, R 5/1/98	8.00

Scottie the Terrier, new tag, R 5/1/98	8.00
Seamore the Seal, old tag, R 10/1/97	120.00
Slither the Snake, old tag, R 12/31/95	800.00
Sly the Fox, brown belly, new tag, D 7/1/96	50.00
Smoochy the Frog, new tag	5.00
Snip the Siamese Cat, new tag	5.00
Snowball the Snowman, new tag, R 12/31/97	10.00
Sparky the Dalmatian, new tag, R 5/11/97	30.00
Spike the Rhino, new tag	5.00
Spinner the Spider, new tag	5.00
Spooky the Ghost, old tag, R 12/31/97	35.00
Spot the Dog, with spot, old tag, R 10/1/97	35.00
Spunky the Cocker Spaniel, new tag	5.00
Steg the Stegosaurus, old tag, R 12/1/96	300.00
Sting the Manta Ray, new tag, R 1/1/97	40.00
Stinky the Skunk, old tag	20.00
Stretch the Ostrich, new tag	5.00
Stripes the Tiger, orange, fuzzy belly, old tag, D	300.00
Stripes the Tiger, orange, old tag, D 7/1/96	150.00
Tabasco the Bull, red feet, new tag, R 1/1/97	65.00
Tank the Armadillo, 7 ridges, old tag, R 7/1/96	95.00
Teddy the 1997 Holiday Bear, new tag, R 12/31/97	20.00
Teddy the Bear, brown, old face, old tag, R 7/1/95	900.00
Teddy the Cranberry Bear, new face, old tag, R 7/1/95	500.00
Tracker the Basset Hound, new tag	5.00
Trap the Mouse, old tag, R 7/1/95	400.00
Tusk (Tuck) the Walrus, new tag, R 1/1/97	40.00
Twigs the Giraffe, old tag, R 5/1/98	25.00
Velvet the Panther, old tag, R 10/1/97	40.00
Waddle the Penguin, old tag, R 5/1/98	20.00
Waves the Whale, new tag, R 5/1/98	8.00
Web the Spider, old tag, R 7/1/95	400.00
Weenie the Dachshund, old tag, R 5/1/98	20.00
Whisper the Deer, new tag	5.00
Wrinkles the Bulldog, new tag	5.00
Ziggy the Zebra, old tag, R 5/1/98	25.00
Zip the Cat, white paws, old tag, R 5/1/98	30.00

BEATLES

Beatlemania took the country by storm in 1964, the year the Beatles appeared on "The Ed Sullivan Show." Members of the Fab Four included George Harrison, John Lennon, Paul McCartney, and Ringo Starr (who replaced original drummer Pete Best in 1962). The most desirable items were produced between 1964 and 1968 and are marked "NEMS."

The group disbanded in 1970 and individual members pursued their own musical careers. John Lennon's tragic murder in New York City in 1980 invoked a new wave of interest in the group and its memorabilia.

References: Jeff Augsburger, Marty Eck, and Rick Rann, *The Beatles Memorabilia Price Guide, Third Edition,* Antique Trader Books, 1997; Perry Cox, *The Official Price Guide to the Beatles, Second Edition,* House of Collectibles, 1999; Barbara Crawford and Michael Stern, *The Beatles: A Reference and Value Guide, Second Edition,* Collector Books, 1998; Courtney McWilliams, *Beatle Mania: An Unauthorized Collector's Guide,* Schiffer Publishing, 1998.

Periodicals: *Beatlefan,* PO Box 33515, Decatur, GA 30033; *Good Day Sunshine,* PO Box 1008, Los Angeles, CA 90066; *Instant*

Karma, PO Box 256, Sault Ste Marie, MI 49783; *Strawberry Fields Forever,* PO Box 880981, San Diego, CA 92168.

Collectors' Clubs: Beatles Connection, PO Box 1066, Pinellas Park, FL 34665; Working Class Hero Club, 3311 Niagara St, Pittsburgh, PA 15213.

REPRODUCTION ALERT: Records, picture sleeves, and album jackets have been counterfeited. Sound quality may be inferior. Printing on labels and picture jackets usually is inferior to the original. Many pieces of memorabilia also have been reproduced, often with some change in size, color, design, etc.

Bobbing Head Dolls, hp, wearing gray collarless suits, playing appropriate instruments, gold colored bases with facsimile signatures, Car Mascots, Inc, 8" h, price for set of 4. . . . . **$920.00**

Catalog, Vox Music Catalogue, front cover photo of John, Paul and Ringo performing on stage, black and white photos, c1960s, 14½ x 22½" **65.00**

Clothes Hanger, stiff diecut cardboard attached to white plastic hanger, George Harrison, ©Henderson/Hoggard, Inc, King Features-Suba Films Ltd, 1968, 16 x 17". **60.00**

Coaster, cardboard, images in center, "With Love From Me To You The Beatles," song names on sides, guitar illus on corners **50.00**

Coin Purse, synthetic fabric, John Lennon illus on sides with facsimile signature on guitar, gold colored metal top rim and closure, unmkd, 1960s **85.00**

Doll, Paul McCartney, molded hard plastic body, soft vinyl head, Remco, ©1964 Nems, 4½" h **175.00**

Fan Club Card, blue pen and ink Paul McCartney signature, matted and framed with color picture of Beatles performing and "gold" single for *Yesterday,* 17 x 20½" . . . **345.00**

Game, Flip Your Wig, Milton Bradley, 1964 . . . . **125.00**

Hairbrush, soft plastic, blue, photos, facsimile signatures, and "The Beatle Brush" in relief, Genco, c1960s, 3¾" l, orig pkg **90.00**

Model Kit, John Lennon, molded plastic, Revell, ©1964, $250.00.

Lunch Box, metal, emb images, Aladdin, ©1965 Nems Enterprises Ltd, 7 x 8 x 4" **200.00**

Paint Set, The Beatles Yellow Submarine Water Color Set, Craft Master **135.00**

Pen, The Beatles Official Ballpoint Pen, silvered metal top, plastic bottom, ©Press Initial Corp 1964, 5" l, orig card **75.00**

Pencil Case, vinyl, "The Beatles" with images and facsimile signatures, zipper closure. **175.00**

Pennant, felt, images in musical notes beneath "The Beatles," names below, "Yeah Yeah Yeah" in blue on right **300.00**

Pin Set, set of 8, hard plastic, hp, figural Beatles, Blue Meanie, and 3 other characters from *Yellow Submarine* movie, 1" l, c1968, MIB **65.00**

Program and Ticket, *The Beatles Show* program matted and framed with ticket from Gaumont Theatre, Taunton, featuring the Beatles, 13 x 17" **345.00**

Puzzle, Yellow Submarine, Jaymar, ©1968 King Features Syndicate, orig box **75.00**

Record, *She Loves You/I'll Get You,* 45 rpm, Swan, black and white photo on front and back of sleeve, 1964. . . . . . . **65.00**

Record Case, Disk-Go-Case, plastic, purple and pink, holds 45 rpm records, black illus and facsimile signatures, ©Charter Industries, Inc 1966 Nems Enterprises, Ltd, 6¾" h, 7½" d **100.00**

Rug, woven fabric, design includes portrait of Beatles, guitar, snare drum, and musical notes, 22 x 34" **200.00**

Scarf, glossy fabric, half corner design, mkd "The Beatles, Copyright by Ramat & Co Ltd, London, ECl," c1964, 25" sq **150.00**

Sweatshirt, cotton, red, Beatles portraits on chest with "Yea Yea Yea/Beatles," used, c1964. . . . . **85.00**

Wallet, vinyl, gray, folding, pinktone group photo on 1 side, black facsimile signatures on other, Standard Plastic Products, ©Rmat & Co, Ltd, London, c1964, 3½ x 4½" **120.00**

BELLEEK, AMERICAN

The American Belleek era spanned from the early 1880s until 1930. Several American firms manufactured porcelain wares resembling Irish Belleek. The first was Ott and Brewer Company of Trenton, New Jersey, from 1884 until 1893. Companies operating between 1920 and 1930 include Cook Pottery (1894–1929), Coxon Belleek Pottery (1926–1930), Lenox, Inc. (1906–1930), Morgan Belleek China Company (1924–1929), and Perlee, Inc. (1920s–c1930).

Reference: Mary Frank Gaston, *American Belleek,* Collector Books, 1984, out of print.

Bowl, white ware, dragon shaped handles, Lenox mark, 13" d. **$100.00**

Candlesticks, pr, white ware, raised scalloped designs on base, Lenox mark **130.00**

Centerpiece Bowl, hp, red tulips, gold trim with red accents, Lenox mark, 4½" h. **120.00**

Coffee Set, 3 pcs, coffeepot, creamer, and sugar bowl, sterling silver overlay, Lenox mark, c1921 . . . . **3,500.00**

Demitasse Cup and Saucer, blue and pink enamelled floral inserts, wide maroon border, Morgan mark **175.00**

Dinner Plate, Bouquet pattern, Coxon mark, 8" d **125.00**

Dinner Plate, peacocks and mixed floral dec, gold trim,
Gordon Belleek mark, 7" d **45.00**

Dish, hp, purple clematis blossoms with green leaves,
gold trim, 5" sq **55.00**

Individual Salt, 3 ftd, hp leaf dec, gold trim, Cook Pottery . . . **135.00**

Lemonade Pitcher, perlized, 6 repeated branched red
apples and leaves on olive green ground, wide gold
band dec, gold molded beaded applied handle, Lenox
mark, 5½" h **220.00**

Mug, hp, red gooseberries, angular handle, sgd "Cline,"
Lenox mark, 4½" h **80.00**

Powder Box, pink, gold wheat on lid, Lenox mark, 4 x 6" **40.00**

Sugar, cov, blue an pink transfer floral design, wide yellow outer border, gold trim, Coxon mark, 6" h **250.00**

Tea Set, 3 pcs, teapot 6½" h, creamer 3¾" h, 4¼" h covered sugar, Hawthorn pattern, Lenox mark. **175.00**

Vase, hp, foilage scenes in shades of green, Lenox mark,
6½" h **50.00**

Vase, multicolored floral at top with black border, white
base, gold trim, Perlee mark, 5" h **80.00**

BELLEEK, IRISH

Belleek is a thin, ivory-colored, almost iridescent-type porcelain. It was first made in 1857 in county Fermanagh, Ireland. Production continued until World War I, was discontinued for a period of time, and then resumed.

Shamrock is the most commonly found pattern, but many patterns were made, including Limpet, Tridacna, and Grasses. Pieces made after 1891 have the word "Ireland" or "Eire" in their mark. Some are marked "Belleek Co., Fermanagh."

The following abbreviations have been used to identify marks:

1BM = 1st Black Mark (1863–1890)
2BM = 2nd Black Mark (1891–1926)
3BM = 3rd Black Mark (1926–1946)
4GM = 4th Green Mark (1946–1955)
5GM = 5th Green Mark (1955–1965)
6GM = 6th Green Mark (1965–c1980)
B/GM = Brown/Gold Mark (1980–present)

References: Susan and Al Bagdade, *Warman's English & Continental Pottery & Porcelain, 3rd Edition,* Krause Publications, 1998; Richard K. Degenhardt, *Belleek: The Complete Collector's Guide and Illustrated Reference, Second Edition,* Wallace-Homestead, Krause Publications, 1993.

Collectors' Club: The Belleek Collectors' International Society, 9893 Georgetown Pike, Ste 525, Great Falls, VA 22066.

Ashtray, Thorn pattern, 3BM, 4¼" d **$18.00**

Bowl, Limpet pattern, 3BM, 4¾" d **28.00**

Bread and Butter Plate, Shamrock pattern, basketweave
ground, 3BM, 7" d **60.00**

Bread Tray, Neptune pattern, 1BM, 11¼" d **100.00**

Butter Plate, open, leaf shape, 3BM **38.00**

Cake Plate, Shamrock pattern, handled, basketweave
ground, 3BM, 10¼" d **110.00**

Coffeepot, Shamrock pattern, basketweave ground, twig
handle, 3BM, 7" h **250.00**

Creamer and Sugar, Lotus pattern, 3BM **80.00**

Creamry and Sugar, Shamrock pattern, 2BM **175.00**

Cup and Saucer, Mask pattern, 3BM **85.00**

Creamer, Shamrock pattern, $75.00. Photo courtesy Collectors Auction Services.

Cup and Saucer, Shamrock pattern, 3BM **100.00**

Cup and Saucer, Tridacna pattern, 3BM **80.00**

Dinner Plate, Shamrock pattern, 3BM, 8½" d **50.00**

Dinner Plate, Shell pattern, 3BM, 8½" d **100.00**

Figure, swan, 3BM, 4½" h **110.00**

Mug, Thorn patten, twig handle, 3BM **18.00**

Nut Dish, Neptune pattern, #0857, 3BM **18.00**

Sandwich Tray, Limpet pattern, 2BM **22.00**

Sandwich Tray, Tridacna pattern, 2BM **22.00**

Tub, handled, 3BM **80.00**

Vase, Aberdeen pattern, ewer shaped, ribbed body,
raised floral relief, loop handle, 3BM, 7" h **500.00**

Vase, cream, lily pad leaf molds on body, lilies in relief
with porcelain stames, ribbed upper half, flared pleat
top, 3BM, 13½" h **385.00**

BESWICK

James Wright Beswick and his son, John Beswick, are well known for their ceramic figures of horses, cats, dogs, birds, and other wildlife. Produced since the 1890s, figures representing specific animal characters from children's stories, such as Winnie the Pooh and Peter Rabbit, have also been modeled. In 1969 the company was bought by Royal Doulton Tableware, Ltd.

References: Diana Callow et al., *The Charlton Standard Catalogue of Beswick Animals, Third Edition,* Charlton Press, 1998; Diana and John Callow, *The Charlton Standard Catalogue of Beswick Pottery,* Charlton Press, 1997.

Newsletter: *Beswick Quarterly,* 10 Holmes Ct, Sayville, NY 11782.

Note: See Royal Doulton for further information.

Ashtray, duck, #755, 1939–69, 4" h **$50.00**

Ashtray, German shepherd, #1918, pale brown, glossy,
1963–71, 11" l **125.00**

Ashtray, Scottie dog, #88, blue, 1934–65, 3¼" h **50.00**

Ashtray, trout, #1599, glossy, 1959–70, 5" h **250.00**

Candle Holder, piglet, #2294, Fun Models series, brown,
1970–72, 11" l **100.00**

Cow Creamer, Daisy the Cow, #2792, Fun Models
series, blue, 1982–89, 5¾" h **125.00**

Figure, Mrs. Tiggy Winkle, #1107, Beatrix Potter series, 1947, 3¹/₄" h, $50.00.

Egg Cup, cat, #2810, Fun Models series, glossy, 1983–
  86, 2¹/₂" h **75.00**
Figure, Arabian foal, #1407, matte, 1979–89, 4¹/₂" h **45.00**
Figure, beagle, #2300, Fireside Models series, glossy,
  1969–83, 12³/₄" h **300.00**
Figure, bear, #1313, brown, glossy, 1953–66, 2¹/₂" h **125.00**
Figure, boxer dog, #1202, brindle, glossy, 1950–89, 5¹/₂" h **85.00**
Figure, Cat Conductor, #1026, Cat Orchestra series,
  glossy, 1945–73, 2" h **100.00**
Figure, dachshund, standing, #3103, Good Companions
  series, black and tan, glossy, 1987–89, 4¹/₄" h **75.00**
Figure, dalmatian, standing, #3385, glossy, 1994–97, 3" h **30.00**
Figure, dog playing accordion, #811, glossy, 1940–70, 4" h **100.00**
Figure, goose, #1471, CM Series 1, 1957–62, 3¹/₂" h **200.00**
Figure, Hereford calf, #1827C, glossy, 1985–97, 3" h **25.00**
Figure, Hide and Seek, pig and piglets, #LL3, Little
  Likables, glossy, 1985–87, 3¹/₄" h **70.00**
Figure, kangaroo, #2312, 1970–73, 5" h **275.00**
Figure, monkey with banjo, #1260, 1952–63, 2¹/₂" h **250.00**
Figure, mounted Indian, #1391, glossy, 1955–90, 8¹/₂" h **450.00**
Figure, Nijinsky, #2345, Connoisseur Horses series,
  matte, 1971–89, 11¹/₄" h **325.00**
Figure, poodle, #1472, CM Series 1, 1957–62, 5³/₄" h **300.00**
Figure, Poodle "Ivanola Gold Digger," #2108, white with
  blue bow, glossy, 1967–71, 5³/₄" h **350.00**
Figure, Puppit Dog, #1002, Fun Models series, glossy,
  1944–69, 4³/₄" h **125.00**
Figure, Sporting Cat, #3012, burgundy striped shirt,
  glossy, 1987, 4¹/₄" h **100.00**
Figure, Watching the World Go By, reclining frog, #LL2,
  Little Likables, glossy, 1985–87, 3³/₄" h **110.00**
Salt and Pepper Shakers, pr, cat on chimney pot, #2761,
  Fun Models series, glossy, 1982–85, 4" h **150.00**
Teapot, Peggoty, #1116, 6" h **60.00**
Trinket Dish, fish, #1304, glossy, 1953–66, 5" l **100.00**
Wall Plaque, Alsatian, #2932, matte, 1986–89 . . . . **50.00**
Wall Plaque, Basset Hound, #2235, glossy, 1968, 6¹/₄" h **150.00**
Wall Plaque, horse's head looking left through horse-
  shoe, #806, second version, glossy, 1939–68, 7¹/₄" h **150.00**
Whiskey Flask, eagle, #2281, glossy, 1969–84, 11" h **150.00**
Whiskey Flask, squirrel, #2636, glossy, 1978–86, 3¹/₂" h **30.00**

BICYCLES & RELATED

The bicycle was introduced in America at the 1876 Centennial. Early bicycles were high wheelers with heavy iron frames and disproportionately sized wooden wheels. By 1892 wooden wheels were replaced by pneumatic air-filled tires, which were later replaced with standard rubber tires with inner tubes. The coaster brake was introduced in 1898.

Early high wheelers and safety bikes made into the 1920s and 1930s are classified as antique bicycles. Highly stylized bicycles from the 1930s and 1940s represent the transitional step to the classic period, beginning in the late 1940s and running through the end of the balloon tire era.

References: Jim Hurd, *Bicycle Blue Book,* Memory Lane Classics, 1997; Jay Pridmore and Jim Hurd, *The American Bicycle,* Motorbooks International, 1995; Jay Pridmore and Jim Hurd, *Schwinn Bicycles,* Motorbooks International, 1996; Neil S. Wood, *Evolution of the Bicycle, Volume 1* (1991, 1994 value update), *Volume 2* (1994) L-W Book Sales.

Periodicals: *Antique/Classic Bicycle News,* PO Box 1049, Ann Arbor, MI 48106; *National Antique & Classic Bicycle,* PO Box 5600, Pittsburgh, PA 15207.

Newsletter: *Classic Bike News,* 5046 E Wilson Rd, Clio, MI 48420.

Collectors' Club: Classic Bicycle and Whizzer Club, 35769 Simon Dr, Clinton Twp, MI 48035.

BICYCLES

Colson Packard, girl's, streamlined, orig saddle, snap in
  "3 rib" tank, headlight, and droop rack, c1939 . . . . **$450.00**
Columbia Five Star Superb, boy's, 3 speed, 2 tone cream
  and maroon, orig paint, 1952. . . . . **875.00**
Crawford, tandem, post-1940s, needs restoration **75.00**
Elgin, girl's, orig pod stoptail light, Stewart Warner floating hub, c1940s **375.00**

Shelby Airflow, 1950, restored, $660.00. Photo courtesy Collectors Auction Services.

Poster, 39½" h, 24" w, $440.00. Photo courtesy Collectors Auction Services.

Clock, electric, "Columbia Built Bicycles Since 1877 America's First Bicycle," 15" d 350.00
Magazine Tear Sheet, Schwinn adv, fold-out, depicts Hollywood stars, framed, 28 x 20" 175.00
Newsletter, *News and Views*, Veteran-Cycle Club, c1988–97, price for lot of 54 . . . . 75.00
Poster, National Amateur Bicycle Championships, Aug 23–24, Furman Kugler photo, 10 x 13½" 15.00
Poster, "World's Fair In New York—1940/Admission Fifty Cents," "Go by all means" above family riding bicycles, S Ekman artist, 30 x 20" 120.00
Rear Carrier, Mead Ranger "Tall Tank," 1922 . . . . 350.00
Sign, electric, "Columbia Since 1877, America's First Bicycle," plastic, ribbed metal frame, c1950–60 . . . . 100.00
Stamp Set, First Day Cover 100th Anniversary Commemorative, c1978 . . . . 35.00
Weather Vane, man and woman riding tandem bike on arrow, directionals, Cape Cod Weathervane Co, late 1950s–60s 160.00

BIG LITTLE BOOKS

Big Little Books is a trademark of the Whitman Publishing Company. In the 1920s Whitman issued a series of books among which were Fairy Tales, Forest Friends, and Boy Adventure. These series set the stage for Big Little Books.

The year 1933 marked Big Little Books' first appearance. Whitman experimented with ten different page lengths and eight different sizes prior to the 1940s. Many Big Little Books were remarketed as advertising premiums for companies such as Cocomalt, Kool Aid, Macy's, and others. Whitman also published a number of similar series, e.g., Big Big Books, Famous Comics, Nickel Books, Penny Books, and Wee Little Books.

In an effort to keep the line alive, Whitman introduced television characters in the Big Little Book format in the 1950s. Success was limited. Eventually, Mattel-owned Western Publishing absorbed Whitman Publishing.

References: Larry Jacobs, *Big Little Books,* Collector Books, 1996; Lawrence F. Lowery, *Lowery's: The Collector's Guide to Big Little Books & Similar Books,* Educational Research and Applications Corp, 1981, out of print; *Price Guide to Big Little Books & Better Little, Jumbo, Tiny Tales, A Fast-Action Story, Etc.,* L-W Books Sales, 1995.

Collectors' Club: Big Little Book Collectors Club of America, PO Box 1242, Danville, CA 94526.

Elgin Deluxe, girl's, horn tank, headlight, illuminated rear rack and skirt guards, orig condition, 1940 . . . . 200.00
Firestone Pilot, boy's, orig red and white paint, basket, and chrome carrier, 26" 165.00
Firestone Super Cruiser, girl's, orig blue and white paint, c1947 . . . . 100.00
Hawthorne Flo-Cycle, 1936, orig condition 2,000.00
JC Higgins, boy's, "Wonderide Spring Fork," c1957, restored 1,000.00
Monark Silver King 26-X, pencil spring fork, streamlined horn light, electric tail light, stainless steel fenders, 26" wheels, 45" wheel base, 1939 . . . . 1,800.00
Schwinn Collegiate Sport, 5 speed, red, new old stock 25.00
Schwinn D97XE, boy's, horn tank, headlight, 9-hole rack and drop stand, orig red and cream paint, Goodyear All Weather white wall tires, 1939 . . . . 1,050.00
Schwinn Fair Lady, girl's, yellow, 1960s 65.00
Schwinn Fiesta, girl's, pnk and white, c1960 . . . . 55.00
Schwinn Jaguar Mark 2, 3 speed, horn tank, phantom rack and tail light, book rack, crashrail seat, Westwind white wall tires, orig condition, 1955 . . . . 450.00
Schwinn Manta-Ray, boy's, 5 speed, yellow, c1969, 24" 225.00
Schwinn Panther, boy's, balloon bicycle, blue and white paint, knee action spring fork, 1960s 200.00
Schwinn Scrambler, boy's, red, c1975 . . . . 50.00
Schwinn Sting Ray Lil Chik, 1970s 130.00
Schwinn Swing bike, orange, new old stock, 1960s 250.00
Silver King Monark, girl's, stepped stainless steel fenders, lobdell saddle, EA headlight, 1936 . . . . 300.00
Sting Ray Tornado, 1970s, orig condition 75.00

RELATED

Bicycle Frame and Fork, 1983 Pan American Games Team Pursuit Gold Medal winning bicycle, red and blue frame, "Raleigh" on down tube, "US Cycling Team" on top tube, fork with built-in aero stem $100.00
Calendar, 1940, cardboard, Kilian and Vopel on Durkopp racing bicycles photo, 8¾ x 11" 15.00
Charm, plastic, blue, world globe inside bike tire, inscribed "Arnold Schwinn & Co, Chicago" on front, "Ride The World's Cycles" on reverse, c1930s 10.00

#734, *Chester Gump at Silver Creek Ranch,* **$35.00; #723,** *Dick Tracy Out West,* **$55.00; #1439,** *Felix the Cat,* **$50.00; #1180,** *New Adventures of Tarzan,* **$40.00.** Photo courtesy of Collectors Auction Services.

#710, *Dick Tracy and Dick Tracy Jr* $65.00
#716, *Little Orphan Annie and Sandy*. 55.00
#719, *Robinson Crusoe*, soft cov 40.00
#759, *Alice in Wonderland* 18.00
#766, *Chester Gump Finds the Hidden Treasure* 35.00
#1107, *Don Winslow USN* 25.00
#1120, *Little Miss Muffet* 20.00
#1125, *Dan Dunn Trail of the Counterfeiters* 20.00
#1130, *Apple Mary and Dennie Foil the Swindlers* 18.00
#1133, *Bringing Up Father* 35.00
#1136, *Sombrero Pete*. 25.00
#1139, *Jungle Jim and the Vampire Wagon* 35.00
#1142, *Radio Patrol* 20.00
#1148, *International Spy, Dr Doom Faces Death at Dawn*. . . . 15.00
#1411, *Kay Darcy and the Mystery Hideout*. 20.00
#1413, *Hal Hardy in the Lost Land of Giants* 25.00
#1430, *Donald Duck Headed for Trouble* 40.00
#1438, *Don O'Dare Finds War* 15.00
#1447, *Blaze Brandon with the Foreign Legion* 10.00
#1465, *Bugs Bunny the Masked Marvel* 40.00
#1473, *Alley Oop in Jungles of Moo* 20.00
#1483, *Big Chief Wahoo and the Magic Lamp* 20.00
#1486, *Buck Jones, the Rough Riders*. 20.00
#1491, *Blondie, Cookie and Daisy's Pups*. 20.00
#1494, *Buffalo Bill Plays a Lone Hand* 10.00

BIG LITTLE BOOK TYPES

Today, Big Little Books is often used as a generic term that describes a host of look-alike titles from publishers such as Dell, Engel-Van Wiseman, Lynn, and Saalfield.

References: Larry Jacobs, *Big Little Books*, Collector Books, 1996; Lawrence F. Lowery, *Lowery's: The Collector's Guide to Big Little Books and Similar Books*, Educational Research and Applications Corp, 1981, out of print; *Price Guide to Big Little Books & Better Little, Jumbo, Tiny Tales, A Fast-Action Story, Etc.*, L-W Book Sales, 1995.

Blue Ribbon Pop-Up, *Dick Tracy, Capture of Boris Arson*,
    3 pop-ups, 1935 . . . . $225.00

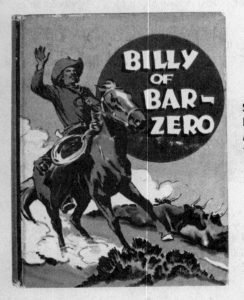

Saalfield, Jumbo
Book, *Billy of
Bar-Zero*, #1178,
1940, $18.00.

Blue Ribbon Pop-Up, *Little Red Ridinghood*, 3 pop-ups,
    1934. . . . . 150.00
Dell Fast-Action Story, *Captain Marvel, the Return of the
    Scorpion* 150.00
Dell Fast-Action Story, *Red Ryder Brings Law to Devils
    Hole* 50.00
Engle Van-Wiseman Five Star Library, *Great Expectations,
    #8*, 1934. . . . . 15.00
Golden Press, Golden Star Book, *Walt Disney's Sleeping
    Beauty and Cinderella*, #6072, 1967 . . . . 10.00
Lynn Book, *Jack London's Call of the Wild*, #L11, 1935 . . . . . . 20.00
Saalfield, Jumbo Book, *Joe Palooka's Great Adventures,
    #1168*, 1939. . . . . 12.00
Saalfield, Little Big Book, *Stan Kent Varsity Man*, #1123,
    1936. . . . . 30.00
Samuel Lowe, *Nevada Jones, Trouble Shooter*, 1949 . . . . 5.00
Whitman 710 Series, *Cinderella and the Magic Wand*,
    #711-10 . . . . 20.00
Whitman Better Little Book, *Brad Turner in Transatlantic
    Flight*, 1939. . . . . 25.00
Whitman Big Big Book, *Little Orphan Annie, The Story
    of*, #4054 . . . . 90.00
Whitman New Little Better Book, *Tarzan and the
    Journey of Terror*, 1950 . . . . 35.00
Whitman Tiny Tales, *Steve the Steam Shovel*, #2952,
    1950. . . . . 10.00

BING & GRØNDAHL

Frederick Grøndahl and brothers Meyer and Jacob Bing founded Bing & Grøndahl in 1853 to create replicas of the work of the famed Danish sculptor Thorvaldsen. The company's initial success led to an expansion of its products that included elegant dinnerware, coffee services, and other tabletop products.

In 1895 Harald Bing decided to test the idea of a plate designed specifically for sale during the Christmas season. F. A. Hallin, a Danish artist, created "Behind the Frozen Window" which appeared on a limited edition of 400 plates with the words "Jule Aften" (Christmas Eve) scrolled across the bottom and decorated in the company's signature blue and white motif. While Bing & Grondahl's annual Christmas plate is its most recognized and collected product, collectors have expanded their focus to include the company's figurines, dinnerware, and other desirables.

References: Pat Owen, *Bing & Grøndahl Christmas Plates: The First 100 Years*, Landfall Press, 1995, distributed by Viking Import House; Rinker Enterprises, *The Official Price Guide to Collector Plates, Seventh Edition*, House of Collectibles, 1996.

Bell, 1985, Christmas Eve at the Farmhouse $50.00
Bell, 1987, Snowman's Christmas Eve 40.00
Bell, 1990, Changing of the Guards. 50.00
Bell, 1992, Christmas at the Rectory 60.00
Dinnerware, cup and saucer, Seagull pattern, gold trim. 60.00
Dinnerware, dish, Blue Lace pattern, leaf shape, white
    ground, handled, 7³/₈" l 50.00
Dinnerware, gravy boat, attached underplate, Seagull
    pattern, gold trim. 150.00
Dinnerware, platter, Seagull pattern, gold trim, 16" l,
    11" w 175.00
Figure, cat, white, #2527. . . . . 50.00
Figure, girl kissing boy, 7" h 135.00
Figure, girl with milk can, #2181, 8³/₄" h 375.00

Bell, 1984, Cathedral of Trier, $90.00.

Plate, 1938, Lighting the Candles, Christmas series, Immanuel Tjerne artist **400.00**

Plate, 1961, Winter Harmony, Christmas series, Kjeld Bonfils artist **75.00**

Plate, 1976, E Pluribus Unum, Bicentennial series **60.00**

Plate, 1977, Yard and Warehouse, Carl Larsson series, price for set of 4 . . . . **150.00**

Plate, 1979, Fox and Cubs, Mother's Day series, Henry Thelander artist **28.00**

Plate, 1987, Manx and Kittens, Cat Portraits series, Angela Sayer artist **40.00**

Plate, 1991, Fun On the Beach, Children's Day series, Sven Vestergaard artist **55.00**

Plate, 1994, Christmas in Church, Centennial Collection series, Henry Thelander artist **60.00**

BLACK MEMORABILIA

Black memorabilia is a generic term covering a wide range of materials from advertising to toys made in the image of a black person or featuring an image of a black person in its artwork. The category also includes materials from the era of slavery, artistic and literary contributions by black people, Civil Rights memorabilia, and material relating to the black experience in America.

Much of the material in this category is derogatory in nature, especially pre-1960s material. Despite this, it is eagerly sought by both white and black collectors.

Interest in Civil Rights memorabilia has increased significantly in the past decade.

References: Douglas Congdon-Martin, *Images in Black: 150 Years of Black Collectibles, 2nd Edition,* Schiffer Publishing, 1999; Patiki Gibbs, *Black Collectibles Sold in America,* Collector Books, 1987, 1996 value update; J. P. Thompson, *Collecting Black Memorabilia,* L-W Book Sales, 1996.

Newsletter: *Lookin Back at Black,* 6087 Glen Harbor Dr, San Jose, CA 95123.

Collectors' Club: Black Memorabilia Collector's Assoc, 2482 Devoe Terrace, Bronx, NY 10468.

Alarm Clock, black face with "Dat Sho Was Good!" across forehead on cardboard face, glass front, metal body, ©1942 Robertshaw Controls Company, Lux Time Division, Lebanon, Tenn, U.S.A., 6" h **$200.00**

Alarm Clock, Little Black Sambo, cardboard face, plastic front, metal housing, ©1946, Made in U.S.A., 3½" h, 2¾" d **225.00**

Arcade Card, Four Mills Brothers, mid 1930s **8.00**

Autograph, Jackson, Jesse, PS, 1970s **50.00**

Bag, Plantation coffee, cloth, Negro illus, 1930s **5.00**

Batter Bowl, mammy handle, Weller Pottery, c1938, 5½" d, 8½" h **750.00**

Candy Box, cardboard, Amos 'n' Andy Um-Um! Ain't Dat Sumpin!, "A Delicious Honey Comb Candy Coated with Rich Chocolate," "5¢," mkd "Williamson Candy Co., Chicago, Brooklyn, San Francisco," 11¾" h, 8½" w **100.00**

Card Game, Snake Eyes, Selchow & Righter, 1930–57 . . . . . . **60.00**

Clock, Aunt Jemima Buckwheat Pancakes, electric, plastic, cardboard face, ©1956, 7" h, 7½" w **500.00**

Clock and Memo Holder, clock is ceramic mammy with white turban and dress with blue trim, holding round clock face, back mkd "Model W, The Session Clock Co, Forestville, Conn, U.S.A." with patent numbers, memo holder is molded plastic and painted mammy with green turban and scarf with red dots, green, brown, and white dress, stamped "Mammy Memo Holder, No. 123" **50.00**

Comic Book, Clean Fun Starring Sugarfoot Jones, 1944 . . . . . **130.00**

Cookie Jar and Cookbook, contemporary, ceramic, mammy with red turban, bow, and dress, and white apron, stirring bowl of cookie dough, base sgd "New Orleans, LA," together with *Southern Cookbook: 322 Old Dixie Recipes,* c1939 . . . . **40.00**

Creamer and Sugar, cov, and pair of syrup containers, promotional, sugar and creamer have yellow plastic bowls, creamer with Uncle Moses handle, sugar with Aunt Jemima handle, each stamped on base "F&F Mold & Die Works, Dayton Ohio" within shield, above "Made in U.S.A.," syrups have mammy in red dress with white shawl and apron carrying a tray, c1950, price for 4 pcs **170.00**

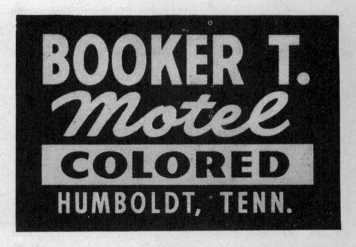

Sign, tin, white lettering, red ground, 15½" h, 24" w, $990.00. Photo courtesy Collectors Auction Services.

Game, Blacks and Whites, *Psychology Today*, 1970–71 . . . . . . **20.00**
Game, The Black Experience, Theme Productions, 1971 . . . . . **15.00**
Magazine, *Ebony*, Sep 1968, Dr Martin Luther King and
   Coretta King cov **25.00**
Serving Tray, litho tin, 2 children getting ready for bed,
   6¼" h, 9" w **275.00**
Sheet Music, *Mammy's Little Coal Black Rose* **30.00**
Sign, adv, cardboard, litho, "Quality Yes-Suh-h," black
   man holding tray with bottles and glasses, "Pabst
   Famous Blue Ribbon Beer" across bottom, ©1938
   Premier Pabst Sales Co, framed, 39½" h, 30" w **275.00**
Wall Plaques, collection of 4, painted chalk, the first a
   boy and girl each eating a slice of watermelon, girl
   with blue bows, boy with green cap, dated 1949, the
   second 2 children sharing slice of watermelon, each
   in yellow attire, girl with red bows and boy with red
   cap, the third a girl with red turban and yellow dress,
   the fourth a mammy with red turban and bow, c1950,
   price for 4 . . . . **50.00**

BLUE RIDGE POTTERY

The Carolina Clinchfield and Ohio Railroad established a pottery
in Erwin, Tennessee, in 1917. J. E. Owens purchased the pottery in
1920 and changed the name to Southern Potteries. The company
changed hands again within a few years, falling under the ownership of Charles W. Foreman.

By 1938 Southern Potteries was producing its famous Blue
Ridge dinnerware featuring hand-painted decoration. Lena Watts,
an Erwin native, designed many of the patterns. In addition, Blue
Ridge made limited production patterns for a number of leading
department stores.

The company experienced a highly successful period during the
1940s and early 1950s, the Golden Age of Blue Ridge. However,
cheap Japanese imports and the increased use of plastic dinnerware in the mid-1950s sapped the company's market strength.
Operations ceased on January 31, 1957.

References: Betty and Bill Newbound, *Collector's Encyclopedia of
Blue Ridge Dinnerware* (1994), *Vol. II* (1998), Collector Books;
Frances and John Ruffin, *Blue Ridge China Today*, Schiffer
Publishing, 1997.

Periodical: *Blue Ridge Beacon Magazine*, PO Box 629, Mountain
City, GA 30562.

Newsletter: *National Blue Ridge Newsletter*, 144 Highland Dr,
Blountville, TN 37617.

Collectors' Club: Blue Ridge Collectors Club, 208 Harris St, Erwin,
TN 37650.

Ashtray, Rise & Shine **$25.00**
Butter Pat, Fruit Fantasy **15.00**
Cake Plate, Chintz, maple leaf shape **50.00**
Cake Plate, French Peasant, maple leaf shape **90.00**
Cake Plate, Verna, maple leaf shape **60.00**
Celery, Chintz **20.00**
Celery, Nove Rose, leaf shape **40.00**
Cereal Bowl, Crab Apple, 6"d **5.00**
Cereal Bowl, Ribbon Plaid **10.00**
Child's Feeding Dish, Jigsaw **90.00**
Chocolate Pot, French Peasant **300.00**

Cigarette Set, Rooster, cov box and 4 ashtrays **180.00**
Creamer, Chintz, pedestal **25.00**
Creamer, Mardi Gras **10.00**
Cup, Crab Apple **9.00**
Cup and Saucer, Crab Apple **12.50**
Cup and Saucer, Spray **8.00**
Cup and Saucer, Strawberry Sundae **5.00**
Demitasse Cup and Saucer, Brittany **30.00**
Demitasse Sugar, Gumdrop **35.00**
Dinner Plate, Crab Apple **13.00**
Dinner Service, Quaker Apple, service for 4 . . . . **150.00**
Eggcup, Sungold #2 . . . . **15.00**
Fruit Bowl, Buttercup, 6" d **10.00**
Gravy Boat, Mardi Gras, matching underplate **20.00**
Jug, Chick **100.00**
Pie Baker, Mardi Gras **25.00**
Pie Plate, 3 large flowers **25.00**
Pie Plate, Cassandra, maroon border **25.00**
Pitcher, Annette's Wild Rose, antique shape, 5" **75.00**
Pitcher, Fairmede Fruit, Alice shape, earthenware, 6¼" **85.00**
Pitcher, Rebecca **195.00**
Plate, Bluebell Bouquet, 6" d **3.50**
Plate, Briar Patch, 10½" d **8.00**
Plate, Carnival, 9" d **8.50**
Plate, Christmas Tree, 10" d **70.00**
Plate, Nocturne, sq **12.50**
Plate, Red Barn, 9" d **22.00**
Platter, Rooster **100.00**
Relish, French Peasant, shell shape **165.00**
Salad Bowl, French Peasant **125.00**
Salt and Pepper Shakers, pr, Rooster, toe flake **90.00**
Soup Bowl, Cherries **5.00**
Sugar, Daffodil **12.00**
Sugar, French Peasant **75.00**
Sugar, Rustic Plaid **8.00**
Teapot, Champagne Pink **100.00**
Teapot, Yellow Nocturne **15.00**
Tidbit Tray, Apple and Pear, 3 tiers **40.00**
Tray, French Peasant, leaf shape **125.00**
Vase, French Peasant, handled **70.00**

Soup Bowl, blue and yellow flowers, 8" d, $17.50.

BOEHM PORCELAIN

Edward and Helen Boehm founded The Boehm Studio in 1950. It quickly became famous for its superb hand-painted, highly detailed sculptures of animals, birds, and flowers. Boehm also licensed his artwork to manufacturers of collector plates.

Boehm porcelains are included in the collections of over 130 museums and institutions throughout the world. Many U.S. presidents used Boehm porcelains as gifts for visiting Heads of States.

Reference: Reese Palley, *The Porcelain Art of Edward Marshall Boehm,* Harrison House, 1988, out of print.

Collectors' Club: Boehm Porcelain Society, 25 Princess Diana Ln, Trenton, NJ 08638.

Amanda with Parasol, #86-01-001	$750.00
Aria, #86-01-002	875.00
Blackburnian Warbler, #84-01-017	965.00
Blue Heron, #200-19	375.00
Calliope Hummingbird, #87-01-039	600.00
Cherries Jubilee Camellia, #86-03-005	625.00
Crested Flycatcher, baby, #458C	185.00
Elephant, white bisque, #85-02-015	575.00
Fledgling Brown Thrashers, #77-01-071	680.00
Fledgling Eastern Bluebird, #442	125.00
Globe of Light Peony, #86-03-022	500.00
Hunter, #52-02-022	1,400.00
Jo, skating, #86-04-008	750.00
Kingfisher, #449, 6" h	150.00
Lady's Slipper Orchid, #84-03-031	575.00
Magnolia Warbler, #84-01-107	1,100.00
Meg with Basket, #86-04-010	625.00
Nuthatch, #71-01-125	1,130.00
Rose, Nancy Reagan, #81-03-069	920.00
Rose, Queen Elizabeth, #82-03-076	1,800.00
Spanish Iris, #78-03-087	760.00
Waterlily, #74-03-097	725.00
White-Tailed Buck, #84-02-034	1,660.00
Yellow-Shafted Flicker, #82-01-196	1,500.00

BOOKENDS

Theme is the most important consideration when placing a value on bookends. In most cases, the manufacturer is unknown, either because the bookends are unmarked or research information about the mark is unavailable. Be alert to basement workshop examples. Collectors prefer mass-produced examples.

References: Louis Kuritzky, *Collector's Guide to Bookends,* Collector Books, 1997; Gerald P. McBride, *A Collector's Guide to Cast Metal Bookends,* Schiffer Publishing, 1997; Robert Seecof, Donna Lee Seecof and Louis Kuritsky, *Bookend Revue,* Schiffer Publishing, 1996.

Collectors' Club: Bookend Collector Club, 4510 NW 17th Pl, Gainesville, FL 32605.

Note: All bookends are priced as pairs.

Angelfish, gray metal, polished stone base, J B Hirsch, c1930, 6" h	$120.00
Blenko Girl, c1970, 8" h	40.00

Angular Elephants, Cowan, #840, designed by Margaret Postgate, glossy caramel glaze, die-stamped circular mark, c1929, 4¹/₂ x 5¹/₂ x 3¹/₂", $550.00. Photo courtesy David Rago Auctions, Inc.

Boy with Sailboat and Dog, Frankart	250.00
Cape Cod Fisherman, iron, Connecticut Foundry, 1928, 5¹/₂" h	65.00
Chariot Horses, gray metal, Frankart, c1934, 5" h	150.00
Crusaders, iron, Hubley, c1926, 5¹/₂" h	75.00
Dutch Girl, holding buckets, iron, c1928, 6¹/₂" h	45.00
Ebony Elks, iron, c1925, 3¹/₂" h	50.00
Flower Urn, soapstone	90.00
German Shepherd, iron, 4³/₄" h	45.00
Kitten on Book, cast iron, Bradley & Hubbard, mkd "B&H"	600.00
Lady Godiva, crystal, KR Haley Glassware Co, 6" h	45.00
Lily Pad, gray metal, Dodge, c1945, 4¹/₂" h	65.00
Lyre, gray metal, PM Craftsman, c1965, 6" h	45.00
Nashville Surgical Supply Co, Bakelite, B&B Remembrance, 4³/₄" h	50.00
Scottie Dog, gray metal, Frankart, 4" h	125.00
Scottish Rite, gray metal, Ronson, 1922, 3¹/₄" h	85.00
Seashell, spring-coiled steel and resin composition, Revere, c1935	45.00
Sir Francis Drake, gray metal, Jennings Brothers, c1925, 3" h	50.00
Spinning Scene, iron, 1930s, 4⁷/₈" h	50.00
St George and the Dragon, iron, Hubley, c1925, 5¹/₂" h	85.00
Swordfish, pressed wood	18.00
The Thinker, iron, Hubley, c1928, 5" h	35.00
Tiger, glass, New Martinsville, 6¹/₂" h	325.00
Town Crier, gray metal, PM Craftsman, c1965, 7¹/₄" h	50.00
Unicorn and Lion, brass, 6" h, 5¹/₂" l	50.00
Whale, gray metal, PM Craftsman, c1965, 7¹/₂" h	50.00

BOOKS

Given the millions of books available, what does a collector do? The answer is specialize. Each edition of this price guide will focus on one or more specialized collecting categories. This edition focuses on first edition books.

References: Allen and Patricia Ahearn, *Collected Books: The Guide to Values,* F. P. Putnam's Sons, 1997; *American Book Prices Current,* Bancroft-Parkman, published annually; Ron Barlow and Ray Reynolds, *The Insider's Guide to Old Books, Magazines, Newspapers, Trade Catalogs,* Windmill Publishing, 1995; Ian C. Ellis, *Book Finds: How to Find, Buy and Sell Used and Rare Books,* Berkley Publishing, 1996; *Huxford's Old Book Value Guide,*

Eleventh Edition, Collector Books, 1999; Marie Tedford and Pat Goudey, *The Official Price Guide to Old Books, Third Edition,* House of Collectibles, 1999; John Wade, *Tomart's Price Guide to 20th Century Books,* Tomart Publications, 1994.

Periodicals: *AB Bookman's Weekly,* PO Box AB, Clifton, NJ 07015; *Firsts: The Book Collector's Magazine,* PO Box 65166, Tucson, AZ 85728; *Book Source Monthly,* 2007 Syosett Dr, PO Box 567, Cazenovia, NY 13035.

Newsletter: *Rare Book Bulletin,* PO Box 201, Peoria, IL 61650.

Collectors' Club: Antiquarian Booksellers Assoc of America, 20 West 44th St, 4th Flr, New York, NY 10036.

Bloch, Robert, *Opener of the Way, The,* Sauk City, 1945, 8vo, cloth, dj **$400.00**
Bradbury, Ray, *R Is For Rocket,* Garden City, 1962, 8vo, cloth, dj, sgd **160.00**
Burroughs, William S, *Dead Fingers Talk,* London, 1963, 8vo, gray cloth, sgd **230.00**
Campbell, John W, Jr, *Moon Is Hell!, The,* Fantasy Press, 1951, 8vo, purple cloth gilt, protective cloth dj with morocco gilt labels and slipcase, sgd **115.00**
Capote, Truman, *Christmas Memory, A,* New York, 1951, 8vo, line, dj, inscribed and sgd **400.00**
Cather, Willa, *Lucy Gayheart,* New York, 1935, 8vo, green cloth, paper title labels, dj **230.00**
Chandler, Raymond, *Long Good-Bye, The,* London, 1953, 8vo, maroon cloth, dj **250.00**
Christie, Agatha, *Hound of Death and Other Stories, The,* London, 1933, 8vo, dj, slightly faded spine, creasing at edges, repairs on verso **630.00**
Clancy, Tom, *Hunt for Red October, The,* Naval Institute Press, Annappolis, 1984, 8vo, red cloth, dj, inscribed and sgd "First Edition" **1,380.00**
Clarke, Tom, *2001: A Space Odyssey,* London, 1968, 8vo, cloth, dj, inscribed and sgd **315.00**
Collier, John, *No Traveller Returns,* London, 1931, 8vo, orig velveteen gilt, sgd, The White Owl Press **175.00**
Crofts, Freeman Wills, *Death on the Way,* London, 1932, 8vo, orange cloth, dj, lightly foxed edges, repaired on verso, slipcase **500.00**
Dahl, Roald, *Some Time Never: A Fable for Supermen,* New York, 1948, 8vo, cloth, dj, repaired tears on verso **115.00**
Eddison, ER, *Worm Ouroboros, The,* London, 1922, 8vo, illus by Keith Henderson, gilt pictorial cloth, dj, small repair on verso, Jonathan Cape **500.00**
Faulkner, William, *Knight's Gambit,* New York, 1949, 8vo, red cloth stamped in gold and black, top edge stained deep gray, dj **140.00**
Ginsberg, Allen, *To Eberhart From Ginsberg: A Letter About Howl 1956,* Penmaen Press, Lincoln, MA, 1976, 4to, cloth, etchings by Jerome Kaplan **125.00**
Goldman, William, *Princess Bride, The,* New York, 1973, 8vo, cloth, dj **175.00**
Haggard, H Rider, *Treasure of the Lake,* Garden City, 1926, 8vo, orig cloth, dj **175.00**
Heinlein, Robert A, *Tunnel in the Sky,* New York, 1955, 8vo, pictorial cloth, dj **200.00**
Horler, Sydney, *False-Face,* London, 1926, 8vo, deep orange calf with gilt rules and spine compartments by Sangorski and Sutcliffe **100.00**

Keller, David H, *Tales From Underwood,* New York, 1952, 8vo, dj, Ellegrini & Cudahy for Arkham House, ... **80.00**
Lee, Harper, *To Kill a Mockingbird,* London, 1960, 8vo, maroon cloth, dj **430.00**
Lovecraft, HP, *At the Mountains of Madness and Other Novels,* Sauk City, 1964, 8vo, cloth, green dj, first printing **230.00**
Milne, AA, *House at Pooh Corner, The,* London, 1928, 8vo, illus by Ernest H Shepard, gilt pictorial cloth, dj **550.00**
O'Flaherty, Liam, *Return of the Brute,* London, 1929, 8vo, tan cloth, dj **175.00**
Pasternak, Boris, *Doctor Zhivago,* 8vo, red cloth, dj, London, 1958 . . . . **200.00**
Petee, FM, *Palgrave Mummy, The,* London, 1929, 8vo, red cloth, dj, repair on verso **175.00**
Salinger, JD, *Catcher in the Rye, The,* London, 1951, 8vo, blue cloth, dj, repair on verso of spine panel **485.00**
Steinbeck, John, *Moon Is Down, The,* New York, 1942, 8vo, blue cloth, dj **90.00**
Walton, Evangeline, *Witch House,* Sauk City, 1945, 8vo, cloth, dj **100.00**
Williams, Tennesse, *Glass Menagerie, The,* New York, 1945, frontispiece, thin 8vo, red cloth, dj **320.00**

BOOKS, CHILDREN'S

Although children's books date as early as the 15th century, it was the appearance of lithographed books from firms such as McLoughlin Brothers and series books for boys and girls at the turn of the 20th century that popularized the concept. The Bobbsey Twins, Nancy Drew, the Hardy Boys, and Tom Swift delighted numerous generations of readers.

The first Newberry Medal for the most distinguished children's book was issued in 1922. In 1938 the Caldecott Medal was introduced to honor the children's picture book.

Most children's book collectors specialize. Award-winning books, ethnic books, first editions, mechanical books, and rag books are just a few of the specialized categories.

Each edition of this price guide will concentrate on one or more specialized collecting categories. This listing focuses on children's books published by P. F. Volland Publishers, a company well known for its high-quality, fully illustrated hardcover books.

References: E. Lee Baumgarten (comp.), *Price Guide and Bibliographic Checklist for Children's & Illustrated Books for the Years 1880–1960, 1996 Edition,* published by author, 1995; David and Virginia Brown, *Whitman Juvenile Books,* Collector Books, 1997; E. Christian Mattson and Thomas B. Davis, *A Collector's Guide to Hardcover Boys' Series Books,* published by authors, 1996; Diane McClure Jones and Rosemary Jones, *Collector's Guide to Children's Books, 1850 to 1950,* Collector Books, 1997.

Periodicals: *Book Source Monthly,* 2007 Syosett Dr, PO Box 467, Cazenovia, NY 13035; *Mystery & Adventure Series Review,* PO Box 3488, Tucson, AZ 85722; *Yellowback Library,* PO Box 36172, Des Moines, IA 50315.

Newsletter: *Martha's KidLit Newsletter,* PO Box 1488, Ames, IA 50010.

Collectors' Clubs: Movable Book Society, PO Box 11645, New Brunswick, NJ 08906; The Society of Phantom Friends, PO Box

1437, North Highlands, CA 95660. There are numerous collectors' clubs for individual authors. Consult the *Encyclopedia of Associations* at your local library for further information

Note: The books listed are all first editions, with color illustrations and illustrated boards. For additional children's book listings see Big Little Books, Big Little Book Types, Little Golden Books, and Little Golden Book Types.

Addington, Sarah, *Tommy Tingle-Tangle*, Gertrude Kay illus, 1927, Sunny Books, square 8vo, 39 pp, pictorial endpapers. **$75.00**

Campbell, Lang, *Dinky Ducklings*, Lang Campbell illus, 1928, Sunny Books, 12mo, 39 pp, pictorial endpapers **70.00**

Campbell, Ruth, *Cat Whose Whiskers Slipped*, VE Cadie illus, 1925, 8vo. **40.00**

Colum, Padriac, *Six Who Were Left in a Shoe*, 1923, Sunny Books, square 8vo, unpg, pictorial endpapers. **45.00**

Gordon, Elizabeth, *Happy Home Children*, Marion Foster illus, ML Foster, Sunny Books, 1924, 12mo, 34 pp, pictorial endpapers **60.00**

Gordon, Elizabeth, *Tale of Johnny Mouse*, MW Enright illus, 1920, Sunny Books, 8vo **90.00**

Gruelle, Johnny, *Beloved Belindy*, Johnny Gruelle illus, 8vo, 95 pp, pictorial endpapers **100.00**

Gruelle, Johnny, *Cheery Scarecrow*, Johnny Gruelle illus, 1929, 12mo, 39 pp, pictorial endpapers, 6 color plates **110.00**

Gruelle, Johnny, *Eddie Elephant*, Johnny Gruelle illus, Sunny Books, 1921, 12mo, 39 pp, pictorial endpapers . . . **100.00**

Gruelle, Johnny, *Little Brown Bear*, Johnny Gruelle illus, Sunny Books, 1920, 12mo, 40 pp, pictorial endpapers **90.00**

Gruelle, Johnny, *Magical Land of Noom*, Johnny Gruelle, illus, 1922, 4to, 157 pp, pictorial endpapers, 12 color plates **250.00**

Gruelle, Johnny, *Marcella Stories*, Johnny Gruelle illus, 1929, 8vo, 94 pp, pictorial endpapers **85.00**

Gruelle, Johnny, *Paper Dragon*, Johnny Gruelle illus, 1926, 8vo, 96 pp, pictorial endpapers **90.00**

Gruelle, Johnny, *Raggedy Andy Stories*, Johnny Gruelle illus, Happy Children Books, 1920, large 8vo, unpg, pictorial endpapers **125.00**

Gruelle, Johnny, *Raggedy Ann in Cookie Land*, Johnny Gruelle illus, Happy Children Books, 1931, large 8vo, 95 pp, pictorial endpapers **75.00**

Gruelle, Johnny, *Wooden Willie*, Johnny Gruelle illus, 1927, 8vo, 95 pp, pictorial endpapers **120.00**

Hankins, Maude, *Daddy Gander*, V Elizabeth Cadie illus, Sunny Books, 1928, 12mo, 40 pp **70.00**

Haynes, Louise Marshall, *Over the Rainbow Bridge*, CL Browne illus, Sunny Books, 1920, square 8vo, 42 pp **80.00**

Holling, HC, *Choo-Me-Shoo*, HC Holling illus, 1928, 8vo, pictorial endpapers **75.00**

Holling, HC, *Little Big-Bye-and-Bye*, HC Holling illus, 1926, 12mo, 40 pp, pictorial indpapers **50.00**

Jacobs-Bond, Carrie, *Tales of Little Dogs*, Katharine Dodge illus, Sunny Books, 1921, small square 8vo, 35 pp, pictorial endpapers **60.00**

Kay, Gertrude, *Friends of Jimmy*, Gertrude Kay illus, 1926, large 8vo, 95 pp, pictorial endpapers **70.00**

Kay, Gertrude, *Helping the Weatherman*, Gertrude Kay illus, 1920, Happy Children Books, 8vo, unpg, pictorial endpapers **60.00**

Kay, Gertrude, *Jolly Old Shadow Man*, Kay Gertrude illus, Sunny Books, 1920, 12mo, 39 pp, pictorial endpapers. **60.00**

Larned, WT, *American Indian Fairy Tales*, John Rae illus, 1921, 8vo, 88 pp, pictorial endpapers **50.00**

Larned, WT, *Fairy Tales from France*, John Rae illus, 1920, Happy Children Books, large 8vo, 93 pp, pictorial endpapers **100.00**

Mee, John L, *Three Little Frogs*, John Rae illus, Sunny Books, 1924, 8vo **65.00**

Mitchell, Edith, *Betty, Bobby and Bubbles*, JL Scott illus, Sunny Books, 1921, 12mo, 40 pp, pictorial endpapers. **50.00**

Rae, John, *Granny Goose*, John Rae illus, 1926, large 4to, 44 pp, 21 full page color illus, pictorial endpapers. **180.00**

Rae, John, *Grasshopper Green/Meadow Mice*, John Rae illus, Sunny Books, 1922, 12mo, 40 pp **70.00**

Reid, Sydney, *How Sing Found the World Was Round*, KS Dodge, Sunny Books, 1921, 12mo, 40 pp **85.00**

Thompson, Ruth Plumly, *Princess of Cozytown*, JL Scott illus, 1922, large 8vo, 96 pp, pictorial endpapers **140.00**

Wright, Isa L, *Remarkable Tale of a Whale*, J Held illus, 1920, Sunny Books, 8vo **75.00**

Wynne, Annette, *Treasure Things*, E Merritt illus, 1922, Sunny Books, 12mo, 39 pp, pictorial endpapers **55.00**

BOTTLE OPENERS

In an age of pull-tab and twist-off tops, many young individuals have never used a bottle opener. Figural openers, primarily those made of cast iron, are the most commonly collected type. They were extremely popular between the late 1940s and early 1960s.

Church keys, a bottle opener with a slightly down-turned "V" shaped end, have a strong following, especially when the opener has some form of advertising. Wall-mounted units, especially examples with soda pop advertising, also are popular.

Collectors' Clubs: Figural Bottle Opener Collectors Club, 3 Avenue A, Latrobe, PA 15650; Just For Openers, 3712 Sunningdale Way, Durham, NC 27707.

ADVERTISING

Canandaigua, wood, bottle shaped, 1930s **$20.00**
Coca-Cola, metal, wall mount, raised lettering, mkd "Patd. Apr. 21, 1925 Stark NPT News Va.," 4¼" h, 2¾" w. **50.00**
Congress Beer, opener/pocketknife, 1930s **25.00**
Dr Pepper, figural lion's head, Crown T&D Co, Chicago, IL, 3" l. **85.00**
Shell, metal, emb logo, 8⅜" l, 3⅜" w, ... **15.00**

FIGURAL

Alligator, cast iron, 5¼" l. **$65.00**
Bulldog, cast iron, 4 x 4". **50.00**
Canada Goose, head extended to ground, brown and black markings, green base, Wilton Products **50.00**
Dachshund, brass **50.00**
Dodo Bird, cast iron, cream, black highlights, red beak, 2¾" **150.00**
Donkey, cast iron, 3½" h. **60.00**

**Brass, 4¹/₄" h,
3³/₄" w, $95.00.**
Photo courtesy
Collectors Auction
Services.

**Soda, "Hellertown Bottling Works,
Quality Beverages, Hellertown,
Penna., All Flavors," green glass,
mountain scene, 1 qt, 11³/₄" h,
$5.00.**

Drunk, leaning against sign post, mkd "Baltimore, MD" **10.00**
Elephant, trunk up, cast iron, John Wright Foundry, 3" h **75.00**
False Teeth, cast iron, wall mount, flesh gums, off-white
 teeth, 2³/₈" h, 3³/₈" w **100.00**
Four-Eyed Woman, cast iron, 4 x 3³/₄" **125.00**
Mr Dry, cast iron, wall mount, man wearing black top
 hat, red hair, blue bags under eyes, red lips, flesh-tone
 face, Wilton Products, 5¹/₂" h, 3¹/₂" w **125.00**
Pretzel, brass **25.00**
Railroad Coupler, cast iron, Case, 3¹/₄" l **75.00**
Sea Gull, cast iron, cream, black, and gray highlight, red
 beak, orange feet, gray and black stump, John Wright
 Co, 3³/₁₆" h **35.00**
Seahorse, cast iron, 4 x 2" **50.00**

BOTTLES

This is a catchall category. Its role is twofold—to list a few specialized bottle collecting areas not strong enough to have their own category and provide the logical place to find information about bottle references, collectors' clubs, and periodicals.

References: Ralph and Terry Kovel, *The Kovels' Bottles Price List, Eleventh Edition,* Crown Publishers, 1999; Jim Megura, *The Official Identification and Price Guide to Bottles, Twelfth Edition,* House of Collectibles, 1997; Michael Polak, *Bottles, Second Edition,* Avon Books, 1997; Carlo and Dorothy Sellari, *The Standard Old Bottle Price Guide,* Collector Books, 1989, 1997 value update.

Periodical: *Antique Bottle and Glass Collector,* PO Box 180, East Greenville, PA 18041.

Collectors' Club: Federation of Historical Bottle Collectors, 88 Sweetbriar Branch, Longwood, FL 32750.

Note: Consult *Maloney's Antiques & Collectibles Resource Directory* by David J. Maloney, Jr., at your local library for additional information on regional bottle clubs.

Hoffman, "Don't Blame Me," policeman with music
 box, Occupation series **$25.00**
Hoffman, Red River Breed, CM Russell Series **25.00**
Hoffman, "Star Spangled Banner," Betsy Ross with music
 box, Bicentennial series **35.00**
Japan, Sake God, bone china, 10" h **10.00**
Japan, White Pagoda **10.00**

Luxardo, duck, green and amber, clear glass base, 1960 . . . . . **25.00**
Miniature, Ballantine's Ale, P Ballantine & Sons,
 Newark, NJ **3.00**
Miniature, Dad's Root Beer **3.00**
Miniature, Fort Pitt Beer, Fort Pitt Brewing Co, Pittsburg **5.00**
Miniature, Old Barton Blend Whiskey, 1930. . . . . **50.00**
Soda, Polak Pak, San Diego, CA, clear, bear sitting on
 iceberg, 1944, 7 oz **20.00**
Soda, Snappy, Los Angeles, CA, green, Eastern woman,
 radio tower and globe, 1937, 6¹/₂ oz **200.00**
Soda, Tower Root Beer, Charleston, MA, amber, castle
 tower illus, 7 oz, 1955 . . . . **100.00**

BOYD CRYSTAL ART GLASS

Boyd Crystal Art Glass, Cambridge, Ohio, traces its heritage back to Bernard C. Boyd and Zackery Thomas Boyd, two glass makers who worked for a number of companies in the Cambridge area. In 1964 Elizabeth Degenhart asked Zack Boyd to assume the management of Degenhart Glass. When Zack died in 1968, Bernard assumed leadership of the company.

In 1978, Bernard C. Boyd and his son, Bernard F., purchased Degenhart Glass. Initially working with the 50 molds acquired from Degenhart, the Boyds began making pieces in a host of new colors. Eventually, John Bernard, son of Bernard F., joined the company. Today Boyd Crystal Art Glass has over 200 molds available for its use including a number of molds purchased from other glass companies such as Imperial.

Reference: *Boyd's Crystal Art Glass: The Tradition Continues,* Boyd's Crystal Art Glass, n.d.

Newsletter: *Jody & Darrell's Glass Collectibles Newsletter,* PO Box 180833, Arlington, TX 76096.

Collectors' Club: Boyd Art Glass Collectors Guild, PO Box 52, Hatboro, PA 19040.

Ashtray, bowling pin, mystique **$3.00**
Basket, handled, 4¹/₂" h **10.00**
Figurine, Angel, crystal carnival **8.50**

Toothpick, gypsy pot, dark brown slag, $6.00.

Calendar, 1954, C&F Motor Sales adv, 33" h, 16" w, $50.00. Photo courtesy Collectors Auction Services.

Figurine, baby shoe, pale orchid **4.00**
Figurine, Bernie the Eagle, banana cream. **4.50**
Figurine, Chuckles the Clown, 26 color series, retired
   Nov 1989 . . . . **7.50**
Figurine, Fuzzy the Teddy Bear, 25 color series, retired
   May 1989 . . . . **5.50**
Figurine, hen, marshmallow, 5" h. **10.00**
Figurine, Miss Cotton the Kitten, milk chocolate **4.00**
Figurine, Pete the Pelican, vaseline **4.50**
Figurine, Zack the Elephant, 40 color series, retired Dec
   1985. . . . . **8.50**
Master Salt, beaded, milk white. **3.00**
Miniature Pitcher, milk white. **4.00**
Mug, milk white **4.00**
Plate, Statue of Liberty, ruby **4.00**
Ring Holder, nile green **4.00**
Salt, cov, lamb, mirage **3.50**
Salt, duck, capri blue **3.50**
Salt, turkey, purple frost. **3.50**
Toothpick Holder, figural basket, citron **4.00**

BOY SCOUTS

William D. Boyce is the father of Boy Scouting in America. Boyce was instrumental in transferring the principles of Baden-Powell's English scouting movement to the United States, merging other American organizations into the Scouting movement, and securing a charter from Congress for the Boy Scouts of America in 1916.

Scouting quickly spread nationwide. Manufacturers developed products to supply the movement. Department stores vied for the rights to sell Scouting equipment.

The first national jamboree in America was held in Washington, D.C., in 1937. Patch trading and collecting began in the early 1950s. The Order of the Arrow, national Scouting centers, e.g., Philmont, and local council activities continually generate new collectible materials.

Reference: George Cuhaj, *Standard Price Guide to U.S. Scouting Collectibles,* Krause Publications, 1998.

Periodical: *Fleur-de-Lis,* 5 Dawes Ct, Novato, CA 94947.

Collectors' Clubs: American Scouting Traders Assoc, PO Box 210013, San Francisco, CA 94121; National Scouting Collectors Society, 806 E Scott St, Tuscola, IL 61953; Scout and Stamps Society International, 20 Cedar Ln, Cornwall, NY 12518.

Collar Insignia, brass, "BSA," screw back posts, 1¼" l **$20.00**
Flashlight, chromed metal, green band around body,
   red, white, and blue stripes, red plastic ring around
   neck, Boy Scout emblem on side **20.00**
Hat Badge, Sr Patrol Leader's, green enameled bars, gilt
   first class BSA emblem, 1940s, 2½" h. **25.00**
Medal, bronze metal, wreath border, engraved "BSA
   Dutchess Co. Pow Wow 1925," rev engraved with
   name and "Tent Pitching," 1¼" d **75.00**
Patch, "National Jamboree Valley Forge 1957," white
   twill, embroidered red, blue, black, brown, and white,
   red border with blue outer ring lettering, red "Onward
   For God And My Country" surrounding image of
   kneeling and praying George Washington, 3" d **20.00**
Patch, Order of the Arrow, gray chenille, arrowhead
   shaped, bow and quill of arrow with red "WWW" in
   center, reverse dated 1979 . . . . **125.00**
Patch, Order of the Arrow, red, white, brown, and green,
   turkey in center, "Unalachtigo WWW 168 Firm
   Bound in Brotherhood," 4" h **25.00**
Patch, Order of the Arrow, yellow twill, keystone
   shaped, red thunderbird in center, blue border, black
   "WWW XI," 3½" h **25.00**

Cub Scout Books, *1937 Jamboree Edition Boy Scout Diary, Camp Aid & Log Book, The Bear Cub Book,* **and** *The Wolf Cub Book,* **price for lot, $16.50.** Photo courtesy Collectors Auction Services.

Pin, First Class, tin plated on brass, hanging knot, safety
pin back, 2" h **25.00**
Pin, Scoutmaster's, green enamel, affixed silver colored
First Class emblem, ³/₄" d **20.00**
Ribbon, woven, red, white, and blue, Flying Eagle Patrol,
1920s, 4¹/₂" h **20.00**
Sash, cloth, complete with 27 tan square cut merit
badges, 1930s **100.00**
Shirt, cloth, olive drab, "Be Prepared" on metal buttons,
"Lexington KY 21" patches on left sleeve, Daniel
Boone on right, 1953 Blue Grass Council Camporee
patch on right pocket, size 34, 1950s **35.00**

BRASTOFF, SASCHA

In 1948, Sascha Brastoff established a small pottery on Speulveda
Boulevard in West Los Angeles. Brastoff's focus was that of designer. Skilled technicians and decorators gave life to his designs.

Brastoff was at the cutting edge of modern design. Figurines
were introduced in the early 1950s to a line that included ashtrays,
bowls, and vases. In 1953 a new studio was opened at 11520 West
Olympic Boulevard. In 1954 production began on the first of ten
fine china dinnerware lines.

Although Brastoff left the studio in 1963, the company survived
another decade thanks to the inspired leadership of plant manager Gerold Schwartz.

Reference: Steve Conti, A. Dewayne Bethany and Bill Seay,
Collector's Encyclopedia of Sascha Brastoff, Collector Books,
1995.

Alaska Series, bowl, C14, 3 ftd, fish shaped, log cabin
motif, 9¹/₂" l **$100.00**
Alaska Series, tray, 054, 7 compartments, female Eskimo
in center, 14¹/₂" l **150.00**
Alaska Series, vase, F20, round, brown seal motif, 5¹/₂" h **80.00**
Aztec, candle holder, 10" h **125.00**
Aztec Jumping Horse, ashtray, C21, 8" w **45.00**
Ballet Dancers, platter, 14³/₄" sq **150.00**
Chi Chi Bird, bowl, 8" d **65.00**
Jewel Bird, ashtray, 7" l **40.00**
Jewel Bird, flowerpot, 6" h **70.00**
Jewel Bird, vase, F20, 6" h **40.00**
Pagodas, ashtray, F2, freeform, rooster backstamp, 8¹/₄" l **55.00**
Pagodas, bowl, F44, rooster backstamp, 12³/₄" d **85.00**
Pagodas, charger, 053, rooster backstamp, 17" d **250.00**
Pagodas, plate, curled lip, 12" d **85.00**
Persian, ashtray, F8, freeform, sgd, rooster backstamp,
17⁵/₈" l **150.00**
Prancing Horse, ashtray, 6¹/₄" sq **35.00**
Rooftops, ashtray, F4, freeform, rooster backstamp, 11" l **55.00**
Rooftops, ashtray, freeform, 8¹/₂" l **40.00**
Rooftops, charger, pastel colored houses, rooster back-
stamp, 17¹/₄" d **250.00**
Rooftops, mug, 076, 4¹/₂" h **40.00**
Rooftops, pipe, 4¹/₂" h **40.00**
Rooftops, plate, freeform, rooster backstamp, 9³/₄" l **50.00**
Rooftops, tea canister, C45, rooster backstamp, 10¹/₂" h **150.00**
Rooftops, vase, F20, 6" h **45.00**
Smoke Tree, dinner plate, 10" d **20.00**
Smoke Tree, salt and pepper shakers, pr, 4" h **35.00**
Surf Ballet, bowl, ftd, yellow gold, applied gold swirls,
sgd "Sasha B" on back, 5¹/₂" d **30.00**

BRAYTON LAGUNA CERAMICS

Durline E. Brayton founded Brayton Laguna, located in South
Laguna Beach, California, in 1927. Hand-crafted earthenware dinnerwares were initially produced. The line soon expanded to
include figurines, flowerpots, tea tiles, vases, and wall plates.

In 1938 Brayton Laguna was licensed to produce Disney figurines. Webb, Durlin's second wife, played an active role in design
and management. A period of prosperity followed.

By the end of World War II, Brayton Laguna ceramics were
being sold across the United States and abroad. In the early and
mid-1960s the company fell on hard times, the result of cheap foreign imports and lack of inspired leadership. The pottery closed in
1968.

Reference: Jack Chipman, *Collector's Encyclopedia of California
Pottery, Second Edition,* Collector Books, 1999.

Candy Jar, cov, hen **$225.00**
Figurine, Chinese boy **100.00**
Figurine, elephant, woodtone, white crackle finish,
c1957, 7¹/₂" h **150.00**
Figurine, fighting pirates, dark brown stained bisque,
colored and crackle glaze, c1956, 9" h **650.00**
Figurine, Mexican peasant couple, textured bisque, in
mold mark, 12¹/₂" h **225.00**
Figurine, Pedro, 6¹/₂" h **100.00**
Figurine, Pluto, sniffing, Walt Disney line, 6" l, 3¹/₄" h **125.00**
Figurine, torso, abstract form, white crackle glaze,
c1950s **200.00**
Figurine, toucan, woodtone, high glaze, 9" h **125.00**
Flower Holder, Swedish peasant woman, incised mark,
c1939, 11¹/₂" h **350.00**
Lady Head Vase, gypsy woman, incised "Brayton Laguna
Pottery," c1939, 9" h **250.00**
Lamp Base, girl holding doll, c1940s **400.00**
Planter, girl with 2 wolfhounds, 11" h **125.00**
Planter, girl with bonnet and basket **70.00**
Planter, shoe **25.00**
Planter, wheelbarrow **35.00**
Salt and Pepper Shakers, pr, granny **65.00**

BREWERIANA

Breweriana is a generic term used to describe any object, from
advertising to giveaway premiums, from bar paraphernalia to beer
cans, associated with the brewing industry. Objects are divided
into pre- and post-Prohibition material.

Breweries were one of the first industries established by early
American settlers. Until Prohibition, the market was dominated by
small to medium size local breweries. When Prohibition ended, a
number of brands, e.g., Budweiser, established themselves nationwide. Advertising, distribution, and production costs plus mergers
resulted in the demise of most regional breweries by the 1970s.

Imported beers arrived in America in the 1960s, often contracting with American breweries to produce their product. In the
1980s and 1990s America experienced a brewing renaissance as
the number of micro-breweries continues to increase.

Collectors tend to be regional and brand loyal. Because of a
strong circuit of regional Breweriana shows and national and
regional clubs, objects move quickly from the general marketplace
into the specialized Breweriana market.

References: Donna Baker, *Vintage Anheuser Busch: An Unofficial Collector's Guide*, Schiffer Publishing, 1999; George J. Baley, *Back Bar Breweriana: A Guide to Advertising Beer Statues and Beer Shelf Signs*, L-W Book Sales, 1992, 1994 value update; *Beer Cans: 1932–1975*, L-W Book Sales, 1976, 1995 value update; Herb and Helen Haydock, *The World of Beer Memorabilia*, Collector Books, 1997; Bill Mugrage, *The Official Price Guide to Beer Cans*, Fifth Edition, House of Collectibles, 1993; Gary Straub, *Collectible Beer Trays With Value Guide*, Schiffer Publishing, 1995; Robert Swinnich, *Contemporary Beer Neon Signs*, L-W Book Sales, 1994; Dale P. Van Wieren, *American Breweries II*, East Coast Breweriana Assoc, 1995.

Periodicals: *All About Beer*, 1627 Marion Ave, Durham, NC 27705; *Suds 'n' Stuff*, 4765 Galacia Way, Oceanside, CA 92056.

Collectors' Clubs: American Breweriana Assoc, Inc, PO Box 11157, Pueblo, CO 81001; Beer Can Collectors of America, 747 Merus Ct, Fenton, MO 63026; National Assoc of Breweriana Advertising, 2343 Met-To-Wee Ln, Milwaukee, WI 53226.

Ashtray, Burger Brown Co, ceramic, brewery illus, 1964 . . . . **$18.00**
Ashtray, Harvard Export Beer, painted glass, 1940s **10.00**
Ashtray, Silver Label Beer, metal, 1950s **6.00**
Back Bar Sign, Schlitz, lighted, metal stand, 1951, 10 x
   11 x 4" **15.00**
Back Bar Statue, Schmidt's of Philadelphia Beer Ale,
   white metal, painted, 9" h **42.00**
Bank, Hamms' Beer, ceramic, figural bear, 1960s, 12" h **85.00**
Banner, Piels Light Beer, silk screened, folded, 1930s, 11
   x 15" **15.00**
Bottle, Beckers Beer, Evanston, WY **10.00**
Bottle, Fehrs XL Beer, tin cap, 1930s, 20 x 5½" **85.00**
Bottle Opener, Storz Beer, Storz Brewing, Omaha, NB,
   wood, metal, 1950s **10.00**
Bottle Opener/Pocketknife, Congress Beer, worn enamel
   on sides, 1930s **45.00**
Cabinet Light, Schoenling, plastic, tin frame, 1940s, 7 x
   26" **90.00**
Calendar, John Eichler Brewing Co, 1934, litho car
   board, 9 x 10" **65.00**

Sign, Heineken, porcelain, 1-sided, 23½" h, 16" w, $275.00. Photo courtesy Collectors Auction Services.

Calendar, Anheuser-Busch Inc., tin over cardboard, hanging chain, 22½" h, 12" w, $250.00. Photo courtesy Collectors Auction Services.

Calendar, Anheuser-Busch Inc., tin over cardboard, hanging chain, 22½" h, 12" w, $250.00. Photo courtesy Collectors Auction Services.

Can, Old Reading Beer, conetop 175.00
Can, Koehler Select Beer, conetop, rolled. 65.00
Clock, Iroquois Beer, lighted, 1960s, 14" sq 40.00
Clock, Michelob Light, lighted globe, clock rotates
   inside, 1970s, 26 x 12" 65.00
Coaster, Burger Brewery, Cincinnati, OH, octagonal, red
   and green, 4" 10.00
Coaster, Miller High Life, ceramic, 1950s 60.00
Coaster, Standard Ale, brass, 1930s 42.00
Cooler, Sterling Beer, galvanized, 1950s, 18 x 12 x 8". 30.00
Corkscrew, Anheuser Busch. 75.00
Crate, Harvard Ale & Beer, wood, 1930s, 19½ x 10½ x
   12¾" 25.00
Display, Budweiser Bud Man, foam rubber, red and blue
   costume, 1970, 17"h 75.00
Doll, Bud Man, foam, 1970s, 19 x 8 x 4". 85.00
Drinking Glass, Nectar Beer, painted blue label, 1950s,
   4½" h 35.00
Drinking Glass, Pabst Blue Ribbon, painted gray label,
   1930s, 7½" h 15.00
Drinking Glass, Storz Beer, 75th anniversary, painted
   white label, 1951, 8½" h 25.00
Fan, Gunther Beer, 3 panel, *Gone With the Wind* river-
   boat scene on reverse, 1930 . . . . 25.00
Foam Scraper, Piel's, metal, 2 dwarfs holding keg 30.00
Foam Scraper Holder, Beverwyck, milk glass, plastic and
   chrome trimmed bar, 1940s 85.00
Foam Scraper Holder, Schaefer, red glass with painted
   white lettering, plastic and chrome trimmed bar 85.00
Label, Old Reading Cream Ale, green, 2 barkeepers
   above product name, 12 oz 12.00
Letterhead, Jackson Brewing, New Orleans, LA, factory
   scene, used 1945 . . . . 6.00
Light, Burgermeister Beer, plastic, chrome plated, 1950s,
   8 x 9" 18.00
Light, Old Dutch Premium Beer, hanging, 1950s 45.00
Mirror, Fell Beer Ale Porter, Fell Brewing, Carbondale,
   PA, reverse glass, 8 x 10". 60.00
Mug, Burgie Beer, ceramic, emb, 1960s, 6½" h 25.00
Necktie, Schlitz Beer, Schlitz Brewing, Milwaukee, WI,
   1950s 18.00
Pinback Button, Miller High Life Beer, multicolored 25.00

Plaque, Hensler Private Label Beer, chalkware, 1950,
  12" d **50.00**
Playing Cards, Moosehead Beer, tin box **12.00**
Poster, Bavarian Rock Beer, 1940s, 12 x 22" **15.00**
Poster, Koehler Pilsener, 1957, 11 x 27" **50.00**
Salt and Pepper Shakers, pr, Bud Man, orig box, 1980s **40.00**
Salt and Pepper Shakers, pr, Flecks Beer, painted label,
  1950s **25.00**
Sign, Budweiser, lighted, 12 x 20" **50.00**
Sign, Murphy's Ale in Bottles, paper, framed, 9 x 28" **20.00**
Sign, Schlitz Malt Syrup, tin, emb, 1929, 12 x 24" **200.00**
Sign, Yuengling Beer, hard rubber, 3-D lettering, plastic
  feet, 1950s, 13 x 4½" **50.00**
Song Book, Wooden Shoe Beer, mug shaped, 1930s **10.00**
Stein, pewter, Bonn relief scenes, Besetzlich Geschutz,
  FM&N Co, 8" h **40.00**
Tap Knob, Billy Bock Beer, glass, 1930s **80.00**
Tap Knob, Erlangers, plastic, enamel insert, 1940s **65.00**
Tap Knob, Gilt Edge Beer, aluminum, 1930s **45.00**
Tap Knob, Koehler's Beer, plastic, 1950s **30.00**
Tap Knob, Yuengling, plastic, enamel insert, 1940s **28.00**
Thermometer, Columbia 5 Star Ale, reverse glass, tin
  frame, 6" d **82.00**
Thermometer, Regal Beer, aluminum, emb, 1950s **210.00**
Thermometer, Shiner Beer, glass dome with metal rim,
  1970s, 12" d **60.00**
Tip Tray, Frank Jones Homestead Ale, 1940s **55.00**
Tip Tray, Standard Scranton Beer, Standard Brewing,
  Scranton, PA, 1930s **55.00**
Tray, Franklin Beer, Franklin Brewing, Wilkes-Barre, PA,
  1950s, 13¼" **35.00**
Tray, Frank's Old Fashioned Beer, M Frank & Son
  Brewing, Mansfield, OH, 1930s, 13½ x 10½" **100.00**
Tray, Free State Supreme, Free State Brewing, Baltimore,
  MD, 1940s, 13¾" **15.00**
Tray, Kaier's Beer Ale Porter, rect, bright red, black,
  white, and gold, 13 x 10½" **130.00**
Tray, Koch's Beer, 1950s, 13¼" d **35.00**
Tray, Miller High Life Beer, Miller Brewing, Milwaukee,
  WI, 1940, 13¼" **25.00**

BREYER HORSES

When founded in 1943, the Breyer Molding Company of Chicago manufactured custom designed thermoset plastics. After WWII, the company shifted production to injection molded radio and television housings. As a sideline, Breyer also produced a few plastic animals based on designs sculpted by Christian Hess.

By 1958 the Breyer line contained a barnyard full of animals — cats, cows, dogs, and horses. In 1959 the company introduced its woodgrain finish. By the end of the 1970s the sale of horses accounted for most of the company's business.

Reeves International, a distributor of European collectibles such as Britains and Corgi, acquired Breyer in 1984. Manufacturing was moved to a state-of-the-art plant in New Jersey.

References: Felicia Browell, *Breyer Animal Collector's Guide*, Collector Books, 1998; Nancy Atkinson Young, *Breyer Molds and Models: Horses, Riders and Animals, 5th Edition*, Schiffer Publishing, 1998.

Periodicals: *The Hobby Horse News*, 2053 Dryehaven Dr, Tallahassee, FL 32311; *Just About Horses*, 14 Industrial Rd,

Pequannock, NJ 07440; *TRR Pony Express*, 71 Aloha Circle, N Little Rock, AR 72120.

Newsletter: *The Model Horse Trader*, 143 Mercer Way, Upland, CA 91786.

Collectors' Club: North American Model Horse Show Assoc, PO Box 50508, Denton, TX 76206.

CLASSIC SCALE

Black Stallion, #3030, matte black, 1983–93 . . . . **$10.00**
Lipizzan Stallion, #620, matte alabaster, 1975–80 . . . . **30.00**
Mustang Foal, #3065, matte chestnut, 1976–90 . . . . **10.00**
Quarter Horse Mare, #3045, matte bay, 1974–93 . . . . **12.00**

LITTLE BITS SCALE

American Saddlebred, #9030, matte palomino, 1985–88 . . . **$10.00**
Morgan Stallion, #9005, matte bay, 1984–88 . . . . **10.00**
Thoroughbred Stallion, #9010, matte red bay, 1984–88 . . . . **10.00**
Unicorn, #1020, white with blue mane, Montgomery
  Ward special issue, 1985 . . . . **30.00**

STABLEMATE SCALE

Arabian Stallion, #5010, matte dapple gray, 1975–76 . . . . . **$32.00**
Draft Horse, #5055, matte light sorrel, 1976–87 . . . . **9.00**
Native Dancer, #5023, matte gray, 1976–94 . . . . **8.00**
Silky Sullivan, #5022, matte dark chestnut, 1976–94 . . . . **7.00**

TRADITIONAL SCALE

Clydesdale Stallion, #80, glossy bay, 1958 . . . . **$120.00**
Family Arabian Mare, #707, matte liver chestnut, 1988 . . . . . . **32.00**
Five Gaiter, Pinto American Saddlebred, #827, matte,
  1990–91 . . . . **35.00**
Foundation Stallion, #64, matte black, 1977 . . . . **30.00**
Grazing Foal, #151, matte bay, 1964–76 . . . . **20.00**
Indian Pony, #175, matte brown pinto, 1970–76 . . . . **65.00**
Man O' War, #47, matte red chestnut, 1969–95 . . . . **20.00**
Mustang, #985, matte woodgrain, 1963–66 . . . . **300.00**
Quarter Horse Gelding, #99, glossy bay, 1959–66 . . . . **100.00**
Shetland Pony, #23, matte bay, 1973–88 . . . . **18.00**
Western Pony, #40, semi-gloss plum brown, pre-1956 . . . . . . **75.00**

Bay Fighting Stallion, matte, stockings, bald face, black mane and tail, Toys "R" Us special issue, 1993, $28.00.

BRIARD, GEORGES

Georges Briard, born Jascha Brojdo, was an industrial designer who worked in a wide range of materials—ceramics, glass, enameled metals, paper, plastic, textiles, and wood. Brojdo emigrated from Poland in 1937. He earned a joint Master of Fine Arts degree from the University of Chicago and the Art Institute of Chicago. In 1947 Brojdo moved to New York where he chose the name Georges Briard as his designer pseudonym.

Columbian Enamel, Glass Guild (The Bent Glass Company), Hyalyn Porcelain, and Woodland were among the early clients of Georges Briard Designs. In the early 1960s Briard designed Pfaltzgraff's Heritage pattern. In 1965 he created sixteen patterns for melamine plastic dinnerware in Allied Chemical's Artisan line, marketed under the Stetson brand name.

Briard continued to create innovative designs for the houseware market through the end of the 1980s. Responding to changing market trends, many of Briard's later products were made overseas.

Reference: Leslie Piña, '50s & '60s Glass, Ceramics, & Enamel Wares Designed & Signed by Georges Briard, Sascha B., Bellaire, Higgins..., Schiffer Publishing, 1996.

REPRODUCTION ALERT: Do not confuse Briard knockoffs, many made in Japan, with licensed Briard products. A high level of quality and the distinctive Briard signature are the mark of a Briard piece.

Bird in Cage, martini pitcher, 9¼" h **$18.00**
Cane Brown, old fashioned glass **4.00**
Hyalyn, vase, rect, gold facade dec, 5½" h **80.00**
Linometric, casserole, brass-plated cov, 11¾" w **25.00**
Mosaic, ashtray, white and gold tiles, Mandarin Orange
   glass insert with Regalia pattern, 9⅝" sq **45.00**
Mosaic, cigarette box, green and blue, 5⅝" l **40.00**
Mosaic, plate, green and blue, 5" sq **20.00**
Mosaic, wall clock, green and blue, 12" sq. **110.00**
Paradise, salad bowl, 10¾" d **15.00**
Paradise, snack bowl, wood and brass center handle, 7" d . . . **12.00**
Peacock White, iced tea glass **5.00**
Porcupine, old fashioned glass, frosted. **6.00**
Spanish Gold, cheese board, 1-dip, 6" tile **30.00**
Topiary Wreath, plate, 7⅝" d **10.00**

BRITISH ROYALTY COMMEMORATIVES

British royalty commemoratives fall into two distinct groups: (1) souvenir pieces purchased during a monarch's reign and (2) pieces associated with specific events such as births, coronations, investitures, jubilees, marriages, or memorials. Items associated with reigning monarchs are the most popular.

Only five monarchs have reigned since 1920 — King George V (May 6, 1910 to January 20, 1936), King Edward VIII (January 20, 1936, abdicated December 10, 1936), King George VI (December 10, 1936 to February 6, 1952), and Queen Elizabeth II (February 6, 1952 to the present).

References: Susan and Al Bagdade, Warman's English & Continental Pottery & Porcelain, Third Edition, Wallace-Homestead, Krause Publications, 1998; Douglas H. Flynn and Alan H. Bolton, British Royalty Commemoratives, Schiffer Publishing, 1994.

Newsletter: British Royalty Commemorative Collectors Newsletter, PO Box 294, Lititz, PA 17543.

Collectors' Club: Commemorative Collector's Society, 25 Farndale Close, Long Eaton, NG-10 3PA, UK.

Bell, Queen Elizabeth II Coronation, brass, inscribed
   "Coronation Of H.M. Queen Elizabeth II 1953," orig
   cardboard display box, Gillette and Johnson, 2½ x
   2½" **$25.00**
Box, cov, Silver Jubilee, jasperware, heart shaped, white
   profile portraits and dec, royal blue ground,
   Wedgwood, 1977 . . . . **120.00**
Coin, Charles and Diana's Royal Wedding, silver tone
   metal, Queen Elizabeth II on reverse, 1981, 1½" d **5.00**
Coloring Book, Queen Elizabeth II Coronation,
   Saalfield, 1953 . . . . **25.00**
Compact, King Edward VIII, silvered metal hinged case
   with tinted color cello insert portrait, silvered int,
   underside of case mkd "Rachel," c1936 . . . . **50.00**
Cup and Saucer, Prince Charles' Investiture as Prince of
   Wales, bone china, red Welsh dragon, gold trim,
   Liverpool Road Pottery, 1969 . . . . **40.00**
Dish, Charles and Diana's Royal Wedding, sterling silver,
   raised portraits, 1981, 3¾" d **125.00**
Goblets, Queen Elizabeth II Silver Jubilee, 1977 . . . . **125.00**
Loving Cup, Prince Henry of Wales, miniature, bone
   china, multicolored roses, gold highlights, Royal
   Crown Derby, 1984, 1¼" h, 2¼" w **85.00**
Photograph, King George V and Elizabeth I with infant,
   real photo, sepia, late 1930s **25.00**
Plate, Queen Mother's 85th Birthday, bone china, color
   portrait and dec, gold rim, limited edition of 2,000,
   Coalport, 1985, 10½" d **100.00**
Tumblers, George VI Coronation, pr, first with portrait
   and inscription "H.M. King George VI Coronation
   May 12, 1937," royalty crown symbol within maple
   leaf design on reverse, second with different portrait
   view within royalty symbols and inscribed "May 1937
   Coronation," both with red finish and clear emb
   flower pattern on bottom, 3¾" h **50.00**

Beaker, Edward VIII Coronation, limited edition of 2,000, Minton, 1937, 4" h, $250.00.

BRUSH POTTERY

The J. W. McCoy Pottery and Brush Pottery joined forces in 1911, resulting in the formation of the Brush-McCoy Pottery. The company produced a wide range of ceramic wares, including art ware, cookie jars, garden wares, kitchen wares, novelty planters, and vases. During the 1930s Brush pottery was sold and distributed by The Carson Crockery Company as "Coronado Art Pottery."

References: Sharon and Bob Huxford, *The Collector's Encyclopedia of Brush-McCoy Pottery,* Collector Books, 1978, 1996 value update; Martha and Steve Sanford, *The Guide to Brush-McCoy Pottery,* published by authors, 1992; Martha and Steve Sanford, *Sanfords Guide to Brush-McCoy Pottery, Book 2,* published by authors, 1996.

REPRODUCTION ALERT: Many reproduction cookie jars are unmarked.

Basket, concentric circles design, white, c1940	$85.00
Carafe, Bronze Line, #928, 9" h	45.00
Cookie Jar, barn, white with gray roof, W31	75.00
Cow Creamer, 1940s	20.00
Decanter, wise bird, 8" h	250.00
Ewer, green, 7" h	30.00
Figure, reclining frog, 10" l	70.00
Flowerpot, Bittersweet, 6½" h	25.00
Jardiniere, Blended Onyx, green and brown, 8½"	135.00
Pitcher, emb water lilies, #30, 5½" h	60.00
Planter, figural conch shell	18.00
Planter, Madonna, white	15.00
Planter, pedestal base, #927, 1957, 4" h	10.00
Planter, Rockcraft, 3" w	35.00
Salt and Pepper Shakers, pr, Cloverleaf, 1955	50.00
Tankard, #609, c1940, 12" h	65.00
Umbrella Stand, moss green, 21" h	600.00
Vase, #212, pink, late 1940s, 12" h	60.00
Vase, #546, 10½" h	25.00
Vase, cobweb design, #074, 8" h	25.00
Vase, Glo-Art, turquoise, #768, 7" h	50.00
Vase, tulip blossom, miniature, c1939	12.00
Vase, Moderne KolorKraft, 12" h	150.00
Vase, Victory, early 1940s, 8" h	75.00
Wall Plaques, pr, African masks, 10½" h	100.00
Wall Pocket, fish	80.00
Window Box, Stardust, 1957, 12" l	80.00

BUSINESS & OFFICE MACHINES

Europeans, especially the Germans, are the leading collectors of business and office equipment. In the United States, decorators buy most examples to use as decorative conversation pieces. It is for this reason that adding machines, check writers, dictating machines, and stock tickers machines are the most eagerly sought after types. Novelty and/or functionality are more important value keys than age.

Reference: Thomas F. Haddock, *A Collector's Guide to Personal Computers and Pocket Calculators,* Books Americana, Krause Publications, 1993.

Collectors' Club: Historical Computer Society, 3649 Herschel St, Jacksonville, FL 32205.

Note: See Calculators and Typewriters for additional listings.

AB Dick, Edison Mimeoscope	$300.00
AB Dick, Edison Model 1	175.00
AB Dick, Edison Model 75	22.00
Compaq Computer, portable, Intel 8088, 4.77 Mhz, 128 K ram expandable to 256 K, 9" black and white monitor displaying 25 lines of 80 characters each, 83-key keyboard with numeric keypad and 10 programmable function keys, double sided 5¼" floppy drives with 320K capacity, c1980s	75.00
Ediphone, dictating machine	40.00
Ediphone, saving machine	40.00
Ediphone, typease typewriter attachment	15.00
Instant Checkwriter	20.00
McCaskey, account register	40.00
Moon Hopkins/Burroughs, accounting machine	350.00
Remington Model 12, bookkeeping machine	350.00
Rotary, Neostyle 8-F duplicator	45.00
Star, adding machine	18.00
Tandy/Radio Shack, computer, TRS-80 Model 1, Zilog Z-80 processor, 16K ram expandable to 64 K, 12" black and white monitor, 53 key keyboard, cassette storage, c1977	75.00
Underwood, bookkeeping machine	400.00

Cookie Jar, brown cow, cat finial, W10, $150.00.

Cipher Machine, Enigma, 1940, $11,000.00. Photo courtesy Auction Team Köln, Breker, Cologne, Germany.

CALCULATORS

The first affordable electronic integrated circuit calculator appeared in the early 1970s. Early pocket calculators cost hundreds of dollars. By the early 1980s the price of a basic pocket calulator was $10 or less. Manufacturers such as HP and Texas Instruments made dozens of different models. First models tend to be the most valuable.

References: Guy Ball and Bruce Flamm, *Collector's Guide to Pocket Calculators,* Wilson/Barnett Publishing, 1997; Thomas F. Haddock, *A Collector's Guide to Personal Computers and Pocket Calculators,* Books Americana, Krause Publications, 1993; W.A.C. Mier-Jadrzejowica, *A Guide to HP Handheld Calculators and Computers, Second Edition,* Wilson/Barnett Publishing, 1996.

Collectors' Club: International Assoc of Calculator Collectors (IACC), 14561 Livingston St, Tustin, CA 92780.

Adler 80C	$30.00
Atlas Rand 260	35.00
Brother 508A	45.00
Calcu-pen 820CD	40.00
Canon Pocketronic, 1971	100.00
Casio 805MR	25.00
Commodore SR7919	40.00
Craig 4516	35.00
Dictaphone 1680	100.00
Figural, avon bottle	15.00
Figural, cordless phone	20.00
Figural, floppy disk	5.00
Figural, heart, 4 functions, LCD, faux jewel buttons	45.00
Hewlett-Packard 45, scientific function, red LED	75.00
JC Penney GL-986R	30.00
Lloyd's 100, 4 functions, LCD, flip-up display cover	60.00
Logitech 1, scientific function, fabric wriststrap, 2-tone case	55.00
Montgomery Ward P8P, c1974	50.00
NCR 1844, c1971–72	200.00
Olivetti BC-D18, c1972	75.00
Olympia CD-100	35.00
Panasonic 805, 1973	35.00
Radio Shack EC-2010	15.00
Sears Digi-matic D-8	40.00
Sharp EL-201	15.00
Texas Instruments TI-1025	15.00
Toy, dog with bone, slide-open type	20.00
Toy, Little Professor	10.00
Toy, My First Calculator Book, 1991	15.00
Toy, Professor Mathics	45.00
Yashica Pickey	70.00

CALENDARS

The 19th-century printing revolution made calendars accessible to everyone. As the century ended, calendars were a popular form of advertising giveaway and remained so through much of the 20th century. Cheesecake calendars enjoyed a Golden Age between 1930 and the mid-1960s.

In the 1980s, the "art" or special theme calendar arrived on the scene. Moderately expensive when purchased new, they are ignored by most calendar collectors.

Today, calendars are collected because of the appeal of their subject matter, the artwork created by a famous illustrator, or because the year matches the birth year of the purchaser. If the monthly pages remain attached value increases 10% to 20%.

Reference: Norman E. Martinus and Harry L. Rinker, *Warman's Paper,* Wallace-Homestead, Krause Publications, 1994.

Collectors' Club: Calendar Collector Society, 18222 Flower Hill Way #299, Gaithersburg, MD 20879.

REPRODUCTION ALERT

1920, Chevrolet Motor Cars	$145.00
1921, Sunshine Bisquits	15.00
1922, Doe Wah Jack, Round Oak Stove, 10½ x 20"	175.00
1924, Calgary Brewing	185.00
1925, Western Ammo, hunting scene	250.00
1926, McCormick-Deering, woman eating cherry	65.00

Casio FX-451, $5.00.

1931, Life's Dog Calendar, cardboard, 14" h, 10" w, $50.00. Photo courtesy Collectors Auction Services.

1927, Winchester Arms, hunter on snowshoes **250.00**
1929, Star Brand Shoes, woman by stained glass window, framed **140.00**
1930, DeLaval, "Story of John & Mary," illus by Norman Price. **150.00**
1935, Bristol Steel Rod Co. **55.00**
1936, Denver & Santa Fe Railroad **30.00**
1937, Centennial Beer, man pointing to ad on wall **350.00**
1939, Johnson Winged Gasoline **18.00**
1940, Travelers Insurance Co, Currier & Ives. **45.00**
1943, Dunkirk Lumber & Co, Maxfield Parrish illus, 12 x 24". **55.00**
1945, McCabe Silversmiths, Will Rogers photo. **325.00**
1947, Gilmore Gasoline, red lion logo, 17 x 7" **20.00**
1949, Princess Elizabeth, 8½ x 4¾". **40.00**
1950, John Deere **90.00**
1950, Wandering Brook Farm, outdoor scene, children and animals **10.00**
1951, Four Seasons, Norman Rockwell illus. **35.00**
1953, Allis Chalmers. **18.00**
1954, Weaterbird Shoes, full pad, 8 x 13½". **25.00**
1959, Girl Scouts **20.00**
1961, Playboy Playmate, 5½ x 6½" **45.00**

CALIFORNIA FAIENCE

William Bradgon and Chauncey Thomas first manufactured art pottery and tiles in 1916. In 1924 they named their products California Faience.

Most art pottery pieces are characterized by cast molding and a monochrome matte glaze. Some pieces had a high gloss glaze. Plaster molds were used to make the polychrome decorated titles. California Faience also produced a commercial floral line and made master molds for other California potteries.

The company was hard hit by the Depresssion. Bradgon bought out Thomas in the late 1930s. He sold the pottery in the early 1950s, working with the new owners until he died in 1959.

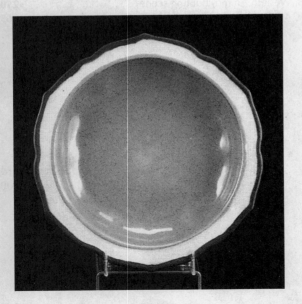

Low Bowl, lotus shaped, matte black glaze with glossy yellow and turquoise interior, incised "California Faience," 9" d, 1½" h, $110.00. Photo courtesy David Rago Auctions, Inc.

Cabinet Vase, raspberry glaze, imp "California Faience," 3½ x 2¾" **$200.00**
Candlesticks, pr, turquoise glaze, imp "California Faience," 4½" h. **200.00**
Console Set, bowl and pr of candlesticks, 12" d matte mustard, semi-matte cobalt and turquoise glaze faceted bowl, 4½" h black and turquoise candlesticks, stamped "California Faience" **200.00**
Lamp Base, bulbous, matte speckled ochre and green glaze, imp "California Porcelain," 8¾ x 7½". **450.00**
Trivet, cuenca, polychrome basket of flowers dec on cobalt ground, stamped "California Faience," 5" d. **200.00**
Trivet, cuenca, polychrome basket of flowers dec on yellow ground, stamped "California Faience," 5" d **300.00**
Trivet, cuenca, stylized blue flowers on white ground, imp "California Faience," 5¼" d. **250.00**
Vase, bulbous, yellow semi-matte glaze, imp "California Faience," 5 x 5¼" **225.00**
Vase, corseted, green glaze, imp "California Faience," 7¼" h **210.00**
Vase, ovoid, medium blue matte glaze, turquoise int, incised mark, 8" h **100.00**
Vessel, classical shape, purple flambé glaze, imp "California Faience," 8" h. **185.00**
Vessel, squat, matte speckled robin's egg blue glaze, imp "California Faience," 2¼ x 4½" **375.00**
Vessel, squat, white semi-matte glaze, imp "California Pottery," 5" h. **175.00**

CAMARK POTTERY

Samuel Jack Carnes founded Camark Pottery, Camden, Arkansas, in 1926. The company made art pottery, earthenware, and decorative accessories. John Lessell, previously employed at Weller, and his wife were among the leading art potters working at Camark.

After Carnes sold the plant in 1966, it was run primarily as a retail operation by Mary Daniels. In January 1986 Gary and Mark Ashcraft purchased the Camark Pottery building in hopes of re-establishing a pottery at the site. At the time of the purchase, they stated they did not intend to reissue pieces using the company's old molds.

References: David Edwin Gifford, *Collector's Guide to Camark Pottery*, (1997), *Book II* (1999), Collector Books; Letitia Landers, *Camark Pottery, Vol. 1* (1994), *Vol. 2* (1996), Colony Publishing.

Collectors' Club: National Society of Arkansas Pottery Collectors Society, PO Box 7617, Little Rock, AR 72217.

Ashtray, rose green overflow, unmkd , 2" h **$20.00**
Basket, matte orange glaze, unmkd, 3¾" h **10.00**
Dish, leaf shape, matte blue glaze, 1½ x 4½" **10.00**
Figure, bear, mirror black glaze, blue Arkansas sticker, 6" h **100.00**
Figure, camel, resting, brown stipple glaze, 6 x 3¼" **140.00**
Figure, frog, open mouth, green and yellow glaze, unmkd, 4 x 3". **80.00**
Ginger Jar, ivory crackle matte glaze, gold Arkansas ink stamp, 9" h **300.00**
Humidor, sea green glaze, unmkd, 6½" h. **120.00**
Jug, "Pure Corn," Arkansas ink stamp, 5" h **60.00**
Pitcher, ivory crackle glaze, parrot handle, gold Arkansas ink stamp, 9" h. **250.00**

Planter, swans, white with gold trim, #521, late 1930s, 7¹/₄" h, $35.00. Photo courtesy Ray Morykan Auctions.

Shot Glass, orange green overflow, 2" h 20.00
Tray, cloverleaf shape, solid matte glaze, 10³/₄" w 60.00
Vase, Barcelona/Spano Ware, Arkansas die stamp, 7" h 140.00
Vase, brown stipple glaze, black "Souvenir of Camden,
   Ark.," unmkd, 3³/₄" h 10.00
Vase, brown stipple glaze, brown Arkansas sticker, 11" h . . . 250.00
Vase, bulbous, celestial blue, 2³/₄" h 20.00
Vase, Coraline, gold Arkansas ink stamp, 4¹/₂" h 180.00
Vase, rose green overflow, unmkd, 4" h 40.00
Wedding Vase, ribbed, matte green glaze, 6³/₄" h 60.00

CAMBRIDGE GLASS

Cambridge Glass, Cambridge, Ohio, was founded in 1901. The company manufactured a wide variety of glass tablewares. After experiencing financial difficulties in 1907, Arthur J. Bennett, previously with the National Glass Company, helped reorganize the company. By the 1930s, the company had over 5,000 glass molds in inventory.

Although five different identification marks are known, not every piece of Cambridge Glass was permanently marked. Paper labels were used between 1935 and 1954.

Cambridge Glass ceased operations in 1954. Its molds were sold. Imperial Glass Company purchased some, a few wound up in private hands.

References: Gene Florence, *Elegant Glassware of the Depression Era, Seventh Edition,* Collector Books, 1997; National Cambridge Collectors, Inc., *The Cambridge Glass Co., Cambridge, Ohio* (reprint of 1930 catalog and supplements through 1934), Collector Books, 1976, 1998 value update; National Cambridge Collectors, Inc., *The Cambridge Glass Co., Cambridge Ohio, 1949 Thru 1953* (catalog reprint), Collector Books, 1976, 1996 value update; National Cambridge Collectors, Inc., *Colors in Cambridge Glass,* Collector Books, 1984, 1997 value update.

Periodical: *The Daze,* PO Box 57, Otisville, MI 48463.

Collectors' Club: National Cambridge Collectors, Inc, PO Box 416, Cambridge, OH 43725.

Ashtray, Gadroon, #3500/124, 3¹/₄" **$5.00**
Ashtray, Gadroon, #3500/126, 4" 55.00
Basket, Wildflower, #3500/55, 2 handles, 6" sq 50.00
Bitters Bottle, Elaine, #1212, no tube 230.00
Bonbon, Elaine, #3400/20 . . . . 55.00
Bonbon, Elaine, 4 toed, #3400/204, 6" 70.00
Bowl, Apple Blossom, 4 toed, #3400/4, 12" 90.00
Bowl, Blossomtime, ftd, #3400/4, 12" 130.00
Bowl, Rose Point, #3400/1185, 2 handles, 10" 140.00
Bread and Butter Plate, Caprice, blue, #20, 5¹/₂" 30.00
Bread and Butter Plate, Portia, #3400/60 . . . . 12.00
Butter, cov, Elaine, #3400/52 . . . . 230.00
Candy Dish, cov, Wildflower, #3400, 3 part 95.00
Candy Dish, Decagon, light blue, #864 . . . . 120.00
Celery/Relish Tray, Apple Blossom, yellow, 5 part 90.00
Celery/Relish Tray, Caprice, blue, 3 part, #124, 8¹/₂" 50.00
Celery Tray, Apple Blossom, pink, #652, 11" 130.00
Cheese and Cracker Set, Blossomtime 190.00
Cheese and Cracker Set, Tally-Ho, gold trim 60.00
Cheese Comport, Apple Blossom, amber 50.00
Cheese Comport, Candlelight, ftd, #3400 . . . . 70.00
Cheese Comport, Rose Point, #3400 . . . . 50.00
Cheese Dish, cov, Elaine, #980, 5" 460.00
Cigarette Box, cov, Caprice, crystal, small 30.00
Cigarette Holder, Caprice, blue, #204 . . . . 60.00
Cigarette Holder, Rose Point, #1337 . . . . 300.00
Claret, Elaine, #3121 . . . . 44.00
Coaster, Caprice, crystal 13.00
Cocktail, Portia, #3130 . . . . 24.00
Cocktail, Tally-Ho, #3900/150, blown, 3¹/₂ oz 32.00
Comport, #3500, 6" 60.00
Comport, #3900/136, 5¹/₂" 70.00
Comport, Apple Blossom, pink, #3400/14, 7" 170.00
Comport, Apple Blossom, yellow, 4 toed, #3400 . . . . 60.00
Comport, Gadroon, #3500/36, 6" 60.00
Comport, Rose Point, #3121/4, blown, 5³/₈" 90.00
Comport, Wildflower, #3500/148, 6" 60.00
Cordial, Caprice, crystal, blown, #300 . . . . 50.00
Corn Dish, Elaine, #477 . . . . 75.00
Corn Dish, Rose Point, #447, gold trim 77.00
Cracker Plate, Rose Point, #3400/6, 11¹/₂" 75.00
Creamer, #3500, individual 30.00
Creamer and Sugar, #3500/14 . . . . 70.00
Creamer and Sugar, Gadroon, #3500/15, individual 70.00
Creamer and Sugar, Tally-Ho, #1402/33 . . . . 70.00
Cup, #3900 . . . . 22.00
Cup and Saucer, #3900 . . . . 30.00
Cup and Saucer, Apple Blossom, crystal 25.00
Cup and Saucer, Caprice, mocha 36.00
Cup and Saucer, Portia, #3400/54 . . . . 24.00
Cup and Saucer, Tally-Ho, cobalt 55.00
Finger Bowl, Caprice, blue, pressed, #16 . . . . 70.00
Fruit Saucer, Caprice, blue, crimped, #19, 5" 75.00
Goblet, Caprice, crystal, blown, #300 . . . . 30.00
Goblet, Decagon, blue, #3077, 9 oz 20.00
Guest Set, Decagon, pink, 4 pcs, #488, 22 oz jug, lid,
   tray and tumbler 160.00
Ice Bucket, Apple Blossom, crystal 100.00
Ice Bucket, Caprice, crystal, with tongs 130.00
Ice Bucket, Tally-Ho, cobalt 177.00
Jug, Apple Blossom, pink, #3400/38, 80 oz 530.00
Mayonnaise, Candlelight, 2 pc, #3400/11 . . . . 130.00
Mayonnaise, Elaine, 2 pc, #3400/11 . . . . 90.00
Mayonnaise, Gadroon, ftd, handled, #3500/59, 6" 77.00

Oil and Vinegar Set, Caprice, crystal, 3 pcs, #99 . . . . **120.00**
Oil and Vinegar Set, Elaine, 3 pcs, #3400/96 . . . . **330.00**
Oil and Vinegar Tray, Decagon, pink, handled, #619 . . . . **40.00**
Oil Cruet, with stopper, #3900/100, 6 oz **130.00**
Parfait, Caprice, pink, #300, 5 oz. **170.00**
Pickle Tray, Apple Blossom, yellow, #3400/59, 9" **70.00**
Plate, #3500, 8½" **25.00**
Plate, #3500/24, 10½" **140.00**
Plate, #3500/39, ftd, round, 12" **190.00**
Plate, #3500/166, 14" **100.00**
Plate, #3900/167, 14½" **160.00**
Plate, Apple Blossom, crystal, #3400, 6" **10.00**
Plate, Caprice, crystal, 9½" **60.00**
Plate, Caprice, crystal, 4 toed, cupped alpine, 14" **70.00**
Plate, Caprice, mocha, 8½" **30.00**
Plate, Everglades, light blue, #56, 3 toed, 13" **130.00**
Plate, Portia, #3400/62, 8" **20.00**
Plate, Portia, #3400/64, 10¼" **140.00**
Plate, Rose Point, #3400, 8½" **25.00**
Plate, Rose Point, #3400, handled, 5". **50.00**
Plate, Wildflower, #3400/1181, 2 handles, 6" **50.00**
Relish, #3500/68, 2 part, 5½" **60.00**
Relish, #3900/124, 2 part, 7" **55.00**
Relish, Apple Blossom, crystal, 3 handles, #3400/91, 8" **60.00**
Relish, Blossomtime, 2 part **60.00**
Relish, Blossomtime, 3 part **90.00**
Relish, Gadroon, 6 pcs, #3500/67, 12". **260.00**
Relish, Rose Point, #3400/90, 2 part, handled, 6" **55.00**
Relish, Tally-Ho, #3900/91, 3 part, 8" **130.00**
Salad Dressing Bowl, with liner, Tally-Ho, #3900/25, 2
    part. **130.00**
Salt and Pepper Shakers, pr, Rose Point, #3400/77, plas-
    tic tops **70.00**
Sandwich Plate, Tally-Ho, #3900/34, 11½". **130.00**
Sauceboat and Liner, Tally-Ho, #3900/17 . . . . **160.00**
Seafood Icer, with liner, Portia **77.00**
Sherbet, Apple Blossom, crystal, #3130 . . . . **20.00**
Sherbet, Caprice, blue, pressed, tall, #2, 7 oz **35.00**
Sherbet, Caprice, crystal, blown, #300, 6 oz **13.00**
Sherbet, Wildflower, #3121, gold trim **20.00**
Sugar, Everglades, light blue, #26 . . . . **130.00**
Sugar, Tally-Ho, cobalt **55.00**

Tea Plate, Apple Blossom, crystal, #3400, 7½" **14.00**
Tray, Gadroon, #3500/67, round, 12" **190.00**
Tumbler, Caprice, blue, barrel, #180, 5 oz **50.00**
Tumbler, Caprice, crystal, ftd, #300/2, 12 oz **22.00**
Tumbler, Elaine, #3400/92, 2½ oz **77.00**
Vase, Caprice, amber, #239, 8⅛" **190.00**
Vase, Caprice, cobalt, #239, 8⅝" **290.00**
Vase, Everglades, light blue, #20, 10½" **360.00**
Vegetable, Cleo, pink, 9½" **120.00**
Water Goblet, Elaine, #3121 . . . . **40.00**
Wine, Decagon, pink, #3700. . . . . **18.00**

CAMERAS & ACCESSORIES

The development of the camera was truly international. Johann Zahn, a German monk, created the first fully portable wood box camera with a movable lens, adjustable aperture, and mirror to project the image in the early 1800s. Joseph Niepce and Louise Daguere perfected the photographic plate. Peter Von Voigtlander, an Austrian, contributed the quality lens. An industry was born.

By the late 19th century, England, France, and Germany all played major roles in the development of camera technology. America's contributions came in the area of film development and marketing.

In 1888 George Eastman introduced the Kodak No. 1, a simple box camera that revolutionized the industry. Model No. 4 was the first folding camera. The Brownie was introduced in 1900.

After World War II, the Japanese made a strong commitment to dominating the camera market. By the 1970s, they had achieved their goal.

Reference: Jim and Joan McKeown (eds.), *Price Guide to Antique and Classic Cameras, 1997–1998, 10th Edition,* Centennial Photo Service, 1996.

Periodical: *Classic Camera,* PO Box 1270, New York, NY 10156.

Collectors' Clubs: American Photographic Historical Society, Inc, 1150 Avenue of the Americas, New York, NY 10036; American Society of Camera Collectors, 7415 Reseda Blvd, Reseda, CA 91335; International Kodak Historical Society, PO Box 21, Flourtown, PA 19301; Leica Historical Society of America, 7611 Dornoch Ln, Dallas, TX 75248; Nikon Historical Society, PO Box 3213, Munster, IN 46321; The Movie Machine Society, 42 Deerhaven Dr, Nashua, NH 03060; Zeiss Historical Society, 300 Waxwing Dr, Cranbury, NJ 08512.

CAMERAS

Ansco Readyset Royal #1, folding, Antar lens, c1926 . . . . . . **$90.00**
Bell & Howell, Stereo Colorist, 35mm, Rodenstock
    Trinar f3.5 lens, c1952. . . . . **145.00**
Eastman Kodak Boy Scout Camera, green vest pocket,
    emb on bed, 127 film, 1930s. **40.00**
Eastman Kodak Instamatic 314, lever wind, light meter,
    uses flash cubes, 1968–71 . . . . **15.00**
Eastman Kodak Pony, 35mm, Kodak Anaston f4.5 lens,
    1950s. **10.00**
Kodak Brownie "Holiday Flash," brown Bakelite, Dakon
    lens, carrying strap **20.00**
Minolta Electro Shot, 35mm, auto range finder, non-
    interchangeable Rokkor QF f1.8/40mm auto shutter
    ¹⁄₁₆-¹⁄₅₀₀, 1965. . . . . **40.00**

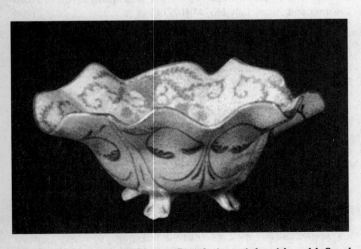

Bowl, Crown Tuscan, oblong, fluted rim, pink with gold floral trim, 11½ x 10½", $165.00. Photo courtesy Jackson's Auctioneers & Appraisers.

Nikon Nikkorex Zoom-8, 8mm movie camers, fl.8 lens, zooms 8 to 32mm, manual zoom **25.00**

Novelty, Donald Duck, Donald, Huey, Dewey and Louie on back, black, 127 film **35.00**

Novelty, Incredible Hulk, 126 film **30.00**

Olympus 35 IV **55.00**

Pentax "ME Super," M1:2 50mm lens, AF 160 flash, auto/manual focus switch, vinyl carry case, instruction booklet **80.00**

Polaroid 420 Instant Camera, folding bellows **20.00**

Polaroid Swinger Sentinel M15, 1965–70 . . . . **10.00**

Sabre 620, black plastic, white plastic carry handle **20.00**

Toy, Kenner Picture-Quick, knob ejects pre-printed pictures through bottom slot, 1977 . . . . **7.00**

Toy, Smurf Musical Camera, blue plastic, plays *Rock-a-bye-Baby*, revolving Smurf head on top, 1982 . . . . **5.00**

ACCESSORIES

Bag, plastic, camera shape, transparent plastic lens and back, Leadworks, c1985 . . . . **$10.00**

Book, *Amateur Carbro Colour Prints*, Viscount Hanworth, Focal Press, London, third ed, dj, 188 pp, 1950–51 . . . . **20.00**

Catalog, Korona, 52 pp, 1926 . . . . **25.00**

Catalog, Leica, 84 pp, 1955 . . . . **15.00**

Catalog, Watson and Sons, Ltd, Camera Lenses and Accessories, 24 pp, 1937 . . . . **20.00**

Exposure Meter, auxiliary cdS, Canon, 1965–67 . . . . **15.00**

Lens, Tele-hentar, 1:3.5 200mm, screw-on, with case **15.00**

Manual, Leica Reflex Housing, 9 pp, 1956 . . . . **5.00**

Manual, Sound Kodascope, FS-10-N, service and parts, large format, 55 pp, c1947 . . . . **8.00**

Mug, Kodak, "You press the button. We do the rest," ivory, brown lettering, illus of woman photographing young girl, made in Korea **15.00**

Range Finder, Nikon, Varifocal **150.00**

Sign, Kodak, Art Deco, enamel, double-sided triangle, red, blue, and yellow, c1930s **200.00**

Timer, Luxor Photo Timer, Burke & James, c1930s **10.00**

CANDLEWICK

Imperial Glass Corporation introduced its No. 400 pattern, Candlewick, in 1936. Over 650 different forms and sets are known. Although produced primarily in cyrstal (clear), other colors exist. The pattern proved extremely popular and remained in production until Imperial closed in 1982.

After a brief period of ownership by the Lancaster-Colony Corporation and Consolidated Stores, Imperial's assets, including its molds, were sold. Various companies, groups, and individuals bought Imperial's Candlewick molds. Mirror Images of Lansing, Michigan, bought more than 200. Boyd Crystal Art Glass, Cambridge, Ohio, bought 18.

References: Mary M. Wetzel-Tomalka, *Candlewick: The Jewel of Imperial, Book II,* published by author, 1995; Mary M. Wetzel-Tomalka, *Candlewick: The Jewel of Imperial, Price Guide '99 and More,* published by author, 1998.

Collectors' Club: The National Candlewick Collector's Club, 275 Milledge Terrace, Athens, GA 30606.

Bell, 400/108, 5" h **$80.00**

Bowl, 400/1F, 5" d **12.00**

Bowl, 400/63B, 10½" d **60.00**

Bowl, 400/84, 2 part, 6½" d **25.00**

Bud Vase, 400/107 . . . . **65.00**

Cake Stand, 400/103D, 11" d **70.00**

Candlestick, 400/80, 3½" h **35.00**

Candlestick, 400/108 . . . . **18.00**

Celery Tray, 400/105, oval, open handles, 13½" l **30.00**

Coaster, 400/78, 4" d. **7.00**

Compote, 400/45, 5½" h **25.00**

Creamer and Sugar, 400/31 . . . . **30.00**

Deviled Egg Tray, 400/154 . . . . **95.00**

Dinner Plate, 400/10D **25.00**

Ice Tub, 400/63 . . . . **85.00**

Juice Pitcher, 400/19, 40 oz **250.00**

Juice Tumbler, 400/19, 5 oz **10.00**

Ladle, 400/130, 3-bead **12.50**

Relish, 400/55, 8½" **22.50**

Relish, 400/56, 10½" **50.00**

Salad Plate, 400/5D, 8" d **8.00**

Shaker, 400/190, ftd **22.00**

Sherbet, 400/19, low, 5 oz. **15.00**

Sherbet, 400/190, 5 oz **18.00**

Sugar Dip/Nut, 400/64 . . . . **12.00**

Tumbler, 400/19, 12 oz **20.00**

Vase, 400/107, ftd, 5¾" h **85.00**

Wine, 400/19, ftd, 3 oz **25.00**

CANDY & GUM COLLECTIBLES

Collecting interest in candy and gum collectibles has reached a level where it deserves its own category. Actually, candy and gum collectibles have figured prominently in several key collecting categories, e.g., advertising and coin-operated, for decades. Several recent publications, ranging from a history of chocolate to one about the Hershey and Mars families, has heightened collector interest.

This category is bigger than chocolate, although chocolate related collectibles certainly sweeten the pot. Candy boxes and candy wrappers are two subcategories gaining in popularity.

Here is something to chew on. Several years ago, a single stick of Coca-Cola gum brought over $3,300 at auction.

Reference: *Candy Containers,* L-W Book Sales, 1996.

Collectors' Clubs: Bubble Gum Charm Collectors, 24 Seafoam St, Staten Island, NY 10306; Candy Container Collectors of America, PO Box 352, Chelmsford, MA 01824.

Blotter, Hershey's Gum, brown lettering and gum pkg on white ground, Hershey's Cocoa adv on reverse, 2⅞ x 5⅜" **$500.00**

Box, Hershey Kisses, cardboard, girl giving Hershey Kiss to boy, 1930s, 7½" h, 10" w, 3" d **7.50**

Box, Reedy's Pineapple Chewing Gum, cardboard with paper label, red and white lettering and 3 pineapples on yellow ground, 1¼ x 8⅝ x 4½" **300.00**

Candy Container, figural Indian motorcycle and rider, clear glass, 5" l **500.00**

Clicker, Pez, "Pez" girl handing candy to boy, litho tin, 2½ x 3½" **275.00**

Vending Machine, Pulver Chewing Gum, wrinkle finish, new old stock, orig cardboard box with keys, 20" h, 8½" w, 4½" d, $1,760.00. Photo courtesy Collectors Auction Services.

Counter Felt, Wrigley's Gum, trademark Wrigley figure and "After Every Meal Wrigley's P.K. Chewing Sweet Peppermint Flavor," yellow ground, 5⅜ x 7¾" **175.00**

Display, Blony Gum, figural truck, cardboard, wood wheels, bed holds gum, 8" h, 13½" w **375.00**

Display Box, Smart Peppermint Gum, True Blue Gum Co, light blue box, yellow globe logo, complete with 20 orig pkgs, new old stock, 1 x 6 x 4¼" **175.00**

Display Rack, Life Savers, litho tin, 3-tier, 4¼ x 9⅞ x 15" . . . **575.00**

Pinback Button, Kis-Me Gum, woman's profile, red and white checkerboard background, ⅞" d **35.00**

Sign, Honey-Fruit Gum, litho tin over cardboard, beveled edge, stick gum pkg and yellow lettering on black ground, 6¼ x 9⅛" **2,750.00**

Tin, Brach's Candies of Quality, square, gold ground, multicolor candies on 2 sides, factory scene other 2 sides, c1940, 5 lbs, 4½" sq, 10⅛" h **65.00**

Tin, Ellis & Helfer H. H. Tablets Confections, tin, red ground, log cabin in center, red and black lettering, gold and black highlights, bail handle, c1940, 5¾" d, 6½" h **20.00**

Tin, FW McNess Fine Confections, square, blue and white plaid ground, red lettering, candy dish, c1930, 4" sq, 7⅝" h **15.00**

Tin, Grand Union Hard Candies, rect, red ground, blue bands, blue and white lettering, c1930, 5 lbs, 6" w, 8⅝" h **30.00**

Tin, Happiness Candy, rect, elephants on lid, animal circus around sides, "Happiness in Every Box," bail handle, c1925, 6" w, 3¾" d, 3¼" h **300.00**

Tin, Hoyt's Selected Sweets, round, black and white checkerboard ground, boy holding candy jar, girl with hand extended, raised lettering on lid, 1920s, 5 lbs, 5" d, 9¾" h **75.00**

Tin, Kid Kandy, yellow ground, black and white Jackie Coogan portrait on front, policeman chasing boy on back, bail handle, c1935, 3¼" d, 3½" h **275.00**

Tin, Sharp's Kreemy Toffee, little girl eating candy bar, "It's Alright," 7" w, 4" d, 5" h **85.00**

Tin, Sharp's Super-Kreem Toffee, Englishman wearing monocle and bowler, parrot, "Speaks for itself," bail handle, 8½" h, 7" d **165.00**

Tin, Sunshine Kisses, light blue ground, yellow and orange sunrise, red, black, and yellow highlights, bail handle, c1930, 9¾" d, 7" h **65.00**

Valentine Card, Beechnut Brand Chewing Gum, mechanical, rosy-cheeked boy and girl, 7 x 5" **55.00**

Whistle, Curtiss Candy Company, Baby Ruth, litho tin, white lettering, red ground **15.00**

CAP GUNS

The first toy cap gun was introduced in 1870. Cap guns experienced two Golden Ages: (1) the era of the cast-iron cap gun from 1870 through 1900 and (2) the era of the diecast metal and plastic cap guns.

Hubley, Kilgore, Mattel, and Nichols are among the leading manufacturers of diecast pistols. Many diecast and plastic pistols were sold as part of holster sets. A large number were associated with television cowboy and detective heroes. The presence of the original box, holster, and other accessories adds as much as 100% to the value of the gun.

References: Rudy D'Angelo, *Cowboy Hero Cap Pistols,* Antique Trader Books, 1997; James L. Dundas, *Cap Guns,* Schiffer Publishing, 1996; Jerrell Little, *Price Guide to Cowboy Cap Guns and Guitars,* L-W Book Sales, 1996; Jim Schleyer, *Backyard Buckaroos: Collecting Western Toy Guns,* Books Americana, Krause Publications, 1996.

Collectors' Club: Toy Gun Collectors of America, 312 Starling Way, Anaheim, CA 92807.

Buck Rogers Atomic Pistol, 1934 . . . . **$275.00**
Buck Rogers Cap Pistol, Kilgore, MIB **125.00**
Derringer Cap Pistol, Nichols **50.00**
Dick Tracy Cap Pistol, NMIB **50.00**
Eagle Cap Gun, Kilgore **40.00**
Early American Flintlock Jr. Cap Pistol, Hubley, MIB **95.00**
Flintlock Jr Cap Gun, Hubley **35.00**
Hawkeye Cap Pistol, Kilgore, MIB **85.00**

Pirate Pistol, #265, Hubley, 9" l, $95.00. Photo courtesy Collectors Auction Services.

Hubley Chief Cap Pistol, 7" l, NMOC	**65.00**
Long Style Double Gun & Holster Set, Hubley	**160.00**
Overland Trail (William Bendix) Kelly's Rifle, Hubley, MIB	**900.00**
Red Ranger Gun, NMIB	**175.00**
Red Ryder 50th Anniversary BB Gun, Daisy	**90.00**
Roy Rogers Classy Guns & Double Holster Set	**900.00**
Roy Rogers Guns, double holsters, Schmidt	**800.00**
Roy Rogers Mini-Cap Gun, with holster and belt, NM	**175.00**
Shootin' Shell Guns, in holsters, Mattel, price for pair	**450.00**
Sportsman 3-in-1 Air Pistol	**195.00**
Western Cap Pistol	**250.00**
Winchester Shootin' Shell Rifle, Mattel	**90.00**
Wyatt Earp Pistol and Holster, NM	**400.00**

CARLTON WARE

Wiltshow and Robinson produced Staffordshire earthenware and porcelains at the Carlton Works, Stoke-on-Trent, beginning in the 1890s. In 1957 the company's name was changed to Carlton Ware, Ltd.

Black was the background color most often used on the company's wares. During the 1920s the line included pieces decorated with Art Deco designs in brightly enameled and gilt flowers and porcelain vases featuring luster decoration in oriental motifs. Walking Ware, introduced in the 1970s, was Carlton's most popular line of novelty footed breakfast dishes and serving pieces recognizable by its brightly decorated socks and Mary Janes.

Reference: Helen Cunningham, *Clarice Cliff and Her Contemporaries: Susie Cooper, Keith Murray, Charlotte Rhead and the Carlton Ware Designers*, Schiffer Publishing, 1999.

Collectors' Club: Carlton Ware Collectors Intl, PO Box 161, Sevenoaks, Kent Tn15 6GA UK.

Bowl, Salad Ware	**$55.00**
Coffeepot, Magnolia line, yellow and green	**40.00**
Condiment Set, salt and pepper shakers, covered mustard, and undertray, yellow conch shell shapes	**75.00**
Figure, comical dog, Pipsqueak and Wilfred series, black and white, 1930s	**95.00**
Figure, Nan, 1930s	**300.00**
Figure, Verona, 1930s	**225.00**
Lamp, Guinness toucan, orig shade	**350.00**
Napkin Ring, figural toy soldier	**50.00**
Pitcher, Fruit Basket	**80.00**
Sugar Bowl, pear shape	**25.00**
Tri-Leaf Dish, green and white	**40.00**
Walking Ware, biscuit jar, cov, 7¼" h, 5½" d	**160.00**
Walking Ware, coffee cup, kneeling, blue vertical striped socks, black shoes, 4½" h	**45.00**
Walking Ware, coffee mug, Adam, bare feet, green fig leaf on white ground, serpeant handle, 5" h	**50.00**
Walking Ware, coffee mug, Eve, bare feet, green fig leaves on white ground, 4½" h	**50.00**
Walking Ware, coffeepot, black and blue vertical striped socks, green shoes, 9¾" h	**85.00**
Walking Ware, eggcup, Caribbean R.J.S. series, green, blue, and yellow beach dec, 3" h	**10.00**
Walking Ware, eggcup, chicken, 2-pc, chicken finial, egg with green sash and dots, yellow shoes, 6" h	**18.00**
Walking Ware, eggcup, polka-dot socks	**12.00**

Pitcher, Art Deco design, blue, pink, and yellow, c1928, 8" h, $300.00.

Walking Ware, eggcup, Wellington, horizontal striped socks, red boots, 3¾" h	**15.00**
Walking Ware, mug, birthday, red hearts on socks, yellow shoes, 4½" h	**40.00**
Walking Ware, plate, blue polka-dot socks, yellow shoes, 10" h, 8¼" d	**100.00**
Walking Ware, salt and pepper shakers, pr, brown checkered socks, blue shoes, 5" h	**75.00**
Walking Ware, soup bowl, open, sitting, purple polka-dot socks, gray shoes, 3½" h	**115.00**
Walking Ware, sugar bowl, cov, crossed legs, blue and yellow vertical striped socks, blue shoes, 6¾" h	**50.00**
Walking Ware, teacup, dark green checkered socks, green shoes, 4¼" h	**35.00**
Walking Ware, teapot, black and blue vertical striped socks, yellow shoes, 7" h	**75.00**

CARNIVAL CHALKWARE

Inexpensive plaster of Paris figurines made from the 1920s through the 1960s are collected under the generic classification of carnival chalkware because they most frequently were given away as prizes at games of chance. Doll and novelty companies produced them in quantity. Cost was as low as a dollar a dozen. While some pieces are marked and dated, most are not.

References: Thomas G. Morris, *The Carnival Chalk Prize I* (1985), *II* (1994), Prize Publishers, 1998 value update; *Price Guide to Carnival Chalkware, Giveaways and Games*, L-W Book Sales, 1995.

Buffalo, bank, c1950, 10½" l	**$28.00**
China Boy, incised "©1948 J.Y. Jenkins," 13" h	**115.00**
Clown, bank, c1950, 13" h	**38.00**
Corn in Hand, Iowa Centennial 1838–1938, c1938, 12" h	**30.00**
Crying Pig, c1940–50, 7" h	**15.00**
Devil's Head, bank, c1950, 6½" h	**70.00**
Donald Duck, c1934, 13" h	**85.00**
Elephant, c1960, 10½" h	**35.00**

Apache Babe, 1936, 14" h, $70.00.

Fat Kewpie, c1935–45, 13" h........................ **50.00**
Ferdinand the Bull, bank, c1940–50, 9" h............... **50.00**
George Washington, c1940, 11" h..................... **38.00**
Horse 'n Saddle, c1940–50, 10½" h.................. **28.00**
Indian with Drum, c1940–50, 12½" h **70.00**
Junior Pig Bank, c1940–50, 9½" h.................... **28.00**
King Kong, c1930–40, 7" h **35.00**
King Kong, c1930–40, 12½" h....................... **60.00**
Majorette, c1940–50, 15½" h....................... **38.00**
Piggy Bank, c1950, 11" l........................... **55.00**
Porky Pig, bank, c1945, 12" h **35.00**
Rider on Horse, c1940, 9" h **85.00**
Sailor Boy, c1934, 9" h **25.00**
Sailor Girl, c1930–40, 14" h **55.00**
Skull with Snake, c1960, 6" h **50.00**
Small Pig, c1935, 6" h............................. **16.00**
Snow White, c1937, 14" h.......................... **50.00**
Tom Boy, c1940, 15½" h........................... **60.00**
Uncle Sam, c1935, 15" h........................... **95.00**
Wolf, c1934, 17" h................................ **28.00**

CARNIVAL GLASS

Carnival glass is iridized pressed glass. When collectors refer to "classic" carnival glass, they are talking about patterns manufactured between 1905 (or 1907— scholars do not agree on the exact date when carnival was first introduced) and 1930. Glass manufacturers in Australia, Czechoslovakia, England, Finland, France, Germany, Sweden, and the United States produced carnival glass. Leading American manufacturers include Dugan, Fenton, Imperial, Millersburg, and Northwood.

Carnival glass has been made continuously since its introduction. American manufacturers of carnival glass in the post-1945 period include Boyd, Fenton, Imperial, Mosser, and L. G. Wright. The Jain Glass Works in India made carnival glass from 1935 until 1986.

Period molds survive and are occasionally used to create reproductions. New patterns abound. David Doty notes: "My personal opinion is that there have been far more patterns made in contemporary carnival glass than there were in the classic era."

References: Carl O. Burns, *Imperial Carnival Glass,* Collector Books, 1996, 1998 value update; David Doty, *A Field Guide to Carnival Glass,* Glass Press, 1998; Fenton Art Glass Collectors of America (comp.), *Fenton Glass: The Third Twenty-Five Years Comprehensive Price Guide, 1998,* Glass Press, 1998; William Heacock, *Fenton Glass, The Third Twenty-Five Years, 1956–1980,* O-Val Advertising (Antique Publications), 1989; William Heacock, James Measell and Berry Wiggins, *Dugan Diamond: The Story of Indiana, Pennsylvania, Glass,* Antique Publications, 1993; James Measell and W. C. Roetteis, *The L. G. Wright Glass Company,* Glass Press, 1997; Margaret Whitmyer and Kenn Whitmyer, *Fenton Art Glass: 1907–1939,* Collector Books, 1996, 1999 value update.

Collectors' Clubs: American Carnival Glass Assoc, 9621 Springwater, Miamisburg, OH 45342; Collectible Carnival Glass Assoc (post-1960), 3103 Brentwood Circle, Grand Island, NE 68801; International Carnival Glass Assoc, PO Box 306, Mentone, IN 46539.

Dugan, Brooklyn Bridge, bowl, marigold, 1930s......... **$300.00**
Dugan, God and Home, tumbler, blue.................. **150.00**
Fenton, Butterfly & Berry, bowl, #8428, peacock tail int,
 ruby, 1976–77.................................. **45.00**
Fenton, Butterfly & Berry, tumbler, #8240, amethyst,
 1972–73...................................... **15.00**
Fenton, Faberge bell, #8466, amethyst, 1977–78 .... **25.00**
Fenton, Grape and Cable, bowl, blue, 1920s, 8".......... **45.00**
Fenton, Grape and Cable, plate, marigold, 1920s, 9" **85.00**
Fenton, Hearts & Flowers, bowl, #8228, flared,
 amethyst, 1971–73 .... **50.00**
Fenton, Mermaid, vase, #8254, 1970–72, amethyst........ **90.00**
Fenton, Orange Tree, compote, #9173, amethyst, 8"....... **45.00**
Fenton, Persian Medallion, compote, #8234, ruby,
 1976–77...................................... **30.00**
Fenton, Pinwheel, compote, #8227, ruby, 1976–77 .... **50.00**
Fenton, Rib and Holly Sprig, compote, flared, royal blue,
 c1925, 6" **50.00**
Fenton, Rib and Holly Sprig, compote, goblet shape,
 golden, c1925.................................. **65.00**
Fenton, Swan, candle holder, #5172, amethyst, 1971–73 .... **30.00**
Imperial, Crackle, candlesticks, pr, marigold, 1930s **20.00**
Imperial, Crackle, candy jar, cov, marigold, 1930s **8.00**
Imperial, Crackle, miniature oil lamp, marigold, 1930s..... **45.00**
Imperial, Crackle, water set, marigold, 1930s **35.00**
Imperial, Daisy, basket, marigold, 1930s **40.00**
Imperial, Floral and Optic, cake plate, marigold **25.00**
Imperial, Floral and Optic, cake plate, smoke............ **125.00**
Imperial, Frosted Block, bowl, square, clambroth **30.00**
Imperial, Frosted Block, compote, clambroth **35.00**
Imperial, Frosted Block, creamer and sugar, marigold **40.00**
Imperial, Frosted Block, plate, marigold, 9" d............ **60.00**
Imperial, Soda Gold, chop plate, marigold, 12" d.......... **50.00**
Imperial, Soda Gold, console bowl, smoke.............. **40.00**
Imperial, Soda Gold, console set, bowl and 2 candle-
 sticks, marigold................................ **90.00**
Imperial, Soda Gold, salt and pepper shakers, pr, light
 blue **90.00**
Imperial, Tree Bark, water pitcher, aqua **30.00**
Imperial, Tree Bark, water set, pitcher and 6 tumblers,
 marigold..................................... **50.00**
Josef Inwald Co, Czechoslovakia, Jacobean Ranger, shot
 glass, marigold, c1925–35 .... **100.00**
LG Wright, Dahlia, pitcher, white, c1977............... **40.00**

LG Wright, Dahlia, tumbler, purple, c1977. . . . . **30.00**
LG Wright, God and Home, pitcher, ruby, c1980 . . . . **125.00**
LG Wright, Grape, rose bowl, purple, c1980 . . . . **45.00**
LG Wright, Grape and Fruit, plate, purple, c1977, 14" d. **90.00**
LG Wright, Iris, tumbler, purple, c1979 . . . . **30.00**
LG Wright, Iris, water pitcher, purple, c1979 . . . . **80.00**
LG Wright, Peacock, bowl, crimped, purple **100.00**
LG Wright, Stork and Rushes, pitcher, marigold, c1975. . . . . **120.00**
LG Wright, Stork and Rushes, spooner, marigold, c1975. . . . . . **40.00**
LG Wright, Stork and Rushes, sugar, cov, marigold, c1975. . . . . **45.00**

CARTOON CHARACTERS

The comic strip was an American institution by the 1920s. Its Golden Age dates from the mid-1930s through the late 1950s. The movie cartoon came of age in the late 1930s and early 1940s as a result of the pioneers at the Disney and Warner Brothers studios. The Saturday morning television cartoon matured through the creative energies of Bill Hanna, Joe Barbera, and Jay Ward.

A successful cartoon character generates hundreds of licensed products. Most collectors focus on a single character or family of characters, e.g., Popeye, Mickey Mouse, or the Flintstones.

References: Bill Bruegman, *Cartoon Friends of the Baby Boom Era: A Pictorial Price Guide,* Cap'n Penny Productions, 1993; *Cartoon & Character Toys of the 50s, 60s, & 70s: Plastic & Vinyl,* L-W Book Sales, 1995; Ted Hake, *Hake's Guide to Comic Character Collectibles,* Wallace-Homestead, Krause Publications, 1993; David Longest, *Cartoon Toys & Collectibles,* Collector Books, 1999; Maxine A. Pinsky, *Marx Toys: Robots, Space, Comic, Disney & TV Characters,* Schiffer Publishing, 1996; Stuart W. Wells III and Alex G. Malloy, *Comics Collectibles and Their Values,* Wallace-Homestead, Krause Publications, 1996.

Newsletter: *Frostbite Falls Far-Flung Flier* (Rocky & Bullwinkle), PO Box 39, Macedonia, OH 44056.

Collectors' Club: Garfield Collectors Society, 7744 Foster Ridge Rd, Memphis, TN 38138.

Note: For additional listings see Disneyana, Hanna-Barbera, Peanuts, Smurfs, and Warner Bros.

Adventures of the Nebbs, game, contains 20 colored numbered wooden counters, 2 dice cups, 2 dice, 4 wooden blocks, Milton Bradley, c1925–27 . . . . **$85.00**
Alvin and The Chipmunks, Alvin "stickles doll," 1984, MOC **8.00**
Alvin and The Chipmunks, figure, plastic, 1984 . . . . **8.00**
Alvin and The Chipmunks, Simon, inflatable doll, plastic, Ideal, 1964, 16" h **15.00**
Archies, game, Pick Up Stix, 1986 . . . . **12.00**
Archies, tattoo sheet and gum, Topps, 1969, 2 x 4" unopened pack **20.00**
Barney Google, album, *Barney Google, The Lates of All Cartoon Comedies,* 16 pp, ©1923 . . . . **50.00**
Barney Google, pull toy, Spark Plug, wood, DeBeck signature, 1928 copyright **150.00**
Barney Google, salt and pepper shakers, pr, Barney and Snuffy, painted plaster, c1940s, 3" h **40.00**
Barney Google, sign, "Boston Sunday Advertiser," cardboard, promoting Sunday comics, c1930s. **200.00**
Beany & Cecil, Cecil the Sea-Sick Serpent in the Music Box, litho tin, crank on side, Mattel, ©1961 Bob Clampett, 5¼ x 5¼ x 5⅝" **85.00**
Beany & Cecil, colorforms, #230, ©1962 Colorforms **65.00**
Beetle Bailey, bank, Sergeant Snorkel, composition, 1960s, 11" h **75.00**
Beetle Bailey, puffy stickers, 1983 . . . . **12.00**
Beetle Bailey, puzzle, Beetle Bailey Picture Puzzle, Potato Artist, diecut cardboard, 63 pcs, Jaymar Specialty Co **12.00**
Betty Boop, alarm clock, animated, 1983, 4½" h **120.00**
Betty Boop, book, *Betty Boop in Snow White,* Whitman Big Little Book, #1119, ©1934. . . . . **90.00**
Betty Boop, pinback button, "16 Pages of Comics Saturday Chicago American," Betty Boop image in center, 1930s, 1⅛" d **40.00**
Betty Boop, playing cards, Betty Boop Co-Ed Bridge Playing Cards, 1935, orig 2½ x 3¾" box. **75.00**
Betty Boop, pocket watch, late 1950s. **250.00**
Blondie, Blondie Paints Water Color Set, tin, 1948 . . . . **25.00**
Blondie, game, Blondie and Dagwood's Race for the Office Game, Jaymar, 1950 . . . . **45.00**
Blondie, greeting card, "Hope Your Christmas Is Like Dagwood's Sandwich," Hallmark, 1939 . . . . **10.00**
Blondie, paperdoll book, Blondie in the Movies, Whitman, 1941 . . . . **200.00**
Bonzo, book, *Bonzo's Annual,* 94 pp, Dean of England, 1950s, 7½ x 10" **35.00**
Bonzo, tablet, "Bonzo—A Dog's Life," 1930s, 5 x 8". **25.00**
Bullwinkle, Bullwinkle's Construction Set, orig blister card containing soft vinyl tools, nuts, bolts, wheels, and parts to construct car, Larami, ©P.A.T. Ward, 1969, 6½ x 14½" **20.00**
Bullwinkle, doll, plush, molded vinyl face, pull string talker, Mattel, 1970, 18" h **75.00**
Bullwinkle, game, Bullwinkle Hide 'N Seek Game, Milton Bradley, 1961. . . . . **75.00**
Bullwinkle, pinback button, "Bullwinkle For President," 1984, 1¾" d **10.00**
Bullwinkle, Play a Tune Bagpipes, 1971 . . . . **22.00**
Bullwinkle, Tru-Vue Magic Eyes Viewer, with film card, yellow diecut card with clear plastic window containing red plastic viewer and 7-scene view card, ©1962 P.A.T. Ward Prod, Inc, 5¾ x 9". **40.00**
Casper the Friendly Ghost, lamp shade, Casper, Wendy, Nightmare, and The Ghostly Trio images, Spooky smiling and riding carousel horse in merry-go-round setting, ©Harvey Famous Cartoons, c1960s, 7 x 7" **45.00**
Casper the Friendly Ghost, palm puzzle, Casper the Friendly Ghost and His TV Pals, Roalex Co, Forest Hills, NY, ©Harvey Famous Cartoons, mid-1960s, 4¾ x 6", MOC **65.00**
Chilly Willy, figure, rubber, c1950s, 6" h **25.00**
Dennis the Menace, action figure, moveable arms, 1954, 5" h. **40.00**
Dennis the Menace, book, *Dennis the Menace Storybook,* 1960 . . . . **25.00**
Dennis the Menace, cup, plastic, figural Dennis as cowboy wearing red hat and kerchief, Kellogg's cereal premium, F & F Mold, ©1962 Kellogg's, 3½" h, 2½" d. **20.00**
Dennis the Menace, Lock 'n Key Set, MOC **12.00**
Dennis the Menace, pinback button, "Cast Your Ballot For Sears Favorite Son," black and white portrait on red and blue ground, ©1968 Hank Ketcham, 1" d. **20.00**

Dennis the Menace, water pistol, figural, plastic, Real Action Toy, Chicago, ©1954 Hank Ketcham, orig box, 2½ x 3⅜ x 6" **40.00**

Dick Tracy, badge, brass, black accent paint on lettering and Tracy portrait, 1938, 2¼" h **75.00**

Dick Tracy, bracelet top, brass, wing shape, shield and airplane in center, 1938, 1½" l **100.00**

Dick Tracy, Caramels candy bar wrapper, Walter H Johnson Co, Chicago, 1930s, 2½ x 3" **85.00**

Dick Tracy, dart gun, Larami, 1930s, orig 6 x 8¼" card **65.00**

Dick Tracy, decoder/membership card, stiff paper folder card joined by small grommet in center holding inner disk dial for decoder, member card on front, back has working disk mechanism for "Standard Alphabet" and Dick Tracy Code Sign secret messages, 1952 ©Chicago Tribune, 2¼ x 3¾" **45.00**

Dick Tracy, Dick Tracy Crime Stoppers Set, nightstick, cuffs, and badge, 1930s, orig 10½ x 8" card **110.00**

Dick Tracy, doll, painted composition, moveable mouth, 1930s, 13½" h **375.00**

Dick Tracy, game, Dick Tracy Master Detective Game, Selchow & Righter, 1961 .... **45.00**

Dick Tracy, salt and pepper shakers, pr, Dick Tracy and Junior, painted plaster, Tracy with red hat and trench coat, black trousers, yellow accents, Junior with red cap and trousers, red necktie dotted in black, black jacket, fleshtone faces, Tracy's name finished in yellow lettering, Junior's name in white, missing cork stopper in bottom, c1940s, 2¾" h **50.00**

Dick Tracy, Secret Service Compartment Ring, brass base, 4-leaf clover and horseshoe designs at top of bands, ring top with high relief Tracy head surrounded by small crescent moon and stars symbols, top lifts off to reveal small inner compartment, 1938 .... **175.00**

Dudley Do-Right, coloring book, #1081, cover shows Dudley on horseback carrying Snidely Whiplash on back tied by rope, 60 pp, Whitman, ©1972 P.A.T. Ward, 8 x 11" **20.00**

Dudley Do-Right, drinking glass, P.A.T. Ward Collector Series, late 1970s, 5" h, $8.00

Felix the Cat, candy container, figural, composition, smiling full figure pose with hands behind back, red cloth ribbon on neck, removable cardboard stopper on underside, printed "Germany" in purple on underside with 3 penciled number notations, mid-1920s, 6" h **75.00**

Felix the Cat, cup, plastic, "Felix the Cat Sip-a-Drink Cup," 1950s, 5" h **40.00**

Felix the Cat, flashlight, plastic, Bantam-Lite, 1960, 4" h, MOC **35.00**

Felix the Cat, tea set, 5" h teapot, covered sugar, creamer, cup and saucer, Villeroy & Boch, c1930s **750.00**

Henry, book, *Henry Goes to a Party*, Wonder Book, #1508, emb cover art, spiral binding, 1955, 6¼ x 8" **15.00**

Henry, doll, painted hard rubber, moveable arms, 1934, 8" h **100.00**

Joe Palooka, basketball set, child's, complete with basketball and inflation pump, orig 12 x 12 x 12" box, 1940s **45.00**

Joe Palooka, book, *Gentleman Joe Palooka*, Saalfield, #1176, 1940 .... **30.00**

Joe Palooka, game, Joe Palooka Boxing Game, Lowell, 1950s, 2 x 12 x 16" box **75.00**

Joe Palooka, lunch box, litho tin, 1948, 4 x 5 x 7" **125.00**

Laurel & Hardy, bank, figural Laurel, 1972, 15" h **15.00**

Laurel & Hardy, record, *Chiller Diller Thriller*, 45 rpm, Peter Pan, 1962, 7 x 7" illus sleeve **12.00**

Li'l Abner, paint set, #311, cover shows Abner playing with Salome the pig as family sits in background, diecut cardboard insert showing Schmoos and Kingmies with various strip characters, complete with contents, Gem Color Co, Patterson, NJ, c1950, 10¾ x 18¼ x ½" **65.00**

Li'l Abner, pinback button, "Get In The Scrap! McKeesport," image of Abner running with his arms in fight position in white and dark blue, small Al Capp facsimile signature on right, 15/16" d **40.00**

Li'l Abner, wristwatch, white face and full color image of Abner saluting American flag which moves back and forth at bottom as watch ticks, chrome cased, dark brown band, c1951, 8½" l **85.00**

Little King, figure, painted composition wood, 1944, 2½" h **150.00**

Little King, ramp walker, plastic, Marx, 1950s **50.00**

Little Lulu, stencil set, Little Lulu & Friends Cartoon-A-Kit, 1948, 1¼ x 10 x 14" box **75.00**

Little Lulu, tissue box, 9" h paper stand-up, Lulu in red band leader's uniform holding box of Kleenex tissues, Kimberly-Clark, 1956 .... **10.00**

Mammy Yocum, doll, vinyl head and body, corncob pipe in mouth, wearing green felt jacket with yellow trim and brass accent buttons, yellow/black plaid felt skirt, pink leggings, brown vinyl shoes, orig Baby Barry cloth label attached to right sleeve, Missouri Meerschaum foil label on underside of pipe, early 1950s, 13½" h **75.00**

Mandrake the Magician, book, *Mandrake the Magician/The Mighty Solver of Mysteries*, Whitman Better Little Book, #1418, 1946 .... **25.00**

Mandrake the Magician, coloring book, Ottenheimer Co, 1965 .... **15.00**

Popeye, fountain pen, yellow plastic, mkd "King Features Syndicate Inc. Epenco," 5" l, $72.00. Photo courtesy Collectors Auction Services.

Mighty Mouse, figure, vinyl and rubber, 1950s, 10" h 55.00

Mighty Mouse, game, Mighty Mouse Presents the Game of Hide 'N Seek Rescue Dinky Duck, 17 x 17" game board with instruction sheet and complete parts, Transogram, ©1961 Terrytoons, orig 9 x 17½ x ¾" box 65.00

Mighty Mouse, sticker book, Whitman, 1967, 10 x 12" 15.00

Moon Mullins, bottle, Uncle Willie, china, cork stopper in neck, 1930s 60.00

Moon Mullins, figure, painted wood, jointed, 1930s, 4" h 125.00

Mr Magoo, drinking glass, blue art accent images around sides of Magoo about to walk into manhole as fire chief looks on, and Magoo sitting on horse backwards yelling "Giddiyap," ©1963 UPA Pictures Inc, 5½" h 15.00

Mr Magoo, figure, vinyl, wearing green overcoat with fur collar and hat, carrying cane, 1958, 12" h 120.00

Mr Magoo, game, Mr Magoo Visits the Zoo, Lowell, ©1961 UPA Pictures Inc 85.00

Mr Peabody, coloring book, #1034, full color front and back covers, 60 pp, Whitman, ©1977 P.A.T. Ward 40.00

Mutt and Jeff, mask, bread premium, 1933, 8 x 10" 10.00

Olive Oyl, hand puppet, cloth body, vinyl head, 10" h 25.00

Olive Oyl, squeaker doll, painted soft hollow rubber, blue eyes, blueish tint on each cheek, red hair bow and blouse, blue skirt, brown shoes and purse, King Features copyright on rear hip, c1940s, 8" h 65.00

Penelope Pitstop, watch, 1971, MOC. 55.00

Phantom, The, comic book, #22, Feature Book, 1936, 8½ x 11½" 200.00

Phantom, The, game, Phantom, Ruler of the Jungle Game, contains clay and skull ring, Transogram, 1965 . . . 110.00

Pink Panther, paint set, 1983, MOC 18.00

Pink Panther, toothbrush holder, figural Pink Panther marching with drum, holds 2 brushes, Avon, 1970s, 5" h, orig 4 x 6" box 15.00

Pogo, mugs, set of 6, plastic, 1960s, 4¼" h 90.00

Pogo, pinback button, "I Go Pogo," litho tin, black and white portrait on orange ground, c1956, ⅞" d 10.00

Popeye, comic strip book, "Popeye In Wild Oats," "Feature Book No. 14," black and white comic strip reprints, 72 pp, David McKay Co, ©1937, 8½ x 11¼". 65.00

Popeye, drinking glass, image of Popeye and Olive Oyl, blue accents, blue lettering, ©1929 King Features, 1930s, 4⅝" h 85.00

Popeye, Pipe Toss Game, 1935 . . . . 65.00

Popeye, pocketknife, silvered steel, ivory white celluloid side panels, one panel showing full figure Popeye image with name, King Features copyright in red, 1 blade mkd "Imperial/Providence, R.I.," c1930s, 3" l 65.00

Popeye, Popeye Pinball, Lido, 1964, 7 x 15½ ". 75.00

Popeye, pull toy, #488, Fisher-Price, c1939 . . . . 375.00

Popeye, rattle, celluloid, hard rubber handle, image of Popeye and friends enjoying country outing, c1920–30s, 3¼" l 75.00

Prince Valiant, dime register bank, tin, 1954. . . . . 100.00

Prince Valiant, game, Prince Valiant, Transogram, 1955. . . . . 35.00

Prince Valiant, playset, Castle Fort, complete, Marx, 1950s 300.00

Schmoo, figure, plaster, unmkd, 1950s, 4¼" h 85.00

Simpsons, sliding tile puzzle, 1989, MOC 15.00

Skippy, Christmas card, personalized greeting at bottom sgd by Pĕrcy Crosby, 1931, 4½ x 6" 75.00

Skippy, mask, paper, Socony Oil premium, 1931, 8 x 10" 30.00

Skippy, sign, "Real Fro-joy Ice Cream in a cup that's a Skippy," Fro-diecut cardboard, 1930s, 24 x 36". 75.00

Sluggo, doll, cloth, stuffed, 1970s, orig box, 6" h 25.00

Smilin' Jack, book, *Smilin' Jack and the Daredevil Girl Pilot*, Whitman, dj, 1942 . . . . 15.00

Smitty, doll, cloth, 1930s, 11½" h 50.00

Snuffy Smith, bank, ceramic, figural whiskey jug, corn-cob stopper, 1950s, 8" h 35.00

Space Ghost, book, *Space Ghost: The Sorceress of Cyba-3*, Whitman Big Little Book, 1968 . . . . 5.00

Teenage Mutant Ninja Turtles, action figure, Hot Spot, Playmates, MIP 50.00

Teenage Mutant Ninja Turtles, doll, stuffed, plush, Playmates, 1989, 14" h 15.00

Teenage Mutant Ninja Turtles, Don's Sewer Squirter, #5681, 1991 . . . . 8.00

Terrytoons, game, Terrytoons Hide & Seek Game, Transogram, 1960 . . . . 45.00

Underdog, game, Underdog's Save Sweet Polly Game, Whitman, 1968 . . . . 30.00

Underdog, harmonica, plastic, emb Underdog and Simon Bar Sinister on each side, "Have no fear...Underdog is here!," Leonardo, 1975, 8" l 15.00

Underdog, wristwatch, full color Underdog image against white ground with name in black text at bottom, chrome accent case, black vinyl simulated alligator skin band, ©1984 P.A.T. Ward, A&M Hollywood, 8¾" l 85.00

Weird-Oh's, puzzle, Weird-Oh's Picture Puzzle, Freddy Flameout: The Way Out Jet Jockey, diecut cardboard, 108 pcs, EE Fairchild, 1963 . . . . 30.00

Wimpy, birthday card, folder card, animated, inner left panel has birthday greeting above inked greeting, ©1934 Hall Brothers, Inc, 4¼ x 5¼" 40.00

Wimpy, squeeze doll, painted hollow soft rubber, brown hat, blue jacket, pale blue tie over white shirt, brown trousers, reddish orange shoes, fleshtone face with black facial markings, rosy tint on cheeks, King Features Syndicate copyright on back, c1940s, 7½" h 65.00

Winky Dink, Little Golden Book, Golden Press, 1956, 7 x 8" 12.00

Woody Woodpecker, Magic Dart Target Game, 1987, MOC 10.00

Woody Woodpecker, pinback button, "Woody Woodpecker Hi Pal!," full color Woody image on white ground, blue lettering, ©1957 Walter Lantz, 1¼" d 40.00

CATALINA POTTERY

The Catalina Pottery, located on Santa Catalina Island, California, was founded in 1927 for the purpose of making clay building products. Decorative and functional pottery was added to the company's line in the early 1930s. A full line of color-glazed dishes was made between 1931 and 1937.

Gladding, McBean and Company bought Catalina Pottery in 1937, moved production to the mainland, and closed the island pottery. Gladding, McBean continued to use the Catalina trademark until 1947.

References: Jack Chipman, *Collector's Encyclopedia of California Pottery, Second Edition,* Collector Books, 1999; Steve and Aisha Hoefs, *Catalina Island Pottery,* published by authors, 1993.

Ashtray, fish, blue glaze, 4½" l	$150.00
Ashtray, goat, 4" h	350.00
Ashtray, hat, white, incised mark	145.00
Bookend, monk, Descanso green glaze, 5 x 4"	225.00
Bowl, shell shape, red, 8¾"	225.00
Candelabra, seal, green, 5 x 10½"	400.00
Cereal Bowl, rope pattern	12.00
Cigarette Box, cov, horsehead finial	200.00
Coaster, yellow	20.00
Coffee Mug, Catalina blue	50.00
Coffee Server, Indian style, Catalina blue, 8¼" h	120.00
Creamer, powder blue matte glaze, rope handle	40.00
Cup and Saucer, green	38.00
Demitasse Cup, pearly white	35.00
Dessert Bowl, red	15.00
Dish, shell shape, scalloped edge, white, 14" d	155.00
Figure, fish, C253	25.00
Head Vase, peasant girl	125.00
Nut Dish, blue	20.00
Pitcher, Toyon red	250.00
Plate, hp scene of Old Mexico, imp mark, 11½" d	600.00
Platter, turquoise, 13" d	85.00
Refrigerator Jar, cov, unmkd, 2¾" h	150.00
Salt and Pepper Shakers, pr, gourd shape, green	70.00
Step Vase, Montery brown, in-mold mark	375.00
Sugar, cov, powder blue matte glaze, rope pattern	50.00
Tray, leaf shape, turquoise and coral	60.00
Tray, rolled edge, turquoise, forged iron handle, 14½" d	150.00
Tumbler, Monterey brown	60.00
Tumbler, orange, 4" h	20.00
Vase, flared, red clay, blue glaze, 6" h	120.00
Vase, fluted, Rhapsody, Catalina blue, 6" h	200.00
Vase, handled, Mandarin yellow, 7½" h	350.00
Vase, Polynesian, #385, 6¾" h	250.00
Wall Pocket, figural seashell, turquoise, incised mark	250.00

CATALOGS

There are three basic types of catalogs: (1) manufacturers' catalogs that are supplied primarily to distributors, (2) trade catalogs supplied to the merchant community and general public, and (3) mail-order catalogs designed for selling directly to the consumer. Montgomery Ward issued its first mail-order catalog in 1872. Sears Roebuck's came out in 1886.

A catalog revolution occurred in the 1980s with the arrival of specialized catalogs and select zip code mailing niche marketing. In the 1990s catalogs began appearing on the Internet. Many predict this will make the printed catalog obsolete by the mid-21st century.

References: Ron Barlow and Ray Reynolds, *The Insider's Guide to Old Books, Magazines, Newspapers and Trade Catalogs,* Windmill Publishing, 1995; Norman E. Martinus and Harry L. Rinker, *Warman's Paper,* Wallace-Homestead, Krause Publications, 1994.

1923, E Ingraham Co, Bristol, CT, watches and clocks, 22 pp, 9 x 12"	$72.00
1925, American Cabinet Co, Two Rivers, WI, dental office furniture, 62 pp, 6 x 9"	55.00
1925, National Livestock & Meat, Chicago, IL, recipes, timetable for cooking meats, illus charts, 48 pp, 5 x 7¾"	10.00
1927, Giftware Publishing Co, New York, NY, giftware, 114 pp, 5¼ x 8"	15.00
1927, Joseph Woodwell Co, Pittsburgh, PA, hardware, tools, and cutlery, 628 pp, 8½ x 11"	72.00
1927, Maytag Co, Newton, IA, 13 pp, 8¾ x 11"	35.00
1928, Crosley Radio Corp, Cincinnati, OH, 8 pp, 3 x 6"	20.00
1929, Atlantic Stamping Co, Rochester, NY, kitchen accessories, 24 pp, 8½ x 11"	30.00
1929, Kalamazoo Loose Leaf Bind, Kalamazoo, MI, supplies, 32 pp, 6¾ x 10"	25.00
1929, Kuempel Co, Guttenberg, IA, Red-I-Cut design book, build your own furniture, 24 pp, 5½ x 8¾"	24.00
1930, Koken Chisholm Corp, New York, NY, barber shop equipment, 93 pp, 10¾ x 13"	300.00
1930, Lionel T Scott, description and explanation of practical tricks and apparatus, illus, 25 pp, 4½ x 7¾"	25.00
1931, George E Day Sons Co, Inc, Springfield, IL, painting supplies, 96 pp, 7 x 10"	12.00
1933, Underwood Elliott Fischer, New York, NY, portable typewriters, 12 pp, 3 x 5"	15.00
1934, Crescent Tool Co, Jamestown, NY, 24 pp, 8½ x 11"	20.00
1935, Milton Bradley Co, Boston, MA, 31 pp, school supplies, 6¾ x 9¾"	25.00
1935, Thurston Supply Co, Anoka, MN, lamps and lighting, 68 pp, 6 x 8¾"	15.00
1937, Abercrombie & Fitch Co, New York, NY, lawn games, playground equipment, picnic accessories, golf accessories, tennis, motor scooters and bikes, 40 pp, 6½ x 9½"	32.00
1937, Miller Electric Co, Utica, NY, lighting equipment, 95 pp, 9 x 12"	42.00
1938, Beckley-Cardy Co, Chicago, IL, school supplies and equipment, 88 pp, 8 x 10½"	20.00
1938, Sears, Roebuck & Co, Chicago, IL, spring and summer, 8¼ x 11"	45.00
1939, Graybar Electric Co, telephones and accessories, 48 pp, 8½ x 11"	45.00
1941, Holgate Brothers Co, Kane, PA, #18, toys, 28 pp, 8½ x 11"	38.00
1941, LL Bean, Inc, Freeport, ME, hunting and camping equipment, 66 pp, 7½ x 9"	35.00
1942, Sears, Roebuck & Co, Chicago, IL, wallpaper samples, 92 pp, 7 x 8¾"	35.00
1945, Animal Trap Co of America, Lititz, PA, 48 pp, 8½ x 11"	40.00
1948, Atlas Boat Supply Co, Inc, New York, NY, marine equipment, 172 pp, 7¾ x 10¾"	25.00
1948, Decca Records Co, 364 pp, 5 x 8¾"	15.00

1948, Pan-Am Navigation, N Hollywood, CA, aeronautical supplies and navigation equipment, 62 pp, 8¾ x 11" **44.00**

1950, Black & Decker Mfg Co, Towson, MD, 40th anniversary, 72 pp, 8½ x 10½" **12.00**

1950, General Merchandise Co, Milwaukee, WI, toys, dolls, and giftware, 326 pp **22.00**

1956, Teleco, Inc, Milwaukee, WI, general merchandise, 48 pp, 8¼ x 11" **12.00**

1961, Old Town Canoe Co, Old Town, ME, 16 pp, 8½ x 11" **50.00**

1964, Gateway Sporting Goods Co, Kansas City, MO, 48 pp, 8¼ x 11" **18.00**

1966, Lionel Toy Corp, Hillside, NJ, Lionel trains, raceways, phonograph, and science sets, 40 pp, 8½ x 11" **20.00**

CAT COLLECTIBLES

Unlike dog collectors who tend to collect objects portraying a single breed, cat collectors collect anything and everything with a cat image or in the shape of a cat. It makes no difference if an object is old or new, realistic or abstract. Cat collectors love it all.

The popularity of cats as pets increased significantly in the 1980s. Many contemporary 1980s cat collectibles, e.g., Kliban's cats and Lowell Davis porcelains featuring cats, are experiencing strong secondary markets. Remember, this market is highly speculative. Serious cat collectors stick to vintage (pre-1965) cat collectibles that have withstood the test of time.

References: Marbena Jean Fyke, *Collectible Cats* (1993, 1995 value update), *Book II* (1996), Collector Books; J. L. Lynnlee, *Purrrfection: The Cat,* Schiffer Publishing, 1990.

Collectors' Club: Cat Collectors, 33161 Wendy Dr, Sterling Heights, MI 48310.

Ashtray, figural calico cat with ash receiver on its back, Japanese mountain scene in bowl, 2½" h **$28.00**

Calendar, Chesapeake & Ohio Railway, Chessie illus, 1957 . . . . **75.00**

Cookie Jar, cat in basket, American Bisque **35.00**

Cookie Jar, cat's head, Metlox **125.00**

Creamer, Calico Cat, Brayton Laguna, 4¼" h **40.00**

Figure, Ambrosia, seated cat, Kay Finch, 10¾" h **200.00**

Figure, seated Siamese cat, Hagen-Renaker, 8⅞" h **75.00**

Figurine, Fluff, seated kitten, Josef Originals, 3⅜" h **45.00**

Figurines, Siamese cats, floral dec, Norcrest, 1965–66, 9" h, price for pair **12.00**

Paperweight, cat on oval base, cast iron, painted black, 4¾" l **300.00**

Pin, cat face, florentined gold, rhinestone whisker tips, c1950 . . . . **20.00**

Pincushion, cat on pillow, beige and orange velvet, glass eyes, red ribbon with bell and 2 wooden spools of thread, 4½" h **225.00**

Pitcher, figural calico kitten wearing blue ribbon collar, Japan, 3½" h **25.00**

Planter, figural kitten, bow is planter, mkd "Purr-Ree," Block Pottery **8.00**

Plate, cat shaped with floral dec, Los Angeles Potteries, 9" l **20.00**

Powder Jar, frosted green glass, figural seated cat finial **100.00**

Figure, papier-mâché, 6½" h, $600.00. Photo courtesy Garth's Auction, Inc.

Reamer, figural kitten wearing reamer hat, "Toronto Exhibition" label, 3½" h **85.00**

Salt and Pepper Shakers, pr, nodders, figural mother cat and kitten, black, Japan, 3¾" h **125.00**

Salt and Pepper Shakers, set, boy and girl cat on pond, mkd "Japan," 5" w base **25.00**

Sheet Music, *I Taut I Taw a Puddy-Tat,* Sylvester and Tweety cov, Alan Livingston, Billy May, and Warren Foster **25.00**

Stuffed Toy, Figaro, jointed, Knickerbocker, c1930–40 . . . . . . **650.00**

Teapot, figural calico cat, Goldcastle, 8" h **75.00**

Toothpick Holder, cat on pillow, glass **45.00**

Toy, Cat Drummer, windup, tin, 7¼" h **175.00**

CD'S

CD technology was first introduced in 1982. Although the technology is recent and many compact discs are still available commercially, a dedicated group of CD collectors has emerged.

Collectors focus on three main categories: (1) promotional issues, including CD singles and radio programs on compact discs, (2) limited edition discs, especially those with creative or innovative packaging, and (3) out-of-print discs. At the moment, American collectors are focused almost exclusively on American manufactured CDs.

As in other emerging collecting categories, prices can vary dramatically. Comparison shopping is advised. Bootleg discs have little to no value. Blues, rock, and pop titles dominate the secondary collecting market. Country and jazz titles follow. Few collectors seek classical titles.

References: Gregory Cooper, *Collectible Compact Disc: Price Guide 2,* Collector Books, 1998; Fred Heggeness, *Goldmine's Promo Record & CD Price Guide, 2nd Edition,* Krause Publications, 1998; Jerry Osborne and Paul Bergquist, *The Official Price Guide to Compact Discs,* House of Collectibles, 1994.

Periodicals: *DISCoveries Magazine,* PO Box 1050, Dubuque, IA 52004; *Goldmine,* 700 E State St, Iola, WI 54990; *ICE,* PO Box 3043-A, Santa Monica, CA 90408.

AC/DC, *Dirty Deeds Done Dirt Cheap,* Atco 4901, promotional, rear insert **$10.00**

Adams, Bryan, *Touch the Hand,* A&M 75021, promotional, silkscreened, picture sleeve, 1991 .... 8.00

Alpert, Herb, *Romance Dance,* A&M 17977, promotional, silkscreened logo, 1989 .... 5.00

Bad Company, *Shake It Up,* Atlantic 2626, promotional, rear insert, 1988 .... 5.00

Beach Boys, *Still Cruisin',* Capitol 79735, promotional, silkscreened red, 1989 .... 10.00

Benetar, Pat, *Please Come Home For Christmas,* Chrysalis 23654, promotional, picture sleeve, 1990 .... 8.00

Blues Traveler, *Sweet Pain,* A&M 75021 7314, promotional, logo on blue, picture sleeve, 1991 .... 5.00

Bon Jovi, Jon, *Blaze of Glory,* Mercury 279, promotional, silkscreened, picture sleeve, 1990 .... 8.00

Brooks, Garth, *The Old Man's Back in Town,* Liberty 79540, promotional, silkscreened, 1992 .... 8.00

Carpenters, *Let Me Be the One,* A&M 75021 7308, promotional, silkscreened, picture sleeve, 1991 .... 8.00

Fleetwood Mac, *Love Is Dangerous,* WB 4302, promotional, 1990 .... 4.00

Hornsby, Bruce, *Set Me in Motion,* RCA 2846, single and lp, promotional, picture sleeve, 1991 .... 4.00

Jagger, Mick, *Wired All Night/Out of Focus,* Atlantic 5020, promotional 8.00

Kiss, *I Love It Loud,* Mercury 882, promotional, logo on red, gatefold hardcover picture sleeve, 1993 .... 8.00

Led Zeppelin, *Stairway to Heaven,* Atlantic 4424, promotional, picture folder with pop-up zeppelin 15.00

Lennon, John, *Jealous Guy,* Capitol 7941, promotional, picture sleeve, silkscreened logo on white, 1988 ..... 10.00

Lynyrd Skynyrd, *Ten From the Swamp,* MCA 2033, promotional, picture sleeve, 1991 .... 15.00

Madonna, *Like a Prayer,* Sire 3448, promotional, picture sleeve, 1989 .... 15.00

McLean, Don, *And I Love You So/American Pie,* Curb 099, promotional, rear insert, 1992 .... 6.00

CERAMIC ARTS STUDIO

Lawrence Rabbett and Ruben Sand founded the Ceramic Arts Studio, Madison, Wisconsin, in January 1941 for the purpose of making wheel-thrown ceramics. During World War II the company began production on a line of high-end molded figurines that were sold in jewelry stores and large department stores. The flood of cheap imported ceramics in the early 1950s led to the demise of the studio in 1955.

Reference: Mike Schneider, *Ceramic Arts Studio,* Schiffer Publishing, 1994.

Collectors' Club: Ceramic Arts Studio Collectors Assoc, PO Box 46, Madison, WI 53701.

Figure, Bali-Fai, price for pair **$145.00**
Figure, cheese 15.00
Figure, Chinese girl, kneeling with fan, yellow pom-poms, blue coat 20.00
Figure, frisky lamb 25.00
Figure, Gay 90's couple, pastel, price for pair 140.00
Figure, Harry, southern gentleman 50.00
Figure, panda bear, holding cub 85.00

Figure, Peter Pan and Wendy, price for pair 120.00
Figure, Pomeranian 40.00
Figure, spaniel puppy 20.00
Figure, Wing Sang 15.00
Salt and Pepper Shakers, pr, mouse and cheese 40.00
Salt and Pepper Shakers, pr, oriental children 40.00
Shelf Sitter, large cat 45.00
Shelf Sitter, oriental girl, price for pair 85.00
Shelf Sitter, Pudgie and Budgie, price for pair 125.00
Wall Plaque, cockatoo 50.00

CEREAL BOXES

Ready-to-eat breakfast cereal appeared around 1900. Until the 1930s, most advertising and packaging was targeted toward mothers. The popularity of children's radio programs and their sponsorship by cereal manufacturers shifted the focus to youngsters.

By the 1950s cereal premiums inside the box and cutouts on cereal box backs were a standard feature. Cereal boxes also were used to promote television shows and the personalities and characters that appeared on them. By the early 1970s, cereal manufacturers issued special promotional boxes, many of which featured local and national sports heroes.

As the 1990s come to a close, cereal box prices are highly speculative. Market manipulators are at work. Crossover collectors are paying premium prices for character and personality boxes whose long-term collectibility is uncertain.

References: Scott Bruce, *Cereal Box Bonanza: The 1950's,* Collector Books, 1995; Scott Bruce, *Cereal Boxes & Prizes; 1960s,* Flake World Publishing, 1998; Scott Bruce and Bill Crawford, *Cerealizing America: The Unsweetened Story of American Breakfast Cereals,* Faber and Faber, 1995.

Periodical: *Flake: The Breakfast Nostalgia Magazine,* PO Box 481, Cambridge, MA 02140.

Collectors' Club: Sugar-Charged Cereal Collectors, 5400 Cheshire Meadows Way, Fairfax, VA 22032.

Note: All boxes are in good condition.

Quaker Puffed Rice Sparkies, 8¹/₂" h, 6" w, $55.00. Photo courtesy Collectors Auction Services.

Cheerios, General Mills, airline hangar cut-out, 1958, 9½" h **$65.00**

Corn-Fetti, Post, Captain Corn front, 1953, 9½" h **75.00**

Corn Flakes, Kellogg's, "The Sweetheart of the Corn" on front, 1953, 10¼" h **45.00**

Grape-Nuts Flakes, Post, scale model Fords offer, 1955, 10" h **175.00**

Jets, General Mills, Pontiac sweepstakes, 1958–59, 8½" h **100.00**

OK's, Kellogg's, Big Otis Catapult Game, 1959–60, 11¼" . . . **100.00**

Pep, Kellogg's, Tom Corbett space goggles offer, 1952, 8½" h **350.00**

Puffed Wheat, Quaker, Gabby Hayes western gun collection offer, 1951, 9" h **200.00**

Raisin Bran, Post, Roy Rogers Western Medal offer, 1953, 8" h **250.00**

Ranger Joe Rice Honnies and Wheat Honnies, 1952–54, 7½" h **100.00**

Rice Krispies, Kellogg's, Woody Woodpecker kazoo offer, 1958, 8½" h **125.00**

Shredded Wheat Juniors, Nabisco, Tobor-Mystery-Action robot, 1959, 7¾" h **100.00**

Sugar Corn Pops, Kellogg's, Wild Bill Hickok, 1952, 6" h . . . **150.00**

Sugar Crisp, Post, Roy Rogers paint set offer, 1954, 9½" h **200.00**

Sugar Jets, General Mills, Major Jet's rocket glider and launcher offer, 1955, 8½" h **150.00**

Sugar Smacks, Kellogg's, Lou Jacobs clown on front, 1953, 9½" h **200.00**

Trix, sample box, 1954, 4¼" h **45.00**

Wheaties, General Mills, license plates offer, 1953, 10" h **50.00**

CHILDREN'S DISHES

Children's dish sets date back to the Victorian era. In the 1920s and 1930s American glass companies manufactured sets of children's dishes in their most popular patterns. Inexpensive ceramic sets came from Germany and Japan. Injection molded plastic sets first appeared in the late 1940s. By the 1950s, miniature melamine plastic sets mimmicked the family's everyday plastic service.

Most children's dish sets were designed to be used by their owners for tea and doll parties. At the moment, collecting emphasis remains on pre-war sets.

References: Maureen Batkin, *Gifts for Good Children Part II: The History of Children's China 1890–1990,* Richard Dennis Publications, n.d., distributed by Antique Collectors' Club; Lorraine Punchard, *Playtime Pottery and Porcelain From the United Kingdom and the United States,* Schiffer Publishing, 1996; Lorraine Punchard, *Playtime Pottery and Porcelain From Europe and Asia,* Schiffer Publishing, 1996.

Collectors' Club: Toy Dish Collectors Club, PO Box 159, Bethlehem, CT 06751.

CHINA

20th Century, creamer and sugar, pink **$20.00**
20th Century, cup, yellow, pink, green, and blue **6.00**
20th Century, plate, green and blue **8.00**
20th Century, saucer, pink, green, and blue **3.00**
Blue Willow, creamer, 1¾ x 2" **18.00**
Blue Willow, creamer, 2 x 1¾" **18.00**

Blue Willow, creamer, 2¼ x 1¾" **18.00**
Blue Willow, creamer, 3¼ x 2¾" **18.00**
Blue Willow, cup, 2" h **12.00**
Blue Willow, cup, 2¼" h **12.00**
Blue Willow, cup, 2¾" h **14.00**
Blue Willow, cup and saucer **15.00**
Blue Willow, gravy boat **25.00**
Blue Willow, plate, 3½" d **9.00**
Blue Willow, plate, 3¾" d **12.00**
Blue Willow, plate, 4½" d **8.75**
Blue Willow, platter, 6¼ x 3¾" l **35.00**
Blue Willow, saucer, 3¼" d **8.00**
Blue Willow, set, service for 6, 23 pcs, 6 cups and saucers, 6 plates, creamer and sugar, cov teapot, complete **285.00**
Blue Willow, sugar, cov, 4¼ x 4¼ x 3½" **25.00**
Blue Willow, teapot, cov, 4" h **50.00**
Homer Laughlin, Lady Alice, demitasse cup and saucer **25.00**
Japan, tea set, 23 pcs, blue lustre, hp, orig box **100.00**
Nippon, tea set, 3¼" teapot, creamer, sugar, 3 cups and saucers, 2 geese, blue bands, Sun mark **275.00**

GLASS

Akro Agate, Chiquita, creamer, cobalt **$9.00**
Akro Agate, Chiquita, cup, opaque green **6.50**
Akro Agate, Chiquita, teapot lid, opaque green **10.00**
Akro Agate, Chiquita, transparent cobalt **14.00**
Akro Agate, Concentric Rib, plate, opaque green **3.00**
Akro Agate, Concentric Rib, saucer, opaque white **55.00**
Akro Agate, Concentric Rib, teapot, open, opaque green **8.00**
Akro Agate, Concentric Ring, cup, lavender **35.00**
Akro Agate, Interior Panel, plate, opaque blue **14.00**
Akro Agate, J Pressman, cereal bowl, fired-on red **5.00**
Akro Agate, J Pressman, demitasse cup and saucer, opaque green **8.00**
Akro Agate, Stacked Disc, set, 16 pcs, white creamer and sugar, blue cup and teapot, green plate, pink saucer and teapot lid **150.00**
Cherry Blossom, Jeannette, plate, delphite blue **15.00**
Cherry Blossom, Jeannette, set, 14 pcs, pink **325.00**
Cherry Blossom, Jeannette, sugar, cov, delphite **30.00**
Doric & Pansy, cup and saucer, teal **57.50**
Doric & Pansy, saucer, teal **8.00**
Fire-King, demitasse cup and saucer, swirl lustre **15.00**

ABC Plate, Three Crown China, Germany, $180.00. Photo courtesy Collectors Auction Services.

Homespun, Jeannette, tea set, pink 250.00
Laurel, McKee, creamer, French ivory, red rim 30.00
Moderntone, Little Hostess, cup, yellow and pink 15.00
Moderntone, Little Hostess Party Set, pastel, 14 pcs 125.00
Moderntone, set, 14 pcs, pastel 135.00
Moderntone, set, 15 pcs, black 350.00
Moderntone, set, 16 pcs, with beige teapot, orig box 375.00
Moderntone, set, 16 pcs, with burgundy teapot 250.00
Moderntone, set, 16 pcs, with turquoise teapot 250.00
Moderntone, teapot, cov, turquoise 125.00
Pyrex, cup, circus, red 10.00
Pyrex, plate, divided, circus, red 12.00

CHINTZ CHINA

Chintz patterned goods owe their origin to Indian chintes, fabrics decorated with richly hued flowers and brightly plumed mythical birds that were imported to England from India in the 17th century. Although English Staffordshire potters produced chintz pattern ceramics as early as the 1820s, the golden age of chintz decorated ceramics dates from 1920 through 1940. Although dozens of post–World War II patterns were made, collectors prefer pre-war examples.

References: Linda Eberle and Susan Scott, *The Charlton Standard Catalogue of Chintz, 2nd Edition*, Charlton Press, 1997; Muriel Miller, *Collecting Royal Winton Chintz*, Francis Joseph Publications, 1996, distributed by Krause Publications; Jo Anne Peterson Welsh, *Chintz Ceramics, 2nd Edition*, Schiffer Publishing, 1998.

Collectors' Clubs: Chintz China Collector's Club, PO Box 50888, Pasadena, CA 91115; Chintz Connection, PO Box 222, Riverdale, MD 20738.

Note: See Royal Winton for additional listings.

Bonbon, Marina, Elijah Cotton, Lord Nelson **$50.00**
Butter Dish, Violet Chintz, #2744, 1/4 lb, 6 5/8" l 15.00
Cake Plate, Apple Blossom, Kendall shape, tab handles,
   cut and shaped corners, James Kent, 10 x 9" 165.00
Cake Plate, Pansy, Kendall shape, open pierced handles,
   cut and shaped corners, Lord Nelson, 10 x 9" 195.00
Cake Plate, Roses and Birds, Bridgewood & Co, 9" sq 165.00
Cake Plate, Rosetime, Elijah Cotton, tab handle, Lord
   Nelson 150.00
Cake Set, Bermuda-Brown, includes 11 3/4 x 10 1/4" cake
   plate with tab handles and shaped corners and 5
   6 1/4" d serving plates, Myott 75.00
Cake Stand and Server, Lorna Doone, Midwinter, 12" d 200.00
Compote, Hydrangea-White, Lily shape, fluted bowl,
   James Kent, 6 1/2 x 3" h 415.00
Condiment Set, Festival, Crown Ducal 160.00
Creamer and Sugar, Florita, James Kent 125.00
Creamer and Sugar, Marina, Elijah Cotton, Lord Nelson 100.00
Cream Jug and Sugar Bowl, Heather, Globe-style shape,
   Lord Nelson, 3" h to spout 165.00
Jam Pot, cov, Apple Blossom, James Kent 125.00
Jam Pot, cov, DuBarry, Diamond shape, flower-shaped
   finial, James Kent 225.00
Jam Pot, cov, with liner, Rosetime, Elijah Cotton, Lord
   Nelson 125.00
Lamp, miniature, Rose Chintz, #686, 5 1/2" h 25.00

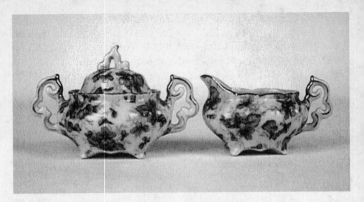

Creamer and Cov Sugar, miniature, Violet Chintz, #663, Lefton, 1 7/8" h, $30.00.

Nut Set, Rapture, includes one 5 1/4" and four 3" dishes,
   ruffled square shape, James Kent 175.00
Plate, Black Beauty, Kendall shape, cut and shaped cor-
   ners, Lord Nelson, 10" sq 190.00
Plate, Rose Chintz, Johnson Brothers, 9 3/4" d 18.00
Relish Dish, Lorna Doone, trefoil shape, silver center
   handle, Midwinter 120.00
Relish Dish, Marina, Ascot shape, 4-part, shaped rim,
   Lord Nelson, 10 1/2" w 320.00
Relish Dish, Rose Chintz, Johnson Brothers, 7 7/8" 25.00
Serving Tray, Rosetime, diamond shaped, Lord Nelson,
   12 1/2 x 6" 250.00
Sugar Bowl, cov, Rose Chintz, Johnson Brothers 45.00
Teapot, cov, Rose Chintz, Johnson Brothers 95.00
Tidbit, Black Marguerite, round, 3-tier, silver center han-
   dle, Empire 165.00
Tidbit, Country Lane, round, 3-tier, silver center handle,
   Lord Nelson 110.00
Tidbit, Modern Mayflower, round, 2-tier, silver center
   handle, AJ Wilkinson 125.00
Tureen, cov, Rose Chintz, Johnson Brothers 300.00
Vase, Oriental Lanterns, flared top and base, Gibsons,
   9" h 100.00
Vegetable Dish, Rose Chintz, Johnson Brothers, 8 1/4" d 32.00

AUCTION PRICES – CROWN DUCAL CHINTZ

Copake Auctions, Inc., North American Chintz Auction, May 2, 1998. Prices include a 10% buyer's premium.

Bud Vase, Marigold, trumpet shape, black int, 5 1/2" h . **$220.00**
Candlestick, Beaumont, straight stick on round
   base, 8 1/2" h 110.00
Center Bowl, Ivory Chintz, Iris shape, black int sides
   with pink roses border, chintz bottom and ext,
   8" d, 3" h 495.00
Plates, Blue Chintz, black trim, 8" d, price for set of 6 . . 852.50
Platter, Florida Chintz, octagonal, black trim, 15 1/4 x
   12" 2,200.00
Tea Set, Blue Chintz, includes 4-cup cov teapot,
   creamer, and cov sugar, white handles and finials
   with black trim 1,485.00
Vase, Purple Chintz, 6-sided with high shoulders
   and trumpet-top opening, narrowing to base,
   9 1/2" h 632.50

CHRISTMAS COLLECTIBLES

The tradition of a month-long Christmas season beginning the day after Thanksgiving was deeply entrenched by the end of the first World War. By the 1930s retailers from small town merchants to large department stores saw Christmas season sales account for 25% and more of their annual sales volume.

Beginning in the 1960s the length of the Christmas season was extended. By the mid-1990s Christmas decorations appeared in many stores and malls the day after Halloween. Today, some Christmas catalogs arrive in mail boxes as early as September.

Light Bulb, figural bird, celluloid, Japan, c1920, $50.00.

References: Robert Brenner, *Christmas Past, 3rd Edition,* Schiffer Publishing, 1996; Robert Brenner, *Christmas Through the Decades,* Schiffer Publishing, 1993; Jill Gallina, *Christmas Pins Past and Present,* Collector Books, 1996; Beth Dees, *Santa's Price Guide to Contemporary Christmas Collectibles,* Krause Publications, 1997; George Johnson, *Christmas Ornaments, Lights & Decorations,* 1987, 1998 value update, *Vol. II* (1997), *Vol. III* (1997), Collector Books; Polly and Pam Judd, *Santa Dolls & Figurines Price Guide: Antique to Contemporary, Revised,* Hobby House Press, 1994; Chris Kirk, *The Joy of Christmas Collecting,* L-W Book Sales, 1994, 1998 value update; Mary Morrison, *Snow Babies, Santas and Elves: Collecting Christmas Bisque Figures,* Schiffer Publishing, 1993; Tim Neely, *Goldmine Christmas Record Price Guide,* Krause Publications, 1997.

Periodical: *The Ornament Collector,* 22341 E Wells Rd, Canton, IL 61520.

Newsletter: *Crèche Herald,* 117 Crosshill Rd, Wynnewood, PA 19096.

Collectors' Clubs: Golden Glow of Christmas Past, 6401 Winsdale St, Minneapolis, MN 55427; Silver Ornament Society, PO Box 903, Laramie, WY 82073.

Note: See Hallmark for additional listings.

Bank, figural, Santa napping in chair, painted plaster, coin slot in upper rear of chair, 1940s, 5½ x 6 x 7" **$65.00**

Bank, figural, standing Santa, painted plaster, white fur trim and beard, coin slot in rear of cap, Mexico, 7 x 8 x 14" **40.00**

Book, Nativity scene, punch-out, #989, Saalfield Publishing Co, designs by Corinne and Bill Bailey, 1933 . . . . **75.00**

Book, *Santa Claus and the Lost Kitten,* Whitman, 1952 . . . . **5.00**

Book, *Santa's Tuney Toy,* Polygraphic Co of America, 1956 . . . . **12.00**

Candy Box, Fanny Farmer, litho cardboard, Santa in chimney **30.00**

Candy Cane Holder, plastic, Santa, white with black and red trim, head moves, 1960s, 4" h **5.00**

Candy Container, snowman, mica cov cardboard, woolen carrot nose, mkd "Made in Germany," 9" h **45.00**

Catalog, Kirkman & Son Inc, Kirkman Products, Brooklyn, NY, "For a Merry Christmas Save Your Kirkman Coupons, They Will Bring Joy and Happiness to the Kiddies," illus, children's toys and novelties, 1920s, 8 pp **15.00**

Chocolate Mold, tin, Santa with basket, double hinged, 8" h **65.00**

Clicker, Santa at fireplace, litho tin, 1930s **40.00**

Clicker, Santa image in center, black "Washington Park National Bank 63rd St & Evans Ave" on sides, 1920s **85.00**

Cookie Jar, holly and ivy dec, Hall China, 8½" h **80.00**

Creamer and Open Sugar, holly dec, mkd "Watt Pottery Company, Christmas 1957" **120.00**

Crèche Figure, Baby Jesus, in manger, plastic, 1950s, 2" h **3.00**

Crèche Figure, shepherd, composition, painted, Italy, 1960, 6" h **5.00**

Crèche Figure, stand alone Infant Jesus in manger with stable roof, ceramic, "Reg. U.S. Pat. Off., Norcrest Japan" pasted label on bottom, 1960s, 5" h **12.00**

Crèche Set, 20 pcs, ceramic, painted, Infant Jesus separate from crib, 1950s, 5" **45.00**

Crèche Set, stable with 12 plaster figures glued to floor, back wall with pasted night scene and Three Magi, "Made in Italy" stamped on back, c1980 . . . . **12.00**

Cup and Saucer, Santa dec, Universal Pottery **25.00**

Decoration, Santa, pressed cardboard, 14" h **20.00**

Decoration, Santa and reindeer, pressed cardboard, 9" l **30.00**

Decoration, wreath and candle, chenille, Occupied Japan **15.00**

Doll, Santa, painted hollow celluloid, Santa holding gifts in 1 arm and toys in other hand, image of fleshtone doll in sack opening at rear, "KT" ship logo marking above "Japan," c1930s, 6¼" h **75.00**

Figure, bisque, painted, hollow, Santa on skis, red outfit, yellow ski pole, single ski base, fur trim on face, unpainted white toy sack, mkd "Japan," c1930s, 1⅞" h **40.00**

Figure, "Rubb'r Nik," Santa with candy cane and Christmas stocking, ©1968 Multiple Toymakers, MOC **20.00**

Figure, Santa, plaster face, cotton beard, wool robe, mkd "Western Germany," 9" h **110.00**

Flag, tissue paper printed on 1 side, image of Santa entering chimney under smiling full moon, mounted on 11" broomstraw rod, 1920–30s, 3 x 4" **60.00**

Game, Santa Claus Game, Milton Bradley, c1920–24 . . . . . . **240.00**

Greeting Card, fold-out, "Merry Christmas," Santa on front, trace picture inside, 1930s, 8" h **5.00**

Lamp, Rudolph the red nosed reindeer, EMC Art, 12" l **45.00**

Lamp, Santa, plastic, red and white, electric, 1950s, 24" h **25.00**

Lamp, wreath and candle, cast iron **60.00**

Light Bulb, Betty Boop, painted milk glass, c1940 . . . . **75.00**

Light Bulb, Bubble Light, rocket ship **5.00**

Light Bulb, duck, wearing shirt and pants, head turned slightly to right, arms crossed, Japan, c1950 . . . . **35.00**

Light Set, Japanese style houses, 1930s **80.00**

Light Set, Santa Claus Xmas Tree Lighting Outfit, Peerless, 1928 . . . . **18.00**

Magazine Tear Sheet, "Don't forget Noma Lights," *Saturday Evening Post*, Dec 11, 1948 .... **5.00**

Ornament, Amelia Earhart, pearly white, black, and pearly blue, German blown glass, c1930, 3½" **275.00**

Ornament, bell, plastic, 4" h **2.00**

Ornament, cockatoo on clip, pearly white with orange crest, black eyes and beak, green wings, and red stripe, spun glass tail, German blown glass, c1920, 3¼" l, 5" l with tail **18.00**

Ornament, frog, pearly white with green shading, black eyes, and red mouth, German blown glass, c1920, 3¼" l **65.00**

Ornament, girl in bag, pearly white face, gold hair, red bag, German blown glass, c1920, 3½" **95.00**

Ornament, house, silver with green shading, matte white, German blown glass, c1920, 2¾" **25.00**

Ornament, lady's slipper, silver with gold bow and buttons, red trim, German blown glass, c1920, 3" **45.00**

Ornament, Santa, red with silver, face with pink blush, some green on tree, chenille legs, composition boots, heavy silvering loss, spotty paint wear, German blown glass, c1920, 4¼" **85.00**

Ornament, seated spaniel, pearly white body with gold shading, black eyes, and red mouth, ribbon, ears, and tail, German blown glass, c1930, 3" **45.00**

Ornament, star, Occupied Japan **10.00**

Pinback Button, "Santa Claus Village Pere Noel/Val David Que," Santa image, made in Montreal, 1950s **85.00**

Pinback Button, "Victor & Co. Toys," multicolored image of Santa holding wreath against black sky studded by tiny stars and eclipse moon, pale blue lettering and rim, c1925 .... **175.00**

Plate, Santa decal, green band, Roseville, 8" d **150.00**

Postcard, "Merry Christmas from Santa Claus/his eyes how they twinkled, his dimples how merry," cat looking at Santa with sack in front of fireplace, 1920s **5.00**

Ring Holder, Santa, 3½" h **10.00**

Sheet Music, *Rudolph the Red Nosed Reindeer*, Johnny Marks, 1949 .... **5.00**

Sign, "Buy Christmas Seals," diecut cardboard, countertop, easel back, image of Santa carrying shoulders sign urging purchase of annual fundraising Christmas Seals of National Tuberculosis Assoc, green and red, white and purple accents, fleshtone face, ©1923 National Tuberculosis Assoc, Edwards & Deutsch Litho Co, 7½ x 10½" **65.00**

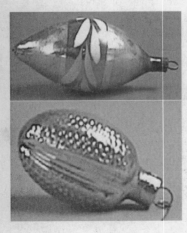

Ornaments, glass, gold with leafy band and pink walnut, Japan, $2.00 each.

Stirrers, set of 8, glass, Christmas trees **8.00**

Toy, battery operated, tin, Santa holding book, turns pages, cotton suit and beard, 7½" h **65.00**

Toy, windup, tin, Santa, Chein, 1920–30s, 5½" h **85.00**

Tree, music box base, heavy wire branches, vinyl needles, 1960s, 13" h **10.00**

Tree, plastic base, cellophane needles, bubble light dec, 1950s, 19" h **50.00**

Tree, wooden base, white tinted vinyl needles, electric base, 1950s, 19" h **15.00**

Tree Stand, cast iron, square, 1930s **50.00**

Tree Topper, angel, satin skirt, braided hair, gold crown, c1950, 6" h **8.00**

CIGAR COLLECTIBLES

Cigars and cigarettes are not synonymous. Cigars have always had an aloofness about them. They were appreciated by a select group of smokers, not the masses. Cigar connoisseurs are as fanatical as wine aficionados concerning the objects of their affection.

The cigar renaissance of the early 1990s has renewed collector interest in cigar collectibles. The primary focus is advertising. Prices remain stable for traditional cigar collectibles such as cutters, molds, and cigar store figures.

References: Tony Hyman, *Handbook of American Cigar Boxes*, Arnet Art Museum, 1979, 1995 value update; Jerry Terranova and Douglas Congdon-Martin, *Great Cigar Stuff for Collectors*, Schiffer Publishing, 1997.

Newsletter: *The Cigar Label Gazette*, PO Box 3, Lake Forest, CA 92630.

Collectors' Clubs: Cigar Label Collectors International, PO Box 66, Sharon Center, OH 44274; International Seal, Label and Cigar Band Society, 8915 E Bellevue St, Tucson, AZ 85715.

Cigar Box, Big Snap, paper litho over wood, "Factory No. 3998 9th District State of Pennsylvania" on bottom, 1½" h, 4½" w, 5" d **$375.00**

Cigar Box, Old Virginia Cheroots, cardboard, 3¾" h, 9¾" w, 4¾" d **38.00**

Cigar Cutter, cast metal, figural ship's wheel, 4½" h **100.00**

Cigar Cutter, sterling silver, swimming fish design on sides, 1¾" l **200.00**

Cigar Lamp, Bossy Brand Cigars, clear glass font, white milk glass globe with black lettering and silhouette cow, White & Son, 7½" h **850.00**

Countertop Change Station, "Buckingham Bros. Fine Cigars, Baltimore, MD.," reverse-painted mirrored glass with tin backing, 12" d **250.00**

Door Push, Nuvana Cigars, aluminum, emb lettering, 6" h, 2" w **85.00**

Humidor, chalkware, glazed int, stoneware lid, 3 busts of Indians in full headdress around sides, 8¾" h **425.00**

Match Dispenser, metal with glass display area and paper adv "Joe Anderson Havana Cigars, Peace Time 5¢," Universal Match Corp, 14½" h, 9" d **875.00**

Pinback Button, Maquoketa Cuban Hand Made Cigars, celluloid over metal, pictures early touring car, 1¾" d **80.00**

Sign, "John Ruskin Cigars, Best and Biggest," emb tin, 1-sided, rect, lit cigar image, 9½" h, 29¾" w **175.00**

Cigar Box Label, Flyer, $40.00.

Sign, Odin 5¢ Cigar, emb tin, rect, cartoon man, yellow ground, 27" h, 19" w 350.00

Sign, "R.G. Sullivan's 7-20-4 Quality 10¢ Cigar," porcelain, 1-sided, rect, 12" h, 30" w 185.00

Sign, "Smoke Nickel King Cigars," painted emb cardboard, black lettering on gray ground, chain hanger, 6" h, 18" w 80.00

Sign, "Smoke the Imperial Club 5cts Cigar, The Best for the Money," emb litho tin, 1-sided, full cigar box, black ground, 10" h, 13³⁄₄" w 185.00

Sign, Van Dam Cigars, emb tin, rect, rect, Dutch master image, "Java Wrapped," 14" h, 28" w 250.00

Tin, Camel 5 ¢ Cigars, rect, man riding camel, green lid, 5¹⁄₄" h, 4¹⁄₂" w 120.00

Tin, La Corona Cigars, litho tin, cylindrical, "Havana Cigar & Tobacco Factories Ltd. Grown in Cuba Blended in Havana, Rolled and Packed in the United States of America, tax stamp dated 1932, 5¹⁄₄" h, 2¹⁄₄" d 40.00

Window Decal, King Edward Cigars, lettering in red shield, 8¹⁄₂" h, 7" w 20.00

AUCTION PRICES – CIGAR LABELS

Cerebro, Antique Label Auction, May 15, 1998.

Cigar Band, Horse Show, EX. **$26.00**
Cigar Band, Mark Twain, EX/M 40.00
Cigar Band, Priscilla, EX. 35.00
Inner Lid Label, Capitolio, HS51309, EX/M 160.00
Inner Lid Label, Indian Maiden (stock), SL, EX 200.00
Inner Lid Label, Lone Trail, 2901 SM1368, EX/M 550.00
Outer Box Label, Blue Ring, HR4156, EX 40.00
Outer Box Label, Handicap, SE6134, EX 60.00
Outer Box Label, Jack of Hearts, SE6032, EX 300.00
Outer Box Label, Massasoit Chief, HM1998, EX 250.00
Outer Box Label, Saturn, HR1599, EX. 170.00
Proof Label, Croaker, 5 colors, VG 400.00
Proof Label, Judge Good, EX/M 275.00
Proof Label, The New Bachelor, Victor Thorsch Co, M . 120.00
Salesman's Sample, Gold Tip, SW5671, VG/EX 40.00
Salesman's Sample, Have Another, SW5218, EX 70.00
Salesman's Sample, Polar Light, HR, EX 2,800.00
Salesman's Sample, Red Hot, HR1133, VG 180.00

CIGARETTE COLLECTIBLES

The number of cigarette smokers grew steadily throughout the 19th century and first two decades of the 20th century. By the 1940s the cigarette was the dominant tobacco product sold in America. In the 1950s cigarette manufacturers were major periodical and television advertisers.

The Surgeon General's Report changed everything. Despite limitations on advertising and repeated non-smoking bans, the cigarette industry has proven highly resourceful in creating public exposure for its product—just watch any televised NASCAR race.

Surprisingly, as the anti-smoking crusade has become stronger, the interest in cigarette collectibles has increased. Cigarette memorabilia, especially advertising dating between 1945 and 1960, is one of the hot collectibles of the 1990s.

References: Douglas Congdon-Martin, *Camel Cigarette Collectibles: The Early Years, 1913–1963,* Schiffer Publishing, 1996; Douglas Congdon-Martin, *Camel Cigarette Collectibles, 1964–1995,* Schiffer Publishing, 1997 Murray Cards International Ltd. (comp.), *Cigarette Card Values: 1994 Catalogue of Cigarette and Other Trade Cards,* Murray Cards International, 1994; Fernando Righini and Marco Papazzoni, *The International Collector's Book of Cigarette Packs,* Schiffer Publishing, 1998; Neil Wood, *Smoking Collectibles: A Price Guide,* L-W Book Sales, 1994.

Collectors' Club: Cigarette Pack Collectors Assoc, 61 Searle St, Georgetown, MA 01833.

Ashtray, plaster, figural Amos 'n Andy standing next to barrel-shaped cigarette holder, 2 slots for matchbooks in front, 7¹⁄₄" h **$275.00**

Blotter, Camel Cigarettes, cigarette pkg and woman wearing polka dots and smoking cigarette, "I'd walk a mile for a CAMEL," red ground, 3¹⁄₂" h, 6¹⁄₂" w 20.00

Cigarette Pack Holder, Cavalier, plastic. **25.00**

Dispenser, figural lady's head, wood with cloth headband, cigarette comes out of woman's mouth, 6¹⁄₂" h, 7" w 350.00

Door Push, Chesterfield Cigarettes, porcelain, "They Satisfy," cigarette pkg, blue ground, 9" h, 4" w 275.00

Poster, Wings King Size Cigarettes, paper, pipe cub airplane and cigarette pkg, 1941, 15" h, 10" w 85.00

Rolling Machine, with tin Zig Zag Cigarette paper dispenser, Golden Grain cigarette papers, and bag of Golden Grain tobacco 35.00

Sidewalk Sign, Piedmont Cigarettes, porcelain, 1-sided, "Piedmont, For Cigarettes Virginia Tobacco is the Best" and cigarette pkg on dark blue ground, wood easel frame, 50" h, 30" w 600.00

Sign, Old Gold Cigarettes, porcelain, 1-sided, 12 x 36", $358.00.
Photo courtesy Collectors Auction Services.

Sign, "Bears' Honeydew Cigarettes, London," porcelain, 1-sided, rect, elephant and palm trees, yellow ground, English, 17½" h, 12½" w **135.00**

Sign, Black Cat Virginia Cigarettes, porcelain, 1-sided, black cat eyeing open cigarette pkg, 36" h, 20½" w **500.00**

Sign, Chesterfield Cigarettes, diecut metal flange, 2-sided, "Buy Chesterfield Here" and 2 cigarette pkgs on red ground, 16¼" h, 11" w **200.00**

Sign, "London Life Turkish Cigarettes, Cork Tip, Plain End," diecut porcelain flange, 2-sided, 3 fox hunters and hound, English, 14½" h, 18" w **1,000.00**

Thermometer, Marvels Cigarettes, tin, "The cigarette of quality," rooster logo and cigarette pkg above thermometer, 12" h, 4" w **175.00**

Tin, Old Gold Cigarettes, cylindrical, red lettering on yellow ground **60.00**

AUCTION PRICES – ROLLING PAPERS

Frank's Antiques & Auctions, Mail Auction Catalog #22, August 20, 1998. Prices include a 10% buyer's premium.

Army Navy, 100 leaves	$14.00
Bugler, 100 leaves	3.00
City Club, name in pencil on front	53.00
Club	6.00
Durham, 5 Cents	19.00
Great Puff	39.00
Greenback	55.00
Half and Half, Lucky Strike	12.00
Pep	107.00
Prince Albert, 15 leaves	2.00
Queen Quality	85.00
Roll 'Em	2.00
Vogue, 100 leaves	35.00
Zig Zag, free sample	14.00

CIRCUS MEMORABILIA

The 1920s through the 1940s marked the golden age of the tent circus. The circus trains for Ringling and Barnum and Bailey often exceeded 100 cars. The advent of television marked the beginning of the tent circus' decline. Mergers occurred. Most small circuses simply vanished. Today, the majority of circus performances occur at civic and institution auditoriums, not under the Big Top.

Most circus collectors are individuals who remember attending a circus under canvas. When this generation dies, what will be the fate of circus collectibles? Categories with crossover potential, e.g., lithographed posters, will hold collector interest. Others will vanish just as did the great circuses they document.

Reference: Norman E. Martinus and Harry L. Rinker, *Warman's Paper*, Wallace-Homestead, Krause Publications, 1994.

Collectors' Clubs: Circus Fans Assoc of America, 1544 Piedmont Ave ME, Ste 41, Atlanta, GA 30324; Circus Historical Society, 3477 Vienna Court, Westerville, OH 43081.

Book, *Schoenhut's Humpty Dumpty Circus Toys Picture Book*, 16 pp, illus, ©1928 A Schoenhut Co, 7 x 10" **$175.00**

Book and Record Set, *Bozo at the Circus*, and *Bozo and His Rocket Ship*, 2 LPs, Capitol Records, 1948 . . . . 20.00

Calendar, "Season's Greetings, Helen and Karl Wallenda," 1977, 7¼ x 12¼" 10.00

Menu, "Ringling Bros. and Barnum & Bailey Combined, The World's Largest Amusement Institution at Home on the Nation's Birthday, Bridgeport, CT, Fourth of July, 1920," 6¼ x 9½" 25.00

Poster, Ringling Bros and Barnum & Bailey Circus, paper, 12 seals in various trained acts, "Seals that exhibit intelligence scarcely less than human, in marvelously skillful performances," P20-120, 36" h, 23½" w 75.00

Poster, Ringling Bros and Barnum & Bailey Combined Shows, paper, "Terrell Jacobs The Lion King Presenting the World's Most Sensational Group of Jungle-Bred Performers," Gargantue the great ape in African scene, "Litho in USA, P-113," 17" h, 24½" w 60.00

Program, souvenir from film *The Greatest Show On Earth*, 16 pp, includes portraits of 6 major stars in roles based on actual Ringling Bros and Barnum & Bailey circus, front and back color cov, 1952, 9 x 12" 45.00

Ticket, Clyde Beatty-Cole Bros Combined Circus, issued by F F R Brown, black and red, 1960 season, 5½ x 2", price for pair 70.00

Toy, 2 In 1 Magic Circus Magnetic Action, litho tin and plastic pavilion with pair of 3-D litho figures, orig box, 1960s, TPS, Japan 40.00

Tray, SP, Ringling Brothers & Barnum & Bailey Circus, 2" silver toned circus elephant seated in center, brown woodgrain-style micarta bottom panel, Ringling Circus emblem affixed to drum in front of elephant, Rogers Silver Co, 14" d 20.00

Tru-Vue Card, "Circus Boy," color photos from show in illus red, white, and yellow sleeve, black and white illus of Circus Boy and Bimbo the Elephant, 3¾ x 5½" 20.00

Window Card, Circus Vargas, cardboard, elephants, horses, and men and women, "Abajo De La Capra Grande," Burbank, Apr 23–27, 22" h, 14" w 30.00

Window Card, Rudy Bros Circus, paper, graphic of elephant with girl sitting on his head, Fri May 29 and Sat May 30, Santa Ana Stadium, sponsored by the Elks, "Majestic Poster Press, Los Angeles, Calif. 102," 35" h, 14" w 30.00

Poster, Elks Circus, paper, 42" h, 28" w, $33.00. Photo courtesy Collectors Auction Services.

CLEWELL POTTERY

Charles Walter Clewell of Canton, Ohio, began his ceramic experiments in 1899. He opened his studio in 1906. His "Clewell Ware" pieces were produced in limited quantities between 1902 and 1955. When Clewell died in 1965, his daughter sold off his remaining stock.

Clewell's emphasis was on decorative techniques which ranged from shaped metal over a ceramic lining to glazes based on historic prototypes, the most famous of which was a blue patina on bronze. He bought his blanks from a variety of potteries including Cambridge, Knowles, Taylor and Knowles, Owens, Rookwood, Roseville, and Weller.

Clewell marks include: (1) impressed mark of "CLEWELL / CANTON O" inside two circles; (2) impressed mark of small "w" inside a large "C"; (3) impressed three line mark "Clewell / Metal Art / Canton, O." inside circle; and (4) incised mark "CLEWELL / CANTON O."

Reference: Ralph and Terry Kovel, *Kovel's American Art Pottery*, Crown, 1993.

Floor Vase, tapered sides, high shoulder, copper-clad with
    deep green patina, etched mark, 17" h, 9½" d **$1,500.00**

Vase, 6-sided cylinder, copper-clad with verdigris and
    bronze patina, incised "Clewell 439-2-6," 10" h, 3½" w . . **2,650.00**

Vase, classically shaped, copper-clad with brown to
    verdigris patina, incised "Clewell 463-26," 8½" h, 7" d . . **2,000.00**

Vase, classically shaped with narrow mouth , copper-
    clad with verdigris patina, incised "Clewell 323-6,"
    8¾" h, 7" d **1,200.00**

Vase, gourd shaped with long tapered neck and bulbous
    bottom, copper-clad with orange to green patina,
    etched mark, 14½" h, 6" d **2,000.00**

Vase, ovoid, copper-clad with verdigirs patina, incised
    "Clewell 331-6," 6" h, 3" d **525.00**

Vase, spherical, copper-clad with verdigris and bronze
    patina, incised "Clewell 300-25," 5" h, 4¼" d **1,200.00**

Vase, spherical squatty body with 2 organic strap han-
    dles, patinated in deep orange to verdigris finish,
    etched mark, 5½" h, 7½" w **875.00**

Vase, tall cylinder with flared squat base, copper-clad
    with verdigirs patina, incised "Clewell 5-2-6," 10¼" h,
    4½" w **1,850.00**

Vase, tall with tapered sides, copper-clad with flat shoul-
    der and verdigris patina, unmkd, 10" h, 5" d **1,100.00**

CLICKERS

These noisemakers were extremely popular from the early 1930s through the late 1950s. Many were distributed to adults and children as advertising premiums. Those touting a particular beer, hotel, political, or household product were meant for adults. Children delighted in receiving clickers when buying Buster Brown or Red Goose shoes. The Halloween season was responsible for more clickers than any other holiday season.

Bonnie Laddie Shoes, emb boy, purple. **$24.00**

Buster Brown Shoes, Buster and Tige, multicolor. **45.00**

Castles Ice Cream, "I'm Chirping For Castles Ice Cream"
    and bird, blue and white **32.00**

Cleo Cola, "Healthy Size," red, white, and green **38.00**

Cracklin' Good, lightning bolt and "Cracklin' Good
    Cookies and Crackers," red and white **24.00**

Felix the Cat, "I'm Surprised At You Felix" and 2 cats, red
    and white **68.00**

Forbes Coffee, "Forbes Quality Brand Coffee" and trade-
    mark logo, red, white, and blue **45.00**

Goodman Shoes, "For Boys, For Girls" and "Goodman
    Shoes" in shield, black and yellow **28.00**

Green Duck, "Green Duck 100% Union Made Buttons
    Badges Emblems," green and white **16.00**

Gunther's Beer, "Just Click For Gunther's Beer, The Beer
    That Clicks," red and white **22.00**

Jack and Jill, Jack and Jill walking arm in arm, "Instantly
    Prepared Gelatin Dessert, Jack and Jill, At Your
    Grocer," multicolor **42.00**

Little Sergeant Shoes, Little Sergeant image, orange,
    black, and white **35.00**

Maxwell House, "Drink Maxwell House Coffee," blue
    and gray **50.00**

Menges for Sheriff, man with sandwich board sign
    inscribed "I Am Chirping For Menges For Sheriff" **16.00**

New & True Coffee, coffee cup, multicolor. **30.00**

Purity Salt, salt canister, multicolor. **38.00**

State Insurance, "Assets Over A Million Dollars,
    Harrisburg, PA." and logo, red, white, and blue **30.00**

Steelco Stainless Steel, "The Greatest Name In Fine
    Cookware" and address, blue and white. **24.00**

Stroehmann Bread, 2 clowns holding "Stroehmann
    Bread" banner, red, white, and yellow **42.00**

Water, frowning man holding bottle labeled "Water,"
    multicolor. **22.00**

Jardiniere, copper-clad, incised "Clewell 418-2-9," 5¼" h, 6½" d, $1,045.00. Photo courtesy David Rago Auctions, Inc.

"Click with Dick" Nixon for President, blue on silver, 2" h, $5.00. Photo courtesy Ray Morykan Auctions.

CLIFF, CLARICE

Clarice Cliff (1899–1972) joined A. J. Wilkinson's Royal Staffordshire Pottery at Burslem, England, in the early 1910s. In 1930 she became the company's art director.

Cliff is one of England's foremost 20th-century ceramic designers. Her influence covered a broad range of shapes, forms, and patterns. Her shape lines include Athens, Biarritz, Chelsea, Conical, Iris, Lynton, and Stamford. Applique, Bizarre, Crocus, Fantasque, and Ravel are among the most popular patterns.

In addition to designer shape and pattern lines, Cliff's signature also appears on a number of inexpensive dinnerware lines manufactured under the Royal Staffordshire label.

References: Susan and Al Bagdade, *Warman's English & Continental Pottery & Porcelain, 3rd Edition,* Wallace-Homestead, Krause Publications, 1998; Helen Cunningham, *Clarice Cliff and Her Contemporaries: Susie Cooper, Keith Murray, Charlotte Rhead and the Carlton Designers,* Schiffer Publishing, 1999; Leonard R. Griffin and Susan Pear Meisel, *Clarice Cliff: The Bizarre Affair,* Harry N. Abrams, 1994.

Collectors' Club: Clarice Cliff Collector's Club, Fantasque House, Tennis Dr, The Park, Nottingham, NG7 1AE, UK.

REPRODUCTION ALERT: Lotus vases.

Bowl, Autumn Balloon Trees, low, black and ocher, 3½" d **$70.00**
Bowl, Tonquin pattern, purple, 5" d **5.00**
Condiment Jar, cov, Crocus pattern, bands of yellow, green, and ochre, crocuses in orange, blue, and purple, mkd "Bizarre by Clarice Cliff," 3½" h **175.00**
Condiment Jar, cov, Rodanthe pattern, yellow and orange flowers, 2½" h **70.00**
Creamer and Open Sugar, Bizarre Ware, Aurea pattern, green, yellow, and pink flowers on brown stems, mkd

Coffee Service, Honeydew pattern, includes coffeepot, creamer, open sugar, and 3 cups and saucers, coffeepot mkd "Clarice Cliff," all other mkd "Made in England," "Wilkinson England," or unmkd, chips on 2 saucers, price for set, $460.00. Photo courtesy Skinner, Inc., Boston, MA.

"Bizarre by Clarice Cliff Wilkinson Ltd. England," "Registration applied for" on creamer, 2¾" h creamer, 2¼" open sugar **200.00**
Dinner Service, Damask-Rose pattern, 21 pcs, 6 cups and saucers, 7 plates, creamer and open sugar, sgd "Bizarre by Clarice Cliff" **230.00**
Dish, yellow, orange, and brown rim bands, mkd "Bizarre by Clarice Cliff," 4" d **70.00**
Gravy Boat and Underplate, Tonquin pattern, purple **25.00**
Honey Pot, cov, Canterbury Bells pattern, hive shaped, applied bee on lid, mkd "Fantastique Bizarre by Clarice Cliff, Newport Pottery," 3¾" h **190.00**
Jam Pot, cov, applied orange and lemon on lid, bands of orange, green, and blue, mkd in gilt "Bizarre by Clarice Cliff, Newport Pottery, England," 3¼" h **185.00**
Jug, Bizarre Ware, border of orange and yellow nasturtium with circular green leaves on brown speckled ground, 12" h **575.00**
Pitcher, Delicia Pansies pattern, pink, yellow, and rose florals with brown stems on cream ground, hp green base and top, splashed green on top int, 8" h **675.00**
Plaque, Bizarre Ware, orange, yellow, and lavender flowers, 13" d **600.00**
Plate, freehand sketched landscape of trees, church, and hillsides in natural colors, rim with colored bands of black, brown, and yellow, mkd "Bizarre by Clarice Cliff," 9" d **400.00**
Plate, stylized prancing horse in dark blue and brown, wide brown rim border with black lines, mkd "designed by John Armstrong, Bizarre by Clarice Cliff, produced in Wilkinson Ltd. England, copyright reserved," 8" d **400.00**
Soup Plate, Tonquin pattern, pink transfer, 8" d **20.00**
Sugar Shaker, Crocus pattern, conical shaped, bands of yellow, green, and ochre, crocuses in orange, blue, and purple, mkd "Bizarre by Clarice Cliff," 5½" h **175.00**
Teapot, cov, Tonquin pattern, reddish brown **100.00**
Vase, Crocus pattern, elongated oval form with flared rim, colored bands of green, brown, and yellow, crocuses in orange, blue, and purple, mkd "Bizarre by Clarice Cliff," 8" h **350.00**
Vase, vine, leaves and clouds in relief in green, brown, and gold, beige ground, mkd "Clarice Cliff Newport Pottery England," 7" h **230.00**

CLOCKS

This collecting category is heavily dominated by character alarm clocks, especially those dating from the 1940s and 50s. Strong collector interest also exists for electric and key wind novelty clocks and clocks featuring advertising.

Generic clocks such as mass-produced Big Ben alarm clocks have little or no collector interest. 1920s' and 30s' wood-cased mantel clocks, banjo-style wall clocks, and period 1950s' wall clocks prove the exception.

References: Hy Brown, *Comic Character Timepieces: Seven Decades of Memories,* Schiffer Publishing, 1992; Michael Bruner, *Advertising Clocks: America's Timeless Heritage,* Schiffer Publishing, 1995.

Collectors' Club: National Assoc of Watch and Clock Collectors, Inc, 514 Poplar St, Columbia, PA 17512.

Advertising, "Atlas Tires Batteries Accessories," white neon light-up, metal body, face, and hands, repainted glass front, 18½ x 18½" $775.00

Advertising, "Buy St. Joseph Aspirin," light-up, metal with glass face and front, Pam Clock Co, dated 1954, metal rim painted black, 14½" d 275.00

Advertising, "Cities Service," light-up, metal with glass face and front, 15" d 450.00

Advertising, "Drink Coca-Cola, Lunch With Us," counter-top model, light-up, metal with reverse painted glass, 9" h, 19½" l, 5" d 1,000.00

Advertising, "Sinclair HC Gasoline," white neon light-up, metal with tin face and glass front, black and red double spinner, 21" d 1,500.00

Advertising, Star Brand Shoes, alarm, Art Deco 50.00

Alarm, electric, yellow Bakelite, flashing light and alarm, Westclox, 1940s 100.00

Alarm, electric, yellow Catalin streamlined case, illuminated face, 1940s, 6½" l 125.00

Character, Amos 'n Andy, windup travel alarm, paper face depicting Amos 'n Andy with taxicab, folding red leatherette case, ©1933, 3¾" h 225.00

Character, Bugs Bunny, alarm, animated, Bugs eating carrot, square metal case, Richie Prem Co, 1940s, 4⅜" h 175.00

Character, Captain Midnight, wall, battery operated, gold wing emblem on dial, round chrome case, 1980s, 10" d 75.00

Character, Donald Duck, alarm, animated, Donald's head moves, his arms are clock's hands, square chrome case, Bayard, late 1930s, 4¾" h 600.00

Character, Joe Lewis, electric, molded copper figure of Louis in boxing stance, "Joe Lewis World Champion," 12" h 550.00

Character, Little Black Sambo, alarm, oval metal case, cardboard face, plastic lens, ©1946, 3½" h 225.00

Character, Lone Ranger, alarm, Clayton Moore as Lone Ranger on dial, round plastic case, 1980s, 4" d 35.00

Chartacter, Roy Rogers, alarm, windup, animated, diecut Roy on galloping Trigger, square metal case, Ingraham, 1950s, 4½" h 200.00

Kitchen, 6-sided red Catalin case, Telechron 65.00

Kitchen, battery operated, red enameled metal case, Gilbert, 7½" sq 30.00

Kitchen, electric, round red metal case, copper trim, West Clock, 7" d 10.00

Kitchen, electric, wall mount, round case with blue numbers on yellow band, General Electric 25.00

Kitchen, electric, wall mount, square chrome case, green Bakelite face, Warren Telechron, c1940, 5" sq 60.00

Planter/Lamp, electric, ceramic green oval planter on metal base with clock insert, Castro Mfg of Hollywood, 6" h 50.00

Table, Art Deco, round glass blue mirror face, chrome hands and balls for hour marks, rect chrome base, Herman Miller, c1932, 10½" h 350.00

Wall, chrome and painted metal, designed by George Nelson, 12 chrome metal rods around black-painted circular works, Herman Miller, 1950s, 24" d 500.00

Wall, sunburst style, battery operated, brown and gold metal "rays," wire trim, 26" d 80.00

CLOTHES SPRINKLERS

Although steam irons have made it unnecessary, many individuals still sprinkle clothing before ironing. In many cases, the sprinkling bottle is merely a soda bottle with an adaptive cap. However, in the middle decades of the 20th century, ceramic and glass bottles designed specifically for sprinkling were made. Many were figural, a primary reason why they have attracted collector interest.

Bottle, "Laundry Sprinkler," white plastic, black lid and lettering, 7" h $5.00

Bottle, plastic, hp floral dec on front, PlasTex Corp, Los Angeles 20.00

Cat, black, china, emb "ESD" on bottom 75.00

Cat, white, glass marble eyes, mkd "Cardinal," 7½" h 150.00

Chinaman, emperor 75.00

Chinaman, Sprinkle Plenty, head is sprinkler 125.00

Chinaman, Sprinkle Plenty, holding sadiron 150.00

Chinaman, white, blue trim, Cleminson Co 55.00

Clothespin, various colors 225.00

Dachshund, wearing green coat tied at neck, red bow, unmkd 300.00

Dearie Is Weary, yellow dress, holding iron, head is sprinkler, rare 350.00

Dutch Boy 250.00

Dutch Girl, plastic 75.00

Dutch Girl, wetter-downer 125.00

Elephant, raised trunk, white, green clover on belly, unmkd 45.00

Fireman, holding hose with sprinkler, cap in front, rare 600.00

Flatiron, woman ironing decal, 1950s 40.00

Kitchen Prayer Lady, Enesco, rare 500.00

Mammy, white dress with red trim, 8" h 225.00

Mary Poppins, clear glass, holding umbrella and purse 90.00

Mary Poppins, wearing hat and dress with striped skirt, Cleminson 300.00

Merry Maid, glass 100.00

Merry Maid, molded plastic, Reliance, 6½" h 15.00

Myrtle, white dress with polka-dot top, sprinkler in back of head, Pfaltzgraff 175.00

Poodle, sitting on hind legs, gray, unmkd 150.00

Poodle, sitting on hind legs, pink, unmkd 190.00

Rooster, long neck, plastic cap, 10" h 175.00

Sadiron, ceramic, ivy 85.00

Sadiron, ceramic, souvenir, theme park adv 95.00

Sadiron, plastic, green 30.00

Siamese Cat, tan, Cardinal China 100.00

Table, electric, television shape, Pennwood Numechron Co, Pittsburgh, PA, 5" h, $40.00.

CLOTHING & ACCESSORIES

Victorian-era clothing is passé. Clothing of the flapper era has lost much of its appeal. Forget pre-1945 entirely. Today's collectors want post-1945 clothing.

1960s' psychedelic-era clothing is challenging 1950s' clothing for front position on sellers' racks. No matter what the era, a major key to clothing's value is a design which screams a specific period. Further, collectors want clothing that is ready to wear. Older collectors still love to play "dress up."

Hollywood-, television-, and movie-personality-related and high-style fashion designer clothing is now steady fare at almost every major American auction house. Prices continue to rise. Many buyers are foreign. Paris may be center stage for the contemporary clothing market, but the American collectibles marketplace is the focus of vintage clothing sales.

References: Mary Bachman, *Collector's Guide to Hair Combs*, Collector Books, 1998; Joanne Dubbs Ball and Dorothy Hehl Torem, *The Art of Fashion Accessories*, Schiffer Publishing, 1993; Maryanne Dolan, *Vintage Clothing: 1880–1980, 3rd Edition*, Books Americana, Krause Publications, 1995; Kate E. Dooner, *Plastic Handbags, 2nd Edition*, Schiffer Publishing, 1998; Ray Ellsworth, *Platform Shoes: A Big Step in Fashion*, Schiffer Publishing, 1998; Roseann Ettinger, *Fifties Forever! Popular Fashions for Men, Women, Boys & Girls*, Schiffer Publishing, 1999; Roseann Ettinger, *Handbags, 2nd Edition*, Schiffer Publishing, 1998; Roseann Ettinger, *Popular and Collectible Neckties: 1955 to Present*, Schiffer Publishing, 1998; Roseann Ettinger, *20th Century Neckties: Pre-1955*, Schiffer Publishing, 1999; Kristina Harris, *Vintage Fashions for Women: 1920s–1940s*, Schiffer Publishing, 1996; Kristina Harris, *Vintage Fashions for Women: The 1950s & 60s*, Schiffer Publishing, 1997.

Ellie Laubner, *Fashions of the Roaring '20s*, Schiffer Publishing, 1996; Jan Lindenberger, *Clothing & Accessories From the '40s, '50s & '60s*, Schiffer Publishing, 1996; Sally C. Luscomb, *The Collector's Encyclopedia of Buttons*, Schiffer Publishing, 1997; J. J. Murphy, *Children's Handkerchiefs*, Schiffer Publishing, 1998; Peggy Anne Osborne, *Button, Button, 2nd Edition*, Schiffer Publishing, 1997; Joe Poltorak, *Fashions in the Groove*, Schiffer Publishing, 1998; Maureen Reilly and Mary Beth Detrich, *Women's Hats of the 20th Century for Designers and Collectors*, Schiffer Publishing, 1997; Trina Robbins, *Tomorrow's Heirlooms: Fashions of the 60s & 70s*, Schiffer Publishing, 1997; Nancy M. Schiffer, *Tropical Shirts & Clothing*, Schiffer Publishing, 1998; Desire Smith, *Vintage Style: 1920–1960*, Schiffer Publishing, 1997; Sheila Steinberg and Kate E. Dooner, *Fabulous Fifties: Designs for Modern Living*, Schiffer Publishing, 1993; Joe Tonelli and Marc Luers, *Bowling Shirts*, Schiffer Publishing, 1998; Debra J. Wisniewski, *Antique & Collectible Buttons*, Collector Books, 1997.

Newsletter: *The Vintage Connection*, 904 N 65th St, Springfield, OR 97478.

Collectors' Clubs: Antique Comb Collectors Club International, 8712 Pleasant View Rd, Bangor, PA 18013; The Costume Society of America, 55 Edgewater Dr, PO Box 73, Earleville, MD 21919; National Button Society, 2733 Juno Pl, Apt 4, Akron, OH 44333.

Apron, cotton, chartreuse and gold print, patch pocket
   trimmed in gold braid **$8.00**
Apron, muslin, bib style, hand embroidered **15.00**

Apron, organdy, bib style, fruit print, red trim **15.00**
Apron, organdy, pink, cotton gingham patch pockets and
   rickrack trim, Gingham Girl **10.00**
Bandanna, cotton, red, printed western motif, 20" sq **20.00**
Belt, suede, pink, orig box, Hickok, 1950s, size 36. . . . . . . **20.00**
Belt, woven metal, plastic pearlized buckle, 1940s. **15.00**
Belt Buckle, brass, 1960s. **20.00**
Button, Bakelite, figural butterfly **4.00**
Button, Bakelite, orange, round **1.00**
Button, cat in relief under plastic, mounted on brass. **2.00**
Button, metal, floral design, scalloped edge, 1940s. **25.00**
Camisole, cotton, blue, elastic waist, 1950. . . . . **15.00**
Cap, with visor, tan cotton twill, black woven label at
   front, yellow "Lee" at front, "Fade proof Sanforized
   Union Made," 1950–60s, size 6⅝ **25.00**
Cape, tan, dark brown chain stitched ornate overall
   designs, 2 slash pockets, button neck fastener, satin
   lined, 1940s **30.00**
Coat, lady's, sateen, pink, wide sleeves,1950s **20.00**
Coat, lady's, wool, black, black satin lining, plastic but-
   ton at neck, 1950s. **30.00**
Coat, man's, wool, tan, single breasted, 2 slot and 2
   flapped pockets, satin lined, Pendleton, size 42 . . . . **20.00**
Coat Dress, black, white, and charcoal wool hound-
   stooth trimmed with flat black braid, jacket double-
   breasted at waist closure, skirt with 2 rows of black
   buttons and mock button holes, labeled "Christian
   Dior Paris 07825 Made in France," size 6 . . . . **575.00**
Cumberbund, satin, black and plaid, c1940 . . . . **10.00**
Dress, 2 pc, loose weave cotton, floral print, sheet floral
   jacket, 1960s. **15.00**
Dress, chiffon, red, sleeveless, scoop neck, feather dec
   on bottom, 1950s **30.00**
Dress, cotton, blue, cotton eyelet trim on pockets, 1940s **30.00**
Dress, cotton, tucked, eyelet trimmed yoke, sleeves,
   skirt, 3½" open work, scalloped hem, 38" l **20.00**
Dress, rayon, cloth flower at base of neckline, velvet
   trim, c1936. . . . . **45.00**
Dress, rayon, cornflower blue, dark blue and white flo-
   ral pattern, 4 bubble button front, Louisa Alcott, 1940. . . . . **40.00**
Dress, wrap-around, floral burgundy print, pleated skirt,
   Bakelite buttons, 1940s **40.00**
Dungarees, child's, blue and white striped bib overalls,
   donut button fly, "Big Smith" label on bib. **25.00**

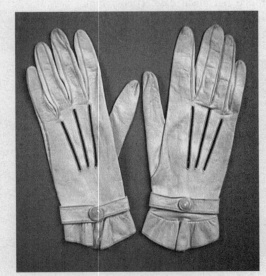

Ivory Kid Gloves, $30.00.

Dungarees, men's, big style, wrench pocket and hammer loop, blue and white "Lee R.M.R." label on bib, blue and white label on yoked back reads "Lee R.M.R. Made in U.S.A.," size 32 x 32 . . . . 50.00

Dungarees, men's, indigo, black Levi tab with big "E," orig paper tag, 1960s, size 28 x 30. . . . . 75.00

Evening Jacket, wool brocaded, beaded front and sleeves, 1940s. 100.00

Fishnet Stockings, white, Hanes, 1970s 5.00

Fur Stole, mink, 4 minks joined together, embroidered initials "MJW," 47" l. 30.00

Gloves, pr, lady's, cotton, metal button trim, 1960s. 10.00

Gloves, pr, lady's, cotton suede, brown, Italy, 1960s 15.00

Gloves, pr, lady's, leather, black, fur trim, 1940s. 15.00

Gloves, pr, lady's, leather, red, 1950s. 15.00

Gloves, pr, lady's, sheer, wide wrist with double fold trim, 1950s 10.00

Gloves, pr, men's, driving, leather, black, c1920s 25.00

Gown, cut velvet, backless, cape sleeves, c1931 . . . . 300.00

Gown, satin, lace trim, c1930s 85.00

Gown, silk, floral print, puffy sleeves, 1940s 75.00

Half Slip, satin, blue and orange, 1940s. 10.00

Handkerchief, children's theme, square, Fruit of the Loom, 9¼" sq 12.00

Handkerchief, floral motif, square, orig label reads "Duchess Handkerchief," 12" 5.00

Handkerchief, months of the year, seasonal illus, hand-rolled edges, orig label reads "Created by Kimball". 8.00

Handkerchief, scalloped edge, floral motif, "Happy Birthday" print, 1940–50s 2.00

Hat, lady's, mink, 1950s 30.00

Hat, lady's, straw, chenille tassel dec, 1960s. 5.00

Hat, lady's, velvet, with brim, feather trim, 1940s 10.00

Jacket, gabardine, single breasted, padded shoulders, rhinestone accent dec at bottom front and neck, 1940s. 20.00

Jacket, lady's, velvet, Peter Pan collar, 1950s. 50.00

Jacket, leather, black, suede fringe, Victoria Leather & Sportswear, Canada, 1970s, size 34 . . . . 40.00

Jacket, leather, black, Talon zipper front, 4 lower pockets, cuffs with leather straps and plastic buttons, red quilted lining, rear belt with plastic buttons, Sears, 1940–50s, size 8 . . . . 100.00

Jacket, suede, olive drab, flight jacket style, knit collar, cuffs, and waist, 2 slash pockets in front, 1940s 40.00

Jacket, wool, pink, gray, and cream colored plaid, single breasted, 2 patch pockets, Western Star, 1950s 50.00

Jacket, wool, red, gray, and white plaid, 2 patch pockets, large buttons at front and at cuffs, 1950s 20.00

Maillot, black wool knit with triangular midriff cutout, labeled "Rudi Gernreich for Harmon Knitwear California" 230.00

Necktie, silk, burnt orange, cream colored design, "Carpaccio's The Dream of Ursula," 1940s 20.00

Necktie, silk, gray, hp abstract designs 20.00

Necktie, silk, hp "George". 20.00

Nightgown, rayon, floral print, c1930–40 . . . . 90.00

Pants Suit, 2 pc, polyester knit, plaid, wide flared legs, boxy jacket, 1960–70s. 10.00

Purse, leather, black, tortoise shell handle, 1950s 35.00

Purse, wicker basket style, 1960s. 8.00

Raincoat, black, double-breasted, white mink polka-dot accents on collar, satin lined, black plastic buttons, 2 flapped slash pockets, 1960s 35.00

Robe, white chiffon, lace trim, front bow, 1950s 30.00

Scarf, sheer silk, floral pattern, 1960s. 15.00

Scarf, silk, polka-dot brown and aqua, sgd "Echo," 1960s 15.00

Scarf, silk, sgd "Tammi Skeef," 1950s. 15.00

Shawl, silk, satin stitch embroidery, 60" sq 45.00

Shirt, boy's, cotton, mint green, multicolored scenes of cowboys roping and branding steer, short sleeve, orig tag, size 16 . . . . 50.00

Shirt, man's, Hawaiian style, rayon, orange, green and brown island scenes, 2 pockets, made in Hong Kong by Raymond 25.00

Shoe Clips, pr, plastic, beaded, 1950s 12.00

Shoes, baby, leather, high top, 1930s 20.00

Shoes, pr, child's, cowboy boots, russet color leather, sewn scroll and pistol designs, pull-on straps, 1940–50s 20.00

Shoes, pr, men's, brown leather, oxford style, Towne Shoes, Wolverine, 1960s 30.00

Shoes, pr, women's, alligator, slingback, open-toe, 1950s. . . . 40.00

Shoes, pr, women's, black leather, tooled design, Miracle Thread, 1940s 75.00

Shoes, pr, women's, brown lizard, platform, open-toe, 1940s. 50.00

Skating Outfit, wool, black, short jacket fastening down front with rhinestone centered buttons, quilted lining, short flared skirt edged with red rickrack, both lined with red taffeta, Abercrombie & Fitch label, 1950, size 6 . . . . 230.00

Slacks, girl's, corduroy, light blue, multicolored floral pattern, orig "Maverick Blue Bell" paper tag, 1970s, size 14 . . . . 50.00

Slacks, wool blend, tan and blue plaid, bell bottom, Talon zipper fly, orig paper tag, 1970s 20.00

Slip, crinoline, pink, layered, 1950s. 25.00

Slip, satin, pink, thin straps, lace trim, 1950s 20.00

Socks, pr, men's, cotton, white, blue and black designs on ankles, orig tag, size 11½ 10.00

Socks, pr, men's, cotton/rayon, brown, white and burnt orange designs on ankles, orig tag, size 10½ 10.00

Stockings, silk, rhinestone design at ankle, c1945 . . . . 25.00

Sunglasses, molded plastic, cat-eyes shape, yellow and red, 1960s. 30.00

Sweater, knit, red, white, and blue cotton piping, 1960s 15.00

Handbag, gold mesh, gate top frame, Whiting & Davis, $80.00.

Sweater, mink collar, c1936. . . . . **45.00**
Sweater, navy blue, pink and white floral designs, silvered ornate metallic buttons, navy blue string tie at neck, "Catalina a California Creator" label, 1940s. **55.00**
Sweater, wool, beaded dec, 1960s. **20.00**
Sweater Guard, goldtone, plastic pearls in center of clips, 1950–60s. **15.00**
Swim Suit, wool, aqua blue, white cloth strap, "pure Zephyr" tag, 1930s **20.00**
Swim Suit, wool, unisex, c1924. **65.00**
Swim Trunks, cotton, paisley, orig paper tags, 1960s. **25.00**
Tennis Shoes, pr, white canvas, oxford style, white rubber toe cap, red stripe trim along sole, 1960s **30.00**
Umbrella, silk, plastic handle, 1960s **5.00**
Umbrella, silk, striped, wooden handle, 1950s. **8.00**

COALPORT FIGURINES

After completing an apprenticeship at Caughley, Robert Rose established a pottery at Coalport, located in Shropshire's Severn Gorge, England, in 1796. The pottery remained in the Rose family until acquired by the Bruff family in 1853.

In 1923 Cauldon Potteries, located in Stoke-on-Trent, Staffordshire, bought Coalport. In 1926 operations were moved from the Shropshire plant to Staffordshire. In 1936 the Crescent potteries of George Jones & Sons acquired Cauldon/Coalport. In 1958 E. Brian and Company, whose Foley China Works were established in 1850, purchased Coalport, maintaining its identity as a separate company. Coalport became part of the Wedgwood Group in 1967.

Although known primarily for its dinnerware, Coalport produced a line of porcelain figurines between 1890 and the present that rival those of Royal Doulton and Lladro. Each figure has a distinctive name. Many are found in multiple variations. Backstamps play a role in value with examples bearing the earliest backstamp having the highest value. As with Royal Doulton, the figurine's designer also impacts on value.

Reference: Tom Power, *The Charlton Standard Catalogue of Coalport Figurines,* Charlton Press, 1997.

Collectors' Club: Coalport Collector Society, PO Box 99, Sudbury CO10 6SN, England.

April, yellow, 1993–97, 5" h **$100.00**
Bedtime Story, pink, yellow, mauve, and green, limited edition of 1,000, 1986, 8" h **400.00**
Blacksmith, brown, limited edition of 1,000, 1974 . . . . **300.00**
Breeze, blue dress, c1949–72, 6¼" h **250.00**
Chelsea, orange and yellow, 1993–95, 5¼" h **125.00**
Christabel, gold, 1976–82, 8½" h. **300.00**
Christmas Kitten, peach dress, limited edition of 5,000, 1993, 7¼" h **150.00**
Daisy, yellow dress, c1920–72, 4½" h **400.00**
Denise, white skirt, 1975–77, 7¾" h **325.00**
Devotion, mother holding daughter, 1980–82, 7¼" h **400.00**
Earth, green and white, limited edition of 1,000, 1989, 10¾" h **400.00**
Edith Cavell, blue, gray, and black, limited edition of 500, 1981, 8½" h **350.00**
Florence Nightingale, pink jacket, blue skirt, 1981–82, 8½" h **600.00**

French Knight, black and purple, 1977. . . . . **475.00**
Girl with Paddington Bear, white, 1979, 10¼" h **400.00**
Her Ladyship, red dress, c1949–72, 4¾" h **625.00**
Holly, green and cream dress, limited edition of 15,000, 1993, 3½" h **125.00**
HRH The Prince of Wales, cream shirt, green kilt, limited edition of 1,000, 1981, 8¾" h **300.00**
Jane, lavender and cream, 1994–95, 5¼" h **125.00**
Jennifer Jane, turquoise dress, 1973–76, 6" h **240.00**
Karen Kain as Snow Queen, white and gold, limited edition of 500, 1986, 9¾" h **300.00**
Lady Rose, pink and green dress, c1949–72, 6¾" h **425.00**
Loretta, lilac, 1987, 5¼" h **90.00**
Marilyn, pink, 1980–82, 8" h. **325.00**
My Pal, boy with dog, limited edition of 7,500, 1996, 6" h. . . . **150.00**
Pedlar, blue jacket, brown trousers, c1920, 6" h **550.00**
Rosie, pink, 1996, 3½" h. **50.00**
Stephanie, yellow, 1984, 8" h **275.00**
Tennis Party, yellow and blue, limited edition of 500, 1997, 5" h. **100.00**
Zara, red, 1986–89, 5" h **170.00**

COCA-COLA

John Pemberton, a pharmacist from Atlanta, Georgia, developed the formula for Coca-Cola. However, credit for making Coca-Cola the world's leading beverage belongs to Asa G. Candler. Candler improved the formula and marketed his product aggressively.

The use of "Coke" in advertising first occurred in 1941. Foreign collectors prefer American Coca-Cola items over those issued in their own countries.

Reproduction and copycat items have plagued Coca-Cola collecting for the past three decades. The problem is compounded by Coca-Cola's licensing the reproduction of many of its classic products. Finally, the number of new products licensed by Coca-Cola appears to increase each year. Their sales represent a significant monetary drain of monies previously spent in the vintage market.

References: B. J. Summers' *Guide to Coca-Cola, Second Edition,* Collector Books, 1998; Gael de Courtivron, *Collectible Coca-Cola Toy Trucks: An Identification and Value Guide,* Collector Books, 1995; Steve Ebner, *Vintage Coca-Cola Machines, Vol. II, 1959–1968,* published by author, 1996; Bob and Debra Henrich, *Coca-Cola Commemorative Bottles,* Collector Books, 1998; Deborah Goldstein Hill, *Price Guide to Vintage Coca-Cola Collectibles, 1896–1965,* Krause Publications, 1999; Allan Petretti, *Petretti's Coca-Cola Collectibles Price Guide, 10th Edition,* Antique Trader Books, 1997; Allan Petretti and Chris Beyer, *Classic Coca-Cola Serving Trays,* Antique Trader Books, 1998; Al and Helen Wilson, *Wilsons' Coca-Cola Price Guide,* Schiffer Publishing, 1997.

Collectors' Clubs: The Coca-Cola Club, PO Box 158715, Nashville, TN 37215; Coca-Cola Collectors Club, 400 Monemar Ave, Baltimore, MD 21228; Coca-Cola Collectors Club, PO Box 49166, Atlanta, GA 30359.

REPRODUCTION ALERT: Coca-Cola trays.

Banner, "...And Take Home" with 6-pack, 1947, 9 x 25". . . . **$40.00**
Banner, "Redeem Coupons Here for Coca-Cola Cartons" with 6-pack, 1940s, 7 x 22" **110.00**
Blotter, 1920s, 6" l. **150.00**

Blotter, "Drink Coca-Cola Delicious and Refreshing" between 2 bottles, framed, 1926 . . . . **60.00**

Booklet, Coca-Cola Bottlers' Current Advertising Price List 1933, illus. **230.00**

Bottle Opener, wall mount, metal, red enamel logo, 1948–50 . . . . **45.00**

Bottle Topper, plastic, "We Let You See The Bottle," 1950s, 7 x 7¹/₂" **850.00**

Calendar, 1937, full pad, boy going fishing, framed **400.00**

Calendar, 1943, 13 x 20" **275.00**

Calendar, 1946, Sprite Boy, "Compliments of your Coca Cola bottler," complete **750.00**

Calendar, 1954, woman holding bottle, basketball player in background **100.00**

Calendar, 1958, "Sign of Good Taste" **130.00**

Calendar, 1959, "The pause that refreshes" **175.00**

Calendar, 1969, "Things go better with Coke," couple sitting at table as man whispers in woman's ear **25.00**

Calendar Holder, tin, emb, 1960s, 13 x 9" **475.00**

Carrier, wire, 6 bottle, litho tin side plates, c1960 . . . . **150.00**

Clock, glass and metal, light-up, 1960s, 11 x 12" **150.00**

Clock, neon, 1940s, 15¹/₂" sq **475.00**

Clock, plastic face under glass, light-up, 1970s, 13 x 16" **55.00**

Coasters, set of 8, colored aluminum, orig box, 1950s **60.00**

Coat Rack, aluminum, emb, gold painted glass bottle affixed to front, 1930–40s, 7¹/₂ x 10" **625.00**

Cooler, Westinghouse style, c1930s, 18 x 26 x 34", restored **775.00**

Cup, printed adv on int for Coca-Cola in Greencastle, IN, 1930s **130.00**

Dispenser, "No-Drip Protection," spring loaded, c1940s, 7¹/₂" h **170.00**

Door Bar, porcelain, "Ice Cold Drink Coca-Cola In Bottles," 1950s, 30" l **525.00**

Door Bar, wrought-iron arms, adjustable, 1930s, 4 x 32" **525.00**

Door Pull, aluminum, figural bottle, 1930s, 11" h **280.00**

Door Push, porcelain, "Come in! Have a Coca-Cola," Canadian, 1941, 17 x 53" **1,150.00**

Door Push, tin, "Pull/Refresh Yourself Drink Coca-Cola In Bottles," 1950s, 3 x 6" **550.00**

Door Push, tin, "Push/Drink Coca-Cola Be Really Refreshed!," 1950–60s, 4 x 8" **525.00**

Toy Truck, metal cab and frame, wood bed, 14 wood block Coca-Cola cases, Smitty Toys, 13¹/₂" l, $715.00. Photo courtesy Collectors Auction Services.

Flange Sign, tin, Drink Coca-Cola" above bottle, 1946, 24 x 20" **775.00**

Fly Swatter, metal, stamped block logo, 1930s **325.00**

Kickplate, porcelain, "Drink Coca-Cola" above "Fountain Service," 1950s, 12 x 28" **1,400.00**

Menu Board, glass, orig metal and cardboard frame, 1960s, 20 x 38" **475.00**

Menu Board, "Specials To-Day" under "Drink Coca-Cola," emb, 1930s **170.00**

Model, cardboard, Cocke Bottling Co, 1950s **25.00**

Napkin, rice paper, matted, woman sitting on chair and "Hot—Tired—Thirsty? Drink Coca-Cola. Delicious— Refreshing—Thirst-Quenching" in circle with arrow, 12" sq **90.00**

Newspaper Advertisement, "Thru 50 Years...the pause that refreshes," "Ice-cold every day in the year," 2 women and "1886/1936," full page, 1936 . . . . **40.00**

Pocket Mirror, "Be Really Refreshed /Drink Coca-Cola/The Coca-Cola Bottling Co Fort Smith, Ark," 1930s, 2¹/₈" d **500.00**

Poster, cardboard, "Delicious Refreshing" with bottle in center, 1950s, 2" sq **300.00**

Poster, cardboard, diecut, figural bottle, 1940–50s, 12" h **210.00**

Poster, cardboard, "I am a Five-Star Coca-Cola Dealer," framed, 12 x 18" **65.00**

Poster, cardboard, "Thirst Knows No Season," man and woman with snowman, 1941 . . . . **90.00**

Pretzel Dish, round, 3 bottles on sides, 1935 . . . . **170.00**

Puzzle, cardboard, diecut, woman holding tray of snacks with bottles on ice, 1950s, 34 x 44" **225.00**

Radio, figural radio, 1950s **425.00**

Sandwich Plate, 1931, 7¹/₄" d **190.00**

Sign, cardboard, bathing girl on rocks, 1938, 30 x 50" **700.00**

Sign, cardboard, Harlem Globetrotters Reece "Goose" Tatum, 1952, 16 x 27" **725.00**

Sign, diecut diamond, "Coca-Cola Cold refreshment" with bottle, orig string hanger, 1937, 21" **725.00**

Sign, diecut, figural bottle, emb, 12 x 36" **130.00**

Sign, "Drink Coca-Cola/Pause Refresh/Lunch," 2-sided, 1950s, 25 x 28" **850.00**

Sign, light-up, countertop, waterfall motion, 1940–50s **1,600.00**

Sign, masonite, diecut, silkscreened, hand on bottle, 1940s, 15" h **35.00**

Sign, metal, plastic front, "Drink Coca-Cola," light-up, 1950–60s, 12 x 24" **190.00**

Cooler, metal with galvanized interior and tray, 19" h, 17" w, 12" d, orig box, $418.00. Photo courtesy Collectors Auction Services.

Sign, plywood, 2-sided, "Slow School Zone/Drink Coca-Cola/Drive Safely," complete with corner brackets and orig metal ring, 1957, 16 x 49" 575.00

Sign, porcelain, bottle with "Coca-Cola" on red button, 24" d 235.00

Sign, porcelain, "Coca-Cola" on red button, 2-sided, orig cutouts at bottom, int ring frame and 2 key posts for mounting, 1940–50s, 48" d.................... 500.00

Sign, tin, bottle on white button, 1940s, 24" d 675.00

Sign, tin, "Drink Coca-Cola," beveled edge, 1930s 130.00

Sign, tin, "Drink Coca-Cola Ice Cold" with bottle, emb, aluminum frame 675.00

Sign, tin, "Wherever You Go Drink Coca-Cola," octagonal, wire accents, snow skiing scene, attached pinecone, 1950s, 14 x 18"...................... 230.00

String Holder, 2-sided, "Take Home Coca-Cola In Cartons," 1930s, 30 x 16" 210.00

Syrup Bottle, aluminum jigger lid, 1920s 475.00

Syrup Jug, 1 gal, orig box, 1930s 275.00

Thermometer, masonite, "Thirst Knows No Season," 1944, 7 x 17" 300.00

Thermometer, silhouette of girl drinking from bottle, 1940, 16" h............................... 210.00

Thermometer, tin, bottle on sides, 1941, 7 x 16"......... 675.00

Towel, "Coca-Cola" above "Delicious And Refreshing" on red ground, 1930–40s, 7 x 18" 40.00

Tray, girl with bottle, 1928....................... 850.00

Tray, soda jerk, 1928............................ 325.00

Tray, woman sitting on bench holding bottle, Spanish text, 1939............................... 100.00

Truck Grill Plate, cast aluminum, "Drink Coca-Cola In Bottles," 1920s, 17" l........................ 200.00

Umbrella, stenciled, "Drink Coca-Cola, The Pause That Refreshes, Ice Cold In Bottles," c1930s............ 900.00

Wall Pocket, pressed composition and cardboard, c1932, 9 x 12" 600.00

Waste Basket, tin, red and white, "Enjoy Coca-Cola, Enjoy Coke," 1970s............................. 10.00

COCKTAIL SHAKERS

The modern cocktail shaker dates from the 1920s, a result of the martini craze. As a form, it inspired designers in glass, ceramics, and metals.

Neither the Depression nor World War II hindered the sale of cocktail shakers. The 1950s was the era of the home bar and outdoor patio. The cocktail shaker played a major role in each. The arrival of the electric blender and the shift in public taste from liquor to wine in the 1960s ended the cocktail shaker's reign.

Reference: Stephen Visakay, *Vintage Bar Ware*, Collector Books, 1997.

Aluminum, cylindrical, black plastic top and base, West Bend, 1934, 11" h............................. $50.00

Chrome, coffeepot shape, etched grapevines, cork-lined spout cover, 1930s, 12" h 70.00

Chrome, cylindrical, black enameled bands, Bakelite finial, Chase Brass & Copper Co, c1930, 11½" h 55.00

Chrome, dumbbell shape, red plastic top, circular foot, 1930s, 12½" h.......................... 100.00

Chrome, electric, maroon enameled cast-iron base, Stevens Electric Co, 1933, 13" h................. 200.00

Glass, clear with aqua and gold geometric design, gold-colored lid and spoon, 1950s, 9" h, $35.00.

Chrome, Manhattan shaker, cylindrical, Revere Copper & Brass Co, c1937, 12¾" h 350.00

Chrome, penguin shape, removable beak for pouring, c1940, 11" h............................. 350.00

Chrome, skyscraper, stepped design, Revere Copper and Brass Co, 1930s, 14" h..................... 200.00

Glass, cylindrical, Tam-o-Shaker, clear with red and blue plaid design, tilted chrome top with red plastic knob resembles tam, Seymour Products, c1935, 13" h 100.00

Glass, spherical, clear upper half with silver stripes, frosted bottom, chrome top, c1940, 5½" d 80.00

Glass, tapered cylinder, amber, chrome top, Cambridge Glass, c1938, 11½" h 60.00

Glass, tapered cylinder, blue with white ship's flags, Hazel Atlas, 10" h.............................. 65.00

Glass, tapered cylinder, clear with pink elephants dec 45.00

Glass, tapered cylinder, clear with white polar bears and blue ice dec, 1930s–40s, 10" h 40.00

Glass, tapered cylinder, red, Spun pattern, chrome top, Imperial Glass, c1955, 14" h 50.00

Glass, tapered cylinder, ruby red with silver-lettered "Martini," chrome top, 1930s, 9½" h 80.00

COINS & CURRENCY

Chances are you have some old coins and currency around the house. Many individuals deposit their pocket change in a large bank or bottle on a daily basis. People who travel return home with foreign change. Most currency exchanges will not convert coinage. Millions of Americans put aside brand new one-dollar silver certificate bills when America went off the silver standard.

Condition plays a critical role in determining the value of any coin or piece of currency. If your coins and currency show signs of heavy use, chances are they are worth little more than face value, even if they date prior to World War II. Circulated American silver dimes, quarters, half dollars, and dollars from before the age of sandwich coins do have a melt value ranging from two-and-one-half to three times face value. In some foreign countries, once a coin or currency has been withdrawn from service, it cannot be redeemed, even for face value.

The first step in valuing your coins and currency is to honestly grade them. Information about how to grade is found in the opening chapters of most reference books. Be a very tough grader. Individuals who are not serious collectors tend to overgrade.

Remember, values found in price guides are retail. Because coin and currency dealers must maintain large inventories, they pay premium prices only for extremely scarce examples.

Coins are far easier to deal with than currency, due to the fact that there are fewer variations. When researching any coin or piece of currency, the reference must match the object being researched on every point.

Allen G. Bergman and Alex G. Malloy's *Warman's Coins & Currency* (Wallace-Homestead, 1995) is a good general reference. It includes the most commonly found material. However, when detailed research is required, use one of the following:

References: American Coins: Coin World (eds.), *The Comprehensive Catalog and Encyclopedia of U.S. Coins, 2nd Edition,* Avon Books, 1998; David Harper (ed.), *1999 North American Coins & Prices, 8th Edition,* Krause Publications, 1998; Thomas E. Hudgeon, Jr. (ed.), *The Official 2000 Blackbook Price Guide of U.S. Coins, 37th Edition,* House of Collectibles, 1999; Scott A. Travers (ed.), *The Official Guide to Coin Grading and Counterfeit Detection,* House of Collectibles, 1997.

American Currency: Thomas Hudgeons, Jr. (ed.), *The Official 2000 Blackbook Price Guide to U.S. Paper Money, 31st Edition,* House of Collectibles, 1999; Robert E. Wihite, *Standard Catalog of United States Paper Money, 17th Edition,* Krause Publications, 1998.

Foreign Coins: Marc Hudgeons, *The Blackbook Price Guide to World Coins, 3rd Edition,* House of Collectibles, 1999; Chester L. Krause and Clifford Mishler, *2000 Standard Catalog of World Coins, 1901-Present, 27th Edition,* Krause Publications, 1999.

Foreign Currency: Colin R. Bruce II and Neil Schafer (eds.), *1998 Standard Catalog of World Paper Money: Modern Issues (1961 to Present), Volume III, 4th Edition,* Krause Publications, 1998; Colin R. Bruce II and Neil Shafer (eds.), *Standard Catalog of World Paper Money, Specialized Issues, 8th Edition,* Krause Publications, 1998; Albert Pick, *Standard Catalog of World Paper Money: General Issues, Volume II, 8th Edition,* Krause Publications, 1997.

Periodicals: *Coin World,* PO Box 150, Sidney, OH 45365; *Coin Prices, Coins, Numismatic News,* and *World Coin News* are all publications from Krause Publications, 700 E State St, Iola, WI 54990.

Collectors' Club: American Numismatic Assoc, 818 N Cascade Ave, Colorado Springs, CO 80903.

COLORING BOOKS

Coloring books emerged as an independent collecting category in the early 1990s, due largely to the publication of several specialized price guides on the subject and the inclusion of the category in general price guides.

The McLoughlin Brothers were one of the first American publishers of coloring books. The Little Folks Painting Books was copyrighted in 1885. Although Binney and Smith introduced crayons in 1903, it was not until the 1930s that coloring books were crayoned rather than painted.

When Saalfield introduced its Shirley Temple coloring book in 1934, it changed a market that traditionally focused on animal, fairy tale, and military themes to one based on characters and personalities. It is for this reason that crossover collectors strongly influence the value for some titles.

Beginning in the 1970s, the number of licensed coloring books began a steady decline. If it were not for Barbie, Disney, and G.I. Joe, today's coloring book rack would consist only of generic titles, primarily because the market focuses on a younger consumer. Further, many of today's coloring books are actually activity books.

Reference: Dian Zillner, *Collectible Coloring Books,* Schiffer Publishing, 1992.

Note: Books are unused unless otherwise noted.

3 Stooges Funny Coloring Book, Samuel Lowe #2855, 1960	**$35.00**
Animal Alphabet to Color, Merrill #M3498, 1935	15.00
Ann Blyth, Merrill #2530, 1952	30.00
Aurora the Sleeping Beauty, Pocket Books, 1958	60.00
Beetle Bailey, Samuel Lowe #2860, 1961	25.00
Bing Crosby, Saalfield #1295, 1954	20.00
Boots and Her Buddies, Saalfield #331, 1941	30.00
Bullwinkle and Dudley Do-Right, Saalfield #5686, 1971	20.00
Car 54 Where Are You?, Whitman #1157, 1962	30.00
Cheerful Tearful, Western Publishing #1851-E, 1966	10.00
Dick Tracy, Saalfield #2536, 1946	50.00
Donald Duck, Whitman, 1957, 32 pg	30.00
Donny & Marie, Western Publishing #1641, 1977	25.00
Elizabeth Taylor, Whitman #1119, 1950	**45.00**
Flash Gordon Mission of Peril, Rand McNally #06538, 1979	15.00
Flying Nun, Saalfield #4672, 1968	20.00
Gloria Jean, Saalfield #158, 1940	35.00
Happy Days, cast photo cov, Playmore Publishing, 1983	10.00
Howdy Doody, Poll Parrot Shoes premium, 8 x 7"	20.00
Johnny Mack Brown, photo cov, Saalfield, 1952	25.00
Jughead, Western Publishing #1045, 1972	10.00
Land of the Lost, Western Publishing #1045, 1975	12.00
Li'l Abner and Daisy Mae, Saalfield #2391, 1942	65.00
Little Dancers, Whitman #1105-22, 1972	8.00
Little Scouts, Whitman #680, 1953	8.00

Batman Forever, Golden Books #8280, DC Comics, 1995, $5.00; Hansel & Gretel, Platt & Munk #15D, $20.00.

Lone Ranger, "Hi-Yo Silver," Funtime, 1953, 24 pgs **12.00**
My Three Sons, Whitman #1113, 1967 . . . . **15.00**
Patience and Prudence, Samuel Lowe #2532, 1957 . . . . **38.00**
Popeye, Samuel Lowe #2834, 1959 . . . . **25.00**
Roger Ramjet, Whitman #1115, 1966 . . . . **40.00**
Skeezix, McLoughlin Brothers #2023, 1929 . . . . **40.00**
Skipper Barbie's Little Sister, Whitman #1115, 1965 . . . . **18.00**
Smitty Color Book, McLoughlin Brothers, 1931 . . . . **35.00**
Terry and the Pirates, Saalfield #398, 1946 . . . . **45.00**
Wendy the Good Little Witch, Rand McNally #06416,
  1959 . . . . **10.00**

COMIC BOOKS

The modern comic book arrived on the scene in the late 1930s.
Led by superheroes such as Batman and Superman, comics quickly became an integral part of growing up. Collectors classifiy
comics from 1938 to the mid-1940s as "Golden Age" comics and
comics from the mid-1950s through the 1960s as "Silver Age"
comics. The Modern Age begins in 1980 and runs to the present.

Comics experienced a renaissance in the 1960s with the introduction of the Fantastic Four and Spider-Man. A second revival
occurred in the 1980s with the arrival of the independent comic.
The number of comic stores nationwide doubled. Speculation in
comics as investments abounded. A period of consolidation and a
bitter distribution rights fight among publishers weakened the market in the mid-1990s and burst the speculative bubble. The comic
book market is in recovery as the decade ends.

References: Grant Geissman, *Collectibly MAD: The MAD and EC
Collectibles Guide,* EC Publications, 1995; Dick Lupoff and Don
Thompson (eds.), *All in Color for a Dime,* Krause Publications,
1997; Alex G. Malloy, *Comics Values Annual, 1999 Edition,*
Antique Trader Books, 1998; Robert M. Overstreet, *The Overstreet
Comic Book Price Guide, 28th Edition,* Avon Books, Gemstone
Publishing, 1998; Robert M. Overstreet and Gary M. Carter, *The
Overstreet Comic Book Grading Guide,* Avon Books, 1992;
Maggie Thompson and Brent Frankenhoff, *Comic Buyer's Guide
1999 Comic Book Checklist and Price Guide: 1961 to Present,
Fifth Edition,* Krause Publications, 1998; Jerry Weist, *Original
Comic Art: Identification and Price Guide,* Avon Books, 1993.

Periodicals: *Comics Buyer's Guide,* 700 E State St, Iola, WI 54990;
Comic Book Marketplace, Gemstone Publishing (West), PO Box
180700, Cornado, CA 92178.

REPRODUCTION ALERT: Publishers often reprint popular stories.
Check the fine print at the bottom of the inside cover or first page
for correct titles. Also, do not confuse 10 x 13" treasury-sized
"Famous First Edition" comics printed in the mid-1970s with original comic book titles.

Note: All comics listed are in near mint condition.

Abbott and Costello, Charlton Comics, #1 . . . . **$60.00**
Aces High, EC Comics, #3 . . . . **75.00**
Actual Confessions, Atlas Comics, #14 . . . . **23.00**
Adlai Stevenson, Dell, Dec 1966 . . . . **25.00**
Adventures of Bob Hope, DC, #24, Dec 1954 . . . . **120.00**
Adventures of Superman, DC, #434, Nov 1987 . . . . **1.00**
After Dark, Sterling Comics, #6, 1955 . . . . **45.00**
Alarming Adventures, Harvey, #1, Oct 1962 . . . . **60.00**

Alice Cooper: The Last Temptation of Alice, Marvel, #2,
  1994 . . . . **6.00**
Aliens, Dark Horse, #4, Mar 1989 . . . . **10.00**
Aquaman, DC, #269, Feb 1960 . . . . **175.00**
Archie Comics, DC, #131 . . . . **8.00**
Atom, The, DC, #22, Jan 1966 . . . . **20.00**
Avengers, Marvel, #18, Jul 1965 . . . . **50.00**
Bamm Bamm and Pebbles Flintstone, Gold Key, #1, Oct
  1964 . . . . **15.00**
Batman Family, The, DC, #2, Dec 1975 . . . . **7.00**
Battlefield, Atlas Comics, #11, May 1963 . . . . **35.00**
Beany and Cecil, Dell, Jan 1955 . . . . **60.00**
Beetle Bailey, Gold Key, #53, May 1966 . . . . **3.00**
Beware the Creeper, DC, #5, Feb 1969 . . . . **35.00**
Blue Devil, DC, #2, Jul 1984 . . . . **1.00**
Bobby Benson's B-Bar-B Riders, Magazine Enterprises,
  #1, 1950 . . . . **350.00**
Boys' Ranch, Harvey, #5 . . . . **140.00**
Brave and the Bold, DC, #45, Strange Sports, Jan 1963 . . . . . **50.00**
Brave Eagle, DC, #705 . . . . **60.00**
Bugs Bunny, Dell, #171 . . . . **3.00**
Bullwinkle & Rocky 3-D, Blackthorne, #1, Mar 1987 . . . . **2.50**
Buster Bunny, Quality Comics, #1, 1953 . . . . **45.00**
Butch Cassidy, Skywald Comics, #1 . . . . **8.00**
Captain Davy Jones, Dell, #598, Nov 1954 . . . . **40.00**
Captain Kangaroo, Dell, #721, Aug 1956 . . . . **145.00**
Captain Marvel, Marvel, #3, Jul 1968 . . . . **15.00**
Care Bear, Marvel/Star, #1, Nov 1985 . . . . **.75**
Casper in Space, Harvey, #6, Jun 1973 . . . . **7.00**
Casper the Friendly Ghost, Harvey, #6, Dec 1958 . . . . **18.00**
Cat, The, Marvel, #1, Nov 1972 . . . . **15.00**
Chilly Willy, Dell, #740, Oct 1956 . . . . **40.00**
Claw the Conquered, DC, #1, Jun 1975 . . . . **2.50**
Combat, Dell, #1, Oct 1961 . . . . **40.00**
Combat Kelly, Atlas Comics, #2 . . . . **75.00**
Comedy Classics, Marvel, #5 . . . . **40.00**
Conan the Barbarian, Marvel, #17, Aug 1972 . . . . **12.00**
Conquest, Famous Funnies, #1, 1955 . . . . **22.00**
Cowboy Romances, Marvel, #3 . . . . **75.00**
Crime and Punishment, Lev Gleason, #2 . . . . **90.00**
Daffy Tunes Comics, Four-Star, #12, Aug 1947 . . . . **16.00**
Dandy Comics, E C Comics, #2 . . . . **165.00**
Date With Debbi, Nation Periodical, #1, Jan 1969 . . . . **35.00**
David and Goliath, Dell, #1205, Jul 1961 . . . . **60.00**
David Cassidy, Charlton Comics, #1, Feb 1972 . . . . **35.00**
Davy Crockett, Charlton Comics, #1, Aug 1955 . . . . **50.00**
Dazey's Diary, Dell, #1, Jun 1962 . . . . **30.00**
Dazzler, The, Marvel, #1, Mar 1981 . . . . **2.50**
Dead Air, Slave Labor Graphics, Jul 1989 . . . . **6.00**
Deadman, DC, #1, Mar 1986 . . . . **1.00**
Dear Beatrice Fairfax, Best/Standard Comics, #5, Nov
  1950 . . . . **45.00**
Death Valley, Charlton Comics, #7 . . . . **28.00**
Demon Dreams, Pacific Comics, #1, Feb 1984 . . . . **1.50**
Dennis the Menace and His Pal Joey, Fawcett, 1961 . . . . **40.00**
Dennis the Menace Triple Feature, Fawcett, 1961 . . . . **50.00**
Detective Comics, DC, #298, Clayface, Dec 1961 . . . . **175.00**
Dexter Comics, Dearfield, #5, Jul 1949 . . . . **10.00**
Diver Dan, Dell, 1962 . . . . **50.00**
Doctor Strange, Marvel, #178, Mar 1969 . . . . **30.00**
Donald and the Wheel, Dell, #1190, Nov 1960 . . . . **70.00**
Dopey Duck Comics, Timely Comics, 1956 . . . . **120.00**
Dracula, Dell, #2 . . . . **25.00**
Dragstrip Hotrodders, Charlton Comics, #1 . . . . **35.00**

Dream of Love, IW Enterprises, 1958 . . . . **10.00**
Dynamic Adventures, IW Enterprises, #8, 1964 . . . . **15.00**
Dynamo, Tower, #3, Mar 1967 . . . . **30.00**
Edge of Chaos, Pacific Comics, #1, Jul 1983 . . . . **2.00**
El Bombo Comics, Standard Comics, 1946 . . . . **70.00**
Enchanting Love, Kirby Publishing, #1, Oct 1949 . . . . **75.00**
Epsilon Wave, Independent Comics, #1, Oct 1985 . . . . **1.50**
Eva the Imp, Red Top Comic, #1, 1957 . . . . **15.00**
Excalibur, Marvel, Nov 1988 . . . . **5.00**
Explorer Joe, Ziff-Davis Comic Group, 1951 . . . . **75.00**
Face, DC, #1, Jan 1995 . . . . **5.00**
Faithful, Marvel, #1, Nov 1949 . . . . **50.00**
Family Affair, Gold Key, #3, Jul 1970 . . . . **12.00**
Famous Indian Tribes, Dell, #12, 1962 . . . . **10.00**
Fantastic Four, Marvel, #62, May 1967 . . . . **25.00**
Fantastic Voyage, Gold Key, #1, Aug 1969 . . . . **33.00**
Fat and Slat, E C Comics, #4, 1948 . . . . **150.00**
FBI, The, Dell, #1 . . . . **18.00**
Fear, Marvel, #1, Nov 1970 . . . . **20.00**
Felix the Cat and His Friends, Toby Press, #1, Dec 1953 . . . . **90.00**
Fightin' Air Force, Charlton Comics, #3, Feb 1956 . . . . **35.00**
Fighting American, Harvey, Oct 1966 . . . . **30.00**
Fighting Undersea Commandos, Men's Publications, #1,
    Aug 1952 . . . . **50.00**
Fight the Enemy, Tower Comics, #1, Aug 1966 . . . . **20.00**
Firestorm, DC, #1 . . . . **6.00**
First Americans, Dell, #843, Sep 1957 . . . . **90.00**
First Kiss, Charlton Comics, #1, Dec 1957 . . . . **30.00**
Flame, The, Ajax/Farrell Publications, #5 . . . . **275.00**
Flash, The, DC, #152, May 1965 . . . . **55.00**
Flash Gordon, Dell, #434 . . . . **85.00**
Flying Cadet, Flying Cadet Publishing, #1, Jan 1943 . . . . **85.00**
Fooey, Scoff Publishing, #1, Feb 1961 . . . . **32.00**
Forever Darling, Dell, $681, Feb 1956 . . . . **110.00**
Freedom Fighters, DC, #1, Apr 1976 . . . . **2.50**
Funny 3-D, Harvey, #1, Dec 1953 . . . . **75.00**
Funny Fables, Decker Publications, #1, Aug 1957 . . . . **25.00**
Gabby Hayes Adventure Comics, Toby Press, Dec 1953 . . . . . **95.00**
Ghost Rider, Marvel, Dec 1976 . . . . **3.50**
Giant-Size Defenders, Marvel, #1, Silver Surfer, Jul 1974 . . . **10.00**
GI Combat, DC, #140, Mar 1970 . . . . **8.00**

GI Jane, Stanhall/Merit, #1, May 1953 . . . . **70.00**
GI Joe, Dark Horse Comics, Dec 1995 . . . . **2.50**
Ginger, Archie Publictions, #10, 1954 . . . . **55.00**
Godzilla, Marvel, Aug 1977 . . . . **4.50**
Goofy Comics, Nedar Publications, #1 . . . . **170.00**
Green Lantern, DC, #18, Jan 1963 . . . . **110.00**
Gunmaster, Charlton Comics, #87 . . . . **12.00**
Gunslinger, Dell, #1220 . . . . **90.00**
Gypsy Colt, Dell, #568, Jun 1954 . . . . **40.00**
Hanna-Barbera Band Wagon, Gold Key, #1, 1962 . . . . **120.00**
Happy Jack Howard, Red Top, 1957 . . . . **24.00**
Haunted Thrills, Ajax/Farrell Publications, #1, Jun 1952 . . . **260.00**
Hawk and Dove, DC, Jun 1969 . . . . **15.00**
Hawkman, DC, #27, Sep 1968 . . . . **24.00**
Heathcliff, Marvel/Star, #1, Apr 1985 . . . . **.65**
Heckle and Jeckle, Gold Key, #1 . . . . **60.00**
Hector Heathcote, Gold Key, #1, Mar 1964 . . . . **60.00**
Henry Aldrich Comics, Dell, #1, Aug 1950 . . . . **80.00**
Hercules Unbound, DC, #1, Nov 1975 . . . . **1.50**
Hi and Lois, Dell, #683 . . . . **25.00**
High Adventure, Dell, #949 . . . . **50.00**
Holiday Digest, Harvey, 1988 . . . . **4.00**
Horrors, The, Star Publications, #11, Jan 1953 . . . . **160.00**
Hot Stuff Sizzlers, Harvey, #1, Jul 1960 . . . . **100.00**
Hot Wheels, DC, #1, 1970 . . . . **75.00**
HR Pufnstuf, Gold Key, #1, Oct 1970 . . . . **180.00**
Huckleberry Finn, Dell, #1114, Jul 1960 . . . . **50.00**
Huckleberry Hound, Charlton Comics, #1, Nov 1970 . . . . . . **30.00**
Huckleberry Hound, Dell/Gold Key, #1050, Dec 1959 . . . . . **80.00**
Hulk, The, Marvel, #1, Jan 1977 . . . . **1.00**
Hunk, Charlton Comics, #1, Aug 1961 . . . . **24.00**
Hurricane Kids, The, R S Callender, 1941 . . . . **60.00**
I Dream of Jeannie, Dell, #1, Apr 1965 . . . . **150.00**
I Met a Handsome Cowboy, Dell, #324, Mar 1951 . . . . **90.00**
Incredible Hulk, Marvel, #139, May 1971 . . . . **3.00**
Indiana Jones and the Last Crusade, Marvel, #1, 1989 . . . . . **1.00**
Indiana Jones and the Temple of Doom, Marvel, #1, Sep
    1984 . . . . **1.00**
Indian Fighter, The, Dell, #687, May 1956 . . . . **80.00**
Inferior Five, The, DC, Apr 1967 . . . . **35.00**
Invaders, The, Marvel, Aug 1975 . . . . **6.00**
Iron Man, Marvel, #41, Slasher, Sep 1971 . . . . **10.00**
Isis, DC, #8, Dec 1977 . . . . **1.00**
I Spy, Gold Key, #1, Aug 1966 . . . . **240.00**
Jeanie Comics, Marvel, #13, Apr 1947 . . . . **95.00**
Jerry Drummer, Charlton Comics, 1957 . . . . **26.00**
Jet Dream, Gold Key, #1, Jun 1968 . . . . **28.00**
Jet Power, I W Enterprises, 1963 . . . . **24.00**
Jetsons, The, Gold Key, #1, Jan 1963 . . . . **220.00**
Johnny Jason, Dell, 1962 . . . . **30.00**
Johnny Thunder, National Periodical Publications, #1,
    1973 . . . . **10.00**
Jonny Quest, Comico, Nov 1986 . . . . **2.50**
Journey Into Mystery, Marvel, #105, Jun 1964 . . . . **45.00**
Judo Joe, Jay-Jay Corp, #1, Aug 1953 . . . . **45.00**
Jughead Jones Comics Digest, The, Archie Publications,
    #1, Jun 1977 . . . . **15.00**
Jungle Cat, Dell, #1136, 1960 . . . . **60.00**
Jungle Jim, Dell, #490 . . . . **60.00**
Justice, Marvel, #1, Nov 1986 . . . . **1.00**
Justice League of America, DC, #41, Dec 1965 . . . . **30.00**
Karate Kid, DC, Apr 1978 . . . . **.75**
Kid Carrots, St John Publishing, Sep 1953 . . . . **30.00**
Kid Eternity, DC, #1, 1991 . . . . **5.00**

Adventures of Sherlock Holmes, Classic Comics #33, Jan 1947, $100.00.

Kid Zoo Comics, Street and Smith, Jul 1948 . . . . 165.00
King Richard and the Crusaders, Dell, #588, Oct 1954 . . . . . 100.00
Kokey Koala, Toby Press, May 1952 . . . . 60.00
Komic Kartoons, Timely Comics, 1945 . . . . 120.00
Kong the Untamed, DC, #1, Jul 1975 . . . . 1.00
Korak, Son of Tarzan, DC, #51, Apr 1973 . . . . 1.50
Labman, Image Comics, Nov 1996 . . . . 4.00
Lady and the Tramp, Dell, #629, 1955 . . . . 60.00
Laffy-Daffy Comics, Rural Home Publications, 1945 . . . . 45.00
Lancelot Link, Secret Chimp, Gold Key, #7, Nov 1972 . . . . 6.00
Last Hunt, The, Dell, #678, Feb 1956 . . . . 70.00
Laugh Comics Digest, #1 . . . . 24.00
Laurel and Hardy, #1, Jan 1967 . . . . 40.00
Lawman, Dell, #970 . . . . 130.00
Leave It to Beaver, Dell, #912 . . . . 190.00
Legend of Wonder Woman, The, DC, May 1986 . . . . 1.00
Legionnaires Three, Jan 1986 . . . . 1.00
Let's Pretend, D S Publishing, #1, 1950 . . . . 90.00
Lieutenant, The, Dell, 1964 . . . . 14.00
Life of Captain Marvel, The, Marvel, Aug 1985 . . . . 2.00
Li'l Menace, Fago Magazine, #1, Dec 1958 . . . . 40.00
Little Bad Wolf, Dell, #403, Jun 1952 . . . . 70.00
Little Beaver, Dell, #211, Jan 1949 . . . . 75.00
Little Dot Dotland, Harvey Publications, #1, Jul 1962 . . . . 75.00
Little Jack Frost, Avon Periodicals, 1951 . . . . 45.00
Little Orphan Annie, Dell, @206, Dec 1948 . . . . 75.00
Loco, Satire Publications, #1, Aug 1958 . . . . 40.00
Lolly and Pepper, Dell, #832, Sep 1957 . . . . 30.00
Looney Tunes, DC, #1, 1994 . . . . 1.50
Love Mystery, Fawcett Publications, #1, 1949 . . . . 130.00
Love Secrets, Marvel, #2, Jan 1950 . . . . 45.00
Luger, Eclipse Comics, Oct 1986 . . . . 2.00
Lyndon B Johnson, Dell, Mar 1965 . . . . 15.00
Machine Man, Marvel, Jun 1978 75
Magic Agent, American Comics Group, #1, 1962 . . . . 18.00
Marco Polo, Charlton Comics, 1962 . . . . 95.00
Marines in Battle, Atlas Comics, #1, Aug 1954 . . . . 100.00
Married...With Children: Quantum Quartet, Now
    Comics, Oct 1993 . . . . 2.00
Marshal Law, Marvel, Oct 1987 . . . . 2.00
Marvel Tales, #3, Torch, Jul 1966 . . . . 40.00
Marvel Two-in-One, Marvel, #6, Dr Strange, Nov 1974 . . . . . 10.00
Masters of the Universe, Marvel/Star, #1, May 1986 75
Mighty Samson, Gold Key, #3, Sep 1965 . . . . 25.00
Mister Miracle, DC, #2, Jun 1971 . . . . 15.00
Mod Love, Western Publishing, 1967 . . . . 24.00
MOD Squad, Dell, #1, jan 1969 . . . . 45.00
Mod Wheels, Gold Key, #1, Mar 1971 . . . . 20.00
Monkees, The, Dell, #2 . . . . 55.00
Monroes, The, Dell, Apr 1967 . . . . 20.00
Monster Menace, Marvel, Dec 1993 . . . . 2.00
Monsters on the Prowl, Marvel, #2, Dec 1968 . . . . 15.00
Monty Hall of the U S Marines, Toby Press, Aug 1951 . . . . 55.00
Moon Mullins, Dell, #81, 1945 . . . . 100.00
Morty Meekle, Dell, #793, May 1957 . . . . 20.00
Ms Marvel, Marvel, #1, Jan 1977 . . . . 5.00
Munsters, The, Gold Key, Jan 1965 . . . . 190.00
My Greatest Adventure, DC, #52, Fab 1961 . . . . 55.00
My Little Margie's Boy Friends, Charlton Comics, #1,
    Aug 1955 . . . . 75.00
My Only Love, Charlton Comics, Jul 1975 . . . . 10.00
My Secret Story, Fox Feature Syndicate, #26, Oct 1949 . . . . . 65.00
Mysterious Suspense, Charlton Comics, Oct 1968 . . . . 42.00
Mystery in Space, DC, #86, Sep 1963 . . . . 50.00

Nature of Things, Dell, #727 . . . . 50.00
Navy Action, Atlas, #4, Feb 1955 . . . . 11.00
Navy Patrol, Key Publications, #1, May 1955 . . . . 35.00
New Adventures of Pinocchio, Dell, 1962 . . . . 85.00
New Adventures of Speed Racer, Now Comics, 1993 . . . . 2.00
New Frontiers, Evolution, #7, Mar 1972 . . . . 20.00
Next Man, Comico, 1985 . . . . 1.50
Nightmare, Marvel, Dec 1994 . . . . 2.00
Nightmask, Marvel, Nov 1986 75
No Sleep 'Til Dawn, Dell, #831, Aug 1957 . . . . 60.00
Omega Man, DC, #7, Oct 1983 . . . . 1.25
One, The, Marvel, Jul 1985 . . . . 1.50
On Stage, Dell, #1336, 1962 . . . . 40.00
Our Army At War, DC, #101, Dec 1962 . . . . 100.00
Our Fighting Forces, DC, #84, May 1964 . . . . 8.00
Outlaw Kid, Marvel, #1, Aug 1970 . . . . 5.00
Outsiders, DC, #2, Dec 1985 . . . . 1.50
Partridge Family, The, Charlton Comics, Mar 1971 . . . . 35.00
Pebbles Flintstone, Gold Key, Sep 1963 . . . . 90.00
Phantom, The, DC, May 1988 . . . . 1.25
Phantom Stranger, DC, 1, Jun 1969 . . . . 60.00
Planet of the Apes, Marvel, #1, Aug 1974 . . . . 5.00
Plastic Man, DC, Mar 1976 . . . . 6.00
Popular Teen-Agers, Star, #9, Oct 1951 . . . . 40.00
Power Man and Iron Fist, Marvel, #51, Jun 1978 . . . . 2.00
Power of the Atom, DC, #1, Aug 1988 . . . . 1.00
Prez, DC, #4, Feb 1974 . . . . 3.00
Ringo Kid, Marvel, #1, Jan 1970 . . . . 2.00
Sea Devils, DC, 9, Feb 1963 . . . . 75.00
Secret Agent, Gold Key, #2, Jan 1968 . . . . 45.00
Secret Origins, DC, #5, Dec 1973 . . . . 5.00
Secret Six, The, DC, #3, Sep 1968 . . . . 15.00
Sgt Fury and His Howling Commandos, Marvel, #43, Jun
    1967 . . . . 30.00
Sgt Rock, DC, #305, Jun 1977 . . . . 10.00
Shadow, The, Archie, Aug 1964 . . . . 20.00
Shazam, DC, Mar 1974 50
Showcase, DC, #48, Cave Carson, Feb 1964 . . . . 35.00
Silver Surfer, Marvel, #7, Aug 1969 . . . . 80.00
Star Spangled War Stories, DC, #91, Jul 1960 . . . . 25.00
Star Trek, Gold Key, #2, Jun 1968 . . . . 320.00
Star Wars, Marvel, #8, Feb 1978 . . . . 25.00
Strange Adventures, #9, Jun 1951 . . . . 420.00
Sugar and Spike, DC, #44, Jan 1963 . . . . 125.00
Superboy, DC, #73, Jun 1959 . . . . 60.00
Super Friends, DC, #2, Dec 1976 . . . . 1.50
Superman, DC, #283, Jan 1975 . . . . 1.50
Superman's Girlfriend Lois Lane, DC, #38, Jan 1963 . . . . 75.00
Superman's Pal Jimmy Olsen, DC, #71, Sep 1963 . . . . 28.00
Swamp Thing, DC, #2, Jan 1973 . . . . 25.00
Thor, Marvel, #139, Apr 1967 . . . . 30.00
Tomahawk, DC, #87, Jul 1963 . . . . 35.00
Tomb of Dracula, Marvel, #13, Oct 1973 . . . . 12.00
Unexpected, The, DC, #124, Apr 1971 . . . . 5.00
Warlord, DC, #2, Apr 1976 . . . . 8.00
Weird War Tales, DC, #2, Nov 1971 . . . . 3.00
Weird Western Tales, DC, #14, Nov 1972 . . . . 5.00
Welcome Back, Kotter, DC, #1, Nov 1976 . . . . 2.00
Western Gunfighters, Marvel, #3, Dec 1970 . . . . 2.00
Where Monsters Dwell, Marvel, #2, May 1970 . . . . 5.00
Wild, Wild West, The, Gold Key, #3, Jun 1968 . . . . 50.00
Witching Hour, DC, #1, May 1969 . . . . 12.00
World's Finest Comics, DC, #115, Feb 1961 . . . . 80.00
World's Unknown, Marvel, #1, May 1973 . . . . 1.00

COMPACTS

Cosmetic use increased significantly in the 1920s as women started playing a major role in the business world. Compacts enabled a woman to freshen her makeup on the run.

Although compacts are still made today, they experienced a Golden Age from the mid-1930s through the late 1950s. Collectors designate compacts manufactured prior to 1960 as "vintage."

Compacts are found in thousands of shapes, styles, and decorative motifs in materials ranging from precious metals to injection molded plastic. Decorative theme, construction material, manufacturer, and novelty are four major collecting themes.

References: Roseann Ettinger, *Compacts and Smoking Accessories, Second Edition,* Schiffer Publishing, 1999; Roselyn Gerson, *Vintage Ladies' Compacts,* Collector Books, 1996, out of print; Roselyn Gerson, *Vintage Vanity Bags and Purses,* Collector Books, 1994; Laura M. Mueller, *Collector's Encyclopedia of Compacts, Carryalls & Face Powder Boxes* (1994, 1999 value update) *Vol. II* (1997), Collector Books; Lynell Schwartz, *Vintage Compacts & Beauty Accessories,* Schiffer Publishing, 1997.

Collectors' Club: Compact Collectors, PO Box 40, Lynbrook, NY 11563.

Alfred Dunhill, vanity, cigarette lighter shape, sterling silver, engine-turned, front opens to beveled mirror, powder, and rouge compartments, sliding lipstick in top, 1⁷/₈" w $260.00
Avon, lip gloss container, Lincoln cent, copper colored. 50.00
Bree, vanity case, square, green enamel with 2 black stripes and small metal woman's profile lid, powder slide, rouge and lipstick compartments, 1930s 125.00
Coty, compact, memo book shape, goldtone with emb basketweave design on lid, matching pencil-shaped combination lipstick/perfume tube, 3¹/₂" l 200.00
Coty, vanity, domino shape, goldtone with black and white enameled dec, int mirror, powder and rouge compartments and puffs, 3³/₄" l 175.00
Elgin, compact, coin shape, silvered metal 175.00
Elgin, compact, round, goldtone with red, yellow, green, and blue enameled swirls and "G.E. Color TV" logo on lid 150.00

Evans, vanity pouch, round, Charlie McCarthy head on black enameled lid 275.00
French, compact, ebony, castanets shape, metal Paris ensignia on lid, orange tasseled carrying cord 225.00
French, compact, hand mirror shape, goldtone with green enamel dec on lid, int and ext mirrors 100.00
German, compact, rectangular, sterling silver, green cloisonné lid, lipstick in upper section, hallmarked 275.00
Illinois Watch Case Co, vanity/watch combination, square, brushed goldtone with small watch face in upper left corner, powder and rouge compartments, 2³/₄" sq 110.00
Kigu, compact, flying saucer shape, metal with blue celestial scene on both sides 375.00
Lucite, compact, square, clear, polished metal medallion with Mexican taking siesta against cactus, 1940s 70.00
Marlowe, compact/bangle bracelet combination, Parisienne, green plastic with sliding metal band to reveal 2 mirrors and 5 compartments 230.00
Novelty, compact, lady bug shape, red with black dots 90.00
Quinto, vanity, rectangular box shape, goldtone, raised squares with inset rhinestones on lid, int powder well and puff, side drawers contain lipstick and perfume bottle, 3" l 90.00
Raquel, vanity, book shape, red emb leather with gold scroll dec cover, metal-framed mirror and powder and rouge compartments inside, 3" l 95.00
Richard Hudnut, Deauville vanity case, round, white and green enamel profiles on lid, powder and rouge compartments, orig presentation box, c1920 . . . . 250.00
Ritz, compact, rectangular, souvenir, brushed goldtone case with polished goldtone Hawaiian Islands map on lid, side clip holds lipstick tube, 3¹/₂" l 75.00
Schuco, compact, teddy bear shape, powder compartment in belly, lipstick tube in head 700.00
Stratton, compact, round, goldtone with scenic transfer of birds on branch, c1950s 50.00
Volupté, compact, artist's palette shape, goldtone with black pallette and multicolor paint splotches, brushes, and paint tube on lid 225.00
Zell, compact, football shape, leather with imp laces on lid, coppertone int with mirror and powder compartment, 4¹/₂" l 80.00

CONSOLIDATED GLASS COMPANY

The Consolidated Glass Company was founded in 1893, the result of a merger between the Wallace and McAfee Company and the Fostoria Shade & Lamp Company. In the mid-1890s, the company built a new factory in Corapolis, Pennsylvania, and quickly became one of the largest lamp, globe, and shade manufacturers in the United States.

The Consolidated Glass Company began making giftware in the mid-1930s. Most collectors focus on the company's late 1920s and early 1930s product lines, e.g., Florentine, Martelé, and Ruba Rombic.

Consolidated closed its operations in 1932, reopening in 1936. In 1962 Dietz Brothers acquired the company. A disastrous fire in 1963 during a labor dispute heralded the end of the company. The last glass was made in 1964.

Reference: Jack D. Wilson, *Phoenix & Consolidated Art Glass: 1926–1980,* Antique Publications, 1989.

Yardley, goldtone vanity case with red, white, and blue emb design on lid, powder and rouge compartments, c1940s, $70.00.

Collectors' Club: Phoenix & Consolidated Glass Collectors' Club, PO Box 159, Burlington, VT 05402.

REPRODUCTION ALERT

Bon Bon, Ruba Rombic, 3-part, flat, green	$250.00
Bottle, Catalonian, blue, 5" h	20.00
Bouillon Bowl, Ruba Rombic, smokey topaz	175.00
Cologne Bottle, Ruba Rombic, crystal frosted, 8" h	125.00
Creamer, Ruba Rombic, green	200.00
Fan Vase, Lovebirds, pink	125.00
Finger Bowl, Ruba Rombic, silver	140.00
Jar, cov, Con-Cora, pleated design with small hp flowers	100.00
Lamp, Lovebirds, 2-lite	315.00
Pin Box, cov, Catalonian, rect, smokey topaz	40.00
Pitcher, Martelé, honey	250.00
Plate, Ruba Rombic, cased yellow, 8"	100.00
Platter, Dancing Nymph, round, blue	750.00
Powder Jar, cov, Ruba Rombic, green	40.00
Puff Box, cov, Bulging Loops, blue	90.00
Snack Set, Martelé, green	50.00
Tumbler, Dancing Nymph, frosted pink, ftd	140.00
Tumbler, Ruba Rombic, flat, smokey topaz, 12 oz	175.00
Vase, Con-Cora, ruffled rim, long neck, and bulbous base, white milk glass with painted ivy dec, 9"	50.00
Vase, Pine Cone, spherical, clear and ruby	200.00

CONSTRUCTION TOYS

Childen love to build things. Modern construction toys trace their origin to the Anchor building block sets of the late 19th and early 20th centuries. A construction toy Hall of Fame includes A. C. Gilbert's Erector Set, Lego, Lincoln Logs, and Tinker Toys.

A construction set must have all its parts, instruction book(s), and period packaging to be considered complete. Collectors pay a premium for sets designed to make a specific object, e.g., a dirigible or locomotive.

References: William M. Bean, *Greenberg's Guide to Gilbert Erector Sets, Vol. One: 1913–1932*, Greenberg Books, 1993; William M. Bean, *Greenberg's Guide to Gilbert Erector Sets, Vol. Two: 1933–1962*, Greenberg Books, 1998; Craig Strange, *Collector's Guide to Tinker Toys*, Collector Books, 1996.

Collectors' Clubs: A. C. Gilbert Heritage Society, 1440 Whalley, Ste 252, New Haven, CT 06515.

AC Gilbert, Erector, 110 Volt Electric Motor Set, #6, 1935	$250.00
AC Gilbert, Erector, Action Conveyer Set, #10063, 1959	120.00
AC Gilbert, Erector, All-Electric Set, #8½, 1951–52	350.00
AC Gilbert, Erector, Amusement Park Set, #10½, 1949–50	400.00
AC Gilbert, Erector, Automotive Set, #9½, 1948	350.00
AC Gilbert, Erector, Electric Engine Set, #7½, 1956	100.00
AC Gilbert, Erector, Engineer's Set, #7½, 1946	300.00
AC Gilbert, Erector, Junior Erector Set, #2, 1949	100.00
AC Gilbert, Erector, Merry-Go-Round-Kit, #12½A, 1949	240.00
AC Gilbert, Erector, Space Age Erector, #18040, 1960–61	200.00
AC Gilbert, Erector, Steam Engine Set, #10062, 1958	120.00
AC Gilbert, Erector, Young Builder's Set, #10021, 1960–61	60.00
Auburn Rubber, Flexible Building Blocks, 1960s	10.00

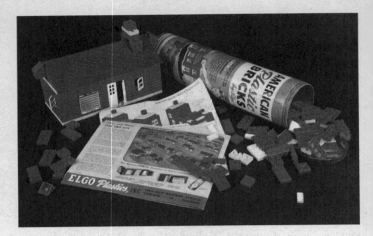

Elgo, American Plastic Bricks #715, 208 pcs, $40.00.

Cozzone Construction Set, #500, electric motor, machined metal parts	225.00
Halsam, Frontierland Logs, #915, 1961	75.00
Kenner, Girder and Panel Bridge and Turnpike Motorized Set, 1960	125.00
Lincoln Logs, #29	125.00
Marx, Riverside Construction Set, 1960s	125.00
Meccano, Engineering Erector Set	20.00
Remco, Jumbo Construction Set, 1968	125.00
Scott Mfg, Bilt-E-Z Skyscraper Building Blocks, c1925	125.00
Spalding, Easy Tinkertoy, complete	15.00
Spalding, Senior Tinkertoy Windlass Drive, complete	30.00
Spalding, Special Tinkertoy Windlass Drive, complete	25.00
Spalding, Tinker Jack and Jill, complete	50.00
Spalding, Tinkertoy, Wonder Builder, complete	25.00
Wannatoy, Construction Kit, 1950s	80.00

COOKBOOKS

The cookbook was firmly entrentched as a basic kitchen utensil by the beginning of the 20th century. *Fannie Farmer's Cookbook* dominated during the first half of the century; *The Joy of Cooking* was the cookbook of choice of the post-1945 generations.

Cookbooks with printings in the hundreds of thousands and millions, e.g., the *White House Cookbook*, generally have little value except for the earliest editions.

Although some cookbooks are purchased by individuals who plan to use the recipes they contain, most are collected because of their subject matter, cover image, and use as advertising premiums. Do not hesitate to shop around for the best price and condition. The survival rate for cookbooks is exceptionally high.

References: Bob Allen, *A Guide to Collecting Cookbooks and Advertising Cookbooks*, Collector Books, 1990, 1998 value update; Mary Barile, *Cookbooks Worth Collecting*, Wallace-Homestead, Krause Publications, 1994; Linda J. Dickinson, *A Price Guide to Cookbooks and Recipe Leaflets*, Collector Books, 1990, 1997 value update; Sandra J. Norman and Karrie K. Andes, *Vintage Cookbooks and Advertising Leaflets*, Schiffer Publishing, 1998.

Collectors' Club: Cook Book Collectors Club of America, PO Box 56, St James, MO 65559.

Baker's Best Chocolate Recipes, Walter Baker & Co,
Dorchester, MA, 60 pp, c1930 . . . . **$10.00**
Blue Ribbon Recipes—Country Fair Winners, Cookbook
Collectors Library, 384 pp, illus, 1968 . . . . **12.00**
Campbell's Book: Canning, Preserving and Pickling,
Campbell, Clyde, 860 pp, revised, NY, 1937 . . . . **45.00**
Chinese Home Cooking, Chinese Committee: YMCA,
90 pp, Honolulu, HI, 1945 . . . . **30.00**
Cook It Outdoors, Beard, James, first ed, NY, 1941 . . . . **30.00**
Elsie's Cookbook, Botsford, Harry, 374 pp, first ed, 1952 . . . . . **35.00**
Encyclopedia of Candy and Ice Cream Making, Leon,
Simon, 454 pp, NY, 1959 . . . . **38.00**
Farmer's Market Cookbook, Beck, Neil and Fred, NY,
first ed, 1951 . . . . **20.00**
Flower Cookery, MacNicol, Mary, 263 pp, Fleet Press
Corp, NY, 1967 . . . . **35.00**
Garden Spice and Wild Pot Herbs, Muenscher, Walter,
211 pp, first ed, Cornell University, Comstock: Ithaca,
1955 . . . . **60.00**
How to Keep Him Cookbook, Kragen, Jinx, first ed, NY,
1968 . . . . **12.00**
It's Fun to Cook, Maltby, Lucy, 397 pp, illus,
Philadelphia, 1938 . . . . **65.00**
Kitchen Manual, A, Hibben, Sheila, 231 pp, first ed,
1941 . . . . **15.00**
Lady's Auxiliary of Amana Recipes, Homestead, IA, 120
pp, 1948 . . . . **20.00**
Let's Set the Table, Lounsbery, Elizabeth, 200 pp, first ed,
cloth, NY, 1938 . . . . **15.00**
McCormick, Spices of the World Cookbook, 328 pp, NY,
1964 . . . . **20.00**
New Good Housekeeping Cookbook, 1963 . . . . **15.00**
New McCall's Cookbook, Eckley, Mary, 1973 . . . . **12.00**
Recipes of All Nations, Morphy, Countess, 821 pp, Wise
Publishing, NY, 1936 . . . . **12.00**
Reynolds Wrap, Creative Cooking with Aluminum Foil,
Lynch, Eleanor, Grosset & Dunlap, 1967 . . . . **6.00**
Simple Salads, Heath, Ambrose, 72 pp, London, 1943 . . . . . . **12.00**
*Soup Manufacture: Canning Dehydration and Quick
Freezing,* Binsted, Raymond, 169 pp, London, 1960 . . . . . **28.00**
Spanish Cooking, Cass, Elizabeth, London, 1957 . . . . **10.00**
Thomas Jefferson's Cookbook, Kimball, Marie, 111 pp,
Garrett & Massie Co, Richmond, VA, 1938 . . . . **60.00**
What to Cook and How to Cook It, Johnson, Nannie,
396 pp, NY, 1923 . . . . **15.00**
Wine and the Wine Lands of the World, Butler, Frank,
271 pp, NY, 1926 . . . . **45.00**

COOKIE JARS

Although cookie jars existed as a form prior to 1945, the cookie
jar's Golden Age began in the late 1940s and ended in the early
1960s. Virtually every American ceramics manufacturer from
Abingdon to Twin Winton produced a line of cookie jars. Foreign
imports were abundant.

There was a major cookie jar collecting craze in the 1980s and
early 1990s that included a great deal of speculative pricing and
some market manipulation. The speculative bubble is in the
process of collapsing in many areas. Reproductions and high-
priced contemporary jars, especially those featuring images of
famous personalities such as Marilyn Monroe, also have contributed to market uncertainty. This major market shakeout is
expected to continue for several more years.

References: Fred Roerig and Joyce Herndon Roerig, *Collector's
Encyclopedia of Cookie Jars, Book I* (1991, 1997 value update),
Book II (1994, 1999 value update), *Book III* (1998), Collector
Books; Mike Schneider, *The Complete Cookie Jar Book, 2nd
Edition,* Schiffer Publishing, 1999; Mark and Ellen Supnick, *The
Wonderful World of Cookie Jars,* L-W Book Sales (1995, 1998
value update); Ermagene Westfall, *An Illustrated Value Guide to
Cookie Jars* (1983, 1997 value update), *Book II* (1993, 1997 value
update), Collector Books.

Newsletter: *Cookie Jarrin',* 1501 Maple Ridge Rd, Walterboro, SC
29488.

Apple, California Originals **$50.00**
Archway Cookie Van **40.00**
Asparagus Bunch, Metlox **75.00**
Ballerina Bear, Metlox **120.00**
Barnum's Animal Crackers, white, McCoy **65.00**
Barrel of Apples, Metlox **80.00**
Baseball Boy, McCoy **225.00**
Basket of Fruit, rope design handle, McCoy **55.00**
Bean Pot, McCoy **55.00**
Bear, red sweater, Metlox **130.00**
Beer Mug, Doranne **35.00**
Big Bird, California Originals, 13³/₄" h **125.00**
Bird on Pinecone, Metlox **200.00**
Black Cook Stove, McCoy **15.00**
Black Engine, McCoy **175.00**
Boy on Football, McCoy **225.00**
Bucky Beaver, Metlox **225.00**
Bulldog, Treasure Craft **175.00**
Burlap Bag, bird finial, McCoy **35.00**
Caboose, McCoy **150.00**
Campbell Soup Kids, mkd "1990 Campbell Soup
Company" **90.00**
Candy House, Twin Winton **75.00**
Care Bear Tenderheart, American Greetings **95.00**
Carousel, Napco **130.00**
Cat in Basket, American Bisque **35.00**
Cat on Beehive, American Bisque **50.00**
Cat with Bow Tie, Doranne **50.00**
Century 21 House, new version **135.00**
Chick, American Bisque, blue, 12¹/₄" h **60.00**
Chipmunk, Twin Winton **120.00**
Cinderella, Napco **225.00**
Circus Tent, Brayton Laguna **375.00**
Circus Wagon, Enesco **75.00**
Clown, Maddux **200.00**
Coffee Grinders, McCoy **50.00**
Coffeepot, DeForest, mkd "DeForest of CA Hand
Painted" **80.00**
Coke Can, McCoy **75.00**
Cookie Bank, McCoy **150.00**
Cookie Barrel, American Bisque **40.00**
Cookie House, McCoy **75.00**
Cookie Time Clock, Abingdon, 9" h **125.00**
Cookie Trolley, Treasure Craft **50.00**
Covered Wagon, McCoy **110.00**
Cow, Treasure Craft **40.00**
Cow, with bell, Clay Art, paper label **55.00**
Cow, yellow, Metlox **350.00**
Daisy, Abingdon **65.00**
Dalmatian, with glass bowl, Treasure Craft **65.00**
Davy Crockett Head, McCoy **400.00**

Cauliflower Mammy, McCoy, $330.00. Photo courtesy Collectors Auction Services.

Dice, red and white, Doranne	45.00
Donkey with Vest and Tie, Twin Winton	80.00
Doranne, olive green	175.00
Elephant, whole trunk on lid, McCoy	100.00
Farmer Pig, American Bisque	125.00
Fireplace, McCoy	125.00
Fire Truck, California Originals	225.00
Flowerpot, Metlox	70.00
Fortune Cookies, McCoy	55.00
Friar Tuck, blue, Red Wing	100.00
Garfield, playing golfing, Enesco	150.00
Gingerbread Boy, brown, Hull	75.00
Girl Chef, deLee	200.00
Grape and Vine, milk glass, #9188, Fenton	85.00
Green Giant Sprout, 12" h	110.00
Gumball Machine, California Originals	155.00
Gypsy Woman, Brayton Laguna	550.00
Harley Davidson Hog, McCoy, 1984	500.00
Hen, mkd "CJ 100", Doranne	140.00
Hippo, white, Abingdon	175.00
Honey Bear, Treasure Craft	110.00
Human Bean, Enesco	125.00
Humpty Dumpty, Abingdon	200.00
Humpty Dumpty, Japan	75.00
Humpty Dumpty, Metlox	250.00
Ice Cream Cone, McCoy	35.00
Jack-in-the-Box, American Bisque, 12" h	180.00
Juggling Clown, California Originals	100.00
Keystone Cop, Twin Winton	100.00
Koala Bear, Metlox	175.00
Kraft Marshmallow Bear, Regal China	175.00
Lantern, Brush	70.00
Liberty Bell, American Bisque, 9¾" h	250.00
Lion, Japan	15.00
Lion, Metlox	225.00
Lion on Circus Wagon, California Originals	60.00
Little Bo Peep, Napco	225.00
Little Bo Peep, Shawnee	75.00
Liv-R-Snaps	50.00
Lollipops, McCoy	40.00
Lunch Box, McCoy	50.00
Milk Can, McCoy	75.00

Monk, McCoy	50.00
Monk, yellow, Red Wing	65.00
Mushroom Cottage, Metlox	200.00
Mushrooms on Stump, McCoy	20.00
Nestle Tollhouse Cookies	70.00
Noah's Ark, American Bisque	60.00
Old Lady in Shoe, Japan	50.00
Oreo, Doranne	45.00
Owl, Brush	110.00
Pagoda, McCoy	30.00
Panda, black and white	45.00
Panda, holding leaf, California Originals	240.00
Parrot, DeForest	200.00
Pear, green, stamped "Red Wing USA"	200.00
Pear, McCoy	65.00
Pelican, California Originals	40.00
Pepperidge Farm	100.00
Peter, Peter, Pumpkin Eater, Japan	65.00
Peter Rabbit, Sigma	300.00
Piano, Vandor	70.00
Picnic Basket, McCoy	75.00
Pillsbury Doughboy, 1973	70.00
Pineapple, Abingdon, 10½" h	180.00
Pineapple, Metlox	125.00
Pinnochio, Metlox	25.00
Poodle, American Bisque	125.00
Precious Moments Bear, Enesco	100.00
Quaker Oats, Regal China	165.00
Rabbit on Stump, McCoy	40.00
Racoon	45.00
Raggedy Ann, Maddux	175.00
Red Riding Hood, Napco	250.00
Robot, Japan	70.00
Rooster, California Originals	40.00
Rooster, Sierra Vista, mkd "Sierra Vista Ca"	80.00
Rose, Metlox	400.00
Santa, Holt-Howard	75.00
Santa, winking, National Potteries, mkd "Napco, Japan KX2352"	150.00
Scarecrow, Japan	45.00
Schnauzer, California Originals	100.00
School Bus, McCoy	50.00
Scottie Dog, white, Metlox	300.00
Sir Francis Drake, Metlox	50.00
Snoopy, olive green	60.00
Snowman, Enesco	45.00
Spool of Thread, American Bisque	35.00
Stagecoach, white, McCoy	1,000.00
Star Trek, Pfaltzgraff	50.00
Strawberry, Sears	35.00
Teepee, Abingdon	800.00
Teepee, McCoy	325.00
Telephone, Napco	50.00
Thinking Dog, McCoy	40.00
Three Bears, Abingdon	120.00
Tigger, California Originals	200.00
Tourist Car, McCoy	130.00
Traffic Light, McCoy	50.00
Treasure Chest, Treasure Craft	120.00
Turkey, McCoy	250.00
Wheelbarrow, Twin Winton	250.00
Windmill, McCoy	65.00
Winnie the Pooh, California Originals	125.00
Woody Woodpecker, Napco	400.00

COOPER, SUSIE

After a brief stint as a designer at A. E. Gray & Co., Hanley Staffordshire, England, Cooper founded the Susie Cooper Pottery in Burslem in 1932. There she designed ceramics that were functional in shape and decorated with bright floral and abstract designs. Cooper introduced the straight-sided "can" shape for coffeepots. Later she was employed by the Wedgwood Group where she developed several lines of bone china tableware.

References: *Collecting Susie Cooper*, Francis Joseph Publications, 1994, distributed by Krause Publications; Helen Cunningham, *Clarice Cliff and Her Contemporaries: Susie Cooper, Keith Murray, Charlotte Rhead and the Carlton Ware Designers*, Schiffer Publishing, 1999.

Collectors' Club: Susie Cooper Collectors Group, PO Box 7436, London N12 7QF U.K.

Charger, litho floral motif	$225.00
Coffeepot, cov, Falcon shape, Elegance pattern, cord and ring transfer print	100.00
Coffeepot, cov, Lustre Ware	150.00
Creamer, woodpecker print	150.00
Cup and Saucer, Dresden Spray, litho floral pattern	75.00
Cup and Saucer, Gardenia	45.00
Cup and Saucer, Gardenia pattern, litho dec	60.00
Cup and Saucer, golfer	125.00
Jug, Paris shape	75.00
Lamp Base, cowboy and horse, orange and yellow bands	300.00
Meat Dish, litho pattern, edge dec	90.00
Plate, Dresden Spray, 5" d	20.00
Plate, leaping ram, sgraffito dec	65.00
Salad Dish, Charcoal Feather pattern, litho dec	70.00
Tea Service, 13 pcs, covered teapot, creamer and sugar, 5 demitasse cups and saucer, blue and black bands on cream ground, mkd "A Susie Cooper Production, Crown Works, Burslem, England"	500.00
Teapot, cov, Kestrel shape, blue, crescent sgraffito	300.00
Teapot, cov, Swansea Spray	200.00
Tray, hp eye motif	250.00
Wall Plaque, leaping deer, hp	200.00

Dinner Service, consisting of eight each dinner plates, salad plates, bread and butter plates, cups and saucers, and handled soups and saucers plus oval platter and vegetable bowl, round casserole, gravy boat, creamer, and sugar, mkd "Susie Cooper Productions, Crown Works, Burslem, England," 62 pcs, $1,265.00. Photo courtesy Skinner, Inc., Boston, MA.

COORS POTTERY

After J. J. Herold went to work for the Western Pottery Company in Denver in 1912, Adolph Coors and the other investors in the Herold China and Pottery Company, Golden, Colorado, kept the factory open and renamed it the Golden Pottery. In 1920 the name was changed to Coors Porcelain Company.

In the 1930s Coors introduced six dinnerware lines: Coorado, Golden Ivory, Golden Rainbow, Mello-Tone, Rock-Mount, and Rosebud Cook-N-Serve. Dinnerware production ceased in 1941. Although the company produced some utilitarian ware such as ashtrays, ovenware, and teapots after the war, it never resumed its dinnerware production.

Reference: Robert H. Schneider, *Coors Rosebud Pottery*, published by author, 1984, 1996 value update.

Newsletter: *Coors Pottery Newsletter*, 3808 Carr Place N, Seattle, WA 98103.

Coorado, casserole, green	$95.00
Coorado, casserole, individual	45.00
Coorado, custard set, metal holder	115.00
Coorado, dinner plate	15.00
Coorado, pie plate	55.00
Coorado, pitcher, large	95.00
Coorado, salt and pepper shakers, pr	65.00
Floree, pitcher, cov	125.00
Hawthorne, cake knife	75.00
Hawthorne, casserole	95.00
Hawthorne, custard	35.00
Hawthorne, pitcher, cov	95.00
Mello-Tone, baker, 8" d	20.00
Mello-Tone, cup and saucer	15.00
Mello-Tone, custard	10.00
Mello-Tone, gravy boat	45.00
Mello-Tone, soup plate, 7¼" d	8.00
Mello-Tone, tumbler	35.00
Mello-Tone, salt and pepper shakers, pr	1.00
Open Window, cake plate	55.00
Open Window, French casserole	95.00
Open Window, pie plate	50.00
Open Window, sugar shaker	65.00
Open Window, water server	150.00
Rosebud, apple baker, cov	45.00
Rosebud, cake knife	60.00
Rosebud, cake plate	35.00
Rosebud, creamer and covered sugar	70.00
Rosebud, cream soup	30.00
Rosebud, cup and saucer	35.00
Rosebud, dinner plate, 8" d	25.00
Rosebud, eggcup	50.00
Rosebud, loaf pan	40.00
Rosebud, mixing bowl, 3½ pt	50.00
Rosebud, muffin set, orange	200.00
Rosebud, pie plate	35.00
Rosebud, ramekin, handled	35.00
Rosebud, refrigerator set, blue	110.00
Rosebud, sugar shaker	50.00
Rosebud, tumbler, ftd	95.00
Tulip, cake plate	55.00
Tulip, pie plate, metal holder	75.00
Tulip, pudding, large	75.00
Tulip, teapot, cov	110.00

COUNTERCULTURE

Counterculture collectibles are the artifacts left behind by the Beatnik and Hippie culture of the 1960s. These range from concert posters to a wealth of pinback "social cause" buttons.

Some collectors prefer to designate this material as psychedelic collectibles. However, the psychedelic movement was only one aspect of the much broader Counterculture environment.

Reference: William A. Sievert, *All For the Cause: Campaign Buttons for Social Change, 1960s–1990s*, For Splash, 1997.

Book, *Beat Generation and the Angry Young Men, The*, Gene and Max Gartenberg, Dell, NY, first ed, paperback, 1959 . . . . **$35.00**
Choker, Peace sign, gold metal, 15½" l **20.00**
Comic Book, *The Forty Year Old Hippie*, No. 2, Rip Off Press, 1979 . . . . **8.00**
Floor Pillow, purple, orange, and blue-green psychedelic motif, 22" sq **50.00**
Magazine, *Life*, Oct 21, 1969, marijuana cover story with photos **20.00**
Magazine, *Ramparts, The Social History of the Hippie*, Mar 1967 . . . . **40.00**
Map, Hippieville, street map of Haight-Asbury area, San Francisco, Samhill, Sausilito, CA, folding, 1967, 17 x 22" **35.00**
Paperweight, ceramic, "LOVE" on sides **15.00**
Pin, Peace symbol, diecut metal, brass luster **10.00**
Pinback Button, "Earth Love It Or Leave It," earth image in shades of green against dark red ground, green letters, ©1970 . . . . **10.00**
Pinback Button, "Getting It Together," symbols of peace, black power, national welfare rights, and gay rights depicted on 4-leaf clover, "Peoples Coalition" on curl **20.00**
Pinback Button, "Kill For Peace," black and white letters on Lyndon Johnson image, c1967 . . . . **15.00**
Pinback Button, "LSD The Only Way To Fly," dark purple letters on bright yellow ground, late 1960s **20.00**
Pinback Button, "Peace Love," black and white stylized letters on deep pink ground **20.00**
Pinback Button, "Schools Not War!," black, white, and red, "May 1 March on Wash. D.C.," and "April 29 Nat'l Day of Student Protest" **10.00**
Poster, "For All Time," silkscreened blacklight, Iwo Jima marines raising peace symbol flag, shades of green, blue, and black, ©1970 Compass Points, 22 x 34" **75.00**
Poster, "Human Be-In," The Bindweed Press, San Francisco, Jan 19, 1967 . . . . **450.00**
Poster, "Peace," line of riot police holding nightsticks and facing line of hippies with swooping white dove in red, white, and blue, ©1970 Dean Eller, Kendrick and Assoc, 22 x 26" **90.00**
Record, *LSD*, Timothy Leary, LP, Pixie Records, NY, 1966 . . . . **120.00**
Record, *San Francisco Poets*, LP, readings by Ginsberg, Ferlinghetti, and McClure, Hanover, NY, 1959 . . . . **65.00**
Ring, Peace symbol, diecut metal, brass luster, adjustable **20.00**
Sheet Music, *San Francisco (Be Sure to Wear Flowers in Your Hair)*, Scott McKenzie, Trousdale Music Publishers, Inc, 1967 . . . . **35.00**
Sticker, "Peace" **2.50**
Switchplate Cover, cardboard, white peace sign on black ground **15.00**

COUNTRY WESTERN

This category is primarily record driven—mainly due to the lack of products licensed by members of the Country Western community. There is not a great deal to collect.

Country Western autographed material, other paper ephemera, and costumes have attracted some collectors. Although fan clubs exist for every major singer, few stress the collecting of personal memorabilia.

References: Fred Heggeness, *Goldmine Country Western Record & CD Price Guide*, Krause Publications, 1996; Jerry Osborne, *The Official Price Guide to Country Music Records*, House of Collectibles, 1996.

Autograph, Barbara Mandrell, PS, color, 8 x 10" **$5.00**
Autograph, Buck Owens, PS, color, gold signature, 8 x 10" **5.00**
Autograph, Dolly Parton, PS, color, 8 x 10" **18.00**
Autograph, Dottie West, LS **5.00**
Autograph, Eddy Arnold, PS, black and white, 8 x 10" **5.00**
Autograph, Grandpa Jones, PS **12.00**
Autograph, Hoyt Axton, AMQS, 8 x 3" music manuscript, "Joy to You Hoyt Axton" **75.00**
Autograph, Kenny Rogers, PS, color, 8 x 10 . . . . **25.00**
Autograph, Mel Tillis, PS, color, 8 x 10" **6.00**
Autograph, Mother Maybelle Carter, PS **80.00**
Autograph, Roger Miller, LS **7.00**
Autograph, Roy Rogers and Dale Evans, PS, publicity pose, black and white, 8 x 10" **250.00**
Bumper Sticker, Jimmie Davis, "Davis for Governor" **15.00**
Catalog, Ernest Tubb Record Shop issue, Nashville, TN, 1972 . . . . **5.00**
Doll, Dolly Parton, vinyl head, plastic body, jointed, painted eyes, orig gown, mkd "Dolly Parton/Eegee Co/Hong Kong" on back of head, "Goldberger Mfg Co" on back, 12" h **40.00**
Lobby Card, Tex Ritter, 27 x 41" **100.00**
Lunch Box, Hee Haw, metal, 1970 . . . . **125.00**
Map, Nashville, TN, sgd by Roy Acuff and other performers, c1948 . . . . **120.00**
Necktie, Ernest Tubb likeness, facsimile signature **15.00**
Paper Dolls, Hee Haw, punch-out, Saalfield, #5139, Gunilla, Lulu, Kathy and Jeannie dolls, uncut, 1971 . . . . . . **12.00**
Paper Dolls, Hootenanny, punch-out, Saalfield, #4440, 4 dolls, uncut, 1964 . . . . **20.00**
Postcard, Cliff Carlisle photo **4.00**
Poster, Chet Atkins and Grand Ole Opry **20.00**
Poster, *Coal Miner's Daughter*, Loretta Lynn, Universal, 1979 . . . . **10.00**
Poster, *Nine to Five*, Dolly Parton, 20th Century, 1980 . . . . . . **10.00**
Record, Chet Atkins, *Finger Style Guitar*, LP **15.00**
Record, Conway Twitty, *We Only Make Believe*, 1971 . . . . **10.00**
Record, Ernest Tubb, *It's Been So Long Darlin'*, 78 rpm **10.00**
Record, Hank Williams, *Ramblin' Man*, 1960 . . . . **25.00**
Record, Johnny Cash, *Johnny Cash's Greatest Hits Vol I*, LP, promotional **15.00**
Record, Kitty Wells, *Burning Memories*, LP **15.00**
Record, Loretta Lynn, *Don't Come Home a Drinkin*, LP **25.00**
Record Jacket, sgd by Chet Atkins **35.00**
Sheet Music, *Jimmie Rogers' Album of Songs*, 1934 . . . . **15.00**
Sheet Music, *Pistol Packin' Mama*, sgd by Al Dexter **18.00**
Sheet Music, *Wabash Cannonball*, Rex Griffin, 1939 . . . . **8.00**

COWAN POTTERY

R. Guy Cowan's first pottery, operating between 1912 and 1917, was located on Nicholson Avenue in Lakewood, Ohio, a Cleveland suburb. When he experienced problems with his gas supply, he moved his operations to Rocky River. The move also resulted in a production switch from a red clay ceramic body to a high-fired porcelain one.

By the mid-1920s Cowan manufactured a number of commercial products including dinnerware, desk sets, and planters. In addition, he made art pottery. In 1931, just a year after establishing an artists' colony, Cowan ceased operations, one of the many victims of the Great Depression.

Reference: Mark Bassett and Victoria Naumann, *Cowan Pottery and the Cleveland School,* Schiffer Publishing, 1997.

Bookend, figural leaping antelope, by Drexel Jacobson, smooth black glaze, imp "Cowan," 8" h, 6" w **$200.00**

Candelabra, "Pavlova," figural dancing nude flanked on either side by an upstretched hand holding a cornucopia, glossy ivory glaze, stamped "Cowan," 7" h, 10" w **300.00**

Candlesticks, pr, figural antelopes, glossy caramel glaze, die-stamped circular mark, 6" h, 6" w. **300.00**

Decanter, figural king, Old Ivory glaze, imp "Waylande Gregory" and "Cowan," 10" h, 5" w **500.00**

Figurines, pr, "Spanish Dancers," by Elizabeth Anderson, male and female, multicolor polychrome glazes, imp "Cowan," 1928, 9" h, 6½" w. **1,325.00**

Flower Frog, "Awakening," stretching woman, flower blossom base, orig ivory glaze, stamped "Cowan," 9½" h, 4" w. **775.00**

Flower Frog, figural dancing nude with scarf, orig ivory glaze, stamped "Cowan," 6¼" h, 4" w **90.00**

Flower Frog, "Flamingo," ivory glaze, stamped "Cowan," 12" h, 6" w **350.00**

Flower Frog, "Swirl Dancer," figural nude, orig ivory glaze, stamped "Cowan," 10½" h, 4" w **1,000.00**

Flower Frog, twirling dancer, glossy white glaze, imp "Cowan," 9½" h, 4½" w. **775.00**

Lamp Base, ginger jar shape, "Starburst," raspberry semi-gloss glaze by R. Guy Cowan, imp "Cowan," 11" h, 7" d **300.00**

Console Bowl, "Pterodactyl" No. 729, by Alexander Blazys, April green glaze interior, ivory exterior, impressed mark, 1927, 5½" h, 14½" l, $150.00. Photo courtesy David Rago Auctions, Inc.

Paperweight, figural elephant, No. D-3, Margaret Postgate, ivory glaze, die-stamped circular mark, c1930, 3¾" h, 2½" w **450.00**

Urn, ribbed body, 2 handles, peacock glaze, stamped "Cowan," 9½" h, 8" w **90.00**

Urn, tall and narrow, fluted body, 2 handles, marigold glaze, stamped "Cowan," 11½" h, 4¾" w **55.00**

Vase, bulbous, emb band of stylized leaves around shoulder, Persian blue crackled glaze, imp "Cowan," 8" h, 8" d **875.00**

Vase, "Chinese Bird," urn form, bird with fancy plumage at base, jade green glaze, stamped "Cowan," 11½" h, 6½" w. **500.00**

Vase, trumpet form with horizontal ribs and pedestal foot, russet brown glaze, stamped "Cowan, 9" h, 6½" d **150.00**

COWBOY HEROES

Cowboy Heroes are divided into eight major categories: (1) silent movie cowboys, (2) "B" movie cowboys, (3) "A" movie cowboys, (4) 1950s' and 60s' TV cowboy heroes, (5) Gene Autry, (6) Hopalong Cassidy, (7) The Lone Ranger, and (8) Roy Rogers.

Silent movie cowboys are in the final stages of the last memory roundup. "B" movie cowboys, comprising individuals such as Buck Jones, Ken Maynard, and Tim McCoy, are just down the trail. Reruns of the old "B" westerns have all but disappeared from television—out of sight, out of mind. "A" movie cowboys such as Clint Eastwood and John Wayne have cult followers, but never achieved the popularity of Gene, Hoppy, or Roy.

Currently the market is strong for 1950s' and 60s' television cowboy heroes. The generations that watched the initial runs of Bonanza, Gunsmoke, Paladin, Rawhide, The Rifleman, and Wagon Train are at their peak earning capacities and willing to pay top dollar to buy back their childhood. Prices for common 1950s' material have been stable for the past few years.

Gene, Hoppy, The Lone Ranger, and Roy are in a class by themselves. Currently, Hoppy collectibles are the hottest of the four with Roy close behind. Gene and The Lone Ranger are starting to eat dust. Look for a major collecting shift involving the collectibles of these four individuals in the next ten years.

References: Joseph J. Caro, *Hopalong Cassidy Collectibles,* Cowboy Collector Publications, 1997; Lee Felbinger, *Collector's Reference & Value Guide to the Lone Ranger,* Collector Books, 1998; Ted Hake, *Hake's Guide to Cowboy Character Collectibles: An Illustrated Price Guide Covering 50 Years of Movie & TV Cowboy Heroes,* Wallace-Homestead, Krause Publications, 1994; Robert Heide and John Gilman, *Box-Office Buckaroos,* Abbeville Press, 1989; Robert W. Philips, *Roy Rogers,* McFarland & Co, 1995; Harry L. Rinker, *Hopalong Cassidy: King of the Cowboy Merchandisers,* Schiffer Publishing, 1995.

Newsletter: *Cowboy Collector Network,* PO Box 7486, Long Beach, CA 90807.

Collectors' Club: Westerns & Serials Fan Club, Rte 1, Box 103, Vernon Center, MN 56090.

Note: For information on fan clubs for individual cowboy heroes, refer to *Maloney's Antiques & Collectibles Resource Directory* by David J. Maloney, Jr., published by Antique Trader Books.

Annie Oakley, flipper badge, cardboard, 1 side with black and white photo of Gail Davis as Annie Oakley and "Annie Oakley Says," other side with "Eat Wonder Bread," mid-1950s, 2½" d **$25.00**

Buck Jones, Big Little Book, *Buck Jones in the Roaring West*, Whitman #1174, ©1935 . . . . **50.00**

Buck Jones, movie slide, *The Overland Express*, glass transparency in cardboard mount, Columbia Pictures, 1938 . . . . **20.00**

Buffalo Bill, Jr, child's outfit, flannel with vinyl fringe and fake fur trim, c1950s, 2 pcs **50.00**

Buffalo Bill, Jr, comic book, Dell, #7, Feb/Apr 1958 . . . . **8.00**

Cisco Kid & Pancho, bread label, waxed paper sticker, sepia tone portrait on yellow ground, red border, Friehofer's Bakery, c1950, 2¾ x 2¾" **8.00**

Cisco Kid & Pancho, postcard, Tip-Top Bread premium, c1953 . . . . **18.00**

Dale Evans, wristwatch, chrome plated metal case, Dale and Buttermilk on dial, Bradley Time-Ingraham, 1950s **75.00**

Davy Crockett, belt buckle, metal, gold luster finish, hinged cover reveals inner compartment, mid-1950s, 1½ x 2½" **80.00**

Davy Crockett, bobbing head, painted composition, Napco Originals by Giftcraft, early 1960s, 5½" h **90.00**

Davy Crockett, wall plaque, plaster, oval bust portrait, Miller Studio, ©1955, 5¾ x 7½" **60.00**

Gene Autry, activity book, "Gene Autry Adventure Comics and Play-Fun Book," horizontal format, color, Pillsbury Pancake Mix premium, ©1947, 6½ x 8" **85.00**

Gene Autry, Better Little Book, *Gene Autry Special Ranger*, Whiman #1428, ©1941 . . . . **60.00**

Gene Autry, bread label album, Series 4, Stroehmann's Bread, early 1950s, 8½ x 10¾" **100.00**

Gene Autry, cap pistol, cast iron, imitation pearl grips, c1938, 8½" l **240.00**

Gene Autry, pennant, purple felt, white outline of Autry on Champ and "Back in the Saddle Again, Gene Autry and Champ," early 1940s, 11 x 28" **75.00**

Hoot Gibson, cartridge belt and holster, leather, c1930s **40.00**

Hoot Gibson, comic book, Fox Features, #5, Jun 1950 . . . . . **40.00**

Hopalong Cassidy, Auto-Magic Picture Gun and Theatre, Stephens Products Co, c1950, 8 x 12½" box **300.00**

Lone Ranger, guitar, 1951, $125.00.

Hopalong Cassidy, bank, hard plastic with copper luster finish, figural bust with removable hat, "Hopalong Cassidy Bank," Hopalong Cassidy Savings Club Program bank premium, c1950, 4¼" h **35.00**

Hopalong Cassidy, book cover, brown paper with red and black printing, c1950, 12 x 18" open size **15.00**

Hopalong Cassidy, figures, Hoppy and Topper, hard plastic, Ideal Toy Corp, c1950, 5½" h **150.00**

Hopalong Cassidy, gum card, Topps, #12, "Dangerous Venture," blue tone, 1950, 2 x 2½" **1.50**

Hopalong Cassidy, handkerchief, white cotton, hand-stitched inscription and Hoppy and Topper images, c1950, 11½" sq **30.00**

Hopalong Cassidy, milk bottle, clear glass, pyroglazed black Hoppy and red Miss Dairylea images, cardboard pull-tab cap with William Boyd portrait and "My Favorite," 1 quart, 8¾" h **100.00**

Hopalong Cassidy, mug, white milk glass, black Hoppy images, litho tin "Big Top Peanut Butter" lid with circus clown, c1950, 3" h **75.00**

Hopalong Cassidy, pencil case, hard plastic, pencil shape, "Hopalong Cassidy Jumbo Pencil," pencil sharpener in removable cap, c1950, 11" l **160.00**

Hopalong Cassidy, valentine card, diecut folder, "To A Grand Boy," Buzza Cardozo, Hollywood, 1950s, 4 x 6" **40.00**

John Wayne, frame tray puzzle, Saalfield, ©1951, 11½ x 15" **55.00**

John Wayne, movie book, *Westward Ho!*, Five Star Library, hardcover, ©1935, 4¼ x 5½" **125.00**

Ken Maynard, cigar band, diecut paper, red, gold, and black design, black and white photo, 1930s, 1 x 3" **20.00**

Kit Carson, book, *Kit Carson*, illustrated biography, Highlights of History Series, World Syndicate Publishing Co, hardcover, ©1933, 200 pgs, 4 x 4½" **18.00**

Lone Ranger, hair brush, wooden, black with Lone Ranger decal, orig box, ©1939, 8½" l **100.00**

Lone Ranger, leaflet, "The Life of Tonto by the Lone Ranger," Merita Bread and Cake premium, ©1940, 3¾ x 6½" **20.00**

Lone Ranger, mechanical pencil, black plastic with clear plastic barrel and brass accents, 1950s, 5¼" l **65.00**

Lone Ranger, newsletter, *Lone Ranger Roundup*, Vol. 1 #1, Aug 1939, Bond Bread Lone Ranger Safety Club, with unclipped membership application coupon, 8 pgs, 8 x 10¾" **70.00**

Lone Ranger, paint book, "Hi-Yo Silver! The Lone Ranger Paint Book," Whitman #621, 11 x 13½" **40.00**

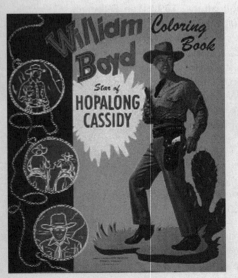

Hopalong Cassidy, coloring book, Samuel Lowe, mid-1950s, $40.00.

Lone Ranger, Picture Printing Set, Stamper Kraft #4092, Superior Type Co, Chicago, ©1939, 4½ x 6¼" box **130.00**

Lone Ranger, pistol, Lone Ranger Smoker, plastic and metal, clicker sound, Marx Toys, c1955, 9½" l **175.00**

Lone Ranger, plate, cup, and saucer, white milk glass, red trim, plate has red Lone Ranger on rearing Trigger image, ©1938, 8¾" d plate, 6" d saucer, 2½" h cup **125.00**

Lone Ranger, posters, paper, 1 Lone Ranger, 1 Tonto, life-size images, 25 x 75", price for pair **160.00**

Lone Ranger, toy, Tonto on Scout windup walker, Durham Industries, 1975, 4¼" h **30.00**

Red Ryder, Better Little Book, *Red Ryder and the Secret Canyon*, Whitman #1454, ©1948. . . . . **45.00**

Rin Tin Tin, doll, plush body, vinyl head and collar, late 1950s, 13" l **75.00**

Rin Tin Tin, pocketknife, black and white grips with Rusty and Rin Tin Tin pictured 1 side, Morse Code alphabet other side, Colonial, late 1950s, 3½" l **40.00**

Rin Tin Tin, Tru-Vue card #T-20, *Indian Ransom*, ©1957, 3½ x 6½". **24.00**

Roy Rogers, binoculars, metal and plastic with tan vinyl strap, mkd "Roy Rogers and Trigger," 1950s, 4½" l **50.00**

Roy Rogers, calendar, paper, "Roy Rogers Ranch Calendar," Nestle premium, 1959, 10 x 14" **75.00**

Roy Rogers, lunch box, emb steel, "Roy Rogers and Dale Evans" and RR Bar Ranch scenes, American Thermos, 1955–56 . . . . **125.00**

Roy Rogers, record album, "Hymns of Faith," Roy and Dale, two 45 rpms in cardboard folder, early 1950s **15.00**

Roy Rogers, Super Beanie, brown felt beanie with white vinyl trim and 1⅝" d litho pinback button with Roy's portrait and "King of the Cowboys, Roy Rogers," Grape-Nuts Flakes premium, orig mailer, 1953 . . . . **850.00**

Tim McCoy, Big Little Book, *Tim McCoy on the Tomahawk Trail*, Whitman #1436, ©1937. . . . . **50.00**

Tom Mix, blotter, "Tom Mix Circus," cardboard, black and white Mix on Tony photo, 1930s, 3 x 6". **30.00**

Tom Mix, holster, brown leather, tooled checkerboard pattern and "Tom Mix Ralston Straight Shooters," premium, 1938, 4 x 8" **200.00**

Tom Mix, movie still, *Fame and Fortune*, Fox Film Corp, 1918, 8 x 10" **175.00**

Tom Mix, pistol, wooden, Ralston Straight Shooters premium, 1933, 9" l **140.00**

Tom Mix, program, "The Life of Tom Mix," Sells-Floto Circus, 1931, 7 x 10". **45.00**

Tom Mix, record, "Original Radio Broadcasts," Vol 1, 33⅓ rpm, ©1982, 12½ x 12½" cardboard album **15.00**

Tom Mix, rope, red, white, and blue, wooden spool grips with "Tom Mix says Eat Ralston The Straight Shooters' Cereal," premium, 1935 . . . . **80.00**

Tom Mix, song book, "Tom Mix Western Songs," published by MM Cole, ©1935, 64 pgs, 9 x 11¾" **50.00**

Tom Mix, wrist cuffs, pr, brown leather with checkerboard emblem and "Tom Mix Ralston Straight Shooters," premium, 1935, 4½ x 10" **250.00**

Tom Tyler, Dixie picture, color, blue margin, biography and *Born to Battle* scenes on back, c1935 . . . . **18.00**

Will Rogers, figure, syroco, dark brown with black accents, name incised on front of base, ©1941, 5¾" h . . . **150.00**

COW COLLECTIBLES

Cow collectors came in from the pasture in the late 1980s, the result of a shift in decorating motif preferences from ducks to cows in Country magazines.

The category is completely image driven. Few collect only a specific breed. Contemporary items are just as popular and desirable as are vintage examples.

Collectors' Club: Cow Observers Worldwide, 240 Wahl Ave, Evans City, PA 16033.

Advertising Trade Card, Domestic Sewing Machine Co, 30,000 Jersey Cow image, printed color **$6.00**

Advertising Trade Card, Eclipse Halter, tethered cow, "Cannot be slipped by any cattle" **30.00**

Advertising Trade Card, Swift's Jersey Butterine, folder, milkmaid and cow image **40.00**

Branding Iron, wrought iron, "D," 21" l **25.00**

Bell, mounted on strap, copper, riveted, painted red, 5½" h **5.00**

Cookie Jar Lid, ceramic, Elsie the cow, unmkd, 4 x 5 x 6". **50.00**

Display, "Spray your team free Cow-Ease Keeps flies off cattle and horses," farmer spraying cow, 34" h, 21" w **825.00**

Greeting Card, color pop-up scene of Elsie and family in various family events, printed greeting "From Elsie, Elmer, Beulah and Beauregard and all of us at Borden's," Christmas tree and gifts on front, Borden Co copyright, c1940, 4¾ x 6½" closed size **50.00**

Lamp Base, ceramic, Elsie and calf, image of Elsie reading book to baby in diaper, 4 x 4 x 7". **100.00**

Pinback Button, "Champion Dairy Cow of the World/The Guernsey Cow May Rilma," sepia cow photo, green letters, white rim, 1920s. **20.00**

Pinback Button, "Golden Guernseys," browntone photo of cow head, yellow letters, blue rim, fabric attachment with metal milk jar hanger, c1930 . . . . **20.00**

Pinback Button, "Stillicious Moo Club," cartoon cow wearing neck bell inscribed "B1" **15.00**

Push Puppet, Elsie the cow, wood, jointed, green base with "Elsie" name in yellow decal, Mespo Products Co, late 1940s, 2½ x 2½ x 5½" **100.00**

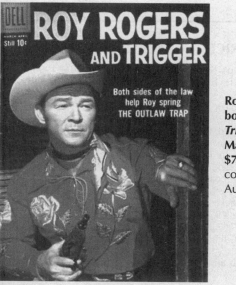

Roy Rogers, comic book, *Roy Rogers & Trigger*, Dell, Vol. 1, Mar/Apr 1944, $75.00. Photo courtesy Collectors Auction Services.

Sign, Hood's Ice Cream, diecut painted metal, 2-sided flange, 19" d, $1,485.00. Photo courtesy Collectors Auction Services.

Left: Whistle, litho tin, red, white, and blue, 2¹/₂" h, $35.00.

Right: Bookmark, litho tin, brown terrier, 1930s, 2³/₄" l, $20.00.

Recipe Book, *108 World's Fair Recipes from Borden,* Elsie the cow cover, Aug 40 reprinted edition for distribution at New York World's Fair, illus, sepia photos, 36 pp, softcover, 6¹/₂ x 9" 20.00

Scrap, holstein, diecut, emb, printed color, 4" w 8.00

Sign, diecut cardboard, Elsie and "M-M-M Look," 10¹/₂ x 11¹/₂" 100.00

Sign, Sharples, milkmaid and cows, matted and framed, 9 x 12" 220.00

CRACKER JACK

Cracker Jack arrived on the scene at the 1893 World's Columbian Exposition in Chicago when F. W. Rueckhaim, a pop store owner, introduced his world famous mixture of popcorn, peanuts, and molasses. The mix was not called "Cracker Jack" until three years later. The 1908 song, *Take Me Out to the Ball Game,* created national recognition for Cracker Jack.

The first prize in the box appeared in 1912. In the past 85 years plus, over 10,000 different prizes have made an appearance. New examples are being discovered every year. Today's prizes, with the exception of the magnifying glass, are made primarily from paper. The Borden Company, owner of Cracker Jack, buys prizes in lots of 25 million and keeps several hundred in circulation at one time.

References: Ravi Piña, *Cracker Jack Collectibles,* Schiffer Publishing, 1995; Larry White, *Cracker Jacks,* Schiffer Publishing, 1999.

Collectors' Club: Cracker Jack Collector's Assoc, 5469 S Dorchester Ave, Chicago, IL 60615.

Advertising Flyer, "Cracker-Jack, 100 packages in case, Trimble, Sides & Co., Phila..." on both sides, red and white, 3¹/₄ x 5³/₄" $165.00

Battleship, silvered metal, 1920s, ... 12.00

Booklet, "Uncle Sam's Famous National Songs," Jackie and Jack on back cover, 2¹/₂ x 3¹/₂" 45.00

Bottle Opener/Cork Screw, metal, "Cracker Jack" 1 side, Angelus Marshmallows other side, 3" l 100.00

Figure, Andy Gump, painted bisque, hollow, mkd "FAS Japan," 2¹/₈" h 40.00

Figure, Herby, painted bisque, hollow, mkd "FAS Japan," 2" h 40.00

Lion Cage, litho tin, multicolor, "Cracker Jack Shows" on top, 1³/₄" l 105.00

Palm Puzzle, cartoon man's face, clear plastic cover, cardboard back, roll balls into eye sockets, 1920s 70.00

Piano, litho tin, red, 1940s 65.00

Pinback Button, "I'm For Cracker Jack," litho tin, Jack and Bingo image, 1¹/₄" d 160.00

Pinback Button, lady's portrait, celluloid, text on back paper, 1¹/₂" d 35.00

Postcard, "The Cracker Jack Bears — No. 11" 35.00

Sedan, gray plastic, 1950s 15.00

Spinner, cardboard, Cracker Jack box 1 side, red, blue, and yellow swirls other side, with strings, 1³/₄" d 90.00

Stand-Up, Chester, diecut litho tin, multicolor, 1930s, 2" h 65.00

Stand-Up, Kayo, diecut litho tin, multicolor, 1930s, 2" h 65.00

Train Set, litho tin, streamline engine and 3 passenger cars, red, yellow, and black, 1940s, each car 2¹/₂" l 125.00

Tray, litho tin, image of Cracker Jack box, red, white, and blue, 1¹/₄ x 1³/₄" 70.00

Truck, litho tin, "Quick Delivery," brown and black, 1930s 55.00

Truck, litho tin, "The More You Eat — The More You Want" on top, 1³/₄" l 60.00

CRACKLE GLASS

Crackle glass, a glass-making technique that results in a multiple-fractured surface appearance, dates back to the 16th century. Martin Bach of Durand Glass is credited with reintroducing the concept in the late 1920s.

Crackle glass achieved widespread popularity in the late 1930s and was produced into the 1970s. Over 500 glass companies made crackle glass. Bischoff Glass, Blenko Glass, Hamon Glass, Kanawha Glass, Pilgrim Glass, Rainbow Art Glass, and Vogelsong Glass are just a few.

References: Judy Alford, *Collecting Crackle Glass,* Schiffer Publishing, 1997; Stan and Arlene Weitman, *Crackle Glass* (1996), *Book II* (1998), Collector Books.

Collectors' Club: Collectors of Crackle Glass, PO Box 1186, Massapequa, NY 11758.

Ashtray, amberina, unknown mfg, 7¼". **$35.00**
Candy Dish, amberina, Kanawha, 3" h **40.00**
Creamer, emerald green, drop over handle, Pilgrim,
    3¾" h **30.00**
Creamer and Sugar, gold, drop over handle, Kanawha,
    3½" h **50.00**
Cruet, amberina, pulled back handle, Rainbow, 7" h. **50.00**
Cruet, ruby, pulled back handle, Pilgrim, 6½" h **50.00**
Cruet, ruby, pulled back handle, Rainbow, 6¼" **45.00**
Cup, amberina, drop over handle, Kanawha, 2¼" h **35.00**
Decanter, crystal, olive green top, Blenko, 10½" h **65.00**
Decanter, topaz, ribbed, crystal drop over handle,
    Pilgrim, 6¼" h, price for pair **100.00**
Glass, blue, drop over handle, Pilgrim, 4" h **40.00**
Jug, amberina, gold drop over handle, Blenko, 8¼" h **75.00**
Jug, topaz, crystal drop over handle, Pilgrim, 6¾" h **65.00**
Miniature Hat, topaz, Blenko, 2¾" h **35.00**
Miniature Jug, blue, drop over handle, Pilgrim, 4" h **30.00**
Miniature Pitcher, amberina, drop over handle, Pilgrim,
    3¾" h **30.00**
Miniature Pitcher, amethyst, drop over handle, Pilgrim,
    3¼" h **35.00**
Miniature Pitcher, blue, pulled back handle, Kanawha,
    4" h **25.00**
Miniature Pitcher, emerald green, pulled back handle,
    Kahawha, 3½" h **30.00**
Miniature Pitcher, gold, drop over handle, Rainbow,
    3½" h **25.00**
Miniature Pitcher, tangerine, pulled back handle,
    Pilgrim, 4" h **30.00**
Miniature Vase, tangerine, Pilgrim, 4½" h **50.00**
Perfume Bottle, blue, crystal top, probably Italian, 7" h **75.00**
Pitcher, green, pulled back handle, Kanawha, 6¼" h **40.00**
Pitcher, green, pulled back handle, Williamsburg Glass
    Co, 4¾" h **55.00**
Pitcher, olive green, pulled back handle, frilled top,
    probably Blenko, 8¼" h. **85.00**
Pitcher, tangerine, drop over handle, Rainbow, 4¾" h **50.00**
Salt and Pepper Shakers, pr, amethyst, unknown mfg,
    3¼" h **50.00**
Vase, amberina, Blenko, 7" h. **75.00**
Vase, crystal with blue rosettes, Blenko, 7" h **75.00**
Vase, dark amber, Pilgrim, 4½" h **50.00**
Vase, olive green, double-neck, Blenko, 4" h **50.00**
Wine Bottle, topaz, unknown mfg, 9" h, 21" l **140.00**

CREDIT CARDS & TOKENS

The charge coin, the forerunner of the credit card, first appeared in the 1890s. Each coin had a different identification number. Charge coins were made in a variety of materials from celluloid to German silver and came in two basic shapes, geometric and diecut. The form survived until the late 1950s.

Metal charge plates, similar to a G.I.'s dog tag, were issued from the 1930s through the 1950s. Paper charge cards also were used. Lamination of the cards to prolong use began in the 1940s.

The plastic credit card arrived on the scene in the late 1950s.

In the 1980s pictorial credit cards became popular. Individuals applied for credit just to get the card. The inclusion of holigrams on the card for security purposes also was introduced during the 1980s. Today institutions from airlines to universities issue credit cards, many of which feature a bonus program. Little wonder America has such a heavy credit card debt.

Reference: Lin Overholt, *The First International Credit Card Catalog, 3rd Edition,* published by author, 1995.

Newsletter: *Credit Cards & Phone Cards News,* PO Box 8481, St Petersburg, FL 33738.

Collectors' Clubs: American Credit Card Collectors Society, PO Box 1992, Midlothian, VA 23112; Token & Medal Society, Inc, 9230 SW 59th St, Miami, FL 33173.

CARDS

American Airlines **$35.00**
Amoco Credit Plate/Speedier Service For You **100.00**
Atlanta Charga-Plate, "Use Your Charga-Plate for Better
    Service" **95.00**
Avis Rent-a-Car/International Credit Card **180.00**
Brett's Department Store **30.00**
Ethan Allen. **125.00**
Fleet, magnetic brown strip **35.00**
JC Penney, "Account for Young Moderns". **95.00**
Lane Bryant, Fifth Avenue, marbelized purple **25.00**
Lion Oil Co, "A Division of Monsanto Chemical Co" **450.00**
Neiman Marcus, "Dallas/Fort Worth/Houston" **60.00**
QVC Network. **30.00**
Super America Convenience Card, "phone 606-329
    5731" **40.00**
Western Airlines Travelcard **50.00**

TOKENS

Abraham & Strauss, scalloped edges **$185.00**
Blaumers, shield shaped, white **45.00**
Brooks, "An Institution of Paris Fashion, 1230 Chestnut
    St, Philadelphia, Pa," rect, beveled corners, 28 x 24". **28.00**
Castle Jewelry, "139 E. Federal St. Youngstown, O.," front
    castle, copper, round. **75.00**
Charles David, "Fashions For The Value-Wise/1008
    Chestnut St/Philadelphia," rect, white metal, 31 x 22". **70.00**
Checker Taxicab Co, red enamel "Sutter/225 Powell St.-
    #400" in center, reverse with "In Charging Give
    Driver/Number/And Your Name," account number in
    center oval, white metal. **325.00**
Crowley Milner & Co, Detroit, MI, "CMCo" monogram
    on front, diamond shape, white metal. **100.00**
Dinkler Hotels, Atlanta, GA, white metal **225.00**

Shell, sample, Canadian, Shell/White Rose and Conoco logos on back, 2 x 3¹/₂", $16.50. Photo courtesy Collectors Auction Services.

Fairmont Hotel, San Francisco, mirrored "F" inside
   draped shield, reverse with Golden Gate Bridge, 1947
   and account number below, white metal, round **300.00**
H Leh & Co, monogram in center, acount number on
   reverse, rect, white metal **170.00**
Pomeroy's, Harrisburg, PA, "Finder Please Return To,"
   account number on reverse, oval, white metal **100.00**
Spiegel Inc, Chicago, "Credit Bank/Account Book/
   Preferred Customer" and account number at top,
   reverse with "Honor Roll/1938," round, brass **85.00**

CROOKSVILLE POTTERY

Founded in 1912, the Crooksville Pottery, Crooksville, Ohio, made semi-porcelain dinnerwares and utilitarian household pottery. Their decal decorated "Pantry Bak-In" line was extremely popular in the 1930s and 40s.

The company's semi-porcelain dinnerware line was marketed as Stinhal China. Most pieces are not marked with a pattern name. Check the reference books. The company ceased operations in 1959, a victim of cheap foreign imports and the popularity of melamine plastic dinnerware.

References: Harvey Duke, *The Official Price Guide to Pottery and Porcelain, Eighth Edition,* House of Collectibles, 1995; Lois Lehner, *Lehner's Encyclopedia of U.S. Marks on Pottery, Porcelain & Clay,* Collector Books, 1988.

Dartmouth, casserole **$28.00**
Dartmouth, cup and saucer **6.00**
Dartmouth, mixing bowls, nesting set of 4 . . . . **60.00**
Dartmouth, plate, 10" d **10.00**
Dawn, after dinner cup and saucer **15.00**
Dawn, gravy **12.00**
Dawn, plate, 7" d **5.00**
Dawn, vegetable bowl, oval **10.00**
Euclid, coffeepot **50.00**
Euclid, creamer and sugar **18.00**
Euclid, pie baker, 9" d **12.00**
Euclid, platter, rect, 11¹/₂" l **15.00**
Ivora, pickle dish **6.00**
Ivora, vegetable, oval, 9" l **20.00**

Pantry Bak-In, bean pot **25.00**
Pantry Bak-In, mixing bowl, 12" d **18.00**
Pantry Bak-In, syrup jug, flat top, floral decal **20.00**
Petit Point House, berry bowl **5.00**
Petit Point House, cup and saucer **8.00**
Petit Point House, salad plate, 7" d **5.00**
Provincial Ware, cup and saucer **5.00**
Provincial Ware, dinner plate **8.00**
Provincial Ware, fruit dish, 5" **2.00**
Quadro, creamer **6.00**
Quadro, dinner plate. **8.00**
Quadro, eggcup **12.00**
Quadro, gravy and liner **20.00**
Rust Bouquet, coffeepot **25.00**
Rust Bouquet, pie baker **15.00**
Rust Bouquet, platter, 11¹/₂" l **8.00**
Silhouette, batter jug, pelican style, Pantry Bak-In **75.00**
Silhouette, soup **18.00**
Silhouette, teapot **70.00**

CUT GLASS

Glass is cut through a grinding process. Metal wheels containing abrasives or stone wheels are used to cut the decoration. Normally, "cut glass" describes glass with deeply cut decorative motifs. "Engraved glass" refers to pieces with lightly cut decorative motifs.

American cut and engraved glass divides into five basic periods: (1) 1740 to 1815; (2) 1815 to 1880; (3) Brilliant period, 1880 to 1915; (4) 1920 to the end of the 1950s, a period during which many pieces featured a combination of pressed and cut designs; and, (5) Contemporary, 1960s to present.

American tastes changed considerably following World War I. While cut glass continued to be a poplar anniversary, birthday, and bridal gift, buyers preferred lightly engraved patterns over the deep cut patterns of the American Brilliant period. Many established cutting firms experienced hard times. J. Hoare ceased operations in 1920, Egginton in 1918, Sinclaire in 1929, and H. C. Fry in 1934. The post–World War I cut glass era effectively ended with the closing of A. H. Heisey & Company in 1958.

Most cut glass sold in the United States today is imported. A few American cut glass studio artisans produce commissioned pieces.

Collectors' Club: American Cut Glass Assoc, PO Box 482, Ramona, CA 92065.

Note: For additional listings see Fry, Heisey, and Stemware.

Bowl, Chantilly pattern, crimped, Duncan & Miller,
   10¹/₂" d **$40.00**
Brandy, Lismore pattern, Waterford Crystal **35.00**
Bread and Butter Plate, Cape Cod pattern, Avon, ruby,
   5³/₄" d **7.00**
Candle, votive, Longchamp pattern, Durand Intl, 3¹/₄ x
   2¹/₂" **10.00**
Candy Dish, cov, Alexis pattern, Fry Glass, 5" h **125.00**
Claret, Star Cut pattern, #3400, Candlewick, 4¹/₂" h **50.00**
Cocktail, Rosewood pattern, Gorham. **55.00**
Cordial, Adonis pattern, #3500, Cambridge, 5" h **65.00**
Cordial, Lily of the Valley pattern, DC-4, Duncan &
   Miller, 5" h **75.00**
Creamer and Open Sugar, flat, Wheat pattern, Fostoria,
   3⁵/₈" creamer, 2³/₄" sugar. **55.00**
Cruet, Beaver pattern, Fry Glass **150.00**

Decanter, Tuilleries/Villandry pattern, Durand Intl **22.00**
Finger Bowl, Hampshire pattern, Stuart Crystal **35.00**
Fruit Bowl, Cape Cod pattern, Line 1602, Imperial Glass,
   4⅛" **10.00**
High Ball, Thistle pattern, Edinburgh Crystal **40.00**
Iced Tea, Harmonie pattern, Baccarat **55.00**
Napkin Rings, set of 4, Cape Cod pattern, Avon, ruby **15.00**
Nappy, Palais Versailles pattern, Tiffin **85.00**
Plate, Nosegay pattern, Fostoria, 8½" d **25.00**
Salt and Pepper Shakers, pr, King Edward pattern,
   Gorham, 4½" h **25.00**
Salt Dip, #1 pattern, Fry Glass, 2" h **70.00**
Sherbet, Orient pattern, Fry Glass **50.00**
Shot Glass, Alana pattern, Waterford Crystal **30.00**
Vase, Longchamp pattern, Durand International, 5¼" h **18.00**
Vase, Poppy pattern, Fry Glass, 4" h **75.00**
Water Tumbler, Ardis Cut 1262, #352, Seneca Glass Co,
   4" h **20.00**

CYBIS

Boleslaw Cybis, a professor at the Academy of Fine Art in Warsaw, Poland, and his wife, Marja, came to the United States in 1939 to paint murals in the Hall of Honor at the New York World's Fair. Unable to return to Poland after war broke out, the couple remained in the United States and opened an artists' studio to create porcelain sculpture.

After a brief stint in New York, the studio moved to Trenton, New Jersey. Sculptures were produced in a variety of themes ranging from the world of nature to elegant historical figures.

Abigale Adams, 9½" h **$1,200.00**
Ballerina on Cue, Princess Christina of Sweden, 12½" l,
   1963–69 . . . . **325.00**
Bathsheba, Portrait in Porcelain **1,500.00**
Bunny, Mr Snowball, Animal Kingdom and Woodland,
   1962 . . . . **70.00**
Bunny, Pat-a-Cake, 1977 . . . . **150.00**
Bunny, Snowflake, 1985 . . . . **75.00**
Burro, Fitzgerald, 1964, 7" h **150.00**
Calla Lily, Bird and Flower, 1968–74 . . . . **900.00**
Clematis with House Wren, 1969 . . . . **315.00**
Dapple Gray Foal, 1986 . . . . **185.00**
Deer Mouse in Clover, 1970 . . . . **150.00**
Duckling, "Baby Brother," 1962 . . . . **140.00**
Easter Egg Hunt, 1972 . . . . **200.00**
George Washington Bust, 1975 . . . . **300.00**
Girl Clown Bust, 1976, 9" h **400.00**
Golden Prince, 8" h **400.00**
Kitten, Tabitha, 1975 . . . . **150.00**
Little Boy Blue, Children to Cherish **350.00**
Madame Butterfly, Portrait in Porcelain **2,400.00**
Nativity Cow, 1984 . . . . **200.00**
Nativity Lamb, 1985 . . . . **125.00**
Nesting Bluebirds, 1978 . . . . **250.00**
Pansies, 1972 . . . . **350.00**
Pierre the Performing Poodle, 1986 . . . . **275.00**
Rebecca, 1964 . . . . **345.00**
Sabbath Morning, 1972 . . . . **200.00**
Valentine, 1985 . . . . **375.00**
Winter, 1972 . . . . **200.00**
Yellow Condesa Rose, 1980 . . . . **250.00**

CZECHOSLOVAKIAN WARES

The country of Czechoslovakia was created in 1918 from the Czech and Solvak regions of the old Austro-Hungarian Empire. Both regions were actively involved in the manufacture of ceramics and glass.

Czechoslovakian ceramics and glassware were imported into the United States in large numbers from the 1920s through the 1950s. Most are stamped "Made in Czechoslovakia." Pieces mirrored the styles of the day. Czechoslovakian Art Deco glass is stylish, colorful, and bright. Canister sets are one of the most popular ceramic forms.

By 1939, Czechoslovakia had fallen under the control of Germany. The country came under communist influence in 1948. Communist domination ended in 1989. On January 1, 1993, Czechoslovakia split into two independent states, the Czech Republic and the Slovak Republic.

References: Dale and Diane Barta and Helen M. Rose, *Czechoslovakian Glass & Collectibles* (1992, 1995 value update), *Book II* (1997), Collector Books; Ruth A. Forsythe, *Made in Czechoslovakia*, Richardson Printing Corp, 1982, 1994–95 value update; Ruth A. Forsythe, *Made in Czechoslovakia, Book 2*, Antique Publications, 1993, 1995–96 value update; Diane E. Foulds, *A Guide to Czech & Slovak Glass, 2nd Edition*, published by author, 1993, 1995 value update, distributed by Antique Publications; Robert and Deborah Truitt, *Collectible Bohemian Glass: 1880–1940*, B & D Glass, 1995, distributed by Antique Publications.

Collectors' Club: Czechoslovakian Collectors Guild International, PO Box 901395, Kansas City, MO 64190.

Ashtray, floral design, orange border, match holder **$25.00**
Ashtray, woman's face **75.00**
Atomizer, red glass, baluster shape, 8¾" h **80.00**
Bell, figural lady, 5" h **30.00**
Cookie Jar, Erphila Art Pottery, rattan handle **100.00**

Vase, pressed glass, cornflower blue, mkd "Czechoslov," 10½" h, $375.00. Photo courtesy Skinner, Inc., Boston, MA.

Creamer, blue and white plaid, 3¼" h **35.00**
Creamer, floral design, green ground, 4½" h. **60.00**
Cup and Saucer, floral design, scalloped edge **20.00**
Dresser Box, cov, clear pressed glass, round. **25.00**
Eggcup, Chelsea pattern, 3" h **35.00**
Figure, crowing rooster, 9" h **85.00**
Figure, sailor, 11½" h **150.00**
Hostess Set, bridge motif, includes 4 snack plates, each
   in the form of a different card suit, and 4 cups, blue
   and tan luster **150.00**
Ice Bucket, crystal overshot base, silver rim band, han-
   dles, and tongs **100.00**
Napkin Ring, figural girl wearing yellow bonnet, Erphila. **25.00**
Perfume Bottle, 6-sided red glass base, clear faceted
   stopper **275.00**
Perfume Bottle, clear glass, cornucopia-shaped bottle,
   frosted butterfly and flower stopper, 7¾" h **350.00**
Perfume Bottle, pressed glass, clear boat-shaped base,
   pink sails stopper. **400.00**
Planter, duck, yellow with red and black trim, 5½" l **80.00**
Salt and Pepper Shakers, pr, flowerpots, 3" h **15.00**
Teapot, figural woman and basket **125.00**
Toothbrush Holder, figural lady, wearing white dress,
   Erphila, 8" h **45.00**
Toothpick Holder, figural elephant, white with green tas-
   seled howdah, 3½" h. **30.00**
Vase, cylindrical, mottled red and black glossy glaze,
   7½" h **40.00**
Vase, figural heron, black and white. **100.00**
Vase, narrow neck, small floral spray on black and white
   striped ground, 4½" h **30.00**
Wall Pocket, bird and pineapple **100.00**
Wall Pocket, bird at well **50.00**
Wall Pocket, Chintz pattern on red ground, 8" h. **60.00**
Wall Pocket, raised peacock and flowers, blue ground,
   7½" h **75.00**
Water Set, pitcher and 6 mugs, red, white, and black
   stripes **250.00**

DAIRY COLLECTIBLES

The mid-20th century was the Golden Age of the American dairy industry. Thousands of small dairies and creameries were located throughout the United States, most serving only a regional market.

Dairy cooperatives, many of which were created in the 1920s and 30s, served a broader market. Borden pursued a national marketing program. Elsie, The Borden Cow, is one of the most widely recognized advertising characters from the 1940s and 50s.

Reference: Dana G. Morykan, *The Official Price Guide to Country Antiques and Collectibles, Fourth Edition,* House of Collectibles, 1999.

Newsletters: *Creamers,* PO Box 11, Lake Villa, IL 60046; *The Udder Collectibles,* HC73 Box 1, Smithville Flats, NY 13841.

Collectors' Clubs: Cream Separator Assoc, Rte 3, Box 189, Arcadia, WI 54612; National Assoc of Milk Bottle Collectors, Inc, 4 Ox Bow Rd, Westport, CT 06880.

Booklet, Windsor Dairy Farm, Denver, CO, *We Pull For Windsor,* 18 pp, early 1930s. **$15.00**
Calendar, 1936, Conewago Dairy, milk maid illus **12.00**

Clock, Beverly Farms Milk, metal and glass, light-up, Pam Clock Co, 14" sq, $165.00. Photo courtesy Collectors Auction Services.

Calendar, 1937, DeLaval Cream Separators **30.00**
Cheese Box, vinyl over sturdy cardboard, dark olive
   green ext with emb gold Elsie head image in center,
   inscribed below cow's head "Borden's/Van Wert,
   Ohio/The World's Largest Cheese Factory," grid pattern background accented by scattered daisies, c1950s. . . . **75.00**
Folder, paper, 3 Elsie images with Trylon and Perisphere
   structures of 1939 New York World's Fair printed on
   outside, inside with pictorial family endorsement with
   recipe and text for "Borden's Chateau" cheese, Aug
   1939 publication date printed on panel, 6¼ x 12"
   open size **20.00**
Paperweight, Borden's Milk, milk carton shape, Elsie
   illus **20.00**
Pinback Button, Ayrshires Milk, "You Can't Go Wrong
   With Ayrshires," center cow illus, maroon and white,
   c1940s **15.00**
Pinback Button, Empire Cream Separator, "I Chirp For
   The Empire Because It Makes The Most Dollars For
   Me," black and white product image, blue rim letter-
   ing on white, attached tin clicker **75.00**
Pinback Button, Ohio Dairy Co, "If You Would Have
   Your Baby Look Like This/Get Your Milk Supply From
   the Ohio Dairy Co," multicolred baby image **50.00**
Postcard, "From Moo To You—With Love Elsie," Elsie sit-
   ting on perisphere, from 1939–40 New York World's
   Fair Borden exhibit, unopened pkg, 3½ x 6", price for
   set of 5 . . . . **35.00**
Sign, Carnation, "Fresh Milk," porcelain, 15" h, 14½" w **235.00**
Sign, DeLaval Cream Separator, porcelain, 12" h, 16" w **70.00**
Sign, "Milk /Food for the Nerves," tin, emb, ©National
   Dairy & Food Bureau, Chicago, 13⅛" h, 19⅞" w **375.00**
Sign, Southern Dairies Ice Cream, porcelain, 20" h,
   28" w **155.00**
Sign, Spring Valley Dairy, painted metal, 12" h, 8" w **140.00**
Stickpin, Omega Cream Separator, multicolored, reverse
   brass inscription "Omega Separator Co./Lansing,
   Mich. U.S.A." **75.00**
Stickpin, Sharples Cream Separator, figural flag, multi-
   colored, oval, reverse brass inscription "The Sharples
   Separator/West Chester, Pa," **75.00**
Thermometer, "Blue Valley Butter is good...that's why
   millions use it," metal, 39" h, 16" w **235.00**
Tip Tray, De Laval Cream Separators, litho tin, product
   illus, 4¼" d **65.00**

DAVID WINTER COTTAGES

David Winter, born in Caterick, Yorkshire, England, is the son of Faith Winter, an internationally recognized sculptor. Working from his garden studio located at his home in Guildford, England, Winter created his first miniature cottage in 1979.

David Winter Cottages received the "Collectible of the Year" award from the National Association of Limited Edition Dealers in 1987 and 1988 and was named NALED "Artist of the Year" in 1991. In 1997 Enesco signed an agreement with David Winter to manufacture David Winter Cottages and operate the David Winter Cottages Collectors' Guild.

The secondary market for David Winter miniature cottages is as strong (perhaps stronger) in England. Be cautious of English price guides that provide a straight conversion from pounds to dollars in their price listings. Taste and emphasis among collectors differs between England and the United States.

References: *Collectors' Information Bureau Market Guide & Price Index, Sixteenth Edition,* Collectors' Information Bureau, 1998, distributed by Krause Publications; Mary Sieber (ed.), *1999 Collector's Mart Magazine Price Guide to Limited Edition Collectibles,* Krause Publications, 1998.

At the Bake House Vignette, David Winter Scenes, 1992	**$35.00**
Audrey's Tea Shop, Main Collection, 1992	**125.00**
Black Bess Inn, Collectors Guild Exclusives, 1988	**95.00**
Coal Miner's Row, Midlands Collection, 1988	**120.00**
Devon Creamery, West Country Collection, 1986	**110.00**
Dower House, Landowners series, 1982	**45.00**
Engine House, English Village series, 1994	**55.00**
Guardian Castle, English Village series, 1994	**95.00**
Hampshire Hutches, Shires Collection, 1993	**30.00**
Ivy Cottage, At the Centre of the Village Collection, closed 1992	**45.00**
Lacemaker's Cottage, Midlands Collection, 1988	**155.00**
Lych Gate, Cameos series, 1992	**15.00**
Meadowbank Cottages, Heart of England series, 1985	**40.00**
Miss Belle, David Winter Scenes, 1993	**35.00**
Mr Fezzwig's Emporium, Christmas series, 1990	**75.00**
Much's Mill, Sherwood Forest Collection, 1995	**45.00**

Only A Span Apart, Irish Collection, 1992	**75.00**
Pen-y-Craig, Welsh Collection, 1993	**90.00**
Scottish Crofter's, Scottish Collection, 1989	**65.00**
Shirehall, Heart of England series, 1985	**50.00**
Single Oast, Regions Collection, 1981	**30.00**
Sweet Dreams, Porridge Pot Alley series, 1995	**75.00**
Sweetheart Haven, Celebration Cottages series, 1994	**60.00**
Tartan Teahouse, Porridge Pot Alley, 1995	**100.00**
There Was a Crooked House, In the Country Collection, 1986	**155.00**
Tom the Street Shoveler, David Winter Scenes, 1993	**60.00**
Waterford Market, Seaside Boardwalk series, 1995	**125.00**
Willow Gardens, Garden Cottages of England series, 1995	**225.00**
Ye Merry Gentlemen's Lodgings, Winterville Collection, 1995	**125.00**

DEDHAM POTTERY

In 1891 a group of influential Bostonians formed Chelsea Pottery, U.S., and hired Hugh C. Robertson, assisted by his son William, to perfect a crackle glaze that he had discovered five years earlier. Crackleware was produced by quickly cooling pieces after they were taken from the glost kiln. The cracking was then rubbed by hand with Cobot's lamp black powder to produce the famous spider-web effect.

The company moved to Dedham in 1895, changing its name to reflect its new location. Although some hand-thrown vases with a high-fired glaze on a high-fired base were made, cracque ware was the company's principal product. Joseph Lindon Smith and Alice Morse designed the famous Dedham rabbit pattern. Over fifty different patterns of tableware were produced.

World War I caused a temporary halt in Dedham's growth. Prosperity returned in the 1920s and 30s. In 1943 J. Milton Robertson, a Commander in the Navy, closed the pottery because of a shortage of skilled workers and increasing costs. Gimbels bought the remaining stock and offered it for sale in its New York store in September 1943.

In the late 1980s The Potting Shed of Concord, Massachusetts, created a series of Dedham reproductions including the 10" dinner plate, 8½" salad plate, and 7½" bread and butter plate in the blue rabbit border motif. Several other companies have also produced reproductions.

Newsletter: *Dedham Pottery Collectors Newsletter,* 248 Highland St, Dedham, MA 02026.

Note: All items listed are marked "Dedham Pottery Registered."

O'Donovan's Castle, Irish Collection, 1992, $75.00.

Bowl, #5, Turkey pattern band, 2⅛" h, 5½" d	**$275.00**
Bowl, Lotus motif with leafy panels, 2" h, 5" d	**715.00**
Butter Pat, 6-sided star shape, blue outline, mkd "1931," 3¼" d	**450.00**
Butter Pat, Wild Rose design, flower-shaped, 3½" d	**350.00**
Charger, Azalea pattern border, 2 imp rabbits, 12" d	**550.00**
Chowder Cup and Saucer, Rabbit pattern band on 2-handled cup, same pattern border on saucer, 2¼" h, 7" d cup, 6½" d saucer	**500.00**
Coaster, Swan medallion and "Silvermine," round with flared lip, 4" d	**700.00**
Coffeepot and Underliner, Rabbit pattern band, squared handle, dome-shaped cover, 2 imp rabbits, 8¾" h	**1,650.00**

Teapot, Horsechestnut pattern border, mkd "Dedham Pottery/1931," 7" h, $1,650.00. Photo courtesy Smith & Jones, Inc. Auctions.

Cup and Saucer, Duck pattern border, 3" h cup, 5¼" d	250.00
Nappie, #2, open, Rabbit pattern border, 2½" h, 11" d	350.00
Plate, Dolphin pattern border, 2 imp rabbits, 8½" d	925.00
Plate, Lion Tapestry pattern border, 2 imp rabbits, 9¾" d	875.00
Plate, Magnolia pattern border, 2 imp rabbits, 6¼" d	200.00
Plate, Polar Bear pattern border, mkd twice, 8¼" d	725.00
Plate, Pond Lily pattern border, 2 imp rabbits, 6" d	200.00
Plate, Rabbit pattern border, 2 imp rabbits, 8¾" d	165.00
Plate, Snowtree pattern border, 2 imp rabbits, 7½" d	200.00
Plate, Swan pattern border, 2 imp rabbits, 8½" d	500.00
Star Dish, Chinese Poppy motif, 5-sided, 7¼" w	500.00
Steak Platter, Elephant and Baby pattern border, oval, 14" l, 8¼" w	2,000.00
Vase, Rabbit pattern band, bulbous body, cylindrical collar neck, 5" h, 4¼" d	600.00

DEGENHART GLASS

John and Elizabeth Degenhart directed the operation of Crystal Art Glass, Cambridge, Ohio, from 1947 until 1978. Pressed glass novelties, such as animal covered dishes, salts, toothpicks, and paperweights were the company's principal products.

Boyd Crystal Art Glass, Cambridge, Ohio, purchased many of the company's molds when operations ceased. Boyd continues to manufacture pieces from these molds in colors different from those used by Degenhart. Most are marked with a "B" in a diamond.

Reference: Gene Florence, *Degenhart Glass & Paperweights, Degenhart Paperweight & Glass Museum, 2nd Edition,* 1991, available from the Degenhart Paperweight & Glass Museum.

Collectors' Club: Friends of Degenhart, Degenhart Paperweight and Glass Museum, Inc, 65323 Highland Hills Rd, PO Box 186, Cambridge, OH 43725.

REPRODUCTION ALERT: Although most Degenhart molds were reproductions themselves, many contemporary pieces made by Kanawha, L. G. Wright, and others are nearly identical.

Animal Dish, cov, chick, powder blue	$25.00
Animal Dish, cov, hen, pigeon blood	50.00
Animal Dish, cov, turkey, amethyst	40.00

Animal Dish, cov, turkey, bittersweet	75.00
Animal Dish, cov, turkey, custard	60.00
Basket, cobalt blue	22.00
Bicentennial Bell, crystal	8.00
Bicentennial Bell, Rose Marie pink	12.00
Candy Dish, Wildflower, amethyst	25.00
Chick, Vaseline	18.00
Child's Mug, Stork & Peacock, baby green	22.00
Coaster, amber	6.00
Coaster, Shamrock	8.00
Cup Plate, Heart & Lyre, blue green	10.00
Cup Plate, Heart & Lyre, mulberry	20.00
Cup Plate, Seal of Ohio, Elizabeth's Blue	25.00
Hand, ivorene	15.00
Hand, sapphire	6.00
Hat, Daisy and Button, frosted jade	15.00
Hat, Daisy and Button, vaseline	15.00
Jewelry Box, Heart, Elizabeth blue	45.00
Owl, bluebell	35.00
Owl, ivorene	50.00
Owl, pearl gray	35.00
Owl, teal	22.00
Paperweight, flowerpot	85.00
Salt, Pottie, white milk	10.00
Salt, Star & Dew Drop, crystal	10.00
Salt and Pepper Shakers, pr, bird, Nile green	35.00
Slipper, Kat, sapphire	15.00
Toothpick Holder, Baby Shoe, cobalt	15.00
Toothpick Holder, Daisy & Button, blue slag	25.00
Toothpick Holder, Elephant Head, blue green	30.00
Toothpick Holder, Forget-Me-Not, caramel	32.00
Toothpick Holder, Forget-Me-Not, lavender blue	25.00
Toothpick Holder, Forget-Me-Not, milk blue	15.00
Toothpick Holder, Forget-Me-Not, misty green	20.00
Toothpick Holder, Forget-Me-Not, toffee	25.00
Toothpick Holder, Gypsy Pot, Bloody Mary	50.00
Toothpick Holder, Heart, buttercup slag	35.00

DELEE ART

While teaching art at Los Angeles' Belmont High School in the 1930s, Jimmie Lee Adair Kohl started a small ceramic figurines business. By the start of 1939, Jimmie Lee had produced over 3,500 salable pieces.

When a shortage of ceramic supplies occurred during World War II, Jimmie Lee borrowed money and moved some production to Cuernavaca, Mexico. Her Los Angeles operations continued on a limited basis. By 1994, Jimmie Lee closed her Mexican facility.

The period from the mid-1940s until the end of the 1950s was deLee's golden age. The company produced high quality giftware figurines. In 1949 a representative from Barnes & Noble asked her to write a ceramic "how to" book. *Ceramics for All*, part of the Everyday Handbook series, was published in 1950.

The arrival of cheap imported reproductions from Japan and elsewhere at the end of the 1950s spelled doom for deLee. The factory closed in 1958.

Reference: Joanne Fulton Schafer, *deLee Art: The Pictorial Story of a California Artist and Her Company, 1937–1958,* published by author, 1997.

Bank, Butch, pig with floral dec, 5" h	$50.00
Bank, Money Bunny, rabbit holding purse, 9" h	80.00

Planter, Nina, #43, 7" h, $25.00.

Candle Holder, Star, angel, 4½" h	20.00
Figure, angel, pink flowers, 6½" h	25.00
Figure, boy and Scottie dog, 5" h	50.00
Figure, Can-Can dancer, 1950s, 14" h	90.00
Figure, Corny, 5¼" h	30.00
Figure, Mickey, white kitten with blue ball, 4" h	30.00
Figure, Mimi, black spaghetti poodle, 1950s, 9" h	100.00
Figure, The Thinker, 2¾" h	35.00
Figure, Zombie Zebra	70.00
Figures, pr, Siamese Dancers, gold trim, 13" h	180.00
Flower Frog, Miss Muffet, 5" h	75.00
Lady Head Vase, Bobby Pin-Up, 1940s	65.00
Planter, Hank, brown and white plaid, 1943, 7½" h	30.00
Planter, Hattie, pink roses, 7½" h	25.00
Planter, Johnny, holding boquet, 8½" h	28.00
Planter, lamb, blue collar and bell, 8" h	50.00
Planter, Sally, green and white dress with red flowers, 7" h	25.00
Planter, seated elephant holding drum, floral dec, 7" h	75.00
Salt and Pepper Shakers, pr, Wiggles and Giggles, pigs with floral dec, 3½" h	25.00
Wall Pocket, mallard duck, 1950s, 7" h	40.00

DEPRESSION GLASS

Depression Glass is a generic term used to describe glassware patterns introduced and manufactured between 1920 and the early 1950s. Most of this glassware was inexpensive and machine made.

In its narrow sense, the term describes a select group of patterns identified by a group of late 1940s and early 1950s collectors as "Depression Glass." Many price guides dealing with the subject have preserved this narrow approach.

Many manufacturers did not name their patterns. The same group of individuals who determined what patterns should and should not be included in this category also assigned names to previously unidentified patterns. Disputes occurred. Hence, some patterns have more than one name.

References: Tom and Neila Bredehoft, *Fifty Years of Collectible Glass: 1920–1970, Vol. I,* Antique Trader Books, 1997; Robert Brenner, *Depression Glass for Collectors,* Schiffer Publishing, 1998; Gene Florence, *Collectible Glassware From the 40s, 50s &*

60s..., *Fourth Edition,* Collector Books, 1998; Gene Florence, *Collector's Encyclopedia of Depression Glass, Fourteenth Edition,* Collector Books, 1999; Gene Florence, *Elegant Glassware of the Depression Era, Eighth Edition,* Collector Books, 1998; Gene Florence, *Kitchen Glassware of the Depression Years, Fifth Edition,* Collector Books, 1995, 1999 value update; Gene Florence, *Very Rare Glassware of the Depression Years, Third Series* (1993, 1995 value update), *Fifth Series* (1997), and *Sixth Series* (1998), Collector Books; Ralph and Terry Kovel, *Kovel's Depression Glass & American Dinnerware Price List, Sixth Edition,* Crown, 1998; Carl F. Luckey, *An Identification & Value Guide to Depression Era Glassware, Third Edition,* Books Americana, Krause Publications, 1994; James Jeasell and Berry Wiggins, *Great American Glass of the Roaring 20s & Depression Era,* Glass Press, 1998; Naomi L. Over, *Ruby Glass of the 20th Century,* Antique Publications, 1990, 1993–94 value update; Ellen T. Schroy, *Warman's Depression Glass,* Krause Publications, 1997; Hazel Marie Weatherman, *Colored Glassware of the Depression Era, Book 2,* published by author, 1974, available in reprint.

Periodical: *The Daze,* PO Box 57, Otisville, MI 48463.

Collectors' Clubs: Canadian Depression Glass Assoc, 119 Wexford Rd, Brampton, Ontario, Canada L62 2T5; National Depression Glass Assoc, PO Box 8264, Wichita, KS 67208.

REPRODUCTION ALERT: Reproductions (exact copies) of several patterns are known. In other cases, fantasy pieces have been made from period molds in non-period colors. Few of these reproductions and fantasy pieces are marked.

The Daze distributes a list of these reproductions and fantasy items. Send a self-addressed, stamped business envelope along with a request for a copy.

American Sweetheart, MacBeth-Evans, bread and butter plate, 6" d, monax	$7.00
American Sweetheart, MacBeth-Evans, bread and butter plate, 6" d, pink	5.00
American Sweetheart, MacBeth-Evans, cereal bowl, 6" d, cremax	10.00
American Sweetheart, MacBeth-Evans, cereal bowl, 6" d, monax	15.00
American Sweetheart, MacBeth-Evans, cereal bowl, 6" d, pink	17.00
American Sweetheart, MacBeth-Evans, chop plate, 11" d, monax	17.00
American Sweetheart, MacBeth-Evans, creamer, monax	10.00
American Sweetheart, MacBeth-Evans, creamer, pink	12.00
American Sweetheart, MacBeth-Evans, creamer, red	85.00
American Sweetheart, MacBeth-Evans, cup and saucer, blue	150.00
American Sweetheart, MacBeth-Evans, cup and saucer, monax	12.50
American Sweetheart, MacBeth-Evans, cup and saucer, pink	21.00
American Sweetheart, MacBeth-Evans, dinner plate, 9¾" d, monax	25.00
American Sweetheart, MacBeth-Evans, dinner plate, 9¾" d, pink	40.00
American Sweetheart, MacBeth-Evans, dinner plate, 9¾" d, smoke	100.00
American Sweetheart, MacBeth-Evans, platter, oval, 13" l, monax	60.00

American Sweetheart, MacBeth-Evans, platter, oval
13" l, pink. 55.00
American Sweetheart, MacBeth-Evans, salad plate, 8" d,
monax 10.00
American Sweetheart, MacBeth-Evans, salad plate, 8" d,
red 80.00
American Sweetheart, MacBeth-Evans, sandwich plate,
12" d, monax 20.00
American Sweetheart, MacBeth-Evans, sherbet, 3³/₄" h,
pink 22.00
American Sweetheart, MacBeth-Evans, sherbet, 4¹/₄" h,
monax 20.00
American Sweetheart, MacBeth-Evans, sherbet, 4¹/₄" h,
pink 18.00
American Sweetheart, MacBeth-Evans, sugar, open,
monax 7.50
American Sweetheart, MacBeth-Evans, sugar, open, red 125.00
American Sweetheart, MacBeth-Evans, vegetable bowl,
oval, 11" l, pink. 65.00
Diana, Federal, bowl, 12" d, crystal, scalloped edge 7.00
Diana, Federal, bread and butter plate, 6" d, pink. 4.00
Diana, Federal, candy lid, crystal 11.00
Diana, Federal, candy lid, pink 24.00
Diana, Federal, cereal bowl, crystal 4.00
Diana, Federal, cereal bowl, pink 9.00
Diana, Federal, coaster, pink 10.00
Diana, Federal, cup and saucer, amber 8.00
Diana, Federal, dinner plate, 9¹/₂" d, pink. 15.00
Diana, Federal, fruit bowl, 11" d, amber. 17.00
Diana, Federal, salad bowl, 9" d, pink 20.00
Diana, Federal, sandwich plate, 11³/₄" d, amber 10.00
Diana, Federal, sherbet, amber 9.00
Diana, Federal, sugar, open, amber 8.00
Diana, Federal, sugar, open, crystal 4.00
Diana, Federal, tumbler, 9 oz, 4¹/₈" h, crystal 25.00
Florentine No 2, Hazel Atlas, berry bowl, 4¹/₂" d, crystal 11.00
Florentine No 2, Hazel Atlas, berry bowl, 4¹/₂" d, green 15.00
Florentine No 2, Hazel Atlas, berry bowl, 8" d, yellow 40.00
Florentine No 2, Hazel Atlas, bread and butter plate,
6" d, crystal. 4.50
Florentine No 2, Hazel Atlas, bread and butter plate,
6" d, green 6.00
Florentine No 2, Hazel Atlas, creamer, crystal 8.00
Florentine No 2, Hazel Atlas, creamer, yellow 14.00
Florentine No 2, Hazel Atlas, cream soup bowl, crystal 10.00
Florentine No 2, Hazel Atlas, cream soup bowl, green 15.00
Florentine No 2, Hazel Atlas, cup and saucer, crystal 9.00
Florentine No 2, Hazel Atlas, dinner plate, 10" d, crystal 9.00
Florentine No 2, Hazel Atlas, pitcher, cone ftd, 28 oz,
crystal. 27.00
Florentine No 2, Hazel Atlas, salad plate, 8¹/₂" d, yellow 7.50
Florentine No 2, Hazel Atlas, sugar, crystal 8.00
Florentine No 2, Hazel Atlas, tumbler, ftd, 5 oz, 4" h,
crystal. 12.00
Florentine No 2, Hazel Atlas, tumbler, flat, 9 oz, 4" h,
green 15.00
Jubilee, Lancaster, bowl, 3-ftd, 8" d, yellow 200.00
Jubilee, Lancaster, bowl, 3-ftd, 11¹/₂" d, yellow 250.00
Jubilee, Lancaster, cake tray, 2-handled, 11" d, pink 60.00
Jubilee, Lancaster, candlesticks, pr, pink 200.00
Jubilee, Lancaster, candy jar, cov, 3-ftd, yellow 300.00
Jubilee, Lancaster, cheese and cracker set, yellow 250.00
Jubilee, Lancaster, creamer and sugar, pink. 70.00
Jubilee, Lancaster, cup and saucer, yellow 15.00

Old Cafe, Hocking, olive dish, 6" l, pink, $7.00.

Jubilee, Lancaster, fruit bowl, handled, 9" d, yellow 125.00
Jubilee, Lancaster, fruit bowl, 11¹/₂" d, pink. 200.00
Jubilee, Lancaster, luncheon plate, 8³/₄" d, pink. 20.00
Jubilee, Lancaster, luncheon plate, 8³/₄" d, yellow 15.00
Jubilee, Lancaster, mayonnaise, underplate, and ladle,
yellow. 250.00
Jubilee, Lancaster, salad plate, 7" d, yellow 14.00
Jubilee, Lancaster, sandwich plate, handled, 13¹/₂" d,
yellow. 50.00
Jubilee, Lancaster, sherbet, 8 oz, 3" h, yellow 75.00
Jubilee, Lancaster, tumbler, ftd, 6 oz, 5" h, yellow. 100.00
Jubilee, Lancaster, vase, 12" h, pink 350.00
Old Cafe, Hocking, bowl, tab handles, 6¹/₄" d, pink 20.00
Old Cafe, Hocking, candy dish, low, 8" d, crystal. 7.00
Old Cafe, Hocking, candy dish, low, 8" d, pink 8.00
Old Cafe, Hocking, candy jar, ruby lid, 5¹/₂" h, crystal 18.00
Old Cafe, Hocking, cereal bowl, tab handles, 5¹/₂" d,
crystal. 9.00
Old Cafe, Hocking, cereal bowl, tab handles, 5¹/₂" d,
royal ruby 24.00
Old Cafe, Hocking, cup, pink 5.00
Old Cafe, Hocking, cup, royal ruby 9.00
Old Cafe, Hocking, dinner plate, 10" d, pink 52.00
Old Cafe, Hocking, olive dish, oblong, 6" l, crystal. 6.00
Old Cafe, Hocking, pitcher, go-with, crystal 18.00
Old Cafe, Hocking, pitcher, go-with, pink 60.00
Old Cafe, Hocking, saucer, pink 3.00
Old Cafe, Hocking, sherbet, pink. 15.00
Old Cafe, Hocking, sherbet, royal ruby 17.00
Old Cafe, Hocking, tumbler, 3" h, royal ruby 22.00
Old Cafe, Hocking, tumbler, 4" h, pink 22.00
Old Cafe, Hocking, tumbler, 4" h, royal ruby 24.00
Old Cafe, Hocking, vase, 7¹/₄" h, crystal. 10.00
Old Colony, Hocking, bowl, plain, 9¹/₂" d, pink 28.00
Old Colony, Hocking, bowl, ribbed, 9¹/₂" d, pink 30.00
Old Colony, Hocking, butter dish, cov, pink. 68.00
Old Colony, Hocking, candlesticks, pr, pink 270.00
Old Colony, Hocking, cereal bowl, 6³/₈" d, pink 25.00
Old Colony, Hocking, comport, cov, ftd, 7", pink 50.00
Old Colony, Hocking, comport, open, 7", pink. 25.00
Old Colony, Hocking, cookie jar, cov, pink 75.00
Old Colony, Hocking, creamer, pink 20.00
Old Colony, Hocking, cup and saucer, pink. 36.00
Old Colony, Hocking, dinner plate, 10¹/₂" d, open lace,
pink 32.00
Old Colony, Hocking, luncheon plate, 8¹/₄" d, pink. 23.00
Old Colony, Hocking, plate, 4-part, solid lace, 13" d,
pink 50.00
Old Colony, Hocking, platter, 5-part, 12³/₄" l, pink 35.00
Old Colony, Hocking, salad bowl, ribbed, 7³/₄" d, pink 40.00
Old Colony, Hocking, sherbet, ftd, pink 110.00
Old Colony, Hocking, sugar, pink 20.00

Old Colony, Hocking, tumbler, flat, 5 oz, 3½" h, pink **100.00**
Old Colony, Hocking, tumbler, flat, 9 oz, 4½" h, pink. **20.00**
Old Colony, Hocking, tumbler, ftd, 10½ oz, 5" h, pink **85.00**
Patrick, Lancaster, candlesticks, pr, yellow **150.00**
Patrick, Lancaster, cheese and cracker set, pink. **150.00**
Patrick, Lancaster, console bowl, 11" d, yellow. **125.00**
Patrick, Lancaster, creamer and sugar, pink. **150.00**
Patrick, Lancaster, fruit bowl, handled, 9" d, yellow **125.00**
Patrick, Lancaster, juice goblet, 6 oz, 4¾" h, yellow **75.00**
Patrick, Lancaster, mayonnaise, underplate, and ladle,
   ftd, yellow. **150.00**
Patrick, Lancaster, salad plate, 7½" d, pink. **25.00**
Patrick, Lancaster, tray, 2-handled, 11" l, pink. **70.00**
Patrick, Lancaster, tray, center handle, 11" l, pink **150.00**
Petalware, MacBeth-Evans, berry bowl, 9" d, cremax,
   brushed gold. **15.00**
Petalware, MacBeth-Evans, berry bowl, 9" d, crystal **7.50**
Petalware, MacBeth-Evans, berry bowl, 9" d, monax. **20.00**
Petalware, MacBeth-Evans, berry bowl, 9" d, pink. **20.00**
Petalware, MacBeth-Evans, bread and butter plate, 6" d,
   monax florette. **6.00**
Petalware, MacBeth-Evans, cereal bowl, 5¾" d, crystal **4.00**
Petalware, MacBeth-Evans, cereal bowl, 5¾" d, monax,
   red floral trim **40.00**
Petalware, MacBeth-Evans, cereal bowl, 5¾" d, pink **10.00**
Petalware, MacBeth-Evans, creamer, crystal **3.00**
Petalware, MacBeth-Evans, creamer, monax florette **14.00**
Petalware, MacBeth-Evans, creamer, pink. **8.00**
Petalware, MacBeth-Evans, cream soup bowl, pink,
   4½" d **12.00**
Petalware, MacBeth-Evans, cup and saucer, cremax, pas-
   tel bands. **18.00**
Petalware, MacBeth-Evans, cup and saucer, monax **8.00**
Petalware, MacBeth-Evans, cup and saucer, pink **20.00**
Petalware, MacBeth-Evans, dinner plate, 9" d, monax. **9.00**
Petalware, MacBeth-Evans, dinner plate, 9" d, pink. **12.00**
Petalware, MacBeth-Evans, mustard, metal cov, cobalt **10.00**
Petalware, MacBeth-Evans, platter, oval, 13" l, pink **15.00**

Petalware, MacBeth-Evans, salad plate, monax, fruit dec, gold trim, $10.00. Photo courtesy Ray Morykan Auctions.

Petalware, MacBeth-Evans, salad plate, 8" d, cremax,
   pastel bands **15.00**
Petalware, MacBeth-Evans, salad plate, 8" d, monax. **5.00**
Petalware, MacBeth-Evans, salad plate, 8" d, monax
   florette **10.00**
Petalware, MacBeth-Evans, salad plate, 8" d, pink. **5.00**
Petalware, MacBeth-Evans, sandwich plate, 11", cremax,
   pastel bands **30.00**
Petalware, MacBeth-Evans, sandwich plate, 11", monax
   florette, red trim **40.00**
Petalware, MacBeth-Evans, sherbet, ftd, low, 4", monax **30.00**
Petalware, MacBeth-Evans, sugar, cremax, gold trim **10.00**
Petalware, MacBeth-Evans, sugar, monax florette **10.00**
Pyramid, Indiana, berry bowl, 4¾" d, crystal **10.00**
Pyramid, Indiana, berry bowl, 4¾" d, green **20.00**
Pyramid, Indiana, bowl, oval, handled, 9½" l, crystal **25.00**
Pyramid, Indiana, creamer and sugar, crystal **20.00**
Pyramid, Indiana, creamer and sugar, pink. **30.00**
Pyramid, Indiana, creamer and sugar tray, crystal **25.00**
Pyramid, Indiana, creamer and sugar tray, pink. **30.00**
Pyramid, Indiana, pitcher, crystal **350.00**
Pyramid, Indiana, pitcher, pink **200.00**
Pyramid, Indiana, relish, 4-part, center handle, pink. **50.00**
Pyramid, Indiana, relish, 4-part, center handle, yellow **70.00**
Pyramid, Indiana, tumbler, ftd, 8 oz, green. **45.00**
Pyramid, Indiana, tumbler, ftd, 11 oz, pink. **50.00**
Pyramid, Indiana, tumbler, ftd, 11 oz, yellow **80.00**
Royal Lace, Hazel Atlas, bowl, 3-ftd, 10" d, pink **50.00**
Royal Lace, Hazel Atlas, bread and butter plate, 6" d,
   blue **12.00**
Royal Lace, Hazel Atlas, butter, cov, crystal **75.00**
Royal Lace, Hazel Atlas, creamer, blue. **50.00**
Royal Lace, Hazel Atlas, cream soup bowl, green. **30.00**
Royal Lace, Hazel Atlas, cup and saucer, crystal. **10.00**
Royal Lace, Hazel Atlas, cup and saucer, pink **20.00**
Royal Lace, Hazel Atlas, pitcher, 48 oz, crystal. **35.00**
Royal Lace, Hazel Atlas, salt and pepper shakers, pr,
   pink **60.00**

Old Colony, Hocking, relish plate, 3-part, 10½" d, pink, $25.00.

Windsor, Jeannette, bowl, handled, 8" d, pink, $18.00.

Royal Lace, Hazel Atlas, salt and pepper shakers, pr, crystal 40.00
Royal Lace, Hazel Atlas, sherbet, ftd, crystal 15.00
Royal Lace, Hazel Atlas, sherbet, ftd, green 25.00
Royal Lace, Hazel Atlas, tumbler, 5 oz, 3½" h, crystal 17.00
Royal Lace, Hazel Atlas, tumbler, 9 oz, 4" h, green 30.00
Royal Ruby, Anchor Hocking, bon bon, 6½" 7.50
Royal Ruby, Anchor Hocking, box, crystal bottom, ruby red cov 60.00
Royal Ruby, Anchor Hocking, coffee cup 5.00
Royal Ruby, Anchor Hocking, creamer and cov sugar, ftd 26.00
Royal Ruby, Anchor Hocking, plate, 9" d 10.00
Royal Ruby, Anchor Hocking, saucer 2.50
Royal Ruby, Anchor Hocking, sugar, open, ftd 6.50
Royal Ruby, Anchor Hocking, tray, 6 x 4½" 12.00
Royal Ruby, Anchor Hocking, tumbler, curved, 3¼" h 3.00
Royal Ruby, Anchor Hocking, tumbler, curved, 4¼" h 3.50
Royal Ruby, Anchor Hocking, tumbler, curved, 5" h 4.00
Royal Ruby, Anchor Hocking, vase, 9" h 15.00
Windsor, Jeannette, ashtray, green 45.00
Windsor, Jeannette, bread and butter plate, 6" d, green 9.00
Windsor, Jeannette, butter dish, cov, crystal 23.00
Windsor, Jeannette, cereal bowl, pink 26.00
Windsor, Jeannette, chop plate, 13½" d, crystal 10.00
Windsor, Jeannette, chop plate, 13½" d, green 40.00
Windsor, Jeannette, chop plate, 13⅝" d, pink 50.00
Windsor, Jeannette, creamer, crystal 5.00
Windsor, Jeannette, creamer, green 15.00
Windsor, Jeannette, cream soup bowl, 5" d, crystal 5.00
Windsor, Jeannette, cup, crystal 2.50
Windsor, Jeannette, cup, pink 11.00
Windsor, Jeannette, dinner plate, 9" d, pink 25.00
Windsor, Jeannette, fruit bowl, 12½" d, pink 150.00
Windsor, Jeannette, pitcher, 16 oz, 4½" h, crystal 20.00
Windsor, Jeannette, pitcher, 16 oz, 4½" h, pink 150.00
Windsor, Jeannette, pitcher, 52 oz, 6¾" h, pink 35.00
Windsor, Jeannette, powder jar, cov, crystal 15.00
Windsor, Jeannette, relish, divided, oval, 11½" l, crystal 15.00
Windsor, Jeannette, relish, divided, oval, 11½" l, pink 275.00
Windsor, Jeannette, salad plate, 7" d, green 30.00
Windsor, Jeannette, salad plate, 7" d, pink 15.00
Windsor, Jeannette, sandwich plate, 10" d, handled, crystal 7.00
Windsor, Jeannette, salt and pepper shakers, pr, green 55.00
Windsor, Jeannette, salt and pepper shakers, pr, pink 35.00
Windsor, Jeannette, saucer, crystal 2.50
Windsor, Jeannette, sherbet, pink 13.00
Windsor, Jeannette, sugar, cov, crystal 12.00

Windsor, Jeannette, sugar, cov, green 35.00
Windsor, Jeannette, sugar, cov, pink 40.00
Windsor, Jeannette, tray, 4 x 4", no handles, pink 75.00
Windsor, Jeannette, tray, 8½" x 9¾", handled, pink 30.00
Windsor, Jeannette, tumbler, 9 oz, 4" h, pink 20.00
Windsor, Jeannette, tumbler, 12 oz, 5" h, crystal 10.00
Windsor, Jeannette, tumbler, 12 oz, 5" h, green 50.00
Windsor, Jeannette, vegetable bowl, oval, pink 25.00

DINNERWARE

This is a catchall category. There are hundreds of American and European dinnerware manufacturers. Several dozen have their own separate listing in this book. It is not fair to ignore the rest.

This category provides a sampling of the patterns and forms from these manufacturers. It is designed to demonstrate the wide variety of material available in the market, especially today when individuals are buying dinnerware primarily for reuse.

References: Susan and Al Bagdade, *Warman's American Pottery and Porcelain,* Wallace-Homestead, Krause Publications, 1994; Jo Cunningham, *The Best of Collectible Dinnerware, 2nd Edition,* Schiffer Publishing, 1999; Jo Cunningham, *The Collector's Encyclopedia of American Dinnerware,* Collector Books, 1982, 1998 value update; Harvey Duke, *The Official Price Guide to Pottery and Porcelain, Eighth Edition,* House of Collectibles, 1995; Joanne Jasper, *Turn of the Century American Dinnerware: 1880s to 1920s,* Collector Books, 1996; Lois Lehner, *Lehner's Encyclopedia of U.S. Marks on Pottery, Porcelain & Clay,* Collector Books, 1988; Raymonde Limoges, *American Limoges: Identification & Value Guide,* Collector Books, 1996; Harry L. Rinker, *Dinnerware of the 20th Century: The Top 500 Patterns,* House of Collectibles, 1997.

Periodical: *The Daze,* PO Box 57, Otisville, MI 48463.

Castleton China, Castleton Rose, gold trim, bread and butter plate, 6½" d $5.00
Castleton China, Castleton Rose, gold trim, creamer 18.00
Castleton China, Castleton Rose, gold trim, cup and saucer 15.00

Castleton China, Castleton Rose, dinner plate, 10¾" d, $12.00.

International China Co, Marmalade. Photo courtesy International China Co.

Castleton China, Castleton Rose, gold trim, fruit bowl, 5⅝" d 7.50
Castleton China, Castleton Rose, gold trim, platter, oval, 15¾" l 50.00
Castleton China, Castleton Rose, gold trim, salad plate, 8" d 6.00
Castleton China, Castleton Rose, gold trim, sugar, cov 25.00
Castleton China, Castleton Rose, gold trim, vegetable, 9⅜" d 40.00
Castleton China, Dolly Madison, bread and butter plate, 6½" d 8.00
Castleton China, Dolly Madison, creamer 20.00
Castleton China, Dolly Madison, cup and saucer, ftd 15.00
Castleton China, Dolly Madison, dinner plate, 10¾" d 15.00
Castleton China, Dolly Madison, fruit bowl, 5⅝" d 10.00
Castleton China, Dolly Madison, gravy boat and liner 45.00
Castleton China, Dolly Madison, platter, oval, 16" l 50.00
Castleton China, Dolly Madison, salad plate, 8" d 10.00
Castleton China, Dolly Madison, sugar, cov 30.00
Castleton China, Dolly Madison, vegetable, oval, 11⅛" l 35.00
Crown Ducal, Bristol, bread and butter plate, 5⅞" d 4.00
Crown Ducal, Bristol, cup and saucer, oversized 12.00
Crown Ducal, Bristol, dinner plate 9.00
Crown Ducal, Bristol, gravy boat, attached liner 30.00
Crown Ducal, Bristol, platter, oval, 12¼" l 20.00
Crown Ducal, Bristol, salad plate 5.00
Crown Ducal, Bristol, vegetable, oval, 9" l 15.00
Flintridge China Co, Miramar, bread and butter plate, 6" d 6.00
Flintridge China Co, Miramar, coffeepot 55.00
Flintridge China Co, Miramar, cup and saucer 18.00
Flintridge China Co, Miramar, dinner plate, 10½" d 12.00
Flintridge China Co, Miramar, salad plate, 8½" d 8.00
Imperial China, Seville, bread and butter plate, 6⅝" d 2.00
Imperial China, Seville, chop plate, 12" d 12.00
Imperial China, Seville, creamer 7.50
Imperial China, Seville, cup and saucer, ftd 6.00
Imperial China, Seville, dinner plate, 10⅜" d 6.00
Imperial China, Seville, fruit bowl, 5½" d 3.00
Imperial China, Seville, platter, oval, 16⅜" l 18.00
Imperial China, Seville, salad plate 4.00
Imperial China, Seville, sugar, cov 7.50
Imperial China, Seville, vegetable, round, 9" d 12.00

International China Co, Marmalade, chip and dip 15.00
International China Co, Marmalade, creamer 5.00
International China Co, Marmalade, cup and saucer, flat 4.00
International China Co, Marmalade, dinner plate, 10¾" d 5.00
International China Co, Marmalade, gravy boat 7.50
International China Co, Marmalade, mixing bowl set 20.00
International China Co, Marmalade, pitcher, 7¼" h 12.00
International China Co, Marmalade, vegetable, cov, 9⅛" d . . . 15.00
Longchamp, Tulip, bread and butter plate 5.00
Longchamp, Tulip, chop plate 25.00
Longchamp, Tulip, coffeepot 40.00
Longchamp, Tulip, creamer 12.00
Longchamp, Tulip, cup and saucer, oversized 8.00
Longchamp, Tulip, dinner plate 12.00
Longchamp, Tulip, jug, 6⅜" h 20.00
Longchamp, Tulip, platter, oval, 13¾" l 25.00
Longchamp, Tulip, salad bowl, 10½" d 30.00
Longchamp, Tulip, salad plate 8.00
Longchamp, Tulip, sugar, cov 15.00
Longchamp, Tulip, teapot, cov 35.00
Longchamp, Tulip, tureen, cov 40.00
Mikasa, Margaux, bread and butter plate, 6½" d 3.50
Mikasa, Margaux, cereal bowl, 6⅝" d 7.50
Mikasa, Margaux, chop plate, 12⅝" d 12.00
Mikasa, Margaux, coffeepot 50.00
Mikasa, Margaux, creamer 10.00
Mikasa, Margaux, cup and saucer 6.00
Mikasa, Margaux, dinner plate 8.00
Mikasa, Margaux, salad plate, 8¼" d 5.00
Mikasa, Margaux, soup bowl, 9⅜" d 8.00
Mikasa, Margaux, sugar, cov 15.00
Mikasa, Margaux, vegetable, 10⅜" d 18.00
Mikasa, Silk Flowers, baker, rect, 12⅝" w 30.00
Mikasa, Silk Flowers, bread and butter plate 4.00
Mikasa, Silk Flowers, cake plate, 12¼" d 15.00
Mikasa, Silk Flowers, chop plate, 12¼" d 18.00
Mikasa, Silk Flowers, creamer 12.00
Mikasa, Silk Flowers, cup and saucer, ftd 10.00
Mikasa, Silk Flowers, dinner plate, 10⅜" d 8.00

Mikasa, Silk Flowers. Photo courtesy Mikasa, Inc.

Spode, Tower, dinner plate, 10⁵⁄₈" d, $12.00.

Mikasa, Silk Flowers, fruit bowl, 4⁵⁄₈" d	5.00
Mikasa, Silk Flowers, salad plate, 8¹⁄₄" d	5.00
Mikasa, Silk Flowers, salt and pepper shakers, pr	15.00
Mikasa, Silk Flowers, soup bowl, 8³⁄₈" d	7.00
Rosenthal, Classic Rose, creamer	15.00
Rosenthal, Classic Rose, cream soup and saucer	18.00
Rosenthal, Classic Rose, demitasse cup and saucer	10.00
Rosenthal, Classic Rose, dinner plate, 10¹⁄₂" d	12.00
Rosenthal, Classic Rose, fruit bowl, 5" d	7.00
Rosenthal, Classic Rose, pitcher, 7³⁄₄" h	30.00
Rosenthal, Classic Rose, platter, oval, 11" l	25.00
Rosenthal, Classic Rose, salad plate, 7⁵⁄₈" d	6.00
Rosenthal, Classic Rose, sandwich tray, 14¹⁄₈" d	30.00
Rosenthal, Classic Rose, sugar, cov	18.00
Rosenthal, Classic Rose, vegetable, 7¹⁄₂" d	20.00
Royal Worcester, Holly Ribbons, bread and butter plate, 6¹⁄₄" d	5.00
Royal Worcester, Holly Ribbons, cereal bowl, 6⁵⁄₈" d	10.00
Royal Worcester, Holly Ribbons, coffeepot	30.00
Royal Worcester, Holly Ribbons, cup and saucer	12.00
Royal Worcester, Holly Ribbons, dinner plate, 10³⁄₄" d	10.00
Royal Worcester, Holly Ribbons, fruit bowl, 5¹⁄₂" d	7.50
Royal Worcester, Holly Ribbons, platter, oval, 15¹⁄₂" l	20.00
Royal Worcester, Holly Ribbons, salad plate, 8" d	7.50
Royal Worcester, Holly Ribbons, soup bowl, 9¹⁄₄" d	14.00
Royal Worcester, Holly Ribbons, teapot	25.00
Spode, Bridal Rose, bread and butter plate, 6¹⁄₄" d	10.00
Spode, Bridal Rose, creamer	18.00
Spode, Bridal Rose, cup and saucer	18.00
Spode, Bridal Rose, dinner plate, 10¹⁄₂" d	20.00
Spode, Bridal Rose, platter, oval, 11¹⁄₄" l	30.00
Spode, Bridal Rose, salad plate, 7⁷⁄₈" d	16.00
Spode, Bridal Rose, sugar, cov	25.00
Spode, Mayflower, bread and butter plate, 6¹⁄₂" d	6.00
Spode, Mayflower, cream soup	25.00
Spode, Mayflower, cup and saucer	15.00
Spode, Mayflower, dinner plate	16.00
Spode, Mayflower, platter, oval, 15" l	45.00
Spode, Mayflower, salad plate, 7³⁄₄" d	12.00
Spode, Mayflower, soup bowl, 7³⁄₄" d	18.00
Spode, Mayflower, vegetable, 9¹⁄₈" sq	35.00
Spode, Tower, bouillon cup	8.00
Spode, Tower, bread and butter plate	5.00
Spode, Tower, cereal bowl	8.00
Spode, Tower, cream soup	15.00
Spode, Tower, cup and saucer, flat	10.00
Spode, Tower, double eggcup	12.00
Spode, Tower, fruit bowl, 5¹⁄₂" d	6.00
Spode, Tower, mug	10.00
Spode, Tower, salad plate, 7³⁄₄" d	8.00
Spode, Tower, sugar, cov	18.00

DIONNE QUINTUPLETS

Annette, Cecile, Emilie, Marie, and Yvonne Dionne were born on May 28, 1934, in rural Canada between the towns of Corbeil and Callander, Ontario. Dr. Dafoe and two midwives delivered the five girls. An agreement to exhibit the babies at the Chicago World's Fair led to the passage of "An Act for the Protection of the Dionne Quintuplets" by the Canadian government.

The Dafoe Hospital, which served as visitor viewing center for thousands of people who traveled to Canada to see the Quints, was built across the street from the family home. The Quints craze lasted into the early 1940s. Hundreds of souvenir and licensed products were manufactured during that period. Emile died in August 1954 and Marie on February 27, 1970.

Reference: John Axe, *The Collectible Dionne Quintuplets,* Hobby House Press, 1977, out of print.

Collectors' Club: Dionne Quint Collectors, PO Box 2527, Woburn, MA 01888.

Book, *Dionne Quintuplets Picture Album*, Dell	**$35.00**
Candy Box, Dionne Pops, Vitamin Candy Co, Providence, RI, 1936, 4 x 10¹⁄₂ x 1"	**135.00**
Doll, mohair wig, painted brown eyes, Madame Alexander, 1936, 7¹⁄₂" h	**275.00**

Fan, cardboard, Davies Funeral Chapel adv on reverse, 1939, 8¹⁄₄" w, $40.00.

Handkerchief, orig box, 9" sq, 1937 . . . . 25.00
Lamp Base, china, hollow, quints pictured seated in high chairs, with additional 2½" h brass bulb socket with electrical on/off depresser switch, ©1936 Leviton mkd on bulb socket, 6" h, 4" d 200.00
Magazine Advertisement Card, cardboard, newsstand promotion card from *Modern Screen* magazine, Jul 1936, color group portrait by Earl Christy, ©1936 NEA Service, 8½ x 11½" 50.00
Paper Dolls, *All Aboard for Shut-Eye-Town,* Colgate-Palmolive-Peet Co premium, orig mailing envelope, 1937 . . . . 75.00
Playing Cards, double deck, orig cellophane and box, 1936 . . . . 155.00
Radio, plastic, decals on front, Stewart-Warner 750.00
Sign, diecut cardboard, color group portrait of quints wearing pastel color dresses with balloon caption "It's the only soap we Quints use!," red lettering on white ground, Palmolive inscription in black on soft green bordered by simulated blue ribbon, c1937, 9 x 12" 75.00
Spoons, set of 5, SP, each depicting 2¼" h quint above her first name in vertical lettering, each in different pose, reverse shows her from back, possibly Palmolive Soap premium, Carlton, 6" l 75.00
Tray, china, "Souvenir of Callander," 2½ x 3" 100.00

DISNEYANA

The Disney era began when *Steamboat Willie*, Walt Disney's first animated cartoon, appeared on theater screens in 1928. The success of Walt Disney and his studio are attributed to two major factors: (1) development of a host of cartoon characters, feature-length cartoons, and feature movies enjoyed throughout the world, and (2) an aggressive marketing and licensing program.

European Disney and Disney theme park collectibles are two strong growth areas within Disneyana. Be especially price conscious when buying post-1975 Disneyana. Large amounts have been hoarded. The number of licensed products increased significantly. Disney shopping-mall stores and mail-order catalog sales have significantly increased the amount of new material available. In fact, products have been created to be sold exclusively through these channels. It is for this reason that many Disneyana collectors concentrate on Disney collectibles licensed before 1965.

References: Bill Cotter, *The Wonderful World of Disney Television: A Complete History,* Hyperion, 1997; Robert Heide and John Gilman, *Disneyana: Classic Collectibles 1928–1958,* Hyperion, 1994; Robert Heide and John Gilman, *The Mickey Mouse Watch: From the Beginning of Time,* Hyperion, 1997; David Longest and Michael Stern, *The Collector's Encyclopedia of Disneyana,* Collector Books (1992, 1996 value update); R. Michael Murray, *The Golden Age of Walt Disney Records, 1933–1988: Price Guide for Disney Fans and Record Collectors,* Antique Trader Books, 1997; Maxine A. Pinsky, *Marx Toys: Robots, Space, Comic, Disney & TV Characters,* Schiffer Publishing, 1996; Dave Smith, *Disney A to Z: The Official Encyclopedia,* Hyperion, 1996; Michael Stern, *Stern's Guide to Disney Collectibles, First Series* (1989, 1992 value update), *Second Series* (1990, 1995 value update), *Third Series* (1995), Collector Books; Tom Tumbusch, *Tomart's Illustrated Disneyana Catalog and Price Guide, Condensed Edition,* Wallace-Homestead, 1990, out of print.

Periodicals: *Storyboard Magazine,* 80 Main St, Nashua, NH 03060; *Tomart's Disneyana Digest,* 3300 Encrete Ln, Dayton, OH 45439.

Collectors' Clubs: National Fantasy Club For Disneyana Collectors & Enthusiasts, PO Box 19212, Irvine, CA 92713; The Mouse Club, 2056 Cirone Way, San Jose, CA 95124.

101 Dalmatians, push puppet, Pongo, orig box, Marx, 1961, 4" h. **$75.00**
Babes in Toyland, TV tray, litho tin, attached collapsible legs on underside, full color soldier illus on white ground, ©1961, 12¼ x 7" **45.00**
Bambi, bank, ceramic, painted and glazed ceramic, Leeds China Co, 1940s, 3 x 4 x 7¼" **45.00**
Bert the Chimney Sweep, toy, 2¼" h hard plastic Bert figure along with chimney base used to launch figure in air, Nabisco Honey Wheats premium, orig sealed cellophane bag, 1964 . . . . **50.00**
Cinderella, watch, chromed metal case with dial illus of Cinderella in blue and purple dress and purple clock tower, complete with 5¼" h plastic figure of Cinderella in blue and white gown with gold stars, orig cardboard illus box, Timex, c1958. . . . . **150.00**
Davy Crockett, box label, "Official Davy Crockett Indian Fighter Hat," glossy paper, c1955, 9 x 13" **175.00**
Davy Crockett, plate, white, center image of Davy and bear, c1955, 7" d. **20.00**
Disneyland, book, *Disneyland,* 72 pp, color photos, hard cover, ©1969, 9½ x 11". **50.00**
Disneyland, book, *Guide to Disneyland,* 28 pp, color photos, ©1964, 8 x 11½". **50.00**
Disneyland, brochure, Disneyland castle on front with "The Home of Disneyland," 4 x 9" **20.00**
Disneyland, magazine, *Family Circle,* Vol 53, #6, Dec 1958, 12 pp, "A Christmas Adventure in Disneyland" by Walt Disney and staff, full color illus, cov with Disney characters gathered around Christmas tree with Disneyland castle in background, 8½ x 11¼" **15.00**
Disneyland, mug, milk glass, "American On Parade," Spirit of '76 design with Goofy, Mickey, and Donald, Disneyland price sticker on underside, 1976, 4¾" h **20.00**
Disneyland, pencil holder, ceramic, Snow White's Doc wearing blue jacket, with red over-the-glaze paint on hat and hands, white base with Disneyland name in black, 2 x 2¼ x 4" **45.00**

Rug, cotton pile, late 1940s, 68" h, 106" w, $2,640.00. Photo courtesy Collectors Auction Services.

Disneyland, pennant, felt, "Disneyland '65/First Fabulous Decade," Disneyland castle illus, 8½ x 24" **20.00**

Donald and Mickey, comic book, Firestone premium, Christmas edition, ©1944 Firestone Tire and Rubber Co, 7¼ x 10¼" **100.00**

Donald Duck, book, *Walt Disney's Donald Duck*, #978, linen, color illus, 12 pp, Whitman, 1935 .... **100.00**

Donald Duck, container, Donald Duck Oats, cardboard, color paper label, front image of Donald holding cereal bowl, back with smaller images of Mickey, Minnie, Goofy, and Pluto, National Oats Co, c1950, 7" h **65.00**

Donald Duck, doll, stuffed, cloth body, oilcloth head, legs, and feet, complete with removable collar and hat, unmkd, 1930s, 5 x 6 x 13" **175.00**

Donald Duck, magazine, *Liberty*, Vol 17, #42, Oct 19, 1940, color cov with Donald in patriotic automobile with Liberty Bell and torch, American Eagle tied to hood, 2-page article by Groucho Marx, 8½ x 11¼" **25.00**

Donald Duck, paint box, litho tin, cov illus of Donald squirting nephews with trick camera, complete with unused paint set, mkd "Made In England By Page Of London," 1970s, 5 x 10 x ½" **20.00**

Donald Duck, pillow, stuffed, velvet-like finish front, plain reddish brown woven fabric back, image of excited Donald in starburst design, 1930s, 16 x 17 x 3½" **100.00**

Donald Duck, sand pail, litho tin, attached handle, wraparound scene of Donald as police officer as nephews speed by on tricycles, ©Ohio Art 1938, 5" h, 5" d **200.00**

Donald Duck, sheet music, *Der Fuehrer's Face*, from film *Donald Duck in Nutzi Land*, cov design of Donald hitting Hitler in the eye with tomato, reverse with brown and white victory symbol and Disney characters, ©1942, 4 pp, 9 x 12" **75.00**

Donald Duck, thermometer, ceramic tile with painted image of Donald as golfer, black text below, glass thermometer attached along right side on gold cardboard backing, reverse with orig cardboard backing with wall hanger tab and "Manufactured By the Kemper-Thomas Company," 1940s, 6 x 6 x ¼" **45.00**

Dopey, book, *Dopey's Christmas Tree*, department store premium, stiff newsprint, 16 pp, 1938, 8½ x 11¼" **100.00**

Dopey, mug, plastic, red, front decal, 1970s, 4¼" h **20.00**

Dopey and Grumpy, hair brush, brown wood brush, black bristles, attached aluminum panel with enameled paint design, ©1938 Hughes-Autograf Brush Co, Inc, 2 x 3½ x 1½" **45.00**

Dumbo, pitcher, ceramic, Dumbo with pink accent on ears, stomach, and cheeks, black accents and bright gold highlights, Leeds China, 1940s, 4 x 4½ x 6" **40.00**

Fantasia, salt and pepper shakers, pr, ceramic, Hop-Low, brown with black eyes, mkd "35," and "36" on bottom, Vernon Kilns, ©1941, 3¼" **175.00**

Figaro, cookie jar, ceramic, giant ball of yarn design, high relief image of Figaro with paw entangled in yarn, removable lid has second Figaro figure as handle, unmkd, 8 x 9 x 10" **65.00**

Geppetto/Lampwick, bowl, clear glass, character images and text in orange, 4¾" d **40.00**

Jiminy Cricket, figure, wood, foil sticker on front of base mkd "United Fund Campaign Award," Multi Products, 1940s, 2¼ x 3 x 5¼" **175.00**

Jiminy Cricket, sign, paper, "Jiminy Cricket! It's A Monstro Soda," float illus of Jiminy at left side, ©1939, 6 x 18" **100.00**

Jungle Book, drinking glass, "King Louie," ©1966, 4¾" h **45.00**

Mary Poppins, book, *Mary Poppins Tell-A-Tale Book*, 28 pp, Whitman, 1963, 5½ x 6¼" **10.00**

Mickey Mouse, book, *Mickey Mouse and the Magic Carpet*, Whitman, soft cov, ©1935 Kay Kamen, Inc, store premium, 3½ x 4" **200.00**

Mickey Mouse, book, *Mickey Mouse Recipe Scrapbook*, premium, front and back cov illus of Mickey, Minnie, nephew and Pluto, back cov with imprint of "Bamby Bread," int pages have repeated character designs around recipe areas where pictures cards can be attached, 48 pp, 1930s, 4¼ x 6¼" **100.00**

Mickey Mouse, eggcup, china, painted, Mickey pulling eggcup wheeled cart, mkd "Made in Japan," 1930s, 1¾ x 3½ x 3¼" **65.00**

Mickey Mouse, hand puppet, velvet, sateen hands, felt ears, oilcloth eyes, string whiskers, all black body, Steiff, 1930s, 10" h, missing ear button and cloth tag. **200.00**

Mickey Mouse, radio, solid wood, pressed wood composition panels on sides, each panel with high relief image of Mickey playing different instrument, attached metal plate on front bottom edge with raised text "Emerson Mickey Mouse," company metal panel attached to back, orig wiring and electric cord with plug, 1930s, 5 x 7¼ x 7¼" **1,000.00**

Mickey Mouse, roly poly, celluloid, figural, black and red, off-white face, 2¼" d, 4" h **100.00**

Mickey Mouse, toothbrush holder, bisque, movable arm, 1930s, 2¼ x 2¾ x 5⅛" **200.00**

Minnie Mouse, Dakin figure, poseable, vinyl, complete with diecut gold cardboard tag and plastic bag, c1970s, 7¾" h. **45.00**

Peter Pan, planter, ceramic, Peter Pan at open treasure chest, Leed China Co, c1953, 2½ x 4 x 4" **100.00**

Peter Pan and Captain Hook, dolls, hard plastic, movable arms and heads, sleep eyes, 6" h Peter in red outfit with gold belt, green felt hat, with metal sword, 7½" h Hook in black felt outfit with red belt and feather in hat, with metal hook hand and felt eye patch, Dutchess Doll Corp, 1950s **75.00**

Pinback Button, Minnie Mouse, red and black on yellow ground, 3" d, $7.00.

Minnie Mouse, bisque figure, hand painted, Japan, 1930s, 3¹/₂" h, $25.00.

DOG COLLECTIBLES

There are over 100 breeds of dogs divided into seven classes: herding, hounds, non-sporting, sporting, terriers, toy breeds, and working dogs. The first modern dog show was held in Newcastle, England, in 1859. The recording of bloodlines soon followed.

Unlike other animal collectors, dog collectors are breed specific. A Scottie collector is highly unlikely to own a Boxer collectible. In most cases, these collections mate with the breed of dog owned by the collector. Finally, dog collectors demand that the collectibles they buy closely resemble their pet. The fact that the collectible portrays a German Shepherd is not enough. It must remind them specifically of their pooch.

References: Edith Butler, *Poodle Collectibles of the 50's & 60's,* L-W Book Sales, 1995; Candace Sten Davis and Patricia Baugh, *A Treasury of Scottie Dog Collectibles,* Collector Books, 1998; Wanda Gessner, *Spaghetti Art Ware: Poodles and Other Collectible Ceramic,* Schiffer Publishing, 1998.

Newsletter: *Collieactively Speaking!,* 428 Philadelphia Rd, Joppa, MD 21085.

Collectors' Clubs: Canine Collectibles Club, 736 N Western Ave, Ste 314, Lake Forest, IL 60045; Wee Scots, PO Box 1597, Winchester, VA 22604.

Ashtray, dog and turtle on rect base, green glaze, Japan **$20.00**
Ashtray, dog seated on heart-shaped base, Japan, 2" h **15.00**
Badge, Texaco Scotties above "Listen," metal, pinback,
    3¹/₄ x 3¹/₄" **575.00**
Calendar, Setter mother and pups, "First Scent," salesman's sample, 1946, 30 x 44" **10.00**
Cigarette Box, Scottie dog finial, rect log-form base **25.00**
Figurine, "Laddie," collie, Robert Simmons, 4³/₄" h **20.00**
Figurine, Scottie dog, bisque, Roselane Sparkler, 4¹/₈" h. **12.00**
Lamp, poodle, ceramic, pink, paper shade **30.00**
Pez Dispenser, dalmatian. **20.00**
Planter, cocker spaniel and dog house, Shawnee **25.00**
Planter, dachshund, Weller, 8¹/₂" h **60.00**
Planter, pouncing dog, green and yellow gingham, Pryde
    & Joy label, Brad Keeler, 6¹/₂" l **25.00**
Planter, puppy, Red Wing **20.00**

Pinocchio, sand pail, litho tin, underwater scene of
    Pinoccio as donkey and Jiminy Cricket along with
    seahorse and fish, ©Ohio Art 1940, 4¹/₄" h, 4¹/₄" d **200.00**
Pluto, coloring book, unused, Whitman, 1971, 8 x 13³/₄" **25.00**
Pluto, salt and pepper shakers, pr, china, cork stoppers,
    black and red, ©1949 Leeds China Co, 3" h **20.00**
Snow White, book, *Snow White and the Seven Dwarfs,*
    #925, linen, color illus, 12 pp, Whitman, ©1938, 9¹/₂
    x 13". **50.00**
Snow White, mug, ceramic, colorful high relief image of
    Snow White holding bluebird, raised name in brown
    wood sign design on left, yellow handle, Enesco foil
    sticker on underside, 3³/₄" h **40.00**
Snow White, record set, "Selections From Walt Disney's
    Feature Production," 78 rpm, Decca, 1944 . . . . **40.00**
Three Pigs, pencil holder, wood, jigsawed wood front
    panel with attached wood block on back designed to
    hold 12 pencils, front image of Practical Pig in blue
    overalls on dark yellow base, blue reverse, unmkd,
    1930s, 1¹/₂ x 4 x 4" **45.00**
Three Pigs, plate, china, scene of Little Red Riding Hood
    playing organ as Practical Pig pumps the bellows,
    Fiddler the Fifer Pigs dancing holding their tails while
    Grandmother knits, Patriot China, 1930s, 7" d **75.00**
Walt Disney, sand pail, plastic, Spirit of '76 design with
    Goofy, Mickey, and Donald repeated design on sides,
    mkd "Made In Italy By Suci For Worcester Toy Corp,"
    1976, 5¹/₂" h, 7" d **75.00**
Winnie the Pooh, drinking glass, "Eeyore Has A
    Birthday," illus of Eeyore, Piglet, and Pooh in orange,
    white, and yellow, ©1965, 4³/₄" h **45.00**
Winnie the Pooh, salt and pepper shakers, pr, ceramic,
    3¹/₄" h Pooh and 3³/₄" h Rabbit, rubber stoppers, hard
    plastic tray with woodgrain design, "Famous Walt
    Disney Characters Salt & Pepper Set On Tray" foil
    sticker, Enesco, 1960s **100.00**
Zorro, candy box, "The Ghost of the Mission," from
    series of boxes featuring different black and white
    comic panel stories on back, Super Novelty Candy
    Co, 2¹/₂ x 3³/₄ x 1" **20.00**
Zorro, lunch box, emb metal, color illus, bright red sky
    design on front panel, Aladdin, 1966 . . . . **100.00**

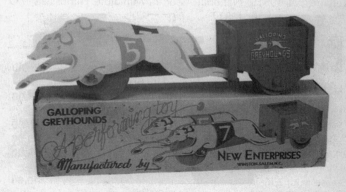

Pull Toy, Galloping Greyhounds, wood, orig box, $95.00. Photo courtesy Collectors Auction Services.

Ring Holder, figural puppy with tail up, white with
brown spots, Cleminsons, 2⁷/₈" h **10.00**
Salt and Pepper Shakers, pr, spotted dogs, Japan, 2³/₄" h **15.00**
Sign, dog's head, diecut tin, feed store adv, 24 x 17"....... **200.00**
Sign, dogs playing poker, "Let Dr. Daniels Be Your Friend
When In Need," cardboard, 14 x 18" **250.00**
Sign, woman and Saint Bernard, "Two Friends 2 Cigars
5¢," cardboard, 2-sided, 7¹/₂" d **600.00**
Toothpick Holder, blue dog, Japan..................... **20.00**
TV Lamp, poodle, chalkware, 1950s................... **40.00**
Valentine, puppy on pile of books, folding card, 1960s....... **1.00**
Vase, 2 Scottie dogs and vase on oval base, Diamond
Cleaners premium, c1925, 5" h **200.00**
Wall Pocket, cocker spaniel head, Royal Copley....... **20.00**
Watch Fob, Bull Dog Tobacco, metal, celluloid insert
with red bulldog image above "Won't Bite, Bull Dog
Cut Plug," 1³/₄" h................................ **185.00**

DOLL HOUSES & FURNISHINGS

Handmade doll house furniture falls into the realm of miniatures. Miniatures are exact copies of their larger counterparts. Depending on the accuracy of detail, material used, and recognition of the maker, these miniatures can quickly jump into the hundreds of dollars. Miniature collectors tend to look down on machine-made material.

Petite Prince, Plastic Art Toy Corporation, Tootsietoy, and Renwal are just four of hundreds of major manufacturers of machine-made doll house furniture. Materials range from wood to injection molded plastic. This furniture was meant to be used, and most surviving examples were. The period packaging and its supporting literature can double the value of a set.

References: Jean Mahan, *Doll Furniture, 1950s–1980s: Identification & Price Guide,* Hobby House Press, 1997; Dian Zillner, *American Dollhouses and Furniture From the 20th Century,* Schiffer Publishing, 1995; Dian Zillner and Patty Cooper, *Antique and Collectible Dollhouses and Their Furnishings,* Schiffer Publishing, 1998.

Periodicals: *Doll Castle News,* PO Box 247, Washington, NJ 07882; *Miniature Collector,* Scott Publications, 30595 Eight Mile, Livonia, MI 48152; *Nutshell News,* PO Box 1612, Waukesha, WI 53187.

Collectors' Clubs: Dollhouse & Miniature Collectors, PO Box 16, Bellaire, MI 49615; National Assoc of Miniature Enthusiasts, PO Box 69, Carmel, IN 46032.

DOLL HOUSES

2-Story, Jayline, 5 rooms, 1949 .... **$50.00**
2-Story, Marx, litho tin, 7 rooms, white clapboard on
multicolored stone, red roof, c1950s, 14 x 38".......... **85.00**
2-Story, Schoenhut, wood, shuttered windows, shin-
gled roof, Colonial style, 1930.................... **750.00**
2-Story, without window boxes, c1963................ **75.00**
2-Story, with window boxes, pink on white, 1959 .... **95.00**
3-Story, Fisher-Price, #0250, 5 rooms, spiral stair-
case, with 2 figures and instructions, late 1970s....... **40.00**
Bungalow, Rich, white, red roof, 4 windows, 2 chimneys, Arts & Crafts style, 1930s.................. **200.00**
Country Cottage, Wolverine, 1986.................... **45.00**

Garage, T Cohn, 1951........................... **145.00**
Little Homemaker Open House, Plasco, fiberboard....... **300.00**
Ranch, 3 rooms, c1967 .... **50.00**
Ranch, Plasco, 4 rooms, plastic.................... **100.00**
Ranch, Plasco, 5 rooms, plastic.................... **200.00**
Ranch, T Cohn, 4 rooms **45.00**
Spanish, T Cohn, 1948 .... **145.00**
Spanish, T Cohn, 1956 .... **75.00**
Split Level, 1959................................ **95.00**
Split Level, Marx, gray siding, yellow brick, white roof,
pool, door bell, complete with furniture **125.00**

FURNISHINGS

Baby, Acme/Thomas **$2.00**
Baby, Ideal **8.00**
Baby Bathinette, Renwal **15.00**
Baby Swing, Acme/Thomas, 3¹/₂" h................ **20.00**
Bed, Superior, 2¹/₂" l **5.00**
Broom, Renwal................................. **40.00**
Chest of Drawers, opening drawers, Jaydon, 2¹/₄" h........ **8.00**
Chest of Drawers, Superior, 3¹/₂" h **5.00**
Chair, Renwal, swivel action **10.00**
Club Chair, Ideal, 2¹/₄" h **15.00**
Club Chair, Plasco, 2¹/₄" h **8.00**
Club Chair, Renwal............................. **8.00**
Club Chair, Superior **5.00**
Cradle, Plasco.................................. **8.00**
Dining Room Chair, Jaydon....................... **2.00**
Father, Renwal, brown............................ **30.00**
Highboy, Plasco, 4¹/₂" h.......................... **8.00**
Ironing Board with Iron, Renwal **22.00**
Kitchen Chair, Ideal.............................. **5.00**
Kitchen Chair, Renwal............................ **3.00**
Kitchen Set, 7 pcs, Colonial style, chestnut wood, cup-
board, table, 4 chairs, 1" scale.................. **55.00**
Kitchen Stool, Renwal **8.00**
Kitchen Table, Ideal............................. **5.00**
Lamp Table, Renwal **8.00**
Living Room Suite, 13 pcs, Renwal, MIB **175.00**
Lounge Chair, Marx.............................. **5.00**
Mantel Clock, Renwal, paper dial **10.00**
Mother, Renwal, red **28.00**
Nightstand, Renwal.............................. **3.00**
Patio Table with Umbrella, Marx **15.00**
Piano with Bench, Jaydon **15.00**
Playpen, Renwal................................ **15.00**
Potty Chair, removable potty, Ideal................. **15.00**
Pump Sink, with 4 dishes, Allied Molding, MIB **45.00**
Radio, Renwal, 2¹/₈" h **8.00**
Refrigerator, Ideal, 3¹/₂" h........................ **15.00**
Refrigerator/Freezer, Princess Patti, Ideal, MIB.......... **150.00**
Seesaw, Acme/Thomas **15.00**
Sewing Machine with Cabinet, Ideal **18.00**
Sewing Machine with Cabinet, Renwal **30.00**
Sink, Ideal, 2¹/₂" h **15.00**
Sofa, Renwal................................... **15.00**
Table Lamp, Renwal **8.00**
Telephone, Renwal.............................. **22.00**
TV/Hi-Fi, Marx **5.00**
TV/Radio/Record Player Console, Mighty Mouse decal
glued to screen, Ideal **40.00**
Vanity with Bench, Plasco........................ **8.00**
Vanity with Bench, Superior, 3¹/₂" h **8.00**

DOLLS

The middle decades of the 20th century witnessed a number of major changes in doll manufacture. New materials (plastic), technology (injection molding), and manufacturing location (the Far East) all played a major role in revolutionizing the industry by the mid-1960s.

Hard, then soft plastic dolls dominated the market by the mid-1950s. Barbie arrived on the scene in 1959. The Cabbage Patch doll was the marketing sensation of the 1970s.

Doll manufacturers are quick to copy any successful doll. Horsman's Dorothy looked surprisingly like Effanbee's Patsy doll. Cosmopolitan's Ginger could easily be mistaken for Vogue's Ginny. Even with a single manufacturer, the same parts were used to make a variety of dolls. Barbie and her friends borrowed body parts from each other.

While condition has always played a major role in doll collecting, it became an obsession in the 1980s, particularly among collectors of contemporary dolls. MIB, mint-in-box, gave way to NRFB, never-removed-from-box.

More and more collectors, especially those under the age of forty-five, are focusing on 1950s and 60s dolls. Many values have doubled in the past five years.

References: J. Michael Augustyniak, *Thirty Years of Mattel Fashion Dolls,* Collector Books, 1998; Kim Avery, *The World of Raggedy Ann Collectibles,* Collector Books, 1997; John Axe, *Effanbee: A Collector's Encyclopedia, 1949–Present, Second Edition,* Hobby House Press, 1994; Carolyn Cook, *Gene,* Hobby House Press, 1998; Carla Marie Cross, *Crissy Family Encyclopedia,* Hobby House Press, 1998; Carla Marie Cross, *Modern Doll Rarities,* Antique Trader Books, 1997; Linda Crowsey, *Madame Alexander: Collector's Dolls Price Guide #24,* Collector Books, 1999; Maryanne Dolan, *The World of Dolls,* Krause Publications, 1998; Jan Foulke, *13th Blue Book of Dolls & Values,* Hobby House Press, 1997; Susan Ann Garrison, *The Raggedy Ann & Andy Family Album, 2nd Edition,* Schiffer Publishing, 1998; Cynthia Gaskill, *More American Dolls from the Post-War Era: 1945–1965,* Hobby House Press, 1996; Beth C. Gunther, *Crissy & Friends: Collector's Guide to Ideal's Girls,* Antique Trader Books, 1998; Beth Gunther, *Crissy Doll and Her Friends,* Antique Trader Books, 1998.

Patricia Hall, *Raggedy Ann and More: Johnny Gruelle's Dolls and Merchandise,* Pelican Publishing, 1999; Dawn Herlocher, *200 Years of Dolls,* Antique Trader Books, 1996; Judith Izen, *Collector's Guide to Ideal Dolls, Second Edition,* Collector Books, 1998; Judith Izen and Carol Stover, *Collector's Guide to Vogue Dolls,* Collector Books, 1998; Polly Judd, *Cloth Dolls of the 1920s and 1930s,* Hobby House Press, 1990; Polly and Pam Judd, *Composition Dolls: 1909–1928, Volume II,* Hobby House Press, 1994; Polly and Pam Judd, *Composition Dolls: 1928–1955,* Hobby House Press, 1991; Polly and Pam Judd, *European Costumed Dolls,* Hobby House Press, 1994; Polly and Pam Judd, *Glamour Dolls of the 1950s & 1960s, Revised Edition,* Hobby House Press, 1993; Polly and Pam Judd, *Hard Plastic Dolls I, Third Revised Edition,* Hobby House Press, 1993; Polly and Pam Judd, *Hard Plastic Dolls II, Revised,* Hobby House Press, 1994.

Michele Karl, *Composition & Wood Dolls and Toys,* Antique Trader Books, 1998; Sean Kettelkamp, *Chatty Cathy and Her Talking Friends,* Schiffer Publishing, 1998; Kathy and Don Lewis, *Chatty Cathy Dolls,* Collector Books, 1994, 1998 value update; Kathy and Don Lewis, *Talking Toys of the 20th Century,* Collector

Books, 1999; A. Glenn Mandeville, *Alexander Dolls Collector's Price Guide, 2nd Edition,* Hobby House Press, 1995; A. Glenn Mandeville, *Ginny: An American Toddler Doll, 3rd Revised Edition,* Hobby House Press, 1998; A. Glenn Mandeville, *Madame Alexander Dolls Value Guide,* Hobby House Press, 1994; A. Glenn Mandeville, *Sensational '60s Doll Album,* Hobby House Press, 1996; Ursula R. Metz, *Collector's Encyclopedia of American Composition Dolls: 1900–1950,* Collector Books, 1999; Marjorie A. Miller, *Nancy Ann Storybook Dolls,* Hobby House Press, 1980, available in reprint; Patsy Moyer, *Doll Values: Antique to Modern, Third Edition,* Collector Books, 1999; Patsy Moyer, *Modern Collectible Dolls* (1997), *Vol. II* (1998), *Vol. III* (1999), Collector Books.

Susan Nettleingham Roberts and Dorothy Bunker, *The Ginny Doll Encyclopedia,* Hobby House Press, 1994; Cindy Sabulis and Susan Weglewski, *Collector's Guide to Tammy,* Collector Books, 1997; Nancy N. Schiffer, *Indian Dolls,* Schiffer Publishing, 1997; Patricia N. Schoonmaker, *Patsy Doll Family Encyclopedia: Vol. II,* Hobby House Press, 1998; Patricia R. Smith, *Collector's Encyclopedia of Madame Alexander Dolls, 1965–1990,* Collector Books, 1991, 1997 value update; Evelyn Robson Strahlendorf, *The Charlton Standard Catalogue of Canadian Dolls, 3rd Edition,* Charlton Press, 1997; Dian Zillner, *Dolls and Accessories of the 1950s,* Schiffer Publishing, 1998.

Periodicals: *Doll Reader,* 6405 Flank Dr, Harrisubrg, PA 17112; *Dolls—The Collector's Magazine,* 170 Fifth Ave, 12th Floor, New York, NY 10010; *Doll World,* PO Box 9002, Big Sandy, TX 75755.

Newsletter: *Rags,* PO Box 823, Atlanta, GA 30301.

Collectors' Clubs: Cabbage Patch Kids Clubs, 1027 Newport Ave, Pawtucket, RI 02862; Chatty Cathy Collectors Club, PO Box 140, Readington, NJ 08870; Dawn Dolls Collectors Club, PO Box 565, Billings, MT 59103; Ginny Doll Club, PO Box 338, Oakdale, CA 95361; Ideal Toy Co Collector's Club, PO Box 623, Lexington, MA 02173; Liddle Kiddles Klub, 3639 Fourth Ave, La Crescenta, CA 91214; Madame Alexander Doll Club (company sponsored), PO Box 330, Mundelein, IL 60060; United Federation of Doll Clubs, 10920 N Ambassador Dr, Kansas City, MO 64153.

Note: For additional listings see Barbie, Kewpies, and Limited Edition Collectibles. Prices listed are for dolls in excellent condition, unless otherwise noted.

Advertising, Buster Brown, stuffed heavy fabric, printed
   color image front, black back, c1930, 13" h **$150.00**
Allied Imported, child, vinyl body, painted eyes, molded
   hair with ribbon, mkd "Allied Grand Doll Mfg Inc,
   1958," and "A," 10" h **20.00**
American Character, Betsy McCall, vinyl, rooted hair,
   blue sleep eyes, 20" h **240.00**
American Character, Eloise, cloth, yarn hair, Christmas
   dress, 1950s, 15" h **325.00**
American Character, Little Miss Echo, talker, 1964, 30" h . . . **200.00**
American Character, Preteen Tressy, plastic and vinyl,
   rooted hair with grow mechanism, sleep eyes, blue
   jumper, mkd "Am.Char. 63" on head, 14" h **50.00**
American Character, Puggy, composition, painted eyes,
   pug nose, mkd "Petite," 1920–31, 12" h **400.00**
American Character, Toni, hard plastic, walker, mkd
   "A.C. Amer. Char. Doll," street dress, 1958, 15" h **200.00**

Arranbee, Angel Skin, vinyl head, stuffed magic skin body and limbs, molded and painted hair, c1954, 13" h 100.00

Arranbee, Kewty, composition, molded hair, mkd "R&B," c1935, 10" h 100.00

Arranbee, Miss Coty, vinyl, mkd with "P" in circle, 1958, 10" h 75.00

Arranbee, Nancy Lee, composition head and limbs, open mouth with upper and lower teeth, 1934–39, 25" h 250.00

Arranbee, Sonja Skater, composition, "Debu-Teen" tag, 1945, 12" h 150.00

Artisan Novelty Co, Raving Beauty, hard plastic, jointed, sleep eyes, open mouth, 1953, 20" h 175.00

Averill Manufacturing Co, Harriet Flanders, composition, jointed, molded hair, painted eyes, mkd "Harriet Flanders/1037," 12" h 225.00

Beehler Arts Ltd, Princess Summerfall Winterspring, hard plastic, jointed arms, sleep eyes, glued-on black braided hair, early 1950s, 7½" h 100.00

Cameo Doll Co, Baby Mine, cloth and vinyl, sleep eyes, 1964, 19" h 80.00

Cameo Doll Co, Marcie, composition, painted hair and eyes, orig French-style outfit, molded and painted socks and shoes, 10" h 275.00

Cameo Doll Co, Miss Peep, vinyl, jointed shoulders and hips, 1960s, 15" h 30.00

Cameo Doll Co, Scootles, composition, sleep eyes, molded hair, 1930s, 21" h 500.00

Cameo Doll Co, Scootles, vinyl, jointed, molded and painted hair, orig cotton dress, matching bonnet, mkd "R7234 Cameo JLK," 8" h 425.00

Cosmopolitan, Little Miss Ginger, vinyl, rooted hair, sleep eyes, orig clothes, 10½" h 105.00

Eegee, Baby Luv, cloth and vinyl, mkd "B.T. Eeegee," 1973, 14" h 25.00

Eegee, Debutante, hard plastic, vinyl head, jointed knees, 1958, 28" h 50.00

Eegee, My Fair Lady, vinyl fashion body, jointed waist, 1956, 10½" h 40.00

Hasbro, Little Miss No Name, vinyl and hard plastic, jointed neck, shoulders, and hips, rooted hair, plastic eyes, real tears, mkd "1965 Hasbro," 15" h, $150.00.

Eegee, Susan Stroller, hard plastic, vinyl head, 1955, 20" h 35.00

Effanbee, Alyssia, walker, hard plastic, vinyl head, c1960, 20" h 150.00

Effanbee, Babyette, cloth and composition, 1946, 16" h 275.00

Effanbee, Betty Brite, composition, fur wig, sleep eyes, mkd "Betty Brite," 1933, 16" h 200.00

Effanbee, Dydee Baby, rubber body and ears, hard plastic head, c1935, 14" h 150.00

Effanbee, Happy Boy, vinyl, molded and painted hair and eyes, jointed, mkd "1960 Effanbee" on back of head and "Effanbee," 10" h 60.00

Effanbee, Howdy Doody, hard plastic head, cloth body, molded and painted hair, sleep eyes, orig cowboy costume with scarf, mkd "Effanbee," 19" h 325.00

Effanbee, Little Sister, composition socket head, shoulder plate, and hands, cloth body and limbs, embroidery floss hair, painted eyes, orig pink and white checkered blouse with pink skirt, 12" h 200.00

Effanbee, Lovums, cloth body, vinyl head and limbs, sleep eyes, rooted hair, 1980 .... 35.00

Effanbee, Patsy Ann, vinyl, jointed, rooted hair, sleep eyes, mkd "Effanbee Patsy Ann.1959," 15" h 200.00

Effanbee, Precious Baby, vinyl flange neck head, cloth body, rooted hair, sleep eyes, 1969, 21" h 90.00

Effanbee, Sugar Plum, vinyl flange neck head, cloth body, vinyl limbs, rooted hair, 1964, 18" h 60.00

Effanbee, Suzanne, composition, mkd "Suzanne," 1940, 14" h 225.00

Effanbee, Thumbkin, vinyl, cloth, rooted hair, mkd "Effanbee/1965/9500 UI," 18" h 90.00

Fisher, Ruth E, Grand-Daughter, bisque, jointed, brown glass eyes, painted oriental features, molded socks and shoes, sleeveless dress, mkd "REF," 1939, 10" h 230.00

Freundlich Novelty Corp, Baby with Scale, composition, jointed, molded and painted hair and features, wearing diaper, in basket on working scale, 9½" h 200.00

Freundlich Novelty Corp, General MacArthur, composition, fabric uniform, paper tag, early 1940s, 18" h 350.00

Georgene Averill, 19" h Raggedy Andy, $150.00; 15" h Raggedy Ann, $100.00.

Freundlich Novelty Corp, Goo Goo Eva, composition, cloth, mohair wig, celluloid floating disc eyes, flowered percale dress, matching bonnet, 15" h **195.00**

Goldberger, Dolly Parton, poseable, complete with orig box, ©1976, 12" h **30.00**

Hasbro, Little Miss No Name, vinyl, hard plastic, jointed, rooted hair, plastic eyes, burlap dress, 1965, 15" h . . **140.00**

hair, orig box, ©1971, 9" h **50.00**

Hasbro, Peace Series, vinyl, jointed, rooted hair, painted eyes, red, white, and blue pantsuit, mkd "6/Hong Kong/Hasbro/US Patented," 9" h **30.00**

Hasbro, Sweet Cookie, plastic, vinyl, rooted hair, painted eyes, freckles, dress with white pinafore with "Sweet Cookie" printed on front, 1972, 18" h **60.00**

Hasbro, That Kid, talking, plastic, vinyl, jointed, battery operated, rooted hair, sleep eyes, cotton shorts outfit, 1967, 21" h **140.00**

Hollywood Doll, Toyland Series, c1950, orig dress and box, c1950 . . . . **50.00**

Horsman, Ballerina, vinyl, jointed elbows, 1957, 18" h **30.00**

Horsman, Bye-Lo Baby, cloth and vinyl, 1972, 14" h **35.00**

Horsman, Little Miss Betty, stuffed vinyl body, vinyl head, rooted hair, sleep eyes, moded lashes, red and white dress, 1954, 8" h **20.00**

Horsman, Mary Poppins, vinyl head, plastic body, rooted hair, painted eyes, mkd "H," 12" h **45.00**

Horsman, Pippi Longstocking, vinyl, cloth, rooted and braided orange hair, painted eyes, 1972, 17" h **80.00**

Horsman, Rosebud, composition and cloth, wig, sleep eyes, 1928, 18" h **200.00**

Horsman & Company, Zodiac Baby, vinyl, jointed, rooted pink hair, black eyes, star-shaped dress and charm bracelet with zodiac signs, with "Your Individual Horoscope" booklet, mkd "Horsman Dolls Inc./ 1968," 6" h **15.00**

Ideal, Belly Button Baby, plastic, 1970, 9½" h **10.00**

Ideal, Betsy Wetsy, composition head, rubber body, c1940, 16" h **150.00**

Ideal, Betsy Wetsy, vinyl, 32" h **200.00**

Ideal, Growing Hair Chrissy, vinyl head, plastic body, rooted hair, 17½" h **120.00**

Ideal, Howdy Doody, cloth body, composition head, floating disc eyes, moving mouth, cowboy outfit, 1940s, 20" h **250.00**

Ideal, Mary Hartline, hard plastic, white dress, 1952, 14" h **350.00**

Ideal, Miss Revlon, vinyl, jointed, rooted hair, sleep eyes, 18" h **225.00**

Ideal, Plassie, hard plastic head, cloth body, latex limbs, sleep eyes, mkd "P-50/Ideal/Made in U.S.A.," 17" h **165.00**

Ideal, Pos'n Pete, vinyl, plastic, 1964, 7¾" h **30.00**

Ideal, Sara Ann, hard plastic, saran wig, mkd "P-90," c1955, 14" h **200.00**

Ideal, Sara Lee, black, vinyl head, cloth body, molded and painted hair, sleep eyes, mkd "Ideal Doll," 17" h **275.00**

Ideal, Saucy Walker, hard plastic, jointed, synthetic hair, sleep eyes, 15" h **145.00**

Ideal, Shirley Temple, vinyl, jointed, rooted dark blonde hair, fixed eyes with lashes, open mouth with painted teeth, mkd "©1972 Ideal Toy Corp. ST-14-H-213" and "©1972 Ideal 2-M-5534," 16¾" h **175.00**

Ideal, Sneezy, stuffed cloth, painted starched linen face, life-like beard, 10½" h **85.00**

Ideal, Toni, hard plastic, synthetic wig, sleep eyes, real upper lashes, 14" h, $450.00.

Ideal, Snow White, stuffed cloth, painted starched linen face, ©1937, 15½" h **200.00**

Ideal, Suzy Playpal, vinyl baby body and limbs, mkd "Ideal O.E.B. 24-3," 1960, 24" h **65.00**

Ideal, Thumbelina, vinyl head, cloth body, rooted hair, painted eyes, mkd "Ideal Toy Corp/©TT-19," 11" h **60.00**

Kenner, Baby Won't Let Go, plastic and vinyl, rooted blonde hair, painted features, mkd "4046 Taiwan K002 G.M.F.I. 1977–93" on head, "G.M.F.I. 1977 Kenner Prod." on back, 17" h **15.00**

Kenner, Baby Yawnie, cloth and vinyl, 1974, 15" h **10.00**

Kenner, Blythe, hard plastic head, jointed body, rooted hair, pull ring to make eyes turn color, orig "mod" style dress, high plastic boots, 12" h **50.00**

Kenner, Gabbigale, vinyl head, plastic body, jointed, rooted hair, painted eyes, pull string in chest, battery operated, orig red jumper, 18" h **55.00**

Knickerbocker, Annie, vinyl head, plastic body, rooted hair, painted eyes, orig red cotton dress with white collar, white socks, black shoes, 1982, 7" h **20.00**

Knickerbocker, Holly Hobbie, cloth, yellow yarn hair, printed features, dress and matching bonnet, 16" h **70.00**

Knickerbocker, Little House on the Prairie Child, vinyl, cloth, rooted hair, painted eyes, orig cotton dress, 12" h **35.00**

Knickerbocker, Orphan Annie, stuffed fabric, curly orange hair, painted facial features, fabric dress, miniature plush puppy in dress pocket, 15½" h **10.00**

Knickerbocker, Raggedy Ann, silk-screen printed face, red yarn hair, 15" h **95.00**

Knickerbocker, Sleeping Beauty, composition, vent right arm, 1939, 18" h **350.00**

Krueger, Pinocchio, cloth body, jointed wooden arms and legs, labeled "Authentic Walt Disney/R. G. Krueger," 15" h **475.00**

Louis Marx, Miss Seventeen, fashion body, blonde hair, painted features, mkd "US Patent 2925784, British Patent 804566, Made in Hong Kong," orig stand and box **200.00**

Madame Alexander, Princess Elizabeth, composition, sleep eyes, blue dress and high button shoes, pink pinafore, head mkd "Princess Elizabeth—Alexander Doll Co.," "McGuffey Ana" clothing tag, 1935–42, 24" h, $750.00.

Madame Alexander, Betty Blue, Alexander-Kins, Storybook Series, hard plastic, c1988, 8" h **60.00**

Madame Alexander, Dionne Quint, composition, toddler body, molded hair, sleep eyes, 1937–38, 11" h **250.00**

Madame Alexander, Flora McFlimsey, vinyl head, inset glass eyes, 1953, 15" h **400.00**

Madame Alexander, Gone With the Wind Scarlett, #1490, 1968–73, 14" h **125.00**

Madame Alexander, Kathy Baby, vinyl, rooted hair, 1954–56, 15" h **75.00**

Madame Alexander, Little Shaver, plastic, painted eyes, 1963–65, 12" h **225.00**

Madame Alexander, Netherland Boy, mkd "Alexander," 1976–89, 8" h **50.00**

Madame Alexander, Renoir Girl, Portrait Children Series, plastic, white dress with red ribbon, 1967–68, 14" h **250.00**

Madame Alexander, Southern Girl, composition, 1940 43, 12" h **400.00**

Mattel, Baby Beans, talking, vinyl head, bean bag body, rooted hair, painted features, pull-string talker, 11" h **18.00**

Mattel, Baby Colleen, talking, vinyl head, cloth body, rooted hair, painted blue eyes, pull-string talker, Sears exclusive, 14" h **30.00**

Mattel, Baby Go Bye Bye, vinyl head, plastic body, rooted hair, painted eyes, mkd "1968 Mattel Inc/Hong Kong," pull-string talker, 10" h **30.00**

Mattel, Chatty Baby, #326, talking, blonde, red pinafore, mkd "Chatty Cathy 1960, Chatty Baby 1961, by Mattel, Inc., U.S. Pat. 3,017,187, Other U.S. & Foreign Pats. Pend.," 18" h **80.00**

Mattel, Chatty Cathy, talking, plastic, long brunette hair, mkd "Chatty Cathy ©1960 Chatty Baby ©1961 By Mattel, Inc. U.S. Pat. 3,017,187 Other U.S. Foreign pats. pend. Pat'd in Canada 1962," 20" h **250.00**

Mattel, Cheerful Tearful, vinyl head, plastic body, rooted hair, painted eyes, 1965, 13" h **30.00**

Mattel, Cynthia, vinyl head, plastic body, rooted hair, painted features, battery operated, 20" h **60.00**

Mattel, Doug Davis, Spaceman, vinyl, molded and painted hair and features, mkd "Mattel Inc/1967/ Hong Kong," 6" h **45.00**

Mattel, Hi Dottie, vinyl head, plastic body, vinyl left arm, plastic right arm, rooted hair, painted features, plug in left hand to connect phone, 17" h **40.00**

Mattel, Julia, black, vinyl, rooted black hair, bendable, painted eyes, mkd "1966 Mattel Inc," 11½" h **240.00**

Mattel, Little Kiddle, Lolli Lemon, vinyl, rooted yellow hair, 2" h **45.00**

Mattel, Miss Beasley, talking, vinyl, cloth, rooted blond hair, painted features, black plastic glasses, pull-string talker, "Mattel Miss Beasley" on cloth tag, 16" h **60.00**

Mattel, Morton Salt Girl, stuffed cloth, yarn hair, yellow dress, 1974 . . . . **20.00**

Mattel, Shopping Sheryl, vinyl head, plastic body, jointed, rooted white hair, painted features, magnetic right hand, 1970, 14" h **30.00**

Mattel, Shrinking Violet, talking, cloth, yellow yarn hair, felt eyes, movable lids and mouth, pull-string talker, cloth label, 15" h **120.00**

Mattel, Sing-A-Song, talking, vinyl head, plastic body, rooted hair, painted eyes, pull-string singer, 17" h **55.00**

Mattel, Sister Small Walk, vinyl head, plastic body, rooted hair, painted eyes, molded-on socks and shoes, 11½" h **22.00**

Mattel, Tippy Toes, vinyl, plastic, rooted hair, painted eyes, battery operated, rides plastic tricycle, 1967, 16" h **40.00**

Mego, Farrah Fashion Doll, poseable, rooted hair, with stand and orig display window box, ©1977, 12¼" h **60.00**

Mego, Growing Hair Cher, poseable, complete with orig box and contents, ©1976, 12¼" h **75.00**

Mollye, bride, hard plastic, floss wig, sleep eyes, closed mouth, 1950s, 18" h **250.00**

Mollye, Raggedy Ann, cloth, red yarn hair, printed features, mkd "Raggedy Ann and Andy Doll Manufactured by Mollye Doll Outfitters," 15" h **350.00**

Nancy Ann Storybook, Debbie, hard plastic, school dress, 10" h **120.00**

Parker, Ann, Alice in Wonderland, sculptured resin, translucent, blond mohair wig, painted eyes, Sir John Tenniel-style outfit, walnut stand, mkd "Alice" on wrist tag, "English Costume Doll by Ann Parker," 8" h **275.00**

Remco, John Lennon, soft vinyl head, life-like hair, with guitar, ©1964 NEMS Enterprises Ltd., 4½" h **75.00**

Remco, Lindalee, cloth and vinyl, 1970, 10" h **12.00**

Remco, Orphan Annie, vinyl, rooted orange hair, plastic jiggle eyes, painted open mouth, fabric dress, mkd "Remco Ind. Inc. Copyright 1967," 15½" h **40.00**

Remco, Sweet April, vinyl, black, 1971, 5½" h **6.00**

Skookums, Squaw with Baby, wool blanket-stuffed body, mask face, wig, suede over wooden feet, 18" h **400.00**

Sports Kids, Inc, New York Mets, vinyl, jointed head, arms, and legs, wearing fabric hat, ©1987, 7¼" h **35.00**

Sun Rubber, So Wee, vinyl, molded hair, inset eyes, mkd "Sunbabe So Wee Ruth Newton New York" on head and "Sun Rubber 1957" on back, 10" h **65.00**

Tudor Games, Minnesota Viking, plush and felt with hard plastic purple helmet, holding football, "NFL Huddles" tag, ©1983, 8" h **15.00**

Uneeda, Baby Sleep Amber, black vinyl head, arms and legs, cloth body, rooted black hair, sleep eyes, mkd "Tony Toy/1970/Made in Hong Kong," 11" h **10.00**

Uneeda, Dollikins, vinyl head, hard plastic body, jointed, rooted hair, sleep eyes, pierced ears, mkd "Uneeda/25" on head, 12" h **60.00**

Uneeda, Freckles, vinyl head, hard plastic body, jointed,
rooted hair, jointed, orig nylon dress, 32" h **120.00**

Uneeda, Glamour Lady Bride Doll, vinyl head, hard
plastic body, jointed, rooted hair, sleep eyes, painted
and real lashes, orig bride gown with lace veil, 20" h **60.00**

Uneeda, Little Sophisticates, vinyl head, plastic body,
vinyl arms, rooted hair, closed eyes, 8½" h **10.00**

Uneeda, Tiny Time Teens, poseable vinyl head, plastic
body, rooted hair, painted features, mkd "U.D. Co.
Inc./1967/ Hong Kong," 5" h **20.00**

Vogue, Baby Dear, vinyl, cloth, rooted hair, painted
eyes, 1960, 13" h **60.00**

Vogue, Brickette, plastic body, vinyl arms and head,
jointed waist, rooted hair, 18" h **45.00**

Vogue, Ginny, vinyl head, plastic body, rooted hair,
sleep eyes, 1963, 8" h **60.00**

Vogue, Jill, hard plastic, jointed, sleep eyes, pierced
ears, mkd "Vogue" on head, and "Jill/Vogue Made in
U.S.A. 1957" on body, 10" h **165.00**

Vogue, Li'l Imp, vinyl head, walker body, jointed, orange
hair, sleep eyes, mkd "R & G" on head, 10½" h **60.00**

Vogue, Littlest Angel, vinyl, rooted hair, mkd "Vogue
Doll/1963" on head and back, 13" h **40.00**

Vogue, Posie Pixie, vinyl head, cloth body, rooted hair,
gauntlet hands, 17" h **45.00**

Webster, Mary Hortence, Flapper Doll, composition,
cloth, black wig, painted eyes, off-the-shoulder gown,
pearl necklace, 1925, 28" h **275.00**

Well-Made Toy Corp, Orphan Annie, yellow hair, paint-
ed facial features, fabric dress, orig box, ©1973, 7" h **12.00**

AUCTION PRICES – MADAME ALEXANDER

Sanford Alderfer Auction Company, Inc., Doll Auction, May 28,
1998. Prices include a 10% buyer's premium.

Abigail Fillmore, #1514, First Ladies Series, 3rd set,
1982–84 . . . . **$55.00**

Blue Boy, #1345, Portrait Children Series, 1972–83,
12" h **38.50**

Caroline Harrison, #1424, First Ladies Series, 4th
set, 1985–87 . . . . **93.50**

Fairy Godmother, #1550, Classic Series, 1983–92,
14" h **44.00**

Heidi, #1580, Classic Series, 1969–85, 14" h **38.50**

Iris, #1112, Portrettes, 1987–88, 10" h **30.25**

Josephine, #1335, Portraits of History Series, 1980–
86, 12" h **22.00**

Juliet, #1370, Portraits of History Series, 1978–87,
12" h **27.50**

Laurie, #1326, Little Men Series, 11" h **33.00**

Lord Fauntleroy, #1390, Portrait Children Series,
1981–83, 12" h **49.50**

Madame Alexander, #2290, 1984–90, 21" h **154.00**

Mark Antony, #1310, Portraits of History Series,
1980–85, 12" h **38.50**

Mary Todd Lincoln, #1517, First Ladies Series, 3rd
set, 1982–84 . . . . **77.00**

McGuffey Ana, #1525, Classic Series, 1977–86,
14" h **44.00**

Rhett, #1380, Portrait Children Series, 1981–85,
12" h **33.00**

Salome, #1412, Opera Series, 1984–86, 14" h **27.50**

Sargent, #1576, Fine Arts Series, 1984–85, 14" h **33.00**

Spain, Internationals, #595, 1973–85, 8" h **30.25**

United States, Internationals, #559, 1974–87, 8" h **22.00**

DOORSTOPS

Prior to the 1920s, the three-dimensional, cast-metal figural
doorstop reigned supreme. After 1920, the flat-back, cast-metal
doorstop gained in popularity. By the late 1930s, it was the dominant form being manufactured. Basement workshop doorstops,
made primarily from wood, were prevalent from the 1930s
through the mid-1950s. By the 1960s the doorstop more often than
not was a simple plastic wedge.

Crossover collectors have a major influence on value. Amount
of surviving period paint also plays a critical role in determining
value.

Beware of restrikes. Many period molds, especially those from
Hubley, have survived. Manufacturers are making modern copies
of period examples.

References: Jeanne Bertoia, *Doorstops: Identification and Values,*
Collector Books, 1985, 1996 value update; Douglas Congdon-
Martin, *Figurative Cast Iron: A Collector's Guide,* Schiffer Publish-
ing, 1994.

Collectors' Club: Doorstop Collectors of America, 2413 Madison
Ave, Vineland, NJ 08630.

Note: All doorstops listed are cast iron unless otherwise noted.

Apple Blossoms Basket, Hubley, 7⅝ x 5⅜" **$100.00**

Aunt Jemima, Littco Products, 13¼ x 8" **600.00**

Bennington Monument, 7¾ x 6½" **125.00**

Black Cat, Eastern Specialty Mfg Co, #62, 7 x 4½" **200.00**

Boston Terrier, 9⅝ x 11¾" **250.00**

Boy Wearing Tuxedo, wood wedge, 7¼ x 4⅜" **300.00**

Cocker Spaniel, mkd "VA. Metalcrafters, Waynesboro
VA Dream Boy 18–7 1949," wedge back, 9 x 7" **165.00**

Colonial Lawyer, mkd "Pat Applied For," Waverly
Studios, 9⅝ x 5¼" **460.00**

Colonial Woman, Hubley, 8 x 4½" **175.00**

Conestoga Wagon, #100, 8 x 11" **100.00**

Covered Wagon, Hubley, 9½ x 5⅛" **125.00**

Donald Duck, ©Walt Disney Productions, 1971, 8⅜ x
5¼" **175.00**

Dutch Boy, mkd "1275," Judd Co, 7½ x 6" **880.00**

**Windmill, emb
"6 Copyright 1926
by AM Greenblatt
Studios, Boston,"
$2,750.00.** Photo
courtesy Bill Bertoia
Auctions.

Dutch Girl, 6 x 3$^{3}/_{4}$" 150.00
Fawn, standing, #6, ©Taylor Cook, 1930, 10 x 6" 150.00
Fisherman in Boat, 6$^{3}/_{4}$ x 4" 175.00
Flower Vase, mkd "Hubley, made in U.S.A. 465," 10$^{3}/_{8}$ x 6$^{1}/_{8}$" 660.00
Fox Terrier, 8$^{1}/_{2}$ x 8$^{3}/_{4}$" 110.00
Fruit and Birds, 6$^{1}/_{2}$ x 5$^{1}/_{2}$" 150.00
Fruit Basket, Albany Foundry, 10$^{1}/_{8}$ x 7$^{1}/_{2}$" 275.00
German Shepherd, Hubley, 9$^{3}/_{4}$ x 13" 100.00
Gladiolus, mkd "489," Hubley, 10 x 8" 275.00
Horse, Hubley, 10 x 12" 100.00
House, mkd "cjo 1288," Judd Co, 8$^{1}/_{8}$ x 4$^{1}/_{2}$" 275.00
House with Woman, emb "Eastern Specialty Mfg. Co. No. 50," 5$^{3}/_{4}$ x 8$^{1}/_{2}$" 550.00
Hummingbird, 4 x 7" 200.00
Iris, mkd "469," Hubley, 10$^{5}/_{8}$ x 6$^{3}/_{4}$" 550.00
Lighthouse, 14 x 9$^{1}/_{4}$" 125.00
Li'l Bo Peep, 6$^{3}/_{4}$ x 5" 175.00
Malamute Dog, mkd "Copr. 1930, C. Co.," Creation Co, 7$^{1}/_{2}$ x 6" 660.00
Man with Cane, 18$^{1}/_{2}$ x 7" 450.00
Organ Grinder, 9$^{7}/_{8}$ x 5$^{3}/_{4}$" 275.00
Owl, Hubley, 10 x 4$^{1}/_{2}$" 175.00
Peacock on Fence, National Foundry, 13 x 7$^{3}/_{8}$" 200.00
Pelican on Dock, Albany Foundry, 8 x 7$^{1}/_{4}$" 200.00
Persian Cat, Hubley, 8$^{1}/_{2}$ x 6$^{1}/_{2}$" 125.00
Peter Rabbit, Hubley, 9$^{1}/_{2}$ x 4$^{3}/_{4}$" 350.00
Police Boy, 10$^{5}/_{8}$ x 7$^{1}/_{4}$" 350.00
Polly Parrot, Hubley, 8$^{1}/_{8}$ x 5$^{1}/_{4}$" 100.00
Poppy Basket, mkd "C.H.F. Co. E110," 10$^{1}/_{2}$ x 8" 600.00
Quail, Hubley, 7$^{1}/_{4}$ x 6$^{1}/_{4}$" 275.00
Rooster, 7 x 5$^{1}/_{2}$" 125.00
Scottie, mkd "Wilton Products Inc. Wrightsville PA," 7$^{3}/_{4}$ x 4$^{1}/_{2}$" 200.00
Ship, National Foundry, 10 x 12" 125.00
Stork, Hubley, 12$^{1}/_{4}$ x 7" 300.00
Swallows, Hubley, 8$^{1}/_{2}$ x 7$^{1}/_{2}$" 275.00
Swan, National Foundry, 5$^{3}/_{4}$ x 4$^{1}/_{2}$" 150.00
White Cockatoo, 11$^{1}/_{4}$ x 9$^{1}/_{2}$" 1,760.00
Whitehaired Fox Terier, Hubley, 10$^{1}/_{2}$ x 12$^{3}/_{4}$" 400.00
Windmill, AA Richardson, 8 x 5$^{5}/_{8}$" 125.00
Woman with Curtsy, mkd "1279," Judd Co, 8$^{1}/_{2}$ x 4$^{1}/_{2}$" 130.00

DRINKING GLASSES, PROMOTIONAL

The first promotional drinking glasses date from 1937 when Walt Disney licensed Libbey to manufacture a set of safety edge tumblers featuring characters from *Snow White and the Seven Dwarfs*. The set was sold in stores and used by food manufacturers for promotional product packaging. In the early 1950s Welch's sold its jelly in jars featuring Howdy Doody and his friends.

The first fast-food promotional glasses appeared in the late 1960s. Gasoline stations also found this premium concept a good trade stimulator. The plastic drinking cup arrived on the scene in the late 1980s. A decade later, they have become collectible.

A never-out-of-the-box appearance is the key value component for any promotional drinking glass, whether made from glass or plastic. Regional collecting preferences affect value. Beware of hoarding. Far more examples survive in excellent to mint condition than most realize.

References: Mark Chase and Michael Kelly, *Collectible Drinking Glasses, Second Edition,* Collector Books, 1999; John Hervey, *Collector's Guide to Cartoon & Promotional Drinking Glasses,* L-W Book Sales, 1990, 1995 value update; Barbara E. Mauzy, *Peanut Butter Glasses,* Schiffer Publishing, 1997.

Periodical: *Collector Glass News,* PO Box 308, Slippery Rock, PA 16057.

Collectors' Club: Promotional Glass Collectors Assoc, PO Box 3212, Post Falls, ID 83877.

All Star Parade, Big Bad Wolf and Three Little Pigs, Disney, 1939 . . . . . . $50.00
Columbine, light turquoise flower with white center, Boscul Peanut Butter 4.00
Creature of the Black Lagoon, Universal, 1960s, 6$^{5}/_{8}$" h 60.00
Davy Crockett, Boscul Peanut Butter, set of 9 . . . . . . 100.00
Freestate Raceway, Terrapin Stakes, Great Nero, Robert Myers, 1983 . . . . . . 5.00
Howdy Doody, Welch's, 1953, 8 oz 50.00
New York World's Fair, "Official Souvenir," 1939 . . . . . . 15.00
Pittsburgh Steelers, Superbowl XIII, Bradshaw, Webster, and Greenwood 5.00
Snow White and the Seven Dwarfs: Sneezy, Disney, 1942 . . . . . . 18.00
Superman, "In Action," 1964, 4$^{1}/_{4}$" h 30.00

AUCTION PRICES – GLASSES, PROMO

Collector Glass News Auction, October 15, 1998.

All Capp, Sneaky Pete's Hot Dog, Daisy Mae, mid-1970s $89.00
Broom Hilda, Sunday Funnies 165.00
Clarabelle Cow, Disney, 1942 . . . . . . 40.00
Dick Tracy, Domino's Pizza 183.00
Freehold Raceway, Raceway Fire, 1984 . . . . . . 20.00
Lady and the Tramp, Walt Disney, Peg, 1960s 55.00
Official Kentucky Derby, 1952 . . . . . . 176.00
Prince of Wales Stakes, Second Jewel of Canada's Triple Crown, 1984 . . . . . . 10.00
Spiderwoman, Marvel, Comics 218.00
Superman, Polomar Jelly, To the Rescue, gray and red, 1964, 5$^{3}/_{4}$" h 69.00
Wizard of Oz, The Wizard, ©S&Co, fluted bottom, 5" h 11.00
Wolfman, Universal Pictures, 1960s 85.00

Sourpuss and Gandy Goose, Terrytoons, 1940s, $386.00. Photo courtesy *Collector Glass News.*

DRUGSTORE COLLECTIBLES

Product type (e.g., laxative), manufacturer (such as Burma Shave), and advertising display value are three standard approaches to drugstore collectibles. Unlike country store collectors, whose desire it is to display their collections in a country store environment, few drugstore collectors recreate a pharmacy in their home or garage.

Emphasis is primarily on products from the first two-thirds of the 20th century. Few individuals collect contemporary chain drugstore, e.g., CVS, memorabilia. Dental and shaving items are two subcategories within drugstore collectibles that are currently seeing value increases.

References: Al Bergevin, *Drugstore Tins & Their Prices,* Wallace-Homestead, 1990, out of print; G. K. Elliott, George Goehring and Dennis O'Brien, *Remember Your Rubbers: Collectible Condom Containers,* Schiffer Publishing, 1998; Patricia McDaniel, *Drugstore Collectibles,* Wallace-Homestead, Krause Publications, 1994.

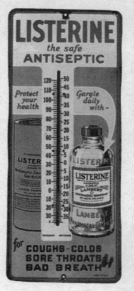

Thermometer, Listerine Antiseptic, porcelain, chips and scratches, thermometer broken, 30" h, 12½" w, $605.00. Photo courtesy Collectors Auction Services.

Absorbent Cotton, Supreme First Aid Co, box, red, yellow, white, and tan box, field workers on label, full unopened box. **$6.00**
Carmen Brand Latex Condoms, tin, round, 1⅝" **450.00**
Chariots Condoms, tin, Goodwear Rubber Co, 2⅛ x 1⅝" . . . **200.00**
Curity Medical Bandages & Supplies, display, plastic Miss Curity figure, c1950. . . . . **130.00**
Davol Anti-Colic Nipples, Davol Rubber Co, full box **4.00**
Derbies Condoms, tin, Killian Mfg Co, 2⅛ x 1⅝" **250.00**
Desitin Baby Lotion, bottle, orig blue and white box with blue, white, and red letters, 4 oz **8.00**
Dickinson's Witch Hazel, cardboard standup, 28 x 19½" **95.00**
Doan's Ointment, tin, round, flat, litho, 2" d. **12.00**
Drug-Pak Condoms, tin, #41, Nutex Sales Co, 2⅛ x 1⅝" . . . **350.00**
Duncan's Exone Cough Syrup, bottle, black metal lid, orig red and yellow cardboard box, 4 oz, ½ full **8.00**
Gensco Condoms, tin, Schaeffer Products Co, 2½ x 1¾". . . . **300.00**
Gillette Blue Blades, dispenser, metal, with key, 18" h, 7½" w. **140.00**
Hush Deodorant, The Gillette Co, Chicago, IL, made in USA, white plastic container, blue, white, and yellow cardboard box, 1959, 1.35 oz **10.00**
Ipana Toothpaste, Bristol-Meyers Co, New York, NY, tube, 4.6 oz **10.00**
Jergens Miss Dainty Talcum, tin, 4½ x 2½". **85.00**
Listerine Antiseptic, thermometer, porcelain, 10" h, 12½" w. **550.00**
Little Warrior Band-Aids, tin, Rexall, litho, 4 x 2¾ x 1". **10.00**
Luden's Cough Drops, sign, tin, 27 x 39" **170.00**
Maybelline Cream Mascara, Maybelline Co, Chicago, IL, clear plastic container, brush, and tube of cream on white card. **12.00**
Pepto-Bismol, sign, stand-up, turkey's head with "If the big bird bites back—Pepto Bismol!," brown, yellow, and red, 16 x 24" **30.00**
Playtex Bib-Smock, International Latex Corp, white, multicolored dots, clear plastic and cardboard pkg, 1956. . . . . **15.00**
Rexall, clock, "Products Of Tomorrow For Better Health Today," metal face and body, glass front, 12¼" d. **85.00**
Shaving Brush, Erskine, red plastic handle, animal hair bristles, 3¼ x 1⅜". **5.50**

Smith Blades, Smith & Smith, Inc, NY, 4 blades, orig 2 x 1 x ¼" orange and blue cardboard box, full box **3.00**
St Joseph's Vitamins for Children, Plough, Inc, clear glass bottle, orig 3⅝ x 1¾ x 1⅝" box, full bottle. **5.00**
Sweetlax, tin, flat, rect, litho **10.00**
Trojans Improved Condoms, tin, #20, Young Rubbers Corp, Inc, 2⅛ x 1⅝" **100.00**
Vicks Vaporub, sign, metal, litho, 10½ x 15½" **170.00**
Vitamins A & D Concentrated Capsules, brown bottle, blue and white label, blue lettering, 100 capsules. **5.00**
Water Bottle, Abbott Laboratories, round, clear glass, rubber stopper, emb measurements, no attachments **9.00**

EASTER COLLECTIBLES

Easter collectibles are the weak sister when it comes to holiday collectibles. The number of collectors is a far cry from those of Valentine, Halloween, or Christmas memorabilia.

Focus is primarily on objects related to the secular side of this important religious holiday. Rabbit (Easter Bunny), chicken, decorated eggs, and Easter baskets head the list of desired objects. While plenty of two-dimensional material exists, most collectors focus primarily on three-dimensional objects.

References: Lissa Bryan-Smith and Richard Smith, *Holiday Collectibles,* Krause Publications, 1998; Pauline and Dan Campanelli, *Holiday Collectibles,* L-W Books, 1997; H. N. Schiffer, *Collectible Rabbits,* Schiffer Publishing, 1990.

Banner, cotton, chicks and bunnies, embroidered, 1930 . . . . **$45.00**
Basket, cane and woven reed, pink, green, and natural, handle, grass filling, Germany, 8" h **15.00**
Basket, woven paper, grass, candy eggs, 1940 . . . . **35.00**
Basket, woven plastic, multicolored. **15.00**
Book, *Peter Cottontail,* 1940 . . . . **10.00**
Candy Box, lihto cardboard, square, bunnies and carrots **10.00**
Candy Container, chicken on nest, molded cardboard, candy eggs inside, 1940. . . . . **100.00**
Candy Container, chick pulling moss cov cart, hp egg, Japan, 1930s. **175.00**

Sheet Music, *Peter Cottontail,* Steve Nelson and Jack Rollins, 1950, $3.00.

EDWIN KNOWLES

In 1900 Edwin M. Knowles founded the Edwin M. Knowles China Company. The company's offices were located in East Liverpool, Ohio, the plant in Chester, West Virginia. Products included dinnerware, kitchenware, specialties, and toilet wares.

In 1913 the company opened a plant in Newell, West Virginia. Harker Pottery purchased the Chester plant in 1931. Knowles continued production at the Newell plant until 1963.

Collectors focus primarily on the company's dinnerware. Three of its popular patterns are: Deanna (introduced 1938); Esquire (1956–1962); and Yorktown (introduced in 1936).

In the 1970s the Bradford Exchange bought the rights to the Knowles name and uses it for marketing purposes as a backstamp on some limited edition collector plates. These plates are manufactured offshore, not in America.

References: Susan and Al Bagdade, *Warman's American Pottery and Porcelain,* Wallace-Homestead, Krause Publications, 1994; Harvey Duke, *The Official Identification and Price Guide to Pottery and Porcelain, Eighth Edition,* House of Collectibles, 1995; Lois Lehner, *Lehner's Encyclopedia of U.S. Marks on Pottery, Porcelain & Clay,* Collector Books, 1988.

Note: See Limited Edition Collectibles for collector plate listings.

Candy Container, rabbit, litho tin, 4" l 10.00
Candy Dish, egg, milk glass, 3 ftd, hp violets and gilt script "Easter" 25.00
Chocolate Mold, chick, hatching from egg, mkd "EPP 7123," 2" h 40.00
Chocolate Mold, rabbit, sitting on fence, dressed, holding basket and smoking pipe, tin, mkd "EPP 4808," 4¼" h 45.00
Chocolate Mold, rabbit, walking and carrying basket, tin, mkd "6629," 12½" h 150.00
Cookie Cutter, egg shape, tin 2.00
Decoration, bunny in basket of eggs, honeycomb, Beistle. 55.00
Display, cardboard, Easter bunny holding colored food dyes 25.00
Egg, blown milk glass, hp green and pink flowers and leaves dec, gold "Easter," 3½" h 30.00
Egg, celluloid, purple, Japan, 5" l 30.00
Figure, chick, celluloid, yellow and red, Japan, 1½" h. 15.00
Figure, rabbit holding carrot, white, cotton batting, "Made in Japan" paper label, 4½" h 45.00
Figure, rabbit wearing flowered hat, Kay Finch, 6" h 125.00
Greeting Card, "Hello There, A Happy Easter," Art Deco, dated 1932, 4" 7.00
Ice Cream Mold, Easter lily, pewter, c1920. .... 50.00
Nut Cup, figural basket, crepe paper, cardboard, cutout chick emerging from egg, 1930 .... 10.00
Planter, bunny and Easter egg, pink 12.00
Postcard, "Easter Greetings," Elvis Presley wearing gray tuxedo, red ground, unused 35.00
Roly Poly, rabbit standing on ball, purple costume, celluloid, Japan, 1920s. 50.00
Sheet Music, *Easter Parade* 10.00
Toy, egg, plastic, tin chick inside, 1950s. 40.00
Toy, hopping rabbit, plush-covered tin, windup, mkd "Japan," 5" h 60.00
Toy, wind-up, celluloid rabbit on litho tin tricycle, yellow and blue litho tin "Happy Easter" balloon attached to handlebars, rabbit and squirrel illus on wheels, Suzuki, Japan, 1960s, 2¼ x 3½ x 5" 50.00

Alice Ann, bread and butter plate, 6¼" d $2.00
Alice Ann, casserole 20.00
Alice Ann, creamer and sugar 12.00
Alice Ann, cup and saucer 5.00
Alice Ann, dish, 5½" d 2.50
Alice Ann, gravy boat 12.00
Alice Ann, plate, 10" d 10.00
Alice Ann, platter, 10" l 10.00
Arcadia, bowl, oval, 9" l 10.00
Arcadia, bread and butter plate, 6" d 2.00
Arcadia, casserole 25.00
Arcadia, creamer and sugar 12.00
Arcadia, cup and saucer 5.00
Arcadia, plate, 9¼" d 8.00
Beverly, bread and butter plate, 6½" d 2.00
Beverly, butter dish, open 15.00
Beverly, creamer and sugar 12.00
Beverly, cream soup cup 12.00
Beverly, cup and saucer 5.00
Beverly, eggcup, double 12.00
Beverly, sherbet. 10.00
Beverly, soup bowl, coupe, 8" 10.00
Beverly, teapot 25.00
Deanna, bowl, 10" d. 18.00
Deanna, bread and butter plate, 6¼" d 2.00
Deanna, butter dish, open, dark blue. 15.00
Deanna, chop plate. 15.00
Deanna, creamer and sugar 12.00
Deanna, double eggcup 10.00
Deanna, gravy boat. 12.00
Deanna, salad bowl, 9" d 15.00
Diana, bread and butter plate, 6" d 2.00
Diana, creamer and sugar 5.00
Diana, gravy boat 12.00
Diana, platter, 11" l 10.00
Diana, vegetable bowl, 9" 10.00
Esquire, bread and butter plate, 6¼" d 5.00

Esquire, cereal bowl, ftd, 6¼" d **10.00**
Esquire, compote, 7½" h, 12½" w **125.00**
Esquire, cup and saucer, Snowflower **22.00**
Esquire, jug, 2 qt. **85.00**
Esquire, platter, 13" l **25.00**
Esquire, vegetable bowl, divided, 13¼" **45.00**
Hostess, bread and butter plate, 6" d **2.00**
Hostess, creamer and sugar **12.00**
Hostess, cup and saucer **5.00**
Hostess, dinner plate, 9¼" d **8.00**
Hostess, soup bowl, 8¼" d **10.00**
Marion, creamer **8.00**
Marion, cup and saucer **5.00**
Marion, plate, 9" d **8.00**
Marion, plate, 10" d **12.00**
Marion, platter, 13¾" l **12.00**
Marion, vegetable bowl, 8¼" d **10.00**
Potomac, butter dish, open, 7½" l **15.00**
Potomac, chop plate **15.00**
Potomac, creamer and sugar **12.00**
Potomac, gravy boat with liner **20.00**
Potomac, platter, 13¼" l **12.00**
Roslyn, casserole **28.00**
Roslyn, creamer and sugar **6.00**
Roslyn, cup and saucer **6.00**
Roslyn, gravy boat **12.00**
Roslyn, platter, 13" l **12.00**
Sylvan, bread and butter plate **2.50**
Sylvan, cup and saucer **5.00**
Sylvan, dinner plate **9.00**
Sylvan, sugar **5.00**
Tempo, rose decal, bread and butter plate **3.00**
Tempo, rose decal, cup and saucer **7.50**
Tempo, rose decal, dinner plate. **8.00**
Tempo, rose decal, platter, 13¾" l **12.00**
Utility Ware, cake server **12.00**
Utility Ware, casserole, 7½" **20.00**
Utility Ware, casserole tray, 10" **10.00**
Utility Ware, leftover, 5" **10.00**
Utility Ware, mixing bowl, 8" **10.00**
Utility Ware, refrigerator jug, 3 pt **35.00**

Tempo, rose decal, fruit dish, 6⅛" d, $2.00.

Yorktown, bread and butter plate, 6½" d **3.00**
Yorktown, chop plate **20.00**
Yorktown, cup and saucer, orange-red **12.00**
Yorktown, custard **8.00**
Yorktown, dish, 6½" d **5.00**
Yorktown, gravy boat, round **15.00**

EGGBEATERS

Kitchen collecting is becoming specialized. A new collecting category often evolves as the result of the publication of a book or formation of a collectors' club. In this instance, eggbeaters became a separate category as the result of the publication of a checklist book on the subject.

Learn to differentiate between commonly found examples and those eggbeaters that are scarce. Novelty and multipurpose beaters are desired. American collectors are expanding their collecting horizons by seeking out beaters from Canada and Europe.

Reference: Don Thornton, *Beat This: The Eggbeater Chronicles*, Off Beat Books, 1994.

AD Foyer & Co, The Dream Cream Whip, 10" l **$40.00**
A&J, metal, "Beats Anything in a Cup or Bowl," 7½" l **15.00**
A&J, metal, Big Bingo, 11¾" l **15.00**
A&J, metal, Bingo No 72, 10¾" l **15.00**
A&J, metal, High Speed Center Drive, 11½" l **10.00**
A&J, metal, round dasher, "A&J Patented Made in USA,"
　13½" l **35.00**
A&J, metal, Super Speed A&J Spinnit Cream and Egg
　Whip, D-handle, 11½" l **30.00**
A&J, stainless steel, Super Center Drive, 11½" l **15.00**
Androck, red plastic coating on beater handle, red bowl **45.00**
Arthur Beck, Archimedes type, Artbeck Whip Beater, orig
　cardboard container, 12¼" l **35.00**
Aurelius, Master Egg Beater, 11½" l **300.00**
Aurelius, metal, wood handles, 11½" l **55.00**
Cassady-Fairbank Co, Chicago, Turbine Egg Beater, 10" l **25.00**
Cassady-Fairbank Co, Chicago, Turbine Egg Beater,
　paper clip bottom, 10" l **60.00**
Dazey Mix-er-ator, 10" h **20.00**
Edlund, plastic handle, 11¾" l **18.00**
EKCO, Flint Mixer Rhythm Beater, wavy blade **10.00**
EKCO, Mary Ann, 11¼" l **10.00**
EKCO, One Hand Beater, 10" l **7.00**
George E Alexander, Whipwell, 11" l **20.00**
Holister, Twin Speed Mixer, 11½" l **20.00**
KC USA, side fold-up handle, curly dasher, 7" l **160.00**
Ladd, #5, Ladd Ball Bearing Beater, tumbler model,
　11½" l **35.00**
Moore, Ram Beater, double disk dasher, 11¾" l **150.00**
SJ&H Dist Co, San Diego, CA, Zip Whip, 13½" l **45.00**
Standard Specialty, cast iron, green glass jar with tin
　screw-on lid, 12" h, 3⅞" d **75.00**
Taplin, Betty Taplin Egg Beater, red 6 oz plastic cup, 6" l **50.00**
Toy, Jr Mixer, push button ratchet, Japan, 5" l **10.00**
Turner & Seymour, Blue Whirl, wood handle, 12½" l **20.00**
Turner & Seymour, cast iron, Merry Whirl, 11½" l **20.00**
Turner & Seymour, metal, 8-hole center drive wheel, 11" l . . . **20.00**
Turner & Seymour, metal, Merry Whirl, 11½" l **15.00**
Ullman, cast and sheet aluminum, 10⅜" l **35.00**
VW Mfg Co, stainless steel, The Best, 11½" l **20.00**
Wallace Brothers, Bakelite handle, 11" l **20.00**

ELEPHANTS

In 1882 when P. T. Barnum bought Jumbo, a 13,000 pound African elephant, from the London Zoo where he resided for seventeen years and brought him to America, the country was swept with elephant mania. When Jumbo was struck by a railway locomotive and died on September 15, 1885, the nation mourned.

America's fascination with the pompous pachyderm dates back to the colonial period. Because of his size, the elephant was considered an exotic creature. Early owners exhibited their elephants in barns and other buildings, moving them at night so that few received a "free" look.

By the first part of the 20th century, most zoological parks featured one or more elephants. The tent circus further increased the pachyderm's visibility. Articles about elephants appeared regularly in periodicals such as National Geographic. Hunters donated record specimens to museums.

By the mid-20th century, the mystery surrounding the elephant disappeared. Elephants were commonplace. The elephant remains in the news today, largely due to the controversy over the excessive killing of elephants for their ivory tusks.

Newsletter: *Jumbo Jargon,* 1002 West 25th St, Erie, PA 16502.

Collectors' Club: The National Elephant Collectors Society, 380 Medford St, Somerville, MA 02145.

Baby Bottle, glass, emb elephant, wide mouth, 1930s,
8 oz **$30.00**
Bank, earthenware, unmkd, 6" h **8.00**
Bank, mechanical, cast iron, Hubley, c1930, 8½" l **400.00**
Bottle Opener, figural elephant sitting on hind legs, trunk
up, mouth open, cast iron, flat, pink, black base **100.00**
Box, ceramic, black figural elephant lid, white base,
Abingdon #608, 6" l **150.00**
Cache Pot, figural elephant, gray with red ears, Japan,
3½" h **20.00**
Carnival Chalkware Statue, 10 x 9" **30.00**
Cheese Cutting Board, elephant shape, cherry hard-
wood, 8 x 13" **85.00**
Clothes Sprinkler, ceramic, gray and pink, 6" h **35.00**

Doorstop, cast iron, raised "Davidson Co. 12" on back,
10¼" h, 11" w **200.00**
Dresser Vanity, figural elephant on triangular base, silvertone, powder, rouge, and lipstick compartments
inside, WB Mfg Co **150.00**
Figurines, 2 elephants playing, carved wood, ivory tusks,
toes, and eyes, 10" h, 13" w **200.00**
Figurines, elephant orchestra, 4 blue elephant figurines,
each playing different instrument, Japan, 2¾" h, price
for set **50.00**
Paperweight, figural elephant, blue, Cowan Pottery,
shape #d-3, mark #9, c1930, 4⅝" h **295.00**
Pinback Button, sq, "Bush Quayle 1992 GOP," black
and white cartoon elephant with black and white
Bush and Quayle photos against red ground, gold let-
tering accent, 2⅛" sq. **25.00**
Poster, "Jumpy? Those Who Keep Their Heads Over Little
Things Make The Biggest Headway, Size It Up And
Keep Cool!," elephant scared by mouse, orange, pur-
ple, brown, Mathes Co, Chicago, 1929. . . . . **225.00**
Powder Jar, figural Jumbo, pink glass, Co-Operative Flint. . . . **65.00**
Rocker Blotter, amethyst glass **85.00**
Salt and Pepper Shakers, pr, Ceramic Arts Studios **35.00**
Tape Measure, figural **30.00**
Teapot, figural elephant, luster glaze, wood handle,
Japan, 5¾" h **65.00**
Whiskey Bottle, Jim Beam, 1956 . . . . **30.00**

ENESCO

Enesco Corporation is a producer and distributor of fine gifts, collectibles, and home decor accessories. Enesco was founded in 1958 as a division of N. Shure Company. Following N. Shure's sale, the import division reorganized as Enesco, formed from the phonic spelling of the prior parent company's initials—N.S.Co. Originally based in Chicago, Enesco relocated it corporate offices to Elk Grove Village in 1975 and to Itasca in 1995. The company's international showroom, warehouse, and distribution facility remains in Elk Grove Village.

The Enesco product line includes more than 12,000 gift, collectible, and home accent items. Enesco markets licensed gifts and collectibles from well-known artists such as Sam Butcher (Precious Moments), Priscilla Hillman (Cherished Teddies and Calico Kittens), David Tate and Ray Day (Lilliput Lane), and David Winter (David Winter Cottages).

In 1983 Enesco became a wholly owned subsidiary of Westfield, Massachusetts-based Stanhome, Inc., a multinational corporation. In 1997 The Bradford Group entered into a long-term licensing agreement to market the product lines of Stanhome's subsidiary, Enesco Giftware Group. In 1998 Stanhome, Inc., changed its name to Enesco Group, Inc. Today, Enesco products are distributed in more than thirty countries.

Note: For additional listings see David Winter Cottages, Limited Edition Collectibles, Music Boxes, Prayer Ladies, and Precious Moments.

KITCHEN AND GIFT WARES

Cookie Jar, Betsy Ross **$225.00**
Figurine, moon girl, green **8.00**
Figurine, Penny the Dalmatian **55.00**

Planter, glossy gray, 8½" l, $10.00.

Precious Moments, mug, 1992, $5.00.

Figurine, turtle, yellow 3.00
Music Box, Mary Poppins, *Spoonful of Sugar,* 8" h 200.00
Napkin Holder, George Washington holding scroll "We
   the people of the United States," 5³/₄" h 20.00
Pencil Holder, ceramic, Mickey Mouse standing beside
   covered barrel holder, metal and plastic sharpener,
   label, 4¹/₂" h 28.00
Salt and Pepper Shakers, pr, Golden Girls, pink 16.00
Salt and Pepper Shakers, pr, Winking Cats 15.00
Spoon Rest, Snappy the Snail. 12.00

LIMITED EDITION COLLECTIBLES

Cherished Teddies, bell, Angel, P Hillman, 1992. . . . . $65.00
Cherished Teddies, figurine, Creche & Quilt, Nativity
   series, 951218, P Hillman, 1992 . . . . 50.00
Cherished Teddies, figurine, Hilary Hugabear, CT952,
   P Hillman, 1995 . . . . 75.00
Cherished Teddies, figurine, Timothy, "A Friend Is
   Forever," 910740, P Hillman, 1993, retired 1996 . . . . 45.00
Cherished Teddies, ornament, Bear in Stocking, 950653,
   1992. . . . . 50.00
David Winter Cottages, ornament, Christmas Carol,
   1991. . . . . 15.00
David Winter Cottages, plate, Cotswold Village, M
   Fisher, 1991 . . . . 30.00
Lilliput Lane, Lighthouse, Countryside Scene Plaques,
   D Simpson, 1989, retired 1991 . . . . 50.00
Lilliput Lane, St Nicholas Church, Christmas Collection,
   D Tate, 1989, retired 1990. . . . . 155.00
Lilliput Lane, Sweet Briar Cottage, Blaise Hamlet
   Classics, 1993, retired 1995. . . . . 150.00
Memories of Yesterday, figurine, Dear Santa, Charter
   1988 series, 115002, M Attwell 50.00
Memories of Yesterday, figurine, I Love My Friends,
   M Attwell, 1991 . . . . 35.00
Memories of Yesterday, figurine, Let's Be Nice Like We
   Was Before, M Attwell, 1989 . . . . 50.00
Miss Martha's Collection, ornament, Baby in Swing,
   421480, M Holcombe, 1992 . . . . 60.00

ERTL

Fred Ertl, Sr., founded Ertl, the world's largest manufacturer of toy farm equipment, in 1945. The company has licenses from most major manufacturers. Located in Dyersville, Iowa, Ertl also manufactures a line of promotional banks, promotional trucks, and toys ranging from airplanes to trucks.

Ertl makes many of its toys in a variety of scales. It also has a line of limited edition, highly detailed models designed for direct sale to the adult collector market. When researching an Ertl toy be certain you are looking in the right scale and quality categories.

Collectors' Club: Ertl Collectors Club, PO Box 500, Dyersville, IA 52040.

Note: All toys listed are in very good condition. Banks are in mint condition. See Farm Toys for additional listings.

Automatic Dump Truck, #3414, 15" l, MIB **$28.00**
Bank, #1667, 1913 Model T Van, red, blue trim, 1983 . . . . . . **75.00**
Bank, #2984UO, American Red Cross #6 Limited
   Edition, 1950 Chevy Panel, red, black trim, 1990 . . . . . . **45.00**
Bank, #9006, Big Bear Family Center, 1905 Ford
   Delivery Van, white, red trim, 1989 . . . . **30.00**
Bank, #9465, Terminix International, #1, 1913 Model T
   Van, white, orange trim, 1986 . . . . **45.00**
Bank, #9505, National Van Lines, #1, 1913 Model
   Model T Van, white, blue trim, 1986 . . . . **65.00**
Bank, #9617, Breyer's Ice Cream, 1905 Ford Delivery
   Van, cream, black trim, 1989. **45.00**
Bank, #9797, Southern States Oil, 1926 Mack Truck,
   gray, red trim, 1988. . . . . **50.00**
Eagle Car Carrier Semi, 23", MIB **16.00**
Ford 8N Utility Tractor, 7" l **35.00**
Ford TW-35 Tractor with Duals, 15" l **50.00**
John Deere Flat Bed Truck, 17" l **44.00**
John Deere Forage Wagon, 12" l **10.00**
John Deere Turbo Combine, 16" l. **16.00**
Oklahoma Crude Semi, 23" l, MIB **22.00**
Shopko Semi, 23" l **16.00**
Shoprite Supermarkets Semi, 23" l **22.00**
Star Train, semi and trailer, 25" l. **16.00**
Toys R Us Semi, 23" l **27.00**
Waterloo Boy Special Edition 1915–1919, 19" l **35.00**
Wonder Bread Semi, 23" l, MIB **27.00**
Zenith Semi, 23" l, MIB. **22.00**

Phillips 66 Truck and Tanker, pressed steel and plastic, 19¹/₂" l, $38.50. Photo courtesy Collectors Auction Services.

FANS, ELECTRIC

While hundreds of companies made electric fans, the market was mostly dominated by Emerson Electric, General Electric, and Westinghouse Electric. Other collectible manufacturers include Berstead Manufacturing, Hunter-Century Gilbert, Menominee, Peerless, Robbins & Meyers, and StarRite/Eskimo.

Montgomery Ward, Sears, Singer, and Western Electric never manufactured electric fans. They put their brand names on fans made by others. Polar Cub electric fans were made for the five-and-dime store trade.

Electric fan collecting came of age in the 1990s. Currently, the focus is primarily on desk fans made prior to 1960. The market for large ceiling fans, with the exception of those of unusual design, is still primarily reuse.

Reference: John M. Witt, *Collector's Guide to Electric Fans*, Collector Books, 1997.

Collectors' Club: American Fan Collectors Assoc, PO Box 5473, Sarasota, FL 34277.

REPRODUCTION ALERT: Beware of assembled fakes. Unscrupulous individuals assemble fictitious fans by using parts from several different fans. Buy only from sellers willing to provide a money-back, no-questions-asked guarantee.

Note: All fans listed are in excellent condition.

Emerson, 3150-B Seabreeze, non-oscillating, 1-speed, 1936, 10" $20.00
Emerson, 73668, cast-iron base and motor housing, brass blades painted gold, spot welded steel guard, 1928–29, 16" 100.00
Emerson, 94646-D, desk, cast-metal base, rounded blades, chrome-plated guards with bullet back, 2-speed push-in switch, 1959, 12". 15.00
Emerson, Emerson B-Junior, brass and black badge, scalloped Parker blades finished in flat black, 2-speed, oscillating, 1936, 10". 50.00

Emerson, Emerson Junior, cast-iron base and motor housing, painted gold blades, 1923, 8". 55.00
Emerson, Northwind, 444A, black and gold painted blades, 2-speed, universal AC/DC motor, 1926, 8" 30.00
General Electric, 49X714, pedestal, cast-iron base, metallic brown finish, 1-speed toggle switch, 1936, 12". 75.00
General Electric, Vortalex, FM10V41, sea green metallic finish, c1950, 10" 20.00
Gilbert, A-54, Art Deco style, cast-iron base, stamped steel elliptical shape motor housing, formed steel guard painted white, 2-speed, oscillating, 1940, 12" 135.00
Hunter/Century, chrome plated, 3-speeds, oscillating, c1948, 12" 50.00
R&M, 6000 Radio Fan, Art Deco style, cast-iron base, stamped steel guard, c1936, 10" 75.00
Westinghouse, 10-A-3 Power-Aire, 1940s, 10" 25.00
Westinghouse, 31575-A, stamped steel base and motor housing, plastic blades, 3-speed slide switch, oscillating, c1925, 12" 45.00
Westinghouse, 457680, desk, stamped steel base, blades, and motor housing, 3-speed slide switch, oscillating, 1924, 10". 25.00

FARM TOYS

Although there are pre–World War I lithograph tin toys with a farm theme, the cast-iron farm toys of the 1920s and 1930s are considered the first "farm toys." Arcade, Hubley, Vindex, and Wilkens are among the earliest manufacturers. Many of these early toys were horse-drawn.

Collecting farm toys became popular in the 1950s and 60s when miniatures by Brubaker, Peterson, and White became available and collectors turned their attention to real tractors. In the late 1950s and 60s, Ertl issued farm toys based upon brand name products such as Allis-Chalmers, Case, John Deere, International, Minneapolis-Moline, Massey-Ferguson, and Oliver.

Claire Scheibe founded the National Farm Toy Show in 1978 in Dyersville, Iowa, home of Ertl and Scale Models. Annual attendance now exceeds 15,000. In addition, over 100 regional farm toy shows are held each year throughout America, with a heavy concentration in the Midwest and Plains states.

Collectors differentiate between industrial models, i.e., highly detailed display models, and toys, objects made specifically for play. Both are collected but the primary emphasis is on toys. Recently, several manufacturers introduced collector model series. These are often as fully detailed as industrial models, and are meant to be displayed. The collector model secondary market is highly speculative at this time.

References: Richard Sonneck, *Dick's Farm Toy Price Guide & Check List*, published by author, 1990; Bill Vossler, *Toy Farm Tractors*, Voyageur Press, 1998.

Periodicals: *Toy Farmer*, 7496 106th Ave SE, Lamoure, ND 58458; *The Toy Tractor Times*, RR3 Box 112-A, Osage, IA 50461.

Collectors' Clubs: Antique Engine, Tractor & Toy Club, 5731 Paradise Rd, Slatington, PA 18080; CTM Farm Toy Collectors Club, PO Box 489, Rocanville, Saskatchewan, S0A 3L0 Canada; Farm Toy Collectors Club, PO Box 38, Boxholm, IA 50040.

General Electric #C83075, 110 volts, cast iron and metal, 16¹/₂" h, $350.00. Photo courtesy Collectors Auction Services.

Note: All toys are in mint condition in their original box. See Ertl for additional listings.

MINIATURES

Agco Allis Tractor, Model 9650, diecast, "Louisville Farm Show," Scale M, stock #FB2363, 1995, 1/16 . . . . **$50.00**

Allis-Chalmers Combine, Model 72 pull type, sand cast aluminum, Baird, 1990, 1/16, limited to 100 . . . . **175.00**

Allis-Chalmers Combine/Gleaner, diecast, open reel supports, fixed head, Ertl, stock #195, 1966, 1/32 . . . . **300.00**

Allis-Chalmers Crawler, Model HD-5, plastic, adjustable blade, Product Miniature, 1955, 1/16 . . . . **580.00**

Allis-Chalmers Scraper-Pan, plastic, orange, Lionel, 1950, 1/48 . . . . **250.00**

Allis-Chalmers Tractor, Model D-21, Series II, diecast, Ertl, stock #1283DO, 1990, 1/16 . . . . **45.00**

Allis-Chalmers Tractor, Model WC, 1940, cast iron, nickel driver, narrow front, Arcade, 7³/₈" l **1,750.00**

Allis-Chalmers Tractor, Model WC, cast iron, painted driver, narrow front, Hubley, 1939, 7" **1,250.00**

Case Agri King, Model 1070, diecast, Ertl, 1969, 1/16 . . . . . **650.00**

Case Tractor, Model SC, plastic, with fenders, narrow front, Monarch Plastics, 1951, 1/16 . . . . **525.00**

Cat Crawler, Model 10, cast iron, steel track plated drive, closed engine, gray, Arcade, 1932, 7¹/₂" **3,000.00**

Cat Grader, plastic, Revell, 1950, 1/24 . . . . **100.00**

Farmhand Hay Stacker, mounted on "M" Farmall, diecast, Scale M, 1985, 1/16 . . . . **225.00**

Ford Post Hole Digger, sand cast aluminum, 3 point, fits 1961, red, Hubley, 1956, 1/12 . . . . **350.00**

Ford Tractor, Model 8-N, diecast, Tootsietoy, 1950s, 1/32 . . . . . **90.00**

International Harvester Disc, pressed steel, 4 gang, no wheels, red, Carter, 1950, 1/16 . . . . **200.00**

International Harvester Tractor, 1917 International Model 8-16, sand cast aluminum, Ebersol, 1984, 1/16 . . . . **45.00**

International Harvester Tractor, Model M, diecast, "Hubley" in raised letters, 1952, 1/12 . . . . **150.00**

John Deere Grain Drill, pressed steel, yellow lids, silver disc openers, Carter, 1960, 1/16 . . . . **500.00**

John Deere Wagon, wood flare box on cast-iron gear, Arcade, 1940, 1/16 . . . . **750.00**

Kenton Ditching Machine, cast iron, 1935 . . . . **1,200.00**

Kubota Lawn and Garden Tractor, Model L-175, diecast, detachable rear rototiller, Japan, 1976, 1/16 . . . . **55.00**

Farmall Pedal Tractor, cast metal, red, 21" h, $1,320.00. Photo courtesy Collectors Auction Services.

Massey Ferguson Cab Tractor, Model 595, diecast, Britains, 1978, 1/32 . . . . **12.00**

Massey Harris Challenger, cast iron, spoke wheels, Bob Gray, 1971, 1/12 . . . . **35.00**

Oliver Tractor, Model 70, cast iron, red, narrow front, all rubber wheels, with driver, Arcade, 1940, 5¹/₂" **300.00**

Scotts Lawn and Garden Tractor, Tonka, 1/16 . . . . **30.00**

PEDAL TRACTORS

Allis-Chalmers Tractor, Model D-14, sand cast aluminum, Eska, 1957, 38" **$1,200.00**

Massey Harris Trailer, for pedal tractor, pressed steel, 2 wheels, straight sided fenders, 1960 . . . . **350.00**

White Tractor with Wagon, diecast, silver colored, Ertl, 1991 . . . . **300.00**

FAST-FOOD COLLECTIBLES

McDonald's dominates the field. In fact, it has become so important that it has its own category. If you have a McDonald's fast-food collectible, look under "M."

Each year dozens of new fast-food franchises are launched. Each year dozens of fast-food franchises fail. Collectors focus primarily on collectibles from those which have achieved national success. National fast-food chains do regional promotions. Collectors' club newsletters are the best way to keep up with these and the premiums that result.

All the major fast-food franchises have gone international. Collectors also are hopping aboard the international bandwagon. Many American collections now contain examples from abroad.

References: Ken Clee and Susan Hufferd, *Tomart's Price Guide to Kid's Meal Collectibles (Non-McDonald's)*, Tomart Publications, 1994; Gail Pope and Keith Hammond, *Fast Food Toys, 3rd Edition*, Schiffer Publishing, 1999; Joyce and Terry Losonsky, *The Encyclopedia of Fast Food Toys, 2 Vols.*, Schiffer Publishing, 1999; Robert J. Sodaro and Alex G. Malloy, *Kiddie Meal Collectibles*, Antique Trader Books, 1998.

Arby's, Babar's Wristpack, vinyl, 1992 . . . . **$3.00**

Arby's, box, Who's Kitten Who?, Looney Tunes series, 1987 . . . . **5.00**

Arby's, bucket, Babar's Bucket of Fun series, school or ghosts theme, 1992 . . . . **5.00**

Arby's, figure, Mr Daydream, Adventures of Mr Men & Little Miss series, 1981 . . . . **4.00**

Arby's, figure, Pepe Le Pew, Looney Tunes, 1987, 2" h **10.00**

Arby's, finger puppet, Babar's World Tour Finger Puppets series, 1990/1993 . . . . **2.00**

Arby's, mug, Yogi & Friends series, 1994 . . . . **3.00**

Arby's, pencil topper, Looney Tunes characters, 1988 . . . . **5.00**

Big Boy, box, Outer Space **4.00**

Big Boy, bucket and shovel, white plastic bucket with scene of Big Boy as underwater diver, red handle, blue plastic shovel, 1992 . . . . **3.00**

Big Boy, Colorforms book, 1992 . . . . **4.00**

Big Boy, figure, race car driver, 1990 . . . . **4.00**

Big Boy, yo-yo, pink, green, or yellow, 1992 . . . . **3.00**

Burger Chef, box, Land Speeder, Star Wars Funmeal series, 1978 . . . . **20.00**

Burger Chef, flying disk, red, 8¹/₂" d **5.00**

Burger Chef, mask, Martian Monster **15.00**

Burger King, activity book, *The Wild West*, heavy cardboard, punch-out handle, Western Publishing, 1985, 6 x 12" 4.00

Burger King, ball, rubber, Nerfuls series, 1989 . . . . 3.00

Burger King, beach ball, Pinnochio series, 1988 . . . . 3.00

Burger King, book, *Ice Escapades*, Purrtenders series, 1988 . . . . 5.00

Burger King, box, Chipmunk Adventure series, 1987 . . . . 6.00

Burger King, bracelet, Barnyard Commandos Commando Cuffs series, 1991 . . . . 2.00

Burger King, bucket, Halloween theme, glow-in-the-dark, 1988 . . . . 3.00

Burger King, calculator disk, Wizard of Fries series, 1981 . . . . . 4.00

Burger King, cassette tape, Christmas Sing-A-Long, 1989 . . . . . 5.00

Burger King, coloring book, Crayola Coloring Mystery Set, 1990 . . . . 3.00

Burger King, cup, plastic, Masters of the Universe series, 1985 . . . . 5.00

Burger King, doorknob card, Alf series, 1987 . . . . 4.00

Burger King, figure, Abu, Aladdin series, 1992 . . . . 3.00

Burger King, figure, Beetlejuice series, 1990 . . . . 3.00

Burger King, figure, Kid Vid 2.00

Burger King, figure, Pepsi, hard rubber, mkd "Russ. China," c1983, 1½" h 3.00

Burger King, light switch plate, Thundercats series, 1986 . . . . . . 5.00

Burger King, pencil topper, Alvin, Chipmunk Adventure series, 1987 . . . . 4.00

Burger King, stuffed toy, plush, Christmas Crayola Bears, 1986, 7" h 5.00

Carl's Jr, bottle topper, Dino-Pour series, 1992 . . . . 5.00

Carl's Jr, canteen, plastic, Camp Carl's Jr series, 1989 . . . . . . 4.00

Carl's Jr, cassette tape, *The Little Rabbit Who Wanted Red Wings*, Easter series, 1989 . . . . 5.00

Carl's Jr, flying disc, Beach Creatures series, 1990 . . . . 4.00

Carl's Jr, pencil case, Back to School series, 1993 . . . . 3.00

Carl's Jr, pencil topper, Thing, Addams Family series, 1993 . . . . 3.00

Chick-Fil-A, Block-A-Saurus Kit, 1994 . . . . 3.00

Chick-Fil-A, box, It's a Kid's World series, 1988 . . . . 5.00

Chick-Fil-A, ornament, Color Your Own Ornaments series, 1992 . . . . 3.00

Chick-Fil-A, sand bucket, The Busy World of Richard Scarry series, 1993 . . . . 3.00

Dairy Queen, box, Circus Train series 4.00

Dairy Queen, felt-tip pen, plastic, "Dairy Queen" printed on barrel, white cap, 1991, 8" l 3.00

Kentucky Fried Chicken, Colonel Sanders display, metal, 2-sided, mounting pipe in center, 55½" h without cane, $415.00. Photo courtesy Collectors Auction Services.

Dairy Queen, figure, Dennis the Menace in fire engine, 1994 . . . . 2.00

Dairy Queen, figure, horse, Bendie 10.00

Dairy Queen, Hackeysack ball, 1993 . . . . 2.00

Dairy Queen, hand puppet, Strawberry Bear, vinyl, 1991 . . . . . 2.00

Dairy Queen, magnet, Butterscotch Beaver, Dairy Queen logo, 1991 . . . . 3.00

Dairy Queen, Silly Putty, Flavor Friends mold top, 1991 . . . . . . 3.00

Dairy Queen, stuffed toy, plush, Chocolate Chimp, 1985, 5" h 5.00

Dairy Queen, watercolor set, teddy bear shape translucent plastic case with 8 watercolor paints, 1993 . . . . 4.00

Denny's, figure, Fred Flintstone in green car, 1991 . . . . 4.00

Denny's, Flintstone Fun Squirter, 1991 . . . . 3.00

Denny's, Jetsons Crayon Fun Game, 1992 . . . . 2.00

Denny's, puzzle/ornament, Jetsons series, 1992 . . . . 2.00

Denny's, rubber ball, Jetsons Planets series, 1992 . . . . 4.00

Domino's, bookmark, Noid, 1989 . . . . 8.00

Domino's, figure, Noid, 1988 . . . . 3.00

Dunkin' Donuts, figure, Captain Planet, 1992 . . . . 5.00

Dunkin' Donuts, figure, Munchkins, 1989 . . . . 5.00

Hardee's, box, Ghostbusters series, 1989 . . . . 5.00

Hardee's, California Raisins, 1987 . . . . 3.00

Hardee's, Days of Thunder Racer, 1990 . . . . 3.00

Hardee's, figure, Beach Bunnies, 1989 . . . . 3.00

Hardee's, Finger Crayon, 1992 . . . . 2.00

International House of Pancakes, figure, Pancake Kids, 1991–92 . . . . 3.00

Jack-in-the-Box, ball, Bouncing Buddies series, 1993 . . . . 3.00

Jack-in-the-Box, card game, Leader of the Pack, 1991 . . . . 3.00

Jack-in-the-Box, finger puppet, Ollie O Ring, 1992 . . . . 5.00

Jack-in-the-Box, frame tray puzzle, Back in Time series, 1993 . . . . 3.00

Little Caesars, doll, Meatsa Man, stuffed, 1990 . . . . 5.00

Long John Silver's, book, paper, *The Gingerbread Man*, Ladybird Well-Loved Tales, Ladybird Books, Inc, 1991/1993, 3 x 4½" 3.00

Long John Silver's, car, metal, Racing Champions series, 1989 . . . . 4.00

Long John Silver's, car, plastic, fish shape, with decals, 1986 . . . . 2.00

Burger King, license plate, 12" l, 6" w, $5.00.

Long John Silver's, pencil topper, Treasure Trolls series, 1993. . . . . **1.00**

Long John Silver's, trading card, Aquatic series, 1993 . . . . **1.00**

Long John Silver's, yo-yo, plastic, name printed on side, sea creature printed on reverse **4.00**

Pizza Hut, comic book, X-Men series, 1993. . . . . **2.00**

Pizza Hut, cup, Nickelodeon series **1.00**

Pizza Hut, cup with trading card, Universal Monsters series, 1991 . . . . **5.00**

Pizza Hut, figure, Aliens series, logo on back of head, 1980s **8.00**

Pizza Hut, magic kit, Aladdin series, 1993 . . . . **4.00**

Pizza Hut, sunglasses, Solar Shades, Back to the Future series, 1989 . . . . **4.00**

Roy Rogers, figure, Critters series, 1990 . . . . **4.00**

Roy Rogers, figure, Dino Meals series, glow-in-the-dark, 1993. . . . . **1.00**

Roy Rogers, figure, Gumby, 1989 . . . . **5.00**

Subway, ring, plastic, Captain Planet series, 1993 . . . . **2.00**

Taco Bell, card, pop-up, Free Willy series, 1993 . . . . **2.00**

Taco Bell, coloring book, Zoobilee Zoo series, 1984. . . . . **5.00**

Taco Bell, cup, Addams Family series, 1992 . . . . **1.00**

Taco Bell, Golden Book, Little Critter's Bedtime Storybooks series, Mercer Mayer, 1987. . . . . **5.00**

Taco Bell, poster, Dinosaur Days series, 1994. . . . . **2.00**

Taco Bell, sand mold, star, 1993 . . . . **1.00**

Taco Bell, stamper, Bullwinkle, Adventures of Rocky and Bullwinkle series, 1993 . . . . **2.00**

Wendy's, Bunny Trail Game, 1984 . . . . **8.00**

Wendy's, car, pull-back spring-powdered, Fast Food Racers series, 1990 . . . . **2.00**

Wendy's, figure, Alien Mix-Ups series, 1990. . . . . **3.00**

Wendy's, puffy stickers, Alvin and the Chipmunks series, 1983. . . . . **5.00**

Wendy's, puzzle/ornament, 1983. . . . . **5.00**

White Castle, Bendy Pen, 1993 . . . . **2.00**

White Castle, figure, Castle Meal Friends series, 1990. . . . . **3.00**

White Castle, Flexiblocks, red and blue, 1993 . . . . **2.00**

White Castle, Pencil Pals, Back to Cool Stuff series, 1988 . . . . . **4.00**

White Castle, sipper bottle, plastic, snap-on lid, built-in drinking spout, 1989 . . . . **3.00**

White Castle, water bottle, Camp White Castle series, 1990. . . . . **2.00**

FENTON GLASS

The Fenton Art Glass Company, founded by Frank L. Fenton in 1905 in Martins Ferry, Ohio, originally offered decorating services to other manufacturers. By 1907 the company had relocated to Williamstown, West Virginia, and was making its own glass.

The company's first products included carnival, chocolate, custard, and opalescent glass. Art glass and stretch glass products were introduced in the 1920s. Production of slag glass began in the 1930s. Decorating techniques ranged from acid etching to hand painting.

Through the 1970s, Fenton marked its products with a variety of paper labels. The company adopted an oval raised trademark in 1970. Recently a date code has been added to the mark.

References: Robert E. Eaton, Jr. (comp.), *Fenton Glass: The First Twenty-Five Years Comprehensive Price Guide 1998*, Glass Press, 1998 Robert E. Eaton, Jr. (comp.), *Fenton Glass: The Second Twenty-Five Years Comprehensive Price Guide 1998*, Glass Press, 1998; Fenton Art Glass Collectors of America (comp.), *Fenton Glass: The Third Twenty-Five Years Comprehensive Price Guide 1998*, Glass Press, 1998; William Heacock, *Fenton Glass: The First Twenty-Five Years*, O-Val Advertising Corp. (Antique Publications), 1978; William Heacock, *Fenton Glass: The Second Twenty-Five Years*, O-Val Advertising Corp. (Antique Publications), 1980, William Heacock, *Fenton Glass: The Third Twenty-Five Years*, O-Val Advertising Corp. (Antique Publications), 1989; James Measell (ed.), *Fenton Glass: The 1980s Decade*, Glass Press, 1996; Margaret and Kenn Whitmeyer, *Fenton Art Glass, 1907–1939* (1996, 1999 value update), *1939–1980* (1999), Collector Books, 1996.

Newsletter: *Butterfly Net,* 302 Pheasant Run, Kaukauna, WI 54130.

Collectors' Clubs: Fenton Art Glass Collectors of America, Inc, PO Box 384, Williamstown, WV 26187; National Fenton Glass Society, PO Box 4008, Marietta, OH 45750.

Aqua Crest, vase, double center, 6" h. **$11.00**

Blue Marble, tobacco jar, Grape & Cable, #9188 . . . . **110.00**

Blue Opalescent, bonbon, ftd, Hobnail, 5½" **14.00**

Blue Opalescent, epergne insert, miniature, Hobnail, #3801. . . . . **14.00**

Blue Opalescent, fan vase, miniature, Hobnail, 4" **12.00**

Blue Opalescent, oil, with stopper, Hobnail **19.50**

Blue Opalescent, vase, ftd, miniature, Hobnail, 4" h **10.00**

Colonial Amber, nut dish, Hobnail, #3650 . . . . **8.00**

Colonial Blue, salt and pepper shakers, pr, Thumbprint, #4409. . . . . **35.00**

Colonial Green, comport, Roses, #9222. . . . . **15.00**

Cranberry Opalescent, basket, Coin Dot, #1437, 7" **80.00**

Cranberry Opalescent, bowl, Coin Dot, #1438, 8½" d **60.00**

Cranberry Opalescent, candle holders, pr, Hobnail, #3870. . . . . **130.00**

Cranberry Opalescent, oil, with stopper, Hobnail **60.00**

Cranberry Opalescent, tumbler, Hobnail, #3947, 12 oz **35.00**

Emerald Crest, compote, 6" **38.00**

French Opalescent, bonbon, Hobnail. **15.00**

French Opalescent, cake stand, low, Diamond Lace **75.00**

Gold Crest, basket, applied handle, 8½" h, $35.00.

French Opalescent, creamer and sugar, Hobnail, #3900 . . . . . **19.00**
French Opalescent, oil cruet, orig stopper, Hobnail. **35.00**
French Opalescent, punch cup, Hobnail **12.00**
French Opalescent, sugar, Hobnail, #3901 . . . . **9.50**
French Opalescent, vase, double crimp, Hobnail, 5¹/₂" h **19.00**
French Opalescent, vase, miniature, #389, Hobnail, 4" **9.00**
Green Opalescent, candy jar, ftd, Hobnail, #3887 . . . . **45.00**
Lavender Satin, bud vase, Water Lily, #8456 . . . . **35.00**
Peach Crest, bowl, ruffled, 6" **18.00**
Pink Opaline, vase, Jacqueline, #9156, 6" **60.00**
Plum Opalescent, basket, oval, Hobnail, #3839, 12" **180.00**
Ruby, juice tumbler, Georgian **14.00**
Ruby, salt and pepper shakers, pr, ftd, Georgian **80.00**
Silver Crest, banana bowl, high **75.00**
Silver Crest, basket, 7¹/₂" h, 8" w **18.00**
Silver Crest, basket, 9" h, 10" w **37.00**
Silver Crest, bowl, ribbed, 11" **50.00**
Silver Crest, cake plate, low, ftd, Spanish Moss, #5813 . . . . . . **15.00**
Silver Crest, candle holder, cov, ftd, Spanish Moss **99.00**
Silver Crest, relish, 2 part. **55.00**
Silver Crest, salt and pepper shakers, pr, ftd **110.00**
Silver Crest, sandwich tray, center handle. **17.00**
Silver Crest, tidbit, 2 tier **26.00**
Silver Crest, tidbit, 2 tier, ruffled bow, #7394 . . . . **65.00**
Silver Crest, vase, bell bottom **85.00**
Topaz Opalescent, basket, Cactus, #3439, 9" **150.00**
Topaz Opalescent, basket, Hobnail, #3837, 7" h, 5" w **50.00**
Topaz Opalescent, compote, Cactus, #3422 . . . . **135.00**
Topaz Opalescent, vase, Coin Dot, #1459, 8" **75.00**
White Milk Glass, basket, Hobnail, 12" **50.00**
White Milk Glass, bell, Hobnail, #3667 . . . . **13.00**
White Milk Glass, bonbon, Hobnail, #3937, 7" **15.00**
White Milk Glass, butter, cov, Hobnail, #3977, ¹/₄ lb. **11.00**
White Milk Glass, candy jar, cov, Hobnail, #3883 . . . . **24.00**
White Milk Glass, cat slipper, Hobnail **12.00**
White Milk Glass, cigarette lighter, Hobnail, 2¹/₄" **14.00**
White Milk Glass, creamer and sugar, Hobnail, #3900 . . . . **7.00**
White Milk Glass, juice pitcher, Hobnail **40.00**
White Milk Glass, mayonnaise plate, Hobnail **5.00**
White Milk Glass, mustard, with spoon, Hobnail, #3889 . . . . **14.00**
White Milk Glass, oil cruet, with stopper, Hobnail, #3889 . . . . **9.50**
White Milk Glass, peanut dish, ftd, Hobnail, #3327 . . . . **5.00**
White Milk Glass, punch set, plain edge, Hobnail, #3527 . . . **400.00**
White Milk Glass, slipper, Hobnail, #3995, 5" h **5.00**

FIESTA

Homer Laughlin began production of its Fiesta line in 1936. Frederick Rhead was the designer. Concentric bands of rings were the only decorative motif besides color. Dark blue, light green, ivory, red, and yellow were the first five colors. Turquoise followed a year later.

Fiesta was restyled in 1969. Antique gold, turf green, and mango red (really the old red retitled) were introduced. These changes were not enough to save Fiesta. Production ceased in 1973.

Wishing to capitalize on the tremendous secondary market interest in Fiesta, Homer Laughlin reintroduced Fiesta in 1986. Several new colors made their appearance at that time.

References: Sharon and Bob Huxford, *Collectors Encyclopedia of Fiesta: Plus Harlequin, Riviera, and Kitchen Kraft, Eighth Edition*, Collector Books, 1998; Jeffrey B. Snyder, *Fiesta, 2nd Edition*, Schiffer Publishing, 1999.

Collectors' Clubs: Fiesta Club of America, PO Box 15383, Loves Park, IL 61115.

After Dinner Cup and Saucer, cobalt **$95.00**
After Dinner Cup and Saucer, green. **85.00**
After Dinner Cup and Saucer, rose **790.00**
Ashtray, medium green **260.00**
Bowl, 4³/₄", medium green **950.00**
Bowl, 5¹/₂", medium green **65.00**
Bud Vase, green **85.00**
Cake Plate, green **1,950.00**
Candle Holders, pr, bulb, cobalt **125.00**
Candle Holders, pr, bulb, ivory **125.00**
Candle Holders, pr, bulb, turquoise **11.00**
Candle Holders, pr, tripod, cobalt **950.00**
Carafe, green **295.00**
Carafe, ivory **650.00**
Carafe, red **475.00**
Casserole, cov, dark green **435.00**
Casserole, cov, gray. **375.00**
Casserole, cov, turquoise **135.00**
Chop Plate, 13", gray **95.00**
Chop Plate, 13", medium green **650.00**
Coffeepot, cobalt. **350.00**
Coffeepot, dark green **750.00**
Coffeepot, rose **850.00**
Coffeepot, turquoise **250.00**
Creamer, individual, yellow. **75.00**
Creamer, medium green **110.00**
Creamer, stick handle, red. **85.00**
Creamer, stick handle, turquoise **115.00**
Cream Soup, chartreuse. **95.00**
Cream Soup, dark green **95.00**
Cream Soup, red. **75.00**
Cream Soup, rose **95.00**
Cup and Saucer, medium green **65.00**
Deep Plate, gray **50.00**
Deep Plate, medium green **135.00**
Disk Pitcher, dark green. **365.00**

Disk Pitcher, chartreuse, $275.00.

Jug, 2 pint, green, $75.00. Photo courtesy Ray Morykan Auctions.

Disk Pitcher, turquoise.	110.00
Eggcup, cobalt	75.00
Eggcup, gray	175.00
French Casserole, yellow	450.00
Fruit Bowl, 11¾", yellow	350.00
Jug, 2 pt, cobalt	120.00
Jug, 2 pt, dark green	215.00
Juice Pitcher, red	750.00
Juice Pitcher, yellow	40.00
Juice Tumbler, cobalt	45.00
Juice Tumbler, gray	375.00
Juice Tumbler, green	30.00
Juice Tumbler, ivory	45.00
Juice Tumbler, rose	60.00
Juice Tumbler, turquoise	40.00
Kitchen Kraft, casserole, cov, 8½", cobalt	110.00
Kitchen Kraft, fork, green	115.00
Kitchen Kraft, fork, yellow	245.00
Kitchen Kraft, jar, cov, small, cobalt	495.00
Kitchen Kraft, spoon, red	195.00
Marmalade, yellow	360.00
Mixing Bowl, #1, cobalt	375.00
Mixing Bowl, #1, green	230.00
Mixing Bowl, #1, red	275.00
Mixing Bowl, #2, cobalt	195.00
Mixing Bowl, #4, green	195.00
Mixing Bowl, #4, ivory	225.00
Mixing Bowl, #4, turquoise	220.00
Mug, chartreuse	90.00
Mug, cobalt	85.00
Mug, gray	95.00
Mug, turquoise	55.00
Mustard, cobalt	325.00
Mustard, green	250.00
Mustard, turquoise	275.00
Onion Soup, cov, ivory	950.00
Pitcher, ice lip, turquoise	195.00
Plate, 6", medium green	35.00
Plate, 9", medium green	65.00
Plate, 10", chartreuse	50.00
Plate, 10", cobalt	55.00
Plate, 10", dark green	65.00
Plate, 10", green	30.00
Plate, 10", ivory	40.00

Plate, 10", medium green	195.00
Plate, 10", red	50.00
Plate, 10", yellow	25.00
Plate, 12", divided, cobalt	75.00
Plate, 12", divided, dark green	95.00
Platter, medium green	175.00
Relish, center, green	55.00
Relish, center, ivory	60.00
Relish, center, turquoise	55.00
Relish, side, green	50.00
Relish, side, red	75.00
Salad Bowl, ftd, yellow	470.00
Salt and Pepper Shakers, pr, medium green	270.00
Salt and Pepper Shakers, pr, turquoise	135.00
Sauceboat, dark green	90.00
Sugar, cov, medium green	265.00
Syrup, Dripcut, turquoise	760.00
Syrup, ivory	600.00
Teapot, large, cobalt	335.00
Teapot, large, turquoise	280.00
Teapot, medium, ivory	245.00
Teapot, medium, rose	350.00
Vase, 8", ivory	895.00
Vase, 12", cobalt	1,500.00
Water Tumbler, turquoise	85.00

FIGURAL PLANTERS & VASES

Initially collected as a form by individuals collecting products of a specific maker, figural planters evolved as a collecting category unto itself in the mid-1990s. Figural baby planters are a major subcategory. Lady head vases command their own category.

Most generic examples and pieces whose design and shape do not speak to a specific time period have little value. Crossover collectors, especially those seeking animal, black, and vehicle images, skew value.

References: Kathleen Deel, *Figural Planters,* Schiffer Publishing, 1996; Betty and Bill Newbound, *Collector's Encyclopedia of Figural Planter & Vases,* Collector Books, 1997.

Note: Refer to specific manufacturers for additional listings.

PLANTERS

Automobile, green, McCoy, Floraline line, 8" l	$25.00
Baby Buggy, dark pink, 4½" h	10.00
Baby Buggy, pink, Haeger, 3280-B, 5½" h, 6" l	15.00
Big Apple, Spaulding/Royal Copley, 6" h	18.00
Birds on Tree Stump, multicolor, Japan, 7¼" h	45.00
Bootees, blue, Kay Finch, #6035	75.00
Boy and Girl on Tricycle, yellow and green, Haeger, 3947, 7½" h	40.00
Bunny House, Lefton, 4½" h	15.00
Cart, yellow, McCoy, Basket line, 10" l	30.00
Chevy Corvette Convertible, pink, Goldor, 9½" l	15.00
Clown, Royal Copley, 8⅜" h	20.00
Cocker Spaniel, light blue, Brush, 6¾" l	18.00
Cradle, pink, Monmouth, 7½" l	8.00
Dancing Lady, Royal Copley, 8¼" h	50.00
Deer, white, Shawnee, 7" h	8.00
Dutch Shoe, light blue, McCoy, 1947, 7½" l	50.00
Fish, yellow, Haeger, #14, c1936, 3½" h	12.00

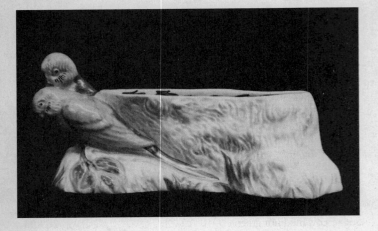

Planter, blue and green lovebirds, gray rocky ground, Clarice Cliff, 10" l, $175.00.

Highchair, pastel colors, Block Pottery, 5½" h **12.00**
Locomotive, pastel colors, Bow of California, 4½" h **12.00**
Peacock, cloudy blue, Haeger, R-453, 10" h **40.00**
Pelican, blue, McCoy, 1940s, 5¾" h **35.00**
Pirate Head, Royal Copley, 8" h **50.00**
Poodle, gray, Royal Copley, 6½" h **60.00**
Puppy, pink, blue, and white, plaid ears, Japan, 4½" h **10.00**
Rearing Horse, green, Shawnee, 6" h **20.00**
Ribbed Star, Royal Windsor, 6½" h **10.00**
Sailfish, green, Haeger, R-271, 9" h **45.00**
Sprinkling Can, white, Shawnee, 5½" h **16.00**
Squirrel on Log, brown, Brush, 6½" l **40.00**
Swan, iridescent black, Stanford, 4¾" h **20.00**
Swan, pink, Kay Finch, 5¾" h **85.00**
Three Fish, green, Japan, 7¼" h **40.00**
Three Owls on Log, Fredericksburg, 5½" l **12.00**
Tugboat, multicolor, American Bisque, 9½" l **25.00**
Turkey, brown and black, Morton Pottery, 4½" h **10.00**
Turtle, brown, McCoy, Floraline line, 5¼" l **12.00**
Violin, mallow, Haeger, R-293, 16" l **80.00**
Woodpecker, Royal Copley **10.00**

VASES

Bird of Paradise, cloudy blue, Haeger, R-186, 13⅛" h **$60.00**
Bird on Sunflower, multicolor, McCoy, 1948, 6½" h **90.00**
Cowboy Boots, brown, McCoy, 1956, 7" h **45.00**
Dancing Girl, green, Haeger, 3105, 8" h **25.00**
Double Tulip Blossoms, white and pink, gold trim,
    McCoy, 1953, 8" w **90.00**
Flower Basket, mauve agate, Haeger, R-386, c1943,
    8½" h, 13 ¼" l **75.00**
Giraffe in Leaves, yellow and green, Hull, 8¼" h **55.00**
Leaf, white, Haeger, D1021, 12¾" h **75.00**
Leaping Gazelle, amber crystal, Haeger, R-706, 15¼" h **40.00**
Leaping Unicorn, flower vase, Hull, 98, 10" h **60.00**
Morning Glories, mauve agate, Haeger, R-452, 16½" h **90.00**
Ram's Head, burgundy, McCoy, 1950s, 9½" h **100.00**
Sea Shell, gray, Haeger, R-701, c1949, 10½" h **60.00**
Siamese Cat, blue, Napco, 8¼" h **8.00**
Snail, blue ext, white int, Haeger, R-299, 7" h **35.00**

FIGURINES

Figurines played a major role in the household decorating decor between the late 1930s and the early 1960s. Those with deep pockets bought Boehm, Lladro, and Royal Doulton. The average consumer was content with generic fare, much of it inexpensive imports, or examples from a host of California figurine manufacturers such as Kay Finch and Florence Ceramics.

Animals were the most popular theme. Human forms came next. Subject matter and the ability of a piece to speak the decorative motifs of a specific time period are as important as manufacturer in determining value.

Note: Refer to Limited Edition Collectibles and specific manufacturer and animal categories for additional listings.

CERAMIC

American Pottery Co, bird, multicolor, 4¾" h **$8.00**
Barbara Willis, horse, crackle finish, 5" h **175.00**
Betty Lou Nichols, Anna, stamped mark, 9½" h **375.00**
Betty Lou Nichols, Pierre Rabbit, 8½" h **275.00**
Brad Keeler, blue jay, 735, in-mold mark, 9¼" h **85.00**
Brad Keeler, cat in basket, 4½ x 5¾" **30.00**
Brad Keeler, flamingo, 10¼" h **35.00**
Brad Keeler, Siamese cat, on red pillow, 946, 3 x 3" **45.00**
Brayton Laguna, Chinese boy **100.00**
Brayton Laguna, elephant, woodtone/white crackle fin-
    ish, 13½" h **225.00**
Brayton Laguna, kissing geese, green, 4⅜" h **25.00**
Brayton Laguna, Pedro, stamped mark, 6½" h **200.00**
Caliente Pottery, goose, 4½" h **65.00**
California Originals, elephant, red, 6⅛" h **15.00**
Cemar Clay Products, horse, yellow, brown base, 4½" h **15.00**
Claire Lerner Studios, oriental mandolin player, 9" h **8.00**
Clay Sketches, bird, inkstamp mark, 12½" h **25.00**
deLee, Dutch boy, paper label, 7¾" h **22.00**
Enesco, kitten, paper label, mkd "©1987/EIC," 4" h **6.00**
Florence, ballerina, lace trim, 22K gold, 7¼" h **250.00**
Florence, mockingbird, W4, attached flowers on base,
    5¼" h **200.00**
Florence, Susann, yellow gown, 9" h **300.00**
Freeman-McFarlin, fox, 145, mkd "Anthony Calif. USA,"
    9" h **65.00**
Freeman-McFarlin, giraffe, woodtone, white crackle
    glaze, in-mold mark, 11" h **85.00**
Freeman-McFarlin, mouse, stoneware, mkd "425 USA,"
    7½" h **45.00**
Hagen-Renaker, reclinging deer, 3½ x 4½" **65.00**
Hagen-Renaker, Scrooge McDuck **300.00**
Hedi Schoop, boy angel, painted mark, 8" h **85.00**
Howard Pierce, boy with pony, 5¼" h **25.00**
Howard Pierce, monkey, stamped mark, 6" h **85.00**
Howard Pierce, owl, 8" h **45.00**
Howard Pierce, rooster, 9¼" h **30.00**
Jane Callender, cocker spaniel, 2⅝" h **30.00**
Japan, boy playing drum, yellow pants, black and white
    coat, red bow tie, 4½" h **10.00**
Japan, calico dog, bandage on face, stripes on shoulder,
    7½" h **10.00**
Japan, cat, playing with ball, multicolor, 2¼" h **8.00**
Japan, colonial couple, pink and green floral dec, gold
    trim, blue paper label, 9½" h, price for pair **40.00**

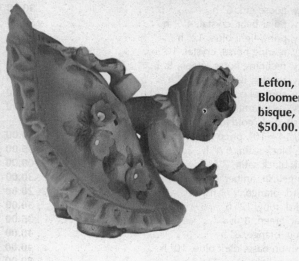

Lefton, Bloomer Girl, bisque, 4" h, $50.00.

Japan, dancing lady, pink and green, 4½" h 40.00
Japan, Elmer elephant, bisque, mkd "Made in Japan," incised on back "S1396," 1½ x 2¼ x 4" 175.00
Japan, lady skier, multicolor matte glaze, 7¾" h 45.00
Japan, pixie on butterfly, multicolor, 3½" h 25.00
Japan, Scottie dogs, cream and tan luster glaze, 1½" h 10.00
Jessie Grimes, girl, white dress, brown hair with pigtails, 6⅛" h 15.00
Josef Originals, Penny, 4½" h 50.00
Kay Finch, afghan, 5016, orange 200.00
Kay Finch, angel, 140A 150.00
Kay Finch, choir boy, 210, 5" h 175.00
Kay Finch, colt, 4806, 11" h 250.00
Kay Finch, cottontail bunny, 152, 2½" h 75.00
Kay Finch, elephant, 4626, sand matte finish 175.00
Kay Finch, little girl, "P.J.," 5002, pigtails, blue hair bows . . . 150.00
Kay Finch, parakeet, 5403, blue, gold trim, 5" h 200.00
Kay Finch, poodle, 5262, white, gold bow, 8" h 300.00
Kay Finch, sky terrier, 5926, orange matte glaze, 6½" h 150.00
Kay Finch, turtle, 126 . . . . 100.00
Kaye of Hollywood, colonial lady, mkd "347-Kaye," 9¼" h . . . 35.00
La Mirada, deer, turquoise crackle glaze, 5" h 25.00
La Mirada, pony, turquoise crackle glaze, 7 x 9½" 65.00
Lefton, parakeet, 5" h 12.00
Maddux, chicken, 8½" h 15.00
Maddux, cockatoo, 9⅛" h 20.00
Marc Bellaire, Bali woman, seated, 8" h 800.00
Metlox, alligator, 8½" l 200.00
Metlox, Indian brave, in-mold mark, 9" h 350.00
Metlox, Prince Charming, paper label, 7½" h 375.00
Modglin's, bunny, 6¾" h 35.00
Modglin's, Janie, 7" h 35.00
Modglin's, Storybook boy, 8" h 45.00
Modglin's, tiger, 4½ x 9" 40.00
Pacific, deer, brown, white spots, 7" h 75.00
Robert Simmons, bird, "Chirpo," 7⅛" h 22.00
Rocky Mountain Art Pottery, buck and doe, price for pr 35.00
Rocky Mountain Art Pottery, poodle, 10" h 25.00
Roselane, fawn, brown on white satin-matte finish, plastic eyes, c1965 . . . . 20.00
Roselane, kangaroo, 2 joeys, 4¼" h 20.00
Royal Copley, cat, brown, gold bow, 8" h 85.00
Royal Copley, cat, brown, pink bow, 8" h 35.00
Royal Copley, cockatoo, 7¾" h 15.00

Royal Copley, dancing lady, brown hair, yellow and blue dress, 8¼" h 50.00
Royal Copley, dog, brown, black ear, 8½" h 20.00
Royal Copley, double parakeets, 7½" h 35.00
Royal Copley, oriental girl, 8" h 10.00
Royal Copley, pheasant, white gold trim, 5¼" h 15.00
Royal Copley, rooster 7½" h 40.00
Royal Copley, spaniel, brown, black nose, 7¾" h 20.00
Royal Copley, swallow, blue, brown back 15.00
Royal Copley, titmouse, multicolor 20.00
Royal Doulton, Autumn Breezes, pink and green 132.00
Royal Doulton, The Little Pig, HN1793, 4" h 135.00
Royal Doulton, The Orange Lady, second version, reen with blue plaid shawl, 8¾" h 192.00
Royal Doulton, Tinkle Bell, HN1677, pink and blue, 4¾" h 55.00
Royal Haeger, bucking bronco, 13" h 150.00
Royal Haeger, bull, 6½" h 225.00
Royal Haeger, cocker spaniel, 3" h 45.00
Royal Haeger, Egyptian cat, 616, mandarin orange, mkd "Royal Haeger ©616 U.S.A.," 1950s, 15½" h 120.00
Royal Haeger, fish, amber, 4" h 85.00
Royal Haeger, gypsy girl, R-1224, brown and green, unmkd, 16½" h 100.00
Royal Haeger, hen, red and green, black accents, 11" h 45.00
Royal Haeger, leopard, chartreuse, 7¾" h 50.00
Royal Haeger, matador, 6343, red, foil crown label, 11⅜" h 125.00
Royal Haeger, mourning dove, 650, rust brown, c1973, 7" h, 10" l 50.00
Royal Haeger, rooster, R-1762, dark brown and white, c1973, 20" h 100.00
Royal Windsor, chickens, price for pair 25.00
Sasha Brastoff, horse, platinum on pink, sgd, 10½" h 250.00
Sleepy Hollow Pottery, reclining deer, 4¾" h 5.00
Squire Ceramics, girl and doll, 6" h 30.00
Stewart McCulloch, peacock, 6½" h, 9½" l 20.00
Stewart of California, pig, 6⅝" h 22.00
Twin Winton, winking lion, unmkd, 3¼" h 40.00
Walker Pottery, reclining dog, 3 x 4¾" 10.00
Will-George, flamingo, stamped mark, 9½" h 150.00
Winfield, deer, 4¼ x 4¾" 150.00

Royal Copley, lark, red, yellow, black, and green, paper label, 5" h, $5.00.

GLASS

Barbini, pigeon, scattered white cane int dec, applied
   red beak and eyes, 6 x 6½" **$55.00**
Cambridge, bashful Charlotte, crystal satin **100.00**
Cambridge, Buddha, amber, 5½" h **225.00**
Cambridge, draped lady, 8½" h **60.00**
Cambridge, heron, crystal, 12" h **85.00**
Cambridge, sea gull, crystal **50.00**
Fenton, alley cat, amethyst carnival **75.00**
Fenton, alley cat, kelley green iridescent **55.00**
Fenton, alley cat, purple slag **55.00**
Fenton, alley cat, ruby slag, 11" h **55.00**
Fenton, alley cat, teal marigold **55.00**
Fenton, fish, ruby, amberina tail and fins, 2½" h **45.00**
Fenton, happiness bird, 6½" l **25.00**
Flint, bear, amber **300.00**
Flint, elephant, crystal, 6 x 13" **125.00**
Fostoria, cat, light blue, 3¾" h **25.00**
Fostoria, duckling, walking, amber, 2⅜" h **10.00**
Fostoria, goldfish, crystal, 4" h **85.00**
Fostoria, Madonna, 10" h **50.00**
Fostoria, mermaid, crystal, 11½" h **120.00**
Fostoria, pelican, amber, 1¼" h **40.00**
Fostoria, pelican, green, 1990 . . . . **65.00**
Fostoria, pelican, opal iridescent **35.00**
Fostoria, penguin, topaz, 4⅝" h **100.00**
Fostoria, polar bear, topaz, 4⅝" h **100.00**
Fostoria, rabbit, light blue **15.00**
Haley, donkey with cart, crystal **10.00**
Haley, jumping horse, crystal, 9½ x 7½" **50.00**
Haley, ringneck pheasant, crystal, 11½" h **20.00**
Haley, seated fawn, crystal, 6" h **12.00**
Haley, thrush, crystal or frosted **10.00**
Heisey, bunny, head down, crystal, 2½" h **150.00**
Heisey, piglet, seated, crystal, 1⅛" h, 1⅛" l **75.00**
Heisey, piglet, walking, crystal, ⅞" h, 1½" l **75.00**
Heisey, Scottie dog, crystal, 3" h **75.00**
Heisey, sparrow, crystal, 2¼" h, 4" l **75.00**
Imperial, duck, caramel slag, 4½" h **40.00**
Imperial, elephant, caramel slag, 4" h **50.00**
Imperial, elephant, pink satin, 4½" h **65.00**
Imperial, gazelle, blue, 11" h **100.00**
Imperial, rooster, milk glass, 5⅝" h **25.00**
Imperial, swan, caramel slag, 4" h **35.00**
Imperial, terrier, amethyst carnival, 3½" h **40.00**
Imperial, woodchuck, caramel slag, 4½" h **50.00**
LE Smith, girl with goose, blue, 8" h **55.00**
LE Smith, rooster, frosted satin, 2¼" h **10.00**
LE Smith, squirrel, frosted satin, 4½" h **12.00**
New Martinsville, bunny, ears up, amber, 1" h **40.00**
New Martinsville, eagle, crystal, 8" h **65.00**
New Martinsville, German shepherd, crystal, 5" h **55.00**
New Martinsville, hen, crystal, 5" h **55.00**
New Martinsville, hunter, crystal, 7⅜" h **80.00**
New Martinsville, papa bear, crystal, 4" h **175.00**
New Martinsville, pelican, crystal, 8" h **75.00**
New Martinsville, porpoise on wave, crystal, 6" h **400.00**
New Martinsville, seal with ball, crystal, 7" h **55.00**
New Martinsville, seal with ball, ruby, 4½" h **40.00**
New Martinsville, squirrel, crystal, 4½" h **35.00**
New Martinsville, tiger, head up, crystal, 6½" h **165.00**
Paden City, bird, light blue, 5" h **100.00**
Paden City, goose, light blue, 5" h **100.00**

Paden City, goose girl, 6" h **30.00**
Paden City, polar bear, crystal, 4½" h **50.00**
Paden City, pony, light blue, 12" h **100.00**
Paden City, rearing horse, crystal, 10" h **150.00**
Paden City, reclining horse, green, 9" l **100.00**
Paden City, rooster, light blue, 11" h **200.00**
Paden City, squirrel on log, crystal, 5½" h **50.00**
Paden City, swan, milk glass, 4" h **15.00**
Seguso, fish, pink, gold foil int under controlled bubbles,
   unmkd, 14 x 10", price for pair **650.00**
Tiffin, cat, black satin, 6¼" h **95.00**
Tiffin, owl, black satin, 7½" h **100.00**
Viking, angelfish, amber, 6½" h **30.00**
Viking, bird, orange, 9½" h **20.00**
Viking, bird, ruby, 12" h **30.00**
Viking, cat, green, 8" h **35.00**
Viking, dog, orange, 8" h **40.00**
Viking, fish on base, dark blue, 10" h **40.00**
Viking, horse, light blue, 11½" h **80.00**
Viking, rabbit, amber, 6½" h **30.00**
Viking, turtle, amber, 5½" l **15.00**
Westmoreland, butterfly, crystal, 4½" w **25.00**
Westmoreland, pouter pigeon, crystal, 2½" h **20.00**
Westmoreland, robin, crystal, 3¼" l **15.00**

FINCH, KAY

After over a decade of ceramic studies, Kay Finch, assisted by her husband Braden, opened her commercial studio in 1939. A whimsical series of pig figurines and hand-decorated banks were the company's first successful products.

An expanded studio and showroom located on the Pacific Coast Highway in Corona del Mar opened on December 7,1941. The business soon had forty employees as it produced a wide variety of novelty items. A line of dog figurines and themed items were introduced in the 1940s. Christmas plates were made from 1950 until 1962.

When Braden died in 1963, Kay Finch ceased operations. Freeman-McFarlin Potteries purchased the molds in the mid-1970s and commissioned Finch to model a new series of dog figurines. Production of these continued through the late 1970s.

References: Devin Frick, Jean Frick and Richard Martinez, *Collectible Kay Finch,* Collector Books, 1997; Mike Nickel and Cindy Horvath, *Kay Finch,* Schiffer Publishing, 1997; Frances Finch Webb and Jack R. Webb, *The New Kay Finch Identification Guide,* published by authors, 1996.

Ashtray, swan, pink, #4958, 4½" l **$50.00**
Bell, white, gold, red bow, #6056, 4" h **75.00**
Canister, emb raspberries, turquoise, #5108 . . . . **30.00**
Cereal Bowl, handled, "For a good boy," #506 . . . . **50.00**
Coaster, holly wreath, #5386, 4½" d **75.00**
Cup and Saucer, Blue Daisy **60.00**
Dish, fan, silver and white, #4960 . . . . **65.00**
Figure, angel, #140a **125.00**
Figure, begging poodle, #5262 . . . . **250.00**
Figure, cat, "Jezzy," #5302 . . . . **125.00**
Figure, duck, white and green, #5006 . . . . **75.00**
Figure, hen, gold, #841 . . . . **250.00**
Figure, lamb, standing on hind legs, #109 . . . . **50.00**
Figure, Socko, monkey, blue jacket, #4841, 4½" h **125.00**
Figure, Yorkie pups, #170 and #171, price for pair **400.00**

Figure, dove, white with gold trim, #5101, 5¼" h, 8¼" l, $125.00. Photo courtesy Ray Morykan Auctions.

Figures, pr, Godey Couple, fall colors, #122	300.00
Flowerpot, square, ivory dec, #508, 3" h	35.00
Mug, Santa Claus, white and gold, #4950, 4" h	50.00
Pin, Afghan head, gold and white, #5081	150.00
Plaque, dachshund, Parade of Champions, #4955	50.00
Salad Plate, emb vegetables, 10" d	30.00
Salt and Pepper Shakers, pr, horse heads	125.00
Stein, poodle handle, #5458	125.00
Tile, Yorkie, blue, 5½" sq	60.00

FIREARMS & ACCESSORIES

Many Americans own firearms, whether a .22 plunking rifle or pistol or a 12-gauge shotgun for hunting. The vast majority were inexpensive when purchased, bought for use and not investment, and have only minor secondary value in today's market. Many firearms sold on the secondary market are purchased for reuse purposes.

Recent federal statutes have placed restrictions on the buying and selling of certain handguns and rifles on the secondary market. Check with your local police department to make certain you are in compliance with state and federal laws before attempting to sell any weapon.

Collector interest in firearm advertising, prints, ammunition boxes, and other firearm accessories has increased significantly in the last decade. Auctioneers such as Dixie Sporting Collectibles (1206 Rama Rd, Charlotte, NC 28211) and Langs (31R Turtle Cove, Raymond, ME 04071) hold several specialized catalog sales each year in this field.

References: Robert H. Balderson, *The Official Price Guide to Antique and Modern Firearms, Eighth Edition,* House of Collectibles, 1996; Robert H. Balderson, *The Official Price Guide to Collector Handguns, Fifth Edition,* House of Collectibles, 1996; John Ogle, *Colt Memorabilia Price Guide,* Krause Publications, 1998; Russell and Steve Quetermous, *Modern Guns, Twelfth Edition,* Collector Books, 1999; Ned Schwing, *Standard Catalog of Firearms, 9th Edition,* Krause Publications, 1999; John Walter, *Rifles of the World,* Krause Publications, 1998.

Periodicals: *Gun List,* 700 E State St, Iola, WI 54990; *Military Trader,* PO Box 1050, Dubuque, IA 52004; *The Gun Report,* PO Box 38, Aledo, IL 61231.

Collectors' Club: The Winchester Arms Collectors Assoc, PO Box 6754, Great Falls, MT 59406.

Note: Prices are for firearms in very good condition.

FIREARMS

Handgun, Beretta Model 318, semi-automatic, 25 caliber, 8-shot magazine, 2½" barrel, 4½" l, fixed sights, blued finish, plastic stocks, 1934–39	**$225.00**
Handgun, Bernardelli Vest Pocket, semi-automatic, 25 caliber, 5- or 8-shot magazine, 2⅛" barrel, 4⅛" l, fixed sights, blued finish, Bakelite stocks, 1945–68	**105.00**
Handgun, Browning BDA 380, double action automatic, 380 caliber, 13-shot magazine, 3¹³⁄₁₆" barrel, 6¾" l, fixed blade front sight, square notch drift adjustable rear sight, nickel finish, 1982–present	**300.00**
Handgun, Browning Classic, 9mm automatic, high-grade engraving, checkered walnut grips with double border, limited to 5,000 production, 1985	**750.00**
Handgun, Charter Arms Undercover 38 Special, double action, 38 caliber, 5-shot cylinder, 2" barrel, 6¼" l, fixed sights, checkered Bulldog stocks, stainless finish, 1965–present,	**175.00**
Handgun, Colt Ace, 22 caliber long rifle, 10-shot magazine, hand-honed action, target barrel, adjustable rear sight, 4¾" barrel, 8¼" l, 1930–40	**1,500.00**
Handgun, Colt Camp Perry Model, 1st issue, single shot, 22 caliber long rifle, 10" barrel, 13¾" l, adjustable target sights, hand-finished action, blued finish, checkered walnut stocks, 1926–34	**750.00**
Handgun, Dan Wesson, Model 738P, 38 Special, single action, 5-shot swing-out cylinder, 2" fixed barrel, stainless steel finish, wooden grips, 6½" l	**160.00**
Handgun, Iver Johnson, Cattleman, single action, 357 magnum, 6-shot cylinder, 4¾" barrel, 7¼" l, fixed sights, blued barrel and cylinder, color-case hardened frame, brass grip frame, 1-pc walnut stock, 1973–78	**150.00**

Handgun, Colt MK IV Series 70, automatic, 45 caliber, 7-shot magazine, 5" barrel, 8⅜" l, fixed rear sight, ramp front sight, blued finish, checkered walnut stocks, 1970–present, $350.00.

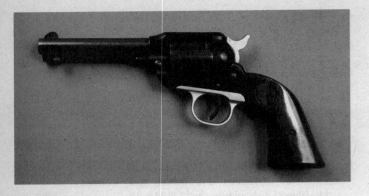

Handgun, Ruger Bearcat, single action, aluminum frame, 22 caliber long rifle, 6-shot cylinder, 4" barrel, 8⁷⁄₈" l, fixed sights, blued finish, smooth walnut stocks, 1958–73, $275.00.

Rifle, Browning Model 52 Ltd Edition, bolt action, adjustable trigger, 5-shot magazine, detachable box, 24" barrel, checkered high grade walnut stock, rosewood fore-end. 280.00

Rifle, Harrington Model 165 Leatherneck Autoloader, 22 caliber long rifle, 10-shot detachable box magazine, 23" barrel, Redfield 70 rear peep sight, blade front sight on ramp, plain pistol-grip stock, swivels, web sling, 1945–61 . . . . 100.00

Rifle, Marlin Model 81 Bolt Action Repeating, takedown, 22 caliber long rifle, 18-shot tubular magazine, 24" barrel, open rear sight, bead front sight, plain pistol-grip stock, 1937–40 . . . . 50.00

Rifle, Remington, Model 591, 5mm Remington rim fire, bolt action, 4-shot removable clip, 24" barrel, Monte Carlo plain 1 pc hardwood pistol grip and forearm 140.00

Shotgun, Remington, Model 870 "All American" Trap Gun, custom grade, engraved receiver, trigger guard, and barrel, walnut, 30" full choke barrel, 1972–77 . . . . . 600.00

Shotgun, Savage, Model 30, hammerless, slide action, 16 gauge, 2³⁄₄" chamber, vent rib barrel, full choke, plain pistol-grip stock, grooved slide handle, 1958–70 . . . 175.00

Shotgun, Stevens Model 124 Cross Bolt Repeater, hammerless, solid frame, 12 gauge, 2-shot tubular magazine, 28" barrel, improved cylinder, modified choke, Tenite stock and forearm, 1947–52 . . . . 150.00

ACCESSORIES

Ammunition Box, U.M.C., "New Club," 12 gauge, 2-pc, empty $60.00

Book, *Colt Guns*, Martin Rywell, 1953 ed, 136 pgs. 16.00

Bullet Mold, 2 cavity, brass, .31 caliber 90.00

Bullet Mold, Winchester .40-82, walnut handles. 60.00

Catalog, Smith and Wesson, red, black, and light brown textured cov, 40 pgs, c1934, 9¹⁄₂ x 7¹⁄₂" 55.00

Counter Display, Winchester "Super Speed 22s," crow image, multicolored, self-frame easel back, 9 x 12". 90.00

Counter Display Case, ¹⁄₂ size, "Remington Hi-Speed 22's," glass front red print, no dividers 200.00

Pinback Button, "Shoot Peters Shells" and image of shot shell, white, black, red, and gold 80.00

Pocketknife, Winchester, 3 blades, black bone handles, nickel silver bolsters, 2³⁄₈" l blade 110.00

Salesman's Sample, Winchester powder shell, leader brass, clear window showing 13 various powders, 6" l . . . 320.00

Shipping Crate, Robin Hood Ammunition Co, wood, dovetailed, black print, mkd "Load No. * B-7, 3¹⁄₄-1-4 load," Robin Hood logo on 2 side panels 300.00

Tin, Dupont Superfine FFg Gunpowder, oval, red with engraved paper label bearing 1924 patent date, screw cap. 45.00

FIRE-KING

Fire-King is an Anchor Hocking product. Anchor Hocking resulted from the 1937 merger of the Anchor Cap Company and Hocking Glass Corporation, each of which had been involved in several previous mergers.

Oven-proof Fire-King glass was made between 1942 and 1976 in a variety of patterns including Alice, Fleurette, Game Bird, Honeysuckle, Laurel, Swirl, and Wheat, and body colors such as azurite, forest green, jadeite, peach luster, ruby red, and white. Non-decorated utilitarian pieces also were made.

Housewives liked Fire-King because the line included matching dinnerware and ovenware. Anchor Hocking's marketing strategy included the aggressive sale of starter sets.

Anchor Hocking used two methods to mark Fire-King—a mark molded directly on the piece and an oval foil paper label.

References: Gene Florence, *Anchor Hocking's Fire-King & More*, Collector Books, 1998; Gary Kilgo et al., *A Collectors Guide to Anchor Hocking's Fire-King Glassware, 2nd Edition*, published by authors, 1997; April M. Tvorak, *Fire-King, Fifth Edition*, published by author, 1997.

Collectors' Club: The Fire-King Collectors Club, 1406 E 14th St, Des Moines, IA 50316.

Alice, cup and saucer, jadeite $9.00

Alice, saucer, blue trim 1.00

Anniversary, pie plate 25.00

Black Dots/Ivory, mixing bowl, 7¹⁄₂" 39.00

Bubble, bowl, 8¹⁄₂" 21.00

Bubble, fruit bowl 15.00

Bubble, soup bowl 15.00

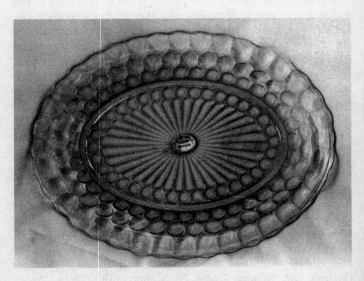

Bubble, platter, 12" l, blue, $14.00.

Charm, creamer and sugar. **16.00**
Charm, saucer, azurite, with label **1.25**
Charm, saucer, jadeite. **1.25**
Fruits, cake pan, sq **38.00**
Fruits, casserole, cov, pt. **27.00**
Fruits, casserole, cov, qt. **34.00**
Fruits, chili bowl, 5" **14.00**
Fruits, custard cup. **11.00**
Fruits, loaf pan, 9". **29.00**
Fruits, refrigerator dish, 4 x 4" **22.00**
Jadeite, batter jug, ³/₄" band **30.00**
Jadeite, batter jug, 1" band **45.00**
Jadeite, bowl, Swedish modern, 5". **135.00**
Jadeite, bowl, swirl, 8". **30.00**
Jadeite, bowl, swirl, 9". **32.00**
Jadeite, bread and butter plate, G-297, 6³/₄" **11.00**
Jadeite, cup and saucer, St Denis **16.00**
Jadeite, chili bowl, G-291 . . . . **13.00**
Jadeite, dinner plate **23.00**
Jadeite, eggcup **46.00**
Jadeite, lunch plate, G-316 . . . . **59.00**
Jadeite, mug **8.00**
Jadeite, pitcher, 20 oz **115.00**
Jadeite, platter, G-308, 9¹/₂ x 11¹/₂". **58.00**
Jadeite, skillet, 1 spout. **150.00**
Jane Ray, bowl, 4¹/₂" **22.00**
Jane Ray, bowl, 8¹/₄" **30.00**
Jane Ray, cereal bowl, 6" **24.00**
Jane Ray, creamer **15.00**
Jane Ray, cup **5.00**
Jane Ray, cup and saucer. **9.00**
Jane Ray, dinner plate **10.00**
Jane Ray, lunch plate. **12.00**
Jane Ray, platter, oval **32.00**
Jane Ray, soup bowl, 7³/₄" **27.50**
Jane Ray, sugar, cov. **12.00**
Kimberly, soup bowl, green **3.00**
Ovenware, baker, cov, 1 pt, 5¹/₂" **15.00**
Ovenware, baker lid, 4¹/₂" **5.00**
Ovenware, baker lid, 7¹/₄" **7.00**
Ovenware, cereal bowl, 5¹/₂" **20.00**
Ovenware, loaf pan, cov **12.75**
Ovenware, nurser, 4 oz **12.75**
Ovenware, refrigerator dish lid, 4¹/₂ x 5". **7.00**
Peach Blossom, casserole, cov, qt **32.00**
Peach Blossom, chili bowl, 5" **14.50**
Peach Blossom, coffee mug **14.00**
Philbe, casserole, cov, individual, sapphire blue, 10 oz. . . . **22.00**
Philbe, casserole, cov, sapphire blue, 2 qt **45.00**
Philbe, custard cup, sapphire blue, 5 oz. **2.50**
Philbe, pie plate, sapphire blue, 8³/₄" **14.00**
Philbe, utility bowl, sapphire blue, 6⁷/₈". **22.00**
Primrose, baking pan, oblong **24.00**
Primrose, cake pan, sq **29.00**
Primrose, creamer. **10.00**
Primrose, cup and saucer **12.00**
Primrose, custard cup **9.00**
Primrose, dessert bowl, 4⁵/₈" **7.00**
Primrose, dinner plate, 9¹/₈" d **13.00**
Primrose, platter, oval, 12". **22.00**
Primrose, salad plate, 7³/₈" **11.00**
Primrose, sugar, cov **20.00**
Red Dots/Ivory, grease jar, cov **45.00**
Red Dots/Ivory, mixing bowl, 8¹/₂" **35.00**

Shell, bowl, jadeite, 4¹/₂" **15.00**
Shell, cereal bowl, jadeite **25.00**
Shell, platter, oval, jadeite **88.00**
Shell, salad plate, jadeite. **17.00**
Shell, sugar, cov, orig label, jadeite **115.00**
Swirl Orange Luster, demitasse cup **10.00**
Swirl Orange Luster, demitasse cup and saucer. **15.00**
Tulips, grease jar **40.00**
Tulips, mixing bowl, 8¹/₂". **42.00**
Turquoise, cereal bowl, 4¹/₂" **15.00**

FISHER-PRICE

Irving L. Price, a retired F. W. Woolworth executive, Herman G. Fisher, previously with Alderman-Fairchild Toy Company, and Helen M. Schelle, a former toy store owner, founded Fisher-Price Toys in 1930. The company was headquartered in East Aurora, New York. Margaret Evans Price, a writer and illustrator of children's books and wife of Irving Price, was the company's first artist and designer.

Toys made prior to 1962 are marked with a black and white rectangular logo. Plastic was introduced for the first time in 1949.

The company remained in private hands until acquired by the Quaker Oats Company in 1969.

Reference: John J. Murray and Bruce R. Fox, *Fisher-Price, 1931–1963: A Historical, Rarity, Value Guide,* Books Americana, Krause Publications, 1991.

Collectors' Club: Fisher-Price Collectors Club, 1442 N Ogden, Mesa, AZ 85205.

Note: Prices listed are for toys in excellent condition.

AllieGator, #653 . . . .**$120.00**
Barky Dog, #462. . . . . **125.00**
Bossy Bell, #656 . . . . **60.00**
Bouncing Bunny Cart, #307. . . . . **60.00**

Squeaky the Clown, #777, $250.00.

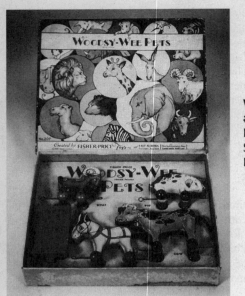

Woodsy-Wee Pets, #207, $860.00. Photo courtesy Skinner, Inc., Boston, MA.

Bucky Burro, #166 . . . . 200.00
Buddy Bullfrog, #728 . . . . 90.00
Bunny Cart, #10 . . . . 135.00
Cackling Hen, #120, white 45.00
Cement Mixer, #926 . . . . 325.00
Chuggy Pop-Up, #616 . . . . 125.00
Donald Duck Drum Major, #400 . . . . 200.00
Ducky Cart, #16 . . . . 125.00
Fido Zilo, #707 . . . . 110.00
Gabby Goofies, #775 . . . . 60.00
Golden Gulch Express, #191 . . . . 100.00
Happy Helicopter, #498 . . . . 200.00
Huffy Puffy Train, #999, with cars 130.00
Jingle Giraffe, #472 . . . . 225.00
Jolly Jumper, #450 . . . . 100.00
Jumbo Rollo, #755 . . . . 300.00
Leo the Drummer, #480 . . . . 200.00
Looky Chug-Chug, #220 . . . . 125.00
Molly Moo Moo, #190 . . . . 275.00
Moo Cow, #155 . . . . 100.00
Mother Goose, #164 . . . . 95.00
Musical Duck, #795 . . . . 75.00
Musical Sweeper, #100 . . . . 180.00
Musical Sweeper, #230 . . . . 125.00
Nosey Pup, #445 . . . . 85.00
Perky Pot, #686 . . . . 110.00
Pluto Pop-Up, #440 . . . . 135.00
Pony Chime, #137 . . . . 60.00
Pudgy Pig, #478 . . . . 60.00
Puffy Engine, #444 . . . . 70.00
Quacky Family, #799 . . . . 45.00
Queen Buzzy Bee, #314 . . . . 65.00
Racing Bowboat, #730 . . . . 150.00
Roller Chimes, #123 . . . . 100.00
Shaggy Zilo, #738 . . . . 120.00
Sleep Sue, #495 . . . . 55.00
Snoopy Sniffer, #180 . . . . 100.00
Snorky Fire Engine, #169, with figures 125.00
Squeaky the Clown, #777 . . . . 250.00
Stoopy Storky, #410 . . . . 375.00
Super-Jet, #415 . . . . 165.00

Tailspin Tabby, #400 . . . . 135.00
Tawny Tiger, #654 . . . . 85.00
Teddy Bear Parade, #195 . . . . 900.00
Timmy Turtle, #150 . . . . 60.00
Tuggy Turtle, #139 . . . . 125.00
Wiggly Woofer, #640 . . . . 120.00
Winky Blinky Fire Truck, #200 . . . . 85.00

FISHING

The modern fishing lure (plug) evolved at the end of the 19th century. Wood was used primarily for the body until replaced by plastic in the mid-1930s. Hundreds of lures, many with dozens of variations, are known to exist.

As lures became more sophisticated so did reels and rods. Improvement occurred in two areas—material and mechanism. Each improvement led to demand for more improvement. Drags and multiplying gears were added to reels. The split bamboo rod was eventually challenged by the modern graphite rod.

Serious collectors only buy examples in virtually unused condition and with their period packaging when possible. The high end of the market has become very investment focused. Many collectors are turning to licenses, paper ephemera, and secondary equipment in an effort to find affordable items within the category.

References: Ralf Coykendall, Jr., *Coykendall's Complete Guide to Sporting Collectibles,* Wallace-Homestead, Krause Publications, 1996; Carl F. Luckey, *Old Fishing Lures and Tackle, 5th Edition,* Krause Publications, 1999; Dudley Murphy and Rick Edmisten, *Fishing Lure Collectibles: An Identification and Value Guide to the Most Collectible Antique Fishing Lures,* Collector Books, 1995; Donald J. Peterson, *Folk Art Fish Decoys,* Schiffer Publishing, 1997; Harold E. Smith, *Collector's Guide to Creek Chub Lures & Collectibles,* Collector Books, 1997; R. L. Streater, *The Fishing Lure Collector's Bible,* Collector Books, 1999; Donna Tonelli, *Top of the Line Fishing Collectibles,* Schiffer Publishing, 1997; Karl T. White, *Fishing Tackle Antiques and Collectibles,* Holli Enterprises, 1995.

Periodical: *Fishing Collectibles Magazine,* 2005 Tree House Ln, Plano, TX 75023.

Newsletter: *The Fisherman's Trader,* PO Box 203, Gillette, NJ 07933.

Collectors' Clubs: American Fish Decoy Assoc, PO Box 252, Boulder Junction, WI 54512; National Fishing Lure Collectors Club, 22325 B Drive S, Marshall, MI 49068; Old Reel Collectors Assoc, 160 Shoreline Walk, Alpharetta, GA 30022.

Book, *Flyfisher & The Trout's Point of View, The,* Harding,
   Col EW, Seeley, London, 1931, first ed, 208 pp, illus $90.00
Book, *Practical Fly Fisherman, The,* McClane, AJ,
   Prentice-Hall, NY, 1953, first ed, 257 pp, color fly
   plates 30.00
Catalog, Heddon, color illus, cut-out "Liar's License for
   Fisherman" intact, 1939, 44 pp 265.00
Catalog, Pflueger Tackle Catalog, #158, unused order
   blank on last page, 1938, 128 pp 190.00
Creel, splint construction, bulbous, center hole circled
   with thin wood strips, form-fitted harness and shoulder strap, rawhide throng strap and splint loop latch,
   7½ x 13½ x 9" 140.00

Hunting and Fishing magazine, May 1938, $18.00.

Creel, split ash, hinged swivel lid, wood lid, small "Brookie" hole, 5½ x 10 x 10" 85.00

Creel, split willow, leather hanging strap 115.00

Creel, willow, large center hole with dowel handle, web handle strap, locking lid, 14 x 21 x 14" 65.00

Creel, willow, web carrying strap, locking lid strap, 10 x 15 x 12" 95.00

Decoy, Drake Pintail, painted eyes, slightly turned head 35.00

Display, Marathon Action Tackle, "The Lures They Like To Strike," molded plastic, stand-up, countertop, molded leaping musky at top, with 13 spoons and spinners, 17" h 30.00

Lure, Abbey & Imbrie Glowbody Minnow, glass tube body of luminous material attached to spinning keels, orig flattened picture box, c1920 . . . . 85.00

Lure, Heddon, Closed Leg Luny Frog, double belly hook, single tail hook, toilet seat hardware. 140.00

Lure, Heddon, Deep Diving Wiggler, #1600, inch worm line tie, side mounted hooks, L-rig hardware, finished in frog. 140.00

Lure, Lockart Water Witch, white with red, 2½" l 82.00

Lure, Thoren Minnow Chaser, minnow and fish attached to wire, fish finished in green scale, silver minnow with black eyes trailing feathers attached to snap 190.00

Lure, Woods Expert Minnow, 5-hook, shaped body, brass holed props, twisted wire hook hangers, glass eyes, dark green back bending to gray on belly, 4" l 225.00

Minnow Bucket, tin, orig green paint, Lucky Floater Co, Chicago decal, spring loaded rod and cover, spring wire latch on lid 90.00

Reel, D Scribner, trout click reel, brass, raised pillar, crank handle, 2⅝" d, ⅞" w spool 165.00

Reel, "Fin-Nor Since 1933-N0. 2," salmon or salt water reel, anti-reverse, gold anodized, 3⅛" d, 1" w spool 215.00

Reel, Hardy, St George Fly Reel, 3-screw latch hub, agate line guide, smooth brass foot, ivorine handle, 3¾" d, ⅞" w spool. 225.00

Reel, Julius Vom Hofe, NY, trout click reel, mkd handle plate, #1, 2⅞" d, 1" wide spool 500.00

Rod, Gary Howells, H006, trout rod, 8 ft, 2 pc, 2 tip, 4⅛ oz, 5-wt line, screw up-locking reel seat, with bag and tube. 1,925.00

Rod, Hardy, "The Wye," salmon rod, 10½ ft, 3 pc, 2 tip, rubbed ball butt button, sliding screw locking band reel seat, thread locking ferrules, agate stripper, turned walnut ferrules, plugs and intermediate winds, light soiling to handle, with orig canvas case with reel seat wrench 415.00

Rod, Pinky Gillum, Serial #1-790, fly rod, 8 ft 9", 2 pc, 2 tip, screw up-locking reel seat, professionally refurbished, with bag and tube. 1,100.00

Rod, WG Scoffler, fly rod, 9 ft, 2 pc, 2 tip, 9-wt line, dark flaming, slide band up-locking reel seat, burl walnut spacer, decorative butt turnings, small removable extension butt with turnings, ferrule plug, and agate stripping guide, with orig bag and tube. 715.00

Shipping Crate, "Pflueger Fishing Tackle, Pronounced Flew-Ger/Akron, Ohio, U.S.A." on both sides in black paint, 21 x 38 x 18". 110.00

Tackle Box, mahogany, cedar lined, leather handle, brass reinforced corners, brass hasp, 2 felt-lined lift-out trays and divided compartment, 9 x 16 x 9" 75.00

Tackle Box, metal, dark green crackle finish, "Heddon-Outing" decal inside lid, cantilevered tray, fold-down handle and black japanned int 165.00

FLASHLIGHTS

The flashlight owes its origin to the search for a suitable bicycle light. The Acme Electric Lamp Company, New York, NY, manufactured the first bicycle light in 1896. Development was rapid. In 1899 Conrad Hubert filed a patent for a tubular hand-held flashlight. Two years later, Hubert had sales offices in Berlin, Chicago, London, Montreal, Paris, and Sydney.

Conrad Hubert's American Eveready company has dominated the flashlight field for the past century. National Carbon purchased the balance of the company in 1914, having bought a half-interest in it in 1906. Aurora, Chase, Franco, and Ray-O-Vac are other collectible companies.

Collectors focus on flashlights from brand name companies, novelty flashlights, and character licensed flashlights.

References: L-W Book Sales, *Flashlights Price Guide*, L-W Book Sales, 1995; Stuart Schneider, *Collecting Flashlights*, Schiffer Publishing, 1997.

Collectors' Club: Flashlight Collectors of America, PO Box 4095, Tustin, CA 92781.

Advertising, Coca-Cola, figural plastic bottle, 1970, 8⅛" $20.00

Advertising, Life Savers, ADI, Inc, NY, made in Hong Kong, 1980, 7¼" l 35.00

Burgess, Model 446, 3 Cell Prefocused Spotlight, orig box, 1950, 9" l 10.00

Burgess, Model 452, 2 cell, orig box, 1945, 7" l 10.00

Challenge, aluminum, 1946, 15" l 10.00

Challenge, brass, 1933, 5½" l 15.00

Character, Donald Duck, Dan Brechner Co, ©Walt Disney Productions, 1948, 6½" l 35.00

Character, Space Patrol, Ray-O-Vac, rocketship shape, metal body, plastic nose cone, rubber tip, bottom plastic band holds exhaust jets and fins with "Official Patrol Rocket Lite" or "Commando Buzz Corry," 4 x 5 x 12". 200.00

Delta, Powerlite lantern, 1937, 6¾" 30.00

Olin Bond & Winchester, 2-cell, metal, 7¹/₂" l, $45.00. Photo courtesy Collectors Auction Services.

Eveready, aluminum, 1923, 6¹/₈" l 15.00
Eveready, Big Jim Masterlite, aluminum, 1961, 10" l 10.00
Eveready, Dayglo lantern, 1930, 3³/₄" 25.00
Eveready, Gaslight Torch, #3266, brass, 1931, 10" l 50.00
Eveready, Masterlite, aluminum, green paint, 1948, 7" l 5.00
Eveready, Official Boy Scouts of America, #2697, plas-
    tic, 1938, 7¹/₂" l 15.00
Eveready, pen light, 1960, 6" l 5.00
Figural, gun, aluminum, 1937, 5³/₈" l 30.00
Keen Kutter, aluminum, 1930, 10" l 40.00
Kwik-Lite, brass, 1932, 14¹/₂" 15.00
Marbo-Lite, combination lighter/flashlight, 1950, 2¹/₂ x
    2¹/₈" 40.00
Montgomery Ward, aluminum, 2-way switches changes
    from spot to flood, 1933, 9¹/₂" l 20.00
Niagara Flashlight Co, aluminum, 1939, 7¹/₄" l 20.00
Niagara Flashlight Co, brass, "B.P.C.E." emblem, 1928,
    3¹/₄" l 15.00
Ranger, aluminum, 1948, 10¹/₂" l 15.00
Ray-O-Vac, copper, 1930, 7¹/₂" l 20.00
Winchester, aluminum, 1940, 7" l 25.00
Winchester, brass, 1940, 6³/₄" l 35.00

FLATWARE

Flatware refers to forks, knives, serving pieces, and spoons. There are four basic types of flatware: (1) sterling silver, (2) silver plated, (3) stainless, and (4) Dirilyte.

Sterling silver flatware has a silver content of 925 parts silver per thousand. Knives have a steel or stainless steel blade. Silver plating refers to the electroplating of a thin coating of pure silver, 1,000 parts silver per thousand, on a base metal such as brass, copper, or nickel silver. While steel only requires the addition of 13% chromium to be classified stainless, most stainless steel flatware is made from an 18/8 formula, i.e., 18% chromium for strength and stain resistance and 8% nickel for a high luster and long-lasting finish. Dirilyte is an extremely hard, solid bronze alloy developed in Sweden in the early 1900s. Although gold in color, it has no gold in it.

Most flatware is purchased by individuals seeking to replace a damaged piece or to expand an existing pattern. Prices vary widely, depending on what the seller had to pay and how he views the importance of the pattern. Prices listed below represent what a modern replacement service quotes a customer.

Abbreviations used in the listings include:

FH	Flat Handle	SS	Sterling Silver
HH	Hollow Handle	ST	Stainless Steel
SP	Silver Plated		

References: Frances M. Bones and Lee Roy Fisher, *Standard Encyclopedia of American Silverplate and Hollow Ware*, Collector Books, 1998; Maryanne Dolan, *American Sterling Silver Flatware, 1830's–1990's*, Books Americana, Krause Publications, 1993; Tere Hagan, *Silverplated Flatware, Revised Fourth Edition*, Collector Books, 1990, 1998 value update; Richard Osterberg, *Sterling Silver Flatware for Dining Elegance*, Schiffer Publishing, 1994; Dorothy T. Rainwater, *Encyclopedia of American Silver Manufacturers, Fourth Edition Revised*, Schiffer Publishing, 1998; Replacements, Ltd., *Stainless Steel Flatware Identification Guide*, Replacements, Ltd., n.d.; Harry L. Rinker, *Silverware of the 20th Century: The Top 250 Patterns*, House of Collectibles, 1997.

Gorham, Colonial Tipt, ST, butter knife, HH, 7" $12.00
Gorham, Colonial Tipt, ST, fork, 8¹/₈" 10.00
Gorham, Colonial Tipt, ST, gravy ladle, 7" 17.00
Gorham, Colonial Tipt, ST, iced tea spoon, 7³/₄" 10.00
Gorham, Colonial Tipt, ST, knife, pistol grip, modern
    blade, 9¹/₄" 15.00
Gorham, Colonial Tipt, ST, salad fork 10.00
Gorham, Colonial Tipt, ST, soup spoon, oval bowl, 7" 10.00
Gorham, Colonial Tipt, ST, tablespoon, 8¹/₂" 15.00
Gorham, Golden Melon Bud, ST, butter serving knife,
    HH, 7" 20.00
Gorham, Golden Melon Bud, ST, cold meat fork, 8⁵/₈" 22.00
Gorham, Golden Melon Bud, ST, fork, 8¹/₈" 15.00
Gorham, Golden Melon Bud, ST, gravy ladle, 7¹/₄" 22.00

Gorham, Colonial Tipt.

International, Joan of Arc.

Gorham, Golden Melon Bud, ST, iced tea spoon, 7⅝" 12.00
Gorham, Golden Melon Bud, ST, knife, HH, modern
  blade, 9¼" 17.00
Gorham, Golden Melon Bud, ST, salad fork, 7⅛" 12.00
Gorham, Golden Melon Bud, ST, soup spoon, oval bowl,
  7" 12.00
Gorham, Golden Melon Bud, ST, sugar spoon, 6⅛" 15.00
Gorham, Golden Melon Bud, ST, tablespoon, 8⅝" 20.00
Gorham, Golden Melon Bud, ST, teaspoon, 6⅛" 10.00
Gorham, Lyric, SS, baby spoon, straight handle, 4½" 32.00
Gorham, Lyric, SS, bonbon spoon, 4¾" 45.00
Gorham, Lyric, SS, butter spreader, FH, 5¾" 25.00
Gorham, Lyric, SS, demitasse spoon, 4⅜" 22.00
Gorham, Lyric, SS, fork, 7⅜" 40.00
Gorham, Lyric, SS, gravy ladle, 6¼" 80.00
Gorham, Lyric, SS, iced tea spoon, 7⅝" 35.00
Gorham, Lyric, SS, jelly spoon, 6¼" 32.00
Gorham, Lyric, SS, salad fork, 6½" 32.00
Gorham, Lyric, SS, sugar spoon, 6" 35.00
Gorham, Lyric, SS, teaspoon, 6" 25.00
Gorham, Ribbon Edge, ST, butter serving knife, HH, 7" 12.00
Gorham, Ribbon Edge, ST, cold meat fork, 8¾" 17.00
Gorham, Ribbon Edge, ST, fork, 8" 10.00
Gorham, Ribbon Edge, ST, gravy ladle, 7⅛" 17.00
Gorham, Ribbon Edge, ST, knife, HH, modern blade,
  9⅛" 15.00
Gorham, Ribbon Edge, ST, salad fork, 7⅛" 10.00
Gorham, Ribbon Edge, ST, soup spoon, oval bowl, 6⅞" 10.00
Gorham, Ribbon Edge, ST, sugar spoon, 6⅛" 10.00
Gorham, Ribbon Edge, ST, tablespoon, 8⅝" 15.00
Gorham, Ribbon Edge, ST, teaspoon 7.00
International, Enchantress, SS, butter serving knife, FH,
  7⅛" 40.00
International, Enchantress, SS, butter spreader, FH, 5¾" 25.00
International, Enchantress, SS, cocktail fork, 5½" 27.00
International, Enchantress, SS, cream soup spoon, round
  bowl, 6½" 37.00
International, Enchantress, SS, fork, 7¼" 45.00
International, Enchantress, SS, jelly spoon, 6½" 35.00
International, Enchantress, SS, knife, HH, New French
  blade, 9⅛" 32.00

International, Enchantress, SS, soup spoon, oval bowl,
  6¾" 40.00
International, Enchantress, SS, teaspoon, 6" 25.00
International, Joan of Arc, SS, butter serving knife, HH,
  7" 32.00
International, Joan of Arc, SS, butter spreader, FH, 5¾" 25.00
International, Joan of Arc, SS, carving knife, ST blade,
  10¾" 50.00
International, Joan of Arc, SS, cream soup spoon, round
  bowl, 6" 40.00
International, Joan of Arc, SS, fork, 7⅜" 35.00
International, Joan of Arc, SS, grapefruit spoon, round
  bowl, 7⅛" 40.00
International, Joan of Arc, SS, gravy ladle, 6½" 90.00
International, Joan of Arc, SS, jelly spoon, 6⅜" 40.00
International, Joan of Arc, SS, knife, HH, modern blade,
  8⅝" 32.00
International, Joan of Arc, SS, knife, New French blade,
  9¼" 32.00
International, Joan of Arc, SS, lemon fork, 6" 37.00
International, Joan of Arc, SS, soup spoon, 7¼" 45.00
International, Joan of Arc, SS, sugar spoon, shell shaped
  bowl, 6⅛" 32.00
International, Joan of Arc, SS, tablespoon, 8¼" 80.00
Kirk Stieff, Golden Winslow, baby fork, 3¾" 45.00
Kirk Stieff, Golden Winslow, baby spoon, straight han-
  dle, 3¾" 45.00
Kirk Stieff, Golden Winslow, fork, 7¼" 60.00
Kirk Stieff, Golden Winslow, fork, 7¾" 75.00
Kirk Stieff, Golden Winslow, knife 45.00
Kirk Stieff, Golden Winslow, salad fork 65.00
Kirk Stieff, Golden Winslow, soup spoon, oval bowl, 6⅛" 70.00
Kirk Stieff, Golden Winslow, tablespoon, 6" 35.00
Oneida, Paul Revere, ST, butter serving knife, HH, 6⅜" 10.00
Oneida, Paul Revere, ST, butter spreader, HH, 6¼" 10.00
Oneida, Paul Revere, ST, casserole spoon, 8⅝" 15.00
Oneida, Paul Revere, ST, cocktail fork, 6" 10.00
Oneida, Paul Revere, ST, cold meat fork, 8½" 12.00
Oneida, Paul Revere, ST, demitasse spoon, 4½" 7.00

Oneida, Silver Artistry.

Reed & Barton, English Chippendale.

Reed & Barton, English Chippendale, SS, teaspoon, 6¼" **30.00**
Whiting, King Albert, SS, bonbon spoon, 4³/₈" **40.00**
Whiting, King Albert, SS, butter serving knife, FH, 6³/₈" **35.00**
Whiting, King Albert, SS, carving fork, ST tines, 9" **55.00**
Whiting, King Albert, SS, cocktail fork, 5³/₈" **27.00**
Whiting, King Albert, SS, cream sauce ladle, 5½" **45.00**
Whiting, King Albert, SS, demitasse spoon, 4¹/₈" **20.00**
Whiting, King Albert, SS, fish fork, 6¼" **45.00**
Whiting, King Albert, SS, fork, 7¼" **45.00**
Whiting, King Albert, SS, fruit fork, ST tines, 6⁷/₈" **32.00**
Whiting, King Albert, SS, fruit knife, ST blade, 8" **32.00**
Whiting, King Albert, SS, fruit spoon, 5⁷/₈" **35.00**
Whiting, King Albert, SS, gravy ladle, 6¼" **80.00**
Whiting, King Albert, SS, iced tea spoon, 7³/₈" **35.00**
Whiting, King Albert, SS, jelly spoon, 6⁵/₈" **30.00**
Whiting, King Albert, SS, lemon fork, 4³/₄" **30.00**
Whiting, King Albert, SS, mayonnaise ladle, 5" **40.00**
Whiting, King Albert, SS, pie server, SP blade, 9½" **60.00**
Whiting, King Albert, SS, salad fork, 6³/₈" **32.00**
Whiting, King Albert, SS, sugar spoon, 6¹/₈" **37.00**
Whiting, King Albert, SS, teaspoon, 5⁷/₈" **25.00**

FLORENCE CERAMICS

Florence Ward of Pasedena, California, began making ceramic objects as a form of therapy in dealing with the loss of a young son. The products she produced and sold from her garage workshop provided pin money during the Second World War.

With the support of Clifford, her husband, and Clifford, Jr., their son, Florence Ward moved her ceramics business to a plant on the east side of Pasadena in 1946. Business boomed after Ward exhibited at several Los Angeles gift shows. In 1949 a state-of-the-art plant was built at 74 South San Gabriel Boulevard, Pasadena.

Florence Ceramics is best known for its figural pieces, often costumed in Colonial and Godey fashions. The company also produced birds, busts, candle holders, lamps, smoking sets, and wall pockets. Betty Davenport Ford joined the company in 1956, designing a line of bisque animal figures. Production ended after two years.

Scripto Corporation bought Florence Ceramics in 1964 following the death of Clifford Ward. Production was shifted to advertising specialty ware. Operations ceased in 1977.

Reference: Doug Fouland, *The Florence Collectibles: The Era of Elegance*, Schiffer Publishing, 1995.

Collectors' Club: Florence Collector's Club, PO Box 122, Richland, WA 99352.

Oneida, Paul Revere, ST, fork, 7¼" **7.00**
Oneida, Paul Revere, ST, fruit spoon, 5⁷/₈" **7.00**
Oneida, Paul Revere, ST, gravy ladle, 7³/₈" **12.00**
Oneida, Paul Revere, ST, iced tea spoon, 7½" **7.00**
Oneida, Paul Revere, ST, knife, HH, modern blade, 8½" **10.00**
Oneida, Paul Revere, ST, pie server, 9³/₄" **15.00**
Oneida, Paul Revere, ST, salad fork, 6½" **7.00**
Oneida, Paul Revere, ST, soup spoon, oval bowl, 6³/₄" **7.00**
Oneida, Paul Revere, ST, sugar spoon, 5⁷/₈" **10.00**
Oneida, Paul Revere, ST, tablespoon, 8½" **12.00**
Oneida, Paul Revere, ST, teaspoon, 6" **7.00**
Oneida, Silver Artistry, SP, baby fork, 7½" **15.00**
Oneida, Silver Artistry, SP, butter serving knife, FH, 6⁵/₈" **15.00**
Oneida, Silver Artistry, SP, demitasse spoon, 4½" **10.00**
Oneida, Silver Artistry, SP, fork, 7½" **15.00**
Oneida, Silver Artistry, SP, gravy ladle, 7³/₄" **25.00**
Oneida, Silver Artistry, SP, iced tea spoon, 7½" **5.00**
Oneida, Silver Artistry, SP, knife, HH, modern blade, 9¼" **15.00**
Oneida, Silver Artistry, SP, pie server, 9³/₄" **45.00**
Oneida, Silver Artistry, SP, salad fork, 6⁷/₈" **12.00**
Oneida, Silver Artistry, SP, soup spoon, oval bowl, 7" **12.00**
Oneida, Silver Artistry, SP, steak knife, 9¹/₈" **17.00**
Oneida, Silver Artistry, SP, sugar spoon, shell shaped
  bowl, 5³/₄" **15.00**
Oneida, Silver Artistry, SP, teaspoon, 6¹/₈" **10.00**
Reed & Barton, English Chippendale, SS, butter serving
  knife, HH, 7³/₈" **40.00**
Reed & Barton, English Chippendale, SS, cold meat fork,
  8³/₄" **95.00**
Reed & Barton, English Chippendale, SS, fish knife, ST
  blade, 8¹/₈" **40.00**
Reed & Barton, English Chippendale, SS, fork, 7½" **60.00**
Reed & Barton, English Chippendale, SS, fruit knife, ST
  blade, 7⁵/₈" **35.00**
Reed & Barton, English Chippendale, SS, knife, HH,
  modern blade, 9" **30.00**
Reed & Barton, English Chippendale, SS, salad fork, 6⁵/₈" **45.00**
Reed & Barton, English Chippendale, SS, soup ladle, ST
  bowl, 11¼" **70.00**
Reed & Barton, English Chippendale, SS, soup spoon,
  oval bowl, 6⁷/₈" **45.00**
Reed & Barton, English Chippendale, SS, tablespoon,
  8⁷/₈" **90.00**

Ashtray, shell. **$60.00**
Figurine, Amber, 9¼" h **275.00**
Figurine, Beth, 7½" h **85.00**
Figurine, Bud, 7½" h **200.00**
Figurine, Catherine, 6³/₄" h **375.00**
Figurine, Charmaine, Godey fashions, 22K gold trim,
  8½" h **275.00**
Figurine, cockatoo, W24, 13¼" **275.00**
Figurine, Colleen, 8" h **145.00**
Figurine, Cynthia, 9¼" h **375.00**
Figurine, David, 7½" h **125.00**
Figurine, Elizabeth, 8¼ x 7" **375.00**
Figurine, Jenette, 7³/₄" h **175.00**
Figurine, John **200.00**

Delia, burgundy, 7³/₄" h, $125.00.

Figurine, Judy, 8³/₄" h 250.00
Figurine, Laura, 7¹/₂" h 130.00
Figurine, Lillian, gray 115.00
Figurine, Marie Antionette, 10" h 350.00
Figurine, Mary 200.00
Figurine, mockingbird, W4, 5¹/₄" h 200.00
Figurine, Patsy, 6" h 40.00
Figurine, Peter, 9¹/₄" h 250.00
Figurine, Priscilla, 7³/₄" h 225.00
Figurine, Rosie, 7" h 100.00
Figurine, Shirley, 8" h 225.00
Floraline Basket 85.00
Floraline Candle Holders, pr 60.00
Floraline Vase 35.00
Floraline Wall Plaque 125.00
Flower Holder, Blossom Girl 100.00
Flower Holder, Lantern Boy 100.00
Flower Holder, May, 6¹/₂" h 40.00
Flower Holder, Polly, turquoise hat 25.00
Flower Holder, Sally 40.00
Flower Holder, Wendy 75.00
Lamp, Clarissa 325.00
Lamp, Genevieve 300.00
Mantel Clock, electric, 13" h 125.00
Vase, shell, pink and gray luster, stamped "Florence
    Ceramics," 6 x 6¹/₂" 75.00
Wall Pocket, Violet, 7" h 150.00
Wall Vase, shell 75.00

FOLK ART

The definition of folk art is fluid, defined by what subcategories contemporary collectors decide are in or out at any given moment. Simply put, folk art is trendy. Edie Clark's "What Really Is Folk Art?" in the December 1986 issue of *Yankee* continues to be one of the most insightful pieces yet written on the subject.

The folk art craze struck with a vengeance in the early 1970s. Auction houses hyped folk art ranging from quilts to weathervanes as great long-term investments. Several market manipulators cornered then touted the work of contemporary artists. The speculative bubble burst in the late 1980s when the market was flooded and excellent reproductions fooled many novice buyers.

References: Chuck and Jan Rosenak, *Contemporary American Folk Art: A Collector's Guide,* Abbeville Press, 1996; Clifford A. Wallach and Michael Cornish, *Tramp Art: One Notch at a Time,* Wallach-Irons Publishing, 1998.

Newsletter: *Folk Art Finder,* One River, Essex, CT 06426.

Collectors' Club: Folk Art Society of America, PO Box 17041, Richmond, VA 23226.

Cane, wood, carved, standing figure of lady with bonnet, umbrella and purse atop carved shaft with entwined snake and frog, 1 pc shaft, no ferrule, 9" l handle **$575.00**
Decoy, Pintail Drake, Al Wragg and Doug Burrell, Canada, carved wing and tail, orig paint, glass eyes, c1960, 17" l 75.00
Figural Group, Pyramid, Reverend Hayes, upright carving consisting of 8 units, crosshatch work, carved children, free-turning figure near center, 1 pc except for base, carved signature "W. Va. 1992 Rev. Hayes," 15" h 175.00
Figure, black bear, Garland and Minnie Adkins, carved and painted wood, 1 pc, black, white, and red, sgd "G & M Adkins 1989," 30" l, 13³/₄" h 345.00
Figure, comical figure, carved wood, initialed "S.T." 45.00
Figure, fish, carved wood, tin fins with orig white paint with black, blue, and red sponging, matching base, 16" l 55.00
Figure, man, Lavell Nickoll, carved poplar, standing man with arms at sides, wearing jacket, painted in black, deep red, yellow, ochre, peach, and white, 1992, 8³/₄" h 90.00
Figure, seated dog, whittled pine, jointed ears and legs, orig white paint with black spots, 11³/₄" h 195.00
Fraktur, drawing, watercolor pen, and ink on paper, David Elliger, red, yellow, and black fantailed rooster beneath arched tulip, c1950 . . . . 750.00
Painting, acrylic on board, Bicycle Race, Paul Lehman, Laureldale, PA, group of high-wheel bicyclers in front of merchants' building/jail, jail located at 5th and Washington, Reading, PA, sgd and dated "P. Lehman '90," 16 x 12" 125.00
Painting, colored pencil on paper, Elephant, Gerald "Creative" DePrie, blue and gray tones, sgd on foam board mount, 23" h 95.00
Painting, oil on canvas, Coney Island, Vestie Davis, children and adults on boardwalk, sgd and dated "Vestie E. Davis, 1977" in lower right, 15¹/₄ x 1³/₈" 2,200.00
Painting, oil on canvas, Farm of the Groves, Blair Streeter, winter scene, 1957, 25 x 29¹/₂" 3,575.00
Painting, oil on canvas, Wash Day, house, tree, wash drying on line, sgd, verso inscribed "Wash Day," 26 x 36", c1940 . . . . 2,640.00
Painting, watercolor on paper, portrait of man and woman, sgd "Holly June Wesley, April 1978," curly maple frame, 17¹/₂" h, 15¹/₂" w 165.00
Plaque, relief carved profile of Abraham Lincoln, natural patina, 6¹/₂" h, 4¹/₂" w 25.00
Plaque, relief carved three-quarter view of "President Elect Herbert Hoover," initialed "F.A.A.," 8" h, 6⁵/₈" w 30.00
Quilt, Tiger Quilt, Garland and Minnie Adkins, pieced and appliquéd, white, yellow, brown, red, black, and green, machine sewn, hand quilted, yellow border and reverse, sgd "G & M Adkins 1991," 78 x 94" 275.00

Redware, candlestick, Isaac Stahl, Powder Valley, PA,
cobalt and slip dec, molded candle socket on flaring
support with incised base and circular molded drip-
pan mounted with rope twist handle, inscribed "Made
by I.S. Stahl / May 13–1938," 5" h **575.00**
Sandstone, seated sheep, "Popeye" Reed, tooled and
carved, incised "E. Reed," 19" l, 12³/₄" h **625.00**
Sewer Tile Art, bank, pig, standing upright, wearing hat,
bow tie, and jacket, incised "W.S.," 8⁷/₈" **65.00**
Sewer Tile Art, flowerpot, tree stump, 6½" **25.00**
Sewer Tile Art, owl, white clay eyes, incised "D.C.
1935," 8³/₄" h **350.00**
Sewer Tile Art, salt and pepper shakers, pr, tooled tree
bark, 3" h **275.00**
Sewer Tile Art, seated dog, hand-molded detail, long
pointed nose, bottom incised ""H.F.D. 1926," repairs
to base and muzzle, 10½" h **1,650.00**
Sewer Tile Art, squirrel eating nut, yellow slip eye,
incised "CM 1980," 6³/₄" h **28.00**
Sewer Tile Art, umbrella stand, ovoid, Art Deco designs
around shoulder, 18½" h **72.00**
Theorem, watercolor on paper, flowers, fruit, and
foliage, framed, 8³/₄" h, 10³/₄" w **500.00**
Theorem, watercolor on paper, TJ Graham, student of
David Elliger, basket of fruit and flowers, bird perched
on vine, painted frame, c1970, 19¼" h, 23¼" w **600.00**
Walking Stick, snake and lizard, Denzil Goodpaster,
carved and painted, 2 coiled snakes in green and yellow extend up each side of handle, brown and ivory
lizard sits on bottom half of stick below coiled snakes,
carved "DG," handle, 35" l, 6³/₄" w **125.00**
Whirligig, airplane, worn and weathered red, black,
green, and silver paint, 20th C, 18" l, 18" h **55.00**

FOOD MOLDS

The earliest food molds were ceramic and cast-iron molds used for
baking. Today most collectors think of food molds in terms of the
cast-iron candy molds, tin chocolate molds, and pewter ice cream
molds used in factories, candy shops, and drugstores throughout
the first half of the 19th century. Many of these chocolate and
pewter molds were imported from Germany and Holland.

A substantial collection of Jell-O and post-1960 metal and plastic molds can be assembled with a minimum of effort and expen-
diture. Collector interest in these items is minimal.

Beware of reproduction chocolate molds. They are old enough
to have developed a patina that matches some period molds.

Butter, cast aluminum, star, R Hall, Burlington, NC, ½ lb,
3½" d **$15.00**
Butter, wood, bee, Germany, 3½ x 1½" **35.00**
Cake, cast aluminum, lamb, 2 pc, Maid of Scandinavia
Co, Minneapolis, MN, 8" h, 13" l **30.00**
Cake, cast iron, lamb, Griswold, #866, 9" l **250.00**
Cake, stamped aluminum, Santa Claus climbing out of
chimney, 2 pc, c1960, 9" h **8.00**
Candy, cast aluminum, 2 rows of 4 egg shaped cups
each, hanging hole at end, 13" l, 4½" w **25.00**
Candy, wood, 5 hearts with cross and 1 circular floral
design, 15" l **325.00**
Cheese, carved wood, cow, 10" d **50.00**
Chocolate, cast aluminum, birds in flight, 7" h **50.00**
Chocolate, cast metal, 14 candy bars, Wilbur Candy Co **20.00**

**Chocolate Mold, tin, mkd "#108 Heille 80 Temple," 6³/₄" l,
$187.00.** Photo courtesy Collectors Auction Services.

Chocolate, metal alloy, duck, 8" h **60.00**
Chocolate, pewter, cupid, 1930 . . . . **40.00**
Chocolate, pewter, turkey **45.00**
Chocolate, steel and copper alloy, lamb, C Weygandt,
#381, 2³/₈" **60.00**
Chocolate, tin, Father Christmas on donkey, Santa with
peaked cap, long robe, and short jacket, 2 pc, 7" h **120.00**
Chocolate, tin, rabbit, 5³/₄" h **40.00**
Doughnut, hinged cast iron, wooden grips, 3-leaf clover
shape, Ace Clover Donut, Ace Co, St Louis, MO **60.00**
Ice Cream, pewter, asparagus, 3⁵/₈" h **35.00**
Ice Cream, pewter, flag, 13 stars **65.00**
Ice Cream, tin, Admiral Byrd bust, 2 pc **150.00**
Ice Cream, tin, bell **18.00**
Jelly, saltglazed stoneware, basket of flowers, German **30.00**
Pudding, tin, cone shape, spiral design **30.00**

FOOTBALL CARDS

Although football cards originated in the 1890s, the 1948
Bowman and Leaf Gum sets mark the birth of the modern football
card. Leaf only produced cards for two seasons. The last Bowman
set dates from 1955.

Topps entered the field in 1950 with a college stars set. It produced a National Football League set each year between 1956 and
1963. Topps lost its National Football League license to the
Philadelphia Gum Company for the 1964 season. Topps produced
only American Football League cards between 1964 and 1967.
Topps recovered the ball in 1968 when it once again was licensed
to produce National Football League cards. It has remained undefeated ever since.

Football cards remain a weaker sister when compared to baseball cards. Many felt the collapse of the baseball market in the
mid-1990s would open the door for a strong surge in the collectibility of football cards. This has not happened.

References: James Beckett, *The Official 2000 Price Guide to
Football Cards, 19th Edition,* House of Collectibles, 1999; James
Beckett and Dan Hitt (eds.), *Beckett Football Price Guide, No. 15,*
Beckett Publications, 1998; Sports Collectors Digest, *1998 Sports
Collectors Almanac,* Krause Publications, 1998.

Periodicals: *Beckett Football Card Magazine,* 15850 Dallas Pkwy,
Dallas, TX 75248; *Sports Cards,* 700 E State St, Iola, WI 54990;
Tuff Stuff, PO Box 569, Dubuque, IA 52004.

Note: Prices listed are for cards in near mint condition.

Bowman, 1948, #11, Jack Wiley **$20.00**
Bowman, 1948, common card (1-108) **18.00**
Bowman, 1950, #2, John Greene. **20.00**
Bowman, 1951, #12, Chuck Bednarik **65.00**
Bowman, 1951, common card (1-144) **18.00**
Bowman, 1952, #16, Frank Gifford, large **450.00**
Bowman, 1952, #133, Bob Williams, small **25.00**
Bowman, 1953, #17, Charley Trippi **40.00**
Bowman, 1953, common card (1-96) **25.00**
Bowman, 1954, #39, Charlie Justice **18.00**
Bowman, 1955, #102, Al Carmichael **8.00**
Bowman, 1991, complete set (561) **5.50**
Bowman, 1992, complete set (573) **200.00**
Bowman, 1993, #170, Michael Irvin **1.50**
Fleer, 1960, common card (1-132) **3.50**
Fleer, 1962, #3, Gino Cappelletti **16.00**
Fleer, 1963, #29, Ken Rice **8.00**
Fleer, 1976, #50, San Francisco, 49ersTeam Action **6.00**
Fleer, 1977, common card (1-56), Team Action **1.00**
Fleer, 1978, #13, Dallas Cowboys, Team Action **6.00**
Fleer, 1979, complete set (69), Team Action **40.00**
Fleer, 1980, complete set (70), Team Action **14.00**
Fleer, 1981, complete set (88), Team Action **18.00**
Fleer, 1990, complete set (400) **3.50**
Leaf, 1948, common card (1-49) **22.00**
Leaf, 1948, common card (50-98) **100.00**
Leaf, 1949, #150, Bulldog Turner **120.00**
McDonald's, 1975, complete set (4), Quarterbacks **8.00**
McDonald's, 1986, #16, Joe Montana, All-Stars **1.00**
McDonald's, 1993, complete set (87), Game Day **18.00**
Pacific, 1984, #1, OJ Simpson, Legends **2.50**
Pacific, 1991, complete set (660) **7.00**
Pacific, 1991, Flash Cards, complete set (1-110) **3.00**
Pacific, 1992, #6, Thurman Thomas, Picks the Pros **1.00**
Pacific, 1992, #14, Don Beebe . . . . **.05**
Pacific, 1993, #5, Brett Favre, Silver Prism Inserts **2.50**
Pacific, 1993, #317, Harold Green . . . . **.05**
Pacific, 1994, #1, Troy Aikman, Gems of the Crown **5.50**
Pacific, 1994, complete set, Knights of the Gridiron (20) **65.00**
Packers, 1961, #18, Bart Starr, Lake to Lake **80.00**
Philadelphia, 1964, #79, Bart Starr **28.00**
Philadelphia, 1966, #69, Alex Karras **10.00**
Philadelphia, 1967, #6, Billy Martin . . . . **.80**
Pinnacle, 1991, #348, Randall Cunningham . . . . **.10**
Pinnacle, 1991, complete set (415) **15.00**
Pinnacle, 1992, #6, Michael Irvin/Eric Allen, Team
  Pinnacle **4.00**
Pinnacle, 1992, #59, Mike Croel, Samples . . . . **.45**
Pinnacle, 1993, #2, Thurman Thomas, Men of Autumn . . . . **.35**
Pinnacle, 1993, #5, Curtis Conway, Rookies **5.50**
Pinnacle, 1993, #15, Dan Marino, Men of Autumn **2.00**
Playoff, 1993, #2, Jim Kelly, Absolute Die Cut Helmets **10.00**
Playoff, 1993, complete set (6), Promos **5.50**
Playoff, 1993, complete set (30), Absolute Die Cut
  Helmets **350.00**
Playoff, 1993, complete set (150), Contenders **18.00**
Power, 1993, #7, John Elway . . . . **.25**
Power, 1993, #21, Deion Sanders . . . . **.25**
Power, 1993, #29, AFC logo, Draft Picks . . . . **.10**
ProLine, 1991, #1, Jim Kelly, Portraits . . . . **.10**
ProLine, 1991, #67, Al Smith, Portraits . . . . **.02**
ProLine, 1992, complete set (16), Portraits Wives . . . . **.45**

Topps, 1970, #90,
OJ Simpson, $75.00.

ProLine, 1992, complete set (495), Profiles **4.50**
Score, 1989, #1, Joe Montana **1.50**
Score, 1989–90, #1A, Franco Harris **35.00**
Score, 1991, #7, Boomer Esiason . . . . **.10**
Score, 1992, #1, Barry Sanders . . . . **.65**
Score, 1992, #6, Richard Dent . . . . **.05**
Score, 1992, #65, Emmitt Smith **1.50**
Score, 1993, #46, Wendell Davis . . . . **.05**
Score, 1993, #265, Dan Marino **1.00**
Score, 1994, complete set (18), Dream Team **80.00**
Score, 1994, complete set (330) **8.00**
Topps, 1950, #7, Bob Bowlby, NC State, Felt Backs **40.00**
Topps, 1951, #47, Bill Putich, Wolverines, Magic **18.00**
Topps, 1955, #64, Benny Friedman, All-American **18.00**
Topps, 1956, #4, Eddie Bell **5.00**
Topps, 1956, #40, Philadelphia Eagles **16.00**
Topps, 1958, common card (1-132) **3.50**
Topps, 1959, #3, Detroit Lion **5.00**
Topps, 1960, complete set (132) **650.00**
Ultra, 1992, common card (1-450) . . . . **.05**
Ultra, 1992, complete set (450) **10.00**
Ultra, 1993, complete set (500) **25.00**
Ultra, 1994, #4, Seth Joyner . . . . **.05**

FOOTBALL MEMORABILIA

Football memorabilia divides into two distinct groups, professional and collegiate, and two distinct categories, equipment and paper ephemera. Collectors of professional football memorabilia far outnumber collectors of collegiate memorabilia. Equipment collectors exceed the number of collectors of paper ephemera.

The category is heavily post-1970 driven, due to availability, and regional in nature. Collectors want game-related material. Team logo material licensed for sale in sports shops has minimal to no appeal.

References: John Carpentier, *Price Guide to Packers Memorabilia,* Krause Publications, 1998; Roderick A. Malloy, *Malloy's Sports Collectibles Value Guide: Up-to-Date Prices for Noncard Sports Memorabilia,* Attic Books, Wallace-Homestead, Krause Publications, 1993; Jim Warren II, *Tuff Stuff's Complete Guide to Starting Lineup,* Antique Trader Books, 1997.

Periodical: *Sports Collectors Digest,* 700 E State St, Iola, WI 54990.

Autograph, Elway, John, PS, 8 x 10" **$18.00**
Autograph, Irvin, Michael, PS, 8 x 10" **20.00**
Autograph, Lombardi, Vince, cut signature **45.00**
Bank, Pittsburgh Steelers, plastic, helmet shape, 1970s,
   6" h **25.00**
Book, *How Champions Play Football*, 98 pp, paperback,
   1948. . . . . **10.00**
Bookends, pr, Knute Rockne, cast iron, incised inscrip-
   tion "The Rock Of Notre Dame," raised portrait,
   c1930s **160.00**
Booklet, Football Book Schedules & Information, Hires
   Root Beer premium, 1940 . . . . **15.00**
Carry Bag, vinyl, black and white, black plastic handle,
   zipper side, black and white newspaper print design
   with Super Bowl headlines, 11 x 13" **25.00**
Cigarette Lighter, San Francisco 49ers Super Bowl XVI
   Champs, silvered metal and plastic **25.00**
Drinking Glass, "Be A Packer Backer," Miller High Life,
   1940s. **30.00**
Drinking Glass, Notre Dame University, blue and gold,
   Victory March on back, 1950s, 5¼" h **15.00**
Figure, Aikman, Troy, Kenner Starting Lineup, 1990 . . . . **20.00**
Figure, Allen, Marcus, Kenner Starting Lineup, 1989. . . . . **15.00**
Figure, Cunningham, Randall, Sports Impressions, 6" h **45.00**
Game, All-American Football Game, Cadaco, 1960 . . . . **30.00**
Game, Arm Chair Quarterback, Novelty Mfg, 1955 . . . . **25.00**
Game, Foto-Electric Football, Cadaco, 1971. . . . . **8.00**
Keychain, Green Bay Packers, plastic, shield shape,
   1960s. **15.00**
Magazine, *Illustrated Football Annual*, 1938 . . . . **40.00**
Magazine, *Kickoff*, O J Simpson, USC, 1968. . . . . **32.00**
Magazine, *Lindy's College Football*, 1988 . . . . **7.00**
Magazine, *Sports All Stars*, Johnny Unitas, 1960 . . . . **38.00**
Magazine, *Stanley Woodward's Football*, 1953 . . . . **4.00**
Pencil Case, National Football League, vinyl, light blue,
   5 x 8½" **25.00**
Pinback Button, "74" in center with "Sack 'Em Dave!
   Dave Roller Fan Club" around rim, 1970s **15.00**
Plate, Lombardi, Vince, Sports Impressions, 8½" d **55.00**
Poster, 1982 Green Bay Packers **5.00**
Poster, Maynard, Don, *Sports Illustrated*, 1968–71 . . . . **18.00**
Poster, Starr, Bart, *Sports Illustrated*, 1968–71 . . . . **30.00**
Press Pin, Super Bowl IX, 1975 . . . . **275.00**

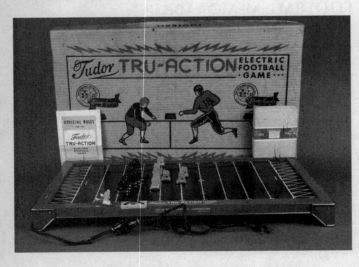

Tru-Action Electric Football Game, Tudor, $40.00.

Program, NFL Championship, Green Bay vs Dallas,
   1966. . . . . **200.00**
Program, *Philadelphia Enquirer* Charities 8th Annual
   Classic, Eagles vs Packers, Sep 13, 1945, Municipal
   Stadium **18.00**
Program, Sugar Bowl, 1958. . . . . **25.00**
Program, Super Bowl XVII, Washington and Miami,
   1982. . . . . **25.00**
Ticket, Ohio State, seating diagram on back, 1978 . . . . **1.50**
Ticket Stub, AFC Championship, 1976 . . . . **6.00**
Ticket Stub, Peach Bowl, Army/Illinois, 1985 . . . . **2.00**
Ticket Stub, Rose Bowl, California/Alabama, 1938 . . . . **30.00**
Wrapper, Bowman's Football, waxed paper, 1954, 5 x 6¼" **10.00**
Yearbook, 1963, Rams. **35.00**
Yearbook, 1965, Naval Academy, Roger Staubach's
   junior and senior years **75.00**
Yearbook, 1972, Dallas Cowboys. **30.00**

FOSTORIA

The Fostoria Glass Company broke ground for a glass factory in Fostoria, Ohio, on January 1, 1888. Within six months the factory was producing a line of glass bottles, shakers, and utilitarian wares. By 1891 Fostoria relocated to Moundsville, West Virginia.

Fostoria's stemware and tableware included a wide variety of products in crystal and colors designed to compete actively against Cambridge, Heisey, and Westmoreland. Fostoria changed with the times. When pressed and needle-etched glass fell from favor, the company turned to plate and master etchings. The role of color was increased. When teas and luncheons were replaced by brunches and cocktail parties, Fostoria added new patterns, shapes, and forms. Fostoria marketed aggressively, especially to the post-1945 bridal market.

Fostoria purchased Morgantown Glass in 1965, moving its operations to Moundsville in 1971. In 1983 Lancaster Colony Corporation purchased Fostoria. The Moundsville factory closed in 1986.

References: Frances Bones, *Fostoria Glassware: 1887–1982*, Collector Books, 1999; Gene Florence, *Elegant Glassware of the Depression Era, Seventh Edition,* Collector Books, 1997; Ann Kerr, *Fostoria: An Identification and Value Guide of Pressed, Blown & Hand Molded Shapes,* Collector Books, 1994, 1997 value update; Ann Kerr, *Fostoria, Volume II: Identification & Value Guide to Etched, Carved & Cut Designs,* Collector Books, 1997; Milbra Long and Emily Seate, *Fostoria Stemware* (1995), *Fostoria Tableware: 1924–1943* (1999), Collector Books; Leslie Piña, *Fostoria Designer George Sakier,* Schiffer Publishing, 1996; Leslie Piña, *Fostoria: Serving the American Table 1887–1986,* Schiffer Publishing, 1995.

Periodical: *The Daze,* PO Box 57, Otisville, MI 48463.

Collectors' Clubs: Fostoria Glass Collectors, Inc, PO Box 1625, Orange, CA 92856; Fostoria Glass Society of America, PO Box 826, Moundsville, WV 26041.

Note: See Stemware for additional listings.

American, almond dish, master, 3¾" **$18.00**
American, ashtray, oval, 3¾" **11.00**
American, ashtray, square, 3" **8.00**

Seascape #2685, creamer and sugar, blue opalescent, $50.00.

American, ashtray with match holder, oval, 5" 27.00
American, bitters bottle 50.00
American, bowl, 7½" d, 3" deep 25.00
American, bowl, round, 8½" d, 4" deep 50.00
American, creamer and sugar, individual 22.00
American, lily pond bowl, 12" d 65.00
American, picture frame, oval 20.00
American, toothpick holder 25.00
Argus, water goblet, red 22.00
Argus, wine goblet, red 21.00
Century, berry bowl, 4¾" 15.00
Century, bowl, round, 3-toe, 7" 18.00
Century, candlesticks, pr, 1-lite, 4½" 32.00
Century, celery/relish, 3-part 27.00
Century, compote 20.00
Century, creamer and sugar 17.00
Century, creamer, sugar, and tray, individual size 35.00
Century, cup and saucer 16.00
Century, float bowl, 9" 30.00
Century, ice bucket, no handle 50.00
Century, mayonnaise, liner, and spoon 40.00
Century, pitcher, ice lip, 7" 95.00
Century, relish, 2-part, 7½" 16.00
Colony, almond dish, 3 ftd 18.00
Colony, cake plate, 2 handles, 10" 25.00
Colony, cake salver 125.00
Colony, candlesticks, pr, lustre, 7½" 195.00
Colony, celery dish, oval, 11½" 30.00
Colony, cocktail goblet 12.00
Colony, compote, cov, 6" 30.00
Colony, cup and saucer 10.00
Colony, fruit bowl, ftd, 10" 125.00
Colony, jelly, cov 35.00
Colony, lunch tray, center handle 35.00
Colony, plate, 8" 13.00
Colony, plate, 15" 70.00
Colony, salt and pepper shakers, pr, 3⅝" 22.00
Colony, salt and pepper shakers, pr, individual 30.00
Colony, water goblet 18.00
Colony, wine goblet 25.00
Fairfax, baker, oval, 9", green 24.00
Fairfax, bonbon, pink 16.00
Fairfax, coaster, green 7.00
Fairfax, creamer and sugar, individual, green 22.00
Fairfax, creamer and sugar, individual, yellow 24.00
Fairfax, nut dish, ftd, individual, green 15.00

Fairfax, pickle, 8½", green 12.00
Fairfax, sugar, individual, pink 20.00
Fairfax, tumbler, ftd, 2 oz, pink 22.00
Fairfax, whipped cream bowl, blue 18.00
Heather, cake plate, 2 handles 30.00
Heather, candy, cov, ftd 55.00
Heather, champagne goblet 18.00
Heather, creamer, ftd 17.00
Heather, creamer, sugar, and tray, individual 48.00
Heather, mayonnaise and spoon, 2-part, ftd 34.00
Heather, relish, 2-part, 2 handles 25.00
Heather, salt and pepper shakers, pr 48.00
Laurel 6017, cocktail goblet 776, crystal 14.00
Laurel 6017, water goblet 776, crystal 22.00
Spartan, champagne, amber with crystal stem 14.00
Spartan, wine goblet, amber with crystal stem 16.00
Sunray, coaster, crystal 8.00
Sunray, nut dish, ftd, individual, crystal 10.00
Sunray, sugar, ftd, individual, crystal 8.00
US Insignia 6023, champagne sherbet, crystal 12.00
US Insignia 6023, water goblet, crystal 16.00

FRANCISCAN

Gladding, McBean and Company, Los Angeles, developed and produced the Franciscan dinnerware line in 1934. The line includes a variety of shapes, forms, and patterns. Coronado, El Patio, Metropolitan, Montecito, Padua, and Rancho are solid color dinnerware lines.

The Franciscan hand-painted, embossed patterns of Apple, Desert Rose, and Ivy dominated the secondary collecting market in the 1980s and early 1990s. Today collectors are seeking out some of the more modern Franciscan decaled patterns such as Oasis and Starburst.

References: Delleen Enge, *Franciscan: Embossed Handpainted,* published by author, 1992; Delleen Enge, *Plain and Fancy Franciscan Made in California,* published by author, 1996; Harry L. Rinker, *Dinnerware of the 20th Century: The Top 500 Patterns,* House of Collectibles, 1997; Jeffrey B. Snyder, *Franciscan Dining Services,* Schiffer Publishing, 1997.

Collectors' Club: Franciscan Collectors Club, 8412 5th Ave NE, Seattle, WA 98115.

Apple, bread and butter plate $3.00
Apple, butter, cov 35.00
Apple, casserole, cov, individual 50.00
Apple, chop plate, 12½" d 50.00
Apple, creamer 20.00
Apple, cup and saucer 8.00
Apple, demitasse cup and saucer 45.00
Apple, dinner plate 12.00
Apple, fruit bowl 8.00
Apple, gravy boat 30.00
Apple, ice lip 125.00
Apple, platter, 12½" l 25.00
Apple, relish, 3 part 50.00
Apple, salad plate 9.00
Apple, salt and pepper shakers, pr 60.00
Apple, spoon rest 75.00
Apple, sugar, cov 30.00
Apple, teapot, cov 125.00

Apple, tumbler 40.00
Apple, tureen, cov, ring base 600.00
Apple, vegetable, 7¹/₂ x 2¹/₈" 30.00
Bouquet #1, cereal bowl 7.00
Bouquet #1, creamer 8.00
Bouquet #1, gravy boat 18.00
Bouquet #1, platter, 12¹/₂" l 15.00
Bouquet #1, sugar 8.00
Chantilly, cup and saucer 6.00
Desert Rose, ashtray 35.00
Desert Rose, bread and butter plate 3.00
Desert Rose, butter, ¹/₄ lb 26.00
Desert Rose, cereal bowl 9.00
Desert Rose, chop plate, 11³/₄" d 45.00
Desert Rose, chop plate, 14" d 120.00
Desert Rose, coffeepot, cov 100.00
Desert Rose, compote, 8¹/₈ x 4" 60.00
Desert Rose, cookie jar, cov 350.00
Desert Rose, creamer 12.00
Desert Rose, cup and saucer 8.00
Desert Rose, cup and saucer, oversize 45.00
Desert Rose, dessert bowl 7.00
Desert Rose, gravy boat, double pour 45.00
Desert Rose, juice tumbler, 3³/₈" h 40.00
Desert Rose, mixing bowl, 7³/₈ x 4¹/₄" 175.00
Desert Rose, mug, 8 oz 20.00
Desert Rose, pepper mill 80.00
Desert Rose, pitcher, 6¹/₂" h 50.00
Desert Rose, pitcher, 9³/₈" h 100.00
Desert Rose, plate, 8" d 7.00
Desert Rose, plate, 9¹/₄" d 9.00
Desert Rose, plate, 10¹/₂" d 10.00
Desert Rose, platter, 12¹/₂" l 30.00
Desert Rose, platter, 14" l 35.00
Desert Rose, platter, 19" l 250.00
Desert Rose, relish, 10⁵/₈" 20.00
Desert Rose, relish, 3-part, 12" 45.00
Desert Rose, salad bowl, 10¹/₂" d 65.00
Desert Rose, salt and pepper shakers, pr, tall 60.00
Desert Rose, sherbet 14.00
Desert Rose, soup bowl, ftd, 5⁵/₈" d 25.00
Desert Rose, sugar, cov 25.00
Desert Rose, teapot, cov 100.00
Desert Rose, tumbler, 5¹/₄" h 40.00
Desert Rose, vegetable, cov, open handle, 9³/₄" d 75.00
Desert Rose, vegetable, divided, oval 26.00
Desert Rose, vegetable, round 24.00
Fruit, bread and butter plate 25.00
Fruit, chop plate, 12" d 295.00
Fruit, chop plate, 14" d 395.00
Fruit, cup 35.00
Fruit, cup and saucer 45.00
Fruit, gravy boat, with liner 225.00
Fruit, plate, 9" d 40.00
Fruit, plate, 10" d 40.00
Fruit, sugar, cov 125.00
Poplar, bread and butter plate 12.00
Poplar, butter, cov 175.00
Poplar, cup and saucer 35.00
Poplar, fruit bowl 40.00
Poplar, gravy boat, without liner 95.00
Poplar, plate, 10" d 45.00
Poplar, salt and pepper shakers, pr 125.00
Poplar, vegetable, cov 125.00

Westwood, dinner plate, 10⁵/₈" d, $7.00.

Poplar, water tumbler 145.00
Westwood, bread and butter plate 3.00
Westwood, cup and saucer 10.00
Westwood, salad plate 6.00
Wild Flower, ashtray, mariposa 95.00
Wild Flower, bread and butter plate 50.00
Wild Flower, cereal bowl 145.00
Wild Flower, chop plate, 14" d 700.00
Wild Flower, fruit bowl 125.00
Wild Flower, luncheon plate 125.00
Wild Flower, platter, 14" l 500.00
Wild Flower, salad bowl 120.00
Wild Flower, saucer 25.00
Wild Flower, vegetable 250.00

FRANKART

Arthur Von Frankenberg founded Frankart, New York, New York, in the mid-1920s. The company mass-produced a wide range of aquariums, ashtrays, bookends, lamps, and vases throughout the 1930s. Frankart nudes are the most desired pieces.

Frankart pieces were cast in white metal. Finishes include bronzoid, cream, French, gun-metal, jap, pear green, and verde. Pieces are usually marked with "Frankart, Inc.," and a patent number or "pat. appl. for." Beware of the possibility of a mismatched ashtray when buying a standing figural.

Collectors' Club: National Coalition of Art Deco Societies, One Murdock Terrace, Brighton, MA 02135.

Ashtray, floor model, nude holding dish in outstretched
 arms, 24" h $750.00
Ashtray, reclining Great Dane, 8¹/₂" h 150.00
Ashtray, stylized duck with outstretched wings support-
 ing green glass ash receiver, 5" h 100.00
Bookends, pr, antelope 145.00
Bookends, pr, begging Scottie dogs 275.00

Bookends, pr, boy with sailboat and dog **100.00**
Bookends, pr, horse heads with flowing manes, 5" h **55.00**
Bookends, pr, seated lions, stylized chip carved, 6" h **125.00**
Incense Burner, female head on burner base, 5" h **195.00**
Lamp, 7" h, 2 nudes sitting back to back, legs out-
stretched, 5" sq crackle glass globe **450.00**
Smoker's Set, seated nude, leaning back, geometric
base, arms resting on removable glass cigarette box,
3" d removable glass ashtray at feet **295.00**
Wall Pocket, seated nude, wrought-iron metal frame-
work, metal pan for flowers, 12" h **300.00**

FRANKOMA

John Frank, a ceramics instructor at Oklahoma University, established Frankoma in 1933. In 1938 he moved his commercial production from Norman to Sapulpa. When a fire destroyed the plant
in 1939, he rebuilt immediately.

A honey-tan colored clay from Ada was used to make Frankoma
pieces prior to 1954. After that date, the company switched to a
red brick clay from Sapulpa. Today some clay is brought into the
plant from other areas.

Fire again struck the Sapulpa plant in September 1983. By July
1984 a new plant was opened. Since the early molds were lost in
the fire, new molds were designed and made.

References: Phyllis and Tom Bess, *Frankoma and Other Oklahoma
Potteries,* Schiffer Publishing, 1995; Gary V. Schaum, *Collector's
Guide to Frankoma Pottery 1933 Through 1990,* L-W Book Sales,
1997.

Collectors' Club: Frankoma Family Collectors Assoc, PO Box
32571, Oklahoma City, OK 73123.

Ashtray, arrowhead shape, turquoise, #453, 7" l **$12.00**
Ashtray, book shape, fawn brown, 3½" l **25.00**
Baker, individual size, Wagon Wheel, #94U, desert gold **40.00**
Bookends, pr, charger horse, desert gold, #111, 6" **150.00**
Bookends, pr, cowboy boots, prairie green, #433, 7" h **40.00**
Boot Mug, white sand **10.00**
Candle Holder, Dogwood, prairie green **12.00**

**Figurines, 9" l reclining puma #116 and 7" h seated puma #114,
prairie green glaze, c1951, price each, $100.00.**

Candle Holders, pr, rock, prairie green, 1970s, 4½" d **45.00**
Creamer and Sugar, Wagon Wheel, prairie green **28.00**
Figure, Gardner Boy **100.00**
Figure, miniature elephant, clay blue **85.00**
Figure, rearing Clydesdale, prairie green, 6¾" h **175.00**
Figure, terrier, #161, 2⅞" h **90.00**
Flower Frog, figural fish, jade green, #404, 4½" **500.00**
Flower Frog, figural swan on 2-tier base, white, 4" h **300.00**
Planter, cornucopia, peach glow **15.00**
Planter, swan, wisteria, #228, 7½" l **15.00**
Salt and Pepper Shakers, pr, Wagon Wheel, prairie green **18.00**
Teapot, Wagon Wheel, prairie green, #94J, 2-cup **30.00**
Trivet, Wagon Wheel, #94TR, prairie green **50.00**
Vase, cornucopia, desert gold, #56, 7" h **20.00**
Vase, miniature, spherical, ribbed, peacock blue **30.00**
Vase, ram's head handles, jade green, #74, 9¼" h **125.00**
Vase, ribbed, leaf handles, blue-gray jade, #71, 10" h **50.00**
Wall Pocket, Dutch shoe, desert gold, #913, 8½" **35.00**
Wall Pocket, Wagon Wheel, desert gold, 7" h **40.00**

FRATERNAL & SERVICE ORGANIZATIONS

Benevolent and fraternal societies from the Odd Fellows to the
Knights of Columbus continued to play a major role in American
life through the first two-thirds of the 20th century. Local service
clubs such as the Lions and Rotary established themselves as a
major force in community life in the 1920s and 30s. Their golden
age spanned the 1950s and 60s. Increasing workplace and family
demands have cut heavily into membership. Membership has stabilized at best in most clubs. In many cases, the average age of
club members is well above 50.

Benevolent & Protective Order of Elks, badge, Atlantic
City, pictures Betty Bacharach Home for Afflicted
Children, 1938 . . . . **$15.00**
Eastern Star, bookends, pr, gray metal, Ronson, 1922,
4¼" h **100.00**
Everett C Benton Lodge AF & AM, plate, purple and
white porcelain, Benton bust in center, gold edging,
Rosenthal, 1930, 10¼" d **35.00**
Knights of Columbus, bookends, pr, emblem, gray metal,
Ronson, 1922, 3¼" h **85.00**
Knights of Templar, shaving mug, shows emblem and
"J.W. Williamson," "T & V Limoges France" stamped
on base, c1885–1925, 3⅝" h **170.00**
Lions Club, license plate attachment, cast metal, Lions
Club emblem at top, "Lions International
Englishtown," 2 plastic screw-on reflectors attached to
2 pre-drilled holes at bottom for mounting, 10½ x 5" **20.00**
Masonic, ashtray, brown and cream, raised depiction of
Mason symbol in center, 6¼ x 5¾" **20.00**
Masonic, bookends, pr, emblem, iron, Judd, c1928,
5¼" h **100.00**
Modern Woodsmen of America, shaving mug, emblem
and "W.D. Wade," mkd "Garrwett K.C.M." in gold gilt
on base, c1890–1925, 3¾" h **130.00**
Odd Fellows, medal, triangular shape, seal and motto of
Grand Lodge on obverse, rings and staff on reverse,
on braided red and purple cord, 1934 . . . . **20.00**
Rotary International, Paul Harris Fellow medal, bronze,
Harris profile obverse, Rotary emblem on reverse,
blue and yellow ribbon, velvet lined presentation case **20.00**
Scottish Rite, bookends, pr, gray metal, Ronson, 3¼" h **85.00**

Shriners, commemorative glass, "Rufus R. Renninger 1970" on front, "Annual Potentate Gold Outing" on reverse, 4³/₈" h, $5.00.

Shriners, bobbing head, hp, Dee Bee Co, Japan, 7" h 45.00
Shriners, bookends, pr, camel, brass, c1930, 4½" h. 110.00
Shriners, bookends, pr, Fez, gray metal, Ronson, 1922,
3¼" h 75.00
Shriners, pin, gold tone finish, Pharoah's head dangling
from scimitar, silver toned sword blade, plush purple
velvet padded case 35.00
United Brotherhood of Carpenters, pinback button,
white lettering on blue rim, gold center with white
"November 1888/Golden anniversary/November
1938". 15.00
Woodsmen of the World, lapel button 10.00

FRISBEES

In 1915 Joseph P. Frisbie built a new bakery in Bridgeport, Connecticut, to produce Frisbie pie. During lunch hour, company employees played catch with the company's pie pans. In the 1920s Yale students picked up the sport. By the 1930s the craze spread to Princeton and the University of Michigan.

In 1937 the Buck Roger's Flying Saucer, the first throw and catch flying disk, appeared for sale. In 1948 Walter (Fred) Morrison and Warren Franscioni created the first plastic flying disc. In the same year, Arthur "Spud" Melin and Rich Knerr started Wham-O to market wooden sling shots. Numerous Frisbee prototypes appeared.

In the mid-1950s Fred Morrison designed the Pluto Platter Flying Saucer, teaming up with Wham-O in 1956 to market the product. The first of over 300 million Wham-O Frisbees was produced on January 23, 1957. By the end of the 1950s, Frisbee mania swept across America.

Wham-O introduced its professional model Frisbee in 1964 and founded the International Frisbee Association in 1967. Membership quickly exceeded 100,000.

In 1982 Kransco, a large toy company, bought Wham-O and its Frisbee trademark. Mattel bought the Frisbee trademark from Kransco in 1994. In 1997 Mattel sold the Frisbee trademark to Charterhouse Group International, a group of New York City investors.

Reference: Victor A. Malafronte, *The Complete Book of Frisbee: The History of the Sport & the First Official Price Guide,* American Trends Publishing, 1998.

Note: Prices listed are for frisbees in very good condition.

Aerial Koit, Cleveland Plastics, 1969 . . . . $40.00
Aerial Sky Surfer, England, 1970s. 35.00
AMF Voit Sailor, Destiny, 1980. . . . . 35.00
Apollo Pilot, Sweden, 1970s 20.00
Australian Frisbee Championships, Wham-O, 1978. . . . . 30.00
Captain Jet Frisbee, Wham-O, 1974 . . . . 70.00
Classic Frisbee, Wham-O, 1973 . . . . 65.00
Flying Saucer, Pipco Products, 1948. . . . . 450.00
Heart Ultimate, Wham-O, 1980s 55.00
Holy Toledo, Auburn Rubber, 1964 . . . . 85.00
Huntington Beach Higher Flyers, Wham-O, 1980s 45.00
Mini Frisbee Olympic Rings, Wham-O, 1967 . . . . 75.00
Moonlighter Mini Frisbee, Wham-O, 1968 . . . . 75.00
Moscow Olympics XXII 1980, Russia. 75.00
Mystery Y Frisbee, Empire Plastics, 1959–60. . . . . 200.00
Mystery Y Frisbee, Wham-O, 1979. . . . . 25.00
Official Twirling Saucer, Knickerbocker, 1958. . . . . 75.00
Raggedy Ann Mini Frisbee, Wham-O, 1974 . . . . 50.00
Royal Wedding 1981, England. 65.00
Sailing Satellite, Wham-O, 1957 . . . . 275.00
Snoopy Tosserino, Aviva, 1970s 18.00
Stitch 'N Toss, Slantzi Craft, 1970s 35.00
U-1 Saucer, space theme decal, Eureka, 1960s 115.00
WFC Signature Disc, Wham-O, 1977. . . . . 20.00
Whizbo, Wham-O, 1976. . . . . 25.00
World Frisbee Champions Signature Disc, Wham-O,
1978. . . . . 25.00
World Frisbee Championships Pasadena Jaycees,
Wham-O, 1975. . . . . 50.00
Zolar Flying Saucer, Empire Plastics, 1958 . . . . 200.00

FRUIT JARS

The canning of fruits and vegetables played a major role in the American household until the late 1950s. Canning jars were recycled year after year. Jars utilizing zinc lids and rubber-sealed metal lids are extremely common. These jars usually sell for about 50¢.

Do not assume the date on a jar indicates the year the jar was made. In almost every case, it is a patent date or the founding date of the company that made the jar.

References: Douglas M. Leybourne, Jr., *The Collector's Guide to Old Fruit Jars, Red Book No. 8,* published by author, 1997; Jerry McCann, *The Guide to Collecting Fruit Jars: Fruit Jar Annual, Vol. 3–1998,* Phoenix Press, 1997; Bill Schroeder, *1000 Fruit Jars: Priced and Illustrated, 5th Edition,* Collector Books, 1987, 1996 value update.

Newsletter: *Fruit Jar Newsletter,* 364 Gregory Ave, West Orange, NJ 07052.

Collectors' Clubs: Ball Collectors Club, 22203 Doncaster, Riverview, MI 48192; Federation of Historical Bottle Collectors, Inc, 88 Sweetbriar Branch, Longwood, FL 32750; Midwest Antique Fruit Jar & Bottle Club, PO Box 38, Flat Rock, IN 47234.

Acme, clear, Union shield, glass lid, wire bail $3.00
Agee Victory, clear, dual side clips 20.00
Anchor, clear, glass insert, zinc screw band 35.00
Atlas Mason, aqua, zinc cap 5.00
Ball Freezer Jar, clear. 3.00

Ball Ideal, clear, glass lid, emb lettering, wire bail, $2.00.

Ball Ideal, blue, Bicentennial Celebration on reverse 1.00
Ball Mason, apple green 30.00
Ball Mason, aqua 1.00
Ball Perfect Mason, clear. 35.00
Ball Sure Seal, blue, beaded neck 2.00
Bernardin Mason, clear, c1940 . . . . 3.00
Brockway Clear-Vu Mason, clear, glass insert 3.00
Brockway Sur-Grip Mason, clear 3.00
Chattanooga Mason, clear. 5.00
Cleveland Fruit Juice Co, Cleveland, OH, clear, ground
    lip, glass lid, ½ gal 5.00
Coles Pure Honey, clear, metal screw cap, pt 10.00
Crown Mason, clear, zinc cap, lid liner emb "Crown,"
    ½ pt 5.00
Double Safety, clear, glass lid, wire bail, ½ pt 5.00
Drey Ever Seal, clear. 2.50
Easi-Pak Mason, clear, c1975. . . . . 1.00
Farm Family Buck Glass Co, Baltimore, MD, clear, c1940. . . . 5.00
Good House Keepers Mason Jar, clear, c1940 . . . . 5.00
Hormel Fine Food, clear 2.50
Household WT Co, clear, c1920 . . . . 300.00
Hygrade, clear, wide mouth Mason cap 35.00
Ideal Wide Mouth Jar, clear, 2 pc Mason cap, c1930 . . . . . . 2.00
Ivanhoe, clear, metal lid, qt. 5.00
Kerr Economy, clear 5.00
Kerr Self-Sealing Mason, cobalt blue streak, reverse mkd
    "65th Anniversary 1903–1968" 25.00
Knox Mason, clear, glass insert, gold lacquered metal
    screw band, c1930 . . . . 5.00
Lamb Mason, clear, glass insert, gold lacquered metal
    screw band, c1930 . . . . 5.00
Liquid Carbonic Company, clear 2.00
Mallinger, clear. 5.00
Mason Fruit Jar, aqua, bead seal 2.00
Mason's, aqua, zinc cap 3.00
Midland Mason, clear, zinc cap, c1975 . . . . 3.00
Mountain Mason, clear, zinc cap, c1920 . . . . 25.00
Pine Deluxe Jar, clear, glass lid, wire bail, c1925 . . . . 10.00
Pine Mason, clear, zinc cap. 5.00
Quick Seal, blue, glass lid, wire bail, c1920. . . . . 5.00
Reliable Home Canning Mason, clear, glass insert,
    c1940. . . . . 5.00
Samco Genuine Mason, clear, white milk glass insert,
    c1940. . . . . 5.00

Samco Super Jar, clear, c1935 . . . . 5.00
San Yeun Co, clear, "822 Washington San Francisco
    California," glass lid, wire bail, c1940, pt 10.00
Security Seal, clear, glass lid, wire bail, qt 6.50
Solidex, green, glass lid, hinged wire clamp, c1950 . . . . . . 50.00
Standard Mason, aqua, zinc cap, c1920. . . . . 5.00
Tight Seal, blue, glass lid, wire bail, c1920. . . . . 5.00
Tropical TF Canners, clear, emb "Florida," c1940 . . . . 15.00
Vacuum, clear, glass lid. 35.00
Whitby Mason, aqua, smooth lip. 5.00
Zetland Airtight, clear, Mason zinc wide mouth cap,
    c1920. . . . . 75.00

FRY GLASS

H. C. Fry Glass, Rochester, Pennsylvania, operated between 1901 and 1933. After an initial production period making Brilliant cut glass, the company turned to manufacturing glass tableware.

Pearl Oven Glass, a heat-resistant opalescent colored glass, was patented in 1922. Most pieces are marked with "Fry" and a model number. For a two-year period, 1926–27, H. C. Fry produced Foval, an art glass line. Its pieces are identified by their pearly opalescent body with an applied trim of jade green or Delft blue. Silver overlay pieces are marked "Rockwell."

Reference: The H. C. Fry Glass Society, *The Collector's Encyclopedia of Fry Glassware*, Collector Books, 1990, 1998 value update.

Collectors' Club: H. C. Fry Glass Society, PO Box 41, Beaver, PA 15009.

REPRODUCTION ALERT: Italian reproductions of Foval, produced in the 1970s, have a teal blue transparent trim.

After Dinner Cup and Saucer, Foval, #2003, Delft blue
    handle $85.00
Baker, Oven Ware, #1919, clear, round, 6" d 20.00
Bean Pot, Oven Ware, #1924, clear, orange trim 75.00
Berry Bowl, Foval, #2503, Delft foot, sgd Rockwell silver
    overlay in Pineapple design, 8" d 300.00
Bowl, ftd, crystal connector, royal blue. 200.00
Cake Plate, emerald, Sunnybrook pattern 50.00
Candle Holders, pr, amber, gold trim, paper label. 65.00
Casserole, cov, Oven Ware, #1954, etched lid, silver
    holder. 55.00
Comport, crystal, gold threading, controlled bubbles
    and teardrop stem 135.00
Creamer, fuchsia. 50.00
Creamer and Open Sugar, rose 75.00
Custard Cup, Oven Ware, #1927, leaf design 20.00
Dinnerware Set, plate, goblet, cup and saucer, fuchsia 65.00
Dinnerware Set, plate, goblet, cup and saucer, royal blue 90.00
Meatloaf Pan, cov, Oven Ware, #1928, clear, emb grape,
    9" l 40.00
Reamer, ruffled edges, canary 220.00
Relish Dish, rose. 35.00
Salad Plate, Pearl, #2504, Delft edge, 8½" d 75.00
Snack Set, royal blue 65.00
Spice Tray, rose 75.00
Teacup and Saucer, azure blue 30.00
Teacup and Saucer, Pearl, #9003, tall. 80.00
Tea Set, cov teapot, cup, and saucer, Foval, #2000, blue
    enamel trim. 400.00

FULPER

Fulper Art Pottery was made by the American Pottery Company, Flemington, New Jersey, beginning around 1910 and ending in 1930. All pieces were molded. Pieces from the 1920s tend to be of higher quality due to less production pressures.

Pieces exhibit a strong Arts and Crafts and/or oriental influence. Glazes differed tremendously as Fulper experimented throughout its production period.

References: John Hibel et al., *The Fulper Book*, published by authors, n.d.; Ralph and Terry Kovel, *Kovel's American Art Pottery: The Collector's Guide to Makers, Marks and Factory Histories*, Crown Publishers, 1993.

Collectors' Club: Stangl/Fulper Collectors Club, PO Box 538, Flemington, NJ 08822.

REPRODUCTION ALERT

Bookends, pr, "Rameses," matte green and gunmetal glaze, felted bottom, 9 x 4¼"	**$550.00**
Bud Vase, leopard skin crystalline glaze, rect ink mark, 8½ x 3"	**1,300.00**
Centerpiece Bowl, "Ibis," ftd, flemington green flambé int, brown flambé over mustard matte ext, rect ink mark, 5¾ x 11"	**850.00**
Chinese Urn, bulbous, mirrored black glaze over hammered body, raised racetrack mark, 11 x 8"	**950.00**
Doorstop, figural cat, cat's-eye flambé glaze, ink race track mark, 6 x 9"	**950.00**
Flower Frog, frog on lilypad, green, ivory, and mahogany flambé glaze, rect ink mark, 3½ x 7½"	**150.00**
Flower Frog, penguin, white, blue, and brown matte glaze, rect ink mark, 7"	**275.00**
Pilgrim Flask, curdled green, mirror black, blue and ivory flambé glaze, rect ink mark, 10 x 7½"	**950.00**
Urn, bulbous, ftd, ochre, mahogany, and pale blue flambé glaze over textured body, raised racetrack mark, 9 x 9"	**850.00**
Urn, classical, scrolled handles and rolled rim, mirror black glaze on hammered body, rect ink mark, 11 x 15½"	**450.00**
Vase, bulbous, frothy wisteria matte glaze, ink racetrack mark, 7½ x 5½"	**325.00**
Vase, classical, frothy cobalt and purple semi-matte glaze, ink racetrack mark, 12 x 4½"	**500.00**

Vase, faceted, frothy cucumber crystalline and ivory flambé glaze, ink racetrack mark, 10 x 5"	**750.00**
Vase, ovoid, dark mirrored green and blue flambé glaze, raised mark, 5½ x 4½"	**300.00**
Vase, tall, cylindrical rim, frothy blue and green flambé glaze, rect ink mark, restoration to rim, 12½ x 6"	**350.00**
Vase, tapering, gunmetal, mahogany, and copperdust crystalline glaze, raised racetrack mark, 13 x 7½"	**600.00**
Vessel, spherical, frothy flemington green flambé glaze, rect ink mark, 5½ x 7"	**425.00**
Vessel, squat, 2 angular handles, copperdust crystalline glaze, incised racetrack mark, 5 x 6"	**500.00**

Vessel, flared rim, banded neck, bulbous base, Moss to Rose glaze, racetrack mark, 10" h, 8" d, $990.00. Photo courtesy David Rago Auctions, Inc.

FURNITURE

The furniture industry experienced tremendous growth immediately following World Wars I and II as America's population ballooned and wartime advances in materials and technology were applied to furniture. Furniture was made in a variety of grades, making the latest styles available to virtually every income level.

Beginning in the 1920s, the American popular taste tended to go in two directions, Colonial Revival and upholstered furniture. Colonial Revival furniture divides into two distinct groups: (1) high-style pieces that closely mirrored their historic counterparts, and (2) generic forms that combined design elements from many different styles in a single piece. Large numbers of upholstered pieces utilized frames that drew their inspiration from English and European revival styles. Buyers with a modern bent fell in love with the Art Deco and Streamlined Modern styles.

While leading designers such as Charles Eames experimented with new materials and forms prior to World War II, it was after the war that modern furniture reached the mass market. Colonial Revival gave way to Early American; upholstered furniture veered off in a sectional direction. Many trendy styles, e.g., tubular, Mediterranean, and Scandinavian, survived less than a decade.

In the post-1945 period designers shifted their focus from household furniture to office and institutional furniture. Design became truly international as English and European design studios replaced America as the major influence for style change.

American tastes became traditional and conservative again in the mid-1970s. Colonial Revival styles made a strong comeback. Modernism was out, except among a select few in large metropolitan areas. Today, many people desiring a modern look are buying pieces manufactured from the mid-1940s through the early 1960s.

Collectors pay a premium for furniture made by major manufacturers based on designs by internationally recognized furniture designers. Name counts heavily, even in mass-produced furniture.

Style Chronology:

Craft Revival	1900–1940
Colonial Revival (High Style and Generic)	1915–1940
International	1920s
Art Deco	1925–1935
Streamlined Modern	1930s/early 1940s
Contemporary/Post-War Modernism	late 1940s/early 1960s
Early American	1950s–1960s
Neo-Modernism and Pop	1960s
Craft Revival	1970s–present
Colonial Revival	1970s–present
Memphis	1980s

References: *American Manufactured Furniture, Furniture Dealers' Reference Book,* reprint by Schiffer Publishing, 1988, 1996 value update; Richard and Eileen Dubrow, *Styles of American Furniture: 1860–1960,* Schiffer Publishing, 1997; *Fine Furniture Reproductions: 18th-Century Revivals of the 1930s and 1940s From Baker Furniture,* Schiffer Publishing, 1996; Oscar Fitzgerald, *Four Centuries of American Furniture,* Wallace-Homestead, Krause Publications, 1995; Philippe Garner, *Twentieth-Century Furniture,* Van Nostrand Reinhold, 1980, out of print; Cara Greenberg, *Mid-Century Modern: Furniture of the 1950s,* Crown Publishers, 1995; *Indiana Cabinets With Prices,* L-W Book Sales, 1997; Emyl Jenkin, *Emyl Jenkin's Reproduction Furniture: Antiques for the Next Generation,* Crown Publishers, 1995; David P. Lindquist and Caroline C. Warren, *Colonial Revival Furniture With Prices,* Wallace-Homestead, Krause Publications, 1993; Karl Mang, *History of Modern Furniture, Translation,* Harry N. Abrams, 1979, out of print.

Leslie Piña, *Classic Herman Miller,* Schiffer Publishing, 1998; Leslie Piña, *Fifties Furniture,* Schiffer Publishing, 1996; Harry L. Rinker, *Warman's Furniture,* Wallace-Homestead, 1993, out of print; Steve Rouland and Roger W. Rouland, *Heywood-Wakefield Modern Furniture,* Collector Books, 1995, 1997 value update; Klaus-Jurgen Sembach, *Modern Furniture Designs: 1950–1980s,* Schiffer Publishing, 1997; Penny Sparke, *Furniture: Twentieth-Century Design,* E. P. Dutton, 1986, out of print; Robert W. and Harriett Swedberg, *Collector's Encyclopedia of American Furniture, Vol. 2,* Collector Books, 1992, 1999 value update; Robert W. and Harriett Swedberg, *Furniture of the Depression Era,* Collector Books, 1987, 1999 value update.

1920s, bed, Table Rock Furniture Co, Morgantown, NC, burl mahogany veneer on gently arched headboard, burl mahogany and bird's-eye maple veneer on conforming footboard with applied roundels and veneered band of triangular designs, ring-turned posts with acorn finials. **$200.00**

1920s, console, American Woodcraft Corp, Evansville, IN, striped mahogany veneer on top and apron, black-painted turned legs **40.00**

1920s, desk, Innes Pearce & Co, Rushville, IN, bird's-eye maple veneer table top and drawer front, single long drawer, maple base with slightly scrolled feet, 36" l **125.00**

1920s, dining chair, Stomps-Burkhardt Co, Dayton, OH, oak, shaped crest rail over simple straight back slat, leather seat with brass studs, 38" h **75.00**

1920s, smoking stand, Metal Stamping Corp, Streator, IL, square top with outset corners, arched handle, bamboo-design side columns, single door in cupboard base, shaped base shelf, ring-turned legs, 10" sq, 31" h **70.00**

1930s, cedar chest, Billington Mfg Co, Sheboygan, WI, waterfall veneer, V-shaped veneer on ends, molded base, French bracket feet, orig paper label **175.00**

1930s, cedar chest, Lane Co, Alta Vista, VA, walnut veneer top and sides, figured walnut veneer front, applied diamond-shaped center dec, applied half spindle columns, bulbous feet **150.00**

1930s, coffee table, Colonial Mfg Co, Zeeland, MI, cloverleaf shaped top with tooled leather surface, solid mahogany frame, 28" w, 19" h **85.00**

1930s, coffee table, Imperial Furniture Co, glass top, hand-painted floral design in center, white ground, blue trim, beaded apron, reeded tapering legs, 18" h, 25" w, 18" d **120.00**

1930s, davenport, Delker Brothers Mfg Co, Henderson, KY, exposed mahogany frame, carved leaf dec on crest rail, 3-section back and seat, spring cushions, webbed bottoms, rolled arms, exposed scrolled arm and triple bowed seat rail, 4 animal-paw front feet centering leaf-carved aprons, velour upholstery, 80" l, 32½" d, 36¼" h. **300.00**

1930s, desk, Colby, Sheraton style, mahogany veneer top and sides, curly maple veneer apron and drawer fronts, ring-turned hardwood legs. **200.00**

1930s, parlor suite, Brandts Furniture Co, Celina, OH, 3 pcs consisting of davenport, club chair, and high back chair, each pc with rounded tufted back, rolled arms, exposed carved scrolled arm and lower rail, slightly bowed seat front, cabriole legs, solid colored mohair upholstery with floral design seat cushions, price for 3-pc suite **750.00**

1940s, chifferobe, Tri-Bond Furniture, Art Deco style, waterfall veneer, narrow center mirrored section, deep drawers one side, cedar-lined short wardrobe above drawers other side **250.00**

1940s, vanity bench, Broyhill Furniture Factories, Lenoir Furniture Corp, Lenoir, NC, bleached and artificially grained mahogany back, birch base, upholstered seat, 31" h, 24" w **50.00**

1950s, chest of drawers, box-like appearance, 5 identical drawers, valance skirt, block leg, 18 x 17 x 44". **85.00**

1950s, desk, Heywood-Wakefield, kneehole, hard rock maple, rect top, pair of 2-drawer pedestals, demilune base, 44" l **300.00**

1950s, desk and chair, ranch style, oak, rect top, 3 center-guided dovetailed drawers to left, drawer beneath writing surface, block and ring legs to right, ox yoke hardware, chair with bowed back slats, plank seat, turned splayed front legs, double stretchers on sides, single stretchers in front, 44 x 16 x 32". **100.00**

1950s, bunk beds, ranch style, maple, ball finials on baluster-turned supports, half wagon wheel headboards and footboards, 39" h, 68" h bunked, $250.00.

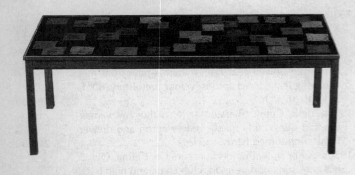

1950s, coffee table, P. Tornenan, enameled top with orange squares on black ground, blonde wood frame, sgd and dated, 53½ x 22" top, 18¾" h, $825.00. Photo courtesy David Rago Auctions, Inc.

1950s, end table, stepped, walnut finished hardwood frame and legs, rect top, splayed round tapered legs, stepped-back shelf raised on 2 spindles on each end, 16 x 24 x 21" 50.00

1950s, high chair, Heywood-Wakefield, folds down to playseat, hard rock maple, kidney-shaped tray, 42" h. 150.00

1950s, sofa, Harmony House (Sears), rectilinear form, hardwood frame, walnut finished legs, orange plastic cover, spring seat base, cotton felt padded button back, welt trim, 68 x 27 x 30" 150.00

1950s, telephone stand, wrought metal, 2 wire grill shelves, pinched paper clip-style side supports, bronze lacquer finish, 12½ x 12 x 17" 15.00

1960s, dinette set, table and 6 chairs, table with 2 leaves and high pressure plastic top in wood grain pattern, tapered black antique finished frame and legs, pillow-back chairs with vinyl plastic covers in abstract tree motif on block grid ground 150.00

1960s, dining table, high pressure plastic top in wood grain pattern, bronze-plated metal tapered block legs, 2 leaves, 42 x 84" 150.00

Art Deco, armchair, attributed to Warren McArthur, tubular frame, 3 slat back, upholstered sling seat, 1948. . . 1,875.00

Art Deco, armchair, KEM Weber, airline style, cantilevered wood and leather, 1934 . . . . 18,000.00

Art Deco, armchair, Paul Frankl, black lacquer, continuous low back and arms formed by square U-slat alternating with inset rect panels, upholstered square seat, 4 straight rect legs, pink brocade upholstery, relacquered, 1925, price for matched pair. 2,500.00

Art Deco, armchair, Russel Wright, bentwood frame, vinyl yellow upholstered seat and back, contrasting blue piping, 1935 . . . . 800.00

Art Deco, bar, attributed to Ray Hille, bleached burl walnut, upright rect center section, fluted doors, illuminated shelved int with mirrored peach glass, sliding shelf fitted with peach glass, 2 cupboard doors, 2 lower rect sections set with cupboard door and shelved int, scrolling H-form support, rect plinth base, c1930, 59¾" h, 56¾" w 1,750.00

Art Deco, cabinet, walnut veneer, center raised lift-top section with 3 long drawers flanked by side cabinets with large cupboard doors, shaped platform base, Bakelite handles. 1,500.00

Art Deco, chaise lounge, black wrought-iron frame with Greek Key motif and chevron pattern armrests, attached channeled gray vinyl cushion, 37" h, 77½" l. . . 1,875.00

Art Deco, club chair, Michael Taylor designer, square back, scroll over arms, upholstered in quilted green and ivory floral china and fringed trim, price for pair . . . 2,500.00

Art Deco, club chair, Paul Frankl, 4-band reed arms with X-form supports, 8-band reed base, reupholstered seat and back in tapestry fabric with leaves, 1930s, unmkd, 31½ x 33 x 32½" 650.00

Art Deco, commode, ivory inlaid and birch, front opening to reveal 2 cabinets, 4 fluted legs tapering to ivory sabots, 35" h, 48" w, 15¾" d 3,200.00

Art Deco, desk, painted, single pedestal, rect top, case of 3 drawers at one end, tall turned tapering leg other end, 1935 . . . . 2,500.00

Art Deco, dining table, maple and ebony, blue rect mirror top, conforming apron, 3 supports base on plinth base, 72" l 2,000.00

Art Deco, end tables, mahogany, quatrefoil-shaped top with blue mirror glass insert, conforming base shelf, 28" h, 18" w top, price for pair. 110.00

Art Deco, mirror, brass with enameled foliate design, 22½" h, 17½" w 175.00

Art Deco, night stand, walnut waterfall veneer, open shelf above single cupboard door, 1935 . . . . 250.00

Art Deco, rocker, Louis Sognot, chromed metal frame, upholstered back and seat, c1930, 36" h 1,200.00

Art Deco, table, burl walnut with black highlights, octagonal top with white animal skin covers, 2 matching small octagonal medial shelves staggered on columnar pedestal, stepped platform base, 26¾" h, 21" w, 15½" d 175.00

Art Deco, vanity, Heywood-Wakefield, C3796, round mirror, large center wll flanked on either side by banks of 2 drawers, wooden X-form pulls, champagne finish, 21½" h, 49" w, 18" d, 44¼" d mirror 300.00

Art Deco, armchair, in the style of Paul Frankl, tubular chrome 6-band arms and 8-band base, orig cushions reupholstered in period charcoal mohair fabric, unmkd, 32 x 34½ x 37½", $3,575.00. Photo courtesy David Rago Auctions, Inc.

Art Deco, armchairs, stained and carved mahogany feet and armposts, heavily padded in contoured and fluted velour upholstery, one blue-gray, other rose colored, c1930, 36 x 38 x 42", price for pair, $495.00. Photo courtesy David Rago Auctions, Inc.

Colonial Revival, Pre-War, bed, Empire style, mahogany, removable pineapple finials, turned and reeded posts, acanthus carving, 60¾" h, 50¾" w, 74¼" l **250.00**

Colonial Revival, Pre-War, bench, Chippendale style, mahogany, slip seat with ivory damask upholstery, cabriole legs, claw and ball feet, 20" h, 44" l, 19" w **150.00**

Colonial Revival, Pre-War, card table, Duncan Phyfe style, Imperial Furniture Co, Grand Rapids, MI, mahogany veneer top and rails, solid mahogany lyre shaped pedestal base, carved downswept legs, carved feet **400.00**

Colonial Revival, Pre-War, china cabinet, Hepplewhite style, inlaid mahogany, 3 urn finials on shaped pediment, glazed cupboard doors, 2 small drawers flanking center drawer over single long drawer, tapering legs, 81" h, 38" w, 17" d **350.00**

Colonial Revival, Pre-War, desk, Chippendale style, Colonial Desk Co, Rockford Il, blister mahogany, slant front, fitted int with valanced pigeonholes, 2 small drawers, flanking open center prospect, 3 drawers, shaped skirt, cabriole legs, eagle brasses, 43" h, 37" w, 20" d **400.00**

Colonial Revival, Pre-War, desk, Hepplewhite style, lady's, inlaid mahogany, tambour door with fitted int, oval brasses, 42½" h, 35" w, 19" d **500.00**

Colonial Revival, Pre-War, dining chairs, Adams style, mahogany, upholstered seats, 2 armchairs, 4 side chairs, price for set of 6 . . . . **600.00**

Colonial Revival, Pre-War, dining table, Hepplewhite style, inlaid mahogany, D-shaped drop leaf ends, 29½" h, 78" l, 46" w **250.00**

Colonial Revival, Pre-War, library table, Empire style, oak, pillar base, scrolled feet, 1920, 28" h, 48" l, 28" d **450.00**

Colonial Revival, Pre-War, nesting table, attributed to Gilbert Rhode, Herman Miller, Hepplewhite style, mahogany, circular top on 3 square tapered legs, circular swing shelf supported by 2 spare tapered legs, brass tag for Herman Miller Clock Co, Zeeland, MI, 23½" h, 11" d **700.00**

Colonial Revival, Pre-War, Pembroke table, Colonial Art Furniture Shop, Grand Rapids, MI, Hepplewhite style, plain cut mahogany veneer top, drop leaves, figured mahogany drawer front, solid mahogany base, 1940s, 10" l leaves, 15" w, 22" d, 27" h **150.00**

Colonial Revival, Pre-War, radio cabinet, Shoers Brothers Co, Bloomfield, IN, designed for Crosley radio, walnut veneer top and sides, pieced burl walnut veneer door panels, bulbous legs, X-stretcher with center carved urn finial, teardrop pulls, 1930s **75.00**

Colonial Revival, Pre-War, secretary/bookcase, Governor Winthrop style, Colonial Desk Co, Rockford, IL, mahogany, broken arched pediment with center finial, glazed mullioned doors, fluted columns, slant front, fitted int with document sleeves, 4 small drawers, center prospect with acanthus carving flanked by columns, 4 graduated drawers, eagle brasses, carved claw and ball feet, 87" h, 41" w, 21" d **1,000.00**

Colonial Revival, Pre-War, settee, Chippendale style, Neoclassical details, mahogany, maroon and gold silk upholstery, 50" l **700.00**

Colonial Revival, Pre-War, tavern table, William and Mary style, oval top, recessed frieze, turned splayed legs joined by box stretcher, 25" h, 34" l, 25" d **500.00**

Colonial Revival, Pre-War, wing chair, Chippendale style, worn green upholstery, claw and ball feet, 40" h **100.00**

Contemporary, armchair, Thonet, laminated bentwood, rect high back and square seat with upholstered foam rubber cushions, bentwood arms continuing to form legs, period finish and paper label, c1955, 40¼" h **300.00**

Contemporary, bed, mahogany frame with cane inserts, 1950, double size, 57" w **100.00**

Contemporary, cabinet, Herman Miller, George Nelson designer, open front arrangement of vertical and horizontal compartments over 4 sections of drawers, 4 chrome legs, 81 x 18½ x 43" **1,750.00**

Contemporary, coffee table, Eero Saarinen, circular mahogany top, cast metal pedestal base, white finish, 1956, 42½" d top, 15" h **500.00**

Contemporary, coffee table, Herman Miller, Noguchi designer, glass and maple, kidney shaped glass top raised on movable maple support, 1945, 15" h **3,000.00**

Colonial Revival, vanity, Sheraton style, walnut, swing mirror, reeded mirror supports, stiles, and legs, 3 drawers, 2 doors, applied molding, on casters, 48" w, $250.00.

Contemporary, armchair, Widdicomb Furniture Co., TH Robsjohn Gibbings designer, wood frame, upholstered seat, loose cushion back, c1952, 33½" h, $715.00. Photo courtesy David Rago Auctions, Inc.

Contemporary, desk, Heywood-Wakefield, kneehole style, rect top, central long drawer with divided int, double pedestal base, drawer front curved toward kneehole, divided file drawer on left, champagne oak finish, stamped with color and maker's mark, c1955, 30¼" h, 50" w, 24" d **1,500.00**

Contemporary, kitchen set, Rachlin Furniture Co, table and 4 chairs, table with rect gray marble Formica top with rounded corners, aluminum apron, chromed tubular steel legs, 1-leaf extension, chairs with chromed handle on top of crest, gray marbleized vinyl butterfly shaped back rest, yellow vinyl slip seat, chromed tubular steel frames and legs, orig paper label under seat, c1960, 47¾" x 35¾" table top, 34¼" h chairs, price for set **300.00**

Contemporary, lounge chair, Herman Miller, Charles Eames designer, #67 lounge chair and matching #671 ottoman, curved laminated rosewood frames with tufted black hide upholstery, swivel base, 1956, 31" h chair, price for set **1,000.00**

Contemporary, lounge chair, Jens Risom, curvilinear seat frame, angular arm and leg supports, 1952, 30" h, 26" d **200.00**

Contemporary, side chair, DCM, Herman Miller, Charles Eames designer, molded plywood seat and back, chrome metal frame, reddish finish, 29" h, 19½" w, 20¼" d **175.00**

Contemporary, side chair, JG Furniture Systems, Ray Komai designer, molded plywood, shaped shell back, chrome plated steel rod legs, c1949 . . . . **175.00**

Contemporary, side table, Knoll, Eero Saarinen designer, circular white plastic laminate top, cast metal pedestal base, 18" d, 20" h **200.00**

Contemporary, sofa, Charles Eames, straight back comprised of 2 slightly angled horizontal rect sections, rect seat, gray vinyl upholstery, chrome steel trestle-type base, 1954, 72" w **1,500.00**

Contemporary, television stand, Heywood-Wakefield, rect top, canted sides, medial shelf, bowed half-round tapered legs, champagne oak finish, color and maker's mark stamped under shelf, refinished, c1955, 26" h, 26" w, 24½" d **350.00**

Craftsman, armchair, Wharton Esherick, Windsor style, 6 spindle back, 2 are arm/rear leg supports, woven black leather seat, pre-1945, 22½ x 20 x 29½" **3,250.00**

Craftsman, bed, George Nakashima, large slab headboard and 2 platform boxes with joinery in contrasting woods, post-1950, king size, 80½ x 115 x 37" **6,000.00**

Craftsman, blanket chest, Wallace Nutting, #909, 17th-C style, oak with black ornamentation, lift top, single drawer, branded mark, 31" h, 48" w, 21" d **1,500.00**

Craftsman, candlestand, cherry stain, circular tilt top, splayed legs, 27¼" h, 25½" w, 16½" d **250.00**

Craftsman, chest of drawers, Stickley, Empire style, cherry, 4 graduated dovetailed drawers, turned feet, "Stickley, Fayetteville, Sytracuse" label, 37" h, 40¾" w, 21" d **500.00**

Craftsman, dining chairs, Widdicomb Furniture, Grand Rapids, MI, George Nakashima designer, turned wood, long narrow gently curved crest rail above 9-spindle back, wide shaped seat, simple turned canted legs joined by high H-form stretcher, branded "George Nakashima 2771," 1955, 36" h, price for set of 6 . . . . **1,500.00**

Craftsman, hat rack, Wallace Nutting, #40, spinning wheel type **500.00**

Craftsman, settee, Kavinsky, carved and laminated walnut, sculptured formed seat and back on abstract trunk-form base, sgd, post-1950, 60 x 23 x 35" **2,000.00**

Craftsman, side chair, Wallace Nutting, #361, Queen Anne style, maple, paper rush seat, old nut brown finish, branded label on bottom back rung, 41¼" h, price for pair. **1,200.00**

Craftsman, washstand, poplar, dovetailed gallery and drawer, base shelf, turned feet and posts, stenciled label "Wm Brown, Successor to Brown & Tate, Manufacturer, Lawrenceburgh, Ind, Warranted," 27¾" h, 24½" w, 16½" d **350.00**

Early American, commode (table), solid maple, autumn brown finish, rect top, single drawer, false front with 2 drawers over 2 drawers, shaped skirt, slightly splayed baluster turned legs, 26 x 21 x 23". **40.00**

Early American, rocker, Beacon Hill, maple frame, finished in Salem (light maple), removable cushions padded with cotton liners, mint green oval motif cotton print cover, ruffled skirt, 25 x 24 x 34" **65.00**

Contemporary, desk, Thonet, bent plywood, laminate top, single drawer, matching chair, paper labels, 30 x 36 x 18" desk, $140.00. Photo courtesy David Rago Auctions, Inc.

Early American, sofa, Harmony House, Chippendale style, upholstered in medium gold tweed fabric, 2 back Serofoam plastic foam cushions with shaped tops, 2 reversible cushions on seat, padded arms and wing sides, pleated shirt, 85 x 37 x 36" **100.00**

International Modern, dinette set, wood, soda fountain table and 4 matching chairs, round drum table with X-form stretcher and square legs, chairs with straight crest and triangular-shaped seats, price for 5-pc set. **400.00**

International Modern, side chairs, Eileen Gray designer, tan leather rect back and seat between framework formed of angular slender chromed steel supports, price for pair **8,500.00**

International Modern, stacking tables, J&J Kohn, Josef Hoffmann designer, bentwood, rect top with rounded corners, multiple sphere handles, inset with fabric panel beneath glass, raised on cylinder spindles continuing to U-form base, price for set of 4 . . . . **4,000.00**

International Modern, vanity, Herman Miller, Gilbert Rhode, 2 circular 2-drawer cabinets flanking central mirror, orig yellow lacquer, dark bands, Bakelite knobs, chrome frame, large vertical center mirror, label, 52 x 16 x 64" **1,750.00**

Memphis, dining table, circular top with abstract design, attached shelving on chrome and metal legs **1,250.00**

Neo-Modern, coffee table, Paul Evans, sq top, block legs, covered in chrome tiles, matching ashtray, etched mark, 1960s, 48" sq top, 15" h **400.00**

Neo-Modern, coffee table, V Kagan style, ceramic tiles set in walnut frame, legs forming long extended arch, 69 x 14 x 19½" **250.00**

Neo-Modern, egg chair, Asko Oy, Eero Aarnio Pastille chair, red glass-reinforced polyester with scooped-out seat, 37" d **1,000.00**

Neo-Modern, globe chair, based on 1966 design by Eero Aarnio for Asko Finn International, white Fiberglas shell, upholstered int, stereo speakers, flared circular base **300.00**

Neo-Modern, lounge chair, Pierre Paulin designer, sculptured bucket form, deep recessed seat, 2 thick rect legs, purple tweed upholstery, 27 x 27½ x 32" **175.00**

International Modern, Herman Miller, George Nelson designer, seating unit consisting of 1-arm sofa with upholstered seat and back cushions, low bench unit with 2 matching seat cushions, and white laminate end table, orig fabric, 1957, 27 x 124 x 30" sofa, $1,210.00. Photo courtesy David Rago Auctions, Inc.

Neo-Modern, side chair, Whilhelm Bofinger, Stuttgart, Helmut Batzner designer, BA1171, stackable, injection molded plastic, 1966 . . . . **50.00**

Neo-Modern, side chair, Herman Miller, Vernon Panton designer, red Fiberglas, cantilevered design, post-1967. . . . . **75.00**

Neo-Modern, umbrella stand, Artemide "Dedalo," designed by Emma Gismondi, thimble motif with 7 holes in top, white ABS plastic, stamped on bottom, 13½" h **175.00**

Pop, chair, Robert Breslau, black leather with multicolored stitching and 2 bull's eyes, 60" w, 48" d **2,000.00**

Pop, sofa, Kim McConnell, upholstered in spray-painted fabric with large scalloped flowers and diagonally striped lines, sgd and dated, 72" w, 36" d, 28" h. **3,500.00**

Scandinavian, chair, Arne Jacobsen designer, egg-form, plastic undulating shell upholstered in yellow worsted wool, raised on X-form chrome swivel base, c1960. . . . . . **500.00**

Scandinavian, coffee table, oak, circular top, tapered legs with brass feet, mkd "Made in Sweden," 15" h, 40" d **75.00**

Scandinavian, dining chairs, Baker Furniture Co, Finn Juhl designer, wood and vinyl, concave wood crest rail, ovoid black vinyl back, oblong curved black vinyl seat, straight seat rail, shaped and turned legs, 2 slender stretchers, 32" h, price for set of 6 . . . . **750.00**

Early American, kneehole desk, Chippendale style, 9 drawers, ogee bracket feet, batwing brasses, $100.00.

Neo-Modern, dining table, in the style of Vladimir Kagan, oblong glass top on mahogany base, 29¼" h, 72" w, 38½" d, $400.00. Photo courtesy David Rago Auctions, Inc.

Scandinavian, occasional table, blond wood, frieze drawer, metal stretchers, branded "Made in Sweden, Factory No. 4". 200.00

Scandinavian, occasional table, Rud Rasmussens, walnut, crossed legs adjust to various heights, "Rud. Rasmussens, Snedkerier, 42 Norre-Brocade, Kobenhaven" paper label, height ranges from 23" to 27½". 300.00

Scandinavian, side chair, Knoll, maple, worsted wool seat and back cushion, c1960 . . . . 100.00

Scandinavian, table, low, Artek, Alvar Aalto, painted black rect top, 4 bentwood supports, refinished, 29 x 21 x 15". 150.00

Streamline Modern, armchair, Berliner Metallgewerbe Joseph Muller, Mies van der Rohe designer, continuous tubular frame beginning with flat shelf-like crest flowing into L-shaped body extending into half-circle leg ending in extended U-form foot, arm attached to back and bottom of leg portion consisting of flat back, right angle bend for arms running parallel to seat and then swept down in quarter circle, continuous band of caning forms seat back, caned arm rests, 1927. . . . . 3,000.00

Streamline Modern, armchair, Heywood-Wakefield and Lloyd Mfg, tubular metal, brown vinyl upholstered back rest and seat, 1935 . . . . 150.00

Streamline Modern, desk, George W Neff, trapezoidal top set on 4 drawers at left and canted support at right, dark stained panels with black bands, mid-20th C, 28" h, 54" l. 1,750.00

Streamline Modern, desk and chair, Conant-Ball Co, Russel Wright designer, maple, desk with rect top above 3 drawers with block-form handles at left and angular support at right, chair with rect upholstered back, curved open arms, square upholstered seat, and straight legs, desk branded "Built by Conant-Ball Co., designed by Russel Wright, American Modern, BC," chair branded "CB. H.," c1935. . . . . 800.00

Scandinavian, lounge chair and ottoman, bentwood teak frame, canvas sling seat and contour fitted brown vinyl cushions, unmkd, 38 x 28 x 30", $825.00. Photo courtesy David Rago Auctions, Inc.

Streamline Modern, 2 armchairs and 2 side chairs, laminated and bent walnut, price for set of 4, $250.00.

Streamline Modern, dining table, Andre Arbus, rect top edged with brass molding, 2 pedestal supports framed in rosewood and enclosing red textured lacquered panels above rect brass base ending in scrolls, sgd on both pedestals "Andre Arbus," 29" h, 96" w, 39¾" d . . . 15,000.00

Streamline Modern, stool, Troy Sunshade, Troy, OH, Gilbert Rhode designer, round black cushion seat, chrome Z-form support, foot rest above circular base ring, 23½" h, 14" d 500.00

GAMBLING COLLECTIBLES

Gambling collectibles divide into two basic groups, those associated with gambling casinos and saloons and gaming materials designed for private "back room" use. Casino material further subdivides into actual material and equipment used on the gambling floors and advertising giveaways and premiums.

Gambling supply houses located throughout the country sold gambling paraphernalia to casinos, saloons, and private individuals through catalogs. Many of the items were "gaffed," meaning fixed in favor of the owner. Obviously, the general public was not meant to see these catalogs.

Gaming tables and punchboards dominated the 1980s collecting market. Gambling chips are today's hot collectible.

Reference: Leonard Schneir, *Gambling Collectibles: A Sure Winner*, Schiffer Publishing, 1994.

Collectors' Club: Casino Chips & Gaming Tokens Collectors Club, PO Box 63, Brick, NJ 08723.

Note: See Punchboards and Slot Machines for additional listings.

Ashtray, Golden Nugget, glass, "Gambling Hall," amber, yellow center, red lettering, 3½" sq $6.00

Ashtray, Harrah's, glass, "Reno and Lake Tahoe," orange center, white lettering, 3⅝" sq 5.00

Ashtray, MGM Grand Hotel, glass, white center with red lion and lettering, 4½" d 8.00

Bingo Cage, metal, red celluloid handle, 11 wood balls, 9 cards, ©1941, 9" h 20.00

Book, *Gamblers Don't Gamble*, Michael MacDougall, and JC Furnas, illus, 1939, 167 pp 35.00

Poker Chips. Left: Elk, inlaid litho, red, white, and blue, 1¹/₂" d, $14.00. Right: New Southport Club, New Orleans, green, black, and white, 1¹/₂" d, $22.00. Photo courtesy Frank's Antiques & Auctions.

Credit Marker, celluloid, red, white, green, and light blue, various sizes and denominations, price for 12 ...... **25.00**

Dice, miniature, bone or composition, brass cylinder with twist-off lid, price for 5. .... **20.00**

Dice, Poker, celluloid, price for set of 5 .... **25.00**

Drinking Glass, Harolds Club, Reno, "Moonshot," spaceship shaped, clear, red, white, and blue lunar shape ship design, 1960–70s, 6" h **20.00**

Matchbook, Lincoln Lake Casino, Michigan, matches removed, 1940s **20.00**

Playing Cards, complete in orig carton with sliding lid, Arrco Playing Card Co, 1940s, 5 x 7" **20.00**

Playing Cards, Crooked Deck, printed and cut in zigzag design, complete in orig carton, A Freed Novelty, Inc, NY **20.00**

Poker Chip Caddy, Bakelite, brown, round **20.00**

Poker Chips, Bakelite, butterscotch colored swirl pattern, price for set of 10, 1¹/₂" d **20.00**

Poker Chips, clay, black, cigar illus in center, M Stachelberg & Co Cigars, price for set of 2 .... **20.00**

Poker Chips, Jack Daniels Tennessee Whiskey, 4 white and 2 red chips, Jack Daniels logo, 1¹/₂" d **20.00**

Punchboard, Diamond Dust, baseball theme, red, yellow, and blue board, 1930s, 8¹/₄ x 5¹/₄". **15.00**

Punchboard, Nickel Special, cigarette packs/cartons as prizes, red, yellow, and blue board, 1930s, 9¹/₄ x 10" **18.00**

Token, brass, Copa Cabana and hat on obverse, $1.00 emblem on reverse, 1¹/₂" d **20.00**

GAMES

This category deals primarily with boxed board games. The board game achieved widespread popularity in the period from 1890 to 1910. After modest sales in the 1920s, board games increased in popularity in the 1930s and experienced a second golden age from the late 1940s through the mid-1960s. Television and movie licensing played a major role in board game development. As a result, crossover collectors frequently skew market values.

Generic board games such as Monopoly have little value except for the earliest editions. The same holds true for games geared to children aged 4 to 8, e.g., Candyland, Go to the Head of the Class, etc. Generic board games dominate toy store shelves in the 1990s. Disney and a few mega-movie licensed games are the exceptions.

References: Mark Cooper, *Baseball Games: Home Versions of the National Pastime 1860s–1960s*, Schiffer Publishing, 1995; L-W Book Sales, *Board Games of the 50's, 60's, and 70's With Prices*, L-W Book Sales, 1994; Alex G. Malloy, *American Games*, Antique Trader Books, 1998; Rick Polizzi, *Baby Boomer Games*, Collector Books, 1995; Harry L. Rinker, *Antique Trader's Guide to Games & Puzzles*, Antique Trader Books, 1997; Desi Scarpone, *Board Games*, Schiffer Publishing, 1995; Bruce Whitehill, *Games: American Boxed Games and Their Makers, 1822–1922*, Wallace-Homestead, Krause Publications, 1992.

Periodicals: *Toy Shop*, 700 E State St, Iola, WI 54990; *Toy Trader*, PO Box 1050, Dubuque, IA 52004.

Collectors' Clubs: American Game Collectors Assoc, PO Box 44, Dresher, PA 19025; Gamers Alliance, PO Box 197, East Meadow, NY 11554.

Note: Unless noted otherwise, prices listed are for complete games in mint condition.

ACME Checkout Game, Milton Bradley, 1959 .... **$35.00**
Across the Continent, Parker Bros, 1960. .... **20.00**
Addams Family Reunion Game, Pressman, 1991 .... **10.00**
Advance to Boardwalk, Parker Bros, 1985 .... **35.00**
Air Mail, The Game of, Milton Bradley, 1927 .... **75.00**
Annie, Parker Bros, 1981. .... **20.00**
Annie Oakley, Milton Bradley, 1950s. **55.00**
Arnold Palmer's Inside Golf, David Bremson Co, 1961 .... **165.00**
As the World Turns, Parker Bros, 1966 .... **20.00**
Astron, Parker Bros, 1955 .... **40.00**
Bamboozle, Milton Bradley, 1962 .... **35.00**
Baretta the Street Detective Game, Milton Bradley, 1976 .... **25.00**
Barrel of Monkeys, Giant, Lakeside, 1969 .... **15.00**
Batman, Hasbro, 1974 .... **40.00**
Battle of the Planets, Milton Bradley, 1979. .... **40.00**
Battleship, Milton Bradley, 1967 .... **40.00**
Battle Stations, John E Burleson, 1952 .... **30.00**
Bermuda Triangle, Milton Bradley, 1975. .... **40.00**
Beverly Hillbillies, Standard Toycraft, 1963. .... **70.00**
Bible Game of New Testament Books, David C Cook Publishing, 1930s **70.00**
Bid It Right, Milton Bradley, 1964 .... **25.00**
Billionaire, Parker Bros, 1973 .... **30.00**
Bing It, Matchbox, 1960s. **15.00**
Bionic Crisis, Parker Bros, 1975 .... **20.00**
Booby-Trap, Parker Bros, 1975. .... **60.00**
Bug-A-Boo Game, Whitman, 1968 .... **15.00**
Bulls and Bears, Parker Bros, 1936. .... **100.00**
Camp Runamuck Game, Ideal, 1965 .... **45.00**
Carrier Strike, Milton Bradley, 1977 .... **50.00**
Car Travel Game, Milton Bradley, 1958 .... **20.00**
Cascade, Matchbox, 1972 .... **15.00**
Casper the Friendly Ghost, Milton Bradley, 1959 .... **28.00**
Cat and Mouse, Game of, Parker Bros, 1964 .... **15.00**
Cheers, Classic Games, Inc, 1992 .... **10.00**
Chopper Strike, Milton Bradley, 1975. .... **50.00**
Citadel, Parker Bros, 1940 .... **35.00**
Cities, Game of, Psychology Today, 1970 .... **25.00**
Clue, Parker Bros, orig issue, no instructions, 1949. ..... **85.00**
Cold Feet, Ideal, 1967 .... **25.00**
Combat Tank Game, Magic Wand Co, 1964. .... **38.00**
Concentration, Milton Bradley, 1958 .... **35.00**
Conflict, Parker Bros, 1940 .... **90.00**

Confucius Say, Milton Bradley, c1937 .... 38.00
Countdown, ES Lowe, 1967......................... 40.00
Countdown Space Game, Transogram, 1959 .... 90.00
Coup D'Etat, Parker Bros, 1966 .... 70.00
Crazy Clock, Ideal, 1964........................... 75.00
Defenders of the Flag, Noble and Noble Publishers,
    1922... 40.00
Detectives, The, Transogram, 1961.................. 45.00
Diner's Club Credit Card Game, Ideal, 1961 .... 45.00
Dino the Dinosaur, Transogram, 1961 .... 50.00
Dream House, Milton Bradley, 1968 .... 115.00
Egg Race Game, Ideal, 1968 .... 18.00
Electric Horserace, Pressman Toy Co, 1950s........ 100.00
Emergency Game, The, Milton Bradley, 1973–74 ...... 15.00
Feeley Meeley, Milton Bradley, 1967 .... 15.00
Finance, Parker Bros, 1956 .... 45.00
Fireball XL5, Milton Bradley, 1964.................. 90.00
Flagship Airfreight, Milton Bradley, 1946 .... 55.00
Flapper Fortunes, The Embossing Co, 1929........... 18.00
Frantic Frogs, Milton Bradley, 1965 .... 20.00
Flying Nun, Milton Bradley, 1968 .... 45.00
General Hospital, The Game of, Cardinal, 1982 ...... 18.00
George of the Jungle, Parker Bros, 1968 .... 50.00
Gettysburg, Avalon Hill, 1958 .... 25.00
Gidget Fortune Teller Game, Milton Bradley, 1966 ... 30.00
Godfather Game, Family Games, Inc, 1971 .... 25.00
Grab A Loop, Milton Bradley, 1968 .... 15.00
Harpoon, Gabriel, 1955 .... 25.00
Headache, Kohner, 1968............................ 8.00
Hickety Pickety, Parker Bros, 1924................. 40.00
Hippety-Hop, Corey Games, 1940................... 65.00
Hit the Beach, Milton Bradley, 1965 .... 55.00
Hokum, Parker Bros, 1927......................... 38.00
Huckleberry Hound, Milton Bradley, 1981, missing 1 pc 20.00
Hullabaloo Electric Teen Game, Remco, 1965 .... 65.00
Hunch, Happy Hour, 1956 .... 15.00
Hunt for Red October, TSR, 1988................... 20.00
In the Chips, Tega, 1980 .... 10.00
Indiana Jones and the Temple of Doom, LJN, 1984........ 38.00

Intercept, Lakeside, 1978.......................... 15.00
Ipcress File, Milton Bradley, 1966 .... 75.00
I've Got A Secret, Lowell, 1956 .... 40.00
Jack and the Beanstalk, Game of, National Games, 1957 .... 35.00
James Bond 007 Assault Game, Victory Games, 1961...... 60.00
Jaws, The Game of, Ideal, 1975 .... 15.00
Jet Race Game, Built-Rite, 1960s................... 15.00
Jig Race, Game Makers, 1940s 30.00
Joker Joker Joker, Milton Bradley, 1979............. 8.00
Jonny Quest Game, Transogram, 1964 .... 600.00
Journey to the Unknown Game, Remco, 1968 .... 95.00
Kings, Akro Agates, 1931.......................... 35.00
Knight Rider, Knight Rider, 1983 .... 20.00
Kooky Karnival Game, Milton Bradley, 1969 .... 20.00
Krull, Parker Bros, 1983 .... 20.00
Land of the Giants, Ideal, 1968 .... 90.00
Last Straw, The, Schaper, 1966 .... 10.00
Leave It to Beaver Money Maker, Hasbro, 1959 ...... 35.00
Lie Detector, Mattel, 1960......................... 40.00
Limbo Legs, Milton Bradley, 1969 .... 32.00
Line Drive, Lord & Freber, 1953.................... 80.00
Little Boy Blue, Cadaco-Ellis, 1955 .... 15.00
Little Red Bushy-Tail, Parker Bros, 1921 .... 50.00
Liz Tyler Hollywood Starlet, Ideal, 1963............ 30.00
Lolli Plop, Milton Bradley, 1962 .... 10.00
Look Out Below, Ideal, 1968....................... 20.00
Lot the Calf, Brown Games, Inc, 1964 .... 20.00
Love Boat, Ungame, 1980.......................... 20.00
Lucky Bingo, Transogram, 1936 .... 15.00
Lucy Show, Transogram, 1962 .... 80.00
Mad Magazine Card Game, Parker Bros, 1980 .... 10.00
Magic Race, Habob, 1940s......................... 70.00
Mail Run, Quality Games, 1960 .... 40.00
Managing Your Money, Cuna Mutual Insurance Society,
    1969.. 10.00
Manhunt, Milton Bradley, 1972 .... 10.00
Marathon Game, Sports Game Co, 1978 .... 20.00
Mask, Parker Bros, 1985 .... 5.00
Mentor, Hasbro, 1961............................. 45.00
Mille Bornes, Parker Bros, 1962..................... 5.00
Mister Ed, Parker Bros, 1962 .... 35.00
Monkeys and Coconuts, Schaper, 1965 .... 12.00
Monster Old Maid, Milton Bradley, 1964............ 35.00
Mr Novak Game, Transogram, 1963................. 35.00
Mr Ree, Selchow & Righter, 1946, missing 1 weapon 28.00
Murder She Wrote, Warren, 1985 .... 28.00
Musingo, Mattel, 1962 .... 20.00
Nemo, Creston Industries, 1969.................... 15.00
New Frontier, Colorful Products, 1962.............. 30.00
Newlywed Game, The, Hasbro, 1967 .... 10.00
Ocean to Ocean Flight Game, Wilder Mfg, 1927 .... 110.00
Old Hogan's Goat, Whitman, 1939 .... 20.00
Ouija, Parker Bros, 1970s 10.00
Over the Garden Wall, Milton Bradley, 1937 .... 15.00
Pathfinder, Milton Bradley, 1977 .... 40.00
Peeko, Watkins-Strathmore, 1964................... 10.00
People's Court, Hoyle Products, 1986 .... 12.00
Peter Gunn, Lowell, 1960 .... 30.00
Pink Panther, The, Cadaco, 1981 .... 8.00
Pirate Plunder, All-Fair, 1950s 40.00
Planet of the Apes, Milton Bradley, 1974 .... 35.00
Playful Trails Game, Lakeside, 1968................. 35.00
Poison Ivy, Ideal, 1969 .... 35.00
Pollyanna, Parker Bros, 1915–20s 30.00

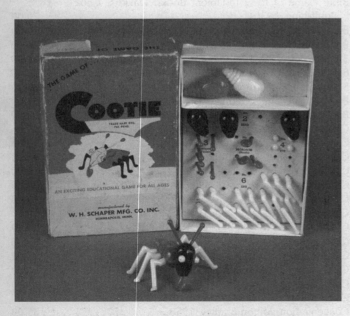

The Game of Cootie, WH Schaper Mfg, $30.00.

Toonerville Trolley Game, Milton Bradley, No. 4838, $120.00.

Pot O'Gold, All-Fair, 1950s	40.00
Price Is Right, The, Lowell, 1958	35.00
Probe, Parker Bros, 1974	5.00
Pro Draft, Parker Bros, 1974	20.00
Pursuit, Aurora, 1973	18.00
Pyramids, Knapp Electric, 1930s	15.00
Quinto, 3M, 1964	10.00
Qwik Quiz Game, Transogram, 1958	25.00
Rack-O, Milton Bradley, 1961	8.00
Radio Amateur Hour Game, Milton Bradley, 1930s	70.00
Raggedy Ann, Milton Bradley, 1954	25.00
Red Rover, Cadaco, 1963	15.00
Robin Hood, Parker Bros, 1973	28.00
Rook, Parker Bros, 1936	8.00
Route 66 Travel Game, Transogram, 1962	85.00
Rummy Royal, Whitman, 1959	10.00
Sale of the Century, Milton Bradley, 1969	15.00
Say When!, Parker Bros, 1961	20.00
Scrabble, Selchow & Righter, 1953	10.00
Scribbage Twin, ES Lowe, 1965	8.00
Secrecy, Universal Games 1965	25.00
Seven-Up Game, Transogram, 1961	15.00
Shadowlord!, Parker Bros, 1983	10.00
Sherlock Holmes, Cadaco, 1982	32.00
Shindig, Remco, 1965	55.00
Shopping Center Game, Whitman, 1957	18.00
Siege Game, Milton Bradley, 1966	25.00
Silly Sidney, Transogram, 1963	35.00
Sinbad, Cadaco, 1978	25.00
Situation 7, Parker Bros, 1969	15.00
Skee Ball, Eldon, 1963	30.00
Skip-A-Cross, Cadaco-Ellis, 1954	20.00
Smitty Game, Milton Bradley, 1930s	110.00
Snake Eyes, Selchow & Righter, 1930–57	55.00
Snake's Alive, The Game of, Ideal, 1966	20.00
Society Today, Dynamic Design, 1971	12.00
Sonar Sub Hunt, Mattel, 1961	45.00
Sorry!, Parker Bros, 1950	20.00
Space Game, Parker Bros, 1953	45.00
Spedem Auto Race, Alderman-Fairchild, 1922	95.00
Spingo and Whirlette, Transogram, 1930s	45.00
Spin It, Milton Bradley, 1926	30.00
Sports Arena, Milton Bradley, 1962	40.00
Sprint, Mattel, 1965	30.00
Spy Detector Game, Mattel, 1963	30.00
Stoney Burke, Transogram, 1963	35.00

Strat-O-Matic Baseball, 1988	35.00
Swahili Game, Milton Bradley, 1968	15.00
Sweeps, All-Fair, 1940	25.00
Taffy's Party Game, Transogram, 1966	12.00
Tarzan to the Rescue, Milton Bradley, 1977	20.00
Taxi, Selchow & Righter, 1960	15.00
Terminator 2—Judgement Day, Milton Bradley, 1991	22.00
Three Men in a Tub, Milton Bradley, 1935–36	35.00
Thunderbirds, Parker Bros, 1967	50.00
Ticker, Glow Products Co, 1929	75.00
Tiltin' Milton, Ideal, 1968	25.00
Time Tunnel Game, The, Ideal, 1966	90.00
Tom & Jerry, Milton Bradley, 1977	20.00
To Tell the Truth, Lowell, 1957	30.00
Traffic, ES Lowe, 1968	15.00
Trap, Ideal, 1972	10.00
Trial Lawyer, James N Vail, 1977	12.00
Trip-Trap, Remco, 1969	40.00
Truth or Consequences, Gabriel, 1955	30.00
TV Guide TV Game, Trivia, Inc, 1984	30.00
Twiggy, Milton Bradley, 1967	35.00
Twister, Milton Bradley, 1966	15.00
Tycoon, Wattson Games, 1976	10.00
Uncle Jim's Question Bee, Lowell, 1938	30.00
Undercover, Cadaco-Ellis, 1960	25.00
Underseas World of Jacques Cousteau, Parker Bros, 1968	20.00
Universe, Parker Bros, 1967	15.00
Uranium Rush, Gardner Games, 1950s	60.00
Varsity, Cadaco-Ellis, 1945	15.00
Venture, 3M, 1968	10.00
Voodoo Doll Game, Schaper, 1967	30.00
Wackiest Ship in the Army Game, The, Standard Toykraft, 1964–65	45.00
Waltons, Milton Bradley, 1974	20.00
Walt & Skeezix Gasoline Alley Game, Milton Bradley, 1920	120.00
Watch On De Rind, Alderman-Fairchild, 1931	250.00
Weird-Ohs Game, Ideal, 1963–64	40.00
What Shall I Be?, Selchow & Righter, 1966	15.00
What's My Name?, Jay Mar Specialty, 1940	35.00
Where's the Beef?, Milton Bradley, 1984	10.00
Whirly Bird, Schaper, 1958	15.00
Who?, Parker Bros, 1951	30.00
Who Did It?, Gardner Games, 1950s	35.00
Why, Milton Bradley, 1961	15.00
Wildlife, ES Lowe, 1971	35.00

What's My Line, Lowell, 1954–55, $40.00.

Willow, Parker Bros, 1988	10.00
Wings, Parker Bros, 1928	20.00
Wizard of Oz, Cadaco, 1974	35.00
Wonderbug, Ideal, 1977	12.00
Wordy, Pressman Toy Corp, 1938	25.00
Wow Pillow Fight Game for Girls, Milton Bradley, 1964	20.00
X-Plor US, Alderman-Fairchild, 1922	85.00
Yacht Race, Parker Bros, 1961	80.00
Yahtzee Challenge, ES Lowe, 1974	10.00
Yankee Doodle, Cadaco-Ellis, 1940	25.00
Yertle, The Game of, Revell, 1960	50.00
You Don't Say Game, Milton Bradley, 1964–69	10.00
Yours For a Song, Lowell, 1961	25.00
Zok, Hasbro, 1967	20.00

GAS STATION COLLECTIBLES

Many of today's drivers no longer remember the independently owned full-service gas station where attendants pumped your gas, checked your oil, and cleaned your windshield. Fortunately, collectors do. Many are recreating golden age (1930s through the 1960s) versions of the independent gas station in their basements and garages.

While pump globes and oil cans remain the principal collecting focus, gasoline station advertising, uniforms, and paper ephemera have all become hot collecting subcategories in the 1990s. Road maps, especially those issued prior to the Interstate system, double in value every few years.

References: Mark Anderton, Encyclopedia of Petroliana, *Krause Publications, 1999;* Mark Anderton and Sherry Mullen, *Gas Station Collectibles,* Wallace-Homestead, Krause Publications, 1994; Robert W. D. Ball, *Texaco Collectibles,* Schiffer Publishing, 1994; Scott Benjamin and Wayne Henderson, *Gas Pump Globes,* Motorbooks International, 1993; Scott Benjamin and Wayne Henderson, *Oil Company Signs,* Motorbooks International, 1995; Scott Benjamin and Wayne Henderson, *Sinclair Collectibles,* Schiffer Publishing, 1997; Mike Bruner, *Gasoline Treasures,* Schiffer Publishing, 1996; Todd P. Helms, *The Conoco Collector's Bible,* Schiffer Publishing, 1995; J. Sam McIntyre, *The Esso Collectibles Handbook,* Schiffer Publishing, 1998; Rick Pease, *Filling Station Collectibles,* Schiffer Publishing, 1994; Rick Pease, *Service Station Collectibles,* Schiffer Publishing, 1996; B. J. Sommers and Wayne Priddy, *Value Guide to Gas Station Memorabilia,* Collector Books, 1995; Sonya Stenzler and Rick Pease, *Gas Station Collectibles,* Schiffer Publishing, 1993; Charles Whitworth, *Gulf Oil Collectibles,* Schiffer Publishing, 1998; Michael Karl Witzel, *Gas Station Memories,* Motorbooks International, 1994.

Newsletter: *Petroleum Collectibles Monthly,* PO Box 556, La Grange, OH 44050.

Collectors' Club: International Petroliana Collectors Assoc, PO Box 937, Powell, OH 43065.

Ashtray, Texaco, metal, litho corners, 4¼" sq	**$180.00**
Attendant's Hat, Mobil, cloth, plastic rim, 5" h, 10" w, 11" l	135.00
Blotter, Esso, cardboard, Standard Service, 1931	6.00
Blotter, Gargoyle Lubricants, leather, gilt letters, 6¾" h, 6¼" w	60.00

Blotter, Sunoco, Donald Duck driving car and "A Quick Start Blue Sunoco Peps Up Cold Motors," Walt Disney Enterprises, c1938	135.00
Credit Card, Texaco, paper, #66574, May, Jun, Jul, and Aug, 1940, with attached coupons, 3½" h, 6¼" w	160.00
Display, Esso, diecut cardboard, countertop, "Sodico Paris Made in France," 15½" h, 10" w	80.00
Display, Mobil attendant, painted wood, life size, easel backed, 72" h, 21" w	650.00
Display Rack, Gulf Valvetop, metal, "Sciuto Signs, Kenton, O. '72," 25" h, 10¾" w	85.00
Gas Globe, Aetna, glass body, 2 lenses, 13½"	275.00
Gas Globe, Crown, glass body, screw base, 13½"	250.00
Gas Globe, Elreco Special Gasoline, glass body, "The El Dorado Refining Co," 13½"	200.00
Gas Globe, Essolene, metal body, 2 lenses, 15"	325.00
Gas Globe, Hi Energee Gasoline, plastic body, 2 lenses, 13½"	190.00
Gas Globe, Mobilgas, metal body, 2 lenses, 16½"	550.00
Gas Globe, Mobilgas Ethyl, metal body, 2 lenses, 16½"	450.00
Gas Globe, Onyx, plastic body, 2 lenses, 13½"	160.00
Gas Globe, Paraland, plastic body, 2 lenses, 16½"	300.00
Gas Globe, Stone's Regular, plastic body, 2 lenses, 13½"	335.00
Gas Globe, Walburn Gasoline, metal body, 1 lens, 15½"	350.00
Gas Nozzle, metal, "K-721-1," 14" lens	60.00
Hat Top, Phillips 66, cloth with cloth and embroidered patch, 4 snaps for mounting on bill	30.00
Keychain, BP, metal, logo	10.00
Keychain, Mobil, plastic, Pegasus horse, inscribed "Mobil"	25.00
License Plate Attachment, Mobil Pegasus horse, diecut tin, emb, 4¼" h, 5¼" w	55.00
Map, Sinclair, New York, Kentucky and Tennessee, 2 Ohio, 1947–51, price for 4	25.00
Map, Sun Oil Co, New York, 1935	15.00
Map Rack, Phillips 66, wood, rotates at base, with 48 maps from 1950s, 22" h, 12" w	650.00
Motor Oil Cup, Independent Gasoline, tin, 2 logos on each side, 2¾" h, 3¾" d	145.00
Oil Bottle, Socony Motor Oil, glass, emb, qt	40.00

Cup, Independent Gasoline Motor Oil, tin, 2¾" h, 3¾" d, $160.00.
Photo courtesy Collectors Auction Services.

Cigarette Lighter, Sinclair Gasoline, Powell Heiskell Sinclair Products, debossed metal, 2¹/₄" h, $105.00. Photo courtesy Collectors Auction Services.

Oil Can, Valvoline Motor Oil, "Valvoline Oil Company, Chicago," gal, 11" h. 185.00
Padlock, Phillips 66, metal, with key, 2¹/₄" h 25.00
Paperweight, St Louis Pumps, cast iron, copper hose and nozzle, emb lettering, 7³/₄" h 500.00
Playing Cards, Mobilgas/Mobiloil, Maidencreek Feed & Supply, Maidencreek, PA. 25.00
Pocket Mirror, Excelsior Gasoline, celluloid over metal, "C.E. Mills Oil Co. Syracuse, N.Y.," 2" d 75.00
Poster, Gulf, paper, "Singing with sweeter power/New No-Nox/New Good Gulf," 42" h, 27³/₄" w 90.00
Poster, Gulfpride, paper, cat in center with "Change to Gulfpride Here!/How About Now?," 42" h, 27³/₄" w 150.00
Poster, Shell, paper, "Best Routes to the Fair/Ask Shell," 53¹/₂" h, 39¹/₄" w 300.00
Poster, Super-Shell, paper, "Saves on 'Stop and Go' Driving," 33" h, 57¹/₂" w 80.00
Price Rack, Gulf, metal, box of prices in 20¢–40¢ range, 62" h, 43" w 350.00
Pump Sign, Fleetwing Super-Flite, painted metal, emb, 8" h, 9¹/₄" w. 350.00
Pump Sign, Husky Hi Power, porcelain, 1-sided, 12" h, 12" w 375.00
Pump Sign, Jetrol Premium, porcelain, 1-sided, 12" h, 12" w 225.00
Pump Sign, Mobilgas Special, porcelain, 1-sided, 12" h, 12¹/₂" l 210.00
Pump Sign, Sky Chief Supreme Petrox, porcelain, 1-sided, "Made in U.S.A. 3–6–59," 18" h, 12" w 100.00
Pump Sign, Texaco Fire Chief Gasoline, porcelain, 1-sided, "Made in U.S.A. 3–6–62," 18" h, 12" w 35.00
Salt and Pepper Shakers, pr, Esso, plastic, "Katko's Service Station, 541 Hamilton St. New Brunswick, N.J.," orig box 65.00
Salt and Pepper Shakers, pr, Philgas, plastic, 1-piece, "Always a Fair Shake Phillips 66/Al Carlstrom Home Oil Company Gowrie, Iowa Dial EL 2-1331" 25.00
Sign, Magic Gasoline, tin, emb, 1-sided, "Ellwood Myers Co., Springfield, O.," 24" h, 18" w 100.00
Sign, Purol Gasoline, porcelain, 1-sided, 15" h, 14" w 175.00
Sign, Red Crown Gasoline, porcelain, 2-sided, 42" d 650.00
Sign, Shell, "No Smoking," porcelain, 1-sided, 12" h, 17¹/₂" w. 50.00

Sign, Wedhams Gas, tin, wood frame, 83¹/₂" h, 18" w 250.00
Soap Dispenser, Shell, cast iron, logo on front plate, 5" h . . . 150.00
Thermometer, Authorized United Motors Service, wood, glass tube, metal holder, "Made by Marshall Mfg. Co. Coshocton, O.," 15" h, 4" w 120.00
Thermometer, Mobil, tin face and body, glass front, ©1957 Pam Clock Co, Inc, New Rochelle, NY, 12" d 400.00
Thermometer, Shell, plastic, metal, and glass, cardboard gauge, glass tube. 10.00

GEISHA GIRL

Geisha Girl is a generic term used to describe Japanese export ceramics made between the 1880s and the present whose decoration incorporates one or more kimono-clad Japanese ladies. Most collectors focus on pre-1940 ware. Geisha Girl ceramics made after 1945 are referred to as "modern" Geisha Girl.

Reference: Elyce Litts, *The Collector's Encyclopedia of Geisha Girl Porcelain,* Collector Books, 1988, out of print.

REPRODUCTION ALERT: Be alert for late 1970s' and early 1980s' Geisha Girl reproductions in forms ranging from ginger jars to sake sets. These contemporary pieces have red borders. Other telltale characteristics include lack of detail, very bright gold highlights, and a white porcelain body.

Czechoslovakian ceramic manufacturers also copied this ware in the 1920s. Some are marked "Czechoslovakia" or have a false Chinese mark. Many are unmarked. Decal decoration was used extensively. However, the real clue is in the faces. The faces on Czechoslovakian Geisha do not have a strong oriental look.

Bowl, Bamboo Trellis, 7¹/₂" d $40.00
Bowl, Ikebana in Rickshaw, 8" d 45.00
Bread and Butter Plate, Bamboo Tree, 6" d 10.00
Bread and Butter Plate, Bamboo Trellis, 6¹/₂" d 12.00
Bread and Butter Plate, Bird Cage, 6" d 12.00
Cocoa Pot, cov 60.00
Cocoa Set, By Land and By Sea, cov chocolate pot with 5 cups and saucers 90.00

Teacup and Saucer, Parasol/Lesson Variant, gold line through scalloped blue border, mkd "Japan," $10.00.

Condiment Set, Duck Watching B, pine green, salt and
  pepper shakers, toothpick holder, mustard pot, and
  cherry blossom shape tray 50.00
Creamer, Long-Stemmed Peony 12.00
Creamer, Porch, Torii Nippon. 25.00
Creamer and Sugar, River's Edge 70.00
Cup and Saucer, Bird Cage 15.00
Eggcup, Child Reaching For Butterfly, Variation A 15.00
Eggcup, squat 12.00
Hair Receiver, Long-Stemmed Peony 35.00
Ice Cream Set, Fan A, red, 6 pcs 100.00
Mint Dish, leaf shape 25.00
Mug, Bamboo Trellis, 4" d 22.00
Pitcher, child's, Garden Bench, red, Variant N, 2¹/₂" h 20.00
Plate, By Land and By Sea, 7" d 15.00
Plate, Child Reaching For Butterfly, red, Variation A, 7" d . . . 15.00
Plate, Ikebana in Rickshaw, 7¹/₄" d 22.00
Powder Jar, Lantern Gateway, red. 30.00
Sake Cup, Meeting B. 15.00
Salt and Pepper Shakers, pr, Ikebana in Rickshaw 20.00
Teacup and Saucer, Bamboo Trellis, Torii, Japan 10.00
Toothpick Holder, River's Edge, mkd "Kutani" 70.00

G.I. JOE

Hasbro introduced G.I. Joe at the February 1964 American
International Toy Fair in New York. Initially, this 12-inch poseable
figure was produced in only four versions, one for each branch of
the military.

A black G.I. Joe joined the line in 1965, followed by a talking
G.I. Joe and female nurse in 1967. The G.I. Joe Adventure Team
introduced this all-American hero to civilian pursuits such as hunting and deep sea diving. The 1976 Arab oil embargo forced
Hasbro to reduce G.I. Joe's size from 12 to 8 inches. Production
stopped in 1977.

Hasbro reintroduced G.I. Joe in 1982 in a 3¹/₄-inch format. In
1994 Hasbro resumed production of the 12-inch figure, targeted
primarily toward the adult collector market. Action Man, G.I. Joe's
British equivalent, was marketed in the United States during the
1996 holiday season.

Collectors concentrate on pre-1977 action figures. Collecting
interest in accessories, especially those with period boxes, continues to grow.

References: John Marshall, *GI Joe and Other Backyard Heroes,*
Schiffer Publishing, 1997; John Michlig, *GI Joe: The Complete
Story of America's Favorite Man of Action,* Chronicle Books, 1998;
Vincent Santelmo, *The Complete Encyclopedia to GI Joe, 2nd
Edition,* Krause Publications, 1997; Vincent Santelmo, *GI Joe,
1964–1994,* Krause Publications, 1999.

Periodical: *GI Joe Patrol,* PO Box 2362, Hot Springs, AR 71914.

Collectors' Clubs: GI Joe Collectors Club, 225 Cattle Barron Park
Dr, Fort Worth, TX 76108; GI Joe: Steel Brigade Club, 8362 Lomay
Ave, Westminster, CA 92683.

Note: All action figures are MOC.

ACCESSORIES

Bayonet $25.00
Binoculars 7.00

Action Figure,
Gung-Ho (U.S. Dress
Marine), #6849, Hall
of Fame, 1993, 12" h,
$45.00.

Cannon Shell 8.00
Canteen and Holster, with strap 28.00
Deep Sea Boot Weights, pr 15.00
Dress Shoes, pr. 30.00
Flare Gun 3.00
Flippers, pr, Hasbro. 4.00
Footlocker, wood, no tray 25.00
Green Beret Bazooka 28.00
Medic Crutch 12.00
Medic Helmet. 20.00
Medic Shoulder Bag, green cloth 35.00
Medic Stretcher, no struts 25.00
Mine Detector Harness, with battery pack 40.00
MP Dufflebag 25.00
MP Helmet. 20.00
Pith Helmet 10.00
Raft, yellow, with loops 40.00
Scuba Tank 5.00
Spare Tire, with hub 15.00

ACTION FIGURES

Ambush $30.00
Astro Viper 50.00
Bazooka 50.00
Beach Head 50.00
Big Boa 50.00
Cobra. 150.00
Cobra Commander 300.00
Cobra LA Team 75.00
Cobra Officer 150.00
Doc 100.00
Duke 250.00
Flash 125.00
Gung Ho 125.00
Hydro Viper 50.00
Recondo. 90.00
Repeater 40.00
Roadblock 125.00
Tipwire 100.00
Torpedo 100.00
Voltar 30.00

CLOTHING

Action Pilot Jumpsuit, with side snaps	$30.00
Air Adventurer Jumpsuit	18.00
Crash Crew Hood	25.00
Crash Crew Jacket	25.00
Crash Crew Pants	20.00
Deep Sea Diver Suit	15.00
Deep Sea Helmet, with mask	20.00
Fatigue Cap, green	7.00
Green Beret Pants	38.00
Marine Dress Shirt	22.00
MP Jacket	25.00
MP Pants	30.00
Scramble Pilot Jumpsuit	28.00
Sea Adventurer Shirt and Pants	25.00
Space Suit, 2 zipper	25.00
Spy Trenchcoat	15.00
West Point Jacket	30.00

PLAYSETS

GI Joe Training Center	$90.00
Secret Mountain Outpost	75.00
Three in One Super Adventure Set	150.00
Training Tower, complete with box, no guns	235.00

VEHICLES

Adventure Team Helicopter Landing Gear	$20.00
Adventure Team Helicopter Module, with shift lever	15.00
Adventure Team Six Wheel ATV, with winch	60.00
CLAW Cobra	12.00
Destro's Despoiler	30.00
Rattler, complete, orig box	65.00
Rolling Thunder	45.00
Pigmy Gorilla Boat, with seat	25.00

GIRL SCOUTS

Juliette Gordon Low of Savannah, Georgia, began the Girl Scout movement in 1912. It grew rapidly. The 1928 Girl Scout manual suggested selling cookies to raise money. Today the annual Girl Scout cookie drive supports local troops and councils.

Girl Scout collectibles enjoy limited collector interest. There is a ready market for flashlights and pocketknives, primarily because they cross over into other collecting fields.

Bookends, pr, eagle emblem, gold enamel painted composition, metal base, 5¼ x 5¾"	$20.00
Doll, Brownie, vinyl, movable legs, arms, and head, open and close glass eyes, rooted hair, painted features, dark brown felt fabric crown cap with orange Brownie symbol, brown fabric uniform dress with orange ribbon neckerchief and brown vinyl belt, dark khaki elastic fabric stockings, white lace under panties, brown vinyl sandal shoes, Effanbee, 1965, 8¼" h	50.00
Flag, Brownie, brown and yellow, emblem in center, sewn-on lettering "Troop 219 Nevada MO," with wooden pole	20.00
Pin, figural Girl Scout, diecut, painted plastic, fleshtone girl with brown hair in green Scout uniform holding collar of dalmatian dog, c1940s, 2¼" h	15.00

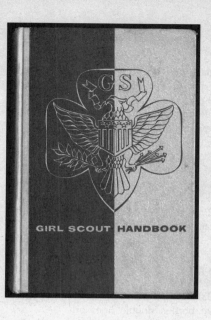

Handbook, Intermediate Program, green and black hard cover, 512 pgs., 5½ x 8¼", $5.00.

Pinback Button, "Girl Scouts Mystery Trip," yellow image of bus above "1977"	10.00
Pinback Button, girl with brown hat and collar on yellow ground, c1920s	15.00
Pinback Button, "USA Girl Scouts Mainland Japan," colored flags of each nation in center, 1970s	10.00
Pocketknife, green plastic grips, gilt emblem, Kutmaster	50.00
Ring, sterling silver, ⅜" Girl Scout emblem, c1930s	20.00
Trivet, iron, painted gold and green enamel, "1912 50th anniversary Girl Scouts of the U.S.A. Honor the Past Serve the Future 1962"	10.00
Uniform, leader's, 4 pcs, green dress with green plastic buttons and "GS" emblem at collar, dark green cap with affixed "GS" device, green canvas web belt, and stamped steel "Girl Scouts Be Prepared" buckle, size 22½	35.00
Whistle, silver tone, lanyard ring, emblem engraved on side, mkd "B&R," 2½" l	20.00

GLASS SHOES

Glass shoe is a generic term for any figural shoe (or slipper, boot, ice skate, etc.) made of glass, ceramic, or metal. Some examples are utilitarian in nature, e.g., the Atterbury shoe night lamp or the ruby glass cocktail shaker in the shape of a leg and foot wearing a metal sandal. Most were made for purely decorative purposes.

Shoes were extremely popular during the Victorian era, when household bric-a-brac from toothpick holders to pincushions to salt cellars were made in the form of footwear. Once the glass shoe entered the form vocabulary, it never went out of production. There was a lull during the Depression, when few families had money for non-essential items.

Several contemporary glass companies including Boyd, Degenhart, Fenton, and Moser have reproduced early designs and introduced new ones. Thanks to several new books on the subject, glass shoes are enjoying a collecting renaissance.

References: Earlene Wheatley, *Collectible Glass Shoes: Including Metal, Pottery Figural & Porcelain Shoes,* Collector Books, 1996, 1998 value update; Libby Yalom, *Shoes of Glass, 2,* Antique Publications, 1998.

Collectors Club: Miniature Shoe Collectors Club, PO Box 2390, Apple Valley, CA 92308.

Baby Bootee, Fenton, milk glass, no logo	$18.00
Boot, crystal, wrinkled, lace dec, c1930, 2³/₄ x 2³/₄"	25.00
Boot, crystal, wrinkled, strap dec, 3 x 2¹/₂"	30.00
Boot, Degenhart, Daisy and Button, amber	30.00
Boot, Fenton, shaded yellow to orange, with logo, #1990	15.00
Boot, green, 6 buttons on left side, c1970, 3¹/₈ x 4³/₄"	10.00
Boot, green, wrinkled, etched "Los Angeles 1936" across foot, c1930, 2³/₄ x 2³/₄"	35.00
Boot, LE Smith, milk glass	15.00
Boot, milk glass, wrinkled, 2³/₄ x 2³/₄"	35.00
Boot, Mosser Glass Co, clear, spur and indentation on sole, with logo, 3⁷/₈ x 3¹/₈"	10.00
Boot, yellow, c1970, 4¹/₄ x 6¹/₂"	10.00
Cat Slipper, Degenhart, milk glass	25.00
Santa Boot, amethyst, 2¹/₂ x 2³/₄"	15.00
Santa Boot, cobalt blue, c1930, 2¹/₂ x 2³/₄"	15.00
Shoe, flashed red, scalloped border, double lines on vamp, hollow sole, solid heel, gilded lettering, c1920, 4¹/₂ x 2¹/₂"	65.00
Shoe, Guernsey Glass Co, Cambridge, OH, light green	15.00
Shoe, Kanawha Glass Co, amber, emb flower, scalloped top, c1968, 6 x 2¹/₂"	15.00
Shoe, stippled, small bow, Cuban heel, c1930, 4¹/₂ x 2¹/₂"	35.00
Shoe, Taiwan, Daisy & Button, blue	5.00
Shoe Skate, Central Glass Co, blue, diamond mesh, 3³/₈ x 4¹/₄"	50.00
Shoe Skate, LE Smith, golden amber, Daisy and Square, c1978, 4¹/₄ x 3¹/₈"	8.00
Shoe Skate, milk glass, alligator pattern, flared and scalloped top, diamond pattern sole, mkd "France," 3¹/₄ x 3⁷/₈"	45.00
Slipper, amber, stippling on upper part of back of shoe and under bow in front, hollow sole, indented heel, England, 4³/₄ x 2¹/₂"	60.00
Slipper, Degenhart, white opalescent	25.00
Slipper, milk glass, beading across toe and shoe, squatty heel, 4³/₄ x 3"	40.00
Slipper, Mosser Glass Co, #109, bow dec, solid sole and heel	10.00

GOEBEL

Franz and William Goebel, father and son, founded the F. D. & W. Goebel Porcelain Works near Coburg, Germany, in 1879. Initially, the firm made dinnerware, utilitarian ware, and beer steins. Marx-Louis, William's son, became president in 1912. He introduced many new porcelain figurine designs and added a pottery figurine line. Franz Goebel, son of Marx-Louis, and Dr. Eugene Stocke, his uncle, assumed control of the company in 1929.

Franz Goebel is responsible for making arrangements to produce the company's famous Hummel figurines. During World War II, Goebel concentrated on the production of dinnerware. Following the war, the company exported large quantities of Hummels and other figurines. Today Goebel manufactures high quality dinnerware, limited edition collectibles, the popular Hummel figurines, and figurine series ranging from Disney characters to Friar Tuck monks.

Collectors' Club: Friar Tuck Collectors Club, PO Box 262, Oswego, NY 13827; Goebel Networkers, PO Box 396, Lemoyne, PA 17043.

Note: This category consists of Goebel's non-Hummel production. See Limited Editions and Hummel Figurines for additional listings.

Ashtray, figural bluebird on rim, 1974	$40.00
Bell, Angel with clarinet, white bisque, 1976	8.00
Bell, Angel with french horn, white bisque, 1982	12.00
Bell, Angel with harp, blue, 1995	20.00
Bell, Angel with saxophone, 1980	12.00
Bell, Angel with teddy bear, 1991	30.00
Bell, Angel with train, white bisque, 1995	38.00
Cookie Jar, cardinal, red robe	150.00
Figurine, Al the Trumpet Player, Co-Boy, 1981	45.00
Figurine, American Goldfinch, miniature, Wildlife Series, 1985	85.00
Figurine, Bachelor Degree, 1970	60.00
Figurine, Bashful, miniature, Disney, 1987	80.00
Figurine, Bert the Soccer Player, Co-Boys Sports, 1994	25.00
Figurine, Blacksmith, miniature, Americana Series, 1989	125.00
Figurine, Boyhood Dreams, N. Rockwell, 1963	325.00
Figurine, Brum the Lawyer, Co-Boy, 1994	25.00
Figurine, Carl the Chef, Co-Boys Culinary, 1980	40.00
Figurine, Cinderella coach with 2 horses, multicolored, c1934, 3" h, 5¹/₂" l	325.00
Figurine, Doc the Doctor, Co-Boys Professionals, 1980	60.00
Figurine, God Bless You, Betsey Clark, 1972	285.00
Figurine, Grandpa, miniature, Children's Series, 1984	75.00
Figurine, Mothers Helper, N. Rockwell, 1963	325.00
Figurine, She Sounds the Deep, miniature, Americana Series, 1983	65.00
Figurine, The Wicked Witch, miniatures, 1987	75.00
Lemon Reamer, 2 pc, green and yellow body, cream top, brown handle, crackle finish, 1927, imp mark, 4¹/₂" h	145.00
Ornament, Angel, 1991	22.00
Pitcher, Boxer dog, miniature	120.00
Planter, swan, 1969	135.00
Salt and Pepper Shakers, pr, cowboy and cowgirl kissing	55.00

Toothpick Holder, red Scottie dog, mkd "EW 224" and "WG" under crown mark, 2¹/₂" h, $35.00.

GOLF COLLECTIBLES

Golf roots rest in 15th-century Scotland. Initially a game played primarily by the aristocracy and gentry, by the mid-19th century the game was accessible to everyone. By 1900, golf courses were located throughout Great Britain and the United States.

Golf collectibles divide into four basic groups: (1) golf books, (2) golf equipment, (3) items associated with a famous golfer, and (4) golf ephemera ranging from tournament programs to golf prints. Golf collecting has become highly specialized. There are several price guides to golf balls. There is even a price guide to golf tees.

References: Chuck Furjanic, *Antique Golf Collectibles,* Krause Publications, 1997; John F. Hotchkiss, *500 Years of Golf Balls,* Antique Trader Books, 1997; John M. Olman and Morton W. Olman, *Golf Antiques & Other Treasures of the Game, Expanded Edition,* Market Street Press, 1993; Beverly Robb, *Collectible Golfing Novelties,* Schiffer Publishing, 1992.

Periodical: *Golfiana Magazine,* 222 Leverette Ln, #4, Edwardsville, IL 62025.

Newsletter: *U.S. Golf Classics & Heritage Hickories,* 5407 Pennock Point Rd, Jupiter, FL 33458.

Collectors' Clubs: Golf Collectors Society, PO Box 241042, Cleveland, OH 44124; The Golf Club Collectors Assoc, 640 E Liberty St, Girard, OH 44420.

Book, *Basis of the Golf Swing, The,* Forrest, James, illus, gilt lettered dark blue cloth, first ed, London, Thomas Murby, 1925 . . . . $50.00
Book, *Golf,* Cotton, Henry, foreword by Bernard Darwin, illus, first American ed, New York, Coward-McCann, 1931 . . . . 100.00
Book, *Golfer's Catechism: A Vade Mecum of the Rules of Golf,* Browning, Robert H K, illus, printed boards, first ed, London, H O Quinn, 1935 . . . . 138.00
Book, *On Learning Golf,* Boomer, Percy, first ed, London, John Lane, 1942 . . . . 195.50

Doorstop, golfer wearing red coat and gray pants with black highlights, green grass, 10" h, $450.00.

Bottle, Fore After Shave, clear glass, paper label with golfer image, 9½" h 65.00
Cookbook, *Golfers Cookbook,* Craft-Zavichas, National Golf Foundation, 1984 . . . . 12.00
Game, Amateur Golf, Parker Bros, 1928 . . . . 65.00
Game, Fore, Artcraft Paper Products, 1954 . . . . 30.00
Game, Tournament Golf, Rigely Banada, 1969 . . . . 15.00
Jim Beam Whiskey Bottle, Bing Crosby National Pro-Am, Regal China, 1979 . . . . 15.00
Magazine, *American Golfer,* 1931 . . . . 8.00
Magazine, *Golf World,* Apr 13, 1951 . . . . 8.00
Miniature Whiskey Bottle, Old St Andrews, figural golf ball, 1980s 6.00
Paperweight, frosted glass, figural golf ball, 2" d 40.00
Postcard, lady golfer photo, 1930–40s 5.00
Program, Bob Hope Desert Classic, 1975 . . . . 15.00
Swizzle Sticks, aluminum, 3 figural golf clubs in leather bag, Chase 100.00
Tee, rubber 10.00
Tee, sterling silver 40.00
Tee, wood 2.00
Tumbler, clear, gold "Womens Open Muskogee, Okla" and emblem, 1970 . . . . 5.00
Tumbler, cobalt blue, white golfers illus, Hazel Atlas, 5" h 30.00

GONDER POTTERY

After a distinguished ceramic career working for American Encaustic Tiling, Cherry Art Tile, Florence Pottery, and Ohio Pottery, Lawton Gonder purchased the Zane Pottery, Zanesville, Ohio, in 1940 and renamed it Gonder Ceramic Arts. The company concentrated on art pottery and decorative accessories. Gonder hired top designers and sculptors to create his products. Gonder's glazes were innovative.

In 1946 Gonder expanded his Zanesville plant and purchased the Elgee Pottery to produce lamp bases. Elgee burned in 1954; operations were moved to Zanesville. Hurt by the flood of cheap foreign imports, Gonder sold his business in 1975 to the Allied Tile Company.

Many Gonder pieces have a double glaze and a pink interior. Most pieces are marked GONDER or GONDER USA in a variety of ways and are numbered. Some pieces were marked with a paper label.

Reference: Ron Hoopes, *The Collector's Guide and History of Gonder Pottery,* L-W Books, 1992, out of print.

Collectors' Club: Gonder Collectors Club, 917 Hurl Dr, Pittsburgh, PA 15236.

Basket, #674, 8" h $40.00
Bookends, pr, #582, horse head 50.00
Butter Warmer, #996 . . . . 20.00
Candle Holder, pr, #501, starfish, 6" h 50.00
Candle Holder, pr, #552, shell 100.00
Candle Holder, pr, E-14, E-14, 5" w 25.00
Candle Holder, pr, J-56, half moon, 6½" h 40.00
Conch Shell, white crackle glaze, 16" 175.00
Console, #505, shell, 16 x 8" 50.00
Console, #556, dolphins on sides 75.00
Cookie Jar, pirate, 12" h 600.00
Cookie Jar, Ye Olde Oaken Bucket, 8" h 50.00

Pitcher, light blue, mkd "Gonder H34 USA," 9" h, $45.00.

Cornucopia Vase, #691, 8" h	25.00
Cup and Saucer, La Gonda	20.00
Ewer, J-25, 11" h	75.00
Ewer, J-54, 11" h	75.00
Figurine, cat, #521, white crackle glaze, 12" h	350.00
Figurine, chinaman, #775, 9" h	25.00
Figurine, coolie, #519, 9" h	25.00
Figurine, deer, #690, 11" h	25.00
Figurine, elephant, #108, 7½ x 10"	250.00
Figurine, panther, 15" l	25.00
Figurine, prancing horse, paper label, 10" h	75.00
Figurine, ram, white crackle glaze, 6" h	35.00
Ginger Jar, #530, 10" h	100.00
Lamp Base, Chinese boat, 11 x 13"	100.00
Lamp Base, giraffe, 18" h	250.00
Lamp Base, horse head, 11" h	50.00
Lamp Base, oak leaves and vines	75.00
Planter, E-44, swan	30.00
Pitcher, #410, 8" h	50.00
Pitcher, H-73, green, 8" h	15.00
Relish Dish, #871, 18 x 11"	75.00
Vase, #513, swan	50.00
Vase, #522, fish, 9" h	175.00
Vase, #523, butterfly, 9" h	175.00
Vase, #604, 10" h	75.00
Vase, H-79, tiger lily, olive green glaze, 8" h	30.00
Vase, J-61, 9" h	50.00
Vase, J-69, 11" h	50.00

GRANITEWARE

Graniteware is a generic term used to describe enamel-coated iron or steel kitchenware. Originating in Germany, the first American graniteware was manufactured in the 1860s. American manufacturers received a major market boost when World War I curtailed German imports.

Graniteware is still being manufactured today. Older examples tend to be heavier. Cast-iron handles date between 1870 and 1890; wood handles between 1900 and 1910.

This market experienced a major price run in the early 1990s as dealers raised their prices to agree with those published by Helen Greguire. At the moment, the category as a whole appears to be greatly overvalued.

References: Helen Greguire, *The Collector's Encyclopedia of Graniteware: Colors, Shapes & Values* (1990, 1994 value update), *Book 2*, (1993, 1997 value update), Collector Books; Dana G. Morykan, *The Official Price Guide to Country Antiques & Collectibles, Fourth Edition,* House of Collectibles, 1999; David T. Pikul and Ellen M. Plante, *Collectible Enameled Ware: American & European,* Schiffer Publishing, 1998.

Collectors' Club: National Graniteware Society, PO Box 10013, Cedar Rapids, IA 52410.

Asparagus Boiler, gray mottled, 7¾" h, 7¾" w, 11" l	$165.00
Basin, green and white swirl ext, white int, cobalt rim and riveted handles, 17½" d, 5½" h	90.00
Casserole, cov, cobalt blue and white swirl	55.00
Cereal Bowl, yellow and white swirl, black rim	45.00
Coffeepot, light blue and white	180.00
Colander, gray mottled, 10¼" d	135.00
Colander, white, 2½" h	60.00
Cup, aqua and white swirl ext, white int, cobalt blue rim	95.00
Custard Cup, gray mottled	10.00
Dipper, gray mottled	65.00
Milk Pitcher, white, green trim and handle, 7¼" h	65.00
Miner's Lunch Kettle, blue and white and solid blue	45.00
Mixing Bowl, yellow and white swirl, black trim	40.00
Muffin Cup, gray mottled, 1¼" h, 3¼" d	85.00
Pail, dark blue and white, matching lid	45.00
Pan, green and white, 3⅜" h, 10 1/16" d	90.00
Percolator, light blue and white, 8¼" h	45.00
Pie Pan, cobalt blue and white marbelized, 6" d	30.00
Pie Plate, dark brown and white mottled, black trim, 8⅞" d	20.00
Pudding Pan, black and white swirl, 7½" h	425.00
Pudding Pan, white, cobalt blue trim, 7" d	35.00
Skimmer, gray mottled, 10" l	30.00
Spoon, Blue Diamond Ware, long handle	50.00
Spoon, brown and white swirl, 13⅜" l	135.00
Spoon, white, red trim on handle, 13¼" l	25.00
Tumbler, yellow and white swirl, black trim	60.00
Wash Basin, blue and white mottled, 12⅜" d	120.00
Water Pitcher, green and white relish pattern, white int, cobalt blue trim, 7¾" h	150.00

Soap Dish, wall mount, gray, $30.00.

GREETING CARDS

The modern greeting card originated in the middle of the 15th century in the Rhine Valley of medieval Germany. Printed New Year greetings gained in popularity during the 17th and 18th centuries. Queen Victoria's interest in holiday and special occasion cards helped establish the sending of greeting cards as a regular event.

Louis Prang, a color lithography printer, was one of the first American manufacturers of greeting cards. The post-1945 era witnessed the growth of a number of card manufacturers who eventually would dominate the industry. The Hall Brothers (Joyce C., Rollie, and William), Kansas City postcard distributors and publishers, began printing greeting cards in 1910. Fred Winslow Rust established Rust Craft Company. Cincinnati's Gibson Art Co. entered the greeting card field. Arthur D. and Jane Norcross formed a mutual partnership in 1915.

Although greeting cards are collected primarily by event or occasion, a growing number of collectors seek specialized type cards, e.g., diecut or mechanical. Holiday and specialized collectors represent the principal buyers of greeting cards in the 1990s.

Reference: Ellen Stern, *The Very Best From Hallmark: Greeting Cards Through the Years,* Harry N. Abrams, 1988, out of print.

Note: See Valentines for additional listings.

Birthday, "Birthday Greetings," jigsaw puzzle, verse beneath arch, 2 knaves carrying cake lower left corner, cover sheet featuring seated dog, "Happy Birthday" in puzzle pcs, and verse, Volland, B-1, 1932, 5¼ x 4¼" **$15.00**
Birthday, Hopalong Cassidy, photo pinback button insert **35.00**
Birthday, Star Trek, "This is your Captain speaking... Have a far-out birthday," punch-out items, Random House, 1976 .... **15.00**
Christmas, "At Christmas time may Peace o'er shadow you," flowers, white fringe, Prang, artist sgd **15.00**
Christmas, Breyer Ice Cream, c1920 .... **20.00**
Christmas, Captain Marvel, 1941 .... **30.00**

Christmas, children and dog playing in snow, Raphael Tuck, artist sgd, 4 x 2" **6.00**
Christmas, golf scene, "May every Christmas joy be Yours!" **50.00**
Christmas, Graceland scene, sepia and blue tones, 1970s **30.00**
Christmas, LG Kelly-Miller Bros Circus, pr, 4 pp, 3 color, early 1940s, 5 x 7" **20.00**
Easter, Donald Duck, flocked body, diecut, Hallmark, 1942 .... **25.00**
First Communion, mechanical, opens to 3-D altar scene, Germany **30.00**
Hanukkah, postcard, Hanukkah Greeting from Cleveland, skyline with menorah, Nu-Vista Prints, 1989 .... **25.00**
Valentine, "Cupid's Temple of Love," honeycomb **15.00**
Valentine, "Will You Be My Valentine?," boy wearing sailor suit and duck, c1920 .... **2.00**

GRINDLEY POTTERY

Arthur Grindley and his son, Arthur Grindley, Jr., established the Grindley Artware Manufacturing Co. in Sebring, Ohio, in 1933. The pottery produced novelty items such as banks and figurines, usually in animal form. A fire destroyed the plant in 1947. Although the plant was rebuilt, economic factors prevented the firm from attaining its earlier level of production. The pottery closed its doors in 1952.

Reference: Mike Schneider, *Grindley Pottery,* Schiffer Publishing, 1996.

Bank, elephant, white, 6½" h **$15.00**
Creamer, Dutch boy, 4¾" h **12.00**
Figurine, Airedale, 3⅝" h **10.00**
Figurine, dachshund, pink, 5" l **10.00**
Figurine, deer, yellow with gold trim, 6½" h **12.00**
Figurine, Egyptian cat, cobalt blue with gold highlights, 6¾" h **28.00**
Figurine, elephant, burgundy, 2¼" h **5.00**
Figurine, English bulldog, 3½" l **8.00**
Figurine, fox, pink, 3¼" h **10.00**
Figurine, goat, green with gold highlights, 4⅞" h **18.00**
Figurine, pelican, pink with gold highlights, 3½" h **8.00**
Figurine, rearing horse, brown, 7½" h **75.00**
Figurine, seated dog, cobalt blue with gold highlights, 4½" h **25.00**
Figurine, standing colt, brown, 5½" l **50.00**
Figurine, standing horse, white with gold highlights, 8½" h **18.00**
Figurine, St Bernard, white, brown, and black, 5" l **12.00**
Salt and Pepper Shakers, pr, begging Scottie dogs, yellow with gold highlights, 2¾" h **10.00**
Salt and Pepper Shakers, pr, chickens, gold, 3¾" h **10.00**
Salt and Pepper Shakers, pr, fish, green with gold highlights, 2¼" h **12.00**
Salt and Pepper Shakers, pr, German shepherds, yellow with gold highlights, 3" h **7.00**
Salt and Pepper Shakers, pr, penguins, blue with gold highlights, 3⅝" h **15.00**
Salt and Pepper Shakers, pr, squirrels holding acorns, pink with gold highlights, 2⅞" h **10.00**
Wall Plaque, horse head, brown, 5" h **35.00**

Birthday Cards, children's ages 1 through 9, heavy gauge paper, Mia Cards, England, 1930s, price for set, $22.00.

GRISWOLD

Griswold Manufacturing was founded in the mid-1860s by Matthew Griswold and John and Samuel Selden. Originally the Selden & Griswold Manufacturing Co., Griswold bought out the Selden family interests in 1884. Since then the company has changed hands several times, including being bought by its major competitor, Wagner Manufacturing Co., in 1957. In August 1969, the General Housewares Corp. acquired all rights to Griswold and Wagner. Cast cookware is still being made.

References: John B. Haussler, *Griswold Muffin Pans*, Schiffer Publishing, 1997; David G. Smith and Charles Wafford, *The Book of Griswold & Wagner: Favorite Piqua, Sidney Hollow Ware, Wapak*, Schiffer Publishing, 1995; *Griswold Cast Iron, Vol. 1* (1993, 1997 value update), *Vol 2.* (1995, 1998 value update), L-W Book Sales.

Newsletter: *Kettles 'n' Cookware*, PO Box 247, Perrysburg, NY 14129.

Collectors' Club: Griswold & Cast-Iron Cookware Assoc, PO Box 243, Perrysburg, NY 14129.

Apple Cake Pan, #32	$40.00
Ashtray, #00	30.00
Corn Stick Pan, #27	250.00
Crispy Corn Stick Pan, #273, pattern #930	35.00
Deep Patty Bowl, #72	50.00
Deep Patty Mold Set, #2, orig box	35.00
Deep Skillet, cov, #8, pattern #777A	110.00
Double Broiler	250.00
Double Skillet, #90, plated	95.00
Dutch Oven, #9, pattern #834, slant logo, Erie	105.00
Dutch Oven Trivet, #11, pattern #209	60.00
Gem Pan, #2, variation 2	170.00
Griddle, #8, pattern #738, Erie	75.00
Griddle, #8, single hole handle	65.00
Griddle, #9, chrome, handle	35.00
Kettle, #0	475.00
Muffin Pan, #8, pattern #946, Erie	110.00
Muffin Pan, #8, slant emblem	165.00
Omelet Pan, pattern #A54, small logo, aluminum	85.00
Patty Mold, #1, orig box	30.00
Popover, #10, pattern #948, Erie	60.00
Popover, #10, pattern #949c	30.00
Popover, #18, variation 5	60.00
Scotch Bowl, flat bottom, slant "Erie, Pa. USA"	90.00
Skillet, #3, medium logo, grooved handle	25.00
Skillet, #3, smooth bottom, large emblem	20.00
Skillet, #3, smooth bottom, small emblem, 709L	15.00
Skillet, #4, smooth bottom, large emblem, 702A	60.00
Skillet, #4, smooth bottom, small emblem, 702C	40.00
Skillet, #5, slant "Erie, Pa. USA"	50.00
Skillet, #5, smooth bottom, small emblem, 2505	20.00
Skillet, #5, smooth bottom, small emblem, hinge	55.00
Skillet, #6, heat ring, large block	80.00
Skillet, #6, smooth bottom, large block	30.00
Skillet, #6, smooth bottom, large emblem	50.00
Skillet, #7, Erie, nickel	15.00
Skillet, #7, heat ring, large block, chrome	60.00
Skillet, #7, inside heat ring, pattern #701H, Erie	75.00
Skillet, #7, smooth bottom, large block	70.00
Skillet, #9, smooth bottom, large emblem, 710F	40.00

Skillet, #11, heat ring, large block	140.00
Skillet, #55, square	45.00
Skillet Lid, #3, high, smooth	225.00
Skillet Lid, #6, high dome, plain	95.00
Skillet Lid, #12, smooth top, pattern #472	225.00
Snack Skillet, #65	65.00
Toy Skillet, #775, square	145.00
Tree Platter, #A1082, aluminum	75.00
Trivet, #7, pattern #205	75.00
Vienna Roll Pan, #6, variation 5	90.00
Waffle Iron, #9, finger hinge	95.00
Wheat Pan, #2700	290.00

GUNDERSON

Robert Gunderson purchased the Pairpoint Corporation, Boston, Massachusetts, in the late 1930s and operated it as the Gunderson Glass Works until his death in 1952. Operating as Gunderson-Pairpoint, the company continued for only five more years.

In the 1950s, the Gunderson Glass Company produced a wide range of reproduction glassware. Its peachblow-type art glass shades from an opaque faint pink tint to a deep rose.

Robert Bryden attempted a revival of the firm in 1970. He moved the manufacturing operations from the old Mount Washington plant in Boston back to New Bedford.

Compote, Camelia Swirl, bubble ball connector, clear base, bell tone flint, 6" h	$475.00
Compote, Morning Glory, acid finish, 5" h	375.00
Cordial, amberina, set of 10	365.00
Decanter, pedestal base, deep rose shading to white, orig stopper, 9½" h	550.00
Goblet, flared, deep rose stem, 7¼" h	175.00
Goblet, matte finish, 6¾" h, 3¾" d	150.00
Hat, Diamond Quilted pattern, satin finish, 3¼" h	150.00
Syrup Pitcher, cased, offset handle, 2¾" h	165.00
Tumbler, acid finish, 4" h	150.00
Tumbler, matte finish, 3¾" h	175.00
Vase, classical shape, sq base, applied serpentine handles, 8½" h	175.00
Vase, ftd, glossy finish, 8" h, 3" d	75.00

Decanters, Peachblow, acid-finished in pink fading to white, mid-20th C, 13³/₄" h, price for pair, $575.00. Photo courtesy Skinner, Inc., Boston, MA.

HAEGER POTTERIES

Haeger Potteries was founded by David H. Haeger in Dundee, Illinois in 1871. The first Haeger Art Pottery was produced in 1914. In 1938, Royal Arden Hickman joined the firm and introduced the Royal Haeger line. The following year the Buckeye Pottery Building in Macomb was purchased for the production of florist trade items. That year also saw the formation of the Royal Haeger Lamp Co.

Many Haeger pieces can be identified by molded model numbers. The first Royal Haeger item was assigned the number R01, with subsequent numbers ascending in chronological order.

Numbers found on giftware from the Studio Haeger line, designed by Helen Conover in 1947–48, are preceded by the letter "S." The Royal Garden Flower-ware line, produced from 1954 until 1963, is numbered RG-1 through RG-198, with the lowest numbers found on the earliest examples.

References: David D. Dilley, *Haeger Potteries,* L-W Book Sales, 1997; Joe and Joyce Paradis, *The House of Haeger: 1914–1944,* Schiffer Publishing, 1999.

Collectors' Club: Haeger Pottery Collectors of America, 5021 Toyon Way, Antioch, CA 94509.

Ashtray, #127, gold tweed, 2" h, 10¼" l, 9½" w	**$20.00**
Ashtray, #153, mandarin orange, 10¾" l	15.00
Bowl, #343, cotton white ext, turquoise int, 3¼" h, 8" d	15.00
Bowl, #364-H, lily, yellow-orange with dark tips, 16¼" l	30.00
Bowl, R-867, figural starfish, pearl gray drip, 2⅜" h, 14½" l	45.00
Candle Holder, R-203, standing double fish, mauve agate, unmkd, 5" h	35.00
Candy Dish, #8044-H, mandarin orange, 6½" h	20.00
Centerpiece Bowl, R-1824, palm leaf shape, pearl shell, 26" l	35.00
Cookie Jar, fire hydrant, red, gold crackle trim, gilded "Fire Plug Cookies," 12" h	300.00
Figurine, #650, mourning dove, rust brown, c1973, 7" h, 10" l	50.00
Figurine, R-103, horse, green briar, unmkd, 8¼" h	35.00
Figurine, R-284, fish, amber, unmkd, 4" h, 3½" l	100.00
Figurine, R-424, bucking bronco, amber, 1940s, 13" h	175.00

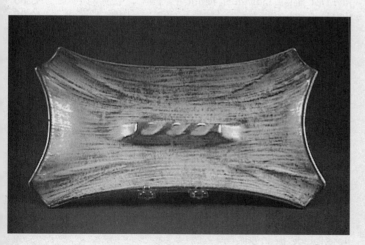

Ashtray, gold tweed, mkd "Royal Haeger© 149-USA," 1967, 13" l, $15.00

Figurine, R-649, lying panther, oxblood, 7¼" l	40.00
Figurine, R-777, cocker spaniel, brown, black tail, unmkd, 3" h, 5½" l	50.00
Figurine, R-1131, leopard, chartreuse, unmkd, 7¾" h	75.00
Lamp, #5190, bucking bronco, cactus finial, unmkd, 26" h	225.00
Planter, #502-H, bull fighter, Haeger red, 13" h	125.00
Planter, #3855, Little Bo Peep, pink, c1959, 8½" h	20.00
Planter, R-453, figural peacock, mauve agate, 10" h	40.00
Television Lamp, leaping gazelle, green and white, unmkd, 10½" h, 13½" l	75.00
Vase, #4165, peasant orange, black int, 11⅜" h	40.00

HALL CHINA

In 1903 Robert Hall founded the Hall China Company in East Liverpool, Ohio. Taggert Hall, his son, became president following Robert's death in 1904. The company initially made jugs, toilet sets, and utilitarian whiteware. Robert T. Hall's major contribution to the firm's growth was the development of an economical, single-fire process for lead-free glazed ware.

Hall acquired a new plant in 1930. In 1933 the Autumn Leaf pattern was introduced as a premium for the Jewel Tea Company. Other premium patterns include Blue Bonnett (Standard Coffee Company), Orange Poppy (Great American Tea Company), and Red Poppy (Grand Union Tea Company).

The company launched a decal-decorated dinnerware line in 1933. Hall's refrigerator ware was marketed to the general public along with specific patterns and shapes manufactured for General Electric, Hotpoint, Montgomery Ward, Sears, and Westinghouse.

Hall made a full range of products, from dinnerware to utilitarian kitchenware. Its figural teapots in the shape of Aladdin lamps, automobiles, etc., are eagerly sought by collectors.

Reference: Margaret and Kenn Whitmyer, *The Collector's Encyclopedia of Hall China, Second Edition,* Collector Books, 1994, 1997 value update.

Collectors' Club: Hall Collector's Club, PO Box 360488, Cleveland, OH 44136.

Note: See Autumn Leaf for additional listings.

Blue Blossom casserole, round, #76	**$40.00**
Blue Blossom, jug, Five Band, 1½ pt	50.00
Blue Bouquet, ball jug, #3	80.00
Blue Bouquet, cereal bowl, D-style, 6" d	12.00
Blue Bouquet, creamer, Boston	10.00
Blue Bouquet, custard, thick rim	12.00
Blue Bouquet, plate, D-style, 9" d	15.00
Blue Bouquet, leftover, rect	60.00
Blue Bouquet, sugar, cov, Boston	18.00
Brown Eyed Susan, baker, ftd	20.00
Cameo Rose, creamer	7.50
Cameo Rose, flat soup, 8" d	10.00
Cameo Rose, platter, oval, 11¼" l	15.00
Cameo Rose, tidbit tray, 3 tier	35.00
Carrot, casserole, Radiance	60.00
Century Fern, gravy	12.00
Coffeepot, French, canary yellow, flower, 4 cup	40.00
Coffeepot, Hollywood, Monterey, green	60.00
Coffeepot, New York, marine blue, 12 cup	40.00
Coffeepot, Orange Poppy, S lid	50.00

Crocus, tidbit, 3-tier, $45.00. Photo courtesy Ray Morykan Auctions.

Coffeepot, pheasant decal, electric	125.00
Coffeepot, Red Poppy, Daniel	50.00
Coffeepot, Red Poppy, New York	110.00
Coffeepot, Washington, cadet blue, 9–10 cup	65.00
Crest, minuet coffee server	45.00
Crocus, ball jug	195.00
Crocus, bean pot, New England, #4	100.00
Crocus, cake plate	30.00
Crocus, casserole, cov	60.00
Crocus, cup, St Denis	35.00
Crocus, cup and saucer	18.00
Crocus, French baker, fluted	20.00
Crocus, gravy boat	35.00
Crocus, mixing bowl	50.00
Crocus, plate, 8¼" d	10.00
Crocus, plate, 9" d	12.00
Crocus, plate, 10" d	35.00
Crocus, pretzel jar	200.00
Crocus, soup tureen	425.00
Fantasy, ball jug, #2	100.00
Fantasy, casserole, rayed	45.00
Fantasy, creamer and sugar	75.00
Five Band, casserole, red, 8" d	30.00
Five Band, jug, ivory, 5" h	18.00
Game Bird, coffee mug	15.00
Game Bird, fruit bowl, 5½" d	7.50
Game Bird, Irish coffee	25.00
Gold Dot, nesting bowls	45.00
Golden Glo, bean pot, #4	90.00
Golden Glo, teapot, sugar and creamer	130.00
Heather Rose, bowl, 6" d	8.00
Heather Rose, cup and saucer	8.00
Heather Rose, pie baker	20.00
Heather Rose, plate, 9" d	10.00
Heather Rose, tureen, cov	18.00
Homewood, bowl, Radiance, 6" d	12.00
Homewood, salt and pepper shakers, pr, handled	20.00
Meadow Flowers, casserole	50.00
Monticello, fruit bowl	8.00
Monticello, platter, oval, 15½" l	18.00
Monticello, vegetable, cov	25.00

Mount Vernon, cereal bowl, E-style, 6¼" d	6.00
Mount Vernon, sugar, cov, E-style	1.00
Mulberry, berry bowl, 5¾" l	8.00
Mulberry, cereal bowl, 6" d	18.00
Mulberry, salt and pepper shakers, pr	25.00
Mulberry, vegetable bowl, open, 9" sq	25.00
Mums, cereal bowl, D-style, 6" d	8.00
Mums, cup, D-style	25.00
Mums, drip jar, open, Kitchenware, #1188	35.00
Mums, jug, Kitchenware, Simplicity	30.00
Mums, saucer, D-style	2.00
New England #4, bean pot, ivory	45.00
No. 488, creamer, New York	18.00
No. 488, drip jar, cov, Radiance	22.00
No. 488, French baker, Kitchenware	20.00
No. 488, leftover, square	70.00
No. 488, shaker, Teardrop	15.00
Orange Poppy, bean pot	165.00
Orange Poppy, bowl, Radiance, 6" d	10.00
Orange Poppy, cake plate	22.00
Orange Poppy, canister, Radiance	275.00
Orange Poppy, casserole, cov, oval, 8" l	65.00
Orange Poppy, casserole, cov, oval, 9" l	55.00
Orange Poppy, cup, C-style	15.00
Orange Poppy, leftover	75.00
Orange Poppy, plate, 6" d	6.00
Orange Poppy, plate, 9" d	15.00
Orange Poppy, platter, oval, 13" l	20.00
Orange Poppy, salt and pepper shakers, pr	65.00
Orange Poppy, sugar, cov	25.00
Pastel Morning Glory, ball jug, #3	75.00
Pastel Morning Glory, bean pot, handled	165.00
Pastel Morning Glory, bowl, oval	40.00
Pastel Morning Glory, cereal bowl, D-style, 6" d	12.00
Pastel Morning Glory, creamer and sugar, D-style	60.00
Pastel Morning Glory, drip jar, cov, Radiance	22.00
Pastel Morning Glory, flat soup	25.00
Pastel Morning Glory, pie baker	25.00
Pastel Morning Glory, plate, 6" d	8.00
Pastel Morning Glory, plate, 7" d	18.00
Pink Rose, teapot, sugar and creamer	50.00
Primrose, creamer	7.50
Primrose, jug, Rayed	25.00
Primrose, sugar, cov	15.00
Red Dot, baker, individual, handled	35.00
Red Dot, bowl, 8¾" d	30.00
Red Dot, cereal bowl, 6" d	20.00
Red Dot, custard	22.00
Red Poppy, cereal bowl, 6" d	20.00
Red Poppy, creamer, Daniel	15.00
Red Poppy, bowl, Radiance	60.00
Red Poppy, cup	10.00
Red Poppy, cup and saucer	15.00
Red Poppy, custard	20.00
Red Poppy, drip jar	20.00
Red Poppy, flat soup	25.00
Red Poppy, mixing bowl, #5, Radiance	10.00
Red Poppy, plate, 9" d	7.00
Red Poppy, shakers, tear drop	45.00
Red Poppy, tumbler, frosted, 5¼" h	22.00
Rose, casserole, white	35.00
Rose Parade, bean pot, cov	75.00
Rose Parade, casserole, cov	38.00
Rose Parade, drip jar	25.00

Rose Parade, sugar **15.00**
Royal Rose, ball jug **125.00**
Royal Rose, casserole, cov. **40.00**
Royal Rose, drip jar, cov **30.00**
Royal Rose, French teapot **125.00**
Royal Rose, salt and pepper shakers, pr **18.00**
Serenade, berry bowl, 5½" d **8.00**
Serenade, bowl, Radiance, 7½" d **15.00**
Serenade, cup and saucer **15.00**
Serenade, fruit bowl, D-style **5.00**
Serenade, plate, 9" d **15.00**
Serenade, salad bowl, 9" d **25.00**
Silhouette, ball jug, #3 . . . . **90.00**
Silhouette, bowl, oval, D-style **25.00**
Silhouette, mug. **35.00**
Silhouette, saucer, St Denis **10.00**
Springtime, cup and saucer **8.00**
Springtime, plate, 9" d **8.00**
Springtime, platter, oval, 13" l **20.00**
Taverne, mug **80.00**
Teapot, Airflow, cobalt. **150.00**
Teapot, Airflow, emerald green **60.00**
Teapot, Baltimore, yellow **50.00**
Teapot, Basket, yellow and gold. **110.00**
Teapot, Boston, canary, 4 cup **45.00**
Teapot, Boston, maroon, ruffled lip, 2 cup **35.00**
Teapot, Bouquet, blue, Aladdin **140.00**
Teapot, Cleveland, green **65.00**
Teapot, Connie, celadon green **55.00**
Teapot, Crocus, banded. **175.00**
Teapot, French, brown with gold daisies, 1 cup **50.00**
Teapot, Globe, emerald green **80.00**
Teapot, Hollywood, pink, gold dec **35.00**
Teapot, Los Angeles, cobalt blue, 6 cup **40.00**
Teapot, Manhattan, blue **65.00**
Teapot, McCormick, maroon, 6 cup **40.00**
Teapot, Melody, blue. **65.00**
Teapot, Moderne, cadet blue **30.00**
Teapot, Moderne, ivory **30.00**
Teapot, Murphy, light blue. **85.00**
Teapot, Nautilus, yellow, gold dec **70.00**
Teapot, New York, black, gold lip, 2 cup **25.00**
Teapot, New York, emerald green, gold, 2 cup . . . **35.00**
Teapot, Ohio, black and gold, 6 cup **150.00**
Teapot, Orange Poppy, Boston **200.00**
Teapot, Orange Poppy, Donut **550.00**
Teapot, Orange Poppy, Melody **240.00**
Teapot, Parade, yellow, gold dec **30.00**
Teapot, Philadelphia, ivory, gold dec, 6 cup **150.00**
Teapot, Red Poppy, New York **75.00**
Teapot, Springtime **45.00**
Teapot, Star, green, gold dec **45.00**
Teapot, Sundial, brown **100.00**
Teapot, Sundial, maroon **95.00**
Teapot, Sundial, yellow, gold trim **55.00**
Teapot, Washington, marine blue, 6 cup **70.00**
Teapot, Windshield, Gold Dot **55.00**
Tulip, creamer and cov sugar. **35.00**
Tulip, cup and saucer **15.00**
Tulip, fruit bowl, 5½" d **10.00**
Tulip, mixing bowl, 6" d **27.00**
Tulip, mixing bowl, 7½" d **36.00**
Tulip, platter, oval, 13¼" l **42.00**
Wildfire, bowl, 5½" d **12.00**

Wildfire, jug #5, Radiance shape, $25.00.

Wildfire, bread and butter plate, 6" d **20.00**
Wildfire, coffee server **70.00**
Wildfire, creamer and sugar. **50.00**
Wildfire, French baker. **25.00**
Wildfire, gravy boat. **35.00**
Wildfire, shaker, teardrop **30.00**
Wildfire, saucer **5.00**

HALLMARK

In 1913 brothers Joyce and Rollie Hall launched a firm to sell Christmas cards. The line soon expanded to all types of holiday cards. In January 1913, a fire destroyed their entire stock of valentines. Undaunted, the Halls purchased a Kansas City engraving firm a year later and began printing and marketing Hallmark cards. Within two years, Hallmark cards were sold nationwide.

Following World War II, Hallmark launched a major expansion. In 1948 Norman Rockwell became the first "name" artist to appear on Hallmark cards. Hallmark's Plans-A-Party line was introduced in 1960. Playing cards appeared a year later. Hallmark introduced a Cookie Cutter line in the early 1960s, its Keepsake Christmas Ornament line in 1973, and its Merry Miniature line in 1974.

Hallmark is a leader in preserving its company's heritage. The Hallmark Historical Collection is one of the finest company archives in America.

References: *Collector's Value Guide: Hallmark Keepsake Ornaments: Secondary Market Price Guide and Collector Handbook,* Collector's Publishing, 1998; *Rosie's Secondary Market Price Guide for Hallmark Ornaments, 13th Edition,* Rosie Wells Enterprises, 1999.

Note: For additional listings see Greeting Cards.

Bell, Fairy Bunny, porcelain, Enchanted Garden,
   E Richardson, 1992 . . . . **$35.00**
Book, *American Psalms,* Peter Max illus, ©Hallmark 1971 . . . **25.00**
Card Holder, paper, fold-up Santa and reindeer, 1940s **18.00**
Figurine, Chipmunk with Kite, Heartland Merry
   Miniatures series, 1994 . . . . **4.00**

Jigsaw Puzzle, "Friendship Is a Special Treat," Springbok, ©1972 Hallmark Cards, Inc., 7" d, $3.00.

Figurine, Hippo in Innertube, At the Beach Merry
  Miniatures series, 1994 . . . . **3.00**
Figurine, Rabbit with Croquet, Easter Egg Hunt
  Miniatures series, 1994 . . . . **4.00**
Figurine, Seal with Earmuffs, North Pole Christmas
  Merry Miniatures series, 1994 . . . . **3.00**
Ornament, Baby's First Christmas, 1976 . . . . **150.00**
Ornament, Calico Kitty, Fabric Ornaments series, 1981 . . . . . . **20.00**
Ornament, Christmas Is Love, Keepsake Collection, 1973 . . . . **80.00**
Ornament, Locomotive, Colors of Christmas series, 1978 . . . . **45.00**
Ornament, Mountains, The Beauty of America series,
  1977 . . . . **15.00**
Ornament, Mrs Claus, Yarn Collection series, 1978 . . . . **22.00**
Ornament, Raggedy Andy, Yarn Ornaments series, 1976 . . . . . **40.00**
Ornament, Reindeer Chimes, Holiday Chimes, 1978 . . . . **60.00**
Ornament, Rocking Horse, Handcrafted Ornaments:
  Nostalgia series, 1975 . . . . **120.00**
Ornament, Snoopy and Friends, Collectible series, 1979 . . . . **125.00**
Ornament, Soldier, Keepsake Yarn Ornaments, 1973 . . . . **22.00**
Ornament, Star, Holiday Highlights series, 1977 . . . . **50.00**
Ornament, Wreath, Christmas Expressions Collection,
  1977 . . . . **65.00**

HALLOWEEN

Halloween collectors divide material into pre- and post-1945 objects. Country of origin—Germany, Japan, or the United States—appears to make little difference. Image is everything. The survival rate of Halloween collectibles is extremely high. Currently, Halloween is second only to Christmas in respect to popularity among holiday collectors.

References: Pamela E. Apkarian-Russell, *Collectible Halloween* (1997), *More Halloween Collectibles* (1998), Schiffer Publishing; Dan and Pauline Campanelli, *Halloween Collectibles: A Price Guide*, L-W Books, 1995; Charlene Pinkerton, *Halloween Favorites in Plastic*, Schiffer Publishing, 1998; Stuart Schneider, *Halloween in America: A Collector's Guide With Prices*, Schiffer Publishing, 1995.

Newsletters: *Boo News*, PO Box 143, Brookfield, IL 60513; *Trick or Treat Trader*, PO Box 499, Winchester, NH 03470.

Candy Box, Baby Ruth Halloween Treats, cardboard, "Be
  Good to Your goblins," 1930s **$55.00**
Candy Container, pumpkin, black cat attached to top by
  spring, painted papier-mâché, removable cardboard
  stopper on underside, ink stamp "Germany," c1930s,
  4³/₄" h, 3¹/₂" d **100.00**
Chocolate Mold, 4 witches, Germany **155.00**
Costume, Cabbage Patch Kids, molded plastic mask,
  Tiny Tot, orig box **20.00**
Costume, Creature From the Black Lagoon, molded plas-
  tic mask, green vinyl outfit with design on chest, rayon
  legs, Collegeville, ©1980 Universal City Studios, Inc,
  orig 8¹/₂ x 11 x 3" box **40.00**
Costume, First Man on the Moon, molded plastic mask,
  "White For Nite," Collegeville, 1969 . . . . **60.00**
Decoration, black and white cat, wearing witch's hat,
  diecut, fuzzy finish,1950–60s **5.00**
Earrings, pr, Trick or Troll, Russ, orig card **4.00**
Fan, paper, cat's face, wooden stick **45.00**
Figure, black cat, celluloid over plaster, thin red painted
  collar, inset reddish orange glass dot eyes, unmkd,
  1930s, 2¹/₂" h **40.00**
Game, Haunted House, Ideal, 1962 . . . . **60.00**
Ice Cream Mold, witch, 2 part **175.00**
Lantern, papier-máché, cat face **125.00**
Mask, Batman, rubber **45.00**
Noisemaker, litho tin, wooden grip, images of black cats,
  white ghosts, and smiling crescent moon on orange
  ground, "Made in U.S.A." symbol, c1940s, 2³/₄" l,
  3¹/₄" d **20.00**
Noisemaker, litho tin, wooden grip, images of jack-o-
  lantern and witch, black and yellow on orange
  ground, mkd "Kirchof 'Life of the Party' Products,"
  1930s, 3¹/₂" l, 2¹/₄" d **20.00**
Party Hat, cardboard, cats dec, c1940 . . . . **5.00**
Pinback Button, center orange pumpkin with "Boost
  the Pumpkin Show/Oct 9-10-11-12/Delaware O" on
  white ground, 1930s **10.00**

Costume, E.T., Collegeville Flag & Mfg Co, 1982, $15.00.

Salt and Pepper Shakers, pr, devils, c1930 . . . . **55.00**
Sheet Music, *Punky Punkin the Happy Pumpkin,* Cy
   Coben, 1940s **10.00**
Sheet Music, *Witch Doctor,* Ross Bagdasarian, Monarch
   Music Co **10.00**
Stickpin, figural black cat, painted composition, tail
   mounted by fire spring, black body, yellow eye
   accent, white opened mouth, molded on brass stick-
   pin **20.00**
Sucker Mold, metal, orig card, Lorann **8.00**
Table Decoration, scarecrow, paper, honeycomb
   haystack and pumpkin, c1950, 8" h **10.00**
Wall Decoration, skeleton, diecut cardboard, 1950s, 60" h **35.00**

HANNA-BARBERA

William Denby Hanna was born on July 14, 1910, in Melrose, New Mexico. A talent for drawing landed him a job at the Harman-Ising animation studio in 1930. Hanna worked there for seven years.

Joseph Roland Barbera was born in New York City in 1911. After a brief stint as a magazine cartoonist, Barbera joined the Van Beuren studio in 1932 where he helped animate and script Tom and Jerry.

In 1938 Hanna and Barbera were teamed together. Their first project was Gallopin' Gals. By 1939 the two were permanently paired, devoting much of their energy to Tom and Jerry shorts.

Twenty years after joining MGM, Hanna and Barbera struck out on their own. Their goal was to develop cartoons for television as well as theatrical release. The success of Huckleberry Hound and Yogi Bear paved the way for The Flintstones, one of the most successful television shows of the 1960s.

In 1966 Taft Communications purchased Hanna-Barbera Productions for a reported 26 million dollars. Hanna and Barbera continued to head the company.

Hanna-Barbera Productions produced over 100 cartoon series and specials. In several cases, a single series produced a host of well-loved cartoon characters. Some of the most popular include Atom Ant, Auggie Doggie and Doggie Daddy, The Flintstones, Huckleberry Hound, The Jetsons, Jonny Quest, Magilla Gorilla, Peter Potamus, Penelope Pitstop, Quick Draw McGraw, Ricochet Rabbit, Ruff and Reddy, Space Ghost, Top Cat, and Yogi Bear.

References: Joseph Barbera, *My Life in 'Toons: From Flatbush to Bedrock in Under a Century,* Turner Publishing, 1994; Bill Hanna, *A Cast of Friends,* Taylor Publishing, 1996.

Atom Ant, doll, soft vinyl head, felt stuffed body, Rushton
   Co, Atlanta, GA, late 1960s, 11" h **$100.00**
Augie Doggie, frame tray puzzle, Whitman, 1960, 11 x
   14" **12.00**
Bamm Bamm, doll, vinyl, felt outfit, vinyl bone attached
   at waist, holding 8" long vinyl club, Ideal, #0721,
   ©Hanna-Barbera Prod, 1963, 12½" h, MIB **200.00**
Flintstones, card game, Pre-Historic Animal Rummy, Ed-
   U-Card, 1960 . . . . **15.00**
Flintstones, drinking glass, clear, white, brown, and yel-
   low art of Fred pouring Barney drink from ladle as
   Wilma and Betty talk, Dino drinking from punch
   bowl, name with palm trees and image of smiling
   Baby Puss on rim, ©Hanna-Barbera Prod, 1962, 5" h **75.00**
Flintstones, frisbee, Flintstone Flyer, sponge, 1980, 9" d **10.00**

Fred Flintstone, alarm clock, ceramic body, dial mkd "Sheffield, The Flinstones Alarm, Western Germany," 8½" h, $150.00.

Flintstones, party cups, "Happy Birthday," orig cellophane pack of 10 cold cups and colorful image of
   party scene as Barney holds birthday cake and Fred
   takes a piece, Wilma gives slice to Dino as Betty
   points, Futura, early 1960s. **20.00**
Flintstones, snow dome, plastic, image of Fred standing
   next to palm tree getting ready to give giant bone to
   running and laughing Dino against Bedrock background, "Bedrock City Kelowana B.C.," ©Hanna-
   Barbera Prod, 1981, 2½ x 3¾ x 2¾" **20.00**
Flintstones, *TV Guide,* Vol 9, #26, Jul 1, 1961, issue
   #431. . . . . **20.00**
Flintstones, wind-up, litho tin, granite rock design roll-
   over-type tank with images of Flintstone characters on
   all sides, underside has diecut flat metal image of Fred
   with hands in air, 1961 . . . . **375.00**
Flintstones, yo-yo, The Flintstones Swirler Flying Barrel,
   Imperial Toy Corp, ©1980 Hanna-Barbera Prod, MOC **20.00**
Fred Flintstone, push puppet, smiling full figure Fred
   making muscles, black base with attached gold foil
   sticker, Kohner, #3991, ©Hanna-Barbera Prod, 3¾" h **45.00**
Funky Phantom, game, The Funky Phantom Game,
   Milton Bradley, 1971 . . . . **12.00**
Huckleberry Hound, bank, vinyl, full figure smiling
   image of Huck, ©Hanna-Barbera,1960s, 15½" h **20.00**
Huckleberry Hound, car, litho tin, soft vinyl Huck head
   on top, orig 4 x 4¼ x 2" box, ©Hanna-Barbera Prod,
   1962. . . . . **200.00**
Huckleberry Hound, doll, red stuffed body, blue felt hat
   and bow tie, colorful soft vinyl face, white soft vinyl
   hands, orig tag attached at neck, box, ©1959 H-B
   Enterprises, Inc, 16" h **100.00**
Huckleberry Hound, drinking glass, Huck, Jinks, Pixie
   and Dixie, and Yakky Doodle playing musical instruments, pink accent notes at top, early 1960s, 5⅛" h **100.00**
Huckleberry Hound, pinback button, "Huckleberry
   Hound For President," litho tin, red, white, and blue,
   pink accent, yellow ground, Huck wearing stars and
   stripes hat, 1960, 3" d **20.00**
Huckleberry Hound, pinball game, 1970s, MOC **20.00**

Yogi Bear, doll, plush, wearing green hat, white collar, and yellow tie, $70.00.

Jetsons, thermos, image of family in spacecraft leaving "Space Burger" restaurant, Aladdin, 1963, 6½" h 175.00

Jonny Quest, game, Jonny Quest Game, Transogram, 1964. .... 75.00

Lippy the Lion, Touché Turtle, and Wally Gator, cup, plastic, paper illus of characters marching with musical instruments sealed inside plastic coating, Gothern Ind, 1964 .... 20.00

Lippy the Lion, Touché Turtle, and Wally Gator, thermos, Cartoon Zoo, characters looking through holes in fence, Universal, 1963, 7½" h 100.00

Magilla Gorilla, change purse, blue vinyl, red and yellow accent art and name at bottom, Estelle Toy Co, mid-1960s 10.00

Mr Jinx, doll, stuffed, black cloth, vinyl face, orange felt bow tie, "Knickerbocker Huckleberry Hound Toy" attached cloth label, 1959, 12" h 50.00

Mush Mouse, figure, hollow white vinyl, holding rifle in left handle, Ideal, ©Hanna-Barbera Prod, 1960s, 7½" h 75.00

Pebbles and Bamm-Bamm, View-Master Set, 3 reels and story booklet, Pebbles and Bamm Bamm swimming underwater with sea serpent, 1964. .... 20.00

Pebbles Flintstone, game, Pebbles Flintstone Live Wire on the Bedrock Exchange, Transogram, #3853, 1962...... 75.00

Peter Potamus, pull toy, painted molded vinyl, Peter Potamus sitting on plastic wagon, Ideal, 1964, 5" h....... 45.00

Pixie and Dixie, coloring book, Whitman, 1865 .... 12.00

Quick Draw McGraw, record, *Quick Draw McGraw as El Kabong*, 45 rpm, colorful sleeve with Quick Draw in disguise looking at viewer as left hoof sticks through guitar on floor, Golden Record, #593, 1960...... 20.00

Ricochet Rabbit, soaky, Ricochet Rabbit Bubble Club, jointed, purple hat, pink nose, black vest with tan star and purple flowers, jointed right arm holding gun, Purex, late 1960s, 11" h............................ 75.00

Ricochet Rabbit, squeeze toy, vinyl, colorful figure of smiling and seated Ricochet Rabbit, "A Magilla Gorilla Toy" stamp on back, Ideal, 1960s, 6" h 75.00

Rosey the Robot, wind-up, litho tin, Marx, 1963.......... 200.00

Scooby Doo, doll, stuffed, "Scooby Doo where are you!" tag, JS Sutton and Sons, 1970, 14" h. 40.00

Secret Squirrel, frame tray puzzle, Whitman, #4559, 1967, 11½ x 14½" 20.00

Squiddly Diddly, soaky, Squiddly Diddly Bubble Club, Purex, late 1960s, 10" h. 75.00

Wacky Races, jigsaw puzzle, Luke, Blabber Bear, and Sawtooth racing scene, 70 pcs, Whitman, 1970 .... 18.00

Wilma Flintstone, push puppet, smiling full figure Wilma holding ear of corn in right hand, blue base, 1960s. 45.00

Yogi Bear, drinking glass, Yogi sleeping as Pixie and Dixie steal apple off his stomach, Yakky and Blabber looking on from right, Boo Boo and snooper look on from left, green accent leaves at top, early 1960s, 5⅛" h 100.00

Yogi Bear, figure, smiling full figure purple Yogi wearing green tie and hat, DMI Toys, Dallas Texas, ©Hanna-Barbera Prod, c1970, MOC 20.00

Yogi Bear, game, Yogi Bear Presents Snagglepuss Fun at the Picnic, Transogram, #3805, ©1961 Hanna-Barbera Prod. 50.00

Yogi Bear, gloves, black cotton, orange cuffs with tan fringe, yellow and white accent picture of Yogi on each side, 4½ x 8¼" 8.00

Yogi Bear, riding toy, molded plastic, Buddy L, 1960, 7½ x 20½ x 19" 75.00

Yogi Bear, thermos, metal, Yogi and Quick Draw McGraw in tug-of-war with Hanna-Barbera charaters, Aladdin, 1961, 6½" h 45.00

Yogi Bear and Boo Boo, birthday candles, figural, Halo, ©1965 Hanna-Barbera Prod. 65.00

HARKER POTTERY

Harker Pottery Co., founded as Harker, Taylor and Co. in 1840, manufactured a wide range of products, beginning with doorknobs, toys, and ceramic hearth and table top tiles. Production soon included Rockingham and yellow wares. In 1879, the company began manufacturing white ironstone toilet wares, tea sets, and dinnerware. A shift to semi-porcelain ware was made in 1890.

By 1931 vitreous hotel ware, toilet sets, advertising novelties, and kitchen and dinnerware lines were produced. Notable patterns include Amy, Cameo Ware, Red Apple, and White Rose.

The Jeannette Glass Company purchased Harker Pottery in 1969. It made reproduction Rebekah-at-the-Well teapots and Toby jugs. Harker ceased operations in 1972.

References: Susan and Al Bagdade, *Warman's American Pottery and Porcelain*, Wallace-Homestead, Krause Publications, 1994; Harvey Duke, *The Official Price Guide to Pottery and Porcelain, Eighth Edition*, House of Collectibles, 1995.

Newsletter: *The Harker Arrow*, 69565 Cresent Rd, St Clairsville, OH 43950.

Amy, bread and butter plate.......................... **$5.00**
Amy, casserole, cov. 30.00
Amy, cup and saucer................................ 12.00
Amy, dinner plate 10.00
Amy, salt and pepper shakers, pr 20.00
Amy, spoon 30.00
Bermuda, dinner plate................................ 7.00
Bermuda, fruit dish 2.00
Bermuda, luncheon plate 5.00
Black-Eyed Susan, bread and butter plate, 6" d........... 2.00

Black-Eyed Susan, cake set, cake plate and 6 serving
plates **18.00**
Black-Eyed Susan, cup and saucer **3.00**
Black-Eyed Susan, dinner plate **6.00**
Black-Eyed Susan, pie lifter **5.00**
Black-Eyed Susan, tidbit tray, 3 tier. **12.00**
Colonial Lady, cereal bowl, lug handle. **10.00**
Colonial Lady, cup and saucer. **12.00**
Colonial Lady, dinner plate **10.00**
Colonial Lady, salad plate **18.00**
Colonial Lady, soup bowl **20.00**
Dainty Flower, Cameoware, casserole, cov. **15.00**
Dainty Flower, Cameoware, cup and saucer. **10.00**
Dainty Flower, Cameoware, dinner plate, 10" d **10.00**
Dainty Flower, Cameoware, fruit dish **4.00**
Dainty Flower, Cameoware, salt and pepper shakers, pr **15.00**
Deco-Dahlia, casserole, cov **35.00**
Deco-Dahlia, pie baker **15.00**
Deco-Dahlia, platter, oval, 11" l. **20.00**
Deco-Dahlia, salt and pepper shakers, pr, Skyscraper **28.00**
Ivy Wreath, creamer and sugar **20.00**
Ivy Wreath, cup and saucer. **6.00**
Ivy Wreath, dinner plate **10.00**
Ivy Wreath, fruit dish, 5" d. **4.00**
Ivy Wreath, luncheon plate **8.00**
Ivy Wreath, platter **15.00**
Ivy Wreath, soup, oval **6.00**
Ivy Wreath, vegetable dish, divided **8.00**
Mallow, Hot Oven, cake plate. **12.00**
Mallow, Hot Oven, custard **4.00**
Mallow, Hot Oven, mixing bowl **28.00**
Mallow, Hot Oven, pie lifter **15.00**
Mallow, Hot Oven, syrup **18.00**
Modern Tulip, bread and butter plate **5.00**
Modern Tulip, creamer **10.00**
Modern Tulip, jug, cov **25.00**
Modern Tulip, pie baker **20.00**
Modern Tulip, teapot. **30.00**
Modern Tulip, utility plate, 11". **15.00**
Monterey, casserole, cov **30.00**
Monterey, coffeepot, aluminum insert **50.00**
Monterey, luncheon plate **8.00**

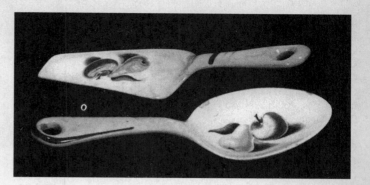

Red Apple II: pie lifter, $25.00; spoon, $20.00.

Monterey, syrup **15.00**
Monterey, utility plate **25.00**
Red Apple II, cheese plate, Modern Age shape **28.00**
Red Apple II, creamer and cov sugar, Zephyr shape **30.00**
Red Apple II, dinner plate **10.00**
Red Apple II, salt and pepper shakers, pr, Modern Age
shape **25.00**
Red Apple II, teapot, Zephyr shape **40.00**
White Rose, Carv-Kraft, bread and butter plate **5.00**
White Rose, Carv-Kraft, cup and saucer **10.00**
White Rose, Carv-Kraft, dinner plate **12.00**
White Rose, Carv-Kraft, salad plate **8.00**
White Rose, Carv-Kraft, salt and pepper shakers, pr **18.00**
White Rose, Carv-Kraft, vegetable **15.00**

HARTLAND FIGURES

Hartland Plastics, located in southern Wisconsin, produced a series of sport and western figures between 1953 and the early 1960s. These painted acetate plastic figures came with removable accessories.

Western figures ranged from generic figures, e.g., Western Champ, to licensed figures, e.g., The Lone Ranger and Wyatt Earp. Hartland occasionally used the same mold for more than one character, e.g., #804 for St. Preston and Sgt. Lance O'Rourke and #817 for Jim Bowie and Davy Crockett. A different paint scheme, accessories, and packaging distinguished one from the other.

The sports series contains thirty different football players (a generic offensive and defensive player for each of the fourteen NFL teams at the time plus two personality figures) and eighteen baseball players (eighteen personality figures and a bat boy).

In 1989 Hartland reissued all nineteen baseball figures in a twenty-fifth anniversary edition. They are identified by a "25" in a circle located on their back just below the belt.

Reference: Elizabeth Stephan (ed.), *O'Brien's Collecting Toys, 9th Edition*, Krause Publications, 1999.

Note: Unless noted otherwise, prices are for mint condition figures with original mint conditon tag and/or box.

Aberdeen Angus, #669, Dairy Cattle **$125.00**
Alkali Ike, #611, Western Wranglers **125.00**
Annie Oakley, #823, Western Figures. **150.00**
Bat Boy, #651, 6", Baseball, white, bubble pkg. **375.00**
Bat Masterson, #769, Gunfighter Series **1,000.00**

**Bermuda,
gray rim,
plate, 8¹/₄" d,
$5.00.**

Bret Maverick, #762, Gunfighter Series 150.00
Cactus Pete, #612, Western Wranglers 125.00
Carl Yastrzemski, #578, BasebalI, 1993–94 . . . . 460.00
Cheyenne, #818, Western Figures 325.00
Chris Colt, #761, Gunfighter Series, 1960s 550.00
Comanche Kid, #613, Western Wranglers. 125.00
Dale Evans, #802, Western Figures. 350.00
Dizzy Dean, Baseball 275.00
Don Drysdale, #546, Baseball 25th Anniversary 60.00
General Custer, #814, Western Figures 75.00
General Robert E Lee, #808, Historical Figures 125.00
George Washington, #815, Historical Figures 300.00
Jim Bowie, #817, Western Figures 500.00
Johnny Unitas, #413, Football 950.00
Jon Arnett, #412, Football 650.00
Lone Ranger, #801, Western Figures. 325.00
Luis Aparicio, #545, Baseball 25th Anniversary 60.00
Nolan Ryan, #554, Missouri, Baseball, 1993–94 . . . . 70.00
Roberto Clemente, #549, Missouri, Baseball, 1993–94 . . . . . 70.00
Roger Maris, #530, Baseball 25th Anniversary 100.00
Roy Rogers, #806, Western Figures 125.00
Safe at Second, #550, Missouri, Baseball, 1993–94. . . . . 140.00
Whitey Ford, Dallas, Baseball 150.00
Wyatt Earp, #709, Gunfighter Series, 1960s 625.00

AUCTION PRICES – HARTLAND FIGURES

Bill Bertoia Auctions, Summer Toy, Train, & Doorstop Sale, June 19–20, 1998. Prices include a 10% buyer's premium. All figures listed are in excellent (E) or near mint (NM) condition.

Babe Ruth holding bat and pointing to fence,
Yankees, 7½" h, NM. **$165.00**
Dick Groat at bat, Pirates, 7³/₈" h, NM. 413.00
Don Drysdale pitching, Dodgers, 7" h, NM. 165.00
Duke Snider at bat, Dodgers, 7" h, NM. 193.00
Eddie Mathews throwing ball, Braves, 7" h, NM 138.00
Ernie Banks at bat, Chicago Cubs, 7" h, NM 165.00
Hank Aaron at bat, Atlanta Braves, 7" h, NM. 165.00
Harmon Killebrew at bat, Twins, 7" h, NM 165.00
Luis Aparicio fielding ball, White Sox, 7" h, E 165.00
Mickey Mantle at bat, Yankees, 6³/₄" h, NM. 193.00
Nellie Fox throwing ball, White Sox, 7" h, NM. 110.00
Rocky Colavito at bat, Tigers, 7" h, NM. 193.00
Roger Maris swinging bat, Yankees, 7¼" h, NM. 193.00
Stan Musial at bat, Cardinals, 7" h, NM 110.00
Ted Williams swinging bat, Red Sox, 7½" h, NM. 165.00
Warren Spahn pitching, Braves, 7½" h, NM 138.00
Willie Mays in fielding position, Giants, 7½" h, NM . . 138.00
Yogi Berra catching, removable mask, 6½" h, E 110.00

Yogi Berra   Rocky Colavito   Don Drysdale
Photo courtesy Bill Bertoia Auctions.

HAVILAND CHINA

There are several Haviland companies. It takes a detailed family tree to understand the complex family relationships that led to their creations.

David and Daniel Haviland, two brothers, were New York china importers. While on a buying trip to France in the early 1840s, David Haviland decided to remain in that country. He brought his family to Limoges where he supervised the purchase, design, and decoration of pieces sent to America. In 1852, Charles Field Haviland, David's nephew, arrived in France to learn the family business. Charles married into the Alluaud family, owner of the Casseaux works in Limoges. Charles Edward and Theodore Haviland, David's sons, entered the firm in 1864. A difference of opinion in 1891 led to the liquidation of the old firm and the establishment of several independent new ones. [Editor's note: I told you it was complicated.]

Today, Haviland generally means ceramics made at the main Casseaux works in Limoges. Charles Edward produced china under the name Haviland et Cie between 1891 and the early 1920s. Theodore Haviland's La Porcelaine Theodore Haviland was made from 1891 until 1952.

References: Harry L. Rinker, *Dinnerware of the 20th Century: The Top 500 Patterns,* House of Collectibles, 1997; Arlene Schleiger, *Two Hundred Patterns of Haviland China, Books I–VI,* now published by Dona L. Schleiger; Nora Travis, *Haviland China,* Schiffer Publishing, 1997, 1998 value update.

Collectors' Club: Haviland Collectors Internationale Foundation, PO Box 802462, Santa Clarita, CA 91380.

Baltimore Rose, Haviland & Co, bone dish, pink and yellow **$45.00**
Baltimore Rose, Haviland & Co, bread and butter plate, pink and yellow 25.00
Baltimore Rose, Haviland & Co, breakfast cup and saucer, pink and yellow 80.00
Baltimore Rose, Haviland & Co, celery tray, pink and yellow, 12" l 125.00
Baltimore Rose, Haviland & Co, chop plate, pink, 13" w 150.00
Baltimore Rose, Haviland & Co, chop plate, violet, 12½" w 190.00
Baltimore Rose, Haviland & Co, coupe bread and butter, pink and yellow 25.00
Baltimore Rose, Haviland & Co, coupe salad, green 15.00
Baltimore Rose, Haviland & Co, coupe salad, pink and yellow 25.00
Baltimore Rose, Haviland & Co, creamer and open sugar, pink and yellow. 165.00
Baltimore Rose, Haviland & Co, dinner plate, pink 45.00
Baltimore Rose, Haviland & Co, dinner service, pink and yellow, service for 6 consisting of 6 each dinner plates, luncheon plates, and salad plates, 2 each teacups and saucers, 4 each bouillon cups and saucers, and 1 each open oval vegetable, oval and round cov vegetable, and gravy, price for 40 pcs 1,100.00
Baltimore Rose, Haviland & Co, favor dish, ball ft, pink and yellow, 3" w 60.00
Baltimore Rose, Haviland & Co, luncheon plate, pink and yellow 30.00
Baltimore Rose, Haviland & Co, platter, pink, 16" l 85.00
Baltimore Rose, Haviland & Co, punch cup 110.00

Baltimore Rose, Haviland & Co, punch bowl, pink, ftd and scalloped, 14¹/₂" d, 7¹/₄" h, $1,250.00. Photo courtesy Gene Harris Antique Auction Center.

Baltimore Rose, Haviland & Co, ramekin and underplate, pink. **50.00**
Baltimore Rose, Haviland & Co, salad plate, violet, 7¹/₂" d **15.00**
Baltimore Rose, Haviland & Co, teacup and saucer, pink and yellow **80.00**
Baltimore Rose, Haviland & Co, vegetable, cov, oval, pink, 11¹/₄" l **150.00**
Baltimore Rose, Haviland & Co, vegetable, cov, round, pink and yellow, 10" d **150.00**
Dropped Rose, Haviland & Co, biscuit tray, fuschia, 13⁵/₈ x 7¹/₄" **250.00**
Dropped Rose, Haviland & Co, bowl, scalloped rim, pink, 7³/₄" d **90.00**
Dropped Rose, Haviland & Co, cake plate, fuschia, 10³/₄" w **130.00**
Dropped Rose, Haviland & Co, chop plate, pink, cobalt and gold trim, 12³/₄" w **250.00**
Dropped Rose, Haviland & Co, coffeepot, pink, 7" h **350.00**
Dropped Rose, Haviland & Co, cup and saucer, fuschia **65.00**
Dropped Rose, Haviland & Co, luncheon plate, lavender, 8¹/₂" d **30.00**
Dropped Rose, Haviland & Co, pitcher, dark pink, 8¹/₈" h **550.00**
Dropped Rose, Haviland & Co, salad plate, pink, green and gold trim **40.00**
Dropped Rose, Haviland & Co, soup tureen, cov, pink **385.00**
Dropped Rose, Haviland & Co, tea and toast **165.00**
Ranson, Haviland & Co, biscuit plate. **25.00**
Ranson, Haviland & Co, bone dish **20.00**
Ranson, Haviland & Co, bowls, nesting set of 3, 7¹/₂" d, 9¹/₂" d, and 10" d **400.00**
Ranson, Haviland & Co, bread tray, 11³/₄" l. **110.00**
Ranson, Haviland & Co, butter chip. **8.00**
Ranson, Haviland & Co, cake plate **135.00**
Ranson, Haviland & Co, celery tray **125.00**
Ranson, Haviland & Co, chocolate pot. **275.00**
Ranson, Haviland & Co, chop plate, 11¹/₂" d **190.00**
Ranson, Haviland & Co, chop plate, 14" d **250.00**
Ranson, Haviland & Co, coffee cup and saucer **15.00**
Ranson, Haviland & Co, coffee set consisting of coffeepot, creamer, sugar, and 12 cups and saucers **500.00**
Ranson, Haviland & Co, creamer, 4" h. **75.00**

Ranson, Haviland & Co, demitasse cup and saucer. **25.00**
Ranson, Haviland & Co, dinner service, complete service for 12 plus creamer, sugar, 3-pc butter, 3 different size platters, and cov vegetable **775.00**
Ranson, Haviland & Co, gravy boat **75.00**
Ranson, Haviland & Co, luncheon plate. **9.00**
Ranson, Haviland & Co, mayonnaise and attached liner **125.00**
Ranson, Haviland & Co, oatmeal bowl. **60.00**
Ranson, Haviland & Co, oyster plate, 5-well. **100.00**
Ranson, Haviland & Co, pitcher, 8⁵/₈" h **235.00**
Ranson, Haviland & Co, platter, 10¹/₂" l **75.00**
Ranson, Haviland & Co, platter, 13¹/₂" l **60.00**
Ranson, Haviland & Co, platter, 18" l **200.00**
Ranson, Haviland & Co, platter, 20" l **400.00**
Ranson, Haviland & Co, relish dish, 7¹/₂" l **125.00**
Ranson, Haviland & Co, salad plate. **15.00**
Ranson, Haviland & Co, sauce dish **12.00**
Ranson, Haviland & Co, sauce tureen and attached liner . . . **250.00**
Ranson, Haviland & Co, soup bowl **30.00**
Ranson, Haviland & Co, sugar, cov **85.00**
Ranson, Haviland & Co, sugar, open **65.00**
Ranson, Haviland & Co, vegetable, cov, round **200.00**
Ranson, Haviland & Co, vegetable, open, oval, 10" l **90.00**

HAZEL ATLAS GLASSWARE

Hazel Atlas resulted from the 1902 merger of the Hazel Glass Company and the Atlas Glass and Metal Company, each located in Washington, Pennsylvania. The company's main offices were located in Wheeling, West Virginia.

The company was a pioneer in automated glassware manufacture. A factory in Clarksburg, West Virginia, specialized in pressed glassware and achieved a reputation in the late 1920s as the "World's Largest Tumbler Factory." Two factories in Zanesville, Ohio, made containers, thin-blown tumblers, and other blown ware. Washington and Wheeling plants made containers and tableware, the latter including many of the Depression-era patterns for which the company is best known among collectors.

Continental Can purchased Hazel-Atlas in 1956. Brockway Glass Company purchased the company in 1964.

References: Gene Florence, *Collectible Glassware From the 40s, 50s, 60s..., Fourth Edition,* Collector Books, 1998; Gene Florence, *Kitchen Glassware of the Depression Years, Fifth Edition,* Collector Books, 1995, 1997 value update.

Note: See Depression Glass for additional listings.

Cloverleaf, creamer, black **$20.00**
Cloverleaf, cup and saucer, black. **25.00**
Cloverleaf, luncheon plate, 8", black **16.00**
Cloverleaf, luncheon plate, 8", pink. **9.00**
Cloverleaf, salad plate, 6", yellow **10.00**
Cloverleaf, salt and pepper shakers, pr, ftd, black **95.00**
Cloverleaf, sherbet, crystal. **8.00**
Cloverleaf, sherbet, green **10.00**
Cloverleaf, sherbet, yellow **12.00**
Cloverleaf, sherbet, ftd, black. **20.00**
Cloverleaf, sherbet, ftd, pink **9.00**
Cloverleaf, sherbet, ftd, yellow **10.00**
Cloverleaf, sugar, black **15.00**
Cloverleaf, sugar, yellow **18.00**
Crisscross, butter dish, cov, ¹/₄ lb, crystal **22.00**

Crisscross, butter dish, cov, 1 lb, cobalt	140.00
Crisscross, butter dish, cov, 1 lb, green	75.00
Crisscross, creamer, crystal	16.00
Crisscross, creamer, pink	150.00
Crisscross, pitcher, 54 oz, crystal	100.00
Crisscross, reamer, green	35.00
Crisscross, reamer, large, crystal	12.00
Crisscross, refrigerator dish, cov, 4 x 4", cobalt	35.00
Crisscross, refrigerator dish, cov, 4 x 4", crystal	12.00
Crisscross, refrigerator dish, cov, 4 x 8", crystal	22.00
Crisscross, refrigerator dish, cov, 4 x 8", green	60.00
Crisscross, refrigerator dish, cov, 8 x 8", cobalt	125.00
Crisscross, sugar, cov, pink	25.00
Crisscross, tumbler, 9 oz, crystal	25.00
Crisscross, water bottle, 8³/₄", crystal	20.00
Florentine No. 1, berry bowl, small, blue	42.00
Florentine No. 1, creamer, green	10.00
Florentine No. 1, cup and saucer, green	12.00
Florentine No. 1, dinner plate, 10", green	16.00
Florentine No. 1, grill plate, 10", green	12.00
Florentine No. 1, juice tumbler, ftd, green	16.00
Florentine No. 1, sherbet, green	10.00
Florentine No. 1, sherbet, pink	6.00
Florentine No. 1, sherbet plate, green	6.00
Florentine No. 1, sugar, cov, green	28.00
Florentine No. 1, sugar, open, green	10.00
Florentine No. 1, sugar, ruffled, blue	50.00
Florentine No. 1, water tumbler, green	22.00
Moderntone, cereal bowl, blue	80.00
Moderntone, creamer, blue	12.00
Moderntone, cream soup, blue	24.00
Moderntone, cup, amethyst	10.00
Moderntone, cup and saucer, blue	16.00
Moderntone, custard cup, blue	24.00
Moderntone, dinner plate, 8⁷/₈" d, blue	20.00
Moderntone, luncheon plate, 7³/₄" d, blue	12.00
Moderntone, salad plate, 6³/₄" d, blue	10.00
Moderntone, salt and pepper shakers, pr, blue	45.00
Moderntone, sherbet, blue	12.00

Moderntone, sherbet plate, amethyst	5.00
Moderntone, sherbet plate, blue	6.00
Moderntone, sugar, amethyst	10.00
Moderntone, sugar, blue	12.00
Moderntone, tumbler, 9 oz, blue	38.00
Moroccan, bowl, oval, 7³/₄", amethyst	16.00
Moroccan, bowl, oval, center handle, 7", amethyst	14.00
Moroccan, bowl, round, 6" d, amethyst	10.00
Moroccan, cup and saucer, amethyst	8.00
Moroccan, dinner plate, octagonal, amethyst	9.00
Moroccan, fruit bowl, octagonal, 4³/₄", amethyst	8.00
Moroccan, juice tumbler, 2¹/₂", amethyst	8.00
Moroccan, old fashion, 3¹/₄", amethyst	12.00
Moroccan, punch set, 15 pcs, amethyst and white milk glass, orig box	135.00
Moroccan, tumbler, 6 oz, 3¹/₂", amethyst	10.00
Moroccan, tumbler, 16 oz, 6¹/₂", amethyst	16.00
Moroccan, wine, 4", amethyst	10.00
Newport, berry bowl, amethyst	17.00
Newport, berry bowl, blue	22.00
Newport, cereal bowl, blue	43.00
Newport, creamer and sugar, amethyst	34.00
Newport, cream soup, amethyst	18.00
Newport, cream soup, blue	23.00
Newport, cup and saucer, amethyst	16.00
Newport, cup and saucer, blue	20.00
Newport, luncheon plate, amethyst	14.00
Newport, luncheon plate, blue	17.00
Newport, platter, oval, amethyst	45.00
Newport, salt and pepper shakers, pr, blue	56.00
Newport, sherbet, amethyst	12.00
Newport, sherbet, blue	18.00
Newport, tumbler, blue	48.00
Royal Lace, bowl, straight edge, 10" d, pink	50.00
Royal Lace, cookie jar, crystal	55.00
Royal Lace, cream soup, crystal	17.00
Royal Lace, cup, pink	15.00
Royal Lace, sugar, crystal	8.00

HEISEY GLASS

In April 1896, Augustus H. Heisey opened a sixteen-pot glass furnace in Newark, Ohio. Eventually the plant expanded to three furnaces and employed over 700 people.

Early production was limited to pressed ware and bar and hotel ware. In the late 1890s, Colonial patterns with flutes, scallops, and panels were introduced.

George Duncan Heisey, a son of Augustus H., designed the famous "Diamond H" trademark in 1900. The company registered it in 1901. In 1914 blown ware was first manufactured. Not content with traditional pulled stemware, the company introduced fancy pressed stemware patterns in the late 1910s.

Edgar Wilson, another son of Augustus H., became president in 1922 following Augustus' death. He was responsible for most of the colored Heisey glass. While some colored glass was made earlier, the first pastel colors and later deeper colors, e.g., cobalt and tangerine, were manufactured in quantity in the 1920s and 30s. By the time of Edgar Wilson's death in 1942, colored glassware had virtually disappeared from the market.

T. Clarence Heisey, another son of Augustus, assumed the presidency of the company. Shortages of manpower and supplies during World War II curtailed production. Many animal figures were

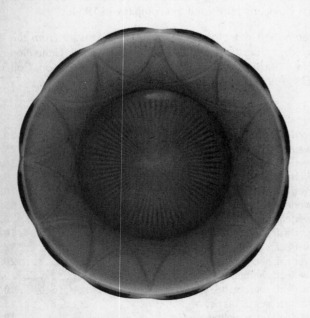

Newport, sandwich plate, 11³/₄" d, $40.00.

introduced in the 1940s. An attempt was made to resurrect colored glass in the 1950s. Increasing production costs and foreign competition eventually resulted in the closing of the Heisey factory in December 1957.

The Imperial Glass Corporation of Bellaire, Ohio, bought the Heisey molds in 1958. Only a small number were kept in production, primarily those of patterns Heisey had in production when it ceased operations. Some pieces still carried the Heisey mark. In January 1968, Imperial announced it would no longer use the Heisey mark.

References: Neila Bredehoft, *The Collector's Encyclopedia of Heisey Glass, 1925–1938,* Collector Books, 1986, 1999 value update; Gene Florence, *Elegant Glassware of the Depression Era, Eighth Edition,* Collector Books, 1999; Frank L. Hahn and Paul Kikeli, *Collector's Guide to Heisey and Heisey By Imperial Glass Animals,* Golden Era Publications, 1991, 1998 value update; Harry L. Rinker, *Stemware of the 20th Century: The Top 200 Patterns,* House of Collectibles, 1997.

Collectors' Club: Heisey Collectors of America, Inc, 169 W Church St, Newark, OH 43055.

Animal, dolphin, candle holder, 3 ftd	$45.00
Animal, fighting rooster, 8" h	145.00
Animal, fish, bookend	145.00
Animal, giraffe	275.00
Animal, goose, 1/2 wings	80.00
Animal, goose, cordial	145.00
Animal, goose, wings up	125.00
Animal, kicking pony	175.00
Animal, mallard, 1/2 wings	125.00
Animal, mallard, wings up	145.00
Animal, plug horse	115.00
Animal, rabbit, milk glass, Imperial, price for pair	28.00
Animal, rabbit, paperweight	165.00
Animal, rearing pony, ultra blue, Imperial	38.00
Animal, ringneck pheasant	145.00
Animal, rooster, cocktail, rooster stem	85.00
Animal, seahorse, cocktail	145.00
Animal, sparrow	100.00
Animal, standing pony	85.00
Animal, swan, nut cup, individual	28.00
Cabochon, champagne/sherbet, crystal	12.00
Cabochon, water, crystal	14.00
Carcassone Sahara, cocktail, ftd, 3 oz	24.00
Colonial, custard cup	10.00
Colonial, plate, crystal, 4 3/4"	5.00
Crystolite, cheese comport, ftd	25.00
Crystolite, cheese plate, 2 handles	45.00
Crystolite, oil cruet, no stopper	30.00
Crystolite, punch cup	10.00
Crystolite, salad bowl	70.00
Danish Princess, cocktail	45.00
Danish Princess, cordial	65.00
Danish Princess, water	32.00
Danish Princess, wine, 2 1/2 oz	55.00
Ipswich, oyster cocktail, ftd, crystal, 4 oz	22.00
Ipswich, tumbler, ftd, 5 oz	30.00
Ipswich, tumbler, ftd, 8 oz	30.00
Ipswich, tumbler, ftd, 10 oz	24.00
Ipswich, tumbler, ftd, 12 oz	24.00

Water Goblets. Left: Minuet, $20.00. Right: Plantation, $25.00.

Minuet, champagne	30.00
Minuet, plate, 8" d	20.00
Narcissus, cocktail	18.00
Narcissus, sherbet/champagne	18.00
Narcissus, water	38.00
Narcissus, wine, 2 oz	38.00
Orchid, candy jar, cov, Bowknot finial, crystal, 6"	225.00
Orchid, candy jar, cov, seahorse handle, crystal	275.00
Orchid, cigarette holder, ftd	16.00
Orchid, comport, crystal, 6"	45.00
Orchid, plate, 7 1/4" d	18.00
Orchid, saucer	15.00
Orchid, water, crystal	48.00
Pied Piper, cocktail, 4 oz	125.00
Pied Piper, water, crystal	28.00
Plantation, candle holders, pr	150.00
Plantation, coaster	60.00
Plantation, tumbler, ftd, pressed, 12 oz	80.00
Rosalie, cocktail, 3 oz	10.00
Rose, cake plate, low pedestal, 14"	325.00
Rose, champagne	26.50
Rose, cocktail	32.50
Rose, goblet, 9 oz	42.00
Rose, sherbet, low	22.00
Rose Etch, sherbet/champagne, crystal	38.00
Rose Etch, tumbler, ftd, crystal, 12 oz	58.00
Rose Etch, water, crystal	48.00
Sahara, tumbler, ftd, 12 oz	45.00
Spanish Stem, champagne, cobalt bowl	110.00
Spanish Stem, water, cobalt bowl, 10 oz	145.00
Spanish Stem, wine, cobalt bowl, 2 1/2 oz	195.00
Twist Green, plate, 7"	10.00
Twist Green, tumbler, ftd, 9 oz	50.00
Victorian, champagne	14.00
Victorian, cocktail, crystal	16.00
Victorian, sherbet/champagne, crystal	14.00
Victorian, wine, crystal, 2 1/2 oz	18.00

HESS TRUCKS

Hess Oil and Chemical Corporation of Perth Amboy, New Jersey, introduced its first toy truck in 1964. The Hess Tank Trailer, with operating headlights and taillights and a fillable cargo tank with drainer hose, sold for $1.29, batteries included. It was reissued, unchanged, in 1965.

These promotions were so well received that vehicles have been distributed annually ever since. Available for initial purchase only at Hess service stations, these limited edition plastic toys are known for their quality construction. Each was issued complete with batteries and instructions in a sturdy cardboard box with superb graphics.

Reference: Michael V. Harwood, *The Hess Toy Collector*, FSBO, 1991.

Note: Prices listed for Hess Trucks MIB.

1977, Tank Truck, large label, $200.00.

1964, Model B Mack Tanker Truck	$2,250.00
1965, Model B Mack Tanker Truck	2,250.00
1966, Voyager Tanker Ship	2,500.00
1967, Split Window Tanker Truck	2,600.00
1968, Split Window Tanker Truck	650.00
1969, Amerada Hess Truck	2,500.00
1969, Split Window Tanker Truck	750.00
1970, Red Pumper Fire Truck	750.00
1971, Red Pumper Fire Truck	2,750.00
1972, Split Window Tanker Truck	375.00
1974, Split Window Tanker Truck	350.00
1975, Box Trailer, with unlabeled oil drums	350.00
1976, Box Trailer, with labeled oil drums	350.00
1977, Tanker Truck, large label	200.00
1978, Tanker Truck, small label	200.00
1980, GMC Training Van	400.00
1982, '33 Chevy, "First Hess Truck"	100.00
1983, '33 Chevy, "First Hess Truck"	100.00
1984, Tanker Truck Bank	85.00
1985, '33 Chevy, "First Hess Truck" bank	100.00
1986, Aerial Ladder Fire Truck, red	125.00
1987, White Box Trailer, with oil drums	75.00
1988, Car Transporter with Race Car	85.00
1989, Aerial Ladder Fire Truck with Siren, white	55.00
1990, Semi-Tanker Truck with Horn	45.00
1991, Car Transporter with Race Car	35.00

1992, 18-Wheeler Box Truck with Race Car	40.00
1993, Patrol Car, with sirens and flashing lights	30.00
1993, Premium Diesel Semi-Tanker Truck, not sold publicly	1,000.00
1994, Rescue Truck	25.00
1995, Hess Truck and Helicopter	30.00
1996, Emergency Truck	25.00
1997, Toy Truck and Racers	25.00
1998, Recreation Van with Dune Buggy and Motorcycle	28.00
1998, Hess Miniature Tanker Truck	45.00

HI-FI EQUIPMENT

1950s and 60s hi-fi equipment is now collectible. Vacuum tube-type amplifiers, pre-amplifiers, AM-FM tuners, and receivers are sought. Look for examples from Acrosound, Altec, Eico, Fisher, McIntosh, Marantz, and Western Electric. Some American and English record turntables and speakers are also collectible. Garrard and Thorens are two leading brand names.

Prices reflect equipment in working order. If a piece of equipment does not work, it has parts value only, usually $25 or less. Because collectors restore equipment, unused tubes in their period boxes have value, albeit modest.

Amplifier, Amperex, EL34, vacuum tube, output, made in France or Holland, new	$3.00
Amplifier, Eico, HF-60, mono, 60 watts, EL34 output tubes	100.00
Amplifier, Fisher, 80AZ, mono, 30 watts, 6L6GC tubes, narrow style chassis	50.00
Amplifier, Marantz, 5, mono, 30 watts, EL34 output tubes, meter	200.00
Amplifier, McIntosh, MC-60, mono, 60 watts, 6550 output tubes	100.00
Pre-Amplifier, Harmon Kardon, Citation I, stereo, tubes, wood case	50.00
Receiver, Fisher, 800C, stereo, AM/FM, 50 watts, walnut case	75.00

Turntable, Thorens TD124, 4-speed, belt drive, $25.00.

Tuner, Marantz, 10-B, stereo, tubes, AM/FM, oscillo-
scope display 300.00
Vacuum Tube, Telefunken, 12AX7, dual triode, flat
plates, made in Germany, new in box 3.00
Vacuum Tube, Westen Electric, 300B, output, triode, new 12.50

HIGGINS GLASS

Michael Higgins and Frances Stewart Higgins were actively
involved in designing and decorating glass in their Chicago studio
by the early 1950s. Between 1958 and 1964, the couple worked
in a studio provided for them by Dearborn Glass, an industrial
glass company located outside Chicago. Pieces were mass produced. A gold signature was screened on the front of each piece
before the final firing. During the period with Dearborn, the
Higgins developed new colors and enamels for their double-lay-
ered pieces and experimented with weaving copper wire into
glass, fusing glass chips to create crystalline forms, and overlaying
colors onto glass panels.

After leaving Dearborn, the Higgins established a studio at
Haeger. In 1966 they re-established their own studio. During the
late 1960s and early 1970s, the Higgins manufactured large quantities of glass plaques, often framed in wood. In 1972 they moved
their studio to Riverside, Illinois. Pieces made after 1972 have an
engraved signature on the back. Michael Higgins passed away on
February 13, 1999.

Reference: Donald-Brian Johnson and Leslie Piña, *Higgins:
Adventures in Glass,* Schiffer Publishing, 1997.

Note: Unless stated otherwise, all pieces have a gold signature.

Ashtray, bird pattern, 7" l **$45.00**
Ashtray, blue and yellow check, gold signature, 7 x 10" 50.00
Ashtray, blue with applied squares, gold signature, 7 x
10" 50.00
Ashtray, blue, yellow, and lavender, gold signature, 4" sq 15.00
Ashtray, lock and keys, gold signature, 7 x 10" 95.00
Ashtray, orange and lavender pulled feathers, gold sig-
nature, 4" d 15.00
Ashtray, orange and yellow ray, gold signature, 5½" d 28.00
Ashtray, purple with blue and green spikes, gold signa-
ture, 7 x 10" 38.00
Bowl, blue blob, etched signature, 10" d 110.00
Bowl, blue puffed leaf, fluted rim, inside signature, 7" d 60.00
Bowl, emerald with applied patches, Stickman signa-
ture, 9½" d 220.00
Bowl, green and orange dot ray, gold signature, 12½" d 82.00
Bowl, orange and green ray, inside signature, 5½" sq 16.00
Bowl, white dot ray, gold signature, 12½" d 60.00
Bowtie Dish, black and gray dot ray, Stickman and
etched signature, 10" l 95.00
Charger, blue, green, and gold ray, inside and gold sig-
nature, 13½" sq 82.00
Charger, green with chartreuse spikes, gold signature,
17½" d 132.00
Charger, orange spike, gold signature, 17" d 110.00
Finger Rings, pr, etched signature, 1" sq 110.00
Pendant, Frank Lloyd Wright window design, etched sig-
nature, 2 x 3" 95.00
Pendant, trees and setting sun, etched signature, 2 x 3" 82.00
Plate, blue scroll, gold signature, 13½" d 82.00
Plate, orange spike, gold signature, 12½" d 55.00

**Trays, matching, orange, red, and amber ornamentals with curvi-
linear geometric devices, edge mkd "higgins" in gold, 17" d
round tray, 14" l rectangular tray, price for pair, $200.00.** Photo
courtesy Skinner, Inc., Boston, MA.

Plate, purple with blue and green spikes, gold signature,
paper label, 12½" d 72.00
Tray, blue and brown waves with gold sand dollar, gold
signature, 7 x 10" 50.00
Tray, blue seaweed, gold Stickman signature, 5 x 10" 72.00
Tray, chartreuse and white stripe with seaweed, 2-part,
Stickman and gold signature, orig paper label, 7 x 14" 72.00
Tray, red, orange, and avocado, Stickman and gold sig-
nature, 7 x 14" 38.00
Tray, white daisy, gold signature, 4½" d 28.00
Tray, white with wildflowers, Stickman and etched sig-
nature, 5" sq 55.00
Wall Pocket, fishtail, white scroll, etched Francis
"Higgins" signature, 24" l 220.00

HOCKEY CARDS

The first hockey cards were three cigarette sets produced between
1910 and 1913. Four candy card sets and one cigarette set were
issued in the 1920s. In the 1930s Canadian chewing gum manufacturers, e.g., World Wide Gum Company, offered hockey cards
as a premium.

The modern hockey card dates from the 1950s. Parkhurst issued
hockey card sets between 1951 and 1964, the exception being the
1956–57 season. Topps produced its first hockey card set in 1954.
Topps sets focused on American teams; Parkhurst on Canadian
teams. Starting with the 1964–65 season, Topps issued card sets
that included players from all teams in the National Hockey
League. O-Pee-Chee, a producer of card sets in the 1930s, re-
entered the market in 1968.

There were five major card sets for the 1990–91 season:
Bowman, O-Pee-Chee Premier, Pro Set, Score, and Upper Deck.
Like trading cards for other sports, current hockey card sets contain special feature cards. This is one collectible that is equally at
home in either Canada or the United States.

References: James Beckett, *Beckett Hockey Card Price Guide & Alphabetical Checklist No. 7*, Beckett Publications, 1997; James Beckett, *Official Price Guide to Hockey Cards 1998*, 7th Edition, House of Collectibles, 1997; Sports Collectors Digest, *1998 Sports Collectors Almanac*, Krause Publications, 1998.

Periodicals: *Beckett Hockey Monthly*, 15850 Dallas Pkwy, Dallas, TX 75248; *Sports Cards*, 700 E State St, Iola, WI 54990.

Note: Prices are for cards in good condition.

Donruss, 1993–94, #152, Wayne Gretzky	$1.50
Donruss, 1993–94, #242, Eric Lindros	1.50
Donruss, 1994–95, #5, Mario Lemieux	.75
Donruss, 1995–96, #338, Patrick Roy	.50
Fleer, 1992–93, #126, Glenn Healy	.05
Fleer, 1993–94, #117, Gilbert Dionne	.10
Fleer, 1993–94, #334, Chris Osgood	1.50
Fleer, 1993–94, #485, Paul Kariya	2.50
Fleer, 1994–95, #283, Bryon Dafoe	.10
Leaf, 1993–94, #117, Gilbert Dionne	.10
Leaf, 1993–94, #200, Mighty Ducks	.55
O-Pee-Chee, 1933–34, common player (1-48)	4.00
O-Pee-Chee, 1933–34, complete set (48)	350.00
O-Pee-Chee, 1934–35, common player (49-72)	4.50
O-Pee-Chee, 1934–35, complete set (24)	150.00
O-Pee-Chee, 1935–36, common player (73-96)	5.00
O-Pee-Chee, 1935–36, complete set (24)	150.00
O-Pee-Chee, 1936–37, common player (97-132)	7.50
O-Pee-Chee, 1936–37, complete set (36)	500.00
O-Pee-Chee, 1937–38, common player (133-180)	4.00
O-Pee-Chee, 1937–38, complete set (48)	250.00
O-Pee-Chee, 1939–40, common player (1-100)	1.50
O-Pee-Chee, 1939–40, complete set (100)	200.00
O-Pee-Chee, 1940–41, complete set (50)	175.00
O-Pee-Chee, 1968–69, common player (1-216)	.20
O-Pee-Chee, 1968–69, complete set (216)	125.00
O-Pee-Chee, 1969–70, common player (1-231)	.15
O-Pee-Chee, 1969–70, complete set (231)	90.00
O-Pee-Chee, 1969–70, common player (1-12)	.35
O-Pee-Chee, 1970–71, complete set (264)	80.00
Parkhurst, 1951–52, complete set (105)	550.00
Parkhurst, 1952–53, #3, Boom Boom Geoffrion	8.00
Parkhurst, 1953–54, #26, Doug Harvey	3.00
Parkhurst, 1955–56, #1, Harry Lumley	2.00
Parkhurst, 1957–58, complete set (50)	125.00
Parkhurst, 1958–59, common player (1-50)	1.00
Parkhurst, 1958–59, complete set (50)	100.00
Parkhurst, 1961–62, #44, Wayne Connelly	5.50
Parkhurst, 1961–62, complete set (51)	90.00
Pinnacle, 1992–93, #200, Brett Hull	.50
Pinnacle, 1993–94, #263, Andrew Moog Mask	.75
Pro Cards, 1988–89, common player (1-348), American Hockey League	.03
Pro Cards, 1988–89, complete set (348), American Hockey League	10.00
Score, 1985–86, #15, Mario Lemieux and Mike Bullard, Seven Eleven Credit Cards series	1.50
Score, 1990–91, complete set (440)	3.00
Score, 1990–91, #1, Wayne Gretzky	.12
Score, 1990–91, #250, Pat LaFontaine	.02
Score, 1991–92, complete set (40),Young Superstars	2.50
Score Young Superstars, 1991–92, complete set, 40 cards	2.50
Topps, 1961–62, #20, Boston Bruins	1.50

Topps, 1961–62, complete set (24), Hockey Bucks	30.00
Topps, 1962–63, #33, Bobby Hull	15.00
Topps, 1963–64, #36, Stan Mikita	5.50
Topps, 1964–65, complete set (110)	400.00
Topps, 1969–70, #24, Bobby Orr	7.50
Topps, 1975–76, common player (1-330)	.02
Topps, 1975–76, complete set (330)	15.00
Topps, 1979–80, #83, Stanley Cup Finals	.45
Upper Deck, 1990–91, #63, Jeremy Roenick	1.25
Upper Deck, 1993–94, #98, Rob Niedermayer	.10

HOCKEY MEMORABILIA

Hockey memorabilia focuses primarily on professional hockey teams. Although the popularity of college hockey is growing rapidly and Canada's Junior Hockey is deeply entrenched, professional teams have generated almost all licensed collectibles.

Collecting is highly regionalized. Most collectors focus on local teams. Even with today's National Hockey League, there is a distinct dividing line between collectors of material related to American and Canadian teams.

Superstar collecting is heavily post-1980 focused. Endorsement opportunities for early Hockey Hall of Famers were limited. Collectors want game-related material. Logo licensed merchandise for sale in sports shops has minimal or no appeal.

Reference: Roderick Malloy, *Malloy's Sports Collectibles Value Guide: Up-to-Date Prices for Noncard Sports Memorabilia*, Attic Books, Wallace-Homestead, Krause Publications, 1993.

Autograph, Hull, Brett, CS, 3 x 5".	$30.00
Autograph, McGee, Frank, hockey stick sgd	60.00
Autograph, LaFontaine, Pat, cut signature	6.00
Autograph, Mikita, Stan, PS, 8 x 10".	85.00
Book, *Official 1932 Field Hockey Guide*, Spaulding's Athletic Library	20.00
Drinking Glass, Buffalo Sabers, Gil Perreault	7.00
Drinking Glass, Detroit Redwings, Klima/Burr, Little Caesar premium	5.00
Drinking Glass, "Philadelphia Flyers 1976–1977 recoup the cup," 3¼" h.	6.00
Drinking Glass, Quebec Nordiques, #16, Michel Goulet, A&W premium	10.00
Game, Box Hockey, Milton Bradley, 1941	50.00
Game, Nip and Tuck Hockey, Parker Bros, 1928	150.00
Game, Slapshot, Avalon Hill, 1982	12.00
Hockey Stick, Brett Hull	275.00
Magazine, *Action Sports Hockey*, Mar 1973, Bobby Hull	12.00
Magazine, *Hockey Digest*, Nov 1975, Bobby Clarke	6.50
Magazine, *Hockey Illustrated*, Feb 1970, Stan Mikita	14.00
Magazine, *Sports Illustrated*, Dec 11, 1967, Bobby Orr cov	15.00
Media Guide, Atlanta Flames, logo, 1972–73	15.00
Media Guide, Blackhawks, mascot, 1972–73	8.00
Media Guide, Bruins, Stanley Cup trophy, 1972–73	10.00
Media Guide, Maple Leafs, 50th anniversary photos, 1981–82	8.00
Nodder, Maple Leafs, square base, 1961–62	60.00
Nodder, Rangers, square base, 1961–62	75.00
Plate, Gretzky, Wayne, Lynel Studios, 8½" d	200.00
Poster, Hull, Bobby, *Sports Illustrated*, 1968–71	45.00
Poster, Orr, Bobby, *Sports Illustrated*, 1968–71	40.00
Program, NHL All-Star Game, 1976	8.00

Program, NHL Stanley Cup Playoffs, 1961 . . . . **20.00**
Ticket Stub, NHL All Star Game, Montreal, 1956 . . . . **25.00**
Ticket Stub, NHL All-Star Game, Philadelphia, 1976. . . . . **4.00**

HOLIDAY COLLECTIBLES

Holiday collectibles can be broken down into three major periods: (1) pre-1940, (2) 1945 to the late 1970s, and (3) contemporary "collector" items. Crossover collectors, e.g., candy container collectors, skew the values on some items.

This is a catchall category for those holiday collectibles that do not have separate category listings. It includes Fourth of July and Thanksgiving collectibles. Look elsewhere for Christmas, Easter, Halloween, and Valentines.

References: Lisa Bryan-Smith and Richard Smith, *Holiday Collectibles*, Krause Publications, 1998; Pauline and Dan Campanelli, *Holiday Collectables: A Price Guide*, L-W Book Sales, 1997.

Periodical: *Pyrofax Magazine*, PO Box 2010, Saratoga, CA 95070.

Newsletter: *St Patrick Notes*, 10802 Greencreek Dr, Ste 703, Houston, TX 77070.

Birthday, candle holders, pastel flowers, molded composition, orig box, 1940s **$10.00**
Birthday, hat, crown, Sweet Sixteen, silver cov cardboard, glitter dec, 1930s **5.00**
Birthday, napkins, clown holding balloons, orig pkg **3.00**
Chanukah, cookie cutter, Star of David, tin **10.00**
Chanukah, streamer, crepe paper, blue and gold, printed "Happy Chanukah" **5.00**
Chanukah, tablecloth, printed paper, Menorah and dreidel border **5.00**
Father's Day, sign, "Father's Day Special," Winchester Arms, 1966 . . . . **15.00**
Fourth of July, bookends, pr, Liberty Bell, bronze patina on pot metal **25.00**
Fourth of July, bowtie, cloth, stars and stripes **10.00**
Fourth of July, candy container, Uncle Sam, composition, removable base **175.00**

Leap Year, postcard, Gabriel, NY, Leap-Year Series, No. 401, sgd "D Wig," $12.00.

Fourth of July, chocolate mold, Liberty Bell, tin. **35.00**
Fourth of July, pinback button, "Spend the 4th In Malden," c1930s **10.00**
Fourth of July, sheet music, *Yankee Doodle Dandy* **20.00**
Labor Day, pinback button, "Labor Day, Labor Omnia Vincit, In Union There Is Strength, Justice For All," celluloid on metal, 2 hands shaking, shield symbol and eagle, Badge and Novelty Co, Baltimore, MD, 1" d **20.00**
Lincoln's Birthday, bookends, pr, bronze colored plaster, Lincoln sitting on bench **35.00**
Lincoln's Birthday, bottle/bank, figural Lincoln, clear glass. **10.00**
Mother's Day, bell, Devotion for Mothers, Hummel, 1976. . . . . **55.00**
Mother's Day, pinback button, "I Am Taking Orders For Whitman's Chocolates Mother's Day May 8," 1920–30s **3.00**
Mother's Day, pinback button, "Remember Mother's Day May 11," mother and red haired children on brown ground, white and yellow lettering, 1940–50s. **10.00**
Mother's Day, plate, Alpine Mother and Children, Mother's Day series, Anri, 1973 . . . . **55.00**
New Year's, banner, "Happy New Year," silver border, 1930. . . . . **10.00**
New Year's, handkerchief, printed cotton, bells and "Happy New Year Greetings," 1940s **5.00**
New Year's, noisemaker, blow-out whistle, cardboard and paper, feather blow-out, 1930 . . . . **5.00**
New Year's, noisemaker, horn, cardboard and paper, silver and black, 1930 . . . . **8.00**
New Year's, photograph, Times Square, New York, New Year's Eve, 1953 . . . . **15.00**
New Year's, postcard, emb cardboard, "Happy New Year," New Year's baby surrounded by flowers **5.00**
St Patrick's Day, candy container, top hat, cardboard, green foil, shamrock and clay pipe on top, Germany, 3" h **60.00**
St Patrick's Day, decoration, dancing Irish girl, green, shamrocks on skirt, mkd "Dennison, USA, 05S," 7" h **10.00**
St Patrick's Day, sheet music, *Danny Boy* **5.00**
St Patrick's Day, stickpin, diecut flag with green 4-leaf clover accent **10.00**
Thanksgiving, candle, figural turkey **10.00**
Thanksgiving, cookie cutter, turkey, aluminum **5.00**
Thanksgiving, decoration, turkey, emb cardboard, black, white, and red, mkd "Made in USA," 9½" h **20.00**
Thanksgiving, figure, turkey, celluloid, red, white, and blue, 4" h **15.00**
Thanksgiving, greeting card, family seated around table **3.00**
Thanksgiving, greeting card, turkey with feather tail, 1930s. **8.00**
Thanksgiving, ice cream mold, cornucopia, pewter. **20.00**
Thanksgiving, magazine, *Home Arts*, woman sewing stuffing in turkey, 1930 . . . . **8.00**
Valentine's Day, nut cup, red and white crepe paper, fringed with foil covered heart and name tag, 1930 . . . . **5.00**
Valentine's Day, recipe booklet, Baker's Chocolates, 1940. . . . . **10.00**
Washington's Birthday, candy container, cardboard log, applied cherries. **75.00**
Washington's Birthday, cookie cutter, hatchet, tin, large **75.00**
Washington's Birthday, ice cream mold, log, pewter, hinged **45.00**

HOLT-HOWARD

A. Grant Holt and brothers John and Robert J. Howard formed the Holt-Howard import company in Stamford, Connecticut in 1948. The firm is best known for its novelty ceramics, including the Cat and Christmas lines and the popular Pixieware line of condiment jars. Designed by Robert J. Howard and produced between 1958 and the early 1960s, these ceramic containers proved to be so successful that knock-offs by Davar, Lefton, Lipper & Mann, M-G, Inc., and Norcrest quickly found their way into the market. Kay Dee Designs purchased Holt-Howard in 1990.

Authentic Pixieware is easily identified by its single-color vertical stripes on a white jar, flat pixie-head stopper (with attached spoon when appropriate), and condiment label with slightly skewed black lettering. An exception is three salad dressing cruets which had round heads. All pieces were marked, either with "HH" or "Holt-Howard," a copyright symbol followed by the year "1958" or "1959," and "Japan." Some pieces may be found with a black and silver label.

Reference: Walter Dworkin, *Price Guide to Holt-Howard Collectibles and Related Ceramic Wares of the '50s & '60s,* Krause Publications, 1998.

Coq Rouge, butter dish, cov, 6³/₄" l	$40.00
Coq Rouge, cereal bowl, 1962, 6" d	12.00
Coq Rouge, coffeepot, cov, 6 cup	60.00
Coq Rouge, dinner plate, 1962, 9¹/₂" d	12.00
Coq Rouge, salt and pepper shakers, pr, 3³/₄" h	8.00
Cozy Kitchen Kitties, Cozy Kittens bud vase, 2-pc set, Tabby and Tom Charmers, 1958, 6³/₄" h	80.00
Cozy Kitchen Kitties, Cozy Kittens butter dish, cov, 7" l	95.00
Cozy Kitchen Kitties, Cozy Kittens caddy, 1958, 6¹/₂" h	55.00
Cozy Kitchen Kitties, Cozy Kittens salt and pepper shakers, pr, 1958, 4¹/₂" h	15.00
Cozy Kitchen Kitties, Cozy Kittens spoon rest, 6" l	65.00
Cozy Kitchen Kitties, kitten string holder, 4¹/₂" h	40.00
Jeeves, ashtray, 4"	45.00
Jeeves, decanter, 10¹/₂" h	150.00
Jeeves, olives jar, 5" h	125.00
Merry Mouse, desk pen pal, 5¹/₂" h	75.00
Pixieware, Bottle Bracelet, 1958	40.00

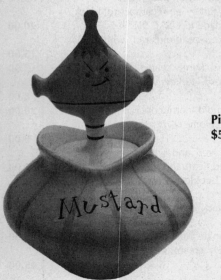

Pixieware, mustard, $50.00.

Pixieware, Cocktail Cherries Jar, 1958	90.00
Pixieware, Hanging Pixie Planter, 1959, 12" l including chains	175.00
Pixieware, Instant Coffee, 1958	150.00
Pixieware, Ketchup Katie, 1959	95.00
Pixieware, Li'l Sugar and Cream Crock, 1958	75.00
Pixieware, Liquor Decanter, 1958	175.00
Pixieware, Mayonnaise Jar, 1959	95.00
Pixieware, Olive Jar, 1958	65.00
Pixieware, Onion Annie, 1959	95.00
Pixieware, Peanut Butter Pat, 1959	95.00
Pixieware, Russian Dressing, 1959	95.00
Pixieware, Salty & Peppy, salt and pepper shakers, pr, 4¹/₂" h	175.00
Pixieware, Sam 'n Sally Salad Set, oil and vinegar, 1958	120.00
Pixieware, Spoon, 1958	50.00
Pixieware, Teapot Candle Holder, with hurricane globe, 1959, 8¹/₄" h	165.00
Pixieware, Towel Hook, 1959	50.00
Santa, Merry Whiskers Beverage Set, pitcher and 6 mugs, 1959	50.00
Santa, Noel Candle Holder, 3" h, 9" l	15.00
Santa, Winking Santa Creamer and Sugar, stackable, 1959, 4¹/₂" h	30.00
Santa, Winking Santa Egg Nog Pitcher, 4¹/₂" h	45.00
Santa, Winking Santa Punch Bowl Set, 10 pc, 3-qt punch bowl, eight 6-oz mugs, candy cane shaped ladle, 1962	115.00

HOMER LAUGHLIN

In 1870 Homer and Shakespeare Laughlin established two pottery kilns in East Liverpool, Ohio. Shakespeare left the company in 1879. The firm made whiteware (ironstone utilitarian products). In 1896 William Wills and a group of Pittsburgh investors, led by Marcus Aaron, purchased the Laughlin firm. The company expanded, building two plants in Laughlin Station, Ohio, and another in Newall, West Virginia. A second plant was built in Newall in 1926.

Cookware, dinnerware, and kitchenware were the company's principal products. Popular dinnerware lines include Fiesta, Harlequin, Rhythm, Riviera, and Virginia Rose.

References: Jo Cunningham, *Homer Laughlin: 1873–1939,* Schiffer Publishing, 1998; Bob and Sharon Huxford, *Collector's Encyclopedia of Fiesta: Plus Harlequin, Riviera, and Kitchen Kraft, Eighth Edition,* Collector Books, 1998; Joanne Jasper, *The Collector's Encyclopedia of Homer Laughlin China,* Collector Books, 1993, 1997 value update; Richard G. Racheter, *Collector's Guide to Homer Laughlin's Virginia Rose,* Collector Books, 1997.

Newsletter: *The Laughlin Eagle,* 1270 63rd Terrace S, St Petersburg, FL 33705.

Collectors' Club: The Homer Laughlin Collector's Club, Inc, PO Box 16174, Loves Park, IL 61132.

Note: See Fiesta for additional listings. See Figurines for Harlequin animals.

Conchita, casserole	$125.00
Conchita, casserole, individual	225.00
Dogwood, bowl, 5¹/₂" d	5.00
Dogwood, dinner plate, 9" d	8.00

Oven Serve, pie baker, No. 602, yellow, 1933, 10½" d, $10.00.

Dogwood, vegetable, oval 10.00
Eggshell Theme, creamer and cov sugar 25.00
Eggshell Theme, cup and saucer 15.00
Eggshell Theme, dinner plate 10.00
Eggshell Theme, gravy, attached underplate 18.00
Eggshell Theme, salad plate 7.00
Epicure, casserole, turquoise 50.00
Epicure, gravy, turquoise 25.00
Hacienda, bowl, 5" d 8.50
Hacienda, bowl, 6" d 28.50
Hacienda, bowl, 8¼" d 25.00
Hacienda, bowl, 9" d 19.50
Hacienda, bread and butter plate, 6¼" d 5.00
Hacienda, casserole, cov 65.00
Hacienda, flat soup, 8" d 26.50
Hacienda, gravy, Yellowstone shape 60.00
Hacienda, plate, 7" d 15.00
Hacienda, plate, 9" d 22.00
Hacienda, platter 22.00
Hacienda, saucer 3.50
Hacienda, sugar lid 6.00
Harlequin, ball pitcher, gray 100.00
Harlequin, ball pitcher, mauve 75.00
Harlequin, ball pitcher, spruce 95.00
Harlequin, bread and butter plate, maroon, 6" d 8.00
Harlequin, casserole, cov, maroon 215.00
Harlequin, casserole, cov, red 125.00
Harlequin, creamer, green, individual 125.00
Harlequin, creamer, maroon, individual 35.00
Harlequin, creamer, red, individual 16.50
Harlequin, cream soup, green 125.00
Harlequin, cream soup, spruce 40.00
Harlequin, cream soup, turquoise 18.50
Harlequin, cup, chartreuse 9.00
Harlequin, demitasse creamer and sugar, green 80.00
Harlequin, demitasse cup and saucer, medium green 100.00
Harlequin, eggcup, double, green 25.00
Harlequin, eggcup, double, maroon 38.00
Harlequin, eggcup, double, rose 45.00
Harlequin, eggcup, double, yellow 15.00
Harlequin, fruit bowl, maroon, 5½" d 125.00
Harlequin, fruit bowl, turquoise, 5½" d 3.50
Harlequin, nut dish, 3 part, mauve blue 8.00
Harlequin, oatmeal bowl, 36's, medium green 25.00
Harlequin, oatmeal bowl, 36's, red 25.00
Harlequin, oatmeal bowl, 36's, yellow 20.00
Harlequin, plate, gray, 10" d 45.00
Harlequin, plate, maroon, 10" d 35.00
Harlequin, plate, mauve, 10" d 35.00
Harlequin, plate, medium green, 9" d 20.00
Harlequin, relish, turquoise plate, yellow, red, blue, and
   rose inserts 280.00

Harlequin, salt, red 9.00
Harlequin, sauceboat, dark green 35.00
Harlequin, sugar, cov, gray 45.00
Harlequin, teacup, turquoise 4.50
Harlequin, teapot, chartreuse, base only 75.00
Harlequin, teapot, gray 185.00
Harlequin, teapot, green 125.00
Harlequin, water tumbler, red 50.00
Jubilee, dinner plate, cream beige 8.00
Jubilee, saucer, celadon green 5.00
Kitchen Kraft, mixing bowl, 8" d 25.00
Kitchen Kraft, salt and pepper shakers, pr 32.00
Mexicana, bowl, 5" d 12.50
Mexicana, casserole 145.00
Mexicana, cup and saucer 15.00
Mexicana, deep plate 45.00
Mexicana, fruit bowl 15.00
Mexicana, plate, 7" d 12.00
Oven Serve, bowl, pumpkin, 4" d, handled 6.00
Oven Serve, bowl, pumpkin, 6" d 6.00
Oven Serve, bowl, pumpkin, 7" d 8.00
Oven Serve, cup and saucer, pumpkin 20.00
Oven Serve, custard, pumpkin, 3" 5.00
Oven Serve, pie plate, pumpkin, 7" d 12.00
Oven Serve, plate, pumpkin, 6" d 7.00
Oven Serve, plate, pumpkin, 7" d 8.00
Oven Serve, plate, pumpkin, 9" d 15.00
Oven Serve, ramekin, 2 handles, 6" d 9.00
Rhythm, saucer, gray 5.00
Rhythm, soup bowl, harlequin yellow, 8" d 10.00
Riviera, butter dish, cov, green, ¼ lb 185.00
Riviera, casserole, cov, yellow 110.00
Riviera, cup, mauve blue 8.00
Riviera, dinner plate, green, 10" d 95.00
Riviera, salt shaker, red 10.00
Riviera, syrup, red 295.00
Riviera, teapot, cov, ivory 225.00
Royal Harvest, bread and butter plate 4.00
Royal Harvest, cup and saucer 8.00

Riviera, Century shape.

Royal Harvest, platter, oval **12.00**
Royal Harvest, salad plate **4.00**
Royal Harvest, vegetable, round **7.50**
Virginia Rose, butter, cov. **45.00**
Virginia Rose, cake plae **17.50**
Virginia Rose, cup and saucer **5.00**
Virginia Rose, gravy **6.50**
Virginia Rose, pickle **10.00**
Virginia Rose, salt and pepper shakers, pr **10.00**
Virginia Rose, vegetable, cov. **48.00**

HORSE COLLECTIBLES

Objects shaped like a horse or featuring an image of a horse are everywhere. Most collectors specialize, e.g., collectors of carousel horses. Horse-related toys, especially horse-drawn cast-iron toys, are bought and sold within the toy collecting community.

Reference: Jan Lindenberger, *501 Collectible Horses*, Schiffer Publishing, 1995.

Note: For additional listings see Breyer Horses.

Blanket, tan wool, pink, black, and green stripes **$20.00**
Calendar, 1950, Dodge Stables and Castleton Farm **50.00**
Catalog, SD Myers Saddle Co, Fine Stock Saddles, Ranch
    Supplies and Art Leather Goods, El Paso, TX, 80 pp,
    c1930. . . . . **55.00**
Comic Book, Francis the Talking Mule, Dell, #4-C-501,
    1953. . . . . **10.00**
Comic Book, Fury, Gold Key, #1, 1962 . . . . **18.00**
Comic Book, Gene Autry's Champion, Dell, #12, 1953 . . . . . . **6.00**
Curry Comb, stamped "Oliver Slant Tooth," 1940s **25.00**
Figure, Appaloosa, Hagen-Renaker, 4³/₄" h **500.00**
Figure, Best of the West Nodding Head Buckskin, plas-
    tic, brown, black accents, saddle, saddle bags, and
    bridle, orig box, Marx, 12¹/₂" h. **50.00**
Figure, prancing horse, carnival chalkware, 11" h **45.00**

Hood Ornament, flying horse, diecast metal, chrome-plated, 6" h, $275.00. Photo courtesy Collectors Auction Services.

Figure, rearing horse, Hagen Renaker, miniature, 4" h **100.00**
Figure, Roan Lady, Hagen Renaker, 7³/₄" h **500.00**
Figure, standing horse, pot metal, 6 x 4". **20.00**
Figure, wagon horse, plastic, cream, Marx, 2¹/₄" h. **3.00**
Figure, Zillo, Hagen Renaker, 5" h **100.00**
Little Golden Book, *Fury Takes a Jump,* 1958 . . . . **8.00**
Pinback Button, "Boys-D-Lite Horse," brown horse head
    on gold ground, black lettering, 1930–40s **15.00**
Rocking Horse, wooden, fur covering, 1930s **170.00**
Watch Fob, diecut brass, horseshoe entwined spear-like
    letter "S" to form "US" initials for "United States
    Horseshoe Co/Erie PA". **20.00**
Whip, leather, braided, russet colored, 9 ft l **20.00**

HORSE RACING

Items associated with Hall of Fame horses, e.g., Dan Patch and Man O'War, bring a premium. Paper ephemera, e.g., postcards and programs, and drinking glasses are two strong areas of focus. A program was issued for the first Belmont Stakes in 1867, the first Preakness Stakes in 1873, and the first Kentucky Derby in 1875. Kentucky Derby glasses date back to 1938, Preakness glasses to 1973, Belmont glasses to 1976, and Breeders Cup glasses to 1985. Pins were introduced at the Kentucky Derby in 1973 and at other major stakes races in the 1980s.

References: *Bill Friedberg's Pictorial Price Guide & Informative Handbook Covering "Official" Kentucky Derby, Preakness, Belmont, Breeder's Cup Glasses and Much More,* published by author, 1996; Roderick A. Malloy, *Malloy's Sports Collectibles Value Guide: Up-to-Date Prices for Noncard Sports Memorabilia,* Attic Books, Wallace-Homestead, Krause Publications, 1993.

Bottle, RC Cola, "RC Salutes 100th Kentucky Derby
    Churchill Downs 1974," 16 oz. **$12.00**
Decanter, Jim Beam, 95th Kentucky Derby Churchill
    Downs **20.00**
Drinking Glass, 1960 Kentucky Derby **45.00**
Drinking Glass, 1964 Kentucky Derby **18.00**
Drinking Glass, 1965 Kentucky Derby **23.00**
Drinking Glass, 1966 Kentucky Derby **25.00**
Drinking Glass, 1967 Kentucky Derby **26.00**
Drinking Glass, 1968 Kentucky Derby **20.00**
Drinking Glass, 1973 Kentucky Derby **20.00**
Drinking Glass, 1979 Preakness. **25.00**
Drinking Glass, 1982 Freehold Raceway, Apr 24, 1982,
    Bruce Cornell Memorial, John Campbell, Willow
    Wiper, gold rim, bubble bottom, red and white dec,
    3³/₈" h **11.00**
Drinking Glass, 1985 Centerbury Derby, Inaugural
    Running, Sep 2, 1985 . . . . **10.00**
Drinking Glass, 1989 Pepsi West Virginia Breeders
    Classic **18.00**
Drinking Glass, 1992 Kentucky Derby **5.00**
Drinking Glass, 1997 Indiana Derby **10.00**
Game, Derby Day, Parker Bros, 1940. . . . . **24.00**
Game, Derby Downs, Great Games, 1973 . . . . **25.00**
Game, Kentucky Derby Racing Game, Whitman, 1938. . . . . . **20.00**
Pin, Belmont Stakes, 1987. . . . . **10.00**
Pin, Breeders Cup, 1988 . . . . **10.00**
Pin, Kentucky Derby, 1976, plastic. **65.00**
Pin, Preakness, 1989. . . . . **10.00**
Program, 77th Kentucky Derby, 1951 . . . . **65.00**

Drinking Glass, Kentucky Derby, Churchill Downs, 1979, 5¼" h, $20.00.

Program, Kentucky Derby, 1942 . . . . 175.00
Program, Preakness Day, May 19, 1979, Pimlico 20.00
Stein, 1988 Canterbury Cup 10.00

HOT WHEELS

Automobile designer Harry Bradley, Mattel designer Howard Newman, Mattel Chairman Elliot Handler, and R & D chief Jack Ryan were the principal guiding forces in the creation of Hot Wheels. The creative process began in 1966 and culminated with the introduction of a diecast metal 16-car line in 1968. Hot Wheels were an immediate success.

Initially, cars were produced in Hong Kong and the United States. Mattel continually changed styling and paint motifs. Copies of modern cars were supplemented with futuristic models. Since the cars were meant to be raced, Mattel produced a variety of track sets. A Hot Wheels licensing program was instituted, resulting in Hot Wheels comic books, lunch kits, etc. In the 1980s Mattel did a number of Hot Wheels promotions with McDonald's and Kellogg's. In 1993 Mattel introduced a reproduction line focused toward the adult collector market. In 1997 Mattel acquired Tyco, bringing Hot Wheels and Matchbox under one roof.

References: Bob Parker, *The Complete & Unauthorized Book of Hot Wheels, 3rd Edition,* Schiffer Publishing, 1999; Michael Thomas Strauss, *Tomart's Price Guide to Hot Wheels, 3rd Edition,* Tomart Publications, 1998.

Periodical: *Toy Cars & Vehicles,* 700 E State St, Iola, WI 54990.

Newsletter: *Hot Wheels Newsletter,* 26 Madera Ave, San Carlos, CA, 94070.

ACCESSORIES

12-Car Collector's Case, yellow $30.00
Automatic Lap Counter 15.00
Cutoff Canyon, 2 cars 90.00
Danger-Changer 2-Pak 25.00
Daredevil Loop Accessory Pak 15.00
Dual-Lane Speedometer 30.00

Fold-Down Service Station, 1968 . . . . 60.00
Full Curve Accessory Pak 12.00
Hot Curves Race Action Set, 2 cars 45.00
Pop-Up Car Collectors Case 45.00
Poster, Snake and Mongoose 75.00
Rod Runner Hand Shift Power-Booster 20.00
Super-Charger Grand Prix Race Set, 4 cars 45.00
Talking Service Center 85.00
Trestle Accessory Pak 12.00
Wipe-Out Race Game 50.00

CARS

'31 Ford Woody, purple $50.00
'57 T-Bird, aqua 45.00
'57 T-Bird, green 50.00
Alive 55, green 22.00
All Tune Lube Viper 20.00
All Tune Lube VW Bus 40.00
American Hauler, blue 8.00
Army Funny Car 25.00
Baja Bruiser, blue 12.00
Blue Angels VW Bus 55.00
Blue Tricar Premium Baggie 10.00
Boss Hoss Chrome Collectors 65.00
Bugeye, red 20.00
Buzz Off, blue, yellow stripes 15.00
CD Rom VW Bus 35.00
Chapparal, white, no fin 10.00
Classic Convertible T-Bird, red 38.00
Classic Nomad, purple 40.00
Classic Nomad, red 32.00
Custom Barracuda, purple 55.00
Custom Camaro, green 28.00
Custom Corvette 15.00
Custom Eldorado, blue 38.00
Custom Fleetside, purple 32.00
Custom Mustang, blue 35.00
Custom T-Bird, blue 48.00
Deamon, green 14.00
Deora, gold 58.00
Dune Daddy 115.00
Fast Food Services Sweet Stocker 25.00
Ferrari 312, red 6.00
Fish Stick VW Bus 40.00
Fleetside, orange 48.00

Turboa, yellow and green, $6.00.

Flintstones Flintmobile	8.00
Ford J, purple	32.00
Highway Rider	23.00
Highway Robber	38.00
Internet Volkswagen Bus	85.00
Iola, purple	15.00
Iola GT 70, green	10.00
JC Whitney VW Bus	150.00
Jet Thret, light green	55.00
Jiffy Lube Race VW Bus	40.00
King Kuda, blue	25.00
Lotus, green	5.00
Mantis, light blue	12.00
Mercedes Benz, green	18.00
Mighty Maverick, green	35.00
Neet Street, chrome	15.00
Paddy Wagon, blue, with windshield	15.00
Porsche Carrera, yellow and blue	35.00
Rash One, blue	95.00
Rock Buster, chrome	8.00
Rolls Royce, gold	60.00
Sand Drifter, yellow, orange flames	12.00
Shelby Turbine, purple	30.00
Shell Promo Yellow Passion	50.00
Silhouette, blue	6.00
Snake, yellow	48.00
Splittin' Image, green	20.00
Steam Roller, white	22.00
Stingray Corvette	12.00
The Hood, light green	38.00
Thunderbired VW Bus	45.00
TNT Bird, brown	22.00
Torero, green	10.00
Twin Mill, chrome	25.00
VW Bus, 1st edition, 1996	85.00
VW Bus, 30th anniversary edition, 1998	50.00
Xploder, red	90.00
Yamaha Limited Hauler	30.00

HULL POTTERY

In 1905 Addis E. Hull purchased the Acme Pottery Company, Crooksville, Ohio, and changed its name to the A. E. Hull Pottery Company. By 1917, Hull's lines included art pottery for gift shops and florists, kitchenware, novelties, and stoneware.

Tile production helped the company weather the economic difficulties of the Depression. Hall's Little Red Riding Hood kitchenware arrived in 1943 and remained in production until 1957.

A 1950 flood and fire destroyed the company's plant. Two years later the company returned as the Hull Pottery Company. It was during this period that Hull added a new line of high-gloss glazed ceramics and developed Floraline and Regal, its product lines for the floral industry. The popularity of the California movement prompted a production shift to kitchen and dinner wares in 1960, with noteable lines including Mirror Brown, Rainbow, Provincial, Heartland, and Blue Belle. The plant closed in 1985.

Hull's early stoneware is marked with an "H." Matte pieces contain pattern numbers. Series numbers identify Open Rose/Camellia pieces (100s), Iris (400s), and Wildflower (W plus a number). Many Hull pieces also are marked with a number indicating their height in inches. Pieces made after 1950, usually featuring the high-gloss glaze, are marked "hull" or "Hull" in a script signature.

References: Barbara Loveless Glick-Burke, *Collector's Guide to Hull Pottery: The Dinnerware Lines,* Collector Books, 1993; Joan Gray Hull, *Hull: The Heavenly Pottery, Sixth Edition,* published by author, 1998; Brenda Roberts, *The Collectors Encyclopedia of Hull Pottery,* Collector Books, 1980, 1999 value update.

Newsletters: *The Hull Pottery News,* 466 Foreston Place, St Louis, MO 63119; *Hull Pottery Newsletter,* 11023 Tunnell Hill NE, New Lexington, OH 43764.

Collectors' Club: Hull Pottery Assoc, 4 Hilltop Rd, Council Bluffs, IA 51503.

Note: See Little Red Riding Hood for additional listings.

Ashtray, Parchment and Pine, S-14	$125.00
Ball Pitcher, Marcrest, pink, 7¹/₂" h	45.00
Bank, Corky Piggy, 5"	50.00
Basket, Bow-Knot, blue and green, B25, 6¹/₂" h	300.00
Basket, Capri, green and yellow, 12" h	12.00
Basket, Dogwood, yellow and green, 501-7¹/₂"	300.00
Bookends, pr, Orchid, pink and blue, 305-7"	1,000.00
Candle Holders, pr, Calla Lily, green and brown, unmkd, 2¹/₄" h	160.00
Candlesticks, pr, Magnolia, 4" h	70.00
Cookie Jar, Floral, 48, 8³/₄" h	100.00
Creamer and Open Sugar, Rosella, R-3-5¹/₂" and R-4-5¹/₂"	100.00
Ewer, Open Rose, pink, 105-7"	250.00
Flowerpot, attached saucer, Sueno Tulip, yellow and blue, 116-33-6"	140.00
Flowerpot, Sunglow, yellow, 98-7¹/₂"	40.00
Jardiniere, Royal Imperial, pink and black, 75-7"	50.00
Leaf Dish, Tuscany, 19	30.00
Mixing Bowls, Nuline Bak-Serve, nesting set of 5	150.00
Planter, figural, 2 ducks, 7¹/₂" h	18.00
Planter, figural, basket girl, 8" h, price for pair	65.00
Planter, figural, poodle, red and green, 8" h	18.00
Planter, figural, woman with flowing skirt, 7" h	30.00

Jardiniere, #536, green and brown glaze, 9", $85.00.

Left: Cornucopia, Wildflower, W-10-8¹/₂" h, $150.00. Right: vase, Serenade, 211, 10¹/₂" h, $125.00.

Planter, Water Lily, pink, with underplate, 6" h **60.00**
Planters, figural, 3 swans, Imperial line, large size F23 is
  6" h, two smaller size F21 are 4" h, price for 3 pcs **20.00**
Rose Bowl, Iris, yellow, 412-7" **175.00**
Salt and Pepper Shakers, pr, Bouquet, 25-3¹/₂" **50.00**
Teapot, Magnolia Matte, pink and blue, 23, 6¹/₂" h **95.00**
Tidbit, Rainbow, tangerine, 2-tier, 10" h **40.00**
Urn Vase, Imperial, 454, 5" h. **18.00**
Vase, Rosella, R-2-5". **75.00**
Vase, Thistle, green, 51-6¹/₂". **125.00**
Vase, Tropicana, 54, 12¹/₂" h **400.00**
Wall Pocket, Poppy, pink and blue, 609-9". **350.00**
Wall Pocket, Rosella, heart shape, R-10-6¹/₂" **150.00**

HUMMEL FIGURINES

Berta Hummel, a German artist, provided the drawings that were the inspiration for W. Goebel's Hummel figurines. Berta Hummel, born in 1909 in Massing, Bavaria, Germany, enrolled at age eighteen in the Academy of Fine Arts in Munich. In 1934 she entered the Convent of Siessen and became Sister Maria Innocentia.

W. Goebel, Rodental, Bavaria, produced its first Hummel figurines in 1935. John Schmid of Schmid Brothers, Randolph, Massachusetts, secured American distribution rights. When Goebel wished to distribute directly to the American market in 1967, the two companies and Berta Hummel's heirs became entangled in a lawsuit. A compromise was reached. Goebel would base its figurines on drawings made by Berta Hummel between 1934 and her death in 1964. Schmid was given the rights to produce pieces based on Hummel's pre-convent drawings.

A Hummel figurine must have the "M. I. Hummel" legend on its base and a Goebel trademark. If either is missing, the figurine is not a Goebel Hummel. Seven different trademarks are used to identify the production period of a figurine:

Trademark 1	Incised Crown Mark	.1935–1949
Trademark 2	Full Bee	.1950–1959
Trademark 3	Stylized Bee	.1957–1972
Trademark 4	Three Line Mark	.1964–1972
Trademark 5	Last Bee Mark	.1972–1979
Trademark 6	Missing Bee Mark	.1979–1991
Trademark 7	Current/New Crown Mark	.1991–Present

References: Ken Armke, *Hummel,* Wallace-Homestead, Krause Publications, 1995; Carl F. Luckey, *Luckey's Hummel Figurines & Plates, 11th Edition,* Krause Publications, 1997; Robert L. Miller, *The No. 1 Price Guide to M. I. Hummel: Figurines, Plates, More...,* Sixth Edition, Portfolio Press, 1995.

Collectors' Clubs: Hummel Collectors Club, 1261 University Dr, Yardley, PA 19067; M I Hummel Club, Goebel Plaza, PO Box 11, Pennington, NJ 08534.

An Apple A Day, 403, trademark 7 . . . . **$150.00**
Angel Duet, 261, trademark 4 . . . . **235.00**
Bashful, 377, trademark 6 . . . . **90.00**
Boy with Toothache, 217, trademark 5 . . . . **190.00**
Brother, 95, trademark 5 . . . . **90.00**
Carnival, 328, trademark 6 . . . . **105.00**
Congratulations, 17/0, trademark 7 . . . . **80.00**
Culprits, 56/A, trademark 3 . . . . **250.00**
Doll Bath, 319, trademark 6 . . . . **165.00**
Easter Greeting, 378, trademark 5 . . . . **110.00**
Feeding Time, 199, trademark 2 . . . . **190.00**
Feeding Time, 199/0, trademark 5 . . . . **135.00**
Goose Girl, 47/0, trademark 5 . . . . **80.00**
Goose Girl, 47/2, trademark 5 . . . . **325.00**
Harmony in Four Parts, 471, trademark 6. . . . . **1,150.00**
Hear Ye, Hear Ye, 15/0, trademark 6. . . . . **85.00**
Hear Ye, Hear Ye, 15/1, trademark 5. . . . . **110.00**
Hello World, 429, trademark 5 . . . . **110.00**
Home From Market, 198/1, trademark 5. . . . . **80.00**
I Didn't Do It, 626, trademark 7 . . . . **80.00**
It's Cold, 421, trademark 6. . . . . **125.00**
I Wonder, 486, trademark 7. . . . . **75.00**
Knitting Lesson, 256, trademark 5 . . . . **200.00**
Land in Sight, 580, trademark 7 . . . . **1,000.00**

Playmates, 58/0, trademark 3, $250.00.

Let's Tell the World, 487, trademark 6 . . . . 465.00
Letter to Santa, 340, trademark 4 . . . . 300.00
Little Goat Herder, 200/1, trademark 5 . . . . 110.00
Lost Sheep, 68/0, trademark 7 . . . . 165.00
Lost Stocking, 374, trademark 6 . . . . 65.00
Morning Concert, 447, trademark 6 . . . . 85.00
My Wish Is Small, 463/0, trademark 7 . . . . 95.00
Out of Danger, 56/B, trademark 5 . . . . 150.00
Postman, 119, trademark 5 . . . . 75.00
Shepherd's Boy, 64, trademark 5 . . . . 105.00
Signs of Spring, 203/1, trademark 6 . . . . 115.00
Sister, 98/0, trademark 5 . . . . 85.00
Sister, 98/2/0, trademark 5 . . . . 65.00
Soldier Boy, 332, trademark 4 . . . . 140.00
Telling Her Secret, 196/0, trademark 6 . . . . 125.00
Telling Her Secret, 196/1, trademark 5 . . . . 250.00
The Little Pair, 449, trademark 7 . . . . 150.00
The Surprise, 431, trademark 6 . . . . 100.00
Timid Little Sister, 394, trademark 6 . . . . 300.00
Wayside Harmony, 111/1, trademark 2 . . . . 160.00
What Now, 442, trademark 6 . . . . 100.00

HUMMEL LOOK-ALIKES

If imitation is the most sincere form of flattery, Berta Hummel and W. Goebel should feel especially honored. Goebel's Hummel figurines have been stylistically copied by ceramic manufacturers around the world.

A Hummel look-alike is a stylistic copy of a Goebel Hummel figurine or a completely new design done in an artistic style that mimics that of Berta Hummel. It does not require much of an alteration to avoid infringing on a design patent. These copycats come from a host of Japanese firms, Herbert Dubler (House of Ars Sacra), Erich Stauffer (Arnart Imports), Decorative Figures Corporation, Beswick, and Coventry Ware.

Reference: Lawrence L. Wonsch, *Hummel Copycats with Values,* Wallace-Homestead, 1987, 2nd printing by Bumblebee Press.

Adoration, Japan, 6½" h **$35.00**
Apple Tree Girl, Hong Kong, 4⅛" h 20.00
Baker, Lefton, 5¼" h 22.00
Band Master, Dubler 95.00
Big Game Hunter, Erich Stauffer, 5½" h 20.00
Boots, Japan, 5⅝" 25.00
Confidentially, Occupied Japan, 5½" h 18.00
Doctor, Occupied Japan, 5" h 65.00
Globe Trotter, Japan, 4⅞" h 25.00
Life On the Farm, Erich Stauffer, 4⅞" h 15.00
Little Hikers, Erich Stauffer, 5½" h 20.00
News Boy, Arnart, 4¼" h 18.00
Picnic, Arnart, 5" h 15.00
Pray Every Day, Erich Stauffer, 5½" h 18.00
Puppy Love, Japan, 5⅜" h 12.00
Rainy Days, Erich Stauffer, 4" h 16.00
Sandy Shoes, Arnart, 5½" h 18.00
School Days, Arnart, 4⅜" h 13.00
Spring Song Boy, Dubler 35.00
Stormy Weather, Coventry Ware, 6½" h 30.00
Summer Time, Erich Stauffer, 5½" h 15.00
To Market, Coventry Ware, 5⅜" h 20.00
Volunteers, 5⅛" h 15.00

AUCTION PRICES – HUMMEL FIGURINES

Ken Farmer Auctions & Estates, LLC, March 13, 1998.

A Fair Measure, 345, trademark 5 . . . . **$137.50**
Apple Tree Boy, 142V, trademark 5 . . . . 495.00
Apple Tree Girl, 141V, trademark 4 . . . . 495.00
Brother, 95, trademark 3 . . . . 99.00
Chicken Licken, 385, trademark 5 . . . . 121.00
Crossroads, #331, trademark 5 . . . . 176.00
Good Hunting, 307, trademark 3 . . . . 275.00
Goodnight, 214/C, trademark 7 . . . . 55.00
Happy Days, 150 2/0, trademark 3 . . . . 110.00
Knitting Lesson, 256, trademark 5 . . . . 154.00
Little Fiddler, 4, trademark 3 . . . . 110.00
Little Shopper, 96, trademark 5 . . . . 66.00
School Girls, 177/1, trademark 4 . . . . 467.50
Stitch In Time, 255, trademark 4 . . . . 143.00
Street Singer, 131, trademark 6 . . . . 77.00
Umbrella Girl, 152/0 B, trademark 6 . . . . 220.00
We Congratulate, 214/E, trademark 7 . . . . 82.50

Feeding Time, AH IH, Napco, 5¾" h, $15.00.

HUNTING

Hunting came into its own as a major collecting category in the 1980s. The initial focus was on hunting advertising and paper ephemera, e.g., books, calendars, and catalogs. Examples from firms such as DuPont, Peters Cartridge Company, Remington, and Winchester command premium prices.

Collectors also have identified a group of illustrators whose hunting scenes and images have become highly desirable. Look for works by G. Muss Arnolt, Phillip Goodwin, Lynn Bogue Hunt, and Edmund Osthaus. Beware of the limited edition hunting prints issued in the 1970s and 80s. The secondary market is volatile—more will decline than rise in value over the next decade.

Hunting licenses and ammunition boxes currently are two hot subcategories. Even some post-1945 decoys have joined the collectible ranks.

References: Ralf Coykendall, Jr., *Coykendall's Complete Guide to Sporting Collectibles,* Wallace-Homestead, Krause Publications, 1996; Henry A. Fleckenstein, Jr., *Decoys of the Mid-Atlantic Region, 2nd Edition,* Schiffer Publishing, 1998; Gene and Linda Kangas, *Collector's Guide to Decoys,* Wallace-Homestead, Krause Publications, 1992; Jim and Vivian Karsnitz, *Sporting Collectibles,* Schiffer Publishing, 1992; Carl F. Luckey, *Collecting Antique Bird and Duck Calls: An Identification and Value Guide, 2nd Edition,* Books Americana, Krause Publications, 1992; Bob and Beverly Strauss, *American Sporting Advertising, Volume 2,* L-W Book Sales, 1992; Donna Tonelli, *Top of the Line Hunting Collectibles,* Schiffer Publishing, 1998.

Periodical: *Sporting Collector's Monthly,* PO Box 305, Camden Wyoming, DE 19934.

Collectors' Clubs: Call & Whistle Collectors Assoc, 2839 E 26th Place, Tulsa, OK 74114; Callmakers & Collectors Assoc of America, 137 Kingswood Dr, Clarksville, TN 37043.

Ammunition, Maynard Carbine, 50 caliber cartridges,
blunt nose, brass cases, price for 6 . . . . **$72.00**
Ammunition Box, Nobel's Ballistite Cartridges, 12
gauge, BB shot size, 2³/₄" h, empty **18.00**
Ammunition Box, Remington, 310 Skeet, 12 gauge, 250
count box, white label with green print, empty **34.00**
Ammunition Box, Winchester Ranger Trap Load, 12
gauge, emtpy **70.00**
Book, *American Game Birds,* Edminster, Frank C, first ed,
1954. . . . . **10.00**
Book, *Chronicles of an African Trip,* Eastman, George,
Smith, Rochester, NY, 1927, 97 pp **25.00**
Booklet, *Score Book for Rifle Shooting,* U S Cartridge Co,
contains 50 individual score sheets **12.00**
Booklet, *Winchester Ammunition Booklet,* 112 pp,
1950, 5¹/₂ x 8". **14.00**
Catalog, Brownell, 167 pp, 1947. **3.00**
Catalog, J Stevens Arms Co, black and white, 24 pp,
illus, 1938, 8¹/₂ x 11". **28.00**
Catalog, Used Guns 1963, Abercrombie and Fitch,
16 pp, 1964, 8¹/₂ x 11" **8.00**
Cocktail Glasses, set of 6, clear, "Winchester" and gold
rider logo, Houze Art Glass CO, MIB **100.00**
Container, Revelation Gun Oil, tin, Western Auto Supply
Co, red, black, white, and yellow, 3 oz. **52.00**
Decoy, dove, hand carved, painted eyes, orig paint **40.00**

Ammunition Box, Peters High Velocity Rustless, 16 gauge, cardboard, with contents, $150.00. Photo courtesy Collectors Auction Services.

Duck Call, Herter's, walnut barrel, plastic stopper call,
4¹/₄" **20.00**
Duck Call, Kumduck, green plastic call, 5". **20.00**
Envelope, Marlin Rifles and Shotguns, hunter and dog in
top left corner, 1920s, 3³/₄ x 6¹/₂" **75.00**
Hunting License Button, New Jersey, Residents' License,
1939. . . . . **18.00**
Magazine, *Field and Stream,* 1955 . . . . **12.00**
Memo Pad, Winchester, red vinyl cover, gold emb logo,
3 x 3³/₄" **5.00**
Pinback Button, "Shoot Peters Shells," white, black, red,
and gold **80.00**
Poster, Western Winchester, rabbit and hunter in snow
scene, dated 1955 at bottom, 26 x 40" **600.00**
Shipping Crate, Winchester "Super Speed," #6 shot size,
20 gauge, wood, nailed construction, red and black
printing. **53.00**
Tin, Remington Gun Oil, red, black, and yellow, 3 oz. **35.00**
Trap, gopher, Crago. **200.00**

ICE CREAM COLLECTIBLES

The street ice cream vendor dates from the 1820s. In 1846 Nancy Johnson invented the hand-cranked ice cream freezer, a standard household fixture by the mid-1850s. The urban ice cream garden arrived on the scene in the middle of the 19th century.

The ice cream parlor was superseded by the drugstore soda fountain in the 1920s and 30s. Improvements in the freezer portions of refrigerators, the development of efficient grocery store freezers, and the spread of chain drugstores in the 1950s, 60s, and 70s slowly lessened the role of the local drugstore soda fountain.

Ice cream collectibles fall into two basic groups: (1) material from the dairy industry, and (2) ice cream and soda fountain items. Beware of reproductions, reputed "warehouse" finds, and fantasy items.

Reference: Wayne Smith, *Ice Cream Dippers,* published by author, 1986.

Collectors' Clubs: National Assoc of Soda Jerks, PO Box 115, Omaha, NE 68101; The Ice Screamers, PO Box 465, Warrington, PA 18976.

Sign, Neilson's Ice Cream, 1-sided diecut porcelain, 23" h, 36" w, $209.00. Photo courtesy Collectors Auction Services.

Can, Borden's Richer Malted Milk, metal, 8½" h, 6" d **$120.00**
Cone Holder, Heisey Glass, individual **50.00**
Decal, Mr Softee Ice Cream Safety Club **10.00**
Dish, glass, Borden Ice Cream, Elsie portrait **30.00**
Display, figural ice cream cone, "Eat-It-All," pink top,
　1950s, 17" h **100.00**
Display, figural ice cream cone, papier-mâché,
　1920–30s, 18" h **425.00**
Flange Sign, Hunt's Economy Ice Cream, 1940–50s, 9 x
　15" **150.00**
Glass, Breyers Ice Cream, ftd, green logo **5.00**
Globe, French Bauer Ice Cream, 13½" d **476.00**
Hot Fudge Dispenser, Boyd's, metal, porcelain int, elec-
　tric, 10" h, 7" d **220.00**
Ice Cream Cone Holder, glass jar with metal lid and
　holder, 14¼" h **467.00**
Milkshake Machine, Gilcrest, orig cup, c1926 . . . . **65.00**
Pin, Sparkle Ice Cream Dessert, aqua and white, hanger,
　c1940, 3½" d **22.00**
Pinback Button, Skippy Ice Cream, litho, red, white, and
　blue, 1930s, 1⅛" d **22.00**
Postcard, Carnation Ice Cream Store **10.00**
Scoop, Gilcrest, #31 . . . . **60.00**
Scoop, Gilcrest, #33 . . . . **50.00**
Scoop, No-Pak, metal, wood handle **60.00**
Sign, Crown Quality Ice Cream emb tin, 1930–40s, 20 x
　28" **325.00**
Sign, Gem City Ice Cream, metal, "Supreme Since
　1901," metal, 2-sided, 20 x 28" **130.00**
Sign, "Enjoy Ice Cream A Refreshing Healthful Treat,"
　diamond shaped, c1940–50s, 10" sq **250.00**
Sign, Johnston Hut Fudge, light-up, bullet shape, glass,
　tin frame, wood base, 1930–40s, 13½" h **1,100.00**
Sign, Pevely Ice Cream, porcelain, 2-sided, 1940s, 30 x
　36" **150.00**
Sign, Quality Dairy Ice Cream, porcelain, "We Serve
　Quality Dairy Ice Cream/None Better," 2-sided, cast-
　iron frame, 1940–50s, 42 x 36" **125.00**
Sign, Sealtest Ice Cream, "Fro-Joy," 2-sided, diecut
　porcelain, 1930–40s, 17 x 17" **275.00**
Sign, "Serve It and You Please All," porcelain, 1920s,
　18" d **525.00**

Sign, Wayne Dairy Ice Cream, porcelain, 2-sided,
　1940–50s, 15 x 20" **140.00**
Tray, Banquet Ice Cream, 10½ x 15" **20.00**
Tray, Elmira Ice Cream, "Cream Supreme," 1920s,
　12½" d **250.00**
Whistle, Dairy Queen, cone shape **15.00**

ILLUSTRATORS

The mass-market printing revolution of the late 19th century marked the advent of the professional illustrator. Illustrators provided artwork for books, calendars, magazines, prints, games, jigsaw puzzles, and a host of advertising and promotional products.

Illustrator art breaks down into three major categories: (1) original art, (2) first strike prints sold as art works, and (3) commercially produced art. While the first two categories are limited, the third is not. Often images were produced in the millions.

Magazines, more than any other medium, were responsible for introducing the illustrator to the general public. Norman Rockwell's covers for *Boy's Life* and *The Saturday Evening Post* are classics. Magazine covers remain one of the easiest and most inexpensive means of collecting illustrator art.

References: Clifford P. Catania, *Boudoir Art,* Schiffer Publishing, 1997; Karen Choppa, *Bessie Pease Gutman,* Schiffer Publishing, 1998; Patricia L. Gibson, *R. Atkinson Fox, William M. Thompson,* Collectors Press, 1995; William Holland, Clifford Catania and Nathan Isen, *Louis Icart: The Complete Etchings, Revised 3rd Edition,* Schiffer Publishing, 1998; Rick and Charlotte Martin, *Vintage Illustration: Discovering America's Calendar Artists, 1900–1960,* Collectors Press, 1997; Norman I. Platnick, *Coles Phillips: A Collector's Guide,* published by author, 1997; Tina Skinner, *Harrison Fisher,* Schiffer Publishing, 1999; Sarah Steiner and Donna Braun, *A Bit of [Frances] Brundage,* Schiffer Publishing, 1999; Jo Ann Havens Wright, *The Life and Art of William McMurray Thompson, American Illustrator…,* published by author, 1995.

Newsletters: *Calendar Art Collectors' Newsletter,* 45 Brown's Ln, Old Lyme, CT 06371; *The Illustrator Collector's News,* PO Box 1958, Sequim, WA 98382.

Collectors' Clubs: Arthur Szyk Society, 1294 Sao Paula Ave, Placentia, CA 92670; The Harrison Fisher Society, 123 N Glassell, Orange, CA 92666; Hy Hintemeister Collector's Group, 5 Pasture Rd, Whitehouse Station, NJ 08889.

Note: For additional listings see Nutting, Wallace; Parrish, Maxfield; Rockwell, Norman; and Children's Books, Kewpies, Pin-Up Art, Postcards and Prints.

Armstrong, Rolf, cabinet card, man with bicycle, "South
　Main St, Rockford, IL," 4¼ x 6½" **$50.00**
Barks, Carl, pencil on tissue, model sheet for comic
　book art, Huey, Louie, and Dewey, inscribed, matted,
　c1955, 7½ x 9½" **1,100.00**
Bralds, Braldt, magazine cover, *US News,* acrylic on
　board, crowd reaching up to bird, 14½ x 11" **250.00**
Brown, Ken, postcard, American Baseball series, green **10.00**
Cady, Harrison, book, *Lightfoot the Deer,* Thornton W
　Burgess author, Little, Brown & Co, 205 pp, first ed,
　1921 . . . . **95.00**

Coffin, Haskell, magazine cover, *Modern Priscilla*, Feb 1929. . . . . **10.00**

Coffin, Haskell, magazine cover, *The Farmer's Wife*, May 1927. . . . . **10.00**

Crandell, John Bradshaw, calendar print, The Gingham Girl, c1932, 9 x 5" **20.00**

Elsley, Arthur, calendar print, A Loyal Guardian, c1926, 12 x 9" **50.00**

Feiffer, Jules Munro, set of 116 drawings, blue and black pencil on storyboard sheets, unframed, 1960, 3 x 4 each. **2,500.00**

Flagg, James Montgomery, poster, "I Want You For The US Army," 27 x 40" **275.00**

Fox, Robert Atkinson, print, Edge of Grand Canyon, c1932, 8 x 10" **150.00**

Fuller, Arthur, calendar, 1920, Hercules Powder Co, A Surprise Party, 13 x 30" **125.00**

Goddard, L, calendar print, 'Neath the Tropic Moon, c1933, 9 x 7" **45.00**

Goodwin, Phillip R, calendar print, Taking the Trail, c1926, 8 x 6" **25.00**

Hall, H Tom, gouache, *Woman's Home Companion*, Aug 1947, sgd, woman and movie studio, 17 x 13¾". **100.00**

Harper, FR, calendar print, Ramona, c1930, 10 x 8". **25.00**

Herriman, George, pen and ink on board, Krazy Kat Daily, sgd, 1938, 4¼ x 20". **880.00**

Hiebel, Adelaide, calendar print, Sweet Baby O' Mine, c1931, 8 x 10" **30.00**

Hintermeister, Hy, calendar print, Bee Ware, c1944, 10 x 8" **10.00**

Humphrey, Maud, puzzle, Parker Bros, c1925, 15 pcs **30.00**

Humphrey, Walter Beach, calendar, 1932, Hercules Powder Co, Stowaways, 13 x 30" **175.00**

Kelly, Ken, painting, oil on board, cover painting for Creepy #6, sgd, 1975, 25 x 17" **770.00**

Kenyon, Zula, calendar print, My Bluebird, c1929, 12 x 9". **50.00**

Kettering, Charles, magazine cover, *Time*, Jan 9, 1933 . . . . . . **10.00**

Leyendecker, FX, magazine cover, *Life*, Jun 2, 1921 . . . . **65.00**

JC Leyendecker, blotter, 1941, $35.00.

Mauldin, Bill, pen, ink, and pencil on pebble paper, military men cartoon, sgd, 1942–45, 10 x 8" **1,320.00**

Nelson, Homer, calendar print, Rising Sun, c1930, 6 x 4". . . . **25.00**

Pressler, Gene, calendar print, Unmatched, c1927, 9 x 7". . . . **35.00**

Price, Garrett, watercolor, End of the Season, *The New Yorker*, 1950s, 11½ x 8¼" **750.00**

Thompson, William McMurray, calendar print, On the Wing, 1944, 12 x 6" **30.00**

Thorne, Diana, book, *Who Goes to the Wood*, Fay Inchfawn author, Winston, 1942, 229 pp **12.00**

Van Nortwick, Chester K, calendar print, Little Bo-Peep, c1927, 5 x 4" **25.00**

Walker, Robert Hollands, painting, A Breezy Day on the Mersey, watercolor and gouache on paperboard, framed, sgd, 7½ x 14½". **525.00**

Wilkinson, JW, blotter, Amoco, Uncle Sam, You Come First, Santa shaking hands with Uncle Sam, 5½ x 2¾". **10.00**

IMPERIAL GLASS

In 1901 a group of investors founded the Imperial Glass Company. Production began on January 13, 1904 and was mass-market directed, e.g., jelly glasses, tumblers, and tableware. Imperial's success was guaranteed by one of its first orders, approximately 20 different items to be supplied to almost 500 F. W. Woolworth stores. McCrory and Kresge were also major customers.

Between 1910 and 1920 Imperial introduced a number of new glassware lines. "Nuart" iridescent ware was followed by "Nucut" crystal, a pressed reproduction of English cut glass pieces which sold well as a premium and was widely distributed by The Grand Union Tea Company. In the 1950s, "Nucut" was reintroduced as "Collectors Crystal."

Imperial declared bankruptcy in 1931 but continued to operate through court-appointed receivers. Imperial Glass Corporation, a new entity, was formed during July and August of 1931. In 1937 Imperial launched Candlewick, its best selling line.

In 1940 Imperial acquired the Central Glass Works. It proved to be the first of a number of acquisitions, including A. H. Heisey and Company in 1958 and the Cambridge Glass Company in 1960.

In 1973, Imperial became a subsidiary of Lenox Glass Corporation. In 1981 Lenox sold the company to Arthur Lorch, a private investor, who in turn sold it to Robert Stahl, a liquidator, in 1982. In October 1982 Imperial declared bankruptcy. Consolidated-Colony, a partnership of Lancaster Colony Corporation and Consolidated International, purchased Imperial in December

Maude Fangel, store sign, adv for *The Ladies' Home Journal*, 1920s, 11 x 13", $40.00.

1984. Most of the company's molds were sold. Maroon Enterprises of Bridgeport, Ohio, purchased the buildings and property in March 1985.

References: Margaret and Douglas Archer, *Imperial Glass: 1904–1938 Catalog,* reprint, Collector Books, 1978, 1998 value update; National Imperial Glass Collectors' Society, *Imperial Glass Encyclopedia, Vol I: A – Cane* (1995), *Vol II: Cape Cod – L* (1998), Antique Publications; Harry L. Rinker, *Stemware of the 20th Century: The Top 200 Patterns,* House of Collectibles, 1997.

Collectors' Club: National Imperial Glass Collectors Society, PO Box 534, Bellaire, OH 43906.

Note: See Candlewick for additional listings.

Beaded Block, square plate, amber, 7³/₄" w, $10.00.

Animal, bulldog, clear	$35.00
Animal, tiger, jade green	18.00
Beaded Block, creamer, pink	16.00
Beaded Block, pickle dish, 2 handles, amber, 6¹/₂"	13.00
Beaded Block, plate, square, green, 7³/₄"	16.00
Beaded Block, sugar, amber	15.00
Cape Cod, basket, #160/73/0	350.00
Cape Cod, bowl, #160/125, divided, 11"	95.00
Cape Cod, bowl, #160/62B, handled, 7¹/₂"	28.00
Cape Cod, butter dish, cov, #160/144	32.00
Cape Cod, cake stand, #160/67D	40.00
Cape Cod, candle holders, pr, #160/80, 5"	40.00
Cape Cod, celery, #160/189	165.00
Cape Cod, center bowl, #160/75L	65.00
Cape Cod, coaster, #160/76, with rest	8.00
Cape Cod, comport, #160/54, 4¹/₄"	28.00
Cape Cod, cordial, #1602	10.00
Cape Cod, creamer and sugar, #160, ftd	35.00
Cape Cod, cruet, #160/119, 4 oz	28.00
Cape Cod, cupped plate, #1608V, 14"	50.00
Cape Cod, decanter, #160/163, 30 oz	62.00
Cape Cod, decanter, #160/212, 24 oz	72.00
Cape Cod, finger bowl, #1604-1/2A	14.00
Cape Cod, float bowl, 8"	100.00
Cape Cod, goblet, #160, 8 oz	10.00
Cape Cod, goblet, #1600, 10 oz	25.00
Cape Cod, goblet, #1602, 11 oz	10.00
Cape Cod, ice lip jug, #160/19, 40 oz	85.00
Cape Cod, juice tumbler, #1602, ftd	9.00
Cape Cod, marmalade, #160/89, 4 pc	45.00
Cape Cod, old fashioned tumbler, 7 oz	15.00
Cape Cod, pepper mill, #160/235	30.00
Cape Cod, pitcher, 160/24, 60 oz	98.00
Cape Cod, pitcher, #160/240, 16 oz	55.00
Cape Cod, punch cup, #160/37	5.00
Cape Cod, relish, #160/55, 3 part, oval	35.00
Cape Cod, relish, #160/102, 5 part, 11"	65.00
Cape Cod, salad plate, #160/5D, 8"	8.00
Cape Cod, shakers, pr, #160/116	20.00
Cape Cod, sherbet, #1602, low	6.00
Cape Cod, whiskey, #160, 21/2 oz.	15.00
Grape, flat tumbler, 4¹/₄"	15.00
Grape, plate, 10"	16.00
Jewels, plate, iridescent pale green, 8" d	48.00
Jewels, plate, white luster, 8" d	60.00
Lace Edge, sugar, cov, green opal	20.00
Monticello, cheese dish, cov	38.00
Mount Vernon, compote, 8"	25.00

Mount Vernon, cup and saucer	14.00
Mount Vernon, goblet, 10 oz	15.00
Mount Vernon, punch set, 15 pc	90.00
Mount Vernon, sherbet, 6¹/₂ oz.	12.00
Nuart, ashtray	20.00
Nuart, berry bowl, tab handles, 4¹/₂" d	18.00
Old Williamsburg, cake stand, 11"	40.00
Old Williamsburg, candlesticks, pr, 7¹/₂"	20.00
Old Williamsburg, candy dish, cov, ftd, 10"	55.00
Old Williamsburg, celery, 13"	25.00
Old Williamsburg, champagne, 4³/₄"	8.00
Old Williamsburg, claret	8.00
Old Williamsburg, cocktail	8.00
Old Williamsburg, compote, 4¹/₂"	15.00
Old Williamsburg, compote, 6"	20.00
Old Williamsburg, creamer and sugar, cov, handled	25.00
Old Williamsburg, creamer and sugar, open	15.00
Old Williamsburg, cruet, with stopper	15.00
Old Williamsburg, finger bowl, 4¹/₂"	7.50
Old Williamsburg, iced tea, flat	10.00
Old Williamsburg, juice, ftd	10.00
Old Williamsburg, nappy, 4"	10.00
Old Williamsburg, plate, 8"	6.00
Old Williamsburg, relish, 3 part, 10"	25.00
Old Williamsburg, salad bowl, 9"	35.00
Old Williamsburg, salt and pepper shakers, pr	12.00
Old Williamsburg, torte plate, 13"	17.00
Old Williamsburg, water goblet, 6³/₄"	8.00
Park Lane, cordial, amber	5.00
Park Lane, wine, amber	5.00
Twist, champagne, 4³/₈"	10.00
Twist, claret, 4⁷/₈"	14.00
Twist, cordial, 3⁵/₈"	10.00
Twist, cup, 2"	11.00
Twist, iced tea, flat	10.00
Twist, iced tea, ftd	11.00
Twist, juice, flat	7.00
Twist, parfait, 6¹/₄"	11.00
Twist, plate, 8³/₈"	10.00
Twist, sherbet	10.00
Twist, tumbler	8.00
Twist, water goblet, 6³/₈"	11.00
Twist, wine, 4¹/₂"	11.00

INSULATORS

The development of glass and ceramic insulators resulted from a need created by the telegraph. In 1844 Ezra Cornell obtained the first insulator patent. Armstrong (1938–69), Brookfield (1865–1922), California (1912–16), Gayner (1920–22), Hemingray (1871–1919), Lynchburg (1923–25), Maydwell (1935–40), McLaughlin (1923–25), and Whitall Tatum (1920–38) are the leading insulator manufacturers.

The first insulators did not contain threads. L. A. Cauvet patented a threaded insulator in the late 1860s. Drip points were added to insulators to prevent water from accumulating and creating a short. A double skirt kept the peg or pin free of moisture.

Insulators are collected by "CD" (consolidated design) numbers as found in N. R. Woodward's *The Glass Insulator in America*. The numbers are based upon the design style of the insulator. Color, name of maker, or lettering are not factors in assigning numbers. Thus far over 500 different design styles have been identified.

References: John and Carol McDougald, *Insulators: A History and Guide to North American Glass Pintype Insulators, Volume 1* (1990), *Volume 2* (1990), *Price Guide* (1995), published by authors; Marion and Evelyn Milholland, *Glass Insulator Reference Book, 4th Revision,* published by authors, 1976, available from C. D. Walsh (granddaughter).

Periodical: *Crown Jewels of the Wire,* PO Box 1003, St Charles, IL 60174.

Collectors' Club: National Insulator Assoc, 1315 Old Mill Path, Broadview Heights, OH 44147.

Note: Insulators are in near mint/mint condition unless otherwise noted.

CD145, HG Co, honey amber, $500.00.

CD 106, no name, grayish tint	$12.00
CD 112, SBT&T Co, aqua	25.00
CD 121, Lynchburg, aqua	10.00
CD 122, Armstrong No 2, off-clear, smooth base	3.50
CD 122, Hemingray-16, clear, smooth base	3.00
CD 122, Whitall Tatum, clear, smooth base	2.50
CD 125, Hemingray/WU #5, aqua	6.00
CD 126, W Brookfield, 55 Fulton St, 3 patent dates, light blue	5.00
CD 126, W Brookfield, NY, aqua	5.00
CD 126, WUT, patent date below wire groove on rear, light aqua	15.00
CD 127, WUT, aqua	7.00
CD 128, Hemingray-42, smooth base, blue	25.00
CD 128, Pyrex, short variation	12.00
CD 129, Armstrong, clear	3.00
CD 134, KCGW, Fairmount, greenish aqua	10.00
CD 138.2, National Insulator Co, blue aqua with milky swirled impurities through skirt and into dome	300.00
CD 145, B, aqua with amber streaks	4.00
CD 145, no name, bubbly aqua	20.00
CD 145, Postal, blue aqua	4.00
CD 145, Postal, green aqua	4.00
CD 154, ESA, deep green	12.00
CD 154, Lynchburg, dark smoky straw	20.00
CD 154, no name (Lynchburg Product), dark smoky straw	75.00
CD 154, Whitall Tatum, peach	5.00
CD 154, Whitall Tatum, pink	12.00
CD 154, Whitall Tatum, purple	22.00
CD 160, Armstrong's, clear	10.00
CD 160, Lynchburg, light aqua	15.00
CD 162, Hemingray/Patented, aqua	12.00
CD 162, star, yellow green	12.00
CD 168, Hemingray D-150, carnival	20.00
CD 170.1, unemb Pennycuick, blue aqua with bubbles	200.00
CD 201, Hemingray No 2 Transposition, HG blot out, blue aqua	5.00
CD 210, Postal, dark aqua	3.00
CD 218, Hemingray-660, clear	4.00
CD 231, Kimble, clear	4.00
CD 231.2, Kimble 820, clear	4.00
CD 238, Hemingray D-514, clear	4.00
CD 239, Kimble 830, light straw	4.00
CD 252, ESS Co, aqua	125.00
CD 252, No 2 Cable, green	20.00
CD 260, star, light green with amber streaks in ears	225.00
CD 287, Locke, No 15, aqua	7.00

IRONS

The modern iron resulted from a series of technological advances that began in the middle of the 19th century. Until the arrival of the electric iron at the beginning of the 20th century, irons were heated by pre-heating a slug put into the iron, burning solid or liquid fuels or by drawing heat from a heated surface such as a stove top.

Pre-electric irons from the late 19th and early 20th centuries are common. Do not overpay. High prices are reserved for novelty irons and irons from lesser known makers.

H. W. Seeley patented the first electric iron in 1882. The first iron, a General Electric with a detachable cord, dates from 1903. Westinghouse introduced the automatic iron in 1924 and Edec the steam iron in 1926. Electric irons are collected more for their body design than their historical importance or age. Check the cord and plug before attempting to use any electric iron.

References: David Irons, *Irons By Irons,* published by author, 1994; David Irons, *More Irons By Irons,* published by author, 1997.

Newsletter: *Iron Talk,* PO Box 68, Waelder, TX 78959.

Williams Corp., Eureka Cordless Automatic, shoe is electric outlet, c1950, $18.00.

Automatic Cordless, electric, 2-iron set with double
   stand, c1930 .... **$25.00**
Bylock Victor Safety Iron, weighted heel, c1950 .... **35.00**
Chicago Flexible Shaft Co (Sunbeam), The Domestic,
   electric, c1920 .... **18.00**
Coleman, Model 38, electric, c1935 .... **12.00**
Duvall Appliance Corp, electric, cordless, c1930 .... **15.00**
Edison Electric, Hotpoint Super-Automatic, electric,
   Calrod heating element, c1930 .... **22.00**
Fada, Wireless Iron, electric contact in trivet, c1930 .... **24.00**
General Electric, Chief Steam Iron, Steemco Model 500,
   aluminum body, AC/DC, c1930 .... **12.00**
General Electric, Hotpoint Special Model, electric,
   adjustable voltage, detachable cord, 1935–36 .... **25.00**
General Electric, Hotpoint Utility Iron, travel, electric,
   with high stand and metal storage box, c1920 .... **18.00**
General Electric, Moderne, electric, AC, 115-125 volts,
   streamline body, 1935–36 .... **20.00**
General Mills Home Appliances, Tru-Heat, electric,
   1948 .... **32.00**
Knapp-Monarch Co, electric, no thermostat, 1936 .... **15.00**
Knapp-Monarch Co, K/M Flatwork ironer, round iron,
   heat indicator, c1930, 6⅛" d **38.00**
Landers, Frary & Clark, Universal, electric, 1925 .... **28.00**
Montgomery Ward, Model No 94, lift top to add water,
   c1940 .... **25.00**
Montgomery Ward, red enamel top and handle, c1930 ...... **22.00**
No Cord Electric Appliance Co, No Cord Electric Iron,
   1922 .... **20.00**
Proctor Electric Co, Windsor Never-Lift, red plastic
   steam attachment, c1950 .... **28.00**
Proctor & Schwartz Electric Co, Never Lift Speed Iron,
   electric, spring-loaded pop-up stand, 1941 .... **25.00**
Proctor & Schwartz Electric Co, Snap-Stand Speed Iron,
   electric, 1935 .... **30.00**
Quality Appliance Co, Quality Iron, white enamel, with
   trivet, c1930 .... **20.00**
Rival Mfg Co, Steam-O-Matic, lift top to add water,
   c1940 .... **18.00**
Sunbeam, electric, metal storage box, c1925 .... **32.00**
Sunbeam, Ironmaster, electric, automatic, chrome finish,
   1940s **30.00**
Westinghouse, Automatic Type-LA-6, electric, c1925 .... **15.00**

JEANNETTE GLASS

The Jeannette Glass Company, Jeannette, Pennsylvania, was founded in 1898. Its first products were glass jars, headlight lenses, and glass brick, known as sidewalk tile. The company supplied glass candy containers to other firms during the 1920s.

Jeannette introduced pressed table and kitchenware in the 1920s. Popular Depression-era patterns include Adam (1932–34), Cherry Blossom (1930–39), Cube (1929–33), Doric (1935–38), Doric and Pansy (1937–38), Hex Optic (1928–32), Homespun (1939–49), Iris and Herringbone (1928–32, 1950s, and 1970s), Swirl (1937–38), and Windsor (1936–46).

The company continued to thrive in the post–World War II era. Anniversary (1947–49, late 1960s to mid-1970s), Floragold (1950s), Harp (1954–1957), Holiday (1947 through mid-1950s), and Shell Pink Milk Glass (1957–1959) were among the most popular patterns. The popularity of Iris was so strong it easily made the transition from pre-war to post-war pattern.

In 1952 Jeannette purchased the McKee Glass Corporation, enabling the company to expand into the production of heat resistant and industrial glass.

The Jeannette Glass Company ceased operations in the mid-1980s.

Note: For additional listings see Depression Glass and Kitchen Glassware.

Adam, grill plate **$22.00**
Adam, iced tea, green **57.50**
Adam, plate, 8" d, pink **15.00**
Adam, sherbet, pink **30.00**
Adam, tumbler, 4½" h, green **28.00**
Cherry Blossom, bowl, 3 ftd, pink **107.00**
Cherry Blossom, bread and butter plate, 6" d, pink **10.00**
Cherry Blossom, cake plate, pink **32.00**
Cherry Blossom, cereal bowl, 5¾" d, pink **50.00**
Cherry Blossom, coaster, green **14.00**
Cherry Blossom, cup and saucer, pink **29.00**
Cherry Blossom, fruit bowl, 3 ftd, 10½", pink **95.00**
Cherry Blossom, grill plate, 9" d, pink **30.00**
Cherry Blossom, juice tumbler, ftd, pink **19.00**
Cherry Blossom, platter, 13" l, pink **70.00**
Cherry Blossom, salad plate, 7" d, green **24.00**
Cherry Blossom, saucer, pink **6.00**
Cherry Blossom, sherbet, ftd, green **20.00**
Cherry Blossom, tumbler, green **35.00**
Cherry Blossom, vegetable bowl, oval, pink **48.00**

Cherry Blossom, covered sugar and creamer, pink, $50.00.

Cube, bowl, 4¹/₂" d, pink, $8.00.

Cube, candy jar, cov, 6¹/₂" h, pink 27.50
Cube, cup and saucer, pink 10.50
Cube, salt and pepper shakers, pr, green 35.00
Cube, tumbler, 4" h, 9 oz, green 65.00
Cube, tumbler, 4" h, 9 oz, pink 60.00
Doric, bowl, 4¹/₂" d, green 11.00
Doric, creamer, green 17.00
Doric, salt and pepper shakers, pr, pink 35.00
Doric, sugar, cov, green 40.00
Floragold, bowl, 4¹/₂" sq, iridescent 7.00
Floragold, butter, cov, iridescent 45.00
Floragold, candy dish, cov, iridescent 52.50
Floragold, creamer, iridescent 8.00
Floragold, cup and saucer, iridescent 18.00
Floragold, deep bowl, 9¹/₂" d, iridescent 45.00
Floragold, dinner plate, 8¹/₂" d 40.00
Floragold, pitcher, 64 oz, iridescent 45.00
Floragold, tumbler, 10 oz, ftd, iridescent 12.50
Floragold, tumbler, 11 oz, iridescent 30.00
Floral, bread and butter plate, 6" d, pink 10.00
Floral, butter, cov, pink 125.00
Floral, coaster, green 11.00
Floral, coaster, pink 16.00
Floral, creamer, green 24.00
Floral, cup and saucer, pink 24.00
Floral, pitcher, ftd, 32 oz, pink 50.00
Floral, relish dish, pink 18.00
Floral, salt and pepper shakers, pr, ftd, pink 45.00
Floral, saucer, pink 13.00
Floral, shaker, pink 24.00
Floral, sherbet, pink 19.00
Floral, sugar, cov, pink 15.00
Floral, sugar, open, pink 8.00
Floral, tumbler, pink 23.00
Floral, vegetable bowl, cov, pink 47.00
Iris, butter, cov, iridescent 45.00
Iris, candlesticks, pr, crystal 50.00
Iris, cereal bowl, 5" d, crystal 125.00
Iris, cocktail, 4¹/₂" h, 4 oz, crystal 28.00
Iris, creamer and sugar, cov, crystal 37.00
Iris, cup and saucer, crystal 27.00
Iris, cup and saucer, iridescent 25.00
Iris, dinner plate, 9" d, crystal 65.00
Iris, fruit bowl, 11", crystal 62.50
Iris, goblet, crystal 30.00
Iris, pitcher, 9¹/₂" h, crystal 37.50

Iris, sherbet, ftd, 2¹/₂", iridescent 15.00
Iris, sherbet, ftd, 4" h, crystal 25.00
Iris, soup bowl, 7¹/₂", iridescent 60.00
Iris, sugar, cov, crystal 23.00
Iris, sugar, cov, iridescent 23.00
Iris, tumbler, 6¹/₂" h, crystal 35.00
Iris, vase, iridescent 25.00
Iris, wine, 4" h, iridescent 22.00
Iris, wine, 5¹/₂" h, 3 oz, crystal 17.00
Jennyware, measuring cup, ¹/₄ size, ultramarine 70.00
Swirl, bowl, 4⁷/₈" d, pink 7.00
Swirl, bowl, 7¹/₄" d, pink 35.00
Swirl, bowl, ftd, closed handle, 10", ultramarine 37.00
Swirl, cereal bowl, 5¹/₂" d, ultramarine 20.00
Swirl, creamer and sugar, ultramarine 32.00
Swirl, cup, ultramarine 16.00
Swirl, cup and saucer, ivory 5.50
Swirl, dinner plate, ivory 4.50
Swirl, salad bowl, ftd, 9", ultramarine 30.00

JEWELRY

Jewelry divides into two basic groups: precious and non-precious (a.k.a., costume after 1920). This category focuses on precious jewelry. While collected, most precious jewelry is purchased to be worn or studied.

U.S. custom laws define antique jewelry as jewelry over one hundred years old. Estate or Heirloom jewelry is generally assumed to be over twenty-five years old.

Craftsmanship, aesthetic design, scarcity, and current market worth of gemstones and the precious metal are the principal value keys. Antique and period jewelry should be set with the cut of stone prevalent at the time the piece was made. Names (manufacturer, designer, or both) also play a major role in value.

Be extremely cautious when buying jewelry. Reproductions, copycats (stylistic reproductions), fantasies (non-period shapes and forms), and fakes abound. Also be alert for married and divorced pieces.

References: Lillian Baker, *Art Nouveau & Art Deco Jewelry*, Collector Books, 1981, 1997 value update; Howard L. Bell, Jr., *Cuff Jewelry: A Historical Account for Collectors and Antique Dealers*, published by author, 1994; Jeanenne Bell, *Answers to Questions About 1840–1950 Old Jewelry, Fourth Edition*, Books Americana, Krause Publications, 1996; Monica Lynn Clements and Patricia Rosser Clements, *Cameos: Classical to Costume*, Schiffer Publishing, 1998.

Arthur Guy Kaplan, *The Official Identification and Price Guide to Antique Jewelry, Sixth Edition*, House of Collectibles, 1990, reprinted 1994; Penny Chittim Morrill and Carol A. Beck, *Mexican Silver: 20th-Century Handwrought Jewelry and Metalwork, Revised 2nd Edition*, Schiffer Publishing, 1998; Dorothy T. Rainwater, *American Jewelry Manufacturers*, Schiffer Publishing, 1988; Christie Romero, *Warman's Jewelry, 2nd Edition*, Krause Publications, 1998; Nancy N. Schiffer, *Silver Jewelry Treasures*, Schiffer Publishing, 1993; Sheryl Gross Shatz, *What's It Made Of?: A Jewelry Materials Identification Guide, Third Edition*, published by author, 1996; Doris J. Snell, *Antique Jewelry With Prices, Second Edition*, Krause Publications, 1997.

Periodicals: *Gems & Gemology*, Gemological Inst of America, 5355 Armada Dr, PO Box 9022, Carlsbad, CA 92008; *Jewelers'*

Circular Keystone/Heritage, 201 King of Prussia Rd, Wayne, PA 19089.

Collectors' Clubs: American Society of Jewelry Historians, Box 103, 1B, Quaker Ridge Rd, New Rochelle, NY 10804; National Cuff Link Society, PO Box 5700, Vernon Hills, IL 60061; Society of Antique & Estate Jewelry, Ltd, 570 Seventh Ave, Ste 1900, New York, NY 10018.

Belt Buckle, Hecktor Agilar, sterling silver layered scales, stamped "Made in Mexico, sterling, HA," 2³/₄ x 6¹/₂" **$50.00**

Bracelet, 14K yellow gold square links, 7" l, 27.1 dwt. . . . **550.00**

Bracelet, eliptical shape, hammered 18K yellow gold **175.00**

Bracelet, hinged bar links alternately set with round diamonds and channel-set baguette-cut sapphires, 14K yellow and white gold, stamped "BH" **500.00**

Bracelet, ropetwist, 18K yellow gold chain twisted with thinner rhodium plated 18K gold chain, 7¹/₂" l, 25.3 dwt **1,050.00**

Bracelet, snake form, flexible coiled design, 18K yellow gold with ruby eyes, 62.5 dwt **1,000.00**

Brooch, 3 oval 14K bicolor gold links, c1940s, 8.7 dwt **375.00**

Brooch, cat, body designed with prong-set round rubies, twisted 18K yellow gold wire face and tail, 1 eye winking, other prong-set round emerald, sgd "Tiffany & Co" **2,500.00**

Brooch, Georg Jensen, hammered sterling silver stylized bell flowers inset with lapis lazuli cabochon, mkd "JG, Denmark, 930S," 1¹/₄ x 1" **275.00**

Brooch, horse and carriage, 14K bicolor gold, carriage holding spray of prong-set colored gemstones, articulated wheels, c1945 . . . . **575.00**

Brooch, Rebajes, cat shape, imp "Rebajes, sterling" **55.00**

Brooch, silver, brass, copper, ivory, coral, and ebony abstract form, Peter Macchiarini, stamped "Macchiarini" **875.00**

Brooch and Earrings, attributed to Mary Gage, sterling silver foliate design around woman's portrait, 2" d brooch, 1" w earrings. **230.00**

Cuff Links, poodles, 14K yellow gold with blue stone eyes, sgd "Ruser," 10.3 dwt **500.00**

Earrings, owls, 18K yellow gold set with sapphire eyes, wiretwist and engraved bodies, English hallmarks, sgd "Cartier," c1963 . . . . **2,500.00**

Necklace, Kalo, 14K yellow gold foliate design around abalone and freshwater pearl pendant, imp "Kalo," 9¹/₄" l **3,165.00**

Necklace, sixty-two 14K yellow gold beads, 15" l, 9.4 dwt **425.00**

Necklace, strand of 53 cultured pearls measuring approx. 7.7 mm, ruby and diamond flowerhead clasp set in 14K yellow gold **2,175.00**

Pendant, sterling silver abstract form centered by tumbled green tourmaline, sliver curb-link chain, pendant sgd Ed Wiener," c1950s, 19" l **450.00**

Pendants, collet-set Biwa baroque pearls with cluster of green jade beads in 18K yellow gold caged detachable pendants, intended to be worn together, sgd "Janiye," c1969–72 . . . . **1,150.00**

Pin, Arts & Crafts, sterling silver grape design around semi-precious design, ¹/₂" h, 2" l **175.00**

Pin, Coro Duette, parrots, pavé rhinestone bodies, blue enamel wings, pastel flowers, sgd, c1930s **150.00**

Pin, fox, textured 18K yellow gold boey, marquise-cut sapphire eyes, 8.8 dwt **300.00**

Pin, mink form, textured 14K yellow gold mink with sapphire eye, standing on 3 baroque pearls, sgd "Rotter," 8.5 dwt **250.00**

Pins, pr, Chanel, enameled, flower shapes, one is lavender and bright green, other is powder blue and green, script signature **350.00**

Ring, Arts & Crafts, sterling silver foliate design around lapis lazuli and freshwater pearls, 1" l **175.00**

Ring, center rectangular prong-set step-cut aquamarine measuring approx 18.61 x 14.44 x 10.68 mm, flanked by two epaulettes containing 42 bead-set single-cut diamonds, platinum mount, c1940, approx 0.53 cts total wt **2,550.00**

Suite, bracelet, pin, and earrings, Arts & Crafts, sterling silver leaf, mkd "T.N.," 6¹/₄" w pin, 2" w earrings. **175.00**

Suite, brooch and earrings, grapevine motif, brooch set with coral, matching coral grape cluster earrings, 14K yellow gold mounts, 1¹/₂" l brooch **300.00**

JEWELRY, COSTUME

Prior to World War I, non-precious jewelry consisted of inexpensive copies of precious jewelry. This changed in the 1920s when Coco Chanel advocated the wearing of faux jewelry as an acceptable part of haute couture. High-style fashion jewelry continued to exercise a strong influence on costume jewelry until the middle of the 20th century.

During the 1930s costume jewelry manufacture benefited from developments such as more efficient casting machines and the creation of Bakelite, one of the first entirely synthetic plastics. Material shortages during World War II promoted the increased use of ceramics and wood. Copper, plastic novelty, and rhinestone crazes marked the 1950s and 60s.

Because of this category's breadth, collectors and dealers focus on named manufacturers and designers. A maker's mark is not a guarantee of quality. Examine pieces objectively. This is a very trendy category. What is in today may be out tomorrow. Just ask anyone who collected rhinestone jewelry in the early 1980s.

Bracelet, woven 14K yellow gold wire studded with 8 diamond-set flowerheads, mounted in platinum, 46.5 dwt., $920.00. Photo courtesy Skinner, Inc., Boston, MA.

References: Lillian Baker, *Fifty Years of Collectible Fashion Jewelry: 1925–1975,* Collector Books, 1986, 1997 value update; Lillian Baker, *100 Years of Collectible Jewelry, 1850–1950,* Collector Books, 1978, 1997 value update; Lillian Baker, *Twentieth-Century Fashionable Plastic Jewelry,* Collector Books, 1992, 1996 value update; Joanne Dubbs Ball, *Costume Jewelers, Second Edition,* Schiffer Publishing, 1997; Dee Battle and Alayne Lesser, *The Best Bakelite and Other Plastic Jewelry,* Schiffer Publishing, 1996; Vivienne Becker, *Fabulous Costume Jewelry,* Schiffer Publishing, 1993; Jeanenne Bell, *Answers to Questions About Old Jewelry, 1840–1950, Fourth Edition,* Books Americana, Krause Publications, 1996; Matthew L. Burkholz and Linda Lictenberg Kaplan, *Copper Art Jewelry,* Schiffer Publishing, 1992.

Deanna Farneti Cera, Costume Jewelery, Antique Collectors' Club, 1997; Monica L. Clements and Patricia Rosser Clements, *Avon Collectible Fashion Jewelry and Awards,* Schiffer Publishing, 1998; Monica L. Clements and Patricia Clements, *Sarah Coventry Jewelry,* Schiffer Publishing, 1999; Maryanne Dolan, *Collecting Rhinestone Jewelry, 4th Edition,* Krause Publications, 1998; Roseann Ettinger, *Forties & Fifties Popular Jewelry,* Schiffer Publishing, 1994; Roseann Ettinger, *Popular Jewelry: 1840–1940, Second Edition,* Schiffer Publishing, 1997; Roseann Ettinger, *Popular Jewelry of the '60s, '70s & '80s,* Schiffer Publishing, 1997; Sandy Fichtner and Lynn Ann Russell, *Rainbow of Rhinestone Jewelry,* Schiffer Publishing, 1996.

Jill Gallina, *Christmas Pins,* Collector Books, 1996; S. Sylvia Henzel, *Collectible Costume Jewelry, Third Edition,* Krause Publications, 1997; Mary Jo Izard, *Wooden Jewelry and Novelties,* Schiffer Publishing, 1998; Sibylle Jargstorf, *Glass in Jewelry, Revised 2nd Edition,* Schiffer Publishing, 1998; Lyngerda Kelley and Nancy Schiffer, *Costume Jewelry, Revised 3rd Edition,* Schiffer Publishing, 1998; Lyngerda Kelley and Nancy Schiffer, *Plastic Jewelry, Third Edition,* Schiffer Publishing, 1996; J. L. Lynnlee, *All That Glitters,* Schiffer Publishing, 1986, 1996 value update; Mary Morrison, *Christmas Jewelry,* Schiffer Publishing, 1999; Fred Rezazadeh, *Costume Jewelry,* Collector Books, 1998.

Christie Romero, *Warman's Jewelry, 2nd Edition,* Krause Publications, 1998; Nancy N. Schiffer, *Costume Jewelry,* Schiffer Publishing, 1988, 1996 value update; Nancy N. Schiffer, *Rhinestones!, 2nd Edition,* Schiffer Publishing, 1997; Cherri Simonds, *Collectible Costume Jewelry,* Collector Books, 1997; Harrice Simons Miller, *Costume Jewelry, Second Edition,* Avon Books, 1994; Sheryl Gross Shatz, *What's It Made Of?: A Jewelry Materials Identification Guide,* published by author, 1991; Nicholas D. Snider, *Sweetheart Jewelry and Collectibles,* Schiffer Publishing, 1995; Donna Wassestrom and Leslie Piña, *Bakelite Jewelry,* Schiffer Publishing, 1997.

Collectors' Club: Vintage Fashion & Costume Jewelry Club, PO Box 265, Glen Oaks, NY 11004.

Bangle Bracelet, plastic, lemon yellow, Monet **$28.00**
Bracelet, Bakelite, yellow and green, relief designs of
  leaves and flowers, 3" d **20.00**
Bracelet, black coral, silver toned detailing on side, 3" d **20.00**
Bracelet, gold toned chain link, Monet **8.00**
Bracelet, Lucite and rhinestones, mottled opaque and
  translucent white, c1950 . . . . **70.00**
Brooch, brass, enamel, convex-sided rect plaque, cloi-
  sonné enameled design, overlapping vasiform shapes
  in shades of periwinkle blue, purple, and pink on red
  ground, counter-enameled reverse, c1950 . . . . **160.00**

Tiara, rhinestone, adjustable band, $100.00.

Brooch, gold toned metal, Art Deco, 3 inset stones **75.00**
Brooch, gold toned metal, Art Deco, large faceted light
  blue glass stone set at center, 2 round deep blue
  stones set at each side, dangling figural bee at bottom
  with deep blue glass bead set at bottom and red
  faceted stone set at head, 2½ x 2½" **60.00**
Brooch, gold toned metal, Art Nouveau, intricate floral
  design down center, amber colored glass stone set at
  center, 2 red glass stones set in heart shaped design at
  ends, 2¾ x 1" **70.00**
Brooch, gold toned metal, figural flower with stem, faux
  pearl at center, Miriam Haskell, 2" l **20.00**
Brooch, rhodium plated, abstract cushion design with
  clear chaton-cut rhinestones, Sarah Coventry **55.00**
Brooch, silver toned metal, figural leaf, Trifari **25.00**
Charm, 14K gold, figural frog **20.00**
Charm, polished finish, figural Derringer pistol, Japan,
  1½" l **20.00**
Choker, 8-strand string strung pearls, silver toned
  "Goldette" fastener, 4½" d **40.00**
Clip, rhodium plated white metal, 5 petaled flower,
  enamel, small rhinestone accents, Trifari, c1940 . . . . **125.00**
Cuff Links, pr, iridescent stones in center, Swank **10.00**
Cuff Links, pr, mother-of-pearl, 5" d **20.00**
Dress Clip, Czechoslovakian, Egyptian Revival, molded
  in sphinx shape, green glass with painted orange
  accents, set in flat-backed gold plated bezel, engraved
  flat-back hinged clip on reverse, c1930 . . . . **65.00**
Earrings, pr, amber colored translucent stones, clip-on **20.00**
Earrings, pr, circular domed red enamel disk with
  applied copper dome at bottom and applied copper
  wires at top forming abstract eye, clip-on, Matisse,
  ¾" d **20.00**
Earrings, pr, gold finish, suspended yellow and orange
  faceted disks, clip-on **20.00**
Earrings, pr, round glass beads, amber, pink, and green,
  clip-on **10.00**
Earrings, pr, thermoset plastic, light blue plastic convex
  oval disks, oval aurora borealis and colorless rhine-
  stones, clip-on, mkd "Weiss," c1955 . . . . **60.00**
Headband, blue celluloid cylindrical band set with blue
  rhinestones overlapping with ivory colored flowerhead shaped adjustable clasp set with blue rhinestones and ovoid pearlescent white tips, clasp mkd
  "pat apld for," c1920 . . . . **180.00**

Necklace, black glass faceted beads, Miriam Haskell, c1950, 60" l 80.00

Necklace, clear and black glass strung beads, screw-barrel closure, 20" l 20.00

Necklace, pink glass, adjustable choker with prong-set links, hook and chain closure, attached metal tag mkd "Vendome," c1950 . . . . 155.00

Necklace, prong mounted rhinestones with 7 faceted rhinestones, hook style fastener, 15" l 20.00

Necklace, strung ivory beads, screw type carved fastener, 6" d 20.00

Necklace, strung red beads, Japan, 5" l 20.00

Pendant, large green stone surrounded by clear rhinestone leaflets, Sarah Coventry. 25.00

Pin, Bakelite, 3 flowers, yellow-green, hinged metal clip on back, 1³/₄" l 20.00

Pin, Bakelite, carved horse, brownish red, dangling horseshoe and cowboys, gold painted bridle, yellow eyes with black pupils, 2¹/₂ x 2³/₄". 175.00

Pin, figural eagle, Lucite, green and white body, amber colored wings, MIB 50.00

Pin, rhodium plated, Art Deco, glued-in clear rhinestone accents, 4 black plastic cabochon, 5 triangular dangles with clear rhinestones, Sarah Coventry, 2¹/₄ x 3¹/₄" 65.00

Ring, Bakelite, marbled blue-green tapered dome, laminated black dot center, c1940 . . . . 60.00

Ring, clear lucite, c1950 . . . . 45.00

Ring, plastic, faux ivory on gold plated white metal, mkd "KJL," 1970s 75.00

Ring, turquoise and silver, oval stone, size 6. . . . . 20.00

Stickpin, SS, figural wolf's head, 2³/₄" l 20.00

Suite, hinged bangle and earrings, pr, wraparound gold plated foliate motif terminating in pr of pear shaped faux pearls, matching ear clips, Tortolani, c1960. . . . . 70.00

Sweater Guard, rhinestone 30.00

Tie Bar, figural fish, silver toned, Anson, 2" l 20.00

Watch Pin, gold plated brass, figural winged griffin, bezel-set with circular peacock eye glass cab, red glass eye, C-catch, upturned hook on reverse, 1 x 1". 85.00

JOHNSON BROTHERS

In 1883 three brothers, Alfred, Frederick, and Henry Johnson, purchased the bankrupt J. W. Pankhurst Company, a tableware manufactory in Hanley, Staffordshire, England and established Johnson Brothers. Although begun on a small scale, the company prospered and expanded.

In 1896, Robert, a fourth brother, joined the firm. Robert, who lived and worked in the United States, was assigned the task of expanding the company's position in the American market. By 1914 Johnson Brothers owned and operated five additional factories scattered throughout Hanley, Tunstall, and Burslem.

Johnson Brothers continued to grow throughout the 1960s with acquisitions of tableware manufacturing plants in Hamilton, Ontario, Canada, and Croydon, Australia. Two additional English plants were acquired in 1960 and 1965.

Johnson Brothers became part of the Wedgwood Group in 1968.

References: Mary J. Finegan, *Johnson Brothers Dinnerware: Pattern Directory & Price Guide,* published by author, 1993; Harry L. Rinker, *Dinnerware of the 20th Century: The Top 500 Patterns,* House of Collectibles, 1997.

Coaching Scenes, blue, cup and saucer, $15.00.

Athena, butter, cov, ¹/₄ lb $30.00
Athena, cereal bowl, coupe, 6¹/₂" d 7.00
Athena, dinner plate, 10" d 12.00
Athena, fruit bowl, 5¹/₄" d 7.00
Athena, soup bowl, coupe, 7³/₈" d 10.00
Coaching Scenes, bread and butter plate, 6¹/₄" d . . 6.00
Coaching Scenes, cereal bowl, coupe, 6" d 12.00
Coaching Scenes, dinner plate, 9⁷/₈" d 15.00
Coaching Scenes, fruit bowl, 5¹/₈" d 8.50
Coaching Scenes, gravy boat with underplate. 45.00
Coaching Scenes, salad plate, 7⁷/₈" d 8.50
Coaching Scenes, sugar, cov 25.00
Friendly Village, bread and butter plate 5.00
Friendly Village, cereal bowl, square 10.00
Friendly Village, creamer 15.00
Friendly Village, dinner plate 10.00
Friendly Village, fruit bowl. 6.00
Friendly Village, salad plate, square 15.00
Friendly Village, salt and pepper shakers, pr 25.00
Friendly Village, sugar 20.00
Friendly Village, teapot 90.00
Friendly Village, vegetable bowl, oval 25.00
Friendly Village, vegetable bowl, round 20.00
His Majesty, cup and saucer 22.50
His Majesty, dessert bowl, square. 18.00
His Majesty, dinner plate. 20.00
His Majesty, gravy boat with underplate. 75.00
His Majesty, turkey platter 295.00
Merry Christmas, coaster 20.00
Merry Christmas, creamer 30.00
Merry Christmas, cup and saucer, flat, 2³/₈" h 16.00
Merry Christmas, dinner plate, 10⁵/₈" d. 14.00
Merry Christmas, sugar, cov. 16.00
Merry Christmas, vegetable, 8¹/₄" d. 30.00
Old Britain Castles, bread and butter plate, 6¹/₄" d 8.00
Old Britain Castles, butter, cov, ¹/₄ lb 45.00
Old Britain Castles, dinner plate, 10"d 12.00
Old Britain Castles, fruit bowl, 5¹/₈" d. 6.00
Old Britain Castles, platter, 11³/₄" l 36.00
Old Britain Castles, salt and pepper shakers, pr 30.00

Sheraton, bread and butter plate, 6³/₈" d 5.00
Sheraton, cereal bowl, square, 6¼" 10.00
Sheraton, chop plate, 12³/₄" d 45.00
Sheraton, creamer 16.00
Sheraton, fruit bowl, 5¼" 8.00

JOSEF FIGURINES

When Muriel Joseph George could no longer obtain Lucite during World War II for her plastic jewelry, she used clay to fashion ceramic jewelry. George loved to model, making a wide variety of serious and whimsical figures for her own amusement.

In 1946 Muriel and her husband, Tom, made their first commercial ceramic figures in their garage. The printer misspelled Joseph, thus inadvertently creating the company's signature name Josef. Despite the company's quick growth, early 1950s' cheap Japanese imitations severely undercut its market.

In 1959 Muriel, Tom, and George Good established George Imports. Production was moved to the Katayama factory in Japan. Muriel created her designs in America, sent them to Japan with production instructions, and approved samples. Once again, the company enjoyed a period of prosperity.

In 1974 the company became George-Good Corporation. When Muriel retired in 1981, George Good purchased her interest in the company. Muriel continued to do design work until 1984. In 1985 George Good sold the company to Applause, Inc.

References: Dee Harris, Jim and Kaye Whitaker, *Josef Originals,* Schiffer Publishing, 1994; Jim and Kaye Whitaker, *Josef Originals: A Second Look,* Schiffer Publishing, 1997.

Newsletter: *Josef Original Newsletter,* PO Box 475, Lynnwood, WA 98046.

Figurine, Birthstone Doll, 4" h **$15.00**
Figurine, bunny, tan and brown, satin finish, 3" h 5.00
Figurine, California Belle, 3" h 35.00
Figurine, Chihauhau, satin finish 25.00
Figurine, Coco, light gray, gold highlights, raised flowers 30.00
Figurine, Denise, 5" h 45.00
Figurine, elephant, baby sprinkling water over back 20.00

Figurine, Mama Elephant, $30.00.

Figurine, Fluff, light blue, raised flowers 30.00
Figurine, Gail, 5" h 45.00
Figurine, Graduation Angel 30.00
Figurine, Heddy, 4" h 40.00
Figurine, Japan Belle, 3¹/₂" h 30.00
Figurine, Mama, 7¹/₂" h 80.00
Figurine, Mary Ann, 3¹/₂" h 35.00
Figurine, mouse, satin finish, 2" h 10.00
Figurine, Nip, light blue, raised flowers 30.00
Figurine, penguin, satin finish, 4³/₄" h 25.00
Figurine, Puff, light blue, raised flowers 30.00
Figurine, Tammy, girl playing piano 30.00
Figurine, Teddy, 4" h 40.00
Figurine, Tuck, light blue, raised flowers 30.00
Music Box, girl in green gown, plays *A Pretty Girl Is Like a Melody* 60.00
Music Box, girl in lavender gown, plays *Anniversary Waltz* 60.00
Music Box, girl playing violin, plays *Fascination* 50.00
Rosary Box 35.00
Salt and Pepper Shakers, pr, Mr & Mrs Claus 10.00
Salt and Pepper Shakers, pr, owls 10.00
Salt and Pepper Shakers, pr, Santa heads 12.00
Salt and Pepper Shakers, pr, snowmen 12.00
Wall Pocket, 3 owls on log with "Bless Our Nest" 35.00

JUKEBOXES

A jukebox is an amplified coin-operated phonograph. The 1940s and early 1950s were its golden age, a period when bubble machines ruled every teenage hangout from dance hall to drugstore. Portable radios, television's growth, and "Top 40" radio were responsible for the jukebox's decline in the 1960s.

Pre-1938 jukeboxes were made primarily of wood and resemble a phonograph or radio cabinet. Wurlitzer and Rock-Ola, whose jukeboxes often featured brightly colored plastic and animation units, made the best of the 78 rpm jukeboxes of the 1938–1948 period. The 45 rpm jukebox, popularized by the television show *Happy Days,* arrived on the scene in 1940 and survived until 1960. Seeburg was the principal manufacturer of these machines. Beginning in 1961, manufacturers often hid the record mechanism. These machines lack the collector appeal of their earlier counterparts.

References: Michael Adams, Jürgen Lukas, and Thomas Maschke, *Jukeboxes,* Schiffer Publishing, 1995; Jerry Ayliffe, *American Premium Guide to Jukeboxes and Slot Machines, Gumballs, Trade Stimulators, Arcade, 3rd Edition,* Books Americana, Krause Publications, 1991; Scott Wood, *A Blast From the Past Jukeboxes,* L-W Book Sales, 1992.

Periodicals: *Always Jukin',* 221 Yesler Way, Seattle, WA 98104; *Antique Amusements, Slot Machines & Jukebox Gazette,* 909 26th St NW, Washington, DC 20037; *Gameroom Magazine,* PO Box 41, Keyport, NJ 07735; *Jukebox Collector,* 2545 SE 60th Court, Des Moines, IA 50317.

AMI, Model XJDB-200 "Continental II," concave glass marquee with song titles above square case with glass bubble dome, restored, 64" h **$3,000.00**
Rock-Ola, Model 1428, red and green plastic panels, Art Deco grill, etched glass front panels, c1948, 60" h **2,500.00**

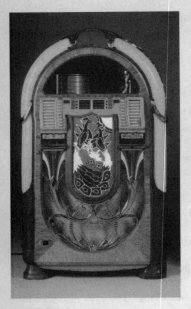

Wurlitzer, "Peacock" Model 850, glazed front revealing 24 song selections, Polarized acetate disks with 3 light bulbs behind each, film interacts with plastic to create prism effect, 1941, 65½" h, $12,650.00. Photo courtesy Sotheby's.

Seeburg, 100 B, 100 song selections, restored, c1950, 54" h 975.00

Seeburg, 100 C, 100 song selections, rotating color inside lower plastic panel, restored, c1952, 54" h 2,500.00

Seeburg 100 Select-O-Matic, pink with chrome and mirrored front, glass bubble top, restored, 54" h 1,725.00

Seeburg Select-O-Matic LPC-1, plays albums (10¢/single or 25¢/album side), rectangular chrome case, c1962..... 300.00

Seeburg, Symphonola "Trash Can," blond simulated woodgrain metal cabinet, restored, c1948, 59" h 2,000.00

Wurlitzer, "Bubbler" Model 1015, Paul Fuller design, glazed front revealing 24 song selection, decorative front panel with white plastic cylinders, walnut veneer case, 1946–47, 59½" h 7,000.00

Wurlitzer, Model 750, glazed front revealing 24 song selection, 2 curved small bubble tubes beneath selector buttons, round face with stylized floral motif encased in walnut veneer case, 55¾" h 5,175.00

Wurlitzer, Model 750E, Paul Fuller design, 24 song selection, electric keyboard, stylized floral motif, c1941 .... 5,175.00

Wurlitzer, 1100, Paul Fuller design, 24 song selection, vertical plastic int light tube in bottom rotates red and yellow colors, dome top, restored, c1947, 59" h 4,000.00

KEMPLE GLASS

In May 1945 John E. and Geraldine Kemple leased two buildings in East Palestine, Ohio, for the purposes of manufacturing tabletop glassware. They acquired many old molds from the 1870–1900 era along with molds from the Mannington Art Glass Company of West Virginia and McKee Glass.

During its twenty five years of operation (1945–1970), Kemple Glass produced a large number of "Authentic Antique Reproductions." Concerned that purchasers not confuse its products with period pieces, Kemple initially used milk glass for its restrikes from earlier molds. Color was added to the line in 1960, again in shades that make Kemple's products easy to distinguish

from earlier examples. Kemple Glass was marked either with a paper sticker or the letter "K," an addition made to earlier molds whenever possible.

Kemple Glass moved to the old Gill Glass Works in Kenova, West Virginia, following a fire at its East Palestine plant in 1956. When John E. Kemple died in 1970, the company was sold and production ended in Kenova. Today, many of the Kemple molds are in the possession of Wheaton Industries, Millville, New Jersey.

Reference: John R. Burkholder and D. Thomas O'Connor, *Kemple Glass: 1945–1970*, Glass Press, 1997.

Ashtray, coal bucket with bail, milk glass $15.00
Ashtray, Gypsy Kettle, milk glass 45.00
Banana Boat, Moon & Star Variant, ftd 18.00
Basket, Lace & Dewdrop, 4" h 25.00
Bonbon, Toltec, handled, 6" d 18.00
Butter, cov, Lace & Dewdrop 18.00
Cake Plate, Moon & Star Variant, ftd, 11" d 8.00
Candlesticks, pr, Narcissus 35.00
Candlesticks, pr, Sawtooth 25.00
Candy Dish, cov, Ivy-in-Snow, ftd 25.00
Celery, Ivy-in-Snow, crimped top 40.00
Celery, Lace & Dewdrop, ftd 18.00
Compote, cov, Ivy-in-Snow, 10" h 10.00
Creamer, Sandwich 45.00
Dresser Box, cov, Scroll with Flower, violet dec 25.00
Eggcup, chick 25.00
Ewer, Lacey Heart, crimped spout 15.00
Goblet, Lace & Dewdrop 20.00
Nut Dish, cov, Lace & Dewdrop 18.00
Pitcher, Lace & Dewdrop 20.00
Plaques, pr, Mary and Jesus 20.00
Plate, Cabbage Leaf, 7" d 25.00
Plate, Ivy-in-Snow, 10" d 45.00
Plate, Lovers' Knot, milk glass 25.00
Sugar, cov, Blackberry 22.00
Vase, Swirl, ruffled mouth and rigaree 28.00
Water Pitcher, Blackberry, 36 oz 15.00
Water Pitcher, Ivy-in-Snow 65.00

Hen on Nest, blue frosted glass, mkd "K" on base, 8½" l, $30.00.

KEWPIES

Rose Cecil O'Neill (1876–1944) created the Kewpie doll. This famous nymph made its debut in the December 1909 issue of *Ladies' Home Journal*. The first doll, designed in part by Joseph L. Kallus, was marketed in 1913. Kallus owned the Cameo Doll Company; Geo. Borgfelt Company owned the Kewpie production and distribution rights.

Most early Kewpie items were manufactured in Germany. American and Japanese manufacturers also played a role. Composition Kewpie dolls did not arrive until after World War II.

O'Neill created a wide variety of Kewpie characters. Do not overlook Ho-Ho, Kewpie-Gal, Kewpie-Kin, Ragsy, and Scootles.

Kewpie licensing continues, especially in the limited edition collectibles area.

References: John Axe, *Kewpies: Dolls & Art of Rose O'Neill & Joseph L. Kallus,* Hobby House Press, 1987, out of print; Cynthia Gaskill, *The Kewpie Kompanion: A Kompendium of Kewpie Knowledge,* Gold Horse Publishing, 1994.

Newsletter: *Traveler,* PO Box 4032, Portland, OR 97208.

Collectors' Club: International Rose O'Neill Club, PO Box 668, Branson, MO 65616.

Bottle, Kewpie Talc, composition figural Kewpie, 7" h $135.00
Candy Container, molded glass container with painted
　Kewpie figure, George Borgfeldt, c1920s, 3 x 3 x 3½" 150.00
Candy Container, tin, litho illus, c1920s, 1¾ x 6" 75.00
Crumb Tray, brass 30.00
Cup and Saucer, multicolored, sgd "Rose O'Neill
　Wilson" 110.00
Doll, bisque, painted, holding parasol and traveling
　case, Japan, 1930s, 2½" h 250.00
Doll, celluloid, hollow, movable arms, name decal on
　chest, Japan, 1930s, 7½" h 150.00

Doll, composition, jointed, name decal on chest, 11" h **200.00**
Doll, composition, jointed arms, 1930s, 12" h **125.00**
Doll, soft rubber, squeaker, Cameo Products, 1930s, 6" h **35.00**
Pillowcase, "The Kewpies in the Moon," c1930, 16 x 29" . . . **160.00**
Postcard, "Tis Christmas dear, I hope you'll see, young
　joys like Kewpies on your tree," c1925, 3½ x 5½" **15.00**
Ring, SS, Kewpie raising hand and kicking foot, c1920s **85.00**
Teacup, white china, full color art, German, 2¼" h **65.00**
Tray, full color, Limoges China, c1920s, 3½ x 5" **50.00**

KEYS & KEY CHAINS

People collect keys and key chains more for their novelty than any other reason. Because they are made in such quantities, few examples are rare. Most collectors specialize, focusing on a specific subject such as automobile, hotel, presentation keys ("Key to the City"), railroad, etc.

Beware of fantasy keys such as keys to the Tower of London, a *Titanic* cabin, or a Hollywood movie star's dressing room.

References: Don Stewart (comp.), *Antique Classic Marque Car Keys: United States 1915–1970, Second Edition,* published by author, 1993; Don Stewart (comp.), *Standard Guide to Key Collecting, 3rd Edition,* published by author, 1990.

Collectors' Club: License Plate Key Chain & Mini License Plate Collectors, 888 Eighth Ave, New York, NY 10019.

KEYS

Cabinet, steel, Art Deco, 2" **$6.00**
Car, auto dealer presentation keys, gold-plated **1.50**
Car, Chrysler Omega, brass, 5 pc set, Yale, 1933 . . . . **15.00**
Clock, steel, iron, Waterbury Clock Co, 2¼" **16.00**
Door, brass, standard bow and bit, 4" **5.00**
Gate, iron, bit type, 8" **6.00**
Hotel, steel, bit type, bronze tag **3.00**
Jail, nickel-silver, pin tumbler, cut, Yale Mogul **15.00**
Jewelers, brass, 6-point **18.00**
Railroad, Baltimore & Ohio, brass **40.00**
Railroad, Erie & Lackawanna Railroad, brass, Adlake **20.00**
Railroad, Long Island Railroad, mkd "LIRR," brass **10.00**
Ship, bronze, bit type, foreign ship tags **6.00**
Ship, pin tumbler type, USN tag **2.00**

KEY CHAINS

Aluminum, Good Luck, penny insert, Parts Boys, Auto
　Specialty Co adv, 1½" h **$10.00**
Brass, Chevrolet, 50th anniversary **15.00**
Brass, Hercules Powder Co, rect, Fiftieth Anniversary
　1912–1962, 1¼" l **15.00**
Enamel, Swift Premium Ham **12.00**
Metal, AC Spark Plug **8.00**
Metal, BP logo **8.00**
Metal, Esso logo and "Put a Tiger in Your Tank," Happy
　Motoring Club serial number, 1960s, 1⅜" d **12.00**
Metal, John F Kennedy, diecut initials, brass finish, brass
　chain **15.00**
Metal, seashells with "Shell" on back **12.00**
Plastic, Avia logo, clear, square **8.00**
Plastic, Castrol **8.00**
Plastic, Mobil logo, clear, square **25.00**

Doll, Cameo Doll Co, composition socket head and body, $250.00.

KITCHEN COLLECTIBLES

Collectors are in love with the kitchen of the 1920s and 30s. A few progressive collectors are focusing on the kitchens of the 50s and 60s. Color and style are the two collecting keys. Bright blue, green, and red enamel handled utensils are in demand, not for use but to display on walls. Everything, from flatware to appliances, in Streamline Modern and Post-War Modern design styles is hot. Do not overlook wall clocks and wall decorations. There are even individuals collecting Tupperware.

References: Ellen Bercovici, Bobbie Zucker Bryson and Deborah Gillham, *Collectibles for the Kitchen, Bath & Beyond,* Antique Trader Books, 1998; Brenda C. Blake, *Egg Cups,* Antique Publications, 1995; Loretta Smith Fehling, *Terrific Tablecloths from the '40s & '50s,* Schiffer Publishing, 1998; Linda Fields, *Four and Twenty Blackbirds (Pie Birds),* published by author, 1998; Linda Campbell Franklin, *300 Years of Housekeeping Collectibles,* Books Americana, Krause Publications, 1992; Linda Campbell Franklin, *300 Years of Kitchen Collectibles, Fourth Edition,* Krause Publications, 1997; Michael J. Goldberg, *Collectible Plastic Kitchenware and Dinnerware: 1935–1965,* Schiffer Publishing, 1995; Michael J. Goldberg, *Groovy Kitchen Designs for Collectors: 1935–1965,* Schiffer Publishing, 1996; Jan Lindenberger, *Black Memorabilia for the Kitchen, 2nd Edition,* Schiffer Publishing, 1999; Jan Lindenberger, *The 50s and 60s Kitchen, 2nd Edition,* Schiffer Publishing, 1999; Barbara Mauzy, *Bakeline in the Kitchen,* Schiffer Publishing, 1998; Barbara Mauzy, *The Complete Book of Kitchen Collecting,* Schiffer Publishing, 1997; Dana G. Morykan and Harry L. Rinker, *Country Antiques & Collectibles, Fourth Edition,* House of Collectibles, 1999; Ellen M. Plante, *Kitchen Collectibles,* Wallace-Homestead, Krause Publications, 1991; Don Thornton, *Apple Parers,* Off Beat Books, 1997.

Newsletters: *Cookies,* 9610 Greenview Ln, Manassas, VA 20109; *Piebirds Unlimited,* 14 Harmony School Rd, Flemington, NJ 08822.

Collectors' Clubs: Cookie Cutter Collectors Club, 1167 Teal Rd SW, Dellroy, OH 44620; Eggcup Collectors' Corner, 67 Stevens Ave, Old Bridge, NJ 08857; Glass Knife Collectors' Club, 4448 Ironwood Ave, Seal Beach, CA 90740; International Society for Apple Parer Enthusiasts, 117 E High, Mount Vernon, OH 43050; Jelly Jammers, 6086 W Boggstown Rd, Boggstown, IN 46110; Kollectors of Old Kitchen Stuff, 501 Market St, Mifflinburg, PA 17844; Pie Bird Collectors Club, 158 Bagsby Hill Ln, Dover, TN 37058.

Note: See Advertising, Appliances, Cookbooks, Cookie Jars, Egg Beaters, Fire-King, Food Molds, Fruit Jars, Graniteware, Griswold, Kitchen Glassware, Pyrex, Reamers, Wagner Ware, Yellow Ware, and individual glass and pottery categories for additional listings.

Apron, cotton, floral print, machine sewn, 1940s	**$20.00**
Bread Box, green and white graniteware, 1920s, 19" l	**95.00**
Bread Box, metal, Betsy Ross Moderne pattern, white with red trim, mkd "Roll-A-Way EM Meder Co," c1930s	**20.00**
Butter, cov, aluminum, copper-toned, West Bend	**4.00**
Canister Set, 4 pc, aluminum, West Bend	**10.00**
Candle Holders, stamped tin flowers, price for set of 10	**15.00**
Casserole Holder, wrought iron	**3.00**

Meat Grinder, Harras No. 52, white enameled, wood plunger and handle, $50.00.

Clock, figural frying pan, electric, enameled iron and tin, white pan, red screw-on handle, red knife and fork minute hands, white numerals, 1950s	**60.00**
Coaster, stamped aluminum, floral design	**4.00**
Coffeepot, electric, Flavo Matic, brown Bakelite handles and feet, West Bend	**10.00**
Cookbook, *Bride in the Kitchen,* Wason, Betty, NY, 1959, 116 pp	**15.00**
Cookie Cutter, stamped aluminum, Mickey Mouse, riveted strap handle, Disney, 4" l	**30.00**
Cookie Cutter, tin, lion, 3½" l	**15.00**
Cookie Gun and Pastry Decorator, Wear-Ever	**5.00**
Cookie Jar, hobo, Treasure Craft	**65.00**
Coupon, Mirro Aluminum Bake Pan, printed, black on pale orange, 20¢ off a 55¢ bake pan, Lundt & Co, Moline, IL, 1920s, 8½ x 11"	**12.00**
Eggcup, bucket shaped, Golliwog illus	**60.00**
Eggcup, double, Chalaine, McKee Glass	**28.00**
Eggcup, double, flared base, opalescent, oval silhouette of courting couple in colonial dress	**12.00**
Eggcup, figural Big Ears character, plastic, Hong Kong, 1960s	**15.00**
Eggcup, figural clown, 3 pc set, cup, bowl, and plate	**60.00**
Eggcup, pink roses, gold trim, Meissen porcelain, Mitterteich Porcelain Factory	**12.00**
Egg Slicer, aluminum, hinged top, 1930s, 5" l	**8.00**
Egg Timer, turned wood, sand bulbs	**20.00**
Electric Fryer, Fri-Well, Dormeyer, 1952	**25.00**
Flatware, 6 pc set, Bakelite handles	**45.00**
Flour Scoop, stamped metal, Trisco Flour, 5⅜" l	**12.00**
Funnel, gray graniteware, crimped bottom, small side handle, 6" h	**25.00**
Knife Sharpener, Handy Hannah, #4950, 1930s, 4½" d	**10.00**
Masher, red wooden handle	**4.00**
Measuring Spoon Holder, ceramic, "#1 Measure Boy," Cardinal China, 1952, 5" h	**15.00**
Measuring Spoon Holder, ceramic, chicken, holds spoons in tail, 4" h	**6.00**
Measuring Spoon Holder, ceramic, duck, holds rectangular shaped spoons, 5" h	**8.00**

Measuring Spoon Holder, ceramic, flowerpot, multicolored spoons, 4" h, 6" w 10.00

Measuring Spoon Holder, ceramic, owl, souvenir, "Spooning for you in Tennessee," spoons inserted into tree stump, 5" h 10.00

Melon Scoop, wooden handle, Ekco 4.00

Napkin Holder, chrome, Bakelite base, Hero Co 8.00

Napkin Lady, blue and white dress, 1940s 27.00

Napkin Lady, cocktail version, complete with 5 rice paper napkins, Holt-Howard, 1958 .... 35.00

Napkin Lady, pink and yellow dress, hp eyes, stamped "Japan," 9¼" h 25.00

Napkin Lady, Rosie, #H-132, Holland Mold Co 30.00

Napkin Lady, Servy-Etta, wood, red skirt, matching hat with silver accents, 11¾" h 18.00

Napkin Lady, Spanish Dancer, basket on head holds toothpicks, napkin slits in rear of skirt, California Originals 35.00

Napkin Lady, wood, Jamaican woman, bowl of fruit on head, jointed arms 20.00

Napkin Lady, wood, "Napkins" on round base, paper label, Japan, 11½" h 15.00

Notepad Holder, celluloid, fruit dec, wall mounted, pencil on string 8.00

Pie Bird, Benny the Baker, holds pie crimper and cake tester, Cardinal China 75.00

Pie Bird, bird, rose, yellow, and white patches, Morton Pottery 20.00

Pie Bird, rooster, Cleminson Pottery 20.00

Pot Holder, handsewn, appliquéd cotton, stuffed 4.00

Recipe Box, Pennsylvania Dutch design, Ohio Art 3.00

Rolling Pin, wood 4.00

Salt and Pepper Shakers, pr, colored aluminum 5.00

Saucepan, Worthmore Aluminum, 7" d 4.00

Scoop, cast aluminum, rounded handle, Wagner Ware, 11¼" l 15.00

Spoon Rest, aluminum, figural black chef head with open mouth, 1930s, 4 x 6" 80.00

Spoon Rest, stainless steel 2.00

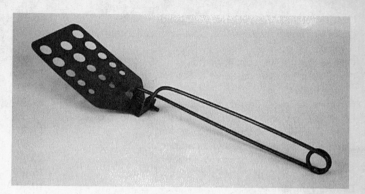

Spatula, metal, squeeze handle to flip spatula, 12" l, $15.00.

Teapot, whimsical man, spout is nose, pastel pink, blue, and yellow, mkd "Japan," 1930 .... 25.00

Trivet, cast-iron, Griswold #204 .... 20.00

Tumbler, colored aluminum, mkd "Bombay India" 5.00

Tupperware, salad tongs, green, 1950s 5.00

Tupperware, Wonderlier bowl 5.00

TV Tray, metal, stylized fish design 6.00

Utility Fork, melamine handle, Provincial design, mkd "Flint" 4.00

KITCHEN GLASSWARE

Depression Glass is a generic term for glass produced in the United States from the early 1920s through the 1960s. Depression Glass patterns make up only a fraction of the thousands of glass patterns and types produced during this period.

Kitchen Glassware is a catchall category for inexpensive kitchen and table glass produced during this period. Hundreds of companies made it. Hocking, Hazel Atlas, McKee, U.S. Glass, and Westmoreland are a few examples.

Kitchen glassware was used on the table and for storage. It usually has a thick body, designed to withstand heavy and daily use. The category is dominated by storage glass and utilitarian items prior to 1940. Following World War II, tabletop glass prevailed. Kitchen glassware was a favored giveaway premium in the 1950s and early 1960s.

Reference: Gene Florence, *Kitchen Glassware of the Depression Years, Fifth Edition,* Collector Books, 1995, 1999 value update.

Newsletter: *Knife Rests of Yesterday & Today,* 4046 Graham St, Pleasanton, CA 94566.

Note: For additional listings see Depression Glass, Drinking Glasses, Fire-King, Pyrex, Reamers, and individual glass company categories.

Batter Bowl, white with fired-on red band at rim $12.00

Batter Jug, Cambridge, pink 85.00

Batter Jug, Jenkins #570, transparent green 140.00

Bowl, Hocking Jad-ite, flower dec, 7½" d 15.00

Butter Dish, cov, McKee, opaque yellow, 1 lb 75.00

Butter Tub, cov, Federal, amber 30.00

Cake Plate, snowflake design, pink 25.00

Candlesticks, pr, double, Tear Drop, Indiana, crystal 30.00

Colander, wire frame and mesh, green painted wooden handles with white stripes, 8⅛" d, 5¼" h, $15.00.

Canister, Hazel Atlas, "Cereal," glass lid, cobalt 80.00
Canister, rooster head finial, clear with red comb and
   wattle 25.00
Cheese Dish, Kraft, cobalt, no lid 12.00
Condiment Set, Medco Serve U Set No. 86, clear with
   green lids 65.00
Creamer, Kellogg's Correct Cereal 20.00
Cruet Set, oil and vinegar, frosted white with rooster
   decal and clear stopper, price for pair 25.00
Curtain Tie Backs, pr, Feathered, amber 25.00
Curtain Tie Backs, pr, Sandwich, amber 20.00
Curtain Tie Backs, pr, Sandwich, peacock blue 25.00
Drawer Pull, amber 10.00
Drawer Pull, crystal, double 10.00
Drawer Pull, double, peacock blue 22.00
Dry Measures, 1/4, 1/3, 1/2, and 1 cup, Jeannette, delphite 180.00
Eggcup, black 18.00
Gravy Boat, Cambridge, double spout, pink 40.00
Grease Jar, Vitrock Red Tulips, red lid 25.00
Knife, Aer-Flo, amber 65.00
Knife, Leaf Dur-X, teal 28.00
Knife, pinwheel, crystal 15.00
Mixing Bowl, Federal, pink, 9 3/4" d 50.00
Knife, Westmoreland, clear with flower dec 25.00
Knife Rest, amber 18.00
Knife Rest, green transparent, flowerhead ends 20.00
Ladle, Cambridge, moonlight blue 40.00
Ladle, Heisey, flamingo 30.00
Measuring Cup, emb "Armour's Extract," side pour,
   1 cup, clear 20.00
Measuring Cup, Federal, 1 cup, amber 35.00
Measuring Cup, McKee, opaque yellow, 2 cup 30.00
Measuring Pitcher, ftd, chalaine blue, 4 cup 400.00
Mixing Bowl, Hazel Atlas, "Restwell," cobalt, 5 3/4" d 28.00
Mixing Bowls, Jeannette, delphite, nesting set of 3 . . . . 200.00
Napkin Holder, "Hy-G Napkins," white 150.00
Napkin Holder, Nar-O-Fold, black 150.00
Napkin Holder, "Serv-All," green clambroth 35.00
Reamer Pitcher, US Glass, pitcher and inverted reamer
   lid, transparent yellow 750.00
Refrigerator Dish, cov, chalaine blue, 4 x 5" 45.00
Refrigerator Dish, cov, wedge shape, jadite 15.00
Rolling Pin, chalaine blue, shaker top 1,500.00
Rolling Pin, forest green, glass handles 125.00
Rolling Pin, peacock blue 250.00

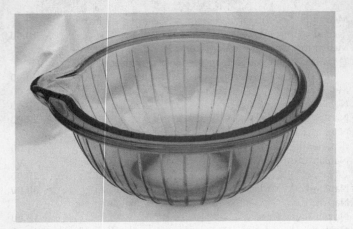

Batter Bowl, green, Hocking, 8 7/8" d, 3 3/4" h, $25.00.

Salad Set, Cavalier Emerald-Glo, serving bowl, fork, and
   spoon 50.00
Salad Set, fork and spoon, black, Cambridge 130.00
Salt and Pepper Shakers, pr, Jeannette, horizontal ribs,
   delphite, range size, 8 oz 100.00
Salt and Pepper Shakers, pr, McKee, Roman Arch shape,
   white with green dots, range size 35.00
Shakers, range set, Hocking, flour, pepper, salt, and
   sugar, opaque yellow, metal threaded lids 75.00
Soap Dish, Holt, green transparent 20.00
Spice Jars and Rack, Griffiths, 10 white jars with green
   threaded lids 90.00
Stack Set, Jeannette, Hex Optic, pink, set of 3 . . . . 60.00
Straw Holder, transparent green, chrome lifter and lid 425.00
Sugar Cube Tray, Cambridge, tab handles, transparent
   yellow 70.00
Sugar Shaker, Tipp City Dutch 22.00
Tea Kettle, Glasbake, glass handle, metal cap 35.00
Toast Rack, clear, knob handle, holds 6 slices 50.00
Tom & Jerry Cup 5.00
Towel Bar, peacock blue 40.00
Towel Bar Holders, pr, green clambroth 25.00
Vinegar Bottle, fired-on red, metal cap 10.00
Water Dispenser, McKee, white 120.00
Water Pitcher, clear with fired-on blue and red Dutch
   children 25.00

KOREAN WAR

The Korean War began on June 25, 1950, when North Korean troops launched an invasion across the 38th parallel into South Korea. The United Nations ordered an immediate cease-fire and withdrawal of the invading forces. On June 27 President Harry Truman ordered U.S. Forces to South Korea to help repel the North Korean invasion. The United Nations Security Council adopted a resolution for armed intervention.

The first American ground forces arrived in Korea on July 1, 1950. General Douglas MacArthur was named commander of the United Nations forces on July 8, 1950. The landing at Inchon took place on September 15, 1950. U.S. troops reached the Yalu River on the Manchurian border in late November.

On November 29, 1950, Chinese Communist troops counterattacked. Seoul was abandoned on January 4, 1951, only to be recaptured on March 21, 1951. On April 11, 1951, President

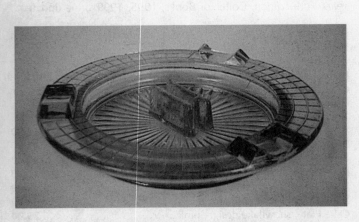

Ashtray, #1102, green, Jeannette, c1934, 5 1/2" d, $12.00.

Truman relieved General MacArthur of his command. General Matthew Ridgway replaced him. By early July a cease-fire had been declared, North Korean troops withdrew above the 38th parallel, and truce talks began. A stalemate was reached.

On November 29, 1952, President-elect Dwight Eisenhower flew to Korea to inspect the United Nations forces. An armistice was signed at Panmunjom by the United Nations, North Korea, and Chinese delegates on July 27, 1953.

References: Richard J. Austin, *The Official Price Guide to Military Collectibles, Sixth Edition,* House of Collectibles, 1998; Ron Manion, *American Military Collectibles Price Guide,* Antique Trader Books, 1995.

Periodical: *Military Trader,* PO Box 1050, Dubuque, IA 52004.

Ammunition Magazine, 30 round, M1 Carbine, black painted steel **$10.00**

Cap, Fatigue, Army, dark olive drab herringbone twill with stitched bill, pleated body, and 1851 dated Quartermaster markings, size 7 . . . . **35.00**

Cap, Visor, Officer, Army, tan worsted wool top with soft roll crown stiffener, russet brown leather visor, front and rear chinstraps, oversize gilt brass device, side button sand satin lining, Bancroft, size 7¹/₂ **30.00**

Cartridge Belt, Army, dark olive drab web with brass fittings, includes 2 dark olive drab web Carlisle bandage pouches, dated 1952 and 1845 . . . . **20.00**

Dog Tags, aluminum, US style, Korean characters and service number **22.00**

Flight Suit, nylon, olive drab, woven specification, diagonal zipper front, pockets, label, size 40S. **35.00**

Helmet, helicopter pilot's, microphone, plug, earphones, strap, and visor, with case **100.00**

Helmet, Navy, aviator's, model H-4, black ext, leather and web head restraints int, size large **50.00**

Jacket, Army, wool, olive drab, Korean made bullion 8th Army patch on left and "Korea" arc on right shoulder, "Korea" leadership loops, woven Sergeant chevrons, 2 bullion overseas bars, collar discs, 3-place ribbon bar with Korean Disinguished Unit Citation ribbon on left chest pocket flap **55.00**

Lensatic Compass, folding, olive drab, mkd "US 1952". **45.00**

Mittens, Army, Arctic, dark olive drab cotton, light brown leather palms with alpaca facing, adjustable straps on wrists and gauntlets, size medium **20.00**

Parachute, backpack style, green nylon case with web straps and aluminum buckles, dated Nov 1952, Switler Parachute Mfg Co. **125.00**

Patch, Army, Military Government of Korea, cloth, red, white, and blue swirl pattern, 2" d **65.00**

Pillowcase, souvenir, red cotton, embroidered 8th Army patch design in center, "11th Evac Hospital Pusan Korea," 17 x 17" **35.00**

Propaganda Leaflet, surrender text with G3 translation letters, dated 1952. . . . . **25.00**

Rifle Case, paratrooper's, olive drab, padded, green case with zipper, rings, and straps **60.00**

Scarf, souvenir, green silk, multicolored embroidered dragon pattern, "Seoul Korea 1952" above dragon **15.00**

Shield, souvenir, blue cloth, paper backing, hand stitched, UN and Korean flags over multicolored dragon, "Returned From Hell, 1951 Korea 1952," made in Korea **25.00**

KREISS CERAMICS

In 1946 Murray Kreiss founded Murray Kreiss and Company as an importer and distributor of Japanese-made ceramic figurines to the five-and-dime-store and souvenir trade. The company changed its name to Kreiss & Company in 1951.

Kreiss contracted for a wide variety of figures ranging from Christmas Santas to a large variety of animals. Copycat examples mimicked Dr. Seuss and Disney characters. In the late 1950s, Kreiss introduced its Beatnik series followed in 1958 by its Psychoceramics series. Ashtrays, mugs, napkin ladies, and planters are Kreiss forms found in addition to figurines.

Norman Kreiss, Murray's son, assumed control of the company as the Sixties ended. He redirected the company's efforts into the sale of fine furniture. While the precise date for the termination of imported figures is unknown, collectors assume it occurred in the early 1970s.

All Kreiss ceramic figurines were made in Japan. Beware of examples stamped on the bottom "West Germany."

Reference: Pat and Larry Aidins, *The World of Kreiss Ceramics,* L-W Book Sales, 1999.

Animal, Boston Terrier, 4⁵/₈" h **$25.00**

Animal, Merry Wolf **20.00**

Animal, Powder Puff Puppy. **15.00**

Animal, Siamese cat, attached bell at neck, 4⁵/₈" h **20.00**

Ashtray, Beatchick, "Cat, I dig you the most," 5¹/₂" sq **80.00**

Ashtray, Beatnik, "Man, you're sick—sick—sick!," 5³/₈" sq **45.00**

Ashtray, Psycho Christmas, "No—that's not my tongue— it's a Christmas tie!!," 5¹/₂" sq **50.00**

Bank, skunk, black, white, pink, and gold, 6³/₈ x 7". **20.00**

Bank, pig, "Cheers Good Health," 5¹/₄" l. **30.00**

Bank, pig, "Save for a Merry Christmas," 4³/₄" l **25.00**

Bank, Psycho, "In case of fire lift up hat," plastic, 5⁷/₈" h **100.00**

Bookend, girl standing on book and talking on telephone, 8¹/₈" h **18.00**

Bookends, pr, Hans and Greta, 6³/₈" h **40.00**

Candle Holder, 4 "NOEL" carolers, 3³/₄" h, 6¹/₄" l **20.00**

Figure, Beatnik, black hair and beard, green pants, red and white shirt and Santa hat, wooden base, 6¹/₂" h **95.00**

Figure, boy fisherman, holding rod in right hand, hat in left, 3¹/₂ x 6¹/₄" **12.00**

Figure, King of Clubs, 6⁵/₈" h **25.00**

Figure, Psycho, "But honey, it was only an innocent Christmas party!," 5¹/₄" h **150.00**

Figure, Psycho, "Looking for someone with a little authority? I have as little as anyone," 4³/₄" h **110.00**

Figure, Psycho, No-Goodnik, holes in head, "Nobody is Perfect," 4¹/₂" h **90.00**

Figure, Sound of Music, 10¹/₂" h. **28.00**

Figures, skunks wearing Santa hats, 3⁵/₈" h, price for pair. **12.00**

Mug, Psycho, "I knew I'd crack up!," 4¹/₂" h **125.00**

Napkin Lady, girl with hat, 8⁷/₈" h. **75.00**

Napkin Lady, gold accent muff, candle holder in hat, 10³/₈" h **100.00**

Napkin Lady, night light, 11¹/₄" h **135.00**

Napkin Lady, set, pr salt and pepper shaker with hors d'oeuvres tray **140.00**

Nodder, Psycho, Bouncing Bum, 9" h. **120.00**

Planter, colonial lady, pink dress, 7¹/₄" h. **35.00**

Planter, Psycho, "I'm a devilish good planter!," 5¹/₄" h **225.00**

Plate, abstract bottles design, Sablo Manchini, 11¹/₄" h **35.00**

Salt and Pepper Shakers, pr, kissing monkeys, 4¼" h 15.00
Salt and Pepper Shakers, pr, Mistletoe Men, 4" h 18.00
Salt and Pepper Shakers, pr, monks, 2¾" h 25.00
Salt and Pepper Shakers, pr, Salty Ma and Peppy Pa,
   6⅞" h 30.00
Salt and Pepper Shakers, pr, Santa and Mrs Claus, 3¾"
   and 3½" 12.00
Teacup, Queen of Clubs, 2⅜" h 20.00
Toothpick Holder, Christmas tree, 6½" h 18.00
Vase, abstract bottles design, Sablo Manchini, 14" h 65.00

K.T. & K. CALIFORNIA

Homer J. Taylor established K.T. & K. California pottery in Burbank, California, in 1937. The son of one of the original founders of the Knowles, Taylor & Knowles pottery in East Liverpool, Ohio, he served as president of that company after his father's death in 1914. Following Knowles, Taylor & Knowles' closing, Homer moved to Burbank and started his own company.

K.T. & K. California produced decorative accessories such as figural planters, vases, and wall pockets. "K.T.K. Calif" was incised on all items. "Hand Made" was sometimes included in the mark.

Reference: Mary Frank Gaston, *Collector's Encyclopedia of Knowles, Taylor & Knowles China: Identification & Values,* Collector Books, 1996, out of print.

Basket, applied twisted rope handle, 6½" w $30.00
Basket, applied twisted rope handle and bow 35.00
Bowl, pear and leaves dec, sgd "M," 6" d 40.00
Bowl, rolled rim, applied rope design handles,
   turquoise, 9" d 70.00
Bowl, twisted rope handles on sides, peach mono-
   chrome finish, 3¼" h, 8½" w 80.00
Candle Holder, bowl form, scalloped body, raspberry
   sprayed finish 25.00
Candle Holders, pr, applied bow on front, 3" h 40.00
Centerpiece Vase, 3 flower holders on pedestal base,
   white, mkd "KT&K cabaña Calif," 5¼" h, 10¼" w 50.00
Cigarette Holder, figural watering can, 3" h 30.00
Coaster Holder, train and car, sgd "E" 100.00
Dish, divided, applied flower and stems form center
   handle, raspberry sprayed finish 55.00
Dish, incised leaves, light blue, raspberry sprayed finish,
   sgd "H," 6" d 30.00
Dish, leaf shape, sgd "L," 6" w 30.00
Dish, shallow, applied bow, 8" w, 1¾" d 35.00
Figure, lamb, applied bow around neck 30.00
Figure, rooster, hollow, 6" h 65.00
Flower Holder, diamond shaped body, elaborate floral
   designs, pedestal base, mkd "KTK S—V,"4" h, 7½" w 80.00
Match Holder, figural wheelbarrow, 3" h 30.00
Pitcher, curved sectional body, twist rope style handle,
   sgd "Eileen 1/21/43," 6¼" h 50.00
Pitcher, triple section rounded body, flared neck, twisted
   rope handle, sgd "B," 4" h 45.00
Vase, abstract design in shades of green, 4¼" h 40.00
Vase, abstract overlapping design body, initials "SS"
   incised with mark, 6¼" h 35.00
Vase, applied flower and leaves, 4" h 55.00
Vase, scalloped neck with front half rolled down,
   applied flower and stem with large incised leaf on
   front, turquoise 45.00

LADY HEAD VASES

The lady head vase craze began in the early 1940s and extended through the early 1960s. They were just one of hundreds of inexpensive ceramic novelties made by American and foreign manufacturers, primarily Japanese, in the period immediately following World War II.

Although designated lady head vase, the category is broadly interpreted to include all planters and vases in the shape of a human head.

References: Kathleen Cole, *The Encyclopedia of Head Vases,* Schiffer Publishing, 1996; Mike Posgay and Ian Warner, *The World of Head Vase Planters,* Antique Publications, 1992, 1996 value update; Mary Zavada, *Lady Head Vases,* Schiffer Publishing, 1988, 1996 value update.

Collectors' Club: Head Vase Society, PO Box 83H, Scarsdale, NY 10583.

Inarco, E1066, Cleveland Ohio 1963 transfer and label,
   missing earrings, 4½" h $45.00
Japan, faint transfer, glossy, blonde ponytail, 5¾" h 15.00
Japan, long blonde hair, crazed, 6¾" h 150.00
Japan, long brown hair with flower, jeweled, lashes,
   label, 5¼" h 90.00
Lefton, 1843 transfer, with hand, necklace, lashes, lustre,
   paper label, 5¾" h 50.00
Lefton, 1955 transfer, glossy green checkered hat and
   bow, label, sgd "Geo. Z. Lefton," 5" h 50.00
Napcoware, 1956 transfer, "National Potteries Co, Made
   in Japan" label, with hand, feather hat, lashes,
   repaired finger, 5¼" h 50.00
Napcoware, C3343A, with hat and hand, necklace and
   earrings, lashes, "National Potteries Co, Made in
   Japan" paper label, 1 earring missing, 4½" h 55.00
Napcoware, C4897C, 1960 transfer, blue hat with rose,
   bonde hair, earrings, lashes, imp mark, 4¾" h 55.00
Napcoware, C5036A, 1960 transfer, lashes, hand on
   upturned collar, coat and hat, "National Potteries Co,
   Cleveland, Made in Japan" paper label, 5½" h 165.00

Norcrest, E-372, blue bonnet, blonde hair, pink flowered dress, silver paper label, 6" h, $40.00.

AUCTION PRICES – LADY HEAD VASES

Gene Harris Antique Auction Center, Inc., Collector's Auction, February 9, 1999. Prices include a 10% buyer's premium.

"Brinnis, Pittsburgh, PA, Made in Japan," 1-182, with hand, pearl earrings and necklace, paper label, 7" h $220.00
Enesco, blue ribbons, pearl earrings, paper label, 7¼" h 297.00
"Fine Quality Japan," 56551/A, glossy, with hand, bonnet, pearl earrings, lashes, paper label, 7" h 176.00
Inarco, E-1068, hair comb, pearl earrings and necklace, lashes, transfer, paper label, 1963, 10" h 368.50
Napcoware Import, Japan, C72-3, pearl earrings and necklace, paper label, 5" h 44.00
Rubins Original, Japan, 499 transfer, pearl flowered shoulders and hat, earrings, lashes, bubble break and factory painted chip on hat, 5¾" h 66.00
Topling Imports, Inc., Japan, 50/425, black ribbon, pearl necklace, paper label, 8½" h 209.00
Trimontware, Japan, with hand, pearl earrings and necklace, lashes, paper label, 7" h 121.00

Napcoware, C7471 transfer, earrings and leaf pendant, partial National label, 4⅝" h 60.00
Napcoware, C7494 transfer, "National Potteries Made in Japan" paper label, blue hat, pearl earrings and necklace, 5¾" h 85.00
Relpo, K1932 transfer, black bows in hair, black shoulders, earrings, paper label, 5¾" h 165.00

LALIQUE

René Lalique (1860–1945) began his career as a designer and jewelry maker. His perfume flacons attracted the attention of M. Francois Coty. Coty contracted with Lalique to design and manufacture perfume bottles for the company. Initially, the bottles were made at Legras & Cie de St. Dennis. In 1909 Lalique opened a glassworks at Combs-la-Ville. Lalique acquired a larger glassworks at Wingen-sur-Moder in Alsace-Lorraine in 1921 and founded Verrerie d'Alsace René Lalique et Cie.

Although René was not involved in the actual production, he designed the majority of the articles manufactured by the firm. Lalique glass is lead glass that is either blown in the mold or pressed. There are also combinations of cutting and casting and some molded designs were treated with acids to produce a frosted, satiny effect. Lalique blown wares were almost all confined to stemware and large bottles. Glass made before 1945 has been found in more than ten colors, including mauve and purple.

Early pieces were of naturalistic design—molded animals, foliage, flowers, or nudes. Later designs became stylized and reflected the angular, geometric characteristics of Art Deco.

Each piece of Lalique glass is marked on the bottom or near the base. It is often marked in several places, in block letters and in script. Marks include: R. LALIQUE FRANCE (engraved and sandblasted block and script); LALIQUE FRANCE (diamond point tool, engraved, sandblasted block and script); and LALIQUE (engraved). The "R" was deleted from the mark following René's death in 1945. Collectors prefer pre-1945 material.

Lalique closed its Combs-la-Ville factory in 1937. The factory at Wingen-sur-Moder was partially destroyed during World War II. Lalique made no glass between 1939 and 1946. Production resumed after the war. In 1965 Lalique made its first limited edition Christmas plate, ending the series in 1976. Marc Lalique and his daughter, Marie-Claude Lalique, have contributed a number of new designs. The company still produces pieces from old molds.

Reference: Robert Prescott-Walker, *Collecting Lalique Glass,* Francis Joseph Publications, 1996, distributed by Krause Publications.

Collectors' Club: Lalique Collectors Society (company-sponsored), 400 Veterans Blvd, Carlstadt, NJ 07072.

REPRODUCTION ALERT: Beware of the Lalique engraved signature and etched mark applied to blanks made in Czechoslovakia, France, and the United States.

Ashtray, Gao, clear and frosted, molded with interlaced motifs, modern, 4" d $115.00
Bowl, Gui, molded in low relief with berried mistletoe branches, gray enamel in recesses, inscribed "R. Lalique France No. 3223, small rim chips, model introduced 1921, 9⅜" d 260.00
Bowl, Nemours, frosted and enameled, molded with flowers, modern, model introduced 1929, 10" d 500.00
Bowl, Bulbes No. 2, shallow, clear opalescent, molded with stylized flowers, model introduced 1935, 10" d 725.00
Box, cov, Mendon, circular, frosted glass molded with flowers, green stain, model introduced 1924, 3¾" d 500.00
Carafe, Phalbourg, clear and frosted, stopper molded with vines, modern, 10" h 185.00
Champagne Glasses, Ange, model #13645, clear and frosted, each stem molded with a winged angel, price for 5 pcs 575.00
Chandelier Panels, Hetre, clear and frosted, molded with flat leaves, model introduced 1924, 13½" l, price for 3 pcs 1,250.00
Cruet, Bourgueil, clear and frosted, stepped motif, model introduced 1933, 5½" h 250.00

Vase, Malesherbes, clear and frosted green, molded with flat leaves, model introduced 1927, 9¼" h, $4,000.00. Photo courtesy William Doyle Galleries.

Figure, Belier, model #1165300, clear and frosted ram's head, designed by Marie Claude Lalique, 1982, 6½" h . . . **750.00**

Lamp, frosted and shaded gray, rectangular form molded with trees, modern, 9" h **1,250.00**

Paperweight, Bison, clear and frosted, modeled as a buffalo, model introduced 1931, 4¾" l **600.00**

Pendant, Lys, rectangular, amber, molded with lilies, model introduced 1920, 2" h **700.00**

Plate, Oursins, clear opalescent, molded with circular motifs, model introduced 1935, 11" d **775.00**

Stemware Service, Argos, crystal, comprising carafe, 8 water goblets, 12 red wine glasses, 7 champagne glasses, and 7 liqueur glasses, modern, price for set **1,500.00**

Vase, Claude, clear and frosted, lobed form cut with ovals, modern, 13½" h, price for pair **975.00**

AUCTION PRICES – LALIQUE

Butterfield & Butterfield, Art Nouveau, Art Deco and Arts & Crafts Auction, May 11, 1998. Prices include a 15% buyer's premium.

Bowl, Sirène, opalescent, low circular dish molded in low relief with mermaid and swirling bubbles, 3 conical feet, "R. Lalique" in relief," inscribed "France," polished chip on rim, model introduced 1920, 14⅜" d **$4,313.00**

Hood Ornament, Grand Libellule, frosted, perching dragonfly with wings raised, "R. Lalique" in relief, inscribed "R. Lalique France" in script, model introduced 1928, 8¼" h, 7¾" l **7,475.00**

Perfume Bottle, Vers Les Jours for Worth, frosted amber, moon-shaped, molded in low relief with 5 bands of chevrons, conforming disc stopper, amber shading to clear at shoulder, "Worth R. Lalique France" in relief, model introduced 1926, 4¼" h **805.00**

Vase, Camaret, spherical vase molded in low relief with 4 continuous bands of fish, traces of gray enamel in recesses, inscribed "R. Lalique France No. 1010" in script, model introduced 1928, 5⅜" h **518.00**

Vase, Sauterelles, ovoid body molded in low and high relief with grasshoppers on tall blades of grass, blue and green enamel in recesses, inscribed "R. Lalique France" in script, base shaved, model introduced 1913, 10½" h **3,738.00**

LAMPS

Kerosene lamps dominated the 19th century and first quarter of the 20th century. Thomas Edison's invention of the electric light bulb in 1879 marked the beginning of the end of the kerosene lamp era.

The 1930s was the Age of Electricity. By the end of the decade electricity was available throughout America. Manufacturers and designers responded quickly to changing styles and tastes. The arrival of the end table and television as major pieces of living room furniture presented a myriad of new design opportunities.

Most lamps are purchased for reuse, not collecting purposes. Lamps whose design speaks to a specific time period or that blend with modern decor have decorative rather than collecting value. Decorative value is significantly higher than collecting value.

With the broad lamp category, there are several lamp groups that are collected. Aladdin lamps, due primarily to an extremely

strong collectors' club, are in a league of their own. Other collecting subcategories include character lamps, figural lamps, novelty, motion or revolving lamps, student lamps, Tiffany and Tiffany-style lamps, and TV lamps.

References: Jan Lindenberger, *Lamps of the 50s & 60s*, Schiffer Publishing, 1997; *Electric Lighting of the 20s–30s, Vol. 1* (1994, 1998 value update), *Vol. 2*, 1994, 1998 value update, L-W Book Sales; L-W Book Sales (ed.), *Better Electric Lamps of the 20's & 30's*, L-W Book Sales, 1997; L-W Book Sales (ed.), *Quality Electric Lamps*, L-W Book Sales, 1992, 1996 value update; Nadja Maril, *American Lighting: 1840–1940*, Schiffer Publishing, 1995; Leland and Crystal Payton, *Turned On: Decorative Lamps of the 'Fifties*, Abbeville Press, 1989.

Note: For additional listings see Aladdin, Motion Lamps, and Television Lamps.

Character, Davy Crockett, ceramic, brown accent Davy Crockett image standing full figure holding rifle next to simulated tree with his name incised in base, bear seated on right side, ©Premco Mfg Co, Chicago, 1955, 11¼" h **$100.00**

Character, Donald Duck, ceramic, Donald atop candlestick holder with arm wrapped around dripping candle, orig electric cord and flame bulb, Leeds China, Co, unmkd, late 1940s, 7¾" h, 5" d base **200.00**

Character, Joe Carioca, ceramic, orig electric cord, American Pottery Co foil sticker on top front edge of base, 1940s, 5½" h, 4½" d base **200.00**

Character, Road Runner, ceramic, purple accent Road Runner resting on green cactus with pink and yellow flowers on top, brown simulated desert base with decal on front, Holiday Fair, made in Japan paper sticker on underside, ©1970 Warner Bros, Inc, 4¾ x 4¾ x 9" **50.00**

Character, Roy Rogers and Trigger, painted plaster on 3¼ x 5" rounded base, no shade, c1950s, Plasto Mfg Co, Chicago **200.00**

Character, spaceman, ceramic, red accent line around base edge with raised "Off To Space" on front, 12½" h, 4½" d base **75.00**

Desk, ceramic, figural panther, fiberglass shade, 16" h **55.00**

Lamp, abstract design, ceramic, turquoise with gold highlights, 2-tier parchment shade, 1960s, 30½" h, price for pair, $75.00.

Desk, ivory enameled metal boomerang arm, bright chrome saucer shade and base, adjustable, Fasi, 18 x 21" **100.00**

Desk, plastic, basketweave design, wood legs, 15" h. **15.00**

Floor, aluminum and Bakelite, torchere style, Art Deco, etched frosted shade, 56 x 17" **100.00**

Floor, brass, mushroom shaped frosted glass shade, Laurel, 56" h **425.00**

Floor, brushed chrome, mushroom shaped frosted glass globe, unmkd, Lanel, 57" h, 14" d globe **650.00**

Floor, brushed chrome, swing-arm, adjustable height, milk glass flaring shade, Nessen Studios, 52 x 14". **100.00**

Floor, ceramic, cylindrical, bold horizontal polychrome stripes, unmkd, Raymor, 22½ x 6" **275.00**

Floor, chrome, circular base and counter weighted arm, semi-spherical shade, adjustable, 63" h **275.00**

Floor, chrome, tubular with 5 large white globe bulbs, 64½ x 13½" **175.00**

Floor, glass, white, flaring top and base joined by chrome cylinder, Italian, 47½ x 16" **400.00**

Floor, glass, white, light bulb shaped, 40 x 15" **400.00**

Floor, wood, torchere style, flaring brushed aluminum fixture and flaring white glass shade, c1950, 66½ x 17½" **275.00**

Hanging, chrome, 5 molecular spheres **320.00**

Table, aluminum, off-center semi-spherical shade resting on broad cylindrical shaft, Laurel, 18" h, 12¼" d. **350.00**

Table, arched chrome base, white spherical shade, paper label, Laurel, 14¼ x 7½" **325.00**

Table, blue, white, and green swirling acanne glass base, Barovier/Milano paper label, 18" h. **350.00**

Table, bright chrome and orange plastic, molded in shape of jai alai basket, Lamperti, 13" h **150.00**

Table, conical walnut base, frosted glass mushroom shade, Laurel, 12 x 13" **225.00**

Table, corseted brushed chrome base, white spherical shade, paper label, Laurel, 18 x 7", price for pair **550.00**

Table, iron, figural dollar sign, 18" h **30.00**

Table, red cordinato oro glass, Barovier & Toso, 13" h. **100.00**

Table, white and clear sommerso glass with controlled bubbles, attributed to Seguso, 20" h **250.00**

LEFTON CHINA

George Zoltan Lefton was the driving force behind Lefton China, a china importing and marketing organization. Following World War II, Lefton, a Hungarian immigrant, began importing giftware made in the Orient into the United States. Lefton passed away on May 29, 1996.

Until the mid-1970s Japanese factories made the vast majority of Lefton China. After that date, China, Malaysia, and Taiwan became the principal supply sources.

Most Lefton pieces are identified by a fired-on trademark or a paper label. Numbers found on pieces are item identification numbers. When letters precede a number, it is a factory code, e.g., "SL" denotes Nippon Art China K.K.

References: Loretta DeLozier, *Collector's Encyclopedia of Lefton China* (1995) and *Book II* (1997), Collector Books; Ruth McCarthy, *Lefton China*, Schiffer Publishing, 1998.

Collectors' Club: National Society of Lefton Collectors, 1101 Polk St, Bedford, IA 50833.

Grouping, urn and 2 vases, #491, green, paper label, 1953–71, 2⅞", $15.00.

After Dinner Cup and Saucer, Elegant Rose, #634 . . . . **$32.00**

Ashtray, Pink Romance, #4963, 7½" d **40.00**

Bank, lion with glasses, #13384, 6" h. **52.00**

Bank, pig with flowers, #1992, 5 x 4" **20.00**

Bank, turtle, #3893, glass eyes **12.00**

Bookends, pr, violin and mandolin, #018, 5½ x 5" **35.00**

Bowl, figural sleigh, White Holly, #6048, 5" l **10.00**

Box, candy, Valentine Girl, #7172, 5¾" h **22.00**

Box, egg shaped, Spring Bouquet, #335, 5" h **40.00**

Candle Holder, pr, lily, #2499, 3¾" h **25.00**

Candy Dish, cov, #365, 7½ x 4¼" **35.00**

Cheese Dish, cov, Miss Priss, #1505, 5½" d **85.00**

Cigarette Set, box and 2 ashtrays, Heavenly Rose, #103 . . . . . **50.00**

Coaster, fruit design, gold trim, #20128, 3" d **10.00**

Coffeepot, cov, Cosmos, #1077 . . . . **110.00**

Compote, Paisley Fantazia, #6802, 7" h **15.00**

Cookie Jar, Dainty Miss, #040, 7½" h. **125.00**

Cookie Jar, Scottish girl **235.00**

Decanter, Santa, #1383, 7¾" h **25.00**

Espresso Line, creamer and sugar, #3160, tangerine, 4" h **32.00**

Espresso Line, cup and saucer, #3250, tangerine. **10.00**

Espresso Line, plate, #3284, 9" d **12.00**

Espresso Line, snack set, #2149, wisteria, 8" l. **15.00**

Figurine, Angel, #2323, bisque, 4¾" h **30.00**

Figurine, Angel of the Month, #1987 . . . . **30.00**

Figurine, ballerina, #444, 5¾" h, price for set of 3 . . . . **95.00**

Figurine, Bobwhite, #300, 5¼" h **35.00**

Figurine, cat on pillow, #2540, 4½" h **10.00**

Figurine, Christmas Angel, #1419, 3¼" h **15.00**

Figurine, dachshund, #3213, with stones, matte, 5" l **15.00**

Figurine, Fifi, #5742, 7½" h. **120.00**

Figurine, Heron, #1532, 5½" h **45.00**

Figurine, Little Miss Mistletoe, #102, 4½" h **35.00**

Figurine, Musical Girl, #149, 3½" h **18.00**

Figurine, otter, #132, 5½" h **32.00**

Figurine, poodle with lilacs, #157, 5" h **40.00**

Figurine, tiger, #8743, black, white, and gold, 8½" l **50.00**

Pitcher, Green Heritage, #4579, 6¼" h **55.00**

Planter, fish, #709, 10¼" l **22.00**

Plate, Holly Garland, #1804, 9" d **30.00**

Powder Box, #550, bone china, 3¼" l **18.00**

Ring Holder, figural hand, #90545, pink bisque, 3½" h. **22.00**

Salt and Pepper Shakers, pr, Fruits of Italy, #1207 . . . . **12.00**

Snack Set, Moss Rose, #3171, 8¼" d **18.00**

Soap Dish, shell shaped, #5066, ftd **10.00**

Toothbrush Holder, French Rose, #2646, 3¾" h **15.00**

LENOX

In 1889, Walter Scott Lenox and Jonathan Coxon, Sr., founded the Ceramic Art Company in Trenton, New Jersey. Lenox acquired sole ownership in 1894. In 1906 he formed Lenox, Inc.

Lenox gained national recognition in 1917 when President Woodrow Wilson ordered a 1,700-piece dinner service. Later, Presidents Franklin D. Roosevelt and Harry S. Truman followed Wilson's lead. First Lady Nancy Reagan ordered a 4,732-piece set of gold-embossed bone china from Lenox in 1981. According to Eric Poehner, the Lenox craftsman who did much of the work, each raised golden seal in the center of the Reagan service plates took two-and-one-half to three hours to hand paint.

During the last two decades, Lenox, Inc., has expanded, acquiring Art Carved, Inc., H. Rosenthal Jewelry Corporation, Imperial Glass Corporation, and many other companies. Operating today as Lenox Brands, the company is a multimillion-dollar enterprise producing a broad range of tabletop and giftware.

References: Susan and Al Bagdade, *Warman's American Pottery and Porcelain,* Wallace-Homestead, Krause Publications, 1994; Harry L. Rinker, *Dinnerware of the 20th Century: The Top 500 Patterns,* House of Collectibles, 1997; Harry L. Rinker, *Stemware of the 20th Century: The Top 200 Patterns,* House of Collectibles, 1997.

Note: For additional listings see Limited Edition Collectibles.

Brookdale, cereal bowl, coupe, 5³/₄" d	$45.00
Brookdale, coffeepot, cov	240.00
Brookdale, creamer	80.00
Brookdale, cup and saucer, ftd, 2¹/₈"	50.00
Brookdale, dinner plate, 10¹/₂" d	40.00
Brookdale, fruit bowl, 5¹/₂" d	40.00
Brookdale, sugar, cov	95.00
Busts, pr, man and woman, Art Deco, porcelain, glossy ivory glaze, imp "A.B.C.O. '35," green stamped mark, 8³/₄ x 3³/₄"	225.00
Charleston, bread and butter plate, 6¹/₂" d	6.00
Charleston, butter, no lid, ¹/₄ lb	30.00

Charleston, cup, ftd, 3¹/₄"	15.00
Charleston, dinner plate, 10³/₄" d	12.00
Charleston, salad plate, 8¹/₄"	10.00
Charleston, vegetable, oval, 9¹/₂" l	50.00
Cinderella, bread and butter plate, 6³/₈" d	20.00
Cinderella, cream soup bowl	80.00
Cinderella, cup and saucer, ftd, 2⁵/₈"	50.00
Cinderella, dinner plate, 10⁷/₈" d	40.00
Cinderella, fruit bowl, flat, 6¹/₂" d	40.00
Cinderella, gravy boat, attached underplate	160.00
Cinderella, salad plate, 8³/₈" d	25.00
Cinderella, soup bowl, flat, 8¹/₂" d	50.00
Fancy Free, bread and butter plate, 6³/₈" d	6.00
Fancy Free, casserole, cov, 6¹/₄" d	65.00
Fancy Free, cereal bowl, coupe, 6¹/₈" d	15.00
Fancy Free, cup and saucer, flat, 2³/₄"	12.00
Fancy Free, dinner plate, 10³/₈" d	20.00
Fancy Free, salad plate, 8" d	15.00
Fancy Free, sugar, cov	22.00
Figurine, girl, porcelain, flowing gown covered in glossy ivory glaze, imp "Lenox/A.B.C. '37," 13³/₄ x 5³/₄"	385.00
Vase, baluster form, emb ivy leaves, celadon, #3170, 9¹/₂" h	45.00
Wall Masks, pr, male and female, stamped mark, 9" h	115.00

L.E. SMITH GLASS

L.E. Smith Glass began when Lewis E. Smith, a gourmet cook, needed glass jars for a mustard he planned to market. Rather than buy jars, he bought a glass factory in Mt. Pleasant, Pennsylvania, and made them himself. Smith remained active in the company from 1908 through 1911. He is credited with inventing the glass top for percolators, the modern-style juice reamer, the glass mixing bowl, and numerous other kitchen implements.

Smith sold his interest in L.E. Smith Glass in 1911. The company continued, making automobile lenses, cookware, fruit jars, kitchenware, novelties, and tableware. Black glass was a popular product in the 1920s and 30s. Giftware and tableware products remain the company's principal focus today.

Reference: Marlena Toohey, *A Collector's Guide to Black Glass,* Antique Publications, 1988, 1998 value update.

Amy, cookie jar, cov, black	$95.00
Do-Si-Do, cake plate, handled	15.00
Do-Si-Do, plate, 6" d	5.00
Do-Si-Do, sugar, cov	8.00
Figure, fighting cock, dark blue, 9"	75.00
Figure, goose girl, amber, 6" h	55.00
Figure, thrush, robin's egg blue, Haley mold	75.00
Homestead, grill plate, 9" d	8.00
Homestead, parfait	8.00
Kent, fern dish, 3 ftd, white opaque	10.00
Kent, mayonnaise	8.00
Kent, sugar, cov	8.00
Melba, bowl, ruffled, green, 10¹/₂" d	12.00
Melba, casserole, cov, oval, 9¹/₂" l	18.00
Melba, cup and saucer, pink	5.00
Melba, plate, amethyst, 6" d	5.00
Moon 'n' Star, compote, cov, amberina	40.00
Moon 'n' Star, creamer, amberina	12.00
Moon 'n' Star, cruet, amberina	12.00
Moon 'n' Star, fairy lamp, ruby	35.00

Figure, Art Deco, girl with greyhound, glossy ivory glaze, imp "Lenox, A.B.C.O. '37," 13¹/₂" h, $468.00. Photo courtesy David Rago Auctions, Inc.

Urn Vase, ftd, veined onyx, 7¹/₂" h, $30.00.

Verna Mae Wright, L.G. Wright's wife, directed the company following Wright's death in 1969. She added custard glass to the company's line in 1969, and carnival in 1972. Verna Mae Wright died in 1990. Dorothy Stephen and Phyllis Stephan Buettner, her daughter, inherited the company. In October 1996 the company opened a museum adjacent to its gift shop and plant in New Martinsville, West Virginia.

Reference: James Measell and W. C. "Red" Roetteis, *The L.G. Wright Glass Company,* Glass Press, 1997.

Apothecary Jar, Thumbprint, 6" h	$125.00
Ashtray, Colonial Carriage	18.00
Ashtray, Moon and Star	35.00
Barber Bottle, Fern	110.00
Barber Bottle, Stars and Stripes, cranberry	275.00
Compote, cov, Stipple Star, 6" h	55.00
Creamer and Sugar, Panel Grape	22.00
Creamer and Sugar, Sweetheart	22.00
Cruet, Fern, satin finish, round	115.00
Cruet, Honeycomb	145.00
Cruet, Thumbprint, fluted, oval	100.00
Decanter, Moon and Star, c1976	400.00
Epergne Vase, Panel Grape	75.00
Finger Bowl, with honeycomb	65.00
Goblet, Panel Grape, blue opalescent	32.00
Pickle Jar, Fern, vaseline opalescent	200.00
Pitcher, Beaded Curtain, yellow overlay	600.00
Pitcher, Fern, blue opalescent	225.00
Plate, Moss Rose, milk glass, lattice open edge	120.00
Rose Bowl, Fern, large	75.00
Rose Bowl, Hobnail, amber	50.00
Sugar Shaker, Thumbprint	65.00
Toothpick Holder, frog, milk glass	32.00
Tumbler, carnival glass, Banded Grape	32.00
Tumbler, cranberry swirl	45.00
Tumbler, Mary Gregory dec	45.00
Vase, fern motif	175.00
Wall Planter, Daisy and Button, blue	32.00
Water Pitcher, Daisy and Fern	350.00
Wine, Panel Grape	18.00

Moon 'n' Star, sugar, cov, amberina	15.00
Moon 'n' Star, water goblet, amberina	18.00
Mt Pleasant, bowl, scalloped, 2-handled, pink, 8" d	20.00
Mt Pleasant, bowl, scalloped, ftd, 9" d, black	30.00
Mt Pleasant, cake plate, 2-handled, coblat, 10¹/₂" w	30.00
Mt Pleasant, cake plate, ftd, black, 10¹/₂" d	38.00
Mt Pleasant, candlestick, double, cobalt	24.00
Mt Pleasant, candlesticks, pr, single, pink	20.00
Mt Pleasant, creamer, black	20.00
Mt Pleasant, cup and saucer, cobalt	17.00
Mt Pleasant, maple leaf dish, cobalt, 8" w	18.00
Mt Pleasant, plate, scalloped, cobalt, 8" d	15.00
Mt Pleasant, rose bowl, scalloped, 3 ftd, cobalt	25.00
Mt Pleasant, salt and pepper shakers, pr, ftd, cobalt	40.00
Mt Pleasant, sherbet, scalloped, cobalt	18.00
Mt Pleasant, sugar, open, scalloped, cobalt	18.00
Mt Pleasant, vase, ruffled rim, cobalt, 7¹/₄" h	35.00
Vase, crimped, 2 handles, 2 ladies dancing inside a heart, 7" h	45.00

L.G. WRIGHT GLASS

L.G. Wright Glass reproduced many types of late 19th- and early 20th-century glass. The company also introduced new forms, shapes, and patterns.

Lawrence Gale Wright (1904 to 1969) began buying and selling glass "seconds" in 1936/37. In 1938 he contracted with Fenton to manufacture a reproduction Hobnail barber bottle in amber and vaseline. As the 1930s ended, Wright was buying glass from Cambridge, Fenton, Morgantown, and Westmoreland. He ordered his first new molds in 1937.

Not all L.G. Wright glass was made from period molds. Although Wright purchased period molds from Northwood and Dugan, the company ordered hundreds of new molds from firms such as Albert Boston's B. Machine & Mould, Island Mould and Machine, National Mould and Machine, and Stiehm & Son.

Wright's early customers included "reproduction" wholesalers such as AA. Sales, Koscherak Brothers, and F. Pavel. The period from 1950 to 1970 was L.G. Wright's golden age. Peachblow was produced between 1955 and 1963. A glass decorating plant opened in early 1968.

LIBBEY GLASS

The Libbey Glass Company traces its origins to the New England Glass Company, founded in 1818 in Boston. In 1888 New England Glass moved to Toledo, Ohio, to be nearer a better fuel source. The company became the Libbey Glass Company in 1892, named for the family that managed it for several decades.

Financial difficulties arising from the move ended when Libbey began producing light bulbs. The company also manufactured a brilliant cut glass line. By the 1920s, Libbey introduced an art glass line (amberina, pomona, peachblow, etc.) and a hotel and restaurant line. In 1925 Libbey acquired the Nonik Glassware Corp., a major tumbler manufacturer.

In 1933, under the direction of Douglas Nash, Libbey re-emphasized its fine glass lines. It also acquired the H. C. Fry Company. In 1935 Owen-Illinois Glass Company purchased Libbey Glass, then billed as the "world's largest producers of glass containers." Owen-Illinois established a separate division and continues to manufacture products using the Libbey name.

References: Carl U. Fauster (comp.), *Libbey Glass Since 1818: Pictorial History & Collector's Guide*, Len Beach Press, 1979, out of print; Bob Page and Dale Fredericksen, *A Collection of American Crystal: A Stemware Identification Guide for Glasonbury/Lotus, Libbey/Rock Sharpe & Hawkes*, Page-Fredericksen Publishing, 1995; Kenneth Wilson, *American Glass 1760–1930; The Toledo Museum of Art*, 2 vols., Hudson Hills Press and The Toledo Museum of Art, 1994.

Bowl, art glass, experimental colorless glass with internal controlled bubble design and pale green powders, base stamped "Libbey," 9" d........................ **$85.00**
Bowl, cut glass, elliptical disk with hobstar and diamond cutting below intaglio-cut border with pears, peaches, and blossoms, ⅛" chip on outer rim, 10¼" d, 3¼" h..... **750.00**
Crow, cocktail.. **8.00**
Drinking Glass, Alice in Wonderland, Libbey Classics....... **12.00**
Drinking Glass, The Wizard of Oz, Libbey Classics......... **28.00**
Drinking Glass, Three Musketeers, Libbey Classics......... **12.00**
Drinking Glass, Treasure Island, Libbey Classics.......... **15.00**
Liberty Bell, sherbet, crystal............................. **22.00**
Silhouette, candlesticks, pr, clear cup, opalescent camel stem... **325.00**
Silhouette, cocktail, clear bowl, black kangaroo stem...... **125.00**
Silhouette, compote, clear bowl, fiery opalescent elephant stem, 7½" h, 11" d..................................... **525.00**
Silhouette, cordial, clear bowl, opalescent greyhound stem... **185.00**
Silhouette, goblet, clear bowl, opalescent cat stem, 7" h.... **150.00**
Silhouette, sherbet, clear bowl, black monkey stem........ **90.00**
Soap Dish, swan, crystal.................................. **25.00**
Stemware, crystal swirled goblets with green disk foot, twelve 3½" h sherbets and twelve 3¼" h wines, price for 24 pcs... **175.00**
Vase, crystal, trumpet shaped, seafoam green zipper dec, 12" h... **345.00**
Vase, Talisman, optic ribbed body with spiraled green internal thread, flared rim, applied foot, mkd "Libbey," 14" h... **225.00**
Vase, Zipper, flared rim, internally dec with green dotted lines, ftd, 6" h... **250.00**

LIBERTY BLUE

In 1973 the Grand Union Company, a retail supermarket chain based in New Jersey, commissioned Liberty Blue dinnerware to be offered as a premium in grocery stores throughout the eastern United States. Ironically, though intended to celebrate America's independence, the dinnerware was produced in Staffordshire, England.

Liberty Blue dinnerware, introduced in 1975, portrayed patriotic scenes in blue on a white background. It combined several elements of traditional Staffordshire dinnerware while remaining unique. The Wild Rose border was reproduced from a design dating back to 1784. Original engravings depicted historic buildings and events from the American Revolutionary period.

Liberty Blue is easy to identify. Most pieces contain the words "Liberty Blue" on the underside and all are marked "Made in England." The back of each dish also contains information about the scene illustrated on it.

Reference: Harry L. Rinker, *Dinnerware of the 20th Century: The Top 500 Patterns*, House of Collectibles, 1997.

Baker, oval.. **$50.00**
Berry Bowl, 4½" d... **5.00**
Bread and Butter Plate.................................... **5.00**
Butter, cov... **65.00**
Cereal Bowl... **12.00**
Coaster, set of 4... **36.00**
Creamer.. **25.00**
Cup and Saucer... **9.00**
Dinner Plate, 10" d....................................... **10.00**
Gravy Boat and Liner..................................... **50.00**
Luncheon Plate... **18.00**
Meat Platter, 12".. **48.00**
Mug.. **14.00**
Mugs, boxed set of 4..................................... **60.00**
Nappy, 5".. **5.00**
Pitcher... **150.00**
Place Marker, boxed set of 4.............................. **100.00**
Place Setting, 5 pcs...................................... **30.00**
Plate, 6½" d.. **12.00**

Silhouette, stemware, crystal with opalescent stems, consisting of 6 polar bear wines, 4 camel candlesticks, and 1 giraffe compote, each stamped "Libbey," price for 11 pcs, $2,300.00. Photo courtesy Skinner, Inc., Boston, MA.

Dinner Plate, 10" d, $10.00.

Platter, 14" **40.00**
Mug **12.00**
Salad Plate, 8½" d **12.00**
Salt and Pepper Shakers, pr **35.00**
Soup, flat, 7½" d **18.00**
Soup Tureen **250.00**
Sugar, cov **30.00**
Teapot, cov **150.00**
Vegetable, cov **150.00**
Vegetable, open, oval **35.00**
Vegetable, open, round **45.00**

LIFE MAGAZINES

The first *Life* magazine appeared in January 1883. Its covers featured artwork by some of America's foremost illustrators between 1898 and 1936. Illustrators include John Held, Jr., F. X. Leyendecker, Maxfield Parrish, Coles Phillips, and Norman Rockwell. Value for these issues is driven more by the cover illustration than the interior content. Covers are often cut from the magazine and sold as tear sheets.

On November 13, 1936, a new oversized *Life* featuring a photographic format cover replaced the old *Life*. Once again, the cover subject matter usually determines value. Interior advertising (especially in full color and personality driven) and key feature stories increase value. Many examples are purchased by crossover collectors, e.g., a Hopalong Cassidy collector seeking the June 12, 1950, issue with William Boyd's picture on the cover.

Collectors want complete issues when purchasing a post-November 1936 magazine. Removal of advertising or featured articles reduces the value by more than half.

Post-November 1936 *Life* magazines survive in extremely high quantities. As a result, only those in fine or better condition command top dollar.

Reference: Denis C. Jackson, *Life Magazines: 1899–1994*, published by author, 1998.

Periodical: *Paper Collectors' Marketplace (PCM)*, PO Box 128, Scandinavia, WI 54977.

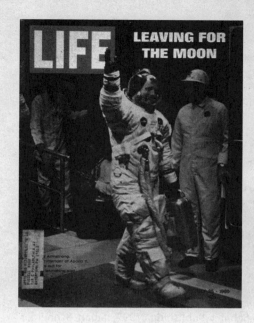

July 25, 1969, Leaving for the Moon, $5.00.

1924, Jan 31, Maxfield Parrish cov and Jell-o adv **$200.00**
1924, Nov 6, Norman Rockwell cov **85.00**
1925, Apr 2, Flapper Kissing Conductor, John Held, Jr
    cov **35.00**
1927, Jul 14, The Call of the Wild, Coles Phillips cov **60.00**
1937, Jun 28, Beach Bather **12.00**
1937, Nov 29, US Capitol Building **10.00**
1938, Oct 31, Raymond Massey **10.00**
1939, Jan 23, Bette Davis **25.00**
1940, Jan 15, Ralph Vaughn **12.00**
1941, Jan 13, Swimsuit Fashions **25.00**
1942, Jan 12, Pacific Coastal Defense **15.00**
1943, Jan 18, Rita Hayworth **18.00**
1944, Jan 24, Margaret Sullivan **15.00**
1945, Jan 15, General Patton **15.00**
1946, Feb 11, Lincoln Memorial **15.00**
1947, Feb 3, Broadway Actresses **10.00**
1948, Feb 23, Skiing **10.00**
1949, Jan 3, Dwight Eisenhower, Jr **15.00**
1950, Jan 30, Childbirth **10.00**
1951, Jan 15, Rose Parade Marshall **10.00**
1951, Oct 15, Zsa Zsa Gabor **45.00**

1952, Feb 18, Queen Elizabeth II **15.00**
1952, Mar 31, Dogpatch **14.00**
1953, Jan 19, Wilson and Humphrey **10.00**
1954, Mar 1, Rita Moreno **10.00**
1955, Jan 10, Greta Garbo **18.00**
1956, Jan 23, Harry Truman **10.00**
1957, Jan 7, Richard Nixon **10.00**
1958, Feb 3, Shirley Temple and Daughter **15.00**
1959, Jan 19, Fidel Castro **10.00**
1960, Feb 29, Olympic Skier **10.00**
1961, Jan 27, JFK Inauguration **15.00**
1961, Sep 22, Hurricane Carla **10.00**
1962, Aug 24, Soviet Capsules **10.00**
1963, Sep 27, Astronauts **15.00**
1964, Feb 21, Lee Harvey Oswald **22.00**
1965, Feb 5, Churchill's Funeral **8.00**
1966, Feb 25, Vietnam Aircraft **8.00**
1967, Dec 15, Heart Transplant **5.00**
1968, Apr 12, Martin Luther King **15.00**
1969, Jun 18, Space Walk **20.00**
1969, Sept 5, Peter Max **35.00**
1970, Dec 18, William Buckley and Family **4.00**
1971, Mar 5, Ali and Frazier **4.00**
1972, Jun 9, Bella Abzug **10.00**
1978, Dec, Prince Charles **4.00**
1979, Apr, Solar Eclipse **3.00**
1980, Aug, Muppets **3.00**
1981, Feb, Windsurfing, John Lennon **15.00**
1982, Dec, Princess Diana **15.00**
1983, Jun, Star Wars **25.00**
1984, Sep, Michael Jackson **10.00**
1985, Dec, Beyond the Stars **2.00**
1986, Jul, Statue of Liberty **2.00**
1987, Aug, Oliver North **2.00**
1988, Mar, Gilda Radner **2.00**
1989, Oct, 101 Collectibles **3.00**
1990, Feb, Child and Candles **2.00**
1991, Jun, Michael Landon **2.00**
1992, Mar, Afterlife . . . . **.75**
1993, Jan, Royal Couple **8.00**
1994, May, Breast Cancer . . . . **.50**

LIGHTERS

By the 1920s the cigarette lighter enjoyed a prominent place in most American homes, even those of non-smokers who kept a lighter handy for guests.

Well-known manufacturers include Bowers, Dunhill, Evans, Marathon, Parker, Ronson, and Zippo. Well over a thousand different manufacturers produced lighters. Although the principal manufacturing centers were Japan and the United States, there was at least one lighter manufacturer in every industrialized country in the 20th century.

Collectors shy away from lighters in less than average condition. It is important that the sparking or lighting mechanism works, whether it be flint, liquid fuel, or gas. Repairing a lighter to working order is accepted among collectors.

References: Larry Clayton, *The Evans Book,* Schiffer Publishing, 1998; Jim Fiorella, *The Viet Nam Zippo Cigarette Lighters,* Schiffer Publishing, 1998; James Flanagan, *Collector's Guide to Cigarette Lighters,* (1995, 1998 value update), *Bk. II* (1999), Collector Books; David Poore, *Zippo,* Schiffer Publishing, 1997; Stuart Schneider and George Fischler, *Cigarette Lighters,* Schiffer Publishing, 1996; Neil S. Wood, *Collecting Cigarette Lighters* (1994) and *Vol. II* (1995), L-W Book Sales.

Collectors' Clubs: International Lighter Collectors, PO Box 536, Quitman, TX 75783; Pocket Lighter Preservation Guild & Historical Society, PO Box 1054, Addison, IL 60101.

Advertising, Dodge, hard plastic barrel with removable metal cap, "Switch to Dodge Trucks," late 1930s **$65.00**
Advertising, Pan Am, chromed metal, hinged lid, blue logo, made in Japan for Penguin distribution, orig box, 1960s **12.00**
Advertising, Philco Hi-Hat Club, chromed metal, incised trademark hat and "Philco Hi-Hat Club," orig mailer box, 1940s **50.00**
Advertising, "Phillips 66," plain case, orange, black, and white logo, Zippo, 1966 . . . . **35.00**
Advertising, Pontiac, brushed finish, Pontiac emblem and black lettering for "Louis Frahm Pontiac Inc., Downey, Calif," orig box, Zippo, 1962 . . . . **90.00**
Advertising, "Purina Kitten Chow," brushed finish, yellow, purple, and orange emblem, orig box, Zippo, 1975 . . . . **60.00**
Commemorative, LBJ, silvered metal case with inset black on silver foil LBJ photo, mkd "Life-Lighter, Ritepoint, U.S.A." **25.00**
Pin-Up, chromed metal, clear plastic wrapper over pinup model on each side, mkd "Pacific, Dragon Mfg. Co.," 1960s **30.00**
Souvenir, 1936 Great Lakes Expo, silvered metal, black and white paper wrapper under clear celluloid with Terminal Tower building **80.00**
Souvenir, 1976 Bicentennial, chrome metal case, Liberty Bell and "1776–1976, 200 Years of Freedom" **20.00**
Souvenir, "Florida, The Sunshine State," brushed stainless case with etched Florida map, palm tree, and oranges, Zippo, 1979 . . . . **25.00**
Zippo, black crackle finish, steel case, 3-barrel hinge, 1943–45 . . . . **165.00**
Zippo, brown woodgrain vinyl wrap with engraved "Dad," orig box, 1979 . . . . **28.00**

Zippo, brushed finish with engraved and enameled man bowling **90.00**
Zippo, plain case with polished finish, 1981 . . . . **50.00**

AUCTION PRICES – ZIPPO LIGHTERS

Manion's International Auction House, Inc. September 15, 1998. Prices include an 18% buyer's premium.

"American General Life Insurance Company," and George Washington on horse, brushed finish with blue enameled engraved design, period white and red factory repair box, 1972 . . . . **$97.00**
"Camel," midnight chrome finish, Joe Camel on motorcycle, with box, 1991 . . . . **45.00**
Eightball design, black matte enameled finish with black, white, blue, and yellow design, 1995 . . . . **38.00**
"Hinde & Dauch Coragated," steel case, brushed finish with red and blue enameled engraved logo, maroon and white diagonal striped box with black bottom, 1953 . . . . **112.00**
"Lockheed," brushed finish with engine-turned vertical line design and engraved winged star emblem, 1964 . . . . **72.00**
Plain Case, brown alligator leather wrap, 1953–57 . . . **173.00**
Plain Case, gold-filled polished finish, base mkd "10K Gold Filled," 1960s **90.00**
Plain Case, steel finish, 3-barrel, wear and some tarnish, WWII era **71.00**
"Springvale Country Club, N. Olmsted, Ohio" and man golfing, brushed finish with 6-color enameled engraved design, period white and red factory repair box, 1973 . . . . **103.00**

LIMITED EDITION COLLECTIBLES

In 1895 Bing and Grøndahl produced its first Christmas plate. Royal Copenhagen followed in 1908 and Rosenthal in 1910. Limited edition art prints, many copies of Old Masters, were popular in the 1920s and 30s.

In the late 1960s and extending through the early 1980s, Americans eagerly purchased large quantities of limited edition bells, eggs, mugs, ornaments, plates, and prints. Many came with a "Certificate of Authenticity," in reality a meaningless document.

With production runs often exceeding 100,000 units, very few of these issues were truly limited. Many individuals purchased them as investments rather than for display. The speculative limited edition bubble burst in the mid-1980s. Today, the vast majority of limited edition collectibles issued between the late 1960s and the early 1980s sell for less than 50¢ on the dollar.

Limited edition collectibles is a broad category. Not all items are numbered. In some cases, limited means produced for a relatively short period of time.

Currently, prices are stable or slowly rising on a few select pieces—those that collectors have identified as desirable or whose image crosses over into other collecting categories.

References: *Collectibles Price Guide & Directory to Secondary Market Dealers, Ninth Edition,* Collectors' Information Bureau, 1999, distributed by Krause Publications; Collectors' Information Bureau, *Collectibles Market Guide & Price Index, 16th Edition,*

Collectors' Information Bureau, 1998, distributed by Krause Publications; Annette Power, *The Charlton Standard Catalog of Lilliput Lane, Second Edition,* Charlton Press, 1998; Rinker Enterprises, *The Official Price Guide to Collector Plates, Seventh Edition,* House of Collectibles, 1999; Mary Sieber (ed.), *Price Guide to Limited Edition Collectibles,* Krause Publications, 1998.

Periodicals: *Collector Editions,* 170 Fifth Ave, 12th Floor, New York, NY 10010; *Collector's Bulletin,* 22341 East Wells Rd, Canton, IL 61520; *Collectors Mart Magazine,* 700 E State St, Iola, WI 54990; *The Treasure Trunk,* PO Box 13554, Arlington, TX 76094.

Collectors' Club: International Plate Collectors Guild, PO Box 487, Artesia, CA 90702.

Note: In addition to company-sponsored collectors' clubs, there are numerous clubs for specific limited edition collectibles. Consult *Maloney's Antiques & Collectibles Resource Directory* by David J. Maloney, Jr., at your local library for further information. For additional listings see individual manufacturers' categories.

Architecture, Band Creations, Inc, Knox, Chester County, PA, America's Covered Bridges Series, 1995 . . . . . **$30.00**
Architecture, Brandywine Collectibles, Bradfield House, Barnsville Collection, M Whiting, 1991 . . . . **32.00**
Architecture, Dave Grossman Creations, Pemaquid Bell House, ME, C Spencer Collin, 1984 . . . . **30.00**
Architecture, Department 56, The Old Curiosity Shop, Christmas in the City Series, 1987 . . . . **42.00**
Architecture, Gift Star, Bavarian Church, Brian Baker's Déjà Vu Collection, B Baker, 1987 . . . . **38.00**
Architecture, Harbor Lights, Marblehead, OH, Great Lakes Region Series, 1992 . . . . **100.00**
Architecture, Hawthorne Village, Grande Dame of Nob Hill, Lost Victorians of Old San Francisco Series, 1991 . . . . **35.00**
Architecture, Lilliput Lane Ltd, Wallace Station, American Collection, D Tate, 1984 . . . . **400.00**
Architecture, Sheila's Collectibles, St Michael's Church, Charleston Series, S Thompson, 1990 . . . . **50.00**
Architecture, The Cat's Meow, Wintrop House, Christmas '84–Nantucket Series, F Jones, 1984 . . . . **250.00**
Bell, Artists of the World, Los Ninos, DeGrazia Bells, T DeGrazia, 1980 . . . . **85.00**
Bell, Belleek, A Partridge in a Pear Tree, Twelve Days of Christmas Series, 1991 . . . . **30.00**
Bell, Dave Grossman Creations, Faces of Christmas, Norman Rockwell Collection, 1975 . . . . **35.00**
Bell, Fenton Art Glass, Christmas Morn, Christmas Series, M Dickinson, 1978 . . . . **25.00**
Bell, Goebel/Hummel, Let's Sing, Annual Bells Series, MI Hummel, 1978 . . . . **75.00**
Bell, Gorham, American Homestead, Currier & Ives Mini Bells Series, 1977 . . . . **25.00**
Bell, Gorham, Sweet Song So Young, N Rockwell, 1975 . . . . . **50.00**
Bell, Kirk Stieff, Santa's Workshop, 1992 . . . . **40.00**
Bell, Lenox Crystal, Angel Bell, Annual Bell Series, 1988 . . . . **45.00**
Bell, Lladró, Christmas Bell Series, 1987 . . . . **60.00**
Bell, Lowell Davis Farm Club, Kate, RFD Bell Series, L Davis, 1979 . . . . **375.00**
Bell, Reed & Barton, Noel Musical Bell Series, 1980 . . . . **60.00**
Bell, Roman Inc, Beach Buddies, F Hook Bells Series, 1985 . . . . **28.00**

Bell, Seymour Mann Inc, Bluebird, Connoisseur Collection, Bernini, 1995 . . . . **15.00**
Doll, Annalee Mobilitee Dolls, Baby Angel, A Thorndike, 1950, 7" h **550.00**
Doll, Annalee Mobilitee Dolls, Baby Mouse, A Thorndike, 1975, 7" h **150.00**
Doll, Annalee Mobilitee Dolls, Unicorn, Animals Series, A Thorndike, 1986, 10" h **350.00**
Doll, Anri, Victoria, Sarah Kay Dolls Series, S Kay, 1988, 14" h **500.00**
Doll, Ashton-Drake, Little Bo Peep, Child of Mother Goose Series, Y Bello, 1987 . . . . **100.00**
Doll, Attic Babies, Flakey Jakey, retired, M Maschino Walker, 1989 . . . . **75.00**
Doll, Department 56, Mr & Mrs Fezziwig, Heritage Village Doll Collection, 1988 . . . . **170.00**
Doll, Dolls by Jerri, Alfalfa, J McCloud, 1986 . . . . **350.00**
Doll, Elke's Originals Ltd, Kricket, E Hutchens, 1990 . . . . . . **400.00**
Doll, Georgetown Collection Inc, Katie, Little Loves Series, B Deval, 1989 . . . . **140.00**
Doll, Goebel/Hummel Chimney Sweep, MI Hummel, 1964 . . . . **200.00**
Doll, Gorham, Molly Melinda Bearkin, Beverly Port Designer Collection, B Port, 1987, 10" h **300.00**
Doll, Hamilton Collection, Melissa, Baby Portrait Dolls Series, B Parker, 1991 . . . . **175.00**
Doll, Ladie and Friends, Christmas Wooly Lamb, The Christmas Pageant Series, B&P Wisber, 1985 . . . . **35.00**
Doll, Lee Middleton Original Dolls, Angel Face, Vinyl Collectors Series, 1985 . . . . **150.00**
Doll, Original Appalachian Artworks, Amethyst, Cabbage Patch Kids Series, X Roberts, 1986 . . . . **200.00**
Doll, Reco, Tommy the Clown, Children's Circus Doll Collection, J McClelland, 1991 . . . . **75.00**
Doll, Sarah's Attic, Holly Black Angel, Heirlooms from the Attic Series, 1986 . . . . **35.00**
Doll, Seymour Mann Inc, Dianna, Connossieur Doll Collection, S Mann, 1990 . . . . **175.00**
Doll, Timeless Creations, Ellen, Barefoot Children Series, A Himstedt, 1987 . . . . **825.00**

Doll, Ashton-Drake Galleries, Edwin M. Knowles, "Mary Had a Little Lamb," Children from Mother Goose, 1987, 14" h, $100.00.

Figurine, Ace Product Management Group Inc, Mainstreet USA, Harley-Davidson Christmas Series, 1990. . . . . 130.00

Figurine, All God's Children, Adam, All God's Children Series, M Root, 1989. . . . . 35.00

Figurine, Amaranth Productions, Holly, Christmas Elves Series, L West, 1988 . . . . 230.00

Figurine, American Artists, Tranquility, F Stone, 1986 . . . . . . 275.00

Figurine, Anri, Admiration, J Ferrandiz, 1983 . . . . 300.00

Figurine, Anri, A Young Man's Fancy, Club Anri Series, S Kay, 1987. . . . . 175..00

Figurine, Anri, Devotion, Shepherd of the Year Series, J Ferrandiz, 1982, 6" h 275.00

Figurine, Armani, Lady Harlequin, Moonlight Masquerade Series, G Armani, 1991 . . . . 465.00

Figurine, Armstrong's, Clem Kadiddlehopper, The Red Skelton Collection, R Skelton, 1981 . . . . 175.00

Figurine, Artaffects, Crazy Horse, The Chieftains Series, G Perillo, 1983 . . . . 200.00

Figurine, Artists of the World, My First Horse, Goebel Miniatures Series, R Olszewski, 1985. . . . . 95.00

Figurine, Artists of the World, Wee Three, T DeGrazia, 1987. . . . . 250.00

Figurine, Band Creations, March, Angel of the Month Series, Richards/Penfield, 1993. . . . . 10.00

Figurine, Boyds Collection Ltd, Neville as Joseph, The Bearstone Collection, GM Lowenthal 30.00

Figurine, Boyds Collection Ltd, Wilson at the Beach, The Bearstone Collection, GM Lowenthall, 1994. . . . . 25.00

Figurine, Byers' Choice Ltd, Traditional Grandparents, Carolers Series, J Byers, 1985. . . . . 45.00

Figurine, Cast Art Industries, Forever Friends, Dreamsicles Series, K Haynes, 1991. . . . . 45.00

Figurine, Crystal World, Alligator, All God's Creatures Series, R Nakai, 1983 . . . . 45.00

Figurine, Dave Grossman Creations, Mammy, Gone With the Wind Series, 1988. . . . . 70.00

Figurine, Department 56, Best Friends, Snowbabies Series, 1986 . . . . 125.00

Figurine, Duncan Royale, Uncle, History of Class Entertainers Series, P Aposit, 1987 . . . . 350.00

Figurine, Enchantica, Gargoyle-Spring Dragon, retired, A Bill, 1988 . . . . 500.00

Figurine, Enesco, Anna, "Hooray For You," Cherished Teddies, P Hillman, 1992. 22.00

Figurine, Flambro Imports, Balancing Act, Emmett Kelly Jr Miniatures Series, 1986 . . . . 150.00

Figurine, Florence-Kitchen Angel, The Folkstone Collection, GM Lowenthal, 1994. . . . . 30.00

Figurine, Franklin Mint, Ride 'em Cowboy, Joys of Childhood Series, N Rockwell, 1976 . . . . 175.00

Figurine, Franklin Mint, The Nurse, N Rockwell, 1987 . . . . . . 75.00

Figurine, Gartlan USA, Kareem Abdul-Jabbar, "The Captain," Kareem Abdul-Jabbar Sky-Hook Collection, sgd, L Heyda, 1989 . . . . 300.00

Figurine, Goebel/Hummel, The Accompanist, MI Hummel Collectibles Figurines Series, MI Hummel, 1988 . . . . 115.00

Figurine, Gorham, At the Vets, Miniatures Series, N Rockwell, 1981 . . . . 40.00

Figurine, Hamilton Collection, Calla Lilly, American Garden Flowers Series, D Fryer, 1988. . . . . 75.00

Figurine, Hudson Creek, Comanche Plains Drummer, Chilmark American West Series, D Polland, 1982 . . . . 115.00

Figurine, Hudson Creek, Giraffe, Chilmark Wildlife Series, D Polland, 1979 . . . . 145.00

Figurine, June McKenna Collectibles Inc, Watermelon Patch Kids, Black Folk Art Series, J McKenna, 1985 . . . . . 100.00

Figurine, Kurt S Adler, Young Arthur, Fabriché Camelot Figure Series, P Mauk, 1994. . . . . 110.00

Figurine, Legends, Grizz Country, pewter, American Heritage Series, D Edwards, 1987. . . . . 370.00

Figurine, Lowell Davis Farm Club, Attic Antics, Davis RFD America Series, L Davis, 1984 . . . . 100.00

Figurine, Lowell Davis Farm Club, The Party's Over, L Davis, 1987 . . . . 175.00

Figurine, Madame Harp, Melody in Motion, S Nakane, 1988. . . . . 130.00

Figurine, Maruri USA, Cherry Blossom, Legendary Flowers of the Orient, Ito, 1985 . . . . 55.00

Figurine, Museum Collections Inc, First Haircut, American Family Series, N Rockwell, 1980. . . . . 150.00

Figurine, Old World Christmas, Black Cat on Wire, Halloween Series, EM Merck, 1988 . . . . 12.00

Figurine, Original Appalachian Artworks, Bedtime Story, Extra Special Series, X Roberts, 1984 . . . . 20.00

Figurine, PenDelfin, Jingle, retired, D Roberts, 1985 . . . . 30.00

Figurine, Polland Studios, The Hunter, Collector Society Series, D Polland, 1988 . . . . 550.00

Figurine, Precious Art, Sneaking A Peak, Krystonia Collector's Club, Panton, 1993 . . . . 45.00

Figurine, Reco Intl, Mr Tip, Clown Figures Series, J McClelland, 1987 . . . . 35.00

Figurine, Rick Cain Studios, Nightmaster, Master Series, R Cain, 1985. . . . . 350.00

Figurine, River Shore, Grandpa's Guardian, N Rockwell, 1982. . . . . 200.00

Figurine, Roman Inc, St Francis, Ceramica Excelsis Series, 1977 . . . . 60.00

Figurine, Ron Lee's World of Clowns, Peek-A-Boo Charlie, Ron Lee Collector's Club Renewal Sculptures, R Lee, 1989 . . . . 150.00

Figurine, Sarah's Attic Inc, Angel Bear, Beary Adorables Collection, 1989 . . . . 25.00

Figurine, Tudor Mint Inc, Infernal Demon, Myth & Magical Standard Series, R Gibbons, 1989 . . . . 400.00

Figurine, United Design Corp, Peaceful Encounter, Angels Collection, D Newburn, 1992. . . . . 100.00

Figurine, Walnut Ridge Collectibles, Tiny Cat, K Bejma, 1991. . . . . 30.00

Ornament, Ace Product Management Group, Harley Davidson Christmas Ornaments Series, 1981 . . . . 5.00

Ornament, Annalee Mobiltee Dolls Inc, Clown Head, A Thorndike, 1985 . . . . 175.00

Ornament, Anri, Heavenly Drummer, Ferrandiz Woodcarvings Series, J Ferrandiz, 1988 . . . . 225.00

Ornament, Artists of the World, Flower Girl, DeGrazia Annual Ornaments Series, 1988. . . . . 90.00

Ornament, Bing & Grøndahl, Christmas Eve at the Farmhouse, E Jensen, 1985 . . . . 20.00

Ornament, Boyd Collection Ltd, Nicholai with Tree, The Folkstone Collection, GM Lowenthal, 1995 . . . . 25.00

Ornament, Brandywine Collectibles, Wigmaker, Williamsburg Ornaments Series, M Whiting, 1988 . . . . 8.00

Ornament, Carlton Cards, O Holy Night, Summit Heirloom Collection, 1988 . . . . 10.00

Ornament, Cazenovia Abroad, Standing Angel, 1968 . . . . 70.00

Ornament, Goebel, West Germany, MI Hummel Annual, "Flying High," 1988, 4¹/₂ x 3³/₄", $75.00.

Ornament, Christopher Radko, Long Icicle, Holiday Collection, 1986, C Radko. **90.00**

Ornament, Dave Grossman Creations, Rhett, Gone With the Wind Ornaments Series, DGeently, 1987 . . . . **45.00**

Ornament, David Winter Cottages/Enesco, Christmas Carol, 1991, D Winter. **15.00**

Ornament, Department 56, Golden Swan Baker, 1984 . . . . . . **45.00**

Ornament, Department 56, Scrooge & Marley Countinghouse, Village Light-Up Series, 1987. . . . . **35.00**

Ornament, Gorham, Sterling Snowflake, Annual Snowflake Ornaments Series, 1986 . . . . **75.00**

Ornament, Hamilton Collection, Angel of Charity, Christmas Angels Series, S Kuck, 1994 . . . . **20.00**

Ornament, Hand & Hammer, Praying Angel, De Matteo, 1984. . . . . **45.00**

Ornament, Harbor Lights, Burrows Island, 1996. . . . . **15.00**

Ornament, June McKenna Collectibles Inc, Amish Girl, blue, 1986 . . . . **100.00**

Ornament, Kirk Stieff, Wythe House, Colonial Williamsburg Series, D Bacorn, 1992. . . . . **10.00**

Ornament, Kurt S Adler Inc, Christina, Christmas in Chelsea Collection, 1992. . . . . **25.00**

Ornament, Lilliput Lane Ltd, Mistletoe Cottage, 1992 . . . . **50.00**

Ornament, Lowell Davis Farm Club, Church, Lowell Davis Farm Club Series, L Davis, 1986 . . . . **50.00**

Ornament, Old World Christmas, Small Bunny, Animals Series, EM Merck, 1985. . . . . **8.00**

Ornament, Roman Inc, Christmas Mourning, Catnippers Series, I Spencer, 1988. . . . . **15.00**

Ornament, The Cat's Meow, Grayling House, F Jones, 1986. . . . . **40.00**

Ornament, United Design Corp, Mary and Dove, Angels Collection, PJ Jonas, 1992 . . . . **20.00**

Ornament, Wallace Silversmiths, Reindeer, Candy Canes Series, 1990 . . . . **35.00**

Plate, American Artists, Sioux, Noble Tribes Series, D Zolan, 1984 . . . . **65.00**

Plate, American Artists, The Eternal Legacy Series, Fred Stone Classics, F Stone, 1987. . . . . **85.00**

Plate, American Commemorative, Monticello, Southern Landmarks Series, 1973. . . . . **95.00**

Plate, American Greetings, A Smile Reflects a Happy Heart, Holly Hobbie Series **18.00**

Plate, American Legacy, Wendy, Children to Love Series, S Etem, 1982. . . . . **125.00**

Plate, American Rose Society, Arizona, All-American Roses Series, 1975. . . . . **140.00**

Plate, Anna-Perenna, Sunday Ride, American Silhouettes III–Valley Life Series, P Buckley Moss, 1983 . . . . **85.00**

Plate, Anri, Santa Claus in Tyrol, Christmas Series, 1981 . . . . **200.00**

Plate, Armstrong's/Crown Parian, Sheena, Beautiful Cats of the World Series, D Van Howd, sgd, 1979 . . . . **80.00**

Plate, Artaffects, Blackfoot Nation, America's Indian Heritage Series, G Perillo, 1988 . . . . **35.00**

Plate, Artaffects, Daddy's Here, Mother's Love Series, B Pease Gutmann, 1984 . . . . **50.00**

Plate, Artists of the World, Navajo Lullaby, Don Ruffin Series, D Ruffin, 1976 . . . . **90.00**

Plate, Art World of Bourgeault, John Bunyan Cottage, Royal Literary Series, R Bourgeault, 1986 . . . . **75.00**

Plate, Bareuther, Stiftskirche, Christmas Series, H Mueller, 1967 . . . . **85.00**

Plate, Belleek Pottery, Celtic Cross, Christmas Series, 1971. . . . . **50.00**

Plate, Bing & Grøndahl, Christmas Eve in Williamsburg, Christmas in America Series, J Woodson, 1986 . . . . **150.00**

Plate, Bing & Grøndahl, Danish Village Church, Christmas Series, K Bonfils, 1960 . . . . **120.00**

Plate, Bing & Grøndahl, Duck and Ducklings, Mother's Day Series, H Thelander, 1973 . . . . **20.00**

Plate, Bing & Grøndahl, Eskimos, Jubilee Five-Year Christmas Series, A Friis, 1950 . . . . **90.00**

Plate, Bing & Grøndahl, The Fir Tree and Hare, Christmas Series, H Thelander, 1964 . . . . **35.00**

Plate, Bing & Grøndahl, Watchman, Sculpture of Town Hall, Christmas Series, M Hyldahl, 1948 . . . . **75.00**

Plate, Boehm Studios, Mr Lincoln Rose, Award-Winning Roses (Hamilton/Boehm), 1979 . . . . **65.00**

Plate, Byliny Porcelain, Winter Idyll, Russian Seasons Series, 1992 . . . . **80.00**

Plate, Calhoun's Collectors Society, In His Image, Creation Series, Y Koutsis, 1977 . . . . **120.00**

Plate, Capo Di Monte, Cherubs, Christmas Series, 1972 . . . . . **90.00**

Plate, Capo Di Monte, Mother's Day Series, 1974. . . . . **70.00**

Plate, Castleton China, Amelia Earhart, Aviation Series, 1972. . . . . **60.00**

Plate, Crown Delft, Two Sleigh Rides, Christmas Series, 1970. . . . . **20.00**

Plate, Danbury Mint, American Winter Evening, Currier & Ives Silver Series, 1976. . . . . **135.00**

Plate, Danbury Mint, First Continental Congress, Bicentennial Silver Series, 1974 . . . . **125.00**

Plate, Dave Grossman, Christmas Carol, Emmett Kelly Christmas Series, B Leighton-Jones, 1986 . . . . **350.00**

Plate, Dave Grossman, Doctor & Doll, Norman Rockwell Bas Relief Series, Rockwell-inspired, 1982, 7¹/₂" d **95.00**

Plate, Delphi, Indiana Jones and His Dad, Adventures of Indiana Jones: The Last Crusade, V Gadino, 1989 . . . . **40.00**

Plate, Dominion China Ltd, The Return Home, Proud Passage Series, 1992 . . . . **50.00**

Plate, Duncan Royale, Medieval, History of Santa Claus I Series, S Morton, 1985 . . . . **75.00**

Plate, Edna Hibel Studios, Compassion, Eroica Series, E Hibel, 1990 . . . . **65.00**

Plate, Edna Hibel Studios, Sayuri and Child, Mother and Child Series, E Hibel, 1974 . . . . **175.00**

Plate, American Express, "Baltimore Oriole," Songbirds of Roger Tory Peterson, 1982, $48.00. Photo courtesy Vincent T. Miscoski.

Plate, Enesco, Nutcracker Suite, Lucy & Me Christmas
Collection, L Rigg, 1988 . . . . **17.00**
Plate, Enesco, Some Bunny Loves You, Cherished
Teddies–Easter Series, P Hillmann, 1996 . . . . **35.00**
Plate, Fenton Art Glass, Little Brown Church in Vale,
Christmas in America Series, blue satin glass, 1970 . . . . . . **50.00**
Plate, Franklin Mint, Cardinal, Birds Series, R Evans
Younger, 1972 . . . . **135.00**
Plate, Frankoma Pottery, Provocations, Bicentennial
Series, J Frank, 1972 . . . . **40.00**
Plate, Fukagawa, Beneath Plum Branch, Warabe No
Haiku, S Suetomi, 1977 . . . . **45.00**
Plate, Furstenberg, Rabbits, Christmas Series, 1971 . . . . **30.00**
Plate, Gartlan USA, Hockey's Golden Boys, Brett and
Bobby Hull Series, sgd, M Taylor, 1992, 10¼" d **150.00**
Plate, Gartlan USA, Joe Montana, sgd, M Taylor, 1991,
10¼" d **275.00**
Plate, George Washington Mint, Coming Through the
Rye, Remington Series, F Remington, 1974 . . . . **365.00**
Plate, Ghent Collection, Cardinals in Snow, Christmas
Wildlife Series, AE Gilbert, 1974 . . . . **55.00**
Plate, Goebel/MI Hummel, Star Steed, Brastoff Series, S
Brastoff, 1979 . . . . **140.00**
Plate, Gorham Collection, April Fool's Day, April Fool
Annual, N Rockwell, 1978 . . . . **50.00**
Plate, Gorham Collection, Little Boatyard, Barrymore
Series, sterling, 1972 . . . . **145.00**
Plate, Hackett American, California Sea Otters,
Endangered Species Series, S Mano, 1980 . . . . **75.00**
Plate, Hackett American, Canadian Harp Seals, Snow
Babies Series, V Parkhurst, 1981 . . . . **65.00**
Plate, Hadley House, Evening Glow, Glow Series,
T Redlin, 1985 . . . . **325.00**
Plate, Hadley House, Heading Home, Annual Christmas
Series, T Redlin, 1991 . . . . **225.00**
Plate, Hamilton Collection, African Shade, Big Cats of
the World Series, D Manning, 1989 . . . . **35.00**

Plate, Hamilton Collection, Happy Dreams, Bundles of
Joy Series, B Pease Gutmann, 1988 . . . . **65.00**
Plate, Hamilton Collection, Mischief Makers, Country
Kitties Series, G Gerardi, 1989 . . . . **45.00**
Plate, Kaiser, Love Birds, Anniversary Series, T Schoener,
1972 . . . . **30.00**
Plate, Kaiser, Signing Declaration, Bicentennial,
J Trumball, 1976 . . . . **150.00**
Plate, Kern Collectibles, Dana and Debbie, Sugar and
Spice Series, L Jansen, 1976 . . . . **130.00**
Plate, Kern Collectibles, Randy and Rex, Portrait of
Innocence Series, L Jansen, 1978 . . . . **65.00**
Plate, Lowell Davis Farm Club, Right Church Wrong
Pew, Davis Cat Tales Series, L Davis, 1982 . . . . **90.00**
Plate, Lynell, Olde Country Inn, Betsy Bates Annual,
1979 . . . . **45.00**
Plate, Reco Intl, Little Jack Horner, McClelland's Mother
Goose Series, J McClelland, 1982 . . . . **30.00**
Plate, River Shore, The Sweetheart Tree, Little House on
the Prairie Series, E Christopherson, 1985 . . . . **45.00**
Plate, Roman Inc, Meal at Home, Father's Day Series,
1972 . . . . **25.00**
Plate, Santa Clara, Christmas Message, 1970 . . . . **40.00**
Plate, Schmid, Cheerful Cherubs, Berta Hummel
Christmas Series, 1988 . . . . **65.00**
Plate, Seeley's Ceramic Service, Alexandre, Antique
French Doll Collection, M Seeley, 1980 . . . . **45.00**
Plate, Signature Collection, Courting, Grandma's
Scrapbook, L Berran, 1983 . . . . **45.00**
Plate, Spode, Dickens, single issue, 1970 . . . . **80.00**
Plate, Sports Impressions, Larry Bird, J Catalano, 1991 . . . . . **195.00**
Plate US Historical Society, Deck the Halls with Boughs
of Holly, Christmas Carol Series, J Landis, 1982 . . . . **65.00**
Plate, Vague Shadows, Texas Night Herder, Masterpieces
of the West (Curator Collection), FT Johnson, 1980 . . . . . . **55.00**
Plate, Vernonware, Jingle Bells, Christmas Series, 1972 . . . . . **30.00**
Plate, Viletta China, Jennifer By Candlelight, Childhood
Memories (Collector's Heirloom), W Bruckner, 1978 . . . . . . **60.00**
Plate, Villeroy and Boch, Holy Family, Christmas Series,
1977 . . . . **200.00**
Plate, WS George, Moonlight Lookout, Alaska: The Last
Frontier Series, H Lambson, 1992 . . . . **55.00**
Plate, WS George, Morning Mischief, Baby Cats of the
World Series, C Fracé, 1992 . . . . **45.00**
Stein, Ace Product Management Group Inc, Roaring Into
the 1920's, Harley-Davidson Decade Series, 1995 . . . . . . **185.00**
Stein, Anheuser-Busch Inc, All I Want For Christmas,
Gerz Saturday Evening Post Collection, JC Leyen-
decker, 1994 . . . . **220.00**
Stein, Anheuser-Busch Inc, Bald Eagle, Endangered
Species Series–Collector Edition, B Kemper, 1989 . . . . **400.00**
Stein, Anheuser-Busch Inc, Bud Man, Specialty Steins,
1975 . . . . **400.00**
Stein, Anheiser-Busch Inc, First Budweiser Champion
Clydesdales, Clydesdales Holiday Series, 1980 . . . . **120.00**
Stein, Anheuser-Busch Inc, John F Kennedy, American
Heritage Collection, Gerz Meisterwerke Collection,
1993 . . . . **220.00**
Stein, Anheuser-Busch Inc, King Cobra, Specialty Steins,
1987 . . . . **250.00**
Stein, Anheuser-Busch Inc, Mallard, Gerz Meisterwerke
Collection, 1994 . . . . **250.00**
Stein, Anheuser-Busch Inc, Smoky Mountains, America
the Beautiful Collector Edition, 1997 . . . . **40.00**

Stein, Hamilton Collection, Healing Spirits, Warriors of
the Plains Tankards, G Stewart, 1995 . . . . **125.00**
Stein, Hamilton Collection, The Legendary Mickey
Mantle, R Tanenbaum, 1996 . . . . **40.00**
Stein, Royal Doulton, Beethoven, Great Composers,
S Taylor, 1996 . . . . **240.00**
Stein, Royal Doulton, Winston Churchill, Character Jug
of the Year, 1992 . . . . **225.00**

LINENS, LACE, CROCHET WORK & OTHER EMBROIDERED HOUSEHOLD TEXTILES

Linen is now a generic term used for any household covering made from cotton, lace, linen, man-made fibers, or silk. Linens experienced two golden ages, the Victorian era and the 1920s–30s. Victorian ladies prided themselves on their household linen handwork of delicate stitchery, lace insertions, fine tucking, and ruffles.

Lace divides into bobbin, embroidered, needlepoint, and machine made (also includes chemical and imitation lace). Machine-made lace dates to the first quarter of the 19th century. By 1840 technology had reached the point where machines were able to produce an imitation lace that was indistinguishable from most handmade laces.

Inexpensive mass-produced linens arrived at the turn of the century. Women turned to pre-stamped embroidery kits. The popularity of bridge and formal dining in the period following World War I brought with it a renewed interest in linens.

Today the vast majority of linens are manufactured in China, Europe, and the United States. Collectors feel modern examples lack the intricate handwork and freshness of design associated with pre-1945 linens.

References: Maryanne Dolan, *Old Lace & Linens Including Crochet,* Books Americana, Krause Publications, 1989; Frances Johnson, *Collecting Antique Linens, Lace, and Needlework,* Wallace-Homestead, Krause Publications, 1991; Frances Johnson, *Collecting Household Linens,* Schiffer Publishing, 1997; Elizabeth M. Kurella, *Guide to Lace and Linens,* Antique Trader Books, 1998; Elizabeth Scofield and Peggy Zalamea, *20th-Century Linens and Lace,* Schiffer Publishing, 1995.

Periodical: *The Lace Collector,* PO Box 222, Plainwell, MI 49080.

Collectors' Club: International Old Lacers, PO Box 481223, Denver, CO 80248.

Bedspread, white sheeting, pink and blue embroidered
colonial lady **$75.00**
Bridge Set, tablecloth and 4 matching napkins, linen,
embroidered **30.00**
Centerpiece, crocheted, rectangular, repeating snow-
flake design **18.00**
Doily, crocheted, pineapple pattern, white, 1920s, 16" d . . **30.00**
Doily, linen center panel with crocheted border, c1925 . . . . . **12.00**
Dresser Scarf, linen, embroidered multicolored basket
design, blue crocheted edging, 1930s **25.00**
Guest Towel, linen towel with embroidered flowers, cro-
cheted hanger, c1930 . . . . **25.00**
Hot Pad, flower-shaped, crocheted, green and white **1.00**
Pillowcase, pink crocheted edging, embroidered roses **20.00**
Tablecloth, cotton, multicolor Amish motif in printed
cross-stitch, white ground **25.00**

Doily, crocheted, blue edging, star pattern, $20.00.

Tablecloth, cotton, multicolor dogwood blossoms on
light blue ground **18.00**
Tablecloth, cotton, red, green, and yellow floral design
on white ground **20.00**
Tablecloth, linen, blue and white checkerboard **12.00**
Tablecloth, linen with crocheted floral design in corners,
1920s, 48" sq **40.00**
Tablecloth, muslin, Autumn Leaf pattern **225.00**
Tea Towel, cotton, multicolor stripes, 1940s **8.00**
Tea Towel, cotton, printed fruit, 1950s **10.00**
Tea Towel, cotton, printed kittens, 1950s **12.00**
Tea Towel, cotton, printed Mexican motif with colorful
donkey, 1950s **15.00**
Tea Towel, linen, green and white with brown Scottie
dog, 1950s **18.00**
Toaster Cover, quilted, fruit motif **5.00**

LITTLE GOLDEN BOOKS

The first Little Golden Books were published in September 1942. George Duplaix and Lucile Olge of the Artist and Writers Guild, a company formed by Western Printing & Publishing in the 1930s to develop new children's books, and Albert Leventhal and Leon Shimkin of Simon & Shuster developed Little Golden Books.

The key to the success of Little Golden Books was their price, 25¢. Within the first five months, 1.5 million copies were printed. Simon & Shuster published the books, the Artists and Writers Guild produced them, and Western Printing and Lithographing printed them. By the 10th anniversary (1952), over 182 million copies had been sold, 4 million of which came from sales of The Night Before Christmas.

The first Walt Disney title was published in 1944. Many of the titles issued in the 1950s and 60s were direct tie-ins with TV shows, especially Westerns and Saturday morning cartoons. In 1958 Western Printing and Lithographing and Pocket Books purchased the rights to Little Golden Books from Simon & Shuster. A Golden Press imprint was introduced. Eventually Western bought out Pocket Books and created Golden Press, Inc.

Little Golden Books are identified by a complex numbering system that experienced several changes over the years. Many titles have remained in print for decades. Value rests primarily in first printing examples in near mint condition. If the book contained a dust jacket or any other special feature, it must be intact for the book to have any retail market value.

Reference: Steve Santi, *Collecting Little Golden Books, Third Edition*, Krause Publications, 1998.

Newsletter: *The Gold Mine Review*, PO Box 209, Hershey, PA 17033.

Collectors' Club: Golden Book Club, 19626 Ricardo Ave, Hayward, CA 94541.

Note: Prices listed are for books in mint condition.

Amazing Mumford Forgets the Magic Words?, The, 1979	**$2.00**
Beach Day, 1988	**1.00**
Buck Rogers and the Children of Hopetown, 1979	**3.00**
Bugs Bunny's Birthday, #98, 1950	**10.00**
But, You're a Duck, 1990	**1.00**
Cars, #566, 1973	**4.00**
Color Kittens, The, #86, 1949	**15.00**
Come Play House, #44, 1948	**15.00**
Count All the Way to Sesame Street, 1985	**2.00**
Daniel Boone, #256, 1956	**6.00**
Danny Beaver's Secret, #160, 1953	**7.00**
Deep Blue Sea, The, #338, 1958	**7.00**
Doctor Dan at the Circus, #399, 1960	**18.00**
Doctor Dan the Bandage Man, #111, 1950	**20.00**
Five Little Firemen, #64, 1948	**12.00**
Fuzzy Duckling, The, #78, 1949	**7.00**
Gene Autry and Champion, #267, 1956	**11.00**
Golden Book of Fairy Tales, The, #9, 1942	**15.00**
Happy Family, The, #35, 1947	**8.00**
Here Comes the Parade, #143, 1951	**8.00**
I Can Fly, #92, 1950	**8.00**
Indian, Indian, #149, 1952	**5.00**
Little Black Sambo, #57, 1948	**50.00**
Little Boy with a Big Horn, #100, 1950	**8.00**
Little Golden Cut-Out Christmas Manger, #176, 1953	**9.00**
Little Golden Paper Dolls, The, #113	**28.00**

***Through the Picture Frame*, #D1, Walt Disney Little Library, 1944, $24.00. *The Little Golden Book of Words*, #45, 1948, $8.00.**

Little Red Riding Hood, #42, 1948	**10.00**
Magic Compass, The, #146, 1953	**12.00**
Marvelous Merry-Go-Round, The, #87, 1950	**9.00**
My Kitten, #163, 1953	**10.00**
My Little Dinosaur, #571, 1971	**5.00**
Night Before Christmas, The, #20, 1946	**25.00**
Noises and Mr. Flibberty-Jib, #29, 1947	**18.00**
Nurse Nancy, #154, 1952	**22.00**
Ookpik the Arctic Owl, #579, 1968	**8.00**
Out of My Window, #245, 1955	**10.00**
Pebbles Flintstone, #531, 1963	**11.00**
Poky Little Puppy, The, #8, 1942	**20.00**
Puss in Boots, #137, 1952	**7.00**
Rainy Day Play Book, #133, 1951	**5.00**
Seven Little Postmen, #134, 1952	**7.00**
Silly Sisters, The, 1989	**1.00**
Susan in the Driver's Seat, #600, 1973	**6.00**
Taxi That Hurried, The, #25, 1946	**12.00**
Timothy Tiger's Terrible Toothache, 1988	**2.00**
Train to Timbuctoo, The, #118, 1951	**8.00**
Two Little Miners, #66, 1949	**12.00**
Walt Disney's Noah's Ark, #D28, 1952	**14.00**
Water Babies, 1990	**1.00**
Where Did the Baby Go, #116, 1974	**5.00**
Wiggles, #166, 1953	**12.00**
Year on the Farm, A, #37, 1948	**10.00**

LITTLE GOLDEN BOOK TYPES

Competitors quickly rose to challenge Little Golden Books. Wonder Books, part of a publishing conglomerate that included Random House, arrived on the scene in 1946. Rand McNally published its first Elf Books in September 1947 and a Hanna-Barbera Character Series between 1975 and 1977.

Golden Press also produced variations of its successful Little Golden Book line. Giant Little Golden Books arrived in 1957, followed by the Ding Dong School Book series in 1959.

Newsletter: *The Gold Mine Review*, PO Box 209, Hershey, PA 17033.

Note: Prices are for books in mint condition.

***Lassie and the Lost Explorer*, #343, 1958, $10.00. *Supercar*, #492, 1962, $20.00.**

Big Golden Book, *Baby's Mother Goose,* 1958 . . . . **$20.00**
Big Golden Book, *Frosty the Snowman,* 1951 . . . . **7.00**
Big Golden Book, *Fuzzy Duckling, The,* 1949 . . . . **5.00**
Big Golden Book, *Sailor Dog, The,* 1952 . . . . **10.00**
Big Golden Book, *Stories from Mary Poppins,* 1952 . . . . **15.00**
Ding Dong School Book, *In My House, #212,* 1954 . . . . **6.00**
Ding Dong School Book, *Mr Meyer's Cow, #DIN2* **8.00**
Ding Dong School Book, *Our Baby, #218* **12.00**
Ding Dong School Book, *Our Baby, #DIN8* **15.00**
Elf Book, *Plump Pig, #542,* 1956 . . . . **6.00**
Elf Book, *Popcorn Party, #468,* 1952 . . . . **5.00**
Elf Book, *Space Ship to the Moon, #473,* 1952 . . . . **12.00**
Elf Book, *Volksy the Little Yellow Car, #8695,* 1965 . . . . **7.00**
Giant Golden Book, *Aviation,* 1959 . . . . **8.00**
Giant Golden Book, *Fun and Nonsense,* 1970 . . . . **15.00**
Giant Little Golden Book, *Mother Goose,* 1957 . . . . **8.00**
Golden Book, *Best Storybook Ever,* 1968 . . . . **8.00**
Golden Book, *Fluppy Dogs Home for a Fanci Flup,* 1986 . . . . . **5.00**
Golden Forty-Niner, *Cowboys,* 1956 . . . . **6.00**
Golden Forty-Niner, *Presidents of the United States,* 1956 . . . . . **4.00**
Golden Funtime Book, *Charmin' Chatty,* paper dolls, 1964 . . . **12.00**
Golden Funtime Book, *Civil War, The,* punch-out **10.00**
Golden Funtime Book, *Dinosaurs,* trading cards, 1961 . . . . . . **12.00**
Golden Funtime Book, *Hokey Wolf,* coloring book **8.00**
Golden Funtime Book, *Wild Animals,* stick-um book, 1960 . . . . **9.00**
Golden Fuzzy Book, *Mouse's House,* 1949 . . . . **15.00**
Golden Giant Sturdy Book, *Baby Farm Animals,* 1958 . . . . **8.00**
Golden Happy Book, *I Am a Mouse,* 1963 . . . . **4.00**
Golden Happy Book, *Numbers,* 1963 . . . . **2.00**
Golden Hours Library, *Heidi,* 1954 . . . . **3.00**
Golden Hours Library, *Hop, Little Kangaroo,* 1965 . . . . **2.00**
Golden Illustrated Classics, *Heidi Grows Up,* small, 1966 . . . . . **7.00**
Golden Illustrated Classics, *King Arthur and the Knights*
  of the Round Table, large, 1963 . . . . **14.00**
Golden Look-Look Book, *Learn to Count,* 1976 . . . . **1.00**
Golden Melody Book, *People in Your Neighborhood,* 1984 . . . **4.00**
Golden Read-It Yourself, *George the Gentle Giant,* 1962 . . . . . **2.00**
Golden Star Book, *Adventures of Henry Rabbit,* 1967 . . . . **8.00**
Golden Star Book, *Walt Disney's Peter Pan,* 1967 . . . . **12.00**
Golden Story Book, *Stagecoach Robber,* 1949 . . . . **6.00**
Golden Story Book, *Train Stories,* 1949 . . . . **8.00**
Golden Storytime Book, *Animal Stories,* 1957 . . . . **7.00**
Golden Tiny Book, *Old McDonald Had a Farm,* 1960 . . . . **30.00**

Giant Little Golden Book, *Plants and Animals,* #5017, 1958,
$13.00. Wonder Book, *Pat Sullivan's Felix the Cat,* #665, 1953,
$15.00.

Golden Treasure Chest, *Tales and Legends,* 1968 . . . . **7.00**
Little Little Golden Book, *Theodore Mouse Goes to Sea,*
  1983 . . . . **2.00**
Little Little Golden Book, *Walt Disney's Pinocchio,* 1989 . . . . . **2.00**
Little Silver Book, *Come Play With Me,* 1948 . . . . **6.00**
Little Silver Book, *Jerry at School,* 1950 . . . . **2.00**
Rand McNally Book, *Hanna-Barbera's Scooby-Doo and*
  the Haunted Doghouse, 1975 . . . . **8.00**
Sandpiper Book, *Lone Ranger's New Deputy, The,* 1951 . . . . . . **7.00**
Sandpiper Book, *Wishing Stick, The,* 1951 . . . . **2.00**
Tell-A-Tale Book, *Barbie and Skipper Go Camping,*
  #2489, 1974 . . . . **6.00**
Tell-A-Tale Book, *Walt Disney's Bambi,* #2548, 1972 . . . . **2.00**
Treasure Books, *Fixit Man, The,* #851, 1952 . . . . **10.00**
Treasure Books, *Tubby the Tuba,* #873, 1954 . . . . **12.00**
Wonder Book, *Babar the King,* #602, 1953 . . . . **15.00**
Wonder Book, *Happy Surprise, The,* #582, 1952 . . . . **6.00**
Wonder Book, *How the Clown Got His Smile,* #566, 1951 . . . . **6.00**
Wonder Book, *Surprise Doll, The,* #519, 1949 . . . . **35.00**
Wonder Book, *Who Does Baby Look Like?,* #525, 1950 . . . . . . **8.00**

LITTLE RED RIDING HOOD

Design Patent #134,889, June 29,1943, for a "Design for a Cookie Jar," was granted to Louise Elizabeth Bauer of Zanesville, Ohio, and assigned to the A. E. Hull Pottery Company. This patent protected the design for Hull's Little Red Riding Hood line, produced between 1943 and 1957.

Hull and the Royal China and Novelty Company, a division of Regal China, made the blanks. Decoration was done almost exclusively at Royal China. Because the pieces were hand painted, many variations in color scheme have been discovered.

Reference: Mark and Ellen Supnick, *Collecting Hull Pottery's Little Red Riding Hood,* L-W Book Sales, 1998.

REPRODUCTION ALERT: Be alert for Little Red Riding Hood cookie jar reproductions. The period piece measures 13" h; the Mexican reproduction is shorter.

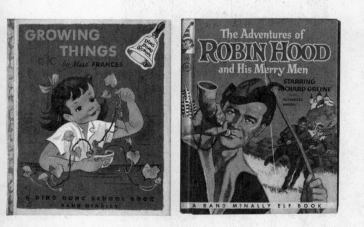

Ding Dong School Book, *Growing Things,* #210, 1954, $6.00.
Elf Book, *The Adventures of Robin Hood and His Merry Men,*
#532, 1955, $12.00.

Batter Pitcher, poppy decal, 6¾" h **$500.00**
Cereal Canister **1,000.00**
Cracker Jar **690.00**

Cookie Jar, open basket, gold stars on apron, 13" h, $400.00. Photo courtesy Gene Harris Antique Auction Center, Inc.

Creamer, ruffled skirt, 5" h 575.00
Creamer, tab handle, 5" h 375.00
Creamer and Sugar, open 690.00
Creamer and Sugar, side pour 325.00
Dresser Jar, 8³⁄₄" h 700.00
Hot Chocolate Mug 2,500.00
Lamp 2,500.00
Match Holder, blue dress, 6" h 1,400.00
Match Holder, plain dress, 6" h 850.00
Milk Pitcher, poppy decal, 8" h 400.00
Mug 2,500.00
Mustard Jar with Spoon, 5¹⁄₂" h 475.00
Popcorn Canister 2,200.00
Salt and Pepper Shakers, pr, 4¹⁄₂" h 1,250.00
Salt and Pepper Shakers, pr, 5¹⁄₈" h 225.00
Salt Canister, 9¹⁄₄" h 2,250.00
Spice Jar, allspice 900.00
Spice Jar, nutmeg 700.00
Teapot 300.00
Teapot, cov 325.00
Tidbit Canister 6,000.00
Toothbrush Holder 75.00

LLADRÓ PORCELAINS

In 1951 José, Juan, and Vincente Lladró established a ceramics factory in Almacera, Spain. Each was educated at the Escuela de Artes y Oficios de San Carlos. José and Juan focused on painting and Vincente on sculpting. The Lladró brothers concentrated on the production of ceramic figurines, initially producing diminutive ceramic flowers.

In 1953 the brothers built a kiln that could produce temperatures sufficient to vitrify porcelain. With it, they began to make porcelain pieces in styles duplicating those of Dresden and Sevres. In 1955 they opened a shop in Valencia, and in 1958 began construction of a factory in the neighboring town of Tavernes Blanques.

In 1985 the company organized the Lladró Society, a collectors' club. Rosa Maria Lladró assumed the presidency of the Society in 1995. She, along with her sister Marie Carmen, and her cousins,

Rosa and Juan Vicente, represent the second generation of the Lladró family to become involved in the business.

References: Collectors' Information Bureau, *Collectibles Market Guide & Price Index, 16th Edition,* Collectors' Information Bureau, 1998, distributed by Krause Publications; Glenn S. Johnson, *The Lladró Collection Reference Guide,* Clear Communications, 1996; Mary L. Sieber (ed.), *Price Guide to Limited Edition Collectibles,* Krause Publications, 1998.

Collectors' Club: Lladró Collectors Society (company sponsored), 1 Lladró Dr, Moonachie, NJ 07074.

Figurine, Afternoon Tea, L1428G, 1982 . . . . **$300.00**
Figurine, Bear, white, L1208G 75.00
Figurine, Bird, L1053G, 1969 . . . . 100.00
Figurine, Clown on Domino, L1179G, 1971 . . . . 375.00
Figurine, Dalmatian, L1260G, 1974 . . . . 350.00
Figurine, Deer, L1064, 1969 . . . . 325.00
Figurine, Dove, L1015G, 1969 . . . . 150.00
Figurine, Eskimo, L1195G, 1972 . . . . 135.00
Figurine, Feeding Time, L1277G, 1974 . . . . 350.00
Figurine, Flying Duck, L1265G, 1974 . . . . 90.00
Figurine, Friendship, L1230M, 1972 . . . . 350.00
Figurine, Frosted Bear, head up, Crystal Sculptures, 1983 . . . 350.00
Figurine, Girl with Bonnet, L1147G, 1971 . . . . 275.00
Figurine, Girl with Geese, L1035M, 1969 . . . . 165.00
Figurine, Hen, L1041G, 1969 . . . . 350.00
Figurine, Julia, L1361G, 1978 . . . . 265.00
Figurine, Kissing Doves, L1170G, 1971 . . . . 250.00
Figurine, Little Jug Magno, L1222.3G, 1972 . . . . 300.00
Figurine, Nature's Bounty, L1417G, 1982 . . . . 400.00
Figurine, Shepherdess with Goats, L1001M, 1969 . . . . . 450.00
Figurine, Woman Carrying Water, L1212G, 1972 . . . . . 475.00
Plate, Boy and Girl, Christmas Series, 1973 . . . . 45.00
Plate, Carolers, Christmas Series, 1974 . . . . 75.00
Plate, Caroling, Christmas Series, 1971 . . . . 27.50
Plate, Kiss of the Child, Mother's Day Series, 1971 . . . . . 75.00
Plate, Nursing Mother, Mother's Day Series, 1974 . . . . . 125.00
Plate, Off to School, Mother's Day Series, 1979 . . . . 90.00

Figurine, Alice in Wonderland, L5740G, 1991, $485.00.

LONGABERGER BASKETS

Dave Longaberger (1934–99) began his business career as the owner of Harry's Dairy Bar and an IGA Foodliner in Dresden, Ohio. John Wendell Longaberger, Dave's father, owned the Ohio Ware Company, a firm making ware baskets for the pottery industry. In 1972 Dave asked his father to make sample baskets for sale to the retail department store trade. Successful initial sales led to Dave's opening J. W.'s Handwoven Baskets later that year.

Today the Longaberger Company has 42,000 independent sales consultants located in all 50 states and the District of Columbia. In 1990 the company opened a new modern facility located just outside Dresden. Its home office is located in a replica seven-story Market Basket located in Newark, Ohio. Tami and Rachel Longaberger, his two daughters, assumed control of the company following Dave's death on March 17, 1999.

Although Longaberger stresses a handmade craft ancestry for its baskets, they are mass produced. The company sold 7.7 million baskets in 1997, indicating that scarcity is not a word that will be used to describe a Longaberger basket, even fifty years from now.

Collectors of antique and vintage baskets will tell you that Longaberger baskets are vastly overrated. While not something Longaberger basket collectors want to hear, they will regret not paying attention when the current speculative bubble, fueled by a market manipulative price guide, company hype, a company controlled collectors' club, and Internet auction prices, finally bursts.

All American, Handle Tie. **$15.00**
All American, Patriot Divided Protector, 1997. . . . . **10.00**
All American, Pie, liner and protector, 1998. . . . . **135.00**
All American, Summertime Combo, 1996 . . . . **60.00**
Bee Basket, Bee, liner, and protector, 1996. . . . . **160.00**
Bee Basket, Bee, liner, and protector, 1997. . . . . **130.00**
Bee Basket, Bee, liner, and protector, 1998. . . . . **100.00**
Booking Basket, Ambrosia, orig liner, protector, 1996. . . . . . . **60.00**
Booking Basket, Ambrosia Tie-On, 1995. . . . . **14.00**
Christmas Collection, Bayberry Combo, 1993. . . . . **80.00**
Christmas Collection, Christmas Cranberry, red, holly
  liner, protector, lid, 1995 . . . . **100.00**
Christmas Collection, Christmas Cranberry, red, protec-
  tor, 1995. . . . . **130.00**
Christmas Collection, Holiday Cheer, liner and protec-
  tor, 1996. . . . . **100.00**
Christmas Collection, Jingle Bell, 1994. . . . . **100.00**
Christmas Collection, Memory Basket, green, 1989 . . . . **90.00**
Christmas Collection, Mistletoe Basket, red, 1989. . . . . **110.00**
Christmas Collection, Pewter Ornament, 1995 . . . . **70.00**
Christmas Collection, Season's Greetings, red, plaid
  liner, protector, 1992. . . . . **120.00**
Christmas Collection, Snowflake, liner and protector,
  1997. . . . . **90.00**
Classics Collection, Laundry Basket, protector, small,
  1998. . . . . **175.00**
Collector's Club, Charter Member Combo with box,
  1996. . . . . **110.00**
Collector's Club, Charter Member Handle Gripper, 1996 . . . . **30.00**
Collector's Club, Charter Membership Renewal Brass
  Splint, with card, 1998 . . . . **5.00**
Collector's Club, Hometown Christmas Ornament, 1997. . . . . **42.00**
Collector's Club, Membership Basket, liner, protector,
  box, and product cards, 1997 . . . . **100.00**
Collector's Club, Mini Market Liner, 1996 . . . . **50.00**
Collector's Club, Mini Market Protector, 1996 . . . . **20.00**

Collector's Club, Mini Waste Liner, 1997 . . . . **25.00**
Collector's Club, Serving Tray Combo, with box, 1996 . . . . . **250.00**
Collector's Club, Serving Tray Protector, 1996. . . . . **25.00**
Collector's Club, Welcome Home, liner, protector, box,
  and product cards, 1997 . . . . **150.00**
Easter Series, Blue Easter, with protector, 1989 . . . . **90.00**
Easter Series, Small Easter Combo, with matching fabric
  lid, 1997. . . . . **45.00**
Father's Day, Finder's Keepers Divided Protector, 1998 . . . . . . **8.00**
Father's Day, Finder's Keepers Regular Protector, 1998 . . . . . . **5.00**
Incentive Basket, Branch Bouquet, 1997. . . . . **119.00**
May Series, Petunia combo, with liner, 1997 . . . . **70.00**
Mother's Day, Mini Chore Combo, 1988 . . . . **100.00**
Mother's Day, Mother's Day Combo, 1992 . . . . **90.00**
Mother's Day, Mother's Day Tie-On, 1996 . . . . **10.00**
Mother's Day, Mother's Day Vanity Combo, with regular
  and divided protectors and lid, 1996 . . . . **85.00**
Shades of Autumn, Bountiful Harvest, with gingham
  liner and lid, 1997. . . . . **100.00**
Shades of Autumn, Maple Leaf Combo, Fall Foliage liner,
  1996. . . . . **65.00**
Special Events, Inaugural Combo, 1997 . . . . **55.00**
Sweetheart Basket, Bee Mine Combo, 1994 . . . . **64.00**
Sweetheart Basket, Bouquet Combo, 1996 . . . . **52.00**
Sweetheart Basket, Hostess Precious Treasures Combo,
  1995. . . . . **160.00**
Sweetheart Basket, Sweet Treats Combo, blue, 1997. . . . . . . **40.00**
Traditions Collection, Fellowship Combo, with box,
  1997. . . . . **100.00**
Traditions Collection, Hospitality Combo, 1998 . . . . **115.00**

LOTTON, CHARLES

Charles Gerald Lotton (born October 21, 1935) is a contemporary glass artist. In 1970 Lotton built a small glass studio behind his house in Sauk Village, Illinois. In June 1971 Lotton sold his first glass to C. D. Peacock, a downtown Chicago jeweler.

A chance meeting with Dr. Ed McConnell during a visit to Corning, New York, resulted in a meeting with Lillian Nassau, a leading New York City art glass dealer. Paul Nassau, Lillian's son, and Lotton signed an exclusive five-year contract in 1972. Lotton leased a former lumber yard in Lansing, Illinois, to serve as his studio. In 1975 he built a new studio in Lynwood, Illinois, eventually building a glassworks behind his home in Crete, Illinois, in 1982.

By 1977 Lotton had achieved a national reputation and wanted the freedom to sell glass directly to his own distributors. Lotton glass is sold through a number of select retailers and at antiques shows. The four Lotton children, Daniel, David, John, and Rachel, are all involved with some aspect of glassmaking.

Reference: D. Thomas O'Connor and Charles G. Lotton, *Lotton Art Glass,* Antique Publications, 1990, out of print.

Bud Vase, baluster form, iridescent purple oil spot finish
  and blue luster pulled drapes, sgd and dated "John
  Lotton 1983," 8½" h **$250.00**
Bud Vase, cylindrical, purple oil spot finish, blue luster
  King Tut dec, sgd and dated "John Lotton 1991," 3" h **165.00**
Toothpick, vasiform, cobalt blue iridescent, sgd and
  dated "Charles Lotton 1981," 2½" h **200.00**
Vase, classical shape, selenium red with green and pur-
  ple leaf design, sgd and dated "Charles Lotton, 1983" **675.00**

Vase, classical shape, verre de soie with multicolor floral design in pink, blue, and green, sgd and dated "Charles Lotton 1983 multi flora," 8½" h 560.00

Vase, cylindrical, opalescent mottled pink with iridescent leaf and vine design, sgd and dated "Lotton 1994," 8½" h 275.00

Vase, flared rim, bulbous body, opalescent with blue luster leaves, purple int, sgd and dated "David Lotton 1995," 5" h 365.00

Vase, flared rim, spherical body, neo-blue with silvery blue leaves and vines on mottled green ground, sgd and dated "David Lotton 1995," 5" h 450.00

Vase, flared rim above bulbous ovoid body, verre de soie with blue and green luster leaves and threaded vines, sgd and dated "Charles Lotton 1983," 8" h 560.00

Vase, flared rim and narrow neck above corseted body, black amethyst with blue leaf and vine design, sgd and dated "Lotton 1991," 8" h 275.00

Vase, narrow flared neck, bulbous body, opalescent with blue pulled drape pattern, sgd and dated "Lotton 1975," 7½" h 400.00

Vase, ovoid, iridescent pulled feather design, sgd and dated "Charles Lotton 1983," 7" h 450.00

Vase, ruffled rim, opalescent with pink leaves, green iridescent vines, and stretched purple iridescent rim, sgd and dated "John Lotton 1990," 10" h 550.00

Vase, short cylindrical neck above ovoid body, selenium red with blue and silver zipper dec, sgd and dated "Charles Lotton 1977 with Love Always Merrie," 5½" h 560.00

Vase, slightly flared rim, bulbous body, mottled pink with pink leaf and green iridescent vine design, sgd and dated "John Lotton 1990," 6" h 450.00

Vase, wide rim, slightly bulging body, cobalt blue Cypriot with blue luster lava draping, sgd and dated "Charles Lotton 1987," 6" h 700.00

LUNCH BOXES

A lunch kit is comprised of a lunch box and a thermos. Both must be present for the unit to be complete.

Although lunch kits date back to the 19th century, collectors focus on the lithographed tin lunch kits made between the mid-1930s and the late 1970s. Gender, Paeschke & Frey's 1935 Mickey Mouse lunch kit launched the modern form. The 1950s and early 1960s was the lunch kit's golden age. Hundreds of different kits were made, many featuring cartoon, movie, and television show images. Aladdin Company, Landers, Frary and Clark, Ohio Art, Thermos/King Seeley, and Universal are among the many companies who made lunch kits during the golden age.

This market went through a speculative craze that extended from the late 1970s through the early 1990s at which point the speculative bubble burst. Prices have dropped from their early 1990s high for most examples. Crossover collectors, rather than lunch kit collectors, are keeping the market alive in the late 1990s.

References: Larry Aikins, *Pictorial Price Guide to Metal Lunch Boxes & Thermoses,* L-W Book Sales, 1992, 1996 value update; Larry Aikins, *Pictorial Price Guide to Vinyl & Plastic Lunch Boxes & Thermoses,* L-W Book Sales, 1992, 1995 value update; Allen Woodall and Sean Brickell, *The Illustrated Encyclopedia of Metal Lunch Boxes,* Schiffer Publishing, 1992.

Periodical: *Paileontologist's Report,* PO Box 3255, Burbank, CA 91508.

Collectors' Club: Step Into the Ring, 829 Jackson St Ext, Sandusky, OH 44870.

Note: Prices listed reflect boxes with thermos, both in near mint condition.

Alice in Wonderland, vinyl, with thermos. $100.00
Annie and Sandy, vinyl, with thermos 95.00
Annie Oakley 85.00
Astronauts, dome 135.00
Atom Ant 75.00
Barbie, metal 295.00
Baseball Scene, metal 65.00
Battle of the Planets 65.00
Battlestar Galactica, with thermos 20.00
Beatles 325.00
Bee Gees 75.00
Beverly Hillbillies, 1963 . . . . 40.00
Bionic Woman, with thermos 20.00
Bobby Sherman, 1972 . . . . 25.00
Brady Bunch 125.00
Buccaneer, dome, 1957 . . . . 50.00
Campus Queen 45.00
Canadian Goose and Duck, metal 60.00
Carnival, with thermos, 1959 . . . . 200.00
Charlie's Angels, vinyl, with thermos 60.00
Chitty Chitty Bang Bang, with thermos, 1968 . . . . 75.00
Circus Wagon, dome, 1958 . . . . 50.00
Cowboy on Horse, litho tin, 1940s 20.00
Curiosity Shop, 1972 . . . . 20.00
Davy Crockett, Holtemp 145.00
Disco Fever, 1980 . . . . 15.00
Disney Fire Fighters, dome 85.00
Disney School Bus, dome 55.00
Disney World, with thermos 15.00
Donny and Marie, vinyl 35.00
Dukes of Hazzard 15.00
Dynomutt 45.00
Early West Oregon Trail 35.00
El Chapulin 45.00

Charlie's Angels, litho tin, Aladdin, 1978, $25.00.

Emergency	25.00
Fat Albert	25.00
Fireball XL5	125.00
Flintstones, orange, 1962	40.00
Frog Flutist, blue vinyl, with thermos	25.00
Frontier Days, 1957	75.00
Funtastic World of Hanna-Barbera, 1977	25.00
Ghostland, with spinner and sticker	20.00
Green Hornet, 1967	125.00
Gremlins, with thermos	15.00
Hansel & Gretel, 1982	20.00
Hector Heathcote	80.00
Hee Haw, 1970	30.00
Hopalong Cassidy, litho tin	95.00
Howdy Doody	275.00
How the West Was Won	45.00
Indiana Jones and the Temple of Doom	50.00
James Bond 007, with thermos	375.00
Julia	95.00
Kid Power, with thermos	15.00
Kiss, with thermos	50.00
Laugh-In, vinyl	50.00
Lawman	75.00
Legend of the Lone Ranger, with thermos	15.00
Looney Tunes TV, 1959	40.00
Lost in Space	150.00
Marvel Comics Super Heroes	75.00
Masters of the Universe, with thermos	10.00
Mickey Mouse Head, with thermos	20.00
Minnie Mouse Head, with thermos	20.00
Mod Floral	50.00
Monkees, collector video and puzzle inside	25.00
Monkees, vinyl, with thermos, 1967	150.00
Monroes	75.00
Mork & Mindy, with thermos	65.00
Mr Merlin, with thermos	70.00
Munsters	95.00
Muppet Babies	15.00
Muppet Show, with thermos	60.00
NFL, with thermos	15.00
Pac-Man, with thermos	15.00
Paisley, vinyl, with thermos	25.00
Peanuts, baseball scene, red, with thermos, 1976	15.00
Peter Pan Sandwich, 1974	75.00
Pink Panther, with thermos	95.00
Pink Panther and Sons	10.00
Play Ball	65.00
Popeye, with thermos	75.00
Porky's Lunch Wagon	110.00
Princess, vinyl, 1963	40.00
Pro-Sports	15.00
Pussycats, vinyl, with thermos	75.00
Rambo, with thermos	45.00
Ringling Bros Circus, vinyl	595.00
Road Runner, with thermos	20.00
Ronald McDonald Sheriff of Cactus Canyon, with thermos	85.00
Roy Rogers	175.00
Satellite	75.00
Scooby Doo, plastic, dome, with thermos	30.00
Sesame Street, litho tin, with thermos	65.00
Sesame Street, vinyl, with thermos	85.00
Sleeping Beauty, vinyl, with thermos, 1970	100.00
Smokey the Bear, vinyl	395.00

Snoopy and Woodstock, 1973	15.00
Space: 1999	85.00
Spider-Man & Hulk, with thermos	15.00
Sport Goofy	30.00
Star Trek, with thermos	25.00
Star Wars, with thermos	15.00
Strawberry Ice Cream, vinyl, with thermos	75.00
Strawberry Shortcake	15.00
Submarine	65.00
Superman, with thermos, 1978	20.00
S.W.A.T., plastic, dome, 1970s	30.00
Thundercats, with thermos	75.00
"V," with thermos	275.00
Welcome Back, Kotter, Barbarino, vinyl, with thermos	65.00
Wild Frontier, 1977	20.00
Wild Wild West, 1969	75.00
Wizard of Oz, with thermos	20.00

MADE IN JAPAN

Prior to 1921, objects made in Japan were marked NIPPON or MADE IN NIPPON. After that date, objects were marked JAPAN or MADE IN JAPAN.

Although MADE IN OCCUPIED JAPAN was the primary mark used between August 1945 and April 28, 1952, some objects from this period were marked JAPAN or MADE IN JAPAN.

This is a catchall category for a wide range of ceramic, glass, and metal items made by Japanese manufacturers for export to the United States. Many were distributed by American import companies who designed the products in America, had them manufactured in Japan, and marketed them in the United States.

References: Carol Bess White, *Collector's Guide to Made in Japan Ceramics* (1994, 1996 value update), *Book II* (1996, 1998 value update), *Book III* (1998), Collector Books.

Note: See Figurines and Occupied Japan for additional listings.

Ashtray, Art Deco, applied cat on rim, multicolored, yellow ground, 2¼' h	$15.00
Ashtray, chicken face, openmouth, calico glaze, 3¾" l	25.00
Ashtray, dog and dish, multicolored luster and shiny glaze, 2½" h	20.00

Biscuit Barrel, pink roses and finials, rattan-wrapped handle, 7¼" h, 8½" w handle to handle, $50.00.

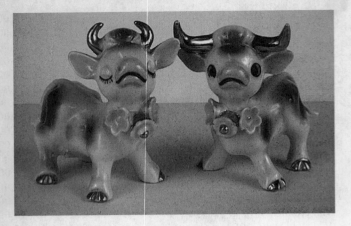

Figurines, cows, 2³/₄" h, price for pair, $10.00.

Biscuit Barrel, cream basketweave design with flower
 finial, 6¹/₄" h **50.00**
Bonbon, multicolored floral motif, white ground, 6¹/₄" d **10.00**
Bookends, pr, multicolored ships, 6³/₄" h **30.00**
Bowl, lug handle, multicolored house motif, teal luster
 glaze, Noritake, 6" d **25.00**
Candlesticks, pr, white shiny glaze, 3¹/₄" h **8.00**
Cigarette Box, cov, multicolored plaid motif, Noritake,
 3¹/₂" l **75.00**
Creamer and Sugar, figural cowboy, multicolored shiny
 glaze **45.00**
Eggcup, hen and basket, multicolored luster and shiny
 glaze, 3¹/₄" h **20.00**
Figurine, bird on stump, multicolored shiny glaze, 4" h **5.00**
Figurine, Pixie playing accordion, multicolored matte
 glaze, 4³/₄" h **20.00**
Fish Bowl Ornament, castle, multicolored shiny glaze,
 2³/₄" h **20.00**
Incense Burner, fireplace, black and red shiny glaze,
 4" h **15.00**
Pincushion, girl in canoe, multicolored shiny glaze,
 2¹/₄" h **30.00**
Salt and Pepper Shakers, pr, figural cat, multicolored
 shiny glaze, gold accents, 5" w tray **35.00**
Sandwich Server, floral motif, tan, lavender, and multicolored luster glaze, gold center handle, 10" d **50.00**
Vase, moon and cherub, blue and yellow shiny glaze,
 5" h **20.00**
Whiskey Decanter, figural brown elephant wearing
 crown, howdah holds 4 mug-shaped shot glasses, 8" l **30.00**

MAGAZINES

In the early 1700s general magazines were a major source of information. Literary magazines such as *Harper's* became popular in
the 19th century. By 1900 the first photo-journal magazines
appeared. Henry Luce started *Life*, the prime example, in 1932.

Magazines created for women featured "how to" articles about
cooking, sewing, decorating, and child care. Many were devoted
to fashion and living a fashionable life. Men's magazines were
directed at masculine skills of the time, such as hunting, fishing,
and woodworking. "Girlie" titles became popular in the 1930s and
enjoyed a golden age in the 1950s and 60s.

Popular magazines, such as *Collier's, Life, Look,* and *Saturday
Evening Post,* survive in vast quantities. So do pulps. Value is driven primarily by cover image, content, and advertisements.

Many magazines are torn apart and the pages sold individually.
The key value component for these "tear sheets" is subject matter.
As a result 99% plus are purchased by crossover collectors. Except
for illustrator collectors, crossover collectors care little if the tear
sheet features a drawing or photograph. The most desirable tear
sheets are in full color and show significant design elements.

References: Ron Barlow and Ray Reynolds, *The Insider's Guide to
Old Books, Magazines, Newspapers, Trade Catalogs,* Windmill
Publishing, 1995; David K. Henkel, *Magazines,* Avon Books,
1993; Denis C. Jackson, *Men's "Girlie" Magazines: Newstanders,
4th Edition,* TICN, 1994; Denis C. Jackson, *Old Magazines, 4th
Edition,* TICN, 1997; *Old Magazine Price Guide,* L-W Book Sales,
1994, 1997 value update; Frank M. Robinson and Lawrence
Davidson, *Pulp Culture: The Art of Fiction Magazines,* Collectors
Press, 1998; Lee Server, *Danger Is My Business: An Illustrated
History of the Fabulous Pulp Magazines: 1896–1953,* Chronicle
Books, 1993.

Periodicals: *Echoes* (pulps), 504 E Morris St, Seymour, TX 76380;
PCM (Paper Collectors' Marketplace), PO Box 128, Scandinavia,
WI 54977.

Newsletters: *The Illustrator Collector's News,* PO Box 1958,
Sequim, WA 98392; *Pulp & Paperback Market Newsletter,* 5813
York Ave, Edina, MN 55410.

Collectors' Club: The Secret Society of the Sanctum (pulps), 10811
Columbus Ave #13, Mission Hills, CA 91345.

Note: For additional listings see *Life, Playboy* and *TV Guide.*

Accent Magazine, 13 issues, 1940–50s **$35.00**
Actual Detective Stories, 1930–40s **8.00**
Adventure, 1930–40 . . . . **5.00**
Aero Digest, 1926–32 . . . . **25.00**
Aeronautics, 9 issues, 1940–41 . . . . **15.00**
Air Life, Mar 1942, Vol 1, #1 . . . . **35.00**
Air Progress, Jun 1943 . . . . **25.00**
American Legion Weekly, 1921, John Held, Jr, cov **10.00**
American Legion Weekly, 1927, Christy cov **10.00**
Automotive Digest, 1920s **10.00**
Automotive Digest, 1930s **5.00**
Avant Garde, 1958, Marilyn Monroe portfolio **40.00**
Battle Stories, Feb 1932 . . . . **15.00**
Beauty Parade, Mar 1955, Bettie Page **30.00**
Bedtime Story, 1932, Vol 1, #1 . . . . **35.00**
Better Homes and Gardens, 1922–40 . . . . **4.00**
Billboard Magazine, 1954 . . . . **10.00**
Black Book Detective, 1940s **25.00**
Boys' Life, Nov 1952, football painting **12.00**
Boys' Life, Apr, 1963, Yogi Berra **23.00**
Boys' Life, Mar 1966, Willie Mays **25.00**
Boys' Life, Mar 1969, Ron Santo **9.00**
Bronze Thrills, Jan 1961 . . . . **5.00**
Car and Driver, 1960–80 . . . . **3.00**
Child's Life Magazine, Dec 1928 . . . . **10.00**
Circus Review, 1950s **5.00**
Classic Photography, Spring 1957 . . . . **15.00**
Colliers, Jan 27, 1945, Franklin D Roosevelt **8.00**

National Geographic,
Vol. 159, No. 3,
March 1981, $.50.

Colliers, Jan 4, 1957, Princess Grace 3.00
Cosmopolitan, 1950s 5.00
Country Gentleman, Aug 1933, lady in flower garden 4.00
Country Gentleman, May 1938, turkeys in tree 4.00
Country Gentleman, Apr 1950, farming 4.00
Deliniator, The, Aug 1922 . . . . 15.00
Dunninger's Popular Magic and Card Tricks Magazine,
   1929 . . . . 100.00
Esquire, Sep 1952, Esther Williams 25.00
Farm Journal, Jun 1932 . . . . 5.00
Farm Life, 1920s 5.00
Flair, 1953 Annual 20.00
Flying Aces, 1936–40 . . . . 20.00
Fortune, Dec 1939 . . . . 20.00
Hollywood Men, 1953, Tony Curtis 15.00
House Beautiful, Oct 1959, Frank Lloyd Wright 10.00
Liberty, 1930s 3.00
Literary Digest, Nov 15, 1930 . . . . 8.00
Look, Jul 28, 1942, Gary Cooper 25.00
Look, Aug 12, 1952, Mickey Mantle/Loraine Day 25.00
Look, Sep 4, 1956, Clark Gable 7.00
Look, May 12, 1959, Perry Como 6.00
Look, May 5, 1960, Marilyn Monroe 18.00
Look, Feb 7, 1967, John F Kennedy 2.00
Look, Feb 20, 1968, swimsuit issue 6.00
Look, Sep 9, 1969, Sex Education/ Joe Namath 8.00
Mademoiselle, 1950s 3.00
Man About Town, Sep 1958 . . . . 15.00
McCall's, Jul 1931 . . . . 20.00
Modern Photography, 1950–53, 30 issues 25.00
Modern Priscilla, Oct 1928 . . . . 10.00
Modern Screen, Apr 1938, Ginger Rogers, Christy cov 15.00
National Geographic, 1920s 10.00
National Geographic, 1930s 8.00
National Geographic, 1940s 8.00
National Geographic, 1950s 6.00
National Geographic, 1960–80 . . . . 4.00
National Historical Magazine, Dec 1938 . . . . 10.00
New Yorker, The, 1961–68 . . . . 3.00
Night and Day, Nov 1954 . . . . 8.00
Outdoor Life, 1950–80s 3.00

Paris Life, 1954, #17 . . . . 12.00
Peep Show, Nov 1957 . . . . 10.00
Penthouse, 1970–83 . . . . 5.00
Phantom Detective, Apr 1946 . . . . 15.00
Photoplay Magazine, Sep 1931, Barbara Stanwick 20.00
Picture Show, Jun 1959 . . . . 10.00
Popular Card Tricks Magazine, c1925 . . . . 100.00
Popular Science, 1930–35, 13 issues 6.00
Psychology Today, 1967–84, 212 issues 300.00
Radio Age, 1926 . . . . 15.00
Radio Amateur Call Book Magazine, Winter 1931 . . . . 50.00
Radio Broadcast, 1928 . . . . 15.00
Radio Craft, 1932 . . . . 10.00
Radio Engineering, 1927 . . . . 10.00
Radio Mirror, Apr 1937, Joan Blondell 10.00
Radio World, 1927 . . . . 10.00
Reader's Digest, 1923–44, 50 issues 55.00
Reader's Digest, 1928–33 . . . . 3.00
Reader's Digest, 1930–40, 7 issues 5.00
Reader's Digest, 1950–70s 1.00
Redbook, 1930–40s 4.00
Redbook, 1950–60s 3.00
Rexall Magazine, 1929–76 . . . . 3.00
Rod & Custom, Oct 1955 . . . . 8.00
Rural New Yorker, 1936–37, 23 issues 60.00
Saturday Evening Post, Mar 2, 1957, Rockwell/Baseball 28.00
Saturday Evening Post, Dec 1, 1962, greed scene 3.00
Saturday Evening Post, Jan 19, 1963, Rockwell 10.00
Saturday Evening Post, Apr 6, 1963, John F Kennedy 8.00
Saturday Evening Post, Apr 20, 1963, Armageddon 3.00
Saturday Evening Post, Jun 29, 1963, soldier 4.00
Saturday Evening Post, Aug 22, 1964, America's Cup 8.00
Saturday Evening Post, Dec 12, 1964, John Unitas 12.00
Saturday Evening Post, Sep 1977, Farrah Fawcett 10.00
Science & Technology International, 1962–69 . . . . 5.00
Scouting, 1930s 3.00
Screen Romances, Jan 1942, Judy Garland 25.00
Screen Stories, Aug 1951, Alice in Wonderland 25.00
Seventeen, 1950s 2.00
Sky Aces, Jun 1938 . . . . 30.00
Sky Aces, Sep 1939 . . . . 15.00
Sky Birds, Jun 1930 . . . . 20.00
Sky Devils, Mar 1938 . . . . 30.00
Sky Fighters, Mar 1938 . . . . 15.00
Song Fan, Mar 1954 . . . . 15.00
Song Hits, Nov 1953, Marilyn Monroe 20.00
Spinning Wheel, 1950–70s 5.00
Sporting News, The, 1959–68, 8 issues 50.00
Sporting News, The, 1967–70, 10 issues 50.00
Sport Magazine, Dec 1966, Gale Sayers 10.00
Sport Magazine, Dec 1968, OJ Simpson 15.00
Sports Illustrated, 1970s 5.00
Successful Farming, 1924–34 . . . . 5.00
Suspense, 1951 . . . . 5.00
Tempo Magazine, 1953–60 . . . . 5.00
Time, Apr 27, 1936, Shirley Temple 25.00
Time, Oct 18, 1937, Ernest Hemingway 10.00
Time, Dec 27, 1937, Walt Disney and Seven Dwarfs 45.00
Time, Jan 17, 1938, Frank Lloyd Wright 25.00
Time, Mar 28, 1938, Bette Davis 10.00
Time, Apr 4, 1938, Einstein 15.00
Time, Jun 19, 1939, Lindbergh 25.00
Time, Dec 15, 1939, Vivien Leigh 75.00
Time, Mar 3, 1941, Gary Cooper 15.00

Saturday Evening Post,
December 4, 1965,
$4.00.

Time, Apr 7, 1941, Bing Crosby 15.00
Time, Nov 10, 1941, Rita Hayworth 20.00
Time, Nov 20, 1944, Edgar Bergen & Charlie McCarthy 15.00
Time, Mar 11, 1946, Danny Kaye 15.00
Time, Jan 12, 1948, Gregory Peck 15.00
Time, Jul 19, 1949, Howard Hughes 15.00
Time, Feb 27, 1950, Arthur Godfrey 15.00
Time, Nov 27, 1950, Hopalong Cassidy 25.00
Time, Dec 31, 1951, Groucho Marx 15.00
Time, May 3, 1952, John Wayne 25.00
Time, May 26, 1952, Lucille Ball 15.00
Time, Dec 27, 1954, Walt Disney 25.00
Time, May 14, 1956, Marilyn Monroe 40.00
Town and Country, Jun 15, 1932 . . . . 10.00
Variety, 1950s 10.00
Venture, 1966–71, 30 issues 85.00

MARBLEHEAD POTTERY

In 1904 Dr. Herbert J. Hall established the Marblehead Pottery as one of several craft projects for his Deveraux Mansion sanitarium patients. Four years later, Arthur Baggs, one of the instructors, established the pottery as a separate business operation. In 1915 Baggs became the pottery's owner.

The pottery was moved to 111 Front Street, Marblehead. After 1920, the pottery only operated in the summer. During the balance of the year, Baggs first taught at the Cleveland School of Art and eventually at Ohio State University. Production ended in 1936.

Baggs attracted a number of leading artists, designers, decorators to his pottery among whom were Annie Aldrich, Rachel Grimwell, Arthur Hennessey, Maude Milner, and Mrs. E. D. (Hannah) Tutt. After an initial design period based primarily on geometric forms, conventional animal, bird, floral, fruit, and marine motifs appeared on pieces.

Many pieces are marked with a ship flanked by the letters "M" and "P."

Reference: Ralph and Terry Kovel, *Kovel's American Art Pottery,* Crown, 1993.

Collectors' Club: American Art Pottery Assoc, PO Box 1226, Westport, MA 02790.

Bookends, pr, carved Egyptian dec, blue and semi-gloss
   matte glaze, mkd **$600.00**
Bowl, flaring, flower frog covered in shaded blue matte
   glaze, imp ship mark, 4 x 7" 275.00
Bowl, low, by Hannah Tutt, carved geometric design in
   dark brown on matte olive-green ground, imp ship
   mark and "HT," 2³⁄₄ x 5" **2,000.00**
Bowl, low, light blue int, smooth dark blue ext, ship
   mark, 2¹⁄₄ x 6¹⁄₄" 200.00
Bud Vase, gray glaze, 7" h 275.00
Match Safe, faceted with striker inside lid, covered in
   smooth matte green glaze, imp ship mark, 3 x 2" 350.00
Pitcher, emb waves around neck, medallions of tall-
   masted ships in gray, ochre, and blue semi-matte
   glaze, imp ship mark, 5 x 6" 700.00
Plate, frieze of camels and nomads in blue and yellow
   on white ground, ship mark, 7¹⁄₂" d 950.00
Tile, cluster of trees in dark green under blue overcast
   sky, ship mark and paper label, 4¹⁄₄" sq 800.00
Tile, landscape of trees in dark green reflected in lake,
   ship mark and paper label, 4¹⁄₄" sq 700.00
Vase, bulbous, bobeche lid covered in smooth matte
   gray glaze, paper label, 4¹⁄₄ x 4³⁄₄" 600.00
Vase, bulbous, red and purple stylized floral pattern on
   semi-matte pink ground, 4¹⁄₄ x 4³⁄₄" 800.00
Vase, bulbous, smooth dark blue matte glaze, ship mark,
   8 x 6¹⁄₂" 700.00
Vase, cylindrical, incised geometric design, dark green
   matte on lighter green matte ground, ship mark
   incised cipher "MT," 8³⁄₄ x 4" 850.00
Vase, flaring, lavender int, matte mauve glaze ext, ship
   mark, 3³⁄₄ x 7¹⁄₂" 350.00
Vase, ovoid, gray matte glaze ext, light blue matte glaze
   int, ship mark, 9 x 6¹⁄₂" 700.00
Vase, ovoid, smooth dark blue matte glaze, ship mark,
   7 x 4¹⁄₄" 600.00
Vessel, bulbous, light blue int, matte blue ext, ship mark,
   4 x 5" 400.00
Vessel, squat, matte gray glaze, imp ship mark and paper
   label, 3³⁄₄ x 4¹⁄₂" 400.00
Vessel, squat, matte pink glaze, imp ship mark, 3³⁄₄ x
   4¹⁄₂" 300.00

Vase, bulbous, incised dark brown stylized blossoms, lighter brown ground, imp ship mark, 6¹⁄₂" h, $9,350.00. Photo courtesy David Rago Auctions, Inc.

Vessel, squat, moss green matte glaze, 2 handles, ship
mark, 2³/₄ x 3³/₄" **450.00**
Vessel, squat, smooth speckled brown glaze, ship mark,
2³/₄ x 5¹/₄" **325.00**
Wall Pocket, flared top, matte green glaze, 5" h, 7" w **300.00**
Wall Pocket, semi-circular rim, blue matte glaze, ship
mark, 5³/₄ x 6¹/₂" **400.00**

MARBLES

Marbles divide into three basic types: (1) machine-made clay, glass, and mineral marbles, (2) handmade glass marbles made for use, and (3) handmade glass marbles made for display. Machine-made marbles usually sell for less than their handmade counterparts, comic strip marbles being one of the few exceptions. Watch for modern reproduction and fantasy comic strip marbles.

The Akro Agate Company, Christensen Agate Company, M. F. Christensen & Son Company, Marble King Company, Master Marble Company, Peltier Glass Company, and Vitro Agate/Gladding-Vitro Company are some of the leading manufacturers of machine-made marbles. Today, collector emphasis is on marble sets in their period packaging.

Handmade marbles are collected by type—Bennington, china (glazed and painted), china (unglazed and painted), clay, end of day, Lutz, mica, sulfide, and swirl—and size. Over a dozen reproduction and fantasy sulfide marbles have appeared during the last decade.

Many contemporary studio glassblowers have made marbles, often imitating earlier styles, for sale to the adult collector market. These marbles show no signs of wear and have not been tested in the secondary resale market. Any value associated with these marbles is highly speculative.

References: Robert Block, *Marbles, 2nd Edition,* Schiffer Publishing, 1998; Stanley Block (ed.), *Marble Mania,* Schiffer Publishing, 1998; Everett Grist, *Antique and Collectible Marbles, Third Edition,* Collector Books, 1992, 1998 value update; *Everett Grist's Big Book of Marbles,* Collector Books, 1993, 1999 value update; *Everett Grist's Machine Made and Contemporary Marbles, Second Edition,* Collector Books, 1998; Dennis Webb, *Greenberg's Guide to Marbles, Second Edition,* Greenberg Books, 1994.

Collectors' Clubs: Marble Collectors Society of America, PO Box 222, Trumbull, CT 06611; National Marble Club of America, 440 Eaton Rd, Drexel Hill, PA 19026.

Akro Agate, Carnelian Agate **$35.00**
Akro Agate, Egg Yolk and Oxblood. **60.00**
Akro Agate, Imperial **25.00**
Akro Agate, Lemonade Corkscrew **25.00**
Akro Agate, Lemonade Corkscrew with Oxblood **80.00**
Akro Agate, Lemonade with Oxblood **80.00**
Akro Agate, Limeade Corkscrew **25.00**
Akro Agate, Opaque Corkscrew. **15.00**
Akro Agate, Oxblood Bricks with White **100.00**
Akro Agate, Popeye Corkscrew **25.00**
Akro Agate, Silver Oxblood. **60.00**
Akro Agate, Sparklers **25.00**
Akro Agate, Tri-Colored Corkscrew **25.00**
Akro Agate, Two-Colored Opaque Corkscrew. **10.00**
Akro Agate, White Marble with Oxblood **100.00**
Christensen Agate Co, Coral **250.00**

Ribbon Swirl, red, white, and blue ribbon, yellow swirl exterior, 2¹/₂" d, $150.00.

Christensen Agate Co, Flame **80.00**
Christensen Agate Co, Guinea **250.00**
Christensen Agate Co, Hurricane **100.00**
Christensen Agate Co, Slag **20.00**
Christensen Agate Co, Turkey. **75.00**
Marble King, 42 marbles with bag **325.00**
Master Made Marble Co, Chicago Worlds Fair, 1933
Century of Progress, moss agates and solid colors **700.00**
MF Christensen & Son, Slag. **40.00**
Peltier Glass Co, Christmas Tree **60.00**
Peltier Glass Co, Comic, "Andy" **85.00**
Peltier Glass Co, Comic, "Annie" **100.00**
Peltier Glass Co, Superman **80.00**
Vitro Agate/Gladding-Vitro, Blackie **50**
Vitro Agate/Gladding-Vitro, Cat's Eye, bag of 100, c1950 . . . . . **2.00**

MATCHBOX

In 1947 Leslie Smith and Rodney Smith, two unrelated Navy friends, founded Lesney (a combination of the first letters in each of their names) in London, England. Joined by John Odell, they established a factory to do die casting.

In 1953, Lesney introduced a miniature toy line packaged in a box that resembled a matchbox. The toys quickly became known as "Matchbox" toys. The earliest Matchbox vehicles had metal wheels. These were eventually replaced with plastic wheels. In 1969 the Superfast plastic wheel was introduced. Slight variations in color and style occurred from the beginning due to paint and parts shortages. In 1956 the Models of Yesteryear series was introduced, followed in 1957 by Major Packs.

Matchbox toys arrived in the United States in 1958 and achieved widespread popularity by the early 1960s. Mattel's Hot Wheels arrived on the scene in 1968, providing Matchbox with a major competitor. Matchbox revamped its models through the 1970s and added the "1-75" numbering system. "Nostalgia" models were introduced in 1992.

In 1982 Universal Group bought Lesney. Production was moved to the Far East. In 1992 Tyco Toys bought Universal Group. In 1997 Mattel, owner of Hot Wheels, acquired Tyco.

References: Dana Johnson, *Matchbox Toys: 1947–1998, Third Edition,* Collector Books, 1999; Charlie Mack, *Lesney's Matchbox Toys: 1969–1982, 2nd Edition,* Schiffer Publishing, 1999; Charlie Mack, *Matchbox Toys: The Universal Years, 1982–1992, 2nd Edition,* Schiffer Publishing, 1999; Charlie Mack, *The Encyclopedia of Matchbox Toys: 1947–1996,* Schiffer Publishing, 1997.

Collectors' Clubs: Matchbox Collectors Club, PO Box 977, Newfield, NJ 08344; Matchbox USA, 62 Saw Mill Rd, Durham, CT 06422; The Matchbox International Collectors Assoc, PO Box 28072, Waterloo, Ontario, Canada N2L 6J8.

1910 Benz Limousine, Y3-B9	$20.00
1911 Model T Ford, Y1-B2	15.00
1911 Renault 2 Seater, Y2-B3	20.00
1914 Prince Henry Vauxhall, Y2-C1	25.00
Allchin Tractor Engine, Y1-A2	80.00
AMX Javelin, 9-E	6.00
Atlantic Trailer, 16-A	40.00
Baja Dune Buggy, 13-F	10.00
Bedford Duplé Long Distance Coach, 21-A	55.00
Big Bull Bulldozer, 12-F	5.00
BMW 3.0 CSL, 45-D	8.00
Boat and Trailer, regular wheels, 9-C	20.00
Bread Bait Press, Lesney	75.00
Case Tractor Bulldozer, 16-D	45.00
Caterpillar D8 Bulldozer with Blade, 18-A	40.00
Coca-Cola Lorry, cases and metal wheels, 37-B	55.00
Commer Milk Truck, 21-C	35.00
Conestoga Wagon, with 6 horses, no barrels	175.00
Corvette T-Roof, 40-F	4.00
Daimler Ambulance, 14-A	55.00
Datsun 126X, 33-E	6.00
Dennis Fire Escape, gray wheels, 9-A	60.00
Dodge Stake Truck, "Matchbox Intl Ltd" on base, 4-Eb	3.00
Dragon Wheels, 43-E	6.00
Dumper, 2-A	60.00
Fire Pumper, regular wheels, 29-C	20.00
Flying Bug, 11-F	6.00
Ford Anglia, 7-B	45.00
Ford Pick-Up, regular wheels, 6-D	12.00
Formula 5000, 36-F	6.00
GMC Refrigerator Truck, regular wheels, 44-C	25.00
Hairy Hustler, 7-E	6.00
Hand Cement Mixer, Lesney	250.00
Hay Trailer, 40-C	15.00
Horse Drawn Milk Cart, Lesney	250.00
Iron Fairy Crane, regular wheels, 42-C	40.00
Jaguar XJ6, 1-K	2.00
Karrier Refuse Truck, 38-A	45.00
Land Rover with Driver, 12-A	50.00

Lincoln Continental Mark V, 28-G	4.00
London Bus, 5-A	60.00
London Bus, 5-B	45.00
London E Class Tramcar, Y3-A2	50.00
Lotus Europa with SF wheels, 5-E	15.00
Lotus Racing Car, spoked wheels, 19-Da	30.00
Mack Dump Truck, regular wheels, 28-D	20.00
Maserati Bora, 32-E	8.00
Massey Harris Tractor with Fenders, 4-A	65.00
Mechanical Horse and Trailer, 10-A	65.00
Mercedes Benz Lorry with regular wheels, 1-E	12.00
Merryweather Fire Engine, 9-B	30.00
MG Midget Sports Car, with driver, 19-A	50.00
Mod Tractor, 25-F	6.00
Police Launch, 52-D	6.00
Pontiac Trans Am, 16-G	4.00
Prime Mover Truck Tractor, 15-A	45.00
Quarry Truck, 6-A	55.00
Railway Passenger Coach, 44-F	8.00
Revin' Rebel Dodge Challenger, 1-I	6.00
Road Roller, 1-B	50.00
Road Tanker, 11-A	55.00
Rolls Royce Phantom V, 44-B	35.00
Rolls Royce Silver Cloud, 44-A	40.00
Rover Sterling, 31-J	3.00
Siva Spider, 41-E	8.00
Soap Box Racer, Lesney	400.00
Stingeroo Cycle, 38-E	6.00
Thames Trader Compressor Truck, 28-B	40.00
US Mail Jeep, 5-G	6.00
Vauxhall Victor Sedan, 45-A	35.00
Volkswagen 1500 Saloon, chrome hubs, 15-D	20.00

MATCHCOVERS

Joshua Pusey, a Philadelphia lawyer who put ten cardboard matches into a plain white board cover, is credited with inventing the matchcover. In 1892 he sold 200 to the Mendelson Opera Company, which hand-printed the cover with its advertisement.

Binghamton Match Company, Binghamton, New York, made the first machine-made matchcover for the Piso Company of Warren, Pennsylvania. Only one example survives, owned by the Diamond Match Company.

Matchcovers dating prior to the early 1930s are scarce. The modern collecting craze dates from the Chicago Century of Progress World's Fair of 1933–34. The matchcover's golden age began in the mid-1940s and extended through the early 1960s.

The introduction of the throw-away lighter in the mid-1960s and rising production costs ended the matchcover era. The per unit cost of diecut matchcovers today falls in the seven to eight cents range. Given this, matchcovers lost their appeal as a free giveaway.

The 1990s saw matchcover prices soar. The $1,000 barrier was broken. Many of these higher prices are being paid by crossover, not matchcover collectors. Trading, usually on a one-for-one basis, remains the principal form of exchange among collectors.

Reference: Bill Retskin, *The Matchcover Collector's Price Guide, 2nd Edition*, Antique Trader Books, 1997.

Collectors' Clubs: Rathkamp Matchcover Society, 432 N Main St, Urbana, OH 43078; The American Matchcover Collecting Club, PO Box 18481, Asheville, NC 28814.

1920 Aveling & Porter Steam Roller, Y-11, green body and canopy supports, red wheels, 3" l, $80.00.

Note: Prices are for matchcovers in mint or near mint condition.

20-Strike, The Sands, Las Vegas, Nevada on front, hotel on back, penguin on each side, "Why be formal?...Come as you Are!" across sticks, Lion Match **$8.00**

21-Feature, Petrullo's, Hackensack, New Jersey, black with orange and white lettering on outside, orange with black lettering inside, orange "Petrullo's" across black sticks **10.00**

Display, beachcomer and island on front and back, "Home of the Zombie" and zombie on front, dancing zombie and drink on display, nude Hawaiian dancer, shipwrecked sailor, and monkey in palm tree across sticks **15.00**

Display, Jack Dempsey's on Broadway on front, oval bar on back, Dempsey photo display, "J.D." on each match, alternating light blue on dark blue and dark blue on light blue, Feature Matchbook, Lion Match. **15.00**

Features, Restaurants Longchamps, New York City, chef on each stick with "Longchamps" across all sticks, orange and white, 20-strike size, Lion Match **10.00**

Lucky Sticks, Flemington Glass Co, Inc, Flemington New Jersey on front, "Factory Showrooms" and wine glass on back, white on magenta ground, play instruction inside, 21 sticks each with card symbols for different poker hand on each stick, Lion Match. **10.00**

Midget, Hutzler's Quixie on front, Baltimore on saddle, No Tipping Please on back, white lettering on pink, Lion Match **5.00**

Midget-Type, Hotel El Tejon, Say "Tay-Hone" Bakersfield California, George Bowser, Mgr on front, "Good Food" on saddle, building, name, and location on back, "200 Delightfully Air-Condition Rooms, Banquet Facilities, Sample Rooms, In the Heart of Bakersfield" inside, black and white, Diamond Match. **5.00**

Military, Coast Guard Training Station, Curtis Bay, MD with USCGA insignia on front, black saddle, marching honor guard on back, blank inside, Lion Match **5.00**

Patriotic, Bond Bread Navy Plane Set, Wildcat Fighter, Lion Match, 1942 . . . . **8.00**

Patriotic, Disney/Pepsi-Cola Set, Type I, Company C 69th Quartermaster Battalion (LM), No 19, running monkey wrench wearing helmet carrying tools, gray, National Match Co, 1942 . . . . **10.00**

20-Strike, Trainer's Seafood, Quakertown, PA, seafood pictures on matches, $8.00. Photo courtesy Ray Morykan Auctions.

Patriotic, Give to the Greater New York Fund, Keep the Home Front Strong, full length, large soldier with arms spread to encompass crowd of civilians, "Give!" superimposed over "V" and "1942 to the Greater New York Fund" inside, National Match. **8.00**

Printed Sticks, Downingtown Inn Resort and Golf Club, aerial view of grounds on front, list of club features on back, printed sticks with black "Gateway To The Pennsylvania Dutch Amish Land," Amish man's head, and horse and buggy, Universal Match. **8.00**

Radio, Faiman's Café adv on front, "Station WOW" and girlie picture on back, "We Never Sleep" on saddle **5.00**

Transportation, "French Line, Normandie, The World's Largest Ship" and drawing of ship on outside, list of 4 ships and their tonnage on inside, Lion Match **10.00**

Transportation, New Jersey Central Railroad, New Jersey Central Terminal Restaurant adv on front, "New Jersey Central Railroad" on saddle, "Ride the 'Crusader' Between New York and Phila, The Blue Comet Between New York and Atlantic City" and drawings of trains on back, "Choice Beer, Wines, Liquors, Excellent Food, Prompt-Courteous Service" inside, Diamond Match **5.00**

MCCOY POTTERY

In 1910 Nelson McCoy, with his father's (J. W. McCoy) support, founded the Nelson McCoy Sanitary Stoneware Company to manufacture crocks, churns, and jugs. Early pieces were marked on the side with a stencil of a clover within a shield with an "M" above. By the mid-1920s, the company also made molded artware in forms ranging from jardinieres to vases.

In 1933 the company became the Nelson McCoy Pottery. Products included cookware, dinnerware, floral industry ware, gardenware, kitchenware, and tableware.

In 1967 Mount Clemens Pottery, owned by David Chase, purchased the company. Some pieces were marked "MCP" on the bottom. In 1974 Chase sold McCoy to Lancaster Colony Corporation, which added its logo to the bottom. Nelson McCoy, Jr., served as president under the Mount Clemens and Lancaster Colony Corporation ownership until 1981. After being sold to Designer Accents in 1985, operations at McCoy ceased in 1990.

References: Bob Hanson, Craig Nissen, and Margaret Hanson, *McCoy Pottery* (1997, 1999 value update), *Vol. II* (1999), Collector Books; Sharon and Bob Huxford, *The Collectors Encyclopedia of McCoy Pottery,* Collector Books, 1980, 1997 value update; Martha and Steve Sanford, *Sanfords Guide to Pottery by McCoy,* Adelmore Press, 1997.

Newsletter: *The NM Express,* 3081 Rock Creek Dr, Broomfield, CO 80020.

REPRODUCTION ALERT: Nelson McCoy Pottery Company reproduced many of its original pieces.

Ashtray, arrowhead shape, $9^3/_4$ x $6^3/_4$" **$20.00**
Ashtray, bird on flower 20.00
Bookends, pr, rearing horses, white, gold trim, 8" h 100.00
Bowl, Stone Craft, 6" d 8.00
Candy Dish, cov, Sunburst Gold Line, 5 x 5" 40.00
Cat Feeder, 6" d 60.00
Cookie Jar, bear with beehive 48.00

Cookie Jar, cabin	125.00
Cookie Jar, Chilly Willy	55.00
Cookie Jar, owl	45.00
Cookie Jar, Smiley Face	14.00
Corn Dish, Brown Drip	10.00
Cornucopia Vase, 7½" h	30.00
Creamer, Brown Drip, 4" h	8.00
Cup and Saucer, Graystone, 4 x 6"	8.00
Dinner Plate, Graystone, 10½" d	10.00
Fernery, Hobnail, 5½" l	20.00
Flower Bowl, Lily Bud Line, 9½" l	30.00
Flower Holder, elephant	20.00
Flower Holder, fish, yellow	60.00
Flower Holder, turtle, rose	60.00
Flower Holder, witch	100.00
Garden Dish, Lily Bud Line, 5½ x 4½"	20.00
Lamp, rearing horse	75.00
Match Holder, Blue Country, speckled finish	30.00
Pitcher, Happytime, 6½ x 4½"	10.00
Planter, alligator, green, 10" l	35.00
Planter, baby crib, 6½ x 4"	50.00
Planter, baby shoes, pink	9.00
Planter, basket, yellow and brown, 9 x 5¼"	35.00
Planter, caterpillar, Floraline, 13½" l	20.00
Planter, cobbler's bench, brown, 8¾" h	30.00
Planter, kitten	35.00
Planter, sheep	35.00
Salt and Pepper Shakers, pr, Brown Drip	25.00
Snack Dish, Rustic Line, 11 x 8"	35.00
Spoon Rest, butterfly	75.00
Spoon Rest, penguin	75.00
Stein, cowboy boot, 8¼" h	35.00
Teapot, ivy dec, 6 cup	40.00
Vase, butterfly, blue, mkd "USA," 7½ x 5½"	50.00
Vase, sunflower, yellow, gold trim, 9" h	65.00
Wall Pocket, apple and leaves, brown leaves	100.00
Wall Pocket, butterfly, pastel	200.00
Wall Pocket, lily bud, 8" h	175.00
Wall Pocket, violin, gold trim	150.00

Lazy Susan, avocado and butterscotch, $35.00.

MCDONALD'S

In 1948 Dick and Mac McDonald opened their first limited menu, self-service McDonald's drive-in restaurant in San Bernadino, California. They began franchising their operation as the Speedee Service System in 1952. In 1955 Ray Kroc became a franchising agent for the McDonald brothers and opened his first McDonald's restaurant in Des Plaines, Illinois.

The 100th McDonald's restaurant opened in 1959 and the 200th in 1960. In 1961 Kroc bought out the McDonald brothers and launched the All American Meal of a hamburger, french fries, and milkshake. The Golden Arches replaced the Speedee logo in 1962. The first "Ronald McDonald," Willard Scott, made his debut in Washington, D.C.'s Cherry Blossom Parade in 1963. The Happy Meal dates from 1977. Toys were introduced in 1982.

By 1983, McDonald's had 7,000 restaurants in the United States and additional restaurants in thirty-one foreign countries. McDonald's has continued to build new restaurants around the world. Promotional tie-ins with movies, television shows, and major toy products have proven highly successful. By 1994, the 15th anniversary of the Happy Meal, McDonald's was serving 25 million customers daily in 70 countries.

References: Gary Henriques and Audre DuVall, *McDonald's Collectibles,* Collector Books, 1997 (1999 value update); Joyce and Terry Losonsky, *McDonald's Happy Meal Toys from the Eighties* (1999), *From the Nineties* (1999), Schiffer Publishing; Joyce and Terry Losonsky, *McDonald's Pre-Happy Meal Toys from the Fifties, Sixties and Seventies,* Schiffer Publishing, 1999; Terry and Joyce Losonsky, *McDonald's Happy Meal Toys Around the World,* Schiffer Publishing, 1995; Terry and Joyce Losonsky, *McDonald's Happy Meal Toys in the U.S.A.,* Schiffer Publishing, 1995; Meredith Williams, *Tomart's Price Guide to McDonald's Happy Meal Collectibles, Revised Edition,* Tomart Publications, 1995.

Newsletter: *Collecting Tips Newsletter,* PO Box 633, Joplin, MO 64802.

Collectors' Club: McDonald's Collectors Club, 1153 S Lee St, Ste 200, Des Plaines, IL 60016.

Activity Book, *Lady and the Tramp,* Disney Favorites, 1987	$2.00
Book, Berenstain Bears Books, 1990	2.00
Book/Cassette Tape, Dinosaurs Talking Storybook, 1989	4.00
Bumper Car Tag Game, Giggles & Games, 1982	10.00
Car, Camaro Z-28, purple, Barbie/Hot Wheels, 1991	3.00
Changeable, 1987	3.00
Colorforms, 1986	3.00
Crayola Washable Ink Drawing Marker, CosMc Crayola, 1988	2.00
Design-O-Saurs, 1987	3.00
Doodler Ruler, Circus Wagon, 1979	8.00
Duck Code Quacker, Duck Tales I, 1988	2.00
Figure, Ariel, *Little Mermaid,* 1989	3.00
Figure, Bambi, 1986	3.00
Figure, Barnyard Happy Meal Series, 1986	8.00
Figure, Big Mac, Adventures of Ronald McDonald, 1981	2.00
Figure, Big Mac Helicopter, green, 3 pcs, 1986	5.00
Figure, Catwoman and Leopard, Batman The Animated Series, 1993	2.00
Figure, Flintstone Kids, 1988	5.00
Figure, French Fry Guy, Fun With Food, 1989	5.00

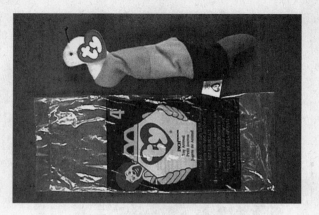

Teenie Beanie Babies, Inch the Worm, 1997, $5.00.

Figure, Garfield on Scooter, 1989 . . . . 2.00
Figure, Papa Berenstain With Wheelbarrow, 1987 . . . . 2.00
Fry Kid Trumpet, McDonaldland Band, 1986 . . . . 2.00
Grimace Bouncin' Beach Ball, test, 1989 . . . . 20.00
Grimace Canteen, 2pcs, blue, Camp McDonaldland,
   1990. . . . . 2.00
Halloween Pail, 1985 . . . . 10.00
Hamburglar Train, Crazy Vehicles, 1991. . . . . 2.00
Happy Meal Box, An American Tail, 1986 . . . . 2.00
Happy Meal Box, Big Top, 1988 . . . . 3.00
Happy Meal Box, Changeables, 1987 . . . . 3.00
Happy Meal Box, Chip 'N Dale Rescue Rangers, 1989. . . . . . . 2.00
Lego Building Set, 1984 . . . . 8.00
Little Golden Book, 1982 . . . . 3.00
Locket Surprise Barbie, Barbie and Friends–World of
   Hot Wheels, Caucasian, 1994 . . . . 2.00
Magic Tablet, Ronald holding tablet, Magic Show, 1985 . . . . . 8.00
McBoo Bag, witch, ghost, or monster, 1991 . . . . 1.00
McDonaldland Dough, 1990. . . . . 3.00
Notepad, apple, Food Fundamentals, 1993 . . . . 2.00
Popoids, Crazy Creatures, 1985. . . . . 5.00
Poster, *E.T.,* 1985. . . . . 10.00
Sand Mold, Castlemaker, 1987 . . . . 20.00
Soap Dish, Feeling Good, 1985 . . . . 3.00
Stencil, Hamburglar, with 4 crayons, Crayola, 1987 . . . . 3.00
Stopwatch, Fitness Fun Challenge, 1992. . . . . 1.00
Stuffed Toy, plush, Amazing Wildlife, 1995, 4" h. 2.00
Toothbrush, Feeling Good, 1985 . . . . 4.00

MCKEE GLASS

McKee and Brothers was founded in Pittsburgh, Pennsylvania, in 1853. In 1888 the factory moved to Jeannette, Pennsylvania. The company reorganized in 1903, renaming itself the McKee Glass Company. It manufactured a wide range of household and industrial glassware. McKee introduced its Glasbake line in the 1910s.

The company is best known for its crystal pressed patterns, Depression glass kitchenware, and opaque ware. Tableware lines in color were first made in the early 1920s. Many older clear patterns, e.g., Aztec and Rock Crystal Flower, became available in color. Between 1923 and the late 1930s, new colors were added to the line each year. The popularity of the colorful opaque ware, made between 1930 and 1940, helped the company weather the hard times of the Depression.

In 1951 Thatcher Glass Company purchased McKee, selling it in 1961 to the Jeannette Glass Corporation. Upon purchasing McKee, Jeannette Glass Corporation closed the manufacturing operations at its plant and moved them to the McKee factory.

References: Gene Florence, *Kitchen Glassware of the Depression Years, 5th Edition,* Collector Books, 1995, 1999 value update; Gene Florence, *Very Rare Glassware of the Depression Years, Fifth Series,* Collector Books, 1997.

Note: For additional listings see Kitchen Glassware and Reamers.

Bottoms Up, carmel tumbler, crystal tray **$145.00**
Eclipse, pitcher, Presscut Yutec 45.00
Glasbake, pie plate, heart with cupids 22.00
Laurel, bowl, 4³/₄", French ivory 8.00
Laurel, bowl, 4³/₄", jadite 9.00
Laurel, bowl, 4³/₄", lustre 6.00
Laurel, bowl, 5³/₄", jadite 140.00
Laurel, bowl, 6", 3 ftd, French ivory 18.00
Laurel, bowl, 6", French ivory 12.00
Laurel, bowl, 9", French ivory 25.00
Laurel, bowl, 9", jadite 40.00
Laurel, bowl, 11", French ivory 40.00
Laurel, bowl, 11", jadite 65.00
Laurel, bowl, flanged rim, 6", jadite 18.00
Laurel, bowl, oval, delphite 75.00
Laurel, candlestick, French ivory 20.00
Laurel, creamer, French ivory 12.00
Laurel, cup, French ivory 8.00
Laurel, cup, jadite 14.00
Laurel, cup, lustre 6.00
Laurel, dinner plate, lustre 4.00
Laurel, plate, 7¹/₂", French ivory 10.00
Laurel, plate, 9", delphite 25.00
Laurel, plate, 9", French ivory 15.00
Laurel, plate, 9", jadite 24.00
Laurel, salad plate, lustre 9.00
Laurel, salt and pepper shakers, pr, French ivory 40.00
Laurel, saucer, delphite 8.00
Laurel, saucer, French ivory 4.00
Laurel, saucer, jadite 6.00
Laurel, sherbet, French ivory 10.00
Laurel, sugar, French ivory 12.00
Red Ships, bowl, 5" d, 3¹/₂" h 35.00

Autumn, console bowl, jadite, 8¹/₂" l, $65.00.

Red Ships, bowl, 6" d, 4½" h 35.00
Red Ships, bowl, flared, 9" d, 5" h 38.00
Red Ships, butter, cov, 1 lb 60.00
Red Ships, mixing bowl, 6" 20.00
Red Ships, mixing bowl, 9" 40.00
Red Ships, mixing bowls, nesting set of 4, orig box 140.00
Red Ships, refrigerator dish, white lid, 4 x 5" 40.00
Red Ships, salt and pepper shakers, pr, square, red lids 50.00
Red Ships, shaker set, salt, pepper, sugar, and flour, orig
  box 125.00
Rock Crystal, bowl, ftd, 12½", clear 75.00
Rock Crystal, cake stand, amber 35.00
Rock Crystal, candelabra, pr, 3-lite, ruby 400.00
Rock Crystal, candlestick, double, clear 16.00
Rock Crystal, candy, cov, amber, emb mint gold band 62.00
Rock Crystal, cheese comport, amber 14.00
Rock Crystal, cocktail, ftd, clear 15.00
Rock Crystal, comport, 11½", amber 60.00
Rock Crystal, cordial, 1 oz, clear 22.00
Rock Crystal, cornucopia vase, 8½", clear 80.00
Rock Crystal, creamer, ftd, clear 20.00
Rock Crystal, goblet, 7 oz, clear 18.00
Rock Crystal, goblet, 8 oz, ruby 40.00
Rock Crystal, pitcher, cov, pink 350.00
Rock Crystal, plate, 7", ruby 18.00
Rock Crystal, plate, 8½", clear 8.00
Rock Crystal, relish, 5-part, clear 30.00
Rock Crystal, sherbet, 3½ oz, clear 13.00
Rock Crystal, sherbet, 3½ oz, ruby 45.00
Rock Crystal, sundae, 6 oz, clear 9.00
Rock Crystal, tumbler, ftd, 7 oz, 5½", pink 25.00
Rock Crystal, water goblet, 8 oz, clear 18.00
Rock Crystal, wine, 3 oz, ruby 40.00
Rock Crystal, wine, 3 oz, clear 50.00

MEDICAL ITEMS

Doctors are the primary collectors of medical apparatus and instruments. Most collect material that relates to their medical specialty. Medical apparatus and instruments are sold by specialist dealers or auctions. This is why so little medical material is found at flea markets and antiques malls, shops, and shows.

Office furniture, especially large wooden storage cabinets with unusual drawer configurations, are popular in the general antiques marketplace. The same holds true for wall charts, ranging from the standard eye examination chart to those dealing with anatomy.

Pharmaceutical items divide into two groups: (1) items used by druggists to prepare medicines and (2) packaging associated with over-the-counter and doctor-prescribed medications. There is little added value if the contents are intact. In fact, most collectors prefer that they are not.

Reference: C. Keith Wilbur, *Antique Medical Instruments,* Schiffer Publishing, 1987, 1998 value update.

Collectors' Club: Medical Collectors Assoc, Montefiore Medical Park, 1695A Eastchester Rd, Bronx, NY 10461.

Note: See Drugstore for additional listings.

Baby Scale, white wicker basket, wooden base, c1930 . . . . . **$52.00**
Book, *The Great Physician,* life of Sir William Osler,
  Oxford University Press, 299 pp, 1934 . . . . 8.00

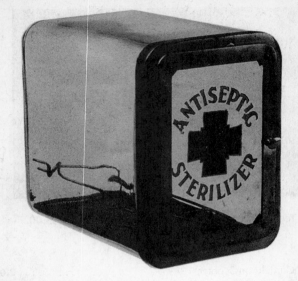

Sterilizer, glass with metal frame, 2 wire racks, 10" h, 7" w, 11" d, **$170.00.** Photo courtesy Collectors Auction Services.

Catalog, Diagnostic Otoscopes, Welch, Allyn, 16 pp,
  1948, 7 x 4" 15.00
Cautery Unit, Bakelite, 5 different electrodes, "National
  Cautery Pistol," c1930s 20.00
Goggles, folding metal mesh side protectors, folds into
  brown metal carry case mkd "Wilson Goggles,"
  c1920 . . . . 18.00
Hearing Aid, Zenith, brown leatherette case, blue velvet
  int with gold battery control case, wire, 2 plastic ear
  inserts, booklet, c1950 . . . . 45.00
Otoscope-Ophthamoloscope Set, 6 pcs, dark blue velvet
  lined int, "Wampler American Cystoscope Makers
  N.Y.," 7 x 5 x 2½" case with gold letters "A.G.S.,"
  complete, c1925 . . . . 55.00
Percussion Hammer, mkd "Kny-Scheerer Germany,"
  chrome plate, c1925 . . . . 27.00
Quack Foot X-ray Machine, mahogany case, step and
  foot insert in back, controls and 3 viewing boxes in
  front, 1930s 1,160.00
Stethoscope, turned hardwood, mkd "medica Bowles
  made in U.S.A.," c1930 . . . . 55.00
Vaginal Speculum, self-retaining, Guttman, mkd "Milex
  Stainless Steel," c1960s 30.00

MELMAC

Thermosetting plastics, principally melamine resins, were used to make dinnerware. Melamine resins result from the interaction of melamine and formaldehyde. A chemical reaction creating permanent hardness occurs when thermosetting plastics are heated.

Melmac is a trade name of American Cyanamid. Like Kleenex and Xerox, it soon became a generic term describing an entire line of products.

The first plastic dinnerware was used in cafeterias, hospitals, restaurants, and other institutional settings. Melamine dinnerware's popularity waned in the early 1960s. Repeated washing caused fading and dullness. Edges chipped, knives scratched surfaces, and foods left stains. Pieces placed too close to heat discolored or scarred. Many early 1960s' designs were too delicate. Pieces actually broke. The final death blow came from the import of inexpensive Asian and European ceramic dinnerware in the late 1960s and early 1970s.

Reference: Gregory R. Zimmer and Alvin Daigle, Jr., *Melmac Dinnerware,* L-W Book Sales, 1997.

Note: Prices listed are for items in mint condition.

ABC Manufacturing Co, salad plate	$2.00
ABC Manufacturing Co, soup bowl	3.00
Air Flite, cup	2.00
Apollo Ware, dinner plate	2.00
Aztec, bread and butter plate	1.00
Aztec, cup and saucer	2.00
Aztec, dinner plate	2.00
Aztec, soup bowl	3.00
Boonton, bread tray	8.00
Boonton, compartment plate	10.00
Boonton, dinner plate	4.00
Boonton, fruit bowl	3.00
Boonton, platter	8.00
Boonton, sugar	6.00
Boontonware, bread and butter plate	2.00
Boontonware, cereal bowl	4.00
Boontonware, dinner plate	4.00
Boontonware, serving bowl	8.00
Branchell, butter, cov	10.00
Branchell, salt and pepper shakers, pr	6.00
Branchell Royale, dinner plate	4.00
Branchell Royale, soup bowl, cov	5.00
Brookpark, butter, cov, Tropicana	10.00
Brookpark, cup, handleless, square	2.00
Brookpark Arrowhead, dinner plate, Desert Flower	4.00
Brookpark Arrowhead, dinner plate, divided	5.00
Debonaire, dinner plate	2.00
Debonaire, sugar, cov	3.00
Flite Lane, tumbler, large	7.00

Flite Lane, tumbler, small	6.00
Fostoria, bread plate	3.00
Fostoria, cereal bowl	7.00
Fostoria, dinner plate	6.00
Harmony House, cup and saucer	3.00
Harmony House, dinner plate, Autumn Leaves	4.00
Holiday, cup and saucer	3.00
Imperial Ware, dinner plate	2.00
Imperial Ware, salad plate	2.00
Lucent, bread and butter plate	3.00
Lucent, platter	12.00
Mallo-Ware, butter, cov	5.00
Mallo-Ware, cup and suacer	2.00
Mar-Crest, cereal bowl	2.00
Mar-Crest, soup bowl	3.00
Monte Carlo, cup and saucer	2.00
Monte Carlo, salt and pepper shakers, pr	4.00
Restraware, cup and saucer	2.00
Restraware, dinner plate	2.00
Royalon, gravy boat	5.00
Royalon, serving bowl	4.00

METLOX

In 1927 T. C. Prouty and Willis, his son, established Metlox Pottery, Manhattan Beach, California, primarily for the purpose of making ceramic outdoor signs. When business declined during the Depression and T. C. died in 1931, Willis converted the plant to the production of ceramic dinnerware. Brightly colored California Pottery was the company's first offering. Between 1934 and the early 1940s, Metlox produced its Poppytrail line of kitchenware and tableware. In 1936 the company adopted the poppy, California's state flower, as its trademark.

Designer Carl Romanelli, who joined Metlox in the late 1930s, created Metlox's miniature line and the Modern Masterpiece line that included bookends, figural vases, figurines, and wall pockets.

The company shifted to war production during the early 1940s. California Ivy, Metlox's first painted dinnerware, was introduced in 1946. That same year, Willis Prouty sold Metlox to Evan Shaw, owner of American Pottery, Los Angeles, a company under contract to Disney for ceramic figurines. Production of Disney figurines continued until 1956. In the 1960s and 70s, Metlox made Colorstax (solid color dinnerware), cookie jars, and Poppet (stoneware flower holders and planters).

In 1958 Metlox purchased Vernon Kiln. The company's Vernon Kiln division made artware in the 1950s and 60s, American Royal Horses, and Nostalgia, a scale model carriage line.

Shaw died in 1980. His family continued the business for another decade, ending operations in 1989.

References: Carl Gibbs, Jr., *Collector's Encyclopedia of Metlox Potteries,* Collector Books, 1995; Harry L. Rinker, *Dinnerware of the 20th Century: The Top 500 Patterns,* House of Collectibles, 1997.

Antique Grape, creamer and sugar	$35.00
Antique Grape, cup and saucer	12.00
Antique Grape, fruit bowl	8.00
Antique Grape, pitcher, 8¼"	70.00
Antique Grape, platter, oval, 12½" l	25.00
Antique Grape, salad plate	12.00
California Provincial, coffee canister	50.00

Oneida Deluxe, cup and saucer, peach-colored cup, white saucer with autumn foliage, mkd "OD," $3.00.

Antique Grape, Poppytrail, dinner plate, white, 10½" d, $15.00.
Photo courtesy Ray Morykan Auctions.

California Provincial, coffee server with warmer	275.00
California Provincial, platter, oval, 11" l	45.00
California Provincial, sugar canister	65.00
California Provincial, tea canister	42.00
Della Robbia, creamer	20.00
Della Robbia, shakers, pr	20.00
Della Robbia, sugar, cov	20.00
Florence, cereal bowl	12.00
Florence, creamer	12.00
Florence, cup and saucer	12.00
Florence, platter	45.00
Florence, sugar bowl	18.00
Florence, vegetable, round, 10½" d	25.00
Homestead Provincial, ashtray, 8" d	60.00
Homestead Provincial, canister set	275.00
Homestead Provincial, coaster	20.00
Homestead Provincial, coffeepot	125.00
Homestead Provincial, creamer	22.00
Homestead Provincial, cup and saucer	12.00
Homestead Provincial, gravy bowl	45.00
Homestead Provincial, match box	75.00
Homestead Provincial, mug, large	45.00
Homestead Provincial, mustard	85.00
Homestead Provincial, plate, 7" d	12.00
Homestead Provincial, soup tureen, with ladle	795.00
Homestead Provincial, stein, cov	65.00
Homestead Provincial, sugar, cov	32.00
Homestead Provincial, teapot	145.00
Homestead Provincial, turkey platter	395.00
Homestead Provincial, vegetable, cov	75.00
Homestead Provincial, vegetable, divided	45.00
Homestead Provincial, vegetable, open	35.00
Ivy, casserole, cov	95.00
Ivy, coaster	22.00
Ivy, cup and saucer	18.00
Ivy, mug, tall	45.00
Ivy, pepper mill	60.00

Ivy, plate, 9" d	15.00
Ivy, salad bowl	75.00
Ivy, salad plate	12.00
Provincial Blue, ashtray, 4¾"	45.00
Provincial Blue, bread dish	65.00
Provincial Blue, canister set	395.00
Provincial Blue, chop plate	65.00
Provincial Blue, coffeepot	95.00
Provincial Blue, cookie jar	225.00
Provincial Blue, creamer	30.00
Provincial Blue, cup and saucer	18.00
Provincial Blue, dinner plate	20.00
Provincial Blue, fruit bowl	14.00
Provincial Blue, gravy bowl	65.00
Provincial Blue, mug, tall	50.00
Provincial Blue, platter, 13" l	55.00
Provincial Blue, rim soup	35.00
Provincial Blue, salad plate	14.00
Provincial Blue, salt and pepper shakers, pr, handle	25.00
Provincial Blue, steeple clock	145.00
Provincial Blue, tidbit, 3-tier	185.00
Provincial Blue, vegetable, 7½"	60.00
Provincial Blue, vegetable, divided	65.00
Red Rooster, tray, 3 pt, rect	100.00
Rose, butter dish	50.00
Rose, coffeepot	70.00
Rose, cookie canister	80.00
Rose, cruet set, 5 pcs	150.00
Rose, gravy boat	28.00
Rose, ice lip pitcher, large	60.00
Rose, lug soup	18.00
Rose, mug	25.00
Rose, pitcher, small	35.00
Rose, platter, 15" l	40.00
Rose, soup bowl	15.00
Rose, vegetable, cov	70.00
Sculptured Daisy, apothecary jar	125.00
Sculptured Daisy, bowl, handled, 7" d	28.00
Sculptured Daisy, bowl, handled, 8" d	35.00
Sculptured Daisy, canister lid	50.00
Sculptured Daisy, coffeepot	95.00
Sculptured Daisy, creamer	9.00
Sculptured Daisy, cup and saucer	12.00
Sculptured Daisy, dinner plate	15.00
Sculptured Daisy, fruit bowl	9.00
Sculptured Daisy, mug, 7 oz	33.00
Sculptured Daisy, plate, 7½" d	8.00
Sculptured Daisy, platter, small	35.00
Sculptured Daisy, salad bowl	95.00
Sculptured Daisy, salad fork/spoon	125.00
Sculptured Daisy, salad plate	12.00
Sculptured Daisy, server, 10"	55.00
Sculptured Daisy, soup bowl, 7" d	12.00
Sculptured Daisy, sugar, cov	30.00
Sculptured Daisy, teapot lid	30.00
Sculptured Daisy, tumbler	38.00
Sculptured Daisy, vegetable, cov, 1 qt	45.00
Sculptured Daisy, vegetable, tab handles, oval	65.00
Strawberry, bread and butter plate	8.00
Strawberry, butter dish	48.00
Strawberry, casserole, cov	12.00
Strawberry, cup and saucer	12.00
Strawberry, dinner plate	12.00
Strawberry, salad plate	10.00

MILK BOTTLES

Hervey Thatcher is recognized as the father of the glass milk bottle. Patents are one of the best research sources for information about early milk bottles. A. V. Whiteman received a milk bottle patent as early as 1880. Patent recipients leased or sold their patents to manufacturers. The golden age of the glass milk bottle spans from the year 1910 to 1950.

Milk bottles are collected by size: gill (quarter pint), half pint, ten ounces (third of a quart), pint, quart, half gallon (two quarts), and gallon.

Paper cartons first appeared in the early 1920s and 30s and achieved popularity after 1950. The late 1950s witnessed the arrival of plastic bottles. Today, few dairies use glass bottles.

References: John Tutton, *Udderly Beautiful: A Pictorial Guide to the Pyroglazed or Painted Milk Bottle,* published by author, no date; John Tutton, *Udderly Delightful: Collecting Milk Bottles & Related Items,* published by author, 1994.

Newsletter: *The Udder Collectibles,* HC73 Box 1, Smithville Flats, NY 13841

Collectors' Club: National Assoc of Milk Bottle Collectors, Inc, 4 Ox Bow Rd, Westport, CT 06880.

Allumbaugh, Idaho's largest dairy serving Boise since
1912, creamer building, red pyroglaze, 1 qt **$45.00**
Atherholt Dairy, Tunkhannock, PA, cow and boy drink-
ing glass of milk, red pyroglaze, 1 qt **32.00**
Ben Jansing Farm Dairy, Licking Pike, Newport, KY, pic-
ture of family on reverse, round, red pyroglaze, 1 qt **38.00**
Curly's Dairy, Salem, OR, Dutch boy with milk buckets,
boy and girl on shoulder, green and brown pyroglaze,
1 qt **38.00**
Duff's Health Products, Walla-Walla, WA, red pyroglaze,
1 qt **22.00**
Edwin P Hartsock Dairy, Duquoin, IL, emb, 1 pt **25.00**

Dairylea, Allentown, PA, red and black pyroglazed Hopalong Cassidy illus, 1/2 pt, $30.00.

Elkhorn Farm, Watsonville, "Elkhorn Farm Dairy Prod.
Phone 224, Reg. Cal.," picture of elk, round, orange
pyroglaze, 1/4 pt **48.00**
Ennes Dairy, H Zupke, Greely, CO, round, black
pyroglaze, 1 qt **35.00**
Farmer's Dairy Assoc, Portland, OR, row of bottles com-
ing out of barn, black pyroglaze **38.00**
HJ Penney, Melrose, MA, emb, 1 qt **30.00**
Independent Creamery, 2158 West Grand Ave, Chicago,
IL, emb, 1 pt **25.00**
JF McAdams and Bros, Chelsea, emb, 1 qt **30.00**
Mansberger's Dairy, Middletown, PA, ice cream sundae,
red pyroglaze, 1 qt **28.00**
Maple Leaf Dairy, Gardner, IL, round, "U.S. needs us
strong" on back, maroon pyroglaze, 1 qt **48.00**
Moons Farm, Catterall, England, shepherd's, red and
blue pyroglaze, 1 pt **20.00**
Mt Desert Island Dairies, Bar Harbor, ME, Indian head,
maroon pyroglaze, 1 qt and 1 pt set **140.00**
Pine Grove Dairy, Skaneateles, NY, pine trees on
reverse, round, green and orange pyroglaze, 1 qt **30.00**
Robinson's Grade A Milk, Denver's Progressive Dairy,
brown pyroglaze, 1 qt **35.00**
Rocky Mountain Dairy Products, Denver, CO, red
pyroglaze, 1 qt **45.00**
Valley Dairy, Grade A Pasteurized Milk & Cream,
LaGrande, OR, red pyroglaze, 1 qt **28.00**
Walnut Dairy Farm, Waterloo, IA, long neck, square,
orange pyroglaze, 1 qt **20.00**

MILK GLASS

Opaque white glass, also known as milk glass, enjoyed its greatest popularity in the period immediately prior to World War I when firms such as Atterbury, Challinor-Taylor, Flaccus, and McKee made a wide range of dinnerware, figural, household, kitchenware, and novelty forms. Despite the decline in popularity of milk glass during the 1920s, several manufacturers continued its production, especially for kitchenware and decorative novelty items.

Milk glass enjoyed a brief renaissance extending from the early 1940s through the early 1960s. Most milk glass offered for sale in today's market dates after 1940 and was produced by Fenton, Imperial, Kemple, and Westmoreland.

References: Frank Chiarenza and James Slater, *The Milk Glass Book,* Schiffer Publishing, 1998; Everett Grist, *Covered Animal Dishes,* Collector Books, 1988, 1996 value update; Betty and Bill Newbound, *Collector's Encyclopedia of Milk Glass,* Collector Books, 1995, 1998 value update.

Collectors' Club: National Milk Glass Collectors Society, 46 Almond Dr, Hershey, PA 17033.

Note: For more information and additional listings see Fenton, Imperial, Kemple, and Westmoreland.

Ashtray, Kool Cigarettes adv, white **$5.00**
Bookends, pr, bear, white **35.00**
Bowl, ftd, Daisy **10.00**
Box, cov, flatiron, white, 7" l **50.00**
Candlesticks, pr, ball edge, Anchor Hocking, white **8.00**
Candy Dish, cov, Bull's Eye, white **25.00**
Child's Mug, bird and wheat, white **5.00**

Compote, grape pattern, Anchor Hocking, unmkd, 1960s–70s, 9¹/₈" d, 5³/₈" h, $8.00.

Child's Mug, duck and swan, white 20.00
Compote, Jenny Lind, blue 85.00
Cookie Jar, cov, tufted pillow, ivy dec, Consolidated, initialed "MD," 8¹/₂" h 65.00
Covered Animal Dish, closed neck swan on basket, Westmoreland, white 75.00
Covered Animal Dish, dog, pointing, possibly Flaccus, standing in grassy field, white, 6⁵/₈" l 325.00
Covered Animal Dish, elephant, walking, white 250.00
Covered Animal Dish, hen on nest, basketweave base, white with blue head, 5¹/₂" l 35.00
Covered Animal Dish, owl, white 65.00
Covered Animal Dish, rooster, standing, white, Kanawha Glass 40.00
Creamer, owl, orig eyes, white 25.00
Creamer and Sugar, cov, cord and tassel, white 30.00
Cup, swan, white 17.50
Cup and Saucer, white, flower dec, gold trim 25.00
Decanter, Victorian Lady, Avon, white 8.00
Dish, cov, baseball, white 35.00
Dish, cov, battleship *Oregon*, white 50.00
Dish, cov, Easter egg, rabbit finial, white, 4³/₄" l 225.00
Dresser Tray, daisy, white 20.00
Dresser Tray, grape cluster, Imperial Glass, white 25.00
Dresser Tray, scroll, gold paint, 11¹/₂" l 25.00
Dresser Tray, sunflower, white, 10¹/₄" l 30.00
Eggcup, kingfisher, white 10.00
Figure, jumping horse, Kemple, white 60.00
Figure, snowman, Mosser, white, black, green, and red paint 15.00
Fruit Bowl, Monroe pattern, white, Fostoria 25.00
Fruit Jar, owl, metal lid, white 100.00
Honey Jar, cov, Jeannette Glass, pink 30.00
Jar, cov, Queen Victoria bust, white 135.00
Jar, cov, Scottie, pink 45.00
Ladle, curved handle, white, 13³/₄" l 40.00
Master Salt, swan, head down, white, 3¹/₄" h, 5¹/₂" l 25.00
Master Salt, turtle, blue 70.00
Match Safe, Bible, blue 25.00
Match Safe, dog's head, white 120.00
Mug, bird and wheat, white 25.00

Pickle Dish, sheaf of wheat, white 12.50
Pin Dish, square, Fleur de Lis & Scroll, white 7.00
Pin Tray, Indian maiden with headdress, white, 7" l 45.00
Pitcher, grazing cows, white 80.00
Plate, 3 kittens, white 15.00
Plate, Angel and Harp, white, gold paint, 7¹/₂" l 7.50
Plate, Easter Bunny and Egg, orig gold border, white 50.00
Plate, keyhole border, white 3.00
Salt, swan, white, 3⁷/₈" l 15.00
Shaker, boy with hat, white 190.00
Shaker, souvenir of Niagara Falls, white, painted scene 30.00
Shakers, acorn, white 25.00
Shakers, owl, white 300.00
Sprinkler, white 30.00
Toothpick, bees in a basket, white 30.00
Toothpick, corset, white 85.00
Trinket Box, cov, actress, white 35.00
Tureen, cov, sleigh, white, 9¹/₄" l 40.00
Vase, horse and foliage, LE Smith, white 15.00
Vase, hp violets, Consolidated Glass, white, 6¹/₂" h 25.00
Wine Set, decanter and 8 glasses, Grape, Imperial Glass, white 40.00

MODEL KITS

Model kits break down into three basic types: (1) wood, (2) plastic, and (3) cast resin. Scratch-built wooden models, whether from magazine plans or model kits, achieved widespread popularity in the 1930s. Airplanes were the most popular form. Because of the skill levels involved, these were built primarily by teenagers.

England's 1/72 Frog Penguin kits of the mid-1930s were the first plastic model kits. After 1945, manufacturers utilized the new plastic injection molding process developed during World War II to produce large quantities of plastic model kits. Automobile model kits quickly replaced airplanes as the market favorite.

Model kits are sold by scale with 1/48, 1/72, and 1/144 among the most common. By the 1960s, some model kit manufacturers introduced snap-together models. The 1970s oil crisis significantly reduced production. However, the market fully recovered by the mid-1980s. While vehicles still dominate model kit sales, monster and other personality kits have gained in popularity.

Resin model kits are designed for the adult market. Gruesome monsters, scantily dressed women, and fantasy creatures abound.

Box art influences the value of a model kit, especially when the cover art is more spectacular than the assembled model. Surprisingly, collectors prefer unassembled models. If the model is assembled, its value declines by 50% or more.

References: Bill Bruegman, *Aurora: History and Price Guide, 3rd Edition,* Cap'n Penny Productions, 1996; Gordon Dutt, *Collectible Figure Kits of the 50's, 60's & 70's,* Gordy's KitBuilders Magazine, 1995; Thomas Graham, *Greenberg's Guide to Aurora Model Kits,* Kalmbach Books, 1998; Rick Polizzi, *Classic Plastic Model Kits,* Collector Books, 1996.

Periodical: *KitBuilders Magazine,* Box 201, Sharon Center, OH 44274.

Collectors' Club: Kit Collectors International, PO Box 38, Stanton, CA 90680.

Note: All model kits are MIB unless noted otherwise.

Historic PT-109, Revell H-310, 1/72 scale, $8.00.

American Buffalo, Aurora	$25.00
Angel Fink, Revell	250.00
Apollo Saturn Rocket, Monogram	65.00
Babe Ruth, Aurora	395.00
Batman, MPC	45.00
Beatles Yellow Submarine, MPC, missing 2 pcs, with box and instructions	200.00
Black Bear and Cubs, Aurora	40.00
Black Fury, Aurora	15.00
Camaro T-Top, AMT	20.00
Captain Action, Aurora	275.00
Captain Kidd, Aurora	145.00
Castle Creatures Frog, Aurora	250.00
Charlie's Angels Van, Revell	45.00
Chinese Mandarin and Girl, Aurora	300.00
Comic Scenes Tonto, Aurora	40.00
Crusader, Aurora	250.00
Dark Shadows Barnabas Collins, MPC, partial assembly, complete, with box and instructions	200.00
Dark Shadows Barnabas Vampire Van, MPC	200.00
Dark Shadows Werewolf, MPC	250.00
D'Artagnan, Aurora	175.00
Dempsey vs Firpo, Aurora, partial assembly, with box and instructions	75.00
Dick Tracy, Aurora	175.00
Dick Tracy, Aurora, 1 pc missing, with box and instructions	150.00
Double Whammy '53 Studebaker, AMT	85.00
Dracula, Aurora	295.00
Dracula's Dragster, Aurora	450.00
Dr Doolittle's Good Ship *Flounder*, Aurora, unassembled, some paint, missing 1 pc, with box and instructions	75.00
Dutch Boy, Aurora	30.00
Dutch Girl, Aurora	25.00
Fantastic Voyage Voyager, Aurora	575.00
Forgotten Prisoner, Aurora, some assembly, no paint, complete	75.00
Frankenstein, Aurora	450.00
Frightening Lightning Forgotten Prisoner, Aurora	295.00
Frightening Lightning Wolfman, Aurora	495.00
General Aldo, Addar	45.00
George Washington, Aurora, 1 pc painted	95.00
Gladiator with Lion, Aurora	175.00
Gladiator with Trident, Aurora	150.00
Glow Mummy, Aurora	125.00
Gold Knight, Aurora, 1957	275.00
Green Beret, Aurora	175.00

Hercules and the Lion, Aurora	295.00
Hunchback, Aurora, disassembled, with box and instructions	195.00
Incredible Hulk, MPC	40.00
Indian Chief & Squaw, Aurora	150.00
Infantryman, Aurora	100.00
Invaders UFO, Aurora	75.00
Jesse James, Aurora	200.00
Jesse James, Aurora, partial assembly, never painted, with box	175.00
John F Kennedy, Aurora	165.00
King Kong, Aurora	495.00
Knight in Shining Armor Sir Galahad, Aurora	65.00
Knight in Shining Armor Sir Kay, Aurora	65.00
Land of the Giants Snake Scene, Aurora, partial assembly, never painted, with box and instructions	175.00
Lost in Space Robot, Aurora	795.00
Luminators Dracula, Monogram	25.00
Mad Doctor, Aurora	150.00
Marine, Aurora	100.00
Mexican Caballero, Aurora	150.00
Mexican Senorita, Aurora	150.00
Model T Ford, AMT	48.00
Monster Scenes Giant Insect, Aurora	895.00
Mummy, Aurora, disassembled, with box and instructions	165.00
Mustang, AMT	48.00
Phantom of the Opera, Aurora	300.00
Phantom of the Opera, Cinemodels	40.00
Pilot, USAF, Aurora	175.00
Planet of the Apes Dr Zaius, Addar	50.00
Rat Patrol, Aurora	95.00
Robin, Aurora	145.00
Scotch Lassie & Lad, Aurora	100.00
Seaview, Voyage to the Bottom of the Sea, Aurora	190.00
Spider-Man, Aurora	450.00
Star Probe Space Base, Lindbergh	65.00
Steve Canyon, Aurora	250.00
Superman, MPC	45.00
Tarzan, Aurora	225.00
Three Knights, Aurora	175.00
Three Musketeers Porthos, Aurora	125.00
U.N.C.L.E. Ilya Kuryakin, Aurora	150.00
US Marshall, Aurora, unassembled, not orig instructions, no box	125.00
US Sailor, Aurora	30.00
White House, Empire	75.00
White Stallion, Aurora	30.00

Columbia and 747, Revell #4715, 1/144 scale, 1980s, $15.00.

MODERNISM

Art Deco is one of the most misused attributions in the current antiques market for both furniture and decorative arts. More than half the Art Deco pieces actually should be attributed to Modernism, a movement little understood by collectors and dealers.

Modernism continued and expanded upon the design style advances of the Arts and Crafts Movement. Perhaps it is easier to understand Modernism by viewing it as Machine Modern, a design period when functionalism and carefully reasoned design were dominant. Architects provided the motivating force for much of the design.

Modernism began in Germany, spreading to the United States in the late 1920s and 30s. Modernist furniture of the 1920s rejected decoration and relied heavily on the use of glass and steel. The 1930s were a decade of eclecticism. Surrealistic furniture enjoyed a brief vogue.

Part of the difficulty involved in understanding Modernism is that the term is used to describe the movement as a whole as well as one of the major components. Establishing a mental decade chronology can help keep the sequence of events straight. International Modernism, the first period, covers the period of conception (1900s through World War I) and the period when the movement was centered in Germany (1920s). Modernism is the period when many of the German designers fled Germany and moved to England and the United States (1930s). After World War II, Modernism reached its zenith in the Contemporary Style (1945 through 1960s) that enjoyed great popularity in the United States. The 1970s Neo-Modernism was a brief attempt to rechannel the movement. Current scholarship continues to refine these basic divisions.

Modernist pieces are listed in their specialized collecting categories. This introduction provides a brief introduction to this important post-1920 design style.

Reference: Marianne Aav, et al., *Finnish Modern Design,* Bard Graduate Center for Studies in the Decorative Arts and Yale University Press, 1998.

Periodicals: *Echoes,* PO Box 155, Cummaquid, MA 02637; *The Modernism Magazine,* 333 N Main St, Lambertville, NJ 08530.

MONROE, MARILYN

Marilyn Monroe was born Norma Jean Mortenson in Los Angeles, California, on June 1, 1926. An illegitimate child, Marilyn spent her early years in a series of foster homes. She was only 16 when she married Jim Doughtery on June 19, 1942. While Jim was in the Merchant Marines, a photographer discovered Marilyn. She soon found work with the Blue Book Modeling Studio.

After a brief flirtation with the movies in 1947–48, Marilyn found herself without a contract. Her life changed dramatically after Tom Kelley's "Golden Dreams" photograph appeared in magazines and calendars across the nation in 1950. By March, Marilyn had signed a seven-year film contract with MGM. In 1953 *How to Marry a Millionaire* and *Gentlemen Prefer Blondes* turned Marilyn into a superstar. *Bus Stop* (1956), *Some Like It Hot!* (1959), and *The Misfits* (1961) are considered among her best films.

Divorced from Doughtery, Marilyn married Joe DiMaggio in January 1951. Divorce followed in October 1954. Her marriage to Arthur Miller in June 1956 ended in 1961 following an affair with Yves Montand. The threat of mental illness and other health problems depressed Marilyn. She died on August 5, 1962, from an overdose of barbiturates.

References: Denis C. Jackson, *The Price & ID Guide to Marilyn Monroe, 3rd Edition,* TICN, 1996; Dian Zillner, *Hollywood Collectibles: The Sequel,* Schiffer Publishing, 1994.

Collectors' Club: All About Marilyn, PO Box 291176, Los Angeles, CA 90029.

Bank, Funtime Savings, battery operated, plastic, mounted vinyl figure 8½" h, movable arms, painted molded hair and facial features, white fabric dress, coin slot on top front center of base, when powered air blows from vent in base below her dress causing dress to blow upward, orig box, Made in China, c1980s, 5 x 5½ x 12½" **$100.00**

Calendar Photo, "Golden Dreams," full color, glossy paper, nude pose on red drapery background, "Posed By Marilyn Monroe," bottom margin with Golden Dreams title and "No. 1427–U.I. Co., N.Y. Made In U.S.A.," early 1950s, 12 x 13¼" 75.00

Cigarette Lighter, chromed metal, plastic wrapper over tinted color photo on each side, Made in Japan, 1950–60s, 1¾ x 1¾" 100.00

Lobby Card, *The Seven Year Itch,* #8, 1955 .... 38.00

Magazine, *Behind the Scenes,* Jul 1955, front cov color photo of Monroe in charcoal black gown, "10 Most Daring Photos of Marilyn," black and white photo, 4 x 5½" 25.00

Magazine, *Escapade's Best,* 1957 Annual, cov photo of man holding Dec 1956 monthly issue, 84 pp, full color double image of Marilyn Monroe calendar at center, 8¼ x 11" 25.00

Magazine, *Laff,* Aug 1946, full color, 32 pp, cov photo and "Cover Girl/Jean Norman" on contents page, 10½ x 13¼" 100.00

Magazine, *People Today,* Dec 2, 1953, full color cov photo of Monroe in red dress embracing architectural column, 4 x 5¾" 25.00

Modern Man magazine, June 1956, cover story, $60.00.

Magazine, *Ray Anthony & Co,* pocket magazine published by Moonlight Music, Inc, 76 pp, captioned photos, Anthony and Monroe in full color front cov photo, 1954, 4 x 5¾" **25.00**

Movie Poster, *Let's Make It Legal,* 20th Century Fox, 1951 ... **150.00**

Paperback Book, *The Misfits,* first ed, Dell Publishing, 224 pp, 8 pp insert of black and white movie stills with Monroe, 1961, 4 x 6¼" **20.00**

Press Book, *River of No Return,* 16 pp, 1954, 14 x 16" **75.00**

Record, *There's No Business Like Show Business,* 45 rpm, 4 songs from movie, front cov with pinktone photo and yellow and white lettering, back cov with black and white Monroe photo, RCA Victor, 7 x 7" cardboard sleeve, 1950s **45.00**

Serving Tray Stamping Sheet, stamped steel, 10¼ x 30" litho tin production sheet with printed image for two 14 x 19" serving trays featuring red drapery nude poses with facsimile signature, early 1950s **200.00**

Sheet Music, *My Heart Belongs to Daddy,* 1938 .... **30.00**

King Kong, Halloween costume, Ben Cooper, ©1976 Paramount Pictures, $45.00.

MONSTERS

Animal monsters played a major role in the movies from the onset. King Kong is the best known of the pre-1945 genre. The Japanese monster epics of the 1950s introduced Godzilla, a huge reptile monster. Godzilla, his foes, and imitators are all very collectible. The 1950s also saw the introduction of a wide range of animal monsters with human characteristics, e.g., the Creature From the Black Lagoon and numerous werewolf variations.

Early film makers were well aware of the ability of film to horrify. Dracula, Frankenstein, and the Mummy have been the subjects of dozens of films.

The Addams Family and The Munsters introduced a comedic aspect to monsters. This was perpetuated by the portrayal of monsters on Saturday morning cartoon shows. The chainsaw-wielding mentally deranged villains of the 1960s to the present are a consequence of this demystification of the monster.

After a period of speculation in monster material from the mid-1980s through the early 1990s, market prices now appear to have stabilized.

References: Dana Cain, *Collecting Godzilla Memorabilia,* Antique Trader Books, 1998; Dana Cain, *Collecting Monsters of Film and TV,* Krause Publications, 1997; Sean Linkenback, *An Unauthorized Guide to Godzilla Collectibles,* Schiffer Publishing, 1998.

Periodical: *Toy Shop,* 700 E State St, Iola, WI 54990.

Addams Family, Addams Family Card Game, 1965 .... **$48.00**

Addams Family, Addams Family Mystery Jigsaw Puzzle, "Ghost At Large" **45.00**

Chaney, Lon, photo, behind the scenes photo of Chaney dressed as soldier, "Lon Chaney And Director," 1920s..... **35.00**

Creature From the Black Lagoon, MIB **18.00**

Creepy, puzzle, Demon Knight, #71, Milton Bradley, MIB.... **45.00**

Creepy, puzzle, Dog-Fighting Demons, #81, Milton Bradley, MIB.. **45.00**

Dark Shadows, Barnabas Collins Dark Shadows Game...... **55.00**

Dark Shadows, Jolietts Music Box, complete **425.00**

Dark Shadows, magazine, *Barnabas Collins Famous Monsters of Filmland,* #59 .... **35.00**

Dracula, comic book, Dracula the Mummy, Dell **80.00**

Dracula, doll, with coffin box and death certificate, Travelers, 1985 .... **75.00**

Dracula, Glow Dracula, Remco, 3¾" h, MOC **40.00**

Dracula, record, *Dinner With Drac,* Peter Pan, 7" d........ **15.00**

Dracula, wind-up, Russ, 2½" h **8.00**

Elvira, display, Coors Beer, stand-up, life-size **45.00**

Frankenstein, comic book, Dell, 1963 .... **45.00**

Frankenstein, jigsaw puzzle, APC, 1974 .... **30.00**

Frankenstein, Monster Flip Book, 1960s................ **35.00**

Frankenstein, wind-up, Russ, 2½" h **8.00**

Godzilla, cup holder, Taco Bell premium, MIP **8.00**

Godzilla, doll, vinyl, Imperial, 1985, 14" h............ **35.00**

Godzilla, movie poster, 1985...................... **15.00**

King Kong, bank, plastic, figural, 1970s **15.00**

King Kong, doll, cloth, 1970s, 20" h **38.00**

King Kong, game, Ideal, 1978, MIB **40.00**

King Kong, jigsaw puzzle, 551 pcs, box cov shows King Kong battling jet fighters, American Publishing, 1976, 18 x 24" completed size **40.00**

King Kong, magazine, *Films in Review,* cov shows King Kong holding Jessica Lange, 1977 .... **15.00**

King Kong, magazine, *Kong,* 1976 .... **20.00**

King Kong, paperback book, *King Kong,* Wallace & Cooper, Bantam, color cov scene, 1965 .... **30.00**

King Kong, trading card pack, Topps, unopened **5.00**

Little Shop of Horrors, press release photo **10.00**

Monster Laffs Trading Cards, Topps, 12 cards, 1963 .... **12.00**

Mummy, comic book, Dell, 1962 .... **45.00**

Mummy, drinking glass, ©Universal Pictures, 1960s, 6⅝" h **75.00**

Munsters, magazine, *Munsters Monster World,* #2 .... **30.00**

Munsters, *TV Guide* **35.00**

Nightmare on Elm Street, The Freddy Game, Cardinal, 1989, MIB...................................... **45.00**

Price, Vincent, Shrunken Head Kit **35.00**

Quasimodo, doll, poseable, Hong Kong, 9½" h **35.00**

Vampirella, comic book, #1, Harris Publishing **15.00**

Wolfman, comic book, Dell, 1963.................... **45.00**

Wolfman, figure, Burger King Universal Monsters.......... **4.00**

Wolfman, glow figure, Remco, 1980, 3¾" h, MOC........ **45.00**

Wolfman, jigsaw puzzle, APC, 1974 .... **20.00**

MOORCROFT POTTERY

After extensive study that included classes at the Wedgwood Institute, Royal College of Art, and British Museum and an initial career at James Macintyre & Company in Burselm, William Moorcroft built a new state-of-the-art pottery, the Washington Works, in Burselm in 1913. Enlargements followed in 1915 and 1919.

Initially, Moorcroft produced pieces that featured simple, bold designs, often incorporating dark colored exotic flowers. In 1928 Moorcroft received a Royal Warrant. A few years later the company introduced its flambe glaze. New decorative motifs, e.g., birds, boats, fish, and fruit, joined the line in the 1930s.

William Moorcroft died in 1945 and was succeeded by his son, Walter. In the 1950s Walter expanded the line by adding Caribbean and marine life motifs and a more dramatic use of color in traditional designs. The use of flambe glaze continued until 1973. Liberty & Co., who helped finance Moorcroft, ended its joint-share ownership in 1961.

In 1984 John, Walter's brother, became managing director and a controlling interest in the first was sold to three Roper brothers. They sold within two years to a consortium of the Dennis and Edwards families. Walter retired in 1987.

Reference: Susan and Al Bagdade, *Warman's English & Continental Pottery & Porcelain, 3rd Edition*, Krause Publications, 1998.

Creamer and Sugar, Pomegranate pattern, celadon
    ground, ink sgd "W. Moorcroft," sugar 4½ x 4½",
    1913–25 .... **$1,100.00**
Floor Vase, Eventide pattern, dec in squeezebag with
    green trees on shaded cobalt sky, copper liner, imp
    "Moorcroft, Made in England," 19½" h, 8" d **7,700.00**
Temple Jar, cov, Eventide pattern, ink signature and die
    stamped "Made in England/760," 11" h, 8½" d **6,500.00**
Vase, baluster shape, Pansy pattern with large pink and
    purple flowers on cobalt ground, imp "Moorcroft,
    Made in England," 13" h, 7¼" d **1,875.00**
Vase, bulbous, flaring rim, Landscape pattern, blue trees
    on mottled blue and yellow ground, script mark, 6" h .. **2,000.00**
Vase, bulbous, Orchid pattern, dark flowers on teal
    green ground, stamped "Moorcroft, Made in England,
    M74," 7" h, 5" d **2,500.00**

Vase, Fresia pattern, blue, mustard, and dark red florals, mustard ground, blue interior, signature mark, c1935, 10½" h, $2,000.00.

Vase, classical shape, 2-handled, Florian Ware, blue and
    yellow anemones on white ground, ink stamped "W.
    Moorcroft, des., Florian Ware, 10" h, 7" w **3,200.00**
Vase, classical shape, Anemone motif, mauve and
    cinnabar flower and green leaves against cobalt blue
    ground, ink sgd "W.M.," die-stamped "Moorcroft,"
    12¼ x 5½" **800.00**
Vase, fruit and leaves dec, shaded blue to green ground,
    ink script mark, 1928–34, 8 x 6" **475.00**
Vase, ovoid, blue Cornflower pattern, imp "Moorcroft
    Made In England 210," 6¼ x 4½" **1,200.00**
Vase, Pansy pattern, Liberty Tudric hammered pewter
    base, stamped "Made in England, Tudric, Moorcroft,
    01516, Made by Liberty & Co.," 6¼" h, 3½" d **875.00**
Vase, Pomegranate pattern, squeezebag dec, orange and
    purple fruit on blue ground, some crazing, die
    stamped "Moorcroft/Made In England," ink signature,
    9¾ x 6" **850.00**
Vase, red Poppy pattern, stamped "Moorcroft," slip sig-
    nature, 10 x 7" **4,000.00**

MORGANTOWN GLASS

In 1903 the Morgantown Glass Works (West Virginia), founded in 1899, changed its name to the Economy Tumbler Company which became the Economy Glass Company in 1924. It marketed its products under the "Old Morgantown" label. In 1929 the company reassumed its original name, Morgantown Glass Works.

Morgantown eventually expanded its line to include household and kitchen glass. The company also made blanks for decorating firms. Morgantown is known for several innovative design and manufacturing techniques, e.g., ornamental open stems, iridization, and application of gold, platinum, and silver decoration.

The company became a victim of the Depression, closing in 1937. In 1939 glassworkers and others associated with the company reopened it as the Morgantown Glassware Guild. In 1965 Fostoria purchased the company and continued to produce most of the Morgantown patterns and colors, marketing them under a Morgantown label. Fostoria closed the plant in 1971. In 1972 Bailey Glass Company purchased the factory and used it primarily to make lamp globes.

References: Jerry Gallagher, *A Handbook of Old Morgantown Glass, Vol. I*, published by author, 1995; Jeffrey B. Snyder, *Morgantown Glass From Depression Glass Through the 1960s*, Schiffer Publishing, 1998.

Collectors' Club: Old Morgantown Glass Collectors' Guild, PO Box 894, Morgantown, WV 26507.

Brandy Snifter, red **$65.00**
Bud Vase, Serenade, #53, 10" h, opaque yellow **250.00**
Candle Holders, pr, Florentine, #9931, 5½" h, Bristol
    blue opaque **65.00**
Champagne, American Beauty, #7668, freshest roses **25.00**
Champagne, Golf Ball, red **39.00**
Claret, Golf Ball, red **45.00**
Cocktail, Golf Ball, #7643, red **32.00**
Cocktail, Monroe, #7690, red stem **32.00**
Cocktail, Old English, #7678, 3½ oz, Stiegel green **30.00**
Cordial, Gypsy Fire, #7685, 1½ oz **60.00**
Cordial, Plantation, Spanish red **99.00**
Creamer, Dancing Girl, pink **45.00**

Goblet, Art Moderne, Ritz Blue bowl, crystal stem and foot, 9 oz, $95.00.

Goblet, American Beauty, #7668, freshest roses 35.00
Goblet, Old Morgantown, amber, cupped, pierced metal
   stem holder. 4.00
Goblet, Old Morgantown, heliotrope, cupped, pierced
   metal stem holder 6.50
Hurricane Lamps, pr, #60, 8" h, amethyst 50.00
Iced Tea, ftd, Carlton, #7711, crystal stem 25.00
Juice, ftd, Carlton, #7711, crystal stem 20.00
Martini Set, #92, 10" h mug and three 3" h cocktail glass-
   es, amethyst 40.00
Martini Set, #9980, 8 pcs, amethyst 65.00
Pitcher, #78, 16 oz, 5" h, amethyst. 19.00
Plate, Anna Rose, #1500, 8½" d, Bramble rose etch 35.00
Plate, Dancing Girl, 7½" d, blue 17.00
Tumbler, Belton, #9074, 12 oz, golden iris, Virginia etch. . . . 40.00
Tumbler, Dancing Girl, 4¼" h, green 30.00
Vase, Old Morgantown, Palm Optic, 6¼" h, green 35.00
Water Goblet, Ballerina, #7630, 9 oz, blue stem 20.00
Water Goblet, Fairwin, #7688½, crystal stem, price for 4 . . . 150.00
Water Goblet, Golf Ball, #7643, cobalt 45.00
Water Goblet, Golf Ball, #7643, crystal 30.00
Wine Goblet, Golf Ball, #7643, blue 40.00
Wine Goblet, Golf Ball, #7643, claret 45.00
Wine Goblet, Golf Ball, #7643, cobalt. 39.00
Wine Goblet, Golf Ball, #7643, red 39.00

MORTON POTTERIES

Morton, Illinois, was home to several major potteries, all of which trace their origins to six Rapp Brothers who emigrated from Germany in 1877 and established the Morton Pottery Works.

   American Art Potteries (1945–1961), Cliftwood Art Potteries (1920–1940), Midwest Potteries, the continuation of Cliftwood (1940–44), Morton Pottery Company (1922–1976), and Morton Pottery Works, also known as Morton Earthenware Company (1877–1917), were all founded and operated by Rapp descendants.

   These companies produced a variety of art, household, novelty, and utilitarian pottery. Morton Pottery Company specialized in kitchenwares, novelty items, and steins. In the 1950s they made a variety of TV lamps ranging from animal figures to personality, e.g., Davy Crockett. Under contract to Sears Roebuck, they produced some of the Vincent Price National Treasures reproductions. The American Art Pottery produced a line of wares marketed through floral and gift shops.

Reference: Doris and Burdell Hall, *Morton's Potteries: 99 Years, 1877–1976, Volume II,* L-W Book Sales, 1995.

American Art Potteries, bunny behind log, 4¾" h $15.00
American Art Potteries, creamer, bird, open mouth 10.00
American Art Potteries, planter, grotesque duck, yellow
   and green, 5½" h 10.00
American Art Potteries, planter, quail, brown and black
   air brushed glaze, 9½" h 25.00
American Art Potteries, TV lamp, conch shell, purple and
   pink spray glaze, 7 x 10" 20.00
Amish Pantry Ware, Colonial beverage set, green 100.00
Amish Pantry Ware, creamer, blue 35.00
Amish Pantry Ware, mixing bowl, green, 12" d 40.00
Amish Pantry Ware, porridge bowl and saucer, green 40.00
Amish Pantry Ware, water pitcher, blue, 2½ qt 60.00
Cliftwood Art Potteries, buttermilk jug, old rose over
   white 30.00
Cliftwood Art Potteries, candlestick, cobalt blue, 10½" h. . . . 25.00
Cliftwood Art Potteries, creamer, chocolate drip, 4" h,
   3" d 30.00
Cliftwood Art Potteries, figurine, cat, gray drip, small 20.00
Cliftwood Art Potteries, flower insert, turtle, #2, dark
   green, 5½" l 15.00
Cliftwood Art Potteries, pretzel jar, barrel shaped, emb
   lettering 50.00
Cliftwood Art Potteries, range shakers, pr, old rose over
   pink and white 20.00
Cliftwood Art Potteries, sweetmeat bowl, cov, green and
   yellow drip 45.00
Midwest Potteries, creamer, figural cow, open mouth,
   pastel glaze, 5" h. 15.00
Midwest Potteries, figurine, cocker spaniel, black, 6 x 4". . . . 28.00

Cliftwood Art Potteries, figurine, police dog, glass eyes, 1920–40, $75.00.

Midwest Potteries, figurine, leaping deer, white, gold
  highlights, 12" h 35.00
Midwest Potteries, figurine, squirrel, brown drip, 9" h 35.00
Midwest Potteries, planter, bird and nest, blue, 6½" h 15.00
Morton Pottery, bank, bulldog, brown 15.00
Morton Pottery, figurine, cat, white, pink ears, small 8.00
Morton Pottery, lamp, teddy bear, pink, blue and brown 20.00
Morton Pottery, planter, Scottish Terrier 8.00

MOSSER GLASS

The glassmaking art has been passed down through three generation of the Mosser family.

Mosser Glass, Cambridge, Ohio, makes reproductions and
copycats of late 19th- and early 20th-century glassware as well as
figurines and decorative accessories. Daisy and Button, Inverted
Thistle, Log Cabin, Rose, Shell, and Thistle are a few of the Mosser
reproduction pattern glass patterns.

Ashtray, amberina, #107 . . . . $2.50
Bath Set, toothbrush holder, tumbler, and soap dish,
  #159, blue milk glass with hp flowers 20.00
Bell, Daisy and Button, #145, green 5.00
Bell, Floral Cut #2, #119-12, crystal, 5¾" h 12.00
Bird Mug, #102-I, iridized cobalt 8 oz 4.50
Boot, #108, crystal, 4" h 3.50
Butter Dish, cov, Cherry, #132B, purple carnival 10.00
Candlesticks, pr, #114, blue milk glass, 8" h 18.00
Child's Table Set, Jennifer, #140, cov butter, creamer, and
  sugar, apple green 15.00
Compote, Queens, #171, vaseline, 8" h, 8" d 15.00
Creamer and Sugar, Log Cabin, #203, crystal 20.00
Cup Plate, Last Supper, #113, blue, 3¼" d 1.50
Fairy Lamp, holly leaf design, #120, green, 5" h 7.50
Figurine, bear, #134, crystal 6.00
Figurine, bird, #175, cobalt, 5¼" h 8.00
Figurine, cat, #101, cobalt, 3" h 3.00
Goblet, Rose, #123, green 5.00
Hen on Basket, #128, vaseline 8.00
Lamp, Santa, #104, crystal satin, 4¾" h 10.00

Cake Plate, Queens, vaseline, 9" d, $14.00.

Pitcher, Diamond Cut, #105P, chocolate 15.00
Plate, lace edge, #135, pink, 5½" d 2.50
Powder Box, doll, #176, crystal, 5" h 10.00
Ring Box, Mt Vernon, #122, blue 3.00
Salt Dip, Hexagon, #106, green 1.50
Salt Dip, Saw Tooth, #116, blue 1.00
Slipper, Rose, #117, amethyst 4.50
Slipper, scroll design, #109, chocolate 4.00
Spoon Holder, miniature, Cherry Thumbprint, #206,
  hand dec 7.50
Toothpick, #110, amethyst 2.00
Toothpick, Panel, #100, red, 2½" h 3.50
Toothpick, Thimble, #130, amethyst 1.50
Toothpick, turkey, #111, amber 4.00

MOTION LAMPS

A motion lamp is a lamp with animation, usually consisting of a
changing scene, which is activitated by the rising heat from the
lamp's bulb. There are three basic types: (1) stationary exterior
cylinder, revolving interior cylinder; (2) revolving exterior cylinder,
stationary interior cylinder; and (3) revolving shade.

Motion lamps first appeared in the 1920s. They disappeared in
the early 1960s. Econolite Corporation (Los Angeles, California), L.
A. Goodman Manufacturing Company (Chicago, Illinois), Ignition
Company (Omaha, Nebraska), Rev-O-Lite (Brunswick, New
Jersey), and Scene in Action Company (Chicago, Illinois) were the
principal manufacturers.

Reference: Sam and Anna Samuelian, *Collector's Guide to Motion
Lamps,* Collector Books, 1998.

Note: All lamps are plastic unless noted otherwise.

Annie, William FB Johnson, 1981 . . . . $50.00
Bellows Whiskey, unknown maker, 1950s 150.00
Butterfly, Econolite, #753, 1954 . . . . 150.00
Cheers, Creative Light Products, 1970s 100.00
Circus, Econolite, #401, 1952 . . . . 175.00
Cook's "500" Ale, unknown maker, 1950s 75.00
Dance at Dawn Rev-o-Lite, #202, 1930s 200.00
Ducks, Econolite, #953, 1955 . . . . 200.00
Fireplace, Gritt, #1023, 1920s, plaster 250.00
Fish Bowl, Econolite, #781, 1960 . . . . 275.00
Flames, Scene-in-Action Corp, #51, 1931 . . . . 200.00
Flying Geese, LA Goodman, 1957 . . . . 150.00
Forest Fire, Econolite, #FF, 1949 . . . . 75.00
Forest Fire, LA Goodman, #2003, 1956 . . . . 100.00
Forest Fire, unknown maker, Bakelite frame, c1940s 150.00
Genesee Beer, Coronet of NY/Genesee Brewing Co of
  NY, psychedelic, 1970s 75.00
Laurel and Hardy, Creative Lighting Division, 1971 . . . . 200.00
Lighthouse, LA Goodman, 1956 . . . . 125.00
Love Lamp, unknown maker, 1970s 50.00
Man and Woman at Fireplace, unknown maker, metal 125.00
Mayflower, National, 1930s 275.00
Merry Christmas, LA Goodman, 1970s 125.00
Miss Liberty, Econolite, #769, 1958 . . . . 350.00
Mother Goose, Econolite, #C-1, blue 150.00
Nature's Splendor, National, 1930s 300.00
NHL, Visual Effects Co, 1970s 100.00
Niagara Falls, Econolite, #NF, 1950 . . . . 75.00
Niagara Falls, Ignition Co, 1948 . . . . 100.00

Antique Autos, Econolite, $200.00.

Niagara Falls, Rev-o-Lite, 1930s.................... 175.00
Nursery Rhymes, Econolite, 1953 .... 150.00
Ocean Creatures, LA Goodman, 1955 .... 200.00
Old Mill, Econolite, #765, 1956 .... 125.00
Oriental Fantasy, LA Goodman, 1957.............. 200.00
Ripples, Scene-in-Action Corp, #52 .... 200.00
Roadrunner and Coyote, Visual Effects Co, 1970......... 125.00
Seven-Up, Creative Lighting Co, 1970s 125.00
Sparkelite Christmas Tree, LA Goodman, #97, 1950s 175.00
The Bar Is Open, Monique, 1970s 100.00
Trains Racing, LA Goodman, 1957................ 150.00
Waterfall, LA Goodman, 1956................... 100.00
Winken, Blynken, and Nod, Lightcraft Co, 1948......... 200.00

MOTORCYCLE COLLECTIBLES

The motorcycle came of age with the dawn of the 20th century. In 1901 Oscar Hedstrom and George Hendee produced the first Indian motorcycles in Springfield, Massachusetts. Indian was quickly challenged by Harley.

The popularizing of the motorcycle followed much the same route as that of the automobile. The Federation of American Motorcyclists was organized in 1903. It became the American Motorcyclist Association in the early 1920s. The years from 1905 to World War I were the golden age of motorcycle racing. Harley and Indian military motorcycles performed yeoman duty in World War I and again in World War II.

Prior to World War I, there were over 300 different motorcycle manufacturers. When Indian ceased production in the early 1950s, Harley-Davidson became the sole remaining American motorcycle manufacturer.

Motorcycle collectibles divide into three basic groups: (1) objects associated with actual motorcycles including sales and promotional material, (2) objects in the shape of motorcycles, e.g., motorcycle toys, and (3) objects featuring the image of a motorcycle. All three groups are heavily collected.

Motorcycle collectibles became a hot ticket item in the mid-1990s. Everything motorcycle, from cast-iron toys to Harley-

Davidson showroom signs, experienced price jump multiples. Prices have stabilized, but speculation remains.

References: Michael Dregni, *Harley-Davidson Collectibles*, Town Square Books, Voyageur Books, 1998; Leila Dunbar, *Motorcycle Collectibles* (1996), *More Motorcycle Collectibles* (1997), Schiffer Publishing.

Ashtray, Harley-Davidson, aluminum, 1950s, 4 x 4" $120.00
Banner, "Harley-Davidson Motor Cycles Cycle Wear Built By Wrangler," denim, yellow lettering, 1960s, 48" h, 36" w 350.00
Belt Buckle, bronze, 1931 Gypsy Tour Rally, enamel AMA logo, stamped "DL Auld Co., Columbus O" on reverse, unused, 1³/₄" h, 2¹/₂" w.................... 300.00
Blotter, Firestone Motorcycle Tires, c1920, 6" h, 3¹/₂" w..... 185.00
Book, *Indian Riders' Instruction Book*, 44 pp, illus, 1937, 7 x 5" 125.00
Business Cards, Westside Motorcycle Shop, Eugene, OR, double sided, 5-card set showing Indian products, unused, 2¹/₈" h, 3¹/₄" w.......................... 130.00
Can, Harley-Davidson AMF Premium Grade Oil, orange, white, and black, full, 1 qt.................... 80.00
Catalog, Excelsior Motorcycles, fold-out, 12 pp, color cov, 1920s, 9¹/₄" h, 15¹/₂" w 225.00
Catalog, Harley-Davidson, "The Sport of 1,000 Joys," includes "74, 45, and 30.50" full color models, centerfold with "The Greatest Sport of Them All" with cycle, plane, and other sports, 9" h, 18" w 65.00
Goggles, Harley-Davidson, aluminum and rubber, Harley bar and shield logos, c1930s, 2" h, 7" l 240.00
Handbook, "The Motorcycle Handbook," Manly, Harold, 320 pp, illus, 1920, 7 x 4³/₄" 65.00
Magazine, *Indian Magazine*, Holiday issue, Vol 1, #2, 1948. .... 130.00
Matchbook, Harley-Davidson Sales, Butler, PA, shows 1942 Knucklehead 100.00
Owner's Manual, Harley-Davidson, 44 pp, illus, 1929, 6³/₄ x 4³/₄" 55.00

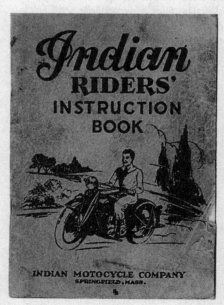

Indian Riders' Instruction Book, 44 pp, 1937, 7 x 5", $138.00. Photo courtesy Collectors Auction Services.

Pin, Harley-Davidson, flying diamond shaped, tank logo, red lettering, 1934, ³/₄" l **200.00**

Poster, "The National Jack Pine...The World's Toughest Endurance Test Won By Harley-Davidson," features William Muehlenbeck, green, black, and white, 24" h, 38" w **170.00**

Tank Emblem, Indian Motorcycles, chief with arrow, plated tin, 4" h, 5" l **125.00**

Toy, rabbit with sidecar, litho tin, Wyandotte, 1930s, 6¼" h, 9¼" l **160.00**

Toy, rider on motorcycle, Auburn Rubber, 1930s, 4" l **55.00**

MOVIE MEMORABILIA

This category includes material related to movies and the individuals who starred in them. Movie collectibles divide into two basic groups, silent and sound era. With the exception of posters, material from the silent era is scarce and collected by only a small number of individuals.

Prior to the 1960s movie licensing was limited. Most collectibles are tied to media advertising and theater promotions. This changed with the blockbuster hits of the 1970s and 80s, e.g., the *Star Wars* series. Licensing, especially in the toy sector, became an important method of generating capital for films.

Many collectors focus on a single movie personality. Regional association plays a major role. Many small communities hold annual film festivals honoring local individuals who went on to fame and glory on the silver screen.

Two-dimensional material abounds. Three-dimensional material is scarce. Pizzazz is a value factor—the greater the display potential, the higher the price.

In the 1980s movie studios and stars began selling their memorabilia through New York and West Coast auction houses. Famous props, such as Dorothy's ruby glass slippers from *The Wizard of Oz*, broke the $10,000 barrier.

References: Dana Cain, *Film & TV Animal Star Collectibles,* Antique Trader Books, 1998; Anthony Curtis, *Lyle Film & Rock 'n' Roll Collectibles,* The Berkley Publishing Group, 1996; Tony Fusco, *Posters: Identification and Price Guide, Second Edition,* Avon Books, 1994; Ephraim Katz, *The Film Encyclopedia, 2nd Edition,* Harper Collins, 1994; John Kisch (ed.), *Movie Poster Almanac: 1997–98,* Spearate Cinema Publications, 1998; Robert Osborne, *65 Years of The Oscar: The Official History of The Academy Awards,* Abbeville, 1994; Christopher Sausville, *Planet of the Apes,* Schiffer Publishing, 1998; Jay Scarfone and William Stillman, *The Wizard of Oz Collector's Treasury,* Schiffer Publishing, 1992; Moe Wadle, *The Movie Tie-In Book: A Collector's Guide to Paperback Movie Editions,* Nostalgia Books, 1994; Jon R. Warren, *Warren's Movie Poster Price Guide, 4th Edition,* American Collectors Exchange, 1997; Dian Zillner, *Hollywood Collectibles,* Schiffer Publishing, 1991; Dian Zillner, *Hollywood Collectibles: The Sequel,* Schiffer Publishing, 1994.

Periodicals: *Big Reel,* PO Box 1050, Dubuque, IA 52004; *Collecting Hollywood Magazine,* PO Box 2512, Chattanooga, TN 37409; *Movie Advertising Collector,* PO Box 28587, Philadelphia, PA 19149; *Movie Collector's World,* Box 309, Fraser, MI 48026.

Collectors' Club: The International Wizard of Oz Club, 1438 N Ullman St, Appleton, WI 54911.

Note: For additional listings see Animation Art, Autographs, Disneyana, Marilyn Monroe, Posters, Shirley Temple, Star Trek, and Star Wars.

Association Cards, Clark Gable, member cards for Screen Actors Guild dated 1959–60, and American Federation of Television and Radio Actors, with actor's card from Academy of Motion Pictures arts and Sciences issued 1960, price for 3 . . . . **$1,600.00**

Autograph, Arnold Schwarzenegger, PS, color, scene from *Terminator,* 8 x 10" **80.00**

Autograph, Cary Grant, PS, black and white, 11 x 14½" glossy black frame holding glass over dark gray mat border, c1940s **75.00**

Autograph, Gene Autry, sgd Stetson hat, inscribed in ink in lining "To Bob My Best Wishes Always, Gene Autry 3–17–78," stamped on inner rim with Stetson logo and "Shuddle Brothers Houston" **700.00**

Autograph, Joan Crawford, PS, black and white closeup, black ink signature "Hello Carolyn from Joan Crawford," c1940s, 5 x 7" **75.00**

Book, *Who's Who at MGM,* photographs, biographies, 119 pp, 1940 . . . . **60.00**

Certificate, Academy of Motion Picture Arts and Sciences Certificate of Nomination, for Best Supporting Actor for *Day of the Locust,* featuring image of Oscar and signature of the president of the Academy, framed, 17 x 12½" **285.00**

Costume, *Planet of the Apes,* military type, green, inset leather-type collar, quasi-military bands on arms, loosely woven inner cuffs that extend beyond sleeves, front zipper closure, with matching pants and ape-like 5-toed boots, jacket features Western Costume Co label mkd "2771-1," 1968 . . . . **1,150.00**

Costume Sketch, *The Swan* starring Grace Kelly, pencil and watercolor on board, Kelly in full length white silk negligee, inscribed "Grace Kelly, The Swan #6," production information and signatures including "Hagedon" on verso, 1956, 22 x 15" **575.00**

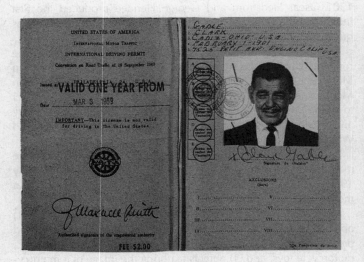

International Driving Permit, Clark Gable, dated March 3, 1959, black and white photo, blue signature, $2,300.00. Photo courtesy Christie's New York.

Hot Water Bottle, Jayne Mansfield, plastic, hat unscrews to fill, orig box, Poynter Products, 22" h, 7" w, $242.00. Photo courtesy Collectors Auction Services.

Hand Puppet, *Wizard of Oz*, The Wizard, plastic, green coat, yellow vest, brown trousers and tie, Scooter Pies premium, ©MGM 1967, 6¼ x 9" **50.00**

Lobby Card, *The Crimson Skull*, starring Billy Pickett, 1921, 11 x 14" **132.00**

Lobby Card, *The Lemon Drop Kid*, Paramount Pictures, 1951, price for set of 8 . . . . **100.00**

Magazine, *Frank Sinatra*, "Story in Pictures," Film Publishing Corp, 36 pp, 1945, 9 x 11¾". **45.00**

Magazine, *Modern Screen*, Apr 1943–Dec 1944, 6 issues. . . . **50.00**

Magazine, *Movie Humor, Hollywood Girls & Gags*, Jul 1935. . . . . **12.00**

Magazine, *Movieland*, May–Nov 1944, 7 issues, 8½ x 11". **50.00**

Magazine, *Sheilah Graham's Hollywood Romances*, Vol 1, #1, 100 pp, black and white photos, front color cov photo of Elizabeth Taylor, ©1951, 8½ x 10½" **20.00**

Movies, 16 mm, group of 5, starring Clark Gable, *Boom Town* (1940), *Combat America* (1940s), *Red Dust* (1932), *Run Silent Run Deep* (1958), and *Soldier of Fortune* (1955) **1,500.00**

Note, Katharine Hepburn, thank you not typewritten on single sheet of Katharine Houghton Hepburn stationary, dated 1–12–1988, "Many Thanks— Looks fascinating—, Katharine," framed, 6½ x 4½" **315.00**

Paperback, *Errol and Me*, Signet, Oct 1960, 1st ed, 176 pp, 8 pp portfolio of 11 black and white photos, 4¼ x 7" **20.00**

Perfume Bottle, *Gone With the Wind*, clear glass, threaded thin brass cap, replica image of Scarlett O'Hara in cap sleeved and floor length gown with closed parasol held at handle by clasped hands at waist, underside mkd "Babs Creations Inc," empty, early 1940s, 1½ x 2 x 4". **75.00**

Postcard, *A Night at the Hollywood Canteen*, linen paper, black and white photo of dance hall filled by servicemen and hostesses dancing, reverse with pencil signatures of Joel McCrea, Burgess Meredith, and Alan Ladd, "Free/Hollywood Canteen" postal permit stamp, unused, early 1940s, 3½ x 5½" **100.00**

Poster, *Alice Doesn't Live Here Anymore*, 14 x 36" **45.00**

Poster, *Empire Strikes Back*, starring Mark Hamill, 27 x 41" **28.00**

Poster, *Road to the Big House*, Somerset Pictures/Screen Guild Productions, features John Shelton, Ann Doran, and Guinn Williams, late 1940s, 27 x 41" **50.00**

Poster, *Some Blonds Are Dangerous*, Universal Pictures, starring Noah Berry Jr, William Gargan, Dorothea Kent, Nan Grey, Roland Drew, and Polly Rowles, Morgan Litho Co, 1937, 27 x 41". **75.00**

Poster, *Street of Chance*, depicting Burgess Meredith and Claire Trevor, framed, 1942, 39 x 26½" **230.00**

Presentation Money Clip, Frank Sinatra, center dollar sign above inscription "Thanks," orig box **700.00**

Press Book, Jerry Lewis, *Don't Raise the Bridge...Lower the River*, 1968 . . . . **25.00**

Program, *Ben Hur*, MGM. **32.00**

Program, *Gone With the Wind*, stiff paper, souvenir from first theater performance, 20 pp, 1939–40, 9 x 12" **75.00**

Prop, magic ticket, *Last Action Hero*, reads "Admit One" with elephant eye and Indian deity illus, 1993 . . . . **170.00**

Scarf, *Gone With the Wind*, sheer printed fabric, single word of movie title at each corner, corner pictures resemble Clark Gable, c1940, 18 x 20" **175.00**

Sheet Music, *April Showers*, from The Jolson Story, cartoon illus on border, blue and red, 1949 . . . . **6.00**

Sheet Music, *Bibbidi-Bobbodi-Boo*, from Disney's Cinderella, Cinderella on cov, 1949 . . . . **15.00**

Sheet Music, *Sweet Dreams, Sweetheart*, from Hollywood Canteen, star photos on cov, 1944 . . . . **10.00**

Souvenir Book, *Beau Geste*, 16 sepiatone pp, 30 stills and captions, back cov pictures cast stars including Gary Cooper, Broderick Crawford, Robert Preston, Ray Milland, Brian Donlevy, and Susan Hayward, 1939, 8 x 11" **20.00**

Souvenir Book, *Since You Went Away*, 20 pp, 1944, 9 x 12". **28.00**

Tablet, lined paper, full color Elizabeth Taylor cov photo with facsimile signature, unused, late 1940s–50s, 5½ x 8¾" **20.00**

Window Card, *Saga of Death Valley*, Roy Rogers, Gabby Hayes, and Doris Day, black and white **15.00**

Window Card, *To the Shores of Tripoli*, 20th Century Fox, cardboard, full color inset still against red, white, and blue shield ground, movie title in red lettering, "Technicolor" printed in 4 colors, information for benefit performance related to WW II war effort in black printing, 1942, 14 x 22". **50.00**

MOXIE

During the height of its popularity, 1920 to 1940, Moxie was distributed in approximately 36 states and even outsold Coca-Cola in many of them. It became so popular that moxie, meaning nervy, became part of the American vocabulary.

Moxie is the oldest continuously produced soft drink in the United States. It celebrated its 100th birthday in 1984. It traces its origin to a Moxie Nerve Food, a concoction developed by Dr. Augustin Thompson of Union, Maine, and first manufactured in Lowell, Massachusetts.

Moxie's fame is due largely to the promotional efforts of Frank Morton Archer, an intrepid entrepreneur endowed with a magnificent imagination. Archer created an advertising campaign as famous as the soda itself. Scarcely an event occurred in the first half of the 20th century that Archer did not exploit. The famous World War I "I Want You For The U.S. Army" Uncle Sam poster has a striking resemblance to the Moxie man pointing at his viewers and commanding them to "Drink Moxie."

Many firms attempted to play upon the Moxie name. Hoxie, Noxie, Proxie, Rixie, and Toxie are just a few. Most of these spurious products were produced in limited quantities, thus making them a prime find for collectors.

Moxie is still produced today, not in New England but Georgia. However, its popularity remains strongest in the Northeast.

Reference: Allan Petretti, *Petretti's Soda Pop Collectibles Price Guide,* Antique Trader Books, 1996.

Collectors' Club: New England Moxie Congress, 445 Wyoming Ave, Millburn, NJ 07041.

Display, diecut cardboard, Moxie bottle, paper label, c1930, 28" h **$185.00**
Drinking Glass, clear, emb lettering, flared rim, 4" h **90.00**
Fan Pull, diecut litho tin, 2-sided, Moxie boy above "Drink Moxie," Frank Archer sign, c1930, 6¼ x 6¼" **575.00**
Hanger Pin, multicolor diecut litho tin, Moxie Girl offering glass of Moxie, 1920s **50.00**
Sign, emb tin, rect, "Drink Moxie," white lettering on red ground, wooden frame, 7½" h, 20¼" w **235.00**
Sign, painted metal, 2-sided flange, "Drink Moxie," white lettering in red oval, 9" h, 18" w **150.00**
Spinner Top, multicolor cardboard disk, Moxie Boy 1 side, Moxiemobile parade car other side, "Drink Moxie" and "Read T.N.T. Cowboy," 1920s, 2" d **85.00**
Thermometer, litho tin, rect, Moxie bottle and Moxie boy on red and green ground, "Drink Moxie, Take Home a Case Tonight" in black button and "Drink Moxie, Good At Any Temperature," c1940, 26" h **4,000.00**
Thermometer, litho tin, rect, Moxie boy on red ground, "Drink Moxie, It's Always a Pleasure to Serve You," 1952, 26" h **1,325.00**
Thermometer, tin, rect, Moxie girl at top, "Tired and Thirsty?, Moxie is your drink, Clean, Wholesome, Refreshing" and Moxie boy at bottom, 26½" h **250.00**
Tip Tray, litho tin, Moxie girl holding glass, "I Just Love Moxie, Don't You?," 6" d **125.00**

Sign, tin, 1956, 34" h, 44" w, $231.00. Photo courtesy Gary Metz's Muddy River Trading Co.

MUSICAL INSTRUMENTS

Most older musical instruments have far more reuse than collectible value. Instrument collecting is still largely confined to string and wind instruments dating prior to 1900. Collectors simply do not give a toot about brass instruments. The same holds true for drums unless the drum head art has collectible value.

Celebrity electric guitars is the current hot musical instrument collecting craze. They are standard offering at rock 'n roll auctions held by leading New York and West Coast auction houses. In the 1980s a number of individuals began buying guitars as investments. Prices skyrocketed. Although the market has appeared to stabilize, it should still be considered highly speculative.

From the 1890s through the 1930s, inexpensive student violins marked with a stamp or paper label featuring the name of a famous violin maker—Amati and Stradivarius are just two examples—were sold in quantity. They were sold door to door and by Sears Roebuck. The advertisements claimed that the owner would have a violin nearly equal in quality to one made by the famous makers of the past. The cheap model sold for $2.45, the expensive model for $15. If cared for and played, these student violins have developed a wonderful, mellow tone and have a value in the $150 to $200 range. If damaged, they are $30 to $40 wall hangers.

References: S. P. Fjestad (ed.), *Blue Book of Guitar Values, Third Edition,* Blue Book Publications, 1996; George Gruhn and Walter Carter, *Electric Guitars and Basses: A Photographic History,* Miller Freeman Books, GPI Books, 1994; Paul Trynka (ed.), *The Electric Guitar,* Chronicle Books, 1993.

Periodicals: *Concertina & Squeezebox,* PO Box 6706, Ithaca, NY 14851; *Vintage Guitar Magazine,* PO Box 7301, Bismarck, ND 58507.

Collectors' Clubs: American Musical Instrument Society, RD 3, Box 205-B, Franklin, PA 16323; Harmonica Collectors International, PO Box 0681, St Louis, MO 63006.

Banjo, tenor, Ludwig, Ambassador Deluxe, gold-plated 1-pc tone ring and pot, gold-plated engraved rim and flange, laminated resonator with decorative inlay, laminated neck with engraved pearl inlay at peghead, ebony fingerboard with engraved pearl inlay, 10¾" d head **$50.00**
Banjo-Mandolin, Tieri, spruce wood top recessed in wood resonator, fretted fruitwood fingerboard with pearl inlay, "Tiere" label at peghead and branded on back, with case, 10" d head **85.00**
Cornet, American, Wurlitzer, silver, 6 crooks and "C" crook, orig case with accessories **300.00**
Cornet, Carl Fisher Coronet, silver, modified shepherd's crook, orig mouthpiece, flat spring missing, no case **95.00**
Cornet, Marceau & Company, solo alto, brass, flat spring, orig mouthpiece, later buttons **175.00**
Cornet, Special New York Model, Franz Weber, Vienna and New York, silver, modified shepherd's crook, flat springs, gold trim, orig case and accessories, 2 mouthpieces, extra crook and lead pipe **275.00**
Guitar, acoustic, black, inscribed "Catch the Wind, Donovan '97" with drawing of mountains and moon **450.00**
Guitar, arch top tenor, Recording King, Gibson, Inc, for Montgomery Ward, mahogany back and sides, spruce top, red-brown varnish, c1935, 18" l back **250.00**

Guitar, tenor, Gibson, Inc, bound mahogany back and sides, fine grain bound top with sunburst finish, mahogany neck with rosewood fingerboard, c1940, 19⁵/₁₆" l back **450.00**

Harmonica, Hohner, American Ace, 10 holes, WWI biplanes or jet fighter shown on box. **20.00**

Harmonica, Hohner, Herb Shriner's Hoosier Boy, 10 holes, gold covers, 4" l **40.00**

Harmonica, Japan, 1,000,000 $ Baby, miniature, 4 holes, cardboard box. **20.00**

Mando-Cello, Gibson Mandolin-Guitar Co, labeled "Gibson Mando-cello Style K-1, Number 57487," 1-pc birch back and sides bound in faux tortoiseshell, top of medium grain bound in celluloid, mahogany neck with "The Gibson" pearl inlay at peghead, bound ebony fingerboard with pearl dot inlay, 18¹/₂" l back. **1,375.00**

Mandolin, Gibson, 2-pc curly maple back and sides, fine grain spruce top, with F holes and bound boey, bround rosewood fingerboard with pearl eyes, with case, c1950, 13⁵/₈" l back. **635.00**

Ukelele, CF Martin and Co, Nazareth, PA, Style O, mahogany body and neck, with soft case, 1925, 9³/₈" l back **375.00**

Violin, child's, labeled "Copie de Antonius Stradivarius," 1-pc plain back, wide to fine grain top, red-yellow varnish, with case and bow, 12¹/₄" l back **450.00**

Violin, labeled "Antonius Stradivarius Cremonensis Faciebat Anno 1717," narrow curl back, similar ribs, scroll with faint curl, medium grain top, yellow-red varnish, 14¹/₄" l back **200.00**

Violin, unlabeled, 2-pc back with faint curl, similar ribs, plain scroll, medium grain top, red-brown varnish, with case, 14" l back **225.00**

MUSIC BOXES

Antoine Favre, a Swiss watchmaker, made the first true music box in 1796. The manufacture of music boxes was largely a cottage industry until Charles Paillard established a factory in Sainte-Croix, Switzerland, in 1875.

The golden age of the music box was from 1880 to 1910. A cylinder or disc music box occupied a place of importance in many Victorian-era parlors. The radio and record player eventually replaced the parlor music box.

Although novelty music boxes date to the Victorian era, they enjoyed increased popularity following World War II. In the case of the novelty box, the musical portion is secondary to the shape of the box itself. This category focuses primarily on these boxes.

References: Collectors' Information Bureau, *Collectibles Market Guide & Price Index, 16th Edition,* Collectors' Information Bureau, 1998, distributed by Krause Publications; Mary Sieber (ed.), *Price Guide to Limited Edition Collectibles,* Krause Publications, 1998.

Collectors' Club: Musical Box Society International, 1209 CR 78 West, LaBelle, FL 33935.

Big Deal, Enesco, plays "The Entertainer" **$15.00**

Children on Merry-Go-Round, wood, figures move, plays "Around the World in 80 Days", 7³/₄" **22.00**

Children on Seesaw, wood, figures move in time to music, 7" **20.00**

Treasure Chest of Toys, Enesco, plays "Toy Symphony," $65.00.

Church, mica cov wood, plays "Silent Night," 1930 . . . . **25.00**

Clock, Mattel, plays "Hickory Dickory Dock," 1952 . . . . **28.00**

Clown, Gorham, plastic, dome, 5¹/₂" **18.00**

Cotillion, Enesco, plays "The Emperor Waltz" **85.00**

Cozy Cup, Enesco, plays "In the Good Old Summertime" **25.00**

Dove, figural, ceramic, 6¹/₄" h **15.00**

Dreamkeeper, Enesco, plays "Memory" from *Cats* **100.00**

Easter Egg, tin **15.00**

Follies, Enesco, plays "There's No Business Like Show Business" **18.00**

Garfield Birthday Musical, Garfield in birthday cake, Enesco, plays "Happy Birthday" **15.00**

Jingle Bell Rock, Santa and jukebox, Enesco, plays "Jingle Bell Rock" **25.00**

Kitten With Ball, ceramic, 5¹/₂" **18.00**

McDonald's Restaurant, plays "Good Times/Good Taste" theme when front door is opened, orig package **17.50**

Melody Maker, parlor piano, Enesco, plays "The Entertainer" **12.00**

Owl, figural, ceramic, 6" h **20.00**

Paddington Bear, Schmid, Christmas, 1981 . . . . **35.00**

Peanuts, Schmid, 30th Anniversary. **18.00**

Player Piano, Enesco, plays "Rhapsody on a Theme of Paganini" **10.00**

Powder Box, metal, silver, litho cov, c1940, 3¹/₂ x 4¹/₄" **25.00**

Radio Days, Enesco, plays "In the Mood" **15.00**

Raggedy Ann, Schmid, 1980 . . . . **15.00**

Sesame Street's Big Bird and Snowman, Gorham, 7" h **24.00**

Snowball, glass, green wood base, Mr and Mrs Santa, 5" h **10.00**

Snowball, glass, green wood base, Santa and Rudolph, 5" h **10.00**

Snowball, glass, red wood base, Frosty the Snowman, 5" h **10.00**

Stein, porcelain, diamond dec, 5" h **35.00**

Yellow Brick Road, Enesco, plays "We're Off to See the Wizard" **25.00**

NAZI ITEMS

Anton Drexler and Adolf Hitler founded The National Socialist German Workers Party (NSDAP) on February 24, 1920. The party advocated a 25-point plan designed to lift the German economy and government from the depths of the Depression.

When the Beer Hall Putsch failed in 1923, Hitler was sentenced to a five-year prison term. Although serving only a year, he used that time to write *Mein Kampf*, a book that became the NSDAP manifesto.

During the early 1930s the NSDAP grew from a regional party based in Southern Germany to a national party. Hitler became Reich's chancellor in 1933. Following the death of President von Hindenberg in 1934, Hitler assumed that title as well.

Nazi items are political items, not military items. Do not confuse the two. Although the Wehrmacht, the German military, was an independent organization, it was subject to numerous controls from the political sector. Nazi memorabilia were popular war souvenirs. Large quantities of armbands, daggers, flags, and copies of *Mein Kampf* survive in the United States.

References: Richard J. Austin, *The Official Price Guide to Military Collectibles, Sixth Edition,* House of Collectibles, 1998; Bob Evans, *Third Reich Belt Buckles,* Schiffer Publishing, 1999; Gary Kirsner, *German Military Steins: 1914 to 1945, Second Edition,* Glentiques Ltd, 1996; Ron Manion, *German Military Collectibles Price Guide,* Antique Publications, 1995.

Periodical: *Military Trader,* PO Box 1050, Dubuque, IA 52004.

Cigarette Card Album, Kampf Um S Dritte Reich, soft bound, 91 pp, color photos of Nazi party and Hitler's early history, color photo of chariot flying the Nazi flag affixed to cov with gold lettering, 9½ x 12½" **$140.00**
Document, SS marriage, granting permission to marry SS officer, large Nazi stamp and ink signature, with postcard size photo of young woman seated by table reading book, 5¾ x 8¼" **145.00**

German Refugee Pass, 1939 . . . . **50.00**
Hitler Youth Pennant, triangular red cotton body, composite centers, large white pole sleeve with tiestring at one end, 16 x 20½" **50.00**
Hitler Youth Plaque, "Hockland Lager 1936" **165.00**
Letter, from concentration camp in Auschwitz **100.00**
Letter, from concentration camp in Dachau **50.00**
Magazine, *Newsweek,* Hitler, Mussolini and Goring on cov, 1937 . . . . **20.00**
Nazi Party Membership Book **85.00**
Newspaper, *Der Kampfruf* **20.00**
Paperweight, swastika, nickel base with green felt, affixed swastika on ball mount **100.00**
Pennant, Woman's RAD **135.00**
Periodical, *Deutsche StudentenZeitung,* Jan 24 and Jan 31, 1934 issues, paper for students by NSDAP, lead article on Hitler's victory in Saarland **45.00**
Periodical, *SS Leitheft,* soft bound, 25 pp, photos and articles on the SS and Nazi propoganda and news of the war, photos of SS troops in action, art of pure Aryan race, crossed sword and battle ax on cov, 1941 . . . . . **45.00**
Postcard, Hitler profile surrounded with his conquests from 1933 to 1939, unused, with Condor Legion cancellation, of 1939 Berlin, no stamp **20.00**
Postcard, Unserre Waffen SS, "Pak setzt uber einen Kanal," group of Waffen SS soldiers on rubber raft with PAK gun **20.00**
Propoganda Book, *Deutschland in Paris* **135.00**
Recruiting Poster, Waffen SS **500.00**
Stein, NSDAP **300.00**

NEWCOMB POTTERY

In 1886 Ellsworth and William Woodward founded the New Orleans Pottery Company. Thirty women from the Ladies Decorative Art League worked at the firm. The company lasted a year. Attempts by the Art League Pottery Club and later the Baronne Street Pottery to keep the pottery tradition alive also met with failure.

In 1895 Ellsworth Woodward convinced Sophie Newcomb College, the women's college of Tulane University, to establish a pottery class and sell its products. Mary G. Sheerer from Cincinnati was hired to teach pottery decoration. Joseph Fortune Meyer became the chief potter in 1896 and remained until 1925. Paul E. Cox, a technician, arrived in 1910.

Sadie Irvine, one of Newcomb's foremost decorators, worked from 1908 to 1952. Kenneth E. Smith and Professor Lota Lee Troy guided the pottery's operations through the 1930s. Robert Field and John Canady succeeded them.

Collectors divide Newcomb College wares into four basic periods: (1) 1895–1899; (2) 1900–1910; (3) 1910–1930, the period of the pale blue and green tree dripping with Spanish moss reflected in the moonlight; and, (4) 1930–1945. Commercial production ended in 1939. The Newcomb Guild was organized to sell students' work. It was dissolved when Sadie Irvine retired in 1952.

References: Ralph and Terry Kovel, *Kovel's American Art Pottery,* Crown, 1993; Jessie Poesch, *Newcomb Pottery,* Schiffer Publishing, 1984.

Collectors' Club: American Art Pottery Assoc, PO Box 1226, Westport, MA 02790.

Medal, Third Reich Russian Front (front and back views), $20.00.

Vase, Sadie Irvine, scenic, oak trees, Spanish moss, and moonlit landscape, denim-blue ground, mkd "NC/250/JM/MS26/SI," 8¼" h, $2,860.00. Photo courtesy David Rago Auctions, Inc.

Low Bowl, green and brown hare's fur glaze, imp "NC/JMF/F/D," 2½" h, 4¾" d **$500.00**

Vase, bulbous form, raspberry matte glaze, imp "NC/JM," 4" h, 3¼" d **500.00**

Vase, Juanita Gonzales, incised line dec, semi-matte gold glaze, sgd "NC/G71/TC47/JH," 7½" h, 4" d **1,200.00**

Vase, Kenneth Smith, tall with flaring rim, ridged body, semi-matte turquoise glaze, sgd "NC/Kenneth Smith," 7½" h, 6" d **600.00**

Vase, Sadie Irvine, band of light blue and yellow flowers with green leaves around shoulder, denim-blue ground, imp "NC/OY 14/19/SI," 1925, 6" h, 3¼" d **1,500.00**

Vase, Sadie Irvine, corseted body, pink berries and long green leaves on faded blue ground, sgd "NC/KZ2/83/ SI," 1920, 10½" h, 4¼" d **2,750.00**

Vase, Sadie Irvine, scenic, carved live oaks, Spanish moss, and moon, mkd "NC/SI/OX28/JM/117," 1925, 12¼" h, 5" d **7,500.00**

Vessel, AF Simpson, scenic, bulbous form, carved with full moon and live oak trees covered in Spanish moss, imp "NC/LV31/JM/183/AFS," 6½" h, 6½" d **5,000.00**

Vessel, bulbous form, incised geometric Art Deco pattern under matte blue-green glaze, mkd with artist cipher only, 1930s, 7¼" h, 7¼" d **1,500.00**

Vessel, C Chalaron, bulbous form, light blue irises with green leaves on light blue ground, sgd "NC/JM/260 N33/CMC," 1925, 5½" h, 6" d **2,500.00**

Vessel, Sadie Irvine, squatty bulbous form, light blue and yellow daffodils on faded blue ground, sgd "NC/SI/ JM/MI38/212," 1922, 4¼" h, 7" d **2,000.00**

NEW MARTINSVILLE/VIKING GLASS

The New Martinsville Glass Manufacturing Company was founded by Mark Douglass and George Matheny in New Martinsville, West Virginia, in 1901. The company's products included colored and plain dishes, lamps, and tumblers. John Webb, a cousin of the famous English glass maker Thomas Webb, joined the firm in December 1901. Within a brief period of time, New Martinsville was making Muranese, a direct copy of Peachblow.

After being destroyed by a major fire in 1907, the glasshouse was rebuilt and production was resumed in 1908. Harry Barth joined the firm in May 1918. He and Ira Clarke guided the company through the difficult years of the Depression. R. M. Rice and Carl Schultz, two New Englanders, bought New Martinsville Glass in July 1938.

New Martinsville Glass Company was renamed Viking Glass in 1944. Post-1945 product lines included handmade cut and etched giftware, novelties, and tableware. Most pieces were marked with a paper label reading "Viking." In 1951 Viking purchased a number of Paden City and Westmoreland molds.

Viking purchased the Rainbow Art Glass Company, Huntington, West Virginia, in the early 1970s, and continued production of its "Rainbow Art" animal figurines.

Kenneth Dalzell, former head of the Fostoria Glass Company, purchased the Viking Glass Company in mid-1986. After closing the plant for renovations, it was reopened in October 1987. The company's name was changed to Dalzell-Viking Glass. Dalzell-Viking, using models in Viking's inventory, reintroduced animal figurines and other items, often using non-period colors.

Reference: James Measell, *New Martinsville Glass: 1900–1944,* Antique Publications, 1994.

Figurine, baby seal **$70.00**
Figurine, elephant, crystal **85.00**
Figurine, hunter, crystal **95.00**
Figurine, pelican, amethyst **160.00**
Figurine, tiger, head up **190.00**
Georgian, butter top, green **30.00**
Georgian, cereal bowl, green **20.00**
Georgian, tumbler, #1611, ftd, 9 oz, 5" h, royal blue **18.00**
Janice, ball vase, 9" h, red **250.00**
Janice, bonbon, 2 handled, 6" **8.00**
Janice, bowl, swan, red **225.00**
Janice, celery, 11" d, crystal **15.00**
Janice, celery, swan, red **125.00**
Janice, cup and saucer, light blue **32.00**
Janice, jam jar, cov, 6" h, blue **40.00**
Janice, plate, 8½" d, light blue **20.00**
Janice, platter, oval, 13" l, crystal **28.00**
Janice, vase, flared, 3 ftd, 8" h, crystal **45.00**
Moondrops, berry bowl, red **30.00**
Moondrops, bowl, oval, cobalt **85.00**
Moondrops, bread and butter plate, 6" d, cobalt **8.50**
Moondrops, bread and butter plate, 6¼" d, red **9.00**
Moondrops, butter, cov, cobalt **550.00**
Moondrops, butter base, cobalt **60.00**
Moondrops, candlestick, ruffled, 5" h, amber **10.00**
Moondrops, candlesticks, pr, #37/2, brocade etching, 4" h . . . **130.00**
Moondrops, compote, 4", red **30.00**
Moondrops, compote, 11½", red **125.00**
Moondrops, cordial, amber, 1 oz, silver dec **25.00**
Moondrops, cordial, metal stem and foot, cobalt **50.00**
Moondrops, creamer, red **16.00**
Moondrops, cup, red **10.00**
Moondrops, cup and saucer, ftd, red **22.00**
Moondrops, dinner plate, 9½" d, cobalt **30.00**
Moondrops, goblet, crystal **18.00**
Moondrops, gravy boat, red **350.00**
Moondrops, luncheon plate, 8½" d, red **10.00**
Moondrops, mint dish, 3 ftd, red **95.00**
Moondrops, pickle, cobalt **55.00**
Moondrops, pickle, red **35.00**
Moondrops, shot glass, 2 oz, red **16.00**

Moondrops, mug, cobalt blue, $35.00.

Moondrops, soup bowl, 6³/₄" d, cobalt 60.00
Moondrops, sugar, 2³/₄" h, red 15.00
Moondrops, sugar, 3¹/₂" h, amethyst 11.00
Moondrops, tumbler, 5 oz, 3⁵/₈" h, red 15.00
Moondrops, tumbler, 9 oz, 4⁷/₈" h, handled, green 17.00
Moondrops, whiskey, amber 8.00
Moondrops, whiskey, cobalt 16.00
Prelude, bowl, 3 ftd, 11" d 55.00
Prelude, cake salver, 5" h 45.00
Prelude, candlesticks, pr, 1-lite, 5" h 130.00
Prelude, champagne 15.00
Prelude, plate, 15" d 70.00
Prelude, relish, 5 part, 13" 45.00
Radiance, butter, red 650.00
Radiance, candlesticks, pr, #42, 2-lite, light blue 229.00
Radiance, candy box, cov, 3 part, etch #26, amber 160.00
Radiance, celery, crystal, floral etch 10.00
Radiance, cheese and cracker, crystal, Meadow Wreath
  etching 25.00
Radiance, console bowl, with 2-lite candles, crystal
  etching, 12" 125.00
Radiance, cordial, red 30.00
Radiance, creamer, amber 12.50
Radiance, creamer and sugar, amber 26.00
Radiance, creamer and sugar on tray, crystal 20.00
Radiance, creamer and sugar on tray, Meadow Wreath
  etching 70.00
Radiance, creamer and sugar on tray, red 112.00
Radiance, cup, amber 8.00
Radiance, decanter, stopper, and 6 cordials, red, silver
  overlay 325.00
Radiance, honey dish, cov, ice blue 275.00
Radiance, honey lid, red 200.00
Radiance, mayonnaise ladle, ice blue 40.00
Radiance, mayonnaise liner, ice blue 18.00
Radiance, plate, 14" d, crystal, leaf cut 20.00
Radiance, punch bowl, ice blue 225.00
Radiance, punch bowl set, with 12 punch cups and
  ladle, ice blue 575.00
Radiance, punch cup, ice blue 12.00
Radiance, relish, 3 part, red 45.00
Radiance, relish, 3 part, 3-handled, red 50.00
Radiance, tray, crystal 13.00
Radiance, vase, #4232, crimped, etch #26, 10" h 140.00

NEWSPAPERS

Newspapers are collected first for their story content and second for their advertising. Volume One, Number One of any newspaper brings a premium because of its crossover value. Beware of assigning too much value to age alone; 18th-century and 19th-century newspapers with weak story content and advertising are frequently framed and used for decorative purposes.

A newspaper must be complete and have a minimal amount of chipping and cracking to be collectible. Newsprint, commonly used after 1880, is made of wood pulp and deteriorates quickly without proper care. Pre-1880 newsprint is made from cotton and/or rag fiber and survives much better. If only the front page of a 20th-century headline newspaper survives, value is reduced by 40% to 50%. Banner headlines, those extending across the full page, are preferred. Add a 10% to 20% premium to headline newspapers from the city where the event occurred.

Two of the most commonly reprinted papers are the January 8, 1880, *Ulster Country Gazette*, announcing the death of George Washington, and the April 15, 1865, issue of the *N.Y. Herald*, announcing Lincoln's death. If you have one of these papers, chances are you have a reprint.

References: Ron Barlow and Ray Reynolds, *The Insider's Guide to Old Books, Magazines, Newspapers, Trade Catalogs,* Windmill Publishing, 1995; Norman E. Martinus and Harry L. Rinker, *Warman's Paper,* Wallace-Homestead, Krause Publications, 1994.

Periodical: *PCM (Paper Collectors' Marketplace),* PO Box 128, Scandinavia, WI 54977.

Collectors' Club: Newspaper Collectors Society of America, 6031 Winterset, Lansing, MI 48911.

1924, Feb 4, *St Paul Pioneer Press,* MN, Woodrow
  Wilson dies $15.00
1924, Sep 9, *New York Daily Times,* Morro Castle burns 25.00
1925, Jan 18, *Lancaster Intelligencer,* Lancaster, PA, gen-
  eral news 5.00
1926, Jun 29, *Stockton Independent,* CA, general news 10.00
1927, May 15, *The Illustrated London News,* King
  George VI crowned 15.00
1927, May 21, *Dayton News,* Dayton, OH, Lindbergh
  over Ireland 23.00
1927, May 29, *St Paul Dispatch,* MN, Lindbergh starts
  Paris flight 25.00
1927, Jun 20, *Riverside Daily Press,* general news 5.00
1928, Nov 7, *St Paul Pioneer Press,* MN, Hoover wins
  White House 10.00
1929, Feb 15, *Washington Observer,* St Valentine's Day
  Massacre 130.00
1932, Mar 6, *St Paul Pioneer Press,* MN, Roosevelt
  orders bank holiday 10.00
1933, Jan 5, *Lancaster Daily Eagle,* Lancaster, OH,
  President Coolidge dies 15.00
1933, Jan 6, *St Paul Pioneer Press,* MN, Coolidge funer-
  al details 10.00
1933, Apr 4, *Pittsburgh Sun-Telegraph,* "Akron Breaks To
  Pieces: 73 Dead" 12.00
1934, Apr 8, *Kingsport Times,* Clyde Barrow sought in
  killing 20.00
1935, Jan 14, *St Paul Dispatch,* Lindbergh kidnapping
  testimony 5.00

1959, Sep 16, *Watertown Daily Times,* comical Khrushchev headline, $10.00.

1936, Jan 18, *Des Moines Register,* Rudyard Kipling dies 10.00
1936, Jan 29, *Minneapolis Star,* news of the day 5.00
1936, Mar 21, *St Paul Pioneer Press,* MN, New England
flood 5.00
1937, Jan 29, *St Paul Dispatch,* MN, Mississippi flood 5.00
1938, Jun 22, *Chicago American,* Chicago, IL, Max
Schmeling vs Joe Lewis 20.00
1939, Jul 3, *Chicago Examiner,* "Chamberlain Warns
Britain Read For War!" 7.00
1939–45, *Buffalo Courier Express,* 10 issues 12.00
1940, Aug 12, *Daily Journal-Gazette,* Mattoon, IL, Nazis
open aerial battle 5.00
1941, Dec 8, *Roanoke World News,* Pearl Harbor attack 25.00
1944, May 30, *Honolulu Advertiser,* Yanks lunge on
Rome 5.00
1944, Jun 6, *Niagara Falls Gazette,* Normandy invasion 25.00
1945, Mar 28, *St Paul Dispatch,* MN, US Army advances
in Europe 10.00
1945, Apr 25, *Oakland Tribune,* Hitler's hideout bombed 5.00
1945, May 2, *St Paul Dispatch,* MN, Nazi Army quits in
Italy 10.00
1945, May 7, *Buffalo Evening News,* Buffalo, NY, War
Victory issue 4.00
1945, Jul 10, *Los Angeles Times,* Los Angeles, CA,
European war ends 30.00
1945, Aug 7, *New York Herald-Tribune,* atom bomb
dropped on Japan 25.00
1945, Aug 8, *Guinea Gold,* New Guinea, GI newspaper,
atom bomb dropped on Japan 25.00
1953, *The Illustrated London News,* Coronation issue 35.00
1956, Jul 27, *San Francisco Examiner,* Andrea Doria
sinks 20.00
1960, Nov 9, *Pasadena Independent,* Kennedy elected 20.00
1962, Feb 21, *The News,* Garden Grove, CA, John Glenn
space flight 10.00
1963, Nov 22, *Sacramento Bee,* Kennedy shot 25.00
1963, Nov 25, *San Francisco Examiner,* Oswald killed 15.00
1965, Jan 21, *New York Daily Times,* Johnson takes
office 15.00

1965, Jan 24, *New York Daily Times,* Winston Churchill
dies 15.00
1967, Superbowl I 12.00
1968, Jun 6, *Williamsport Gazette,* PA, Robert Kennedy
killed 15.00
1969, Jul 21, *New York Daily News,* moon landing 40.00
1976, Apr 6, *San Jose Mercury,* CA, Howard Hughes dies 15.00
1977, Aug 17, *Commercial Appeal,* Memphis, TN, Elvis
Presley dies 25.00
1977, Oct 15, *San Francisco Examiner,* Bing Crosby dies 10.00
1980, Dec 19, *San Jose News,* John Lennon killed 15.00
1981, Mar 31, *New York Daily Times,* Reagan shot 65.00
1982, Mar 7, *San Francisco Chronicle,* John Belushi dies 10.00
1982, Aug 30, *Peninsula Times Tribune,* Palo Alto, CA,
Ingrid Bergman dies 15.00

NICODEMUS POTTERY

After attending the Cleveland Art School where he studied under Herman Matzen and Frank Wilcox, Chester Roland Nicodemus served as instructor and head of the sculpture department of the Dayton Art Institute (1925–1930) and then head of the sculpture department and later dean of the Columbus Art School (1930–1943). In 1943 Nicodemus left teaching to establish Ferro-Stone Ceramics.

Between 1943 and 1973 Nicodemus supplied fountain figures, portrait heads, and other sculptural forms to the retail trade. He continued to sell privately after ending his retail business.

Ferro-Stone ceramics were made from an Ohio clay with a high iron content. Fired between 2,000 and 2,500 degrees Fahrenheit, the finished products had a russet brown body and were stone hard. Favorite glaze colors were deep blue, mottled green, antique ivory, pussy willow, turquoise, and dark yellow. Products include specialized advertising pieces, Christmas cards, dinnerware, figurines (especially animals and birds), fountain pieces, medallions, plaques, statues, and vases.

In January 1990 Nicodemus fell and broke his hip. He died in November of the same year.

Nicodemus used a variety of markets including an incised "Nicodemus" and a two-tone paper label reading "NICODEMUS/FERRO-STONE."

Reference: Jim Ribel, *Sanfords Guide to Nicodemus: His Pottery and Art,* Adelmore Press, 1998.

Ashtray, #558, green, 6 x 4" **$50.00**
Ashtray, fraternity souvenir, green **25.00**
Ashtray, pelican, #106, ivory, 4½" **200.00**
Bank, elephant, #37, green, 4½" l **300.00**
Bookends, pr, giraffe, #122, yellow, 6½" h **600.00**
Candle Holder, scroll design, pedestal foot, green, 4¾" d **75.00**
Christmas Card, "Glad Tidings," 1968, 2¾ x 2¾" **75.00**
Christmas Ornament, Santa mask, 3" h **75.00**
Cigarette Holder, #218, ivory, 4½" d **75.00**
Cup, #235, green, 7 oz **50.00**
Figure, American bison, #14, yellow, 8" l **450.00**
Figure, collie, #24, green, 7" **250.00**
Figure, goldfinch, #592, yellow and black, 4½" **150.00**
Figure, kitten, #133, turquoise, 3" l **100.00**
Figure, pelican, #255, yellow, 8" h **450.00**
Figure, penguin, "The Pessimist," green, 8½" **75.00**
Figure, Pomeranian, #98, green, 6" h **225.00**

Flower Block, penguin, #27, yellow, 7" h 300.00
Flower Frog, mermaid, green, 7 x 6" 400.00
Jardiniere, #95, turquoise, 5" h 75.00
Pitcher, #88, cobalt, 8 oz, 3¹/₂" 75.00
Planter, cornucopia, #81, gray, 10" l 125.00
Planter, rabbit, #134, gray, 2¹/₂" 100.00
Salad Bowl, #260, green, 6¹/₂" d 50.00
Teapot, #224, dripless, yellow, 1¹/₄ qt 200.00
Vase, 2-handled, #44, gray, 4" h 75.00
Wall Pocket, flower design, #210, green 400.00

NILOAK POTTERY

In 1910 Hyten Bros. Pottery, Benton, Arkansas, introduced Mission, a marbleized art pottery line based on a swirl ware developed by Arthur Dovey when he worked at Ouachita Pottery. It was an immediate success.

In 1911 the company name was changed to the Niloak (kaolin spelled backwards) Pottery Company and Dovey left to pursue other interests. Money was raised for a new plant. Niloak produced stoneware and decorated glazed wares in addition to its colored-clay, marbleized pieces. Charles D. "Bullet" Hyten bought control of the company in 1918. During the 1920s, production reach an annual high of fifty thousand pieces.

Niloak sales fell during the Depression. The company survived by making hand-thrown and cast wares in high and matte finishes. These pieces are marked "Hywood Art Pottery," "Hywood by Niloak, Benton, Arkansas," "Hywood by Niloak," or simply "Niloak." Heavily mortgaging the pottery, Hyten eventually lost control in the early 1940s. Production was sporadic through 1947, when the plant was converted and became the Winburn Tile Company.

References: David Edwin Gifford, *The Collector's Encyclopedia of Niloak*, Collector Books, 1993, out of print; Ralph and Terry Kovel, *Kovel's American Art Pottery*, Crown, 1993.

Collectors' Clubs: American Art Pottery Assoc, PO Box 1226, Westport, MA 02790; Arkansas Pottery Collectors Society, PO Box 7617, Little Rock, AR 72217.

Bud Vase, Hywood line, leaf, blue glaze, 6" h $15.00
Candlesticks, pr, Hywood Art Pottery, double cornu-
    copia, white, unmkd, 6³/₄" h 100.00
Cornucopia, light pink, 3" 5.00
Ewer, eagle, 9¹/₂" w 45.00
Figure, frog 20.00
Figure, squirrel 20.00
Pitcher, yellow, 3¹/₄" 15.00
Planter, camel, 3" 25.00
Planter, duck, pink and white, 5" 20.00
Planter, log, white, 7" 15.00
Planter, rabbit, green, 3" 15.00
Rose Bowl, Mission ware, closed-in rim, brown, blue,
    terra cotta, and sand, stamped "Niloak" and paper
    label, 5³/₄" h, 7" d 250.00
Salt and Pepper Shakers, pr, penguin 65.00
Vase, maroon, handles, 7" h 15.00
Vase, Mission ware, baluster shape, brown, blue, terra
    cotta, and sand, stamped "Niloak," 9¹/₂" h, 5" d 300.00
Vase, Mission ware, brown, rust, white, and blue,
    stamped "Niloak," 10" h, 4³/₄" d 450.00

Candlesticks, pr, Mission ware, blue, terra cotta, and sand, stamped "Niloak," 8" h, 5" d, $325.00. Photo courtesy David Rago Auctions, Inc.

Vase, Mission ware, classical shape, brown, ivory, and
    terra cotta, stamped "Niloak" and paper label," 12" h 500.00
Vase, Mission ware, conical, flared foot, brown, blue,
    and terra cotta, stamped "Niloak," 8¹/₂" h, 4¹/₂" d 175.00
Vase, Mission ware, corseted, brown, blue, and terra
    cotta, stamped "Niloak," 10" h, 4¹/₂" d 225.00
Vase, Mission ware, corseted, brown, blue, terra cotta,
    and purple, stamped "Niloak," 9¹/₂" h, 5¹/₂" d 350.00
Vase, Mission ware, cylindrical, flared foot, brown, blue,
    and terra cotta, stamped "Niloak" and paper label,
    10" h, 4¹/₂" d 375.00
Vase, Mission ware, rolled rim, brown, blue, terra cotta,
    and purple, stamped "niloak" and paper label, 14" h,
    7" d 875.00

NODDERS & BOBBIN' HEADS

A nodder consists of two separate molded parts. A pin is used as the fulcrum to balance one piece on the other. A true nodder works by gravity, a counterbalance weight attached to the fulcrum located in the base piece. Eventually, electrical, frictional, mechanical, and windup mechanisms were used. While bisque nodders are the most common, nodders were made from almost every medium imaginable.

Most nodders are characterizations, often somewhat grotesque. Buddhas, 18th-century courtiers, ethnic and professional types, cartoon figures, and animals are just a few examples. Most collectors specialize, e.g., nodding salt and pepper shakers or holiday theme nodders.

Bobbin' heads have no weight. Their motion comes from a spring or other mechanism inside their head. While most individuals think of bobbin' heads in respect to the Beatles, Peanuts, and Sports Mascot series from the 1960s, papier-mâché cartoon and holiday figures date from the early decades of the 20th century.

Reference: Hilma R. Irtz, *Figural Nodders*, Collector Books, 1997.

Collectors' Club: Bobbin' Head National Club, PO Box 9297, Lakeland, FL 32120.

American Indian, papier-mâché **$200.00**
Best Husband Award, man wearing black rim glasses, white shirt, blue coat and trousers, red and white tie, pottery painted head, glazed body, Vari-Vue Co, Mount Vernon, NY, c1950s, 5" h **20.00**
Bunny, chalkware, spring neck, 5" h **30.00**
Bunny, flocked, glass eyes, Japan **65.00**
Colonel Sanders, 7" h **75.00**
Golfer, holding tee in mouth, spring neck, 7" h. **25.00**
Green Bay Packers, papier-mâché, Sports Specialties CA/Japan, 1968, 8" h **45.00**
Happy Hooligan, papier-mâché, Germany, early 1930s, 6" h **90.00**
Hobo, papier-mâché and composition, wood base, 8½" h . . . **25.00**
Keystone Kop, painted composition, white sq base inscribed "Movieland," Japan, c1960s, 7½" h **100.00**
Portland Trailblazers Basketball Player, papier-mâché, c1967–71 . . . . **100.00**
Reindeer, flocked, 5½" h **45.00**
Salt and Pepper Shakers, pr, bull and matador, souvenir from Mexico, complete with condiment lid and spoon, Japan **100.00**
Salt and Pepper Shakers, pr, donkeys, sq base, Japan **45.00**
Salt and Pepper Shakers, pr, hen and rooster on stump, Japan **50.00**
Salt and Pepper Shakers, pr, Rock 'n Roll Santa, Holt-Howard, 6" h **60.00**
Salt and Pepper Shakers, pr, swans, white, multicolored floral holder **50.00**
Salt and Pepper Shakers, pr, yellow canaries, hanging from tree branch, Japan **15.00**
Santa, pipe cleaner hands, fur beard, Western Germany **50.00**
Shriner, Japan, 6¾" h **50.00**
Topo Gigio, painted composition, orig box, Ross Products, Inc, ©Maria Perego, early 1960s, 5" h **75.00**
Watergate Bug, orange plastic, wearing earphones with decaled bloodshot eyes, 6¼" h **100.00**
Woodstock, Korea, c1965–72 . . . . **85.00**

Mickey Mantle, c1962, 7" h, $600.00. Photo courtesy Gene Harris Antique Auction Center.

NON-SPORT TRADING CARDS

Tobacco insert cards of the late 19th century are the historical antecedents of the modern trading (bubble gum) card. Over 500 sets, with only 25 devoted to sports, were issued between 1885 and 1894. Tobacco cards lost popularity following World War I.

In 1933 Indian Gum marketed a piece of gum and a card inside a waxed paper package, launching the era of the modern trading card. Goudey Gum and National Chicle controlled the market until the arrival of Gum, Inc., in 1936. In 1948 Bowman entered the picture, followed a year later by Topps. The Bowman-Topps rivalry continued until 1957 when Topps bought Bowman.

Although Topps enjoyed a dominant position in the baseball trading card market, Frank Fleer Company and Philadelphia Chewing Gum provided strong competition in the non-sport trading card sector in the 1960s. Eventually Donruss also became a major player in the non-sport trading card arena.

Non-sport trading cards benefited from the decline of the sport trading card in the early 1990s. Fueled by a strong comic book store market, many companies issued non-sport trading card sets covering a wide range of topics from current hit movies to pin-up girls of the past. Dozens of new issues arrived each month. As the 1990s end, the craze appears to be over. High prices, too many sets, and the introduction of chase and other gimmick cards have had a negative impact. Secondary market value for these post-1990 sets is highly speculative, a situation not likely to change within the next ten to fifteen years.

References: Christopher Benjamin, *The Sport Americana Price Guide to Non-Sports Cards: 1930–1960, No. 2,* Edgewater Books, 1993, out of print; Christopher Benjamin, *The Sport Americana Price Guide to Non-Sports Cards: 1961–1992, No. 4,* Edgewater Books, 1992, out of print; Timothy Brown and Tony Lee, *The Official Price Guide to Role Playing Games,* House of Collectibles, 1998.

Periodicals: *Non-Sport Update,* 4019 Green St, PO Box 5858, Harrisburg, PA 17110; *Collect!,* PO Box 569, Dubuque, IA 52004; *The Wrapper,* 1811 Moore Ct, St Charles, IL 60174.

Collectors' Club: United States Cartophilic Society, PO Box 4020, St Augustine, FL 32085.

Bowman, America Salutes the FBI, 1949, 36 cards **$650.00**
Bowman, Antique Autos, 1953, 48 cards **350.00**
Bowman, Movie Stars, 1948, 36 cards **500.00**
Cardz, San Diego Zoo, 1993, 110 cards. **15.00**
Cardz, Tales From the Crypt, 1993, 110 cards. **15.00**
Collect-A-Card, American Bandstand, 1993, 100 cards. **12.00**
Comic Images, Marvel Universe Trading Cards, 90 cards. **50.00**
Dart, Beetlejuice, 1990, 100 cards. **10.00**
Diamond, Teenage Mutant Ninja Turtles III, 1993, 88 cards, 11 stickers. **10.00**
Donruss, Ace Ventura: When Nature Calls, 1995, 90 cards **12.00**
Donruss, Addams Family, 1964, 66 cards **280.00**
Donruss, All Pro Skateboard, 1978, 44 stickers and cards **12.00**
Donruss, Awesome All-Stars, 1988, 127 stickers and cards **18.00**
Donruss, Bionic Woman, 1976, 44 cards **50.00**
Donruss, CB Convoy Code, 1978, 44 sticker cards **30.00**
Donruss, Chips, 1977, 66 stickers **40.00**

Donruss, Combat, 1964, 66 cards **165.00**
Donruss, Disneyland, 1965, 66 cards. **150.00**
Donruss, Elvis Presley, 1978, 66 cards **550.00**
Donruss, Fantastic Odd Rods, 1973, 66 sticker cards **160.00**
Donruss, Green Hornet, 1966, 44 cards. **270.00**
Donruss, King Kong, 1965, 55 cards **325.00**
Donruss, Kiss, 1978, 66 cards, Series I **50.00**
Donruss, Monkees, 1966, 44 cards, Series A **125.00**
Donruss, Odd Rods, 1970, 44 sticker cards **110.00**
Donruss, Saturday Night Fever, 1978, 66 cards. **20.00**
Donruss, Sgt Pepper's Lonely Hearts Club Band, 1978,
    66 cards **10.00**
Duo Cards, Abbott & Costello, 1996, 72 cards **15.00**
Eclipse, Rotten to the Core, 1989, 36 cards **10.00**
Enesco, Precious Moments, 1993, 16 cards **15.00**
Fleer, Cracked Magazine, 1978, 56 cards, 10 stickers **30.00**
Fleer, Drag Nationals, 1972, 70 cards **210.00**
Fleer, Race USA, 1972, 74 cards **170.00**
Frostick, Animal Cards, 1930s, 44 cards. **185.00**
Gum, Inc, Adventure, 100 cards with #86 . . . . **550.00**
Gum, Inc, American Beauties, 1941, 24 cards **750.00**
Gum, Inc, Superman, 1941, 72 cards. **125.00**
Hasbro, GI Joe, 1986, 192 cards **50.00**
Imagine, Night of the Living Dead, 1987, 60 cards, 1st
    printing. **25.00**
Leaf, Munsters, 1966, 72 cards **475.00**
Leaf, Pirate Cards, 1948, 49 cards **450.00**
Philly, Dark Shadows, 66 cards, Series I **375.00**
SkyBox, Aladdin, 1993, 90 cards **12.00**
SkyBox, Star Trek: The Next Generation Episode Series,
    1994, 108 cards **18.00**
SkyBox, Three Musketeers, 1993, 90 cards. **112.00**
Star Pics, All My Children, 1991, 72 cards **18.00**
Topps, Alf, 1987, 69 cards, 18 stickers **15.00**
Topps, Alien, 1979, 84 cards, 22 stickers **30.00**
Topps, Animals of the World, 1951, 100 cards **500.00**
Topps, Astronauts, 1963, 55 cards, 3-D backs. **260.00**
Topps, A-Team, 1983, 66 cards, 12 stickers **8.00**
Topps, Autos of 1977, 99 cards, 20 stickers **115.00**
Topps, Baby, 1984, 66 cards, 11 stickers **10.00**

Topps, Back to the Future II, 1989, 88 cards, 11 stickers **12.00**
Topps, Battle, 1965, 66 cards. **600.00**
Topps, Battlestar Galactica, 1978, 132 cards, 22 stickers. **40.00**
Topps, Bay City Rollers, 1975, 66 cards **140.00**
Topps, Beverly Hillbillies, 1963, 66 cards. **475.00**
Topps, Black Hole, 1979, 88 cards, 22 stickers. **18.00**
Topps, Buck Rogers, 1979, 88 cards, 22 stickers. **20.00**
Topps, Casey and Kildare, 1962, 110 cards **200.00**
Topps, Charlie's Angels, 1977–78, 55 cards, 11 stickers **50.00**
Topps, Civil War News, 1962, 88 cards **450.00**
Topps, Crazy Cards, 1961, 66 cards **200.00**
Topps, Creature Feature, 1980, 88 cards, 22 stickers **45.00**
Topps, Evel Knievel, 1974, 60 cards. **140.00**
Topps, Fighting Marines, 1953, 96 cards **700.00**
Topps, Flags of the World, 1956, 80 cards **175.00**
Topps, Fright Flicks, 1988, 90 cards, 11 stickers **15.00**
Topps, Funny Doors, 1970, 24 cards **180.00**
Topps, Garbage Pail Kids, 1985–88, #1 sticker, 88 cards **145.00**
Topps, Get Smart, 1966, 66 cards **380.00**
Topps, Gilligan's Island, 1965, 55 cards **825.00**
Topps, Good Times, 1975, 55 cards, 21 stickers **70.00**
Topps, Incredible Hulk, 1979, 88 cards, 22 stickers **18.00**
Topps, Johnson vs Goldwater, 1964, 66 cards **180.00**
Topps, Kung Fu, 1973, 60 cards. **125.00**
Topps, Laugh-In, 1968, 77 cards **175.00**
Topps, Man From U.N.C.L.E., 1966, 55 cards **125.00**
Topps, Maya, 1967, 55 cards. **35.00**
Topps, Michael Jackson, 1984, Series I, 33 cards and
    stickers **12.00**
Topps, Monster Laffs-Midgee, 1963, 153 cards **250.00**
Topps, Partridge Family, 1971, 55 cards, yellow border **75.00**
Topps, Presidents & Famous Americans, 1965, 44 cards **195.00**
Topps, Rails & Sails, 1955, 200 cards **1,150.00**
Topps, Rambo, 1985, 66 cards, 22 stickers. **18.00**
Topps, Rat Patrol, 1966, 66 cards. **110.00**
Topps, Roger Rabbit, 1988, 132 cards, 22 stickers **20.00**
Topps, Scoop, 1954, 156 cards. **1,300.00**
Topps, Shock Theater, 1975, 51 cards. **475.00**
Weber Bros, Animals, 1920s, 80 cards **230.00**
Weber Bros, Indian Pictures, 1920s, 50 cards. **250.00**
Yazoo, Pioneers of Country Music, 1985, 40 cards **10.00**

NORITAKE AZALEA

Azalea is a Noritake hand-painted china pattern first produced in the early 1900s. Because the pieces are hand painted, subtle variations are common.

The Larkin Company, Buffalo, New York, used Azalea as one of its "Larkin Plan" premiums. In 1931 Larkin billed it as "Our Most Popular China." Some Azalea accessory pieces appeared in Larkin catalogs for three or four years, others for up to nineteen consecutive years. Azalea decorated glass and other coordinating items were made, but never achieved the popularity of the dinnerware.

Reference: Walter Ayars, *Larkin China, Catalog Reprint,* Echo Publishing, 1990.

Note: All items listed are china, unless otherwise noted. For additional information see Noritake China.

Topps, Davy Crockett, Series I, card #1, 1956, 80 card set, $325.00

Berry Creamer. **$55.00**
Bouillon Cup and Saucer. **25.00**
Bread and Butter Plate, 6½". **8.00**

Creamer, $20.00.

Butter Dish, cov, round	80.00
Cake Plate, handled, 9³/₄" w	42.00
Celery, 12¹/₂"	35.00
Compote, 2³/₄"	80.00
Cranberry Bowl, 5¹/₄"	50.00
Cup and Saucer	17.00
Dinner Plate, 10"	28.00
Eggcup, single	40.00
Fruit Bowl, 5¹/₄"	10.00
Gravy Boat, attached liner	40.00
Lemon Tray, handled	24.00
Luncheon Plate, 8¹/₂"	18.00
Olive Dish, 7¹/₈"	65.00
Platter, oval, 11³/₄"	40.00
Platter, oval, 13⁵/₈"	60.00
Relish, 2-part	40.00
Relish, 8¹/₄"	18.00
Salad Plate, 7⁵/₈"	12.00
Salt and Pepper Shakers, pr, bell shape	24.00
Salt and Pepper Shakers, pr, bulbous	32.00
Snack Set, plate and cup	38.00
Sugar, cov, gold finial	60.00
Syrup	70.00
Teapot, cov	95.00
Toothpick Holder	80.00
Vegetable, cov, round	90.00
Whipped Cream Ladle	15.00

NORITAKE CHINA

Ichizaemon Morimura, one of the founders of Noritake, established Morimura-kumi, a Japanese exporting company located in Tokyo in 1867. An import shop was also founded in New York to sell Japanese traditional goods. In 1904 he founded Nippon Toki Kaisha Ltd., the forerunner of Noritake, in Nagoya, Japan.

The Larkin Company, Buffalo, New York, was one of the principal distributors for Noritake China in the 1920s. The Azalea, Braircliff, Linden, Modjeska, Savory, Sheriden, and Tree in the Meadow patterns were utilized as Larkin premiums.

The factory was heavily damaged during World War II and production was greatly reduced. The company sold its china under the "Rose China" mark between 1946 and 1948 because the quality did not match that of earlier Noritake China. High quality was achieved once again by early 1949.

Noritake Company was established for selling tableware in the United States. Over the next thirty years, companies were created in Australia, Canada, the United Kingdom, Sri Lanka, Guam, the Philippines, and Ireland for the manufacture and distribution of Noritake products.

In 1956 Noritake began an expansion program that eventually resulted in a full line of tabletop products. Crystal glassware joined the line in 1961, earthenware and stoneware dinnerware and accessories in 1971. The company's name was changed to Noritake Company, Ltd. in 1981.

Close to 100 different Noritake marks have been identified. Most pieces are marked with "Noritake," a wreath, "M," "N," or "Nippon."

References: Aimee Neff Alden, *Collector's Encyclopedia of Early Noritake*, Collector Books, 1995; Joan Van Patten, *Collector's Encyclopedia of Noritake* (1984, 1997 value update), *Second Series* (1994), Collector Books; Harry L. Rinker, *Dinnerware of the 20th Century: The Top 500 Patterns*, House of Collectibles, 1997; David Spain, *Collecting Noritake A to Z*, Schiffer Publishing, 1999.

Collectors' Club: Noritake Collectors' Society, 145 Andover Pl, West Hempstead, NY 11552.

Note: For additional listings see Noritake Azalea and Noritake Tree in the Meadow.

Amenity, bread and butter plate, 6³/₈"	$7.00
Amenity, creamer	20.00
Amenity, cup and saucer, ftd, 3"	15.00
Amenity, dinner plate, 10⁵/₈"	17.00
Amenity, gravy boat, attached liner	45.00
Amenity, platter, oval, 13⁵/₈"	45.00
Amenity, salad plate, 8³/₈"	10.00
Amenity, sugar, cov	25.00
Amenity, vegetable, oval, 10¹/₈"	35.00
Anticipation, bread and butter plate, 6¹/₄"	6.00
Anticipation, coffeepot, cov	75.00
Anticipation, creamer	20.00
Anticipation, cream soup and saucer	25.00
Anticipation, cup and saucer, ftd, 3¹/₄"	12.50
Anticipation, dinner plate, 10⁵/₈"	12.00
Anticipation, fruit dish, 5¹/₂"	7.50
Anticipation, gravy boat and liner	40.00
Anticipation, platter, oval, 13⁵/₈"	50.00
Anticipation, platter, oval, 15⁵/₈"	70.00
Anticipation, relish, 9¹/₄"	12.00
Anticipation, salad plate	8.00
Anticipation, salt and pepper shakers, pr	25.00
Anticipation, soup bowl, flat, 9" d	12.50
Anticipation, sugar, cov	25.00
Anticipation, teapot, cov	75.00
Anticipation, vegetable, cov, round	75.00
Anticipation, vegetable, oval, 10¹/₈"	30.00
Barrymore, bread and butter plate, 6¹/₂"	6.00
Barrymore, cake plate, handled, 11⁷/₈" w	45.00
Barrymore, canape, 10⁵/₈"	35.00
Barrymore, coffeepot, cov	80.00
Barrymore, creamer	20.00
Barrymore, cup and saucer, ftd	15.00
Barrymore, dinner plate, 10⁵/₈"	8.00
Barrymore, platter, oval, 14¹/₄"	35.00
Barrymore, relish, 7⁷/₈"	14.00

Barrymore, salad plate, 8¼". 9.00
Barrymore, salt and pepper shakers, pr. 20.00
Chatham, bread and butter plate, 6½". 4.00
Chatham, cereal bowl, lug handle. 7.50
Chatham, creamer. 16.00
Chatham, cream soup and saucer 20.00
Chatham, cup and saucer 10.00
Chatham, fruit dish, 5½" 5.00
Chatham, platter, oval, 12⅜". 25.00
Chatham, platter, oval, 14¼". 30.00
Chatham, salad plate, 8¼". 7.00
Chatham, teapot, cov 50.00
Chatham, vegetable, oval, 9¾". 20.00
Etienne, bread and butter plate, 6⅜" 5.00
Etienne, creamer. 20.00
Etienne, cup and saucer, ftd. 16.00
Etienne, demitasse cup 12.00
Etienne, dinner plate, 10½". 15.00
Etienne, fruit dish, 5¾" 7.50
Etienne, gravy boat and liner 35.00
Etienne, napkin ring 6.00
Etienne, platter, oval, 12⅛". 30.00
Etienne, salad plate, 8¼". 75.00
Etienne, salt and pepper shakers, pr 20.00
Etienne, soup bowl, coupe, 7¾" 12.00
Etienne, teapot, cov. 65.00
Etienne, vegetable, oval, 10" l 35.00
Margot, bread and butter plate, 6⅜". 5.00
Margot, creamer 15.00
Margot, cup and saucer, flat 12.00
Margot, demitasse cup and saucer 10.00
Margot, dinner plate 12.00
Margot, fruit dish, 5½". 6.00
Margot, platter, oval, 12¼" l 25.00
Margot, salad plate, 8¼". 8.00
Margot, snack set, plate and cup 15.00
Margot, sugar, open 18.00
Margot, vegetable, 8⅞" d 24.00

Somerset, bread and butter plate, 6¼" 5.00
Somerset, creamer. 15.00
Somerset, cup and saucer 12.50
Somerset, dinner plate, 10½" d 12.00
Somerset, fruit dish, 5½". 6.00
Somerset, platter, oval, 13¾". 25.00
Somerset, salad plate, 7½". 6.00
Somerset, soup bowl, 7½". 12.00
Somerset, sugar, cov 20.00
Somerset, vegetable, oval, 10⅝" l 25.00

NORITAKE TREE IN THE MEADOW

Tree in the Meadow is another popular hand-painted Noritake pattern. The basic scene includes a meandering stream (usually in the foreground), a peasant cottage, and a large tree. Muted tones of brown and yellow are the principal colors.

Noritake exported the first Tree in the Meadow pieces to the United States in the early 1920s. Several different backstamps were used for marking purposes. The Larkin Company distributed the pattern in the 1920s and 30s.

Reference: Walter Ayars, *Larkin China, Catalog Reprint,* Echo Publishing, 1990.

Bread and Butter Plate, 6½" d $10.00
Butter Dish, cov, insert 65.00
Cake Plate, 10" d 40.00
Celery Dish, 12" l 35.00
Coffeepot, cov 185.00
Creamer and Sugar, cov 50.00
Lemon Dish, handled, 5½" d 25.00
Luncheon Plate, 8½" d 15.00
Nappy 15.00
Platter, oval, 10" l 85.00
Salt and Pepper Shakers, pr 30.00
Sugar Shaker. 30.00
Syrup 50.00
Teapot, cov. 100.00
Toothpick Holder, 2½" h 55.00
Vase, fan, 5¾" h 115.00
Vegetable Bowl, oval, 9¼" l 30.00

NORTH DAKOTA SCHOOL OF MINES

Earle J. Babcock, a University of North Dakota chemistry instructor, was instrumental in promoting the use of North Dakota clay with the pottery industry. The first experiment pieces produced at the North Dakota School of Mines date from 1904. In 1910 a Ceramics Department was established.

Margaret Kelly Cable, department director from 1910 to 1949, was the driving force behind North Dakota School of Mines pottery. Pottery was exhibited at numerous fairs and expositions. Flora Cable Huckfield, Margaret's sister, arrived in 1924 as a decorator. By 1930 she was in charge of marketing the pottery's wares. Freida Louise Hammers, Julia Edna Mattson, Margaret Davis Pachl are other women who played a prominent role in the success of North Dakota School of Mines Pottery. Pachl succeeded Margaret Cable when she retired in 1949. Commercial production lessened. Pachl retired in 1970.

A cobalt blue university seal was used to mark wares produced between 1913 and 1963. Other early marks include a stamped or

Chatham, dinner plate, 10⅝", $12.00.

hand-printed "UND" or "U.N.D. Grand Forks, N.D." Only student names appear on pieces made after 1963.

Reference: Darlene Hurst Dommel, *Collector's Encyclopedia of the Dakota Potteries,* Collector Books, 1996.

Collectors' Club: North Dakota Pottery Collectors Society, PO Box 14, Beach, ND 58621.

Cabinet Vase, Julia Mattson, green stripes on mustard
body, ink stamp and "M," 3¼" h, 3¼" d **$350.00**
Low Bowl, Julia Mattson, straight-sided, hp and lightly
tooled scene of oxen and covered wagons on prairie
with blue sky against brown ground, circular ink
stamp and incised "JM#6-121-Huck," 2" h, 6½" d **1,000.00**
Pitcher, Margaret Cable, squat, "Red River Ox Carts,"
emb frieze under glossy ivory glaze, buff clay body,
stamp mark, emb signature and title and "140," 5" h,
8½" w **1,000.00**
Trivet, Julia Mattson, Bentonite, carved stylized eagle in
black on brick ground, ink stamp mark and "JM 58,"
1958, 4¾" d **275.00**
Vase, Flora Huckfield, bulbous, "N.D. Sioux," carved
with Indian warriors on horseback, dark brown matte
ground, ink stamp mark and incised "151" and title,
5¾" h, 5½" d **2,000.00**
Vase, Flora Huckfield, "Trees/Thorne," hand-carved with
large excised oak trees, matte green glaze, ink stamp
and incised signature, 10¾" h, 5½" d **4,500.00**
Vase, Julia Mattson, bulbous, stylized flowers in purple
and green on beige ground, ink stamp, dated "1925,"
and incised "M," 7¼" h, 7½" d **7,150.00**
Vase, Ruth Skyberg, excised with brown daffodils, dark
brown ground, ink stamp and incised signature, 1949,
7¾" h, 5½" d **2,000.00**
Vessel, Margaret Cable, spherical, "Covered Wagon,"
matte brown glaze, mkd with circular stamp and title,
and "186, M. Cable," 6¼" h, 7" d **2,500.00**

Vessel, Julia Mattson, bulbous, purple and green stylized flowers on beige ground, ink stamp, incised "M," 1925, 7¼" h, 7½" d, $7,150.00. Photo courtesy David Rago Auctions, Inc.

NUTCRACKERS

Lever-action cast-iron nutcrackers, often in the shape of animals, appeared in the mid-19th century. Designs mirrored the popular design styles of each era. Art Deco and 1950s-era nutcrackers and sets are eagerly sought by collectors. Beginning in the 1960s, wooden nutcrackers from Germany's Erzgebirger region began flooding the American market. These Erzgebirger-style figures are now being made around the world, especially in the Far East, and from a wide variety of materials.

Reference: James Rollband, *American Nutcrackers: A Patent History and Value Guide,* Off Beat Books, 1996.

Collectors' Club: Nutcracker Collectors' Club, 12204 Fox Run Dr, Chesterland, OH 44026.

Anvil and Blacksmith's Hammer, cast iron, black paint
John Wright, 4" l **$15.00**
Bearded Man with Hat, wood, lacquered, 8¾" l **150.00**
Big Ben, brass, English **55.00**
Clown, cast iron, painted, 5¾" l. **40.00**
Dog, cast iron, green paint, 4¼" h, 11" l **100.00**
Eagle, wood, glass eyes, 7½" l **125.00**
Elephant, cast iron, painted red and black, 10" l **130.00**
Hammer, brass, silver-plated, walnut shaped base, 6½" l **125.00**
Jester and Knight, cast brass, plier type. **40.00**
Kangaroo, cast iron, brass plated, Nestor, 5½" h **150.00**
Krag's Whole Kernel Nut Cracker, nickel-plated metal,
ratchet mechanism and lever, black enameled metal
tray, orig box, 7" l **60.00**
Parrot, cast brass, 5½" l **30.00**
Peasant, attached undertray, wood, painted, 10½" h **200.00**
Rooster, cast brass **25.00**
Skull and Bones, cast iron, 6" l **125.00**
Squirrel, cast aluminum, black paint, sitting on hind legs
on grape leaf, 7½" l. **30.00**
Squirrel, cast iron, black, 4½" h, 5½" l, c1970 . . . . **15.00**
Toy Soldier, wood, China, 10½" h **10.00**
Woman's Legs, high heels, cast aluminum, 6⅞" l **100.00**

NUTTING, WALLACE

Wallace Nutting was born in 1861 in Rockingham, Massachusetts. He attended Harvard University and the Hartford Theological Seminary and Union Theological Seminary in New York. In 1904 Nutting opened a photography studio in New York. Within a year, he moved to Southby, Connecticut and opened a larger studio. His pictures sold well. In 1907 he opened a branch office in Toronto, Canada. By 1913 Nutting's operation was located in Framingham, Massachusetts. Business boomed. At its peak, Nutting employed over 200 colorists, framers, salesmen, and support staff.

Nutting took all his own pictures. However, printing, coloring, framing, and even signing his name were the work of his employees. Over 10,000 photographs in an assortment of sizes have been identified.

In the 1920s when the sale of pictures declined, Nutting explored a host of other business opportunities. His books, especially the *States Beautiful and Furniture Treasury* series, were the most successful.

Wallace Nutting died on July 19, 1941. His wife continued the business. When Mrs. Nutting died in 1944, she willed the business to Ernest John Donnelly and Esther Svenson. In 1946, Svenson bought out Donnelly. In 1971 Svenson entered a nursing home and ordered the destruction of all of the Nutting glass negatives. A few were not destroyed and are in the hands of private collectors.

References: Michael Ivankovich, *Collector's Guide to Wallace Nutting Pictures,* Collector Books, 1997; Michael Ivankovich, *The Alphabetical & Numerical Index to Wallace Nutting Pictures,* Diamond Press, 1988; Michael Ivankovich, *The Guide to Wallace Nutting Furniture,* Diamond Press, 1990; *Colonial Reproductions* (reprint of 1921 catalog), Diamond Press, 1992; Wallace Nutting (reprint of 1915 catalog), Diamond Press, 1987; Wallace Nutting, *Wallace Nutting General Catalog, Supreme Edition* (reprint of 1930 catalog), Schiffer Publishing, 1977; Wallace Nutting, *Windsors* (reprint of 1918 catalog), Diamond Press, 1992.

Collectors' Club: Wallace Nutting Collector's Club, 2944 Ivanhoe Glen, Madison, WI 53711.

Book, *England Beautiful,* 2nd ed	**$45.00**
Book, *Pathways of the Puritans,* 1st ed, 1930	75.00
Book, *Wallace Nutting Biography,* 1st ed, 1936	100.00
Chair, #390, ladderback	500.00
Print, A Hawthorn Dell, 10 x 12"	150.00
Print, A New Market Belle	275.00
Print, A Sip of Tea, 14 x 17"	285.00
Print, Birch Bend, 16 x 20"	300.00
Print, Brookside Blooms, 10 x 12"	150.00
Print, Decked as a Bride, 12 x 16"	175.00
Print, Dell Blossoms, 14 x 17"	185.00
Print, Easter in Washington, 13 x 16"	375.00
Print, Feathered Elms, 10 x 12"	160.00
Print, Flower Bower, 11 x 14"	160.00
Print, Honeymoon Drive, 10 x 12"	160.00
Print, Larkspur, 14 x 16"	235.00
Print, Mirror with Man Scene, 9 x 26"	700.00
Print, Old Wentworth Days, 14 x 17"	375.00
Print, On the Slope, 11 x 14"	350.00
Print, Spring Red & Greens, 11 x 14"	165.00
Print, Story of Chivalry, 10 x 12"	275.00
Print, The Corner Cupboard, 10 x 16"	325.00
Print, The Swimming Pool, 20 x 30"	350.00

Print, View from Casino, Funchal, Funchal Harbor, Madeira, 12 x 16", $1,540.00. Photo courtesy Michael Ivankovich Antiques, Inc.

Print, The Whirling Candlestand, 11 x 14"	400.00
Print, Twin Sentinels, 10 x 12"	150.00
Print, Yellow Gowned, 16 x 20"	275.00
Silhouette, girl sewing, sitting in rocker, 4 x 4"	45.00

NUTTING-LIKE PHOTOGRAPHS

The commercial success of Wallace Nutting's hand-colored, framed photographs spawned a series of imitators. David Davidson (1881–1967), Charles Higgins (1867–1930), Charles Sawyer (born 1904) and his Sawyer Picture Company, and Fred Thompson (1844–1923) are only a few of the dozens of individuals and businesses that attempted to ride Nutting's coattails.

Most of these photographers followed the same procedure as Nutting. They took their own photographs, usually with a glass plate camera. Prints were made on special platinum paper. Substitute paper was used during World War I. Each picture was titled and numbered, usually by the photographer. A model picture was colored. Colorists then finished the remainder of the prints. Finally, the print was matted, titled, signed, and sold.

References: Carol Begley Gray, *The History of the Sawyer Pictures,* published by author, 1995; Michael Ivankovich, *Collector's Value Guide to Early Twentieth Century American Prints,* Collector Books, 1998.

Bicknell, J Carleton, State House, Augusta, Maine, 10 x 16"	**$250.00**
Bicknell, J Carleton, untitled exterior, close-framed, blue lake nestled between grassy green banks, 5 x 7"	65.00
Carlock, Royal, Capitol Building, close-framed, 5 x 7"	75.00
Carlock, Royal, Jefferson Memorial, close-framed, 4 x 6"	50.00
Davidson, David, A Berkshire Sunset, 7 x 9"	65.00
Davidson, David, Echo Lake Drive to Plymouth, VT, 10 x 12"	110.00
Davidson, David, Golden Sunset, 10 x 12"	110.00
Davidson, David, Jack Frost Palette, 9 x 16"	200.00
Davidson, David, Mary's Garden, 13 x 16"	175.00
Davidson, David, Plymouth, VT, Pres Coolidge's Home, 5 x 7"	85.00
Davidson, David, The Porch Beautiful, 14 x 17"	200.00
Davidson, David, Winooski Palisades, 6 x 8"	125.00
Davidson, David, Ye Olden Tyme, 10 x 12"	110.00
Harris, St Augustine Street, close-framed, 9 x 15"	175.00
Hayward, Stuart, Shin Bone Alley, Bermuda, 1915, 10 x 12"	85.00
Higgins, Charles, Apple Blossom Lane, 8 x 12"	35.00
Higgins, Charles, A Rocky Shore, 8 x 14"	55.00
Higgins, Charles, By the Fireplace, 11 x 14"	125.00
Higgins, Charles, untitled seascape, 7 x 11"	65.00
Sawyer, A Fleet of Boats, Bailey Island, 9 x 16"	175.00
Sawyer, Burke Mountain, 7 x 9"	175.00
Sawyer, Camel's Hump & the Winooski, 9 x 11"	110.00
Sawyer, Echo Lake, 7 x 9"	75.00
Sawyer, Echo Lake, Franconia Notch, 11 x 14"	110.00
Sawyer, Old Man in the Mountains, close-framed, 4 x 6"	65.00
Sawyer, The Old Boat Landing on the Messalonskee, 11 x 14"	150.00
Sawyer, The Swimming Pool, 13 x 16"	145.00
Sawyer, Waterfalls, close-framed, 7 x 11"	75.00
Thompson, Fred, Spinning Days, 7 x 9"	75.00
Thompson, Fred, Ye Duette, 7 x 9"	95.00
Yates, Paul, Digby Basin and Pier, 8 x 12"	110.00

OCCUPIED JAPAN

America occupied Japan from August 1945 until April 28, 1952. World War II devastated the Japanese economy. The Japanese ceramics industry was one of the first to be revitalized. Thousands of inexpensive figurines and knickknacks were exported to the United States and elsewhere in the late 1940s and 1950s.

Not all products made in Japan between 1946 and April 1952 are marked "Occupied Japan." Some pieces simply were marked "Japan" or "Made in Japan." However, collectors of Occupied Japan material insist that "Occupied" be found in the mark for an item to be considered a true Occupied Japan collectible.

Beware of Occupied Japan reproductions, copycats, fantasy pieces, and fakes. Period marks tend to be underglaze. They will not scratch off. Rubber-stamped fake marks will. The marks on recent reproductions are excellent. Shape, form, color, and aging characteristics are now the primary means of distinguishing period pieces from later examples.

References: Florence Archambault, *Occupied Japan For Collectors,* Schiffer Publishing, 1992; Gene Florence, *The Collector's Encyclopedia of Occupied Japan Collectibles, First Series* (1976), *Second Series* (1979), *Third Series* (1987), *Fourth Series* (1990), *Fifth Series* (1992), (1999 value update for series I–V), Collector Books; Anthony Marsella, *Toys From Occupied Japan,* Schiffer Publishing, 1995; Lynette Palmer, *Collecting Occupied Japan,* Schiffer Publishing, 1997.

Collectors' Club: The Occupied Japan Club, 29 Freeborn St, Newport, RI 02840.

Ashtray, Florida state shaped, blue lettering on white
   ground, gold trim $12.00
Berry Bowl, Blue Willow, 4½" d 8.00
Bookends, pr, lady, porcelain. 20.00
Bowl, cov, ceramic, Capo Di Monte style, double han-
   dled, wooded scene with winged cherubs 20.00
Box, figural piano, metal, emb dec 10.00
Candle Holders, pr, bisque, mkd "Ucago," 5" h 25.00
Chocolate Pot, cov, floral dec, mkd "Royal Sealey," 7½" h . . . 20.00
Cigarette Box, blue floral design, gold "Rossetti Chicago" 10.00
Cigarette Dispenser, inlaid wood, mechanical, spring-
   operated sliding drawer dispenses cigarette into bird's
   beak. 55.00
Clock, bisque, double figure, Colonial dancing couple
   atop floral-encrusted case, 10½" h 250.00
Cornucopia, applied roses, Lamore China 30.00
Creamer, cottage scene, Ucagco emblem, 2" h. 10.00
Creamer, white, floral band, gold trim, Aichi China 5.00
Creamer and Sugar, tomato 25.00
Crumb Pan, metal, emb New York scenes. 10.00
Cup, white, pink and green floral dec, gold trim, Hadson
   Chinaware 4.00
Cup and Saucer, Blue Willow 10.00
Cup and Saucer, daisy motif, ftd, Orato China 5.00
Cup and Saucer, dragon motif, blue and white 25.00
Demitasse Cup and Saucer, green, gold and blue floral
   dec, mkd "Ucago China" in silver 15.00
Demitasse Cup and Saucer, pink and white, Colonial
   scene, gold handle, Shofu China 20.00
Demitasse Cup and Saucer, white, floral dec, Chata
   China. 8.00
Demitasse Teapot, cov, red Ucagco emblem. 65.00

Cup and Saucer, multicolor floral dec, white center, pale yellow ground, gold trim, mkd "Noritake, Made in Occupied Japan," 1949, 2⅛" h cup, 5⅝" d saucer, $25.00.

Dish, ceramic, Indian profile, 4½ x 4½". 15.00
Dish, divided, brown, floral dec 6.00
Dish, fish shape, circle "K" mark 8.00
Figurine, angel laying tambourine, Ucagco China, 7¼" h 50.00
Figurine, black musician playing instrument, 2¾" h 10.00
Figurine, Chinese boy and girl coolie, 7¾" h 60.00
Figurine, cow, celluloid, emb cloverleaf design 6.00
Figurine, cowboy, metal, on rearing horse, 3¾" h 15.00
Figurine, Dutch girl with yellow buckets, blue delft, 4½" h . . . 25.00
Figurine, girl with feather in hair, 4⅜" h 12.00
Figurine, girl with song book, Ucagco China 20.00
Figurine, hula dancer 6.00
Figurine, ladybug with lantern, Ucagco China 8.00
Figurine, lady with umbrella, blue delft, 5" h 22.00
Figurine, man with violin, pink and white, gold trim,
   6½" h 25.00
Figurine, organ grinder 10.00
Figurine, wheelbarrow, white, multicolored floral dec,
   1⅝ x 5" 8.00
Fish Bowl Ornament, pagoda with palm trees. 10.00
Harmonica, metal, figual butterfly 25.00
Incense Burner, porcelain, cobalt blue, floral dec, gold
   trim 20.00
Kazoo, tin, stamped "Japan Occupied," 2½" l. 8.00
Lady Head Vase, Oriental girl 10.00
Lamp, Oriental reading book, multicolored 25.00
Lantern, paper, pink with painted flowers, 9½" d 8.00
Lantern, paper, pink with painted red and blue flowers,
   6½" d 6.00
Mug, cowgirl handle, 5½" h 20.00
Necklace, plastic, figural charms, sports motif, 25" l 75.00
Nut Dish, metal, floral border, 6" d 15.00
Oriental Shelfsitters, wooden bench. 20.00
Parasol, paper, Stars and Stripes, 10" d, MIP 12.00
Planter, boy playing guitar, dog at heel, 4⅛" h 10.00
Planter, figural angel, bisque, 5" h, 6" l. 65.00
Planter, girl playing mandolin, 3⅝" h 8.00
Planter, Oriental boy with basket. 5.00

Planter, sleeping musician **6.00**
Planter, swan, white, orange, gold trim. **8.00**
Plate, fruits and flowers design, latticed border **10.00**
Plate, lake in front, shoreline on both sides with pine
  trees and rocks, mountain in background, hp, mkd
  with blue seal, 9" d **35.00**
Plate, sailboat on water with building on shore, moun-
  tains in background, hp, sgd "Y Mezutabi," 9" d **35.00**
Plate, souvenir, souvenir of New Orleans, red **6.00**
Platter, crab apples dec, Ucgco China, 15" l **20.00**
Purse, faux pearl dec **50.00**
Ring Box, metal, heart shaped, emb dec **10.00**
Saki Cup, metal, emb **5.00**
Salt and Pepper Shakers, pr, coffeepots, cobalt blue
  glass, red Bakelite handles, metla tray, orig box. **25.00**
Salt and Pepper Shakers, pr, Dutch boy **12.00**
Salt and Pepper Shakers, pr, gondola, 3 pc **35.00**
Salt and Pepper Shakers, pr, strawberry **20.00**
Salt and Pepper Shakers, pr, totem pole, gold trim **10.00**
Saucer, green, floral dec, Gold China **2.00**
Saucer, red, floral dec, sq, Trimont China **2.00**
Snack Set, ivy dec **12.00**
Tape Measure, celluloid, pig, 2³⁄₈" h **45.00**
Teapot, cov, beehive, ivy dec, Ucagco emblem **22.00**
Toby Mug, man with glasses, 3¹⁄₂" h **20.00**
Vase, ceramic, boy reading book, Hummel type, 5¹⁄₄" h **25.00**
Vase, ceramic, cat watching bird **12.00**
Wind-up, boy on bicycle, celluloid **70.00**
Wind-up, circus elephant, tin, Modern Toys **75.00**
Wind-up, mouse, tin **40.00**

OCEAN LINER COLLECTIBLES

This category is devoted to collectibles from the era of the diesel-powered ocean liner, whose golden age dates between 1910 and the mid-1950s. It is dominated by legendary companies, e.g., Cunard and Holland-American, and ships, e.g., *Queen Elizabeth* and *Queen Elizabeth II*. Many World War II servicemen and women have fond memories of their voyage overseas on a fabulous ocean liner.

Collectors focus primarily on pre-1960 material. Shipboard stores sold a wide range of souvenirs. Printed menus, daily newspapers, and postcards are popular. The category is very much fame driven—the more famous, the more valuable.

References: Myra Yellin Outwater, *Ocean Liner Collectibles,* Schiffer Publishing, 1999; Karl D. Spence, *How to Identify and Price Ocean Liner Collectibles,* published by author, 1991; Karl D. Spence, *Oceanliner Collectibles* (1992), *Vol. 2* (1996), published by author; James Steele, *Queen Mary,* Phaidon, 1995.

Baggage Tag, *Cunard-Anchor Lines,* celluloid, color illus,
  "Fastest Ocean Passenger Service In The World,"
  applied identification on reverse, 1920s **$75.00**
Baggage Tag, *Cunard Line,* color illus of ocean liner
  against setting sun background, insciption "World
  Renowned Services/America/Europe," 1920s **75.00**
Box, *RMS Caronia,* textured silver metal, black enamel
  painted bottom, top engraved "R.M.S. Caronia World
  Cruise 1964," wood lining, with card, Harman Bros
  Ltd, 4 x 4 x 1" **75.00**
Brochure, *Alaska Line,* browntone photos of shipboard **25.00**

Spoon, Red Star Lines, German silver, 5¹⁄₂" l, $75.00.

Calendar, *Aquatania,* diecut celluloid, front with full
  color art depicting *Aquatania* with black and white
  imprint at bottom for local travel office in MI, reverse
  lists US and international ports, 1930, 2 x 4" **50.00**
Deck Plan, *SS Scynthia,* fold-up, color coded layout of
  rooms, black and white photos of sections of ship,
  dated 1925, 10¹⁄₂ x 5¹⁄₄" **15.00**
Keychain, *Home Lines,* gold luster metal spring clip and
  chain suspending pendant depicting cruise ship,
  "M.V. Atlantic," and "Home Lines" on front and rear,
  c1960s **10.00**
Pen, *RMS Queen Elizabeth,* ballpoint, hard molded plas-
  tic and gold toned metal, inset "R.M.S. Queen
  Elizabeth" on side, clear molded plastic end depicts
  colorful plastic ocean liner, orig box with instructions **20.00**
Pinback Button, *Queen Mary,* black and white **20.00**
Pinback Button, *SS Normandie* **20.00**
Playing Cards, Cunard Steamship Company, full color
  Cunard crest logo, complete deck, De La Rue & Co,
  London, 1920–30s, 1 x 2¹⁄₂ x 3³⁄₄" **50.00**
Postcard, *RMS Aquitania,* sepia toned, specs on back **10.00**
Salt and Pepper Shakers, pr, *Cunard,* white, gold border,
  Royal Doulton **25.00**
Vegetable Dish, *Delta Line,* Shenango **8.00**

OLYMPIC MEMORABILIA

Athens, Greece, was the site of the first modern Olympic games in 1896. Baron Pieree de Coubertin, who created the Olympic rings symbol, is the father of the modern games. The first flag featuring the Olympic rings appeared at the 1914 Paris games. The first torch run, carrying the Olympic flame from Greece to the site of the games, occurred in 1936.

Collectors seek anything and everything associated with the games from athletes' medals to officials' badges. Posters are among the high-end items; contemporary "pins" rank at the bottom.

Reference: Roderick A. Malloy, *Malloy's Sports Collectibles Value Guide: Up-to-Date Prices for Noncard Sports Memorabilia,* Attic Books, Wallace-Homestead, Krause Publications, 1993.

Collectors' Club: Olympic Pin Collector's Club, 1836 Fifth St, Schenectady, NY 12303.

1924 Paris VIII Summer, gold winner's IOC pin, silver
  gilt, Olympic rings over laurel wreath and "1924,"
  black presentation case **$145.00**
1928 Amsterdam IX Summer, US Olympic Tryouts tick-
  et, June 16, 1928 session in LA Coliseum, used **60.00**

1932 Lake Placid III Winter, winner's diploma, unassigned **865.00**

1936 Garmisch-Partenkirchen IV Winter, souvenir pinback button, skiing fund raiser, plastic and metal, "Washington Ski Club Olympic Ski Fund, 1936" **65.00**

1938 Berlin XI Summer, official NOC badge, gilt bronze, Olympic rings and Brandenburg Gate, "XI Olympiade Berlin 1936, N.O.K.," dark blue and multicolor fabric ribbon **1,200.00**

1940 Helsinki XII Summer, weightlifting official commemorative pin, cloisonné, colored Olympic rings and "US Olympic 1940," suspended medallion with weightlifter and American flag **300.00**

1948 St. Mortiz V Winter, third place bronze winner's medal, hand holding raised torch, rings, and snow crystals **5,600.00**

1952 Helsinki XV Summer, pennant, colored Olympic rings, "Helsinki 1952," and stadium tower in blue on white ground **70.00**

1952 Oslo VI Winter, official press badge, silvered bronze, "De Vi. Olympiske Vinterleker, Oslo 1952" encircling Olympic emblem within Norwegian legend on blue enamel ground, "Presse" on ID plaque below **500.00**

1956 Melbourne XVI Summer, souvenir scarf, hand rolled, made in Japan, map of Australia behind Olympic torch and colored Olympic rings, events depicted in squares all around, yellow border, "Olympic Games, Melbourne, 22 Nov – 8 Dec 1956" . . . **125.00**

1960 Rome XVII Summer, keychain, bronze, head of Victory on suspended medallion and "Alitalia" **38.00**

1960 Squaw Valley VIII Winter, ashtray, blue ceramic, ski jumper and "Winter Games, Squaw Valley" **112.00**

1968 Grenoble X Winter, mascot, plastic, ©Shuss/JIM **150.00**

1972 Munich XX Summer, ashtray, blue Bakelite sphere, silver lettering "München 1972" around top, 2 hinged chrome lids **40.00**

1928 Amsterdam IX Summer, souvenir plate, mkd "ONT W.W.J. Rozendaal, Petrus Regout & Co., Maastricht, Made in Holland, N.O.C. Officiffi Bord," $275.00. Photo courtesy GVL Enterprises.

1976 Montreal XXI Summer, Quebec license plate, red lettering and Olympic rings on white ground **40.00**

1984 Los Angeles XXIII Summer, baseball batt, 125 Louisville Slugger engraved with "1984 TEAM USA," sgd by all team members, orig plastic tube **250.00**

AUCTION PRICES – NOC TEAM PINS

GVL Enterprises, Olympic Memorabilia Auction, June 1998. Prices include a 12% buyer's premium.

1932 Los Angeles X Summer, cloisonné, Hungarian enameled emblem attached to globe over South America silhouette, 25mm diameter **$220.00**

1936 Berlin XI Summer, cloisonné, Swedish fencing, 2 crossed swords over Olympic rings on dark blue ground, 27 x 42mm **176.00**

1948 London XIV Summer, metal, Czechoslovakian, Bohemian lion on red ground, legend above, 35 x 25mm **165.00**

1956 Melbourne XVI Summer, plastic and metal, Australian Hockey, green Australian logo and legend on yellow ground, 32mm diameter **113.00**

1968 Grenoble X Winter, cloisonné, Soviet athletes, legend within stylized snowflake, flat surface and plain back, 31 x 31mm **77.00**

1976 Montreal XXI Summer, metal, Yugoslavia, rect, Olympic rings above red star on Yugoslav flag with "Jugoslavija, Montreal" below, 41 x 67mm . . . **160.00**

1988 Calgary XV Winter, enamel, Jamaica Bobsleigh, shield shape with 2-man bobsled over stylized mountain, palm trees below, 19 x 11mm . . . **46.20**

PADEN CITY GLASS

The Paden City Glass Manufacturing Company, Paden City, West Virginia, was founded in 1916. David Fisher, formerly president and general manager of the New Martinsville Glass Company, headed the company. When he died in 1933, Sam Fisher, David's son, assumed the presidency.

Initially the company produced pressed lamps, tableware, and vases. Later the company expanded its lines to include hotel and restaurant glassware. The company also acted as a jobber, doing mold work for other glass companies.

Color was one of Paden City's strong points. It offered a wide range of colored glasswares, e.g., amber, blue, cheriglo, dark green, ebony, mulberry, and opal. Thus far over 35 etchings have been identified as being done at Paden City.

In 1949 Paden City purchased the fully automated American Glass Company, continuing production of ashtrays, containers, and novelties. The American Glass acquisition proved disastrous. Paden City Glass ceased operations in 1951.

Reference: Gene Florence, *Very Rare Glassware of the Depression Years, Fifth Series,* Collector Books, 1997.

Ardith, bowl, ftd, 11" **$57.00**

Ardith, candle holders, pr, #555, 1-lite, medallion center, etched, gold trim, 6¼" h **190.00**

Ardith, candy dish, square, green **165.00**

Ardith, cup, yellow **35.00**

Ardith, water set, pitcher with 6 tumblers **550.00**

Black Forest, bowl, rolled edge, 11³/₄" d, pink 250.00
Black Forest, bowl, rolled edge, 13¹/₄" d, green 300.00
Black Forest, cake plate, ftd, pink 80.00
Black Forest, cup, ruby 120.00
Black Forest, ice bucket, pink 200.00
Black Forest, tray, center handle, green 80.00
Crow's Foot, candlesticks, pr, black, silver etch 170.00
Crow's Foot, console bowl and candlestick, 12", black 300.00
Crow's Foot, cup and saucer, ruby 14.00
Crow's Foot, gravy boat, black 70.00
Crow's Foot, tumbler, flat, black 100.00
Cupid, bowl, rolled edge, 11" d, pink 400.00
Cupid, candlestick, pink 175.00
Cupid, comport, pink 325.00
Cupid, ice tub, green 325.00
Cupid, mayonnaise with underplate, green 230.00
Cupid, tray, oval, pink 375.00
Gothic Garden, cake stand, ftd, #411, yellow 100.00
Gothic Garden, comport, ftd, yellow, 6¹/₂" 90.00
Largo, bowl, handled, 11¹/₄" d, ruby 22.00
Lela Bird, cheese plate, green 64.00
Lela Bird, tray, center handle, pink 120.00
Nora Bird, candy dish, cov, flat, pink 325.00
Nora Bird, candy dish, cov, ftd, green 350.00
Nora Bird, mayonnaise with spoon, green 120.00
Nora Bird, plate, 8¹/₂" d, pink 60.00
Orchid, bowl, oval, 2 handled, ruby 250.00
Orchid, candlesticks, pr, ruby 250.00
Orchid, comport, 6⁵/₈" h, ruby 160.00
Orchid, console bowl, ruby 225.00
Orchid, mayonnaise with underplate and spoon, yellow 160.00
Orchid, plate, 10" sq, ruby 85.00
Peacock & Wild Rose, bowl, ftd, 9" d, pink 175.00
Peacock & Wild Rose, bowl, ftd, flared, 11" d, green 175.00
Peacock & Wild Rose, bowl, ftd, rolled, 11" d, pink 175.00
Peacock & Wild Rose, cake plate, ftd, pink 155.00
Peacock & Wild Rose, plate, 10" d, green 120.00
Peacock & Wild Rose, plate, 10" d, pink 120.00
Peacock & Wild Rose, tray, ftd, 10⁷/₈" l, green 150.00
Peacock & Wild Rose, vase, 6¹/₄" h, black 100.00
Peacock & Wild Rose, vase, 8¹/₄" h, elliptical, green 375.00
Peacock & Wild Rose, vase, 10" h, black 325.00
Peacock & Wild Rose, vase, 12" h, green 175.00
Penny Line, cup, amethyst 5.00
Penny Line, goblet 10.00

PADEN CITY POTTERY

Paden City Pottery, located near Sisterville, West Virginia, was founded in 1914. The company manufactured high quality, semi-porcelain dinnerware. The quality of Paden City's decals was such that their ware often was assumed to be hand painted.

The company's Shenandoah Ware shape line was made with six different applied patterns. Sears Roebuck featured Paden City's Nasturtium pattern in the 1940s. Bak-Serv, a 1930s kitchenware line, was produced in solid colors and with decal patterns. Paden City also made Caliente, a line of single-color glazed ware introduced in 1936. Russel Wright designed the company's Highlight pattern, manufactured in five colors between 1951 and 1952. Paden City Pottery ceased operation in November 1963.

Reference: Harvey Duke, *The Official Price Guide to Pottery & Porcelain, Eighth Edition,* House of Collectibles, 1995.

Shenandoah, Poppy pattern, soup bowl, 8" d, $8.00.

Bak-Serv, ball jug $15.00
Bak-Serv, casserole, ribbed bottom, sunken knob, 8¹/₄" d 20.00
Bak-Serv, fruit bowl, ftd, 10" 20.00
Bak-Serv, mixing bowl, 7" d 10.00
Bookends, pr, pouter pigeon 60.00
Elite, creamer and sugar 12.00
Elite, cup and saucer 5.00
Elite, gravy boat 12.00
Elite, plate, 9¹/₄" d 8.00
Highlight, bread and butter plate 8.00
Highlight, creamer and sugar 50.00
Highlight, dinner plate 20.00
Highlight, platter, oval 35.00
Highlight, vegetable bowl, oval 35.00
Manhattan, bread and butter plate, 6" d 1.00
Manhattan, casserole 20.00
Manhattan, cup and saucer 5.00
Manhattan, dish, 6" d 3.00
Manhattan, platter, 12¹/₂" l 12.00
New Virginia, creamer and sugar 12.00
New Virginia, dinner plate 10.00
New Virginia, salad bowl 15.00
New Virginia, teapot 25.00
Papoco, creamer and sugar 12.00
Papoco, cup and saucer 5.00
Papoco, plate, 8¹/₄" d 5.00
Patio, creamer and cov sugar 14.00
Patio, platter 10.00
Patio, salt and pepper shakers, pr 12.00
Regina, casserole 20.00
Regina, creamer and sugar 12.00
Regina, platter, 11¹/₂" l 10.00
Regina, soup bowl, 8" d 10.00
Sally Paden, dish, 6" d 3.00
Sally Paden, platter, 11¹/₂" l 10.00
Shell Crest, casserole, ftd 30.00
Shell Crest, chop plate, 12¹/₂" d 20.00
Shell Crest, cream soup cup and saucer 20.00
Shell Crest, dish, 6¹/₄" d 4.00
Shenandoah, bread and butter plate, 6¹/₄" d 1.00

Shenandoah, creamer and sugar **12.00**
Shenandoah, cup and saucer. **5.00**
Shenandoah, gravy boat with liner. **18.00**
Virginia, casserole. **20.00**
Virginia, plate, 9" d. **8.00**

PAINT BY NUMBER SETS

Paint By Number sets achieved widespread popularity in the early 1950s. They claimed to turn rank amateurs into accomplished painters overnight. Virtually every generic scene, from a winter landscape to horse or clown portraits, was reduced to an outlined canvas with each section having a number that corresponded to one of the paints that came with the set.

Craft House Corporation (Toledo, Ohio), Craft Master (Toledo, Ohio, a division of General Mills), and Standard Toykraft (New York, New York) were among the leading manufacturers. Hassenfeld Brothers (Hasbro) did a number of licensed sets, e.g., Popeye and Superman.

Contemporary licensed paint by number sets, sometimes employing acrylic crayons rather than paint, can be found in today's toy stores. Rose Art Industries makes many of them.

Angela Cartwright Paint By Number Set, Transogram,
1970. . . . . **$30.00**
Batman Sparkle Paint Set, Kenner, 6 pre-numbered
sketches of Batman, 1966 . . . . **45.00**
Buck Rogers, Craft Master, 1980s. **10.00**
Bullwinkle and Rocky Presto Sparkle Painting Set, 6 pic-
tures, 2 comic strip panels, Kenner, 1962 . . . . **35.00**
Darth Vader Glow-In-The-Dark Paint Set, ... **10.00**
Flipper "Stardust" Paint Set, Hasbro, two 7 x 11" pic-
tures, 6 paint vials, application, and instruction sheet,
1966. . . . . **20.00**
Flying Nun Paint By Number Set, Hasbro, 1967 . . . . **50.00**
Fountain Brush Paint Set, Kenner, No 100, 6 brushes, 10
refills, 6 pre-numbered pictures, and animal stencils,
1950s **45.00**
Green Hornet Paint By Number Set, Hasbro, 1966 . . . . **90.00**
Herman & Katnip Deep View Paint Set, Pressman, box
contains 3-D picture with painted background, 6
paints, water bowl, and brush, 1961. . . . . **55.00**

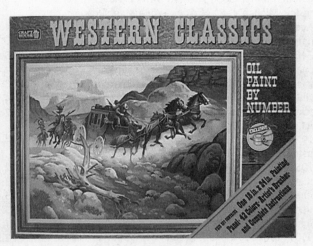

Western Classics, Craft House, $12.00.

Howdy Doody Paint Set, Milton Bradley, 1950s **50.00**
Hulk Comics Paint By Number Set, Hasbro, No. 1, 1982 . . . . **15.00**
Land of the Giants, Hasbro, 1969 . . . . **45.00**
Pebbles and Bamm Bamm Paint By Numbering Coloring
Set, Transogram, 8 inlaid paint tablets, plastic paint
tray, 8 pre-numbered sketches, and brush, 1965 . . . . **55.00**
Snoopy Paint By Number Set, Craft House, 1980s. **20.00**
Space Traveler Paint-By-Number Set, Standard Toykraft,
1950s **100.00**
Star Trek Paint By Number Set, Hasbro, 1972 . . . . **30.00**
Wizard of Oz, Craft Master, 1968 . . . . **20.00**
Wonderful World of Color Pencil and Paint By Numbers,
Hasbro, pre-sketched character boards, colored pen-
cils, and watercolors, 1960s. **30.00**
Wyatt Earp Paint By Number Set, Transogram, 1958 . . . . **60.00**
Yellow Submarine Water Color Set, Craft Master, 1960s **80.00**
Yogi Bear Paint 'em Pals, Craft Master, 1978 . . . . **20.00**

PAIRPOINT

The Pairpoint Manufacturing Company, a silver plating firm, was founded in New Bedford, Massachusetts, in 1880. In 1894 Pairpoint merged with Mount Washington Glass Company and became Pairpoint Corporation. The company produced a wide range of glass products, often encased in silver-plated holders or frames.

In 1938 the Kenner Salvage Company purchased Pairpoint, selling it in 1939 to Isaac N. Babbitt. Babbitt reorganized the company and named it the Gundersen Glass Works. Robert Gundersen, a master glass blower at Pairpoint, guided the new company.

When Gundersen died in 1952, Edwin V. Babbitt, president of National Pairpoint Company, a manufacturer of aluminum windows, chemical ordinance, glass, and toys, purchased Gundersen Glass Works and renamed it Gundersen-Pairpoint Glass Works. The company made a full line of plain and engraved lead crystal.

In 1957 old equipment and a decline in sales forced a closure. Robert Bryden was assigned the task of moving the plant from New Bedford to Wareham, Massachusetts. The Wareham plant closed in February 1958.

Desiring to fill existing orders, Bryden leased facilities in Spain and moved Pairpoint there. In 1968 Bryden, along with a group of Scottish glassworks, returned to Massachusetts. In 1970 Pairpoint opened a new, two-pot factory in Sagamore, Massachusetts.

When Bryden retired in 1988, Robert Bancroft bought the company. Production of lead crystal continues.

References: Edward and Sheila Malakoff, *Pairpoint Lamps,* Schiffer Publishing, 1990; Leonard E. Padgett, *Pairpoint Glass,* Wallace-Homestead, 1979, out of print; John A. Shumann III, *The Collector's Encyclopedia of American Art Glass,* Collector Books, 1988, 1996 value update.

Collectors' Club: Pairpoint Cup Plate Collectors, Box 52D, E Weymouth, MA 02189.

Basket, quadruple silver plated fluted, ftd, with
gadrooned edge, twisted handle with open work, sgd,
8" h, 9¼" d **$82.00**
Bowl, swan, rosaria and crystal glass, shallow, 9½" h,
10¼" w. **100.00**
Calling Card Receiver, clear bubble ball connected to
base, engraved floral dec, 5" d **110.00**

Vase, etched grape pattern, controlled bubble spherical standard, canaria color, 12" h, $250.00.

Dresser Jar, cov, clear green ground, cranberry cov, clear finial, orig label, 4" h **110.00**

Mantel Lamp, 2-arm candelabra form composed of elaborate silver plated metal fittings joined by controlled bubble ball stems and finials, imp "Pairpoint" marks under candlecups, 14" h, 10½" w, price for pair . . . **690.00**

Mantel Vase, goblet form, rosaria, raised on colorless twisted ball, stem, and foot, flame finials, 17" h, price for pair **632.00**

Table Lamp, domed Copley glass shade, hp int with broad landscape scene, mounted on silver plated 2-socket base, 21" h, 16" d **1,092.00**

Table Lamp, reverse painted dome top, Art Deco style, burnished bronze base, sgd, 17½" h **1,760.00**

Tray, china insert with courting couple in 18th-C garb, blue ground, sgd, 8" l, 5½" w **250.00**

PAPERBACK BOOKS

The mass-market paperback arrived on the scene in 1938. Selling for between 15¢ and 25¢, the concept was an instant success. World War II gave paperback book sales a tremendous boost. Hundreds of publishers rushed into the marketplace.

The mid-1940s through the end of the 1950s was the golden age of paperback books.

Price is a key factor in dating paperback books. Collectors focus on titles that sold initially for 75¢ or less. Huge collections still enter the market on a regular basis. Further, many paperbacks were printed on inexpensive pulp paper that has turned brown and brittle over time. Although books in excellent condition are difficult to find, they are available.

Most collections are assembled around one or more unifying themes, e.g., author, cover artist, fictional genre, or publisher.

References: Gary Lovisi, *Collecting Science Fiction and Fantasy,* Alliance Publishing, 1997; Kurt Peer, *TV Tie-Ins: A Bibliography of American TV Tie-In Paperbacks,* Neptune Publishing, 1997; Dawn E. Reno, *Collecting Romance Novels,* Alliance Publishers, 1995; Lee Server, *Over My Dead Body: The Sensational Age of the*

American Paperback: 1945–1955, Chronicle Books, 1994; Moe Wadle, *The Movie Tie-In Book: A Collector's Guide to Paperback Movie Editions,* Nostalgia Books, 1994.

Periodical: *Paperback Parade,* PO Box 209, Brooklyn, NY 11228.

Note: Prices listed are for paperback books in fine conditon.

Arthur, Burt, *Buckaroo,* Signet 782, 1950 . . . . **$5.50**
Asimov, Isaac, *Currents of Space,* Signet 1082, 1953 . . . . **6.00**
Bishop, Sheilah, *House With Two Faces,* Ace K192, 1st printing, 1963 . . . . **1.00**
Bradbury, Ray, *Something Wicked This Way Comes,* Bantam H 2630, 1963 . . . . **3.00**
Buck, Pearl, *Good Earth,* Pocket 11, 13th printing **7.00**
Caldwell, Erskine, *Tobacco Road,* Pan G 159, 3rd printing, 1959 . . . . **7.00**
Cogswell, Theodore, *Third Eye,* Belmont B 50-840, 1st ed, 1968 . . . . **10.00**
Corbin, Gary, *Ringside Tarts,* Pillow 501, 1962 . . . . **5.00**
Davis, Frederick, *Let the Skeletons Rattle,* Hillman 78 . . . . **4.50**
Dexter, William, *Children of the Void,* PB Library 52-357, 1966 . . . . **11.00**
Dickens, Charles, *Christmas Carol,* Pocket 29, 1939 . . . . **20.00**
Ellis, Joan, *Campur Jungle,* Midwood 182, 1st ed, 1962 . . . . . **20.00**
Fair, AA, *Kept Women Can't Quit,* Pocket 4602 . . . . **5.50**
Faulkner, William, *Long Hot Summer,* Signet S 1501, 1958 . . . . **9.00**
Gardner, Erle Stanley, *Case of the Injured Parrot,* Cardinal C 379, 1959 . . . . **3.00**
Gehman, Richard, *Driven,* Gold Medal 387 . . . . **4.50**
Halliday, Brett, *Bodies Are Where You Find Them,* Dell 668 . . . . **5.50**
Hamilton, Bruce, *Hanging Judge,* Hillman 15 . . . . **5.00**
Hitchcock, Alfred, *Hangman's Dozen,* Dell 3428, 1st printing, 1962 . . . . **1.50**
Hopley, George, *Night Has 1000 Eyes,* Dell 679, 1st printing **18.00**
Jakes, John, *Witch of the Dark Gate,* Lancer 75-415 . . . . **5.00**
James, J, *Nympho Nurse,* Gold Star 75 . . . . **4.00**
Kane, Henry, *Who Killed Sweet Sue?,* Signet 2575, 1st revised ed, 1965 . . . . **10.00**
Keating, EP, *Hard-Boiled Mistress,* Magazine Village 7, 1948 . . . . **24.00**
Ketchum, Phillip, *Good Night for Murder,* Dagger 22 . . . . **5.00**
Kingsley, Michael J, *Black Man, White Man, Dead Man,* Ace 06610 . . . . **4.50**
Lariar, Lawrence, *Girl With the Frightened Eyes,* Avon 746, 1956 . . . . **5.00**
Leonard, Elmore, *Bounty Hunters,* Bantam 13295 . . . . **4.00**
Lesser, Milton, *Secret of the Black Planet,* Belmont 01054 . . . . . **3.50**
Levin, Ira, *Kiss Before Dying,* Signet 1147, 1954 . . . . **4.50**
Mackendrick, *Passion for Honor,* Leisure 467, 1977 . . . . **7.50**
MacLean, Alistair, *Puppet on a Chain,* Crest M 1482, 1970 . . . . **4.00**
Marsten, Richard, *Murder in the Navy,* Gold Medal 507, 1955 . . . . **12.50**
McGerr, Patricia, *Seven Deadly Sisters,* Dell 412 . . . . **3.00**
Michener, James A, *Return to Paradise,* Bantam 999 . . . . **5.00**
Miller, M, *Broadwalk,* Nightstand 1851 . . . . **5.50**
Mitchell, Margaret, *Gone With the Wind,* Perma M 9501, 1961 . . . . **2.50**
Munroe, James, *Die Rich Die Happy,* Bantam S 3401, 1st printing, 1967 . . . . **4.50**

Norton, Andre, *Galactic Derelict,* Ace F310 . . . . **1.50**
O'Brien, Robert C, *Mrs. Frisby & the Rats of Nihm,*
    Scholastic 10228. . . . . **3.00**
O'Donnell, Lillian, *No Business Being a Cop,* Crest
    21322, 1987. . . . . **3.50**
Packer, Vin, *Thrill Kids,* Gold Medal 510. . . . . **10.00**
Parker, Robert B., *Passport to Peril,* Dell 568. . . . . **4.00**
Patterson, Rod, *Whip Hand,* Lion 203, 1954. . . . . **4.00**
Powell, Richard, *Shot in the Dark,* Graphic 55 . . . . **7.00**
Prather, Richard S, *Meandering Corpse,* Pocket 55024,
    7th ed, 1969. . . . . **4.00**
Preston, Lillian, *Sex Habits of Single Women,* Beacon
    748, 1964. . . . . **6.00**
Price, Jeramie, *Blackbeard's Bride,* Cardinal C 393, 1st
    printing, 1959. . . . . **3.50**
Rhodan, Perry, *Death Waits in Semi-Space,* Ace 66044 . . . . **1.50**
Robeson, Kenneth, *Mystery Under the Sea,* Bantam
    23648, 1983. . . . . **4.00**
Russell, W, *Berlin Embassy,* MacFadden 50-129 . . . . **5.00**
Ruth, Babe, *Babe Ruth Story,* Pocket 562 . . . . **5.00**
Schneck, Stephen, *Nighclerk,* Grove Press 6376, 1st ed,
    1966. . . . . **10.00**
Sciacca, Tony, *Kennedy & His Women,* Manor 19110,
    1st printing, 1976 . . . . **4.00**
Seeley, ES, *Sorority Sin,* Beacon 278, 1st printing, 1959 . . . . . . **9.00**
Silverberg, Robert, *Time Hoppers,* Avon S 372, 1968 . . . . **2.00**
Steinbeck, John, *Red Pony,* Bantam 402, 1948 . . . . **35.00**
Sturgeon, Theodore, *Baby Is Three,* Magabook 3, 1965. . . . . . . **8.00**
Thorndike, Russell, *Dr. Syn Returns,* Ballantine 23785,
    1974. . . . . **5.00**
Tracy, Don, *Big X,* Pocket 80773, 1st ed, 1976 . . . . **10.00**
Updike, John, *Poorhouse Fair,* Crest R 1177, 1st printing,
    1968. . . . . **4.00**
Van Druffen, John, *Voice of the Turtle,* Armed Services 815. . . . **4.50**
Ward, William, *Jeff Clayton's Thunderbolt,* Westbrook
    46, 1910. . . . . **18.00**
West, Tom, *Bucking for Boot Hill,* Ace 08360, 1st ed, 1970. . . . **8.00**
Weverka, Robert, *Moonrock,* Bantam N 8306, 1973. . . . . **6.00**
Wheeler, Keith, *Reef,* Popular 403, 1st printing, 1952 . . . . **5.00**
Yates, Peter, *If a Body,* Dell 159, 1947 . . . . **10.00**

Agatha Christie,
Crooked House,
Pocket Book 753,
1950, $5.00.

PAPER DOLLS

Paper dolls were used as advertising and promotional premiums. *Good Housekeeping, Ladies' Home Journal,* and *McCall's* are just a few of the magazines that included paper doll pages as part of their monthly fare. Children's magazines, such as *Jack and Jill,* also featured paper doll pages.

The first paper doll books appeared in the 1920s. Lowe, Merrill, Saalfield, and Whitman were leading publishers. These inexpensive stiffboard covered books became extremely popular. Celebrity paper dolls first appeared in the 1940s. Entertainment personalities from movies, radio, and television were the primary focus.

Most paper dolls are collected in uncut books, sheets, or boxed sets. Cut sets are valued at 50% of the price of an uncut set if all dolls, clothing, and accessories are present.

Many paper doll books have been reprinted. An identical reprint is just slightly lower in value. If the dolls have been redrawn, the price is reduced significantly.

References: Lorraine Mieszala, *Collector's Guide to Barbie Doll Paper Dolls,* Collector Books, 1997; Mary Young, *Tomart's Price Guide to Lowe and Whitman Paper Dolls,* Tomart Publications, 1993.

Newsletter: *Paper Doll News,* PO Box 807, Vivian, LA 71082.

Collectors' Club: Original Paper Doll Artist Guild, PO Box 14, Kingsfield, ME 04947.

Note: Prices listed are for paper doll books and sets in unused condition.

Airline Pilot and Stewardess, Merrill, 1953 . . . . **$15.00**
Annie Laurie, Lowe, 1941 . . . . **50.00**
Arlene Dahl, Saalfield, 1953 . . . . **50.00**
Baby Brother, Whitman, 1929 . . . . **50.00**
Baby Dreams, Whitman, 1976. . . . . **5.00**
Baby Nancy, Whitman, 1931. . . . . **50.00**
Baby Sister and Baby Brother, Merrill, 1950 . . . . **10.00**
Barbie, Whitman, 1969. . . . . **25.00**
Bedknobs and Broomsticks, Whitman, 1971. . . . . **25.00**
Betty and Bobby, Saalfield, 1970 . . . . **8.00**
Betty Blue and Patty Pink, Merrill, 1949 . . . . **20.00**
Boarding School, Merrill, 1942 . . . . **30.00**
Bobby Socks, Whitman, 1945 . . . . **45.00**
Bob Hope and Dorothy Lamour, Whitman, 1942 . . . . **200.00**
Brady Bunch, Whitman, 1973 . . . . **45.00**
Bride and Groom, Whitman, 1970. **12.00**
Buffy, Whitman, 1968 . . . . **50.00**
Candy Stripers, Saalfield, 1973 . . . . **8.00**
Cathy Goes to Camp, Merrill, 1954 . . . . **10.00**
Children 'Round the World, Merrill, 1955 . . . . **20.00**
College Style, Merrill, 1941. . . . . **30.00**
Country and Western, Warren Built-Rite Toys, 1950s. **25.00**
Cynthia Pepper Featured on the Margie Television Show,
    Watkins-Strathmore, 1963 . . . . **25.00**
Dennis the Menace Back-Yard Picnic, Whitman, 1960 . . . . . . **40.00**
Donna Reed, Saalfield, 1959. . . . . **30.00**
Donny and Marie, Whitman, 1977 . . . . **15.00**
Dr Kildare and Nurse Susan, Lowe, 1960s **50.00**
Dude Ranch, Lowe, 1943 . . . . **20.00**
Flying Nun, Artcraft, ©1969 Screen Gems, Inc **45.00**
Four Baby Dolls, Whitman, 1953. . . . . **15.00**

Baby Dolls with Cloth-Like Clothes, designed by Kathryn Taylor, Whitman, 1944, $30.00.

Peepul Pals, Whitman, 1967 . . . . 15.00
Peter and Pam, Whitman, 1961 . . . . 20.00
Pixie Doll and Pup, Lowe, 1968 . . . . 25.00
Playmates, Whitman, 1952 . . . . 25.00
Polly and Her Playmates, Merrill, 1951 . . . . 10.00
Portrait Girls, Whitman, 1947 . . . . 50.00
Pretty Changes Barbie, Whitman, 1981 . . . . 8.00
Rainbow Brite, Whitman, 1984 . . . . 2.00
Sabrina and The Archies, Whitman, 1971 . . . . 20.00
Shari Lewis and Her Puppets, Saalfield, 1960 . . . . 30.00
Sleeping Beauty, Whitman, 1959 . . . . 75.00
Storybook Kiddles, Whitman, 1968 . . . . 20.00
Tender Love 'n Kisses, Whitman, 1978 . . . . 5.00
This Is Peggy, Whitman, 1939 . . . . 40.00
Three Sisters, Whitman, 1942 . . . . 35.00
Tini Go-Along, Whitman, 1969 . . . . 10.00
Tony and Tina, Lowe, 1940 . . . . 35.00
Tricia Paper Doll Book, Saalfield, 1970 . . . . 25.00
Tutti, Whitman, 1968 . . . . 20.00
TV Tap Stars, Lowe, 1952 . . . . 20.00
Twiggy, Whitman, 1967 . . . . 75.00
Walt Disney's Cinderella, Whitman, 1989 . . . . 2.00
Wee Wee Baby Doll Book, Lowe, 1945 . . . . 35.00

PAPER EPHEMERA

This is a catchall category. Maurice Richards, author of *Collecting Paper Ephemera,* defines ephemera as the "minor transient documents of everyday life," i.e., material destined for the wastebasket but never quite making it.

Ephemera collecting has a distinguished history, tracing its origins back to English pioneers such as John Bagford (1650–1716), Samuel Pepys (1633–1703), and John Seldon (1584–1654). The Museum of the City of New York and the Wadsworth Athenaeum, Hartford, Connecticut, are two American museums with outstanding ephemera collections. The libraries at Harvard and Yale also have superior collections.

It is wrong to think of ephemera only in terms of paper objects, e.g., billhead, bookplates, documents, tickets, etc. Many three-dimensional items also have a transient quality to them. Advertising tins and pinback buttons are two examples.

References: Norman E. Martinus and Harry L. Rinker, *Warman's Paper,* Wallace-Homestead, Krause Publications, 1994; Gordon T. McClelland and Jay T. Last, *Fruit Box Labels,* Hillcrest Press, 1995; Craig A. Tuttle, *An Ounce of Preservation: A Guide to the Care of Papers and Photographs,* Rainbow Books, 1995; Gene Utz, *Collecting Paper,* Books Americana, Krause Publications, 1993.

Periodicals: *Bank Note Reporter,* 700 E State St, Iola, WI 54990; *PCM (Paper Collectors' Marketplace),* PO Box 128, Scandinavia, WI 54977; *Paper & Advertising Collector (PAC),* PO Box 500, Mount Joy, PA 17552.

Collectors' Clubs: American Society of Check Collectors, PO Box 577, Garrett Park, MD 20896; Fruit Crate Label Society, Rt 2, Box 695 Chelan, WA 98816; The Citrus Label Society, 131 Miramonte Dr, Fullerton, CA 92365; The Ephemera Society of America, Inc, PO Box 95, Cazenovia, NY 13035.

Note: For additional listings see Advertising, Autographs, Catalogs, Cigar Collectibles, Photographs, Postcards, and Posters.

Girl Friends, Whitman, 1944 . . . . 35.00
Glenn Miller Marion Hutton Turnabout Doll Book,
    Lowe, 1942 . . . . 300.00
Goldilocks and the Three Bears, Lowe, 1955 . . . . 20.00
Groovy World of Barbie, Whitman, 1971 . . . . 20.00
Grown-Up Paper Dolls, Merrill, 1936 . . . . 40.00
Here Comes the Bride, Whitman, 1952 . . . . 35.00
Historic Costume Paper Doll Cut-Outs, Whitman, 1934 . . . . 45.00
I Love Lucy, Whitman, 1953 . . . . 175.00
It's a Date, Whitman, 1956 . . . . 30.00
Jean and Her Twin Brother Bob, Lowe, 1940 . . . . 35.00
Juliet Jones, Saalfield, 1964 . . . . 45.00
Junior Miss, Lowe, 1958 . . . . 20.00
Lady Lovely Locks, Whitman, 1987 . . . . 2.00
Laugh-In Party, Saalfield, 1969, MIB 25.00
Little Audrey's Dress Designers Kit, Saalfield, 1962 . . . . . 30.00
Little Ballerina, Whitman, 1959 . . . . 25.00
Little Dolls, Lowe, 1972 . . . . 6.00
Little Girls, Lowe, 1969 . . . . 6.00
Little Miss Christmas and Holly Belle, Merrill, 1965 . . . . . 20.00
Lucy and Her TV Family, Whitman, 1963 . . . . 50.00
Marie Osmond, Saalfield, 1973 . . . . 15.00
Marilyn Monroe, Saalfield, 1953 . . . . 100.00
Mary Poppins, Whitman, 1963 . . . . 25.00
Masquerade Party, Lowe, 1955 . . . . 6.00
Meet Francie, Whitman, 1966 . . . . 20.00
Missy Go-Along, Whitman, 1970 . . . . 8.00
Mod Fashions Starring Marlo Thomas, Saalfield, 1967 . . . 15.00
Molly Dolly, Lowe, 1962 . . . . 15.00
Mother and Daughter, Whitman, 1940 . . . . 50.00
Mrs Beasley, Whitman, 1972 . . . . 45.00
My Fair Lady, Standard Toykraft, ©Columbia Broadcast-
    ing Systems, mid 1960s, orig box 50.00
Nancy and Sluggo, Whitman, 1974 . . . . 15.00
Nanny and the Professor, Artcraft, 1970 . . . . 45.00
New 'N' Groovy PJ, Whitman, 1981 . . . . 10.00
Original Monchhichi, Whitman, 198 . . . . 2.00
Partridge Family, Artcraft, ©1972 Columbia Pictures 45.00
Partridge Family Susan Dey As Laurie, Artcraft, ©1973
    Columbia Pictures 45.00
Patchwork Paper Dolls, Saalfield, 1971 . . . . 6.00

Baptismal Certificate, #60, Abingdon Press, New York
and Cincinnatti, 1925 . . . . **$5.00**

Bill of Sale, Bentley Auto, 1926 . . . . **2.00**

Blotter, Amoco, "Looks Good for '48," baby looking
through telescope, 5½ x 2¾" **10.00**

Blotter, Atlantic Hi-Arc for Driving Power, football play-
ers, 6 x 3" **8.00**

Blotter, Goodrich, "Zippers are made only by
Goodrich," fashionable women and shoes, 6¼ x 3½" **5.00**

Blotter, Green River Whiskey "Blots Out All Your
Troubles," vignette with man and horse, whiskey bot-
tle, 9½ x 4" **50.00**

Blotter, Sweet Wheat Chewing Gum, boy and girl hold-
ing oversized chewing gum pkg, ... **75.00**

Booklet, American Asphalt Paint Co, 1931, 8 x 11" **8.00**

Booklet, Boston, published by Convention Bureau of the
Chamber of Commerce, 1928, 64 pp, 7 x 10" **10.00**

Booklet, Facts You Should Know About Furs, Boston
Better Business National Association Better Business
Bureaus, 1936, 12 pp **5.00**

Booklet, Fleischmann's Recipes, 1924, 48 pp **6.00**

Booklet, Hartford Trial Range, Hartford Electric Light Co,
1930, 12 pp **3.00**

Booklet, Know Your Money, US Secret Service, 1943,
32 pp **10.00**

Booklet, Leyland Motor Corp, Triumph Herald 12/50
model, 1950, 8 pp, 11½ x 9" **10.00**

Booklet, Making Bread, Northwestern Yeast Co, 1939
New York World's Fair **12.00**

Booklet, Pocket Facts About the New '59 Ford **15.00**

Booklet, Salt Lake City, 7 Wonderful 1-Day Trips, 1930,
8 pp, 8 x 9" **7.00**

Booklet, The Latest Books, book buyer's guide, June
1930, 34 pp, 3½ x 6" **8.00**

Booklet, Yosemite Park, National Park Services, 1933,
62 pp **10.00**

Certificate, "A Loving Tribute to the Memory of Rudolph
Valentino," with photo, 1926, 7 x 11" **15.00**

Certificate, appointment to Postmaster General, 1936,
10½ x 13½" **25.00**

Certificate, Guarantee National Trust, 1st United Trust,
1965–66 . . . . **4.00**

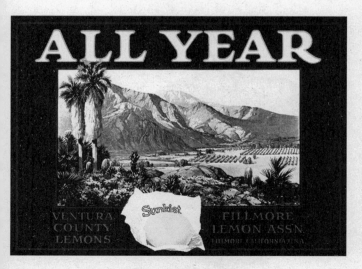

Label, All Year Lemons, 8¾ x 12½", $2.00.

Certificate, Oak Park Republican Committeemen's
Organization, State of Illinois, Office of Secretary of
State, March 5, 1937, engraved, 8½ x 14" **25.00**

Certificate, Pupils Reading Circle, printed, butterflies
and moths, 1933 . . . . **10.00**

Check, Pepsi-Cola, American State Bank, 1946, 10 x 3" **10.00**

Check, Sonoma Vineyards, L M Martinia Grape
Products, Kingsburg, CA, canceled, 1939 . . . . **8.00**

Decal, Triple AAA Root Beer, cartoon girl drinking
through straw, "Just Say Triple 'AAA' Your Favorite Root
Beer, 5¢" 9 x 7" **5.00**

Directory, Gehrig Hotel Directory & Tourist Guide...US
& Canada, 60 pp of black and white road maps, 1927,
256 pp total **10.00**

Directory, Plant Production Directory, Industry's Buying
Guide, Spring 1944, 12 x 11" **18.00**

Fishing License, black lettering on pink ground, 1960,
2½ x 4" **4.00**

Gift Stamps, Weatherbird Shoes, set of 10 . . . . **5.00**

Hunting License, antlerless deer, Warren County, black
and white, 1937 . . . . **5.00**

Label, Bellows Club Bourbon, green, black, and cream . . . . **.75**

Label, Black Hawk Lime Rickey Soda, Indian chief . . . . **.50**

Label, Blue Hill White Corn, house and river **3.00**

Label, Country Maid Evaporated Milk, milk maid carry-
ing pail, blue and red ground **2.00**

Label, Defender Tomato, yacht at sea **1.00**

Label, Del Monte Sliced Yellow Cling Peaches, sliced
peaches in bowl **1.00**

Label, Electric Kidney Beans, gilt dec **2.00**

Label, Elkay Cocoa, emb, cup of cocoa, dark blue, gold,
and white **10.00**

Label, Farmer's Pride Catsup . . . . **.25**

Label, Forest City Lima Beans, autumn leaves, 1920s **2.00**

Label, Shave Rite, blue striped dec . . . . **.25**

Label, Silver Lake Red Beets, sailboat on lake, train,
beets in bowl **3.00**

Label, Three P's Pork & Beans, red, blue, and green **15.00**

Label, Tube City Red Alaska Salmon, fish, white, red, and
blue **7.00**

Letter, Herbert Hoover, letter of thanks, Herbert Hoover
letterhead, dated June 28, 1943 . . . . **125.00**

Letterhead, Case Power Farming Machinery, color, used,
1929 . . . . **18.00**

Letterhead, Floto-Johnson Cycle Co, Steubenville, OH,
black and white, used, 1928 . . . . **20.00**

Letterhead, Winchester Repeating Arms Co, New Haven,
CT, black and white, no picture **10.00**

Liquor License, Railroad Car, New York State Railroad,
early 1960s, 8 x 11" **10.00**

Manual, Ford Model "A" Instruction Book, 1930 . . . . **10.00**

Manual, "How To Invest," Wall Street Investigator, 1923,
16 pp **7.50**

Manuscript, Arthur Conan Doyle, text for article titled
"Notes from a Strange Mailbag," revisions and editor-
ial mark, autographed, 25 pp, 1930, 8 x 10" **7,500.00**

Map, Baron Munchausen (Jack Pearl) Presents His Olde
Mappe of Radio Land As It Lies, folder, 1935, 19 x 14" **15.00**

Map, New York City streets, foldout, 1922, 8½ x 17"
open size **10.00**

Membership Card, Captain Battle Boy's Brigade, 1941–42 . . . . **60.00**

Menu, Down Under Restaurant, Rockfeller Center, red,
white, and blue cov, 4 pp, 1942, 7 x 11" **10.00**

Owner's Manual, Volkswagen, 1965 . . . . **6.00**

Timetable, New England Transportation Co, bus schedule, 1955, 3 x 4¹/₂" folded size, $12.00.

Postcard, Allen-A Silk Stockings adv, 5¹/₂ x 3¹/₄" **4.00**
Poster, Dr Pepper, woman carrying grocery bag, reaching for soda bottle, "frosty, man – frosty!, The Friendly 'Pepper – Upper,'" 1957, 25 x 15" **80.00**
Program, Annual Christmas Dinner, Bank of California, Fairmont Hotel, Dec 15, 1927 . . . . **8.00**
Program, Ringling Bros & Barnum & Bailey Circus, 1953 . . . . **12.00**
Receipt, Hygeia Bottling Works, Pensacola, FL, Bottlers of Soda Water & Coca-Cola **10.00**
Scrap Book, Europe, photos, menus, billheads, booklets, steamships, 1930–31, 50 pp **20.00**
Ticket, 32nd International Bowling Tournament, Detroit, MI, 1932, 5 x 3" **6.00**
Ticket, Cab Calloway & His Cotton Club Orchestra, 1935. . . . . **12.00**
Ticket, Elvis Presley Concert, San Antonio Convention Center, Oct 8, 1974, unused **50.00**
Trapping License, non-resident, white, black ink stamped "1951," red letters and numbers **10.00**

PAPERWEIGHTS

The paperweights found in this category divide into three basic types: (1) advertising, (2) souvenir or commemorative, and (3) contemporary glass. Advertising paperweights were popular giveaway premiums between 1920 and the late 1950s. Cast-iron figural paperweights are the most eagerly sought.

Souvenir paperweights are valued highest by regional collectors. Most were cheaply made. Many are nothing more than a plastic disk with information stenciled on the top or a colored photograph applied to the bottom. No wonder collector interest is limited.

Paperweights enjoyed a renaissance in the 1970s and 80s. Baccarat, Perthshire, and Saint Louis are leading contemporary manufacturers. Many studio glassmakers, e.g. Ray and Bob Banford, Paul Stankard, and Victor Trabucco, make paperweights.

References: Andrew H. Dohan, *Paperweight Signature Canes: Identification and Dating,* Paperweight Press, 1997; Monika Flemming and Peter Pommerencke, *Paperweights of the World,*

2nd Edition, Schiffer Publishing, 1998; John D. Hawley, *The Glass Menagerie: A Study of Silhouette Canes in Antique Paperweights,* Paperweight Press, 1995; Paul Hollister, Jr., *The Encyclopedia of Glass Paperweights,* Paperweight Press, 1969; Sibylle Jargstorf, *Paperweights,* Schiffer Publishing, 1991; Lawrence H. Selman, *All About Paperweights,* Paperweight Press, 1992.

Collectors' Clubs: International Paperweight Society, 761 Chestnut St, Santa Cruz, CA 95060; Paperweight Collectors Assoc, Inc, PO Box 1059, Easthampton, MA 01027.

Advertising, American Oil Products, domed glass, red on white design picturing elephant within circular title of sponsor located in Somerville, MA, inscription "We Want To Do Business With The Man On The Other Side," 1920–30s, 3" d **$75.00**
Advertising, AP Smith Mfg Co, East Orange, NJ, metal, figural fire hydrant, Van Gytenbeek, Inc, NY, 1920s, 3¹/₂ x 6" **75.00**
Advertising, ATA Nelson Co, manufacturers of cut leather, pole, shaft, and auto straps, rect, naked woman hiding behind her hide, 2¹/₂ x 4". **145.00**
Advertising, Badger Insurance, cast iron, figural crouching badger on base, inscribed "The Badger Mutual," and "Fire Insurance Co" on sides, engraved 1887–1937 anniversary dates, dark luster, 2¹/₄ x 3³/₄ x 1³/₄" **75.00**
Advertising, Coates Clipper Mfg Co, Worcester, MA, glass, 2 clippers scene, rect **85.00**
Advertising, JR Leeson & Co, Boston, MA, Linen Thread Importers, vintage spinning wheel, 2¹/₂ x 4" **85.00**
Advertising, Karg Bros, Johnson, NY, metal, figural boar, "Originators of Pigskin Leathers for Fine Gloves" inscribed on base, c1920–30s, 5" l **75.00**
Advertising, Lovell Diamond Cycles, John P Lovell Arms Co, manufacturers of firearms, bicycles, and sporting goods, rect, vintage bicycle, 2¹/₂ x 4" **115.00**
Commemorative, United Nations, NY, brass luster over white metal, 3-D likeness of United Nations complex, green felt bottom, 1950s, 3 x 5 x ³/₄" **20.00**

Apple, red glass, applied green stem, c1970, 4" h, $20.00.

Commemorative, United States Marine Corps, metal, raised Marine Corps symbol circled by raised inscription and outer border, 2½" d **20.00**

Contemporary, Baccarat, clematis, with ruby striped white petals, around pink and yellow millefiori center, blooms on stalk with variegated green leaves, over cerulean blue ground, sgd and dated, acid etched, 1970, 3¹⁄₁₆" d **350.00**

Contemporary, Bob Banford, double yellow blossoms, with trumpet-shaped centers, on stems with pr of buds and slender emerald green leaves, 6 and 1 faceting with fancy diamond cutting around base, signature cane, 2⅞" d **500.00**

Contemporary, Czechoslovakian, morning glories, 3 trumpet shaped blossoms with red, white, and blue stripes, growing from green cushion, beneath cobalt blue, pink, yellow, white, and amber lily, 3" d **180.00**

Contemporary, Daniel Salazar, Lundberg Studios, white fantasy flower, flower with 5 heart-shaped petals around yellow stamens, on dark green stalk with slender green leaves, over iridescent blue ground, sgd and dated, 1982, 3" d **250.00**

Contemporary, Drew Ebelhare, bull's-eye, center complex signature cane encircled by ring of blue and white star canes, set inside sea of white bull's-eye canes, studded with green cogs, yellow and white pastry mold canes, set in red and white stave basket, sgd and dated, 2⅛" d **325.00**

Contemporary, Gordon Smith, pink rose, furled blossom unfolds on stalk with pr of large closed buds and yellow-green leaves, sgd and date, 1987, 3" d **475.00**

Contemporary, Ken Rosenfeld, upright fantasy flower, containing 3 pink blossoms with white stamens, 2 blue blossoms with yellow stamens, and bud on stalk with yellow-green leaves, stem extends down to base, sgd and dated, 1987, 2¾" **200.00**

Contemporary, Perthshire Paperweights, Christmas rose, heart shaped yellow striped white petals around green signature cane center and emerald sepals, blooms on stem with opening bud, over star-cut ground, circular top facet, Limited Edition of 347, 1975, 2½" d **300.00**

Contemporary, Ysart, double clematis garland, flower with gold aventurine striped tomato petals around pink complex cog cane, on stalk with ridged green leaves, flower floats on opaque cobalt blue ground, inside spaced garland of complex cobalt blue, white and lime cog canes, sgd, 2¹⁵⁄₁₆" d **475.00**

PARRISH, MAXFIELD

Maxfield Parrish was born in Philadelphia on July 25, 1870. Originally named Frederick Parrish, he later adopted his mother's maiden name, Maxfield, as his middle name.

Parrish received his academic training at Haverford College and the Pennsylvania Academy of Fine Arts, and spent a brief period as a pupil of Howard Pyle at Drexel. His first art exhibit was held at the Philadelphia Art Club in 1893; his first magazine cover illustration appeared on an 1895 issue of *Harper's Bazaar*. He soon received commissions from *Century Magazine, Collier's, Ladies' Home Journal, Life,* and *Scribners*. In 1897 Parrish was elected to the Society of American Artists.

Parrish established a studio, The Oaks, in Cornish, New Hampshire. He painted a large number of works for advertise-

ments, book illustrations, and calendars. He is best known for the work he did between 1900 and 1940.

Maxfield Parrish died on March 30, 1966.

References: Erwin Flacks, *Maxfield Parrish, 3rd Edition,* Collectors Press, 1998; *Maxfield Parrish: A Price Guide,* L-W Book Sales, 1993, 1996 value update.

Newsletter: *The Illustrator Collector's News,* PO Box 1958, Sequim, WA 98382.

Book, *The Ruby Story Book, Duffield & Co,* color frontispiece, 1921 . . . . **$100.00**

Booklet Advertisement, "New Hampshire," 1942 . . . . **50.00**

Calendar, "Early Autumn," Brown & Bigelow, cropped, 1939, 11 x 16" **250.00**

Calendar, "Golden Hours," Edison Mazda, small, 1929 . . . **1,500.00**

Calendar, "Peaceful Country," Brown & Bigelow, 1963, 8 x 11" **275.00**

Calendar, "Peaceful Night," Brown & Bigelow, 1953 . . . . **250.00**

Calendar, "The Rocks and Rills," Brown & Bigelow, 1944, 16½ x 22" **550.00**

Calendar, "The Village Brook," Our Beautiful America, Brown & Bigelow, 1942 . . . . **150.00**

Calendar, "Twilight," Brown & Bigelow, 1937, 3¼ x 4" **50.00**

Magazine Advertisement, *Century Magazine,* Jun 1921, Hires Root Beer ad **50.00**

Magazine Advertisement, *Hearst's Magazine,* Mar 1922, Jello adv, "The King and Queen" **80.00**

Magazine Advertisement, *Ladies' Home Journal,* Jul 1925, Maxwell House Coffee, "The Broadmoor" **60.00**

Magazine Cover, *Collier's,* Jan 5, 1929, "The End" **95.00**

Magazine Cover, *Ladies' Home Journal,* Jan 1931, woman skiing **100.00**

Magazine Cover, *Life,* Jan 5, 1922, "A Man of Letters" **100.00**

Poster, "Jack and the Beanstalk," Ferry's Seeds, 1923, 19 x 27" **2,000.00**

Print, "Dreaming," 1928, 10 x 18" **500.00**

Print, "Jack Frost," 1936, 12½ x 13" **275.00**

Print, "Spirit of Transportation," 1923, 16½ x 20" **700.00**

Print, "Stars," 6 x 10" **300.00**

Print, "The Canyon," 1924, 6 x 10" **125.00**

Advertising Display, Edison Mazda Bulb Tester, litho metal, c1921, 23¼" h, $3,350.00. Photo courtesy Wm. Morford.

PATRIOTIC COLLECTIBLES

Uncle Sam became a national symbol during the Civil War. His modern day appearance resulted from drawings by Thomas Nast in *Harper's Weekly* and portraits by the artist, James Montgomery Flagg. Uncle Sam played a major role in military recruiting during World Wars I and II.

Other important symbols of American patriotism include Columbia and the Goddess of Liberty, the eagle, the flag, the Liberty Bell, and the Statue of Liberty. Today they are most prevalent during national holidays, such as Memorial Day and the Fourth of July, and centennial celebrations. They often appear subtley in print advertising and television commercials.

Reference: Gerald E. Czulewicz, Sr., *The Foremost Guide to Uncle Sam Collectibles,* Collector Books, 1995.

Collectors' Club: Statue of Liberty Collectors' Club, 26601 Bernwood Rd, Cleveland, OH 44122.

Constitution, bread and butter plate, clear glass, Constitution signer's names, emb "1776–1876" **$80.00**
Eagle, fan, diecut cardboard, eagle image on front, ad for Ontario Drill Co Baltimore on reverse, wooden handle, 8¼ x 9" **70.00**
Eagle, license plate attachment, litho tin, emb "We Serve," red, white, and blue, gold eagle, 4½ x 10" **25.00**
Flag, automobile mount, tin, Universal Fixture Corp, NY. **10.00**
Flag, Cracker Jack premium, litho tin, red, white, and blue, patriotic inscription on base, 1940s **20.00**
Flag, figurine, "Free Speech Mike," plaster, upper torso formed in image of radio microphone in matching patriotic finish to hat crown, each side of base with "KMPC," base mke "710 KC," late 1960s, 5¾" h. **175.00**
Flag, matchcover, "I am Proud to Be an American," soldier saluting, red, white, and blue **10.00**
Flag, stickpin, brass, emb gold bug, red, white, and blue cloth flag **70.00**
Flag, tie, red, white, and blue, black, white embroidered "Wilson/Marshall," 47" l **50.00**
Flag and Shield, window sticker, "Hoover & Curtis," diecut, red, white, and blue, 1932, 5 x 7½" **45.00**

Independence Hall, postcard, sepia **5.00**
Liberty Bell, bank, cast metal, coin slot at top, "Wallace '68," 3¾" h **20.00**
Liberty Bell, paperweight, glass, full color scene of White House, souvenir of 1926 Sesqui-Centennial, 2½ x 4 x 1". **20.00**
Statue of Liberty, tie slide, Boy Scout, emb brass, detailed raised Statue, scroll banner at base, c1930 . . . . **22.00**
Uncle Sam, bank, cast iron, c1974 . . . . **15.00**
Uncle Sam, creamer, Royal Winton, c1920 . . . . **75.00**
Uncle Sam, jigsaw puzzle, hound dog dressed as Uncle Sam, Wolverine World-Wide, 19 x 12¾" **10.00**
Uncle Sam, paper dolls, Uncle Sam's Little Helpers, Ann Kovach, 1943 . . . . **15.00**
Uncle Sam, sign, Dolly Varden Chocolates, cardboard, Uncle Sam in chair holding newspaper, 1920s, 10 x 14¾" **75.00**
Uncle Sam, stamp machine, #4819, automatic, red, white and blue, Uncle Sam illus on front, nickel and dime slots, c1945 . . . . **100.00**
US Capitol, bowl, Capitol in relief, Syroco, oval **12.00**

PEANUTS

In 1950 Charles M. Schulz launched Peanuts, a comic strip about kids and a beagle named Snoopy. Charlie Brown, Lucy, Linus, and the Peanuts gang have become a national institution. They have been featured in over sixty television specials, translated in over a dozen languages.

Charles M. Schulz Creative Associates and United Features Syndicate have pursued an aggressive licensing program. Almost no aspect of a child's life has escaped the licensing process.

Given this, why is the number of Peanuts collectors relatively small? The reason is that the strip's humor is targeted primarily toward adults. Children do not actively follow it during the formative years, i.e., ages seven to fourteen, that influence their adult collecting.

References: Jan Lindenberger, *The Unauthorized Guide to Snoopy Collectibles, 2nd Edition* (1998), *More Snoopy Collectibles* (1997), *Peanut Gang Collectibles* (1998), Schiffer Publishing.

Collectors' Club: Peanuts Collector Club, 539 Sudden Valley, Bellingham, WA 98226.

Bank, plastic, Snoopy, holding football, 16" h **$20.00**
Book, *Happiness Is a Warm Puppy,* Schulz, Charles M, 60 pp, 1962 . . . . **8.00**
Bubble Pipe, hard molded plastic, Snoopy sitting in bathtub full of bubbles, shower pipe as mouthpiece and paddle wheel in tub as bubble mechanism, Chemtoy, 1958 . . . . **20.00**
Doll, Belle, molded plastic, black fabric ears, wearing colorful jumper, purse, and hard molded plastic roller skates, complete with change of clothing, Knickerbocker, 1966, 7½" h. **35.00**
Doll, Charlie Brown, molded plastic and soft molded rubber, fabric outfit, c1960s, 6¾" h **40.00**
Drinking Glass, Camp Snoopy, McDonald's premium **6.00**
Figure, Snoopy, asleep on top red vinyl dog house, Chex premium **10.00**
Film, 16mm, color, sound, orig TV commercial for "Race For Your Life Charlie Brown," with box **15.00**

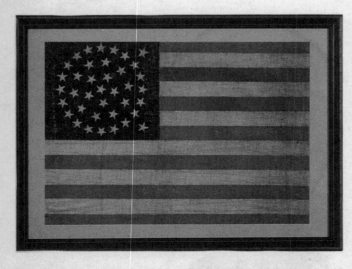

Civil War Flag, cloth, 37 states, fading and repair, framed, 31" h, 22" w, $440.00. Photo courtesy Collectors Auction Services.

Collector Plate, Peanuts Mother's Day series, "Linus," Schmid, Japan, limited to 15,000, 1972, $10.00.

Hair Brush, Snoopy, white hard molded plastic, black
and red details, Avon, 1970, 5³/₄" l **20.00**
Lunch Box, Lunchtime with Snoopy, orange, hard mold-
ed plastic, dome type, depicts Snoopy and Woodstock
on sides, thermos depicts Woodstock and Snoopy eat-
ing lunch by doghouse, Thermos **15.00**
Matchcover, Snoopy, 1961 Ford Falcon adv **5.00**
Music Box, Flying Ace Snoopy on doghouse, wood,
Schmid **85.00**
Paperweight, Snoopy dancing in front of hearts, "Love
Me Now & Beat The Crowd" **10.00**
Playset, Snoopy's Beagle Scouts Colorforms Stand-Up
Playset **35.00**
Press Photo, Snoopy with Easter basket **5.00**
Press Release, with photo from 1996 premiere broadcast
of "Charlie Brown's All-Stars" **20.00**
Puzzle, frame tray, Charlie Brown, Lucy, Sally, and
Schroeder having party, ©1960 Golden **10.00**
Radio, figural Snoopy, plastic, Determined #351, 1975 . . . . . **18.00**
Ramp Walker, Snoopy, plastic, Aviva **10.00**
Ramp Walker, Woodstock, plastic, yellow, feather in
band on head, Avia **10.00**
Record, radio commercials for "A Boy Named Charlie
Brown" **20.00**
Shampoo Bottle, Charlie Brown hugging Snoopy, Avon,
1971 . . . . **10.00**
Snoopy Sno-Cone Maker, complete **25.00**
Soap Dish, Snoopy lying on back, Avon, 7¹/₂" l **20.00**
Toothbrush, Snoopy on doghouse stand, plastic, battery
operated, Kenner #30301, 1972 . . . . **40.00**
Toy, Snoopy in the Music Box, litho tin box, white plas-
tic fabric Snoopy inside, Mattel, 1966 . . . . **35.00**
Toy, Snoopy's Airplane, diecast metal, molded plastic
Snoopy figure as Flying Ace in bi-winged airplane,
Aviva, 1975, MIB **85.00**
Wall Decoration, molded plastic, 3-D Snoopy in profile,
aqua ground, 1965 . . . . **45.00**
Watch, Snoopy face on blue ground, arms serve as hour
and minute hands, Timex, 1958 . . . . **35.00**

PEDAL CARS

Pedal car is a generic term used to describe any pedal-driven toy. Automobiles were only one form. There are also pedal airplanes, fire engines, motorcycles, and tractors.

By the mid-1910s pedal cars resembling their full-sized counterparts were being made. Buick, Dodge, Overland, and Packard are just a few examples. American National, Garton, Gendron, Steelcraft, and Toledo Wheel were the five principal pedal car manufacturers in the 1920s and 30s. Ertl, Garton, and Murray made pedal cars in the post-1945 period. Many mail-order catalogs, e.g., Sears, Roebuck, sold pedal cars. Several television shows issued pedal car licenses during the mid-1950s and 60s.

Pedal car collecting is serious business in the 1990s. The $10,000 barrier has been broken. Many pedal cars are being stripped down and completely restored to look as though they just came off the assembly line. Some feel this emphasis, especially when it destroys surviving paint, goes too far.

References: *Evolution of the Pedal Car, Vol. 1* (1989, 1996 value update), *Vol. 2* (1990, 1997 value update), *Vol. 3* (1992), *Vol. 4* (1993, 1997 value update), *Vol. 5* (1999), L-W Book Sales; Andrew G. Gurka, *Pedal Car Restoration and Price Guide,* Krause Publications, 1996.

Newsletter: *The Wheel Goods Trader,* PO Box 435, Fraser, MI 48026.

Collectors' Club: National Pedal Vehicle Assoc, 1720 Rupert NE, Grand Rapids, MI 49505.

Airplane, pressed steel, painted red, rubber tires, single
propellor, hinged wings flip up, 53" l, 26" h **$2,500.00**
Case Agri King, missing steering shaft and steering wheel . . . **525.00**
JDA, coffin block, traces of orig red paint still visible **25,000.00**
Murray Champion, metal, black with white trim, hard
rubber wheels and pedals, straight side, professional-
ly restored, 34" l, 22" h, 15" w **1,200.00**
Murray "Sad Face" No. 7 Sand & Gravel Dump Truck,
pressed steel, rubber tires, Murray decal in seat, lift
lever and back dumps, 49" l, 23" h **1,200.00**

Farmall 560, 95% original, $1,500.00. Photo courtesy Aumann Auctions.

Oliver 1800 Checkerboard **4,400.00**
Oscar Mayer Weinermobile, plastic with metal mecha-
nism, 46" l, 21" h **200.00**
Racer #9, Miracle Pedal Car Co, red aluminum body,
plush upholstery, pneumatic tires, cast aluminum grill,
chrome exhaust, simulated gauges on dash, 60" l,
31" h **3,410.00**
Racer, pressed steel, rubber tires, horn, orig green with
yellow trim, 32" l, 20" h, 20" w **1,600.00**
Tru-matic Hand Pedal Tractor. **475.00**

AUCTION PRICES – PEDAL CARS

Aumann Auctions, Inc., Lee Richardson Estate Auction,
March 13–15, 1998. All vehicles are complete.

AC D-17.	**$1,500.00**
Case 400	**2,500.00**
Case 800	**1,400.00**
Cat Dozer.	**1,800.00**
Farmall 450.	**950.00**
Fire Ball, pedal racer	**450.00**
Ford 6000 Commander, blue and white	**1,700.00**
Hiesler Tractor, pressed steel, red, large	**3,500.00**
IH 856	**750.00**
JD 10, 3-hole.	**750.00**
JD 620	**900.00**
JD LG 60 Tractor, green, #440	**800.00**
MM TOT, orig condition	**1,050.00**
Oliver Super 88	**2,000.00**
Pedal Mustang.	**450.00**
Silver King Tractor, silver, red trim, NOS.	**3,100.00**
Stelber Super Trak, red, yellow trim, NOS.	**1,350.00**
Tractall, with loader	**625.00**

PENNANTS

Felt pennants were popular souvenirs from the 1920s through the end of the 1950s. College sports pennants decorated the walls of dormitory rooms during this period. Pennants graced the radio antenna of hot rods and street rods. A pennant served as a pleasant reminder of a trip to the mountains, shore, or an historic site.

Most commercial pennants were stenciled. Once a pennant's paint cracks and peels, its value is gone. Handmade pennants, some exhibiting talented design and sewing work, are common.

Ali-Frazier Fight, "World's Heavyweight Championship
Fight," white felt, red and black lettering and crown,
black and white screened photos of Frazier and Ali,
1974, 21" l, 8" h **$50.00**
Baseball Teams, set of 10 miniature felt pennants, tradi-
tional team colors, various logos, American Nut &
Chocolate Co premium, 1940s, each measures 3¼" l,
1½" h, price for 10 . . . . **85.00**
Chicago White Sox, "White Sox, Zeke Bonura," navy
blue felt, white lettering, 1937s, 4¼" l, 2¼" h **18.00**
Coney Island, "Souvenir of Coney Island," dark red felt,
female sunbather, white lettering, dark blue end strip,
1940s, 11" l, 4½" h **20.00**
FDR, "I Was At the 1st Third Term Inauguration, January
20, 1941," red felt, white FDR portrait, Capitol build-
ing, and lettering, yellow end strip, 12" l, 4½" h **75.00**
Gene Autry and Champ, "Back in the Saddle Again,
Gene Autry and Champ," purple felt, white image of
Autry on rearing Champ, white lettering and end strip,
early 1940s, 28" l, 11" h **60.00**
Green Hornet, images of Green Hornet, Kato, and Black
Beauty, orange felt, green and white lettering, ©1966
Greenway Products, Inc., 8½" l, 4½" h **50.00**
Humphrey/Muskie, "Vote Democrat," blue felt, black
and white jugate photos, 20" l, 9" h **12.00**
Indianapolis Speedway, "Indianapolis, Souvenir of
Speedway, May 30th 1939," green felt, crossed check-
ered flags and race car, white lettering, red end strip,
26½" l, 11½" h **75.00**
New York World's Fair, "I Was There Closing Day,
October 27, 1940, New York World's Fair," cornflower
yellow felt, dark blue ink Trylon and Perisphere and
lettering, 1940, 8½" l, 3½" h **40.00**
Seattle '62 Expo, "Seattle World's Fair," black felt, white
lettering, blue, yellow, lavender, and orange circular
Century 21 Exposition design, gold end strip and
streamer strips, 27" l, 9" h **15.00**
War Effort, "Remember Pearl Harbor, Let's Go
Americans," blue felt, white lettering, image of Uncle
Sam flanked by civilian workers on left and military
personnel on right, 23" l, 7" h **60.00**
World War II, "Target for 1943 from the Boys Down
Under," dark blue felt, white lettering, Australian sol-
dier and US sailor riding kangaroo and holding spear
aimed at Japanese flag target on trouser seat of fleeing
Japanese soldier, banner attached to spear reads
"AUS**USA," 24½" l, 9½" h **100.00**

Gettysburg, PA, orange felt, multicolored screened images of historic landmarks, gold end strip and streamer strips, 28" l, 11¾" h, $10.00.

Walt Disney World, purple felt, multicolored castle, gold flocked lettering, gold end strip and streamer strips, 24" l, 8¾" h, $15.00.

PENNSBURY POTTERY

In 1950 Henry Below, a ceramic engineer and mold maker, and Lee Below, a ceramic designer and modeler, founded Pennsbury Pottery. The pottery was located near Morrisville, Pennsylvania, the location of William Penn's estate, Pennsbury.

Henry and Lee Below previously worked for Stangl, explaining why so many forms, manufacturing techniques, and motifs are similar to those used at Stangl. A series of bird figurines were Pennsbury's first products.

Although Pennsbury is best known for its brown wash background, other background colors were used. In addition to Christmas plates (1960–70), commemorative pieces, and special order pieces, Pennsbury made several dinnerware lines, most reflecting the strong German heritage of eastern Pennsylvania.

The company employed local housewives and young ladies as decorators, many of whom initialed their work or added the initials of the designer. At its peak in 1963, Pennsbury had 46 employees.

Henry Below died on December 21, 1959; Lee Below on December 12, 1968. Attempts to continue operations proved unsuccessful. The company filed for bankruptcy in October 1970 and the property was auctioned in December. The pottery and its supporting buildings were destroyed by fire on May 18, 1971.

References: Harvey Duke, *The Official Price Guide to Pottery and Porcelain, Eighth Edition,* House of Collectibles, 1995; Lucile Henzke, *Pennsbury Pottery,* Schiffer Publishing, 1990; Mike Schneider, *Stangl and Pennsbury Birds,* Schiffer Publishing, 1994.

REPRODUCTION ALERT: Some Pennsbury pieces (many with Pennsbury markings) have been reproduced from original molds purchased by Lewis Brothers Pottery in Trenton, New Jersey. Glen View in Langhorne, Pennsylvania, marketed the 1970s' Angel Christmas plate with Pennsbury markings and continued the Christmas plate line into the 1970s. Lenape Products, a division of Pennington, bought Glen View in 1975 and continued making products with a Pennsbury feel.

Amish, ashtray, "St Wonders Me"	$30.00
Amish, bread plate, "Give Us This Day," 8" d	28.00
Amish, creamer and sugar, 4" h	28.00
Amish Woman, pitcher, 5" h	28.00
Beer Mug, Amish couple	40.00
Beer Mug, Quartet	40.00
Bird, gold finch, #102, sgd "K"	245.00
Bird, wren, #109, sgd "K"	125.00
Birds, tray, octagonal, 5 x 3"	18.00
Black Rooster, butter dish	50.00
Black Rooster, cake stand	82.00
Black Rooster, coffee mug	30.00
Black Rooster, eggcup	10.00
Black Rooster, salt and pepper shakers, pr, black tops	28.00
Boy and Girl, pie pan, 9½" d	242.00
Commemorative, tray, Fidelity Mutual Life	14.00
Courting Buggy, plate, 8" d	75.00
Dutch Talk, bowl, 11" d	275.00
Gay Ninety, beer mug	40.00
Gay Ninety, creamer and sugar	40.00
Hex, creamer and sugar, 4" h	45.00
Making Pie, cookie jar	190.00
Mother Serving Pie, pie pan, 9" d	160.00
Red Barn, coffee mug	30.00
Red Barn, pitcher, 6¼" h	45.00

Pennsylvania Railroad, dish, "1856 Tiger," 7⅞" l, $45.00.

Red Rooster, bowl, piecrust, 6" d	10.00
Red Rooster, bowl, plain edge, 6" d	8.00
Red Rooster, butter, ¼ lb	50.00
Red Rooster, creamer, 4" h	25.00
Red Rooster, cup	6.00
Red Rooster, dinner plate	20.00
Red Rooster, pitcher, 2" h	30.00
Red Rooster, plate, 6" d	10.00
Red Rooster, plate, 8" d	8.00
Red Rooster, platter, 13" l	15.00
Red Rooster, salad bowl	35.00
Red Rooster, saucer	6.00
Red Rooster, sugar, 4" h	25.00
Red Rooster, teapot	65.00
Red Rooster, vegetable, 2 pt	35.00

PENS & PENCILS

Fountain pens are far more collectible than mechanical pencils. While a few individuals are beginning to collect ballpoint pens, most are valued by collectors more for their advertising than historical importance. Defects, e.g., dents, mechanical damage, missing parts, or scratches, cause a rapid decline in value. Surprisingly, engraved initials, a monogram, or name has little impact on value.

Lewis Waterman developed the fountain pen in the 1880s. Parker, Sheaffer, and Wahl-Eversharp refined the product. Conklin, Eversharp, Moore, Parker, Sheaffer, Wahl, and Waterman were leading manufacturers. Reynolds' introduction of the ballpoint pen in late 1945 signaled the end for the nib fountain pen.

Sampson Mordan patented the mechanical pencil in 1822. Early mechanical pencils used a slide action mechanism. It was eventually replaced by a spiral mechanism. Wahl-Eversharp developed the automatic "click" mechanism used on pens as well as pencils.

Fountain pen values rose dramatically from the late 1970s through the early 1990s. Many of these values were speculative. The speculative bubble burst in the mid-1990s. Today, prices are extremely stable with common fountain pens a very difficult sell.

References: Paul Erano, *Fountain Pens,* Collector Books, 1999; George Fischler and Stuart Schneider, *Fountain Pens and Pencils, 2nd Edition,* Schiffer Publishing, 1998; Henry Gostony and Stuart

Schneider, *The Incredible Ball Point Pen,* Schiffer Publishing, 1998; Regina Martini, *Pens & Pencils, 2nd Edition,* Schiffer Publishing, 1998; Stuart Schneider and George Fischler, *The Illustrated Guide to Antique Writing Instruments, Second Edition,* Schiffer Publishing, 1997.

Periodical: *Pen World Magazine,* PO Box 6007, Kingwood, TX 77325.

Newsletter: *Float About* (floaty pens), 1676 Millsboro Rd, Mansfield, OH 44906.

Collectors' Clubs: American Pencil Collectors Society, 7640 Evergreen Dr, Mountain View, WY 82939; Pen Collectors of America, PO Box 821449, Houston, TX 77282.

PENS

Durabilt Ribbon, black pearl marbleized, gold-filled trim, lever filled, 1930	**$50.00**
Gold Medal, blue marbleized, gold-filled trim, lever filled, 1934	225.00
Grieshaber #016, Ambassador, burgundy, gold-filled trim, lever filled, 1929	250.00
Maroon, stainless steel cap, chrome-plated trim, 1950	32.00
Parker, Blue Diamond Vacumatic, gold pearl stripes, 1940	90.00
Parker, Hopalong Cassidy, black plastic and silvered metal, 3-D plastic portrait, c1950, 6" l	50.00
Parker, Parkette, red, nickel silver cap, chromium-plated trim, lever filled, 1951	20.00
Sheaffer's, #74TR Lifetime, black, gold-filled trim, lever filled, 1928	150.00
Sheaffer's, emerald pearl stripes, 1939	60.00
Wahl-Eversharp Gold Seal Doric, black, gold-filled trim, lever filled, 1931	300.00
Waterman, Corinth Taperite, blue, chrome cap, gold-filled trim, lever filled, 1949	50.00
Waterman, Ideal #452, SS, 1925	150.00

PENCILS

American Foundry and Mfg Co, St. Louis, MO, mechanical, red, white, and blue, 1950s	**$50.00**
Eversharp, repeating, dark blue, gold-filled trim, 1941	50.00
Kendall Oil adv, "The 2000 Mile Oil," mechanical, metal and plastic	15.00
"Remember Pearl Harbor, United We Stand, We Will Win," red, white, and blue plastic, local business sponsor adv, 5" l	65.00
Secretary Pen Co, Elsie, ©Borden Co, mechanical, 1930–40, 5" l	60.00

Pencil, Lion Head Motor Oil, black and orange on cream ground, calendar on end, 5³/₄" l, $72.00. Photo courtesy Collectors Auction Services.

PEN/PENCIL COMBINATIONS

Diamond Medal Diplomat, black and green pearl marbleized, gold-filled trim, lever filled, 1932	**$350.00**
Sheaffer's, 5-30, black, gold-filled trim, lever filled, 1936	225.00

PEPSI-COLA

Caleb D. Bradham, a pharmacist and drugstore owner in New Bern, North Carolina, developed "Brad's Drink," a soda mix, in the mid-1890s. By 1898, Brad's Drink had become Pepsi-Cola. By 1902 Bradham was promoting Pepsi-Cola on a full-time basis. Two years later he sold his first franchise.

In 1910 the Pepsi-Cola network consisted of 250 bottlers in 24 states. Investing in the sugar market, Pepsi-Cola found itself in deep financial difficulties when the market collapsed immediately following World War I. Roy Megargel, a Wall Street financier, rescued and guided the company out of its difficulties. Pepsi-Cola survived a second bankruptcy in 1931.

In 1933 Pepsi-Cola's fortunes soared when the company doubled its bottle size and held its price to a nickel. Walter Mack (1938 to 1951) provided the leadership that enabled Pepsi to challenge Coca-Cola for the number one spot in the soda market. "Pepsi-Cola Hits The Spot, Twelve Full Ounces That's A Lot" was one of the most popular advertising jingles of the 1950s.

Pepsi Co., a division of Beatrice, enjoys a worldwide reputation, outselling Cola-Cola in a number of foreign countries. This is one reason why many foreign buyers have an interest in Pepsi-Cola memorabilia.

Beware of a wide range of Pepsi-Cola reproductions, copycats, fantasy items, and fakes. The 1970s Pepsi and Pete pillow, a Pepsi double bed quilt, and a 12" high ceramic statute of a woman holding a glass of Pepsi are a few examples.

Collectors place little secondary market value on contemporary licensed products.

References: James C. Ayers, *Pepsi-Cola Bottles Collectors Guide,* RJM Enterprises, 1995 (1999 value update); Everette and Mary Lloyd, *Pepsi-Cola Collectibles,* Schiffer Publishing, 1993; Bill Vehling and Michael Hunt, *Pepsi-Cola Collectibles, Vol. 3* (1993, 1995 value update), L-W Book Sales.

Collectors' Club: Pepsi-Cola Collectors Club, PO Box 1275, Covina, CA 91722.

Blotter, "Pepsi and Pete," "5¢," bottle illus with comical
   figures, 1930s **$55.00**
Booklet, *Hospitality Recipes Out of a Pepsi-Cola Bottle,*
   1940s **20.00**
Can, aluminum, lift tab, "Seasons Greetings" **5.00**
Clock, plastic, light-up, metal case, "Say Pepsi Please
   Pepsi-Cola," 1960s, 16" sq **75.00**
Cone Cup Holder, Bakelite, complete with straw and
   cone cup, 1940s **85.00**
Cooler, salesman's sample, cast aluminum, blue, logo on
   sides, 1940s, 12 x 7½ x 11½" **2,600.00**
Display, diecut cardboard, "Pepsi-Cola Double Size,
   5¢," wih refilled and recapped 1930s Pepsi bottle,
   1930s **650.00**
Dispenser, counter top, probably mfg by Multiplex,
   1950s **525.00**
Drinking Glasses, set of 9, red lettering on white, with
   syrup line, 10 oz, 1930–40s **120.00**
Fan Pull, cardboard, 2-sided, Pepsi cop holding 6-pack
   bottles, 1940, 4 x 7¾" **1,000.00**
Festoon, cardboard, 7 pc, diecut, 2-sided, Pepsi and Pete
   illus, 1930s **1,400.00**
Flange Sign, aluminum, diecut, bottle cap and hand,
   c1940s, 17 x 15" **450.00**
Kickplate, tin, emb, "Enjoy Pepsi-Cola America's Biggest
   Nickels Worth," 1940s, 10 x 30" **550.00**
Letterhead, Pepsi-Cola Bottling Company, Jackson, TN,
   1940s **10.00**
Radio, Bakelite, figural radio, orig decals, 1947, 24" h **280.00**
Salt and Pepper Shakers, 2-in-one, orig box **170.00**
Sign, laminated wood, 2-sided, arrow, "Pepsi-Cola Sold
   Here Beverage Dept," 1940s **650.00**
Sign, metal, "5¢," with "Pepsi-Cola Refreshing
   Healthful" on bottle, 1930s, 16 x 48" **500.00**

Chalkboard, painted tin, 30" h, 19½" w, $275.00. Photo courtesy Collectors Auction Services.

Sign, plastic, light-up, wood frame, Pepsi polar bear with
   "Ice Cold Drinks," 1950s, 14 x 24" **950.00**
Sign, plastic and tin, light-up, figural Diet Pepsi 6-pack,
   1960–70s, 7 x 7" **975.00**
Sign, "Say Pepsi Please" with bottle and cap, 1960s, 18
   x 48" **160.00**
Sign, silk screen and decals on glass, wood base, bottle
   cap, "20¢, 10¢," 1950–60s **210.00**
Sign, tin, diecut bottle with "5¢," 1940s, 29" h **500.00**
Sign, tin, emb, "Curb Service Pepsi-Cola Ice Cold Bigger
   Better," 1939 . . . . **325.00**
Sign, tin, figural bottle cap, slant top, 1950s, 30" d **170.00**
Thermometer, metal frame, plexiglass front, "Diet
   Pepsi" in center, 1960–70s, 32 x 46" **90.00**
Thermometer, tin, emb, "Pepsi-Cola The Light
   Refreshment," raised cap top, 1950s, 7 x 27" **200.00**
Thermometer, tin, woman drinking from straw in bottle,
   "Pepsi-Cola Hits the Spot," 1941, 7 x 27" **925.00**
Toy, truck, balsa wood, cab over engine, hand-carved
   parts, orig box with instructions, Ting, 1940s, 5¼" l **200.00**
Toy, truck, metal, flat bed, blue, 1940s, 6" l **185.00**

PERFUME BOTTLES

Perfume manufacturers discovered that packaging is almost as important a selling factor for a perfume as its scent. Coty contracted with Lalique to produce exquisitely designed bottles for many of its perfumes. Many Czechoslovakian perfume bottles manufactured between the 1920s and 1960s are architectural miniatures reflecting the very best in design styles of the period.

A perfume bottle is a bottle with a stopper, often elongated, that serves as an applicator. A cologne bottle is usually larger than a perfume bottle. Its stopper also serves as an applicator. An atomizer is a bottle with a spray mechanism.

After a period of speculation and rapidly escalating prices in the 1980s and early 1990s, perfume bottle prices have stabilized, especially for common and middle range examples. Large countertop display bottles enjoyed a brief speculative price run in the early 1990s. They are tough sells today, largely because most collectors consider them overvalued.

References: Joanne Dubbs Ball and Dorothy Hehl Torem, *Commercial Fragrance Bottles,* Schiffer Publishing, 1993; Glinda Bowman, *Miniature Perfume Bottles,* Schiffer Publishing, 1994; Jacquelyne Jones-North, *Commercial Perfume Bottles, Third Edition,* Schiffer Publishing, 1996; Jacquelyne Y. Jones North, *Perfume, Cologne and Scent Bottles, 3rd Edition,* Schiffer Publishing, 1999; Tirza True Latimer, *The Perfume Atomizer,* Schiffer Publishing, 1991; Sue Mattioli, *Evening in Paris by Bourjois,* published by author, 1997; Beverly Nelson (comp.), *A Guide for the Collector of the Fragrances of the Bourjois Company,* published by author, 1996; Jeri Lyn Ringblum, *A Collector's Handbook of Miniature Perfume Bottles,* Schiffer Publishing, 1996.

Collectors' Clubs: International Perfume Bottle Assoc, 3314 Shamrock Rd, Tampa, F 33629; Miniature Perfume Bottle Collectors, 28227 Paseo El Siena, Laguna Niguel, CA 92677.

Atomizer, Czechoslovakian, mottled blue waves over
   orange, no bulb, 3½" h **$30.00**
Atomizer, Czechoslovakian, red, mottled colors, 7½" h **65.00**

Perfume Bottle, Fenton, Dusty Rose color, 1994, 8¹/₂" h, $20.00.

Atomizer, Czechoslovakian, yellow, blue band, white enamel dec, 6" h 40.00

Atomizer, Japan, figural poodle, pump spray, c1960, 4³/₄" h 20.00

Atomizer, Moser, sapphire blue, melon ribbed, gold flowers, leaves, and swirls, gold top and bulb, 4¹/₂" h 250.00

Atomizer, Steuben, De Vilbiss, clear engraved glass bottle, enameled foot, c1925, 6¹/₂" h 150.00

Cologne, Dana, Tabu, violin shaped bottle, c1930s, 2" h 15.00

Cologne, Nash Glass, chintz, paperweight stopper 225.00

Cologne, Pairpoint, applied vertical cranberry ribbing, flower form cranberry and clear stopper, 8" h 110.00

Perfume, Cartier, Art Deco, ovoid body, blue-black glass acid-etched as geometric designs, tapered cylindrical glass stopper, inscribed "Cartier CA6 8430," 4¹/₄" h 425.00

Perfume, Czechoslovakian, colorless glass bottle in wide stepped design, topped with elaborate oval stopper engraved and etched as kneeling woman gathering flowers, 8¹/₄" h 400.00

Perfume, Czechoslovakian, Red Butterfly, mold-blown red glass in form of woman with butterfly wings, enhanced frosting design, frosted and polished colorless glass lily stopper, 9³/₄" h 750.00

Perfume, Elizabeth Arden, On Dit, emb woman's face on frosted glass bottle, 4" h 150.00

Perfume, Lalique, Nina Ricci, pr of spiral ribbed colorless glass, 1 with frosted glass stopper of pr of doves, and 1 with single dove stopper, acid stamp at base "Lalique France," 1 with script "Lalique," sold together with third miniature bottle of similar design with acrylic dove stopper, 4¹/₄, 3¹/₂, and ³/₄" h 250.00

Perfume, Schiaparelli, Zut, colorless and frosted glass bottle in form of woman's lower torso in a wave base, highlighted with gold enamel stars, fringe, and ribbon, gilded stopper with green enamel "Zut," 4³/₄" h 300.00

Perfume, Steuben, Rosaline, teardrop shaped vessel in cloudy pink with applied alabaster glass foot, c1925, 5³/₈" h, price for pair 425.00

Scent, Czechoslovakian, green malachite glass with elaborate cherub and foliate design, conforming stopper with floral bouquet, polished base, 6¹/₄" h, price for pair 250.00

PEZ

Eduard Haas, an Austrian food manufacturer, developed the PEZ formula in 1927. He added peppermint (Pffefferminz in German) oil to a candy formula, pressed it into small rectangular pellets, and sold it as an adult breath mint and cigarette substitute.

World War II halted the production of PEZ. When it reappeared in the late 1940s it was packaged in a rectangular dispenser. An initial foray into the United States market in 1952 was only modestly successful. Evaluating the situation, Haas added fruit flavors and novelty dispensers, thus enabling PEZ to make a major impact on the children's candy market.

Because the company carefully guards its design and production records, information regarding the first appearance of a particular dispenser and dispenser variations is open to interpretation. PEZ Candy, Inc., is located in Connecticut. A second, independent company with distribution rights to the rest of the world, including Canada, is located in Linz, Austria. Although the two cooperate, it is common for each company to issue dispensers with different heads or the same dispenser in different packaging.

There are three basic types of dispensers—generic, licensed, and seasonal. New dispensers appear regularly. Further, the company is quite willing to modify an existing design. The Mickey Mouse dispenser has gone through at least a dozen changes.

Pez has been made in Austria (current), Czechoslovakia (closed), Germany (closed), Hungary (current), Mexico (closed), United States (current), and Yugoslavia (current). Plants in Austria, China, Hong Kong, Hungary, and Slovenia make dispensers.

References: Richard Geary, *More PEZ For Collectors, 2nd Edition* (1998), *PEZ Collectibles, 3rd Edition* (1999), Schiffer Publishing; David Welch, *Collecting Pez*, Bubba Scrubba Publications, 1994.

Newsletter: *PEZ Collector's News*, PO Box 124, Sea Cliff, NY 11579.

Note: Prices listed are for Pez containers in mint condition.

Air Spirit, soft head $265.00
Angel, no feet 80.00
Annie 180.00
Astronaut B, aqua 195.00
Astronaut B, white 180.00
Baloo, royal blue 135.00
Bambi 60.00
Barney Bear, with feet 40.00
Baseball Glove and Ball 235.00
Batman, with cape, no feet 100.00
Betsy Ross, with feet 190.00
Bouncer Beagle 6.00
Boy, no feet 20.00
Bubbleman 20.00
Bullwinkle, yellow stem 350.00
Camel, whistle 50.00
Candy Shooter, black 135.00
Candy Shooter, orange 80.00
Candy Shooter, red 100.00
Captain America, blue mask 100.00
Captain Hook 90.00
Chip, brown 115.00
Chip, pink 100.00
Clown, whistle 10.00
Clown Totem 35.00

Coach, whistle	45.00
Cockatoo, blue, yellow beak, with feet	65.00
Cocoa Marsh	300.00
Cool Cat, with feet	75.00
Cow A, orange	95.00
Cow B, blue face, horns	95.00
Cowboy, Club Med face	350.00
Cowboy, tan hat	300.00
Creature from the Black Lagoon A, with feet	425.00
Daffy, plastic eyes, with feet	20.00
Dalmatian, with feet	55.00
Dewey	7.00
Doctor	265.00
Dog, whistle	25.00
Donkey, whistle, no feet	30.00
Dopey	275.00
Droopy Dog A, with feet	25.00
Duck with Flower	125.00
Dumbo, blue, gray trunk, no feet	50.00
Elephant, blue hair	195.00
Elephant, gray, red hair, with feet	250.00
Engineer	235.00
Fireman	100.00
Foghorn Leghorn, with feet	95.00
Football Player	175.00
Frog, whistle, with feet	45.00
Girl, no feet, MIB	20.00
Gorilla	90.00
Green Hornet	250.00
Groom, flat side	650.00
Gyro Gearloose	6.00
Henry Hawk, no feet	95.00
Henry Hawk, with feet	65.00
Huey	7.00
Icee Bear #2	20.00
Icee Bear #3, purple stem	10.00
Icee Bear #3, white stem	12.00
Indian Brave, reddish face	185.00
Indian Chief, marbleized	170.00
Indian Chief, rubber headdress	125.00
Indian Maiden	175.00
Jack in the Box	30.00
Jerry B, 2-pc head, with feet	20.00
Jiminy Cricket	300.00
King Louie, no feet	40.00
Koala, whistle	30.00
Li'l Bad Wolf, with feet	20.00
Li'l Lion, no feet	75.00
Lamb, no feet	15.00
Louie	7.00
Maharajah	50.00
Merlin Mouse, with feet	20.00
Mexican, no hat or moustache, 2 earrings	150.00
Mimic, light blue head	45.00
Mimic, orange head, with feet	35.00
Mimic, yellow head	45.00
Monkey, whistle	25.00
Monkey Sailor	65.00
Mowgli	20.00
Neurmal	3.00
Octopus, orange, no feet	95.00
Olympic Wolf	900.00
One-Eyed Monster, black	100.00
Orange	275.00

Panda A, MIB	35.00
Panda Totem	35.00
Parrot, whistle	10.00
Penguin, soft head	190.00
Peter Pan	200.00
Peter PEZ, orig	65.00
Petunia Pig, no feet	40.00
Petunia Pig, with feet	35.00
PEZ Pen, 1970s	50.00
PEZ Truck #2	65.00
Pig, whistle, with feet	50.00
Pilot	230.00
Pink Panther, with feet, MOC	4.00
Pinocchio B, with feet	200.00
Pirate	60.00
Pluto, no feet	15.00
Policeman	60.00
Popeye B	125.00
Power Pez A	6.00
Practical Pig A, with feet	30.00
Practical Pig B, fat cheeks	45.00
Pumpkin A, with feet, MIP	10.00
Raven, with feet	70.00
Rhino, whistle	10.00
Roadrunner A, MIB	45.00
Rooster, whistle, white, with feet	45.00
Rooster, yellow, no feet	55.00
Rudolph, no feet	70.00
Sailor	225.00
Santa A, with feet	140.00
Santa B, red head	150.00
Santa B, white head	135.00
Scarewolf, soft head	265.00
Scrooge McDuck	6.00
Sheik, black band	100.00
Sheik, red band	50.00
Smurf A, with feet	5.00
Smurfette A, with feet	5.00
Snowman, orange face, with feet, MOC	25.00
Space Gun, maroon, 1950s	950.00
Space Gun, red, 1980s	90.00
Space Gun, silver, 1980s	185.00
Space Trooper, red	500.00
Speedy Gonzalez, with feet	35.00
Spike A, painted eyes, with feet	30.00
Stewardess	240.00
Sylvester, with whiskers	10.00
Thumper, with feet	50.00
Tinkerbell, with feet	300.00
Tuffy A, multi-piece, with feet	5.00
Tuffy C, with feet	5.00
Tyke A, painted eyes, with feet	25.00
Vamp, soft head	300.00
Webby	6.00
Winnie the Pooh, with feet	80.00
Witch, orange face, green hat	150.00
Witch, plum hat, no feet	600.00
Wounded Soldier	200.00
Wylie Coyote	55.00
Yappy Dog, green, with feet	60.00
Yappy Dog, orange head, with feet	70.00
Yosemite Sam, short whiskers	7.00
Zorro, no logo, with feet	70.00
Zorro, with logo	85.00

PFALTZGRAFF

The name Pfaltzgraff is derived from a famous Rhine River castle, still standing today, in the Pfalz region of Germany. In 1811 George Pfaltzgraff, a German immigrant potter, began producing salt-glazed stoneware in York, Pennsylvania.

The Pfaltzgraff Pottery Company initially produced stoneware storage crocks and jugs. When the demand for stoneware diminished, the company shifted its production to animal and poultry feeders and red clay flowerpots. The production focus changed again in the late 1940s and early 1950s as the company produced more and more household products, including its first dinnerware line, and giftwares.

In 1964 the company became The Pfaltzgraff Company. Over the next fifteen years, Pfaltzgraff expanded via construction of a new manufacturing plant and distribution center at Thomasville, North Carolina, the purchase of the Stangl Pottery of Trenton, New Jersey, and the acquisition of factories in Dover, Aspers, and Bendersville, Pennsylvania. Retail stores were opened in York County, Pennsylvania; Flemington, New Jersey; and Fairfax, Virginia.

References: Susan and Al Bagdade, *Warman's American Pottery and Porcelain,* Wallace-Homestead, Krause Publications, 1994; Harvey Duke, *The Official Price Guide to Pottery and Porcelain, Eighth Edition,* House of Collectibles, 1995; Harry L. Rinker, *Dinnerware of the 20th Century: The Top 500 Patterns,* House of Collectibles, 1997.

Collectors' Club: Pfaltzgraff America Collectors Club, 2536 Quint Ln, Columbia, IL 62236.

Christmas Heirloom, creamer	**$15.00**
Christmas Heirloom, cup and saucer	**15.00**
Christmas Heirloom, dinner plate	**15.00**
Christmas Heirloom, salt and pepper shakers, pr	**20.00**
Gourmet, baker, 10" l	**22.00**
Gourmet, deviled egg plate	**20.00**
Gourmet, flour canister	**32.00**
Gourmet, gravy boat	**25.00**
Gourmet, sugar, cov	**15.00**
Heirloom, augratin	**25.00**
Heirloom, cup and saucer	**7.00**
Heirloom, gravy boat, no underplate	**25.00**
Heirloom, salt and pepper shakers, pr	**15.00**
Heritage, augratin, 8" d	**7.00**
Heritage, baker, oval, 9⅝" l	**8.00**
Heritage, butter, cov	**7.00**
Heritage, chip and dip, no bowl	**12.00**
Heritage, gravy boat and underplate	**12.00**
Heritage, mug, 4¼" h	**4.00**
Heritage, onion soup, open	**6.00**
Heritage, salt and pepper shakers, pr	**7.00**
Heritage, soup bowl	**5.00**
Heritage, sugar canister	**10.00**
Village, baker, oval	**5.00**
Village, beverage server	**20.00**
Village, butter	**8.00**
Village, candlesticks, pr	**14.00**
Village, canister set	**50.00**
Village, casserole, cov	**15.00**
Village, cup and saucer	**3.50**
Village, dinner plate	**3.00**

Yorktowne, cup and saucer, $4.00.

Village, mug, ftd	**7.00**
Village, tureen, cov, with ladle	**65.00**
Windsong, butter, cov, ¼ lb	**20.00**
Windsong, cereal bowl, 6⅛" d	**7.00**
Windsong, coffee canister, 6½" h	**20.00**
Windsong, cup and saucer	**8.00**
Windsong, dinner plate	**12.00**
Windsong, sugar, cov	**15.00**
Yorktowne, augratin, 8¼" d	**8.00**
Yorktowne, baker, individual	**7.00**
Yorktowne, butter, cov, ¼ lb	**7.00**
Yorktowne, cereal bowl, 6⅛" d	**3.00**
Yorktowne, dinner plate, 10⅜" d	**4.00**
Yorktowne, measuring cup, 4¾"	**5.00**
Yorktowne, salt and pepper shakers, pr, 4" h	**7.00**

PHOENIX BIRD CHINA

The Phoenix Bird pattern features a Phoenix Bird facing back over its left wing, its chest spotted and wings spread upward. Although produced predominantly in blue and white, pieces have been found in celadon (green).

There are a number of Phoenix Bird pattern variations: (1) Firebird with its downward tail, (2) Flying Dragon typified by six Chinese characters and a pinwheel-like design, (3) Flying Turkey with no spots on its chest and one wing only partially visible, (4) Howo with no feet and a peony-like flower, and (5) Twin Phoenix with two birds facing each other. Pieces with a cloud and mountain border are the most common. Pieces with a heart-like border are known as HO-O for identification purposes.

Phoenix Bird china was manufactured by a number of companies and made available in a wide variety of markets. Beginning in the 1970s many new pieces of Phoenix Bird arrived on the market. The shapes are more modern, the blues more brilliant, and most lack an identifying backstamp.

References: Joan Collett Oates, *Phoenix Bird Chinaware, Book 1* (1984), *Book II* (1985), *Book III* (1986), *Book IV* (1989), 1996 value update, published by author.

Collectors' Club: Phoenix Bird Collectors of America, 685 S Washington, Constantine, MI 49042.

After Dinner Cup and Saucer, hp Flying Turkey $30.00
Berry Server and Underplate, Flying Turkey transfer print. . . . 100.00
Celery Tray, hp Flying Turkey, 12" l 90.00
Child's Cup and Saucer, Flying Turkey transfer print 20.00
Chop Plate, Flying Turkey transfer print, 12¼" d 150.00
Coaster, 3" d 20.00
Coffeepot, cov, #26-B, 8" h 75.00
Coffeepot, cov, HO-O, hexagonal base, 7⅝" h 100.00
Cracker Jar 40.00
Cracker Jar, cov, Flying Turkey transfer print, 3 ftd 150.00
Creamer, #52, HO-O 20.00
Creamer and Sugar, #49 . . . . 50.00
Creamer and Sugar, Flying Turkey transfer print 40.00
Cream Soup, cov, with underplate, hp Flying Turkey 60.00
Dresser Tray, 8¼" l 50.00
Farmer's Cup, #4, HO-O 20.00
Farmer's Cup and Saucer 30.00
Flower Bowl, HO-O 50.00
Ginger Jar Lamp, #3, 15½" total height with shade 55.00
Luncheon Plate, HO-O, 8¾" d. 40.00
Luncheon Plate, hp Flying Turkey, scalloped rim, 8¾" d 40.00
Mayonnaise Bowl, with ladle, HO-O 40.00
Mustard Jar, cov, Flying Turkey transfer print 50.00
Platter, HO-O, 10¾" l 125.00
Reamer 175.00
Relish, #3, square ends, 7⅛" l 30.00
Salt and Pepper Shakers, pr, hp Flying Turkey 40.00
Salt Dip, #1-B, HO-O 30.00
Salt Shaker, #16, HO-O. 15.00
Sauce Bowl, #2, HO-O 40.00
Souffle Dish, Flying Turkey transfer print, 3" h, 8¾" w 90.00
Sugar, #54 . . . . 30.00
Teacup and Saucer, #8 . . . . 20.00
Teapot, cov, #2, HO-O 110.00
Teapot, cov, #34, HO-O 50.00
Tea Strainer, #2-B 75.00
Tea Strainer, with stand, Flying Turkey transfer print 70.00
Vegetable Tureen, #3B-1, HO-O 80.00

PHOENIX GLASS

In 1880 Andrew Howard founded the Phoenix Glass Company in Phillispburg (later Monaca), Pennsylvania, to manufacture glass tubes for the new electrical wires in houses. Phoenix bought J. A. Bergun, Charles Challinor's decorating business, in 1882. A year later Phoenix signed a contract with Joseph Webb to produce Victorian art glass. Phoenix began producing light bulbs in the early 1890s. In 1893 Phoenix and General Electric collaborated on an exhibit at the Columbian Exposition.

In 1933 the company introduced its Reuben and Sculptured lines. Phoenix acquired the Co-Operative Flint molds in 1937. Using these molds, Phoenix began manufacturing Early American, a pressed milk glass line in 1938.

In 1970 Anchor Hocking acquired Phoenix Glass. The construction of Phoenix's new plant coincided with the company's 100th anniversary in 1980. In 1987 Newell Corporation acquired Anchor Hocking.

Reference: Jack D. Wilson, *Phoenix & Consolidated Art Glass, 1926–1980,* Antique Publications, 1989.

Collectors' Club: Phoenix & Consolidated Glass Collectors Club, 41 River View Dr, Essex Junction, VT 05452.

Banana Boat, Diving Girl, tan pearlized $325.00
Bowl, Lacy Dewdrop, caramel iridescence. 125.00
Bowl, Tiger Lily, amethyst frosted 350.00
Candlesticks, pr, Lily, amethyst. 250.00
Candlesticks, pr, Sawtooth, caramel iridesence 300.00
Cigarette Box, Phlox, brown over milk glass 150.00
Cigarette Box, Phlox, deep burgundy pealized 180.00
Compote, Blackberry, pink dec on milk glass 150.00
Console Bowl, lily, frosted design on green wash 425.00
Fruit Holder, Moon and Stars, caramel iridescence 250.00
Pitcher, Lacy Dewdrop, caramel iridesence 700.00
Pitcher, Water Lily, green relief design on gold ground 400.00
Plate, Dancing Nudes, relief design on yellow ground, 8¼" d 60.00
Tumbler, Lacy Dewdrop, gray highlights on milk glass 50.00
Umbrella Vase, Thistle, burgundy pearlized 500.00
Umbrella Vase, Thistle, lime green pearlized. 425.00
Umbrella Vase, Thistle, slate blue pearlized 500.00
Vase, Aster, pearlized design on deep burgundy ground 125.00
Vase, Blue Bell, deep burgundy pearlized. 125.00
Vase, Cosmos, purple pearlized 185.00
Vase, Dancing Girl, green, over milk glass 350.00
Vase, Madonna, pearlized design on pink ground. 200.00
Vase, Madonna, satin white deisng on slate blue ground. . . . 200.00
Vase, Philodendron, pearlized design on burgundy ground 185.00
Vase, Wild Geese, frosted design on pink ground 150.00
Vase, Wild Rose, milk glass design on blue ground. 200.00
Vase, Wild Rose, white frost. 100.00
Vase, Zodiac, deep rose over milk glass 650.00
Wine Glass, Blackberry, iridized 150.00

PHOTOGRAPHS

In 1830 J. M. Daugerre of France patented a process of covering a copper plate with silver salts, sandwiching the plate between glass for protection, and exposing the plate to light and mercury vapors to imprint an image. The process produced Daguerreotypes. Fox Talbot of Britain patented the method for making paper negatives and prints (calotypes) in 1841. Frederick Scott Archer introduced the wet collodion process in 1851. Dr. Maddox developed dry plates in 1871. When George Eastman produced roll film in 1888, the photographic industry reached maturity.

Cartes de visite (calling card) photographs flourished from 1857 to 1910 and survived into the 1920s. In 1866 the cabinet card first appeared in England. The format quickly spread to the United States. It was the preferred form by the 1890s.

The family photo album was second only to the Bible in importance to late 19th- and early 20th-century families. The principal downfall of family albums is that the vast majority of their photographs are unidentified. Professional photographers produced and sold "art" folios. Two post-1945 developments produced profound changes. The 35 mm "slide" camera and home video equipment decreased the importance of the photographic print.

Before discarding family photos, check them carefully. A photograph showing a child playing with a toy or dressed in a costume or an adult at work, in military garb, or shopping in a store has modest value. Collectors prefer black and white over color prints, as the latter deteriorate over time.

References: Norman E. Martinus and Harry L. Rinker, *Warman's Paper,* Wallace-Homestead, Krause Publications, 1994; Susan

Theran, *Prints, Posters & Photographs: Identification and Price Guide,* Avon Books, 1993; John S. Waldsmith, *Stereo Views: An Illustrated History and Price Guide,* Wallace-Homestead, Krause Publications, 1991.

Periodicals: *On Paper,* 39 E 78th St, #601, New York, NY 10021; *The Photograph Collector,* 301 Hill Ave, Langhorne, PA 19047.

Collectors' Clubs: American Photographic Historical Society, 1150 Ave of the Americas, New York, NY 10036; National Stereoscopic Assoc, PO Box 14801, Columbus, OH 43214; The Photographic Historical Society, PO Box 39563, Rochester, NY 14604.

Note: See Wallace Nutting and Nutting-Like Photographs for additional listings.

Movie Still, *Anna Christie,* Greta Garbo and Charles Bickford, MGM, 1930 . . . . **$25.00**
Movie Still, *Citizen Kane,* black and white, RKO, 1941, 8 x 10" **75.00**
Professional Photographer, Ernie Pyle, post-mortem of Ernie Pyle, silver print, 1945, 7½ x 9½" **800.00**
Professional Photographer, Eugene Richards, village elder with river blindness, Mali, silver print, sgd and titled by photographer in pencil on verso, framed, 1988, 13 x 8½" **575.00**
Professional Photographer, Godfrey Frankel, Martinsburg, WV, silver print, with photographer's New York City handstamp and title and date written in ink on verso, 1943, 9¾ x 7¾" **860.00**
Professional Photographer, Harry Warnecke, portrait of actress Dorothy Dandridge, color carbo print, photographer's signature, date, and caption on verso, 1959, 13½ x 10½" **575.00**
Professional Photographer, Harry Warnecke, portrait of Vice Presidential candidate Richard M Nixon, color carbo print, sgd, dated, caption on verso, 1952, 16½ x 12¾" **975.00**

Professional Photographer, Lord Snowdon, portrait of Prince Charles on his 8th birthday, silver print, notations on reverse of mat, 1956, 9¾ x 7¾" **1,500.00**
Professional Photographer, Margaret Rhodes Peattie, portrait of Norman Rockwell painting, toned silver print, sgd by photographer twice in pencil on recto, c1920, 8 x 5½" **750.00**
Professional Photographer, Max Alpert, combat, Red Army Officer leading his command into an attack, silver print, photographer's signature on verso, 1942, printed later, 9 x 11¼" **575.00**
Professional Photographer, Olive Cotton, Max Dupain after surfing, silver print, sgd, titled, and dated by photographer, in pencil, on recto and verso, 1939, printed later, 10½ x 7¾" **700.00**
Professional Photographer, Philippe Halsman, portrait of Edward Steichen, silver print, Halsman's handstamp and penciled notation on verso, 1959, 13½ x 10¾" **750.00**
Professional Photographer, PH Oleman, nude behind lace, toned silver print, with photographer's penciled signature on mount recto, 1940, 8½ x 6¾", tipped to orig mount **520.00**
Professional Photographer, Thomas McAvoy, portrait of Franklin D Roosevelt standing, silver print, Thomas McAvoy handstamp on verso, mid-1940s, 13½ x 10½" **920.00**
Snapshot, Carole Lombard, Paramount Pictures promo, automatic pen signature, 1938 . . . . **15.00**
Snapshot, destruction caused by crazed maniac, dead horses, Bath, MI, May 18, 1927 . . . . **20.00**
Snapshot, dog in buggy **8.00**
Snapshot, farm machinery, thresher and wagons **6.00**
Snapshot, girl with doll, 5 x 7" **10.00**
Snapshot, Harley-Davidson cycle and rider, 1921, 3 x 5" **15.00**
Snapshot, Mae West, half-length pose, wearing white furs, black and white glossy, inscribed and sgd in purple ink, 8 x 10" **60.00**
Snapshot, ventriloquist with dummy, black and white **35.00**

Snapshot, Frank Sinatra, black and white glossy, sgd, 1988, $400.00. Photo courtesy Gene Harris Antique Auction Center, Inc.

PICKARD CHINA

In 1894 Willard Pickard founded Pickard China in Chicago, Illinois. Until 1938, the company was a decorating firm; it did not manufacture the ceramics it decorated. Blanks were bought from foreign manufacturers, primarily French prior to World War I and German after the war.

Most of Pickard's early decorators were trained at Chicago's famed Art Institute. The company's reputation for quality soon attracted top ceramic painters from around the world. Many artists signed their work. Edward S. Challinor, noted for his bird, floral, fruit, and scenic designs, began working at Pickard in 1902 and remained with the company until his death in 1952. By 1908 Pickard offered more than 1,000 shapes and designs. In 1911 the company introduced gold-encrusted and gold-etched china.

In 1938 Pickard opened its own pottery in Antioch, Illinois. Pickard made china for the Navy during World War II. Decal patterns were introduced after the war. The company entered the limited edition bell and plate market in 1970 and introduced its first Christmas plate in 1976. In 1977 the U.S. Department of State selected Pickard to manufacture the official china services used at embassies and diplomatic missions around the world.

References: Susan and Al Bagdade, *Warman's American Pottery and Porcelain,* Wallace-Homestead, Krause Publications, 1994; Alan B. Reed, *Collector's Encyclopedia of Pickard China With Additional Section on Other Chicago China Studios,* Collector Books, 1995.

Collectors' Club: Pickard Collectors Club, 300 E Grove St, Bloomington, IL 61701.

Note: AOG stands for "all over gold."

Bonbon, Rose and Daisy AOG, shallow, fan-perforated handles, star wreath, RS, Tillowitz Silesia blank 1919–22 .... **$65.00**
Bowl, ring ftd, scalloped rim, planets AOG with mint green inner bowl scattered with stars, unsgd, 1925–30, 6½" d **65.00**
Bud Vase, Rose and Daisy AOG, unsgd, 6" h **95.00**
1919–22 .... **115.00**
Charger, perforated tab handles, green airbrushed leaf silhouettes on green ground, unsgd, Hutschenreuther Selb oval lion LHS blank, 1930–38, 10¾" d **100.00**
Creamer and Covered Sugar, flowered festoon with alternate blue ribbon festoons on white, sgd "Tol." ZS & Co Bavaria blank, 1925–38 .... **90.00**
Limited Edition Plate, Green-Winged Teal and Mallard, Lockhart Wildlife Series, J Lockhart, price for pair **170.00**
Limited Edition Plate, Maria, Children of Mexico Series, J Sanchez, 1981 .... **85.00**
Limited Edition Plate, Merlin the Magician, Legends of Camelot Series, D Palladini, 1982 .... **62.00**
Plate, all over roses, sgd "E. Challinor," Rosenthal Selb Bavaria blank, 1930–38, 9" d **175.00**
Plate, Yellow Botany/Gladiolus, sgd "Challinor," Pickard blank, 1938–present, 10½" d **85.00**
Souvenir Plate, Century of Progress, 1933, 8" d **35.00**
Tea Set, covered teapot, creamer and covered sugar, Indian Tree, sgd "Samuelson," crown Wreath Union T Made In Czecho-Slovakia blank, 1925–30 .... **275.00**
Vase, long-necked, Rose and Daisy AOG, style 843, Pickard blank, 1938–present, 7¾" h **50.00**

Mug, Poinsettia, gold banding and trim, oil-style glaze on white ground, artist sgd, 6⅞" h, $200.00.

PICTURE FRAMES

Until the early 1990s most picture frames were sold at auction in boxed lots. This is no longer true. Collectors discovered that picture frames are an excellent indication of changing design styles and that the manufacturing quality of many picture frames, whether handmade or mass produced, was quite high.

Tabletop frames are the "hot" portion of the market in the late 1990s. Beware of placing too much credence in the prices on frames associated with a licensed movie or television character. Crossover collectors are the group forcing these values upward.

Collectors' Club: International Institute for Frame Study, 443 I St NW, PO Box 50156, Washington, DC 20091.

Blue Glass, metal corners, cardboard back, c1948, 4 x 5" ... **$25.00**
Brass, Egyptian motif, 3½ x 6" **100.00**
Brass, linking rings, c1920, 3½ x 4¾" **150.00**
Brass, plain, 2¾ x 3½" **10.00**
Brass, Steps to the Cathedral, 7 x 8" **45.00**
Cast Brass, ivy vine pattern, 4½ x 5½" **100.00**
Glass, twisted glass with red internal stripe, Italian **195.00**
Ivory, pierced and carved floral design, 1¼ x 2¼"........ **70.00**
Silver Plated, dragon motif, Japan, 6 x 8" **200.00**
Silver Plated, rough textured finish, 2" w border, 9¾ x 17½" **100.00**
Silver Plated Brass, beaded edge with applied corners, 3¾ x 6" **60.00**
Sterling Silver, table top, compact, English, 2⅛ x 2½" **175.00**
Thermoplastic, overall mother-of-pearl effect, c1937, 5 x 5" **120.00**
Trench Art, made from machine gun shells and wood, 10½ x 14¼" **150.00**
Wood, Art Deco, black inset corners, c1928, 3⅝ x 4⅝" **50.00**
Wood, Art Deco, swings on 2 outer pillars, c1928, 8¼ x 8½" **20.00**
Wood, curly maple, refinished, 16¾ x 20½" **90.00**
Wood, mahogany, deep well, black inner edge, 12½ x 15" **40.00**
Wood, walnut, chip carved edge, applied hearts, 16 x 19½" **50.00**

PIERCE, HOWARD

After working for William Manker Ceramics in Claremont, California, and doing freelance work for other California potteries such as Kay Finch Ceramics, Howard Webster Pierce established his La Verne, California, studio in 1941. His initial efforts focused on the production of pewter and copper finished pins.

Although producing some dinnerware and high gloss planters and vases, Pierce is best know for his bird, human, marine, and wildlife figurines. Numbers of some pieces are limited. Although in production for over fifty years, Pierce remained a small, home-based business.

In 1941 Howard married Ellen Van Voorhis, an art teacher and graduate of the Chicago Art Institute. They worked together as a team. The Pierce children, Janet, Linda, and Jerry, also worked at the pottery. In 1968 the Pierces moved to a new home/studio in Joshua Tree, near Palm Springs.

Reference: Darlene Hurst Dommel, *Collector's Encyclopedia of Howard Pierce Porcelain,* Collector Books, 1998.

Ashtray, free-form, ebony black, 4" l, unmkd **$18.00**

Bowl, fluted, metallic blue with black highlights, "Howard Pierce" black ink stamp, 4¹/₂ x 7" 100.00

Bowl, rect, sunburst effect, aqua int, black ext, "Howard Pierce Porcelains" black ink stamp, 2¹/₂ x 7¹/₂" 75.00

Dish, triangular, aqua int shading from light to dark, black ext, black ink stamp "Howard Pierce Porcelain," 9¹/" l 75.00

Figurine, cat, bluish black glaze, imp "Howard Pierce Claremont Calif," 14 x 6" 250.00

Figurine, chipmunk, glossy gray flecked glaze, 4 stripes, unmkd, 2¹/₄ x 7" 25.00

Figurine, dachshund, "Howard Pierce" black ink stamp, 3¹/₄ x 10" 85.00

Figurine, female native, black and white matte glaze, "Howard Pierce" black ink stamp, 7¹/₄ x 2¹/₂" 60.00

Figurine, girl playing mandolin, "Howard Pierce" black ink stamp, 8 x 4" 150.00

Figurine, horse with flying mane, "Howard Pierce" black ink stamp, 8¹/₂ x 7¹/₂" 125.00

Figurine, pigeon, black matte glaze, "Howard Pierce" black ink stamp, 7¹/₄ x 5¹/₂" 50.00

Figurine, porcupine, "Howard Pierce" black ink stamp, 4¹/₂ x 6" 75.00

Figurine, raccoon, textured glaze, "Howard Pierce" black ink stamp, 5 x 5¹/₄" 60.00

Figurines, angel fish, multicolored, "Howard Pierce" black ink stamp, 4¹/₂ x 5 and 3 x 4", price for pair 125.00

Figurines, fawn and doe, "Howard Pierce" black ink stamp, price for pair 75.00

Planter, rect, emb holly leaves, green, unmkd, 5¹/₂ x 12" 65.00

Strawberry Planter, yellow and brown matte glaze, incised "Pierce," 5 x 5" 100.00

Vase, cylindrical, 7" h, 4" d 50.00

Vase, owl and foliage motif, glossy mottled glaze, "Howard Pierce Porcelain" black ink stamp, 5 x 4" 50.00

PIG COLLECTIBLES

Austrian, English, and German bisque and hand-painted glazed ceramic pig figurines and planters were popular souvenirs and fair prizes at the turn of the century. So many early banks were in the shape of a pig that "Piggy Bank" became a generic term for a child's bank in the early 20th century.

As an important food source, the pig was featured prominently in farm advertising. Warner Brothers' Porky Pig and Walt Disney's The Three Little Pigs are among the most recognized cartoon characters of the mid-20th century.

A pig collecting craze swept across America in the late 1970s and early 1980s, eventually displaced by cow mania.

Three German bisque pig figurines have been reproduced—a pig by an outhouse, a pig playing a piano, and a pig poking his head out of a large purse. Their darker green color distinguishes them from period pieces.

Collectors' Club: The Happy Pig Collectors Club, PO Box 17, Oneida, IL 61467.

Note: Shawnee Pottery produced Smiley Pig and Winnie Pig kitchen accessories, figural pigs with various decorative motifs.

Ashtray, ceramic, bride and groom pigs on top, Germany, 3¹/₂ x 4¹/₂" **$125.00**

Sign, Dennis's Pig Powders, litho tin, 12 x 18", $412.00. Photo courtesy Collectors Auction Services.

Bank, composition, Love & Peace, pink sleeping pig, coin slot at back, "Love" on side, "Peace" dog tag and zodiac emblem pinback button, 7" l 20.00

Bank, litho tin, mechanical, off-white, wind-up tail with spinning action, Mikuni, Japan, 1950s 110.00

Bank, plastic, Porky Pig 25.00

Bookends, pr, metal, full figure Porky Pig wearing red vest, blue bow tie atop green base, name in orange on front next to brown accent tree, 3 x 3³/₄ x 4¹/₂" 100.00

Cookie Jar, lady pig, gold trim, unmkd 75.00

Figurine, black pig sitting by green purse, bisque, 2³/₄" h 70.00

Figurine, carnival chalkware, 1950s, 7" h 45.00

Figurine, chef pig standing by barrel, blue hat and jacket 95.00

Figurine, mama pig wheeling piglets, "The Heavenly Twins," incised "Made in Germany," 3 x 3³/₄" 85.00

Figurine, pig in canoe 75.00

Figurine, pig in cradle 60.00

Figurine, pig looking in outhouse, "Engaged," 4 x 2¹/₂" w 75.00

Figurine, pig sitting by windmill, orange roof 80.00

Figurine, pig wheeling piglets in cart, "The More The Merrier" 75.00

Figurine, pig with camera 50.00

Figurine, pigs at end of caboose 80.00

Game, Three Little Pigs, Einson-Freeman Co, 1933 . . . . 75.00

Inkwell, pig sitting on top, 3" h 100.00

Matchsafe, pig poking head through fence, 4¹/₂" w 65.00

Pail, litho tin, Three Little Pigs illus, 1930s, 3" h, 6¹/₂" d 75.00

Planter, Miss Piggy, Sigma 25.00

Playing Cards, Three Little Pigs, complete deck, orig box mkd "By Special Permission Walt Disney Enterprises," 1930s 50.00

Push Puppet, Porky Pig 40.00

Salt and Pepper Shakers, pr, 1 pig playing accordion, other pig playing saxophone, glazed and painted, mkd "Japan," c1930, 4" h 45.00

Salt Dish, 3 pigs around water trough, 2¹/₂" h 50.00

Tape Measure, figural pig, celluloid 25.00

Toothpick Holder, pig pushing wheelbarrow 65.00

Toothpick Holder, pig with mug in hand leaning on fence, 3" h 60.00

Vase, pigs looking out of shoe, Germany 60.00

PINBACK BUTTONS

In 1896 Whitehead & Hoag Company, Newark, New Jersey, obtained the first celluloid button patent. The celluloid buttons golden age stretched from 1896 through the early 1920s. Hundreds of manufacturers made thousands of buttons.

J. Lynch Company of Chicago introduced the first lithograph tin pinback buttons during World War I. Although lithograph buttons could be printed in multiple colors, the process did not produce the wide color range found in celluloid buttons. This mattered little. Lithograph tin buttons were much less costly to produce.

The lithograph tin pinback button played a major role in political campaigns from the early 1930s through the 1980s. Advertising buttons increased in size. Social cause buttons were dominant in the 1960s, colorful rock group buttons in the 1970s.

As the cost of lithograph tin pinback buttons rose, their popularity diminished. Today pinback buttons are sold primarily by greeting card manufacturers and retail gift shops.

Reference: William A. Sievert, *All For the Cause: Campaign Buttons For Social Change, 1960s–1990s,* Decoy Magazine/For Splash, 1997.

Buster Brown Bread, celluloid, multicolored, 1¹/₂" d, $7.00.

Bedtime Stories Club, Peter Rabbit in white on light blue ground, 1930s, ¹³/₁₆". **$45.00**

Bye-Lo Baby, blue and white, used on dolls by K&K, designed by Grace S Putnam, c1930s, 1" d. **45.00**

CIO Shipyard Workers Union, litho tin, cream lettering on dark blue ground, c1940s. **5.00**

Earth Love It Or Leave It, earth in shades of green against dark red ground, 1970. . . . . **10.00**

For President John F Kennedy, smiling black and white photo on white, red lettering at top, white on blue lettering at bottom, ⁷/₈" d. **5.00**

Forward With Stevenson, litho tin, black and white portrait on black ground, 1952, 1¹/₈" d. **10.00**

Good Humor Safety Club, "Use Your Eyes—Look!". **20.00**

Grass Rooters For Nixon, white on bright green ground, 1¹/₂" d. **10.00**

Greetings From Santa Claus At CDS, multicolored close-up portrait, gold lettering rim inscription, "Made in Canada" on rim curl, 1920–30s. **65.00**

I Am A Buick Man, litho tin, blue lettering on white ground, 1930–40s. **20.00**

Impeach Nixon/Agnew—Watergate Kickbacks, red caricatures on bright yellow ground. **10.00**

International Black Expo, red and black lettering against dark green ground, c1971. . . . . **5.00**

I Voted For Lassie, browntone photo on bright yellow ground, c1960s, 1" d. **20.00**

Jerry Brown/The Times Are Changing, bluetone photo with red lettering on white ground, center flanked by dark red rose panels left and right, 1980s. **5.00**

March, Rally To End The War Now, red arrow surrounding blue type against white ground, "Sat Oct 31, New York Peace Action Coalition". **20.00**

Maryland Freedom Union/Breaking Free At Last, black and white, black hands breaking chain, c1970s. **10.00**

Member Happy Home Village Theater Club-Mills Baking Company, theater stage with footlights and curtains design in red, clown figure in black and white costume with red buttons, inscription printed against black area at center, 1930s, 1¹/₄" d. **10.00**

Mr Perky's, litho tin, yellow and blue symbol figure for Perkins Pancake House chain holding platter stacked by brown pancakes, c1960s. **10.00**

Nature's Toothbrush, figural red apple with gold colored inscription "1938". **10.00**

Nickles' Butternut Bread, red lettering on white ground, 1930s. **10.00**

No Beer/No Work, black on cream, Statue of Liberty illus, 1920s. **20.00**

Roosevelt, Teddy Roosevelt in tan uniform with blue collar wearing gray hat with yellow military insignia and bright red hat band, gold ground, 1¹/₄" d. **175.00**

Roosevelt/Garner, blue and white portraits against red, white, and blue star and stripe ground, 1¹/₄" d. **20.00**

Smokey Bear Is Alive & Well, brown text on yellow ground, 1980s, 1¹/₂" d. **5.00**

Tastykake Magic Lamp Club, blue, white, and yellow, genie emerging in vapor form from magic lamp, 1930s. **20.00**

The Lady Is Back, full color Diana Ross photo, 3" d. **10.00**

Tom Mix Circus, black and white photo on black ground, 1³/₄" d. **45.00**

What Makes Emmett Smile? Econo-Car, litho tin, black and white Emmett Kelly photo at center accented by red nose against red and white ground, white lettering, c1960s, 2¹/₄" d. **20.00**

Winky Dink, litho tin, black and white figure with yellow star shaped hair on black ground, 1¹/₈" d. **45.00**

Wisconsin Football Golden Jubilee, red silhouette image of football punter on gold ground, black and red "50 Years of Football," late 1940s. **10.00**

Witness For Peace Easter–1961, white lettering on blue ground. **5.00**

Woodsy Owl Says…Don't Pollute/Give A Hoot!, flicker, full color Woodsy cartoon figure holding whistle then blowing as hat flies off, c1970s, Vari-Vue, 2¹/₂" d. **15.00**

Zenith Data Systems, black and white Ziggy cartoon figure next to his computer on bright yellow ground, c1980s, 1³/₈" d. **10.00**

PINBALL MACHINES

The introduction of Gottlieb's "Baffle Ball" in 1931 marked the beginning of the modern pinball machine era. Pre-1940 pinball machines typically had production runs of 25,000 to 50,000 machines. After 1945 production runs fell within the 500 to 2,000 range with an occasional machine reaching 10,000. Some scholars suggest that over 200 manufacturers made over 10,000 models, a result of a machine's high attrition rate. Several companies released a new model every three weeks during the 1950s.

The first electric machine appeared in 1933. Bumpers were added in 1936. Flippers arrived in 1947, kicking rubbers in 1950, score totalizers in 1950, multiple player machines in 1954, and solid state electronics in 1977. Machines by D. Gottlieb are considered the best of the pinballs, primarily because of their superior play and graphics.

The entire pinball machine was collected through the mid-1980s. More recently, collecting back glasses has become popular. Manufacturers were not concerned with longevity when making these glasses. Flaking paint is a restoration nightmare.

References: Richard M. Bueschel, *Collector's Guide to Vintage Coin Machines, 2nd Edition,* Schiffer Publishing, 1998; Richard M. Bueschel, *Encyclopedia of Pinball: Contact to Bumper, 1934–1936, Vol. 2,* Silverball Amusements, 1997; Heirbert Eiden and Jürgen Lukas, *Pinball Machines,* Schiffer Publishing, 1992, 1997 value update; Bill Kurtz, *Arcade Treasures,* Schiffer Publishing, 1994.

Periodicals: *Coin Drop International,* 5815 W 52nd Ave, Denver, CO 80212; *PinGame Journal,* 31937 Olde Franklin Dr, Farmington Hills, MI 48334.

Note: Prices are for machines in near mint to excellent condition.

Atari, Superman, 1979. . . . . **$400.00**
Automatic Games, Fifty Grand, 1933 . . . . **600.00**
Automatic Industries, Baby Whiffle, 1931. . . . . **400.00**
Baker, On Deck, 1940. . . . . **350.00**
Bally, Bally Booster, 1937 . . . . **500.00**
Bally, Dolly Parton, 1978. . . . . **200.00**
Bally, Jumbo, 1935 . . . . **450.00**
Buckley, Favorite, 1932 . . . . **250.00**
Chicago Coin, Beam Lite, 1935 . . . . **350.00**
Chicago Coin, Leland Standard, 1933 . . . . **250.00**
Chicago Coin, Sound Stage, 1976 . . . . **300.00**
Exhibit Supply, Play Ball, 1932 . . . . **300.00**
Exhibit Supply, Smoky, 1947 . . . . **250.00**
Genco, Base Ball, 1935. . . . . **500.00**
Genco, Cheer Leader, 1935. . . . . **300.00**
Genco, Spit Fire, 1935 . . . . **350.00**
Gottlieb, Arabian Knights, 1953. **500.00**
Gottlieb, Electric Scoreboard, 1937 . . . . **450.00**
Gottlieb, Five Star Final, 1932 . . . . **300.00**
Gottlieb, Hi-Diver, 1959 . . . . **850.00**
Gottlieb, Queen of Diamonds, 1959 . . . . **650.00**
Gottlieb, Sunshine Derby, 1936. **350.00**
Houston Showcase, Sweetheart Double, 1933 . . . . **350.00**
Hutchison, Scram, 1932 . . . . **400.00**
Midway, Race Way, 1963 . . . . **350.00**
Midway, Rodeo, 1964 . . . . **200.00**
National Pin, The Pilot, 1932. . . . . **300.00**
Pacific, Lite-A-Line, 1934. . . . . **450.00**

Pacific, Pamco Palooka, 1936 . . . . **400.00**
Rock-Ola, Army Navy, 1934 . . . . **550.00**
Rock-Ola, Totalite, 1936 . . . . **450.00**
Rock-Ola, Wings, 1933 . . . . **350.00**
Rock-Ola, World Series, 1934 . . . . **250.00**
Rube Gross, Fury, 1935 . . . . **400.00**
Stoner, Cavalcade, 1935 . . . . **350.00**
Williams, Aces & Kings, 1970 . . . . **300.00**
Williams, Hayburners, 1951 . . . . **500.00**
Williams, Jolly Roger, 1967 . . . . **250.00**
Williams, Suspense, 1946 . . . . **300.00**

PIN-UP ART

The pin-up beauty owes her origin to 1920s' film magazines such as *Film Fun* and *Real Screen* whose front covers showed women with a fair amount of exposed skin. Artists such as Cardwell Higgins, George Petty, and Charles Sheldon continued to refine the concept through the 1930s. Petty's first gatefold appeared in *Esquire* in 1939.

Pin-up art reached its zenith in the 1940s. Joyce Ballantyne, Billy DeVorss, Gillete Elvgren, Earl Moran, and Alberto Vargas (the "s" was dropped at Esquire's request) were among the leading artists of the period. Their pin-up girls appeared everywhere—blotters, calendars, jigsaw puzzles, matchcovers, magazine covers, posters, punchboards, etc.

The reign of the pin-up girl ended in the early 1960s when the photograph replaced the artist sketch as the preferred illustration for magazines.

References: Max Allen Collins and Drake Elvgren, *Elvgren: His Life & Art,* Collectors Press, 1998; Denis C. Jackson, *The Price & ID Guide to Pin-Ups & Glamour Art,* TICN, 1996; Charles G. Martignette and Louis K. Meisel, *The Great American Pin-Up,* Taschen, 1996.

Newsletters: *Glamour Girls: Then and Now,* PO Box 34501, Washington, DC 20043; *The Illustrator Collector's News,* PO Box 1958, Sequim, WA 98382.

Blotter, Earl Moran, WWII theme, "Don't Try Any Pincer Movements On Me," $3\frac{1}{2}$ x $6\frac{1}{4}$" **$10.00**
Calendar, 1945, Varga, spiral bound, sgd "A. Varga," Esquire copyright symbol and descriptive verse by Phil Stack, $8\frac{3}{4}$ x 12", orig $9\frac{1}{4}$ x $12\frac{1}{4}$" envelope. **100.00**
Calendar, 1947, Alfred Buell, "All American Girl," cardboard, full color art of blonde ice skater in red outfit, "Litho U.S.A." copyright, $9\frac{1}{2}$ x $15\frac{1}{2}$" **45.00**
Calendar, 1948, George Petty, "Petty Girl," spiral bound, sgd, $9\frac{1}{4}$ x $12\frac{1}{2}$", orig 9 x 12" envelope **75.00**
Calendar, 1948, Varga, "The Varga Girl," spiral bound, full color portrait, each page with calendar title, Varga signature, and short descriptive verse by Earl Wilson, ©1947 Varga Enterprises, Inc, $8\frac{1}{2}$ x 12" **100.00**
Calendar, 1951, Al Moore, "Esquire Girl," spiral bound, sgd, $8\frac{1}{2}$ x 12", orig 9 x $12\frac{1}{2}$" envelope **45.00**
Calendar, 1951, Freeman Elliott, "Artist's Sketch Pad," spiral bound, pages imprinted for local sponsor at bottom right, $8\frac{3}{4}$ x 14" **45.00**
Calendar, 1954, MacPherson, "Hunter's Guide," spiral bound, $9\frac{1}{2}$ x $12\frac{1}{2}$", orig 10 x 13" envelope **75.00**
Calendar, 1955, Thompson, "Studio Sketches," spiral bound, 9 x 12", orig $8\frac{1}{4}$ x $11\frac{1}{4}$" envelope **75.00**

Ashtrays, Texaco Service, litho metal, 4¹/₄" sq, set of 3, $198.00. Photo courtesy Collectors Auction Services.

Calendar Cards, Earl Moran, set of 4, 1942, April, May, Jun, and Sept, "Two Lip Time," "Hard To Beat," "Sox Appeal," and "Figures Don't Lie," imprinted for local sponsor, full color art with diecut contour of figure design to stand away from background, assembled by diecut tabs and slots, Brown & Bigelow, 4³/₄ x 10" **50.00**

Calendar Print, Moran, "When Shadows Fall," sgd, 1940s, 17¹/₂ x 21¹/₂" framed size **20.00**

Greeting Card, MacPherson, fold-out, holiday greeting message in red lettering, ©Brown & Bigelow, 1942, 6¹/₄ x 8¹/₄" closed size **45.00**

Greeting Card, Munson, fold-out, reclining model in sheer transparent gown posed by award trophy, text about proper diet with New Year's greeting, ©1944 Brown & Bigelow **45.00**

Magazine, *Esquire,* Jan 1942, "Holiday Issue," 196 pp, 12 pp bound full color folio, sgd Varga portraits with short descriptive verse by Phil Stack, 10 x 14" **75.00**

Matchcover, Petty, "Hold the Phone," "Hot as a Firecracker," "Perfect Form for Fun," "Pistol Packin' Mamma," and "Will You Bait my Hook?," GMC adv on front, Superior Match Co, 1948 . . . . **15.00**

Matchcover, Thompson, "Glamour Girls Facing a Heat Wave!," "In Perfect Shape!," "South of the Border," "Strictly for the See!," and "To Be...or Not to Be!," GMC adv on front, Superior Match Co, 1956 . . . . **15.00**

Note Pads, Elvgren, set of 4, "I'm Game," "A Winner," "Stepping Out," and "Budding Out," Elgvren signature and Brown & Bigelow copyright, imprinted for local sponsor, 3¹/₄ x 6" **45.00**

Playing Cards, Elvgren, complete deck, blonde model in sheer pale blue/black lingerie holding ribbon toyed by kitten on light pink ground, each card imprinted at bottom margin for local Esso dealer sponsor, 1940–50s **75.00**

Portfolio, Devorss, "Six Gorgeous Glamazons," 2 sgd Elvgren themes of blonde model in bathroom setting, other with glamour pose in large brimmed hat and swimsuit sgd by Devorss, front cover with diecut view opening, c1940s, 5¹/₂" **75.00**

Postcard, Varga, "The Varga Girl," set #12, complete set of 6, published by *Esquire* magazine, with orig envelope **300.00**

Print, Earl Moran, nude model in dramatic pose, artist signature lower left, 12 x 16¹/₂" wooden frame, c1940s . . . **100.00**

Print, Rolf Armstrong, brunette in bibbed shorts and yellow shirt, matted and framed, 11 x 14" **32.00**

Program, Elvgren, "A Live Wire," full color, sgd, inner agenda for Jan 24, 1946 Royal Order of Jesters Buffalo Court meeting, 5¹/₂ x 8" **20.00**

Program, Vargas, "Skating Vanities of 1947," blonde roller skater wearing pink outfit, 8 x 11" **35.00**

Punchboard, reclining nude basking in sun, 5,000 punch options, 1 punch used, Brewer Boards, c1960s **20.00**

Sample Calendar, Walt Otto, "Sweetheart of the Ranger," cowgirl in red and white outfit with matching tan western boots and hat accented in red, beside brown horse, night sky background, mkd "Made in U.S.A.," 16 x 32" **75.00**

PLANTERS PEANUTS

In 1906 Amedeo Obici, known as a peanut specialist, and Mario Peruzzi founded the Planters Nut and Chocolate Company, Wilkes-Barre, Pennsylvania. Initially, the company sold Spanish salted red skins priced at 10¢ a pound.

The Mr. Peanut trademark evolved from a 1916 contest. A young Italian boy submitted a rough sketch of a monocled Peanut figure. Hundreds of Mr. Peanut advertising and promotional items have been issued.

References: Jan Lindenberger, *Planters Peanut Collectibles Since 1961,* Schiffer Publishing, 1995; Mark Woodson, *Mr. Peanut Collectibles,* published by author, 1992.

Collectors' Club: Peanut Pals, PO Box 4465, Huntsville, AL 35815.

Bank, plastic, full figure Mr Peanut, lime green, 8¹/₂ x 4 x 3¹/₄" **$350.00**

Bank, red plastic, figural penny operated "Planters Peanuts Vender-Bank," inside hat holds peanuts which are dispensed through neck area, coin trap in bottom, orig instructions, c1950s, 8³/₄ x 5¹/₂" **375.00**

Book, *Mr Peanut,* Mr Peanut crossing finish line, 1970s **10.00**

Box, Planters Clean Crisp 1¢ Peanut Bars, 2 pc, covered with Mr Peanut circus images, c1920s, 3 x 11¹/₄ x 5¹/₄" . . . **525.00**

Costume, Mr Peanut, plastic top, cloth bottom, 1974 . . . . **25.00**

Dispenser, Planters Honey Roast, plastic, 1986 . . . . **12.00**

Display Box, Planters Salted Peanuts, waxy cardboard, holds 5¢ bags, covered with images of Mr Peanut engaged in various activities including flying airplane, playing baseball, parachuting, and flying kite, missing insert pc, 1920s, 10¹/₄ x 7¹/₂ x 3⁵/₈" **850.00**

Doll, cloth, Mr Peanut, 1970s **5.00**

Drinking Glass, red and yellow enameled images of Mr Peanut doing circus acts, 5 x 2³/₄" **140.00**

Hand Puppet, rubber, Mr Peanut, 6¹/₂ x 6¹/₂" **1,100.00**

Ice Cream Scoop Set, 2 pc, metal, Mr Peanut on handle, orig box, 1985 . . . . **20.00**

Jar, Planters Peanut Butter, clear glass, paper label with Mr Peanut image on front and premium mail-in offers on back, 5¹/₂ x 3¹/₂" **100.00**

Jar, Planters Salted Peanuts, oval front and back, rect base, emb text on oval panels, glass lid with peanut finial, 9" h to top of finial **250.00**

Letter Opener, metal, flat peanut handle with cloisonné Mr Peanut image, "Planters" on blade, 9 x 1³/₈" **1,815.00**

Mask, Mr Peanut face, cardboard, no rubber band, 7³/₄ x 8¹/₄" **360.00**

Matchcover, Mr Peanut with Planters Dry Roasted Peanuts, 1970s **20.00**

Mug, ceramic, peanut shell textured surface with joined peanuts for handle, Mr Peanut image above "Mr. Peanut," Japan, 4 x 5½" **525.00**

Nut Tray, painted bisque, figural Mr Peanut at center, Japan, 1930s, 4" h **100.00**

Paint Book, Colorful Story of Peanuts As Told By Mr Peanut, 1957, 28 pp **35.00**

Pencil Holder, green plastic, Mr Peanut Pencil Pack, 1968 . . . . **40.00**

Pin, painted wood, figural Mr Peanut with Trylon and Perisphere, "1939 World's Fair" on Trylon **40.00**

Pinback Button, black and white Mr Peanut image, "Vote For Mr Peanut, The People's Choice," white lettering on red rim, c1940, 1¼" d **25.00**

Pinback Button, tan and black Mr Peanut image on yellow ground, red lettering, 1940s **20.00**

Planter, blue plastic, tin replica **20.00**

Radio, Planter Cocktail Peanuts can shape, 1978 . . . . **30.00**

Ring, beige plastic, raised Mr Peanut image, 1950s **12.00**

Salt and Pepper Shakers, pr, green plastic, Mr Peanut figures, removable shaker top hat, orig box, 1950s, 3" h shaker **50.00**

Sign, metal, "Planters, The Name for Quality!," 24 x 12½" **45.00**

Tin, Planters Hi-Hat Peanut Oil, Planters Edible Oil Co, Suffolk, VA, rect, pictures fried foods along sides, Star of David and Hebrew writing on front and back, small Mr Peanut image on front, unopened can, 1 gal **450.00**

Tin, Planters Popcorn Oil, 1970s, 1 gal **30.00**

Toy, stake body truck, Pyro Toy Co, 2 pc, red cab, yellow sides, blue bed with "Planters Peanuts" on side, 1950s, 1¾ x 5½" **200.00**

Toy, tractor trailer, Pyro Toy Co, 2 pc, red cab, yellow and blue trailer with "Planters Peanuts" and Mr Peanut image, 1950s, 1¾ x 5½" **225.00**

Toy, walker, plastic, figural Mr Peanut wind-up, 8½" h **350.00**

Wastebasket, metal, Mr Peanut with "Planters Cocktail Peanuts," 1968 . . . . **15.00**

Whistle, red plastic, figural Mr Peanut, 1950s, 2½" l **8.00**

Jar, slant front, tin lid, emb "Planters," 8½" h, 5¼" w, 10" l, $302.00. Photo courtesy Collectors Auction Services.

PLASTICS

There are hundreds of different natural, semi-synthetic, and synthetic plastics known. Collectors focus on three basic types: celluloid, Bakelite, and melamine. Celluloid, made from cellulose nitrate and camphor, is a thin, tough, flammable material. It was used in the late 1880s and through the first four decades of the 20th century to make a wide range of objects from toilet articles to toys. Celluloid's ability to mimic other materials, e.g., amber, ivory, and tortoiseshell, made it extremely popular.

In 1913 L. H. Baekeland invented Bakelite, a synthetic resinous material made from formaldehyde and phenol. It proved to be a viable substitute for celluloid and rubber. Easily dyed and molded, Bakelite found multiple uses from radio cases to jewelry. Often it was a secondary element, e.g., it was commonly used for handles.

Although injection molding was developed prior to World War II, its major impact occurred during and after the war. Many new plastics, e.g., melamine, were developed to take advantage of this new technology. The 1950s through the 1960s was the golden age of plastic. It was found everywhere, from the furniture in which one sat to the dashboard of a car.

This is a catchall category. It includes objects made from plastic that do not quite fit into other collecting categories.

References: Shirley Dunn, *Celluloid Collectibles,* Collector Books, 1996; Michael J. Goldberg, *Collectible Plastic Kitchenware and Dinnerware: 1935–1965,* Schiffer Publishing, 1995; Bill Hanlon, *Plastic Toys: Dimestore Dreams of the '40s & '50s,* Schiffer Publishing, 1993; Keith Lauer and Julie Robinson, *Celluloid,* Collector Books, 1999; Jan Lindenberger, *More Plastics for Collectors,* Schiffer Publishing, 1996; Barbara Mauzy, *Bakelite in the Kitchen,* Schiffer Publishing, 1998; Lyndi Stewart McNulty, *Wallace-Homestead Price Guide to Plastic Collectibles,* Wallace-Homestead, Krause Publications, 1987, 1992 value update; Holly Wahlberg, *Everyday Elegance: 1950s Plastic Design,* 2nd Edition, Schiffer Publishing, 1999.

Note: For additional listings see Costume Jewelry and Melmac.

Bakelite, bangle bracelet, brown, carved designs **$8.00**

Bakelite, bangle bracelet, green, carved designs, ½ x 3" **35.00**

Bakelite, bangle bracelet, wide **65.00**

Bakelite, belt buckle, cream colored **30.00**

Bakelite, clock, Telechron, black, octagonal **38.00**

Bakelite, coat pin, figural horse, dark amber, incised detailing, 3" l **225.00**

Bakelite, coat pin, jockey motif, amber, 3" l **165.00**

Bakelite, corn holders, pr, red Bakelite handles **15.00**

Bakelite, earrings, pr, yellow hoops **25.00**

Bakelite, flashlight, swivel head **20.00**

Bakelite, flatware, Sta-Brite, set of 10, ST knives and forks, Bakelite handles **80.00**

Bakelite, horsehead and shoe, amber painted details and brass studs, 2½" h **225.00**

Bakelite, iron, General Electric, red Bakelite handle **25.00**

Bakelite, ladle, tortoiseshell Bakelite handle **25.00**

Bakelite, napkin ring, rocking horse, rodded eyes **75.00**

Bakelite, necklace, multicolored fruit **95.00**

Bakelite, pastry server, 2-tone handle **75.00**

Bakelite, pin, amber **8.00**

Bakelite, pin, brown cat **55.00**

Bakelite, potato masher, red handle **25.00**

Bakelite, radio, RCA Victor, police band **65.00**

Bakelite, spoon, Scotty handle........................**50.00**
Bakelite, tea strainer, red Bakelite knob at end of handle.....**50.00**
Bakelite, telephone, black, Signal Corp, US Army.........**125.00**
Catalin, drink stirrer, Cato Mixer.....................**30.00**
Catalin, radio, Crosley, brown.......................**30.00**
Celluloid, bookends, pr, plaster-weighted, mottled pink,
  emb with ornamental gold drape, unmkd, c1930........**35.00**
Celluloid, box, rect, mottled opaque amber, painted
  engraving and amber rhinestones dec................**20.00**
Celluloid, compact, round, cream pearlescent, mono-
  grammed, c1930.................................**25.00**
Celluloid, doll, Kewpie-type bride and groom, crepe
  paper clothes, 3¼" h, price for pair.................**42.00**
Celluloid, dresser set, Arch Amerith, Melano pattern,
  laminated translucent amber and ivory, embellished
  with pink celluloid oval and molded cameo profile,
  c1930...**175.00**
Celluloid, figure, cat, cream colored, black spots, pink
  bow, ears, and mouth, Sekiguchi Kako Co, Japan, 3" l.....**25.00**
Celluloid, figure, flamingo, pink, mkd "Japan," 2" h.......**15.00**
Celluloid, figure, leopard, cream colored, black spots,
  orange highlights, Occupied Japan, 4" l...............**35.00**
Celluloid, finger pick, imitation grained ivory............**2.00**
Celluloid, finger pick, mosaic colors, D'Andrea, c1950......**2.00**
Celluloid, folding comb, Art Deco style, cream and
  black...**25.00**
Celluloid, hair comb, black, 3 prong, Art Deco plume......**25.00**
Celluloid, jewelry suite, pendant and earrings, black, Art
  Deco style feather motif in rhinestones with red, blue,
  and topaz enamel paint, c1925....................**125.00**
Celluloid, rattle, dumbbell, old blue paint floral design,
  6" l...**30.00**
Celluloid, salt and pepper shakers, pr, figural skyscrap-
  ers, black and red...............................**25.00**
Celluloid, shoe horn, DuPont Viscoloid Corp, Navarre
  pattern dec.....................................**12.00**
Celluloid, tape measure, figural fish, souvenir from Cape
  Cod, Royal Co Ltd, Japan, 4¼" l....................**45.00**
Celluloid, toy, elephant, standing, white, red jacket,
  orange highlights, movable arms and legs, makes rat-
  tle sound, 5¾" h................................**45.00**
Celluloid, toy, wind-up cat, cream colored, bright pink
  stripes, jointed limbs, missing key, Made in Occupied
  Japan..**55.00**
Celluloid, watch holder, laminated amber and pearles-
  cent, grayish pink pearlized effect, late 1920s..........**15.00**
Plastic, ashtray, Willert Home Products.................**3.00**
Plastic, bank, figural pig, clear, Japan..................**8.00**
Plastic, bank, First Federal Savings and Loan.............**5.00**
Plastic, bottle opener, chrome and red plastic............**8.00**
Plastic, child's cup and plate, Campbell's Soup adv........**15.00**
Plastic, child's flatware, Joy-Toy, 6 pcs, Banner Plastics......**8.00**
Plastic, clock, electric, Seth Thomas Speed Read..........**20.00**
Plastic, clothes sprinkler, mkd "USA Plastic".............**8.00**
Plastic, coasters, set of 4, fish shaped, cork lined.........**6.00**
Plastic, doll house furniture, 3 pcs, Marx...............**15.00**
Plastic, dresser box, cov, oriental motif.................**20.00**
Plastic, dresser set, 3 pc, floral dec, Schwarz Bros Plastics....**15.00**
Plastic, earrings, pr, plastic and pearl beads, clip-on.......**8.00**
Plastic, fan, Air Flight, black, electric.................**125.00**
Plastic, grapefruit peeler, red........................**5.00**
Plastic, ice cream scoop, red, 1970s...................**8.00**
Plastic, letter opener, red...........................**10.00**

Plastic, clock, red case, chrome colored trim, General Electric Telechron, $25.00.

Plastic, measuring cup, E-Z Scoop, yellow, mkd
  "Advertising Slogan" on bottom.....................**4.00**
Plastic, napkin holder, figural pineapple, 1960–70s.........**15.00**
Plastic, napkin ring, heart shaped, 1970s................**8.00**
Plastic, poker chip holder, Tri State Plastic, 1960s.........**15.00**
Plastic, powder box, cov, rhinestones and plastic flowers
  dec, Menda Co, Pasadena, CA, 1950s................**10.00**
Plastic, purse, pill box style, 1950s...................**40.00**
Plastic, radio, Motorola, aqua.......................**75.00**
Plastic, rattle, figural telephone.....................**6.00**
Plastic, rattle, yellow chick, Knickerbocker..............**8.00**
Plastic, reamer, red, no rim, Westland Plastics...........**8.00**
Plastic, salt and pepper shakers, pr, cornucopia, ivory......**18.00**
Plastic, serving tray, floral design center, latticed edge......**15.00**
Plastic, silverware tray, pink flecked..................**6.00**
Plastic, thermometer, adv..........................**5.00**
Plastic, wall plaque, red rooster.....................**4.00**

PLAYBOY

Hugh M. Hefner launched the first issue of *Playboy,* featuring the now famous calendar photograph of Marilyn Monroe, in December 1953. There was no cover date. Hefner was not certain the concept would work. *Playboy* grew at a phenomenal rate.

During the 1960s and 70s, Hefner opened a series of Playboy Clubs, launched several foreign editions, operated several gambling casinos, and organized a Hollywood production company. *Playboy* went public in 1971 and was listed on the New York and Pacific stock exchanges. *Oui* was launched in October 1972.

Christie Hefner became president of Playboy Enterprises in 1982. In the mid-1980s more than sixty companies were licensed to market products bearing the Playboy, Playmate, and Rabbit Head trademarks.

Reference: Denis C. Jackson, *The Price & ID Guide to Playboy Magazines, 3rd Edition,* TICN, 1997.

Collectors' Club: Playboy Collectors Assoc, PO Box 653, Phillipsburg, MO 65722.

Book, *I Was a Negro Playboy Bunny*, paperback, Novel
  Books, 1964, 122 pp **$12.00**
Book, *Playboy's Little Annie Fanny*, soft cover, comic
  strip adventures, preface by Hugh Hefner, 1st ed,
  1972, 8½ x 11" **35.00**
Calendar, Playmate, spiral bound, glossy, orig envelope,
  1975, 8¼ x 12½" **18.00**
Candle Holder, glass, red frosted, 2 Femlin symbols,
  repeating inscription "The Playboy Club," and "Please
  Do Not Talk During Show, Your Curtesy is Appreciated
  By Others," 1960s, 6¼" h **35.00**
Key Ring, rabbit head charm, metal, gold luster finish,
  orig box and tags, c1980 . . . . **24.00**
Martini Pitcher, clear glass, cylindrical, 2 black rabbit
  head symbols, with 10" l clear glass stir rod, unmkd,
  1960s, 7¾" h **50.00**
Mug, clear glass, "Atlantic City Playboy Hotel & Casino,
  2500 Boardwalk," 5 rabbit head symbols, 1960s, 5½" h **20.00**
Mug, glass, charcoal color, 2 gold Femlin symbols and
  repeating inscription "The Playboy Club," clear bot-
  tom inscribed "The Playboy Club," 1960s, 6¼" h **25.00**
Playboy Magazine, Sep 1954 . . . . **150.00**
Playboy Magazine, Dec 1955 . . . . **45.00**
Playboy Magazine, May 1957 . . . . **25.00**
Playboy Magazine, Aug 1960 . . . . **15.00**
Playboy Magazine, Sep 1962 . . . . **22.00**
Playboy Magazine, Apr 1965 . . . . **15.00**
Playboy Magazine, Nov 1968 . . . . **7.00**
Playboy Magazine, Oct 1970 . . . . **7.00**
Playboy Magazine, Nov 1973 . . . . **6.00**
Playboy Magazine, Oct 1975 . . . . **6.00**
Playboy Magazine, Nov 1978 . . . . **6.00**
Playboy Magazine, Aug 1982 . . . . **6.00**
Playboy Magazine, Jun 1988 . . . . **4.00**
Playing Card Set, black leather wallet folder contains 2
  sealed card decks, Bridge scoring tablet, gold luster
  metal mechanical pencil, and extra scoring tablet,
  orig box, 1960s **45.00**
Puzzle, Playmate, Miss March, Bonnie Large, 1973, 5½" h
  canister **20.00**
Whistle, rabbit head, silvered metal, 1960s, 2½" l **15.00**

**Magazine, College
Issue, Oct 1956,
$125.00.** Photo
courtesy Frank's
Antiques & Auctions.

PLAYING CARDS

Playing cards came to America with the colonists. They were European in origin. The first American playing cards did not arrive on the scene until after the American Revolution. Caleb Bartlett (New York), Thomas Crehore (Dorchester, Massachusetts), David Felt (New York), the Ford (Foord) family (Milton, Massachusetts), and Amos and Daniel Whitney printed some of the first playing cards made in America. A. Dougherty, The New York Consolidated Card Company, and the United States Playing Card Company were the leading American manufacturers of playing cards. U.S. Playing Card introduced its Bicycle Brand in 1885. American card manufacturers are credited with introducing the classic joker, slick finish for shuffling, standard size, and upper corner indexes.

Card collectors specialize. Advertising, children's card games, miniature decks, novelty decks, and souvenir decks are just a few examples. Some collectors only collect one type of card, e.g., jokers. Although play is the primary focus of most playing cards, cards also have been used for fortune telling, instruction, e.g., World War II airplane spotting, and aiding travelers, e.g., a language set. These sets also appeal to collectors.

Always count the cards to make certain you are buying complete decks. American poker decks have 52 cards plus one or two jokers, pinochle decks have 48 cards, and Tarot decks 78 cards.

References: Everett Grist, *Advertising Playing Cards,* Collector Books, 1992, out of print; Norman E. Martinus and Harry L. Rinker, *Warman's Paper,* Wallace-Homestead, Krause Publication, 1994.

Collectors' Clubs: Chicago Playing Card Collectors, 1826 Mallard Lake Dr, Marietta, GA 30068; 52 Plus Joker, 204 Gorham Ave, Hamden, CT 06514; International Playing Card Society, 3570 Delaware Common, Indianapolis, IN 46220.

Beau Belle, 52 cards plus 2 jokers, different black and
  white nude photos on backs, boxed "pocket size" set,
  1950s **$60.00**
Bowlers Victory Legion, 52 cards, pin-up art of woman
  bowler, red, white, and blue emblem, and
  "Compliments Of The Bowlers Of America" on backs,
  boxed set, 1945 . . . . **65.00**
Chesapeake & Ohio Railroad, 2 decks, each deck has 52
  cards and 2 jokers, sleeping Chessie on 1 deck, Peake
  on other, "Purr-fect Transportation" on both, unmkd
  clear plastic case, boxed set, used, 1950s **75.00**
Cunard Line, 52 cards plus 2 Jokers, black, yellow, and
  silver symbolic crowned lion holding globe, boxed
  set, 1950s **25.00**
Flying A Service, black and white basset hound and
  logo, "When it comes to your car...ooooh, do we
  worry!," sealed box, 1950s **20.00**
Gaiety 54 Models, 52 cards plus 2 Jokers, different nude
  color photos on faces, generic backs, Hong Kong,
  1960s **18.00**
JFK Airforce One, 2 sealed decks, black, white, and gold
  presidential seal, plane, and world background on
  backs, gold cardboard slipcase box with blue flocking . . . **700.00**
Marilyn Monroe, 2 sealed decks, classic nude pose on
  drapery, boxed card and coaster set with 4 litho tin
  coasters with same illus and suede-like finish box,
  mid-1950s **400.00**

Amalgamated Meat Cutters/Butcher Workmen of America, mid-1950s, $10.00.

Planters Peanuts, 52 cards, linen finished cards with image of Mr Peanut paddling pretty lady in peanut canoe, no box, c1920s 850.00

Reddy Kilowatt, 2 decks of 52 cards, Reddy on backs and as Ace of Spades, velveteen finish slipcase, 1960s 75.00

Vargas Pin-ups, 2 decks of 52 cards plus 2 jokers each deck, sgd Vargas portraits on backs and 2 jokers, Vargas biography on other 2 jokers, mahogany leather over pressed wood box, made in Italy, 1950s 100.00

Western Railroads, 52 cards plus joker, different tinted color scenic photos on faces, scenic railroad photo and state seal emblems on backs, boxed set, 1920s 50.00

POCKETKNIVES

American manufacturers such as Samuel Mason and C. W. Platts of the Northfield Knife Company began making pocketknives in the 1840s. Numerous design, manufacturing, and marketing advances occurred. Collectors consider the period between the 1880s and 1940 as the pocketknife's golden age. American manufacturers received favorable tariff protection beginning in the 1890s. Before 1940, the best factory knives were handmade in a wide variety of designs and with the best material available.

The period between 1945 and the early 1960s is considered a dark age. Many pre-war manufacturers went out of business. A renaissance occurred in the 1970s as individual knife craftsmen began making pocketknives geared more for collecting and display than use. Bob Hayes, Jess Horn, Ron Lake, Jimmy Lile, Paul Pehlmann, Robert Ogg, and Barry Wood were leaders in the craftsman revival. Recently, collector and limited edition knives have flooded the market.

Pocketknives divide into three main groups: (1) utilitarian and functional knives, (2) advertising, character, and other promotional knives, and (3) craftsman knives. Alcas, Case, Colonial, Ka-Bar, Queen, Remington, Schrade, and Winchester are the best known manufacturers of the first group. Aerial Cutlery, Canton Cutlery, Golden Rule Cutlery, Imperial Knife Company, and Novelty Cutlery made many of the knives in the second group.

References: Jacob N. Jarrett, *Price Guide to Pocket Knives, 1890–1970*, L-W Books, 1993, 1998 value update; Bernard Levine, *Levine's Guide to Knives and Their Values, 4th Edition*, Krause Publications, 1997; C. Houston Price, *The Official Price Guide to*

Collector Knives, Eleventh Edition, House of Collectibles, 1996; Roy Ritchie and Ron Stewart, *The Standard Knife Collector's Guide, 3rd Edition,* Collector Books, 1997; Jim Sargent, *Sargent's American Premium Guide to Pocket Knives & Razors, 4th Edition,* Books Americana, Krause Publications, 1995; J. Bruce Voyles, *The International Blade Collectors Association Price Guide to Antique Knives, 2nd Edition,* Krause Publications, 1995; Richard D. White, *Advertising Cutlery,* Schiffer Publishing, 1999.

Periodicals: *Blade Magazine*, 700 E State St, Iola, WI 54990; *Edges*, PO Box 22007, Chattanooga, TN 37422.

Note: Prices are for pocketknives in mint condition.

Advertising, Coca-Cola, inscribed "Drink Coca-Cola" on side, 2 blades, second blade is nail file, stainless steel spring clipcase, c1950s $40.00

Advertising, Reddy Kilowatt, Zippo, 2 blades, second blade is nail file, stainless steel case with Reddy Kilowatt image and name, mid-1960s. 45.00

Boker, Lockback, stainless steel blade, brown plastic handle, tree medallion inlays, 3¼" l 20.00

Camco, single blade, with screwdriver and bottle opener tool, 2¾" l. 6.00

Case, Banana, 1139, walnut handle, 1955–65 . . . . 160.00

Case, Bow Tie, B1051, celluloid handle 375.00

Case, Daddy Barlow, 6143, bone handle, 1940–65 . . . . 75.00

Case, Doctor's, 6185, red bone handle, 1940–65 . . . . 150.00

Case, Greenskeeper, 4247K, white composition handle, 1965–70 . . . . 350.00

Case, Jack, 11031SH, walnut handle, 1940–65. . . . . 35.00

Case, Shark Tooth, folding, brass ends on case, leather sheath, orig box, 3½" l 55.00

Cattaraugus Cutlery, Bartender's Knife, 43263 . . . . 200.00

Cattaraugus Cutlery, Congress Whittler, 32449 . . . . 200.00

Character, FBI Jr Utility Pocketknife, silvered metal case, plastic insert panels with investigator portrait and title, swing-out single steel blade, complete with plastic whistle, and clear plastic magnifying glass, Imperial, Providence, R I, 1930–40, 3" l 75.00

Character, Popeye, silvered steel, ivory white celluloid side panels with Popeye image, name, King Features copyright in red, 2 blades, 1 blade mkd "Imperial Providence, RI," c1930s, 3" l 75.00

Character, Tom Mix, Ralston Straight Shooters, white pearlized grips, "TM" checkerboard logo with bright red lettering, 1939, 3" l 100.00

Character, Walt Disney's Davy Crockett, miniature, single blade, grip with black and silver photo at center of crossed rifle and hatchet on yellow ground, "Fess Parker as Davy Crockett," complete with loop and keychain, 1955, 2¼" l 45.00

Commemorative, 1939 New York World's Fair, Fish-Knife, steel, dark red and black marbled plastic grip handles, 1 panel incised "New York World's Fair" with insert metal title plate incised "Fish-Knife," 4" swing-out blade, with sharp edge lower side and serrated upper edge, Colonial, Providence, RI, 5" l 75.00

Commemorative, Marilyn Monroe, Golden Dreams pose, black plastic with clear plastic over color litho face, single blade, 3½" l folded size 20.00

Ka-Bar, Barlow, 5223, composition handle, 3¼" l 80.00

Ka-Bar, Boot, double edge blade, brass guard, ivory-like plastic grip, leather sheath with metal boot clip, 5" l 20.00

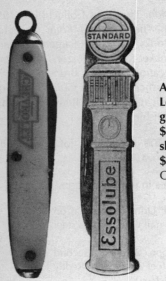

**Advertising Pocketknives.
Left: Chevrolet, yellow plastic
grips with red logo, 3" l,
$82.00. Right: Esso, gas pump
shape, debossed metal, 2½" l,
$165.00.** Photos courtesy
Collectors Auction Services.

Ka-Bar, Equal End Pen, T200RG, celluloid handle, 2½" l **50.00**
Ka-Bar, Jumbo Jack, 62701/2, Delrin handle, 4½" l **40.00**
Ka-Bar, Navy, 6175RG, bone handle, Union Cut Co,
4½" l **70.00**
Red Ryder, A Boy's First Knife, stainless steel blade, red
rubber handle, buckskin style fringed leather sheath,
with comic style handbook on knife care, safety, and
sharpening, 11¼" l, MIB **20.00**
Remington, Boy's Jack, 2848, bone handle, 3½" l **175.00**
Remington, Dog Groomer, R4733, bone handle **325.00**
Remington, Easy Open, R1671, redwood handle **85.00**
Remington, Premium Jack, RC803, bone handle **65.00**
Remington, Premium Stock, R3133, 4 blades, bone han-
dle **450.00**
Remington, Scout Utility, R3335, red, white, and blue
flag handle **375.00**
Remington, Teardrop Jack, R1752, black composition
handle **100.00**
Schrade Cutlery Corp, The Old-Timer, single lock style
blade, Staglon handles, orig box, 1¾" l **20.00**
United Cutlery, Elite Forces, bowie knife, "Desert Storm"
inscription on blade, black rubber grip, leather
sheath, MIB. **25.00**

POLITICAL & CAMPAIGN

Collectors prefer three-dimensional items. Material associated
with winning candidates is more desirable than that associated
with individuals who lost. While there are third party collectors,
their number is small.

The period from the late 1890s through the mid-1960s is the
golden age of political and campaign material. Today candidates
spend most of their money on television advertising. The 1996
presidential election was noteworthy for its lack of political collectibles.

Political and campaign item collectors were one of the first specialty collector groups to organize. As a result, large hoards of
post-1970 material exist. This is why most collectors concentrate
on material dating prior to the 1970s.

Reference: Ted Hake, *Hake's Guide to Presidential Campaign
Collectibles,* Wallace-Homestead, Krause Publications, 1992.

Periodical: *The Political Collector,* PO Box 5171, York, PA 17405.

Newsletter: *The Political Bandwagon,* PO Box 348, Leola, PA
17540.

Collectors' Club: American Political Items Collectors, PO Box
340339, San Antonio, TX 78234.

REPRODUCTION ALERT: Campaign buttons have been widely
reproduced. Examine the curl for evidence of modern identification marks having been scratched out. The backs of most early buttons were bare or had a paper label. Beware of any button with a
painted back. Buttons made prior to 1896 were celluloid. Any lithograph button from an election earlier than 1896 is incorrect.
Celluloid buttons need a collar since they are made in a sandwich
fashion. Lithograph buttons have a one-piece construction.

Bush, squeaker dolls, Bush and Gorbachev, vinyl,
labeled "It's A Glasnost Christmas," each dressed as
Santa, Ethical Products, NJ, c1990, 5" h, price for pair . . . **$15.00**
Clinton, satirical badge, "Camp Pain Traveling Press,"
used by reporters on 1992 campaign tour, encased in
plastic with bar pin hanger, 2½ x 4". **30.00**
Eisenhower, earrings, rhinestones spell out "IKE," silver
metal mountings, mounted on orig card, 1956, ⅝" h. **30.00**
Eisenhower, poster, "Win With Ike!," cardboard, black
and white photo, 9½ x 10¼" **20.00**
Eisenhower, woven silk, black and white Eisenhower
image at top and white silhouette of state of New York
on yellow ground, inscribed "We Like Ike!," made in
Austria, c1956. . . . . **45.00**
Goldwater, tie clip, brass bar with spring clip, diecut let-
tering "Goldwater" on front, 1¼" l **15.00**
Hoover, breakfast menu folder, cardboard cover,
inscribed "Trip Of The President To Detroit Michigan
And Return October 21st To October 23rd 1932,
Pennsylvania Railroad," red fabric spine sash, emb
gold-colored eagle at top, 6¼ x 8½". **125.00**
Hoover, flag, red, white, and blue, attached to black
wooden dowel with gold painted tip, c1928, 8 x 11"
flag **100.00**
Hoover, skill puzzle, wooden block pieces, "Hoover
Wins!, Prove It!," Republican Party platform planks
from 1929, orig box, 5½" sq box **80.00**
Kennedy, John, bust, black vinyl, inscribed with name
and birth and death dates, c1963, 5½" h **40.00**

**Roosevelt, admission ticket, "Democratic National Convention,
Philadelphia, June 1936," $25.00.**

Landon/Knox, thimble whistle, 1936, $25.00.

Kennedy, John, pinback button, red, white, and blue with black and white JFK and LBJ jugate photos, gold and white presidential seal between photos, easel back, 6" w. **70.00**

Kennedy, John, record album, "Sing Along with JFK, Laugh Along with Nixon," red, white, and blue sleeve with black and white caricature drawing of JFK in rocking chair by Al Burns, 1961 promo **28.00**

Kennedy, John and Robert, commemorative tile, white porcelain with bluetone images of JFK and RFK, gold lettered quotes "Ask not..." and "Some men see things as they are...," and names, birth and death dates, Screen Craft, 6" sq **70.00**

Kennedy, Robert, magazine, *Bobby Kennedy Next President of the United States,* 64 pp, 1965, 8½ x 11" **35.00**

Kennedy, Robert, mug, red, white, and blue with black and white caricature portrait and "Bobby For President," mkd "Mann Made Mugs," 1968, 4" h **25.00**

Nixon, ashtray, raised "The Watergate Hotel, Washington, D.C.," cast aluminum, Artograph, 1972, 4" d **30.00**

Nixon, inflatable bag, "Keep Kicking Nixon!!," white vinyl, red, white, and blue image of Nixon giving peace sign, orig pkg with "Kick It Around; It Always Makes A Comeback!," 1972, 16 x 11" **60.00**

Nixon, poster, psychedelic, "Nixon's the One," issued by "Youth For Nixon, Washington, D.C.," 14 x 20" **40.00**

Nixon, waste can, tin, oval, sepia-colored presidents' images from Washington to Nixon, 1970s, 12½" h **30.00**

Reagan/Bush, second inauguration medal, miniature of official medal, bronze, orig box, 1½" d **25.00**

Roosevelt, Franklin, pinback button, black and white photo, white fabric ribbon with red and blue lettering "Register Democratic," 1936, 1¾" d **50.00**

Roosevelt, Franklin, ribbon, red fabric, silver lettering "I'm For Roosevelt in '44," 2½ x 10" **40.00**

Roosevelt, Franklin, second inauguration medal, bronze, raised image of FDR 1 side, "John Nace Garner" other side, dated "Jan. 20, 1937," 3" d **200.00**

Roosevelt/Garner, parade ticket, orange stock, black type, issued for address on Pennsylvania Ave, second floor window seat, 2 x 4½" **25.00**

Smith, Al, photo, autographed to early APIC member, white paper stock, c1920, 9½ x 13" **100.00**

Truman, inaugural program, glossy cover, "United We Stand, Divided We Fall," orig mailing envelope, 72 pp, 1949, 8¼ x 11½" **90.00**

Willkie, license emblem, steel, portrait, red and blue on tan ground, orig envelope, 4 x 4½" **200.00**

PORCELIER PORCELAIN

The Porcelier Manufacturing Company was incorporated on October 14, 1926, with business offices in Pittsburgh, Pennsylvania, and a manufacturing plant in East Liverpool, Ohio. In 1930 Porcelier purchased the vacant plant of the American China Company in South Greensburg, Westmoreland County, Pennsylvania.

Initially, Porcelier produced light fixtures. Electrical kitchen appliances were added by the mid-1930s. Some credit Porcelier with making the first all-ceramic electrical appliances. In the course of its history, Porcelier made over 100 patterns of kitchenware and over 100 different light fixtures.

Sears, Roebuck and Company and Montgomery Ward were among Porcelier's biggest customers. Many products appear with brand names such as Heatmaster and Harmony House.

In March 1954 Pittsburgh Plate Glass Industries bought the Porcelier plant and adjacent land. The company was dissolved in the summer of 1954.

Reference: Susan E. Grindberg, *Collector's Guide to Porcelier China,* Collector Books, 1996.

Collectors' Club: Porcelier Collectors Club, 21 Tamarac Swamp Rd, Wallingford, CT 06492.

American Beauty Rose, creamer and sugar **$25.00**
Antique Rose, creamer **10.00**
Antique Rose, table lamp **45.00**
Arrow, dresser lamp **60.00**
Barock-Colonial, cookie jar, 2015, gold dots **95.00**
Barock-Colonial, syrup jar, 2012, red dots **45.00**
Basketweave Cameo, flour canister **35.00**
Basketweave Wild Flowers, spaghetti bowl. **85.00**
Black-Eyed Susan, double teapot, 6 cup, Colonial shape. **75.00**
Cattail, creamer and sugar. **30.00**
Cattail, urn, electric. **100.00**
Country Life, casserole, cov, 9½" d **85.00**
Country Life, sugar, cov. **15.00**
Deco Ribbed, coffeepot, 6 cup **35.00**
Dutch Boy and Girl, teapot, 6 cup **30.00**
Field Flowers, tankard, 6 cup. **35.00**
Flamingo, creamer and sugar. **20.00**
Floral Panel, creamer and sugar **25.00**
Floral Panel, percolator, 70, electric. **75.00**
Golden Wheat, percolator, 120, electric. **70.00**
Goldfinches, creamer and sugar. **25.00**
Nautical, creamer and sugar **40.00**
Nautical, coffeepot, 8 cup. **35.00**
New York World's Fair, ashtray **100.00**
New York World's Fair, creamer and sugar **160.00**
Pears, coffeepot, 2 cup **30.00**
Rope Bow, creamer and sugar **25.00**
Scalloped Wild Flowers, creamer. **15.00**
Scalloped Wild Flowers, waffle iron **225.00**
Serv-All Line, batter pitcher, 3014, platinum dec **35.00**
Serv-All Line, coffeepot, 576-D, gold dec **35.00**
Serv-All Line, waffle iron, 451, platinum dec **120.00**
Silhouette, teapot, 6 cup, Colonial shape **45.00**
Silhouette Hostess, percolator, electric **75.00**
Tree Trunk, teapot, 6 cup. **35.00**
Tulips, creamer and sugar **35.00**
White Flower Platinum, urn, electric **95.00**

POSTCARDS

In 1869 the Austrian government introduced the first government-issued postcard. The postal card concept quickly spread across Europe, arriving in the United States in 1873.

The period from 1898 until 1918 is considered the golden age of postcards. English and German publishers produced most of the cards during the golden age. Detroit Publishing and John Winsch were leading American publishers.

The postcard collecting mania that engulfed Americans ended at the beginning of World War I. Although greeting cards replaced many postcards on sales racks, the postcard survived. Linen cards dominated the period between 1930 and the end of the 1940s. Chromolithograph cards were popular in the 1950s and 60s. Postcards experienced a brief renaissance in the 1970s and 80s with the introduction of the continental size format (4 x 6") and the use of contemporary designs.

Are the stamps on postcards valuable? The answer is no 99.9% of the time. If you have doubts, consult a philatelic price guide. A postcard's postmark may be an added value factor. There are individuals who collect obscure postmarks.

References: Diane Allmen, *The Official Price Guide to Postcards,* House of Collectibles, 1990; J. L. Mashburn, *Black Americana: A Century of History Preserved on Postcards,* Colonial House, 1996; J. L. Mashburn, *Fantasy Postcards,* Colonial House, 1996; J. L. Mashburn, *The Artist-Signed Postcard Price Guide,* Colonial House, 1993; J. L. Mashburn, *The Postcard Price Guide, Third Edition,* Colonial House, 1997; J. L. Mashburn, *Sports Postcard Price Guide,* Colonial House, 1998; J. L. Mashburn, *The Super Rare Postcards of Harrison Fisher With Price Guide,* Colonial House, 1992; Susan Brown Nicholson, *The Encyclopedia of Antique Postcards,* Wallace-Homestead, Krause Publications, 1994; Robert Ward, *Investment Guide to North American Real Photo Postcards,* Antique Paper Guide, 1991; Jane Wood, *The Collectors' Guide to Post Cards,* L-W Books, 1984, 1997 value update.

Periodicals: *Barr's Post Card News,* 70 S Sixth St, Lansing, IA 52151; *Postcard Collector,* PO Box 1050, Dubuque, IA 52004.

Collectors' Clubs: Deltiologists of America, PO Box 8, Norwood, PA 19074; Postcard History Society, PO Box 1765, Manassas, VA 22110.

Note: *Barr's Post Card News* and the *Postcard Collector* publish lists of over fifty regional clubs in the United States and Canada. Prices listed are for postcards in excellent condition.

Advertising, August Schell Brewing Co, New Ulm, MN, view of brewery and elk, adv text on back **$50.00**

Advertising, Ford Motor Co exhibit building at 1939 New York World's Fair, published by The Albertype Co, Brooklyn. **35.00**

Advertising, Gloria Bicycles and Motorcycles, young couple taking break together from riding, Italian adv, Mosca, sgd, 1953, used **50.00**

Advertising, RoLee Photographers, Des Moines, IA, portrait of woman with adv text, real photo, 1949, used. **40.00**

Advertising, throat lozenges, "Frog in Your Throat? For Public Speakers," frog giving lecture to audience of frogs **40.00**

New York State Barge Canal Terminal, Genesee River, Rochester, NY, published by The Rochester News Company, 1929 postmark, $6.00.

Amsterdam Olympics 1928, runner with Olympics flag and stadium in background **75.00**

Art Deco, man and woman in pierrot costumes dancing at party, Italian, Chiostri, sgd **40.00**

Atlantic City Pageant, New Jersey, 1921, woman performing dive in front of Neptune and his trident, and other characters and onlookers of the pageant **75.00**

"Atoms For Peace," mobile exhibit truck of US Atomic Energy Commission, "Have been in St Louis two days attending an Atomic Energy Commission meeting...," St Louis, 1958, used **30.00**

Boy Scout Jamboree, Bad Ischl, Austria, Austrian scout with 2 Indian scouts, real photo, used, with Jamboree stamp and cancel, 1951. . . . . **60.00**

California Pacific International Expo, San Diego, "Arabian horse and rider at Saladin show on Midway," Nielsen, Cincinnati, OH, real photo, 1935 . . . . **45.00**

Child with Doll, portrait of girl with dressed doll in her doll carriage, real photo, British **40.00**

Christmas, family gathered in front of tree, German, real photo **65.00**

Circus Workers, posed in front of Minnelli Brothers tent, real photo **50.00**

Crowds of Blacks, gathered in boats on shore, "Negro Baptism, near Norfolk, Virginia," 1924, Norfolk, used **30.00**

Donald Duck, with nephews and Pluto, "It has the air of truth that sugar causes pain in the teeth!," French text. **50.00**

Dorsey, Tommy, portrait of Dorsey with King Liberty Trombone, adv for trombones by HN White Co, Cleveland, OH, real photo. **65.00**

Fallas De San Jose, Valencia, Spain, dancers on stilts atop giant donuts, flames behind, S Carrilero Abad, sgd, 1961 . . . . **35.00**

Famous American Indians, complete set of 8, including Joseph, Geronimo, Sitting Bull, Curley, Rain-in-the Face, Gall, Red Cloud, and Keokuk, history of each printed on back, ©1941 G I Groves, brown and white **80.00**

Hawaiian Maidens, portrait of 2 hula girls, real photo. **65.00**

Hold to Light, Christmas, child chasing turkey, "A Happy Christmas to you," fruit, clothing, and decorative elements illuminate **150.00**

"Greetings from New Jersey," 1946 postmark, $4.00.

Hold to Light, Easter, dressed rabbit family painting Easter eggs, "Easter Greetings," eggs, lantern, and light rays illuminate. **75.00**

Holy Cross Central School of Nursing in Indiana and Illinois, "In the heart of the Midwest close to home," c1960. . . . . **35.00**

Ice Hockey, "At Madison Square Garden between the Atlantic City Sea Gulls and the Crescent-Hamilton Athletic Club of Brooklyn," real photo by "Jack Frank of the New York Herald-Tribune, made with Kalart Photoflash, Synchronizer..." adv text on back for Synchronizer camera equipment, by Kalart Co, New York City, black and white, 1935 . . . . **325.00**

Man in Shriner's Cap, notation on back "John Gerb Karom Sanctorum Lodge No 195, Hartford, Connecticut, 1922," real photo **40.00**

Nevada Club, Las Vegas, NV, women at slot machines, real photo, 1955 . . . . **50.00**

New York World's Fair, complete set of 6, blue, orange, and metallic gold depictions of exhibit buildings. **200.00**

"Noodles," mother preparing food, with daughter watching, published by Block Pub, NY, #23, Alph Levy, sgd, black and white. **60.00**

Novelty, "Cross Word Puzzling," girl working on crossword puzzle, bubble eyes with moving pellet irises, British. **30.00**

Novelty, photo of woman with real hair attached, tinted, real photo, French. **40.00**

Pan American Airliner, "Aboard a Luxurious Airliner of Pan American Airways, Inc," int view of seated passengers, linen, PA, 1953, used, stamp removed. **85.00**

San Francisco Synagogue, ext view of Temple Emanu-El, San Francisco, CA, real photo, 1945. . . . . **35.00**

Sports, portrait of wrestlers from different countries, each person numbered in pen with corresponding list of names and countries on back, includes black wrestler V Thomson from US, real photo, black and white, dated 1930 . . . . **100.00**

The Sioux, portrait of mother and child, real photo, c1930. . . . . **50.00**

Woman Golfer, portrait of woman with golf clubs, real photo, tinted, British **45.00**

Yankee Clipper Takeoff, La Guardia Field, New York City, W Hoff, real photo, 1942, used **75.00**

POSTERS

The full color poster arrived on the scene in the 1880s, the result of the lithographic printing revolution. Posters by Courier and Strobridge are considered some of the finest examples of American lithography ever printed. Philadelphia was the center of the poster printing industry in America prior to 1945.

Almost from its inception, collectors were fascinated with this colorful art form. Printers began overprinting their commercial runs and selling the extra posters through print dealers and galleries. Editions Sagot in Paris offered posters for sale featuring the art of Toulouse-Lautrec. Posters were an inexpensive advertising form and played a major role during World Wars I and II.

Scarce is a term that must be used very carefully when referring to posters. Print runs into the millions are known. Yet, most were destroyed. The poster collecting community was relatively small and heavily art-focused until the 1970s.

Carefully check the date mark on movie posters. An "R," usually located in the lower right corner near the border in the white area, followed by slash and the date denotes a later release of a movie. These posters generally are not as valuable as posters associated with the initial release.

References: Tony Fusco, *Posters, Second Edition*, Avon Books, 1994; Janet Gleeson, *Miller's Collecting Prints and Posters*, Millers Publications, 1997; Susan Theran, *Prints, Posters & Photographs: Identification and Price Guide*, Avon Books, 1993.

American Airlines/San Francisco, Golden Gate Bridge spanning across horizon with San Francisco and Bay Bridge in background, white lettering, 1948, 40 x 30". . . **$550.00**

Anthony Adverse, Warner Bros, Frederic March, Olivia de Havilland, 1936, 27 x 41". **320.00**

Bally Ski, Orell Fussli, Zurich, photomontage of ski boot and binding against blue ground, red lettering, 50¼ x 35¾" **375.00**

Boost!/Boy Scout Week/June 8th to 14th, Norman Rockwell, smiling Boy Scout in khaki green hat within dark blue circle, red bandanna hangs down into red and blue text, Lutz & Sheinkman, NY, 28 x 21". **525.00**

Conquest, MGM, Greta Garbo, Charles Boyer, 1937, 14 x 22". **325.00**

Disneyland, David, rocket with electric pink markings rising into sky, sights and attractions of amusement park in orange, red, brown, green, and purple, bright orange and pink lettering, tie-dyed purple and blue ground, 40¼ x 25" **550.00**

Dr Meyer's Foot Soap, farmers, policemen, hockey players, football players, and priest dressed in reds, blues, and purples on green ground, green and tan lettering, 38 x 25¼" **260.00**

Flying Is the Way to Travel/TWA, view of Grand Canyon seen through window of plane, purple, orange, yellow, brown, and blue, 40 x 25⅛" **630.00**

For a Few Dollars More, United Artists, Clint Eastwood, 1967, 81 x 81" **460.00**

Give 'em Both Barrels, Jean Carlu, c1941, 15 x 22". . . . **130.00**

Gulf/Happy New Year, paper, with archival backing, form SS 57, for posting all divisions Dec 31–Jan 15, 1940, 42 x 27¾" **85.00**

Hoover Dam and Lake Mead, family motorboating on blue water in shadow of dam under orange sky and brown cliffs, green and red lettering, 32½ x 24½" **525.00**

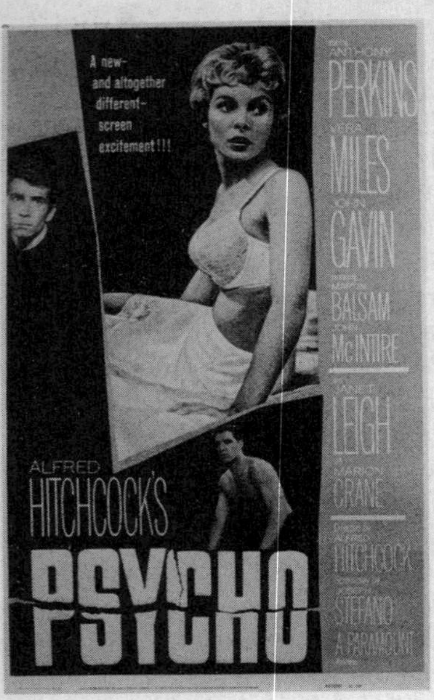

***Psycho*, Paramount, Janet Leigh, Anthony Perkins, 1960, 60 x 40", $800.00.**

Illinois Central/Come to Mardi Gras, costumed reveler, street party with train, black, red, and pink, 41½ x 28" ... 260.00

Ivory Soap, linen back, "Ivory Soap. It Floats," white lettering on black ground, 17" h, 56½" w ... 50.00

Las Vegas/Fly TWA, stylized image of woman in half pink evening dress and half yellow striped swimsuit straddling day and night, with collage of different day and night events, 40 x 25" ... 325.00

Liberte, Edouard Collin, colorful signal hanging in front of black ship with red funnel blowing steam into red, light blue, and violet sky, gray and blue lettering, 38¾ x 24" ... 460.00

Look Who's Laughing, RKO Radio, linen, Fibber McGee and Molly, 1941, 27 x 41" ... 460.00

Los Angeles, Jebary, Charlie Chaplin in light blue behind green, brown, blue, yellow, and orange camera, orange and fuchsia lettering, 1967, 40¼ x 25" ... 260.00

Maxwell House Coffee, Norman Rockwell illus, 1931–32 ... 325.00

Protect His Future Buy and Keep War Bonds, man holding boy up with hands, US Government Printing Office, 1942, 5½ x 33" ... 35.00

Ringling Bros and Barnum & Bailey Combined Shows Circus, features "Terrell Jacobs, the lion king," lion with tamer, "Erie Litho & Prt Co, Erie, PA, No 849," 17 x 24¼" ... 175.00

Rose Marie, MGM, linen, Joan Crawford, 1928, 27 x 41" ... 575.00

Royal Baking Powder, product illus, 1920s, 25 x 20" ... 40.00

The High and the Mighty, John Wayne, 27 x 41" ... 75.00

The Man Who Knew Too Much, Paramount, linen, James Stewart, 1956, 41 x 81" ... 230.00

White Stag Ski Togs, family with red faces, skis and poles making their way up slope, black ground, white and red lettering, 34½ x 23^{3}/" ... 260.00

You Buy 'Em We'll Fly 'Em!, Wilkinsons, smiling pilot in open cockpit with thumbs-up, US Government Printing Office, 1942, 60 x 40¼" ... 485.00

You Don't Have to Be Jewish to Love Levy's, Italian mother with sandwich standing over table with red checkered tablecloth laden with food on blue ground, 1971, 45½ x 29¼" ... 400.00

POTTERIES, REGIONAL

There were thousands of pottery factories scattered across the United States. Many existed only for a brief period of time.

Recent scholarship by individuals such as Phyllis and Tom Bess on the Oklahoma potteries, Carol and Jim Carlton on Colorado pottery, Jack Chipman on California pottery, and Darlene Dommel on the Dakota potteries have demonstrated how rich America's ceramic heritage is. This is only the tip of the iceberg.

This is a catchall category for all those companies that have not reached a strong enough collecting status to deserve their own category. Eventually, some will achieve this level. Collectors collect what they know. Thanks to today's scholarship, collectors are learning more about these obscure potteries.

References: California: Jack Chipman, *Collector's Encyclopedia of California Pottery, Second Edition,* Collector Books, 1998; Michael L. Ellis, *Collector's Guide to Don Winton Designs,* Collector Books, 1998; Michael Schneider, *California Potteries,* Schiffer Publishing, 1995; Bernice Stamper, *Vallona Starr Ceramics,* Schiffer Publishing, 1995. Colorado: Carol and Jim Carlton, *Collector's Encyclopedia of Colorado Pottery,* Collector Books, 1994, out of print. North Dakota: Darlene Hurst Dommel, *Collector's Encyclopedia of the Dakota Potteries,* Collector Books, 1996. Oklahoma: Phyllis and Tom Bess, *Frankoma and Other Oklahoma Potteries,* Schiffer Publishing, 1995.

Collectors' Clubs: Arkansas: Arkansas Pottery Collectors Society, PO Box 7617, Little Rock, AR 72217; Minnesota: Nemadji Pottery Collectors Club, 4310 Old Co Rd 8, Moose Lake, MN 55767; North Dakota: North Dakota Pottery Collectors Society, PO Box 14, Beach, ND 58621.

California, American Pottery Co, figurine, bird on twig, multicolored glaze, paper label, 4¾" h ... $8.00

California, Batchelder, vase, #49, 6 x 8½" ... 150.00

California, Bellaire, ashtray, asymmetric, Bird Isle, sgd "Bellaire," 7 x 14" ... 100.00

California, Bellaire, charger, stylized bird on branch motif, sgd "Marc Bellaire," 15" d ... 165.00

California, Bellaire, dish, divided, Jamaica, Line, sgd "Bellaire Calif./Jamaica" in sgraffito on underside, 10" ... 175.00

California, Bellaire, platter, jungle dancer scene, oval, sgd, 18 x 13" ... 250.00

California, Bellaire, vase, asymmetrical, Mardi Gras painted scene, 18" h ... 350.00

California, Betty Lou Nichols Ceramics, planter, Gretel, 5½" ... 30.00

California, Block of California, planter, highchair, imp mark, 5½" h ... 10.00

California, Brahm, candy box, cov, applied rose dec on lid, in-mold mark ... 65.00

California, California Originals, stylized long-neck bird, multicolored, 16" h ... 15.00

California, Callender, figurine, English setter ... 65.00

California, Capistrano Ceramics, figurine, Oriental lady ... 25.00

California, Cemar, condiment jar, notched cov, fish shaped, in-mold mark ... 65.00

California, Cemar, figurine, fish, polychrome glaze, "Cemar 564" in-mold mark, 9¼" h ... 125.00

California, Cemar, figurine, phoenix bird, 9½" h ... 65.00

California, Ceramicraft, cotton holder, figural whale, yellow and black, 3¼ x 6" ... 10.00

California Originals, dresser set, covered box and 2 pin trays, applied lace and pink rose, mkd "Heirlooms of Tomorrow," c1950, $12.00.

California, Claire Lerner Studios, figurine, Oriental mandolin player, 9" h. 8.00

California, Clay Sketches, planter, frog pulling snail, 3 x 7½" 30.00

California, Cleminsons, bread tray, Distlefink pattern, 12½" l 35.00

California, Cleminsons, butter, cov, Distlefink pattern 50.00

California, Cleminsons, figurine, goose, green body, yellow beak, 4¼" h 25.00

California, Cleminsons, plate, crowing rooster center, 9½" d 30.00

California, Cleminsons, ring holder, dog, white body, tan spots, black highlights, 2⅞" l 10.00

California, Cleminsons, spoon rest, gray, gold, and purple leaf design, 8½" l 8.00

California, Cleminsons, wall pocket, frying pan, "Them that works hard eats hearty," 11⅜" h 25.00

California, Decora Ceramics, wall plaques, Dutch boy and girl, mkd "2111," and "DeCora Ceramics, Inc," 6" h boy, 6½" h girl, price of pair 50.00

California, Doranne, cookie jar, tortoise and hare, woodtone, 1970s. 50.00

California, Flintridge China, dinner plate 30.00

California, Freeman-McFarlin, figurine, Arabian stallion, 9 x 11¼". 90.00

California, Goldhammer Ceramics, planter, rabbit, pink, 7¼" h 18.00

California, Hagen-Renaker, figurine, Siamese cat, 8⅞" h 75.00

California, Hagen-Renaker, flower bowl, applied roses, 9½ x 11¼" 15.00

California, Haldeman, candle holder, green, 1½ x 4½". 5.00

California, Haldeman, figure, monkey, dressed as bellboy, 2¾" h 25.00

California, Haldeman, planter, figural swan, sand lined with turquoise, 5 x 7" 40.00

California, Kaye of Hollywood, figurine, basket lady, 3130, 8½" h 25.00

California, Kaye of Hollywood, soap dish, woman sitting with hands folded, 8" h 75.00

California, Keeler, figurine, begging Cocker Spaniel, #735, 6" h. 10.00

California, Keeler, figurine, kitten in basket, 4½ x 5¾" 30.00

California, Keeler, figurine, Little Red Riding Hood, 5½" h 35.00

California, Kim Ward, figurine, Mimi, 5¼" h. 25.00

California, La Mirada Pottery, wall pocket, fish, chartreuse crackle glaze. 75.00

California, Manker, cup and saucer, leaf shape 30.00

California, Manker, plate, leaf shape, 7½" d 25.00

California, Manker, vase, fluted, powder blue ext, light rose int, 6" h 150.00

California, Pacific, baby plate, divided, bunny design border, 9" d 200.00

California, Pacific, baking dish, delphinium blue, clip-on wood handle, 8¾" d 35.00

California, Pacific, fish platter, oval, Hostess Ware, 15" l 165.00

California, Pacific, pitcher, Hostess Ware, 2 qt 28.00

California, Pacific, pretzel jar, jade green 500.00

California, Pacific, vase, bird motif, 8¼" h 18.00

California, Poinsettia Studios, shot glass/bell, figural man, "A Measure of Cheer" on top hat. 15.00

California, Rio Hondo, planter, rabbit pulling cart, 2¾" h 5.00

California, Roselane, bowl, pedestal, square, Chinese Modern, 2½ x 6¼" 10.00

California, Roselane, figurine, Bali dancer, 11" h 18.00

California, Roselane, figurine, "Sparkler" kangaroo with joeys, 4¼" h 20.00

California, Sara Hume, bank, shoe, 3⅜ x 5¼" 25.00

California, Treasure Craft, planter/wall pocket, pixie sitting under tree, 5" h 7.00

California, Twin Winton, figurine, squirrel, 3½ x 5¼" 30.00

California, Twin Winton, pitcher, Open Range Line. 28.00

California, Weil, vase, sailor boy, 10¾" h 15.00

California, Winfield China, cheese dish, cov, Blue Pacific 65.00

California, Winfield China, coffeepot, Desert Dawn 55.00

California, Winfield China, mug, Bird of Paradise 25.00

Colorado, Broadmoor, ashtray, applied bird, 4" d 50.00

Colorado, Broadmoor, bean pot. 65.00

Colorado, Broadmoor, cornucopia vase, blue and mauve glaze, 6" l 45.00

Colorado, Broadmoor, planter, turquoise, 18" h 110.00

Colorado, Denver White, bowl, gray, 3 x 5" 55.00

Colorado, Denver White, vase, blue, crimped edge, 6" h 95.00

Colorado, Denver White, vase, pine cone dec, 6" h 125.00

Colorado, Hopkins, figurine, tree with birds, 12" h 65.00

Colorado, Indian Hills, wedding jug, blue 35.00

Colorado, Johnson, bowl, brown swirl, 8" d 55.00

Colorado, Loveland, condiment tray, applied deer, 10" d. 10.00

Colorado, Loveland, salt and pepper shakers, pr, 3" h. 6.00

Colorado, Morrison, vase, blue matte, 8" h. 40.00

Colorado, Rocky Mountain, figurine, poodle, 10" h 25.00

North Dakota, Dickinson Clay Products, ashtray, marine blue, white flowing overglaze, 4¼" d 28.00

North Dakota, Dickinson Clay Products, bookends, pr, mountain sheep, green 350.00

North Dakota, Dickinson Clay Products, vase, orange gloss glaze, gold and black overglaze, 4" h 45.00

North Dakota, Messer, figurine, burro, 3 x 4¾". 50.00

North Dakota, Messer, figurine, prairie dog, 2¼" h 100.00

North Dakota, Pine Ridge, hanging basket, geometric motif, 5 x 7½". 250.00

North Dakota, Pine Ridge, plate, geometric star motif, 7" d 200.00

North Dakota, Rushmore, ashtray, relief pine cone motif, blue, 4½"l 65.00

North Dakota, Rushmore, pitcher, swirl design, uranium orange, 7" h 125.00

North Dakota, Rushmore, trivet, Art Deco style floral design, mint green. 110.00

North Dakota, Rushmore, vase, concentric rings, blue, 3½" h 25.00
North Dakota, University of North Dakota, bowl, sgraffito mule design, 3¾ x 5¾" 380.00
North Dakota, University of North Dakota, figurine, horse, turquoise, 6" h................................. 180.00
North Dakota, University of North Dakota, Julia Mattson, modernistic cone woman, 6" h 150.00
North Dakota, University of North Dakota, pitcher, white clay, blue stencil, 2¼ x 4½" 200.00
North Dakota, University of North Dakota, wall plaque, oxen pulling covered wagon, 5" d 225.00
North Dakota, WPA Ceramics, bowl, Native American motif, black and tan sgraffito dec, 3½ x 7" 700.00
Oklahoma, Cherokee, bank, buffalo nickel, 7½" h 10.00
Oklahoma, Cherokee, bottle, ring handled, mottled, 12" h 8.00
Oklahoma, Cherokee, bust, Indian head, 15" h............ 25.00
Oklahoma, Creek, eggcup, red, 3½" h 5.00
Oklahoma, Creek, figurine, mallard, 7½ x 9" 15.00
Oklahoma, Gracetone, ashtray, #2AT1, jade, 7" d........ 15.00
Oklahoma, Gracetone, bowl, pedestal base, #100P, gunmetal, 6" h.. 20.00
Oklahoma, Gracetone, figurine, English Setter, cinnamon, 5½" l 175.00
Oklahoma, Gracetone, salt and pepper shakers, pr, pink champagne finish 10.00
Oklahoma, Hammat Originals, ashtray, banana leaf, 7" l..... 10.00
Oklahoma, Hammat Originals, bowl, conch shell, 5" d...... 15.00
Oklahoma, Hammat Originals, compote, cabbage leaf, 4½" h 15.00
Oklahoma, Hammat Originals, mug, coconut, 7 oz 4.00
Oklahoma, Hammat Originals, tumbler, western motif, 4½" h 20.00
Oklahoma, Hammat Originals, wall mask, Indian maiden, 4½" h 15.00
Oklahoma, Hilsmeyer, vase, wildlife scene, 5" h........... 25.00
Oklahoma, NYA, bottle vase, blue int, 5½" h 25.00

Oklahoma, NYA, pitcher, yellow ware, 20 oz............. 25.00
Oklahoma, Sequoyah, ashtray, 5" d 30.00
Oklahoma, Sequoyah, kneeling potter, mkd "Patty Vineyard, 1943," 8" h 80.00
Oklahoma, Sequoyah, pitcher, frog handle, red, 5" h 65.00
Oklahoma, Sequoyah, pitcher, thunderbird dec, green, beige, 3½" h 20.00
Oklahoma, Sequoyah, planter, mkd "Krouse Welling Okla. U.S.A. #10," 2¾" h, 6" l 65.00
Oklahoma, Sequoyah, urn, red, 10" h 160.00
Oklahoma, Sequoyah, vase, mkd "Lucille Works 1939 Sequoyah #20," 4¾" h 100.00
Oklahoma, Sequoyah, vase, straight neck, mkd "Winnie Simmer 1938–39 Sequoyah," 6½" h 45.00
Oklahoma, Synar Ceramics, basket, woodpine ext, aqua int, 7½" h 15.00
Oklahoma, Synar Ceramics, lotus bowl, wintergreen, 5½" 5.00
Oklahoma, Synar Ceramics, vase, wheat design, 10" h 10.00
Oklahoma, Tamac, ashtray, frosty fudge 10.00
Oklahoma, Tamac, coffeepot, cov, 24 oz, frosty fudge....... 70.00
Oklahoma, Tamac, dinner plate, avocado, 10" d 8.00
Oklahoma, Tamac, juice tumbler, 4 oz, frosty pine 8.00
Oklahoma, Tamac, mantel planter, raspberry, 18" l 25.00
Oklahoma, Tamac, relish dish, divided, avocado, 7" l 15.00
Oklahoma, Tamac, spoonrest, raspberry, "For My Stirring Spoon," 6" h 5.00
Oklahoma, Winart, chip 'n dip plate, persimmon with frost, 13" d 10.00
Oklahoma, Winart, decanter, pink with brown overglaze, 1 qt, 8" h. 30.00
Oklahoma, Winart, juice tumbler set, carousel tray with 6 tumblers, persimmon with frost 30.00
Oklahoma, Winart, Lazy Susan, persimmon with frost, 16" d 25.00
Oklahoma, Winart, pitcher, 16 oz, #46, blue with frost........ 10.00
Oklahoma, Winart, salt and pepper shakers, pr, ball, #23H, persimmon with frost 8.00
Oklahoma, Winart, teapot, individual, 12 oz, #52, brown with frost 15.00
Oklahoma, Winart, tidbit tray, 2-tier, pink, frost rim, 10" d 18.00

PRAYER LADIES

Prayer Ladies are kitchen items in the shape of a woman wearing an apron with a prayer printed on it. More often than not, the woman has her eyes closed and hands folded in prayer.

Prayer ladies are found in a wide variety of forms, e.g., bud vases, cookie jars, egg timers, napkin holders, salt and pepper shakers, scouring pad holders, string holders, and toothpick holders. The most commonly found examples wear a pink dress.

Prayer ladies date from the 1960s and 70s. Enesco, one of the chief importers, called its line "Mother in the Kitchen."

Reference: April Tvorak, *Prayer Lady – Enesco Price Guide*, published by author, 1998.

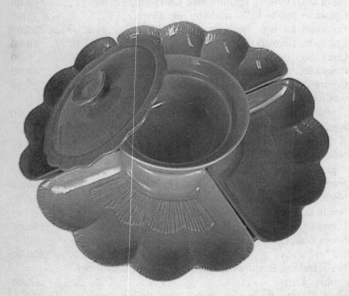

California, Marsh Industries, Lazy Susan, bright yellow and orange, center piece mkd "CALIF USA," other sections mkd "CALIF USA L69," c1970, $15.00.

Air Freshener, pink $150.00
Bank, "Mother's Pin Money," blue 175.00
Bank, "Mother's Pin Money," pink 145.00
Bell, blue 95.00
Bell, pink 85.00
Bud Vase, pink 125.00

Tea Set, blue, 6¹/₂" h teapot (illus), 4¹/₄" h creamer, and 4¹/₄" h sugar, price for set, $275.00.

Candle Holders, pr, pink	125.00
Canister, pink	300.00
Cookie Jar, blue	495.00
Cookie Jar, pink	295.00
Cookie Jar, white, blue trim	425.00
Crumb Sweeper Set, brush and tray, pink	145.00
Egg Timer, pink	135.00
Instant Coffee, blue	145.00
Instant Coffee, pink	125.00
Instant Coffee, white, blue trim	160.00
Mug, blue	145.99
Mug, pink	135.00
Napkin Holder, blue	35.00
Napkin Holder, pink	25.00
Napkin Holder, white, blue trim	40.00
Photo Holder, pink	135.00
Planter, kitchen prayer, pink	65.00
Ring Holder, blue	50.00
Ring Holder, pink	48.00
Salt and Pepper Shakers, pr, blue	20.00
Salt and Pepper Shakers, pr, pink	15.00
Salt and Pepper Shakers, pr, white, blue trim	22.00
Soap Dish, blue	45.00
Soap Dish, pink	38.00
Spoon Holder, slotted skirt holds 4 spoons, blue	50.00
Spoon Holder, slotted skirt holds 4 spoons, pink	45.00
Spoonrest, flat, blue	45.00
Spoonrest, flat, pink	35.00
Spoonrest, flat, white, blue trim	50.00
Sprinkler Bottle, holding iron, blue	350.00
Sprinkler Bottle, holding iron, pink	200.00
String Holder, blue	145.00
String Holder, pink	135.00
Tea Set, teapot, creamer and sugar, blue	400.00
Tea Set, teapot, creamer and sugar, pink	250.00
Toothpick Holder, blue	28.00
Toothpick Holder, pink	20.00
Toothpick Holder, white, blue trim	32.00
Wall Plaque, pink	100.00

PRECIOUS MOMENTS

During a visit to the Los Angeles Gift Show in 1978, Eugene Freeman, president of Enesco, saw some cards and posters featuring the drawings of Samuel J. Butcher. At first, Butcher and Bill Biel, his partner in Jonathan and David, were not thrilled with the idea of having Butcher's art transformed into three-dimensional form. However, after seeing a prototype sculpted by Yashei Fojioka of Japan, Butcher and Biel agreed.

Initially twenty-one pieces were made. Early figures are darker in color than those made today. Pieces produced between 1978 and 1984 and licensed by Jonathan & David Company have smaller heads than pieces relicensed by the Samuel J. Butcher Company and Precious Moments. Jonathan & David closed in 1988.

The Enesco Precious Moments Club was established in 1981. In 1989, Butcher opened the Precious Moments Chapel in Carthage, Missouri. In 1995 Goebel introduced hand-painted bronze miniatures. The year 1995 also saw Enesco launch its Century Circle Retailers, a group of 35 retailers selling a limited edition line of Precious Moments material.

References: Collectors Information Bureau, *Collectibles Market Guide & Price Index, 16th Edition*, Collector's Information Bureau, 1998, distributed by Krause Publications; Rosie Wells (ed.), *Rosie's Secondary Market Price Guide for Enesco's Precious Moments Collection, 15th Edition*, Rosie Wells Enterprises, 1997.

Collectors' Club: Enesco Precious Moments Collectors' Club, PO Box 99, Itasca, IL 60143.

Note: For additional listings see Enesco and Limited Edition Collectibles.

Bell, I'll Play My Drum for Him, Annual Bells Series, 1982	$75.00
Bell, Jesus Is Born, 1981	50.00
Figurine, A Perfect Display of 15 Happy Years, 15th Anniversary Commemorative Edition, 1993	115.00
Figurine, A Smile's a Cymbal of Joy, Birthday Club Welcome Gift Series, 1987	55.00
Figurine, Baby's First Step, 1984	75.00
Figurine, Bless Those Who Serve Their Country (Army), 1991	50.00
Figurine, Christmas Is a Time to Share, Musical Figurines Series, 1979	150.00
Figurine, Dog With Slippers, Animal Collection, 1983	20.00
Figurine, God Bless Our Years Together, 5th Anniversary Commemoritive Edition, 1985	300.00
Figurine, God Bless Our Years Together With So Much Love and Happiness, 1984	50.00
Figurine, He Upholdeth Those Who Fall, 1983	75.00
Figurine, He Walks With Me, Easter Seal Series, 1987	50.00
Figurine, I Love to Tell the Story, Special Edition Members' Only, 1985	60.00
Figurine, I'm Nuts Over My Collection, Birthday Club Figurines Series, 1990	40.00
Figurine, Isn't Eight Just Great, Birthday Train Figurines Series, 1988	25.00
Figurine, Join In On the Blessings, Inscribed Charter Member Renewal Gift, 1984	50.00
Figurine, Katie, Sammy's Circus Series, 1994	15.00
Figurine, Let Us Call the Club to Order, Collectors Club Welcome Gift Series, 1983	50.00

Figurine, God Loveth a Cheerful Giver, 1978, $800.00.

Figurine, Lord Keep Me On the Ball, Clown Series, 1986 .... **50.00**
Figurine, March, Calendar Girl Series, 1988 .... **40.00**
Figurine, Sam Butcher, Sugartown Series, 1992 .... **125.00**
Figurine, Sharing Our Christmas Together, Growing In
    Grace Series, 1986 .... **75.00**
Figurine, Showers of Blessings, Birthday Series, 1987 ...... **65.00**
Figurine, So Glad I Picked You As a Friend, Spring
    Catalog Series, 1994 .... **40.00**
Figurine, The Good Lord Has Blessed Us Tenfold, 10th
    Anniversary Commemorative Edition, 1988. .... **200.00**
Figurine, There's a Song In My Heart, Rejoice In the
    Lord Series, 1985 .... **40.00**
Figurine, The Sweetest Club Around, Inscribed Charter
    Membership Renewal Gift Series, 1988 .... **65.00**
Figurine, The Voice of Spring, The Four Seasons Series,
    1985. .... **200.00**
Figurine, This Land Is Our Land, Commemorative 500th
    Columbus Anniversary, 1992 .... **400.00**
Figurine, Wedding Arch, Bridal Party Series, 1987. .... **50.00**
Ornament, Baby's First Christmas, 1995 .... **18.00**
Ornament, Blessed Are the Pure In Heart, 1984 .... **40.00**
Ornament, It's a Perfect Boy, 1986 .... **30.00**
Ornament, Love Is Patient, E0536, 1983. .... **60.00**
Ornament, Mother Sew Deer, 1983 .... **25.00**
Ornament, Rocking Horse, 1986 .... **25.00**
Ornament, We Have Seen His Star, 1981 .... **50.00**
Ornament, Wishing You a Merry Christmas, 1984. .... **35.00**
Plate, But the Greatest Of These Is Love, Christmas
    Blessings Series, 1992 .... **50.00**
Plate, Christmastime Is For Sharing, Joy of Christmas
    Series, 1983 .... **60.00**
Plate, I Believe In Miracles, Inspired Thoughts Series,
    1983. .... **40.00**
Plate, Merry Christmas Deer, Christmas Love Series,
    1988. .... **55.00**
Plate, Our First Christmas Together, 1982 .... **50.00**
Plate, Summer's Joy, The Four Season's Series, 1985 ...... **100.00**
Plate, The Purr-fect Grandma, Mother's Love Series,
    1982. .... **40.00**
Plate, Thinking of You Is Really What I Like to Do,
    Mother's Day Series, 1993 .... **50.00**
Plate, Unto Us A Child Is Born, Christmas Collection,
    1984. .... **40.00**
Plate, You're As Pretty As a Christmas Tree, Beauty of
    Christmas Collection, 1994 .... **50.00**

PREMIUMS

A premium is an object given free or at a reduced price with the purchase of a product or service. Premiums divide into two groups: (1) point of purchase (you obtain your premium when you make the purchase) or (2) proof of purchase (you send proof of purchase, often box labels or seals, to a distribution point which then sends the premium to you).

Premiums are generational. The fifty-, sixty- and seventy-something generations think of radio premiums. The forty- and older thirty-something generations identify with cereal and radio premiums. Younger generations collect fast-food premiums.

Collectors place a premium on three-dimensional premiums. However, many of these premiums arrived in paper containers and envelopes and contained paper instruction sheets. A premium is considered complete only if it has its period packaging and everything that came with it.

Ovaltine's offer of a "Little Orphan Annie" music sheet was one of the earliest radio premiums. Jack Armstrong, Lone Ranger, and Tom Mix premiums soon followed. By the middle of the 1930s every child eagerly awaited the phrase "Now, an important word from our sponsor" with pad in hand, ready to write down the address for the latest premium offer. Thousands of radio premiums were offered in the 1930s, 40s, and 50s.

Cereal manufacturers found that the inclusion of a premium in the box was enough of an incentive to stimulate extra sales. Cereal premiums flourished in the post-1945 period. Although television premiums were offered, they never matched in numbers those offered over the radio.

The arrival of the fast-food restaurant and eventual competition between chains led to the use of premiums to attract customers. Many premiums were tied to television shows and movies. Although not a premium, fast-food packaging has also attracted the interest of collectors.

Not all premiums originated via cereal boxes, fast-food chains, radio, or television. Local and national food manufacturers and merchants used premiums to attract customers. Cracker Jack is the most obvious example.

References: Scott Bruce, *Cereal Box Bonanza: The 1950's,* Collector Books, 1995; Ted Hake, *Hake's Price Guide to Character Toys, 2nd Edition,* Avon Books, Gemstone Publishing, 1998; Jim Harmon, *Radio & TV Premiums,* Krause Publications, 1997; Robert M. Overstreet, *Overstreet Premium Ring Price Guide, Third Edition,* Gemstone Publishing, 1997; Tom Tumbusch, *Tomart's Price Guide to Radio Premiums and Cereal Box Collectibles,* Wallace-Homestead, 1991.

Newsletters: *The Premium Watch Watch,* 24 San Rafael Dr, Rochester, NY 14618; *The Toy Ring Journal,* PO Box 544, Birmingham, MI 48012.

Note: See Cracker Jack, Fast-Food Collectibles, and McDonald's for additional listings.

REPRODUCTION ALERT

Apple Jacks, Crater Creatures From Outer Space, soft
    plastic, 1969, 1¼" h **$20.00**
Bazooka, Exploding Battleship and Submarine, 6½" l
    plastic ship, 3¾" l submarine with firing mechanism
    and torpedoes, with instruction sheet and box, 1960s **75.00**

Beech-Nut Gum, Chandu the Magician, magic trick, Chinese coin on string, orig mailer envelope, 1930s **30.00**

Belle Meade Shoe Co, *Sky Rider's Pilot's Handbook,* "For Rider Shoes For Boys," 12 pp, imprint for Allentown, PA store at bottom front, aviation related illus, 1930s, 4 x 8¾" **45.00**

Blue Bonnet Margarine, doll, Blue Bonnet Sue, stuffed, orig paper tag, Dakin **10.00**

Blue Bonnet Margarine, hand puppet, Blue Bonnet Buttercup, plush, orig paper tag, Dakin **10.00**

Bond Bread, blotter, "Plastic Means Progress In Design," inset illus of Bond Bread loaf, 1950s, 3¾ x 6¼" **10.00**

Boo Berry, poster and figural monster crayons, General Mills, 1988 . . . . **20.00**

Butter-Nut Bread, badge, "Lone Ranger Safety Club," goldtone, raised depiction of Lone Ranger at top on rearing Silver, blue and red enamel painted, 1½" d **50.00**

Canada Dry, handbill, "Terry and the Pirates" comic books, full color paper, includes text on 3 different comics, illus of Terry holding soda bottle with ad for TV show, ©1953 *Chicago Tribune,* 6¾ x 8" **40.00**

Cap'n Crunch, Sea Cycle, rubber band powered, with Cap'n Crunch and Seadog figures, unused, 1960s **60.00**

Cap'n Crunch, Treasure Chest Bank, plastic, 1970s **20.00**

Cap'n Crunch, wiggle figure, red hard plastic, complete with coil spring and foam sticker mounting pads, c1969, 2½ x 3½" **20.00**

Chase and Sanborn, Eddie Cantor booklet, "How to Make a Quack-Quack," 1932 . . . . **25.00**

Cheerios, postcard, Cheerios Kid and Donald Duck, Huey, Louie, and Disneyland, black and white, 1957, 3½ x 6". **10.00**

Cocomalt, Buck Rogers Cut-Out Adventure Book Order Folder, full color, 1933, 9 x 13" **150.00**

Count Chocula, airplane, plastic, dark brown, depicts Count Chocula in cockpit on both sides, 2¼" l brown propeller, plastic ring protruding from each side of plane, 1970s, 3½" l **15.00**

Count Chocula, figure, molded plastic, brown, black, and white painted suit and details, orig cellophane bag, 7½" h **30.00**

Diamond Crystal Salt, recipe booklet, *Kate Smith's Collection of Famous Dishes from Famous Places/ Authentic Recipes from New York's Foremost Eating Places,* 28 pp, different recipe on each page with illus and address of restaurant, 1939, 3½ x 5½" **20.00**

Dow, squeeze toy, Scrubbing Bubble, hard plastic, blue and white, 7 x 3" **10.00**

Frosted Flakes, US Army Swamp Glider, complete with instructions and box, 1955. . . . . **75.00**

General Electric, Mr Magoo Flicker Keychain Tag, plastic, 1961. . . . . **20.00**

General Mills, Map of the Old West, 1940s, 20 x 28" **50.00**

Grape Nuts Flakes, Hop Harrigan Para-Plane, four 5 x 13¼" stiff paper punch-out sheets, pr of Code Signal Blinkers and instruction sheet, orig 5½ x 14" illus mailing envelope, 1965 . . . . **175.00**

Honey Nut Cheerios, bee doll, stuffed, plush, black, white, and yellow, felt wings, antenna, red tongue, plastic and vinyl eyes, attached tag mkd "Manufactured Exclusively For General Mills/Animal Fair Inc.," 1970s, 4 x 9 x 14" **20.00**

Ivory Soap, booklet, *Spies I Have Known,* Captain Tim Healy, 1936 . . . . **15.00**

Ovaltine, Radio Orphan Annie, Tri-Tone Signaler Badge, member's kit whistle, litho tin, 2½" l, $40.00.

Jack Pearl Show, Baron Munchausen's Old Mappe of Radio Land, illus and text describing different US cities and attractions, 1932, 19 x 23½". **200.00**

Jello, hand puppet, Sweet Tooth Sam, soft vinyl head, fabric body, black top hat, green face, white eyeballs dotted in black, single white fang tooth extending from opened black inner mouth, 1960s, 10½" h **75.00**

Jif Peanut Butter, Jifaroo Periscope, yellow cardboard, colorful depictions of child using periscope on sides, unpunched, ©Proctor & Gamble, 20 x 4" **20.00**

Johnson's Wax, spinner top, Fibber McGee and Molly, wood peg, 1936 . . . . **65.00**

Kellogg's, bank, Tony the Tiger, plastic, 1967 . . . . **30.00**

Kellogg's, book, *Mother Goose as Told by Kellogg's Singing Lady,* 32 pp, full color illus by Vernon Grant for nursery rhyme characters, includes text stories "Kellogg's Supper Song," and information on Kellogg's products, ©1933 Kellogg Co, 6½ x 9" **20.00**

Kellogg's, Don Winslow Periscope, cardboard, unassembled, orig mailing envelope, 1939 . . . . **175.00**

Kellogg's, figure, Huckleberry Hound, plastic, removable head with secret storage space, 1960s **30.00**

Kellogg's, pinback button, "Huck Hound for President," 1960, 3" d. **15.00**

Kellogg's, Presidents Album, 36 pp, 1949. . . . . **20.00**

Kellogg's, puppet, Banana Splits "Bingo," plastic, 1969 . . . . . **10.00**

Kellogg's, Tony the Tiger Swimmer, soft plastic, complete, unused, orig mailing envelope, 1967 . . . . **100.00**

Kellogg's, TV Viewer with Films, hard plastic "RCA Victor" television set replica and set of 4 black and white film disks, issued by Kellogg's of Toronto Canada, orig mailing box, c1950 . . . . **45.00**

Kellogg's, Walky-Talky, unassembled, complete with 8¼ x 10½" brown envelope. **175.00**

Ken-L-Ration, Rin-Tin-Tin, booklet, *Training Your Dog/What Every Dog Should Know,* 1931 . . . . **25.00**

Kraft, Robin Hood Nottingham Castle Playset, 3 full color 10½ x 15" stiff paper sheets with punch-out castle, forest scene, and 16 figures, includes additional unused illus order blank, back of envelope features "The Story of Robin Hood," complete and unused, 1957. . . . . **200.00**

Roi-Tan Cigars, Sophie Tucker Radio Show, toy car promoting 1939 Chevrolet giveaway, 4¼" l, $209.00. Photo courtesy Past Tyme Pleasures.

Libby's Tomato Juice, Terry's Official Victory Airplane Spotter, portrait illus on front of Terry, Pat, April, Burman, and Connie, diecut window moved to reveal different silhouette plane images, reverse features plane images with statistics, orig 8¼ x 9¼" illus envelope, ©1942 F A S **200.00**

Log Cabin Bread, postcard, Jimmie Allen, c1934 . . . . **15.00**

Lucky Charms, Pot o' Gold Musical Bank, 5" h **5.00**

Merlita Bread, Lone Ranger Safety Club Card, 1948 . . . . **45.00**

Merlita Bread, Silver Bullet Pencil Sharpener, gray metal bullet shaped sharpener with opening under base, front has white on red decal, 1940s, 1⅜" h **20.00**

Morrell Meats, flicker button/decoder, red, white, and blue, "Happy Hearts Club/Morrell Meats" text on button, center portrait images which change from King Fuddle and Clarissa to Sir Sedley and Mr Crafty, numbers 1–26 attached along bottom rim in thin plastic disk with red alphabet letters, 1970s, 3" d **45.00**

Nabisco, Cook Out With Sky King Recipe Folder, 1950s **65.00**

Nabisco, Spoonman "Munchy," vinyl, light blue, 1950, 2" h **45.00**

Nabisco Shredded Wheat, Straight Arrow War Drum, 5" d cardboard drum, complete with pr of 5½" l beaters and orig plain cardboard mailing box, 1949 . . . . **75.00**

Nabisco Wheat Honeys, Buffalo Bee Flicker Ring, gray plastic base, 1950s **20.00**

National Biscuit Co, Munchie "The Spoonman" Pillow, stuffed cotton, figural, attached tag mkd "Albert Pillow Co. Inc.," 1958, 9½ x 15" **375.00**

Ovaltine, Radio Orphan Annie "Flying W" Bandanna, red and white printed fabric with brown accents, border of horseshoe motifs and circular background of portraits of Radio Orphan Annie, Sandy, Joe corntassel, and Ginger, 1934, 17 x 18½" **75.00**

Ovaltine, Radio Orphan Annie Mug, ceramic, reverse with Sandy "Running For His Ovaltine" with balloon caption "Arf!," 1932, 3" h **75.00**

Ovaltine, sheet music, *Little Orphan Annie's Song*, 1931 . . . . . **18.00**

Oxydol, Ma Perkins Seeds, instructions on packets, with mailer, 1935 . . . . **50.00**

Pep, beanie, orange and white felt, 1943 . . . . **25.00**

Pep, model warplane, #21, "Curtiss Seagull Scout Observation," thin balsa sheet with printed parts, in orig glassine envelope with instructions, back of envelope with text including ad for "The Adventures of Superman" radio program, c1942 . . . . **20.00**

Pepsodent, Amos 'n Andy, puzzle, illus of Amos, Andy, Kingfish, Brother Crawford, and Lightnin', ©1932, 8 x 10" **75.00**

Philco, Philco Hi-Hat Lighter, 2¼" h chromed metal lighter with incised design on front including trademark hat and text "Philco Hi-Hat Club," orig box with insert mkd "Birthday Greetings Today and All 'Round," insert mkd with name of Philco distributor, 1940s **45.00**

Pillsbury, Choo Choo Cherry Pillow, cloth, 1970 . . . . **15.00**

Pillsbury, Funny Face Mugs, set of 6, plastic, Freckle Face Strawberry, Goofy Grape, Jolly Olly Orange, Choo-Choo Cherry, Lefty Lemon, and Loud Mouth Punch, 1969–70 . . . . **75.00**

Pink Panther Cereal, BMX Race Car, 1973 . . . . **80.00**

Popsicle, booklet, *Popsicle Gift List*, 8 pp, full color "Popsicle Pete," features sports equipment, train set, jewelry, and model kits, 1950–60, 5 x 8½" **20.00**

Popsicle, contest poster, Bob Hope, 1961, 8 x 20" **30.00**

Post, spoon, Mickey Mouse, 1930s **10.00**

Post Sugar Crisp, Bears Mug and Bowl Set, with instructions and mailer, 1954 . . . . **75.00**

Post Sugar Crisp, hand puppet, 1953 . . . . **30.00**

Quaker, badge, "Member Dick Tracy Secret Service Patrol," emb brass, 1⅜" h **45.00**

Quaker, Dick Tracy Secret Service Patrol Promotion Certificate, without stickers, 1938 . . . . **30.00**

Quaker, Roy Rogers Microscope Ring, 1949 . . . . **80.00**

Quaker, Sgt Preston Coloring Contest Photo, color, glossy photo of Preston and Yukon King, 1957, 7¾ x 9" **45.00**

Quaker Puffed Wheat and Rice Sparkies, comic book, "The Adventures of Little Orphan Annie," 20 pp, contains "Magic Morro" story and Capt Sparks adventure centerfold, illus ads on inside cov showing offered premiums, back cov includes Secret Guard Club membership offer in full color, 1941 . . . . **100.00**

Quisp, bank, painted composition, figural, with rubber trap, mkd "Taiwan," 1960–70s, 3 x 4 x 6½" **375.00**

Quisp, fire truck, hard plastic body, metal wheel on underside, missing rip-cord and ladder, JV Zimmerman Co, 1960–70s, 2 x 6 x 2½" **75.00**

Quisp, propeller, 4" l blue soft plastic propeller in 4 x 6" sealed cellophane pkg, 1960–70s **20.00**

Quisp, Space Match Card Game, 1968 . . . . **25.00**

Raid, wind-up, green blended to yellow hard plastic vicious bug symbol, complete with green vinyl antennas sprouting from top of head, mkd "SC Johnson & Son Hong Kong," orig 3 x 3 x 3½" mailing carton, 1980s **75.00**

Ralston Straight Shooters, Tom Mix Comic Book, 33 pp, cover shows Mix involved in big fight with Indians holding chief over his head, 1941 . . . . **75.00**

Sky Birds Chewing Gum, Sky Birds Escadrille Official Handbook, 12 pp, "Aviation Lingo" and small airplane illus, 3¾ x 6¼" **100.00**

Sugar Corn Pops and Sugar Frosted Flakes, Kellogg's US Navy Frogmen, orig mailing env contains three 3½" h soft plastic frogmen, unopened pkg of "High Pressure Propellant," and 8½ x 11" instruction sheet, figures include Obstacle Scout, Torch Man, and Demolitions Expert, complete with instruction sheet with order blank for additional frogmen and "Nautilus Atomic Sub," 1950s.. **100.00**

Sugar Frosted Flakes, Tony the Tiger Radio, figural, plastic, 1980... **10.00**

Sugar Smacks, Superman Duel in Space Comic Book, 1955... **150.00**

Sunbeam Bread, pinback button, Gene Autry photo, c1950.. **12.00**

Superman Bread, shield badge, cardboard, 1942........ **500.00**

Tip-Top Bread, punch-out sheet, 8 x 11" stiff paper sheet with punch-out parts for bread truck and miniature bread loaves, ©1955–56 Spec-y Adv Serv, Inc........... **10.00**

Town Talk Bread, Jimmie Allen Wings Badge, brass, 1930s.. **65.00**

Trix, pinback button, litho tin, "No! Trix Are For Kids!," 1970s... **5.00**

Wheaties, Jack Armstrong Stampo Game, 2 sheets, uncut, orig mailer, 1930s........................... **100.00**

Wheat Krispies, Squadron of Peace Membership Card, 1939... **18.00**

Wheato-Nuts, Voodoo Eye Pendant, metal, with envelope, 1930s.. **80.00**

White King Soap, magic trick set, "Chandu White King of Magic," complete, 1930s...................... **150.00**

Wonder Bread, fan club newsletter, "Bachelor's Children," c1945.................................. **12.00**

AUCTION PRICES – PREMIUM RINGS

Frank's Antiques & Auctions, Mail Auction #22, August 20, 1998. Prices include a 10% buyer's premium.

Buffalo Bill Jr., metal, 1950 .... **$33.00**
Buster Brown Club, 1940s, metal **39.60**
Captain Frank's Air Hawks, metal, 1930s........... **93.50**
Captain Midnight, Skelly Oil, metal, 1940s......... **110.00**
Davy Crockett, head, gold colored plastic, 1950s **18.70**
Davy Crockett, figure, plastic, 1960s **3.30**
Davy Crockett, rifle, silvered metal, 1950s **22.00**
Have Gun Will Travel, 1960s **33.00**
Lone Ranger, 6-shooter, metal, 1947............. **77.00**
Lone Ranger, atomic bomb, Kix Cereal, 1946 .... **38.50**
Lone Ranger, movie film, metal, 1949............. **145.20**
Lone Ranger, secret compartment, Army, metal,
   with photo............................... **82.50**
Mack Bulldog, Mack Trucks, bronzed metal, 1940s.... **38.50**
Mickey Mantle, photo, metal **49.50**
Poll Parrot, parrot face, gold colored metal, 1950 ..... **18.70**
Rin Tin Tin, magic ring with paper, 1950s **165.00**
Romper Room, silvered aluminum, 1960s........... **5.50**
Sky King, radar, metal, 1940s................... **79.20**
Smile, Orange Flavored Drink, aluminum, 1950s **24.20**
Straight Arrow, good luck ring, metal, Nabisco
   Shredded Wheat, 1950...................... **57.20**
Superman, emblem, metal, 1970s **5.50**
Tom Mix, sliding whistle, metal, 1940s............. **36.30**
Tom Mix Straight Shooters, gold colored metal **86.90**
Weather Bird Shoes, metal, 1950s **110.00**

PRESLEY, ELVIS

Elvis died on August 17, 1977. Or, did he? The first Elvis license material dates from the mid-1950s. Vintage Elvis dates prior to 1965.

Collectors divide Elvis material into two periods: items licensed prior to Elvis' death and those licensed by his estate, known to collectors as fantasy items. Some Elvis price guides refuse to cover fantasy pieces. Special items manufactured and marketed solely for Elvis fan club members are a third category of material and should not be overlooked.

Reference: Jerry Osborne, *The Official Price Guide to Elvis Presley, Second Edition,* House of Collectibles, 1998.

Collectors' Club: Elvis Forever TCB Fan Club, PO Box 1066, Pinellas Park, FL 33281.

Autograph, PS, blue felt pen signature, inscription "To Jay Best Wishes," matted and framed, c1970s, 15½ x 12½".. **$460.00**

Booklet, *Elvis' Television Special,* 28 pp, promo for Elvis's NBC-TV special for Dec 3, 1968 presented by Singer Co, color cover pictures Elvis in gold lame suit on front and Colonel dressed as Santa on back, 4 x 9"....... **45.00**

Catalog, Elvis RCA Victor Records, lists LPs and 45 rpms, 3½ x 7"... **20.00**

Charm Bracelet, metal, goldtone finish, includes charms of hound dog, broken heart, guitar, and picture frame, heart has red accent with "Heartbreak," picture frame has black and white photo of Elvis with facsimile signature and clear plastic cover, 2 x 7½" cardboard display card with "Exclusive RCA Victor Record Star," ©1956 Elvis Presley Enterprises **100.00**

Christmas Card, color photo of Elvis in red jacket, white shirt, and black pants, green and red holly leaves and berries around photo with "Seasons Greetings Elvis And The Colonel 1966," reverse blank, 5¼ x 8¼"......... **50.00**

Dog Tag Bracelet, metal link bracelet and dog tag, bright silver luster, with facsimile signature and portrait, on 2 x 8" pink and white cardboard card, ©1956 Elvis Presley Enterprises................................... **20.00**

Flicker Button, color illus changes from portrait on blue ground to image of Elvis standing behind microphone holding guitar on yellow ground, "Elvis Presley" in red at bottom, Vari-Vue, c1956, 2½" d.................. **20.00**

Flicker Keychain, plastic, full figure image of Elvis, 2 x 2¾"... **20.00**

Magazine, *Teen,* Jun 1958, Vol 2, features 5 pp "Will The Army Change Elvis" article, black and white photos, color cover illus of Elvis in Army uniform, 8½ x 11"...... **20.00**

Memorial Candle, white, "Elvis 1935–1977," clear sticker wrapped around center with portrait image and text in black, 5" h **20.00**

Pillow, cotton, stuffed, blue printed portrait, "Love Me Tender," Personality Products Co, ©Elvis Presley Enterprises.. **250.00**

Pinback Button, full color photo of Elvis in green jacket with facsimile signature in blue, "©1956 Elvis Presley Enterprises" on curl, 3" d........................... **75.00**

Poster, "Give Elvis for Christmas," RCA, 1959............. **40.00**

Record, *Love Me Tender,* 45 rpm, EP, black label with dog on top, 7 x 7" stiff cardboard sleeve with color photo of Elvis, reverse with text about film, 1956 .... **20.00**

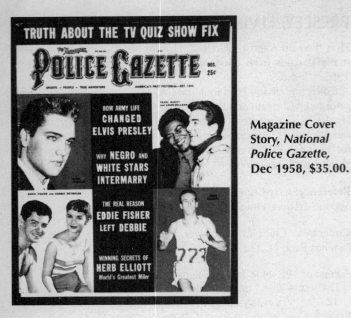

Magazine Cover Story, *National Police Gazette*, Dec 1958, $35.00.

Record, *Stay Away, Joe*, 45 rpm, 7 x 7" glossy paper sleeve includes browntone photo of Elvis in cowboy hat, RCA Victor, 1968 .... **20.00**

Record Player, RCA Victor, paper covered wood, Elvis signature on top, 1950s, 12 x 12½ x 7" **350.00**

Salt and Pepper Shakers, pr, Elvis on TV screen........... **15.00**

Scarf, sheer silk-like material, includes large torso image of Elvis with facsimile signature with smaller figures of Elvis playing guitar and singing with musical notes and records, shows several song titles and small hound dog illus, ©1956 Elvis Presley Enterprises, 30½ x 32"... **200.00**

Sheet Music, *I Want You, I Need You, I Love You*, blue-tone, ©Elvis Presley Music, Inc, 1956................ **15.00**

Song Folio, "The Elvis Presley Album of Juke Box Favorites No 1," 36 pp, contains words and music to 15 songs with black and white photos, ©1956 Hill and Range Songs, Inc, 9 x 12".................... **75.00**

TV Guide, Sep 29, 1956, Vol 4, #39, Cleveland edition, featuring part 3 of a 3-part series, 4 pp, full page color photo, Jackie Gleason cover article **45.00**

PRINTS

Prints serve many purposes. They can be reproductions of an artist's paintings, drawings, or designs, original art forms, or developed for mass appeal as opposed to aesthetic statement. Much of the production of Currier & Ives fits this last category. Currier & Ives concentrated on genre, urban, patriotic, and nostalgic scenes.

Prints were inexpensive, meaning they could be changed every few years. Instead of throwing them out, they went into storage. Most prints were framed. In today's market, check the frame. It could be more valuable than the print.

References: Janet Gleeson, *Miller's Collecting Prints and Posters*, Millers Publications, 1997; Martin Gordon, *Gordon's Print Price Annual*, Gordon Art Reference, published annually; Michael Ivankovich, *Collector's Value Guide to Early 20th Century American Prints*, Collector Books, 1998; Susan Theran, *Prints & Photographs: Identification and Price Guide*, Avon Books, 1993.

Periodicals: *Journal of the Print World*, 1008 Winona Rd, Meredith, NH 03253; *On Paper*, 39 E 78th St, #601, New York, NY 10021.

Newsletter: *The Illustrator Collector's News*, PO Box 1958, Sequim, WA 98382.

Note: For additional listings see Illustrators, Wallace Nutting, Nutting-Like Photographs, Maxfield Parrish, and Norman Rockwell.

Arms, John Taylor, "Venetian Filigree" alternatively titled "Ca D'Oro Venetia," 1931, etching on paper, sgd and dated "John Taylor Arms–1931" in pencil lower right, numbered "Ed.100" in pencil lower left, 10¾ x 11" plate, framed **$3,225.00**

Avery, Milton, "Dawn," 1952, 2nd state, edition of 100, color woodcut on tissue, sgd and dated "Milton Avery 1952" in pencil lower left, inscribed "artist proof" in pencil lower right, initialed in block lower right, annotated and identified on label on reverse, 7 x 9" image, framed **1,725.00**

Fink, Aaron, "Smoker," c1983, litho in yellow and black on gray paper, sgd "Aaron Fink" in pencil lower right, inscribed "B.A.T." in pencil lower left, 14¾ x 11½" image, matted **250.00**

Gorman, RC, "The Earring," 1975, edition of 50, litho in brown, blue, and black on paper, sgd and dated "R.C. Gorman 1975" in pencil lower left, numbered "44/50" in pencil lower right, drystamps lower center, 30 x 21¾" sheet, framed **450.00**

Johns, Jasper, "Cup 4 Picasso," 1973, color litho on paper, edition of 39, printed/published by Universal Limited Art Edition, West Islip, NY, sgd, dated, and numbered "29/39 J. Johns '73" in pencil lower right, printer's drystamp lower right, 21½ x 31½" image, framed **6,325.00**

Mazur, Michael, "Bird's Nest Fern," 1975, monotype in green and brown on paper, sgd "Mazur" in pencil lower right, titled in pencil lower left, inscribed and dated in pencil lower center, 17½ x 25½" image, framed **550.00**

Milton, Peter Winslow, "A Sky-Blue Life," 1976, edition of 160, etching and engraving on paper, sgd and dated "PWMilton 76" in pencil lower right, titled in pencil lower center, numbered "72/160" in pencil lower left, identified on label from the Alpha Galleries, Boston, on reverse, 25½ x 32⅝" image, framed **1,150.00**

Motherwell, Robert, "Untitled" from the New York Portfolio, 1982, edition of 250 plus proofs, color photolitho with embossing on paper, sgd and inscribed "Motherwell/TP" in pencil lower right, printer's/publisher's drystamp lower right, 30 x 22½" image **520.00**

Rauschenberg, Robert, "Statue of Liberty," 1983, edition of 250, color photo-screenprint with collage on charcoal handmade paper, sgd, numbered and dated "RAUSCHENBERG 202/250 85" in pencil lower left, 35½ x 24" image................................ **635.00**

Sultan, Donald, "Four Oranges," 1993, edition of 108, color screenprint on paper, published by Lincoln Center/List Art Program, initialed and dated "April 2, 1993 DS" in pencil within left margin, numbered "83/108" in pencil lower right, 30½ x 30¼" image, framed...................................... **1,600.00**

Andy Warhol, "Turtle," 1985, edition of 250, color screenprint on paper, sgd and numbered "235/250 Andy Warhol" in pencil lower right, 31¹⁄₂ x 39¹⁄₂" image, framed, $4,025.00. Photo courtesy Skinner, Inc., Boston, MA.

Tworkov, Jack, "L.F. – S.F. – E#4," 1979, edition of 100, etching with aquatint on BFK Rives paper with watermark, printed and published by Landfall Press, Inc., Chicago, sgd and dated "Tworkov/79" in pencil lower right, titled in pencil lower center, numbered "53/100" in pencil lower left, printer's drystamp lower left, 14¹⁄₂ x 14¹⁄₂" plate **425.00**

Warhol, Andy, "Marilyn," 1967, edition of 250, color screenprint on paper, stamped "Andy Warhol/103 250" and dedicated "To: Jackie 'O' Best Always XOX Andy Warhol 68" on reverse, 36 x 36" image, shrink-wrapped. **6,900.00**

Wood, Grant, "March," 1941, edition of 250, litho on paper, published by Associated American Artists, sgd in pencil lower right, AAA label on reverse, 8⁷⁄₈ x 11³⁄₄" image, framed **3,675.00**

PSYCHEDELIC COLLECTIBLES

Psychedelic collectibles describes a group of objects made during the 1960s and 70s that are highly innovative in their use of colors and design. American Indian tribal art, the artworks of Toulouse Lautrec and Alphonse Mucha, the color reversal approach of Joseph Albers, dancer Loie Fuller's diaphanous material, late 19th-century graphics, paisley fabrics, and quilts are just a few of the objects and techniques that are the roots of psychedelic design.

The period is marked by eclecticism, not unity—there were no limits on design. Psychedelic artists and manufacturers drew heavily on new technologies, e.g., inflatable plastic furniture. Coverings such as polyester and vinyl were heavily used.

Peter Max is the most famous designer associated with the psychedelic era. His artwork graced hundreds of objects. Although mass produced, some items are hard to find.

References: Eric King, *The Collector's Guide to Psychedelic Rock Concert Posters, Postcards and Handbills,* Svaha Press, 1996; Susanne White, *Psychedelic Collectibles of the 1960s & 1970s,* Wallace-Homestead, 1990, out of print.

Ashtray, white china, center color design depicting different color rings plus black and white checkerboard pattern, mkd "China By Iroquois," c1970 Peter Max, 5" d **$75.00**

Beach Ball, vinyl, inflatable, Peter Max illus of alternating solid blue segments and white segments, bright color illus of doves, cats, circles, stars, and portrait image, 8 x 10" display bag with full color insert, Mego, ©1971, 24" d **20.00**

Charm Bracelet, 6" l gold-colored metal link bracelet with five 3-D charms, 2³⁄₄ x 7¹⁄₂" display cad with multicolored psychedelic designs. **20.00**

Go Go Belt, series of silvered metal loops connecting 1³⁄₄" d celluloid covered disks, 17 disks with illus of planets and small Peter Max logo at bottom, slotted bar on reverse of each disk to attach to metal loops, small clip to attach belt around waist, c1970s, 40" l **100.00**

Handbill, "Electric Lotus," 308 East Sixth Street, NY, psychedelic design on front includes photo of Buddha brightly colored in purple, green, orange, and blue, small Peter Max name at corner, reverse with ink stamp address, c1970, 4¹⁄₄ x 8" **20.00**

Ice Bucket, litho tin body, plastic and metal lid, white plastic int, pr of large plastic sunglasses serve as handles and can be flipped down on each side to go along with facial illus, 1 side depicts woman with large lips and beauty mark while other depicts man with mustache, each side with "Love You" in psychedelic style, unmkd, early 1970s, 10" h, 8" d **100.00**

Peter Max Super Poster Book, 36 pp, illus, black and white photos and text, bound into back of book is 16 x 32" fold-out double sided sheet with color design on 1 side and comic panel story "Mister Mouse Meets Peter Max" on other, Crown Publishers, Inc, ©1971 Peter Max, 11¹⁄₄ x 16" **50.00**

Pillow Case, white cotton, profile of woman along with light rays, stars, and planets, design printed on both sides, purple, orange blue, yellow, and pink, Peter Max, 20 x 30" **50.00**

Pinback Button, 4-H Club, "Clover Power," bright green psychedelic lettering on deep pink ground, 1970, 2" d **20.00**

Poster, John Lennon for *Look* magazine, by Richard Avedon, 1968, 31 x 22¹⁄₂", $220.00. Photo courtesy David Rago Auction, Inc.

Pinback Button, "Flower Power," psychedelic style red against bright yellow flower design on dark green ground, c1970 . . . . **20.00**

Plate, china, black, brown, green, orange, blue, and pink abstract design, mkd "Genuine China By Iroquois," ©1970 Peter Max, 10" d **75.00**

Poster, Cream, stiff paper, portrait images of band members with center text "Fare Thee Well Cream," pair of hands at bottom including 1 holding cigarette, day-glo colors, ©1969 Denhams, 35 x 46" **50.00**

Poster, Grateful Dead, stiff glossy paper for 1988 Spring tour, Peter Max design of large skull image being separated by lightning bolt around top half of skull, 24 x 34" **75.00**

Sleeping Bag, UFO illus, in pouch, Peter Max **90.00**

Sneakers, pr, lightning bolt illus on sides, women's, Peter Max, size 8½ **85.00**

Off We Go!, 10 x 12½", $20.00.

PUNCHBOARDS

Punchboards are self-contained games of chance that are made of pressed paper and contain holes with a coded ticket inside each hole. After paying an agreed upon amount, the player uses a "punch" to extract the ticket of his choice. Cost to play ranged from 1¢ to $1.00.

Animal and fruit symbols, cards, dominos, and words were used as well as numbers to indicate prizes. While some punchboards had no printing, most contained elaborate letters and/or pictures.

Punchboards initially paid the winner in cash. In an effort to appease the anti-gambling crowd, some punchboards paid off in cameras, candy, cigar, cigarettes, clocks, jewelry, radios, sporting goods, toys, etc.

The 1920s through the 1950s was the golden age of the punchboard. An endless variety were made. Many had catchy names or featured pin-up girls. Negative publicity resulting from the movie *The Flim Flam Man* hurt the punchboard industry.

Value rests with unpunched boards. Most boards sell for $15 to $30, although some have broken the $100 barrier.

Reference: Norman E. Martinus and Harry L. Rinker, *Warman's Paper,* Wallace-Homestead, Krause Publications, 1994.

Ace High, 13 x 17 . . . . **$90.00**
Barrel of Cigarettes, 10 x 10" **45.00**
Bars & Bells, 13 x 18½" **135.00**
Baseball, push card, 1¢ for candy, 7 x 10" **10.00**
Beat the Seven, 10 x 10" **35.00**
Best Hand, 6½ x 11" **40.00**
Big Game, 8 x 10½" **30.00**
Bowling Club, 10 x 13" **4.00**
Candy Special, 4½ x 7½" **25.00**
Cash In, 8½ x 9" **18.00**
Double or Nothing, 9 x 10" **35.00**
Extra Bonus, 13 x 12" **40.00**
Fin Baby, folding pull tab game, 19 x 6" **32.00**
Five On One, 11 x 11" **18.00**
Five Tens, 10 x 13" **18.00**
Glades Chocolates, 7 x 9" **25.00**
Home Run Derby, 10 x 12" **75.00**
Jackpot Bingo, 10 x 8" **10.00**
Joe's Special, 11 x 14" **20.00**
Johnson's Chocolates, Elvgren girl, 9 x 11" **35.00**
Lu Lu Board, 10 x 11" **28.00**

More Smokes, 10½ x 10½" **24.00**
Nestle's Chocolate, 2¢ board, 9 x 8½" **45.00**
Nickel Charley, 10 x 9" **18.00**
No Losers, push card, 7 x 9½" **5.00**
Palm Chart, with enveloe, 20 x 11½" **8.00**
Perry's Prize, 9½ x 13" **60.00**
Positive Prizes, 12 x 17" **25.00**
Pots A Plenty, 11 x 17½" **25.00**
Premium Prizes, 10 x 12" **20.00**
Section Play, 8½ x 10" **18.00**
So Sweet, 13½ x 13" **40.00**
Speedy Tens, 10 x 13" **18.00**
Stars & Stripes, 9 x 14" **25.00**
Take It or Leave It, 12 x 14" **85.00**
Tavern Maid, 9½ x 13½" **55.00**
Three Sure Hits, 10 x 14" **25.00**
Tu Pots, 12 x 18" **45.00**
Valuable Prizes, 12 x 16" **15.00**
Win a Seal, 13½ x 16" **70.00**

PUPPETS

Oriental string puppets date from 1,000 B.C. Clay, leather, and terra-cotta puppets have been found in archeological sites in the Far East, Greece, and Persia.

Puppet shows and theaters were commonplace in Europe by the 18th century. The first marionette toys date from the late 19th century. In 1920 Tony Sarg designed the first commercial marionettes sold in the United States for New York's B. Altman Company. By the 1930s over half a dozen American firms were producing marionette toys.

Television shows from the 1940s and 50s such as The Howdy Doody Show and The Mouseketeer Club popularized the marionette. Two dozen different companies made marionettes. Hand puppets made their arrival on the toy scene.

Marionettes declined in popularity in the 1960s and 1970s.

Reference: Daniel E. Hodges, *Marionettes and String Puppets Collector's Reference Guide,* Antique Trader Books, 1998.

Hand Puppets, Jerry Mahoney and Knucklehead Smiff, plastic heads, vinyl bodies, ©1966 by Paul Winchell, price each, $135.00.

FINGER

Bamm Bamm, Knickerbocker, 1972	$12.00
California Raisins, Bendy Toys, 1987	15.00
Fred Flintstone, Knickerbocker, 1972	15.00
Lamb Chop, 1960	30.00
Monkees, The, Remco, 1960s	115.00
Peanuts Showtime Finger Puppets, Ideal, 1977	35.00
Popeye Finger Puppet Family, Denmark Plastics, 1960s	35.00
Prince Charming, Mego, 1977	30.00
Spiderman, Ideal, 1965	85.00

HAND

Bamm Bamm, Ideal, 1964, 10"h	$20.00
Batman, vinyl head, plastic body, Ideal, 1966	70.00
Beetle Bailey, Gund	65.00
Bozo the Clown, Capital, 1962	25.00
Bugs Bunny, rubber head, Zany, 1940s	50.00
Captain Hook, Gund, 1950s, 9" h	50.00
Casper, 8" h	20.00
Cecil, pull-string talker, Mattel, 1961	50.00
Dick Tracy, fabric, vinyl, record, Ideal, 1960s, 10½" h	75.00
Dishonest John, pull-string talker, Mattel, 1961	100.00
Dopey, Gund, 1950s	15.00
Dr Dolittle, pull-string talker, Mattel, 1967	50.00
Droop-A-Long, Ideal	45.00
Lily Munster	150.00
Lone Ranger, The, Ideal, 1966	40.00
Mad Hatter, cloth body, 1960s	20.00
Magilla Gorilla, Ideal, 1960s, 19" h	140.00
Mahoney, Jerry, rubber head, vinyl body, 1960s	65.00
Minnie Mouse, Peter Puppet Playthings, 1952	120.00
Mr Magoo, vinyl head, cloth body, 1960s	55.00
Mushmouse, Ideal, vinyl head, cloth body, 10" h, 1964	30.00
Olive Oyl, Gund, 1960s	30.00
Peter Pan, Oak Rubber, 1953	75.00
Pluto, Gund, 9" h, 1950s	40.00
Prince Charming, Gund, 1959, 10" h	40.00
Superman, Ideal, 11" h	45.00

Swee' Pea, cloth body, bonnet, Gund, 1960s	20.00
Tonto, Ideal, 1966	35.00
Uncle Fester, vinyl, 1960s	100.00
Wimpy, fabric body, vinyl squeaker head, Gund, 1950s	30.00
Wonder Woman, Ideal, 1960s	150.00
Woody Woodpecker, pull-string talker, Mattel, 1963	65.00
Yogi Bear, Knickerbocker	30.00

MARIONETTE

Alice In Wonderland, Peter Puppet, 1950s	$60.00
Clarabelle, Peter Puppet Playthings, 1950s	220.00
Donald Duck, Peter Puppet Playthings, 1950s, 6½" h	55.00
Flub-A-Dub, Peter Puppet Playthings, 1950s	185.00
Howdy Doody, 16" h	225.00
Mad Hatter, Peter Puppet Playthings, 1950s	70.00
March Hare, Peter Puppet Playthings	65.00
Mickey Mouse, Peter Puppet Playthings, 1952, 14" h	60.00
Snoopy, Pelham/Tiderider, 1979	40.00

PUSH BUTTON

Atom Ant, Kohner	$50.00
Batman, Kohner, 1966, 3" h	45.00
Bozo, Knickerbocker, 1962	50.00
Charlie Brown, Ideal, 1977	45.00
Davy Crockett, wood and plastic, Kohner, 1956	65.00
Dino, Kohner, 1964	20.00
Donald Duck, Kohner, 1950s	85.00
Joe Cool, Ideal, 1977	35.00
Magilla Gorilla, Kohner, 1960s	40.00
Mr Jinx, plastic, Kohner, 3" h	20.00
Peter Pan, Kohner, 1950s, 6" h	45.00
Robin, plastic, Kohner, 1966, 3" h	65.00
Robot, plastic, silver, red plastic facial features, dome on top of head, dial on chest, Modern Toys, 1960s	75.00
Rocky Squirrel, 1965	40.00
Secret Squirrel, Kohner, 1960s	30.00
Wally Gator, Kohner, 1964	25.00

PURINTON POTTERY

Bernard Purinton founded Purinton Pottery, Wellsville, Ohio, in 1936. The company produced dinnerware and special order pieces. In 1940 Purinton moved to Shippenville, Pennsylvania.

Dorothy Purinton and William H. Blair, her brother, were the company's principal designers. Dorothy designed Maywood, Plaid, and several Pennsylvania German theme lines. Blair is responsible for Apple and Intaglio.

Purinton hand painted its wares. Because of this, variations within a pattern are common. Purinton made a complete dinnerware service including accessory pieces for each of its patterns.

The company utilized an open stock marketing approach. Purinton products were sold nationwide. Some were exported.

In 1958 the company ceased operations, reopened briefly, and then closed for good in 1959. Cheap foreign imports were the principal reason for the company's demise.

References: Jamie Bero-Johnson and Jamie Johnston, *Purinton Pottery,* Schiffer Publishing, 1997.

Newsletter: *Purinton Pastimes,* PO Box 9394, Arlington, VA 22219.

Apple, salad plate, 6⁷/₈" w, $15.00.

Apple, beer mug	$115.00
Apple, breakfast plate	14.00
Apple, canister, coffee, half oval	60.00
Apple, canister, salt, half oval	85.00
Apple, cookie jar, narrow oval	75.00
Apple, cookie jar, wide oval	55.00
Apple, creamer and sugar, mini	22.00
Apple, cup and saucer	10.00
Apple, Dutch jug, 5 pint	28.00
Apple, juice mug	12.00
Apple, oil and vinegar, bottle cruets	75.00
Apple, oil and vinegar, square cruets	55.00
Apple, pitcher	35.00
Apple, relish, 3-part	22.00
Apple, salt and pepper shakers, range size	30.00
Apple, teapot, 6 cup	25.00
Apple, tumbler	10.00
Brown Intaglio, candy dish, ring handle	60.00
Brown Intaglio, coffee mug	25.00
Brown Intaglio, coffeepot, 8 cup	45.00
Brown Intaglio, honey jug	110.00
Brown Intaglio, jam/jelly	25.00
Brown Intaglio, Kent jug	45.00
Chartreuse, candy dish, ring handle	90.00
Chartreuse, chop plate	55.00
Chartreuse, cookie jar, wide oval	120.00
Chartreuse, creamer and sugar	48.00
Chartreuse, Dutch jug, 5 pint	70.00
Fruit, canister, half oval, red trim	15.00
Fruit, canister, tall oval, blue trim	32.00
Fruit, creamer and sugar, mini	25.00
Fruit, Dutch jug, 5 pint	25.00
Fruit, Kent jug, oversized	130.00
Fruit, Kent jug, regular	15.00
Heather Plaid, chop plate	60.00
Heather Plaid, cookie jar, wide oval	110.00
Heather Plaid, creamer, mini	38.00
Heather Plaid, salt and pepper shakers, mini jug	25.00

Heather Plaid, spaghetti bowl	125.00
Normandy Plaid, bean cup, individual	30.00
Normandy Plaid, beer mug	35.00
Normandy Plaid, candle holder, round, with insert	475.00
Normandy Plaid, chop plate	26.00
Normandy Plaid, coffee cup	5.00
Normandy Plaid, coffee mug	45.00
Normandy Plaid, coffeepot, 8 cup	50.00
Normandy Plaid, cookie jar	65.00
Normandy Plaid, creamer and sugar, mini	35.00
Normandy Plaid, creamer and sugar, regular	18.00
Normandy Plaid, Dutch jug, 1 pint	32.00
Normandy Plaid, Dutch jug, 5 pint	50.00
Normandy Plaid, Kent jug	45.00
Normandy Plaid, marmalade	60.00
Normandy Plaid, oil and vinegar cruets, square	22.00
Normandy Plaid, pitcher	45.00
Normandy Plaid, platter, 12"	14.00
Normandy Plaid, roll tray	25.00
Normandy Plaid, Rum jug	115.00
Normandy Plaid, spaghetti bowl	95.00
Normandy Plaid, tea and toast set	12.00
Normandy Plaid, tumbler	9.00
Normandy Plaid, vegetable bowl, covered	45.00
Normandy Plaid, wall pocket	80.00
Palm Tree, dinner plate	375.00
Palm Tree, honey jug	120.00
Peasant Lady, candle holder, sgd "William Blair"	1,425.00
Peasant Lady, candle holder, unsgd	1,050.00
Pennsylvania Dutch, dinner plate, oversized	290.00
Pennsylvania Dutch, salt and pepper shakers, mini jug	105.00
Petals, breakfast plate	45.00
Petals, cereal bowl	15.00
Petals, cup and saucer	30.00
Petals, dessert bowl	20.00
Petals, dinner plate	45.00
Petals, salad plate	38.00
Petals, salt and pepper shakers, mini jug	60.00
Red Ivy, cookie jar	40.00
Red Ivy, creamer and sugar, mini	35.00
Red Ivy, salt and pepper shakers, range size	15.00
Red Ivy, teapot, 6 cup	15.00

PUZZLES

Puzzles divide into two groups: (1) jigsaw and (2) mechanical. American and English collectors focus primarily on jigsaw puzzles. European collectors love mechanical puzzles.

The jigsaw puzzle first appeared in the mid-18th century in Europe. John Silbury, a London map maker, offered dissected map jigsaw puzzles for sale by the early 1760s. The first jigsaw puzzles in America were English and European imports and designed primarily for use by children.

Prior to the mid-1920s, the vast majority of jigsaw puzzles were cut from wood for the adult market and composition board for the children's market. In the 1920s the diecut, cardboard jigsaw puzzle evolved.

Avoid puzzles whose manufacturer cannot be determined, unless the puzzle has especially attractive graphics or craftsmanship. Diecut cardboard puzzles in excess of 500 pieces remain primarily garage sale items. Some collector interest exists for early Springbok puzzles.

References: *Dexterity Games and Other Hand-Held Puzzles,* L-W Books Sales, 1995; Chris McCann, *Master Pieces: The Art History of Jigsaw Puzzles,* Collectors Press, 1998; Harry L. Rinker, *Antique Trader's Guide to Games & Puzzles,* Antique Trader Books, 1997; Anne D. Williams, *Jigsaw Puzzles,* Wallace-Homestead, 1990, out of print.

Collectors' Clubs: American Game Collectors Assoc, PO Box 44, Dresher, PA 19025; National Puzzler's League, PO Box 82289, Portland, OR 97282.

Dexterity, duck, wearing clown hat, cardboard and plastic, Japan, 1½" d, 1950 . . . . **$20.00**

Dexterity, Nancy, holding ice cream cone, United Features Syndicate, 2¼" d **25.00**

Jigsaw, adult, diecut cardboard, American News Co and Branches, Miss America Puzzle Series, #4, "In Blossom Time," over 300 pcs, 13¼ x 10", 1933 . . . . **25.00**

Jigsaw, adult, diecut cardboard, Consolidated Paper Box Co, Big Star, "School Patrol," #1010, approx 10 x 13½", late 1930s **8.00**

Jigsaw, adult, diecut cardboard, Hallmark Cards, Springbok, "Super Bowl Sunday," 500+ pcs, 18 x 23½", boxed **5.00**

Jigsaw, adult, diecut cardboard, J Pressman & Co, Victory Picture Puzzle #20, "Flying Fortresses Bombing Enemy Base," 375+ pcs, c1945, 19¼ x 15¼" **35.00**

Jigsaw, adult, diecut cardboard, Milton Bradley, Piccadilly Jig Picture Puzzle, #81, "On the Loire," 200+ pcs, 1930s **12.00**

Jigsaw, adult, diecut cardboard, Movie Cut-Up #7, "Bitter Tea of General Yen," 225+ pcs, 9⅞ x 13⅛" **35.00**

Jigsaw, adult, diecut cardboard, Tuco, Upson, Peonies, 357 pcs, 14¾ x 19", ©1937 . . . . **10.00**

Jigsaw, adult, hand cut cardboard, Bliss, RW, Wallaston, MA, "The Flower Market," Van Vreeland print of Dutch flower market, 200 pcs, 9 x 12", c1930 . . . . **25.00**

Jigsaw, adult, hand cut, Cotton, Robert, "Soldier Boy," 76 pcs, cut Jan 22, 1942, back of puzzle is cigar box lid **25.00**

Jigsaw, adult, hand cut, Glencraft/Glendex, "Fishing Pier," 720 pcs, 22 x 15", 1960s **85.00**

Jigsaw, children's frame tray, Yogi Bear, Whitman Publishing, #4420, ©1961 by Hanna-Barbera, $20.00.

Jigsaw, adult, hand cut, Huvanco Jig Saw Puzzle, English, "A Stream In the Highlands," random cut, 203 pcs, 10 x 14", c1940s **20.00**

Jigsaw, adult, hand cut, Joseph K Straus, "Calf of Night," 300 pcs, 12 x 16", 1940s, orig box **28.00**

Jigsaw, adult, hand cut, Kingsbridge by Atlantic, "The Arrival (A Hunting Morn)," L Cury Fox artist, 400 pcs, 15 x 11", 1960s **38.00**

Jigsaw, adult, hand cut, Milton Bradley, Premiere Jigsaw Puzzle, "Tyrolean Waters," 300 pcs, 15 x 11", 1937 . . . . . . **40.00**

Jigsaw, adult, hand cut, Parker Brothers, Pastime Picture Puzzle, "A Pioneer Christmas," wood, 104 pcs, 7 x 5", 1932 . . . . **25.00**

Jigsaw, adult, hand cut, "The Birth of Our Nation," Hy Hintermeister illus, 80 pcs, c1920, 13 x 9" **40.00**

Jigsaw, adv, frame tray, American Bakers Assoc, "What Enriched Bread Does For Me," 9½ x 5½", ©1955, orig packaging missing **15.00**

Jigsaw, adv, frame tray, Poll-Parrot, "Howdy Doody Magic Show," 8¼ x 7¼", c1950s, paper envelope with guide picture **50.00**

Jigsaw, children's, diecut cardboard, Jaymar Specialty Co, NY, "King of the Royal Mounted" Jig Saw Puzzle, large pcs, c1950 . . . . **25.00**

Jigsaw, children's, diecut cardboard, Madmar Quality Co, Utica, NY, "Air Fleet Picture Puzzle," set of 3, 1930s, 10 x 8" box **60.00**

Jigsaw, children's, diecut cardboard, Milton Bradley, "Old Mother Hubbard Puzzle Box," #4212, 3-puzzle set, 1913–35, 9 x 13" box **100.00**

Jigsaw, children's, diecut cardboard, Parker Brothers, "Old Dobbin Picture Puzzles," set of 2, c1925, 12 x 9" box **25.00**

Jigsaw, children's, diecut cardboard, Saalfield Publishing Co, "Mother Goose," set of 3, 1943, 12 x 10" box **20.00**

Jigsaw, children's, diecut cardboard, Whitman Publishing, "Tarzan Big Little Book Picture Puzzles," 1938, 11 x 8" box **150.00**

Jigsaw, children's, frame tray, Built-Rite Sta-N-Place Inlaid Puzzle #1129, Blondie and Dagwood, early 1960s, 13½ x 10⅝" **20.00**

Jigsaw, children's, frame tray, Jaymar Specialty Co, "Li'l Abner," 35 diecut pcs, 14 x 11" **20.00**

Jigsaw, children's, frame tray, Milton Bradley, "Son of Hercules," #4572-X8, 43 pcs, 14¼ x 10⅛", 1966 . . . . **20.00**

Jigsaw, multipurpose, book, *Sam See, Let's Play Together: The Second Eye-Cue Builder Book,* S C Platt, Series 200, 4-puzzle set, diecut frame tray format, 9½ x 11¾", 1945, plastic spiral bound **30.00**

Jigsaw, multipurpose, game, Ideal Toy Corp, #2017-2-100, "Skooz-It Heckle and Jeckle Pick-A-Picture Game," 1963, 8¼" h, 4¼" d, cardboard and metal cylinder **50.00**

Jigsaw, multipurpose, mystery, Einson-Freeman Lithograph Co, Mystery-Jig Puzzle, #2 in series of 4, "By Whose Hand," approx 300 pcs, 19⅞ x 14", booklet enclosed, 1933 cardboard box **30.00**

Skill, head and tail, Calumet Baking Powder, match colors and 4 sides of baking powder cans **25.00**

Skill, sequential movement, Puzzle-Peg, Lubbers & Bell Mfg Co, 1920s **15.00**

Skill, sliced or dissected, Pratt Food Co, "Pratt's Cut Up Puzzle," 2 Puzzles in 1, 10 pcs, 9 x 6¼", 6⅛ x 4⅝" paper envelope **65.00**

PYREX

The origins of Corning Glass begin with Amory Houghton and the Bay State Glass Company, East Cambridge, Massachusetts, founded in 1851. In 1854 Houghton established the Union Glass Company, a leading producer of consumer and specialty glass, in Sommerville, Massachusetts. In 1864 Houghton purchased the Brooklyn Flint Glass Works and moved it to Sommerville. In 1868 Houghton moved his company to Corning, New York, and renamed it the Corning Flint Glass Works. After an initial period focused on producing tabletop glassware, the company's main product became hand-blown glass light bulbs.

In 1908 Dr. Eugene C. Sullivan established a research laboratory at Corning. Dr. William C. Taylor joined Sullivan that same year. In the early 1910s Sullivan and Taylor developed Nonex, a heat resistant glass. Dr. Jesse T. Littleton joined Corning around 1912 and began experiments on glass suitable for baking vessels.

Corning Glass created a consumer products business in 1915, launching a 12-piece Pyrex line. In 1920 Corning granted Fry Glass Company, Rochester, Pennsylvania, a license to produce Pyrex cooking glass under its Fry Oven Glass label. The 200-inch glass disk for the Hale telescope at the California Institute of Technology is one of the most famous uses for Pyrex.

Reference: Susan Tobier Rogove and Marcie Buan Steinhauer, *Pyrex By Corning,* Antique Publications, 1993, 1997–98 value update.

Baker, open, Gold Acorn, 2½ qt	$15.00
Beverage Server, etched, 4 cup	10.00
Bowl, delphite, 222-1-1	24.00
Bowl, delphite, 222-1-1, round base, 7" d	17.00
Cake Dish, 8¼" d	8.00
Casserole, cov, Bluebird, 1½ qt	15.00
Casserole, cov, Blue Stripe, 2½ qt	20.00
Casserole, cov, Constellation, 1½ qt.	15.00
Casserole, cov, Daisy, 2½ qt	20.00
Casserole, cov, Gold Acorn, 1½ qt.	15.00
Casserole, cov, Gooseberry, 1 qt	10.00
Casserole, cov, Holiday, 2 qt	15.00
Casserole, cov, Hostess, 1½ qt.	15.00
Casserole, cov, Medallion, with candle warmer, 2½ qt	20.00
Casserole, cov, Town & Country, 1½ qt	15.00
Double Boiler, Flameware, #6763, 1½ qt.	35.00
Freezer Server, Snowflake, 1¼ qt	10.00
Measure Cup, 1 cup, 2 spout.	8.00
Mixing Bowl Set, Bluebelle, 1½ pt, 1½ qt, 2½ qt	20.00
Nesting Bowl, Americana, #402	8.00
Nesting Bowl, Blue Dot, #403	8.00
Nesting Bowl, Butterprint, #401	5.00
Nesting Bowl, Butterprint Cinderella, #443	8.00
Nesting Bowl, Early American, #403	8.00
Nesting Bowl, Gooseberry Cinderella, #443	8.00
Nesting Bowl, red, #402	5.00
Nesting Bowl, Terra, #401	4.00
Nesting Bowl, yellow rainbow stripes, #403	8.00
Percolator, Flameware, #7824, 4 cup, black handle	15.00
Ramekin, red, 12 oz	4.00
Refrigerator Dish, clear, #501	5.00
Refrigerator Dish, Daisy, #502, 1½ pt	5.00
Saucepan, Flameware, #834-B, 2 qt.	20.00
Serving Bowl, Cinderella, 2½ qt	15.00
Serving Dish, Bluebelle, 1½ qt	15.00
Serving Dish, Royal Wheat, divided, 1½ qt.	15.00
Tea Kettle, Flameware, #7125, 2½ qt.	20.00
Teapot, Deluxe, spouted, #6406, 6 cup	10.00
Utility Dish, oblong, flamingo, 2 qt	10.00
Utility Platter, oval, #812, 12" l	8.00

QUILTS

In the 18th century quilting was used for garments. Quilted curtains and bedcovers also enjoyed widespread popularity. Lap quilts and covers were common during the Victorian era. World War I had a negative effect on quilting as women worked in factories during wartime. A quilting revival occurred in the late 1920s and 1930s. World War II ended this quilting renaissance.

A quilt exhibition at the Cooper Hewitt Museum in New York in 1971 reawakened interest in historic quilts and revitalized the art of quilt making. Many of today's contemporary quilts are done as works of art, never intended to grace the top of a bed.

Beginning in the 1920s, most patchwork quilts were made using silk-screened fabrics. Cherry Basket, Dresden Plate, Grandmother's Flower Garden, Nursery Rhyme blocks, and Sunbonnet Babies were popular patterns of the 1920–30s period.

Periodical: *Quilters Newsletter,* PO Box 4101, Golden, CO 80401.

Collectors' Clubs: American Quilter's Society, PO Box 3290, Paducah, KY 42001; The National Quilting Assoc, Inc, PO Box 393, Ellicott City, MD 21043.

Around the World, Mennonite, pieced and appliquéd, cotton, concentric rows in blues, reds, yellows, orange, soft green, and off-white within royal blue and yellow sawtooth border, early 20th C, 67 x 77½"	$400.00
Bar and Patch, Amish, pieced, cotton, worked in black and lavender, patches worked in shades of lavender, yellow, green, and blue, early 20th C, 64 x 71".	350.00
Crazy Quilt, embroidered, silk and satin, multicolored irregular blocks, early 20th C, 73 x 82".	175.00
Double Wedding Ring, pieced, cotton, varied pastel shades of red, pink, green, lilac, blue, and yellow on quilted ground, early 20th C, 76¾ x 93".	600.00

Pie Baker, clear glass, orig label, $5.00.

Flower Garden, pieced, by Frances Hill, 1928, 60" h, 73" w, $258.00. Photo courtesy Collectors Auction Services.

Floral and Sawtooth Variant, pieced, cotton, pink on white ground, central sawtooth square and floral wreath within floral and sawtooth border, serpentine edges, early 20th C, 80 x 80" 350.00

Floral Bouquet, pieced and appliquéd, cotton, blue and red thread on white ground centering rows of oval rose, peony, tulip, and lilac bouquets, checkerboard frame, banded edge border, early 20th C, 95 x 69" 175.00

Indian Maiden, pieced and appliquéd, cotton, each block depicting back view of woman with long black hair tied with multicolored ribbon, black and white checkerboard quilted ground, 20th C, 68 x 93" 125.00

Kaleidescopic Theme, pieced, cotton, orange, black, pink, yellow, blue, and gray centering large square with kaleidescopic patches, banded border, 20th C, 62 x 55" 120.00

Log Cabin Variant, pieced, cotton, irradiating bars worked in light ecru and dark ecru with gray blocks within quilted border, early 20th C, 104 x 104" 180.00

Nine Patch, pieced, cotton, shades of red and dark blue on off-white printed ground, flying geese borders, early 20th C, 64½ x 67" 150.00

Patchwork, pieced, silk, blocks of various sizes and colors, early 20th C, 58 x 73½" 115.00

Presentation, pieced and appliquéd, cotton, red, yellow, and gray on white ground, centering 9 circular floral wreaths, each embroidered with 3 rows of names, all within banded border, early 20th C, 91 x 89" 300.00

Religious Theme, pieced and appliquéd, polychrome palette, central landscape scene with Jesus, tulips, and lamb, flanked by children playing within landscape, animals frolicking, tulip buds, and doves in flight, diamond patch border, contemporary, crib size, 59 x 57" 115.00

Sampler, printed felt, rect blocks with figures, Persian rug design, animals, and flags, early 20th C, 62 x 63" 175.00

Signature Quilt, pieced and appliquéd, cotton, Los Angeles Rams, appliquéd football helmets and central football, random rect outlines with each player's signature and number on light blue ground, gold and royal blue outline, dated 1977, 85 x 62" 125.00

Star, pieced and embroidered, cotton, shades of brown, each star embroidered with repeating circles and chains, 20th C, 120 x 110" 110.00

RADIO CHARACTERS & PERSONALITIES

Radio's golden age began in the 1920s and extended through the 1950s. Families gathered around the radio in the evening to listen to a favorite program. American Movie Classics' *Remember WENN* television show provides an accurate portrayal of the early days of radio.

Sponsors and manufacturers provided a wide variety of material ranging from cookbooks to photographs directed toward the adult audience. Magazines devoted exclusively to radio appeared on newsstand racks.

When collecting radio material, do not overlook objects relating to the shows themselves. Props, publicity kits, and scripts are a few examples. Many Big Little Book titles also focused on radio shows.

Reference: Jon D. Swartz and Robert C. Reinehr, *Handbook of Old-Time Radio: A Comprehensive Guide to Golden Age Radio Listening and Collecting*, Scarecrow Press, 1993.

Periodical: *Old Time Radio Digest*, 10280 Gunpowder Rd, Florence, KY 41042.

Newsletter: *Hello Again*, PO Box 4321, Hamden, CT 06514.

Collectors' Clubs: Friends of Vic & Sade, 7232 N Keystone Ave, Lincolnwood, IL 60646; National Lum 'n' Abner Society, #81 Sharon Blvd, Dora, AL 35062; North American Radio Archives, 134 Vincewood Dr, Nicholasville, KY 40356; Pow-Wow (Nabisco Straight Arrow), PO Box 24751, Minneapolis, MN 55424; Radio Collectors of America, 8 Ardsley Circle, Brockton, MA 02402.

Note: For additional listings see Premiums.

Amos 'n Andy, leaflet, "Amos 'n Andy on the Screen," RKO Pictures, 1930 . . . . **$50.00**

Amos 'n Andy, sign, "Don't Miss It!, Amos 'n Andy's 10,000 Broadcast," 1940s 200.00

Amos 'n Andy, ticket, green stiff paper, black printing for CBS TV show dated Apr 27, 1951, 1¾ x 4" 20.00

Amos 'n Andy, ticket holder, slots at center to hold radio show ticket, Amos and Andy image with text in cartoon balloons referring to tickets for Friday night show, Rinso ad on back, c1943–44, 3¾ x 6" 25.00

Amos 'n Andy, toy, sparkler, emb litho tin, glass eyes, German, c1930, 6½" h 500.00

Amos 'n Andy Card Party, ©1930, $60.00. Photo courtesy Collectors Auction Services.

Aunt Jemima Breakfast Club, kitchen scale, metal, cardboard face under glass, mkd "Old Kentucky Home Belknap How & Mfg. Co. Louisville, Ky.," 8" h, 6¼" w, 8¼" d, $385.00. Photo courtesy Collectors Auction Services.

Amos 'n Andy, wind-up, Amos, litho tin, facsimile Amos signature, ©Correll & Godsen 1930/Made by Louis Marx & New York U.S.A., 11¼" h 470.00

Bergen, Edgar and Charlie McCarthy, Christmas card, front shows Bergen, McCarthy, and Mortimer Snerd in Revolutionary War style clothing, Bergen playing mandolin as McCarthy plays accordion and Snerd holds Christmas carol book, inside red text "Season's Greetings Edgar, Charlie and Mortimer," Chayson's Hollywood USA imprint on back, 1¼ x 6⅛" 75.00

Bergen, Edgar and Charlie McCarthy, magazine article, *Time*, Nov 20, 1944, 104 pp, cover shows Edgar Bergen with Charlie, Mortimer, and Effie, 3-pp article "Bergen & Mouthpieces," photos, 8 x 10¾" 20.00

Bergen, Edgar and Charlie McCarthy, matchcover, "The Tournament of Roses Starring Edgar Bergen & Charlie McCarthy," black and white photo on front accented by red and green roses with parade name in red, dated "January 1, 1957/CBS-TV," and "With Mrs. Bergen As Your Hostess," reverse with "...Mortimer Snerd, Effie Clinker And The Whole Bergen Gang," sponsored by The Quaker Oats Co on inside, unused, 2 x 2⅛" 20.00

Big John Arthur & Sparkie, fan card, "Hi, Hey Hello There...," American Broadcasting Corp, 1950s 35.00

Booklet, *Radio Stars and Stations*, 36 pp, color cover illus of Eddie Cantor, contents include biography pages of radio stars with portrait illus, advertising for RCA products, list of broadcasting station for US, Canada, and rest of the world, stars include Jack Benny, Bing Crosby, and Kate Smith, ©1933 RCA Radiotron Co, Inc, 6 x 8" 20.00

Bringing Up Father, paint book, #663, Whitman, 1942, 8½ x 11½" 35.00

Bringing Up Father, Whitman Big Little Book, #1133, 1936. . . . . 30.00

Buck Rogers, radio guide, Dec 1937, Vol 8, #9, 2-pp article "What Is Wrong?" with views of children's radio programs, black and white photo of Wilma and Buck, c1933, 10½ x 13½" 100.00

Cantor, Eddie, sign, "Strike Me Pink If I Don't Think New Pebeco Is Swell," 12 x 19" 45.00

Counter-Spy, sign, "Listen To Counter-Spy Pepsi's Radio Thriller!," glossy paper, red, white, and blue, 1949–50 . . . . 75.00

Duffy's Tavern Preview, ticket, stiff green paper, black printing for NBC radio program starring Ed Garner, 1940s, 1½ x 4" 20.00

Fibber McGee and Molly, game, The Merry Game of Fibber McGee and the Wistful Vista Mystery, Milton Bradley, 1940 . . . . 25.00

Fibber McGee and Molly, record set, *Fibber McGee and Molly with Teeny*, three 78 rpm records, features reading of "On the Night Before Christmas," Christmas scene on front and back covers, 1930s 75.00

Fibber McGee and Molly, ticket, stiff gray paper, black printing for NBC radio program sponsored by Johnson's Wax, late 1940–50s, 1½ x 4" 20.00

Happy Hollow, flyer, with recipes, orig mailer, 1936. . . . . . . 20.00

I Want a Divorce, Happy Marriage Game, with punch-outs, game spinner, and mailer, 1938 . . . . 200.00

Jack Pearl Show, game, The Baron Munchausen Game, Parker Bros, 1933 . . . . 25.00

Little Orphan Annie, book, *Little Orphan Annie and Jumbo the Circus Elephant*, pop-up, 13 pp, black and white illus, Blue Ribbon Press, Pleasure Books, Inc, ©1935, 8 x 9¼" 200.00

Little Orphan Annie, dolls, Annie and Sandy, stuffed, full color oilcloth front and back image, reverse side with name and Harold Gray Famous Artists Syndicate, 10" h Annie, 7 x 7½" h Sandy 200.00

Little Orphan Annie, game, Orphan Annie to the Rescue, 1930s 75.00

Little Orphan Annie, jack set, rubber ball and metal jacks on 5 x 7" card, 1930s 50.00

McCarthy, Charlie, figure, plaster, smiling seated figure, unmkd, 1940s, 12¼" h 200.00

McCarthy, Charlie, pencil sharpener, catalin, dark yellow, full color decal on front, 1¾" h 75.00

McCarthy, Charlie, pin, plastic, black and white, ¾" d 20.00

Monk and Sam, radio show kit, complete with photo, mailer, songbook, and 1936 "Monkalendar" 50.00

Mortimer Snerd, publicity photo, smiling Snerd in heart shaped valentine with blue paper, reverse with black text promotion film, "You Can't Cheat An Honest Man," black and white, 8 x 10" 20.00

No School Today, coloring book, Sparkie In Who Am I?, 32 pp, Saalfield Publishing, ©1952 Arthur-Sampson Enterprises Inc, 10¾ x 15¼" 50.00

The Great Gildersleeve, ticket, stiff red paper, black printing for NBC radio program, late 1940s, 1½ x 4". 20.00

The Rochester Show, ticket, stiff cream paper, blue printing for Feb 18, 1950 program, 1½ x 3¾" 20.00

The Shadow, radio broadcasts schedule folder, with folder, Perfect-O-Lite, lists 27 stations in 3 time zones, 1932 . . . . 200.00

The Shadow, secret message letter, paper sheet, directions printed at top margin, lower right facsimile signature "The Shadow," contains secret message which is revealed by dipping sheet of paper in water, 1930s, 8½ x 11" 200.00

The Shadow, sticker, "The Shadow Is Back On The Air," "Presented by Blue Coal," 1930s 120.00

The Tuttle Parlor Show, Sara and Aggie's Cook Book, 32 pp, 1936. . . . . 20.00

Up In Arms, postcard, Dinah Shore promotional photo, 1940s 30.00

RADIOS

Marconi, who designed and perfected the transmission and reception instruments that permitted the sending of electrical messages without the use of direct communication, is considered the father of radio. By the end of the 1890s, the Marconi "Wireless" was being used for ship-to-shore communications.

Significant technological developments took place rapidly. By the mid-1920s the cost and quality of radios had reached a point where they were within the budget of most American households. The radio was transformed from a black box with knobs, dials, and a messy battery to a piece of stylized console furniture. The table-top radio arrived on the scene in the 1930s.

Although the transistor was invented in 1927, it was not until the post-1945 period that it was used heavily in the production of radios. Today transistors are a major subcategory of radio collecting. The transistor also made possible the novelty radio, another popular collecting subcategory.

The value of any radio is directly related to its playability. If components, parts, or tubes are missing or if the radio needs repair, its value is lowered by 50% or more. Parts are readily available to restore radios. In fact, the collecting of radio accessories, ephemera, and parts is increasing.

References: Robert Breed and Marty Bunis, *Collector's Guide to Novelty Radios, Bk II,* Collector Books, 1998; John H. Bryant and Harold N. Cones, *The Zenith Trans-Oceanic,* Schiffer Publishing, 1995; Marty and Sue Bunis, *Collector's Guide to Antique Radios, Fourth Edition,* Collector Books, 1997; Marty and Sue Bunis, *Collector's Guide to Transistor Radios, Second Edition,* Collector Books, 1996; Marty Bunis and Robert F. Breed, *Collector's Guide to Novelty Radios,* Collector Books, 1995; Harold Cones and John Bryant, *Zenith Radio: The Early Years, 1919–1935,* Schiffer Publishing, 1997; Chuck Dachis, *Radios By Hallicrafters, 2nd Edition,* Schiffer Publishing, 1999.

David and Betty Johnson, *Guide to Old Radios, Second Edition,* Wallace-Homestead, Krause Publications, 1995; Ken Jupp and Leslie Piña, *Genuine Plastic Radios of the Mid-Century,* Schiffer Publishing, 1998; Ron Ramirez, *Philco Radio: 1928–1942,* Schiffer Publishing, 1993; Norman R. Smith, *Transistor Radios: 1954–1968* (1998), *Zenith Transistor Radios* (1998), Schiffer Publishing; Scott Wood (ed.), *Evolution of the Radio, Vol. 1* (1991, 1994 value update), *Vol. 2* (1993), L-W Books Sales.

Periodicals: *Antique Radio Classified,* PO Box 2, Carlisle, MA 01741; *The Horn Speaker,* PO Box 1193, Mabank, TX 75147.

Newsletter: *Transistor Network,* 32 West Main St, Bradford, NH 03221.

Collectors' Clubs: Antique Radio Club of America, 81 Steeplechase Rd, Devon, PA 19113; Antique Wireless Assoc, 59 Main St, Bloomfield, NY 14469.

Character, Donald Duck, Philgee International, Hong Kong, transistor, smiling Donald wearing blue sailor cap, 1970s **$50.00**

Character, GI Joe, ©Hasbro, Nastra Industries, transistor, 1980s **20.00**

Character, Huckleberry Hound, transistor, figural, plastic, ©Hanna-Barbera Productions, Marksons' Radio, Chicago, IL, c1970, orig 7 x 7 x 1½" box **75.00**

Coca-Cola Radio, cooler-shaped, red plastic, works, 1950s, 3" w, chip on side with piece missing, $546.00. Photo courtesy Gary Metz's Muddy River Trading Co.

Character, James Bond 007 Secret Earphone Wrist Watch Radio, Vanity Fair, 1970s **200.00**

Character, Jimmy Carter, "The New Peanut Radio," plastic, Carter head and peanut body, orig box **50.00**

Character, Mickey Mouse, solid wood with pressed wood composition panels on sides, each panel has high relief image of Mickey playing different instrument, "Emerson Mickey Mouse" and company information on metal label, 5 x 7¼ x 7¼" **1,000.00**

Character, Spider-Man, Amoco ©1978 Marvel Comics Group **50.00**

Clock Radio, General Electric, Model 560, square, large circular clock face in center with radio tuner on right side, 1953 . . . . **25.00**

Clock Radio, Motorola, Model 5C1, plastic, ribs separate dial and clock face, 1950 . . . . **25.00**

Clock Radio, RCA, Model 2C521, square-lined, 1952 . . . . . . **15.00**

Console, Westinghouse, Model 169, 4 band, phono behind doors, 1948 . . . . **15.00**

Novelty, bass guitar, Windsor, Hong Kong, brown, 1970s **40.00**

Novelty, camera, Stewart, Hong Kong, black and silver, includes radio, light, and mirror, with wrist strap **25.00**

Novelty, Camus Cognac Bottle, Hong Kong, 1970s **20.00**

Novelty, dice, Sanyo, red, numerals on 5 sides, controls on other, 1970s **25.00**

Novelty, Folger's Coffee Can, Hong Kong, 1980s **30.00**

Novelty, Gulden's Mustard Jar, Hong Kong, 1980s **45.00**

Novelty, Hershey's Syrup Bottle, Hong Kong, 1980s **35.00**

Novelty, Moonship, Amico, Japan, 1960s **25.00**

Novelty, Shell Oil Gas Pump, Synanon, China, orig box, 1985 . . . . **75.00**

Novelty, Smiley Face, Power Tronic, Hong Kong, yellow and black, 1970s **20.00**

Novelty, Star-Lite Super World Radio, Japan, 1960s **75.00**

Portable, Bendix, Model 687-A, 5 tube, leatherette and plastic, drop down front, 1946 . . . . **15.00**

Portable, Fada, Model 32 Series, leatherette cov, Catalin knobs, front opens to expose metal face plate, 1930s **45.00**

Portable, Motorola, Model 5M1, Music Box, plastic, 2
   large circular controls on front, 1950 . . . . **35.00**
Portable, Zenith, Model 4K402, leatherette covered,
   drop down front door exposes controls, 1940 . . . . **15.00**
Tabletop, Air King, Model A-400, Minstrel, Bakelite,
   rounded top, large turning pointer at right front, 1947 . . . . . **25.00**
Tabletop, Continental, Model 44, plastic, grill wraps
   around left side, large circular dial and knob at right,
   1955 . . . . **25.00**
Tabletop, Crosley, Model 9-113, brown plastic, elongat-
   ed dial under oversized speaker cloth, 1949 . . . . **15.00**
Tabletop, General Electric, Model 219, AM/short wave
   bands, 1940s **25.00**
Tabletop, Philco, Model 37-630T, 6 tubes, 3 bands with
   circular dial above tuning lever and 3 knobs, 1937 . . . . . . **75.00**
Transistor, Aiwa, Model AR-854, vertical painted plastic
   grill bars, upper 2 knobs, large round dial, leather
   case, top strap handle, 1964 . . . . **12.00**
Transistor, Arvin, Model 61R13, pink plastic, shirt pock-
   et, grill below offset V-shaped metal area with large
   tuner, 1961 . . . . **20.00**
Transistor, DeWald, Model K-701-A, swirled plastic,
   large dial at front below grill, collapsible handle on
   top, 1955 . . . . **200.00**
Transistor, Emerson, Galaxy, upper peephole dial, lower
   lattice chrome grill with logo, top tuning and right volume thumbwheels, 1963 . . . . **50.00**
Transistor, Lloyd's, Model TR-6T, upper left peephole
   dial, right thumbwheel volume, lower perforated
   chrome grill, 1964 . . . . **7.00**
Transistor, Motorola, Ranger 1000, right round dial, left
   volume knob, "rototenna" swiveling top handle,
   lower horizontal grill bars, 1959 . . . . **35.00**
Transistor, Western Auto, Model D-3614A, peach col-
   ored plastic case, gray plastic front panel, brass col-
   ored tuner dial, 1950–60s **40.00**

RAILROADIANA

Canals and railroads competed head to head for right-of-ways in the 1830s. By the early 1840s, the railroad was the clear victor. The Civil War showed the importance and value of railroads. Immediately following the war, America went on a railroad build-ing spree. The transcontinental railroad was completed. Robber barons such as Gould and Vanderbilt created huge financial for-tunes from their railroad activities. A period of mergers occurred as the 19th century came to a close.

The period from the 1880s through the end of World War II is considered the golden age of railroads. The Interstate Highway sys-tem, a car in every garage, and the growing importance of air transportation ended the steel highway's dominance. Poor man-agement and a bloated labor force added to its decline.

In the 1970s the federal government became actively involved in railroad management through Amtrak and Conrail. Thousands of miles of track were abandoned. Passenger service, except for a few key corridors, disappeared. Mergers continued into the 1990s. Even Conrail became a victim of consolidation.

References: Stanley L. Baker, *Railroad Collectibles, 4th Edition*, Collector Books, 1990, 1996 value update; Richard C. Barrett, *The Illustrated Encyclopedia of Railroad Lighting, Volume 1: The Railroad Lantern*, Railroad Research Publications, 1994; Barbara J.

Conroy, *Restaurant China: An Identification & Value Guide for Restaurant, Airline, Ship & Railroad Dinnerware, Vol. I*, Collector Books, 1998; Brad S. Lomazzi, *Railroad Timetables, Travel Brochures & Posters*, Golden Hills Press, 1995; Richard W. Luckin, *Butter Pat World: Transportation Collector's Guide Book*, RK Publishing, 1995; Richard W. Luckin, *Mimbres to Mimbreño: A Study of Santa Fe's Famous China Pattern*, RK Publishing, 1992; Richard W. Luckin, *Teapot Treasury and Related Items*, RK Publishing, 1987; Everett L. Maffet, *Silver Banquet II: A Compendium on Railroad Dining Car Silver Serving Pieces*, Silver Press, 1990; Douglas W. McIntyre, *The Official Guide to Railroad Dining Car China*, published by author, 1990.

Periodical: *The Main Line Journal*, PO Box 121, Steamwood, IL 60107.

Collectors' Clubs: Key, Lock and Lantern, Inc, PO Box 66, Penfield, NY 14526; Railroadiana Collectors Assoc, PO Box 8051, Rowland Heights, CA 91748.

Ashtray, The Pullman Co, brown Bakelite, "The Pullman
   Company" in white, 4¼" d. **$15.00**
Blanket, The Pullman Co, salmon colored, navy printed
   logo at center, 86 x 58" **70.00**
Blotter, Chicago Great Western, logo, steam train,
   "Chances are even we can save money for you,
   Chicago Great Western," Mar 1931, 3¾ x 8½" **20.00**
Book, Rock Island, *Uniform Code of Operating Rules,*
   effective May 1, 1950, gold on maroon **8.00**
Brochure, Illinois Central Green Diamond, 1936 . . . . **60.00**
Brochure, Overland Limited, 1930 . . . . **40.00**
Brochure, The Santa Fe Super Chief, 1935 . . . . **75.00**
Calendar, C&O, 50th Golden Anniversary, Chessie cat
   photos, 9½ x 16" open size **8.00**
Desk Pad Holder, Reading Railway, copper-toned metal,
   depicts Reading Railway engine, "Reading Lines
   Reading Railway System" **30.00**
Handbook, *The New York Visitor*, issued by NY Central
   System, Jan 1942 issue, 4 x 9" **20.00**
Lapel Pin, Burlington Route, "40 Years" service, red and
   black enamel painted logo **55.00**
Magazine, *Great Northern Goat*, Vol 8, #7, Dec-Jan,
   1940–41 . . . . **4.00**

Chocolate Pot, Santa Fe Railway, Membreño pattern, mkd "Ancient Mimbreño Indian Designs, Made Expressly for Santa Fe Dining Car Service, Old Ivory Syracuse China, Copyrighted by Santa Fe Railway," missing lid, 5⅛" h, $85.00.

Map, "Tourist's Map of Canada," issued by Canadian
National Railways, 1952 . . . . **10.00**

Matchcover, Union Pacific Railroad, gold-toned logo,
unused **5.00**

Menu, Illinois Central, Centennial Medallion and
1851–1951 in upper right corner, 8 x 11". **6.00**

Mug, Burlington Northern, green "BN Burlington
Northern," black "Transportation Needs You," "JA"
emblem in black and red on sides, 1972, 5½" h **10.00**

Pinback Button, Baltimore & Ohio Railroad, "Daniel
Willard Day," sepia, 1920–30s **20.00**

Plate, Gulf, Mobile, & Ohio Railroad, white with pale
pink border and rose "GM&O" Gulf, Mobile & Ohio
Railroad logo at top, mkd "3-HH Syracuse China
USA," 6½" d **60.00**

Playing Cards, Chicago & North Western Railway, 2
decks, Congress, yellow and green diesel engine **40.00**

Playing Cards, Hiawatha Railroad, 52 cards, 1940s **20.00**

Postcard, The Pullman Co, cardboard, "Travel in
Pullman Safety and Comfort to Your Favorite Winter
Resort," 1936, 23 x 29" **40.00**

Route Map, Wabash Railroad, black wooden guides on
top and bottom, 1957, 40 x 57". **35.00**

Sheet Music, *I've Been Working on the Railroad*,
Calumet Music Co, Chicago, 1935. . . . . **10.00**

Ticket Punch, conductor's, nickel plated metal, mkd
"McGill Utility Punch," 5¼" l **20.00**

Timetable, Missouri Pacific Railroad, #1, Omaha
Division, Oct 18, 1959 . . . . **5.00**

REAMERS

A reamer is a device used to extract juice from fruits. Reamers are collected primarily by composition, i.e., ceramic, glass, and metal. In an attempt to bring order to reamer collecting, Ken and Linda Ricketts and Mary Walker assigned reamers an identification number. These numbers are used by most collectors.

There are two basic types of reamers: (1) hand operated and (2) mechanical. Reamers were extremely popular in the period between World War I and II. Only a few were made in the post-1945 period, a result of the popularity of frozen juice concentrates and pre-packaged fruit juices.

In the early 1980s Edna Barnes reproduced a number of old reamers from molds belonging to the Jenkins Glass Company and Imperial Glass Company. These reproductions are marked with a "B" in a circle.

Reference: Gene Florence, *Kitchen Glassware of the Depression Years, Fifth Edition*, Collector Books, 1995, 1999 value update.

Collectors' Club: National Reamer Collectors Assoc, 47 Midline Ct, Gaithersburg, MD 20878.

Cambridge, glass, green. **$200.00**

Czechoslovakia, ceramic, 2-pc, orange shape, white
with green leaves, mkd "Erphila," 6" h **32.00**

Fry, glass, amber **375.00**

Fry, glass, pearlized fluted, jello mold. **110.00**

Fry, glass, pearl opalescent, straight side, grapefruit. **65.00**

Gem Squeezer, aluminum, 2-pc, crank handle, table
model. **10.00**

Handy Andy, table model, aluminum, crank handle, red
base **18.00**

Juice Set, reamer, pitcher, and 5 tumblers, mkd "Made in Japan," price for set, $75.00.

Hazel Atlas, glass, blue tab handle. **325.00**

Hazel Atlas, glass, Crisscross, blue **300.00**

Hazel Atlas, glass, Crisscross, pink, orange juice. **240.00**

Japan, ceramic, yellow with white flowers and green
leaves, lemon, 4¾" d **40.00**

Jeannette, glass, delphite, lemon **100.00**

Jeannette, glass, ultramarine. **185.00**

Kwicky Juicer, aluminum, pan style, Quan-Nichols Co **6.50**

McCoy, ceramic, green, 8" d **42.00**

Nasco-Royal, metal, scissor type **6.50**

Occupied Japan, ceramic, 2-pc, strawberry shape, 3¾" h **65.00**

Paden City, glass, cocktail with reamer top **125.00**

Sunkist, glass, black. **800.00**

Sunkist, glass, blue, gray tint **150.00**

Sunkist, glass, carmel **375.00**

Sunkist, glass, crown tuscan **375.00**

Sunkist, glass, crystal, emb bottom **38.00**

Sunkist, glass, custard **65.00**

Sunkist, glass, opalescent. **200.00**

Sunkist, glass, transparent green. **45.00**

Sunkist, glass, white milk glass. **20.00**

Sunkist, glass, white milk glass, light green tint **195.00**

US Glass, glass, grapefruit, green **575.00**

Wagner Ware, cast aluminum, skillet shape, 2 spouts **20.00**

RECORDS

Thomas Edison is credited with the invention of the phonograph. In 1877 Edison demonstrated a phonograph he designed that played wax cylinder records. Although patenting his phonograph in 1878, Edison did not pursue the concept, preferring instead to concentrate on further development of the light bulb.

Alexander Graham Bell created the graphaphone, successfully marketing it by the end of the 1880s. Emile Berliner developed the flat disc phonograph in 1900. Discs replaced cylinders as the most popular record form by the end of the decade.

Initially records were played at a speed of 78 revolutions per minute (rpm). 45 rpm records became the dominant form in the late 1940s and 50s, eventually being replaced by the 33⅓ rpm format. Most phonographs, more frequently referred to as record players in the post-1945 period, could play 33⅓, 45, and 78 rpm records. The arrival of the compact disc in the early 1980s made the turntable obsolete.

Most records have relatively little value, especially those without their dust jackets or album covers. The more popular a song title, the less likely it is to have value. Many records were released in several pressings. Find out exactly which pressing you own. If a record is scratched or warped, its value disappears.

References: Mark Brown, Thomas Conner and John Wooley, *Forever Lounge*, Antique Trader Books, 1999; Les Docks, *American Premium Record Guide, 1900–1965: Identification and Value Guide to 78s, 45s and LPs, Fifth Edition*, Books Americana, Krause Publications, 1997; Anthony J. Gribin and Matthew M. Schiff, *Doo-Wop*, Krause Publications, 1992; Fred Heggeness, *Goldmine Country Western Record & CD Price Guide*, Krause Publications, 1996; Fred Heggeness, *Goldmine's Promo Record & CD Price Guide, 2nd Edition*, Krause Publications, 1998; Ron Lofman, *Goldmine's Celebrity Vocals*, Krause Publications, 1994; Vito R. Marino and Anthony C. Furfero, *The Official Price Guide to Frank Sinatra Records and CDs*, House of Collectibles, 1993; R. Michael Murray, *The Golden Age of Walt Disney Records: 1933–1988*, Antique Trader Books, 1997.

Tim Neely, *Goldmine Christmas Record Price Guide*, Krause Publications, 1997; Tim Neely, *Goldmine Price Guide to Alternative Records*, Krause Publications, 1996; Tim Neely (ed.), *Goldmine Price Guide to 45 RPM Records*, Krause Publications, 1996; Tim Neely, *Standard Catalog of American Records*, Schiffer Publishing, 1998; Tim Neely and Dave Thompson, *Goldmine British Invasion Record Price Guide*, Krause Publications, 1997; Jerry Osborne, *Rockin' Records*, Antique Trader Books, 1998; Jerry Osborne, *The Official Guide to the Money Records*, House of Collectibles, 1998; Jerry Osborne, *The Official Price Guide to Country Music*, House of Collectibles, 1996; Jerry Osborne, *The Official Price Guide to Movie/TV Soudtracks & Original Cast Albums, Second Edition*, House of Collectibles, 1997; Jerry Osborne, *The Official Price Guide to Records, Thirteenth Edition*, House of Collectibles, 1999.

Ronald L. Smith, *Goldmine Comedy Record Price Guide*, Krause Publications, 1996; Charles Szabala, *Goldmine 45 RPM Picture Sleeve Price Guide*, Krause Publications, 1998; Neal Umphred, *Goldmine's Price Guide to Collectible Jazz Albums, 1949–1969, 2nd Edition*, Krause Publications, 1994; Neal Umphred, *Goldmine's Price Guide to Collectible Record Albums, 5th Edition*, Krause Publications, 1996.

Periodicals: *DISCoveries Magazine*, PO Box 1050, Dubuque, IA 52004; *Goldmine*, 700 E State St, Iola, WI 54990.

Collectors' Clubs: Assoc of Independent Record Collectors, PO Box 222, Northford, CT 06472; International Assoc of Jazz Record Collectors, 15745 W Birchwood Ln, Libertyville, IL 60048.

CHILDREN'S

Banana Splits, *We're The Banana Splits*, LP, Decca
   DL-75075, 1969 . . . . **$55.00**
Cattanooga Cats, Forward STF-1018, 1969 . . . . **50.00**
Chipmunks, The, *Sing Again With the Chipmunks*, LP,
   Liberty LST-7159, 1961 . . . . **8.00**
Dream Along With Bozo, Golden GLP-96, 1963 . . . . **40.00**
Hitchcock, Alfred, *Alfred Hitchcock's Ghost Stories For
   Young People*, Golden GLP-89, 1962 . . . . **75.00**
Huckleberry Hound and the Ghost Ship, Colpix
   CP-210, 1962 . . . . **100.00**

Ives, Burl, *Rudolph the Red-Nosed Reindeer*, Decca
   DL-4815, 1966 . . . . **30.00**
Josie and the Pussycats, Capitol ST-665, 1970 . . . . **200.00**
Marx, Harpo, *Harpo in Hi-Fi*, Mercury MG-20232, 1957 . . . . . **50.00**
Mr Ed the Talking Horse, Colpix CP-209, 1961 . . . . **250.00**
Officer Gunther Toody Tells Toody Tales, Golden
   GLP-91, 1963 . . . . **50.00**
Sparky's Magic Piano, Capitol J-3254, 1961 . . . . **50.00**
Woody Woodpecker's Picnic, Capitol J-3263, 1962 . . . . **50.00**

COMEDY

Adams, Don, *The Detective*, Roulette R-25317, 1966 . . . . . . **$20.00**
Benny, Jack, *Jack Benny Plays the Bee (With Mel Blanc)*,
   Capitol T-3241, 1950s **60.00**
Cosby, Bill, *I Started Out As a Child*, orig sleeve **15.00**
Hope, Bob, *Bob Hope in Russia and Other Places*,
   Decca DL-4396, 1963 . . . . **20.00**
Knotts, Don, *An Evening With Me*, United Artists
   UAL-4090, 1961 . . . . **20.00**
Linkletter, Art, *Howlers, Boners and Shockers*, Columbia
   CL-703, 1955 . . . . **35.00**
Rowan, Dan and Dick Martin, *Rowan & Martin At Work*,
   Trey T-901, 1960 . . . . **25.00**

COUNTRY

Acuff, Roy, *Songs of the Smokey Mountains*, Columbia
   HL-9004, 1949 . . . . **$150.00**
Arnold, Eddy, *The Chapel On the Hill*, RCA Victor
   LPM-1225, 1955 . . . . **50.00**
Atkins, Chet, *A Session With Chet Atkins*, RCA Victor
   LPM-1090, 1961 . . . . **20.00**
Blue Ridge Mountain Boys, The, *Hootenanny and
   Bluegrass*, Time T-2083, 1963 . . . . **20.00**
Cash, Johnny, *Orange Blossom Special*, Columbia
   CS-2309, 1965 . . . . **20.00**

Comedy, Spike Jones and His City Slickers, "I Saw Mommy Kissing Santa Claus/Winter," RCA Victor 47-5067, 1953, $25.00.

Foley, Red and Ernest Tubb, *Red and Ernie,* Decca
DL-8298, 1956 . . . . **60.00**
Jones, George, *George Jones Sings His Greatest Hits,*
Starday SLP-150, 1962 . . . . **50.00**
Lee, Brenda, *Merry Christmas From Brenda Lee,* Decca
DL-74583, 1964 . . . . **25.00**
Lynn, Loretta, *Loretta Lynn Sings,* Decca, DL-74457,
1963 . . . . **50.00**
Orbison, Roy, *Crying,* Monument M-4007, 1962 . . . . **100.00**
Parton, Dolly, *Hello, I'm Dolly Parton,* Monument
MLP-8085, 1967 . . . . **30.00**
Perkins, Carl, *Country Boy's Dream,* Dollie 4001, 1960s **30.00**
Wagoner, Porter & The Wagonmasters, *The Porter
Wagner Show,* RCA Victor LPM-2650, 1963 . . . . **40.00**

JAZZ

Armstrong, Louis, *New Orleans to New York,* Decca
DL-5225, 1950 . . . . **$60.00**
Bishop Jr, Walter, *The Walter Bishop Trio,* Prestige
PRST-7730, 1969 . . . . **20.00**
Clooney, Rosemary, *Tenderly,* Columbia CL-2525, 1956 . . . . . **50.00**
Dukes of Dixieland, *Struttin' At the World's Fair,*
Columbia CS-8994, 1964 . . . . **12.00**
Ellington, Duke, *Duke Ellington Jazz Party,* Columbia
CS-8127, 1959 . . . . **20.00**
Fitzgerald, Ella, *Ella and Her Fellas,* Decca DL-8477,
1957 . . . . **40.00**
Gillespie, Dizzy, *Dizzier and Dizzier,* RCA Victor
LJM-1009, 1954 . . . . **100.00**
Hampton, Lionel, *Just Jazz,* Decca DL-7013, 1952 . . . . **60.00**
Jones, Quincy, *Bossa Nova,* Mercury MG-20751, 1962 . . . . . . **15.00**
Torme, Mel, *Back in Town,* Verve MGV-2120, 1959 . . . . **40.00**

ROCK 'N' ROLL

Annette, *Teenage Wedding,* 45 rpm, Buena Vista Records
BVF-414, wedding dress sleeve **$375.00**
Beatles, The, *Ain't She Sweet,* 45 rpm, ATCO Records
6308, illus sleeve **275.00**
Belmonts, The, includes *Carnival of Hits,* LP, Sabina
Records SALP 5001 . . . . **70.00**
Bob-B-Sox and The Blue Jeans, includes *Zip-A-Dee-Doo
Dah,* LP, Philles Records PHLP-4002 . . . . **185.00**
Chartbusters, The, *Why (Doncha Be My Girl),* 45 rpm,
Mutual Records 508, orig paper sleeve **80.00**
Dells, The, *Oh, What a Nite,* LP, Vee Jay Record LP 1010 . . . **200.00**
Holly, Buddy, *Peggy Sue,* 45 rpm, Coral Records
9-61885 . . . . **315.00**
Martha and the Vandellas, *Dancing in the Street,* 45 rpm,
Gordy Records 7033, picture sleeve **125.00**
Miracles, The, *Way Over There,* 45 rpm, Tamla Records
T-54028, paper sleeve **60.00**
Nelson, Ricky, *Songs By Ricky,* EP, Imperial Records
IMP-162, orig picture sleeve **40.00**
Powers, Johnny and His Rockets, *Honey, Let's Go (To a
Rock and Roll Show),* 45 rpm, Fortune Records **90.00**
Presley, Elvis, *It's Now or Never,* 45 rpm, RCA Victor
61-7777, paper sleeve **315.00**
Priest, Judas, *Rocka-Rolla,* Visa IMP-7001, 1974 . . . . **25.00**
Rolling Stones, The, *Heart of Stone,* 45 rpm, London
Records 45-9725, picture sleeve **345.00**
Ronettes, The, *Walking in the Rain,* 45 rpm, Philles
Records 123, picture sleeve **80.00**

Vogue Picture Record, *The Whiffenpoof Song/If That Phone Ever
Rings (and It's You),* **Art Kassel Orchestra, R770, $60.00.**

Teenagers, The, *Go Rock'n,* EP, Gee Records, GEP-601,
orig picture jacket **80.00**
Ward, Billy and The Dominoes, *Will You Remember,* EP,
Decca Records ED 2549, orig picture jacket **50.00**

SOUNDTRACK

Airport 1975, MCA 2082, 1975 . . . . **$10.00**
Barefoot in the Park, Dot DLP-25803, 1967 . . . . **25.00**
Bobo, The, Peter Sellers, Warner Bros W-1711 . . . . **10.00**
Carousel, original cast, Decca ED-804, 1945 . . . . **20.00**
Cats, original London cast, Polydor CATX-001, 1981 . . . . . . **10.00**
Davy Crockett, TV soundtrack, Columbia B-2031, 1955 . . . . . **40.00**
Doctor Zhivago, MGM 1E-6, 1965 . . . . **12.00**
Elmer Gantry, United Artists UAL-4069, 1960 . . . . **45.00**
Every Which Way But Loose, Elektra 5E-503, 1979 . . . . **10.00**
Hang 'Em High, United Artists UAS-5179, 1968 . . . . **18.00**
Harper Valley PTA, Plantation PLP-700, 1978 . . . . **10.00**
Incredible Worl of James Bond, Unart M-20010, 1965 . . . . . . **15.00**
Inside Daisy Clover, Warner Bros W-1616, 1965 . . . . **20.00**
King and I, original cast, Decca DA-876, 1951 . . . . **25.00**
Lady and the Tramp, Capitol DBX-3056, 1955 . . . . **50.00**
Nutcracker, Vanguard 168SD, 1966 . . . . **15.00**
Oklahoma!, original cast, Vol 1, Decca DA-359, 1943 . . . . . . **15.00**
Pajama Game, Columbia A-5210, 1957 . . . . **20.00**
Shaft, Enterprise ENS-2-5002, 1971 . . . . **25.00**

VOGUE PICTURE RECORDS

Doodle Doo Doo/All I Do Is Wantcha, Art Kassel & His
Orchestra, R714 . . . . **$55.00**
Rhumba Lesson No. 1/Rhumba Lesson No. 3, Paul
Shahin, R737 . . . . **55.00**
She's Funny That Way/Dizzy's Dilemma, The Charlie
Shavers Quintet, R754 . . . . **80.00**
So It Goes/The Minute Samba, Enric Madriguera and His
Orchestra, R760 . . . . **65.00**
Sugar Blues/Basin Street Blues, Clyde McCoy & His
Orchestra, R707 . . . . **40.00**
Sweetheart/A Little Consideration, Art Kassel & His
Orchestra, R734 . . . . **75.00**
The Bells of St. Mary's/Star Dust, The Don Large Chorus,
R710 . . . . **65.00**
*You're Only in My Arms/When I Gets to Where I'm
Goin',* Patsy Montana, R721 . . . . **85.00**

RED WING POTTERY

The Red Wing Stoneware Company, Minnesota Stoneware Company (1883–1906), and North Star Stoneware Company (1892–96) were located in Red Wing, Minnesota. David Hallem founded the Red Wing Stoneware Company in 1868. By the 1880s Red Wing was the largest American producer of stoneware storage vessels.

In 1894 the Union Stoneware Company was established as a selling agency for Minnesota, North Star, and Red Wing. Minnesota and Red Wing bought out North Star in 1896. In 1906 production was merged into one location and the Red Wing Union Stoneware Company created. The company made stoneware until introducing an art pottery line in the 1920s. During the 1930s Red Wing created several popular lines of hand-painted dinnerware that were sold through department stores, gift stamp redemption centers, and Sears.

In 1936 the company became Red Wing Potteries, Inc. Stoneware production ended in 1947. In the early 1960s the company began producing hotel and restaurant china. Financial difficulties that began in the 1950s continued. Red Wing ceased operations in 1967.

References: Dan and Gail DePasquale and Larry Peterson, *Red Wing Collectibles,* Collector Books, 1985, 1997 value update; B. L. Dollen, *Red Wing Art Pottery,* Collector Books, 1997; B. L. and R. L. Dollen, *Red Wing Art Pottery, Book II,* Collector Books, 1998; Ray Reiss, *Red Wing Art Pottery: Including Pottery Made for RumRill,* Property Publishing, 1996; Ray Reiss, *Red Wing Dinnerware,* Property Publishing, 1997.

Collectors' Clubs: Red Wing Collectors Society, 200 W Main St, Ste 300, Red Wing, MN 55066; The RumRill Society, PO Box 2161, Hudson, OH 44236.

Belle, compote, #848, ftd, glossy peacock blue ext, emerald green int, 10" d **$25.00**
Birch Bark, planter, #730, 11" l **45.00**
Blossom Time, casserole, cov, Concord shape **30.00**
Blossom Time, dinner plate, Concord shape, 10½" d **10.00**
Blossom Time, salt and pepper shakers, pr, Concord shape **10.00**
Bob White, casserole, cov, 13" l **38.00**
Bob White, cup and saucer, Casual shape **12.00**
Bob White, dinner plate, Casual shape **10.00**
Bob White, dinnerware service, 64-pc set consisting of 12 each 11" dinner plates, 6½" plates, cups and saucers, and salad bowls, and 1 each 9" vegetable bowl, 13" platter, and covered sugar and creamer **200.00**
Bob White, dish, divided, 2-part, 14" **22.00**
Bob White, water pitcher, Casual shape **60.00**
Brittany, candle holders, pr, Provincial shape **70.00**
Brittany, salt and pepper shakers, pr, Provincial shape **30.00**
Compote, #690, fluted, semi-matte white glaze, 9" h **35.00**
Console Bowl, #1620, scalloped edges, semi-matte white glaze, silver wing label, 10" d **40.00**
Cornucopia Vase, #1097, glossy blue ext, yellow int, silver wing label, 5¾" h **30.00**
Delta Blue, baking dish, cov, Village Green shape **35.00**
Delta Blue, cereal bowl, Village Green shape **15.00**
Driftwood, dinner plate, Anniversary shape, 10½" d **12.00**
Driftwood, water pitcher, Anniversary shape **50.00**

English Garden, candle holder, #1190, ivory/brown wipe, 6" h **25.00**
Fan Vase, #892, semi-matte white ext, green int, 7½" h **35.00**
Floraline, bowl, #M1572, glossy fleck zephyr pink glaze, handled, 10 x 7" **25.00**
Floraline, bowl, #M5010, ftd, glossy fleck orchid glaze, 8" d **25.00**
Floraline, cornucopia vase, #635, ftd, glossy cinnamon glaze, 11½ x 7" **30.00**
Floraline, fan vase, #892, glossy zephyr pink fleck glaze, silver wing label, 7½" h **45.00**
Floraline, gladiola vase, #416, semi-matte coral ext, colonial buff int, 10" h **60.00**
Harvest, cereal bowl, Concord shape **25.00**
Harvest, nappy, Concord shape **30.00**
Lanterns, chop plate, Concord shape **12.00**
Lanterns, sugar, cov, Concord shape **10.00**
Magnolia, bowl, #1223, ivory/brown wipe, oblong, 12½" l **50.00**
Magnolia, candle holders, pr, #1029, ivory/brown wipe, 7½" h **40.00**
Magnolia, pitcher vase, #1012, ivory/brown wipe, handled, 7" h **30.00**
Midnight Rose, bread and butter plate, Anniversary shape, 6½" d **10.00**
Normandy, nappy, Provincial shape, 9" **25.00**
Normandy, teapot, cov, Provincial shape **90.00**
Planter, cart, #M1531, semi-matte celadon yellow glaze, 9 x 7" **50.00**
Planter, deer, #1338, glossy turquoise glaze, 5½" h **35.00**
Planter, violin, #1484, semi-matte black glaze, 13" h **50.00**
Prismatique, compote, #796, glossy Persian blue ext, white int, 8 x 9½" **50.00**
Random Harvest, sugar, cov, Futura shape **20.00**
Random Harvest, teacup and saucer, Futura shape **15.00**
Renaissance, bowl, #526, ivory/brown wipe, 12" l **50.00**
Renaissance, candle holders, pr, #529, ivory/brown wipe, 6" h **25.00**
RumRill, bowl, #276, grooved, semi-matte eggshell ext, turquoise int, 6" **40.00**
RumRill, planter, #259, swan, semi-matte white glaze, 6" **50.00**
RumRill, vase, #K8, horn of plenty, semi-matte glaze, 12" **40.00**
Smart Set, gravy, cov, Casual shape **60.00**
Smart Set, vegetable dish, divided, Casual shape **30.00**
Stereoline, compote, #665, glossy burnt orange glaze, 11" d **30.00**
Stereoline, hanging planter, #1467, glossy fleck Nile blue glaze, silver wing label, 10½" h **30.00**
Sylvan, candle holders, pr, #397, ivory/brown wipe, 5½" h **25.00**
Tropicana, planter, #B2017, glossy forest green ext, lemon yellow int, 8" l **25.00**
Vase, #1092, garden club style, semi-matte white ext, green int, 10½" l **30.00**
Vase, #1202, leaf motif, pink ext, white int, 10½" h **30.00**
Vase, #1301, glossy blue crackle ext, gun metal int, 5" h **50.00**
Vase, #1360, emb flowers, semi-matte green ext, white int, 7½" h **30.00**
Vase, #M1609, leaf shape brass handled, semi-matte white glaze, 10" h **40.00**
Vintage, urn, #616, semi-matte ivory/brown wipe, 11" h **100.00**
Zinnia, relish dish, Concord shape **25.00**
Zinnia, sugar, cov, Concord shape **25.00**
Zinnia, supper tray, Concord shape **35.00**

REGAL CHINA

Regal China Corporation, Antioch, Illinois, was established in 1938. In the 1940s, Regal was purchased by Royal China and Novelty Company, a distribution and sales organization. Royal used Regal to make the ceramic products that it sold.

Ruth Van Tellingen Bendel designed Snuggle Hugs in the shape of bears, bunnies, pigs, etc., in 1948. She also designed cookie jars, other figurines, and salt and pepper shaker sets.

Regal did large amounts of decorating for other firms, e.g., Hull's Red Riding Hood pieces. Regal has not sold to the retail trade since 1968, continuing to operate on a contract basis only. In 1976 it produced a cookie jar for Quaker Oat in 1976; 1983 products include a milk pitcher for Ovaltine and a ship decanter and coffee mugs for Old Spice. Regal currently is a wholly owned subsidiary of Jim Beam Distilleries.

Reference; Harvey Duke, *The Official Price Guide to Pottery and Porcelain, Eighth Edition,* House of Collectibles, 1995.

Butter, cov, cow, Old McDonald	$200.00
Clove Jar, cov, Old McDonald	110.00
Coffee Canister, cov, Old McDonald	210.00
Cookie Jar, barn, Old McDonald	300.00
Creamer, white rabbit, Alice in Wonderland	385.00
Creamer and Sugar, Old McDonald	220.00
Grease Jar, pig, Old McDonald	165.00
Milk Pitcher, cow, Old McDonald	425.00
Peanut Canister, cov, Old McDonald	250.00
Salt and Pepper Shakers, pr, Alice, Alice in Wonderland, white and gold	485.00
Salt and Pepper Shakers, pr, boy and girl, Old McDonald	65.00
Salt and Pepper Shakers, pr, churn, Old McDonald	55.00
Salt and Pepper Shakers, pr, feed sack, Old McDonald	160.00
Shaker, Peek-A-Boo, white and red, small	265.00
Snuggle Hugs, bunny, green	15.00
Snuggle Hugs, Dutch girl and boy, white	25.00
Tea Canister, cov, Old McDonald	210.00
Teapot, cov, duck, Old McDonald	300.00

ROBOTS

Robot toys of the late 1940s and early 1950s were friction or windup powered. Many of these lithographed tin beauties were made from recycled material. By the mid-1950s, most robots were battery powered. Japanese manufacturers produced several hundred models. Model variations are common, the result of manufacturers freely interchanging parts. Plastic replaced lithographed tin as the material of choice in the late 1960s.

Robot models responded to changing Space Age motifs. The Japanese Atomic Robot Man, made between 1948 and 1949, heralded the arrival of the Atomic age. Movies, such as *Destination Moon* (1950) and *Forbidden Planet* (1956), featuring Robbie the Robot, provided the inspiration for robot toys in the early and mid-1950s. Space theme television programs, e.g., *Lost in Space* (1965–1968), played a similar role in the 1960s. Ideal and Marx entered the toy robot market in the late 1960s.

Markings can be confusing. Many of the marks are those of importers and/or distributors, not manufacturers. Cragston is an importer, not a maker. Reproductions and fantasy items are a major problem in the late 1990s. Because of the high desirability and secondary market cost of robots such as Mr. Atomic

($10,000+), modern copies costing between $250 and $750 new are being made. Inexpensive Chinese and Taiwanese robots made in shapes that never existed historically are flooding the market.

Reference: Maxine A. Pinsky, *Marx Toys: Robots, Space, Comic & TV Characters,* Schiffer Publishing, 1996.

Periodicals: *Toy Shop,* 700 E State St, Iola, WI 54990; *Toy Trader,* PO Box 1050, Dubuque, IA 52004.

Astronaut, litho tin, battery operated, soft vinyl arms, clear plastic dome cover over head, plastic tubes attach to chest and extend back to pr of oxygen tanks, wire antennas on sides of head hold litho tin walkie talkie unit in hand with spring antenna, Rosko, 1960s, 13" h	**$950.00**
Atom Robot, litho tin, crank lever operation, orig box, KO, Japan, 6½" h	630.00
Atomic Robot Man, advances with waddling motions, Japan, 5" h	750.00
Blink-A-Gear Robot, litho tin, plastic arms and feet, strides with swinging arms, lighted blinking eyes, colored gears spin in chest with machine noise, light behind clear plastic chestplate, orig box, Taiyo, Japan, 15" h	**1,285.00**
Chief Robotman, tin, radar antennas on head, plastic accent pieces on chest, eyes and top of head, bump-and-go action, head turns back and forth, antennas spin and plastic cover on top of head flashes, orig box, KO, Japan, 1950s, 11¾" h	950.00
Cragstan Astronaut, litho tin, advances with moving arms using crank handle, face behind clear plastic visor, Yonezawa, Japan, 10" h	535.00
Earth Man, astronaut type, tin, yellow, walks, lifts gun with lighting barrel and fires, wears oxygen tank with telescoping antenna, Normura, 1950s, 9½" h	975.00
Fighting Robot, gray and red, gun in circuit panel litho tin chest screen, Horikawa	350.00
Fighting Spaceman, tin, advances with swinging arms, blinking light on helmet, stops as gun in chest fires while moving back and forth, litho chest plate with electronics, orig box, SH, Japan, 12" h	500.00

Lavender Robot, Modern Toys, Japan, battery operated, stop-and-go action, blinking lights, orig box and inserts, late 1950s, 15" h, $4,900.00.

Giant Sonic Train Robot, red, black arms and head, battery operated, moves forward emitting train-like sound as eyes light up and arms swing back and forth, Masudaya, 1950s, 15" h **1,600.00**

Golden Gear Robot, tin, advances with moving legs and arms, flashing light atop head, clear chest reveals moving gears and flashing bullet shaped plastic eyes, SH, Japan, 9" h **575.00**

High-Wheel 6 Gear Robot, tin, plastic hands, advances while sparking in chest as 6 plastic gears revolve, telescopic antenna is on/off switch, orig box, KO, Japan, 10" h **715.00**

Jupiter Robot, plastic, windup, built-in key, Robbie style, litho tin panel on chest and back, metal face plate and antennas on head, walks forward, 1960s, KO, Japan, 7" h **100.00**

Lost in Space Robot, hard plastic, cardboard panels on each side of base, replaced plastic battery strap on underside, moves forward as chest lights, manually operated arms and upper body can be turned, Remco, ©1966 Space Productions, 12" h **375.00**

Mars King Robot, litho tin, advances on black rubber treads, stops, raises arms and screeches as TV screen in chest lights and shows Mars landscape, orig box, SH, Japan, 10" h **465.00**

Mirror Man, tin, Shugun with movable vinyl head, advances with arms moving in unison, orig box, Bullmark, Japan, 9½" h **575.00**

Moon Doctor, tin, plastic glasses and arms, advances with moving "X-25" feet, orig box, Japan, 7" h **1,700.00**

Moon Explorer, litho tin, advances with crank action, litho tin face under clear plastic dome, "spin ray counter" revolves as robot advances, orig box, KO, Japan, 7½" h **1,200.00**

Mr Brain the Tru-Smoke Robot With a Memory, hard plastic, complete with 6 memory disks, small empty tube of "Tru-Smoke" and instruction sheet, ©1969 Remco Industries, Inc, 13" h **200.00**

Mr Machine, windup, red plastic head, arms, and legs, yellow plastic transparent body with interior mechanism, metal eyes, nose, and bell attached to front of body, walks forward as arms swing, opens and closes mouth, with plastic wrench and instruction sheet, orig box, ©1960 Ideal Toy Corp, 18" h **100.00**

Mr Mercury, tin and plastic, remote battery operated, light blue, bends and picks up objects, control room at helmet visor, light on helmet, Yonezawa/Linemar, 1955–60s, 13" h **1,150.00**

Planet Robot, litho tin, olive green, Robbie type, metal claws, red tinted plastic insert windows, Japan, 9" h **585.00**

R-35 Robot, litho tin, advances forward and back, remote control, lighted eyes, orig box, Japan, 9" h. **865.00**

Radar Hunter Robot, hard plastic, windup, built-in key, orig box, mkd "Made in Hong Kong," 1970s, 6¼" h **75.00**

Radar Robot, olive gray torso, light gray litho tin legs and face, light-bulb eyes, purple feet, adjustable rear radar screen with light bulb, claw hands clutching wrench, remote control battery box in shape of robot's head, Nomura, 1950s, 8" h **2,600.00**

Ray Robot, plastic, windup, built-in key, blue, bright silver panel on front upper body, red transparent cover over face, walks forward as it produces sparks, orig box, 1970s, 4" h **75.00**

Dino Robot, Horikawa, battery operated, 5 actions, black and red tinplate and plastic, headpiece opens to reveal dinosaur head with lighted mouth, 1950s/60s, 11" h, $750.00. Photo courtesy Sotheby's New York.

RC Planet Robot, litho tin, metal claw hands, advances in realistic movement, antenna spins, radar inside mask circulates and lights, orig box, KO, Japan, 9" h . . . **1,500.00**

Robbie Robot Bulldozer, litho tin, friction, 3-D robot figure holding flag, seat behind robot mkd "Robot Bulldozer/12/Diesel," Marusan, 1960s, 3½ x 6½ x 4½" **200.00**

Robot Captain, windup, built-in key, litho tin, dark gray, various dials and gauges on chest, small diecut opening for viewing sparking mechanism, walks forward as it produces sparks, orig box, 1970s, Yone, Japan, 5½" h **100.00**

Roto Robot, litho tin, plastic, advances, body rotates 360 degrees and shoots with sound and flash, orig box, SH, Japan, 9" h **325.00**

Son of Garloo, windup, built-in key, hard plastic body, painted tin legs, walks forward as arms move, Marx, 1960s, 5¾" h **200.00**

Space Explorer, battery operated, astronaut face plate, antenna, and chest screen display "Apollo flight," orig box, Horikawa **350.00**

Space Scout, litho tin, plastic, strides with flashing light, lighted TV chest image, orig box, SH, Japan, 9½" h **160.00**

Sparky Robot, tin, windup, built-in key, silver, red ear covers and feet, red transparent plastic insert at diecut eyes and mouth, walks forward, antenna on top of head is on/off switch, KO, Japan, 1950s, 7½" h **200.00**

ST 1 Robot, litho tin, coil across top of head and chest opening with sparking action, orig box, Germany, 7" h . . **1,250.00**

Star Mission Robot, hard plastic, windup, built-in key, blue body, black arms, red hands, silver and clear plastic accents on head, color panel chest sticker, rotating head and movable arms, Durham Industries, Inc, 1978, on 7½ x 10" blister card **50.00**

Star Strider, battery operated, astronaut walks forward, body rotates as guns fire from chest, Japan, 1970s, 12½" h **175.00**

Talking Dalek, hard plastic, battery operated, freewheeling, silver body with raised blue dots on lower half, blue transparent insert inside head, with 3 removable attachments, Tomy, 1970s, 4 x 5 x 6" **100.00**

Talking Robot, litho tin, skirted, broadcasts 4 different
messages, orig box, Cragstan/NGS, Japan, 11½" h **1,800.00**

Venus Robot, red and black plastic, clockwork mecha-
nism, Yoshiya, 1965–70, 5½" h **315.00**

Video Robot, blue, battery operated, screen in chest
lights up to reveal moon scene, orig box, Horikawa **350.00**

Voltron Giant Commander Robot, plastic and vinyl,
removable sword and attached remote control battery
box, moves forward and backward, spring-loaded
mechanism hands, orig box, LJN Toys, 1984, 26" h **100.00**

Zintar Robot, plastic, battery operated, performs karate
smashes, forward and reverse actions, with 3 acces-
sories and instruction sheet, Ideal, 1971, 6" h **285.00**

Zoomer the Robot, litho tin, coil on head holding
wrench, advances, red window see-through inserts,
eyes and mouth light up as robot advances, orig box,
TN, Japan, 8" h. **1,050.00**

ROCK 'N' ROLL

In spite of its outward appearance, the rock 'n' roll field tends to
be traditionalist. Material from short-lived new wave or punk
groups of the 1970s, e.g., The Damned and Generation X, do not
appear to be attracting large numbers of collectors.

Collectors are specializing. Memorabilia from the girl groups of
the late 1950s and early 1960s has become hot. The field is trendy.
Autographs, guitars, and stage costumes are three categories that
have gotten hot, cooled off, and show signs of resurgence. Hard
Rock Cafés have spread around the world, creating an international interest in this topic. The top end of this market is documented by the values received at rock 'n' roll auctions held in
London, Los Angeles, and New York.

References: Mark A. Baker, *Goldmine Price Guide to Rock 'N' Roll
Memorabilia*, Krause Publications, 1997; Marty Eck, *The Monkees
Collectibles Price Guide*, Antique Trader Books, 1998; David K.
Henkel, *The Official Price Guide to Rock and Roll*, House of
Collectibles, 1992; Joe Hilton and Greg Moore, *Rock-N-Roll
Treasures*, Collector Books, 1999; Eric King, *The Collector's Guide
to Psychedelic Rock Concert Posters, Postcards and Handbills*,
Svaha Press, 1996; Karen and John Lesniewski, *Kiss Collectibles*,
Avon Books, 1993.

Collectors' Club: Kissaholics, PO Box 22334, Nashville, TN
37202.

REPRODUCTION ALERT: Records, picture sleeves, and album
jackets, especially for the Beatles, have been counterfeited. Sound
may be inferior. Printing on labels and picture jackets usually is
inferior to the original. Many pieces of memorabilia also have
been reproduced, often with some change in size, color, and
design.

Note: See Autographs, Beatles, Elvis Presley, Psychedelic, and
Records for additional listings.

Avalon, Frankie, pillow, stuffed cotton, black and white
portrait, facsimile signature, 1950s, 10½ x 11" **$50.00**

BB King, guitar, sgd, Gibson Epiphone, red finish, felt tip
pen signature on body **1,035.00**

Beach Boys, handbill, sgd, blue paper, for Aug 23, 1963
concert at Le Sourdsville Lake, OH, features early

Bill Haley and the
Comets, sheet music,
*(We're Gonna) Rock
Around the Clock*,
$5.00.

bluetone group photo on front with Brian Wilson
inked signature, reverse with 40 hits for the week of
Aug 1973 compiled by radio station WING, 3¾ x 8½" **50.00**

Beach Boys, PS, black and white machine print photograph, blue ballpoint pen signatures, inscribed "Beach
Boys" by Al Jardine, framed, 16¾ x 10¾" **800.00**

Belafonte, Harry, magazine, *The Belafonte Story*,
Almanac Picture Book, Apr 1957, Vol 2, 68 pp **25.00**

Belafonte, Harry, pinback button, portrait and facsimile
signature, 2½" d **25.00**

Blind Faith, album cover, sgd in different colored inks,
matted and framed with a "silver" copy of record and
machine print advertisement for album and Blind
Faith tour program **575.00**

Byrds, The, song books, set of 2, *The Byrds Bag*, and
Younger Than Yesterday, Tickson Music Co, ©1967
Ludlow Music Inc, 9 x 12" **50.00**

Clark, Dick, yearbook, 1957, 42 pp, black and white
and color photos with text about American Bandstand
show, complete with full color centerfold pin-up, 8½
x 11" **20.00**

Collins, Phil, jacket, worn in video "Jesus He Knows
Me," orange manmade fibers, breast pocket decorated
with yellow, purple, and red embroidered "Gtv" logo
sgd in black felt pen by Phil Collins, Tony Banks and
Mike Rutherford, additional inscription on lapel
"Jesus He Knows Me Video!," c1991 . . . . **690.00**

Dave Clark Five, poster, for film *Having A Wild
Weekend*, photo collage design with black and white
and orangetone images, ©1965 Warner Bros, 27 x 41" **75.00**

Dion and The Belmonts, pinback button, "Dion Is The
Boss Guy," blue text on white ground, red rim, c1960 . . . . . **20.00**

Doors, The, postcard, for Nov 16–18, 1967 concert at
Fillmore Auditorium/Winterland, featuring The Doors,
Procol Harem, and Mt Rushmore, Bill Graham #93,
color art by Jim Blashfield **20.00**

Doors, The, tickets, set of 8, for 1967 concert at KRNT
Theater, Des Moines, IA **345.00**

Dylan, Bob, guitar strap, brown leather, adjustable lac-
ing, matted with color machine print photograph of
Dylan, with letter concerning provenance from
Cesar Diaz, 19 x 22" **1,035.00**

Dylan, Bob, poster, sgd, promoting album *Dylan,* sgd in black felt pen, matted and framed with "silver" copy of record and machine print advertisement for single *A Fool Such As I,* with promotional copy of album, 32½ x 40½" framed size **400.00**

Fleetwood Mac, certificate, nomination in the 20th Annual Grammy Awards for *Rumours* for album of the year, matted, with black and white promotional photograph, 10 x 7½" **800.00**

Fleetwood Mac, poster, stiff paper, for Sat, May 7, 1977 concert presented by Bill Graham held at Oakland Stadium, group photo with design by Tuten/Bostedt, 16½ x 28 . . . . **50.00**

Grateful Dead, The, album, sgd by group, green or black felt pen signatures, mounted and framed, 14¼ x 1¼" **1,150.00**

Grateful Dead, The, poster, stiff paper, for Jun 4–7, 1970 concert at Fillmore West, featuring The Grateful Dead, New Riders of the Purple Sage, and Southern Comfort, Bill Graham #237, design by David Singer, 14 x 21" **50.00**

Haley, Bill, PS, sepia, Haley dressed in cowboy outfit, sgd "Bill Haley W.T.I.C.," matted, 20 x 14½" **345.00**

Jefferson Airplane, guitar, Harmony, electric, cream finish with double cutaway body, 21 fret fingerboard with dot inlays, 3 pickups, selector switch, 3 rotary controls, tremolo bridge/tailpiece and pickguard, sgd on body and pickguard by Grace Slick, Marty Balin, Paul Kantner, Jorma, Jack Casady, and Spencer Dryden . . . **690.00**

John, Elton, CD single sleeve, *Candle in the Wind,* sgd, gold ink inscription "With love," matted with copy of CD **345.00**

Kinks, The, guitar, Yamaha Pacifica, electric, sunburst finished, 22 fret rosewood fingerboard with dot inlays, 1 pickup, 2 rotary controls, selector switch, white pickguard, sgd on body and pickguard by Ray Davies with "You Really Got Me," Dave Davies, Ian Gibbons, Jim Rodford, and Bob Henrit, with machine print photograph of Dave Davies signing guitar **460.00**

Kiss, belt buckle, cast metal, silver prismatic logo on black, Paradise Mfg ©1976–77, 2½ x 3½" **10.00**

Kiss, jacket, thin fiberglass material, shades of red, orange, yellow, and purple, large group logo on front with lightning bolts, flames, and stars, reverse with black and white portrait images and additional logo, sleeves feature flame and star designs, Rockrollium Corp ©1978 Aucoin, size medium **50.00**

Kiss, poster, Paul Stanley with guitar on stage, Boutwell Inc ©1977 Aucoin Management Inc, 22 x 34" **25.00**

Lennon, John, coin purse, synthetic fabric, gold colored metal top rim and closure, sides with Lennon illus and facsimile signature on guitar, unmkd, 1960s, 3½ x 4" **100.00**

Madonna, autograph, black ink inscription "thanks Madonna," decorated with lipstick kiss, matted with machine print photograph, 12 x 15" **690.00**

Monkees, The, song folio, *The Birds, The Bees & The Monkees,* 32 pp, Monkees photos on front and back, Hansen Publications Inc ©1968 Screen Gems Inc, 8½ x 11". **25.00**

Monkees, The, sweatshirt, lined cotton, short sleeve, front portrait images and facsimile signatures for each member, ©1967 Raybert Productions Inc **100.00**

Moody Blues, poster, for Apr 1, 1970 concert at Terrace Ballroom, Salt Lake City, UT, 18½ x 25½" **50.00**

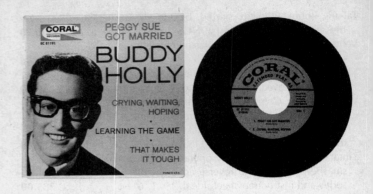

Buddy Holly, record, *Peggy Sue Got Married,* extended play, Coral Records EC 81191, orig picture jacket, $288.00. Photo courtesy William Doyle Galleries.

Presley, Elvis, pennant, blue felt with red stripe along left edge, "I Love Elvis" in white, small star and heart designs, 1960s, 12 x 29" **25.00**

Queen, PS, group seated on long black leather couch with pr of penguins between band members, Roger Taylor, Brian May, John Decon, and Freddie Mercury gold felt-tip pen signatures, with group name, "1991," and Parliphone logo on bottom margin, 8 x 10" **200.00**

Rolling Stones, album cover, sgd, "Some Girls," blue marker signatures, matted and framed, 16 x 16" **630.00**

Rolling Stones, belt buckle, cast metal, silver luster, glossy prismatic sticker on front in red, blue, and silver depicting tongue image, ©1978 Rainbow Productions Inc, 2¼ x 3½". **25.00**

Rolling Stones, pennant, "Souvenir of the Rolling Stones," large group logo and 4 small stars, 1960s, 12 x 29½" **50.00**

Rolling Stones, postcard, sgd on front by group in blue or black ballpoint pen, reverse ink inscription "22nd November '1965' Greenwich Town Hall Meet...," c1963, 4½ x 5½" **690.00**

Rolling Stones, sign, stiff paper, Framus Guitars promo, "Bill Wyman Plays and Praises Framus/The Rolling Stones," center photo of Wyman holding guitar with band photo including Brian Jones, 1960s, 19 x 25" **75.00**

Santana, poster, sgd, stiff paper, for Jan 30, 1977 concert at Long Beach Arena, litho collage of golden statue surrounded by snakes, inside large flower design with repeated "Santana" name, Tea Lautrec Litho, 23 x 29" **100.00**

Sonny & Cher, pennant, dark blue felt, "I Love Sonny & Cher," red trim, white stars and hearts design, 12 x 29" **25.00**

Springsteen, Bruce, autograph, sgd *Born in the USA* album cover, black felt-tip pen signature. **575.00**

Stewart, Rod, program, "Blondes Have More Fun," world tour 1978–79, 96 pp **10.00**

Sting, guitar, sgd, Fender Jazz Bass guitar, serial #MN5132283, cream finish, double cutaway body, 20 fret rosewood fingerboard with dot inlays, 2 pickups, 3 rotary controls, tremolo bridge/tailblock and white pickguard, sgd on body in blue felt pen and inscribed "If You Love Somebody Set Them Free" **920.00**

Zappa, Frank, album cover, sgd "F. Zappa" in red marker signature **370.00**

ROCKWELL, NORMAN

Norman Rockwell was born on February 3, 1894. His first professional drawing appeared in *Tell Me Why Stories.* Rockwell was eighteen at the time. Rockwell is best known for his magazine covers, the most recognized appearing on *Boy's Life* and the *Saturday Evening Post* (over 320 covers). Advertising, books, and calendars are only a few of the additional media where his artwork appeared. His artistic legacy includes more than 2,000 paintings.

Rockwell is one of America's foremost genre painters. He specialized in capturing a moment in the life of the average American. His approach ranged from serious to humorous, from social commentary to inspirational. He used those he knew for inspiration. His subjects ranged from New England villagers to presidents.

Rockwell's artwork continues to be heavily reproduced. Do not confuse contemporary with period pieces. His estate continues to license the use of his images. Buy modern collectibles for display and enjoyment. Their long-term value is minimal.

Reference: Denis C. Jackson, *The Norman Rockwell Identification and Value Guide to Magazines, Posters, Calendars, Books, 2nd Edition,* TICN, 1985.

Collectors' Club: Rockwell Society of America, 597 Saw Mill River Rd, PO Box 705, Ardsley, NY 10502.

REPRODUCTION ALERT

Note: For additional listings see Limited Edition Collectibles.

Book, *Tom Sawyer,* Heritage Press, 1936 . . . . **$20.00**
Calendar, 1920, De La Val, Painting the Kite. **325.00**
Calendar, 1934, Coca-Cola, southerm gentleman, 12 x 24" **400.00**
Calendar, 1941, Hercules Powder Co, boy and dog, 13 x 30¼" **180.00**
Catalog, Winchester Western Sporting Arms, 1966 . . . . **35.00**
Coin, Ford Motor Co, 50th Anniversary **35.00**
Ingot, Charles Dickens, 1977. . . . . **50.00**
Limited Edition Bell, Sweet Song So Young, Gorham, 1975. . . . . **50.00**
Limited Edition Figurine, Looking Out to Sea, River Shore, 1981 . . . . **200.00**
Limited Edition Plate, A Dollhouse For Sis, Classic Plate Series, Rockwell Museum, 1982. . . . . **25.00**
Limited Edition Plate, Christmas Story, Christmas Series, Rockwell Collectors Club, 1978. . . . . **25.00**
Limited Edition Plate, Flirting in the Parlor, Rockwell's Rediscovered Women Series, Rockwell Society, 1983 . . . . . **23.00**
Limited Edition Plate, Memories, Norman Rockwell Mother's Day Series, Lynell, 1982. . . . . **30.00**
Limited Edition Plate, Somebody's Up There, Christmas Series, Rockwell Society, 1979. . . . . **25.00**
Limited Edition Plate, The Country Store, Rockwell's Main Street Series, Rockwell Gallery, 1994. . . . . **45.00**
Limited Edition Plate, The Lighthouse Keeper's Daughter, Rockwell's Centennial Series, Rockwell Gallery, 1994 . . . . . **45.00**
Lithograph, Weighing In, #14/100, sgd, 23½ x 13" **700.00**
Magazine Cover, *American Magazine,* Jul–Dec 1940 . . . . **7.50**
Magazine Cover, *Life,* Jun 1, 1945 . . . . **60.00**
Magazine Cover, *Parents,* May 1951 . . . . **10.00**
Magazine Cover, *Saturday Evening Post,* Jun 20, 1932. . . , . . . **30.00**
Magazine Cover, *Saturday Evening Post,* Jun 27, 1942. . . . . . . **20.00**

Poster, "Save Freedom of Speech," Rockwell illus, distributed by Office of War Information," 28 x 20", $40.00.

Magazine Cover, *Saturday Evening Post,* Dec 29, 1956 . . . . . . **25.00**
Magazine Cover, *TV Guide,* 1970 . . . . **50.00**
Magazine Tear Sheet, *Country Gentleman,* Jell-O adv, 1922. . . . . **10.00**
Postcard, Amoco adv, "Wishing you a smooth running 1939". **175.00**
Poster, "Freedom of Speech," WWII, 1943 . . . . **35.00**
Poster, "Maxwell House Coffee," 1931–32 . . . . **325.00**
Sheet Music, *Family Sing-a-long with Mitch,* 1962. . . . . **15.00**

ROOKWOOD

In 1880 Cincinnatian Maria Longworth Nichols established Rookwood, a pottery named after her father's estate. She and a number of other Cincinnati society women designed and produced the first forms and decorative motifs.

Standard Ware was extremely popular in the 1880s and 90s. It was produced by applying an underglaze slip painting to a white or yellow clay body and then glazing the entire piece with a glossy, yellow-tinted glaze.

In 1904 Stanley Burt developed Vellum ware, a glaze that was a cross between high glaze and matte glaze. By 1905 a matte glaze replaced the company's high-glazed wares. Ombroso, a matte-glaze line, was introduced in 1910 to mark the company's 30th anniversary. In 1915 the company introduced a soft porcelain line featuring gloss and matte glazes.

By the early 1930s, the company was experiencing financial difficulties and filed for bankruptcy in 1941. A group of investors bought the company. A shortage of supplies during World War II forced ownership to be transferred to the Institution Divi Thomae Foundation of the Roman Catholic Archdiocese of Cincinnati in 1941. Sperti, Inc., operated the company for the Archdiocese. By the end of the 1940s the company was again experiencing financial difficulties.

In 1954 Edgar Heltman took over, shifting production to commercial ware and accessory pieces. Production ceased briefly in 1955. In 1956 James Smith bought the company from Sperti. Herschede Hall Clock Company bought Rookwood in 1959, moved its operations to Starksville, Missouri, and finally ceased operations for good in 1967.

Rookwood pieces are well marked. Many have five marking symbols: (1) clay or body mark, (2) size mark, (3) decorator mark, (4) date mark, and (5) factory mark.

References: Anita J. Ellis, *Rookwood Pottery: The Glaze Lines,* Schiffer Publishing, 1995; Ralph and Terry Kovel, *Kovels' American Art Pottery,* Crown Publishers, 1993; L-W Book Sales (ed.), *A Price Guide to Rookwood,* L-W Book Sales, 1993.

Collectors' Club: American Art Pottery Assoc, PO Box 1226, Westport, MA 02790.

Compote, Sara Sax, porcelain-style, ivory floral painting with cobalt blue flowers and mauve and buttercup yellow accents, deep brown over gray ground, sea green pedestal base with emb tulips, imp flame, incised "G/2707" and initials, 1926, 4½" h, 9¾" d **$110.00**

Vase, Elizabeth Lincoln, wax matte, fuschia pink swaying flowers with yellow stamens and maroon accents on long leafed stems, rose pink ground shading to mottled green-pink to mottled cobalt over pink base, imp flame and "1918/LNL," 1927, 9¼" h **1,100.00**

Vase, Kataro Shirayamadani, hexagonal cylinder, aqua flambé drip glaze over deep sea blue-green matte glaze, white stripe glaze effect at panel corners, imp flame and "2794," 1925, 9¾" h **350.00**

Vase, Katherine Jones, anniversary, wax matte, repeating berry and branched leaf painting cascading around shoulder, clusters of maroon berries, hunter green leaves lined in cobalt blue, and deep brown branches, lavender ground shading to deep mottled plum at base, cerulean matte int extending to neck, imp flame, "900g," and half circle mark denoting 50th anniversary year, 1930, 8¾" h, 4½" d **1,325.00**

Vase, milk bottle shape, emb repeating cascading floral and leaf design around shoulder, matte canary yellow glaze, imp flame and "2108," 1927, 6¼" h, 2¾" d **250.00**

Vase, Sara Sax, jewel porcelain, ivory dogwood blossoms on mottled taupe ground, flame mark, "XXVII/927D," and artist cipher, 9½" h, 6½" d **3,300.00**

Vase, Janet Harris, wax matte glaze with red flowers and green leaves on pink and blue butterfat ground, flame mark and "XXIX/JH/614," 1929, 10½" h, 5¾" d, $1,430.00. Photo courtesy David Rago Auctions, Inc.

Vase, Vera Tischler, vellum, large wild roses with maroon petals and mottled yellow and seafoam green stamens, abstract sage green leaves lined in black, smooth black vertical drip glaze over deep plum ground, imp flame, "134-3/V/P/VT," 1923, 5" h, 4¾" d **550.00**

AUCTION PRICES – ROOKWOOD VASES

Smith & Jones, Inc. Auctions, American Art Pottery & European Ceramics Auction #118, March 11–25, 1999. Prices include the 10% buyer's premium.

Bottle Shape, bulbous upper body, pinched waist, and svelte base with long incised vertical panels, scarab blue matte glaze, flame mark, "XXV," and obscured numbers, 1925, 7" h **$247.50**

Cylindrical, closed mouth, cobalt blue mottling on midnight blue ground, stylized magnolia-type flower outlined in black with spattered yellow int, raised and textured leaflet painting cascading in different directions executed in multi-shaded green, Catherine Crabtree, flame mark, "XXIII/2103," and painted initials, 1923, 5½" h **715.00**

Horizontal recessed band with repeating large stylized sunflowers with incised circular centers, bulging leaves at stems and between flowers, dusty pink glaze, imp flame and "XLVII/2591," 1947, 5½" h **137.50**

Ovoid with flared lip, mauve oriental poppies with maroon and green spattered interiors, sage green leaves covering base, plum band at mouth and neck, midsection shades from mauve to ivory to green at base, Kataro Shirayamadani, imp flame mark, "XLIV/6184C/KS," and ground "x," 1944, 9¾" h, 7" d **3,575.00**

Paneled, rect body with narrow panel at each corner, light chicory to scarab blue matte glaze, flame mark and "XXV/2841," 1925, 5" h **165.00**

ROSE BOWLS

A rose bowl is a small round or ovoid shaped bowl with a crimped, petaled, pinched, or scalloped opening at its top. It served as a container for fragrant potpourri or rose pedals.

Rose bowls are found in a wide variety of material with glass being the most common. A favorite giftware accessory, rose bowls often incorporate the best design qualities and materials of their era. Rose bowls are found in virtually every type of art glass.

The popularity of rose bowls extended from the second half of the Victorian era through the 1950s. The form is still made today.

Reference: Sean and Johanna S. Billings, *Collectible Rose Bowls,* Antique Trader Books, 1999.

Collectors' Club: Rose Bowl Collectors, PO Box 244, Danielsville, PA 18038.

Bagerly, pressed, amber, c1950 . . . . **$25.00**
Belleek, ribbed pattern, yellow int **45.00**
Blue Satin World's Fair **395.00**
Cranberry, opalescent swirl **90.00**
Crown Milano, white, with clusters of enameled florals **250.00**
Czechoslovakian, custard, chipped applied flowers **65.00**

LE Smith, Double Shield, black amethyst with silver bands, 1920s–34, 3¹/₂" h, $25.00.

Daisy & Fern, blue opalescent 100.00
Fenton, Beatty Honeycomb pattern 40.00
Fenton, pink overlay 25.00
Fenton, Silver Crest, Beaded Melon 30.00
Fenton, Valtec Sunburst, green, orig sticker 20.00
Imperial, Art Deco style 20.00
Italian, dark base color with sparse millefiori, 1960s 165.00
LG Wright, red overlay Maize 85.00
LG Wright, squat, green opalescent Hobnail 50.00
Moser, ftd, yellow and green cut-to-clear, etched flowers . . 350.00
Mount Joye, acenthus leaf dec, 12" 575.00
Murano, lavender, crystal rigaree foot, c1960 . . . . 65.00
Northwood, Beaded Drape, white opalescent 50.00
Northwood, pink and brown swirl candycane striped,
  2¹/₂" 950.00
Northwood, Spanish Lace, blue 80.00
Pressed Glass, clear, 2¹/₂" 10.00
Rubina Verde, decorated, square mouth, 6" 275.00
Satin Glass, blue 35.00
Van Briggle, acorn pattern, blue and green 110.00
Vaseline, Coin Spot 50.00
Victorian, cranberry spangle 90.00
Viking Glass, blue, orig sticker 28.00
Viking Glass, clear, 3 toes and flower frog 25.00
Webb, brown satin with prunus blossom dec, 3" 160.00
Westmoreland, English Hobnail, white milk glass 12.00
Westmoreland, Moonstar, lilac 25.00
Westmoreland, Wildflower & Lace, ice blue 28.00

ROSEMEADE

Rosemeade's origins began with Laura Taylor, a North Dakota studio potter who demonstrated her skills at the North Dakota Building at the 1939 New York World's Fair. Robert J. Hughes, president of the Greater North Dakota Association, saw Taylor's demonstration and organized the Wahpeton Pottery Company in 1940. Laura Taylor, a partner, was secretary/treasurer.

The company's products were marketed under the trade name Rosemeade in honor of Rosemeade Township, Taylor's birthplace. Vera Gethman and Taylor were the company's two principal designers. Glaze development fell under the watchful eyes of Howard Lewis and Taylor. The company produced a wide range of objects from commemorative and souvenir pieces to household and kitchenware.

In 1953 the company became Rosemeade Potteries. Howard Lewis left Rosemeade in 1956, replaced by Joe McLaughlin, who previously worked for Red Wing Potteries. McLaughlin began importing clay from Kentucky, introduced decal decoration, and incorporated the artistic designs of Les Kouba into the line.

Laura Taylor died in 1959. The company continued operating until 1961. Cheap Japanese copies made from molds cast from Rosemeade pieces and a new minimum wage law contributed to the company's closing. The salesroom remained open until 1964.

References: Darlene Hurst Dommel, *Collector's Encyclopedia of the Dakota Potteries: Identification & Values,* Collector Books, 1996; Harvey Duke, *The Official Price Guide to Pottery and Porcelain, Eighth Edition,* House of Collectibles, 1995.

Ashtray, attached gopher, "Gopher State Minnesota," 5" . . . $150.00
Ashtray, "Dakota Territory Centennial," 7" d 65.00
Bank, black bear, brown muzzle, 3" h 450.00
Bell, flamingo 80.00
Bookend, bear, 4" h 185.00
Candle Holder, heart shape 25.00
Creamer and Sugar, turkeys 140.00
Dish, cov, turkey 40.00
Figurine, bear 25.00
Figurine, elephant, 1¹/₄" h 60.00
Figurine, goose, 4" h 65.00
Figurine, hen pheasant, 3¹/₂ x 11¹/₂" 200.00
Figurine, mule, 5" h 85.00
Figurine, penguin, price for pair 30.00
Figurine, pony, brown and black, 4" h 125.00
Figurine, rocky mountain goat, on base, 2³/₄" h 150.00
Figurine, skunk 10.00
Hors d'oeuvre Holder, fish, 2¹/₄ x 3³/₄" 50.00
Incense Burner, log cabin 65.00
Jam Jar, barrel shape 45.00
Mug, Minnesota Centennial, brown 40.00
Pin, horse head 30.00
Pin, mallard duck 375.00
Pin, meadowlark 375.00
Pitcher, yellow and brown swirl, 3¹/₄" h 110.00
Planter, deer, standing by stump, 8" h 50.00
Planter, peacock, 7¹/₂" h 150.00
Planter, swan, 4³/₄" h 40.00
Salt and Pepper Shakers, pr, brussel sprouts 40.00
Salt and Pepper Shakers, pr, cat 60.00
Salt and Pepper Shakers, pr, chicken, 3¹/₄" h 70.00
Salt and Pepper Shakers, pr, Chinese ring-necked pheas-
  ant, 2³/₄" h 25.00
Salt and Pepper Shakers, pr, dog head 50.00
Salt and Pepper Shakers, pr, flamingos, 3³/₄" h 70.00
Salt and Pepper Shakers, pr, Paul Bunyan and Babe the
  Blue Ox 75.00
Salt and Pepper Shakers, pr, pink fish, 2³/₄" h 50.00
Salt and Pepper Shakers, pr, quail, 3¹/₂" h 55.00
Shoe, Dutch type, wooden-like, 2 x 5¹/₂" 40.00
Shoe, ranger's boot, wrinkled, bronze, 6¹/₂" h 65.00
Shoe, slipper, blue, buttons, 1³/₄ x 4¹/₄" 40.00
Spoon Rest, elephant 40.00
Spoon Rest, flying pheasant, 3¹/₄ x 5¹/₂" 50.00
Spoon Rest, wild rose, 4" 50.00
Tea Bell, Art Nouveau tulip, 3³/₄" 125.00
TV Lamp, Palomino, 9¹/₂" h 450.00
Vase, hand thrown, pinkish peach, ruffled rim, 6" h 45.00
Wall Pocket, deer 5.00
Wall Vase, Egyptian playing instrument motif, antique
  gray, lined with porous bisque planter, 5¹/₂" 150.00

ROSEVILLE POTTERY

George Young purchased the J. B. Owens Pottery, renaming it the Roseville Pottery, in 1892. Cooking utensils, cuspidors, flowerpots, and umbrella stands were among the company's earliest products. Around the turn of the century, Roseville purchased the Midland Pottery plant in Roseville (1898), moved the company's main office to Zanesville, Ohio, bought Peters and Reed, and acquired the Muskingum Stoneware plant (1901).

Rozane, the company's first artware line, evolved into a general term used to describe all the company's art or prestige lines. John Herold established Roseville's commercial artware department in 1903. Artware, including dresser sets, juvenile ware, tea sets, and smoker sets dominated production until the late 1910s.

Roseville closed two of its factories in 1910. Fire destroyed another in 1917. In 1918 Russell Young replaced his father as manager; Frank Ferrel replaced Harry Rhead as art director. Ferrel shifted the company's production into industrial artware, resulting in the introduction of more than 80 new lines.

In 1932 the firm became Roseville Pottery, Inc. The company experienced a major slump in sales following World War II. New industrial artware lines failed to halt the decline. Mosaic Tile Company bought the Roseville plant in 1954. Production of Roseville ceased.

References: Jack and Nancy Bomm, *Roseville in All Its Splendor,* L-W Book Sales, 1998; Virginia Buxton, *Roseville Pottery For Love...Or Money,* Tymbre Hill Publishing, 1996; John W. Humphries, *Roseville By the Numbers,* published by author, 1999; Sharon and Bob Huxford, *The Collectors Encyclopedia of Roseville Pottery, First Series* (1976, 1997 value update), *Second Series* (1980, 1997 value update), Collector Books; Randall B. Monsen, *Collectors' Compendium of Roseville Pottery and Price Guide, Vol. 1* (1995), *Vol. 2* (1997), Monsen and Baer.

Collectors' Clubs: American Art Pottery Assoc, PO Box 1226, Westport, MA 02790; Rosevilles of the Past, PO Box 656, Clarcona, FL 32710.

REPRODUCTION ALERT: Cheap reproduction Roseville pieces are surfacing at auctions and flea markets. Distinguishing characteristics include glaze colors and crude decorative techniques.

Ashtray, Bushberry, russet, #26, 5½" d	$100.00
Ashtray, Magnolia, tan, #28	110.00
Ashtray, Snowberry, blue, 5½" d	110.00
Ashtray, Snowberry, tan and green, 5½" d	80.00
Basket, Apple Blossom, green, #309, 8½" h	190.00
Basket, Bushberry, green, #369, 7" h	160.00
Basket, Bushberry, russet, #370, 8½" h	180.00
Basket, Cosmos, green, handled, #358, 11" h	230.00
Basket, Freesia, blue, handled, #390, 7" h	140.00
Basket, Snowberry, blue, #IBK, 12½" h	250.00
Basket, Water Lily, tan and brown, #380, 8" h	115.00
Basket, Zephyr Lily, Bermuda blue, handled, #395, 10" h	225.00
Bookends, pr, Freesia, tangerine, #16, 5" h	100.00
Bookends, pr, Zephyr Lily, Bermuda blue, #16	100.00
Bowl, Bleeding Heart, pink, handled, #377	200.00
Bowl, Columbine, blue, #655	90.00
Bowl, Florentine, brown, 8½" d	60.00
Bowl, Magnolia, tan, #665, 3" h	40.00
Bowl, Pinecone, brown, #279, 11" h	225.00
Bowl, Rozane 1917, ivory, ftd, 9" d	40.00

Bowl, White Rose, tan and green, low, #389, 7" d	65.00
Bowl Vase, White Rose, blue, #388, 7½" h	190.00
Bowl Vase, Wisteria, brown, handled, green vines and lavender wisteria, 4" h	350.00
Bud Vase, Apple Blossom, blue, #379, 7½" h	100.00
Bud Vase, Apple Blossom, green, #379, 7½" h	125.00
Candle Holders, pr, Bushberry, russet, #114, 2" h	100.00
Candle Holders, pr, Moss, pink and green, 3 socket, 1108, 7" h	500.00
Candle Holders, pr, Peony, blue and brown, #651, 2" h	80.00
Candle Holders, pr, Peony, pink, #1151, 2" h	75.00
Candle Holders, pr, Thornapple, green, #TC17, 2½" h	110.00
Cider Set, Bushberry, 5 pc, blue, 9" h pitcher #1325 and four 3½" h #1 mugs	500.00
Console Bowl, Snowberry, blue, #IBL2, 16½" l	125.00
Console Bowl, Snowberry, pink, #BLI, 12½" l	65.00
Console Bowl, Zephyr Lily, Bermuda blue, #478, 15" l	40.00
Console Set, Bushberry, 3 pc, blue, #415, 11" d	200.00
Cookie Jar, Zephyr Lily, Bermuda blue, #5, 10" h	685.00
Cornucopia Vase, Clematis, blue, #193, 6" h	100.00
Cornucopia Vase, Freesia, delft blue, #197, 6½" h	75.00
Cornucopia Vase, Magnolia, green, #182, 5" h	65.00
Cornucopia Vase, Snowberry, blue, #ICC, 6" h	45.00
Cornucopia Vase, Zephyr Lily, Bermuda blue, #203, 6" h, price for pair	190.00
Creamer, Clematis, green, #5C	35.00
Creamer and Sugar, Bushberry, blue, #2, 2" h	140.00
Creamer and Sugar, Snowberry, blue	35.00
Dealer Sign, pink, 7½" h	1,925.00
Double Bud Vase, Clematis, green, #194, 5" h	65.00
Double Bud Vase, Cosmos, blue, #134, 5" h	275.00
Double Bud Vase, Donatello, 5" h	80.00
Double Bud Vase, Foxglove, blue, #160, 5" h	140.00
Ewer, Magnolia, tan, #15, 16" h	140.00
Ewer, Snowberry, blue, #TK	110.00

Left: Jardiniere (303-10") and Pedestal (306-10"), Apple Blossom, pink, 2 flakes on bottom of jardiniere, $605.00. Right: Umbrella Stand, Vista, unmkd, minute rim chip, glaze flake to base, 20" h, 10" d, $1,705.00. Photos courtesy David Rago Auctions, Inc.

Ewer, Zephyr Lily, Bermuda blue, #130, 10½" h **190.00**
Ewer, Zephyr Lily, green, #22, 6½" h **115.00**
Fan Vase, Silhouette, rose, nude dec, #783, 7½" h **415.00**
Floor Vase, Water Lily, blue, handled, #85, 18½" h **225.00**
Flower Bowl, Zephyr Lily, green and tan, #475, 14" l **100.00**
Flower Frog, Cosmos, blue, #39, 3½" h **225.00**
Hanging Basket, Magnolia, green, 11" l **135.00**
Jardiniere, Bleeding Heart, blue, #651, 3½" h **140.00**
Jardiniere, Freesia, blue, #669, 6" h **110.00**
Jardiniere, Magnolia, blue, #665, 3" h **75.00**
Jardiniere, Peony, pink and green, #661, 7" d **120.00**
Jardiniere, Pinecone, brown, #632, 5" h **225.00**
Jardiniere, Rozane 1917, ivory, 11" d **80.00**
Mug, Bushberry, green, 3½" h **85.00**
Mug, Elk Head, 4½" h **75.00**
Pillow Vase, Moss, tan and blue, #781, 8½" h **275.00**
Pitcher, Freesia, delft blue, #20, 10½" h **175.00**
Planter, Apple Blossom, pink, #329, 12" l **75.00**
Planter, Foxglove, green, #426, 4½" h **190.00**
Rose Bowl, Columbine, blue, #655, 5½" d **90.00**
Rose Bowl, Moss, tan and blue, #289, 4½" h **165.00**
Rose Bowl, Rosecraft, brown, 3½" h **110.00**
Rose Bowl, Thornapple, blue, #305, 6½" d **140.00**
Teapot, cov, Freesia, tangerine, #6, 7" h **115.00**
Tea Set, Snowberry, 3 pc, blue, 7" h teapot #TP, 3½" h
  creamer and sugar **225.00**
Tray, Foxglove, blue, 11" l **100.00**
Tumbler, Pinecone, green, #414, 5" h **150.00**
Urn, Freesia, delft blue, handled, #196, 8" h **80.00**
Urn, Rozane 1917, yellow ftd, 6" h **50.00**
Vase, Apple Blossom, pink, #390, 12" h **190.00**
Vase, Baneda, green and blue, handled, 6½" h **450.00**
Vase, Blackberry, green, 5" h **450.00**
Vase, Bushberry, green, handled, #39, 14½" h **525.00**
Vase, Clematis, tan, #103, 6" h **65.00**
Vase, Columbine, blue, #655, 3" h **105.00**
Vase, Cosmos, green, handled, #944, 4" h **85.00**
Vase, Florentine, brown, 6" h **60.00**
Vase, Freesia, delft blue, 2 handled, #122, 8" h **75.00**
Vase, Ixia, green, #864, 12½" h **225.00**
Vase, Laurel, persimmon, 6" h **250.00**
Vase, Magnolia, green, #183, 6" h **110.00**
Vase, Mostique, tan, 6" h **80.00**
Vase, Peony, pink and green, #57, 4" h **60.00**
Vase, Pinecone, green, #839, 6½" h **250.00**
Vase, Rozane, turquoise, #11, 15" h **325.00**
Vase, Snowberry, blue, #1FH, 6½" h **140.00**
Vase, Snowberry, blue, handled, #VI, 8½" h **80.00**
Vase, Water Lily, blue, 2 handled, #76, 8" h **110.00**
Vase, Water Lily, pink to green, #75, 7½" h **140.00**
Vase, Water Lily, tan and brown, #74, 7" h **160.00**
Vase, White Rose, blue, #978, 4½" h **75.00**
Vase, White Rose, blue, handled, #982, 7" h **110.00**
Vase, Zephyr Lily, Bermuda blue, #133, 8½" h **150.00**
Vase, Zephyr Lily, evergreen, #204 . . . . **140.00**
Vessel, Velmoss, bulbous, 2-handled, blue, 6½" h, 8¼" d . . . **250.00**
Wall Planter, Snowberry, blue, #IWP, 5½" h, price for
  pair **325.00**
Wall Planter, Wincraft, 9" l **30.00**
Wall Pocket, Apple Blossom, green, #366, 9" h **195.00**
Wall Pocket, Snowberry, blue, #IWP, 7½" l **165.00**
Wall Pocket, Zephyr Lily, Bermuda blue, #1297, 8½" h **275.00**
Window Planter, Freesia, tangerine, #1392, 10½" l **85.00**
Window Planter, Peony, pink and green, #386, 8" l **110.00**

AUCTION PRICES – ROSEVILLE POTTERY

David Rago Auctions, Inc., Roseville/Zanesville Pottery Auction, June 28, 1998. Prices include the 10% buyer's premium.

Basket, Cosmos, blue, 357-10" **$275.00**
Candlesticks, pr, Freesia, blue, 1161-1½" **165.00**
Compote, Donatello, 4¾ x 6¼" **137.50**
Console Bowl, Bleeding Heart, scalloped rim,
  green, 382-10" **137.50**
Fan Vase, Snowberry, corseted, pink, IV2-9" **110.00**
Flower Frog, Moss, green, 24, 4½" h **330.00**
Flower Pot, Pinecone, flaring, green, 633-5" **88.00**
Tray, Peony, green, 10½ x 10" **77.00**
Umbrella Stand, Bushberry, orange, 779-21" **550.00**
Urn, Water Lily, blue, 175-8" **110.00**
Vase, Magnolia, bulbous, 2-handled, green, 91-8" **77.00**
Vase, Zephyr Lily, 2-handled, green, 131-7" **110.00**
Window Box, Wincraft, chartreuse and brown, 268-
  12" **88.00**

ROYAL CHINA

Although the Royal China Company purchased the former E. H. Sebring Company (Sebring, Ohio) plant in 1933, extensive renovation delayed production until 1934. Initially, Royal China produced mainly overglaze decal ware. Kenneth Doyle's underglaze stamping machine, developed for Royal China in 1948, revolutionized the industry, allowing for the inexpensive production of underglaze ware. By 1950 Royal China eliminated its decal ware.

The company produced a wide range of dinnerware lines. Colonial Homestead (early 1950s), Currier and Ives (1949/50), Old Curiosity Shop, and Willow Ware (1940s) are among the most popular. Royal Oven Ware was introduced in the 1940s.

In 1964 Royal China purchased the French-Saxon China Company, operating it as a wholly owned subsidiary. The Jeannette Corporation acquired Royal China in 1969. In 1970 fire destroyed the plant and Royal China's operations were moved to the French-Saxon plant, also located in Sebring, Ohio.

The company changed hands several times in the 1970s and 80s, being purchased by the Coca-Cola Bottling Company (1976), J. Corporation of Boston (1981), and Nordic Capitol of New York (1984). Each owner continued to manufacture ware under the Royal China brand name. Operations ceased in 1986.

References: Eldon R. Aupperle, *A Collector's Guide For Currier & Ives Dinnerware*, published by author, 1996; Susan and Al Bagdade, *Warman's American Pottery and Porcelain*, Wallace-Homestead, Krause Publications, 1994; Harvey Duke, *The Official Price Guide to Pottery and Porcelain, Eighth Edition*, House of Collectibles, 1995.

Collectors' Club: Currier & Ives Dinnerware Collectors Club, 29470 Saxon Rd, Toulon, IL 61483.

Colonial Homestead, ashtray **$15.00**
Colonial Homestead, bread and butter plate **2.50**
Colonial Homestead, creamer and cov sugar **16.00**
Colonial Homestead, cup and saucer **4.00**
Colonial Homestead, dinner plate **4.00**
Colonial Homestead, gravy bowl **15.00**
Colonial Homestead, salt and pepper shakers, pr **20.00**

Currier & Ives, dinner plate, 10¼" d, $6.00.

ROYAL COPENHAGEN

In the mid-18th century Europe's royal families competed with each other to see who would be the first to develop a porcelain formula. In 1772 Franz Heinrich Muller, a Danish pharmacist and chemist, discovered a formula for hard paste porcelain. Muller submitted his samples to the Queen Dowager. She was so delighted that she christened his firm "The Danish Porcelain Factory." Although founded privately in 1775, the Danish monarchy fully controlled the firm by 1779. Three wavy lines were chosen as the firm's trademark to symbolize the seafaring tradition of the Danes.

The company proved a drain on the Danish monarchy's finances. In 1867 A. Falch purchased the company under the condition that he be allowed to retain the use of "Royal" in the firm's title. Falch sold the company to Philip Schou in 1882.

In 1885 Arnold Krog became art director of Royal Copenhagen and developed underglaze painting. Only one color is used. Shading is achieved by varying the thickness of the pigment layers and firing the painted plate at a temperature of 2,640 degrees Fahrenheit. Krog revitalized the company. In 1902 Dalgas became art director and introduced the blue and white Christmas Plate series in 1908.

Today the Royal Copenhagen Group also includes Bing and Grondahl. The firm is noted for its extensive dinnerware and giftware lines.

Reference: Robert J. Heritage, *Royal Copenhagen Porcelain: Animals and Figurines,* Schiffer Publishing, 1997.

Note: For additional references see Limited Edition Collectibles.

Figurine, barking fox, 5½ x 3"	**$120.00**
Figurine, barn owl, 8¾" h	200.00
Figurine, boy on rock, 12 x 9"	450.00
Figurine, catfish, open mouth, 3¼ x 6"	150.00
Figurine, curled fox, 3 x 7"	200.00
Figurine, desert fox, 10 x 6½"	600.00

Colonial Homestead, soup bowl	6.00
Colonial Homestead, teapot, cov	60.00
Colonial Homestead, vegetable bowl, 10" d	20.00
Currier & Ives, bread and butter plate, 6" d	2.50
Currier & Ives, butter, cov, ¼ lb	35.00
Currier & Ives, cake plate, tab handle	18.00
Currier & Ives, cereal bowl	18.00
Currier & Ives, chop plate, 12" d	28.00
Currier & Ives, creamer and cov sugar	25.00
Currier & Ives, cup and saucer	4.50
Currier & Ives, flat soup	10.00
Currier & Ives, fruit bowl	1.00
Currier & Ives, gravy, with underplate	30.00
Currier & Ives, juice tumbler	12.00
Currier & Ives, lunch plate	18.00
Currier & Ives, mug	25.00
Currier & Ives, platter, oval	30.00
Currier & Ives, salad plate	12.00
Currier & Ives, salt and pepper shakers, pr	20.00
Currier & Ives, teapot, cov	145.00
Currier & Ives, vegetable bowl, 9" d	20.00
Currier & Ives, vegetable bowl, cov, handled	95.00
Currier & Ives, water tumbler	14.00
Memory Lane, berry bowl	3.50
Memory Lane, bread and butter plate	6.00
Memory Lane, creamer and cov sugar	25.00
Memory Lane, dinner plate	6.00
Memory Lane, platter, oval	30.00
Memory Lane, soup bowl	6.00
Memory Lane, tumbler	10.00
Old Curiosity Shop, bread and butter plate	2.50
Old Curiosity Shop, creamer	8.00
Old Curiosity Shop, cup and saucer	4.00
Old Curiosity Shop, dinner plate	4.00
Old Curiosity Shop, fruit bowl	5.00
Old Curiosity Shop, salad bowl	5.00
Old Curiosity Shop, salt and pepper shakers, pr	15.00
Old Curiosity Shop, soup bowl	6.00
Old Curiosity Shop, sugar, cov	15.00
Old Curiosity Shop, vegetable bowl	18.00

Collector Plate, Aabenraa Marketplace, Christmas Series, 1921, $180.00.

Figurine, English bulldog, seated, 5 x 4" **120.00**
Figurine, farmer with sheep, 7³/₄ x 5" **300.00**
Figurine, faun playing syrinx, 5¹/₂ x 4¹/₂" **220.00**
Figurine, faun with cat, 5 x 7" **300.00**
Figurine, faun with goat, 8¹/₄ x 8" **300.00**
Figurine, goose thief, 6¹/₂ x 4¹/₂" **250.00**
Figurine, guillemot, 10¹/₂ x 7" **300.00**
Figurine, Labrador puppy, 5¹/₂ x 8¹/₄" **200.00**
Figurine, parrot on pedestal, 11" h **500.00**
Figurine, The Proposal, 10 x 5" **150.00**
Figurine, Victorian couple, 11¹/₂ x 8¹/₂" **550.00**
Limited Edition Plate, Christmas Memories, Christmas
    Jubilee Series, 1983 . . . . **95.00**
Limited Edition Plate, Christmas Rose and Cat, Christmas
    Series, K Lange, 1970 . . . . **35.00**
Limited Edition Plate, Mermaid, Hans Christian
    Anderson Fairy Tales Series, S Vestergaard, 1985 . . . . **45.00**
Limited Edition Plate, Mother Robin With Babies,
    Motherhood Series, S Vestergaard, 1982 . . . . **30.00**
Limited Edition Plate, Our Lady's Cathedral Copenhagen,
    Christmas Series, Hans H Hansen, 1949 . . . . **190.00**
Limited Edition Plate, Royal Copenhagen 75th
    Anniversary, Historical Series, 1983 . . . . **95.00**
Limited Edition Plate, The Good Shepherd, Christmas
    Series, Hans H Hansen, 1957 . . . . **125.00**
Limited Edition Plate, Yosemite, National Parks of
    America Series, 1981 . . . . **75.00**
Limited Edition Plate, Virgin Islands, Special Issue, 1967 . . . . . **25.00**

ROYAL COPLEY

Royal Copley and Royal Windsor are tradenames of the Spaulding China Company. Royal Copley, representing approximately 85% of all Spaulding production, was sold mostly through chain stores. Royal Windsor items were sold to the florist trade.

Spaulding China, Sebring, Ohio, began operations in 1942. The company chose names that had an English air, e.g., Royal Copley and Royal Windsor. Even marketing terms such as Crown Assortment and Oxford Assortment continued this theme.

Birds, piggy banks, oriental boy and girl wall pockets, and roosters were among Royal Copley's biggest sellers. The small birds originally retailed for 25¢. Pieces were marked with a paper label.

Cheap Japanese imports and labor difficulties plagued Spaulding throughout the post-war period. In 1957 Morris Feinberg retired, contracting with nearby China Craft to fill Spaulding's remaining orders. Initially Spaudling was sold to a Mr. Shiffman, who made small sinks for mobile homes. After being closed for several years Eugene Meskil of Holiday Designs bought the plant. The company made kitchen ware. Richard C. Durstein of Pittsburgh bought the plant in 1982.

References: Joe Devine, *Collector's Guide to Royal Copley Plus Royal Windsor & Spaulding, Bk I* (1999), *Bk II* (1999), Collector Books; Mike Schneider, *Royal Copley*, Schiffer Publishing, 1995.

Newsletter: *The Copley Courier*, 1639 N Catalina St, Burbank, CA 91505.

Ashtray, duck, Royal Windsor paper label, 3¹/₄ x 6" **$15.00**
Ashtray, straw hat with bow, 5³/₈" d **5.00**
Bank, pig, "For My Mink," 8¹/₈" h **35.00**
Bank, teddy bear, gold dec, 7¹/₂" h **65.00**

Stub Handle Vase, pink, blue, and yellow floral decal, white ground, gold stamped "Royal Copley" in wreath, 4¹/₈" h, 4" d, $8.00.

Cornucopia Vase, floral motif, gold highlights, Spaulding
    paper label, 8" h **15.00**
Figurine, cat, 8" h **25.00**
Figurine, cockatoo, 7¹/₄" h **30.00**
Figurine, cocker spaniel, 6" h **15.00**
Figurine, deer on sled, 6¹/₂" h **22.00**
Figurine, finch on branch, 5¹/₈" h **20.00**
Figurine, flycatcher on stump **25.00**
Figurine, kingfisher **20.00**
Figurine, kitten with ball of yarn, 6⁷/₈" h **35.00**
Figurine, parrot, yellow, 5" h **12.00**
Figurine, rooster, paper label, 7" h **25.00**
Figurine, teddy bear, 5¹/₂" h **35.00**
Lamp Base, double parakeet **45.00**
Lamp Base, pig, 6¹/₈" h **45.00**
Pitcher, emb fruit, 8" h **15.00**
Pitcher, floral decal, 6¹/₄" h **5.00**
Planter, Book of Remembrance **5.00**
Planter, coach **10.00**
Planter, Colonial Old Woman, 8¹/₈" h **35.00**
Planter, cub on stump, 8¹/₄" h **30.00**
Planter, deer with fawn, gold dec, 9¹/₂" h **20.00**
Planter, dog with mailbox, 8¹/₈" h **15.00**
Planter, dog with string bass, 7¹/₄" h **70.00**
Planter, elephant with ball, 6¹/₄" h **20.00**
Planter, hummingbird, 5³/₈" h **30.00**
Planter, kitten with ball of yarn, 8" h **25.00**
Planter, kitten with book, 6⁵/₈" h **20.00**
Planter, kitten with moccasin, paper label, 8⁵/₈" h **30.00**
Planter, recumbent cat, 5³/₄" h **35.00**
Planter, recumbent poodle, gray, gold dec **75.00**
Planter, rocking lamb, white, blue trim, gold highlights,
    6¹/₄" h **45.00**
Planter, rooster, 8³/₈" h **15.00**
Planter, salmon jumping above waves, 8¹/₂" h, 11¹/₈" l **85.00**
Planter, teddy bear, black and white, pink bowl, paper
    label, 8" h **85.00**
Planter, teddy bear with basket, brown and yellow, 5¹/₂" l **30.00**

ROYAL DOULTON

In 1815 John Doulton founded the Doulton Lambeth Pottery in Lambeth, London. The firm was known as Doulton and Watts between 1820 and 1853. Henry Doulton, John's second son, joined the firm in 1835. In 1887 he was knighted by Queen Victoria for his achievements in the ceramic arts.

Henry Doulton acquired the Niles Street pottery in Burslem, Staffordshire in 1877, changing the name to Doulton & Co. in 1882. This plant made high quality porcelain and inexpensive earthenware tableware. In 1901 King Edward VII granted the Royal Warrant of appointment to Doulton. "Royal" has appeared on the company's ware since that date.

Whereas production increased at the Burslem plant during the 20th century, it decreased at the Lambeth plant. By 1925 only twenty-four artists were employed, one of whom was Leslie Harradine, noted for his famed Dickens' characters. Commemorative wares were produced at Lambeth in the 1920s and 30s. Agnete Hoy, famous for her cat figures, worked at Lambeth between 1951 and 1956. Production at the Lambeth plant ended in 1956.

Although Royal Doulton made a full line of tabletop ware, it is best known for its figurines and character jugs. Most figurines were made at Burslem. The HN numbers, named for Harry Nixon, were introduced in 1913. HN numbers were chronological until 1949 after which each modeler received a block of numbers. Noke introduced the first character jugs in 1934. Noke also created series ware, a line that utilizes a standard blank decorated with a wide range of scenes.

Today the Royal Doulton Group includes John Beswick, Colclough, Webb Corbett, Minton, Paragon, Ridgway, Royal Adderley, Royal Albert, and Royal Crown Derby. It is the largest manufacturer of ceramic products in the United Kingdom.

References: Jean Dale, *The Charlton Standard Catalogue of Royal Doulton Animals, Second Edition,* Charlton Press, 1998; Jean Dale, *The Charlton Standard Catalogue of Royal Doulton Beswick Figurines, Sixth Edition,* Charlton Press, 1998; Jean Dale, *The Charlton Standard Catalogue of Royal Doulton Beswick Storybook Figurines, Fifth Edition,* Charlton Press, 1999; Jean Dale, *The Charlton Standard Catalogue of Royal Doulton Beswick Jugs, Fourth Edition,* Charlton Press, 1997; Jean Dale and Louise Irvine, *The Charlton Standard Catalogue of Royal Doulton Bunnykins,* Charlton Press, 1999; Harry L. Rinker, *Dinnerware of the 20th Century: The Top 500 Patterns,* House of Collectibles, 1997.

Periodicals: *Collecting Doulton,* PO Box 310, Richmond, Surrey TW9 1FS; *Doulton Divvy,* PO Box 2434, Joliet, IL 60434.

Collectors' Clubs: Chintz China Collector's Club, PO Box 50888, Pasadena, CA 91115; Royal Doulton International Collectors Club, 701 Cottontail Ln, Somerset, NJ 08873; Royal Doulton International Collectors Club (company-sponsored), 850 Progress Ave, Scarborough Ontario M1H 3C4 Canada.

Adrian, demitasse saucer, 2¼"	**$5.00**
Adrian, dinner plate	25.00
Adrian, salad plate, 8⅛" d	15.00
Angelique, coffeepot, cov	165.00
Angelique, cup and saucer, flat, 2⅞"	25.00
Angelique, luncheon plate, 9" d	20.00
Angelique, platter, oval, 13½" l	120.00

Pitcher, Veteran Motorist, 1972, 7½" h, $132.00. Photo courtesy Collectors Auction Services.

Biscay, Lambethware, creamer	25.00
Biscay, Lambethware, coffeepot, cov	65.00
Biscay, Lambethware, platter, oval, 13⅜" l	60.00
Bunnykins, ABC, plate, 8" d	30.00
Bunnykins, Apple Picking, cereal bowl, Walter Hayward, unsgd	25.00
Bunnykins, Art Class, plate, 8½" d	100.00
Bunnykins, Bedtime with Dollies, eggcup, style 1	35.00
Bunnykins, Beware of the Bull, plate, oval	75.00
Bunnykins, Birthday Cake, plate, with inscription	85.00
Bunnykins, Camp Site, cake stand	150.00
Bunnykins, Camp Site, cereal bowl	25.00
Bunnykins, Camp Site, plate, 8" d	20.00
Bunnykins, Christmas Party, baby plate, oval	125.00
Bunnykins, Christmas Party, bread and butter plate, handled	200.00
Bunnykins, Christmas Party, plate, 8½" d	85.00
Bunnykins, commemorative mug, "To Celebrate the Birth of the First Child of T.R.H. The Prince & Princess of Wales 1982"	75.00
Bunnykins, Dog Carriage, baby plate, oval	275.00
Bunnykins, Dog Carriage, bread and butter plate, handle	250.00
Bunnykins, Dog Carriage, plate, 8½" d	225.00
Bunnykins, Family Cycling, baby plate, round	200.00
Bunnykins, Family Cycling, cereal bowl	95.00
Bunnykins, Family Cycling, hot water plate	175.00
Bunnykins, Family Cycling, porridge bowl	150.00
Bunnykins, Mrs Piggly's Stores, bread and butter plate, handle	200.00
Bunnykins, Mrs Piggly's Stores, cereal bowl	40.00
Bunnykins, Mrs Piggly's Stores, porridge bowl	100.00
Burgundy, coffeepot, cov	100.00
Burgundy, creamer, miniature	15.00
Burgundy, salad plate, 8" d	14.00
Burgundy, platter, oval, 16" l	100.00
Burgundy, soup bowl, flat, 8"	20.00
Cambridge, bud vase, 5¾" h	40.00
Cambridge, cream soup and saucer	50.00
Cambridge, cream soup bowl	35.00
Cambridge, cup and saucer, flat, 2⅜"	35.00
Cambridge, rice bowl, 4½"	30.00
Cambridge, salad serving bowl, 10⅜"	120.00
Cambridge, sugar, cov	75.00
Cambridge, trinket box, cov	40.00

Carlyle, cake plate, handled, 10⅝" d 50.00
Carlyle, dinner plate, 10⅝" d 30.00
Carlyle, salad plate 20.00
Carlyle, teapot lid 80.00
Character Jug, Bill Sykes, D6684, 1982, 1½" h . . . 35.00
Character Jug, BuzFuz, D5383, 5½" h 275.00
Character Jug, David Copperfield, D6680, 1½" h 60.00
Character Jug, Fagin, D6679, 1½" h 85.00
Character Jug, The Fortune Teller, D6497, 6¾" h 850.00
Character Jug, The Gardener, D6630, 7¾" h 275.00
Character Jug, The Gladiator, D6550, 7¾" h 950.00
Character Jug, The Mikado, D6501, 6½" h 850.00
Clarendon, bread and butter plate, 6½" d 20.00
Clarendon, dinner plate, 10⅝" d 40.00
Clarendon, fruit bowl, 5¼" 40.00
Clarendon, gravy boat 175.00
Cornwall, Lambethware, casserole, no lid, 8" l 70.00
Cornwall, Lambethware, cup and saucer, flat, 2⅞" 20.00
Cornwall, Lambethware, dinner plate 25.00
Cornwall, Lambethware, salad plate 20.00
Cornwall, Lambethware, sugar, cov, 3⅜" 40.00
Coronet, bread and butter plate, 6¼" d 16.00
Coronet, dinner plate, 10⅜" d 35.00
Coronet, salad plate, 8⅜" d 25.00
Figurine, Autumn Breezes, pink with green, 1934, 8" h 132.00
Figurine, Little Boy Blue, HN 2062, 5½" h 66.00
Figurine, Mary Mary, HN 2044, 5½" h 115.00
Figurine, My Love, HN 2339, 6¼" h 93.00
Figurine, The Rag Doll, HN 2142, 4¾" h 82.00
Fireglow, bread and butter plate 14.00
Fireglow, cup and saucer 25.00
Fireglow, dinner plate 25.00
Fireglow, platter, oval, 13¼" l 75.00
Fireglow, salad plate 18.00
Glen Audlyn, creamer and covered sugar 120.00
Glen Audlyn, demitasse cup and saucer 40.00
Glen Audlyn, dinner plate, 10⅝" d 35.00
Glen Audlyn, salad plate, 8⅛" d 25.00
Old Colony, cup and saucer, ftd, 2¾" 30.00
Old Colony, dinner plate, 10⅝" d 20.00

ROYAL WINTON

In 1885 Edward, Leonard, and Sidney, three brothers, were instrumental in founding Grimwade Brothers, also known as the Winton Pottery, a firm located in Stoke-on-Trent, Staffordshire, England. Several expansions followed including the purchase of the Winton Pottery Company and Stoke Pottery in 1900. The three firms were combined as Grimwades Limited.

In 1907 Grimwades acquired Atlas China of Stoke, Heron Cross Pottery of Fenton, Rubian Art Pottery, and Upper Hanley Pottery. The company specialized in the production of chinaware and earthenware household and toilet articles as well as British Royalty commemoratives.

In 1913 King George V and Queen Mary visited Winton Potteries. Although formal permission was not granted to use the "Royal" name, it appeared regularly in the company's advertisements following that date.

Royal Winton introduced its chintz patterns and relief wares in the 1930s. Royal Winton's golden age ended with the 1964 death of James Plant, Jr., who introduced a wide range of new chintz, luster, pastel, commemorative, and hand-decorated, artist-signed lines. Today the firm produces tabletop ware, giftware, and limited edition reissues of its chintz patterns.

Reference: Eileen Rose Busby, *Royal Winton Porcelain*, Glass Press, 1998.

Collectors' Club: Royal Winton International Collectors Club, 600 Columbia St, Pasadena, CA 08873.

Cheadle, bonbon, Grimwades **$55.00**
Cheadle, butter dish, Grimwades 175.00
Cheadle, egg cup, ftd, Grimwades 65.00
Chelsea, cake stand, 2-tier, Grimwades 200.00
Chelsea, coaster, Grimwades 55.00
Clevedon, nut dish, Grimwades 60.00
Eleanor, bud vase, Grimwades 80.00
Eleanor, teapot, Grimwades, 4 cup 350.00
English Rose, relish, Grimwades 190.00
Estelle, sandwich tray, Grimwades, 10 x 6" 100.00
Floral Feast, salad bowl, chrome rim, Grimwades 125.00
Hazel, bowl, Ascot shape, rect, flat rim, 9 x 7" 300.00
Hazel, compote, Eton shape, 4 pierced corners, pedestal base, 6¼" w, 2½" h 400.00
Hazel, creamer and sugar, matching tray, Ascot shape 390.00
Hazel, cruet set, Fife shape, salt, pepper, and cov mustard on elongated tray 525.00
Hazel, hot water pot, cov, Countess shape 800.00
Hazel, platter, Ascot shape, 10 x 7" 400.00
Hazel, salad plate, Ascot shape, 8" sq, set of 8 . . . . 875.00
Kinver, compote, ftd, Grimwades 200.00
Old Cottage Chintz, bowl, Ascot shape, flat shaped rim, 9½" d 240.00
Old Cottage Chintz, butter dish, cov, Ascot shape, rect 175.00
Old Cottage Chintz, cake plate, Ascot shape, open pierced handles, 11 x 10" 225.00
Old Cottage Chintz, cake stand, Ascot shape, pedestal base, 8" sq, 2" h 140.00
Old Cottage Chintz, cereal bowl, Ascot shape, 6½" d 40.00

Summertime, stacking tea set, creamer, sugar, and teapot, $650.00.

Old Cottage Chintz, compote, Greek shape, knobbed
pedestal, 5½" d, 3½" h 350.00
Old Cottage Chintz, creamer and sugar, Athena shape,
Ascot shape tray 175.00
Old Cottage Chintz, creamer and sugar, Globe shape,
Ascot shape tray 125.00
Old Cottage Chintz, cup and saucer, Kings shape 50.00
Old Cottage Chintz, jam pot, with liner and silverplated
lid, Squat Rheims shape 175.00
Old Cottage Chintz, plate, Ascot shape, 6" sq 40.00
Old Cottage Chintz, plate, Ascot shape, 10" sq 85.00
Old Cottage Chintz, platter, Ascot shape, rect, flat rim,
13 x 10" 375.00
Old Cottage Chintz, relish dish, Marina shape, 5-part 300.00
Summertime, bud vase, Neme shape, 3½" h 225.00
Summertime, gravy boat, Ascot shape, with liner, 7½" l 190.00
Summertime, lamp, round body with 2 curved handles
and slender neck, brass base, 11" h 1,325.00
Summertime, salt and pepper shakers, pr, Acme shape 275.00
Summertime, sauceboat, Era shape, with liner 225.00
Summertime, trivet, Ascot shape, 5¾" sq 300.00

English Village, dinner plate, 9⅞" d, $10.00.

SALEM CHINA

Biddam Smith, John McNichol, and Dan Cronin, formerly with Standard Pottery in East Liverpool, Ohio, founded the Salem China Company in Salem, Ohio, in 1898. Due to financial problems, it was sold to F. A. Sebring in 1918. Under the management of Frank McKee and Sebring's son, Frank Jr., the company became very successful through the sale of fine dinnerware, much of which was trimmed with 22K gold.

Viktor Schenckengost created many of Salem's shapes and designs during the 1930s and 40s. Salem China continued to manufacture dinnerware until 1967. Beginning in 1968, Salem was exclusively a distribution and sales business.

References: Susan and Al Bagdade, *Warman's American Pottery and Porcelain,* Wallace-Homestead, Krause Publications, 1994; Harvey Duke, *The Official Price Guide to Pottery and Porcelain, Eighth Edition,* House of Collectibles, 1995.

Bonjour, bowl, oval, 9" $10.00
Bonjour, creamer and sugar 12.00
Bonjour, gravy boat 12.00
Briar Rose, butter, open 15.00
Briar Rose, cake plate, 10" d 10.00
Briar Rose, casserole 20.00
Century, bowl, 36s 8.00
Century, bread and butter plate, 6" d 2.00
Century, casserole 15.00
English Village, bread and butter plate 4.00
English Village, creamer and sugar 24.00
English Village, cup and saucer 12.00
English Village, fruit dish, 5¼" d 6.00
English Village, salad plate 18.00
English Village, platter, oval, 12¼" l 18.00
English Village, vegetable, 8½" d 20.00
Free-Form, bowl, ftd 15.00
Free-Form, coffee server 6.00
Free-Form, fruit dish 2.00
Heirloom, casserole 20.00
Heirloom, creamer and sugar 12.00
Heirloom, gravy boat 12.00

Heirloom, platter, 11" l 10.00
Heirloom, salad bowl, 9" d 15.00
Hotco, ashtray 6.00
Hotco, cake server 12.00
Hotco, casserole 25.00
Hotco, chop plate 15.00
Lotus Bud, bowl, oval, 9" l 10.00
Lotus Bud, creamer and sugar 12.00
Lotus Bud, cup and saucer 5.00
New Yorker, ashtray 6.00
New Yorker, creamer and sugar 12.00
New Yorker, dish, 5½" d 2.00
New Yorker, soup bowl, 8" d 10.00
Symphony, bread and butter plate, 6½" d 1.00
Symphony, dinner plate, 10" d 10.00
Symphony, salad plate, 7" d 4.00
Symphony, sugar, 3 point finial 8.00
Tricorne, coffeepot 50.00
Tricorne, nut dish, 3¾" 12.00
Tricorne, sandwich plate, 11½" d 12.00

SALT & PEPPER SHAKERS

The salt and pepper shaker emerged during the latter half of the Victorian era. Fine ceramic and glass shakers slowly replaced individual and master salts. These early shakers were documented by Arthur G. Peterson in *Glass Salt Shakers: 1,000 Patterns* (Wallace-Homestead, 1970).

Although pre–World War I figural salt shakers do exist, the figural salt and pepper shaker gained in popularity during the 1920s and 30s, and reached its zenith in the 1940s and 50s. By the 1960s, inexpensive plastic salt and pepper shakers had replaced their ceramic and glass counterparts.

Salt and pepper shaker collectors specialize. Salt and pepper shakers that included mechanical devices to loosen salt were popular in the 1960s and 70s. Depression-era glass sets also enjoyed strong collector interest during that period. Currently, figural salt and pepper shakers are hot, having experienced a 100% price increase during the past five years.

References: Larry Carey and Sylvia Tompkins, *1003 Salt & Pepper Shakers* (1997), *1004 Salt & Pepper Shakers* (1998), Schiffer Publishing; Melva Davern, *The Collector's Encyclopedia of Salt & Pepper Shakers: Figural and Novelty, Second Series,* Collector Books, 1990, 1995 value update; Helene Guarnaccia, *Salt & Pepper Shakers, Vol. 1* (1985, 1996 value update), *Vol. II* (1989, 1998 value update), *Vol. III* (1991, 1998 value update), *Vol. IV* (1993, 1999 value update), Collector Books; Mike Schneider, *The Complete Salt and Pepper Shaker Book,* Schiffer Publishing, 1993; Irene Thornburg, *Collecting Salt & Pepper Shaker Series,* Schiffer Publishing, 1998.

Collectors' Club: Novelty Salt & Pepper Shakers Club, PO Box 3617, Lantana, FL 33465.

Note: All shakers listed are ceramic unless noted otherwise. Prices are for sets. For additional listings refer to Depression Glass and individual ceramics and glass manufacturer's categories.

Aunt Jemima & Uncle Mose, painted plastic, F&F Mold & Dye Works, Dayton, OH, 1950s, 5" h **$75.00**
Bears, black and white **15.00**
Black Cat, painted accents, magnet on side, wooden **6.00**
Black Cats and Fishbowls **150.00**
Black Chef, holding wooden salt and pepper pots. **20.00**
Black Leapfrogging Kids **75.00**
Blondie & Dagwood, hp plaster, Blondie wearing blue bath robe with name in red on pink base, Dagwood wearing yellow pajamas with name in black above flesh colored feet with red toes, 1940s, 3¼" h. **75.00**
Bonzo, white, dark brown accent on body and ears, pink accent face, green collar, underside incised Goebel stamp, 1920s, 2½" h **75.00**
Book Worm **6.00**
Boxing Glove and Bag **6.00**
Campbell's Soup Can **15.00**
Chef & Mammy, wearing white apron, orange hat and bandanna, matching orange spoon image and mouth dot, cork stopper, 1940s, 4" h chef, 3¾" h mammy **50.00**
Chicken, white and red, red metal basket holder, Italy **6.00**
Chicken and Egg, wooden. **6.00**
Christmas Mice and Cheese. **10.00**
Cowboy and Horse, cowboy wearing brown hat and chaps, peach colored shirt, blue checked pattern on white bandanna lower face mask, brown and white horse with gray mane, red saddle over yellow blanket, cork stopper, Japan, 1930s. **20.00**
Dairy Queen, blonde hair Dutch girl wearing apron, plastic stopper, 1960s, 4" h **75.00**
Deep Sea Diver **8.00**
Deer, nodders. **65.00**
Dick Tracy & Junior, painted plaster, Tracy wearing red hat and trench coat, black trousers, yellow accents, Junior wearing red cap and trousers, red necktie dotted in black, black jacket, fleshtone faces, Tracy's name in yellow lettering, "Junior" in white, cork stopper, 1940s. **75.00**
Elephant, gray, blue trim, trunk forms letter "S" or "P," Ceramic Arts Studios **35.00**
Esso Gasoline Pump, plastic, decal gauge details, orig box, 1950s, 2¾" h. **50.00**
Feet, red painted nails, souvenir from Maine **6.00**
Firestone Tires. **55.00**

Flamingo, souvenir from Florida **10.00**
Fort Pitt Beer, figural bottle, clear brown amber, silvered tin shaker caps, colorful replica labels, 1940–50s, 3" h **20.00**
Greyhound Bus. **75.00**
Indian Chief and Squaw, syroco-like brown composition wood, ©1947 Multi Products, 3¼" h **20.00**
Iron, floral dec, blue handle **6.00**
John F Kennedy and Jackie, color photo of "President John F. Kennedy," and "Mrs. John F. Kennedy," c1961, 2" h **20.00**
Kangaroo and Joey **18.00**
Kewpie, hp accents, mkd cork stopper, "M/K Hand Painted/Japan," 1950s, 2¼" h. **75.00**
Key and Lock **6.00**
Kissing Strawberries, plastic. **8.00**
Laurel & Hardy, mkd "Beswick Ware, Made In England," 4" h Laurel pepper shaker, 3" h Hardy salt shaker, each on 2½ x 3¾" base, 1930s **200.00**
Lennie Lenox, painted plaster, name decal on chest, shaker holes in top of head form letters "S" and "P," 4½" h **200.00**
Lobster, red, claws held above head attached by sprints, green base **25.00**
Nun, plastic **3.00**
Oswald Rabbit & Wally Walrus, ©1958 Walter Lantz Prod Inc, 3⅞" h. **200.00**
Penguin, wearing hat and bow tie **6.00**
Pillsbury Dough Boy. **35.00**
Popcorn and Pop Bottle. **8.00**
Raggedy Ann and Andy. **10.00**
RCA Nipper, black accents, 3" h **100.00**
Schmoo Boy and Girl, 4" h smiling boy with black accents, 3½" h smiling girl with green accents, 1940s **100.00**
Smiley Face, composition, yellow, raised black face markings on both sides, plastic stopper, mkd "Japan," 1970s, 3" d **20.00**
Snoopy and Woodstock, black and white Snoopy wearing chef hat, yellow Woodstock wearing chef hat and sitting on can **10.00**
Snowman, red and white, red tree shaped tray **15.00**

Amish Couple, painted cast iron, $8.00.

Space Rocket, silvered plastic, 4 shaker holes at nose of
  each rocket, Hong Kong, 1960s, 4¼" h. **20.00**
Surfer Girl and Surfboard. **200.00**
TV Set, plastic, dark brown and black marbleized TV
  with gold accents and white screen, removable salt
  and pepper boxes set in top and raise up when on/off
  knob is turned, orig box with instructions, 1950s **20.00**
Tweety, figural coffeepot with image of Tweety with
  flowers on front, ©Warner Bros Inc, 1980, 3" h. **20.00**
Victory Symbol Bombs, painted plaster, upended bomb
  with "V" symbol 1 side and victory code markings
  other side, red, white, and blue, cork stopper, 2½" h. **50.00**
Violin and Case **8.00**
Westinghouse Washer and Dryer **30.00**
Whale on Beach Ball **6.00**
Winking Cat, Enesco. **15.00**
Winnie the Pooh and Rabbit, wood-grained plastic tray,
  "Famous Walt Disney Character Salt and Pepper Sets
  On Tray," foil sticker, Enesco, 1960s, 3¼" h Pooh,
  3¾" h Rabbit. **200.00**

SAND PAILS

Pre-1900 tin sand pails were japanned, a technique involving layers of paint with a final lacquer coating. Lithographed tin pails
arrived on the scene in the first two decades of the 20th century.

The golden age of lithographed tin sand pails began in the late
1930s and extended into the 1960s. After World War II, the four
leading manufacturers were J. Chein & Co., T. Cohn, The Ohio Art
Company, and U.S. Metal Toy Manufacturing. Character-licensed
pails arrived on the scene in the late 1940s and early 1950s. By the
mid-1960s, almost all sand pails were made of plastic.

Many sand pails were sold as sets. Sets could include sand
molds, a sifter, spade, and/or sprinkling can.

Reference: Carole and Richard Smyth, *Sand Pails & Other Sand
Toys,* published by authors, 1996.

Collectors' Club: Ohio Art Collectors Club, 18203 Kristi Rd West,
Liberty, MO 64068.

J Chein, children at zoo, 5¼" h **$75.00**
T Cohn, animals and birds dressed as children and blow-
  ing bubbles, red ground, mkd "T. Cohn, made in
  U.S.A." in circle enclosed in black rings, 3½" h **100.00**
T Cohn, diapered baby confronting calf, piglet, and
  lamb, emb ship on bottom, 4¼" h **100.00**
Happynak, animal musical band, mkd "Happynak
  Seaside Pail No. 4/Made in England, 3½" h. **100.00**
Happynak, Mickey and Donald, emb dolphin and 2
  water bubbles on bottom, mkd "Happynak Sand Pail
  No. 105/Made in England by Permission Walt Disney
  Mickey Mouse Ltd.," 4⅛" h **125.00**
Kiddie Metal Toys, Jack & Jill Wishing Well, 4 nursery
  rhyme scenes with text, litho around base, 1923, 7" h. . . . **250.00**
Ohio Art, children making music scene, artist sgd Elaine
  Ends Hileman, #135, mkd, 4¼" h. **125.00**
Ohio Art, children playing on the beach, artist sgd Elaine
  Ends Hileman, mkd "180" on bottom, 1940s, 8" h **125.00**
Ohio Art, cowboy and Indian on horses, "10 cents" ink
  stamped on bottom, mkd, 4¼" h **100.00**
Ohio Art, Donald Duck Mini Pail, © 1939 Walt Disney
  Productions and Ohio Art Co, 3" h. **225.00**

**J. Chein, cowboy
theme, 4¼" h,
$100.00.**

Ohio Art, frog reading, surrounded by fish, sgd "Fern
  Bisel Peat," mkd "Ohio Art Co./Made in U.S.A.," emb
  with concentric circles, 11" h. **125.00**
US Metal Toy Mfg Co, Treasure Island, pirates on scrap
  tin bottom, 7½" h **125.00**
Wolverine, children riding carousel, emb, wire bail and
  wooden handle, mkd "Wolverine Supply & Mfg. Co.,
  Pittsburgh, Pa.," 1936, 7" h **75.00**

SCANDINAVIAN GLASS

Scandinavian Glass is a generic term for glassware made in
Denmark, Finland, and Sweden from the 1920s through the 1960s
and heavily exported to the United States. Collectors assign a high
aesthetic value to Scandinavian glass. Focus at the moment is on
key companies, e.g., Kosta Glasbruk and Orrefors, and designers
such as Edward Held, Nils Landberg, Vicke Lindstrand, Tyra
Lundgren, Ingeborg Lundin, Sven Palmqvist, Sven Erik Skawonius.

In the 1920s and '30s, Orrefors produced engraved crystal that
combined Modern abstractionism with classicism. In the 1940s
Orrefors' forms became heavier, decoration spare, and the inher-
ent refractive properties of glass were emphasized. Designers at
Kosta Glasbruk were moving in this direction in the 1930s. The
1950s saw an emphasis on simple light softly contoured forms.
Following a period of "Pop" influence in the 1960s, Orrefors'
pieces became sculptural in approach. It was also during this period that color entered the Scandinavian glass design vocabulary
and design links were established between Scandinavian and
Italian glass designers.

Currently, interest in Scandinavian glass is strongest in metropolitan regions in the Middle Atlantic States and West Coast. It is
now regularly featured in 20th Century Modern auction catalog
sales across the United States.

Boda, bowl, colorless glass with belted lime green stripe
  and blue rim wrap, inscribed "Boda Ulrica 52237,"
  4¼" h **$60.00**
Boda, bowl, designed by Bertil Vallien, wide flared rim
  on cylindrical body with radiating trapped bubble pattern in colorless and opaque white glass, inscribed
  "Boda afors B Vallien" on base, c1963, 3½" h, 7½" d **285.00**

Boda, vase, designed by Bertil Vallien, opaque white on colorless vessel enhanced by multicolored vertical dec, inscribed "Boda/Vallien," 9½" h 250.00

Holmegaard, bowl, designed by Per Lutken, freeform tricon bowl of heavy walled blue tinted colorless glass, inscribed at base "Holmegaard/4825" and with artist's insignia, mid-20th C, 5" h, 13¼" d. 300.00

Holmegaard, bowl, designed by Per Lutken, oval with pulled handle, inscribed "Holmegaard" and dated on base with artist's initials, c1955, 2¾" h 100.00

Holmegaard, bowl, designed by Per Lutken, shallow freeform with rolled handle, inscribed "Holmegaard" and dated on base with artist's initials, c1955, 2½" h 100.00

Holmegaard, vase, designed by Per Lutken, oviform, with freeform rim in pale blue crystal, inscribed "Holmegaard" and dated on base with artist's initials, c1955, 8" h. 100.00

Iittala, vase, designed by Tapio Wirkkala, egg shaped vessel with small opening, boat shape form, decorated with vertical engraved linear pattern, inscribed on base "Tapio Wirkkala Iittala," c1952, 6⅛" h, 2⅜" d, price for pair. 500.00

Kosta, bowl, colorless half round internally decorated by opaque white horizontal threading, base inscribed "LH 1004," stamped "Kosta/Lind/Strand," 5⅜" d 225.00

Kosta, center bowl, clear colorless glass with cut radiating leaf dec on extended flared rim, incised "Kosta LS 5614" on base, 12½" d 300.00

Kosta, paperweight, designed by Ann Warff, colorless cap revealing internal bubbles above amber colored stem, base inscribed "Kosta 97323/Warff," 3¾" h 285.00

Kosta, sculpture, aquamarine glass iceberg with etched elk at center, base edge inscribed "Kosta V. Lindstrand W.L. 90002," 6" h 200.00

Leerdam, bowl, designed by Floris Meydam, freeform low bowl with spiraled ribbons of white, smoky amethyst, and colorless glass, inscribed "Leerdam, M" on pontil, paper label, c1950, 1¾" h, 10" l 250.00

Leerdam, vase, egg shaped, cased with orange, white, and colorless glass, 1946, 5⅜" h 200.00

Leerdam, vase, horizontal flattened oval striped in green, yellow, and colorless cased glass, 1946, 3¼" h 200.00

Leerdam, vase, tapered cylindrical form in colorless glass, 1946, 7" h 200.00

Nuutajarvi, vase, cylindrical body with flared base and extended dropped rim of heavy colorless glass encasing amber, inscribed "J. Niemi Nuutajarvi 62" on base, 1962, 5¾" h. 250.00

Nuutajarvi, vase, designed by Kaj Franck, tall, flaring, cylindrical form in amber and colorless glass, inscribed "K. F. Nuutajarvi 64" on base, 1950–76, 10¼" h 300.00

Orrefors, bowl, Graal, designed by Edward Hald, thick walled half-sphere form in colorless glass enclosing brown and white overlaid and patterned int, inscribed "Orrefors J. Graal 1862 L" with artist's signature on base 800.00

Orrefors, decanter, clear colorless glass with cut dec of gondolier playing guitar, flattened oviform with stopper, incised "Orrefors P 2902. B8. RR" on base, 9¼" h . . . 300.00

Orrefors, decanter, engraved, cylindrical form with flattened sides of colorless glass with sailing ship motif, inscribed on base "Orrefors/P 2574/ Lees," 10⅞" h 300.00

Orrefors, vase, designed by Simon Gate, clear colorless glass with copper wheel engraved dec of dancing female nude and snake, flared cylinder form, incised "Orrefors Gate 128J. 03. XR," 7" h 375.00

Orrefors, vase, etched crystal, tapered oviform in colorless crystal, 2 flattened sides, 1 etched nude maiden seated on shoreline rock, inscribed on base "Orrefors 2532. C.S.S.," 11⅜" h 200.00

Plus Glasshyte, vase, designed by Benny Motzfeldt, tapered cylindrical form of amethyst colored glass, with freeform glass fiber gauze inclusions, etched stamp mark "Plus/Bm/ Norway," c1975, 5½" h, 6" d 300.00

Rut Bryk, ceramic plaque, Madonna and Child, 2-part, woman in yellow dress with wreath of roses surrounding her head and young child on dark blue glossy glaze ground, sgd "Bryk" on top of plaque portion, mid-20th C, 27¼" h, 13⅝" w 525.00

SCHOENHUT

In 1872 Albert Schoenhut, a German immigrant, founded his own company to manufacture a toy piano he perfected. The company quickly expanded, its line including a host of musical percussion instruments, military toys, novelty toys, and children's play equipment. Beginning in the 1890s, Schoenhut's sons (there were six) started working for the company.

In 1902 Schoenhut purchased Fritz Meinecke's patent rights for a toy animal whose parts were held together by elastic. The first Humpty Dumpty Circus items appeared in 1903. In 1908 the Rolly Dolly was introduced. Schoenhut received a patent for a swivel, spring-jointed doll in 1911. Walking dolls were added in 1919 and sleep-eye dolls in 1921.

In the late 1920s Schoenhut manufactured a line of comic character jointed toys for George Borgfelt & Co. The Depression hit the company hard. Several new games, colorful wagons and pull toys, and a line of diecut, cardboard jigsaw puzzles were introduced. Schoenhut's catalog dropped from 85 (late 1920s) to 39 pages (1934).

Orrefors, centerbowl, frosted spotted leopards peering through cut and faceted crystal bars, applied dark blue disk base inscribed "Orrefors 4688-13 Gunnar Cyren," 6" h, 8" d, $1,380.00. Photo courtesy Skinner, Inc., Boston, MA.

The company went into bankruptcy in 1935. Albert F. and his son Frederick Carl created the Schoenhut Manufacturing Company to continue making toy pianos. In 1950 Nelson Delavan purchased the manufacturing rights and reproduced several animals and personnel.

Reference: Carol Corson, *Schoenhut Dolls*, Hobby House Press, 1993; Elizabeth Stephan (ed.), *O'Brien's Collecting Toys, 9th Edition*, Krause Publications, 1999.

Collectors' Club: Schoenhut Collectors Club, 1003 W Huron St, Ann Arbor, MI 48103.

Note: All figures are full size and in good condition unless noted otherwise.

Alligator, painted eyes	$300.00
Baby Doll, original labels, 11½" h seated	225.00
Buffalo, carved mane, painted eyes	300.00
Buffalo, cloth mane, glass eyes	575.00
Bulldog, glass eyes	1,100.00
Camel, 1 hump, glass eyes	475.00
Camel, 2 humps, reduced size	325.00
Cat, painted eyes	1,100.00
Chinaman, 1-part head	450.00
Clown, reduced size	110.00
Cow, glass eyes	650.00
Donkey, painted eyes	100.00
Elephant, reduced size	100.00
Girl Doll, head and hair carved with blue headband ribbon, label on back, crazing and paint loss to face and heavy on back of head, 16" h	715.00
Horse, brown, glass eyes	325.00
Horse, white, painted eyes	200.00
Kangaroo, painted eyes	750.00
Lady Acrobat, 1-part head	400.00
Lady Circus Rider, reduced size	225.00
Lion, carved mane, reduced eyes	300.00

Lion, cloth mane, glass eyes	550.00
Lion Tamer, 1-part head	450.00
Moritz Doll, no clothing, 14" h	9,350.00
Poodle, carved mane, painted eyes	200.00
Poodle, cloth mane, glass eyes	275.00
Rabbit, painted eyes	650.00

AUCTION PRICES – SCHOENHUT

Gene Harris Antique Auction Center, Inc., Schoenhuts & Doll Auction, October 13, 1998. Prices include the 10% buyer's premium.

African Native, 2-part face, missing ear	$2,805.00
Black Bear, glass eyes, some paint loss to legs	462.00
Clown, 2-part face	303.00
Deer, painted eyes, minor paint rubs	605.00
Driver, no hat	440.00
Giraffe, painted eyes, minor paint loss	275.00
Goose, painted eyes, minor paint rubs	314.00
Hippopotamus, glass eyes, minor paint rubs	908.00
Hobo, 2-part face	550.00
Leopard, painted eyes, minor paint rubs	330.00
Monkey, black face	440.00
Negro Dude	935.00
Ostrich, painted eyes, minor paint rubs	440.00
Pig, painted eyes	182.00
Polar Bear, painted eyes, scattered paint loss	358.00
Ring Master, with whip	413.00
Tiger, glass eyes, minor paint rubs	495.00
Wolf, glass eyes, partial label, paint rubs	1,870.00
Zebra, glass eyes, scattered paint loss and rubs	550.00

SCHOOP, HEDI

Hedi Schoop, born in Switzerland in 1906, was educated at Vienna's Kunstgewerbeschule and Berlin's Reimann Institute. In the early 1930s she and her husband, Frederick Hollander, a well-known composer, emigrated to America.

After arriving in Los Angeles, Schoop began making and marketing a line of plaster of Paris dolls dressed in contemporary fashions. Discovered by a representative of Barker Brothers, she was advised to scrap the textile clothing and do figures that were entirely ceramic.

Hedi's mother financed a plant in North Hollywood. Schoop employed many displaced European actors, dancers, and musicians as decorators. In 1942 the company became Hedi Schoop Art Creations. Business was strong in the late 1940s and early 1950s. The company introduced a line of TV lamps in the mid-1950s. A fire ended production in 1958. Schoop did not rebuild. Instead, she worked as a free-lance designer for several Los Angeles area firms. She retired permanently from the ceramics business in the 1960s, devoting her time after that to painting.

References: Jack Chipman, *Collector's Encyclopedia of California Pottery, Second Edition*, Collector Books, 1999; Mike Schneider, *California Potteries*, Schiffer Publishing, 1995.

Ashtray, fish shaped, silver and gold overglaze, stamped mark	$45.00
Candle Holder, mermaid, stamped mark, c1950, 13½" h	500.00
Figurine, clown playing cello, mkd, c1943, 12½" h	125.00
Figurine, Conchita, 12½" h	165.00

Cracker-Jack Clown, $743.00. Photo courtesy Gene Harris Antique Auction Center, Inc.

Figurine, Debutante, 12½" h **165.00**
Figurine, French peasant couple, 13" h. **195.00**
Figurine, girl walking collie, 9½" h. **125.00**
Figurine, Margie, 12" h **75.00**
Figurine, Repose, tinted bisque, stamped mark, 1949 . . . . . . **165.00**
Figurine, Vienna, mkd "Hedi Schoop Hollywood, Cal,"
   13½" h **175.00**
Flower Frog, dancing girls, 8" h **250.00**
Flower Holder, Gardening Girl, 7 x 6" **85.00**
Flower Holder, Josephine, stamped mark, 13" h **250.00**
Flower Holder, Tyrolean Girl, 11½" h. **125.00**
Lamp, Colbert, woman holding 2 baskets, c1940, 11½" h **125.00**
Planter, hobby horse **40.00**
Tray, King of Diamonds, in-mold mark **100.00**
Vase, crowing rooster, tinted clay body with transparent
   highglaze and gold overglaze, stamped mark, c1949,
   12" h **150.00**

SCIENTIFIC INSTRUMENTS

Scientific instruments is a broad category that encompasses astrological, calculating, educational, engineering, mathematical, medical, nautical, surveying, and weather instruments along with supporting paper collectibles, e.g., books. Although 18th- and 19th-century instruments have been and remain the principal collector focus, interest is growing in post-1920 instruments, due in part to affordability.

English and European examples command a premium price. Completeness is a major value consideration. The period box is required for an object to be considered complete. Toy scientific kits, e.g., chemistry, electricity, erector, and microscope sets, especially by A. C. Gilbert Company of New Haven, Connecticut, are rising steadily in value.

The appearance of specialized shows, e.g., the Maryland Science and Microscope Society's annual April show and sale, indicates the depth and strength of the market.

Collectors' Club: Oughtred Society (slide rules), PO Box 99077, Emeryville, CA 94662.

Boyden's Hook Gauge, nickel silver gauge with brass
   hooks, mahogany frame, c1920 . . . . **$145.00**
Dipping Refractometer/Saccharimeter, Carl Zeiss, Jena,
   Germany, with focusable eyepiece, optical equidivi-
   sion scale, internal compensator prisms with microm-
   eter screws, and prism mount, nickel-plated leather
   covered brass, case with 2 thermometers, c1930. . . . . . . **115.00**
Facit C1-13 Mechanical Calculator, Atuidaberg-Facit,
   Sweden, 838399, with 8-digit and 13-digit registers,
   10 setting keys, 3 clearing levers, 2 carriage shift keys,
   1 tabulator, and 24-pp instruction manual and cover,
   c1940. . . . . **345.00**
Folding Compound Monocular Microscope, Bausch &
   Lomb Optical Co, Rochester, NY, USA, 170782,
   ¹⁵/₁₆" d tube opens to 11" h, square table, double mirror, orig morocco case, japanned black, c1920,
   6½" h, 4¼" l **345.00**
Fowler's Calculator and Long Scale Calculator, Fowler &
   Co, Manchester, England, 6978m circular logarithmic
   scales on both faces, 2 stems for rotating faces and
   cursor, nickel-plated, with sq velvet lined case, c1920 . . . **375.00**
Handy Shrinkage Rule, thick boxwood with brass end
   covers, graduated on 4 edges, c1930 . . . . **30.00**

Analytical Beam Balance, "W. Ainsworth & Sons Inc. Denver Co.," DLB type with chain weight and notched beam, glass-sided case with counter poised removable door and drawer, 200 g capacity, 1/20 mg sensitivity, 3" non-corrosive pans, c1950, 18" l, 9" w, 18" h, $144.00. Photo courtesy Skinner, Inc., Boston, MA.

High Post Plane Table Alidade, Keufel & Esser Co, NY,
   73903, model 5093A, with 10" telescope on 3 x 18"
   blade with beveled edge, with strider level, 2" radiu,
   Beaman Stadia Arc, trough compass and bull's-eye
   vial on blade, japanned and leather black finish on
   brass, with orig case, c1940, 7½" h **460.00**

SEBASTIAN MINIATURES

Sebastian Miniatures, hand-painted, lightly glazed figurines, are the creation of Prescott W. Baston (1909–1984). He organized the Sebastian Miniature Company in 1940. Production initially was located in Marblehead, Massachusetts, eventually moving to Hudson, Massachusetts.

Sebastian Miniatures range in size from three to four inches. Production was limited. Baston also produced special commission advertising and souvenir figurines. Over 900 different figures have been documented. Pewter miniatures were introduced in 1969. In 1976, the Lance Corporation produced 100 of Baston's most popular designs for national distribution.

Prescott Baston died on May 25, 1984. His son, Woody, continued in his father's footsteps. The Sebastian Collectors Society plays a far greater role in determining secondary market pricing than normally expected from a collectors' club.

References: Collectors' Information Bureau, *Collectibles Market Guide & Price Index, 16th Edition,* Collectors' Information Bureau, 1998, distributed by Krause Publications; Mary Sieber (ed.), *Price Guide to Limited Edition Collectibles,* Krause Publications, 1998.

Collectors' Clubs: The Sebastian Exchange Collectors Assoc, PO Box 10905, Lancaster, PA 17605; Sebastian Miniatures

Collectors Society, (company sponsored), 321 Central St, Hudson, MA 01749.

America Salutes Desert Storm	$200.00
Amish Man	20.00
Betsy Ross, #129	85.00
Buffalo Bill	100.00
Captain Doliber	300.00
Christmas Plaque	50.00
Cleopatra, version 1, 1950–62	200.00
Evangeline	150.00
Fisherman's Wife	100.00
Gathering Tulips	125.00
George Washington	40.00
Gibson Girl, #316-A	175.00
In Candy Store	38.00
Jamestown Fort	250.00
John Alden	45.00
John Harvard	140.00
Juliet	70.00
Kennel Fresh, ashtray, #239	300.00
Little Mother	38.00
Lost Kitchen Jell-O	425.00
Manager	50.00
Margaret Houston	100.00
Mark Twain, #315	100.00
Martha Washington	40.00
Mary Lyons	250.00
Mayflower with Clouds	200.00
Mr Beacon Hill	125.00
Mr Obocell	175.00
Parade Rest, #216	100.00
Priscilla Alden	45.00
Raphael's Madonna	20.00
Romeo	70.00
Sam Houston	100.00
Sampling the Stew	60.00
Shaker Lady	70.00
Shaker Man	70.00
Sir Francis Drake	250.00
Slalom	175.00
Swedish Girl	200.00
The Clown	75.00
Williamsburg Governor	55.00
Williamsburg Lady	55.00
Wisemen	60.00
Yankee Sea Captain	65.00

SEWING COLLECTIBLES

The ability to sew and to sew well was considered a basic household skill in the 18th century, 19th century, and first two-thirds of the 20th century. In addition to utilitarian sewing, many individuals sewed for pleasure, producing work ranging from samplers to elaborately embroidered table coverings.

The number of sewing implements, some practical and some whimsical, multiplied during the Victorian era. Crochet hooks, pincushions, and tape measures were among the new forms. Metals, including gold and silver, were used. Thimbles were a popular courting and anniversary gift. Sewing birds attached to the edge of the table helped the sewer keep fabric taut.

As America became more mobile, the sewing industry responded. Many advertisers used needle threaders, tape measures, and

sewing kits as premiums. A matchcover-like sewing kit became a popular feature in hotels and motels in the post-1945 era. While collectors eagerly seek sewing items made of celluloid, they have shown little interest thus far for post-1960 plastic sewing items.

References: *Advertising & Figural Tape Measures,* L-W Book Sales, 1995; Elizabeth Arbittier, et al., *Collecting Figural Tape Measures,* Schiffer Publishing, 1995; Wade Laboissonniere, *Blueprints of Fashion: Home Sewing Patterns of the 1940s,* Schiffer Publishing, 1997; Sally C. Luscomb, *The Collector's Encyclopedia of Buttons,* Schiffer Publishing, 1997; Averil Mathias, *Antique and Collectible Thimbles and Accessories,* Collector Books, 1986, 1997 value update; Wayne Muller, *Darn It!, The History and Romance of Darners,* L-W Book Sales, 1995; Glenda Thomas, *Toy and Miniature Sewing Machines* (1995), *Book II* (1997), Collector Books; Helen Lester Thompson, *Sewing Tools & Trinkets,* Collector Books, 1997; Estelle Zalkin, *Zalkin's Handbook of Thimbles & Sewing Implements,* Warman Publishing Co, 1988, distributed by Krause Publications.

Collectors' Clubs: International Sewing Machine Collectors Society, 551 Kelmore St, Moss Beach, CA 94038; Toy Stitchers, 623 Santa Florita Ave, Millbrae, CA 94030.

Note: See Thimbles for additional listings.

Brochure, "How to Make Children's Clothes, The Modern Singer Way," Singer Service Library #3, 1928	$5.00
Crochet Hook, plastic, Susan Bates, c1950	1.00
Crochet Hook, steel, Boye Co, c1930	3.00
Darner, wood, double glove, c1920	5.00
Darning Kit, J P Coats, 6 spools darning thread, aluminum thimble, 2 needles, painted, c1930	30.00
Embroidery Hoop, wood, handmade, 16" d	6.00
Knit-Count Mechanical Counter, diecut plastic, Yam Co, 1940s	15.00
Latch Hook, wood handle, c1950	5.00
Magazine, *Needlecraft,* 1939	1.50
Needle Book, Dix Rands "Queen Victoria," #3/9 Sharps, Occupied Japan	5.00
Needle Book, Kentucky, Lexington Ice Co, c1920	5.00
Needle Case, brass, velvet lining, spring closure, c1930	25.00
Needle Case, suede, cross stitch dec, wool pages, c1920	10.00

Needle Book, New York, 5 needle pkgs, Occupied Japan, 1940s, 3¹/₂ x 6", $15.00.

Pincushion, bisque, girl with basket, multicolored matte glaze, Japan, 3" h 30.00

Pincushion, ceramic, parrot, multicolored luster and shiny glaze, Japan, 3³/₄" h.......................... 25.00

Sewing Bag, green, pink, and black carpet bag, natural wood carrying handle, 13 x 15" 20.00

Sewing Kit, celluloid, silver gilt design overlay, with needle holder and thread, c1920...................... 25.00

Sewing Kit, hard plastic, figural spark plug with brass firing tip removable cap from needle storage area, bottom is threaded removable thimble over storage area holding small spool of black and white thread, mkd "S.E.V. Marchal," c1950s, 3¹/₄" h................... 15.00

Sewing Kit, hard plastic container, yellow lower part and threaded green thimble cap removable from storage of plastic spool holding black and white thread, mkd "Germany," 1950s.................................... 15.00

Sewing Kit, silvered metal canister, black and white celluloid wrapper depicting "New York To Chicago" passenger bus of "Frank Martz Coach Co," end cap removes from storage area holding metal spool of black and white thread, 1930s...................... 75.00

Sewing Kit, wooden case, 3 pc, leather sewing kit with sinew thread and tools, bottom unscrews with attachment storage, c1940 .... 15.00

Tape Measure, Atlantic City, silvered tin canister, multicolored scene of "Young's Million Dollar Pier/Atlantic City, N.J.," cloth tape.......................... 20.00

Tape Measure, Dr Caldwell's Syrup Pepsin, celluloid canister, yellow product box illus printed on each side, 1920s...................................... 50.00

Tape Measure, figural, basket of fruit, celluloid, silver handled, Germany............................ 100.00

Tape Measure, figural, Billiken, celluloid, cream, applied brown highlights, Japan.................. 175.00

Tape Measure, Hawk Work Clothes, celluloid canister, full color illus of brown hawk holding red, white, and blue sign from beak on yellow ground with blue rim, reverse with local imprint in blue on yellow for "Miller Co," c1920s.......................... 20.00

Tape Measure, Indian Head National Bank, celluloid canister, 1 side shows profile of Indian head surrounded by bank title and Nashau, NH location, other side with slogan text for bank, 1920s 20.00

Tape Measure, Knickerbocker Portland Cement Co, NY, silvered metal canister, thin metal measuring tape mkd for maker "Lufkin," 1930s................... 20.00

Tape Measure, Nashau Blankets, celluloid canister, red, white, and blue printing on both sides, 1 side with blue eagle symbol of NRA, other side with art and text for other fabric products, cloth tape, c1933 .... 20.00

Thimble, aluminum, White Sewing Machine 2.00

Thimble, SS, relief designs of birds and leaves, mkd inside with star and "8" 20.00

Thread Holder, wood, dachshund, c1930.............. 15.00

Thread Holder, wood, desk style, slant top lifts, inkwell is thimble holder, c1925 .... 12.00

Toy Sewing Machine, Betsy Ross, model 707, electric, wooden plaid case, Gibraltar Mfg Co, 1950s, 8³/₄ x 6¹/₄ x 8¹/₂".................................... 75.00

Toy Sewing Machine, KayanEE, light green, sheet metal body, rose decal, manual operation, 4¹/₄ x 4¹/₄ x 7" 75.00

Toy Sewing Machine, Little Mother, Artcraft Metal Products, 1940s, 8 x 4¹/₈ x 8¹/₄" 100.00

SHAWNEE POTTERY

Addis E. Hull, Jr., Robert C. Shilling, and a group of investors established the Shawnee Pottery Company, Zanesville, Ohio, in 1937. It was named for an Indian tribe that lived in the area.

Shawnee manufactured inexpensive, high-quality kitchen and utilitarian earthenware. The company perfected a bisque drying method that enabled decorating and glazing to be achieved in a single firing. In the late 1930s and early 1940s, Shawnee supplied products to large chain stores. Valencia, a dinnerware and kitchenware line, was created for Sears.

Robert Ganz joined Shawnee as a designer in 1938, creating some of the company's most popular cookie jars, e.g., Puss 'n Boots and Smiley. Designer Robert Heckman arrived in 1945 and was responsible for the King Corn line and numerous pieces featuring a Pennsylvania German motif.

Hull left Shawnee in 1950. In 1954 John Bonistall became president and shifted production from kitchenware to decorative accessories. He created the Kenwood Ceramics division to market the remaining kitchenware products. Chantilly, Cameo, Elegance, Fernwood, Petit Point, and Touché are several art lines introduced in the late 1950s. The company prospered in the late 1950s.

A decision was made to cease operations in 1961. Bonistall purchased Shawnee's molds and established Terrace Ceramics, Marietta, Ohio.

References: Pam Curran, *Shawnee Pottery,* Schiffer Publishing, 1995; Jim and Bev Mangus, *Shawnee Pottery,* Collector Books, 1994, 1998 value update; Mark Supnick, *Collecting Shawnee Pottery,* L-W Book Sales, 1989, 1997 value update; Duane and Janice Vanderbilt, *The Collector's Guide to Shawnee Pottery,* Collector Books, 1992, 1998 value update.

Collectors' Club: Shawnee Pottery Collectors Club, PO Box 713, New Smyrna Beach, FL 32170.

Ball Jug, Quill, USA 12 .... **$40.00**
Cookie Jar, drum major, gold trim, #10................ 300.00
Cookie Jar, Dutch girl, decals, gold dec 200.00
Cookie Jar, Muggsy 450.00
Cookie Jar, owl 200.00
Cookie Jar, Puss 'n Boots 150.00

Creamer, elephant, 4¹/₄" h, $45.00. Photo courtesy Ray Morykan Auctions.

Cookie Jar, seated elephant, decals, gold dec **250.00**
Creamer, cat **40.00**
Creamer, Puss 'n Boots **65.00**
Creamer, Smiley Pig, yellow and blue, #86 . . . . **85.00**
Creamer, yellow pig, blue bib **95.00**
Figurine, boy at stump, #533 . . . . **14.00**
Figurine, doe and fawn, #624 . . . . **34.00**
Figurine, dog and jug, #610 . . . . **14.00**
Figurine, dog on shoe, green **32.00**
Figurine, Dutch children at well, #710 . . . . **24.00**
Figurine, elephant on base, black and pink **65.00**
Figurine, elf on shoe, green **32.00**
Figurine, flying goose, #820 . . . . **25.00**
Figurine, girl with basket of flowers, #616 . . . . **32.00**
Figurine, hound dog and peking, #611 . . . . **37.00**
Figurine, open-mouth fish **12.00**
Figurine, Oriental boy with flowerpot, #701 . . . . **15.00**
Figurine, Oriental with umbrella, #617 . . . . **25.00**
Figurine, owl **50.00**
Figurine, Smiley Pig, flower dec **110.00**
Figurine, squirrel, #664 . . . . **24.00**
Figurine, squirrel with nut, #239 . . . . **35.00**
King Corn, butter, cov, #72 . . . . **50.00**
King Corn, casserole **90.00**
King Corn, cereal bowl, #95 . . . . **32.00**
King Corn, cookie jar, #66 . . . . **140.00**
King Corn, creamer and covered sugar **45.00**
King Corn, demitasse pot, no lid **75.00**
King Corn, mug, #69 . . . . **45.00**
King Corn, range shakers, pr **45.00**
King Corn, salt and pepper shakers, pr **38.00**
King Corn, salt shaker, small **18.00**
King Corn, snack set, 8 pc **300.00**
Pitcher, Bo Peep **110.00**
Pitcher, Fruit, gold dec, #80 . . . . **100.00**
Pitcher, Pennsylvania Dutch, USA 64 . . . . **90.00**
Pitcher, Sunflower, USA **75.00**
Planter, cockatiel, #535 . . . . **15.00**
Planter, conestoga wagon, #733 . . . . **50.00**
Planter, doe, yellow and green **35.00**
Planter, donkey with basket, #722 . . . . **25.00**

Planter, fawn, #535 . . . . **15.00**
Planter, hound dog **35.00**
Planter, lovebird **18.00**
Planter, Oriental girl with mandolin, #576 . . . . **15.00**
Planter, rickshaw, #539 . . . . **18.00**
Planting Dish, #422 . . . . **32.00**
Queen Corn, cookie jar, #66 . . . . **150.00**
Queen Corn, mixing bowl, #8 . . . . **35.00**
Queen Corn, platter, #96, 12" l **45.00**
Queen Corn, saucer, #91 . . . . **15.00**
Queen Corn, sugar, cov **30.00**
Queen Corn, vegetable bowl, #95 . . . . **32.00**
Salt and Pepper Shakers, pr, claw **50.00**
Salt and Pepper Shakers, pr, Dutch girl with braids **30.00**
Salt and Pepper Shakers, pr, flowerpot **25.00**
Salt and Pepper Shakers, pr, watering cans **25.00**
Sugar, cov, Sunflower **32.00**
Vase, Bowknot, #819 . . . . **24.00**
Vase, Southern Belle, #218 . . . . **32.00**
Vase, swan, yellow, gold trim **35.00**
Wall Pocket, wheat **35.00**
White Corn, grease jar, gold dec **150.00**
White Corn, pitcher, gold trim, USA **100.00**
White Corn, salt and pepper shakers, pr, large, gold trim **150.00**
White Corn, sugar shaker, gold trim **90.00**

SHEET MUSIC

Sheet music is collected primarily for its cover art. The late 1880s through the early 1950s is considered the golden age of sheet music cover art. Every conceivable theme was illustrated. Leading illustrators lent their talents to sheet music covers.

Covers frequently featured a picture of the singer, group, or orchestra responsible for introducing the song to the public. Photographic covers followed the times. Radio stars, movie stars, and television stars appeared on sheet music covers to promote their show or latest screen epic.

Sheet music's popularity is closely related to the popularity of piano playing. When interest in piano playing declined in the 1950s, sheet music covers no longer exhibited the artistic and design creativity of former times. Collector interest in post-1960s sheet music, with the exception of TV show themes and rock 'n' roll sheets, is minimal.

Most sheet music is worth between $1.00 and $3.00, provided it is in near mint condition. In spite of this, many dealers ask an average $5.00 to $10.00 per sheet for mundane titles. Part of the reason for this discrepancy in pricing is the crossover influence of subject collectors. These collectors have little patience with the hunt. Not realizing how easy it is to find copies, they pay high prices and fuel the unrealistic expectations of the general dealer.

Further complicating the picture is the inaccurate, highly manipulative values in the Pafik and Guiheen price guide (Collector Books, 1995). The book has been roundly criticized, and rightly so, within the sheet music collecting community.

References: Debbie Dillon, *Collectors Guide to Sheet Music,* L-W Book Promotions, 1988, 1995 value update; Marion Short, *The Gold in Your Piano Bench* (1997), *Covers of Gold* (1998), *Hollywood Movie Songs* (1999), Schiffer Publishing.

Newsletter: *The Rag Times,* 15522 Ricky Ct, Grass Valley, CA 95949.

Pitcher, Chanticleer, $50.00. Photo courtesy Ray Morykan Auctions.

Collectors' Clubs: National Music Society, 1597 Fair Park Ave, Los Angeles, CA 90041; Remember That Song, 5623 N 64th Ave, Glendale, AZ 85301; Sonneck Society for American Music & Music in America, PO Box 476, Canton, MA 02021.

Advisor: Wayland Bunnell, 199 Tarrytown Rd, Manchester, NH 03103.

About a Quarter to Nine, Warren/Dubin, *Go Into Your Dance,* photo of Al Jolson, Ruby Keeler, circle of chorus men, 1935. . . . . **$6.00**

Big Bad Bill Is Sweet William Now, Ager/Yellen/Politzer, blue and orange checked background, man kissing woman's hand, left inset of Jack Sidney, 1924. . . . . **8.00**

Bugle Call Rag, Pettis/Meyers/Schoebel, *The Benny Goodman Story,* drawing of Goodman, inset of Steve Allen, Donna Reed, 1951 . . . . **8.00**

Carolina's Calling Me, Charles, drawing of home, picture of Alice Joy, back page with Prince Albert adv, 1931. . . . . **5.00**

Cowboy, The, Warren, wide yellow borders, large drawing of western man on horse, 1933 . . . . **6.00**

Crazy, Willie Nelson, full color photos of 3 seasons and trees, 1961 . . . . **5.00**

Don't Take Your Love From Me, Nemo, brown silhouette of woman on blue concentric profiles, inset of Dinah Shore, 1941 . . . . **3.00**

Dream a Little Dream of Me, Schwandt/Andree/Kahn, black and yellow picture of woman reclining, left inset of Wayne King, 1931. . . . . **4.00**

Entertainer, The, Joplin, *The Sting,* reproduction of orig cov, 1974 . . . . **5.00**

Happy Together, Gordon/Bonner, large photo of The Turtles, 1967. . . . . **6.00**

Hello Baby, Cleary/Magidson/Washington, *Forward Pass,* Loretta Young, Douglas Fairbanks, football scene, 1930 . . . . **3.00**

I've Got My Eye on You, Stept/Green, *Show Girl In Hollywood,* Alice White, concentric circles behind, 1930. . . . . **10.00**

I've Waited a Lifetime For You, Edwards/Goodwin, *Our Modern Maidens,* vivid drawing of Joan Crawford in dance pose, 1929 . . . . **7.00**

Jungle Love, Robin/Rainger, *Her Jungle Love,* Dorothy Lamour and Ray Milland, 1938 . . . . **12.00**

La Cucaracha, arranged by Manoloff/Field, published by Calumet, Spanish and English lyrics, simple red graphics, inset of Art Kassel, 1935 . . . . **3.00**

Love Me, Styne/Cahn, *The Stork Club,* Betty Hutton, Don DeFore, Barry Fitzgerald, and Andy Russell, blue and yellow, 1945. . . . . **5.00**

Melody In Spring, Gensler/Thompson, romantic circle photo of Lanny Ross and Ann Sothern, 1934. . . . . **10.00**

My Defenses Are Down, Berlin, *Annie Get Your Gun,* drawing of Betty Hutton shooting rifle, 1946. . . . . **12.00**

Ramblin' Rose, Sherman/Sherman, full page photo of Nat King Cole, 1962 . . . . **5.00**

She'll Be Comin' Round the Mountain, Frank/Manoloff, published by Calument, large mountain, train running through valley, right inset of Ben Bernie, 1935 . . . . **4.00**

Singing a Happy Song, Stern/Meskill, *Folies Bergere De Paris,* Chevalier caricature, 1935 . . . . **10.00**

Sinner Kissed an Angel, Joseph/David, white on blue line drawings of halos, wings, and pitchforks, 1941. . . . . **4.00**

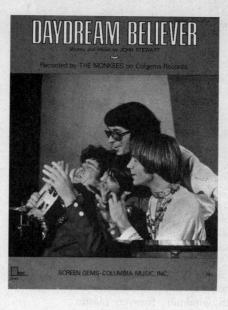

Daydream Believer, **The Monkees, Screen Gems – Columbia Music, $10.00.**

Somewhere in Your Heart, Faith/Kehner, full page grainy black and white photo of Frank Sinatra, 1964 . . . . **4.00**

Thank Heaven For You, Rainger/Robin, *International House,* large head photo of Rudy Vallee, 1933 . . . . **8.00**

They Can't Take That Away From Me, Gershwin, *Shall We Dance,* Fred Astaire, Ginger Rogers at rail with dogs, 1937 . . . . **6.00**

Tom Thumb's Tune, Lee, *Tom Thumb,* drawing of Russ Tamblyn on huge hand, 1958 . . . . **12.00**

Twenty Million People, Johnston/Coslow, *Hello, Everybody,* Kate Smith at piano with song sheet, 1932 . . . . **12.00**

Yodeling Cowboy, Rodgers/Elsie McWilliams, drawing of western man on horse with guitar, singing, left inset of Jimmie Rodgers, 1930 . . . . **5.00**

You Forgot About Me, Robertson/Hanley/Mysels, *Let's Make Music,* Bob Crosby and Jean Rogers, 1940s **6.00**

SILHOUETTE PICTURES

Silhouettes, named for Etienne de Silhouette, the French Minister of Finance responsible for their introduction, were popular in the 18th and early 19th centuries. They lost their appeal when the photograph arrived on the scene in the mid-19th century. Brief revivals occurred in the 1930s and 1950s, when silhouette stands were commonly found resort attractions.

In the 1920s, a new type of silhouette was introduced. This consisted of a black or colored picture that was painted on the back of a piece of flat or convex glass. A paper scenic, tinted, or textured foil background was used to enhance the picture.

Leading manufacturers included Art Publishing Co. (Chicago), Benton Glass Company (Benton, MI), The Buckbee-Brehm Company (Minneapolis), Newton Manufacturing (Newton, IA), Reliance Products (New York/Chicago), and West Coast Picture Company (Portland). Forms ranged from simple two-dimensional pictures to jewelry boxes and were popular promotional giveaways. Stock forms were imprinted with advertisements for local merchants.

Reference: Shirley Mace, *Encyclopedia of Silhouette Collectibles on Glass,* Shadow Enterprises, 1992.

Note: All examples listed are pictures with the silhouette painted on glass.

Boy fishing while dog watches, black silhouette, pressed
   flower background, Fisher $18.00
Butterflies and flowers, black and white silhouette, foil
   background, Reliance 25.00
Colonial man and waving woman walking near tree,
   black silhouette, color background with thatched cot-
   tage, Benton 22.00
Colonial woman holding parasol, walking with small
   boy and girl, color silhouette on white ground, Art
   Pub Co, 1930s 20.00
Colonial woman seated at spinning wheel, black silhou-
   ette, foil ground, Art Pub Co #268, 1930s 20.00
Cowboys at campfire, black silhouette with red and
   white flames, color background of Rocky Mountains,
   Newton Mfg 20.00
Dutch boy and girl with ducks and tulips, red, yellow,
   black, and white silhouette, color background of
   Dutch landscape with windmill, Forever, plastic
   frame, 1950 calendar, 4½" h, 5½" w 20.00
Girl chasing doll-stealing dog, black silhouette, pressed
   flower background, Fisher 18.00
Gondolier, black silhouette, color Venice background,
   Benton 30.00
"Good Night," man and woman kissing at iron gate,
   Buckbee-Brehm, 1932 . . . . 25.00
"Happy in Her Garden," woman watering flowers, black
   silhouette with yellow flowers, white background,
   Plaquette Art Co 25.00
Kittens at duck pond, black silhouette, white ground,
   Benton 25.00
"Knitting," interior scene with woman seated in armchair
   next to window with flowered drapes, she knits while
   kittens play with yarn, interior room silhouette in
   brown and black, window looks out on village landscape background, with thermometer and 1951 cal-
   endar pad, Forever #6842, 6 x 8" 20.00
Man and woman building snowman, black silhouette,
   color background with snowy landscape, Benton 25.00

"Oh, For a Strike," boy fishing as dog watches, black and brown silhouette, color background with house and pond, with 1950 calendar pad, Forever #6817, 6" h, 8" w, $20.00.

Parlor scene with woman playing piano while girl
   dances, blue silhouette, white ground, Benton 60.00
"The Answer," girl mailing letter, black silhouette, white
   ground, Buckbee-Brehm, c1930 . . . . 24.00
Two Scottie dogs playing tug of war, black silhouette,
   white ground 20.00
White lace silhouette framing background color portrait
   of Grecian woman, 1941, Donald Art Co 25.00
Woman and Afghan standing at river's edge, black silhouette, silver foil ground, Deltex, 1933 . . . . 45.00
Woman at spinning wheel, black silhouette, red, white,
   and black background with kettle and brick hearth,
   Newton Mfg, 1961 calendar 12.00
Woman walking Scottie while reaching for wind-blown
   hat, city skyline in background, black silhouette, silver
   foil ground, Deltex, 1933 . . . . 45.00

SILVER, PLATED & STERLING

Sterling silver contains 925 parts of silver per 1,000. The remaining 75 parts consist of additional metals, primarily copper, that add strength and hardness to the silver. Silver plate, developed in England in the late 1860s, is achieved through electrolysis. A thin layer of silver is added to a base metal, usually britannia (an alloy of antimony, copper, and tin), copper, or white metal (an alloy of bismuth, copper, lead, and tin).

Silver plated ware achieved great popularity in the period between 1880 and 1915. Alvin, Gorham, International Silver Company (the result of a series of mergers), Oneida, Reed & Barton, William Rogers, and Wallace are among the principal manufacturers.

Silverware can be divided into three distinct categories: (1) flatware, (2) hollowware, and (3) giftware. This category includes hollowware and giftware. Currently silverware collecting is enjoying a number of renaissances. Plated pieces from the late Victorian era, especially small accessories such as napkin rings, benefited from the Victorian revival of the 1980s. The return to more formal dining has created renewed interest in tabletop accessory pieces.

References: Janet Drucker, *Georg Jensen,* Schiffer Publishing, 1997; Penny Chittim Morrill and Carole A. Berk, *Mexican Silver: 20th Century Handwrought Jewelry & Metalwork, 2nd Edition,* Schiffer Publishing, 1999; Dorothy T. Rainwater, *Encyclopedia of American Silver Manufacturers, 4th Edition,* Schiffer Publishing, 1998.

Periodical: *Silver Magazine,* PO Box 9690, Rancho Santa Fe, CA 92067.

Note: See Flatware for additional silver listings.

SILVER PLATED

Cake Plate, engraved leafy scrolls and fruit, spreading ft,
   Reed & Barton, 1¾" h, 10½" d $175.00
Creamer and Sugar, shaped edge, shell feet, with similar
   undertray by another maker, Gorham 85.00
Dresser Set, 3-pc, consisting of 2 jars and perfume, black
   glass bodies, jars with silver lids with black enameled
   finials, perfume with silver base and lid similarly
   styled as jars, enclosing silver and glass stopper,
   International Silver Co, 2½" and 4½" h jars, 8½" h
   perfume, 1920s–30s 200.00

Serving Box, 3-tier, comprising cov with bone handle, hammered cook pot, and 2 silver plated serving trays, Christian Dior **140.00**

Tea and Coffee Service, 6-pc, comprising teapot, coffeepot, cream jug, 2-handled cov sugar bowl, waste bowl, and tray, each of flaring chamfered rect form with pendant bellflowers at each corner, shaped oval tray with cutout handles, monogrammed, Gorham Mfg Co, 23" l tray **350.00**

Tea Service, 3-pc, comprising teapot, sugar, and creamer, ovoid lobed form, ball ft, English, 5½" h teapot **175.00**

Tea Service, 3-pc, each pc with incised fern and vine motifs **160.00**

Tureen, cov, ovoid, reeded ft, cast handles, domed lid with reeded edge and flower-form finial, monogrammed, Christofle, 20th C, 12" h, 18" l **550.00**

STERLING SILVER

Bowl, stylized flowers on sides, Tiffany & Co, 9¼" d, approx 27 oz **$1,500.00**

Candelabra, pr, Danish style, 2-lite, blossoms dec, American, 8" h, approx 38 oz total weight **1,375.00**

Candlesticks, pr, canted square standard raised on spreading conforming base, engraved with birds and foliage, English, 9" h, approx 43 oz total weight **1,250.00**

Cocktail Shaker, cylindrical, spreading circular base, Crichton Bros, 11" h, approx 38 oz **700.00**

Creamer and Sugar, stylized leaves on sides, Georg Jensen, 4" h creamer, approx 16 oz total weight **1,250.00**

Cup Sleeves, set of 8 sleeves with Lenox porcelain liners and fitted case, approx 13 oz **700.00**

Dresser Set, comprising 3 brushes, mirror, nail buffer, scissors, shoehorn, and 3 jars, each with engine-turned design, American **575.00**

Punch Bowl, Paul Revere style, with 8 matching cups and silver plated ladle, International, 14" d, approx 100 oz total weight **800.00**

Tea and Coffee Service, Danish style, Blossom pattern, comprising teapot, coffeepot, hot water kettle, cov sugar, creamer, and waste bowl, carved ivory handles, American, 16" h teapot, approx 235 oz total **4,500.00**

Teapot and Coffeepot, shield-shaped body dec with scrolls and foliage, American, 11½" h coffeepot, approx 66 oz total weight **900.00**

Trophy Cup, shield-shaped body surrounded by 3 handles, spreading cirular foot, Tiffany & Co., 11" h, approx 70 oz **2,750.00**

Water Pitcher, shield-shaped body, paneled sides, American, 10½" h, approx 23 oz **350.00**

AUCTION PRICES – STERLING SILVER

Wedding Gifts Auction, William Doyle Galleries, April 28, 1998. Prices include the 15% buyer's premium.

Basket, Rococo style, openwork design with central cartouche, flared ft, Howard & Co, approx 14 oz . . . **$345.00**

Bonbon Dish, openwork design, ftd, Shreve & Co, approx 7 oz **161.00**

Bowl, repoussé flowered rim, tripod ftd, S Kirk & Son, approx 7 oz **92.00**

Bread Basket, pierced scalloped rim, approx 7 oz **115.00**

Cake Dish, chased and pierced foliate border, ftd, approx 22 oz **172.00**

Candlesticks, Georgian style, weighted, price for 4 . . . **460.00**

Chocolate Pot, wooden handle, Crichton & Co, approx 22 oz **1,150.00**

Dish, Francis I style, repoussé, oval form, foliate and vine motifs, Reed & Barton, approx 14 oz **207.00**

Dish, wide pierced rim of shells, vines, and latticework, Tiffany & Co, approx 5 oz **258.00**

Mirror, Victorian style repoussé **126.00**

Travel Clock, repoussé case with vine dec, Swiss movement, Black, Starr & Frost **138.00**

SIZZLERS

Mattel produced Sizzlers between 1970 and 1978. Actually, Sizzlers disappeared during 1974, 1975, and 1977. George Soulakis and General Electric developed a nickel-cadmium rechargeable battery that could run for four to five minutes on a 90-second charge. Sizzlers had a hard plastic body and were painted in a variety of colors. Sizzler body types are divided into American cars, Grand Prix types, and exotics. Sizzler variants include Earthshakers, Hotline Trains, and Chopcycles.

Three different chargers were made: (1) a battery Juice Machine (resembling a 1970s gas pump), (2) a battery Goose Pump, revamped in 1978 as the Super Charger, and (3) the Power Pit, an AC charger (resembling a gasoline service station) that plugged into the wall.

Unrestored cars are worth between 20 and 25% of the value of the identical car in restored condition. Complete race sets and accessories still in period packaging are highly desirable.

Mattel failed to protect the Sizzler brand name. Contemporary Sizzlers are manufactured by Playing Mantis of South Bend, Indiana.

Reference: Mike Grove, *A Pictorial Guide to Sizzlers,* published by author, 1995.

Note: Prices listed are for cars in unrestored condition.

Sterling, tea and coffee service, Georgian style, comprising coffeepot, teapot, cov sugar, creamer, and waste bowl, approx 82 oz, $920.00. Photo courtesy William Doyle Galleries.

#2353, Dark Shadow, 1978. . . . . $15.00
#4944, Needle Nose, 1973 . . . . 75.00
#4946, Highway Hauler, 1973. . . . . 75.00
#4947, Red Baron, 1973 . . . . 25.00
#4948, Law Mill, 1973 . . . . 75.00
#5630, Steering Trailer Set, 1973 . . . . 120.00
#5360, Steering Trailer, 1073 . . . . 100.00
#5885, Double Boiler, 1972 . . . . 15.00
#6501, Angeleno M-70, 1970 . . . . 5.00
#6504, Revvin' Heaven, 1970 . . . . 5.00
#6505, Hot Head, 1970 . . . . 5.00
#6520, Spoil Sport, 1971. . . . . 10.00
#6526, Backfire, 1971. . . . . 10.00
#6527, Anteater, 1971. . . . . 10.00
#6532, Indy Eagle, 1971 . . . . 15.00
#6535, March F-1, 1971 . . . . 15.00
#6538, Ferrari 5125, 1971. . . . . 15.00
#6551, Straight Scoop, 1971 . . . . 10.00
#6552, Hot Wings, 1971. . . . . 15.00
#6553, Co-Motion, 1972. . . . . 15.00
#9373, Boss Hoss II, 1976. . . . . 10.00
#9378, Vantom, 1976 . . . . 5.00
#9383, Sideburn II, 1976. . . . . 5.00
#9863, Lamborghini Countache, 1978. . . . . 20.00
#9864, Corvette 4-Rotor, 1978. 25.00
#9866, Long Count, 1978 . . . . 20.00

SLEDS

Sledding or coasting is over 200 years old. Clippers, sleds for boys, had pointed runners. Cutters, sleds for girls, had runners that curled upward in a bow-like fashion.

In 1889 Samuel Leeds Allen applied for a patent for a steerable sled. His Flexible Flyer revolutionized sledding. In 1936 Walt Disney Enterprises licensed Flexible Flyer to produce a Mickey Mouse sled. Other Flexible Flyer lines include The Airline Series, the Yankee Clipper, Ski Racer, and Flexy Racer. The company's headquarters were in Philadelphia, PA.

In 1968 Flexible Flyer became part of the Leisure Group, Inc. In 1973 a group of employees and investors created Balzon-Flexible Flyer. Two years later the company was in Chapter 11 bankruptcy. Roadmaster Corporation bought Blazon-Flexible Flyer in 1993 and continues to manufacture sleds.

A number of other American manufacturers also made sleds: (1) American Toy and Novelty Works/American Acme (Emigsville, PA); (2) Buffalo Sled Company/Auto Wheel Coaster (North Tonawanda, NY); (3) Ellington Turning Co. (South Paris, ME); (4) Garton Toy Company (Sheboygan, WI); (5) Hunt, Helm and Farris/Starline (Harvard, IL); (6) Kalamazoo Sled Company (Kalamazoo, MI); (7) Paris Manufacturing Co. (South Paris, ME); and, (8) Standard Novelty Works (Duncannon, PA).

Reference: Joan Palicia, *Flexible Flyer and Other Great Sleds for Collectors*, Schiffer Publishing, 1997.

American National, Sno-Plane, 1933, 53" l. $125.00
Challenger, 1930s, 36" l 75.00
Fleetwing, Fleetwing Racer, c1940, 51½" l. 25.00
Flexible Flyer, Admiral Byrd Model, 1928, 63" l 100.00
Flexible Flyer, Airline Ace, Model 37H, 1955, 37" l 25.00
Flexible Flyer, Airline Pursuit, 1935, 47" l. 100.00
Flexible Flyer, Baby Sleigh, Model 28W-2 . . . . 100.00

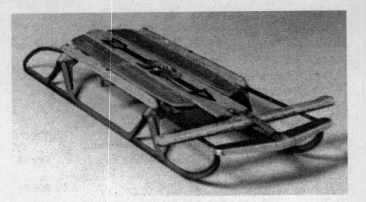

Flexible Flyer, c1974, 45" l, $15.00.

Flexible Flyer, Flexy Racer, Model 100, hand brake on
side, 1921. . . . . 500.00
Flexible Flyer, Model 3E, 1921, 47" l 100.00
Flexible Flyer, "Wee" Racer, 1927, 42" l. 150.00
Flexible Flyer, Yankee Clipper #10, 1936, 36" l. 20.00
Garton, Eskimo, c1930, 31" l. 15.00
King Of The Hill, c1935, 32" l 50.00
Lightning Guider Bob, c1927, 45" l 100.00
Lightning Speedster, c1939, 47" l. 100.00

SLOT CARS

Aurora Plastics Corporation, founded in March 1950, introduced a line of plastic model airplane kits in the fall of 1952. In December 1953, Aurora moved into a new plant in West Hempstead, Long Island, New York. Shortly thereafter Aurora began making a line of hobby craft products. In 1960 Aurora purchased K & B Allyn, a California manufacturer of gas-powered airplane motors.

Aurora launched the electric slot car in 1960. They were an overnight success. From their inception slot cars were noted for the attention paid to details—they looked like the real thing. The slot car's golden age extends from 1962 through the mid-1970s. New models, scales, and track sets and accessories appeared on a regular basis. However, by the mid-1970s, many of the Aurora slot car innovators no longer worked for Aurora. The company changed hands several times during the 1970s and 1980s. By the 1980s, Tyco assumed the leadership role in the slot car field.

References: John A. Clark, *HO Slot Car Identification and Price Guide*, L-W Book Sales, 1995; Thomas Graham, *Greenberg's Guide to Aurora Slot Cars*, Greenberg Books, 1995.

Periodical: *HO Slot Car Journal*, PO Box 2051, Redmond, WA 98073.

Newsletter: *H.O. USA Newsletter*, 435½ S Orange St, Orange, CA 92866.

Note: Prices listed are for slot cars in mint in box (MIB) condition.

Cox, 1:24 scale, La Cucaracha IFC, aluminum chassis,
reddish orange plastic body, 1960s. $125.00
Cox, 1:32 scale, Ford GT 40, blue plastic body, molded
magnesium inline frame, magnesium rims, 1960s 95.00

Eldon, 1:24 scale, Ford GT 40, factory metallic blue painted Lexan body, smoked windows, chrome plated steel chassis, inline motor, 1960s **75.00**

Eldon, 1:24 scale, Porsche Carrera 6, factory painted silver Lexan body, smoked windows, chrome plated steel chassis, inline motor, 1960s **75.00**

Eldon, 1:32 scale, Chaparral 2D, dark blue plastic body, smoked windows, plastic adjustable inline frame, 1960s **35.00**

Eldon, 1:32 scale, Mustang GT, white plastic body, adjustable inline plastic frame, 1960s **35.00**

Eldon, 1:32 scale, Porsche Carrera, silver plastic body, smoked windows, plastic adjustable inline frame, 1960s **35.00**

K&B (Aurora), 1:24 scale, Ferrari 275 LM, red plastic body, aluminum adjustable sidewinder chassis, 1966 . . . . **150.00**

K&B (Aurora), Ford Cobra Coupe, blue plastic body, adjustable aluminum sidewinder chassis, 1960s **300.00**

K&B (Aurora), Screecher, Super Chief, white, red flames **10.00**

K&B (Aurora), Speedline, Stingray, purple chrome. **15.00**

Monogram, 1:24 scale, McLaren Elva, blue plastic body, 1-pc brass chassis, sidewinder motor mount, 1960s **275.00**

Monogram, 1:24 scale, Scarab, #14, blue metallic plastic body, aluminum adjustable inline chassis, X220 motor, 1960s **100.00**

Revell, 1:24 scale, Lotus 23, red or orange plastic body, aluminum adjustable inline frame, SP 600 motor, 1960s **100.00**

Revell, 1:25 scale, BRM, green or blue plastic body, adjustable aluminum inline chassis, 1960s **50.00**

Revell, 1:32 scale, Cobra, blue plastic body, adjustable aluminum inline frame, SP 500 motor, 1960s **300.00**

Revell, 1:32 scale, Lola T 70, orange plastic body, aluminum pan inline chassis, 1960s **100.00**

Strombecker, 1:24 scale, Brabbam F1, green plastic body, suspended scorcher type motor, 1960s **250.00**

Strombecker, 1:24 scale, Lotus Ford 1, white plastic body, suspended scorcher type motor, 1960s **250.00**

Strombecker, 1:32 scale, Cheetah, blue or red plastic body, aluminum or black plastic chassis, late 1960s **40.00**

Strombecker, 1:32 scale, Ferrari Testarossa, red copper or red plastic body, gray plastic inline frame, 1960s **25.00**

Strombecker, 1:32 scale, Jaguar XKE, black plastic body, red plastic int, black plastic inline frame, 1960s **48.00**

Tyco, Autoworld Carrera, white, red, and blue stripes **8.00**

Marx, DC Motor Race, Lynx #22, plastic, 1960s and Mercedes Benz #5, 1950, 5³/₄" l, price for lot, $72.00. Photo courtesy Collectors Auction Services.

SLOT MACHINES

In 1905 Charles Frey of San Francisco invented the first three-reel slot machine, known as the Liberty Bell. An example survives at the Liberty Bell Saloon, an establishment owned by Frey's grandson in Reno, Nevada.

Although the Mills Novelty Company copyrighted the famous fruit symbols in 1910, they were quickly copied by other manufacturers. They are still one of the most popular slot machine symbols. The jackpot was added in 1928.

Early slot machines featured wooden cabinets. Cast-iron cabinets appeared in the mid-1910s. Aluminum fronts arrived in the early 1920s. Mechanical improvements, such as variations in coin entry and detection of slugs, occurred during the 1930s. Additional security devices to prevent cheating and tampering were added in the 1940s. The 1950s marked the introduction of electricity, for operation as well as illumination.

The 1920s and 30s is the golden age of slot machines. Machines featured elaborate castings, ornate decoration, and numerous gimmicks. Caille, Jennings, Mill, Pace, and Watling are among the leading manufacturers.

References: Jerry Ayliff, *American Premium Guide to Jukeboxes and Slot Machines, Third Edition,* Books Americana, Krause Publications, 1991; Richard M. Bueschel, *Collector's Guide to Vintage Coin Machines,* Schiffer Publishing, 1995; Richard M. Bueschel, *Lemons, Cherries and Bell-Fruit-Gum: Illustrated History of Automatic Payout Slot Machines,* Royal Ben Books, 1995; Marshal Fey, *Slot Machines: A Pictorial History of the First 100 Years, Fourth Edition,* published by author.

Periodicals: *Antique Amusements, Slot Machines & Jukebox Gazette,* 909 26th St NW, Washington, DC 20037; *Coin Drop International,* 5815 W 52nd Ave, Denver, CO 80212; *Loose Change,* 1515 S Commerce St, Las Vegas, NV 89102.

Ace, Special Award, 25¢, 1964 . . . . **$850.00**

Baker, Baker's Pacers, 5¢, 1930s **1,600.00**

Bally, Clover Bell, 1949. . . . . **800.00**

Bally, Deluxe Draw Bell, 1947. . . . . **500.00**

Bally, Money Honey, 25¢, 1964 . . . . **1,400.00**

Benton Harbor, New Imp, 1031. . . . . **900.00**

Brainerd, Vend-N-Slot, 1964 . . . . **500.00**

Caille, Superior Grand Prize, 1931 . . . . **1,600.00**

Caille, Victory Mint, center pull handle, 1924 . . . . **2,750.00**

Fields, 4 Jacks, 1930 . . . . **650.00**

Jennings, Century Tripl-Jack, 1933 . . . . **1,500.00**

Jennings, Little Duke, 1¢, 1935 . . . . **1,150.00**

Jennings, Perfected Jackpot, 10¢, 1930 . . . . **1,400.00**

Jennings, Primer Jackpot Vender, 5¢, 1929. . . . . **1,600.00**

Jennings, Selective Little Duke Jackpot, 1933 . . . . **1,500.00**

Jennings, Silver Moon Chief, 1940 . . . . **1,500.00**

Keeney, Two-Way Bonus Super Bell, 5¢, 1946 . . . . **650.00**

Mills, Bell-O-Matic Model M, 25¢, 1968 . . . . **850.00**

Mills, Futurity, 5¢, 1936 . . . . **1,500.00**

Mills, Golden Falls, 50¢, 1946 . . . . **1,500.00**

Mills, Jewel, 25¢, 1947. . . . . **1,400.00**

Mills, Mystery, 1933. . . . . **1,200.00**

Mills, QT, 1934, 1¢, 1934 . . . . **1,000.00**

Mills, Silent Gooseneck, 1931. . . . . **1,400.00**

Mills, Wild Deuce, 1950 . . . . **1,400.00**

Pace, Bantam Ever-Full Jak-Pot, 1930. . . . . **1,200.00**

Pace, Bantam Jak-Pot, 1930 . . . . **1,200.00**

Olympia Bunny XO, electric, metal and plastic, #0101801 and #039348, 32" h, 19" w, 13" d, $330.00. Photo courtesy Collectors Auction Services.

Pace, Bantam Mint Vender, 1933 . . . . **1,400.00**
Pace, Comet Vender, 1933 . . . . **1,400.00**
Pace, Super Jackpot 4th Reel, $1, 1950 . . . . **2,000.00**
Rock-Ola, Four Aces Ball Gum Vender, 1932 . . . . **900.00**
Vendet, Midget, 1932 . . . . **1,250.00**
Watling, Baby Gold Award Vender, 1934 . . . . **1,700.00**
Watling, Blue Seal, twin jackpot, 1930 . . . . **1,000.00**
Watling, Twin Jackpot, 1931 . . . . **1,400.00**
Watling, Wonder Vender, 1934 . . . . **1,400.00**

SMURFS

Pierro "Peyo" Culliford, a Belgian cartoonist, created the Smurfs. The name is a shortening of "Schtroumpf," a French colloquialism meaning "watchamacallit." Over 100 characters are known.

The Smurfs first appeared as a comic strip. Soon the strips were collected into books and a line of toys licensed. In 1965 Schleich, a German firm, began marketing a line of two-inch high, PVC Smurf figures. A full collection numbers in the hundreds, the result of numerous decorating variations and discontinued markings. The first Smurf figures arrived in the United States in 1979.

After appearing in the movie *Smurfs and the Magic Flute* in 1975, Smurfs secured a permanent place in the collecting field when Hanna-Barbera launched its Smurf Saturday morning cartoon show in 1981.

References: Jan Lindenberger, *Smurf Collectibles: A Handbook & Price Guide* (1996), *More Smurf Collectibles* (1998), Schiffer Publishing.

Collectors' Club: Smurf Collectors Club International, 24 Cabot Rd W, Massapequa, NY 11758.

Birthday Candle, PaPa Smurf with number "4" **$4.00**
Book, *Romeo and Smurfette and 12 Other Smurfy Stories*, soft cover, 1978 . . . . **10.00**
Christmas Stocking, cotton felt, "Have A Smurfy Christmas," 17" h **5.00**
Costume, plastic mask and outfit, Ben Cooper **25.00**
Figure, Doctor, #20037, 1978 . . . . **5.00**
Figure, Gargamel, holding lab glass, #20232, 1992 . . . . **6.00**

Figure, Hiker, #20041, 1978 . . . . **6.00**
Figure, Singers, #20038, 1978 . . . . **5.00**
Hand Puppet, PaPa Smurf, Korea, 1981 . . . . **15.00**
Mug, Sporty Smurf, 1981 . . . . **10.00**
Puzzle, "Hiking Smurfs," diecut cardboard, 100 pcs, Milton Bradley, 1983, 11 x 16" **3.00**
Puzzle, "Spring Beauty," wooden, 12 pcs, Playskool, 1982 . . . . **8.00**
Record, *Smurfing Sing Along,* Sessions Records, 1980 . . . . . **12.00**
Stuffed Toy, Baby Smurf, plastic rattle and eyes, 8" l **6.00**
Stuffed Toy, Brainy, 1984 . . . . **5.00**

SNACK SETS

A snack set consists of two pieces, a cup and a matching underplate. Although glass was the most commonly used material, they also were made in ceramics and plastic. Dating back to the 1920s, the snack set achieved its greatest popularity in the 1950s and 60s. Snack sets were ideal for informal entertaining.

Most snack sets were sold in services consisting of four cups and four plates. Collectors pay a slight premium for a service of four sets in their period box. Some snack sets have become quite expensive, not because they are snack sets but because of their crossover value. Many chintz sets exceed $250.

Newsletter: *Snack Set Searchers,* PO Box 158, Hallock, MN 56728.

Note: Unless noted otherwise, prices are for sets consisting of one cup and one plate.

Anchor Hocking, Blue Mosaic, 8 pcs, MIB **$25.00**
Anchor Hocking, Wexford **3.00**
Blue Ridge, Crab Apple **25.00**
Blue Ridge, Pink Spiderweb, 8 pcs **55.00**
Brockway, Concord Ware, crystal, 8 pcs **10.00**
Federal, Homestead, 8 pcs **7.00**
Federal, Rosecrest, 8 pcs, MIB **10.00**
Hazel Atlas, Apple, white plates, black cups, 8 pcs **10.00**
Hazel Atlas, Seashell, Capri blue, 8 pcs **30.00**
Imperial, Candlewick, 400/98, 8 pcs **20.00**

Federal, black, blue, pink, and yellow flowers on white, 8 pcs, $10.00.

Indiana, Harvest, Carnival green, 8 pcs, MIB	30.00
Indiana, Harvest, milk white, 10 pcs	12.00
Indiana, Sandwich, Chantilly green, for Tiara Home Products, 4 pcs	15.00
Indiana, Snowflake, 8 pcs, MIB	45.00
Japan, blue lustre, white flowers, peach colored cup int	6.00
Japan, green	6.00
Jeannette, Dewdrop, 8 pcs, MIB	20.00
Lefton, Christmas Trees, 22K gold, 8 pcs.	50.00
Lefton, Fruits, 4 pcs.	40.00
Lefton, Rose Chintz, 8 pcs.	45.00
Noritake, Azalea, 4 pcs	140.00
Noritake, floral, gold trim, palette shaped plate, 12 pcs.	50.00
Royal Albert, Braemar	12.00
Royal Albert, Forget-Me-Not	18.00
Sphinx Import Co, 1957 Blue Dresden, shell shaped plate, 16 pcs.	25.00

SNOW BABIES

Snow babies, also known as sugar dolls, are small bisque figurines whose bodies are spattered with glitter sand, thus giving them the appearance of being coated in snow. Most are German or Japanese in origin and date between 1900 and 1940.

The exact origin of these figurines is unknown. The favored theory is that they were developed to honor Admiral Peary's daughter, Marie, born in Greenland on September 12, 1893. The Eskimos named the baby "Ah-Poo-Mickaninny," meaning snow baby. However, it is far more likely they were copied from traditional German sugar candy Christmas ornaments.

Babies, children at play, and Santa Claus are the most commonly found forms. Animal figures also are known. It is estimated that over 1,000 snow baby figurines were made. Many collections number in the hundreds. Do not overlook paper items—snow babies also appeared on postcards and in advertising.

Reference: Mary Morrison, *Snow Babies, Santas, and Elves: Collecting Christmas Bisque Figures*, Schiffer Publishing, 1993.

Are All These Mine?, Department 56, 7977-4, 1988	**$12.00**
Bear, sliding on back, Japan, 2" h.	75.00

Penguin Parade, Department 56, 7986-3, 1992, $32.00.

Bear, walking, Japan, 1" h	50.00
Best Friends, Department 56, 7958-8, 1986	125.00
Boy, ice skating, Japan.	20.00
Boy Skier, carrying poles, 4" h.	10.00
Child Carolers, Japan, 2" h	25.00
Church, with Santa, Japan, 2" h	20.00
Dwarf, playing saxophone, Germany, 2¼" h.	30.00
Girl, with ski poles, Japan	12.00
House, with bird, Germany, 2¾" h.	50.00
Monkey, Japan, 1" h	10.00
Read Me a Story, Department 56, 7945-6, 1990	25.00
Santa, at toy shop, Occupied Japan, 1½" h.	40.00
Santa, hands on belt, Japan, 3" h	50.00
Santa, on roof, Japan, 2¼" h	120.00
Santa, pulling sled, Japan, 2" h	50.00
Santa, with tree, Germany, 2" h	50.00
Skier, plaid shirt, Japan, 3" h	20.00
Snowman, sitting, Japan, 2" h	40.00
Snowman, traffic cop, Japan, 2¾" h	40.00
Woman Skater, Occupied Japan, 2½" h	30.00
Woman Skier, red, Germany, 2¼" h.	40.00
Woman Sledder, winking, Japan, 1¾" h	25.00

SNOW GLOBES

Snow globes originated in Europe in the mid-18th century. Manufacturing was primarily a cottage industry. Constantly gaining in popularity during the later decades of the Victorian era and the first three decades of the 20th century, the snow globe became extremely popular in the 1930s and early 1940s. Although the first American patent dates from the late 1920s, most globes sold in the 1930s were imported from Germany and Japan. They consisted primarily of a round ball on a ceramic or plastic base.

William M. Snyder founded Atlas Crystal Works, first located in Trenton, New Jersey, and later Covington, Tennessee, in the early 1940s to fill the snow globe void created by World War II. Driss Company of Chicago and Progressive Products of Union, New Jersey, were American firms making snow globes in the post-war period. Driss manufactured a series based on four popular characters (Davy Crockett, Frosty the Snowman, The Lone Ranger, and Rudoph the Red Nosed Reindeer); Progressive made advertising and award products.

The plastic domed snow globe arrived on the scene in the early 1950s. Initially German in origin, the concept was quickly copied by Japanese manufacturers. After a period of decline in the late 1960s and 70s, a snow globe renaissance occurred in the 1980s, the result of snow globes designed for the giftware market.

References: Nancy McMichael, *Snowdomes*, Abbeville Press, 1990; Connie A. Moore and Harry L. Rinker, *Snow Globes*, Courage Books, 1993.

Newsletter: *Roadside Attractions*, 7553 Norton Ave, Apt 4, Los Angeles, CA 90046.

Collectors' Club: Snowdome Collectors Club, PO Box 53262, Washington, DC 20009.

Archies Lobster House, glass globe, plastic base, fishing boat above metallic blue fish and 2 red lobsters, opposite view of female swimmer beneath boat, Roanoke, VA	**$100.00**

Snowman, plastic dome, mkd "China," 1980s, 5¹/₂" h, $15.00.

SOAKIES

Soakies, plastic figural character bubble bath bottles, were developed to entice children into the bathtub. Soakies, now a generic term for all plastic bubble bath bottles, originates from "Soaky," a product of the Colgate Palmolive Company.

Colgate Palmolive licensed numerous popular characters, e.g., Rocky and Bullwinkle, Felix the Cat, and Universal Monsters. Colgate Palmolive's success was soon copied, e.g., Purex's Bubble Club. Purex licensed the popular Hanna-Barbera characters. Avon, DuCair Bioessence, Koscot, Lander Company, and Stephen Reiley are other companies who have produced Soakies.

Soakies arrived on the scene in the early 1960s and have remained in production since. Most are 10" high. Over a hundred different Soakies have been produced. Many are found in two or more variations, e.g., there are five versions of Bullwinkle.

Reference: Gregg Moore and Joe Pizzo, *Collector's Guide to Bubble Bath Containers*, Collector Books, 1999.

Atom Ant, Purex, 1965 . . . . $60.00
Baloo Bear, Purex, 1966 . . . . 20.00
Batman, Purex 75.00
Bullwinkle, Colgate-Palmolive, 1966 . . . . 45.00
Casper, Colgate-Palmolive, 1960s 30.00
Cinderella, Purex, 1960s 15.00
El Cabong, Purex, 1964 . . . . 70.00
Explosives Truck, Colgate-Palmolive, 1960s 25.00
Frankenstein, Colgate-Palmolive, 1965 . . . . 75.00
Gravel Truck, Colgate-Palmolive, 1960s 25.00
Huckleberry Hound, Purex, 1960s 25.00
Little Orphan Annie, Lander, 1977 . . . . 25.00
Magilla Gorilla, Purex, 1960s 70.00
Morocco Mole, Purex, 1966 . . . . 75.00
Mr Magoo, Colgate-Palmolive, 1960s. 30.00
Mush Mouse, Purex, 1960s 45.00
Paul McCartney, Colgate-Palmolive, 1965. . . . . 100.00
Punkin' Puss, Purex, 1966 . . . . 45.00
Quick Draw McGraw, Purex, 1960s. 25.00
Ricochet Rabbit, Purex, 1964 . . . . 45.00
Rocky, Colgate-Palmolive, 1962 . . . . 25.00

Bedrock City, plastic dome, Fred standing next to palm tree ready to give bone to Dino, Bedrock and mountains background, "Bedrock City Kelowana B.C.," ©Hanna-Barbera Prod, Inc, 1981 . . . . 20.00
Disneyland Pirates of the Caribbean, bottle shaped, 1960s, 2 x 5 x 2¹/₄" 100.00
Dunlop Tire Distributors, glass dome, plastic base, Dunlop whitewall tire near building scene of distributorship building, front of base with distributor name and Brighton, MA, 1950s, orig box. 100.00
Fighter Plane, glass globe, black ceramic base, 1940s 100.00
Michelin, plastic dome and base, Mr Bib as snowman wearing blue jacket, yellow neck scarf, cap, gloves and boots, beside him is brown groundhog holding green sprig, snow covered pine trees and mountains background. 50.00
Nautilus Atomic Sub, glass globe, red plastic base, Driss Co, Chicago, mid-1950s 100.00
Newspaper "Oscar" Newsboy Award, glass dome, plastic base, striding newsboy figure, "Oscar Award For Outstanding Achievement/The Patriot/The Evening News/Sunday Patriot News," 1950s 50.00
Rudolph the Red-Nosed Reindeer, glass dome, Rudolph atop green plastic base with name on front decal, Driss Co, Chicago, 1950s 50.00
Santa, plastic dome and base, Santa in red and white outfit with sack over his shoulders, Hong Kong 50.00
The Lone Ranger Round-Up, glass globe, black plastic base, Lone Ranger holding string in right hand which is attached to white ring which can be manipulated to go over jumping calf, right side with yellow and black decal with image of Lone Ranger and name in rope design, Driss Co, Chicago, ©LR, Inc, 1940s 75.00
The Wizard of Oz, plastic dome and base, characters on Yellow Brick Road, 1970s 50.00
Winnepeg Jets, plastic dome, hockey puck positioned in front of plastic netted goal cage with loose puck, orig box, from 1989 series for the 21 National Hockey League teams 20.00
Wonderful World of Disney, plastic dome, Mickey and Minnie in front of Sleeping Beauty's castle, front panel with "The Wonderful World of Disney," 1970s 50.00

Top Cat, 10¹/₈" h, $20.00.

Secret Squirrel, Purex, 1966 . . . . **75.00**
Smokey the Bear, Lander. **25.00**
Snow White, Colgate-Palmolive, movable arms, 1960s **20.00**
Speedy Gonzales, Colgate-Palmolive, 1960s. **30.00**
Spider-Man, Colgate-Palmolive, 1977. . . . . **20.00**
Squiddly Diddly Bubble Club, Purex, 1960s **75.00**
Superman, Colgate-Palmolive, 1965. . . . . **50.00**
Tennessee Tuxedo, Colgate-Palmolive, 1965 . . . . **30.00**
Tidy Toys Race Car, Colgate-Palmolive, 1960s. **25.00**
Wolfman, Colgate-Palmolive, 1963 . . . . **80.00**
Woodsy Owl, Lander **60.00**
Woody Woodpecker, Colgate, 1977. . . . . **40.00**
Yogi Bear, Purex, 1960s. **20.00**

SODA POP COLLECTIBLES

In addition to Coca-Cola, Pepsi, and Moxie, there are thousands of soda brands, ranging from regional to national, attracting collector interest. In the 1920s Americans became enamored with buying soda in a bottle to consume at their leisure. Tens of thousands of local bottling plants sprang up across America, producing flavors ranging from cream to sarsaparilla. Some brands achieved national popularity, e.g., Grapette and Hires.

Capitalizing on the increased consumption of soda pop during World War II, manufacturers launched a major advertising blitz in the late 1940s and early 1950s. From elaborate signs to promotional premiums, the soda industry was determined to make its influence felt. The soda bubble burst in the early 1970s. Most local and regional bottling plants ceased operations or were purchased by larger corporations. A few national brands survived and dominate the market.

References: Thomas E. Marsh, *The Official Guide to Collecting Applied Color Label Soda Bottles, Vol. II,* published by author, 1995; Tom Morrison, *Root Beer* (1992), *More Root Beer* (1997), Schiffer Publishing; Allan Petretti, *Petretti's Soda Pop Collectibles Price Guide, 2nd Edition,* Antique Trader Books, 1999; Jeff Walters, *The Complete Guide to Collectible Picnic Coolers & Ice Chests,* Memory Lane, 1994.

Periodical: *Club Soda,* PO Box 489, Troy, ID 83871.

Collectors' Clubs: The Cola Club, PO Box 158715, Nashville, TN 37215; Dr. Pepper 10-2-4 Collectors Club, 3100 Monticello, Ste 890, Dallas, TX 75205; Grapette Collectors Club, 2240 Hwy 27N, Nashville, AR 71852; National Pop Can Collectors, 19201 Sherwood Green Way, Gaithersburg, MD 20879; Painted Soda Bottle Collectors Assoc, 9418 Hilmer Dr, La Mesa, CA 91942.

Note: For additional listings see Coca-Cola, Moxie, and Pepsi-Cola.

Ashtray, 7-Up, green glass, bottle shaped, red and white
   label, 8" l **$10.00**
Ashtray, B1 Lemon Lime Soda, red center, white lettering, 3½" sq **6.00**
Backbar Sign, "Orange Crush Carbonated Beverage,"
   glass, later frame and chain hanger, 9" d **160.00**
Backbar Syrup Bottle, Liggett's Cherriade, heavy chrome
   over base metal, orig cap, c1920s **150.00**
Barrel Tag, Hire's Root Beer, painted stainless steel, 4 x 6". . . . **100.00**
Barrel Tag, Richardson's Root Beer, aluminum, c1940s **55.00**
Barrel Tag, Smith-Junior Root Beer, tin, curved, 16" w **90.00**

Chalkboard, Whistle, emb tin, 1948, 27" h, 20" w, NOS, **$825.00.** Photo courtesy Collectors Auction Services.

Belt Buckle, Dr Pepper, enameled, 1930s. **200.00**
Blotter, Canada Dry, 1930s **12.00**
Blotter, Dr Pepper, c1930s. **110.00**
Bottle, Canada Dry, miniature **15.00**
Bottle, Frostie, miniature **10.00**
Bottle, Hi-Fi Beverages, applied color label **4.00**
Bottle Bag, Hires, 1940s **20.00**
Bottle Cap, Kist Grapefruit. **4.00**
Bottle Cap, Mason's Root Beer. **4.00**
Bottle Carrier, Barq's Root Beer, cardboard, 1950s **150.00**
Bottle Carrier, Nehi, wire, 1930s **90.00**
Bottle Opener, Canada Dry, metal, wall mount, gray and
   red raised lettering, Starr X Brown Co, 3¼" h, 2¼" w **50.00**
Bottle Topper, Dr Pepper, cardboard, 1940s, 6 x 8" **1,500.00**
Calendar, 7-Up, 1961 . . . . **30.00**
Calendar, Double Cola, 1953 . . . . **75.00**
Calendar, Dr Pepper, 1955. . . . . **180.00**
Calendar, Dr Pepper, 1976 . . . . **40.00**
Calendar, Grapette, 1949 . . . . **24.00**
Calendar, Mission Orange, 1953 . . . . **65.00**
Calendar, Nehi, 1937 . . . . **350.00**
Calendar, NuGrape, 1949, woman lying on sled **70.00**
Calendar, NuGrape, 1955 . . . . **65.00**
Calendar, Orange Crush, 1932, girl in swimsuit **75.00**
Calendar, Orange Crush, 1946. . . . . **250.00**
Calendar, Royal Crown Cola, 1950, Wanda Hendrix
   photo **35.00**
Calendar, Royal Crown Cola, 1968 . . . . **75.00**
Calendar, Squirt, 1949, smiling woman holding bottle to
   mouth. **55.00**
Calendar, Squirt, 1953. . . . . **50.00**
Calendar, Sun Crest Soda, 1953. . . . . **45.00**
Can, Fresca, aluminum, pull tab **6.00**
Can, Old Fashioned Ma's Root Beer, steel, cone top **40.00**
Clicker, Smile, tin, 1930s. **25.00**
Clock, Dr Pepper, light-up, fiberboard, c1940s, 15" d **425.00**
Cooler, Squirt, yellow enamel, red "Drink Squirt" on
   front and back, handle forms locking mechanism,
   Progress Refrigerating Co, 17½ x 13¼ x 17". **130.00**
Cooler, Whistle, metal, red, "Thirsty? Just Whistle" and
   logo, bail handles, Progress Refrigerator Co, 11¾" h **160.00**
Door Push, Squirt, emb tin, 1941. **210.00**

Figure, Squirt, boy with bottle, c1947, 13" h **1,000.00**

Flange Sign, Nehi, tin, "Drink Nehi Ice Cold," c1940s,
18 x 13" **525.00**

Game, Dr Pepper, Skill Dice, 1943 . . . . **40.00**

Globe, Rochester Root Beer, white milk glass, 8" d **90.00**

Menu Board, Orange Crush, "Ask for Orange-Crush
Carbonated Beverage," scoreboard scene, 1940s, 23 x
36" **85.00**

Menu Board, Teem, rect, emb painted tin, bottle and
"Enjoy Teem a Lemon-Lime Drink," 22" h, 26" w **20.00**

Mirror, Grapette, "Thirsty Or Not…You'll Enjoy Grapette
Soda," 1930–40s, 8 x 16". **170.00**

Mug, Hire's Root Beer, clear glass, applied color label **20.00**

Needle Case, Nu Grape, 1930s **45.00**

Pinback Button, Spur, "Drink Spur Big Bottle 5¢," cellu-
loid, 1950s, 2" d **5.00**

Pocketknife, Pop Kola, 1950s **40.00**

Poster, Double Cola, woman in red cap holding bottle,
1940s, framed and matted under glass **170.00**

Push Plate, 7-Up, tin, 1940s **25.00**

Push Plate, Dr Pepper, 1950s **125.00**

Screen Door Brace, Bubble Up, emb tin, 12 x 6" **120.00**

Serving Tray, Canada Dry, logo center, 1950 . . . . **45.00**

Sidewalk Marker, 7-Up, brass **40.00**

Sidewalk Marker, Grapette, brass, 1940–50s **45.00**

Sign, Blue Bird, "let's drink Blue Bird More delicious
than Grape Juice!," tin over cardboard, with string
hanger, 6 x 9" **75.00**

Sign, Busch Ginger Ale, porcelain, 1920s, 11 x 21" **475.00**

Sign, Canada Dry Spur 5¢, bottle illus, emb tin, 3½ x 12". . . . **35.00**

Sign, Donald Duck Soft Drinks, celluloid, 1940–50s,
9" d **50.00**

Sign, Drink Bireley's For Real Fruit Taste, tin, 13" l **10.00**

Sign, Dr Pepper, celluloid over tin over cardboard,
1930–40s, 8 x 11" **1,000.00**

Sign, Frostie Root Beer, figural cap, emb tin, c1940s,
12" d **360.00**

Sign, Mission Orange, emb tin, "Ice Cold," c1940s, 11 x
28" **170.00**

Toy Truck, Squirt, friction, litho tin, rubber tires, Japan, 8" l, $192.00. Photo courtesy Collectors Auction Services.

Sign, Nesbitt's Orange, button, tin over cardboard, self-
framed, professor with bottle at blackboard, "Don't
Say orange Say Nesbitt's, a soft drink made from real
Oranges," c1950, 9¼" d **65.00**

Sign, NuGrape, diecut cardboard, laminated, 6 x 11" **70.00**

Sign, NuGrape, tin, emb tin, framed under glass,
c1930s, 4½ x 12" **150.00**

Sign, Old Colony Lemonade, celluloid, 9" d **30.00**

Sign, Orange Crush, emb plastic, 1950–60s, 10 x 12". **35.00**

Sign, Red Rock Cola, emb tin, "Drink," "Red Rock
Cola/Enjoy Red Rock Cola" on bottle, 1939, 8 x 32" **250.00**

Sign, Royal Crown Cola, emb tin, "Drink Royal Crown
Cola Best By Taste-Test," 1952, 22 x 34" **180.00**

Sign, Wonder Orange, "For Fresh Fruity Flavor Drink
Wonder Orange Delicious-Refreshing," tin, 1930s–
40s, 6 x 9" **350.00**

Sign, Zippp's Cherri-O, framed under glass, c1930s, 7 x
16" **110.00**

Soda Jerk Cap, Orange-Crush, 1939 . . . . **20.00**

Straw Box, Whistle, full, 1949–50 . . . . **185.00**

Syrup Dispenser, Cherry Smash, dec on both sides, "5¢"
on ends, gold stripes trim, c1920 . . . . **1,300.00**

Syrup Dispenser, Howel's Orange-Julep, ceramic, ball
shaped, adv both sides, 15½" h **2,100.00**

Syrup Dispenser, Ward's Lemon Crush, figural lemon,
reproduction ball pump, 1920s **700.00**

Thermometer, Dr Pepper, plastic, figural bottle cap,
1950–60s, 11" d **80.00**

Thermometer, Dr Pepper, tin, "frosty, man, frosty!,"
1950–60s, 6 x 16" **800.00**

Thermometer, Kist, tin, "Did you get Kist Today?," 1950s **175.00**

Thermometer, Mason's Root Beer, tin, "Keg Brewed
Flavor," 1950s **50.00**

Thermometer, Orange Crush, "Naturally—It Tastes
Better! It's The Natural Fresh Fruit Flavor," 1930–40s,
6 x 15" **290.00**

Thermometer, Whistle, "Thirsty? Just Whistle," 1940s,
12" d **325.00**

Thermometer, Wishing Well Orange, tin, self-framed,
bottle, "Drink Wishing Well Orange," c1961, 40½" h,
10½" w **195.00**

Tray, Major Cola, majorette and marching band, "Keep
In Step With Major Cola," 1940s, 10 x 15" **125.00**

Whistle, Whistle Soda, tin, 1940s **25.00**

Clock, Royal Crown Cola, orange neon light-up, metal and plastic with glass insert at top, 34" h, 37" w, $1,100.00. Photo courtesy Collectors Auction Services.

SOUVENIRS

Novelty souvenirs featuring historical or natural landmarks with identifying names were popular keepsakes prior to World War I. Commemorative pieces include plates issued during anniversary celebrations and store premiums, many of which featured calendars. Souvenirs tend to be from carnivals, fairs, popular tourist attractions and hotels, and world's fairs.

The souvenir spoon arrived on the scene in the late 1880s. In the 1920s the demitasse spoon replaced the teaspoon as the favored size. The souvenir spoon craze finally ended in the 1950s, albeit the form can still be found today.

Plastic souvenir items dominate the post–World War II period. Many pieces were generic with only the name of the town, site, or state changed from one piece to another. In the late 1960s ceramic commemorative plates enjoyed a renaissance.

The vast majority of items sold in today's souvenir shops have nothing on them to indicate their origin. Souvenir shops are gift shops, designed to appeal to the universal taste of the buyer.

References: Pamela E. Apkarian-Russell, *A Collector's Guide to Salem Witchcraft & Souvenirs,* Schiffer Publishing, 1998; Wayne Bednersh, *Collectible Souvenir Spoons,* Collector Books, 1998; Monica Lynn Clements and Patricia Rosser Clements, *Popular Souvenir Plates,* Schiffer Publishing, 1998; Dorothy T. Rainwater and Donna H. Felger, *American Spoons, Souvenir and Historical,* Everybodys Press, Schiffer Publishing, 1977; Dorothy T. Rainwater and Donna H. Felger, *Spoons From Around the World,* Schiffer Publishing, 1992; David Weingarten and Margaret Majua, *Monumental Miniatures,* Antique Trader Books, 1998; Laurence W. Williams, *Collector's Guide to Souvenir China,* Collector Books, 1998.

Newsletter: *Antique Souvenir Collector,* Box 562, Great Barrington, MA 01230.

Collectors' Clubs: American Spoon Collectors, 7408 Englewood Ln, Raytown, MO 64133; The Scoop Club, 84 Oak Ave, Shelton, CT 06484; Souvenir Building Collectors Society, PO Box 70, Nellysford, VA 22958; Statue of Liberty Collectors' Club, 26601 Bernwood Rd, Cleveland, OH 44122.

Note: See Advertising, British Royal Commemoratives, Patriotic, Postcards, and World's Fair for additional listings.

Ashtray, Arizona, ceramic, yellow and brown, "The Grand Canyon State," map and picture in center, 8³/₄" w. **$7.00**
Ashtray, Florida, compressed wood, 4" d **4.00**
Ashtray, London, ceramic, blue, cream bottom, white letters in center **6.00**
Ashtray, Minnesota, ceramic, state shape, white **4.00**
Ashtray, Plains, Georgia, ceramic, peanut shaped, tan, "Went Nuts in Plains Georgia" **6.00**
Ashtray, San Francisco, ceramic, foot shaped, tan, "We get a kick out of San Francisco" **5.00**
Bank, Dime Savings Bank of Brooklyn, ceramic, depicts Liberty head dime, rear has slotted ceramic coin reservoir and extends forward to tray front, tray has recesses for pencils and paper clips, underside has applied cork skid pad plus metal trap, cork imprinted "Dime Savings Bank Of Brooklyn" with addresses of 6 branch offices, 1950s **50.00**

Bank, Empire State Building, 7³/₄" h **68.00**
Brochure, Illustrated Souvenir of New York, 48 pp, story of New York and view guide, 169 photos, color Art Deco cover with Indians in foreground and sailing ship in bay, 1946. . . . . **15.00**
Brochure, Pictorial Souvenir of New York, 64 pp, over 160 photos, 2-pp picture map of NY, map of theatre and transportation map of Greater New York, Art Deco cover, 1948. . . . . **18.00**
Building, American Fletcher National Bank **110.00**
Building, Chrysler Building, NY, 5³/₄" h. **95.00**
Building, Eiffel Tower, Paris, 4¹/₈" h **55.00**
Building, The White House, Made in Japan, 1¹/₄" h **28.00**
Drinking Glass, Coney Island, frosted, red and blue illus of amusement rides Cyclone, Parachute Jump, and Wonder Wheel, 1950s, 4⁷/₈" h **50.00**
Drinking Glass, Illinois, frosted **8.00**
Drinking Glass, Minnesota, "Hello Shorewood Lounge, Fridley, Minn.," black dec, Libbey, orig box **7.00**
Flicker, Mt Rushmore, depicts "before" rocky cliff and "after" completed rock carvings, 1960s **20.00**
Keychain, figural palm tree, celluloid, attached tag "Here Is The Palm Tree I Promised You From Florida," 2" h **20.00**
Pencil Sharpener, Niagara Falls, Canada, celluloid boat with white hull, blue insert figural upper deck topped by white smokestack, Germany, c1930s **20.00**
Pennant, Freedomland USA, felt, red, white printing, multicolored park views, 8¹/₂ x 26". **18.00**
Pinback Button, Ocean City, black and white photo of toddler girl for observance week, "Ocean City Seashore Home for Babies," 1930s. **15.00**
Pinback Button, "Visit Bermuda," white lily with green stem, red inscription, dark blue ground, 1920s **15.00**
Plate, California, scenic landmarks, mkd "Made in Japan," 1950s **10.00**
Plate, Cheyenne, WY, coupe, multi-scene. **50.00**

Plate, Souvenir of Indianapolis, "Made in Staffordshire England Imported Exclusively for Acme Novelty Co. Indianapolis, Ind." backstamp, 7³/₄" d, $82.00. Photo courtesy Collectors Auction Services.

Plate, Elizabethtown, NY, coupe, multicolor scene **30.00**

Pocket Comb, with case, celluloid, Indian profile,
Niagara Falls, Canada **12.00**

Postcard, "Greetings From Coney Island," butcher slicing
tail from dog as another dog with bandage over
removed tail serves as waiter for frankfurters, 1940s **20.00**

Salt and Pepper Shakers, pr, different states, Milford
Pottery State series. **10.00**

Salt and Pepper Shakers, pr, Mt Hood, OR, mountains
and flower scene. **15.00**

Salt Shaker, Mt Vernon Mansion, VA, rose decals flank-
ing scene, Germany. **15.00**

Snow Globe, Florida, plastic, flamingo by palm tree **20.00**

Spoon, Clifford Park, sterling, poppy flower blooms on
single sided handle, 4" l. **20.00**

Tape Measure, Florida, silvered metal canister with identical multicolored celluloid caps on each side depicting ripened oranges with white blossoms and green
stem leaves on blue ground, "Souvenir of Florida,"
cloth tape, 1930s. **20.00**

Tape Measure, Niagara Falls, silver luster metal canister,
multicolored celluloid insert depicting sunset with
rainbow on foreground waterfall, "Twilight Over
American And Horseshoe Falls," cloth tape, 1930s **15.00**

Tea Cloth, scenes of New York landmarks. **145.00**

Ticket, United States Auto Club Races, Trenton, NJ
Speedway, Sun, Apr 27, 1969 . . . . **8.00**

Ticket, Young's Pier, Atlantic City, celluloid, for 10¢ ride,
color photo of "Flip-Flap Railway" amusement ride. **75.00**

SPACE ADVENTURERS, FICTIONAL

Philip Francis Nowland and John F. Dille launched *Buck Rogers 2429 A.D.* in January 1929. The late 1930s was the golden age of this famous space explorer. Buck Rogers in the 25th Century, a television program airing between September 1979 and April 1981, created a renewed interest in Buck.

Flash Gordon was Buck Rogers' main rival in the 1930s. The 1940s was Flash's golden age. A second generation became hooked on Flash when the movie serials were repeated dozens of times on television in the late 1940s and 50s.

Americans were enamored by space in the early 1950s. Television responded with Captain Video and His Video Rangers, Flash Gordon, Rocky Jones Space Ranger, Space Patrol, and Tom Corbett, Space Cadet. A second generation of space adventure series, e.g., Lost in Space and Star Trek, was launched in the 1960s and 70s. Spinoffs such as Deep Space Nine and Babylon 5 have kept the legend of the space adventurer alive on television.

Reference: Stuart W. Wells III, *Science Fiction Collectibles*, Krause Publications, 1999.

Collectors' Club: Galaxy Patrol, 22 Colton St, Worcester, MA 01610.

Note: For additional listings see Premiums, Space Toys, Star Trek and Star Wars.

Battlestar Galactica, action figure, Cylon Centurian,
black and silver, with laser pistol and backpack unit,
clicking noise produced and gun flashes when button
on backpack pressed, Mattel, ©1978 Universal City
Studios, orig box **$75.00**

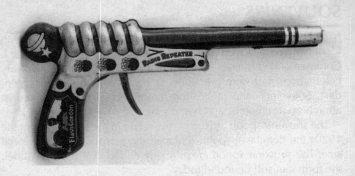

Flash Gordon, Radio Repeater, litho tin, silver and red, Marx, $85.00.

Buck Rogers, Flash Blast Attack Ship, red and white cast
metal body, Tootsietoy, 1937, 4½" l **75.00**

Buck Rogers, rubber band gun, stiff paper sheet with
punch-outs, includes gun with portraits of Buck and
Wilma on handle and targets of spaceship, sea monster and Wing Bat Wu, orig rubber bands attached at
lower right corner, Onward School Supplies, ©1940
John F Dille Co, 5 x 10". **100.00**

Captain Marvel, watch, full figure image of Captain
Marvel, orig green vinyl straps, glow-in-the-dark
hands, ©1958 Fawcett Pub, orig 1¼ x 1⅝" case **200.00**

Captain Video, flying saucer ring, Powerhouse Candy
Bars premium, night and day saucers, instructions
sheets, mailer box, c1951 . . . . **375.00**

ET, calendar, 1983. . . . . **15.00**

ET, doll, Talking ET, plastic, pull string talker, 1982, 7" h **20.00**

ET, finger light, wearable, glows when pressed,
Knickerbocker, 1982 . . . . **15.00**

ET, game, ET Card Game, Parker Bros, 1982. . . . . **15.00**

ET, postcard, Steven Spielberg with ET **2.00**

Flash Gordon, book, *Flash Gordon in the Ice World of
Mongo,* Whitman Better Little Book, #1433, ©1942
King Features Syndicate, Inc. **75.00**

Flash Gordon, Dixie lid, purpletone photo of "Buster
Crabbe Starring In the Universal Chapter Play Flash
Gordon," 1936 . . . . **20.00**

Flash Gordon, figure, wood composition, mkd "1944
King Features copyright" on back of base, 5" h **375.00**

Lost in Space, cast publicity photo, black and white
glossy, 1960s, 8 x 10" **50.00**

Lost in Space, helmet and gun set, Remco, 1967 . . . . **300.00**

Lost in Space, writing tablet, cov with June Lockhart as
Maureen Robinson wearing silver flight uniform,
unused, 8 x 10". **25.00**

Matt Mason, jigsaw puzzle, "Round Jigsaw Puzzle," 20"
d, color illus of Mason and friends on lunar surface,
gathered around fire bolt space cannon with 2 spacemen attacking them from above, Earth in background,
Whitman, ©1969 Mattel, orig 11 x 11 x 2½" box **20.00**

Matt Mason, Satellite Launch Pak, white hard plastic
launcher unit with 4 different colored "Communications Satellite" and sticker sheet, ©1967 Mattel, orig
8½ x 12" blister card **50.00**

Planet of the Apes, book, *Beneath the Planet of the Apes* **1.00**

Planet of the Apes, costume, Warrior, plastic mask, 1-pc
vinyl rayon outfit, orig 8 x 11 x 3½" box, Ben Cooper,
©1974 20th Century Fox Film Corp **50.00**

Planet of the Apes, figure, Soldier Ape, flexible rubber, brown, black and yellow accents, green eyes, holding white knife in hand, ©1963 Apjac Productions, Inc, 6" h **20.00**

Planet of the Apes, kite, vinyl, image of Cornelius in shades of brown, black, and blue, Hi-Flyer Mfg Co, ©Apjac Productions, Inc, c1974, orig 4¼ x 30" display bag with header card **50.00**

Space: 1999, Adventure Playset, diecut cardboard pcs form Moon Base Alpha building, with working elevator, 2 Eagle spacecraft, moon buggy, and complete cast of astronauts, alien people, and sea monsters, Amsco, ©1975 ATV Licensing Ltd, orig 13½ x 20 x 1" box. **75.00**

Space: 1999, Eagle Transporter, hard plastic, friction motor, metallic green, white, and silver with logo stickers atop lunar landscape cardboard base, on 3½ x 8 x 6½" blister card, Ahi, ©1976 ATV Licensing Ltd **75.00**

Space: 1999, Moon Base Survival Kit, hard plastic Swiss Army knife, white case with metallic red logo, 7 different retractable silver utensil/tools, on 3½ 8 x 6½" blister card, ©1976 ATV Licensing Ltd **75.00**

Space Patrol, Chart of the Universe, paper, illus of planets with "Space Distances From Earth To Planetary Orbits," orig came with Buzz Corey Space Patrol wristwatch from US Time, 1951, 8½ x 10¾". **75.00**

Space Patrol, rocketship card, stiff paper, black and white glossy front, illus of Terra IV with customized Ralston design and Buzz Corey facsimile signature, reverse with Top Secret information on ship, issued by Ralston, c1953 . . . . **20.00**

Tom Corbett Space Cadet, frame tray puzzle, color illus, Saalfield Publishing Co, ©1952 Rockhill Productions, 10 x 11¼". **50.00**

Tom Corbett Space Cadet, lunch box, metal, decal on front, Aladdin Industries, ©1952 Rockhill Radio, 7 x 8 x 4". **100.00**

V, action figure, red and black suit, "lizard" head with extendible tongue, complete with human mask and gun, orig box, LJN, ©1984 Warner Bros, 12" h **50.00**

SPACE EXPLORATION

Collector interest in artifacts relating to the manned space program began in the early 1980s. After a brief fascination with autographed material, collectors moved to three-dimensional objects.

The collapse of the Soviet Union coupled with Russia's and several cosmonauts' need for capital has resulted in the sale of space memorabilia by several leading auction houses around the world. Everything from capsules to space suits are available for purchase.

This category focuses primarily on material associated with manned space flight. Collector interest in material from unmanned flights is extremely limited.

Reference: Stuart Schneider, *Collecting the Space Race,* Schiffer Publishing, 1993.

Newsletter: *Space Autograph News,* 862 Thomas Ave, San Diego, CA 92109.

Ashtray, ceramic, white, center image of astronaut and moon surface, Leonard Jed Co 100th Anniversary commemorative, 1970, 6¾" d **$20.00**

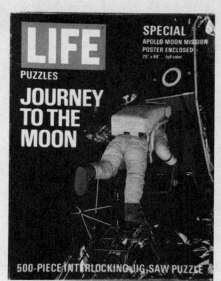

Jigsaw Puzzle, *Life* magazine cover, "Journey to the Moon" Apollo moon mission poster, 500 pcs, 1969 ©Schisgall Enterprises and Time, Inc., $20.00.

Bank, *Sputnik,* litho tin, satellite shape, c1959 . . . . **125.00**

Book, *American Space Digest,* paperback, Schick Safety Razor premium, 64 pp, 1963 . . . . **25.00**

Book, *First On the Moon,* Neil Armstrong, Michael Collins, and Edwin E Aldrin Jr, 1970 . . . . **50.00**

Booklet, Pictorial Record of the American Space Explorations," reprint from *New York Times,* glossy, NASA photos and diagrams, 24 pp, 1969, 8¼ x 10¾". **25.00**

Brochure, Congressional Space Committee, historical review of space program, 8 pp, 1970, 9½ x 14" **18.00**

Brochure, "Space Shuttle," details space shuttle program, 12 pp, 1972, 9¼ x 11¾" **15.00**

Coin, Space Magic, paper insert with astronauts pictured on 1 side and text on back, plastic rims, Krun-Chee Potato Chips premium, mid-1960s, 1⅜" d **4.00**

Drinking Glass, clear glass, command module shape, "Apollo 11, Man On The Moon," 6" h **10.00**

Magazine, *Newsweek,* Apr 27, 1981 . . . . **5.00**

Matchcover, rocket launch and lunar landing scenes, 1969. . . . . **6.00**

Medal, sterling silver, commemorates moon landing, "One Small Step" inscription, acrylic case, 1½" d **35.00**

Mug, ceramic, white, "Kennedy Space Center, Florida" and color emblems from missions 7 through 17, c1973, 4¾" h **20.00**

Patch, cloth, Space Shuttle *Columbia,* 1981 . . . . **8.00**

Photograph, Grodon Cooper, sgd, 1961 . . . . **125.00**

Pinback Button, center photo of Sally Ride and *Challenger,* "Sally Ride, First American Woman In Space, June 18–24, 1983" rim inscription, 3½" d **12.00**

Poster, Space Shuttle, Postal Service issue, 1981 . . . . **20.00**

Record, *Lunar Landing/Man on the Moon,* 33⅓ rpm, *Apollo 11* highlights, Metropolitan Life premium, with sleeve, 1969 . . . . **15.00**

Scrapbook, Space Pak Album, with cards, 1962, 7 x 12½" **75.00**

Spoon, silver, moon landing commemorative, "Armstrong, Aldrin, Collins" engraved in bowl, "Apollo 11, July 20 1969, Man On The Moon" and astronaut saluting flag on handle, display box, 6" l **25.00**

View-Master Reel, Moon Rockets and Guided Missiles, "Cape Canaveral and the Navaho," "Atlas and Titan," and "The Moon Rockets," 1959, set of 3 . . . . **25.00**

SPACE TOYS

Space toys divide into three basic groups: (1) astronauts and spacemen, (2) spacecraft (capsules, flying saucers, rockets, and satellites), and (3) tanks and vehicles. Robots are excluded. They have reached the level of independent collecting status.

The toy industry, especially the Japanese, responded quickly to the growing worldwide interest in manned space flight. The first lithographed tin toys arrived on the market in the late 1940s. Toys became increasingly sophisticated during the 1950s. The number of parts that lit up or made sounds increased.

Plastic became the principal construction material by the early 1970s. Production shifted from Japan to China and Taiwan, a move that collectors view as having cheapened the toys. The decline in public interest in the space program in the mid-1970s also led to a decline in the production of space toys. Most collectors focus on space toys made prior to 1970.

The period box is an essential component of value, often adding 25% to 40% to the toy's value. The artwork on the box often is more impressive than the toy itself. Further, the box may contain information about the name of the toy, manufacturer, and/or distributor not found on the toy itself.

References: Dana Cain, *UFO & Alien Collectibles Price Guide*, Krause Publications, 1998; Dennis Way Nicholson (comp.), *The Gerry Anderson Memorabilia Guide*, Cooee Concepts Pty (Australia), 1994; Maxine A. Pinsky, *Marx Toys: Robots, Space, Comic, Disney & TV Characters*, Schiffer Publishing, 1996; Stuart W. Wells III, *Science Fiction Collectibles*, Krause Publications, 1999.

Periodicals: *Toy Shop*, 700 E State St, Iola, WI 54990; *Toy Trader*, PO Box 1050, Dubuque, IA 52004.

Note: For additional listings see Robots, Space Adventurers, Star Trek and Star Wars.

Apollo Spacecraft, litho tin, battery operated, astronaut head bobs up and down as ship moves, Daiya, Japan, 1960s, 11" l. **$100.00**

Archer Space Gun, gray plastic, clicking sound, 1950s, 5½" l **55.00**

Astronaut Air Pump, litho tin, depicts astronaut holding air pump standing next to rocket, Japan, 7½" h **100.00**

Astronaut Space Helmet, plastic, NASA decal and attached "Space Mike," green tinted retractable visor, Dekker, England, orig box, 12" h **200.00**

Atomic Ball Gun, plastic, spring loaded, 3 plastic balls, M&L Toy, orig box **85.00**

Atomic Cap Firing Rocket, plastic, screaming sound, Ideal, orig box, 14" l **225.00**

Cosmic Ray Gun, plastic, red, blue, and amber, transparent barrel, sparking action, Ranger Steel Products, orig box, 1950s, 8" l **40.00**

Explorer Spaceship, Japan, 1950s, 4½" l **100.00**

Flashy-Ray Gun, litho tin, makes noise, flash appears within celluloid and tin barrel, TN, Japan, orig box, 1950s, 18" l **250.00**

Floating Satellite Target Game, battery operated, tin gun, rubber tipped darts, and balls, SH, Japan, orig box, 1960s, 8½" h **250.00**

Flying Saucer, tin, battery operated, spaceman with oxygen tanks shifting controls, Cragstan, Japan, orig box, 1950s, 7½" d **385.00**

Super Robot Space Tank, friction, litho tin, Horikawa, 1950s, 8³⁄₄" l, $1,275.00.

Friendship 7 Space Capsule, litho tin, friction, transparent plastic windows, hard plastic exhaust jets, mkd "Friendship 7, United States," int features detailed control panel with screen showing lunar landscape with 3-D astronaut, Yone, Japan, 1960s **75.00**

Interplanetary Spaceship Atom Rocket-15, litho tin and plastic, battery operated, Yone, Japan, orig box, 1970s, 13" h **150.00**

Jupiter Flying Saucer, litho tin top, plastic bottom, battery operated, KO, Japan, 1960s, 8" w **235.00**

Jupiter Rocket, friction, Japan, 6" l **175.00**

Jupiter Rocket Truck, litho tin, friction, Marx, 1950s, 15" l **125.00**

King Flying Saucer, litho tin, battery operated, 4 actions, orig box, Modern Toys, Japan, 7" d **275.00**

Mars Gun, litho tin, friction, transparent red plastic insert windows, sparking action, siren noise, orig box, 9" l **100.00**

Moon Globe Orbiter, battery operated, rotating rocket with moon landscape, orig box, Mego, Japan, 1960s **150.00**

Moon Orbiter Windup, 2 pc, plastic "Apollo" capsule with built-in key and vinyl astronaut attached to metal rod, Yone, Japan, orig box, 1960s **75.00**

Moon Ranger Mercury Mark IV, plastic, battery operated, 5 separate domes, Hong Kong, 1960s, 8" d **175.00**

Moon Rocket, litho tin, battery operated, tin astronaut on observation tower, Modern Toys, Japan, 1950s, 9½" l **285.00**

Morse Code Signaling Set, heavy gauge tin, orig box **65.00**

Parks Plastic Guided Missile Base, with rocket launcher, rockets, spinners, and microphone, orig box, 1950–60s **75.00**

Patrol Disk Saucer, litho tin, friction, mkd "Made in Japan," c1950s, 1" h, 2½" d **50.00**

Rocket Car X, litho tin, astronaut at controls, boy and girl passengers, orig box, MT, Japan, 6" l **325.00**

Rocket Launching Truck, plastic, with rocket launching device and 2 rockets, orig box, Ideal, 12" l **100.00**

Rockets to the Moon Game, bagatelle, litho tin space scenes, Wolverine Toys, 1950–60s, 1½" l **125.00**

Rocket with Sparks, litho tin, friction, Linemar, orig box, 6" l **235.00**

Rocket X-6, litho tin, friction, Modern Toys, Japan, 1950s, 4" h **160.00**

Satellite Launching Truck, friction, launching mechanism, 4 satellites, radar scope control, spaceman under dome, Yonezawa, Japan, 1962, 16" l **700.00**

Sky Patrol Space Cruiser, litho tin, battery operating, rotating space gun firing astronaut at helm, TN, Japan, orig box, 1950s, 13" l 900.00

Sonicon Rocket, tin, battery operated, instruction sheet, orig box, Modern Toys, Japan, 1950s, 14" l 800.00

Space Bank, litho tin, planet with coin slot sitting atop base with litho of futuristic city, Japan, 7" l 500.00

Space Boy Bobbing Head, Japan, 1950s, 6" h 200.00

Space Bus, litho tin, depictions of capsules, planets, rockets, and comets, clear plastic window inserts, destination plate reads "Space," 3" l Robbie Robot look alike on roof, Usagayi, Japan, orig box, 1960s, 14½" l . . 1,865.00

Space Capsule Bank, robot shaped, space graphics of astronaut at controls, 2 spring wire antennas with ball ends, dome on top features skill ball game with planet names, Japan, 5" h 425.00

Space Commander X-15, orig box, Japan 200.00

Spacecraft Jupiter with Spark, litho tin, windup, astronaut under plastic dome, K, Japan, 1950s, 4½" d 60.00

Space Explorer Gun, plastic, Palmer, 5½" l 185.00

Space Gun, battery operated, Remco, 1950–60s 75.00

Space Gun, litho tin, plastic barrel, friction, silver chrome with space capsule litho, Japan, 1960s 100.00

Space Patrol Round Rocket, windup, litho tin, raised pilot's helmet in cockpit, Ashitoy, orig box, 5½" l 175.00

Space Patrol Walkie Talkie, battery operated, plastic microphone, J&L Randall, England, orig box, 1955 . . . . . . 150.00

Space Pilot X-Ray Gun, plastic, friction, gold, simulated satellite openings, 2 sounds, flashing barrel, KO, Japan, orig box, 8½" l 95.00

Space Radar Scout Pioneer, litho tin, friction, astronaut under dome, red and blue spinners on back, Japan, 1950s, 7" l 175.00

Space Ray Gun, litho tin, friction, sparking action, Japan, 1960s, 10" l 65.00

Space Rocket Pistol, battery operated, noise and flash, celluloid bulb tip, Earth Man robot graphics on box, 1950s, TN, Japan, 10" l 275.00

Space Saucer Z-26, litho tin, friction, astronaut under dome, KO, Japan, 1950s, 6" d 200.00

Space Scout S-17, litho tin, battery operated, 2 domes Yonezawa, Japan, 10" l 165.00

Space Ship 1, litho tin, astronaut at controls, advances with non-stop action, flashing lights, orig box, MT, Japan, 12" d 850.00

Space Ship X-5, tin top, plastic bottom, battery operated, 4 actions, Japan, 1960s, 8" d 190.00

Space Super Jet Gun, litho tin, transparent green barrel, sparking light, sound, orig box, KO, Japan, 9½" l 75.00

Space Surveillant X-07, triangular shape, battery operated, flashing lights, Modern Toys, Japan, 1960s, 9" l 150.00

Space Survey Z-09, litho tin, battery operated, astronaut under dome, Modern Toys, Japan, 1960s, 9" l 265.00

Space Vehicle, with floating ball, battery operated, Japan, 7" l 400.00

Space Whale Pioneer PX3, tin windup, sparking action, litho illus of robot and spaceman in windows, KO, Japan, 1950s, 9" l 475.00

Spitz Junior Planetarium, orig box with instructions, 1954 . . . . 100.00

Strange Explorer Space Ship, litho tin, battery operated, King Kong figure picks up tank, DSK, Japan, 1960s 100.00

Thunderbird, battery operated, JR Toys, orig box, 1950s, 10" l 100.00

X-07 Space Surveillant, bump-and-go action, astronaut pilot under bubble dome, flashing lights, Cragstan, Masudaya, 9" l, $175.00. Photo courtesy James D. Julia, Inc.

Walking Astronaut, plastic, hp features, 2 oxygen tanks, movable arms, 1960s, Alps, Japan, 6" h 230.00

Wind-Up Motor Space Dog, litho tin, silver, red accents, advances, flapping ears, opens and closes mouth, plastic ball tail end, orig box, KO, Japan, ... 1,150.00

Zoom-Lite Outer Space Flashlight Projector, litho tin, periscope with inner tube that slides in and out to change projected geometric patterns, Thompson Co, 1950s, 7" l, 1½" d 100.00

SPORTS COLLECTIBLES

This category includes memorabilia from sports that do not have separate categories, e.g., baseball, basketball, football, and hockey. The listings include amateur and professional material.

Sports memorabilia has attracted collector interest for two reasons. First, collectors grew tired of two-dimensional trading cards. They wanted three-dimensional material, especially items used to play the sport. Second, decorators began creating sports theme restaurants and bars in the 1980s. Collectors were amazed at the variety of material available.

When buying any game-related object, obtain a written provenance. Beware of sports autographs. The FBI reports that forgeries are as high as 70% and more in some sports categories. The only way to make certain the signature is authentic is to see the person sign it. One hot area in the late 1990s is trophies.

References: Mark Allen Baker, *Sports Collectors Digest Complete Guide to Boxing Collectibles,* Krause Publications, 1995; Roderick A. Malloy, *Malloy's Sports Collectibles Value Guide, Up-to-Date Prices For Noncard Sports Memorabilia,* Attic Books, Wallace-Homestead, Krause Publications, 1994; J. L. Mashburn, *Sports Postcard Price Guide,* Colonial House, 1998.

Periodical: *Boxing Collectors News,* 3316 Luallen Dr, Carrollton, TX 75007.

Collectors' Club: Boxiana & Pugilistica Collectors International, PO Box 83135, Portland, OR 97203.

Note: For additional listings see Auto & Drag Racing, Baseball Cards, Baseball Memorabilia, Basketball Cards, Basketball Memorabilia, Football Cards, Football Memorabilia, Golf Collectibles, Hockey Cards, Hockey Memorabilia, Horse Racing, Hunting, Olympic Memorabilia, and Tennis Collectibles.

Bowling, caricature figure, painted plaster, lady bowler in backswing, hitting male bowler in head with her bowling ball, Rittgers, 1941, 6½" h. $175.00

Bowling, snow globe, amber glass globe with 3 gold bowling pins and black ball, black hard plastic base, "York County Lions, Team-High Average, 1959," 3" h 150.00

Boxing, Big Little Book, *Joe Louis the Brown Bomber*, Whitman #1105, late 1930s. 25.00

Boxing, photograph, black and white glossy, Jack Dempsey and Joe Jouis, news photo, captioned "Two Fisted Champs," 1956, 7 x 9". 24.00

Boxing, photograph, sepia, "Tommy Loughran, Retired Undefeated Light Heavyweight Champion of the World" and signature at bottom, 1927–29, 4½ x 6". 60.00

Boxing, postcard, Jack Dempsey Restaurant, sepia photo of Dempsey and inscription, restaurant adv on back, unused, 1930s–40s, 3½ x 5½". 18.00

Boxing, poster, Patterson/Liston fight, Allied Artists film ©1962, 27 x 41". 200.00

Boxing, program, Ali/Foreman fight, Zaire, Oct 30, 1974, 52 pp, 8½ x 10¾". 75.00

Boxing, ring, Joe Louis portait, silvered metal, 1940s 750.00

Cycling, The Bike Race Game, Master Toy Co, 1930s 45.00

Gymnastics, autograph, Olga Korbut 8.00

Gymnastics, photograph, Bart Conner, sgd, 8 x 10". 18.00

Ice Skating, autograph, Dorothy Hamill 10.00

Roller Derby, hair bows, "Queens of the Roller Derby," rayon, roller derby picture, 1950s, MOC 8.00

Sailing, game, Clipper Race, Gabriel, 1930s. 85.00

Sailing, magazine cov, *Sports Illus*, Sep 6, 1954 . . . . 10.00

Scuba Diving, magazine cov, *Sports Illus*, Aug 11, 1958 . . . . . . 3.50

Skiing, game, Ski Gammon, American Publishing Corp, 1962. . . . . 5.00

Soccer, figurine, Pat Bonner, Kenner Starting Lineup, 1989. . . . . 30.00

Swimming, statuette, white plastic, female swimmer in starter pose, Rugby Sportwear premium, Marx, c1956. . . . . . 20.00

Boxing, arcade card, John Gonsalves, green tone real photo, 1940s, 3³⁄₈ x 5³⁄₈", $10.00.

Track and Field, comic book, True Comics, Track & Field, Apr 1941, Parents' Magazine Press. 65.00

Wresting, comic book, WWF Battlemania, WWF Action, Valiant 1.50

Wrestling, paperback book, *Wrestling Fan's Book*, 1st issue, 96 pp, 1952. . . . . 20.00

STAMPS

Stamp collecting as a hobby was extremely popular throughout the middle decades of the 20th century. After a speculation period in the 1960s and 70s, when stamps became an investment commodity, the bubble burst in the 1980s. Middle- and low-end stamps experienced major price declines. To its credit, Scott Publishing adjusted the prices within its guides to reflect true market sales. Since this meant reducing the value for many stamps, the results sent shock waves through the market.

Stamp collecting is still in a period of recovery. Many question whether stamp collecting will ever recover its former popularity. Today's market is almost exclusively adult-driven. Investment continues to be the dominant collecting motivation. The overall feeling within the market is positive. Attendance is up at stamp shows. Modestly priced stamps are selling strongly. Interest in foreign issues is rising.

Condition, scarcity, and desirability (popularity) are the three pricing keys. Before researching the value of any stamps, carefully read the front matter of the book you are using, especially information relating to catalog values, grade, and condition. Make certain you understand the condition grade being used for pricing. Most stamp collectors want examples graded at very fine or above.

Book values are retail value. Valuable stamps are far easier to sell than lesser valued stamps. Expect to have to discount commonly found stamps by 60% to 70% when selling them. It may make far more sense to use recently issued United States stamps for postage than to try to sell them on the secondary market.

Most catalogs provide unused and used (canceled) values. In some cases, the postmark and/or cancellation may have more value than the stamp.

Bowling, postcard, "Bowl Down Our Alley, Oceanside Bowling Center," linen, $250.00. Photo courtesy Postcards International.

The five-volume *Scott Standard Postage Stamp Catalogue* (Scott Publishing Co., 911 Vandemark Rd., Sidney, OH 45365) is the basic reference used by most collectors to determine values. Volume 1 contains information about United States stamps. If the collection you are evaluating only contains United States stamps, also consult Marc Hudgeons' *The Official 2000 Blackbook Price Guide to United States Postage Stamps, Nineteenth Edition* (House of Collectibles, 1999).

Over the past few years, numerous advertisements from the International Collectors Society have appeared in newspapers and magazines offering stamps featuring prominent personalities issued by countries such as Grenada. These stamps are being printed specifically for sale to unknowledgeable collectors who believe they are purchasing a bargain and long-term collectible. Nothing is further from the truth. They are not the "Hot New Collectible" claimed by the International Collectors Society. Both philatelic and regular collectors are shunning these stamps now and will do so in the future.

Periodicals: *Linn's Stamp News,* PO Box 29, Sidney, OH 45365; *Scott Stamp Monthly,* 911 Vandemark Rd, PO Box 828, Sidney, OH 45365; *Stamp Collector,* 700 E State St, Iola, WI 54990.

Collectors' Club: American Philatelic Society, PO Box 8000, State College, PA 16803.

Note: David J. Maloney, Jr.'s *Maloney's Antique & Collectibles Resource Directory* (found at your local library) contains the names of many specialized collectors' clubs.

STANGL

Stangl Pottery is a continuation of Fulper Pottery. In 1928 Johann Martin Stangl, a former chemist and plant manager at Fulper Pottery, became president of the Fulper pottery located in Flemington, New Jersey. In 1929 he purchased Fulper. Stangl continued to produce some pieces under the Fulper trademark until around 1955. Stangl made inexpensive artware, dinnerware, and utilitarian ware.

In 1940 Stangl introduced a line of bird figurines, inspired by images from Audubon prints. Auguste Jacob designed and created the models for the birds. Initially, twelve birds were produced. A few out-of-production birds were reissued between 1972 and 1977. These are clearly dated on the bottom. When production ceased in 1978, over a hundred different shapes and varieties had been made. In addition, more than fifty dinnerware patterns were introduced between 1942 and 1968.

Johann Martin Stangl died in 1972. Frank Wheaton, Jr., bought Stangl and sold it to Pfaltzgraff Pottery in 1978. Pfaltzgraff ended production.

References: Susan and Al Bagdade, *Warman's American Pottery and Porcelain,* Wallace-Homestead, Krause Publications, 1994; Harvey Duke, *The Official Identification and Price Guide to Pottery and Porcelain, Eighth Edition,* House of Collectibles, 1995; Harvey Duke, *Stangl Pottery,* Wallace-Homestead, Krause Publications, 1992; Mike Schneider, *Stangl and Pennsbury Birds,* Schiffer Publishing, 1994.

Collectors' Club: Stangl/Fulper Collectors Club, PO Box 538, Flemington, NJ 08822.

Passenger Pigeon, #3450, 1,325.00. Photo courtesy David Rago Auctions, Inc.

BIRDS

Allen Hummingbird, #3634	$100.00
Audubon Warbler, #3755	225.00
Audubon Warbler, #3756, group	415.00
Bird of Paradise, #3408	65.00
Blue Jay, #3716	525.00
Carolina Wren, #3590	165.00
Cockatoo, #3580, medium size	195.00
Cockatoo, #3584, large	175.00
Flying Duck, #3443	200.00
Golden-Crowned Kinglets, #3853, group	715.00
Goldfinch, #3814	135.00
Goldfinch, #3849, group	165.00
Hummingbirds, #3599, double	250.00
Owl, #3407	525.00
Magpie-Jay, #3758	1,100.00
Painted Bunting, #3452	75.00
Parrot, #3449	100.00
Passenger Pigeon, #3450	1,325.00
Penguin, #3274	500.00
Pheasants, #3491 and #3492, male and female	300.00
Prothonotary Warbler, #3447	50.00
Running Duck, #3432	500.00
Quail, #3458	1,500.00
Quail Dove, #3454	250.00
Red-Headed Woodpecker, #3751	300.00
Red Starts, #3490D, double	110.00
Rooster and Hen, #3445 and #3446	250.00
Rufous Hummingbird, #3585	195.00
Turkey, #3275	350.00
Western Bluebird, #3815	465.00
Yellow Canaries, #3746 and #3747, male and female	350.00
Yellow Rooster, #3445	100.00

DINNERWARE

Chartreuse, coffee warmer	$18.00
Country Garden, cereal bowl, 5½" d	10.00
Country Garden, chop plate, 12½" d	35.00
Country Garden, coffee warmer	18.00
Country Garden, cup	10.00
Country Garden, platter, oval, 14¾" d	40.00
Country Garden, serving plate, center handle	8.00
Country Life, bread and butter plate	5.00
Country Life, chop plate, farmer, 11¼"	100.00

Country Life, coaster, rooster	3.50
Country Life, cup	10.00
Country Life, dinner plate, farmer's wife	25.00
Country Life, luncheon plate, pig, 8¼"	12.00
Fruits, bowl, 12" d.	35.00
Fruits, platter, oval, 14¾" d	40.00
Fruits, salad bowl, 7" d	6.00
Fruits, serving plate, center handle	7.00
Fruits, tidbit, 2-tier.	25.00
Garden Flower, casserole, Balloon Flower, 8" d	50.00
Garden Flower, cereal bowl, Morning Glory, 5½" d	12.00
Garden Flower, creamer, individual, Rose	12.00
Garden Flower, luncheon plate, Tiger Lily, 9" d	10.00
Garden Flower, saucer, Leaves.	3.50
Garden Flower, teapot, Sunflower	45.00
Golden Blossom, creamer and cov sugar	20.00
Golden Blossom, serving plate, center handle	8.00
Golden Grape, serving plate, center handle	8.00
Golden Harvest, cup and saucer	9.00
Golden Harvest, salt and pepper shakers, pr.	15.00
Magnolia, bread and butter plate, 6" d	2.50
Magnolia, chop plate, 12½"	20.00
Magnolia, creamer and cov sugar	16.00
Magnolia, cup	4.50
Magnolia, dinner plate, 10" d	8.50
Magnolia, platter.	24.00
Orchard Song, salad plate, 8" d	8.00
Orchard Song, serving tray, center handle	8.00
Prelude, dinner plate, 10" d	10.00
Sculptured Fruit, bowl, pedestal base, 8"	27.00
Sculptured Fruit, snack plate and cup.	14.00
Starflower, salad bowl, 12" d	45.00
Town and Country, bowl, blue, 26 oz	30.00
Town and Country, bread and butter plate, 6" d	6.00
Town and Country, creamer, blue.	15.00
Town and Country, ladle	20.00

GIFTWARE

Basket, blue satin, #3251, 11"	$75.00
Bowl, double apple, gray and green, #3550, 9½"	20.00
Kiddieware, 3-part oval dish and cup	150.00
Pitcher, light green, #4054, 12" h.	40.00
Vase, blue, #3214, 8"	55.00
Vase, dark blue, #3214, 4¼"	35.00

Candle Holders, pr, Caribbean, #5069, periwinkle and green, 1950s–60s, 4¼" d, 2³/₁₆" h, $28.00. Photo courtesy Ray Morykan Auctions.

STAR TREK

Gene Roddenberry's Star Trek appeared on TV beginning in September 1966 and ending on June 3, 1969. The show's initial success was modest. NBC reversed a decision to cancel the show in 1968 when fans rose in protest. A move to Friday evenings in its final season spelled doom for the show in the ratings war.

NBC syndicated Star Trek. By 1978 it had been translated in 42 languages and shown in 51 countries. Over 125 stations carried it in the United States. There were more than 350 local fan clubs.

The first Star Trek convention was held in 1972, drawing 3,000 fans. A dispute between the professional and fan managers of the convention resulted in two separate conventions in 1974. Before long, dozens of individuals were organizing Star Trek conventions around the country.

In 1979 Paramount released Star Trek: The Motion Picture. Its success led to additional films and television series starring the crew of the Enterprise. In September 1987 Star Trek: The Next Generation was launched. Deep Space Nine and Star Trek: Voyager followed. The Generations movie appeared in 1994 and First Contact in 1996.

References: Ursula Augustin, *Star Trek Collectibles: Classic Series, Next Generation, Deep Space Nine, Voyager,* Schiffer Publishing, 1997; Sue Cornwell and Mike Kott, *House of Collectibles Price Guide to Star Trek Collectibles, Fourth Edition,* House of Collectibles, 1996; Christine Gentry and Sally Gibson-Downs, *Greenberg's Guide to Star Trek Collectibles, Vol. 1* (1991), *Vol. 2* (1992), *Vol. 3* (1992), Greenberg Books, Kalmbach Publishing; Jerry B. Snyder, *A Trekker's Guide to Collectibles, 2nd Edition,* Schiffer Publishing, 1999.

Collectors' Clubs: International Federation of Trekkers, PO Box 84, Groveport, OH 43125; Starfleet, 200 Hiawatha Blvd, Oakland, NJ 07436; Star Trek: The Official Fan Club, PO Box 111000, Aurora, CO 80042.

Action Figure, Dr McCoy (Bones), blue shirt, black boots and pants, belt with communicator and phaser, Mego, ©1974 Paramount Pictures Corp, 8" h.	$75.00
Action Figure, Klingon, brown and dark maroon outfit, belt holds phaser and communicator, Mego	50.00
Action Figure, Lt Uhura, red dress, with tricorder and life-like hair, Mego	75.00
Action Figure, Mr Spock, black and blue outfit, complete with belt, phaser, communicator, and tricorder, Mego	50.00
Action Figure, Scotty, red shirt, black pants and boots, belt with phaser and communicator, Mego, 8" h, MOC	75.00
Activity Book, "Star Trek Action Toy Book," 16 stiff paper punch-out pages, Random House, ©1976 Paramount Pictures Corp, 8½ x 12".	20.00
Belt Buckle, Kirk and Spock, brass, enamel trim, 1979	10.00
Blueprints, set of 7, black and white paper sheets, official plans from the drawing board of Matt Jeffries, art director for TV series, Enterprise, Galileo, and hangar deck, 1968, 8½ x 11"	25.00
Book, *Trillions of Trilligs,* pop-up, Random House, hardback, 1977	10.00
Bop Bag, inflatable, full color image of Spock with space scene and Enterprise background, orig box, Azrak-Hamway International, Inc, ©1975 Paramount Pictures Corp, 50" h	50.00

Greeting Card, Mr. Spock, bi-fold, Random House Greetings, 1976, 5³/₄ x 7³/₄", $10.00.

Calendar, 1976, Kirk and Spock cov, color stills inside, Ballantine Books, 1976 . . . . **40.00**

Certificate, parchment-like paper, black and white, "United Federation of Planets," includes inked "Star Date" and name of orig recipient plus facsimile signature of Gene Roddenberry, issued in 1968 with annual dues to Star Trek Interstellar Fan Club, 8¹/₂ x 11" **20.00**

Cookie Jar, *USS Enterprise,* NCC-1701-A, Pfaltzgraff **30.00**

Costume, Klingon, Ben Cooper, 1975. . . . . **15.00**

Costume, Mr Spock, plastic mask, 1-pc rayon/vinyl outfit, orig box, Ben Cooper, ©1978 Paramount Pictures Corp. **20.00**

Decanter, Mr Spock, figural, ceramic bust, orig box, Grenadier, ©1979 Paramount Pictures Corp, 9¹/₄" h **75.00**

Drinking Glass, *USS Enterprise,* Dr Pepper, 6¹/₄" h **75.00**

Fan Letter, Star Trek letterhead with black and white *Enterprise* on blue ground, welcomes recipient to "Star Trek Interstellar" and mentions "Inside Star Trek Official Fan Newsletter" with NBC reference "Twisting the Peacock's Tail," includes facsimile signature of Gene Roddenberry, late 1960s, 8¹/₂ x 11" **50.00**

Game, Star Trek Game, includes board, "Star and Mission Cards," and 3-D *Enterprise* playing pcs, Milton Bradley, ©1979 Paramount Pictures Corp, MIB **50.00**

Game, *Star Trek The Motion Picture,* Milton Bradley, 1979. . . . . **85.00**

Greeting Card, Kirk and McCoy with punch-out phaser gun, birthday greeting, mailing envelope, Random House, ©1976 Paramount Pictures Corp, 5 x 10" **20.00**

Jigsaw Puzzle, *Star Trek The Motion Picture,* 551 pcs, Aviva, 1979, 18 x 24" **25.00**

Keychain, *Enterprise,* oval blue ground, Aviva, 1979 . . . . **3.50**

Kite, vinyl, images of *Enterprise* and Klingon Cruiser, Hi-Flyer, ©1975 Paramount Pictures Corp, 36" l unopened pkg. **15.00**

Limited Edition Plate, "Beam Us Down Scotty," Hamilton/Ernst, 1986, 8¹/₂" d **45.00**

Lunch Box, *Star Trek The Motion Picture,* metal box, 6¹/₂" h purple plastic thermos, King-Seeley, ©1979 Paramount Pictures Corp **50.00**

Lunch Box, *Star Trek The Next Generation,* blue plastic, sticker front with color cast photo on silver ground, blue thermos with white cap and *Enterprise* decal, Thermos, ©1988 Paramount Pictures Corp **20.00**

Model, *USS Enterprise,* AMT, ©1966 Desilu Productions, 10 x 14¹/₂ x 2¹/₂" box **200.00**

Model, *USS Enterprise* Command Bridge, AMT, ©1975 Paramount Pictures Corp, 8¹/₂ x 10¹/₂ x 3" box **50.00**

Movie Viewer, black and red hard plastic viewer with 2 boxed films, Chemtoy Corp, ©1967 Desilu Productions, Inc, on 5¹/₂ x 7¹/₂" blister card **50.00**

Napkins, set of 16, depicting Spock, Kirk, and McCoy, Tuttle Press, ©1976 Paramount Pictures Corp, sealed 6¹/₂ x 6¹/₂" pkg **15.00**

Pennant, felt, "Paramount Pictures Star Trek Adventure, Universal Studios Tour," multicolored, *Enterprise* and planet, 9 x 12¹/₂" **10.00**

Phaser Ray Gun/Space Flashlight, battery operated, black hard plastic with silver accents, click action noise, raised logo on side, Azrak-Hamway, ©1976 Paramount Pictures Corp, 3¹/₂" l **50.00**

Record, *William Shatner The Transformed Man,* 33¹/₃ rpm, Decca, 1970 . . . . **20.00**

Ring, McDonald's Happy Meal premium, blue plastic, emb designs on secret compartment lid, ©McDonald's, 1979, 1¹/₂ x 4" **25.00**

Star Trek Communicator Set, battery operated, 2-tone hard plastic, pull-out metal antennae, flip-up top reveals simulated buttons and speaker cover, front with Star Trek insignia sticker and Communicator plate, reverse belt clip, Mego, ©1974 Paramount Pictures Corp, 1 x 2¹/₂ x 6¹/₂" **50.00**

Vehicle, Klingon Battle Cruiser, plastic, metallic blue, white attachments, color decals, "3-Shot Photon Projector Missile-Firing Mechanism," with bag of 8 projectiles, orig box, ©1977 Paramount Pictures Corp. **50.00**

View-Master Reels, *Star Trek The Motion Picture,* ©1979 Paramount Pictures Corp, MIP, set of 3 . . . . **15.00**

Water Pistol, *Star Trek The Motion Picture,* hard plastic, silver, Aviva Enterprises, Inc, ©1970 Paramount Pictures Corp, MOC **20.00**

STAR WARS

Star Wars: A New Hope, George Lucas' 1977 movie epic, changed the history of film making. Luke Skywalker, Princess Leia, Hans Solo, Chewbacca, Ben (Obi-Wan) Kenobi, Darth Vadar, R2-D2, and C-3PO have become cultural icons. Their adventures in the *Star Wars* trilogy were eagerly followed.

Much of the success of the *Star Wars* trilogy is credited to the special effects created by Lucas' Industrial Light and Magic Company. John Williams' score and Ben Burtt's sound effects also contributed. Twentieth Century Fox granted a broad license to the Kenner Toy Company. Approximately 80% of *Star Wars* merchandise sold in Canada and the United States is made by Kenner. Almost every Kenner product was available in England, Europe, and other English-speaking countries through Palitoy of London.

The logo on the box is a good dating tool. Licensing rights associated with the release of *Star Wars* were retained by Twentieth Century Fox. Lucasfilm Ltd. owns the licensing rights to the sequels and regained the right to the *Stars War* name before releasing *The Empire Strikes Back.*

References: Sue Cornwell and Mike Kott, *House of Collectibles Price Guide to Star Wars Collectibles, Fourth Edition*, House of Collectibles, 1997; John Kellerman, *Star Wars Vintage Action Figures*, Krause Publications, 1998; Jeffrey B. Snyder, *Collecting Star Wars Toys 1977–1997*, Schiffer Publishing, 1998; Stuart W. Wells III, *The Galaxy's Greatest Star Wars Collectibles Price Guide*, Antique Trader Books, 1998.

Newsletter: *The Star Wars Collector*, 20982 Homecrest Ct, Ashburn, VA 20147.

Collectors' Club: Official Star Wars Fan Club, PO Box 111000, Aurora, CO 80042.

Note: See Star Wars – Exclusive Report for additional listings.

Action Figure, Admiral Ackbar, on "Jedi" card with "65" back, Kenner, ©1983 20th Century Fox, 3³/₄" h **$20.00**

Action Figure, Amanaman, on "Power of the Force" card, with collector's coin and "92" back, green and yellow, with accessories, Kenner, ©1984 Lucasfilm Ltd, 4¹/₂" h **100.00**

Action Figure, A-Wing Pilot, *Power of the Force*, MOC **120.00**

Action Figure, Barada, with weapon, on "Power of the Force" card with collector's coin, 3³/₄" h, on 6 x 9" blister card **75.00**

Action Figure, Ben Kenobi, cloth hooded cloak, light saber, orig box, Kenner, ©1979 20th Century Fox Film Corp, 12" h **175.00**

Action Figure, Bespin Guard, *Return of the Jedi*, MOC **75.00**

Action Figure, Bib Fortuna, *Return of the Jedi*, MOC **30.00**

Action Figure, Biker Scout, *Power of the Force*, MOC **135.00**

Action Figure, C-3PO, hard plastic, poseable, orig box, Kenner, ©1978 20th Century Fox, 12" h **100.00**

Action Figure, C-3PO, *Return of the Jedi*, removable limbs, MOC **35.00**

Action Figure, Chewbacca, *Empire Strikes Back*, MOC **75.00**

Action Figure, Darth Vader, removable black fabric cape, red light saber, orig box, Kenner, ©1978 20th Century Fox Film Corp, 15" h **175.00**

Action Figure, Death Star Droid, bright silver, black accents, Kenner, ©1979 20th Century Fox, 3³/₄" h **100.00**

Action Figure, Gammorrean Guard, *Return of the Jedi*, MOC **25.00**

Action Figure, Greedo, Kenner, ©1979 20th Century Fox Film Corp, 3³/₄" h, MOC **100.00**

Action Figure, Hammerhead, Kenner, ©1979 20th Century Film Corp, 4" h **75.00**

Action Figure, Han Carbonite, *Power of the Force*, MOC . . . **275.00**

Action Figure, Imperial Coom, *Empire Strikes Back* **65.00**

Action Figure, Imperial Dignitary, *Power of the Force*, MOC **100.00**

Action Figure, Imperial Gunner, *Power of the Force* **160.00**

Action Figure, Jawa, dressed in hooded cloak, removable ammunition belt, laser rifle, with Kenner catalog, orig box, Kenner, ©1977 20th Century Fox, 8" h **175.00**

Action Figure, Lando, *Empire Strikes Back* **75.00**

Action Figure, Leia Organa, *Empire Strikes Back* **300.00**

Action Figure, Luke Skywalker, Imperial Stormtrooper outfit, removable helmet and gun, Kenner, ©1984 Lucasfilm Ltd, 3³/₄" h **75.00**

Action Figure, Luke Skywalker, Jedi Knight outfit, on "Jedi" card with "65" back, Kenner, ©1983 Lucasfilm Ltd, 3³/₄" h **50.00**

Action Figure, Luke Skywalker, white shirt and boots, brown pants, light saber, grappling hook, and utility belt, orig box, Kenner, ©1978 20th Century Fox, 12" h **100.00**

Action Figure, Teebo, *Power of the Force* **200.00**

Action Figure, Tie Pilot, *Return of the Jedi*, MOC **65.00**

Action Figure, Tusken Raider, on Jedi card with "65" back, Kenner, ©1983 Lucasfilm Ltd, 3³/₄" h **50.00**

Action Figure, Walrus Man, 21 card back, Kenner, ©1979 20th Century Fox, 3³/₄" h **75.00**

Action Figure, Walrus Man, *Empire Strikes Back* **150.00**

Action Figure Accessory, Ben Kenobi Cape **4.00**

Action Figure Accessory, Ben Light Saber **8.00**

Action Figure Accessory, Bespin Blaster **7.00**

Action Figure Accessory, Biker Scout Guns **8.00**

Action Figure Accessory, B-Wing Gun **7.00**

Action Figure Accessory, General Madine Staff **4.00**

Action Figure Accessory, Jawa Blaster **6.00**

Action Figure Accessory, Lando General Cape **12.00**

Action Figure Accessory, Lando Skiff Staff **6.50**

Action Figure Accessory, Leia Blaster **8.50**

Action Figure Accessory, Luke Hoth Rifle **5.00**

Action Figure Accessory, R2-D2 Pop-Up Saber **10.00**

Action Figure Accessory, Royal Guard Cape **4.00**

Action Figure Accessory, Royal Guard Staff **6.50**

Action Figure Accessory, Sandpeople Cape **4.00**

Action Figure Accessory, Snowtrooper Cape **4.00**

Action Figure Accessory, Solo Blaster **6.00**

Action Figure Accessory, Stormtrooper Blaster **6.00**

Action Figure Accessory, Stormtrooper Rifle **5.00**

Action Figure Accessory, Vader Cape **4.50**

Action Figure Accessory, Vader Light Saber **8.00**

Action Figure Accessory, Warok Bow **6.00**

Action Figure Pack, Cantina Showdown **25.00**

Action Figure Pack, Death Star Escape **35.00**

Action Figure Pack, Final Jedi Duel **20.00**

Action Figure Pack, Jabba's Dancers **35.00**

Action Figure Pack, Mynock Hunt **35.00**

Activity Set, Presto Magix, includes 18 x 20" full color "Action Poster" and set of color character transfers, American Publishing Corp, ©1982 Lucasfilm Ltd **15.00**

Structors Action Walker All Terrain Scout Transport, windup, gray plastic, MPC, $12.00.

Trading Card, No. 207, C-3PO (Anthony Daniels), ©1977 20th Century Fox, $1.50.

Bank, Darth Vader, ceramic, Darth Vader bust, Roman
  Ceramics Corp, ©1977 20th Century Fox, 6¼" h. 45.00
Bank, Jabba the Hut, ceramic, figural Jabba smoking
  pipe, orig box, Sigma, ©1983 Lucasfilm Ltd, 6¼" h. 50.00
Bank, Princess Kneesaa, hard vinyl, figural, orig box,
  Adam Joseph Industries, Inc, ©1983 Lucasfilm Ltd 50.00
Bank, R2-D2, ceramic. 30.00
Bank, Yoda, Sigma. 60.00
Bed Sheet, cotton, multicolored character and spaceship
  illus against outer space background with repeated
  logo, ©1977 20th Century Fox, 65 x 92" 20.00
Calendar, 1978, Star Wars 10.00
Carrying Case, Star Wars 60.00
Coin, Power of the Force, Bib Fortuna 125.00
Coin, Power of the Force, Princess Leia with R2-D2 . . . . . . 125.00
Coloring Book, Return of the Jedi: The Max Rebo Band,
  Kenner 2.50
Display Sign, "Star Wars Action Figures," diecut card-
  board, 2-sided, each side with photos of "Original 12"
  and "#9 New" action figures, "Collect All 21,"
  Kenner, ©1979 20th Century Fox, 18¼ x 20¼". 100.00
Doll, R2-D2, cloth, stuffed, shiny fabric top with black,
  red and blue designs, white body with black, silver,
  and blue designs, movable legs, makes squeaking
  noise, orig tag, Kenner, ©1978 20th Century Fox, 5 x
  9 x 8½". 50.00
Earrings, clip-on, C-3PO 8.00
Fan Club Kit, The Official Star Wars Lucasfilm Fan Club
  Kit, stiff paper folder containing checklist, welcome
  letter, membership card, six 8 x 10" photos including
  color photo of George Lucas, black and white photos
  from each Star Wars film plus 2 for Indiana Jones, Star
  Wars product brochure and flier, issues 26 and 27 of
  "Bantha Tracks" fan club journal publication and
  Indiana Jones fabric patch, ©1984, 9 x 11½" folder 50.00
Figurine, Luke Skywalker, Sigma 20.00
Game, Adventures of R2-D2, Kenner, ©1978 20th
  Century Fox, MIB 20.00
Game, Electronic Laser Battle Game, battery operated,
  Kenner, ©1977 20th Century Fox 100.00

Game, Star Wars Destry Death Star Game, Kenner,
  ©1977 20th Century Fox, MIB 25.00
Hand Puppet, Yoda, vinyl, full figure Yoda with white
  life-like hair, molded tan tunic outfit with brown
  wood cane, orig box, Kenner, ©1980 Lucasfilm Ltd,
  10" h 50.00
Lunch Box, Return of the Jedi, metal box, color illus,
  6½" h red plastic thermos with color decal and white
  cup, Thermos Co, ©1983 Lucasfilm Ltd, unused 25.00
Mask, Darth Vader, molded black plastic, transparent
  plastic eyes, silver accent on nose and respirator
  points, velcro strip for attaching, Don Post, ©1978
  20th Century Fox, 10 x 10½ x 11½" 75.00
Mask, Yoda, rubber, Ben Cooper 5.00
Model, Darth Vader, battery operated, makes rasping
  breathing sound with illuminated eyes, orig box,
  MPC, ©1978 20th Century Fox 50.00
Model, Millennium Falcon, MPC, 1983 . . . . 50.00
Model, The Empire Strikes Back AT-AT, movable control
  center, poseable legs, accessories including snow
  speeders, MPC, ©1981 Lucasfilm Ltd, MIB 30.00
Mug, Chewie, figural, ceramic, brown, black and dark
  brown accents, blue eyes, blue int, matte finish,
  reverse with raised Star Wars logo and "Chewie,"
  underside mkd "1977 20th Century Fox, ©Calif.
  Originals," sculpted by Jim Rumph, 5 x 7 x 6½" 75.00
Music Box, Wicket and Kneesa, Sigma. 45.00
Playset, Creature Cantina Action Playset, includes plastic cantina base with battle action levers, opening
  front door, circular bar and backdrop with scene
  including cantina band, orig box, Kenner, ©1979 20th
  Century Fox 75.00
Playset, Dagobah Playset, MIB. 85.00
Playset, Darth Vader's Star Destroyer Action Playset,
  Empire Strikes Back, vehicle/playset designed with
  mediation chamber, swiveling command pod, remote
  operated laser cannon, and simulated hologram, orig
  box, Kenner, ©1980 Lucasfilm Ltd 100.00
Playset, Droid Factory, hard plastic base with swivel
  boom, accessory pcs to "Build Up To Five Different
  Roberts At The Same Time," orig box, Kenner, ©1979
  20th Century Fox. 100.00
Playset, Endor Ambush 25.00
Playset, Ewok Village. 55.00
Playset, Hoth Battle. 25.00
Playset, Jabba the Hutt Action Playset, includes Jabba
  figure with movable head and arms, sits on hard plas-
  tic platform base with hidden dungeon, orig box,
  Kenner, ©1983 Lucasfilm Ltd. 75.00
Playset, Turret & Probot, Empire Strikes Back, includes
  Probot figure, turret, and base with action levers, orig
  box, Kenner 100.00
Radio Controlled R2-D2, plastic, remote control, moves
  forward and backward, head turns, eye lights up and
  produces electronic "beep" sounds, orig box, Kenner,
  ©1978 20th Century Fox 20.00
Radio Watch, with headphones, Bradley, ©1982
  Lucasfilm Ltd. 75.00
Sheet Music, Star Wars Medley, Williams, Star Wars,
  man and woman in space suits dancing, disco ver-
  sion, 1977 . . . . 4.00
Toothbrush, battery operated, figural light saber handle,
  with 2 toothbrush attachments, Kenner, ©1977 20th
  Century Fox, MOC 50.00

Toy, Light Saber, black, hard plastic, battery operated, light saber handle with yellow vinyl inflatable sword, sticker on handle with simulated buttons and images of Luke and Leia, Kenner, ©1977 20th Century Fox, 35" l overall when inflated **75.00**

Vehicle, Imperial Shuttle, *Return of the Jedi* **150.00**

Vehicle, Imperial Tie Fighter, hard plastic, battery operated, flashing laser light and space sound, orig box, Kenner, ©1977 20th Century Fox **100.00**

Vehicle, Landspeeder, hard plastic, orig box, Kenner, ©1979 20th Century Fox **50.00**

Vehicle, Luke Speeder Bike **15.00**

Vehicle, Millennium Falcon, *Empire Strikes Back*, orig box, Kenner, ©Lucasfilm Ltd **200.00**

Vehicle, Rebel Armored Snowspeeder, *Empire Strikes Back*, battery operated, orig box, Kenner, ©1980 Lucasfilm Ltd. **75.00**

Vehicle, Rebel Transport, *Empire Strikes Back* *50.00*

Vehicle, Swoop Bike, *Shadows of the Empire* **12.00**

Watch, Bradley Official Star Wars Watch, chromed metal case, blue vinyl straps, color illus on dial of C-3PO, and R2-D2 against outer space background, ©1977 20th Century Fox **75.00**

STEIFF

Giegen on the Benz, Bad Wurtemburg, Germany, is the birthplace and home of Steiff. In the 1880s, Margarette Steiff, a clothing manufacturer, made animal-theme pincushions for her nephews and their friends. Fritz, Margarette's brother, took some to a county fair and sold them all. In 1893 an agent representing Steiff appeared at the Leipzig Toy Fair.

Margarette's nephew, Richard, suggested making a small bear with movable head and joints. It appeared for the first time in Steiff's 1903 catalog. The bear was an instant success. An American buyer placed an order for 3,000. It was first called the "teddy" bear in the 1908 catalog.

In 1905 the famous "button in the ear" was added to Steiff toys. The first buttons were small tin circles with the name in raised block letters. The familiar script logo was introduced in 1932, about the same time a shiny, possibly chrome, button was first used. Brass ear buttons date after 1980.

The earliest Steiff toys were made entirely of felt. Mohair plush was not used until 1903. When fabrics were in scarce supply during World War I and World War II, other materials were used. None proved successful.

By 1903–04 the Steiff catalog included several character dolls. The speedway monkey on wooden wheels appeared in the 1913 catalog. Character dolls were discontinued in the mid-1910s. Cardboard tags were added in the late 1920s. Teddy Babies were introduced in 1929.

Steiff's popularity increased tremendously following World War II. A line of miniatures was introduced. After a period of uncertainty in the 1970s, due in part to currency fluctuation, Steiff enjoyed a renaissance when it introduced its 1980 Limited Edition "Papa" Centennial Bear. More than 5,000 were sold in the United States. Steiff collectors organized. A series of other limited edition pieces followed. Many credit the sale of the "Papa" Bear with creating the teddy bear craze that swept America in the 1980s.

References: Jürgen and Marianne Cieslik, *Button in Ear: The History of Teddy Bear and His Friends,* distributed by Theriault's,

1989; Jürgen and Marianne Cieslik, *Steiff Teddy Bears,* Steiff USA, 1994; Margaret Fox Mandel, *Teddy Bears and Steiff Animals* (1984, 1997 value update), *Second Series* (1987, 1996 value update), Collector Books; Margaret Fox Mandel, *Teddy Bears, Annalee Animals & Steiff Animals, Third Series,* Collector Books, 1990, 1996 value update; Linda Mullins, *Teddy Bear & Friends Price Guide, Fourth Edition,* Hobby House Press, 1993; Christel and Rolf Pistorius, *Steiff: Sensational Teddy Bear, Animals & Dolls,* Hobby House Press, 1991.

Collectors' Clubs: Steiff Club USA (company sponsored), 31 E 28th St, 9th Flr, New York, NY 10016; Steiff Collectors Club, PO Box 798, Holland, OH 43528.

Bear on Wheels, brown mohair, excelsior stuffing, steel frame on wheels, eyes and button missing, fur loss on muzzle and front feet, nose embroidery worn, early 20th C, 6½" h, 9¼" l **$200.00**

Brontosaurus Brosus, gray and yellow mohair, orange felt back bone, glass eyes, c1960, 11½" h **300.00**

Bulldog, probably store display, blonde plush with brown and black spots, poseable wire ears, articulated head, wrinkled forehead over wooden eyes, stitched snout, dewlap jaws, and blonde mane surrounding collar, c1958, 24" h, 35" l **630.00**

Dinosaur Dinos, blue and green multi-fur, felt fins, glass, eyes, c1960 12" l **300.00**

Donkey Five-Member Family, beige mohair, black accents on mane and tip of tail, black eyes, leather or leatherette bridles, 3 have bells, 1 has ear button, spotty fur loss, chest tags missing, 1950s, 12½", 11", 8", 7½", and 7½" l **600.00**

Frog Footrest, green and tan plush with brown froggy spots concealing 4 legged metal superstructure, with button on flipper, frog is poised in leaping position, c1958, 12" h, 22" l **1,380.00**

Giraffe, orange and tan plush, glass eyes, articulated neck and roached mane, restitching on ear, post-1945, 59" h **1,500.00**

Giraffe, plush mohair, air brushed spots, felt ears, glass eyes, ear button and chest tag, 1950s, 12½" h **130.00**

Leo Lion, mohair, recumbent, unjointed, glass eyes, partial chest tag, button missing, 1950s, 16" l **75.00**

Okapi, velveteen, airbrushed coat, glass eyes, mohair mane and accents on ears and tail, ear button, 1960s, 11" h, $288.00. Photo courtesy Skinner, Inc., Boston, MA.

Mallard Drake, Stanic, airbrushed Dralon fur, yellow felt
   bill, black plastic eyes, button wing, c1973, 13½" l **300.00**
Monkey Cart Toy, monkey steering cart fitted with bel-
   lows and 4 wooden wheels stamped "Steiff," c1938 . . . . . **350.00**
Opaki, velveteen, mohair mane and accents on ears and
   tail, airbrushed coat, glass eyes, ear button, 1960s,
   11" h **300.00**
Ride-On Elephant, gray mohair, white felt tusks, steel
   frame, rubber tired metal wheels, red leather harness,
   red and yellow felt blanket, mid-20th C, 24½" l **425.00**
Sitting Dog, yellow mohair, glass eyes, black embroi-
   dered nose, mouth, and claws, spotty fur loss, button
   missing, 5½" h **175.00**
Spider, mohair, multicolored plush back, gold furry
   underbody, legs, antenna, and mouth, black glass
   eyes, button and tag missing, 1960s, 9" l **400.00**
St Bernard Rocking Dog, synthetic fur, dark brown and
   white, plastic eyes, ear button, black embroidered
   nose, steel frame and rocker base, fur matted on back,
   mid-20th C, 23" h, 50" l **175.00**
Teddy Bear, golden mohair, embroidered nose, mouth,
   and claws, excelsior stuffing, felt pads, glass eyes,
   fully jointed, 9" h **150.00**
Teddy Bear, honey beige mohair, embroidered nose,
   mouth, and claws, felt pads, fully jointed, fur and fiber
   loss, button missing, 13" h **225.00**
Teddy Bear, "Teddy Baby," dark brown mohair, beige
   velveteen muzzle and feet, embroidered nose and
   mouth, glass eyes, fully jointed, button missing, 3½" h **325.00**
Tyrannosaurus, yellow and blue mohair, glass eyes, ear
   button, tag missing, c1960, 7½" l **300.00**
Yes/No Elephant, Jumbo, gray mohair, standing on hind
   legs, jointed head and shoulders, jersey pads, felt
   tusks, glass eyes, ear button and chest tag, 1970s,
   10" h **200.00**
Zebra, mohair, glass eyes, unjointed, ear button missing,
   1950s, 11" l **75.00**

STEMWARE

There are two basic types of stemware: (1) soda-based glass and (2)
lead- or flint-based glass, also known as crystal. Early glass was
made from a soda-based formula, which was costly and therefore
available only to the rich. In the mid-19th century, a soda-lime
glass was perfected, which was lighter and less expensive, but
lacked the clarity and brilliance of crystal glass. This advance
made glassware available to the common man.

   The pricipal ingredients of crystal are silica (sand), litharge (a
fused lead monoxide), and potash or potassium carbonate. The
exact formula differs from manufacturer to manufacturer and is a
closely guarded secret. Crystal can be plain or decorated, hand
blown or machine made. Its association with quality is assumed.

   There are three basic methods used to make glass—free blown,
mold blown, or pressed. Furthermore, stemware can be decorated
in a variety of ways. It may be cut or etched, or the bowl, stem or
both may be made of colored glass. The varieties are as endless as
the manufacturers. Notable manufacturers include Baccarat,
Fostoria, Lenox, Orrefors, and Waterford.

References: Gene Florence, *Stemware Identification: Featuring
Cordials With Values, 1920s–1960s,* Collector Books, 1997; Bob
Page and Dale Frederiksen, *Crystal Stemware Identification Guide,*
Collector Books, 1998; Bob Page and Dale Frederiksen, *Seneca
Glass Company: 1891–1983,* Replacements, Ltd., 1995; Harry L.
Rinker, *Stemware of the 20th Century: The Top 200 Patterns,*
House of Collectibles, 1997.

Note: See individual manufacturers' categories for additional listings.

Baccarat, Capri, champagne, 5¼" h **$30.00**
Baccarat, Capri, claret, 6" h **40.00**
Baccarat, Capri, cordial, 3⅝" h **35.00**
Baccarat, Capri, water goblet, 7¼" h **35.00**
Baccarat, Massena, claret, 6⅜" h **70.00**
Baccarat, Massena, fluted champagne, 8½" h **75.00**
Baccarat, Massena, old fashioned, 3⅝" h **60.00**
Baccarat, Massena, water goblet, high, 7½" h. **80.00**
Baccarat, Massena, water goblet, low, 7" h **70.00**
Cambridge, Statuesque, brandy, royal blue bowl, 6" h **125.00**
Cambridge, Statuesque, champagne, royal blue bowl,
   7¼" h **125.00**
Cambridge, Statuesque, claret, royal blue bowl, 7⅝" h **125.00**
Cambridge, Statuesque, cocktail, round royal blue bowl,
   6⅜" h **100.00**
Cambridge, Statuesque, cocktail, tulip-shaped royal blue
   bowl, 6½" h **425.00**
Cambridge, Statuesque, cocktail, v-shaped royal blue
   bowl, 6⅜" h **400.00**
Cambridge, Statuesque, cordial, royal blue bowl, 5¾" h **450.00**
Cambridge, Statuesque, hock, royal blue bowl, 7¾" h **350.00**
Cambridge, Statuesque, sauterne, royal blue bowl, 6½" h **325.00**
Cambridge, Statuesque, water goblet, royal blue bowl,
   9½" h **150.00**
Cambridge, Statuesque, wine, royal blue bowl, 6½" h **250.00**
Duncan & Miller, Canterbury, champagne, 4¼" h **8.00**
Duncan & Miller, Canterbury, claret, 5" h **15.00**
Duncan & Miller, Canterbury, cocktail, 4¼" h **8.00**
Duncan & Miller, Canterbury, cordial **10.00**
Duncan & Miller, Canterbury, iced tea, ftd, 6¼" h **10.00**
Duncan & Miller, Canterbury, juice, ftd, 4¼" h **8.00**
Duncan & Miller, Canterbury, old fashioned, 3¼" h **7.00**
Duncan & Miller, Canterbury, oyster cocktail, 4" h **8.00**
Duncan & Miller, Canterbury, tumbler, 3¾" h **5.00**
Duncan & Miller, Canterbury, tumbler, 6¼" h **8.00**
Duncan & Miller, Canterbury, water goblet, 6" h **8.00**
Duncan & Miller, Canterbury, wine **15.00**
Duncan & Miller, Teardrop, champagne, 5" h **15.00**
Duncan & Miller, Teardrop, cocktail, 4½" h **15.00**
Duncan & Miller, Teardrop, iced tea, ftd, 6" h **17.00**
Duncan & Miller, Teardrop, juice, ftd, 4" h **12.00**
Duncan & Miller, Teardrop, sherbet, 2¼" h **12.00**
Duncan & Miller, Teardrop, tumbler, ftd, 5" h **12.00**
Duncan & Miller, Teardrop, water goblet, 7¼" h **15.00**
Gorham, Florentine, champagne, 5⅜" h **30.00**
Gorham, Florentine, fluted champagne, 8½" h **38.00**
Gorham, Florentine, iced tea, ftd **35.00**
Gorham, Florentine, water goblet. **35.00**
Gorham, Florentine, wine **38.00**
Gorham, King Edward, brandy. **20.00**
Gorham, King Edward, fluted champagne, 7⅜" h **18.00**
Gorham, King Edward, iced tea, ftd, 7⅛" h. **18.00**
Gorham, King Edward, water goblet, 7⅛" h **15.00**
Gorham, King Edward, wine, 6" h **18.00**
Lenox, Antique, champagne, blue, 5" h **10.00**
Lenox, Antique, champagne, clear, 5" h **15.00**

Lenox, Antique, highball, clear, 5" h 17.00
Lenox, Antique, iced tea, blue, 6⅝" h 12.00
Lenox, Antique, iced tea, clear, 6¾" h 17.00
Lenox, Antique, juice, clear, 6" h..................... 15.00
Lenox, Antique, old fashioned, clear, 3⅜" h 17.00
Lenox, Antique, water goblet, blue, 6¾" h 12.00
Lenox, Antique, water goblet, clear, 6¾" h 15.00
Lenox, Antique, wine, blue, 5" h 12.00
Lenox, Antique, wine, clear, 5" h 17.00
Lenox, Blue Mist, champagne, 5" h 8.00
Lenox, Blue Mist, fluted champagne 10.00
Lenox, Blue Mist, iced tea, 6⅜" h 12.00
Lenox, Blue Mist, water goblet, 7⅛" h 12.00
Lenox, Blue Mist, wine, 6¼" h 12.00
Lenox, Castle Garden, champagne..................... 22.00
Lenox, Castle Garden, fluted champagne 25.00
Lenox, Castle Garden, iced tea, 6⅝" h 25.00
Lenox, Castle Garden, water goblet, 7⅝" h............. 22.00
Lenox, Castle Garden, wine, 6¾" h 25.00
Lenox, Moonspun, champagne 22.00
Lenox, Moonspun, fluted champagne, 7⅝" h 25.00
Lenox, Moonspun, iced tea, 6¼" h 25.00
Lenox, Moonspun, water goblet, 7⅛" h 20.00
Lenox, Moonspun, wine, 6⅜" h 22.00
Lenox, Windswept, champagne........................ 12.00
Lenox, Windswept, fluted champagne, 9½" h 12.00
Lenox, Windswept, highball, 6" h 8.00
Lenox, Windswept, iced tea, 8¼" h 15.00
Lenox, Windswept, water goblet, 8⅝" h 12.00
Mikasa, Versailles, champagne, 6" h................... 17.00
Mikasa, Versailles, cordial, 5¼" h 15.00
Mikasa, Versailles, fluted champagne 17.00
Mikasa, Versailles, iced tea, 7" h 20.00
Mikasa, Versailles, old fashioned, 3½" h.............. 17.00
Mikasa, Versailles, water goblet, 8" h 17.00
Mikasa, Versailles, wine, 71/8" h 20.00
Orrefors, Illusion, champagne, 5¼" h 15.00
Orrefors, Illusion, claret, 7¼" h 18.00
Orrefors, Illusion, cordial, 5" h...................... 15.00
Orrefors, Illusion, iced tea, ftd, 9⅜" h 18.00
Orrefors, Illusion, wine, 6½" h 17.00
Orrefors, Rhapsody, champagne, clear, 5⅜" h.......... 15.00
Orrefors, Rhapsody, champagne, smoke, 5⅜" h 12.00
Orrefors, Rhapsody, claret, clear, 6" h 20.00
Orrefors, Rhapsody, claret, smoke, 6" h 17.00
Orrefors, Rhapsody, cocktail, smoke, 4⅛" h 12.00
Orrefors, Rhapsody, cordial, clear, 4¼" h............. 17.00
Orrefors, Rhapsody, cordial, smoke, 4¼" h............ 12.00
Orrefors, Rhapsody, double old fashioned, smoke, 3½" h 12.00
Orrefors, Rhapsody, iced tea, clear.................... 20.00
Orrefors, Rhapsody, iced tea, smoke 18.00
Orrefors, Rhapsody, old fashioned, smoke, 3¼" h........ 12.00
Orrefors, Rhapsody, sherry, smoke, 5" h 12.00
Orrefors, Rhapsody, water goblet, clear, 7¼" h 20.00
Orrefors, Rhapsody, water coblet, smoke, 7⅜" h 17.00
Orrefors, Rhapsody, wine, clear, 5¼" h 17.00
Sasaki, Wings, cocktail, 4⅛" h 25.00
Sasaki, Wings, iced tea, 6⅜" h 25.00
Sasaki, Wings, juice, 3⅞" h 20.00
Sasaki, Wings, port, 4⅞" h 25.00
Sasaki, Wings, sherbet, 4" h 25.00
Sasaki, Wings, sherry, 4⅞" h 28.00
Sasaki, Wings, water goblet.......................... 20.00
Stuart Crystal, Hampshire, champagne, 4½" h 30.00
Stuart Crystal, Hampshire, claret 30.00
Stuart Crystal, Hampshire, cordial 30.00
Stuart Crystal, Hampshire, iced tea, ftd................ 44.00
Stuart Crystal, Hampshire, old fashioned 40.00
Stuart Crystal, Hampshire, sherry 30.00
Stuart Crystal, Hampshire, tumbler.................... 35.00
Stuart Crystal, Hampshire, water goblet 40.00

STEUBEN GLASS

Frederick Carder and Thomas Hawkes founded the Steuben Glass Works in 1903. Initially Steuben made blanks for Hawkes. The company also made Art Nouveau ornamental and colored glass. Steuben Glass had trouble securing raw materials during World War I. In 1918 Corning purchased Steuben Glass from Carder and Hawkes. Carder became art director at Corning.

Steuben experienced numerous financial difficulties in the 1920s, reorganizing several times. When Corning threatened to close its Steuben division, Arthur Houghton, Jr., led the move to save it. Steuben Glass Incorporated was established. All earlier glass formulas were abandoned. The company concentrated on producing crystal products.

In 1937 Steuben produced the first in a series of crystal pieces featuring engraved designs from famous artists. Despite production cutbacks during World War II, Steuben emerged in the post-war period as a major manufacturer of crystal products. The company's first crystal animals were introduced in 1949. Special series, incorporating the works of Asian and British painters, and a group of 31 Collector's pieces, each an interpretation of a poem commissioned by Steuben, were produced during the 1950s and 60s.

Reference: Thomas P. Dimitroff, et al., *Frederick Carder and Steuben Glass,* Schiffer Publishing, 1998.

Bowl, alabaster, acid-etched, broad oval, Chippendale
    pattern dec, ftd, c1925, 5¼" h, 10" w **$1,500.00**
Candlesticks, pr, catalog #2956, amber, baluster-shaped
    stem, wide disk ft, c1925, 11¾" h **700.00**
Candlesticks, pr, catalog #7093, wisteria, dichroic-lead-
    ed and engraved Pillar pattern, reverse-engraved dot
    on base, fleur-de-lis stamp on polished pontil, 1927,
    8¼" h. **1,000.00**

Cocktail Set, catalog #7056, crystal with applied mirror black threads, jug monogrammed "H.W.N.," with 6 matching cups (1 cracked), fleur-de-lis on pitcher base, 9½" h, $403.00. Photo courtesy Skinner, Inc., Boston, MA.

Candlesticks, set of 4, celeste blue, applied foliate-form bobeche and cup, bulbed shaft, 1920–33, 11½" h **2,300.00**

Center Bowl, catalog #112, celeste blue, swirled optic-ribbed borad bowl with rolled rim, applied fluted ft, partially polished pontil, c1925, 4¼" h, 16¼" d **400.00**

Figure, dove, sgd **400.00**

Figure, elephant, sgd **630.00**

Figure, polar bear, sgd **860.00**

Goblets, catalog #7182, wisteria, dichroic-leaded bell-shaped bowls with engraved Pillar pattern, stems with reverse-engraved dots on base, 1927, 9" h, set of 4 . . . . **1,150.00**

Lamp Base, bulbous base with long flared neck and rolled rim, green jade dec with applied alabaster spiral ending with rosettes, silvered-metal fittings, c1925, 11" h **800.00**

Lamp Base, catalog #8023, urn-form, swirled purple, blue, and red moss agate, gilt-metal fittings with acanthus leaf dec, purple glass jewel finial, c1930, 10¼" h . . **2,500.00**

Lamp Shade, shape #2320, bell-shaped, ribbed, silver fleur-de-lis paint stamp, c1925, 4⅜" h **200.00**

Luncheon Plates, Kensington pattern variant, molded celeste blue body with engraved leaves and dots border, c1918–32, 8½" d, set of 12 . . . . **550.00**

Perfume, Rosaline, catalog #6412, teardrop-shaped, cloudy pink with applied alabaster glass ft, c1925 . . . . . . **215.00**

Serving Plate, catalog #3579, Bristol yellow, shallow bowl with broad convex and folded rim, slight optic ribbing, c1925, 2" h, 14¼" d **200.00**

Wall Pocket, Cluthra, half-round flared bowl of black and white cluthra glass cut and mounted in foliate gilt-metal frame, polished pontil, c1930, 8" h, 15½" w . . . **500.00**

STEUBENVILLE POTTERY

The Steubenville Pottery Company, Steubenville, Ohio, operated from 1879 to 1959. The company manufactured household utilitarian wares ranging from dinnerware to toilet sets.

In 1939 Steubenville began the production of Russel Wright's American Modern shape line. Woodfield Leaf with its distinctive leaf pattern on the body and leaf finials on covered pieces was another of the company's popular shape lines. Other body shapes include Antique Adam, Contempora (designed by Ben Seibel), Monticello (distributed by Herman Kupper), and Olivia.

Barium Chemicals, parent company of Canonsburg Pottery, bought Steubenville in 1959 and moved the company's molds and equipment to Canonsburg. Canonsburg Pottery continued to use the Steubenville name during much of the 1960s.

Reference: Harvey Duke, *The Official Price Guide to Pottery and Porcelain, Eighth Edition,* House of Collectibles, 1995.

Note: See Russell Wright for American Modern dinnerware by Steubenville.

Adam Antique, candlesticks, pr **$20.00**

Adam Antique, coffeepot **35.00**

Adam Antique, creamer and sugar **12.00**

Adam Antique, gravy boat **20.00**

Adam Antique, jug, 1 qt **15.00**

Adam Antique, shaker **4.00**

Betty Pepper, creamer **4.00**

Betty Pepper, dish, 5½" d **2.00**

Betty Pepper, plate, 9" d **5.00**

Betty Pepper, platter, 13½" l **12.00**

Betty Pepper, saucer **2.00**

Betty Pepper, teapot, 2 cup **15.00**

Contempora, casserole **45.00**

Contempora, chop plate, 14¼" d **35.00**

Contempora, creamer and sugar **30.00**

Contempora, fruit dish, 6" d **5.00**

Contempora, jug **90.00**

Contempora, plate, 8¼" d **6.00**

Contempora, salad bowl, 11" d **50.00**

Contempora, shaker **10.00**

Monticello, bread and butter plate, 6¼" d **2.00**

Monticello, casserole **20.00**

Monticello, soup bowl, lug **10.00**

Monticello, sugar **8.00**

Monticello, vegetable bowl, oval, 9" l **10.00**

Olivia, butter, cov **20.00**

Olivia, cake plate, emb lug, 10¾" d **8.00**

Olivia, casserole **20.00**

Olivia, eggcup **10.00**

Olivia, gravy boat **12.00**

Olivia, platter, 11" l **10.00**

Olivia, platter, 15" l **15.00**

Olivia, salad bowl, 8½" d **15.00**

Olivia, soup bowl, 8¼" d **10.00**

Shalimar, coffeepot **35.00**

Shalimar, creamer **4.00**

Shalimar, dish, 5½" d **2.00**

Shalimar, platter, oval, 11" l **10.00**

Woodfield, platter, oval, 13½" l **12.00**

Woodfield, relish, 2 part, 9½" **30.00**

Woodfield, tea and toast plate, 9" **6.00**

Woodfield, utility tray, 10¼" **15.00**

STOCKS & BONDS

A stock certificate is a financial document that shows the amount of capital on a per share basis that the owner has invested in a company. Gain is achieved through dividends and an increase in unit value. A bond is an interest bearing certificate of public or private indebtedness. The interest is generally paid on a fixed schedule with the principal being repaid when the bond is due.

Joint stock companies were used to finance world exploration in the 16th, 17th, and 18th centuries. Several American colonies received financial backing from joint stock companies. Bonds and stocks help spread financial risk. The New York Stock Exchange was founded in the late 18th century.

In the middle of the 19th century, engraving firms such as the American Bank Note Company and Rawdon, Wright & Hatch created a wide variety of financial instruments ranging from bank notes to stock certificates. Most featured one or more ornately engraved vignettes. While some generic vignettes were used repeatedly, vignettes often provided a detailed picture of a manufacturing facility or product associated with the company.

Stocks and bonds are collected primarily for their subject matter, e.g., automobile, mining, railroad, public utilities, etc. Date is a value factor. Pre-1850 stocks and bonds command the highest price provided they have nice vignettes. Stocks and bonds issued between 1850 and 1915 tend to be more valuable than those issued after 1920.

Before paying top dollar attempt to ascertain how many examples of the certificate you are buying have survived. The survival rate is higher than most realize. Unused stock and bond certificates are less desirable than issued certificates. Finally, check the signatures on all pre-1915 stocks. Many important personages served as company presidents.

References: Norman E. Martinus and Harry L. Rinker, *Warman's Paper,* Wallace-Homestead, Krause Publications, 1994; Gene Utz, *Collecting Paper,* Books Americana, Krause Publications, 1993.

Periodical: *Bank Note Reporter,* 700 E State St, Iola, WI 54990.

Collectors' Clubs: Bond and Share Society, 26 Broadway at Bowling Green, Rm 200, New York, NY 10004; Old Certificates Collector's Club, 4761 W Waterbuck Dr, Tucson, AZ 85742.

BONDS

Black Mountain Railroad, Kentucky Short Line Railroad,
  $1,000 gold bond, 40 coupons, blue border, 1921 ...... $30.00
Consolidated Edison Co, NY, $1,000, blue, tower,
  Brooklyn Bridge, and New York City background
  vignette, issued, 1963 .... 5.00
Denver & Rio Grande Western Railroad, engraved,
  orange, $1,000 bond, coupons, vignette of 2 trains at
  station, 1924.. 125.00
Gulf Mobile & Ohio, $1,000, diesel locomotive vignette,
  orange border, 1957 .... 6.00
Southern Bell Telephone & Telegraph, $1,000, person
  speaking on telephone, city and rural landscapes
  vignette, coupons, issued, 1947 .... 15.00

STOCKS

Belt Railroad & Stock Yard, black and white, vignette of
  train at station, 1930s $20.00
Chicago & Eastern Illinois Railway, engraved, green,
  vignette of large old train, 1924 .... 12.00
Commonwealth & Southern Corp, engraved, blue,
  vignette of man and seated woman looking out over
  industrial factories, 1934 .... 3.50
Corona Typewriter Co, blue border, early typewriter
  vignette, 1920s 40.00
Four Seasons Nursing Centers of America, Inc, 4 cherubs
  vignette, 1970s 2.50
Glenmore Productions, Inc, brown border, eagle
  vignette, issued to and sgd by Billy Rose, 1948–50 ...... 165.00
Green Bay & Western Railroad, engraved, brown,
  vignette of man on horseback watching train crossing
  bridge, 1920s 20.00
Key System Transit Co, San Francisco, orange, large,
  vignette of seated lady and shield, 1920s 165.00
Pennsylvania-Ohio Electric, engraved, green, vignette of
  standing goddess, generator, and trolley car, 1920s........ 8.00
Pittsburgh McKeesport & Youghiogheny Railroad, train
  vignette, sgd by Cornelius Vanderbilt for Lake Shore &
  Michigan Southern Railroad which guaranteed stock,
  purple, issued 250.00
Seatrain Lines, Inc, engraved, vignette of man, company
  symbol, and 2 world globes........................... 3.50
Tom Reed Gold Mines, AZ, brown, 3 mining vignettes,
  1920s.. 20.00

STRING HOLDERS

Commercial cast-iron string holders, designed to assist merchants and manufacturers in the wrapping of packages, date to the middle of the 19th century. Smaller household models appeared as the century ended.

The 1920s through the 1950s is the golden age of the household string holder. Several Depression glass patterns included a string holder. Hull's Little Red Riding Hood series included an example. Ceramic and chalkware string holders in the shape of a human face, animal, and fruit were common, often selling for less than fifty cents at a five-and-dime store.

Most string holders are unmarked. Many examples were imported from Japan. A few, e.g., Universal Statuary Company, are American made.

Several mail-order catalog companies offered reproduction and new ceramic string holders. Do not confuse them with their historic antecedents.

Reference: Sharon Ray Jacobs, *A Collector's Guide to Stringholders,* L-W Book Sales, 1996.

Apple, bird after worm, chalkware................... $110.00
Apple, stem to left, chalkware 25.00
Apple, stem to right, chalkware 40.00
Apple House, with centipede, chalkware 25.00
Art Nouveau Lady, chalkware 90.00
Bear, with bee on tummy, ceramic.................... 225.00
Bird, scissors through head, Royal Copley, ceramic......... 50.00
Black Cat, red ball of string, chalkware 25.00
Black Lady, turbin, chalkware 170.00
Boy, gold hat and pipe, chalkware................... 35.00
Boy, yellow tie and pipe, chalkware................. 45.00
Bride and 2 Bridesmaids, ceramic 125.00
Bride, Groom, and Bridesmaid, ceramic.............. 70.00
Bridesmaid, blue dress, ceramic..................... 85.00
Bridesmaid, green dress, ceramic.................... 80.00
Bridesmaid, maroon dress, ceramic 90.00
Cat, polka-dot collar with scissors, ceramic 150.00
Chef, with flowers, chalkware 350.00
Clown, chalkware.................................. 225.00

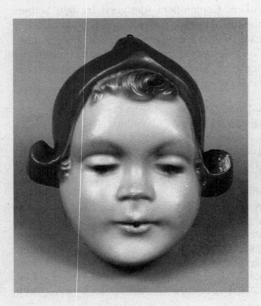

Dutch Girl, green hat, chalkware, $45.00.

Dutch Boy, with cap, chalkware........................ 200.00
Dutch Girl, green polka dot, chalkware 50.00
Dutch Girl, red hat, chalkware 40.00
Girl, maroon bonnet, chalkware 75.00
Girl, red and yellow bonnet, chalkware 45.00
Girl, red bonnet, chalkware.......................... 50.00
Girl, yellow bonnet, chalkware 45.00
Heart with Flowers, "You'll always have pull with me,"
   ceramic 75.00
Lemon, ceramic 125.00
Mammy, scissors in apron, ceramic 350.00
Mammy, with flowers, ceramic 350.00
Pear, chalkware................................... 35.00
Pineapple with Face, chalkware..................... 150.00
Red Riding Hood, chalkware........................ 275.00
Sailor Boy, chalkware 100.00
Sailor with Pipe, chalkware 50.00
Scottie Dog, ceramic.............................. 225.00
Señor, chalkware.................................. 50.00
Siamese Cat, plaid collar with scissors, dated 1958,
   ceramic 50.00
Smiling Mammy Face, red scarf, chalkware 425.00
Strawberry, with blossom, chalkware 65.00
Strawberry Face, chalkware 50.00
Tiger Cat, red ball of string, chalkware 45.00
Tomato Chef, chalkware 140.00
Victorian Lady in Chair, ceramic 200.00
Winking Witch, in pumpkin, ceramic................. 180.00

STUFFED TOYS

The bear is only one of dozens of animals that have been made into stuffed toys. In fact, Margarette Steiff's first stuffed toy was not a bear but an elephant. The stuffed toy animal was a toy/department store fixture by the early 1920s.

    Many companies, e.g., Ideal and Knickerbocker, competed with Steiff for market share. Following World War II, stuffed toys became a favorite prize of carnival games of chance. Most of these toys were inexpensive imports from China and Taiwan.

    Many characters from Disney animated cartoons, e.g., *Jungle Book* and *The Lion King,* appear as stuffed toys. A major collection could be assembled focusing solely on Disney-licensed products. The 1970s stuffed toys of R. Dakin Company, San Francisco, are a modern favorite among collectors.

    The current Beanie Baby craze has focused interest on the miniature stuffed toy. As with any fad, the market already is flooded with imitations. The Beanie Baby market is highly speculative. Expect a major price collapse in a relatively short period of time.

References: Dee Hockenberry, *Collectible German Animals Value Guide: 1948–1968,* Hobby House Press, 1988; Carol J. Smith, *Identification & Price Guide to Winnie the Pooh Collectibles, I* (1994), *II* (1996), Hobby House Press.

Periodical: *Soft Dolls & Animals,* 30595 Eight Mile, Livonia, MI 48152.

Note: For additional listings see Beanie Babies, Steiff and Teddy Bears.

Monkey, Dakin, mohair, glass eyes, velvet astronaut uniform rocket, 1961 .... $100.00

Toohey Owl, Kamar, plush, c1974, 6" h, $5.00.

Musical Dog, German, white and caramel mohair, large
   glass eyes, red felt tongue, unjointed body, swivel
   head, excelsior stuffing, small cylinder-type music box
   encased in bellows concealed in tummy, c1930, 10" h 500.00
Peck-Peck Bird, Schuco, mohair, metal form, black metal
   eyes, tan metal beak, black or tan metal feet, assorted
   colors, 2½" h, 4½" l............................ 150.00
Penguin, Schuco, white mohair, metal head and body,
   airbrushed gray features, black metal eyes, c1950,
   2½" h 175.00
Rabbit, unknown maker, gray mohair, unjointed, glass
   eyes, embroidered nose and mouth, wearing red felt
   jacket and gray felt trousers, some moth damage,
   1920–30s, 13" h 75.00
Rudolph the Red-Nosed Reindeer, unknown maker, cotton plush with brown marking, unjointed, excelsior
   stuffing, brown and black plastic button encased in
   disc eyes, pink velveteen lined ears, green felt horns,
   red plastic bulbous nose, red felt tongue, c1950, 15" h 30.00
Spaniel Puppy, Knickerbocker, sitting, golden brown
   mohair, glass eyes, felt nose and tongue, jointed head,
   cloth chest tag, 1930–40s, 10¾" h 85.00
Squirrel, Schuco, brown and beige mohair, metal head
   and body pipe cleaner legs, black metal eyes, c1950,
   2½" h 150.00
Tiger, Schuco, short beige mohair, airbrushed stripes,
   metal body, green glass eyes, c1950, 3" h 875.00
Turtle, Schuco, beige plush, cardboard form, airbrushed
   design, pipe cleaner legs, black metal eyes, c1950
   2" h 150.00
Wirehaired Fox Terrier, unknown maker, mohair, jointed
   head, glass eyes, embroidered glass and cloth nose,
   1930s, 12" h 40.00
Yes/No Monkey Bellhop, Schuco, on settee, painted
   metal face, metal eyes, ginger mohair head and tail,
   red and black felt outfit and hands, 1930s, 8½" h 215.00
Yes/No Rabbit, Schuco, white and beige mohair head,
   beige mohair arms, cotton fabric body, glass eyes, red
   stitched nose and mouth, fully jointed, excelsior stuffing, wearing felt vest and slippers, cotton shirt and
   pants, red plastic tag sewn onto clothing, c1950, 15" h 600.00

SUPER HEROES

Early super heroes such as Batman and Superman were individuals who possessed extraordinary strength and/or cunning, yet led normal lives as private citizens. They dominated the world of comic books, movie serials, newspaper cartoon strips, radio, and television from the late 1930s through the end of the 1950s. Captain Marvel, Captain Midnight, The Green Lantern, and Wonder Woman are other leading examples of the genre.

The 1960s introduced a new form of super hero, the mutant. The Fantastic Four (Mr. Fantastic, The Human Torch, The Invisible Girl, and The Thing) initiated an era that included a host of characters ranging from Spiderman to The Teenage Mutant Ninja Turtles. Most mutant super heroes are found only in comic books. A few achieved fame on television and the big screen.

In the 1990s comic book storytellers and movie directors began blurring the line between these two distinct groups of super heroes. The death of Superman and his resurrection as a person more attune with the mutant super heroes and the dark approach of the Batman movies are two classic examples.

Collectors prefer three-dimensional objects over two-dimensional material. Carefully research an object's date. Age as a value factor plays a greater role in this category than it does in other collectibles categories.

References: Bill Bruegman, *Superhero Collectibles*, Toy Scouts, 1996; Alan J. Porter, *Batman Unauthorized Collectors' Guide,* Schiffer Publishing, 1999.

Newsletter: *The Adventures Continue* (Superman), 935 Fruitsville Pike, #105, Lancaster, PA 17601.

Collectors' Clubs: Air Heroes Fan Club (Captain Midnight), 19205 Seneca Ridge Club, Gaithersburg, MD 20879; Batman TV Series Fan Club, PO Box 107, Venice, CA 90294; Rocketeer Fan Club, 10 Halick Ct, East Brunswick, NJ 08816.

Note: For additional listings see Action Figures, Comic Books, and Model Kits.

Batman, Cartoon Kit Colorforms, 1966, 8 x 12¹/₂", $30.00.

Batman, hand puppet, vinyl body, molded vinyl head, 9¹/₂ x 16" display bag with colorful header card and illus of Batman and Superman, Ideal, ©1965 National Periodical Publications Inc, 11" h **$75.00**

Batman, Jokermobile, diecast metal, white, color Joker stickers, 4 x 5¹/₄" blister card, Corgi, ©1978 DC Comics Inc, 2³/₄" l **20.00**

Batman, license plates, Batman and Robin, litho tin, emb, Batman name in yellow with image in black and red on green, Robin name in white with color image on orange, Marx, 4 x 4¹/₂" display bags **50.00**

Batman, milk bottle cap, set of 4, Batman, Robin, Riddler, and Penguin, ©1966 National Periodical Publications Inc, 1¹/₄" d **20.00**

Batman, record, 45 rpm, Batman theme and 11 other "Bat Songs" composed and conducted by Neal Hefti, 7 x 7" cardboard sleeve, RCA Victor, c1966 . . . . **50.00**

Batman, toothbrush, plastic, base with attached 3-D Batman figure, Robin next to him serves as battery operated toothbrush handle, with pr of brush attachments, front of base mkd "Brush Each Day/Pow/Zing," Janex Corp, ©1977 DC Comics Inc, 7¹/₄ x 10 x 2" box **75.00**

Batman, wall display, figural, black plastic body frame with applied diecut plastic segments forming Batman's image, body segments are reflective silver, blue, and yellow, Creative Accessories Ltd, ©1987 DC Comics Inc, 9 x 18" overall **50.00**

Captain Marvel, lobby card, "Adventures of Captain Marvel," Captain Marvel illus and text in dark green with greentone photos, ©1941 Fawcett Publications Inc, 11 x 14" **30.00**

Green Hornet, coloring book, "Kato's Revenge," color cov with Kato and Green Hornet, back with cut-out Green Hornet mask, Watkins-Strathmore Co, ©1966 Greenway Productions Inc, unused, 8 x 10³/₄". **75.00**

Green Hornet, drinking glass, Green Hornet, hornet insect and Black Beauty illus, ©1966 Greenway Productions Inc, 4³/₄" h **200.00**

Green Hornet, matchbook cover, glossy color front design featuring cov for Al Hirt album *The Horn Meets the Hornet,* back with name and trumpet design with New Orleans club location, black and white inside with additional Hirt information, complete, unused, 2 x 2" **15.00**

Green Hornet, paperback book, *The Green Hornet in the Infernal Light,* 128 pp, color cov of Green Hornet and insect design, back shows black and white illus of Green Hornet with Kato and Black Beauty, Dell Publishing Co Inc, ©1966 Greenway Productions Inc, 4¹/₄ x 7" **20.00**

Isis, action figure, rooted black hair, white dress with gold and black collar, belt and armbands, sandals, ©1976 Filmation Associates, MOC **50.00**

Masters of the Universe, lunch box, emb metal, 6¹/₂" h plastic thermos, both with color illus, Aladdin Industries Inc, ©1983 Mattel Inc **20.00**

Mighty Thor, pinback button, "Official Member Super Hero Club," #9, Button World Mfg Inc, ©1966 Marvel Comics Group, 3¹/₂" d **20.00**

Phantom, accessory set, purple, blue, and black suit, face mask with hood, black boots, belt with holsters, rifle with scope, knife and skull brass knuckle press, ©1966 Ideal **75.00**

Phantom, book, *Son of Phantom, The,* 248 pp, black and white illus, color dj, Whitman, ©1956 King Features Syndicate, 5½ x 8" 75.00

Spider-Man, brush and comb set, black plastic, Spider-Man sticker on top of brush, Standard Corp, ©1978 Marvel Comics Group, 4¾ x 7 x 1½" box with display window, unused 20.00

Spider-Man, paper plates and napkins, set of eight 7" d paper plates and twenty 6½ x 7" napkins, Reed, ©1978 Marvel Comics Group 20.00

Spider-Man, playing cards, "The Amazing Spider-Man," box with Spider-Man portrait, card backs with similar design and standard fronts, Nasta Industries, ©1979 Marvel Comics Group, 5 x 7" blister card 20.00

Superman, cereal box, Kellogg's Corn Flakes, Superman pictured on front and back panels along with space gun with whirling satellites, adv for Superman's Space Satellite Launcher set, ©1956, 11½ x 16½" 375.00

Superman, comic book, "The Superman Time Capsule," Kellogg's Sugar Smacks premium 200.00

Superman, costume, 4 pcs, fabric shirt, pants, and cape in red, yellow and blue, yellow vinyl belt with gold-tone metal buckle, large "S" emblem on front of shirt and along bottom margin is yellow illus of Superman and young boy with text "Remember—This Suit Won't Make You Fly. Only Superman Can Fly," Ben Cooper, ©1958 Superman Inc, orig box 200.00

Superman, drinking glass, red action illus, Superman name at bottom in gray, ©1964 National Periodical Publications, 5¾" h 50.00

Superman, game, Calling Superman Game of News Reporting, Transogram, ©1954 National Comics Publications Inc, 9 x 17½ x 1¾" box 100.00

Superman, greeting card, get well, front diecut design of Superman flying above young girl's house and designed with pr of red felt boots attached to image, card opens to reveal smaller image of Superman flying above young girl who appears to have recovered with short poem that includes his name, blank back with inked inscription, Quality Cards, ©Superman Inc, c1940, 1½ x 5½" 100.00

Superman, costume and mask, ©DC Comics 1976, Ben Cooper, $50.00.

Superman, slot car, hard plastic, blue, 3-D rubber Superman figure with vinyl cape and color stickers, red plastic dome designed to light up when in use, orig 2½ x 6 x 5½" box with display window shows Superman and Batman on back panel, Polistil, ©1980 . . . . 75.00

Superman, *TV Guide,* Vol 1, #26, Sep 25, 1953, New York edition, 3-pp article on Superman TV series starring George Reeves, color and black and white photos, color cov photo. 200.00

Superman, valentine, diecut stiff paper, color illus of young boy and girl, puppy, and Superman breaking through heart, ©1940 Superman Inc, 4½ x 6¾" 100.00

Tarzan, action figure, set of 9, Tarzan and 8 different jungle animals, Aurora, ©1967, MOC 200.00

Tarzan, Big Little Book, *New Adventures of Tarzan,* #1180, black and white photos, Whitman, ©1935, 4¾ x 5¼" 50.00

Tarzan, comic book, "Tarzan March of Comics," Poll-Parrot Shoes premium, #125, cov photo of Lex Barker as Tarzan, ©1954 K K Publications Inc, 5¼ x 7¼". 20.00

Tarzan, flip book, *Tom McAn Tarzan in Motion Pictures,* Tom McAn Shoes premium, black and white photos showing child getting pr of matching shoes from his dad, illus black and white scene of Tarzan spearing an ape, c1940s, 2¼ x 3". 200.00

Tarzan, watch, chromed metal case, black leather straps, orig cream and clear plastic display case, with warranty paper, Bradley 75.00

The Flash, Color-A-Deck Card Game, contains deck of cards and 5 colored pencils, Russell Mfg Co, ©1970 DC Comics Inc, 6 x 8" blister card 20.00

Ultraman, figure, vinyl, light blue, squid-like creature with tentacle hands, movable arms and large elongated head, red, yellow, and green painted accents, black and silver eyes, mkd under foot with "Bullmark" logo with copyright and "Made in Japan" sticker, 1960s, 2½ x 4 x 8½" h 75.00

Wonder Woman, cake pan set, large silver metal cake pan depicting Wonder Woman from waist up holding magic lasso, 1 arm raised, includes instruction book and hard plastic color face attachment, Wilton, ©1978 DC Comics Inc, MIB 20.00

Marvel Comics' Super Heroes, lunch box, metal, with thermos, Aladdin, $75.00.

SWANKYSWIGS

A Swankyswig is a decorated glass container used as packaging for Kraft Cheese which doubled as a juice glass once the cheese was consumed. The earliest Swankyswigs date from the 1930s. They proved extremely popular during the Depression.

Initial designs were hand stenciled. Eventually machines were developed to apply the decoration. Kraft test marketed designs. As a result, some designs are very difficult to find. Unfortunately, Kraft does not have a list of all the designs it produced.

Production was discontinued briefly during World War II when the paint used for decoration was needed for the war effort. Bicentennial Tulip (1975) was the last Swankyswig pattern.

Beware of Swankyswig imitators from the 1970s and early 1980s. These come from other companies, including at least one Canadian firm. Cherry, Diamond over Triangle, Rooster's Head, Sportsman series, and Wildlife series are a few of the later themes. In order to be considered a true Swankyswig, the glass has to be a Kraft product.

References: Gene Florence, *Collectible Glassware From the 40's, 50's, 60's, 4th Edition,* Collector Books, 1998; Jan Warner, *Swankyswigs, A Pattern Guide Checklist, Revised,* The Daze, 1988, 1992 value update.

Collectors' Club: Swankyswig's Unlimited, 201 Alvena, Wichita, KS 67203.

Antique, churn and cradle, orange, 3³/₄" h	$5.00
Antique, lamp and kettle, black, 3³/₄" h	5.00
Atlantic City, cobalt, 5" h	25.00
Bear and Pig, black, 3³/₄" h	5.00
Bicentennial, yellow, 1938 tulip type, 1975	8.00
Bird and Elephant, red, 3³/₄" h	5.00
Bustling Betsy, brown, 3³/₄" h	5.00
Bustling Betsy, green, 3¹/₂" h	5.00
Carnival, fired-on color, 1939	5.00
Cat and Rabbit, green, 3³/₄" h	5.00
Cornflower, #1, light blue, 3¹/₂" h	5.00
Cornflower, #2, dark blue	3.50
Daisy, jelly jar, 5⁵/₈" h	18.00
Davy Crockett, yellow, 3¹/₂" h	15.00
Dog and Rooster, orange, 3³/₄" h	5.00
Duck and Horse, black, 3³/₄" h	5.00
Forget-Me-Not, dark blue, 3¹/₂" h	4.00
Forget-Me-Not, red, 3¹/₂" h	4.00
Forget-Me-Not, red tulip, #1, 3¹/₂" h	4.00
Forget-Me-Not, yellow	4.00
Kiddie Kup, black, 1956	3.00
Lady and Black Butterfly, red, 3¹/₂" h	4.00
Posy, cornflower, #2, light blue	3.00
Posy, jonquil, 3¹/₂" h	5.00
Posy, tulip, red	3.00
Posy, violet, 3¹/₂" h	15.00
Rooster Head (Kellogg's), red, 3¹/₂" h	12.00
Sailboat, #2, red	8.00
Sailboat, blue, 4⁷/₈" h	10.00
Scottie/Red Check, black, 3¹/₂" h	10.00
Squirrel and Doe, brown, 3³/₄" h	5.00
Stars, green	4.00
Tavern, silver	12.00
Tulip, #3, dark blue, 3³/₄" h	4.00
Tulip, bachelor's button	3.00

SWAROVSKI CRYSTAL

Daniel Swarovski founded D. Swarovski & Co. in Georgenthal, Bohemia, in 1895. Initially the company produced high quality abrasives, crystal stones for the costume jewelry industry, and optical items. The company continues to produce several accessory and jewelry lines including the inexpensive Savvy line and the high-end Daniel Swarovski boutique collection.

In 1977 Swarovski introduced a line of collectible figurines and desk items. A crystal mouse and a spiny hedgehog were the first two figurines. Swarovski figurines have a 30% or more lead content. In 1987 the International Swarovski Collectors Society was formed. Swarovski produces an annual figurine available only to Society members. Every three years a new theme is introduced, e.g., "Mother and Child," three annual figures featuring a mother sea mammal and her offspring.

Initially Swarovski crystal figurines were marked with a block-style SC. In 1989 Swarovski began using a mark that included a swan. Swarovski was included in the mark on larger pieces. Pieces made for the Swarovski Collectors Society are marked with an SCS logo, the initials of the designer, and the year. The first SCS logo included an edelweiss flower above the SCS.

Regional issues are common. Some items were produced in two versions, one for Europe and one for the United States. Many items with metal trim are available in rhodium (white metal) or gold.

A Swarovski figurine is considered incomplete on the secondary market if it does not include its period box, product identification sticker, and any period paper work. Society items should be accompanied by a certificate of authenticity.

Today the Daniel Swarovski Corporation is headquartered in Zurich, Switzerland. Production and design is based in Wattens, Austria. Swarovski has manufacturing facilities in 11 countries, including a plant in Cranston, Rhode Island. The company employs more than 8,000 people worldwide.

Be alert to Swarovski imitations with a lower lead content which often contain flaws in the crystal and lack the Swarovski logo.

References: Jane Warner, *Warner's Blue Ribbon Book on Swarovski: Beyond Silver Crystal,* published by author, 1999; Tom and Jane Warner, *Warner's Blue Ribbon Book on Swarovski Silver Crystal, Fourth Edition,* published by authors, 1999.

Newsletter: *The Crystal Report,* 1322 N Barron St, Eaton, OH 45320.

Collectors' Club: Swarovski Collectors Society (company sponsored), 2 Slater Rd, Cranston, RI 02920.

Angel, #7475NR000009, retired 1/1/94	$130.00
Ashtray, #7461NR100, retired 1/1/91	240.00
Bear, #7670NR32, retired, 1/1/89	330.00
Beaver Mother, #7616NR000001, retired 12/31/96	145.00
Candle Holders, pr, baroque, #7600NR121, retired 1/1/87	480.00
Cat, #7634NR70, retired 1/1/92	70.00
Chicken, #7651NR20, retired 1/1/89	75.00
Dachshund, frosted tail, #7672NR042, retired 1/1/96	80.00
Dinner Bell, #7467NR071000, retired 1/1/92	170.00
Duck, #7653NR55, retired 7/1/88	160.00
Elephant, #7640NR55, retired 1/1/90	215.00
Hedgehog, #7630NR50, retired 12/1/87	150.00
Kingfisher, #7621NR000001, retired 12/31/92	150.00

Dolphin, #7644NR000001, $210.00.

Kitten, #7634NR028000, retired 1/1/96 . . . . 75.00
Kiwi, #7617NR43000, retired 12/31/96 . . . . 60.00
Lion, Annual Edition, D01X951, retired 12/31/95 . . . . 450.00
Mallard, #7647NR80, retired 12/31/94 . . . . 160.00
Mouse, #7631NR50, retired 12/1/87 . . . . 630.00
Owl, #7621NR000003, retired 12/31/92 . . . . 240.00
Parrot, #7621NR000004, retired 12/31/92 . . . . 210.00
Partridge, #7625NR50, retired 1/1/91 . . . . 145.00
Pig, #7638NR65, retired 12/1/87 . . . . 475.00
Prince Frog, black eyes, #7642NR48B, retired 12/31/92 . . . . 125.00
Rabbit, lying, #7678NR030, retired 1/1/96 . . . . 80.00
Scottish Terrier, #7619NR000002, retired 12/31/96 . . . . 100.00
Sparrow, #7650NR20, retired 1/1/92 . . . . 70.00
Squirrel, small ears, #7662NR42v2, retired 12/31/94 . . . . . . 110.00
Swan, #7658NR27, retired 1/1/89 . . . . 150.00
Treasure Box, butterfly, round, #7464NR50/100 . . . . 235.00
Turtle, #7632NR30, retired 12/31/96 . . . . 70.00
Unicorn, Annual Edition, DO1X961, retired 12/31/96 . . . . . . 475.00

SYRACUSE CHINA

Syracuse China traces its origins to W. H. Farrar, who established a pottery in Syracuse, New York, in 1841. The plant moved from Genessee Street to Fayette Street in 1855 and operated as the Empire Pottery. The Empire Pottery became the Onondaga Pottery Company after a reorganization in 1871, retaining that name until 1966 when the company became the Syracuse China Company. Few noticed the change because Onondaga Pottery had marketed its dinnerware under a Syracuse China brand name since as early as 1879.

Onondaga introduced a high-fired, semi-vitreous ware in the mid-1880s that was guaranteed against crackling and crazing. In 1888 James Pass introduced Imperial Geddo, a translucent, vitrified china. By the early 1890s, the company offered a full line of fine china ware.

Onondaga made commercial as well as household china. In 1921 a new plant, devoted exclusively to commercial production, was opened. In 1959 Onondaga Pottery acquired Vandesca—Syracuse, Joliette, Quebec, Canada, a producer of vitrified hotel china. In 1984 Syracuse China absorbed the Mayer China Company.

After manufacturing fine dinnerware for 99 years, Syracuse China discontinued its household china line in 1970, devoting its production efforts exclusively to airline, commercial, hotel, and restaurant china.

References: Cleota Reed and Stan Skoczen, *Syracuse China,* Syracuse University Press, 1997; Harry L. Rinker, *Dinnerware of the 20th Century: The Top 500 Patterns,* House of Collectibles, 1997.

Celeste, cup and saucer, ftd, 2" h $25.00
Celeste, dinner plate, 10¼" d 20.00
Celeste, platter, oval, 12" l 60.00
Celeste, salad plate, 8" d 15.00
Celeste, sugar, cov 40.00
Coralbel, cereal bowl, flat, 6⅜" d 15.00
Coralbel, fruit bowl, 5" d 15.00
Coralbel, gravy boat, attached underplate 65.00
Coralbel, salad plate, 8" d 15.00
Coralbel, teapot, cov 100.00
Coralbel, vegetable bowl, round, 9" d 60.00
Meadow Breeze, cup and saucer, ftd, 2" h 35.00
Meadow Breeze, dinner plate, 10¾" d 20.00
Meadow Breeze, salad plate, 8" d 15.00
Meadow Breeze, sugar, cov 40.00
Sweetheart, cup and saucer, ftd, 2⅞" h 40.00
Sweetheart, dinner plate, 10½" d 35.00
Sweetheart, salad plate, 8¼" d 20.00
Sweetheart, sugar, cov 60.00
Sweetheart, vegetable, oval, 10" l 85.00
Victoria, creamer and sugar 70.00
Victoria, cream soup and saucer 40.00
Victoria, cream soup saucer 10.00
Victoria, dinner plate, 10" d 20.00
Victoria, gravy boat, attached underplate 95.00
Victoria, platter, 12⅛" l 60.00
Victoria, salad plate, 8" d 15.00
Victoria, vegetable bowl, oval, 10⅝" l 60.00
Wayside, gravy boat, attached underplate 60.00
Wayside, platter, oval, 11⅜" l 40.00

Wayside, dinner plate, 10⅛" d, $30.00; cup and saucer, $25.00. Photo courtesy Syracuse China Co.

TAYLOR, SMITH & TAYLOR

Around 1900 Joseph G. Lee, W. L. Smith, John N. Taylor, W. L. Taylor, and Homer J. Taylor founded the firm that eventually became Taylor, Smith & Taylor. The Taylors purchased Lee's interests in 1903, only to sell their interests to the Smiths in 1906. The company's plant was located in Chester, West Virginia, the corporate offices in East Liverpool, Ohio.

Taylor, Smith & Taylor made a wide range of plain and painted semi-porcelain wares, e.g., dinnerware, hotel and restaurant ware, and toilet sets. Lu-Ray (introduced in 1930), Pebbleford, and Vistosa are three of the company's most popular dinnerware shapes. In the 1960s a line of cooking and oven ware was produced. Special commission work ranged from dinnerware premiums for Mother's Oats to Gigi and Holly Hobbie plates for American Greetings Corp.

Anchor Hocking purchased Taylor, Smith & Taylor in 1973. The plant closed in January 1982.

References: Susan and Al Bagdade, *Warman's American Pottery and Porcelain*, Wallace-Homestead, 1994; Harvey Duke, *The Official Identification and Price Guide to Pottery and Porcelain, Eighth Edition*, House of Collectibles, 1995; Kathy and Bill Meehan, *Collector's Guide to Lu-Ray Pastels*, Collector Books, 1995.

Hand-painted fruit and leaves design, chop plate, 14¼" d, $15.00. Photo courtesy Ray Morykan Auctions.

Beverly, bread and butter plate, 6¼" d	$2.00
Beverly, butter, cov	20.00
Beverly, casserole	20.00
Beverly, dinner plate, 10¼" d	10.00
Beverly, gravy boat	12.00
Delphian, casserole	20.00
Delphian, cup and saucer	5.00
Delphian, sugar	8.00
Empire, bowl, 36s	8.00
Empire, bread and butter plate, 6¼" d	2.00
Empire, creamer and sugar	12.00
Empire, dinner plate, 10" d	10.00
Empire, salad plate, 8¼" d	4.00
Fairway, casserole	20.00
Fairway, creamer and sugar	12.00
Fairway, cup and saucer	5.00
Fairway, dinner plate, 10" d	10.00
Garland, cream soup cup	12.00
Garland, dinner plate, lug, 10¼" d	10.00
Garland, soup bowl, 7¾" d	10.00
Laurel, bowl, 36s	8.00
Laurel, bread and butte plate, 6¼" d	2.00
Laurel, butter, cov	20.00
Laurel, cream soup cup	12.00
Laurel, dinner plate, 10" d	10.00
Laurel, gravy boat	12.00
Laurel, platter, 7 x 5" l	8.00
Laurel, salad plate, 7¼" d	4.00
Laurel, teapot	30.00
Lu-Ray, bowl, tab handles, 7"	13.00
Lu-Ray, bread and butter plate, 6½" d	4.00
Lu-Ray, casserole, 8" d	85.00
Lu-Ray, chop plate, 15" d	20.00
Lu-Ray, coaster, 3" d	25.00
Lu-Ray, cream soup cup	40.00
Lu-Ray, cup and saucer	8.00
Lu-Ray, dinner plate, 9" d	10.00

Lu-Ray, eggcup	12.00
Lu-Ray, gravy boat	15.00
Lu-Ray, grill plate, 10" d	15.00
Lu-Ray, luncheon plate, 8¼" d	16.00
Lu-Ray, mixing bowl, 6¾" d	55.00
Lu-Ray, nut dish	40.00
Lu-Ray, platter, oval, green, 11½" l	15.00
Lu-Ray, salt and pepper shakers, pr, pink	16.00
Lu-Ray, soup bowl, 7¾" d	10.00
Lu-Ray, sugar, cov, pink	18.00
Lu-Ray, vegetable bowl, oval, 10½" l	8.00
Lu-Ray, water jug, ftd, 76 oz	35.00
Marvel, casserole	20.00
Marvel, eggcup	10.00
Marvel, teapot	20.00
Paramount, batter jug	35.00
Paramount, butter, cov	20.00
Paramount, syrup jug	30.00
Pebbleford, butter, cov	20.00
Pebbleford, casserole	20.00
Pebbleford, dinner plate, 10" d	10.00
Plymouth, creamer and sugar	12.00
Plymouth, teapot, 2 cup	20.00
Taverne, casserole, Laurel shape	45.00
Taverne, cup and saucer, Laurel shape	18.00
Taverne, salad plate, Vogue shape	30.00
Taverne, soup bowl, Laurel shape, 7½" d	20.00
Taverne, St Denis cup and saucer	45.00
Vistosa, bowl, 36s	8.00
Vistosa, casserole, ftd, handled	20.00
Vistosa, dinner plate, 10" d	12.00
Vistosa, gravy boat	125.00
Vistosa, shaker	8.00
Vistosa, teapot	30.00
Vogue, casserole	20.00
Vogue, creamer	4.00
Vogue, dinner plate, 10" d	10.00
Vogue, soup bowl, 8" d	10.00

TEAPOTS

Tea drinking was firmly established in England and its American colonies by the middle of the 18th century. The earliest teapots were modeled after their Far Eastern ancestors. Teapot shapes and decorative motifs kept pace with the ceramic and new design styles of the 19th century. The whimsical, figural teapot was around from the start.

Teapots were a common product of American ceramic, glass, and metal manufacturers. The "Rebekah at the Well" teapot appeared in the mid-1850s. Hall China of East Liverpool, Ohio, was one of the leading teapot manufacturers of the 1920s and 30s. Figural teapots were extremely popular in the 1930s. The first etched Pyrex teapot was made in the late 1930s.

Reference: Garth Clark, *The Eccentric Teapot: 400 Years of Invention,* Abbeville Press, 1989.

Periodical: *Tea Talk,* PO Box 860, Sausalito, CA 94966.

Note: All teapots listed are ceramic. See Hall China and individual manufacturers for additional listings.

Clarice Cliff, "Greetings From Canada," teepee shape,
Indian spout, totem pole handle, c1950, 5⅞" h **$150.00**
Commemorative, Queen Elizabeth 90th Birthday, white
china, color transfer picture, 2 cup **50.00**
England, Dartmouth Potteries, Queen Elizabeth
Coronation, dark brown profile, crown finial, 5" h **125.00**
Fiesta, yellow, 6½" h **150.00**
Germany, US Capitol, Washington, DC, square, scenic,
gold trim, 4½" h **20.00**
Japan, black cat, red bow around neck, red and yellow
accents, 1950s, 5½" **50.00**
Japan, figural camel, yellow, multicolored shiny glazes,
6" h **50.00**
Japan, Satsuma style, green shiny glaze, gold luster
blown-out elephants, dragon spout, elephant finial,
5½" h **50.00**
Japan, windmill motif, multicolored luster glaze, 7¾" h **35.00**
Lefton, Dainty Miss **150.00**

Sadler, glossy gray with gold dec, mkd "Sadler, Made in England," 5¾" h, 9½" w, $35.00. Photo courtesy Ray Morykan Auctions.

Lefton, figural bluebird, 6 cup **30.00**
Lefton, Green Heritage **100.00**
McCoy, dark brown, white mottling on spout, top of
handle, and rim, 6 cup **15.00**
Noritake, blue, red handle and finial, floral band, 5" h **65.00**
Ohio Art, child's tea set, litho tin, Circus, 31-pc set,
c1953 . . . . **200.00**
Torquay Pottery, sailboat scene, "Take a Cup of Tea Its
Very Refreshing," 4½" h **95.00**
Universal, individual, brown, white flowers motif, mkd
"Stoneware U.S.A.' **10.00**
Victoria Ceramics, Japan, tea set, 3 pcs, California
Redwoods, Chandelier Drive-Thru Tree, 2" h **20.00**
Wade, England, Scottie Man, nose spout, cap lid, brown,
yellow, or green **40.00**

TECO POTTERY a.k.a. The Gates Potteries

In 1881 William Gates founded the Spring Valley Tile Works, Terra Cotta (Crystal Lake), Illinois. Renamed the Terra Cotta Tile Works in 1885, the plant was destroyed by fire in 1887. The plant was rebuilt; and, the firm became the American Terra Cotta and Ceramic Company.

In 1902 the company introduced Teco ("te" from terra and "co" from cotta), its art pottery line. Experimental pieces date as early as 1895. The firm employed a large number of artists and architects as designers. Many pieces were designed for specific architectural projects. Glaze experiments were continuous. In 1911 the company's shape vocabulary exceeded 500 pieces.

The 1929 stock market crash led to the demise of the company. George Berry purchased the buildings in 1930 and created the American Terra Cotta Company to make architectural terra cotta, ornamental pottery, and decorative ceramic wares. In 1972 American Terra Cotta Company merged with TC Industries.

Reference: Ralph and Terry Kovel, *Kovel's American Art Pottery,* Crown, 1993.

Collectors' Club: American Art Pottery Assoc, PO Box 1226, Westport, MA 02790.

Coaster, Cubs, oatmeal ground, team insignia, imp
mark, 4¼" d **$150.00**
Jardiniere, 3 ftd, classically shaped, smooth matte green
glaze, 3½ x 6¾" **375.00**
Jardiniere, ftd, closed-in rim, matte green and charcoal
glaze, imp "Teco," 4 x 7" **600.00**
Saucer, 2 handled vessel, matte pink glaze, stamped,
2¼" and 5¼" d **200.00**
Vase, 2 buttressed handles, dripping blue gray over
brown matte glaze, imp "Teco," 7 x 4" **600.00**
Vase, amphora, 2 handles, smooth green matte glaze,
die-stamped "Teco," 9 x 5" **900.00**
Vase, beaker shaped, 2 buttressed handles, smooth
green matte glaze, die-stamped "Teco," 11½ x 4¾" **2,300.00**
Vase, bulbous, bulging form with protruding mouth,
green matte glaze, 5⅛" h, 4½" d **550.00**
Vase, bulbous with flaring, scalloped rim, matte green
and charcoal glaze, imp "Teco," 5 x 4½" **400.00**
Vase, cylindrical, ribbed, smooth matte green glaze, imp
"Teco," 5 x 4" **450.00**
Vase, matte green and charcoal glaze, imp "Teco," 6¼ x
3¼" **375.00**

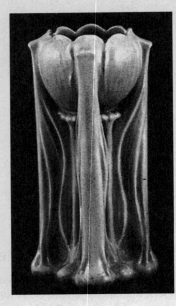

Buttressed tulip-shaped vase, designed by F. Moreau, smooth matte green glaze, stamped "Teco/463," 12 x 5", $4,125.00. Photo courtesy David Rago Auctions, Inc.

Vase, ovoid, smooth matte green glaze, imp "Teco," 4¼
   x 3½" 300.00
Vase, scalloped mouth, outer embossment resembling
   petals, soft dove gray matte glaze, 1¼" h, 4" d 350.00
Vase, squat, ribbed, dark matte green glaze, imp
   "Teco/5," 4 x 4" 350.00
Vessel Vase, squared shoulder covered in curdled green
   matte glaze, 4½" h, 4" d 500.00

TEDDY BEARS

The teddy bear, named for President Theodore Roosevelt, arrived on the scene in late 1902 or early 1903. The Ideal Toy Corporation (American) and Margarette Steiff (German) are among the earliest firms to include a bear in their stuffed toy lines.

Early teddy bears are identified by the humps in their backs, elongated muzzles, jointed limbs, mohair bodies (some exceptions), and glass, pinback, or black shoe button eyes. Stuffing materials include excelsior, the most popular, kapok, and wood-wool. Elongated limbs, oversized feet, felt paws, and a black embroidered nose and mouth are other indicators of a quality early bear.

Teddy bear manufacturers closely copied each other. Once the manufacturer's identification label or marking is lost it is impossible to tell one maker's bear from another.

America went teddy bear crazy in the 1980s. A strong secondary market for older bears developed. Many stuffed (plush) toy manufacturers reintroduced teddy bears to their line. Dozens of teddy bear artisans marketed their hand-crafted creations. Some examples sold in the hundreds of dollars.

The speculative fever of the 1980s has subsided. Sale of the hand-crafted artisan bears on the secondary market has met with mixed results. While the market is still strong enough to support its own literature, magazines, and show circuit, the number of collectors has diminished. Those that remain are extremely passionate about their favorite collectible.

References: Pauline Cockrill, *Teddy Bear Encyclopedia,* Dorling Kindersley, 1993, distributed by Hobby House Press; Ann

Gehlbach, *Muffy VanderBear,* Hobby House Press, 1997; Dee Hockenberry, *The Big Bear Book,* Schiffer Publishing, 1996; Margaret Fox Mandel, *Teddy Bears and Steiff Animals* (1984, 1997 value update), *Second Series* (1987, 1996 value update), Collector Books; Margaret Fox Mandel, *Teddy Bears, Annalee Animals & Steiff Animals, Third Series,* Collector Books, 1990, 1996 value update; Linda Mullins, *American Teddy Bear Encyclopedia,* Hobby House Press, 1995; Linda Mullins, *Teddy Bear & Friends Price Guide, 4th Edition,* Hobby House Press, 1993; Linda Mullins, *Teddy Bears Past & Present, Vol. II,* Hobby House Press, 1992; Jesse Murray, *Teddy Bear Figurines Price Guide,* Hobby House Press, 1996; Cynthia Powell, *Collector's Guide to Miniature Teddy Bears,* Collector Books, 1994; Carol J. Smith, *Identification & Price Guide to Winnie the Pooh Collectibles, I* (1994), *II* (1996), Hobby House Press.

Periodicals: *National Doll & Teddy Bear Collector,* PO Box 4032, Portland, OR 97208; *Teddy Bear & Friends,* PO Box 420235, II Commerce Blvd, Palm Coast, FL, 32142; *Teddy Bear Review,* 170 Fifth Ave, 12th Flr, New York, NY 10010.

Collectors' Clubs: Good Bears of the World, PO Box 13097, Toledo, OH 43613; Teddy Bear Boosters Club, 19750 SW Peavine Mtn Rd, McMinnville, OR 97128.

Note: See Steiff and Stuffed Toys for additional listings.

Character Novelty Co, white mohair, fully jointed, blue
   glass eyes, black airbrushed claws, label in ear,
   c1950, 23" h $300.00
Clemens, cinnamon mohair, fully jointed, glass eyes,
   excelsior stuffing, c1940, 17" h 250.00
Clemens, light tan mohair, straw and soft stuffed, fully
   jointed, glass eyes, black floss nose and mouth, no
   claws, peach velour pads, late 1960s, 8" h 125.00
Gund, Cubbie Bear, cinnamon and gold synthetic plush,
   soft vinyl molded face, painted eyes, label sewn into
   seam, c1950, 12" h 75.00
Ideal, white cotton plush, hard stuffed cotton, unjointed,
   legs supported with wire armature, glass eyes, velveteen nose and pads, open mouth with rubber teeth,
   tagged, c1950s, 10" h 125.00
Ideal, yellow mohair, fully jointed, excelsior stuffing,
   football shaped body, short limbs, black embroidered
   nose, mouth, and claws, tan felt pads, replaced shoe
   button eyes, spotty fur loss, moth damage on pad, late
   1910s–early 1920s, 15" h................................ 230.00
Knickerbocker, blonde mohair, fully jointed, embroidered nose and mouth, plastic eyes, clipped mohair
   inset muzzle, clipped mohair feet, excelsior stuffing,
   spotty fur loss, 1940s, 19" h............................ 225.00
Schuco, beige mohair, fully jointed, glass eyes, embroidered nose, mouth, and claws, shaved mohair
   pads, mid-20th C, 18" h................................. 290.00
Schuco, Yes/No Bear, beige mohair, fully jointed, excelsior stuffing, black and brown glass eyes, black
   embroidered nose, mouth, and claws, felt pads, spotty fur loss, 1950s, 13" h................................. 350.00
Steevans Mfg Co, pink mohair, fully jointed, glass eyes,
   embroidered nose, mouth, and claws, excelsior stuffing, felt pads, 2 pads replaced, some facing and spotty fur loss, 1920s, 20" h................................. 425.00

TELEPHONES & RELATED MEMORABILIA

Until the mid-1990s, telephone collecting centered primarily on candlestick telephones and single, double, and triple wall-mounted, oak case telephones. Avant-garde collectors concentrated on colored, rotary-dial telephones from the Art Deco period. The Automatic Telephone Company (General Telephone) and Western Electric (Bell System) were the two principal manufacturers of this later group. Kellogg, Leich, and Stromberg Carlson also made colored case telephones.

Recently collector interest has increased in three new areas: (1) the desk sets of the late 1930s and 40s, typified by Western Electric Model 302 A-G dial cradle telephone (1937–1954 and designated the "Perry Mason" phone by collectors), (2) colored plastic phones of the 1950s and 60s, e.g., the Princess, and (3) figural telephones, popular in the late 1970s and throughout the 1980s.

References: James David Davis, *Collectible Novelty Phones*, Schiffer Publishing, 1998; Kate Dooner, *Telephones: Antique to Modern, 2nd Edition*, Schiffer Publishing, 1998; Kate Dooner, *Telephone Collecting: Seven Decades of Design*, Schiffer Publishing, 1993; Richard D. Mountjoy, *One Hundred Years of Bell Telephone*, Schiffer Publishing, 1995.

Periodical: *Credit Cards & Phone Card News*, PO Box 8481, St Petersburg, FL 33738.

Collectors' Clubs: Antique Telephone Collectors Assoc, PO Box 94, Abilene, KS 67410; International Phone Card Collectors, PO Box 632, Millwood, NY 10546; Mini-Phone Exchange, 5412 Tilden Rd, Bladensburg, MD 20710; Telephone Collectors International, PO Box 142, Newark, IL 60541.

TELEPHONE

AT&T, experimental phone, clear bulbous shape, red base, rotary dial, c1960s **$200.00**
Gray Mfg, payphone, GTE Automatic Electric, Model 120-A, "semi post pay," 21 x 6" **125.00**
Leich Electric, desk set, greenish clear plastic, c1935 . . . . **50.00**
Novelty, Budweiser Beer Can, Model 1071, touch tone or pulse, desk set, Tectel Inc, Taiwan, 1980s **40.00**

Pay Telephone, metal, 17" h, 9" w, $330.00. Photo courtesy Collectors Auction Services.

Novelty, ear of corn, Model CP-8000, touch tone or pulse dialing switch, made in China for Terra Seed Corp, 1980s **25.00**
Novelty, Ghostbusters, Model ST-738, plastic, touch tone, desk set or wall mount, RCA Columbia Pictures Home Video, 1985 . . . . **125.00**
Novelty, Pac Man, Model DEIF-8410, plastic, touch tone, desk set, American Telecommunications Corp, Hong Kong, 1980s. **50.00**
Novelty, Snoopy and Woodstock, touch tone, table model, white, yellow, red, and brown, AT&T **80.00**
Stromberg-Carlson, dial upright desk stand, mid-1920s **150.00**
Western Electric, black dial upright desk stand, porcelain adv mouthpiece, brass painted black, c1920–30s, 12" h **150.00**
Western Electric, black wall phone, Model 354, 1950–54 . . . . **100.00**
Western Electric, cradle style, Model 202, c1935 . . . . **200.00**

RELATED

Magazine, *Telephony*, 1955. . . . . **$.50**
Paperweight, Bell System, New York Telephone Co, figural, bell, glass, dark blue, gold lettering, c1920, 3¼" h **70.00**
Sign, New England Telephone & Telegraph System, square, early roped "Local and Long Distance Telephone," bell in center of Bell Systems circle, blue and white, 11" sq **80.00**
Telephone Card, ACMI, birthday card. **12.00**
Telephone Card, Ameritech, snowflake, $2 value, 1st ed **5.00**
Telephone Card, AT&T, Golden Gate Bridge, 10 units **18.00**
Telephone Card, Bell Atlantic, James Earl Jones, $2 value **5.00**
Telephone Card, GTI Telecom, Budweiser Clydesdale **8.00**
Telephone Card, Hallmark, red phone **15.00**
Telephone Card, NYNEX, King Kong, $1 value **10.00**
Telephone Card, Sprint, Popsicle Pup. **40.00**
Telephone Card, Western Union, Wright Brothers **10.00**

TELEVISION CHARACTERS & PERSONALITIES

Television programming is only fifty years old. Prior to World War II, television viewing was largely centered in the New York market. In 1946 the first network was established, linking WNBT, NBC's New York station, with Schenectady and Philadelphia.

Networks were organized, and programming ordered. By 1949 Americans were purchasing televisions at the rate of 100,000 units a week. In 1955 one-third of all American homes had a television. In the mid-1980s virtually every home included one or more sets.

The 1950s and 60s are the golden age of television licensing. Many early space and western programs licensed over fifty different products. The vast majority of the licensed products were directed toward the infant and juvenile markets.

Television licensing fell off significantly in the 1970s and 80s, the result of increased adult programming, higher fees, and demands by stars for a portion of the licensing fees. Most television shows have no licensed products.

References: Paul Anderson, *The Davy Crockett Craze*, R & G Productions, 1996; Tim Brooks and Earle Marsh, *The Complete Directory to Prime Time Network and Cable TV Shows: 1946–*

Present, Sixth Edition, Ballantine Books, 1995; Dana Cain, *Film & TV Animal Star Collectibles,* Antique Trader Books, 1998; Greg Davis and Bill Morgan, *Collector's Guide to TV Memorabilia: 1960s & 1970s, Second Edition,* Collector Books, 1998; Marty Eck, *The Monkees Collectibles Price Guide,* Antique Trader Books, 1998; Glenn Erardi, *Guide to Tarzan Collectibles,* Schiffer Publishing, 1998; Robert W. Getz, *The Unauthorized Guide to the Simpsons,* Schiffer Publishing, 1998; Ted Hake, *Hake's Guide to TV Collectibles,* Wallace-Homestead, Krause Publications, 1990; Jack Koch, *Howdy Doody,* Collector Books, 1996; Cynthia Boris Liljeblad, *TV Toys and the Shows That Inspired Them,* Krause Publications, 1996; Kurt Peer, *TV Tie-Ins: A Bibliography of American TV Tie-In Paperbacks,* Neptune Publishing, 1997; Christopher Sausville, *Planet of the Apes Collectibles,* Schiffer Publishing, 1998; Dian Zillner, *Collectible Television Memorabilia,* Schiffer Publishing, 1996.

Periodicals: *Big Reel,* PO Box 1050, Dubuque, IA 52004; *Television Chronicles,* 10061 Riverside Dr #171, North Hollywood, CA 91602; *The TV Collector,* PO Box 1088, Easton, MA 02334.

Note: For additional listings see Autographs, Cartoon Characters, Coloring Books, Comic Books, Cowboy Heroes, Hanna-Barbera, Games, Little Golden Books, Lunch Boxes, Movie Memorabilia, Pez, Smurfs, Space Adventurers, Star Trek, Super Heroes, TV Guide, Warner Bros., and Whitman TV Books.

Addams Family, magazine, *TV Week,* with Ted Cassidy (Lurch), Sep 29–Oct 5, 1968 issue of "Sunday News TV Week," 2-pp story on "New Adventures of Huck Finn" TV show, includes bluetone photo of show's main stars, 7¼ x 10½" **$15.00**

Andy Griffith Show, Ron Howard of the Andy Griffith Show Pictures to Color, #5344, 224 pp, cover art repeated on front and back, Saalfield, ©1962 Mayberry Enterprises Inc, 8 x 10¾" **75.00**

A-Team, vehicle set, set of 3, diecast metal and plastic, includes 2¾" l red and white sports car, black and red van, plus 4½" l red and white helicopter, orig box with color photos from show, Ertl, ©1983 Stephen J Cannell Productions **25.00**

Ben Casey, jigsaw puzzle, "No 4–The Ordeal Is Over," operating room scene, with 12 x 4" color portrait, Milton Bradley, ©1962 Bing Crosby Productions Inc **25.00**

Ben Casey, notebook, vinyl covered cardboard, 2-ring binder, front has insert under clear vinyl cover with full color photo of Ben Casey, Hasbro, ©1962 Bing Crosby Productions, 10 x 11½" **25.00**

Beverly Hillbillies, magazine, *Saturday Evening Post,* Feb 2, 1963, 5-pp article, color cover, 10¾ x 13½" **15.00**

Bewitched, book, "Fun and Activity Book," 64 pp, puzzles, games, and cut-outs, "Honorary Bewitched Witch," and "Bewitched Fan Club" certificates, Treasure Books, ©1965 Screen Gems Inc, 8¼ x 11" **20.00**

Bewitched, doll, plastic and vinyl body, life-like hair, velvet-like outfit with multicolored sparkle accents, missing broom, Ideal, ©1965, 12" h **175.00**

Bionic Woman, coloring book, "The Bionic Woman Good Time Coloring Book," 128 pp, color cover repeated on front and back, Treasure Books, ©1977 Universal City Studios Inc, 8 x 10¾" **20.00**

Bozo the Clown, record, *Bozo Has a Party,* 78 rpm, 20 pp booklet, Capitol, 1952 .... **18.00**

Brady Bunch, record, *Meet The Brady Bunch,* 33⅓ rpm, cover color photo with individual black and white photos of Brady Kids on reverse, Paramount Records, ©1972 .... **20.00**

Caesar, Sid, sign, "The Saturday Evening Post," stiff cardboard sign adv Caesar's appearance in this week's Saturday Evening Post, article titled "TV Gives Him Nightmares," c1953, 10½ x 13½" **75.00**

Captain Kangaroo, cup, soft plastic, figural Captain Kangaroo head, black and white flicker eyes, ©Robert Keeshan Associates, 1950s, 3½" h **25.00**

Captain Kangaroo, Little Golden Book, *Captain Kangaroo and the Panda,* 24 pp, 1st printing, Simon & Schuster, ©1957–58 Keeshan, 6¾ x 8" **10.00**

Captain Kangaroo, thermos, metal, tan cup, color illus, King-Seeley Thermos Co, ©1964 Robert Keeshan Associates Inc, 8" h **75.00**

Car 54, Where Are You?, record, 33⅓ rpm, *Toody and Muldoon on Patrol,* 6 x 6" stiff cardboard with black and white front and blank reverse, Allison, ©1961 Eupolis Productions Inc **25.00**

Charlie's Angels, Charlie's Angels Cosmetic Beauty Kit, box lid has diecut design with cast photo, contents include orange plastic mirror, small compact, and beauty accessories, tan cosmetic bag with repeated Angels' names, full color photo card with beauty tips, HG Toys, ©1977 Spelling-Goldberg Productions, 12 x 15½ x 2¼" **50.00**

Charlie's Angels, mug, hard plastic, brown handle and int, clear plastic cover on outside with full color paper photo insert repeated 3 times of Farrah Fawcett in white t-shirt and jeans holding red flower, facsimile signature in black, ©1977 Pro Arts Inc, 6¼" h **20.00**

Charlie's Angels, poster, full color glossy, "Farrah Fawcett-Majors As Jill," Bi-Rite Enterprises Inc, ©1976 Spelling-Goldberg Productions, 23 x 35" **25.00**

Charlie's Angels, travel case, vinyl covered cardboard case with carrying handle and snap closure on front, repeated large "Charlie's Angels" name and smaller names of "Jill/Sabrina/Kelly," c1977, 4¼ x 8 x 3½" **20.00**

Cox, Wally, record, 45 rpm, *What a Crazy Guy (Dufo)/ Tavern in the Town,* 1950s, 7 x 7" paper sleeve **25.00**

Dark Shadows, cookbook, paperback, 176 pp, color cover photo of Barnabas and book, contains "More Than 150 Unusual Recipes," Ace Publishing Corp, ©1970 Dan Curtis Productions Inc, 4¼ x 7" **20.00**

Davy Crockett, keychain, plastic, transparent orange, depicts Crockett riding horse while holding gun, identification space on reverse, 1950s, 1½ x 2" **10.00**

Dennis the Menace, PS, Dennis and Margaret, glossy, blue felt tip pen signature by Jay North and Jeanne Russell, 8 x 10" **25.00**

Dobie Gillis, bobbing head, composition, 7" h **110.00**

Donna Reed Show, postcard, sgd, black and white cast photo, reverse had brief text on show's stars and postmark of 1959, inked message from Paul Peterson reads "Hi-Here's The Picture You Requested. Hope You Like It, Your Pal Paul," 4¾ x 6½" **25.00**

Donna Reed Show, record, *Favorite Christmas Songs From Singer,* 33⅓ rpm, Donna Reed Show color cast photo, Singer Records, 1964 .... **25.00**

Dragnet, ID Card and Badge, black vinyl holder opens to reveal attached emb tin "Badge 714," and membership card with facsimile Jack Webb signature, card reverse features rules and regulations, ©1955 Sherry TV Inc 50.00

Dr Kildare, candy bar wrapper, waxed paper wrapper for chocolate nut bar by Fair Play Caramels, red, yellow, and brown with color photo of Kildare, ©1963 MGM, 4¾ x 7¾" 50.00

Dr Kildare, coloring book, "Dr Kildare Story," 80 pp, color art repeated on front and back, 12 neatly colored pp, Saalfield Publishing Co, ©1963 MGM Inc, 8¼ x 10¾" 25.00

Dr Kildare, Junior Doctor Kit Punch-Out Book, 4 pp, "A Doctor's Bag With Complete Accessories," including stethoscope, headband with reflector, syringe, desk nameplate, health chart, pills, etc, Golden Press Inc, ©1962 MGM Inc, 7½ x 13" 75.00

Dr Kildare, paper dolls, stiff paper cover and 4 inside pp, back cov has punch-out dolls of Dr Kildare and 2 different for Nurse Susan, 8¼ x 11¾" 50.00

Dukes of Hazzard, General Lee Car, diecast metal, orange, red, white, and blue "General Lee" sticker on roof, on 5 x 7" blister card with color photo, Ertl ©1981 Warner Bros Inc 25.00

Dukes of Hazzard, paint-by-number set, contains 8 x 10" panel with paints and brush, Craft Master, ©1980 Warner Bros Inc, 8½ x 10¼ x 1" 10.00

Evans, Linda, PS, glossy black and white, black felt tip pen signature, with flyer from local celebrity auction event and orig mailing envelope, postmarked 1997, 5 x 7" 20.00

Family Affair, jigsaw puzzle, color illus of Buffy and Jodie tending to sick Bill Davis who sits next to bandaged Mrs Beasley, Whitman, ©1970 Family Affair Co 20.00

Flipper, figurine, ceramic, Flipper coming out of wave, "Flipper" on side, 2 x 4 x 5" 75.00

Flying Nun, doll, vinyl, rooted life-like brown hair, wearing white cloth nun outfit with plastic hat, orig box, Hasbro, ©1967 Screen Gems Inc, 12" h 175.00

Howdy Doody, Wonder Bread adv, heavy paper, jointed, NOS, 13" h, 6" w, $302.00. Photo courtesy Collectors Auction Services.

Foxx, Redd, doll, stuffed cloth, different image printed on each side, Shindana Toys Inc, ©1975 Red Foxx Enterprises, 16" h 20.00

Garrison's Gorillas, coloring book, 96 pp, front cover art repeated on back, Whitman, ©1968 Selmur Productions Inc 15.00

Get Smart, jigsaw puzzle, color cover of Maxwell Smart holding fire hydrant while standing next to his dog which holds a gun in his mouth, text on box reads "Would You Believe Over 101 Pieces? Would You Believe100?," Jaymar, ©1966 Talent Associates, 8 x 9½ x 2" box 25.00

Get Smart, poster, Maxwell Smart and Agent 99 surrounded by weapons and gadgets, art by Jack Davis, 21 x 24" 50.00

Gleason, Jackie, book, *The Golden Ham/A Candid Biography of Jackie Gleason*, Bishop, Jim, 300 pp, soft cover, Simon & Schuster, 1st printing from 1956, color cover photo of Gleason, 5¼ x 8" 15.00

Gleason, Jackie, coloring book, Jackie Gleason Funny TV Coloring Book, 16 pp, color cov repeated front and back while pictures to color depict Gleason as several of his characters including Ralph Cramden and The Poor Soul, 4 pp colored, Abbott, ©1956 VIP Corp, 11 x 12¼" 25.00

Gleason, Jackie, sheet music, *My Love Song to You/Introduced on the Jackie Gleason Show*, color cover photo of Gleason as bus driver with facsimile signature, ©1954, 9 x 11¾" 50.00

Godfrey, Arthur, magazine, *1000 Jokes Magazine*, issue #86, Fall 1953, 2-pp article on Arthur Godfrey with 3 photos, color cover illus of Godfrey playing ukulele, 8½ x 10¾" 25.00

Happy Days, Fonzie's Jalopy, plastic, yellow and black, with 2 unopened bags of parts to complete car's assembly, for use with Mego action figures, ©1977 Paramount Pictures Corp, 14" l 75.00

Howdy Doody, display, hp wood diecut, 1970s, 32" h 900.00

Howdy Doody, hand puppet, Johnny Jupiter, created by Scott Brinker, molded composition head with hp features, brown and red felt body, with orig 13 x 15" pencil design approved by Kagran, used on 1953–54 TV show 2,150.00

The Honeymooners, collector plate, The Hamilton Collection, 1987, $20.00.

Howdy Doody, merchandising catalog, features Howdy lunch boxes, puppets, records, shows, food, phono-doodle, watches, etc, 20 plus pp, 1955 . . . . **750.00**

Howdy Doodle, plates, china, Howdy image as cowboy swinging lariat, mkd "Taylor, Smith, Taylor, USA," 1950s, 8½" d, price for set of 5 . . . . **370.00**

Howdy Doody, premium, Luden's, Howdy Doody Magic Kit, uncut cut-outs, cutting Mr Bluster in half trick and more, with orig envelope. **215.00**

Howdy Doody, tie, silk, repeating images of Howdy with "Howdy Doody" above **965.00**

Howdy Doody, TV show prop, candlestick telephone, gold painted wood with metal fittings, early 1950s, 12" h **1,415.00**

Howdy Doody, TV show prop, Clarabell's Spray Bottle, copper colored with black top, late 1950s, 13" h **1,825.00**

I Dream of Jeannie, costume, plastic mask, vinyl top and red rayon bottom, orig box, Ben Cooper, ©1974 Hanna-Barbera Productions Inc **50.00**

I Dream of Jeannie, doll, life-like rooted hair, poseable, fabric outfit, with plastic purse and display stand, orig box, Remco, ©1977 Screen Gems **25.00**

I Dream of Jeannie, liquor bottle, dark transparent green glass, removable top with cork stopper inside, under-side mkd "Federal Law Forbids Sale Or Re-Use Of This Bottle," 1960s, 13½" h. **50.00**

I Dream of Jeannie, magazine, *TV Week*, with Barbara Eden, Jul 27, 1969, supplement issued in Baltimore MD newspaper *The Sun*, color cover photo of Barbara Eden in red bathing suit, 8¼ x 10¼". **20.00**

I Dream of Jeannie, party invitations, full color illus of Jeannie, Babu, and bottle, Contempo, ©1973 Columbia Pictures Industries Inc, MIP **20.00**

I Love Lucy, book, *I Love Lucy 3 Dimension Picture Storybook*, 24 pp, 4 pp of 3-D photos, rest are black and white, inside front cover is small attached enve-lope that held the "Photo Magic 3-D Specs," back cover color photo of Ricky Jr, 3 Dimension Publications Inc, ©1953 Lucille Ball/Desi Arnaz, 8 x 10". **100.00**

I Love Lucy, coloring book, "Lucille Ball/Desi Arnaz Coloring Book," 64 pp, cover design repeated front and back including illus of pr of lockets with small black and white photos of each holding baby Ricky, 14 pp colored, Whitman, ©1953, 11 x 15". **75.00**

I Love Lucy, comic book, Dell, #535, Four-Color Series. **100.00**

I Spy, poster, color art, action illus plus portraits, 21x 24". **50.00**

Jones, James Earl, PS, glossy, color, black felt-tip pen sig-nature, with orig mailing envelope from public rela-tions office, 8 x 10" **25.00**

Julia, thermos, metal, blue cup, illus, King-Seeley Thermos Co, ©1969 Savannah Productions Inc, 6½" h **20.00**

Kaye, Danny, pinback button, celluloid, black and white, for TV event "Look-In At The Metropolitan Opera" special, 4" d **15.00**

Kung Fu, playset 6 diecut windows containing various figures and parts including horse and rider, frontier building, cowboys, buckboard, etc, ©1975 Multiple Toymakers. **75.00**

Land of the Giants, flip flashlight, hard plastic, sticker on top, orig attached keychain, when button on side is pressed, top cover opens to reveal bulb inside, com-plete with spring, end cap, and orig battery, Bantamlite, ©1968 Kent Productions, 3" l. **45.00**

Land of the Giants, publicity photo, glossy black and white, illus of giant with cast members in giant's hand as well as test tubes, with attached "ABC Press infor-mation" paper, dated 1968, 7¼ x 9". **25.00**

Lassie, bank, painted plaster, raised name "Lassie" on front edge of base, coin slot on back of head, unmkd, c1950s, 6 x 11 x 16½" **100.00**

Lassie, coloring book, 96 pp, Whitman, ©1968 Wrather Corp, 8 x 10¾" **25.00**

Lassie, typed contract, sgd, dated Apr 18, 1961, issued for Jon Provost, states extension has been added to orig agreement of Apr 23, 1957 for "Services As An Actor In Television Programs And Otherwise," blue felt-tip pen signature by Provost and his parents, Bion and Cecile, and representative of Lassie Television Inc, 8½ x 11". **100.00**

Lawman, photograph, Peter Brown and John Russell, black and white, facsimile signatures, early 1960s, 6¼ x 7¼" **22.00**

Lawrence Welk Show, puzzle, "The Lawrence Welk Show Picture Puzzle," color photo of Sheila, Sherri, David, and Roger, orig box, Jaymar, ©Teleklew Productions, 1970s, 13 x 18" assembled size **25.00**

Leave It to Beaver, record, 78 rpm, yellow vinyl, sleeve has color illus with inset black and white illus of Beaver, Golden Records, ©1978 Gomalco **25.00**

Lee, Pinkie, figure, soft vinyl, designed to "blow his top" head and long neck are separate piece from body and when his stomach is squeezed his head pops off, Stern Toy Co, 1950, 8½" h **75.00**

Little House on the Prairie, Colorforms Playset, diecut design with house that opens and closes to reveal int, 2 large sheets of diecut vinyl pcs of cast members and accessories, complete with color cast photo, orig box, © Ed Friendly Productions Inc **25.00**

Man From U.N.C.L.E., Secret Agent Watch, dial illus depicting Napoleon Solo holding communicator, glow-in-the-dark, blue vinyl straps, Bradley, ©1966 MGM **100.00**

Marx, Groucho, napkins, "That's Me Groucho Marx Cocktail Napkins," complete set of 36 different nap-kins featuring Groucho plus and additional 37th nap-kin adv 1955 DeSoto, orig box, ©1954 Monogram **50.00**

Milton Berle, Danny O'Day ventriloquist dummy, plastic head and hands, cloth body, mkd "Juro Novelty Co., Inc. 1964," with instruction booklet, 30" h, $182.00. Photo courtesy Collectors Auction Services.

M*A*S*H, stethoscope, plastic and vinyl, logo sticker and card, on 6 x 12" blister card, Ja-Ru, ©1981 20th Century Fox Film Corp. **20.00**

McHale's Navy, game, diecut playing pc representing PT boats at each corner, Transogram, ©1962 Sto-Rev Co **50.00**

Miss Piggy, trinket box, ceramic, depicting Miss Piggy in purple dress atop large egg shaped base, with small repeated accent design in purple and green, Sigma, 1980s, 4 x 6 x 6¼" **75.00**

Mod Squad, publicity photo, psychedelic black and white illus of Mod Squad members, with "ABC Press information" paper, 7¼ x 9" **15.00**

Mork and Mindy, card game, deck of 84 cards with character illus, plus four 3" h white styrofoam eggs, Milton Bradley, ©1978 Paramount Pictures Corp **25.00**

Munsters, jigsaw puzzle, scene of Munster's in Grandpa's laboratory, Whitman, ©1965 Kayro-Vue Productions, 8½ x 11 x 1½" box **50.00**

Munsters, movie poster, *Munster Go Home*, Munster family in center, lower left corner has smaller illus of Herman, Lily and Grandpa in race, ©Universal Pictures Co Inc, 1966, 27 x 41" **100.00**

My Mother the Car, coloring book, color cover art repeated on front and back, Saalfield Publishing Co, ©1965 Cottage Industries Inc, 8½ x 11" **20.00**

Pee Wee Herman, marionette, Pee Wee's Pal Billy Balogne, stuffed body, hard vinyl head, hands, and feet, wearing plaid jacket with white shirt, gray pants, red tie emb "B," orig box, Matchbox, ©1988 Herman Toys Inc, 18" h **75.00**

Petticoat Junction, game, overhead view of railroad tracks with "Shady Rest Hotel" at center, Standard Toykraft, ©Wayfilms, 1960s **45.00**

Rat Patrol, thermos, metal, yellow cup, illus, Aladdin, ©1967 Cambridge Publications Inc, 6½" h **50.00**

Sales, Soupy, pinback button, litho tin, black and white photo of Soupy with hands in air, facsimile signature, ©1965 Soupy Sales, 3½" d **20.00**

Sgt Bilko, coloring book, 64 pp, color cover photo repeated front and back, 10 pp colored, Treasure Books Inc, ©1959 CBS Inc, 8¼ x 10¾" **45.00**

Sgt Bilko, game, Phil Silvers, Sgt Bilko—CBS Television's "You'll Never Get Rich" Game, Gardner, 1955 . . . . **50.00**

Sgt Bilko, record, *Phil Silvers and Swinging Brass*, 33⅓ rpm, front color cover photo of Silvers as Sgt Bilko with text about him and the record on reverse, Columbia, 1950s **25.00**

Six Million Dollar Man, activity book, 24 pp, color stiff paper cover, inside page with Steve Austin punch-out plaque and "Race In Space" game board and playing pieces, other pages with games and puzzles, unused, Rand McNally, ©1974 Universal City Studios Inc, 10 x 12½" **15.00**

Six Million Dollar Man, Dip Dots Painting Design Book, 16 pp, Kenner, ©1976 Universal City Studios Inc, 9 x 14 x 1" **20.00**

Smothers Brothers, yo-yo, red wood, design in gold on top of Smothers Brothers silhouette with name, reverse mkd "Kodak," 2¼" d **20.00**

Starsky & Hutch, Torino car, diecast metal and plastic, red, white accent sticker, Corgi, ©1977 Spelling-Goldberg Productions, on 4 x 5¼" blister cad with color photos **20.00**

Pee Wee Herman, Colorforms, ©1987 Herman Toys, $12.00.

Third Rock From the Sun, script, sgd, 49 pp, 50th episode titled "Dick-In-Law," final draft dated 9/5/97, front cover sgd by 8 cast members in black felt-tip pen, orig envelope with "3rd Rock From The Sun" mailing label, 8½ x 11" **200.00**

Virginian, The, movie viewer, image of smiling cast members, clear plastic window containing black and red viewer with 2 films in boxes, Chemtoy, #25, ©1966 Universal TV **20.00**

Welcome Back Kotter, bank, Welcome Back Kotter Sweathogs Action Back, hard plastic, built-in key, full color paper labels including Sweathog photos, front panel mkd "Sweathogs Scholarship Fund," bank has designated area for placement of coin on small peg, door opens and 3-D plastic pc depicting Barbarino and Epstein reaches out and grabs coin, orig box, Fleetwood Toys Inc, ©1976 The Wolper Organization **75.00**

Williams, Robin, PS, glossy black and white, black felt-tip pen signature, "Make Fun Not War Robin Williams," 8 x 10" **25.00**

TELEVISION LAMPS

"You will go blind if you watch television in the dark" was a common warning in the early 1950s. American lamp manufacturers responded by creating lamps designed to sit atop the television set and provide the correct amount of indirect lighting necessary to preserve the viewer's eyesight.

The need was simple. The solutions were imaginative and of questionable taste in more than a few cases. Most television lamps were ceramic and back-lit. Motifs ranged from leaping gazelles to a prancing horse with a clock in the middle of his body graced by a red Venetian blind, pagoda-like shade.

References: Leland and Crystal Payton, *Turned On: Decorative Lamps of the Fifties*, Abbeville Press, 1989; Tom Santiso, *TV Lamps*, Collector Books, 1999; Calvin Shepherd, *'50s TV Lamps*, Schiffer Publishing, 1998.

Angel Fish, Royal Haeger, 13¾" h **$80.00**
Basset Hound, Maddux of California, 11½" h **65.00**

Siamese Cats, Midwest Potteries, Kron Line, 1940–44, 13¼" h, $40.00.

Big Horn Sheep, 12½" h 55.00
Black Panther, gold collar, Lane, 15" l 80.00
Black Panther, red eyes, 22" l 65.00
Boxer Dog, fiberglass shade, 10" l 75.00
Boxer Dog, Royal of California, 15" h 70.00
Buffalo, Morton Pottery 75.00
Cocker Spaniel, lucite, plastic base 75.00
Colonial Couple, candy dish base, 12½" h 85.00
Comedy and Tragedy Masks, Royal Haeger, 9½" h 50.00
Covered Wagon, Marcia of California, 11" l 55.00
Crane in Flight, California Original 75.00
Crowing Rooster, Lane, 15" h. 15.00
Dachshund, fiberglass shade, 10" l. 75.00
Double Calla Lily Planter, Morton Pottery. 30.00
Double Deer, oxblood and white, Royal Haeger, 5½" h 175.00
Double Deer Head, Gilner Co, 13" h 50.00
Double Fish Planter, 10½" l 45.00
Elephant, 6½" h 45.00
Fan Vase, turquoise and white, 22K gold trim, La Velle
   of California, 9½" h. 50.00
Fighting Black Panthers, 12" h 75.00
Flamingos Planter, Lane. 50.00
Frogs on Lily Pad, Royal of California, 7" h 45.00
Gazelle Planter, ebony cascade, Royal Haeger, 25½" h 100.00
Gondola Planter, Morton Pottery 40.00
Greyhound Planter, brown, Royal Haeger, 6¼" h,
   11½" l 75.00
Hawaiian Woman, paddling canoe, ceramic, gold
   splash, 8" l 75.00
Horse Head, Morton Pottery, 28" h 45.00
Horse Head and Colt, Made in USA, 11½" h 75.00
Irish Setter Planter, bird in mouth, Morton Pottery, small 45.00
Island Girl, leaning against palm tree, ceramic, green,
   screen background 40.00
Leaf Planter, green, 8" h. 35.00
Mallards in Flight, Maddux 45.00
Mermaid on Shell, Comer Creations, 8½" h 40.00
Oriental Couple, sitting on junk, plastic shade, 10" h 40.00
Oriental Couple, sitting on junk, venetian blind shade,
   19" h 75.00
Owl, Kron of Texas, 11½" h 100.00

Panther Planter, green, Hollywood Ceramics, 8½" h 50.00
Panther Planter, maroon, 6½" h 40.00
Pink Poodle, candy dish base, Lane, 13" h 150.00
Polynesian Woman, plaster, 13" h 75.00
Poodle, chalkware. 40.00
Poodle and Pug, Kron of Texas 50.00
Prancing Horse, candy dish base, Lane, 13½" h 80.00
Prancing Horse, Royal Haeger, 11½" l 40.00
Prancing Ram, green, gold highlights, 14" h 40.00
Roadrunner, Maddux, 9½" h 70.00
Sailboat, painted plaster, Garland Creations, 13½" h 50.00
Sailboat, solid bronze, 13" h 50.00
Sailfish, silver spray, Royal Haeger, 9" h, 9¼" l 40.00
Siamese Cat and Kittens, Lane, 12½" h 75.00
Siamese Cats, black and cream, Claes, 12" h 50.00
Stage Coach, green, gold highlights, 6" h 40.00
Stalking Panther, chartreuse and ebony cascade, venet-
   ian blind shade, Royal Haeger, 5" h, 17½" l 125.00
Swan Planter, Maddux of California, 10" h 70.00
Swordfish and Seashell, green 40.00
Tulip Vase, Ceramic Arts, 9½" h 50.00
Vase, dragon motif, Walco, 10" h 60.00
Vase, horse head motif, 8" h 40.00
Vase, hp floral motif, 10" h 60.00
White Horse, Maddux of California, 12½" h. 65.00
White Panther, Kron of Texas, 16½" l 95.00
White Swan, Maddux of California, 12" h 55.00

TELEVISIONS

Television sets are divided into three groups: (1) mechanical era sets, 1925 to 1932, (2) pre-World War II sets, 1938–1941, and (3) post-1946 sets. Mechanical era sets, also known as radiovisors, were used in conjunction with the radio. Reception was limited to the Chicago and New York area.

The electronic picture tube was introduced in 1938. The smaller the tube, the older the set is a good general rule. Early electric sets provided for a maximum of five channels, 1 through 5. Many sets made prior to 1941 combined the television with a multiband radio. Fewer than 20,000 sets were produced. Many of the sets were sold in kit form.

Production of television sets significantly increased following World War II. Channels 6 to 13 were added between 1946 and 1948. Channel 1 was dropped in 1949, replaced with V.H.F. channels 2 through 13. The U.H.F. band was added in 1953.

Collectors focus primarily on the black and white sets from the 1940s and 1950s. There is some interest in color sets made prior to 1955. Brand and model numbers are essential to researching value. Cabinet condition also is critical to value, sometimes more important than whether or not the set is operational. Sets made after 1960 have more reuse than collectible value.

References: Bryan Durbal and Glann Bubenheimer, *Collector's Guide to Vintage Televisions,* Collector Books, 1999; Scott Wood (ed.), *Classic TVs With Price Guide: Pre-War Thru 1950s,* L-W Book Sales, 1992, 1997 value update.

Periodical: *Antique Radio Classified,* PO Box 2, Carlisle, MA 01741.

Collectors' Club: Antique Wireless Assoc, 59 Main St, Holcomb, NY 14469.

Admiral, 4H126, combination TV and pull-out phono plus AM/FM radio, 1949, 10" screen. **$15.00**

Admiral, 20X11, Bakelite tabletop, sq lines, ribs molded into sides, 10" screen. **65.00**

Air King, A-1001A, console, flat front, screen over 4 knobs, large grill cloth, 1949, 10" screen **75.00**

Andrea, T-VK12, wide wooden table, continuous 13 channel tuner, FM radio dial on right side of screen, 1948, 12" screen **100.00**

Ansley, 701, Beacon, wooden tabletop, 13 channel tuner, grill cloth and mesh on left and right panels, 4 knobs at bottom, 10" screen. **75.00**

Arvin, 15-1550, color console, plain front, 15" round picture tube, 1954. . . . . **450.00**

Bendix, 2001, tabletop, rounded corners, 3 knobs below screen, 1950, 10" screen **100.00**

Capehart/Farnsworth, 4001, combination with AM/FM radio and phono, 12" screen **65.00**

CBS-Columbia, 20C3, console, French Provincial style, double doors, 1951, 20" screen **25.00**

Crosley, 9-409M, console, double doors, controls to left and right of screen, 1949, 12" screen **35.00**

DuMont, ET-140, sq tabletop, 14" picture tube, 1950 . . . . . . **20.00**

Emerson, 611, table, sq lines and flat top, painted glass screen, 4 knobs across bottom, 1948, 10" screen **75.00**

FADA, 800, projection model, sq lines, flat front and top **45.00**

General Electric, 810, wooden tabletop, screen offset to right front, 4 knobs below, 1949, 10" screen. **65.00**

Hallicrafters, 1005, mahogany set, 4 thin legs, 2 large knobs and small controls under screen, 1952, 10" screen. **15.00**

Hallicrafters, T-64, custom chassis with push buttons below porthole-type screen, 1949, 10" screen. **25.00**

JVC, 3240, Video Sphere, oval plastic cover on front of screen, chain on top, simple base, 1972. . . . . **100.00**

Motorola, 27K2, console, 2 large knobs below, 24" screen. **35.00**

Motorola, VK-101, 13 channel console, lower area tilts forward to expose AM/FM radio, 1948, 10" screen **125.00**

Norelco, PT 200, console, fixed plastic projection screen, 1948. . . . . **50.00**

Olympic, TV-947, console, simple style, double doors, 1950s, 16" screen **25.00**

Philco, 48-1001, tabletop, screen above and to left of cabinet, tube within cabinet lines, 10" screen **100.00**

RCA, 4T112, 1951, 17" screen. **20.00**

RCA, 9T246, metal tabletop, grill around screen, imitation mahogany finish, 1949, 10" screen **25.00**

Sentinel, 431-CV, console, double doors conceal screen and 2 knobs, 1951 . . . . **15.00**

Silvertone, 133, wooden console, pull-out phono beneath screen, 1949, 12" screen. **50.00**

Sony, TV-500U, portable, screen at left, UHF dial and controls at right, 1961, 5" screen **20.00**

Sparton, 4900 TV, mirror-in-lid credenza, sq lines, phono behind right door, AM/FM radio behind right doors, TV beneath center lid, 1949, 12" screen **150.00**

Stewart-Warner, AVT-1, consolette, direct vision 10" screen, 1949. . . . . **45.00**

Stromberg-Carlson, TV-125-LA, console, porthole look screen, controls at bottom left and right of 12" screen, 1949. . . . . **85.00**

Sylvania, 21C405, Halolight console, light flush around 21" screen. **100.00**

Philco, 4242, Predicta Holiday, with swivel stand and blonde cabinet, 1958, $248.00. Photo courtesy Gene Harris Antique Auction Center, Inc.

Westinghouse, H-216, console, lid on top at left lifts up and tube pulls up, controls behind right front door, 1949, 16" screen **175.00**

Zenith, G2957, double door combination, 21" porthole look screen **75.00**

Zenith, T2250, wooden console, 21" rect screen. **25.00**

TEMPLE, SHIRLEY

Born on April 23, 1928, in Santa Monica, California, Shirley Temple was the most successful child movie star of all time. She was discovered while attending dance class at the Meglin Dance Studios in Los Angeles. Fox Film's *Stand Up and Cheer* (1934) was her first starring role. She made a total of twelve pictures that year.

Gertrude George, Shirley's mother, played a major role in creating Shirley's image and directing her licensing program. Requests for endorsements and licenses were immediate. Hundreds of products were marketed.

By 1935 Temple was the number one box office star, a spot she retained through 1938. In 1940 Temple starred in *The Blue Bird* and *Young People,* her last films for Fox. She immediately signed a $100,000 a year contract with MGM and starred in *Kathleen* in 1941, her first teenage/adult movie role. Shirley married for the first time in 1945. She retired from films in 1950, the same year she divorced her husband and married Charles Black.

In 1957 Shirley was host of the *Shirley Temple Storybook.* In the 1960s Shirley Temple Black became active in Republican politics. After serving as a U.S. Delegate to the United Nations and Ambassador to Ghana, she became Chief of Protocol in Washington. Her final government service was as Ambassador to Czechoslovakia in 1989.

References: Edward R. Pardella, *Shirley Temple Dolls and Fashion,* Schiffer Publishing, 1992; Dian Zillner, *Hollywood Collectibles: The Sequel,* Schiffer Publishing, 1994.

Book, *Just a Little Girl*, boxed set of 5, black and white, 16 pp, photos, Saalfield, 1936 . . . . **$100.00**

Book, *Story of Shirley Temple, The*, 160 pp, black and white photos, Saalfield, 1934, 4½ x 5¼" **50.00**

Doll, Curly Top, composition, orig clothes and box, 1935, 16" h **150.00**

Fan, "I'll Be Seeing You," R Cola adv **25.00**

Magazine, *Look*, Vol 1, #7, May 25, 1937, front cover design includes black and white photo of Mae West as "Highest Paid Woman," color double centerfold photo of West and Shirley Temple who mimics, 10½ x 13½" **50.00**

Movie Book, *Poor Little Rich Girl*, 32 pp, 27 black and white film scenes, full color front cover, Saalfield, 1936, 9½ x 10" **50.00**

Movie Book, *The Little Colonel*, 150 pp, Saalfield, 1934, 4½ x 5¼" **25.00**

Paper Dolls, Shirley Temple Snap-On Paperdoll Set, Gabriel Sons Co, 1959, 12 x 12½" **75.00**

Photo, Ferndal Dairy adv, black and white, Shirley sipping bottled milk through straws, facsimile signature and 1937 20th Century Fox copyright, back has green on white text for local dairy, 8 x 10" **25.00**

Pinback Button, "Chicago Times Shirley Temple Club," litho tin, blue and white with bluetone photo, ⅞" d **100.00**

Pinback Button, "Genuine Shirley Temple Doll," browntone photo, orange tint on hair bow, ©Ideal Novelty, 1¼" d **75.00**

Pocket Mirror, celluloid, brown photo, pale pink ground, 1¾" d **45.00**

Postcard, *Captain January* scene, glossy sepia picture, unused, 1936, 3½ x 5½" **15.00**

Ring, celluloid, red, white, and black, diecut Shirley head, Japan **25.00**

Sewing Cards, Saalfield, 6 black and white cards, yarn, 1936, 5 x 7" box **45.00**

Souvenir Book, Tournament of Roses Parade, Temple as Grand Marshal, 32 pp, 1939, 9 x 12" **25.00**

Movie Poster, *Susannah of the Mounties*, 20th Century Fox, linen-backed, 1939, 41 x 27", $650.00.

TENNIS COLLECTIBLES

Tennis came to America in the mid-1870s. After a tennis craze in the 1880s, the sport went into a decline. International play led to a revival in the early 1900s. The period from 1919 to 1940 is viewed by many tennis scholars as the sport's golden age.

Tennis collectibles are divided into two periods: (1) pre-1945 and (2) post-1945. There is little collector interest in post-1945 material. There are three basic groups of collectibles: (1) items associated with play such as tennis balls, ball cans, rackets, and fashions, (2) paper ephemera ranging from books to photographs, and (3) objects decorated with a tennis image or in a tennis shape. Because tennis collecting is in its infancy, some areas remain highly affordable (rackets) while others (tennis ball cans) already are in the middle of a price run.

Reference: Jeanne Cherry, *Tennis Antiques & Collectibles*, Amaryllis Press, 1995.

Collectors' Club: The Tennis Collectors Society, Guildhall Orchard, Great Bromley, Colchester, CO7 7TU U.K.

Ball Can, Chemold, Tony Roche on red can with Australian flag **$30.00**

Ball Can, Court, red with white ball, English **80.00**

Ball Can, Davega, cardboard, yellow and black **175.00**

Ball Can, Dunhill, mostly green, some red, English **80.00**

Ball Can, Ellsworth Vines, blue and yellow or blue and green, flat lid **75.00**

Ball Can, Imperial, green with racket and ball, English **75.00**

Ball Can, Oxford, purple, 12 ball can **125.00**

Ball Can, Pennsylvania, "Allcort Championship," yellow and black, dome lid **25.00**

Ball Can, Pennsylvania, "Centre Court," mostly black with white ball, USA dome lid **20.00**

Ball Can, Pennsylvania, yellow, black, and white paper label, 12-ball can, 1940s **400.00**

Ball Can, Spalding, mostly white with red and blue on front, USA dome lid **20.00**

Ball Can, Wilson, "Jack Kramer," red and white, English **75.00**

Ball Can, Wisden, olive green with white ball, disc lid, English **150.00**

Ball Can, X-Pert, blue and red with white ball, dome lid **38.00**

Book, *Match Play and the Spin of the Ball*, Tilden, William T, 1st edition, hardbound, 1923 . . . . **45.00**

Charm, tennis racquet, sterling silver **10.00**

Game, Set Point, Tennis Strategy Game, SV Productions, 1971 . . . . **30.00**

Game, Wide World of Sports—Tennis, cover shows film strip with slide of game name and slide of player serving tennis ball, players on court background, Milton Bradley, 1974 . . . . **15.00**

Magazine, *Sports Illustrated*, Jul 15, 1974, Jimmy Connors and Chris Evert **7.50**

Net, turned wood posts **50.00**

Photograph, Don Budge and Ellsworth Vines, rackets at net, 1939, 7 x 9" **12.00**

Postcard, woman playing tennis with cupid, figural heart tennis ball **30.00**

Poster, "The Light Blue Tennis Ball," Grays of Cambridge, tennis racket and ball, green and blue ground, Affiches Marci, c1947, 24 x 39" **225.00**

Program, Wimbledon, All England Lawn Tennis Club,
  1950s **4.00**
Racquet, Famous Player Series, Don Budge, 1940s **10.00**
Racquet, Hazell's Streamline, 3-shaft construction,
  England, 1930s **90.00**
Racquet, Wilson, "Comet," wooden, 4³/₈" **15.00**
Racquet, Winchester, wooden, trademark decal, 1930s **40.00**

THIMBLES

By the middle of the 19th century, the American thimble industry was able to produce finely worked thimbles. Gold and silver thimbles were restricted to the upper class. Utilitarian thimbles were made of brass or steel. In 1880 William Halsey patented a process to make celluloid thimbles. Aluminum thimbles made their appearance in the second quarter of the 20th century.

A thimble was one of the few gifts considered appropriate for an unmarried man to give to a lady. Many of these fancy thimbles show little wear, possibly a result of both inappropriate sizing and the desire to preseve the memento.

Advertising thimbles were popular between 1920 and the mid-1950s. Early examples were made from celluloid or aluminum. Plastic was the popular post-war medium. The first political thimbles appeared shortly after ratification of the nineteenth amendment. They proved to be popular campaign giveaways through the early 1960s.

References: Averil Mathis, *Antique and Collectible Thimbles and Accessories,* Collector Books, 1986, 1997 value update; Estelle Zalkin, *Zalkin's Handbook of Thimbles & Sewing Implements,* Warman Publishing, 1988, distributed by Krause Publications.

Newsletter: *Thimbletter,* 93 Walnut Hill Rd, Newton Highlands, MA 02161.

Collectors' Clubs: The Thimble Guild, PO Box 381807, Duncanville, TX 75138; Thimble Collectors International, 8289 Northgate Dr, Rome, NY 13440.

Note: For additional sewing listings refer to Sewing Items.

Advertising, Coca-Cola, leaded glass, red, white letter-
  ing, Western Germany **$8.00**
Advertising, Drink Orange Crush For Health, aluminum,
  whistle **30.00**
Advertising, Eveready Flashlight Batteries, plastic **1.00**
Advertising, Hoover, aluminum **4.00**
Advertising, John Deere, plastic **2.00**
Advertising, Prudential Life Insurance, brass **8.00**
Advertising, Sew & Save the Singer Way, plastic **2.00**
Advertising, Star Brand Shoes, aluminum **4.00**
Bone China, Charles and Diana, Theodore Paul, England **6.00**
Bone China, white, gold trim, Noritake, Japan **15.00**
Brass, basketweave design, Austria **12.00**
Brass, bluebells, dark ground **8.00**
Brass, Florida Orange Bird, Walt Disney Productions **6.00**
Brass, grapes motif **8.00**
Brass, leaf band **10.00**
Brass, plain band **3.00**
China, Christmas 1982, Caverswall, England **12.00**
China, Norman Rockwell illus, Japan **10.00**
Enameled Metal, floral spray, "Bicentennial 1976," Betsy
  Ross and US flag, Holland **40.00**

Advertising, Orange-Crush, emb orange band, ⁷/₈ x ⁵/₈", $66.00. Photo courtesy Wm. Morford.

Glass, clear, etched bells **8.00**
Glass, clear, painted dec **8.00**
Glass, spun crystal, hummingbird and blossom finial,
  gold trim **10.00**
Gold, semi-precious stones on band **200.00**
Pewter, figural stein, 1982 World's Fair souvenir **6.00**
Plastic, "Re-elect d'Alesandro for Mayor '86" **1.50**
Sterling Silver, cherubs **125.00**
Sterling Silver, enameled band **75.00**
Sterling Silver, hand-punched knurling top **18.00**
Sterling Silver, Palm Beach souvenir **150.00**
Wood, painted scene, Anri **10.00**

TIFFANY

Charles L. Tiffany and John B. Young founded Tiffany & Young, a stationery and gift store, in 1837. In 1841 Tiffany & Young became Tiffany, Young & Ellis. The name was changed to Tiffany & Company in 1853.

In 1852 Tiffany insisted that its silver comply with the English sterling silver standard of 925/1000. Charles Lewis Tiffany was one of the leaders in the fight that resulted in the federal government adopting this standard, passing a 1906 statute that set 925/1000 as the minimum requirement for articles marked "sterling."

During the 1850s Tiffany & Company produced some electro-plated wares. Production increased significantly following the Civil War. The manufacture of electroplated ware ended in 1931.

Tiffany incorporated as Tiffany & Co., Inc., in 1868, the same year the company acquired the Moore silverware factory. Tiffany's silver studio became America's first school of design. Beginning in 1868, Tiffany silverware was marked with "Tiffany & Co." and the letter "M" for Edward C. Moore, head of the studio. The company continued to mark its silverware with the initial of its incumbent president until the practice was discontinued in 1965.

Tiffany's jewelry, especially its botanical brooches and use of semi-precious gemstones, captured the world's attention at the Paris Exposition Universelle in 1878. Louis Comfort Tiffany, son of Charles Tiffany, became the company's first Design Director. Under his leadership, the company manufactured a wealth of Art Nouveau objects, especially jewelry and lamps.

Recognized as one of the world's most respected sources of diamonds and other jewelry, Tiffany craftsmanship extends to a broad range of items including fine china, clocks, flatware, leather goods, perfume, scarves, silver, stationery, and watches. Tiffany opened its New York Corporate Division 1960. The Vince Lombardi Trophy for the National Football League Super Bowl Championship is one of its most famous commissions.

References: John A. Shuman III, *The Collector's Encyclopedia of American Art Glass,* Collector Books, 1988, 1996 value update; Moise S. Steeg, Jr., *Tiffany Favrile Art Glass,* Schiffer Publishing, 1997; Kenneth Wilson, *American Glass 1760–1930: The Toledo Museum of Art,* 2 vols., Hudson Hills Press and The Toledo Museum of Art, 1994.

REPRODUCTION ALERT: Brass belt buckles, and badges marked "Tiffany" have been widely reproduced.

BRONZE

Box, gilt-bronze, shallow, circular, raised geometric border and red coloring on lower recessed surfaces, stamped "Tiffany Studios, New York 1759," 1¼" h, 8¾" d **$115.00**

Box, gilt-bronze and enamel, Zodiac pattern, imp "Tiffany Studios, New York 166" on base, 2" h, 4½" w, 3½" w **925.00**

Cigarette Box, gilt-bronze and enamel, etched finished on rect cedar-lined hinged box, with enamel dec border in blue and green, imp "Louis C. Tiffany Furnaces Inc. Favrile 130" on base, 2⅛" h **750.00**

Compote, gilt-bronze, allover etched surface on circular dish flaring to round base, imp "Louis C. Tiffany Furnaces Inc., Favrile 527" on base, New York, c1925, 4¼" h, 6" d **230.00**

Letter Holder, gilt-bronze, Bookmark pattern, 2-tier, imp "Tiffany Studios New York 1920," 5¼" h, 9¼" w **500.00**

Pen Tray, brown patina, rect, zodiac medallions on each end, base stamped "Tiffany Studios," 10" l, 3¼" w **175.00**

Picture Frame, gilt-bronze, etched, repeating freeform zigzag border in relief with recesses finished in patinated brown, easel back imp Tiffany Furnaces mark, "Louis C. Tiffany Furnaces, Inc. Favrile 66," New York, 1919–28, 10" h, 8" w **750.00**

Picture Frame, gilt-bronze, Heraldic pattern, lower recesses finished in patinated brown, easel back, imp mark, "Louis C. Tiffany Furnaces Inc.," New York, 1919–28, 12" h, 10¼" w **1,035.00**

Inkwell, Pine Needle pattern, #844, gold doré finish, etched metal and amber slag glass, imp mark, $200.00. Photo courtesy Gene Harris Antique Auction Center, Inc.

Table Lamp, gilt-bronze, 12-paneled favrile-fabrique golden amber glass shade, gold doré 3-socket paneled lamp base, base and shade imp "Tiffany Studios New York" and numbered, 24" h, 14½" d shade, price for pair, $24,150.00. Photo courtesy Skinner, Inc., Boston, MA.

Serving Tray, gilt-bronze, rolled rim on rondel, fire-polished random design, sgd with Tiffany Glass & Decorating monogram and "Tiffany Studios New York/8/9064," 14¾" d **975.00**

Stand, gilt-bronze, Chinese pattern, 5-ftd pedestal stand, imp "Louis C. Tiffany Furnaces Inc," 1919–28, 1½" h, 3½" d **175.00**

Tray, silvered-bronze, circular form, extended rim dec with border of alternating panels of stylized flowers and leaves in relief, stamped "Tiffany Studios, New York 1612," 10" d **175.00**

GLASS

Bonbon, engraved gold iridescent, intaglio cut leaf border on lustrous golden amber bowl with 3 applied shell feet, inscribed "L. C. Tiffany-Favrile," 3¾" h, 4¾" d **$850.00**

Bowl, blue iridescent, ruffled rim on 10-ribbed blue Favrile glass, base inscribed "L.C.T. Favrile," 6" d, 2" h . . . **700.00**

Bowl, gold spotted opal dish with emerald green and blue border rim, 3 applied reeded shell feet, button pontil, inscribed "L.C. Tiffany-Favrile," 6" d **920.00**

Compote, blue iridescent optic, 10-rib scalloped bowl on tapered stem above folded foot, lustrous purple-blue surface overall, inscribed "L. C. T." and labeled, 6¾" h **400.00**

Flower Bowl, opal and blue pastel, bright cornflower blue rolled rim on white opal bowl, int dec in Tiffany's molded herringbone leaf design, unsgd, 2¾" h, 7¼" d **900.00**

Shade, bronze and amber linenfold, 2-sided flared shade with amber glass panels, bordered by rect matching drapery glass, frame imp "Tiffany Studios New York pat. Applied for 1927," 7¼" h, 19¼" w **8,625.00**

Vase, green leaves on translucent opalescent glass with peach/pink color, inscribed "L.C. Tiffany Favrile 7394C," 6½" h **1,750.00**

Vase, oval, light amber glass with iridescent pink and green hooked swirls, base inscribed "L.C.T. Favrile 7582C," 2¾" h **1,375.00**

Vase, oyster white and opalescent glass dec with ric-rac band, white stripes, hooked design, and 2 iridescent bands, inscribed "Louis C. Tiffany 1050G," 7" h **800.00**

Vase, urn shape, applied scrolling, shell handles, overall golden lustre, base inscribed "L.C. Tiffany-Favrile 13H," 6½" h **1,275.00**

LAMPS

Boudoir, dome shaped amber cased to opal shade, subtle iridescent surface, gold Favrile baluster form lamp, leaf form lamp inclusions, lightly engraved outlines, glass foot inscribed "L. C. Tiffany Favrile," 15" h, 8" d . . . **$825.00**
Desk, doré, molded with signs of zodiac on single socket shade above oval platform base, imp "Tiffany Studios New York 414," 10" d, 10¼" w **2,000.00**
Floor, counterbalance, gold doré finish, bulbed 5-ftd base, adjustable ball lever socket, sgd "Tiffany Studios" on foot, 54" h **825.00**

STERLING SILVER

Bowl, on spreading foot, with incised bands to center, everted rim, 1907–38, 3" h, 5⅝" d, approx 9 troy oz **$175.00**
Bowl, raised on 5 stylized floral feet, 3 incised lines running up length of bowl from each, with pr of matching candlesticks, bowl 10¼" d, candlesticks 8½" h, 1947–56, 61 troy oz **2,415.00**
Dresser Set, 8 pcs, consisting of hairbrush, comb, shoehorn, nail file, nail clippers, nail buff, hand mirror, and small tray, monogrammed, 1907–38, approx 12 oz **250.00**
Picture Frame, enameled, red and black geometric design, Italian made, 5⅛" h, 7⅛" w, approx 6 oz weighable silver, price for pair **800.00**
Serving Dish, oval, guilloche band at rim, 1⅝" d and 8⅝" d, approx 38 troy oz, price for pair **1,035.00**

TIFFIN GLASS

J. Beatty and Sons built a large glass works in Tiffin, Ohio, in 1888. In 1892 Tiffin Glass Company became part of the U.S. Glass Company, a combine based in Pittsburgh, Pennsylvania.

During the Depression, Tiffin made hundreds of patterns, its output twice that of Cambridge and A. H. Heisey. Tiffin purchased Heisey blanks to meet its production requirements. The company's famed "Lady Stems" were made between 1939 and 1956.

Tiffin's profits carried many other plants in the U.S. Glass Company. Several plants making inexpensive glassware were closed or sold during the Depression. By 1951 Tiffin was the only U.S. Glass plant remaining in operation. U.S. Glass Company purchased Duncan & Miller in 1955. In 1962 U.S. Glass declared bankruptcy and closed the Tiffin factory.

Production resumed under the name "Tiffin Art Glass Corporation," a firm created by former Tiffin employees. Tiffin Art Glass produced high quality, etched stemware and glass accent pieces. The company also offered a pattern matching program, annually manufacturing retired patterns.

Tiffin purchased the molds and equipment of the T. G. Hawkes Cut Glass Company, Corning, New York, in 1964. Continental Can purchased the Tiffin factory in 1966, selling it in 1968 to the Interpace Corporation, a holding company of Franciscan china. Tiffin was sold once again in 1980, this time to Towle Silversmiths. Towle began importing blanks from Eastern Europe. In 1984 Towle closed the Tiffin factory and donated the land and buildings to the city of Tiffin. Jim Maxwell, a former Tiffin glass cutter, bought the Tiffin molds and equipment. The Tiffin trademark is now a registered trademark of Maxwell Crystal, Inc. In 1992 Maxwell placed four Hawkes and Tiffin patterns back into production.

References: Fred Bickenheuser, *Tiffin Glassmasters, Book I* (1979, 1994–95 value update), *Book II* (1981, 1994–95 value update), *Book III* (1985), Glassmasters Publications; Ed Goshe, Ruth Hemminger and Leslie Piña, *Depression Era Stems & Tableware: Tiffin,* Schiffer Publishing, 1998; Bob Page and Dale Fredericksen, *Tiffin Is Forever: A Stemware Identification Guide,* Page-Fredericksen, 1994; Ruth Hemminger, Ed Goshe and Leslie Piña, *Tiffin Modern: Mid-Century Art Glass,* Schiffer Publishing, 1997; Leslie Piña, *Tiffin Glass: 1914–1940,* Schiffer Publishing, 1997; Harry L. Rinker, *Stemware of the 20th Century: The Top 200 Patterns,* House of Collectibles, 1997.

Collectors' Club: Tiffin Glass Collectors' Club, PO Box 554, Tiffin, OH 44883.

Athens Diana, champagne **$25.00**
Athens Diana, cocktail **18.00**
Athens Diana, cup and saucer **24.00**
Athens Diana, jug, #128 . . . . **260.00**
Athens Diana, oyster cocktail **18.00**
Byzantine, cocktail, #15048, crystal **18.00**
Byzantine, cocktail, #15048, yellow **15.00**
Byzantine, iced tea, ftd, crystal, 6½" h **15.00**
Byzantine, platter, oval, yellow, 12¾" l **35.00**
Byzantine, salad plate, yellow, 7½" d **15.00**
Byzantine, sherbet, low, crystal **12.00**
Byzantine, water goblet, crystal **22.00**
Cadena, bread and butter plate, yellow, 6" d **12.00**
Cadena, console bowl, 12" d **30.00**
Cadena, creamer, yellow **40.00**
Cadena, cream soup bowl, pink **35.00**
Cadena, sugar, cov, yellow **30.00**
Celestial, cordial, #17707, ebony **30.00**
Celestial, cordial, #17707, turquoise **30.00**
Cerice, cordial, #15071 . . . . **40.00**
Cerice, wine **30.00**
Chalet, dessert/champagne **40.00**
Chalet, goblet **50.00**
Chalet, wine **55.00**
Cherokee Rose, bud vase, 8" h **45.00**
Cherokee Rose, candlesticks, pr, 2-lite, #5902 . . . . **160.00**
Cherokee Rose, claret, #17403, 4 oz, 6" h **50.00**
Cherokee Rose, cordial, #17378 . . . . **55.00**
Cherokee Rose, cordial, #17399 . . . . **50.00**
Cherokee Rose, creamer **22.00**
Cherokee Rose, creamer and sugar, beaded **60.00**
Cherokee Rose, iced tea, #17403 . . . . **35.00**
Cherokee Rose, water goblet, #17403 . . . . **35.00**
Classic, cafe parfait, #185 . . . . **70.00**
Classic, cordial, #185 . . . . **70.00**
Classic, goblet, #185 . . . . **35.00**
Classic, tumbler, flat, 8 oz **45.00**
Classic, whiskey, ftd, 2 oz, #185 . . . . **75.00**
Coventry, cordial, #17623 . . . . **30.00**
Fantasy, cordial, #17687 . . . . **30.00**
Flanders, bread and butter plate, pink, 6" d **14.00**
Flanders, candlesticks, pr, crystal **95.00**
Flanders, cordial, #196, crystal **55.00**

Left to right: June Night, water goblet, crystal, etched, 1940s-50s, 7⁷/₈" h, $20.00; Wistaria, water goblet, pink bowl, 6" h, $25.00.

Flanders, creamer and sugar, flat, pink	265.00
Flanders, finger bowl, crystal	40.00
Flanders, iced tea, ftd, pink	75.00
Flanders, pitcher, cov, #194, pink	600.00
Flanders, salad plate, crystal	9.00
Fuchsia, bud vase, 10¹/₂" h	45.00
Fuchsia, cocktail	20.00
Fuchsia, cordial, #15083	40.00
Fuchsia, creamer and sugar, #5902	55.00
Fuchsia, iced tea, ftd, #15083	25.00
Fuchsia, trophy vase, handled, 11" h	230.00
Fuchsia, water, ftd, 9 oz	20.00
June Night, bread and butter plate, crystal, 6" d	16.00
June Night, bud vase, crystal, 10¹/₂" h	45.00
June Night, champagne, #17403	20.00
June Night, claret	38.00
June Night, creamer and sugar	55.00
June Night, iced tea tumbler, ftd	35.00
Killarney Green, candlesticks, pr, 1-lite, #6364	95.00
Killarney Green, champagne, #15074	25.00
Killarney Green, goblet, #15074	35.00
Killarney Green, iced tea, #15074	30.00
King's Crown, goblet, ftd, 9 oz, ruby flashed	35.00
King's Crown, iced tea, flat, 12 oz, ruby flashed	14.00
King's Crown, juice, ftd, 4 oz, ruby flashed	12.00
King's Crown, torte plate, 14" d, ruby flashed	70.00
King's Crown, wedding bowl, cov, ftd, 7¹/₂" d, ruby flashed	90.00
Luciana Green, dessert plate, 8" d	30.00
Majal, cordial, #17594	30.00
Persian Pheasant, champagne, #17358	25.00
Persian Pheasant, claret, 4¹/₂ oz	40.00
Persian Pheasant, cordial, #17392	60.00
Rose Point, bowl, ftd, 3400, 12" d	95.00
Rose Point, celery, 3400/64, 12" d	100.00
Rose Point, comport, 3400/7, 5¹/₂" d	45.00

TONKA

Mound Metalcraft, located on the banks of Lake Minnetonka in Mound, Minnesota, was incorporated in September 1946 to manufacture garden tools and household products. Absorbing the toy business of L. E. Streeter Company, Tonka introduced two pressed steel toys at the 1947 New York Toy Fair. By 1949 the line included fourteen different products including a doll hospital bed.

In 1956 Mound Metalcraft changed its name to Tonka and introduced its line of Hi-Way trucks. Tonka gained a reputation for producing nicely designed, realistic-looking vehicles.

In 1961 Tonka purchased a plastics company and began producing plastic accessories for its vehicles. Tonka acquired Kenner in 1988. Hasbro purchased the combined company in 1991.

The year 1963 is the major divider between younger and older Tonka collectors. Restoration of early examples is common and often unreported by the seller. Beware.

Reference: Don and Barb DeSalle, *Tonka Trucks: 1947–1963*, L-W Book Sales, 1994, 1996 value update.

Note: Prices listed are for vehicles in mint condition.

Aerial Fire Truck, 26"	$14.00
Aerial Ladder Fire Truck, 25"	22.00
Air Express	225.00
Allied Van Lines, #739	125.00
Back Hoe, 17¹/₈"	120.00
Boat Transport, 38" l	180.00
Bottom Dump Truck, 29"	28.00
Car Carrier, 43"	28.00
Carnation Milk Delivery Van	250.00
Carnation Milk Step Van, 11³/₄"	250.00
Cement Truck, 15"	125.00
Crane and Clam, #150, 24"	130.00
Dump Truck, 20"	14.00
Dump Truck, red and blue, 1962, 13"	38.00
Dump Truck, tan and white, 1974, 13"	35.00
Farm Stake and Hose Trailer	150.00
Farm Stake Truck, #404	75.00
Grader, #600	100.00
Grain Hauler Semi, #550, 22¹/₄"	200.00
Hook and Ladder	250.00
Hose Truck, 16"	38.00
Hydraulic Dump	80.00
Jeep Commander, 10¹/₂"	40.00
Jeep Dispatcher, 9³/₄"	50.00
Jeep Universal, #249	55.00
Ladder Fire Truck, 36"	50.00
Livestock Truck	150.00
Loader, #352	50.00
Loboy and Shovel	300.00
Logger, #08	165.00
Logger Semi, #575, 22¹/₄"	200.00
Lumber Truck, 18³/₄"	120.00
Military Jeep Universal, #251	50.00
Military Tractor, #250	100.00
Mini Tonka Livestock Van, 16"	75.00
Mini Tonka Mixer, 9"	75.00
Mini Tonka Van, 16"	50.00
Minute Maid Orange Juice Van	300.00
Mobile Clam, 27¹/₄"	150.00
Mobile Crane, 10"	5.00

Roadster, c1930, 14¹/₂" l, $121.00. Photo courtesy Collectors Auction Services.

Mobile Dragline	125.00
Pickup, #580	185.00
Pickup, #880	225.00
Pickup with Stock Box, 14"	45.00
Pumper, #926	185.00
Rescue Squad Van, 11³/₄"	250.00
Road Grader, #600, 17"	120.00
Rovin' Wrecker, #2202, 14"	22.00
Sanitary Truck	400.00
Service Truck, 12³/₄"	140.00
Snorkel Fire Truck, 17"	65.00
Sportsman	140.00
Steam Shovel, #50, 20³/₄"	175.00
Steam Shovel Deluxe, #100, 22"	125.00
State Hi-Way Department Dump & Plow Truck, 16"	350.00
Steel Carrier Semi, #145, 22"	250.00
Thunderbird Express, #37	250.00
Tow Truck, 15"	22.00
Trailer Fleet Set, 2 tractors, #675	550.00
Trencher, 18¹/₄"	80.00
Utility Truck	170.00
Wrecker Truck, #18, 1958	200.00
Wrecker Truck, 1949–53, 10"	150.00

TOOLS

From the 1920s through the end of the 1950s, the basement workshop was a standard fixture in many homes. Manufacturers quickly developed hand and machine tools for this specific market. The do-it-yourself, fix-it-yourself attitude of the late 1940s through the 1960s resulted in strong tool sales.

Tool collectors collect primarily by brand or tool type. Most focus on tools made before 1940. Quality is critical. Most collectors want nothing to do with cheap foreign imports. Interest is building in power tools and some specialized tool groups, e.g., Snap-on-Tools.

References: Ronald S. Barlow, *The Anique Tool Collector's Guide to Value*, L-W Book Sales, 1999; *The Catalogue of Antique Tools, 1998 Edition*, Martin J. Donnelly Antique Tools, 1998; Herbert P. Kean and Emil S. Pollak, *A Price Guide to Antique Tools*, Astragal Press, 1992; Herbert P. Kean and Emil S. Pollak, *Collecting Antique Tools*, Astragal Press, 1990; Kathryn McNerney, *Antique Tools*, Collector Books, 1979, 1998 value update; Emil and Martyl Pollak, *A Guide to American Wooden Planes and Their Makers,*

Third Edition The Astragal Press, 1994; R. A. Salaman, *Dictionary of Tools*, Charles Scribner's Sons, 1974; John Walter, *Antique & Collectible Stanley Tools, Second Edition,* Tool Merchants, 1996; Jack P. Wood, *Early 20th Century Stanley Tools*, catalog reprint, L-W Book Sales, 1996 value update; Jack P. Wood, *Town-Country Old Tools and Locks, Keys and Closures*, L-W Books, 1990, 1999 value update.

Collectors' Clubs: Early American Industries Assoc, 167 Bakersville Rd, South Dartmouth, MA 02748; Tool Group of Canada, 7 Tottenham Rd, Ontario MC3 2J3 Canada.

Angle Divider Bevel, General Hardware Mfg Co, No 835, orig box, 7¹/₂" l	$25.00
Auger Bit Depth Gauge, Stanley, No 47, orig factory card, 6" l	25.00
Auger Bits, set of 6, Peck, Stow & Wilcox, No 56, orig paper label and box, 10¹/₂" l	55.00
Axe, Keen Kutter, hand, 3" blade	25.00
Axe, Winchester, diamond edge broad axe	60.00
Bench Rule, DB&S, graduated in 50ths, 3" l	35.00
Butt Chisels, Greenlee, No 403C-1, plastic handles, orig box	45.00
Combination Square, Stanley, No 122, "Defiance," nickel-plated, 1930s, 12" l	45.00
Corner Chisel, Norton, heavy socket, new handle, ³/₄" size, 11¹/₂" l	45.00
Dowel Jig, Stanley, cast iron, nickel-plated finish	20.00
Fore Plane, Stanley, No 6, type "20," blue finish	45.00
Hammer, Stanley, No 100, "Golden Hammer of Merit," velvet-lined box, presentation plaque	130.00
Hammer, Winchester, claw	40.00
Hand Drill, Goodell-Pratt, No 385, high speed, aluminum body, 15¹/₂" l	300.00
Hand Saw, Keen Kutter, No 816, applewood handle	55.00
Hand Saw, Winchester	35.00
Hermaphrodite Calipers, Millers Falls, No 530, 5" size, orig box, 7" l	45.00
Jointer Plane, Stanley, No 8C, type "17", orig box, unused	350.00
Level, Stanley, No 0, cherry, orig decal, "Sweetheart" trademark, 30" l	45.00
Level, Union Factory, CT, No 294, laminated mahogany, with single plumb, early trademark, 28" l	55.00

Block Plane, Winchester, No. 5, adjustable, never used, with Winchester store price tag and orig box, 13¹/₂" l, $495.00. Photo courtesy Wm. Morford.

Machinist's Center Gauge, Darling Brown & Sharpe,
standard type, 2¹/₂" l **25.00**
Machinist's Clamps, pr, Starrett Co, No 161D, blued
steel finish, orig box, 4¹/₂" l **45.00**
Machinist's Pocket Rule, Almond Mfg Co, 6" l **15.00**
Machinist's Precision Depth Gauge, Sawyer Tool Co,
optional side mount, 4" l **65.00**
Monkey Wrench, Winchester, wooden handle, 6" l **50.00**
Oilstone, Behr-Manning, No HB14, Arkansas stone,
4¹/₂" l **25.00**
Pipe Burring Reamer, Union Tool Co, No 28, for bit
brace, orig box, 5¹/₂" l **35.00**
Plumb and Level, Eden Specialty Co, patented 1924,
orig box, 6" l **65.00**
Pocket Wrench, Keen Kutter, #93, 4" l **12.00**
Precision Combination Square, Starrett Co, 1920s, 12" l **115.00**
Push Drill, Millers Falls, No 188A, automatic, Bakelite
handle, orig box, 10" l **35.00**
Rule and Level, Rabone & Sons, Birmingham, No 1370,
English and metric, 24" l **225.00**
Rule and Level, Stanley, No 93, nickel-plated, adjustable
marking gauge, "Sweetheart" trademark, 4" l **75.00**
Saw Set, Disston & Sons, "Triumph," Precision
adjustable, 7" l **25.00**
Saw Set, Goodell-Pratt, No 201, tempered steel, red and
black enamel, orig box, 8¹/₂" l **125.00**
Screwdriver, Keen Kutter, Blue Brand, steel, hardwood
handle, rosewood finish, nickel-plated steel ferrule **20.00**
Screwdriver, Millers Falls, No 61A, spiral ratchet, orig
box, 7¹/₂" l **45.00**
Screwdriver, Stanley, Yankee Handyman, reversible
direction, plastic magazine handle, orig box **25.00**
Screwdrivers, set of 7, Plomb Tool Co, phillips and slot-
ted, 1930s–40s, price for set **75.00**
Smooth Plane, Stanley, Victor, No 1104, gray frame,
red frog, stained red handle and knob, orig box **100.00**
Standing Vernier Caliper, Brown & Sharpe Mfg, No 585,
orig leather and velvet fitted case, 13" l **45.00**
Tape Measure and Rule, Stanley, International Retail
Hardware Assoc Hardware Week promotion, 1950s **125.00**
Torpedo Level, Stanley, No 264, aluminum, orig
Christmas box, 9" l **95.00**

TOOTHPICK HOLDERS

When is a toothpick holder not a toothpick holder? When it is a match holder, miniature spoon holder for a toy table setting, a salt shaker with a ground-off top, a small rose bowl, shot glass, an individual open sugar, a vase, or a whimsy. A toothpick is designed to hold toothpicks. Toothpicks have a flat bottom and allow enough of the toothpick to extend above the top so one can be extracted with no problem. If the toothpicks do not extend above the top or stand erect, chances are the object is not a toothpick holder.

References: Neila Bredehoft, et. al., *Glass Toothpick Holders,* Collector Books, 1999; William Heacock, *Encyclopedia of Victorian Colored Pattern Glass, Book 1, Toothpick Holders From A to Z, Second Edition,* Antique Publications, 1976, 1992 value update; National Toothpick Holders Collectors Society, *Toothpick Holders: China, Glass, and Metal,* Antique Publications, 1992.

Collector's Club: National Toothpick Holders Collectors Society, PO Box 417, Safety Harbor, FL 34695.

Glass, Mosser, #168, amber, $2.00.

Aluminum, tumble-up, Niagara Falls souvenir **$40.00**
Art Glass, Crider, threaded dec, iridized **25.00**
Art Glass, Kelsey/Pilgrim, cameo glass, sailboat design
on reverse **25.00**
Art Glass, Lotton, Leafy, cameo glass **25.00**
Bisque, Geisha, blue rim, 2¹/₂" h **15.00**
Bisque, Occupied Japan, girl with barrel holder, 4¹/₂" h **40.00**
Brass, enamel design **35.00**
Brass, top hat, umbrella **20.00**
Ceramic, Japan, figural fish, yellow **5.00**
Ceramic, Occupied Japan, donkey pulling cart **7.50**
China, vase, floral dec on white ground, applied han-
dles, mkd "Made in Czechoslovakia" **45.00**
Glass, amber, frosted, Gonterman Swirl **150.00**
Glass, Fenton, Daisy & Button hat **25.00**
Glass, Indiana Glass, Tea Room **20.00**
Glass, Jenkins Glass Co, Three Fruits, 1920s **40.00**
Glass, Kemple, tapered block hat, clear, vaseline, light
blue and blue-green, 1950–60 . . . . **30.00**
Glass, Puritan, McKee **45.00**
Glass, shoe, gold, 1972 . . . . **10.00**
Pattern Glass, Daisy and Button, blue **70.00**
Pattern Glass, Feather, clear **65.00**
Pattern Glass, Melon, opalescent **50.00**
Pot Metal, figural fish, c1920 . . . . **45.00**
Pressed Glass, milk glass, metal filigree **50.00**
Silver Plate, rooser, engraved "Picks," 2" h **50.00**
White Milk Glass, barrel, metal hoops **25.00**
White Milk Glass, horseshoe and clover **22.00**
White Milk Glass, scrolled shell, goofus dec **12.00**

TORQUAY POTTERY

Pottery manufacturing came to the Torquay district of South Devon, England, in the 1870s following G. J. Allen's discovery of a red terra-cotta potting clay in 1869. Allen organized the Watcombe Pottery, producing a wealth of art pottery terra-cotta products.

In 1875 Dr. Gillow founded the Torquay Terra-Cotta Company. Its products were similar to those of Watcombe Pottery. It closed in 1905, only to be reopened by Enoch Staddon in 1908. Staddon produced pottery rather than terra-cotta ware.

John Philips established the Aller Vale Pottery in 1881. The company specialized in souvenir pieces. Designs were painted on pieces with a thick colored slip that contrasted with the color of the ground slip coat. This "motto" ware achieved widespread popularity by 1900. In 1902 Aller Vale and Watcombe merged and became Royal Aller Vale and Watcombe Art Potteries. The new company produced commemorative and motto ware.

Burton, Daison, and Longpark pottery are examples of numerous small companies that sprang up in the Torquay District and made wares similar to those produced by Aller Vale and Watcombe. Longpark, the last of these companies, closed in 1957. When Royal Aller Vale and Watcombe closed in 1962, the era of red pottery production in Torquay ended.

Reference: Susan and Al Bagdade, *Warman's English & Continental Pottery & Porcelain, 3rd Edition,* Krause Publications, 1998.

Collectors' Clubs: North American Torquay Society, 12 Stanton, Madison, CT 06443; Torquay Pottery Collectors Society, 23 Holland Ave, Cheam, Sutton, Surrey SM2 6HW U.K.

Bowl, "May the Hinges of Friendship Never Go Rusty," Longpark Torquay mark, 4¼" d $50.00
Bread and Butter Plate, "A Thing of Beauty is a Joy Forever," cottage, Watcombe Torquay, 6" d 45.00
Candlestick, "Be the Day Weary or Be the Day Long at Last it Ringeth to Evensong," Watcombe mark, 7½" h 150.00
Chamberstick, "Be the Day Weary or Be the Day Long at Last it ringeth to Evensong, 5½" h 100.00
Chamberstick, "Snore and You Sleep Alone," black cockerel, Longpark Torquay, 4" h 80.00
Compote, ftd, "Do Not Stain Todays Blue Sky With Tomorows Clouds," 5" h, 7" d 120.00
Creamer, "Be Aisy With Tha Crain," colored cockerel, Longpark Torquay, 2¾" h 40.00
Creamer, "From Lynmouth Fresh From the Dairy," cottage, Longpark Torquay 35.00
Eggcup, with saucer, "Fine Words Will Not Fill," cottage, Watcombe Torquay, 3" h 40.00
Hair Tidy, "Save While You Have and Give While You Live, " Watcombe Torquay, scandy, 4" h 100.00
Mug, "A Stitch in Time Saves Nine," scandy, Watcombe Torquay, 3" h 60.00
Pitcher, "Land Ends," sailboat scene, Watcombe Torquay, 4" h 25.00
Sugar Bowl, "Elp Yerzel Tu Sugar," scalloped edge, Longpark Torquay, 3" h 60.00
Teapot, "Now Ladies All I Pray Make Free and Tell Me How You Like Your Tea," primrose, 4½" h 100.00

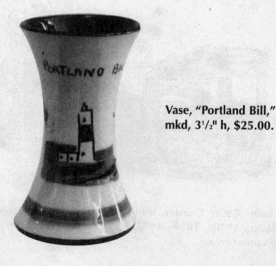

Vase, "Portland Bill," mkd, 3½" h, $25.00.

TOYS

Toys drive the 20th-century collectibles market. The standards for condition, scarcity, and desirability established by the toy community are now being applied throughout the antiques marketplace.

The toy market of the 1990s is highly sophisticated. In fact, some question if there is a single toy market any longer. Many categories within the toy market have broken away and become independent collecting categories. This category covers manufacturers and toy types still located within the general toy category.

Currently, the post-1945 period is the hot period among toy collectors. Prices for pre-1920 cast-iron and penny toys are stable and, in some cases, in decline. Pressed steel dominates vehicle collecting with a small cadre of collectors beginning to look at plastic. Diecast toys, the darlings of the 1970s and 80s, have lost some of their luster. Vehicles remain the toy of choice among collectors aged thirty-five and above. Young collectors focus on action figures and licensed toys.

With so many toys of the post-1945 era of Far Eastern origin, the national collecting prejudice for toys made in one's own country has diminished. What it is rather than where it was made is the key today. One result is a lowering of quality standards for more recently issued toys. The pre-1960s toy market remains heavily quality-driven.

The contemporary toy market is cursed by two groups of individuals—toy speculators and toy scalpers—whose activities badly distort pricing reality. Toy speculators hoard toys, thus upsetting the traditional supply and demand cycle. Toy scalpers created artificial shortages for modern toys. They accept no financial or moral responsibility for their actions when the speculative bubble they created bursts. And, it always does.

References: General: Sharon and Bob Huxford (eds.), *Schroeder's Collectible Toys: Antique to Modern Price Guide, Fifth Edition,* Collector Books, 1999; Sharon Korbeck (ed.), *Toys & Prices, 6th Edition,* Krause Publications, 1998.

Generational: Ronald S. Barlow (ed.), *The Great American Antique Toy Bazaar, 1879–1945: 5,000 Old Engravings from Original Trade Catalogs,* Windmill Publishing, 1998; Robert E. Birkenes, *White Knob Wind Up Collectible Toys,* Schiffer Publishing, 1999; Bill Bruegman, *Toys of the Sixties,* Cap'n Penny Productions, 1991; Tom Frey, *Toy Bop: Kid Classics of the 50's & 60's,* Fuzzy Dice Productions, 1994; Robin Sommer, *I Had One of Those: Toys of Our Generation,* Crescent Books, 1992; Elizabeth Stephan (ed.), *O'Brien's Collecting Toys, 9th Edition,* Krause Publications, 1999; Carol Turpen, *Baby Boomer Toys and Collectibles, Second Edition,* Schiffer Publishing, 1998.

Juvenile: *Price Guide to Pull Toys,* L-W Book Sales, 1996; *Tops and Yo-Yos and Other Spinning Toys,* L-W Book Sales, 1995.

Lithograph Tin: Alan Jaffe, *J. Chein & Co.,* Schiffer Publishing, 1997; Lisa Kerr, *American Tin-Litho Toys,* Collectors Press, 1995; Lisa Kerr, *Ohio Art: The World of Toys,* Schiffer Publishing, 1998; Maxine A. Pinsky, *Greenberg's Guide to Marx Toys, Vol. I* (1988) and *Vol. II* (1990), Greenberg Publishing.

Miscellaneous: Raymond V. Brandes, *Big Bang Cannons,* Ray-Vin Publishing, 1993; Christopher Cook, *Collectible American Yo-Yos, 1920s–1970s,* Collector Books, 1997; James L. Dundas, *Toys That Shoot and Other Neat Stuff,* Schiffer Publishing, 1998; David Gould and Donna Crevar-Donaldson, *Occupied Japan Toys With Prices,* L-W Book Sales, 1993; Morton A. Hirschberg, *Steamtoys,* Schiffer Publishing, 1996; Jay Horowitz, *Marx Western*

Playsets, Greenberg Publishing, 1992; Don Hultzman, *Collector's Guide to Battery Toys,* Collector Books, 1998; Charles M. Jacobs, *Kenton Cast Iron Toys,* Schiffer Publishing, 1996; Kathy and Don Lewis, *Talking Toys of the 20th Century,* Collector Books, 1999; L. H. MacKenzie, *Squeaky Toys,* Schiffer Publishing, 1998; Anthony Marsella, *Toys From Occupied Japan,* Schiffer Publishing, 1995; Jack Matthews, *Toys Go to War: World War II Military Toys, Games, Puzzles & Books,* Pictorial Histories Publishing, 1994; Albert W. McCollough, *The New Book of Buddy "L" Toys, Vol. I* (1991), *Vol. II* (1991), Greenberg Publishing; Harry A. and Joyce A. Whitworth, *G-Men and FBI Toys and Collectibles,* Collector Books, 1998.

Plastic: Bill Hanlon, *Plastic Toys: Dimestore Dreams of the '40s & '50s,* Schiffer Publishing, 1993.

Vehicles: Don and Barb DeSalle, *The DeSalle Collection of Smith-Miller & Doepke Trucks,* L-W Book Sales, 1997; Charles F. Donovan, Jr., *Renwal, World's Finest Toys: Vol. 2, Transportation Toys & Accessories,* published by author, 1996; Edward Force, *Corgi Toys,* Schiffer Publishing, 1984, 1997 value update; Edward Force, *Dinky Toys,* Schiffer Publishing, 1988, 1992 value update; Edward Force, *Solido Toys,* Schiffer Publishing, 1993; Joe and Sharon Freed, *Collector's Guide to American Transportation Toys, 1895–1941,* Freedom Press, 1995; Sally Gibson-Downs and Christine Gentry, *Motorcycle Toys,* Collector Books, 1995.

Kurt Guile, Mike Willyard and Gary Konow, *Wyandotte Toys Are Good and Safe: 1920–1957,* Wyandotte Toys Publishing, 1996; Jeffrey C. Gurski, *Greenberg's Guide to Cadillac Models and Toys,* Greenberg Publishing, 1992; Ken Hutchison and Greg Johnson, *The Golden Age of Automotive Toys: 1925–1941,* Collector Books, 1996; Dana Johnson, *Collector's Guide to Diecast Toys & Scale Models, 2nd Edition,* Collector Books, 1998; Douglas P. Kelly, *The Die Cast Price Guide Post-War: 1946 to Present,* Antique Trader Books, 1997; Raymond R. Klein, *Greenberg's Guide to Tootsietoys, 1945–1969,* Greenberg Publishing, 1993; Bill Manzke, *The Unauthorized Encyclopedia of Corgi Toys,* Schiffer Publishing, 1997; Richard O'Brien, *Toy Cars & Trucks, 2nd Edition,* Krause Publications, 1997; R & B Collectibles & Marketing, *Texaco Collectors 1997 Price Guide,* published by authors, 1997; David Richter, *Collector's Guide to Tootsietoys, Second Edition,* Collector Books, 1996; Ron Smith, *Collecting Toy Airplanes,* Books Americana, Krause Publications, 1995; Gerhard G. Walter, *Tin Dream Machines: German Tin Toy Cars and Motorcycles of the 1950s and 1960s,* New Cavendish, 1998.

Periodicals: *Antique Toy World,* PO Box 34509, Chicago, IL 60634; *Master Collector,* 225 Cattle Baron Parc Dr, Fort Worth, TX 76108; *Toy Shop,* 700 E State St, Iola, WI 54490; *Toy Cars & Vehicles,* 700 E State St, Iola, WI 54990; *Toy Trader,* PO Box 1050, Dubuque, IA 52004.

Collectors' Clubs: Antique Toy Collectors of America, Two Wall St, 13th Flr, New York, NY 10005; Canadian Toy Collectors Society, 67 Alpine Ave, Hamilton, Ontario L9A1A7 Canada.

Maloney's Antiques & Collectibles Resource Directory by David J. Maloney, Jr., lists many collectors' clubs for specific types of toys. Check your local library for the most recent edition.

Note: For additional toy listings see Action Figures, Barbie, Bicycles, Breyer Horses, Cap Guns, Cartoon Characters, Coloring Books, Construction Toys, Cowboy Heroes, Disneyana, Dolls, Ertl, Farm Toys, Fisher-Price, Games, GI Joe, Hanna-Barbera, Hess Trucks, Hot Wheels, Matchbox, Model Kits, Monsters, Occupied

Japan, Paint By Number Sets, Paper Dolls, Pedal Cars, Premiums, Puppets, Puzzles, Radio Characters and Personalities, Robots, Sand Pails, Sizzlers, Slot Cars, Smurfs, Space Adventurers, Space Toys, Star Trek, Star Wars, Steiff, Stuffed Toys, Super Heroes, Teddy Bears, Television Characters & Personalities, Tonka, Toy Soldiers, Toy Train Accessories, Toy Trains, Trolls, View-Master, and Warner Bros.

Acme Plastics Mfg Co, Helicopter, plastic, purple and white marble design top, blue bottom, white propeller blades and wheels, attached orig blue and yellow pull-string, 2" h, 1950s. **$55.00**

AHI, Japan, Power Command-Radio Controlled Batmobile, battery operated, plastic, forward, reverse, and turning action, operating dome light, orig box **430.00**

AHI, Japan, School Bus with Fidgety Driver, friction, litho tin, children at windows, animated driver, moving eye grille, orig box, 9" l **145.00**

Alps, Japan, Baseball Player Monkey, windup, hard vinyl figure, rubber tail, 1970s, 5½" h. **50.00**

Alps, Japan, Miss Bruin the Typist, windup, litho tin and plush, animated arms type on page, orig box, 5½" h. **135.00**

Argentina, Champion Racer, friction, open-wheeled #6 Indy type racer with helmeted driver behind windscreen, mkd "Rapid" with raised pistons and fine details, 9¼" l. **300.00**

Argentina, Fire Engine with Flag and Ladder, friction, litho tin, 3 figural attached uniformed firemen, 1 holds flag upright and drops it down while moving, orig box, 7½" l. **165.00**

Argo Industries Corp, Aircraft Carrier, #415, plane elevator, rotating radar screen, 3 jet planes, guns, drop bombs, 1950s, 36" l **80.00**

Asahi Toy Co, Japan, Fodor Ranch Wagon, #3594, opening rear window, 1962. . . . . **65.00**

ATC, Japan, Ferrari Berlinetta 250/Lemans, battery operated, litho tin, mkd "24 Heures Le Mans," bump-and-go action, engine sound, orig box, 11" l **110.00**

Auburn Rubber, Farm Tractor, 8⅝" l **120.00**

Auburn Rubber, Garrison's Gorilla Gear, plastic accessories include mess kit, belt with attachments, and knife in sheath, ©ABC 1968, orig 9 x 14" box. **100.00**

Chein, Roller Coaster, litho tin, with cars, belt replaced with elastic, 1950s, 10" h, 19" l, $253.00. Photo courtesy Collectors Auction Services.

Arcade, Texas Centennial Bus, rust and paint loss, 1936, 10³/₄" l, $1,300.00. Photo courtesy Gene Harris Antique Auction Center, Inc.

Auburn Rubber, Hondo Frontier Fort Set, Auburn complete with building, 3 fence sections, 12 Indians, 8 cowboys, 2 women, 6 horses, 23 farm animals, and 18 accessory pcs, 1967 . . . . **200.00**

Auburn Rubber, Police Motorcycle, red, drive chain, 1950s, 6" l **35.00**

Automatic Toys, Spiral Speedway, windup, litho tin, highway track with 2 windup 3" l buses, orig 4 x 11" box, 1 bus not working **30.00**

Bandai, Japan, Cadillac Sedan with Wipers, battery operated, litho tin, mounted front mirrors, advances, working wipers, orig box, 11" l **150.00**

Bandai, Japan, Mercedes Benz 220, battery operated, litho tin, detailed int, hubs and front hood ornament, advances with forward and reverse actions, orig box, 10¹/₂" l **200.00**

Bandai, Japan, MG Car, friction, litho tin, greenish blue, red and cream int, retractable windshield with clear plastic insert, each hubcap mkd "MG," 1955 . . . . **100.00**

Bandai, Japan, Plymouth Valiant Sedan, litho tin, detailed int, rear "1963" plate, orig box, 8¹/₄" l **85.00**

Bandai, Japan, Volkswagen Sedan, tin, vinyl driver at wheel, bump-and-go action, clear plastic cover on top reveals lighted rear working engine, orig box, 10" l **175.00**

Banner Plastics, Metaltone Table Ware, 6 knives, forks, and spoons, cake server, salt and pepper shaker, 1952 . . . . **45.00**

Brice Toy & Novelty, Fireman Dog in Truck, pull toy, wooden, paper labels, stiff cardboard attachments, dog's arms move up and down when pulled, drumstick strikes against metal bell, 1950s, 4 x 14 x 9¹/₂" **75.00**

B&S, US Zone Germany, Flying Aero Car, windup, metal, futuristic aero car, advances, when lever is activated hidden wings and propeller emerge, orig box, 8" l **775.00**

B&U, Germany, Happy Jack Musical Toy, litho tin, features Jack doing jig to music on top of platform mkd with his name, crank action produces movement and sound, 8" l **475.00**

Buddy L, Anti-Aircraft Unit, 15" **60.00**

Buddy L, Big Brute Car Hauler Semi, 22", MIB **15.00**

Buddy L, Highway Maintenance Dump Truck, 14" **110.00**

Buddy L, Ladder Fire Truck, 31" **80.00**

Buddy L, Red Hook and Ladder Truck, open cab, rubber tires, 4 ladders, ladder lift mechanism, 1929, 27⁵/₈" l **775.00**

Buddy L, Telephone Maintenance Repair Truck and Trailer, metal, 2 side decals, with ladder, rope, and 10" l trailer, orig box **425.00**

Chein, Beach Toy Set, litho tin, animal molds, sifter, and shovel, in orig sieve set pkg, 8¹/₂ x 11" **225.00**

Chein, Fish, windup, litho tin, red and yellow fish flaps back tail fin, 11¹/₂" l **40.00**

Chein, Gnome, windup, litho tin, shakes when wound, 1930s, 5¹/₄" h **200.00**

Chein, Holly Hobbie Tea Set, metal teapot, 4 blue plastic cups, 4 metal plates and saucers, set of 4 plastic knives, forks, and spoons, 1970s **35.00**

Chein, Ignatz Mouse Tricycle, windup, wooden Ignatz mouse driving tinplate tricycle, legs move up and down on pedals as back wheels operate a squeaking bellows, 1930s **1,150.00**

Chein, Mickey Mouse Ferris Wheel, windup, litho tin, carnival depictions at base, 6 gondolas with lithoed children riders circle bell, orig box, 17" h **475.00**

Chein, Organ, litho tin, built-in crank handle, right and left sides depict outside of church with stained glass windows, stone walls and roof, front and back have same depiction of interior depicting pipe organ with stained glass windows in background, 4¹/₂ x 7¹/₂ x 9¹/₂", 1950s **75.00**

CKO, US Zone Germany, Signal Fire Truck, windup, litho tin, metallic red with illus and detailing in silver and black, firemen depicted at windows, manually operated ladder extends 9", mechanism inside engine produces clanging signal noise when moving, orig box, 1950s **200.00**

Commonwealth Plastics, Jack-in-the-Camera Sr, hard plastic, black, with illus box, 1950s, 2 x 3 x 2¹/₄" **25.00**

Corgi, Avengers Gift Set, #40, diecast metal vintage Bentley and Lotus Elan S2 autos, John Steed and Emma Peel figures, Bentley needs steering wheel, orig box, 1966 . . . . **150.00**

Corgi, Chipperfields Circus, diecast and plastic, red and blue, with plastic figures of clown with microphone and chimpanzee with skirt, orig box, 1960s, 3³/₄" l **100.00**

Corgi, Junior Service Station Set, hard plastic, with 2 sets of plastic gas pumps and 3 diecast metal vehicles, orig box, 1960–70s **75.00**

Corgi, Kennel Club Chevrolet Impala, diecast and plastic, "Kennel Club" stickers on sides, flicker picture on front depicting dachshund against blue ground, opening tailgate and sliding clear plastic doors on sides, complete with 4 plastic dogs, orig box, 1960s **75.00**

Cortland, US Army Tank Car, friction, litho tin, hood mounted plastic weapons, orig box, 7" l **110.00**

Corgi, Mercedes-Benz 240D, metallic silver with light blue plastic interior, 285-A, 1975-81, 5" l, $30.00.

Daiya, Japan, Boeing 707, friction, litho tin, depicts logos, orig box, 10" l 100.00

Daiya, Japan, Cradle Bus, friction, litho tin bonnet bus mkd "Cradle Bus" on sides, black rubber tires, siren sound, orig box, 7½" l 415.00

Daiya, Japan, General Patton M-107 Tank, battery operated, litho tin, forward and reverse actions, firing turret gun swivels in direction while flashing from barrel, orig box, 8" l 150.00

Doepke, Heiliner Scraper, #2011, 29" l, 1952 . . . . 300.00

Duncan, O-Boy Whistling Yo-Yo, litho tin, four ¼" whistle holes on each side, black logo, 1930s 125.00

Duncan, Shrieking Sonic Satellite Yo-Yo, wood, flying saucer shape with air "portholes" around each rim and metal whistles inserted in each side, solid color or 2-tone glitter paint on each side, gold die-stamp logo, 1962 . . . . 60.00

Ed-U-Card, Sew-Up Animal Circus, 4 thin cardboard sheets with full color punch-outs depicting circus animal scenes, 1 panel forms arena, complete with different colored yarn laces, orig box, 1953 . . . . 20.00

England, Happy Dan the Eccentric Milkman, windup, litho tin, Dan carrying basket of milk bottles in each hand, advances, orig box, 4" h 300.00

Gabriel, Box of Crafts, #T419, clay, leather, foil, muslin, pipe cleaners, yarn, and instructions, 1956–57 . . . . 20.00

General Molds & Plastics Corp, Power Dump Truck, #128, battery operated, plastic, metal base, remote control, 1950s 50.00

Germany, KLM-Intercontinental, friction, litho tin, plastic accessories, mkd "CA-ILS," rocket shaped top tailfin and extending engines, orig box, 13½" l 125.00

Germany, Mechanical Elf on Snail, windup, litho tin, figural elf holding onto reins, advances while elf holds on and uses his animated arms in up-and-down motion, 10" l 575.00

Germany, Penny Toy Train, litho tin, 6 units, #291 engine, orig box 275.00

Hasbro, Cookie the Cucumber, complete with figures of Cookie and Mr. Potato Head, instruction form, and order sheet, 1966 . . . . 50.00

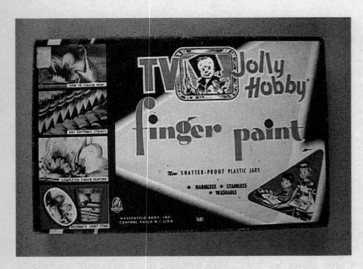

Hasbro, TV Jolly Hobby Finger Paint, No. 1681, $12.00.

Hubley, Harley-Davidson Solo Motorcycle, cast iron, olive with gold accents, black rubber tires, c1930s, 9" l, $1,650.00. Photo courtesy Dunbar's Gallery.

Hasbro, Katie the Carrot with Mr Potato Head, complete with figure, accessory pcs, and instruction sheet, orig box, 1960s 50.00

Hong Kong, Happy Doll, friction, plastic, 1970s, 4" h 75.00

Hubley, Action Road Grader, #1951, Mighty Metal Toy series, pressed steel, emb "Hubly and Diesel," orig box, 13" l 85.00

Hubley, Dump Truck, #1850, Mighty Metal Toy series, pressed steel, decals on doors, orig box, 12" l 85.00

Hubley, Jumbo Pull Toy, "Jumbo" elephant on wheels with name in raised letters on blanket, orig box, 5" l 185.00

Hubley, Mighty Metal Farm Set, 5 diecast metal farm vehicles and equipment, with assortment of 6 plastic farm animals, MIB 165.00

Hubley, P-38 Fighter, diecast metal fighter, raised depiction of bomb on each wing, orig box, 9 x 12" 125.00

Ichiko, Japan, Ford Gyron, Mystery Car of the Future, battery operated, litho tin, black rubber tires, 2 rear antennae, non-stop action, cockpit opens and closes, orig box, 11" l 425.00

Ideal, Danger Patrol Truck, #3300, friction motor, microphone, stretcher, oxygen tank, extension ladder, and tool chest with tools, 1950s 100.00

Ideal, Fire Boat, #4714, rising lifeboat and anchor, siren, 1950s 125.00

Ideal, Hickory Dickory Clock, talking, red, yellow, blue, and black, 1950s, MIB 50.00

Ideal, Roy Rogers Fix-It Stagecoach, plastic, complete decal and team of 2 horses and Roy driving, incomplete accessories, orig box 250.00

Irwin, Talking Fire Chief's Control Car, plastic, automatic windshield wipers, turn crank at rooftop for sound, with Irwin hang tag that stipulates the words to the record, orig box, 9" l 150.00

IY Metal Toys, Japan, Eagle Racer, friction, litho tin, orig box, 11" l 965.00

Japan, Baby Race Car, friction, litho in, open-wheeled #5 racer with helmeted driver, orig box, 4" l 80.00

Japan, Chevrolet Convertible with U-Haul Trailer, friction, litho tin, 7" l vehicle, 5" l trailer with separate litho tin side plate reading "U-Haul Trailer," orig box 200.00

Japan, Cycling Robot, windup, litho tin and plastic, full figure robot driver with dual oxygen tanks, advances with ringing bell sound, orig box, 5" h 950.00

Japan, Fire Engine, battery operated, litho tin, with 3 firemen and driver, remote control action produces blinking light and bell, automatic ladder action, forward and reverse actions, orig box, 7" l 250.00

Japan, Indianapolis 500 Racer, battery operated, remote control, forward and reverse actions, with 4 spare-tired wheels, orig box, c1960s, 15" l 925.00

Japan, International Air Terminal, litho tin, features terminal, radar screen, revolving control tower, friction American Airlines plane, aviation gasoline truck, ramp, and luggage carrier, orig box 825.00

Japan, Lighted Piston Action Tractor, battery operated, figural driver, advances forward and backwards with lighted piston action, orig box, 6½" l 160.00

Japan, Mama Kangaroo, windup, litho tin, mama holding leaves in mouth as baby jumps up and down, orig box, 6½" h 265.00

Japan, Santa Trike with Reindeer, windup, litho tin, cycle advances with bell ringing sound, full figure 4" h Santa with gift sack is driver, full figure celluloid reindeer runs alongside trike 250.00

Japan, Satellites Rotating Earth, windup, litho tin, globe with rotating plastic satellites, 5" d globe 60.00

Japan, Shooting Fighter, battery operated, litho tin, "Phoenix" jet with spinning plastic prop, firing trigger with noise and light, orig box, 9" l 125.00

Japan, Skater Bunny, windup, cloth and plush, on tin skis, advances with bobbing motions, orig box, 9" h 120.00

Japan, Sunbeam Army Jeep, battery operated, litho tin, driver and 2 passengers looking at control panels, fold-down windshield, advances with forward and reverse actions, orig box, 9½" l 325.00

Japan, Teddy the Manager, battery operated, litho tin, plush and plastic, bear at desk, telephone lights with ringing bell sound as he picks up receiver, orig box 475.00

Japan, Tiger Tractor, friction, litho tin, Tiger at front, farmer driver, orig box, Japan, 6½" l 130.00

JNF, West Germany, Packard Convertible, windup and battery operated, red, cardboard fitted luggage in trunk, multi-function mechanism for working gear lights and drive train, orig box, 11½" l 385.00

K, Japan, Mighty Mike the Barbell Lifter Bear, battery operated, litho tin and plush, warms up and lifts his barbells over his head as they light up, orig box, 12" h 350.00

Keystone, Service Station, "Keystone Garage," litho wood, with plastic pump, lights, and rubber hose, 4½" l plastic car, 5 x 7 x 16" 275.00

KO, Japan, Ice Cream Vender Truck, friction, litho tin, "Good Flavor" ice cream truck with awning, crank operated action, orig box, 7" l 325.00

KO, Japan, Volkswagen Sedan, friction, litho tin, detailed int, orig box, 6¼" l 75.00

KW, Germany, Carousel, windup, women in Victorian dress swing around 9" carousel 350.00

Kyoei, Japan, Pan Am Airport Service Car, litho tin, orig box, 1960s 50.00

Lehmann, Climbing Monkey, tin, hat tassel, orig box 130.00

Lehmann, Garage and Auto, #771, litho tin, #765 Sedan and red roofed garage with litho flowers and children playing, c1935 . . . . 800.00

Linemar, Popeye Tricycle Rider, windup, litho tin, 1930s, 6¾" h, $1,000.00.

Linemar, Barber Bear, battery operated, litho tin and plush, bear with swaying head cuts hair of young customer with moving comb and scissors, baby bear looks into mirror as he kicks feet and moves arms, orig box, 11" h 475.00

Linemar, Calypso Joe, battery operated, tin and cloth black man, advances with moving head and lighted eyes as he beats on drum with hands, rubber ears and arms, orig box, 10½" h 775.00

Linemar, Donald Duck Fire Chief Truck, windup, litho tin, miniature nephew sits at front as hood ornament while Donald drives, with side ladders, 5½" l 600.00

Linemar, Jeep and Artillery Gun, friction, litho tin jeep, artillery gun with spring load action fires pellets, orig box, 11½" l 125.00

Linemar, Rocket with Sparks, friction, litho tin, "X-059" with lithoed details, orig box 225.00

LJN, Scooby-Doo Van, diecast metal, green, orange flower decals on sides, MOC 25.00

M, Japan, San Francisco Cable Car, #514, friction, litho tin, roof plates mkd "Powell & Mason Sts," black passengers and conductor, orig box mkd "An exact replica of Andrew Hollidies famous cable car," 8" l 150.00

Mak's, Hong Kong, Mercedes Benz Hard Top, friction, scale model, plastic, emb "300SL," orig box, 6" l 100.00

Marx, A&P Super Market Horse and Wagon, #2684, plastic, 8" l wagon with opening rear gate, pulled by 8" l horse, orig box 160.00

Marx, Army Troop Carrier, 18" 165.00

Marx, Busy Miners, windup, litho tin, images of busy working day at railroad, scoots back and forth with spring action, orig box 235.00

Marx, Captain Maddox and Commanche Horse Set, complete, unused, orig box, 1967 . . . . 100.00

Marx, Cirko the Clown Cyclist, windup, litho tin, orig box 1,500.00

Marx, Coast to Coast Low Boy, 25" 110.00

Marx, Deluxe Delivery Truck, litho tin, orig box, 11" l 350.00

Marx, Deluxe Hauler & Van Trailer, litho tin, large "American Continental Express" truck with double opening rear gates, with supply of cardboard adv boxes, orig box, 21" l 350.00

Marx, Orphan Annie Skipping Rope, keywind, tinplate, 1930s, 5" h, $400.00.

Marx, Disneyland Jeep, friction, litho tin, fold-down windshield, plastic steering wheel, orig box, 9½" l **275.00**

Marx, Fighting Marine Combat Unit Truck and Figures, #1172, pressed steel truck with canvas "USMC" litho, with full set of six 6" h soldiers, orig box **350.00**

Marx, Fix-All Willys Jeep, battery operated, pressed steel, opening hood, fold-down windshield, electric horn, canvas top, wrench and screw jack, orig box, 11" l **125.00**

Marx, Flintstone's Rubbles Wreck, friction, litho tin vehicle, figural Barney driver, 1962, 7½" l **350.00**

Marx, Lazy Days Farms Truck with Steer, litho tin, two 6" l plastic steer **175.00**

Marx, Mechanical Taxi, windup, litho tin "Yellow Cab Co" taxi, litho people in windows, orig box, 11" l **300.00**

Marx, Merry Makers Band, windup, litho tin, mouse conductor, drummer, fiddler, and dancer, orig box, 8" h **1,600.00**

Marx, Mickey Mouse Twirly Tail, windup, plastic Mickey advances with twirly tail action and vibrating movements, orig box, 7½" h **300.00**

Marx, Miniature Fort Apache Playset, plastic, complete with figures, fort, canoe, and supplies, 7 x 10" orig box **100.00**

Marx, Range Rider Rocking Cowboy Toy, windup, litho tin, rocks side to side as pistol carrying cowboy swings metal lasso, base mkd, Range Rider," 11" l **225.00**

Marx, Sunny Side Service Station, litho tin, hinged door garage with 2 gas pumps, lift, and air pump, fitted with battery to illuminate lifts and gas pumps, complete with oil and watering can, orig box, c1938, 5½" h, 13½" w **575.00**

Marx, Universal Gas Service Station, litho tin, platform has built-up "Blue Bird Garage," gas pump, free air pump, orig box **300.00**

Marx, Wee Scottie, windup, litho tin, orig box, 5" l **135.00**

Marx, Worker With Wheelbarrow, ramp walker, plastic, 1950s, 4½" h **25.00**

Marx/Sears, Happitime Roy Rogers Rodeo Ranch, #3990, litho tin, plastic accessories, orig paper bags and instructions, orig box **325.00**

Mattel, Wild-Fire Rapid Fire Rifle, hard plastic, black and brown simulated wood grain, has "High Power Scope," and produces loud firing noise, orig box, 1968, 24" l **75.00**

Meccano, Boat Tail Racer, built from constructor set series, red with cream running boards, rubber tires, rear mounted spare, license plate bracket, head lamps, litho woodgrain dash, hand brake releases clockwork motor, working steering wheel, chrome grill, and bumper, orig label, c1939, 13½" l **1,265.00**

Modern Toys, Patrol 95 Helicopter, litho tin and plastic, detachable propellers, 3-D litho tin pilot, mkd "made in Japan," 1960s **45.00**

Modern Toys, Policeman on Motorcycle, battery operated, litho tin, figure mounts and dismounts bike, not working, 12" l **260.00**

Modern Toys, Santa Copter, battery operated, litho tin, hard plastic propellers and Santa figure, sides mkd "Merry Christmas" with reindeer and snowflake illus, non-fall action, produces pinging sound, orig box, 1970s, 4¾" h **100.00**

MT, Japan, Magic Fire Car, friction, litho tin, vinyl headed animal driver, advances with bell ringing sound and extended front bumper, orig box, 7" l **75.00**

MT, Japan, Tom & Jerry Locomotive, battery operated, litho tin and plastic, advances with bump-and-go action, whistle sound and chugging noise, vinyl Jerry moves while holding lighted lantern, orig box, 9½" l **165.00**

Nomura Toys, Japan, Musical Clown, windup, vinyl head, life-like hair, fabric outfit, litho tin shoes, rubber hands holding cymbals, orig box, 1960s, 6½" h **75.00**

Nylint, Ford Pickup Truck with Trailer, pressed steel, orange, 1960s **75.00**

Occupied Japan, Blacksmith, windup, litho tin, animated arms slam down rubber anvil on horseshoe, 6" h **350.00**

Occupied Japan, Circus Elephant, celluloid, pink, red and gold blanket, blue hat, yellow and red barrel, 1940s, 4½" h **20.00**

Occupied Japan, Fop Monkey, windup, celluloid monkey with spinning tail, stares into mirror as he brushes his hair with animated arm action, orig box, 4½" h **200.00**

Ohio Art, Beach and Sand Box Set, litho tin sieve with molded hard plastic mold set, missing shovel, 1960s **20.00**

Ohio Art, Fido's Musical Doghouse, litho tin, crank handle on back, plays "Where Oh Where Has My Little Dog Gone," 1950s **50.00**

Ohio Art, Musical Top, train theme, 1962, 8½" d, 10¼" h, $50.00.

Structo, Bearcat Roadster, clockwork, pressed steel, orange and black, cast-iron spoke wheels, 15" l, $770.00. Photo courtesy Bill Bertoia Auctions.

PN, West Germany, Thunderbird, litho tin convertible, hp composition driver, working horn and windshield wipers, orig box, 13" l **150.00**

Remco, Barracuda Motorized Atomic Sub, battery operated, hard plastic, with accessories, orig box, 1962 . . . . . . **100.00**

Remco, Flintstones Motorized Paddy Wagon, battery operated, plastic, orig box **475.00**

Remco, Flying Dutchman Antique Car, battery operated, plastic, black and yellow car with decals, gold accents, clear plastic windshield, 8" h diecut cardboard driver, orig box, 1960s, 19" l **100.00**

Remco, Gallant Gladiator Roman Warship, hard plastic, boat with raised images on front and back, yellow plastic oars on each side with stiff paper attachments of various coat of arms designs, removable wood and plastic mast/look-out platform with stiff paper sail in picture of dual lions, complete with 10 fighting warriors, orig box, 4 x 16½ x 11" **100.00**

Renwal, The Busy Mechanic, plastic, from Educational Construction Kit series, contains 2-door sedan, fire truck, taxicab, motorcycle with side car, and flying boat, orig box, 11 x 15" **300.00**

Revell, Caterpillar with Attachment, molded plastic, 4 black wheels, attachment hooks on back, 1950s, 5" l **20.00**

San, Japan, Continental III, friction, tin, plastic steering wheel and front windshield, orig box, 1950s, 9" l **150.00**

San, Japan, Tugboat, battery operated, litho tin, boat with pilothouse and puffing smoke stack, orig box, 13" l **170.00**

Saunders-Swadar, Bell Aircraft Anti-Submarine Helicopter Kit, plastic helicopter with tandem rotors, orig box **85.00**

Schuco, US Zone Germany, Limousine Sedan, windup, #1010, 2-tone, orig key, advances with non-fall action, orig box, 6" l **300.00**

Schuco, US Zone Germany, Micro Racer Ford, windup, #1045, "Ford Custom 300," gray tires, orig instruction sheet, orig box, 4½" l **130.00**

Schuco, US Zone Germany, Mirakomot Motorcycle, windup, litho tin, orig key, 5" l **225.00**

Schuco, US Zone Germany, Mouse Wagon, windup, with 2 mice, tumbling front mouse with rear mouse riding on wheeled dolly, c1932 . . . . **775.00**

S&E, Japan, Dentist Bear, battery operated, litho tin and plush, dentist drilling on young patient, stops as young bear spits, drill lights and both heads move, orig box, 9½" h **550.00**

Serugo Rubber Co, Rinky Ringtail the Monkey, squeeze toy, rubber, gray, painted facial features, holding banana with yellow peel at his feet, orig box, 1950s, 6" h **25.00**

Spain, Coca-Cola Delivery Truck, vinyl, hook on front fender reads "Tome Coca-Cola" on each side, 7½" l **100.00**

Structo, Steel Dump Truck, #141, metal, enamel finish, treaded rubber tires, side decals, orig box **65.00**

Superior, All Metal Service Station, metal, plastic cars, figures, and equipment, orig 15 x 26" litho cardboard box **230.00**

Swader-Aurora, Bell Aircraft Helicopter Construction Kit, plastic, unused, 12" l orig box **85.00**

T Cohn, Superior Service Station, litho tin, with accessories, 10 x 14 x 24" **230.00**

TN, Japan, Blacksmith Teddy, windup, litho tin and plush, bear sits on base and hits horseshoe with hammer, orig box, 6" h **165.00**

TN, Japan, Mother Goose, windup, litho tin and plush, red beak, yellow and white wings, plastic feet, red plastic eyes, black and red polka-dot handkerchief wrapped around head, orig box, 1960s **50.00**

TN, Japan, Shooting Fighter, battery operated, litho tin gun designed like airplane, jet fighters illus on grips, eagle on each side of plane along with word "Phoenix," clear plastic canopy over pilot, white plastic propeller rotates as engine noise is produced, machine gun on top of plane in front of cockpit lights red as clicking sound is produced, orig box, 1960s **75.00**

TN, Japan, Skipping Puppy, windup, litho tin, skipping rope action, orig box, 6" h **160.00**

TN, Japan, Sports Car Benz, friction, litho tin, louvered sides, Mercedes logo on front grille, orig box, 8½" l **110.00**

Tootsietoy, 6-Wheel Army Cannon, 1950s, MIB **50.00**

Tootsietoy, Battleship, silver, 1939, 6" l, MIB **35.00**

Tootsietoy, Buick Estate Wagon, yellow and maroon, black wheels, 1948, 6" l, MIB **50.00**

Schuco, Western Germany, Fox and Goose, windup, #969, fox with fur head and felt clothing, goose with celluloid head and neck in litho tin carrier, 5" h, $1,210.00. Photo courtesy Collectors Auction Services.

Wolverine, Adding Machine, red, white, and blue, 1940s, 7" l, $40.00.

Tootsietoy, Caterpillar Scraper, yellow, black wheels, silver blade, 1956, 6" l, MIB 40.00

Tootsietoy, Chevrolet Bel Air, yellow, black wheels, 1955, 3" l 50.00

Tootsietoy, Chrysler New Yorker, blue, black wheels, 4 door, 1953, 6" l, MIB...................... 55.00

Tootsietoy, Cross Country Bus, MIB 65.00

Tootsietoy, Jaguar XK 140 Coupe, blue, black wheels, 3" l, MIB 50.00

Tootsietoy, Midget Series, green cannon, blue tank, green armored car, green tow truck, green camelback van, 1936–41, 1" l, MIB....................... 60.00

Tootsietoy, Passenger Train Set, 4 pc, 1925, MIB 160.00

Tootsietoy, Restaurant Trailer, yellow, black tread wheels, 2-wheel, open sides, MIB........................ 65.00

Tootsietoy, Stratocruiser, MIB 110.00

Topper, Johnny Lightning Fire Leap Set, complete with diecut cardboard bridge base with separate cardboard and plastic fire loop plus track sections and clamp, instruction sheet, orig box, 1970s.................. 50.00

TPS, Japan, Champs on Ice-Bear Skating Trio, windup, litho tin, orig box, 9" l...................... 850.00

TPS, Japan, Clown on Roller Skates, windup, litho tin, cloth outfit, realistic action, 6½" h 450.00

TPS, Japan, Fishing Monkey on Whales, windup, litho tin, monkey on back of whale has fishing rod in hand attached to 2 fish, travels back and forth with rocking motion as fish moves, orig box, 9" l 325.00

Transogram, Embroidery Set, centerpiece, napkins, hoop, and embroidery implements, 1970............. 30.00

TS, Japan, Mechanical Circus Parade, windup, litho tin, walking elephant tows 3 animated clowns, orig box, 12" l 260.00

TT, Japan, Indian Motorcycle, friction, litho tin, red, 2 x 6 x 4" 100.00

Unique Art, GI Joe and his Jouncing Jeep, windup, tin, 1940s jeep with figure, 8" l 200.00

Unique Art, Kiddie Cyclists, windup, litho tin, 1930s, 8¾" h 120.00

Unique Art, Li'l Abner & His Dogpatch Band, windup, litho tin, depicts characters around piano, clockwork mechanism, orig box, 5¾ x 9".................. 715.00

Unique Art, Sky Rangers, windup, litho tin, suspended airplane and hot air balloon encircle base, orig box, 27" l when extended 550.00

Unknown Mfg, Duck, windup, litho tin, multicolored, silvered tin feet, moves head and feet back and forth when wound, 1950s, 4½" h....................... 50.00

Unknown Mfg, Liberty Sportster Speedboat, windup, wooden bottom, litho tin top with raised designs and half figure driver, mkd "Liberty Sportster," 16" l 175.00

Unknown Mfg, Red Cross Limousine, litho tin, diecut wounded soldier at rear window, nurse at opposite window, full figure driver at wheel, 6" l 200.00

Unknown Mfg, United Airlines Airplane, friction, litho tin, blue, gray, and white, orig box.................. 575.00

US Zone Germany, Space Ride Track Toy, windup, litho tin, futuristic car navigates around graphic color space scenes, 19" l 325.00

Western Germany, Sedan, windup, litho tin, passengers at window, advances as door opens and plastic man emerges carrying suitcase, orig box, 6" l 185.00

Western Germany, Service Station, windup, litho tin, Esso gas pump and station, orig box, 6 x 9" base 130.00

Wham-O, Aqua Jet Plane, plastic plane, connector tubing, and launching tower, orig box shows children playing outdoors with aqua jet, 1962 .... 25.00

Wham-O, Boomerang, red plastic with black and white striped decals, MOC, 1970, 17" l................. 40.00

Wolverine, Drum Major, windup, litho tin, #27, 1930s, 13¼" h 120.00

Wyandotte, Auto Carrier with Vehicles, litho tin, carries two 4" l plastic cars 200.00

Wyandotte, Sambo Target Game, litho tin 14 x 23" Sambo board, complete with easel, orig box........... 175.00

Yone, Japan, Walking Guardsman, windup, litho tin, plastic feet, forward action, orig box, 1970s, 4" h........ 50.00

Yonezawa, Japan, Arrow Locomotive Train, friction, litho tin, Indian motif designs, plunger on back produces squeaking noise simulating train whistle, 1950s 50.00

Yonezawa, Japan, Indianapolis Champion's Racer, friction, litho tin, tinplate racer, chrome exhaust pipe, helmeted driver behind wheel, 1950s, 18" l 1,725.00

Yonezawa, Japan, Jet Racer, friction, litho tin, figural driver at wheel, orig litho paper box, 11½" l............. 775.00

Yonezawa, Japan, Sun Deck Convertible XL500, friction, turquoise car with tinted plastic roof, orig box, 7" l...... 975.00

Y Co, Piggy Cook, battery operated, #10621, orig box, 1950s, 9½" h, $175.00.

TOY SOLDIERS

Toy soldier is a generic term. The category includes animal, civilian, holiday, and western figures in addition to military figures. Military figures are preferred.

The earliest toy soldiers were two-dimensional paper soldiers, often printed in sheets that were cut apart for play. Hilperts of Nuremberg, Germany, introduced the first three-dimensional toy soldiers near the end of the 18th century.

Britains and Mignot are the leading manufacturers of 20th-century toy soldiers. Mignot offered models of more than 20,000 different soldiers in the 1950s. Britains introduced its first hollow-cast figures in 1893. Many figures had movable arms. Britains quality is the standard by which collectors judge all other mass-produced figures.

The American dime store soldier arrived on the scene in the 1930s and remained popular through the early 1950s. Barclay and Manoil dominated the market primarily because of their realistic castings and originality of poses. Pre-1941 Barclay soldiers have helmets that are glued or clipped on.

Recently adult collectors have been speculating heavily in limited production toy soldiers made by a small group of toy soldier craftsman. Others are buying unpainted castings and painting them. The result is an increased variety of material on the market. Make certain you know exactly what you are buying.

Toy soldier collectors place a premium of 20% to 40% on set boxes. Beware of repainted pieces. Undocumented touch-up is a major problem in the market.

References: Norman Joplin, *The Great Book of Hollow-Cast Figures,* New Cavendish Books, 1992; Henry I. Kurtz and Burtt R. Ehrlich, *The Art of the Toy Soldier,* Abbeville Press, 1987; Richard O'Brien, *Collecting American-Made Toy Soldiers, No. 3,* Books Americana, Krause Publications, 1997; Richard O'Brien, *Collecting Foreign-Made Toy Soldiers,* Krause Publications, 1997; James Opie, *Collecting Toy Soldiers,* Pincushion Press, 1992; James Opie, *The Great Book of Britains,* New Cavendish, 1993; Edward Ryan, *Paper Soldiers: The Illustrated History of Printed Paper Armies of the 18th, 19th & 20th Centuries,* Golden Age Editions, 1995, distributed by P.E.I. International; Joe Wallis, *Armies of the World, Britains Ltd. Lead Soldiers 1925–1941,* published by author, 1993.

Periodicals: *Old Toy Soldier,* 209 N Lombard, Oak Park, IL 60302; *Plastic Warrior,* 815 North 12th St, Allentown, PA 18102; *Toy Soldier Review,* PO Box 4809, North Bergen, NJ 07047.

Collectors' Clubs: American Model Soldier Society, 1390 El Camino Real, San Carlos, CA 94070; Miniature Figure Collectors of America, 102 St Paul's Rd, Ardmore, PA 19003; Toy Soldier Collectors of America, 6924 Stone's Throw Circle #8202, St Petersburg, FL 33710.

Britains, Prince Albert's Own 11th Hussars, trooper, #12, early 1930s, $25.00.

American Alloy, soldier advancing with rifle	**$100.00**
American Metal Toys, doctor in white	**175.00**
American Metal Toys, horse, gray, "228"	**12.00**
Auburn Rubber, bugler, khaki, oval base	**30.00**
Auburn Rubber, collie, large	**20.00**
Auburn Rubber, doctor in white	**48.00**
Auburn Rubber, farmer, white with blue shirt	**25.00**
Auburn Rubber, goose	**15.00**
Auburn Rubber, hen	**9.00**
Auburn Rubber, machine gunner, charging, early version	**45.00**
Auburn Rubber, officer on horse	**50.00**
Auburn Rubber, soldier advancing with tommygun	**22.00**
Auburn Rubber, turkey	**9.00**
Auburn Rubber, US infantry officer, khaki	**18.00**
Auburn Rubber, US infantry private	**15.00**
Barclay, aviator, green	**30.00**
Barclay, conductor	**18.00**
Barclay, cowboy with rifle	**20.00**
Barclay, flagbearer, knaki	**16.00**
Barclay, girl skater, red and blue	**14.00**
Barclay, HO porter	**12.00**
Barclay, Indian with rifle	**75.00**
Barclay, knight with shield	**24.00**
Barclay, mailman	**18.00**
Barclay, man in overcoat	**15.00**
Barclay, man pulling kids on sled	**60.00**
Barclay, man speed skater	**20.00**
Barclay, marine	**20.00**
Barclay, mechanic with airplane engine	**65.00**
Barclay, minister holding hat	**25.00**
Barclay, newsboy	**16.00**
Barclay, nurse, blond hair	**24.00**
Barclay, old man with cane	**18.00**
Barclay, policeman, figure 8 base	**20.00**
Barclay, porter with whisk broom	**25.00**
Barclay, sailor in white	**20.00**
Barclay, Santa on lead skis	**58.00**
Barclay, Santa seated with holly wreath	**80.00**
Barclay, shoeshine boy	**30.00**
Barclay, soldier, range finder	**30.00**
Barclay, soldier charging, green	**20.00**
Barclay, soldier crawling with pistol, green	**35.00**
Barclay, soldier kneeling at anti-tank gun	**28.00**
Barclay, stretcher bearer, closed hand	**24.00**
Britains, D-Day Landing Set, #8931	**195.00**
Britains, Home Farm, yard set, #8705	**80.00**
Britains, Lifeguards Mounted Band, set #1	**220.00**

Britains, Mounted Royal Artillery Officer, #8910 . . . . **48.00**
Britains, Royal Artillery Mountain Battery, #8857 . . . . **250.00**
Britains, Vickers Anti-Aircraft Gun, #8911 . . . . **55.00**
Grey Iron, bugler, at attention **6.00**
Grey Iron, drummer, marching **7.00**
Grey Iron, officer, charging **6.00**
Grey Iron, officer, marching **7.00**
Grey Iron, pilot **18.00**
Grey Iron, rifleman, at attention **4.00**
Grey Iron, rifleman, marching **5.00**
Manoil, AA-gunner with range finder **35.00**
Manoil, anti-tank gun **50.00**
Manoil, aviator holding bomb **50.00**
Manoil, bench **15.00**
Manoil, blacksmith with wheel **30.00**
Manoil, bugler **25.00**
Manoil, cactus, small, FW Woolworth price tag **32.00**
Manoil, flagbearer, 3rd version **32.00**
Manoil, girl in white dress **12.00**
Manoil, hod carrier with bricks **38.00**
Manoil, hound, tan and brown spots **26.00**
Manoil, machine gunner, sitting **30.00**
Manoil, man carrying sack on back **28.00**
Manoil, marine, 2nd version **35.00**
Manoil, observer with periscope **40.00**
Manoil, scarecrow wearing top hat **25.00**
Manoil, sniper, firing in air **40.00**
Manoil, stack of sheaves **25.00**
Miller, horse, small **9.00**
Miller, stretcher bearer **30.00**
Molded Products, aviator, X-type harness **18.00**
Molded Products, flagbearer **25.00**
Molded Products, horse, black and white **10.00**
Molded Products, marine in blue **15.00**
Molded Products, officer on horse, WWII helmet **24.00**
Molded Products, soldier marching, WWI helmet **15.00**
Molded Products, soldier with parachute **18.00**
Molded Products, stretcher bearer **25.00**

TOY TRAIN ACCESSORIES

Toy train accessories and boxed train sets are two of the hottest toy train collecting categories in the 1990s. Toy train accessories divide into two main groups: (1) those made by toy train manufacturers and (2) those made by others. Many of the latter were in kit form.

As with toy trains, toy train accessories are sized by gauge. An HO building on a Lionel train platform appears very much out of place. O and S gauge accessories are the most desired. The period box adds 15% to 25% to the value.

Bachmann Brothers, a manufacturer of eyeglasses, produced its first plastic train accessory, a picket fence, in 1949. A log cabin followed in 1950. By the mid-1950s Bachmann's Plasticville O/S gauge buildings were found on the vast majority of America's toy train platforms. An HO line was introduced in 1955, an N gauge line in 1968. Plasticville houses are marked with a "BB" on a banner in a circle.

Bachmann ended a challenge to its market supremacy by Unlimited Plastics' Littletown when it acquired the company in 1956. Bachmann carefully stores its Plasticville dies, giving it the ability to put any model back into production when sufficient demand occurs.

References: Frank C. Hare, *Plasticville, 3rd Edition,* Kalmbach Publishing, 1993; Alan Stewart, *Greenberg's Guide to Lionel Trains, 1945–1969, Vol VI: Accessories,* Kalmbach Publishing, 1994.

AMERICAN FLYER

Aircraft Beacon, 769A, orig box **$95.00**
Bumper, 730 . . . . **18.00**
Bungalow, 161 . . . . **250.00**
Crossing Gate, 592, with track trip and orig box **110.00**
Crossover, 725 . . . . **12.00**
Factory, 162 . . . . **325.00**
Grain Elevator, 165, orig box **435.00**
Log Loader, 751 . . . . **350.00**
Oil Drum Loader, 779, orig box **325.00**
Shell Oil Depot, 768 . . . . **135.00**
Station, 90 . . . . **150.00**
Station Platform, 274 . . . . **195.00**
Transformer, 15B, 110 watt, 1952 . . . . **100.00**
Union Talking Station, 799 . . . . **350.00**
Water Tower, 516 . . . . **55.00**
Wayside Station, 586, orig box **145.00**
Whistle Stop Set, 271 . . . . **175.00**
Whistling Billboard, 568, orig box **75.00**

LIONEL

Animated Freight Station, 12818 . . . . **$42.00**
Beacon, 494 . . . . **60.00**
Blinking Signal, 154, 1950 . . . . **100.00**
Coaling Station, 2315 . . . . **195.00**
Coal Ramp Set, 456 . . . . **300.00**
Crossing Gate, 152, metal, 1947 . . . . **100.00**
Dispatch Board, 334 . . . . **300.00**
Fork Lift Loader Station, 12798 . . . . **38.00**
Ice Station, with car, 352 . . . . **140.00**
Illuminated Stop Station, 132 . . . . **80.00**
Mail Pick-up Set, 12729 . . . . **16.00**
NYC Gantry Crane, 12922 . . . . **140.00**
Oil Derrick, 12848 . . . . **180.00**
Operating Control Tower, 12878 . . . . **80.00**
Operating Flag Man, 1045, 1942 . . . . **100.00**
Pumping Water Tower, 38 . . . . **500.00**
Roadside Lionelville Diner, 12722 . . . . **70.00**
Signal Bridge, 450 . . . . **70.00**
Stop Station, 115 . . . . **425.00**
Track Cleaning Car, 3927, 1955 . . . . **150.00**
Transformer, KW, 190 watt, 1955 . . . . **200.00**
Transformer, LW, 125 watt **125.00**
Transformer, R, 150 watt, 1941 . . . . **200.00**
Transformer, SW, 1961 . . . . **275.00**
Transformer, TW, 175 watt, 1955 . . . . **175.00**
Transformer, ZW, 275 watt **325.00**
Trestle Bridge, 317 . . . . **80.00**
Wayside Station, 256, 1965 . . . . **95.00**

PLASTICVILLE

2-Story House, LH-4, white and blue, orig box **$50.00**
Barn, BN-1, orig box **20.00**
Barnyard Animals, BY-4, orig box **30.00**
Bird Bath, CB, orig box **8.00**
Cape Cod, HP-9, orig box **20.00**

Frosty Bar, FB-1, 1952, $20.00.

Church, CC-9, orig box	20.00
Fire House, FH-4, orig box	30.00
Gas Station, GO-2, orig box	25.00
Hardware/Pharmacy, DH-2, orig box	35.00
New England Ranch, MH-2, orig box	30.00
Outhouse, SA-7, orig box	4.00
Passenger Station, RS-7, orig box	25.00
Police Department, PD-3, orig box	40.00
Post Office, PO-1, orig box	30.00
Ranch House, RH-1, white and blue, orig box	20.00
Road Signs, 12-A, orig box	15.00
School House, SC-4, orig box	25.00
Supermarket, SM-6, orig box	35.00
Town Hall, PH-1, orig box	95.00
Trellis, GT-1, orig box	10.00

TOY TRAINS

The mid-1920s through the late 1950s is the golden age of toy trains. American Flyer, Ives, and Lionel produced electric model trains that featured highly detailed castings and markings. A slow conversion to plastic occurred within the industry in the late 1950s and early 1960s. Most collectors shun plastic like the plague.

Trains are collected first by company and second by gauge. Lionel is king of the hill, followed by American Flyer. As a result, O, O27, and S are the three most popular gauges among collectors. Collector interest in HO gauge trains has increased significantly in the past five years. Many toy train auctions now include HO trains among their offerings. Interest is minimal in N gauge.

The 1990s witnessed several major shifts in collecting emphasis. First, post–World War II replaced pre–World War II trains as the hot chronological collecting period. Pre-1945 prices have stabilized. In the case of cast-iron trains, some decline has been noted. Second, accessories and sets are the hot post-1945 collecting areas. Prices on most engines and rolling stock have stabilized. Third, the speculative bubble in mass-produced trains of the 1970s and 1980s has burst. With some exceptions, most of these trains are selling below their initial retail cost on the secondary market. Fourth, adult collectors currently are investing heavily in limited edition reproductions and special model issues. These pieces have not been strongly tested on the secondary market.

Fifth, there are initial signs of a growing collector interest in HO material, primarily the better grade German trains, and inexpensive lithographed tin windup trains.

References: General: Tim Blaisdell and Ed Urmston Sr., *Standard Guide to Athearn Model Trains*, Krause Publications, 1998; John Grams, *Toy Train Collecting and Operating*, Kalmbach Publishing, 1999; *Greenberg's Pocket Price Guide, LGB, 1968–1996*, Third Edition, Kalmbach Publishing, 1996; *Greenberg's Pocket Price Guide, Lionel Trains, 1901–1999*, Kalmbach Publishing, 1998; *Greenberg's Pocket Price Guide: Marx Trains, 7th Edition*, Kalmbach Publishing, 1999; *Greenberg's Pocket Price Guide, American Flyer S Gauge*, Kalmbach Publishing, 1998; Richard O'Brien, *Collecting Toy Trains, No. 4*, Krause Publishing, 1997; Peter H. Riddle, *America's Standard Gauge Electric Trains*, Antique Trader Books, 1998.

American Flyer: Greenberg Books, three-volume set.

Lionel: Greenberg Books, four volumes dealing with Lionel trains made between 1901 and 1942, seven volumes covering the 1945 to 1969 period, and two volumes for the 1970 to 1991 period. Also check Lionel Book Committee, Train Collectors Association, *Lionel Trains: Standard of the World, 1900–1943*, Second Edition, Train Collectors Association, 1989.

Miscellaneous: Greenberg Books has one or more price guides for Athearn, Kusan, Ives, Marx, and Varney.

Note: For a complete list of toy train titles from Greenberg Books, a division of Kalmbach Publishing Co., write PO Box 1612, Waukesha, WI 53187, and request a copy of their latest catalog. If you are a serious collector, ask to be put on their mailing list.

Periodicals: *Classic Toy Trains*, PO Box 1612, Waukesha, WI 53187; *LGB Telegram*, 1573 Landvater, Hummelstown, PA 17036; *O Gauge Railroading*, PO Box 239, Nazareth, PA 18064.

Collectors' Clubs: American Flyer Collectors Club, PO Box 13269, Pittsburgh, PA 15243; The Ives Train Society, PO Box 59, 6714 Madison Rd, Thompson, OH 44086; LGB Model Railroad Club, 1854 Erin Dr, Altoona, PA 16602; Lionel Collectors Club of America, PO Box 479, LaSalle, IL 61301; Marklin Club—North America, PO Box 51559, New Berlin, WI 53151; The National Model Railroad Assoc, 4121 Cromwell Rd, Chattanooga, TN 37421; Toy Train Operating Society, 25 W Walnut St, Ste 308, Pasadena, CA 91103; Train Collectors Assoc, PO Box 248, Strasburg, PA 17579.

AMERICAN FLYER

Boxcar, 639, yellow, orig box	$32.00
Boxed Set, #5108W	750.00
Caboose, 930, orig box	55.00
CB&Q Hopper, 921	35.00
Crane, 644, brown	150.00
Flatcar with Derrick, 49009	38.00
Flatcar with Farm Tractors, 48509	45.00
Frisco Gondola, 941, orig box	32.00
Gilbert Tanker, 48407	35.00
Gondola, 931	32.00
Hamilton Vista Dome, 962, 1955	150.00
Hopper, 924, orig box	42.00
Hopper, 24209	75.00
Horse Car, 49010	32.00
Katy Boxcar, 937	55.00

American Flyer, engine and tender, #4663, black, 23" l, $330.00.
Photo courtesy Collectors Auction Services.

MOPAC Stock Car, 629, orig box **50.00**
MP Stock Car, 929 . . . . **45.00**
New Haven Boxcar, 984 . . . . **110.00**
NH Boxcar, 24036 . . . . **110.00**
NW Reefer, 989, orig box **350.00**
Reading Caboose, 630 . . . . **24.00**
REA Reefer, 48806 . . . . **35.00**
Red Stripe Combo Passenger, 24773, 1960 . . . . **200.00**
Red Stripe Observation Car, 24833, 1960 . . . . **200.00**
Rio Grande Boxcar, 20439, 1959 . . . . **125.00**
SF Alco A Diesel, 21927, 1960 . . . . **400.00**
Shell Tank, 625, orig box **45.00**
T&P Gondola, 631, orig box **24.00**
Wabash Hopper, 940, orig box **40.00**

DORFAN

Baggage Car, 492, green maroon, brass trim **$40.00**
Box Car, 517953, orange, brown, O gauge **20.00**
Caboose, 5 . . . . **40.00**
Caboose, 600, narrow gauge **25.00**
Coach, 493, Seattle **35.00**
Engine, 3919, orange, wide gauge **340.00**
Locomotive, electric, 3931, green **550.00**
Observation Car, 773, orange and black **70.00**

GILBERT

Caboose, 930 . . . . **$40.00**
Caboose, 24631 . . . . **35.00**
Caboose, 24634, orig box **125.00**
Locomotive and Tender, 283 . . . . **125.00**
Locomotive and Tender, 287 . . . . **125.00**
Locomotive and Tender, 21004 . . . . **400.00**
Locomotive and Tender, 21084 . . . . **175.00**
Locomotive and Tender, 21085 . . . . **150.00**
Locomotive and Tender, 21160 . . . . **65.00**
Wabash Hopper, 940 . . . . **30.00**

IVES

Baggage Car, #70, 1923–25 . . . . **$45.00**
Buffet, #130, 1930 . . . . **75.00**
Caboose, #67, red-orange, green roof, yellow lettering,
 1929–30 . . . . **50.00**
Cattle Car, #1678, green, 1931–32 . . . . **35.00**
Drawing Room Car, #129, The Ives Railway Lines, green,
 gray roof, 1918–24 . . . . **85.00**
Gondola, #1512, blue, 1931–32 . . . . **50.00**
Gravel Car, #63, gray, 1930 . . . . **45.00**
Livestock Car, #20-193, orange, red roof, 1930 . . . . **100.00**

Locomotive, #6, cast iron, "Ives No. 6," 1926–28 . . . . **100.00**
Locomotive, #1506, mechanical, 1931–32 . . . . **130.00**
Locomotive, #1661, black, red trim, 1932 . . . . **110.00**
Locomotive, #1694, electric, maroon roof, brass trim,
 1932 . . . . **500.00**
Merchandise Car, #192, yellow, 1930 . . . . **100.00**
Parlor Car, #62, "The Ives Railway Lines, 62 Parlor Car,"
 1924–30 . . . . **95.00**
Tank Car, orange, "190" and "Texas Oil," 1923–28 . . . . **100.00**

LIONEL

Alaska Hopper, 0836, red, 1958 . . . . **$65.00**
Auto Boxcar, 2758, 1940 . . . . **150.00**
Auto Car, 2458, metal, 1947 . . . . **150.00**
Baby Ruth Boxcar, 1679, 1940 . . . . **100.00**
Baby Ruth Boxcar, 2454, 1947 . . . . **95.00**
Baggage Car, 310, 1932, restored **350.00**
Boat Car, 6801, 1958 . . . . **100.00**
Boxcar, 214, large, 1932, restored **500.00**
Boxcar, Chessie, Waffle-side, 15002 . . . . **25.00**
Boxcar, "I Love Arizona," 19932 . . . . **27.00**
Broadway Ltd Passenger Set, 1487, 1974 . . . . **700.00**
Caboose, 817, red, 1938 . . . . **200.00**
Caboose, 2682, metal, 1940 . . . . **75.00**
Caboose, 6457, 1950 . . . . **75.00**
Cooper-Jarratt Van Car, 6430, 1956 . . . . **150.00**
Diesel Engine, Jersey Central, 18932 . . . . **95.00**
Flatcar with Steam Shovel, 6827, 1960, orig box **500.00**
Floodlight Car, 520, 1932 . . . . **300.00**
Gondola, 512, green, 1932 . . . . **175.00**
Gulf Tank Car, 6025, black, 1955 . . . . **100.00**
Helicopter Car, 3419, 1958 . . . . **150.00**
HO Lionel Race Car, #7, 1959 . . . . **275.00**
HO Operating Milk Car, 0366, 1958 . . . . **100.00**
HO Rocket Fuel Tank Car, 0816, 1964, orig box **100.00**
Hopper Car, 116, 1920 . . . . **225.00**
Illuminated Caboose, 2357, 1946, orig box **150.00**
Lake Shore Gondola, 112, 1924 . . . . **125.00**
Liberty Bicentennial Set, 1577, 1975 . . . . **650.00**
NJC Gondola, 16943 . . . . **18.00**
Observation Car, 190, large, 1925 . . . . **200.00**
Operating Milk Car with Platform, 3482, 1950, orig box **200.00**
Pennsylvania Caboose, 2472, metal, 1946, orig box **125.00**
Pennsylvania Caboose, 2757, metal, 1940 . . . . **125.00**
Pennsylvania Gondola Car, 2452, 1947 . . . . **100.00**
Pipe Car, 6411, 1949, diecast **75.00**
Pullman, 2440, blue/silver, 1946, restored **125.00**
Rocket Launcher Car, 6650, 1959, orig box **195.00**
Scale Detail Sunoco Tank, 2755, 1942 . . . . **150.00**
Slopeback Tender, 1615T, 1955 . . . . **100.00**
Southern Bulkhead Flatcar, 16951 . . . . **35.00**
Steam Locomotive, 637, 2-6-4, 1957 . . . . **300.00**
Steam Locomotive, 1835, 1932, restored **950.00**
Steam Locomotive, 2026, 2-6-4, tender **275.00**
Sunoco #6315 Tank Car, 19607 . . . . **32.00**
Sunoco Tank Car, 6555, metal, 1949, orig box **150.00**
TCA Boxcar, 6464, 1970 . . . . **300.00**
TCA Hopper Car, 6436, 1969, orig box **200.00**
Tennessee Central 2-Bay Hopper, 16419 . . . . **18.00**
Turbine/Tender, 671, 6-8-6, 1946, restored **450.00**
Turbine/Tender, 2020, 6-8-6, 1946, restored **400.00**
USMC Flatcar, 6806, 1957, orig box **475.00**
Wabash RR Steam Loco 4-6-4 Hudson, 18046 . . . . **500.00**

MARX

Boxcar, #817, Colorado & Southern, yellow and black **$12.00**
Caboose, #234, olive drab, white "USA" **25.00**
Diesel Locomotive, diesel, #54, red, yellow, and black,
    yellow and white lettering **30.00**
Flatcar, #2824, missile launcher, olive drab, white letter-
    ing **15.00**
Gondola, Joy Line, mkd "Bunny Express" **60.00**
Shell Tank Car, #652, orange, red lettering **8.00**
Steam Locomotive, #90, Lumar Lines, streamlined, black
    and blue, yellow lettering **30.00**

TRANSPORTATION

America is a highly mobile society. America's expansion and growth is linked to its transportation system, whether road, canal, rail, or sky. Few communities have escaped the impact of one or more transportation systems. As a result, transportation memorabilia has a strong regional collecting base.

Further, collectors are fascinated with anything relating to transportation vehicles and systems. This is a catchall category for those transportation categories, e.g., bus, canal, and trolley, not found elsewhere in the book.

Reference: Alex Roggero and Tony Beadle, *Greyhound: A Pictorial Tribute to an American Icon*, Motorbooks International, 1995.

Collectors' Clubs: Bus History Assoc, 965 McEwan, Windsor, Ontario N9B 2G1 Canada; International Bus Collectors Club, 1518 "C" Trailee Dr, Charleston, SC 29407; National Assoc of Timetable Collectors, 125 American Inn Rd, Villa Ridge, MO 63089.

Note: For additional listings see Automobiles, Automobilia, Aviation Collectibles, Bicycles, Ocean Liner Collectibles, and Railroad Collectibles.

Badge, Burns Cab Service, silvered brass, inscription
    identifying driver "Lee," raised image of taxi cab
    accented by black enamel, tiny white enamel accents
    on window areas, 1930s **$75.00**
Badge, Crescent Taxi, metal, silver luster, slightly con-
    vex, inscription and telephone number incised in
    black, small profile image of c1950s taxi accented in
    blue **75.00**
Badge, Flint Taxi, silvered brass, inscribed "1063-64
    Taxicab Driver/City of Flint," and "339" operator num-
    ber **25.00**
Badge, Tulsa Taxi Driver's, silvered brass, engraved
    "421," 1940 . . . . **75.00**
Badge, Yellow Cab, metal, silver luster, slightly convex,
    yellow enamel car image, 1940–50s **50.00**
Book, *Trolley Car Treasury*, Rowsome, Frank, 200 pp,
    over 300 photos, 1946, dj **30.00**
Hat Badge, Stockton City Lines, silvered brass, orange
    enamel ground, for "City Lines" inscription band,
    inscription Safety/Courtesy/Service" plus engraved
    "5" operator, back names Chicago maker, threaded
    post and wheel fastener at each side, 1930s **50.00**
Keychain Fob, Yellow Cab Co, figural, diecut brass,
    enameled taxi cab, reverse engraved "Phone 8800
    Gaspee" with "653" **75.00**

Bus Station Sign, 2-sided, porcelain in iron frame, 20" h, 16" w, $390.00. Photo courtesy Collectors Auction Services.

Map, Metro Map of Paris, bus routes on 1 side and sub-
    way lines on other, 1982 . . . . **2.00**
Map, New York City subway, issued by Metropolitan
    Transit Authority, 1988. . . . . **1.00**
Pinback Button, Boatmen's Reunion, sepia, single day
    issue for Aug 27, depicting barges in canal locks of
    Rolling Green Park, PA **25.00**
Pinback Button, Gotfredson Truck, truck illus,
    1920–30s **100.00**
Pinback Button, "I Rode The First Skyway," blue on sil-
    ver, depicting passenger car of "Monorail Pilot
    Project/Houston, Texas 1956" **25.00**
Pinback Button, Neighborhood Line, green trolley car
    against small city buildings ground, "If The Street Cars
    Carry It—We Carry It," back paper has White & Hoag
    label plus "Eastern Advertising Company/Street Car
    Advertising All Over New England" **75.00**
Pinback Button, Oregon Speedboat Event, gold on blue,
    for 1971 Oregon Emerald Cup competitor at Dexter
    Lake, OR **15.00**
Pinback Button, Reading Transportation Co, oncoming
    bus illus, 1940s. **25.00**
Pinback Button, Soap Box Derby, 1972, red, white, and
    blue, Akron, OH, sponsored by Warren Jaycees **20.00**
Pinback Button, Washington Tour Bus Service, black and
    white, yellow rim, "The International Auto Sight
    Seeing Transit Co./Touring Interior Public Building,"
    loaded open-air tour bus in front of US Capitol dome **50.00**
Poster, Trolleybus to Kingstone, doubledecker bus and
    cityscape image, Grey Brown, c1930, 25 x 40". **385.00**
Schedule, Travel By Motor Coach Richmond,
    Fredericksburg, Washington, blue and white, 1927 . . . . **8.50**
Sign, "Call A Checker Taxi," and "Extra Passengers Free,
    Also Cadillac Limousines," taxicab illus, 11 x 7". **75.00**
Stickpin, Apperson Motor Car, brass, brass image of rab-
    bit running at full speed with product name on
    image side, c1920–26 . . . . **50.00**
Timetable, Greyhound Transcontinental Bus, centerfold
    map of US and strip maps of western routes, 1940 . . . . . . **12.00**
Timetable, Trailways Bus, Florida West Coast, includes
    map showing bus routes through the Sunshine State,
    1945. . . . . **10.00**
Trolley Card, Chesterfield Cigarettes, "Joan Bennett star-
    ring in *Twin Beds*," 21 x 11" **40.00**

TROLLS

Trolls originated in Scandinavian folklore. In the late 1950s Helena and Martii Kuuskoski, a Finnish couple, began marketing cloth troll dolls. Thomas Dam, a Danish woodcarver, also started selling troll figurines. A troll craze developed. By the early 1960s, Dam-designed trolls were being produced in Denmark, New Zealand, and the United States (Hialeah, Florida).

Dozens of manufacturers, many failing to permanently mark their products, hopped aboard the troll bandwagon. Dam filed a copyright infringement suit against Scandia House Enterprises, a division of Royalty Designs of Florida. The court ruled that the troll image was in the public domain. Eventually Dam signed an agreement with Scandia House to distribute his designs in America. Troll collectors take a negative approach to cheap foreign troll imports from Hong Kong and Japan.

A second major troll craze occurred in the early 1990s. Thomas Dam trolls were distributed by EFS Marketing Associates during this period under the Norfin trademark. Ace Novelty, Applause Toys, Russ Berrie & Company, and Uneeda Doll Company also manufactured troll lines. China and Korea replaced Hong Kong and Japan as the source for inexpensive, often unmarked trolls.

References: Debra Clark, *Trolls*, Hobby House Press, 1993; Pat Peterson, *Collector's Guide to Trolls*, Collector Books, 1995.

Newsletters: *Troll Monthly*, 216 Washington St, Canton, MA 02021; *Troll'n*, PO Box 601292, Sacramento, CA 95860.

Activity Book, Hobnobbins Paint with Water, Golden **$1.50**
Activity Book, Wishnik Color and Play Book, Uneeda Doll Co ©1966, Whitman Publishing **20.00**
Bank, Dam, boy in raincoat, yellow hair, aqua cape, dark blue felt trousers, mkd "Made in Denmark Thomas Dam," 7½" h **40.00**
Bank, Dam, Santa Troll, red and white outfit, black belt, gold buckle, green eyes, mkd "Thomas Dam Made In Denmark" on back, 7" h **50.00**
Bank, Dam, white hair, reddish amber eyes, green and red outfit mkd "Made in Denmark Thomas Dam," 7" h **40.00**
Case, molded plastic, 3-D cave scene with waterfall, Ideal **25.00**
Cookie Cutter, aluminum, mail-in offer, 3½" h **20.00**
Doll, Dam, blue hair, blue felt off-the-shoulder outfit, mkd "Made In Denmark Thomas Dam" on back, 7" h **35.00**
Doll, Dam, girl, dark pink hair, pink and white outfit, felt hair ribbons, mkd "Made in Denmark Thomas Dam," 7½" h **40.00**
Doll, Dam, girl, orange hair, orange frayed outfit, amber eyes, mkd "Dam," 3"h **12.00**
Doll, Dam, Hula Girl, fringe skirt, plastic lei, 6" h **10.00**
Doll, Dam, Iggy-normous, blonde hair, oversized blue tie knotted sailor style over white outfit, mkd "Dam Things Originals (C) 1964–65 Dam Things Est. Mfg by Royalty Designs of Fla, Inc" on paper tag, 12" h **125.00**
Doll, Sweden, Furball, orange hair, wooden eyes and body, 4" h **20.00**
Doll, Uneeda, Double-Nik, short green and yellow hair, red, black, and white plaid outfit, red tinged amber eyes, mkd "Uneeda 19(C)65" on head, 4" h **45.00**
Doll, Wishnik, cowboy, yellow hair, light blue jeans, red checked shirt, tulip design scarf, thin plastic hat, horseshoes mark on feet, 3½" h **15.00**
Doll, Wishnik, pink hair, yellow felt nightshirt with embroidered "Good Night" in orange, amber eyes, 1 blackened eye, unmkd, 5" h **20.00**
Doll, Wishnik, salt and pepper hair, blush pink cheeks, amber eyes, naked, Uneeda horseshoes mark on both feet, 3" h **12.00**
Nodder, Bobblehead Buddies, bright red hair, molded vinyl body, "Chicago Cubs" on base, mkd "Russ (C) MLB 1992 China" on head, 8½" h **10.00**
Ornament, Norfin Santa, painted features, red felt hat, mkd "Dam," 2½" h **3.00**
Premium, Burger King, Jaws, lime green hair, painted molded outfit, rotating head, mkd "Burger King Kids Klub—Jaws" on back, "©1993 Burger King Corp, Made in China" on feet, 3" h **5.00**

TV GUIDE

TV Guide first appeared as *Tele-Vision Guide* on June 14, 1948. Its title was shortened to *TV Guide* on March 18, 1950. Published in New York, *Tele-Vision Guide* was one of a number of regional weekly, digest-sized TV log magazines.

Walter Annenberg bought *TV Guide* near the end of 1952 and went national with the April 3, 1953 issue whose cover featured a picture of Lucy Ricardo (Lucille Ball) and baby Ricky.

Value rests primarily with cover images. Issues #26 (9/25–10/1/53) with George Reeves as Superman and #179 (9/1–7/56) with Elvis are two of the most sought-after issues. Occasionally an inside story is the key. The April 19–25, 1969 issue includes a story of the Beatles. Early fall premier issues command a small premium. Condition is critical. The survival rate is high. Collecting emphasis rests primarily with issues pre-dating 1980.

Reference: Ron Barlow and Ray Reynolds, *The Insider's Guide to Old Books, Magazines, Newspapers, Trade Catalogs*, Windmill Publishing, 1995.

Periodical: *PCM (Paper Collectors' Marketplace)*, PO Box 128, Scandinavia, WI 54977.

Left: Jan 16, 1953, Vol. 6, #3, Ed Sullivan, $25.00. Right: Aug 1, 1964, Vol. 12, #31, "Today" cast, $8.00.

1950, Apr 8, Vol 3, #14, Easter Parade **$75.00**

1950, Jul 8, Ted Williams and Joe DiMaggio cov, All-Star Game **200.00**

1952, Jul 18, Vol 5, #29, Groucho Marx. **25.00**

1952, Dec 12, Vol 5, #50, Lucy's TV Baby **25.00**

1952, Dec 19, Vol 5, #51, winners of the 1952 TV Guide Gold Medal Awards. **75.00**

1953, Jan 2, Vol 6, #1, Jackie Gleason **25.00**

1953, Jan 23, sidebar photo of Marilyn Monroe on cov, "Marilyn Monroe/She'll be on your home screen". **100.00**

1953, Feb 13, Vol 6, #7, Kukla, Fran, and Ollie **50.00**

1953, Mar 5, Vol 6, #9, Groucho Marx **25.00**

1953, May 22, Vol 1, #8, Red Buttons cov, Howdy Doody article, color photo of Buffalo Bob, Clarabell, Princess, and Peanut Gallery **50.00**

1953, Apr 2, Vol 6, #13, "I Want To Get Married," includes photos of Charlton Heston and John Forsythe, article of TV's heartthrobs **50.00**

1953, Jun 5, Vol 1, #10, Martin & Lewis. **50.00**

1953, Jul 24, Vol 1, #17, Groucho Marx and Hopalong Cassidy. **50.00**

1953, Aug 14, "Range Rider" star Jack Mahoney **50.00**

1953, Sep 18, Vol 1, #25, 1953–54 Shows. **50.00**

1953, Sep 25, Vol 1, #26, "Superman" star George Reeves . . **200.00**

1953, Dec 1, Vol 1, #37, Dragnet **25.00**

1954, Jun 25, Howdy Doody & Buffalo Bob Smith **50.00**

1955, Jul 30, Vol 3, #3, "The Whiting Girls With Lucy & Desi" **50.00**

1956, Sep 29, Vol 4, #39, Jackie Gleason cov, Elvis Presley article and full page color photo. **50.00**

1957, Jun 8, Vol 5, #23, Lassie. **25.00**

1957, Sep 14, Vol 5, #37, Wagon Train, 1957–58 Fall Preview **50.00**

1957, Nov 2, Vol 5, #4, Lucille Ball. **25.00**

1958, Jan 18, Restless Gun, John Payne **25.00**

1959, Jan 17, "Maverick" stars James Garner and Jack Kelly. **25.00**

1960, May 7, Vol 8, #9, Elvis Presley and Frank Sinatra. **25.00**

1961, Jul 1, Vol 9, #26, The Flintstones **25.00**

1965, Oct 30, Vol 13, #44, Addams Family **25.00**

1966, Feb 5, Vol 14, #6, Barbara Eden **25.00**

1966, Mar 26, Vol 14, #13, "Batman" star Adam West **75.00**

1966, Sep 10, Vol 14, #37, 1966–67 Fall Preview. **50.00**

1993, Dec 11, Bette Midler, sgd **25.00**

TYPEWRITERS

E. Remington & Son's Sholes & Glidden typewriter, introduced in 1874, was the first commercially produced typewriter in the United States. The keyboard consisted only of capital letters.

The earliest typewriters are known as blind models, i.e., the carriage had to be lifted away from the machine to see what had been written. Five major manufacturers joined forces in 1893 to form the Union Typewriter Company. Their monopoly was soon challenged by L. C. Smith & Brothers and the Underwood Typewriter Company. These companies led the field in typewriter innovation in the pre-1940 period.

Electric typewriters appeared briefly in the 1900s. It was not until the 1930s that IBM introduced the first commercially successful electric typewriter. The electric typewriter replaced the manual typewriter by the late 1960s, only to lose its market position to the home computer in the late 1980s.

Advanced typewriter collectors focus primarily on pre-1920 models. Post-1920 typewriters with unusual features are the exception. The keyboard is a good barometer. If the letter placement, i.e., QWERTY, is the same as a modern typewriter or computer keyboard, chances are strong the machine has little value.

Europe, particularly Germany, is the center of typewriter collecting. The number of American collectors remains small.

References: Michael Adler, *Antique Typewriters: From Creed to QWERTY*, Schiffer Publishing, 1997; Darryl Rehr, *Antique Typewriters & Office Collectibles*, Collector Books, 1997.

Newsletters: *Ribbon Tin News*, 28 The Green, Watertown, CT 06795; *The Typewriter Exchange*, PO Box 52607, Philadelphia, PA 19115.

Collectors' Club: Early Typewriter Collectors Assoc, 2591 Military Ave, Los Angeles, CA 90064.

Bing Student, 4-row, oblique frontstrike **$35.00**

Brochure, Oliver Co, 1922 . . . . **8.50**

Burroughs Electric. **50.00**

Carissima, Bakelite housing and lid, 1934 . . . . **200.00**

Corona, 4-row **10.00**

Corona, 4-row, animal keyboard **100.00**

Corona, sterling silver covering. **1,000.00**

IBM Selectric **25.00**

Macy's Portable, 4-row, 1920. . . . . **50.00**

Mignon, Model 4, black, 1924. . . . . **100.00**

Olivetti Praxis 48, electric1958 . . . . **248.00**

Olivetti Valentine, portable, red, manual **300.00**

Remington Electric, 1925 . . . . **150.00**

Remington Portable, 1929 . . . . **30.00**

Ribbon Tin, Bundy, ³⁄₄ x 2⁵⁄₈" **40.00**

Ribbon Tin, Osborn. **5.00**

Ribbon Tin, Remtico **8.00**

Royal Portable, Quiet De Luxe, gold plated, 4-row, frontstrike **250.00**

Sampson Permagraph **250.00**

Toy, Western Stamping, 1950s **40.00**

Underwood Noiseless **30.00**

Ribbon Tin, Pilot Brand, litho tin, red, black, and white, 2⁵⁄₈" d, $176.00. Photo courtesy Wm. Morford.

UNIVERSAL POTTERY

In 1926 the Atlas China Company (Niles, Ohio) and the Globe Pottery Company (Cambridge, Ohio), both owned by A. O. C. Ahrendts, were consolidated and renamed the Atlas Globe China Company. Financial pressures resulted in another reorganization in the early 1930s. The factory in Niles closed. Globe was liquidated, its assets becoming part of the Oxford Pottery, also owned by Ahrendts.

In 1934 the company became Universal Pottery. Universal made baking dishes, a fine grade of semi-porcelain dinnerware, and utilitarian kitchenware. Tile manufacturing was introduced in 1956, and the company became The Oxford Tile Company. It continued to make dinnerware until 1960. Universal Promotions distributed Universal. It subcontracted with Hull, Homer Laughlin, and Taylor, Smith & Taylor to continue manufacturing Universal patterned pieces with a Universal backstamp into the 1960s.

References: Susan and Al Bagdade, *Warman's American Pottery and Porcelain,* Wallace-Homestead, Krause Publications, 1994; Harvey Duke, *The Official Identification and Price Guide to Pottery and Porcelain, Eighth Edition,* House of Collectibles, 1995.

America, bean pot, lug handle **$15.00**
America, bowl, 4¼" d **6.00**
America, casserole, 8¼" d **20.00**
America, cookie jar **30.00**
America, leftover, 6" d **15.00**
Ballerina, bowl, 36s, pink **8.00**
Ballerina, bread and butter plate, periwinkle blue, 6¼" d **2.00**
Ballerina, butter, cov, burgundy, ¼ lb **20.00**
Ballerina, casserole, charcoal, 10¼" d **20.00**
Ballerina, coffee server, 64 oz, forest green **35.00**
Ballerina, cream soup, cup, jonquil yellow, 6⅞" **12.00**
Ballerina, dinner plate, forest green, 10" d **8.00**
Ballerina, dish, burgundy, 6" d **3.00**
Ballerina, drip jar, periwinkle blue **12.00**
Ballerina, eggcup, dove gray **10.00**
Ballerina, gravy, dove gray **12.00**
Ballerina, luncheon plate, chartreuse, 9⅛" d **8.00**

Ballerina, platter, round, jonquil yellow, 13¼" d **12.00**
Ballerina, salad bowl, individual, dove gray, 7¾" d **12.00**
Ballerina, salad plate, burgundy, 7⅜" d **4.00**
Ballerina, teapot, 6 cup, burgundy **25.00**
Ballerina, vegetable bowl, round, chartreuse, 7¾" d **10.00**
Bittersweet, cup **5.00**
Bittersweet, dish, 6" d **5.00**
Bittersweet, mixing bowl set, 3 pc **40.00**
Bittersweet, stack set, 4 pc **40.00**
Bittersweet, vegetable bowl, 8½" d **18.00**
Calico Fruit, bread and butter plate, 6" d **3.00**
Calico Fruit, custard, 5 oz **8.00**
Calico Fruit, refrigerator jug, 3 qt **10.00**
Calico Fruit, soup bowl **4.00**
Calico Fruit, utility plate, 11½" l **15.00**
Calico Fruit, utility shakers, pr **15.00**
Camwood, bread and butter plate, 6⅛" d **2.00**
Camwood, butter, cov **20.00**
Camwood, creamer and sugar **12.00**
Camwood, dinner plate, 9¾" d **10.00**
Camwood, dish, 5¼" d **2.00**
Camwood, gravy boat **12.00**
Camwood, platter, oval, 7⅛" l **6.00**
Camwood, salad plate, 8" d **5.00**
Camwood, teapot, cov **25.00**
Cattail, bean pot, handled, America **30.00**
Cattail, cup and saucer, Ballerina **8.00**
Cattail, dinner plate, Camwood, 9¾" **8.00**
Cattail, jug **25.00**
Cattail, salad set, 3 pc **60.00**
Cattail, stack set, cov **20.00**
Netherlands, creamer and sugar **12.00**
Netherlands, dinner plate, 10" d **10.00**
Netherlands, dish, 5⅝" d **5.00**
Netherlands, platter, 11¼" l **12.00**
Oxford, new style, ball jug, green **15.00**
Oxford, new style, custard, red **5.00**
Oxford, new style, range shakers, pr, yellow **15.00**
Oxford, new style, teapot, 4 cup, Cattail decal **20.00**
Oxford, old style, jug, Cattail decal, 2 pt, 6" h **15.00**
Oxford, old style, teapot, 4 cup, Circus decal **20.00**
Rambler Rose, gravy boat **6.00**
Rambler Rose, utility shaker **4.00**
Rodeo, bread and butter plate, 6¼" d **2.00**
Rodeo, creamer and sugar **12.00**
Rodeo, platter, 11" l **10.00**
Rodeo, soup bowl, 9" d **10.00**
Upico, ball jug **15.00**
Upico, bean pot, individual **6.00**
Upico, bread and butter plate, 6¼" d **2.00**
Upico, butter, cov, ¼ lb **20.00**
Upico, creamer and sugar **12.00**
Upico, gravy boat **12.00**
Upico, leftover, 4¾" d **8.00**
Upico, nesting bowl, 5⅛" d **6.00**
Upico, salad bowl, 9¼" d **15.00**
Upico, teapot **40.00**
Upico, tumbler **5.00**
Woodvine, gravy boat **8.00**
Woodvine, gravy liner **6.00**
Woodvine, luncheon plate **4.00**
Woodvine, utility jar, cov **17.00**
Woodvine, utility tray **10.00**
Woodvine, vegetable bowl **6.00**

Ballerina, cup and saucer, burgundy, $6.00.

U.S. GLASS

United States Glass resulted from the merger of eighteen different glass companies in 1891. The company's headquarters were in Pittsburgh. Plants were scattered throughout Indiana, Ohio, Pennsylvania, and West Virginia.

Most plants continued to manufacture the same products that they made before the merger. Older trademarks and pattern names were retained. Some new shapes and patterns used a U.S. Glass trademark. New plants were built in Gas City, Indiana, and Tiffin, Ohio. The Gas City plant made machine-made dinnerware, kitchenware, and tabletop items in colors that included amber, black, canary, green, and pink. The Tiffin plant made delicate pressed dinnerware and blown stemware in crystal and a host of other colors. U.S. Glass' main decorating facility was in Pittsburgh.

During the first three decades of the 20th century, several plants closed, the result of strikes, organizational mismanagement, and/or economic difficulties. In 1938, following the appointment of C. W. Carlson, Sr., as president, the corporate headquarters moved from Pittsburgh to Tiffin. Only the Pittsburgh and Tiffin plants were still operating. Carlson, along with C. W. Carlson, Jr., his son, revived the company by adding several new shapes and colors to the line. The company prospered until the late 1950s.

By 1951 all production was located in Tiffin. U.S. Glass bought the Duncan and Miller molds in 1955. Some former Duncan and Miller employees moved to Tiffin. U.S. Glass created a Duncan and Miller Division.

C. W. Carlson, Sr., retired in 1959. U.S. Glass profits declined. In 1962 U.S. Glass was in bankruptcy. Production resumed when C. W. Carlson, Jr. and some former Tiffin workers founded Tiffin Art Glass Corporation.

Reference: Gene Florence, *Collector's Encyclopedia of Depression Glass, Thirteenth Edition,* Collector Books, 1998.

Aunt Polly, bowl, blue, 4³/₈"	**$20.00**
Aunt Polly, berry bowl, blue, 4³/₈"	**20.00**
Aunt Polly, bread and butter plate, blue, 6"	**16.00**
Aunt Polly, candy dish, blue, handled, ftd.	**50.00**
Aunt Polly, sherbet, blue	**15.00**
Aunt Polly, tumbler, blue, 8 oz, 3⁵/₈"	**30.00**
Aunt Polly, vase, blue, 6¹/₂"	**70.00**
Cherryberry, berry bowl, deep	**24.00**
Cherryberry, bowl, iridescent, 7¹/₂"	**17.88**
Cherryberry, bread and butter plate, green, 6"	**10.00**
Cherryberry, sugar lid, green	**17.00**
Floral & Diamond, berry bowl, green 8¹/₂"	**12.00**
Floral & Diamond, butter dish, cov, green	**125.00**
Floral & Diamond, iced tea tumbler, pink, 5"	**50.00**
Floral & Diamond, pitcher, green	**150.00**
Floral & Diamond, pitcher, pink	**135.00**
Floral & Diamond, salad plate, green, 8"	**45.00**
Floral & Diamond, sherbet, green	**10.00**
Floral & Diamond, tumbler, green, 9 oz	**25.00**
Floral & Diamond, tumbler, pink, 5"	**50.00**
Flower Garden with Butterflies, candlesticks, pr, green, 8"	**110.00**
Flower Garden with Butterflies, candy dish, cov, blue	**430.00**
Flower Garden with Butterflies, candy dish, cov, green	**160.00**
Flower Garden with Butterflies, comport, ftd, green, 10¹/₄ x 4³/₄"	**75.00**
Flower Garden with Butterflies, cup and saucer, green	**90.00**
Flower Garden with Butterflies, mayonnaise, ftd, green, gold trim, 6¹/₄ x 4³/₄"	**35.00**
Flower Garden with Butterflies, salad plate, green, 8"	**20.00**
Flower Garden with Butterflies, tray, rect, green, 7³/₄ x 11³/₄"	**60.00**
Flower Garden with Butterflies, vase, cupped, black, 8"	**300.00**
Flower Garden with Butterflies, wall vase, black, 9"	**575.00**
Primo, bowl, yellow, 4¹/₂"	**18.00**
Primo, bowl, yellow, 7³/₄"	**32.00**
Primo, cake plate, 3-ftd, green	**30.00**
Primo, cup, green	**10.00**
Primo, grill plate, green	**12.00**
Primo, sherbet, green	**12.00**
Primo, tumbler, green	**22.00**
Primo, tumbler, yellow	**22.00**
Strawberry, berry bowl, pink, 4"	**16.00**
Strawberry, butter dish, green	**165.00**
Strawberry, sherbet, green	**7.50**
Strawberry, tumbler, green, 9 oz, 3⁵/₈"	**48.00**

VALENTINES

The valentine experienced several major changes in the early decades of the 20th century. Fold or pull out, lithograph novelty, mechanical action, and postcard valentines replaced lacy valentines as the preferred form. Diecut cards became common. Chromolithography brightened the color scheme.

The candy, card, flower, and giftware industry hopped aboard the valentine bandwagon big time following 1920. Elementary schools introduced valentine exchanges when inexpensive mass-produced valentine packs became available. Companies and stars licensed their images for valentine use.

Valentine collectors specialize. Many 20th-century valentines, especially post-1945 examples, are purchased by crossover collectors more interested in the card's subject matter than the fact that it is a valentine. Valentine survival rate is high. Never assume any post-1920 valentine is in short supply.

References: Robert Brenner, *Valentine Treasury,* Schiffer Publishing, 1997; Dan and Pauline Campanelli, *Romantic Valentines,* L-W Book Sales, 1996; Katherine Kreider, *One Hundred Years of Valentines,* Schiffer Publishing, 1999.

Collectors' Club: National Valentine Collectors Assoc, PO Box 1404, Santa Ana, CA 92702.

Mechanical, 1930s, 4 x 6", $6.50.

Greeting Card, diecut stiff paper, full figure image of Superman flying along with young girl and text "Not Even Superman Could Take Me Away From You, Valentine," ©1940 Superman Publications Inc, 4½ x 5" **$75.00**

Greeting Card, diecut stiff paper, Wizard of Oz Tin Man, easel tabs on front bottom, back mkd "Licensed by Loew's Incorporated from Motion Picture Wizard of Oz" plus logo for American Colortype Co, 4¾ x 6¾" **100.00**

Greeting Card, fold-out, Hopalong Cassidy, full color diecut front exposing greeting "To a Grand Boy," front cov accented by inserted string lasso for theme "Tie Your Heart," and inner theme "Rope you in," Buzza Cardozo, Hollywood, 4 x 6" **50.00**

Greeting Card, fold-out, Mickey Mouse, stiff brown filiament paper, black and orange illus, Hall Brothers Inc, 1930s, 5 x 6" folded size **100.00**

Greeting Card, honeycomb, "Cupid's Temple of Love," c1928... **15.50**

Greeting Card, honeycomb, "To My Love," easel back, Saxony, c1920–30, 6 x 8" **25.00**

Greeting Card, mechanical, diecut, Clarabelle, movable head, ©1939, 2¾ x 5" **25.00**

Greeting Card, mechanical, diecut, Figaro, movable paw and ear, inscription on reverse, ©1939 .... **10.00**

Greeting Card, mechanical, diecut, Pinocchio, heart shaped, depicts Pinocchio and Blue Fairy with movable wand, inscription on reverse, ©1939, 5 x 5" **10.00**

Greeting Card, mechanical, diecut, Snow White and Seven Dwarfs, 4¾" h **15.00**

Greeting Card, mechanical, "Reflecting my Love for You," girl looking at herself in mirror, arm moves up and down, Carrington, Co, Chicago, IL, c1930–40, 4 x 6" **4.50**

Greeting Card, mechanical, "Such Is Married Life," c1950... **45.00**

Greeting Card, paper sheet, Television Bug, illus above text references to Milton Berle and Howdy Doody, late 1940s, 8 x 11" **15.00**

Greeting Card, "To My Sweet Valentine," woman greeting 3 cupids, sepia tones **1.50**

Postcard, "Love's Greetings," sgd "Ellen H. Clapsaddle," 1922... **5.00**

Postcard, "To My Valentine," pumpkin head man and woman sitting on bench, verse on top **5.00**

VAN BRIGGLE POTTERY

Artus Van Briggle established the Van Briggle Pottery Company in 1900. His pottery won numerous awards including one from the 1903 Paris Exhibition.

Following Van Briggle's death in 1904, his wife, Anne, became president of the company, reorganized, and built a new plant. Van Briggle produced a wide range of products including art pottery, garden pottery, novelty items, and utilitarian ware. Artware produced between 1901 and 1912 is recognized for its high quality of design and glaze. Van Briggle's Lorelei vase is a classic.

A reorganization in 1910 produced the Van Briggle Pottery and Tile Company. By 1912 the pottery was leased to Edwin DeForest Curtis who in turn sold it to Charles B. Lansing in 1915. Lansing sold the company to I. F. and J. H. Lewis in 1920, who renamed the company Van Briggle Art Pottery. Kenneth Stevenson acquired the company in 1969. He continued the production of art pottery,

introducing some new designs and glazes. Upon his death in 1990, Bertha (his wife) and Craig (his son) continued production.

The Stevensons use a mark similar to the interlocking "AA" mark used by Artus and Anne. Because they also make the same shapes and glazes, novice collectors frequently confuse newly made ware for older pieces. Because the Stevensons only selectively release their wholesale list, discovering which older shapes and glazes are in current production is difficult.

Prior to 1907 all pieces had the "AA" mark and "Van Briggle." These marks also were used occasionally during the 1910s and 20s. "Colorado Springs" or an abbreviation often appears on pieces made after 1920. Some early pieces were dated. Value rises considerably when a date mark is present.

Reference: Richard Sasicki and Josie Fania, *Collector's Encyclopedia of Van Briggle Art Pottery*, Collector Books, 1993, 1998 value update.

Collectors' Club: American Art Pottery Assoc, PO Box 1226, Westport, MA 02790.

REPRODUCTION ALERT: Van Briggle pottery is still being produced today. Modern glazes include Midnight (black), Moonglo (off-white), Russet, and Turquoise Ming.

Bookends, pr, Pug dog, mulberry matte glaze, 1920s **$175.00**
Bowl, emb moth pattern, mulberry matte glaze **50.00**
Bud Vase, emb repeating 3-leaf flower design, stem extends from mouth to base, mulberry matte glaze, mkd with logo, 4-digit date, and artist's initials, 5¾" h, 2⅛" d **225.00**
Candlestick, tapered, turquoise matte glaze with blue overspray, mkd with logo, name, and "U.S.A.," later fitted as lamp, 1920s, 9" h **150.00**
Creamer, melon-ribbed body, turquoise matte glaze, #291, 1970s **15.00**
Ewer, turquoise matte glaze, #71, c1955 .... **30.00**

Vase, 2-handled, emb stylized leaf design around shoulder, mulberry matte glaze with blue-green overspray, shape #780, incised with logo, name, and "Colo Spgs," 1920s, 7½" h, $325.00. Photo courtesy Jackson's Auctioneers & Appraisers.

Figurine, cat, brown, 1950s, 15" h **85.00**
Floor Vase, emb ibis birds, mocha-sand matte glaze with
hint of blue overspray to birds, mkd with logo, name,
"Colo Spgs Co.," and initials "AO," 17" h, 8" d **525.00**
Lamp, Damsel of Damascus, c1950 . . . . **250.00**
Paperweight, rabbit, mulberry matte glaze, c1925, 3" l **125.00**
Vase, 2-handled, emb stylized leaves, mulberry matte
glaze with blue overspray, incised logo, name, and
"U.S.A.," 1920s, 8¾" h **300.00**
Vase, cylindrical, emb daisies, matte turquoise glaze,
imp "AA, USA," 1920s, 7¼" h, 3¾" d **200.00**
Vase, Persian Rose, incised logo, name, and "Colo
Spgs," c1930s, 3½" h **85.00**
Vase, slightly ovoid cylinder shape, emb poppy and leaf
design with incised veins, mulberry matte glaze with
blue overspray, mkd with logo and name, 8⅛" h, 4" d **110.00**
Vase, tall, emb daffodils, matte turquoise and blue glaze,
incised "AA Van Briggle Colo Spgs.," 1920s, 13 x 5" **775.00**
Vase, trumpet shape, emb stylized leaves, turquoise blue
matte glaze with blue overspray, mkd with logo,
name, and "Colo. Spgs.," 1930s, 9½" h **250.00**

VENDING MACHINES

Vending machines were silent salesmen. They worked 24 hours a
day. Thomas Adams of Adams Gum is created with popularizing
the vending machine. In 1888 his Tutti-Frutti gum machines were
placed on elevated train platforms in New York City. The wedding
of the gumball and vending machine occurred around 1910.

Leading vending machine manufacturers from its golden age,
1920 through the end of the 1950s, include Ad-Lee Novelty,
Bluebird Products, Columbus Vending, Northwestern, Pulver,
Volkmann, Stollwerck and Co., and Victor Vending. Figural
machines and those incorporating unusual mechanical action are
among the most desirable.

Today's vending machine collectors collect either globe-type
machines or lithograph tin counter top models dating prior to
1960. While period paint is considered an added value factor,
retention of period decals and labels and workability are the main
value keys. Since the average life of many vending machines is
measured in decades, collectors expect machines to be touched
up or repainted.

Vending machines are collected either by type or by material
dispensed. Crossover collectors can skew pricing.

References: Richard M. Bueschel, *Collector's Guide to Vintage
Coin Machines,* Schiffer Publishing, 1995; Richard M. Bueschel,
Guide to Vintage Trade Stimulators & Counter Games, Schiffer
Publishing, 1997; Bill Enes, *Silent Salesmen: An Encyclopedia of
Collectible Gum, Candy & Nut Machines,* published by author,
1987; Bill Enes, *Silent Salesman Too: The Encyclopedia of
Collectible Vending Machines,* published by author, 1995.

Newsletter: *Around the Vending Wheel,* 5417 Castana Ave,
Lakewood, CA 90712.

Beech-Nut Chewing Gum, interchangeable for either
penny stick gum or nickel pack gum, c1947, 13½" h . . . **$450.00**
Cebco Hut Nut Machine, cast aluminum, salesman's
sample, 2 globes and 2 mechanisms for vending 2
types of nuts, light bulb lights up red glass bulls-eye in
body, side cup dispenser, c1930, 18" h **500.00**

**Ko-Pak-Ta Toasted
Peanuts, metal and
glass, electric,
16½" h, $412.00.**
Photo courtesy
Collectors Auction
Services.

Columbus Model 34 Gambler, gumball, receive gumball
for 25¢ and compare numbered or colored gum
ball to award card, c1936, 15" h **350.00**
Empire Vendor, Empire State Building emb on front of
base and chute cover, D Robbins Co, Brooklyn, NY,
c1932, 16½" h **250.00**
Four in One, Art Deco style, chromium finish, rotates on
base, 4 separate compartments with own mechanism,
8-sided globe, c1935, 17½" h **475.00**
Gilette Razor Blades, white-painted metal, metal, paper
label, "Modern Merchandising Corp. St. Louis,
MO.," wall mount, 19" h, 2½" w **85.00**
Hit the Target, gumball, 1¢, cast-iron stand, c1950,
19" h with stand **85.00**
In the Bag Machine, peanut, 5¢, dispenses peanuts in
sanitary glassine bag, O D Jennings & Co, c1934,
26" h with marquis **250.00**
Library Booster Pencils, Parker Pencil Co, aluminum,
c1927, 11" h **250.00**
Lucky Strike, cigarette, 1¢, 6 column, glass and metal,
c1935 . . . . **250.00**
Magic Vendor, gumball, "Al Hoff" emb on coin door,
Townsend Mfg Co, c1939, 15" h **325.00**
Malkin Phillies, cigar, 10¢, steel, c1930 . . . . **85.00**
Match Vendor, Number 4 Perfection, match, cast iron, 2
fire-breathing dragons and Art Nouveau castings,
cigar cutter, Specialty Mfg Co, 1920s, 13" h **725.00**
Northwestern Match Vendor, 2 column, dispenses book
of matches, 1930s, 13½" h **70.00**
Penny King, gumball, chrome case, Art Deco motif, 4
sections, c1935 . . . . **575.00**
Puritan Cup Dispenser, wall mount, glass dome, APG
Co, 1930s, 35" h **250.00**
Serv-A-Liter, lighter fluid, gas pump shaped, pre-mea-
sured amount of lighter fluid for a penny, Serv-A-Liter
Co, Indianapolis, c1920, 17½" h **475.00**
Silver King Hot Nut, aluminum, flashing ruby hobnail
glass dome, c1947, 15½" h **250.00**
The Twin Merchandiser, cast iron, 2 globes sit atop base,
Stoner Corp, c1941, 13" h **400.00**
US Postage Stamps, cast-iron, Anderson Die & Model
Co, c1920, 13" h **225.00**

VENETIAN GLASS

Italian glass is a generic term for glassware made in Italy from the 1920s into the early 1960s and heavily exported to the United States. Pieces range from vases with multicolored internal thick and thin filigree threads to figural clowns and fish.

The glass was made in Murano, the center of Italy's glass blowing industry. Beginning in the 1920s many firms hired art directors and engaged the services of internationally known artists and designers. The 1950s was a second golden age following the flurry of high-style pieces made from the mid-1920s through the mid-1930s.

Reference: Rosa Barovier Mentasti, *Venetian Glass: 1890–1990*, Arsenale Editrice, 1992, distributed by Antique Collectors' Club.

Newsletter: *Vertri: Italian Glass News,* PO Box 191, Fort Lee, NJ 07024.

Vase, attributed to Gino Forte, flaring pezzati sommerso, amber, turquoise, and clear, unmkd, 11 x 6¹/₄", $1,760.00. Photo courtesy David Rago Auctions, Inc.

Archimede Seguso, vase, bottle-shaped rose glass and gold leaf, flaring rim, dimpled body, unmkd, 8 x 3³/₄" . . . **$500.00**

Aureliano Toso, table lamp, swirling white, aventurine acanne glass, unmkd, 17 x 7¹/₂" **175.00**

Aureliano Toso, vase, Dino Martens, 3-sided, orienta glass, unmkd, 3 x 4" **225.00**

Aureliano Toso, vase, Dino Martens, corseted, pink and white zamfirico glass, unmkd, 8¹/₂ x 6¹/₂" **150.00**

Aureliano Toso, vase, Dino Martens, fazzoletto, pink, white, and aventurine zamfirico glass, unmkd, 9¹/₂ x 12" **500.00**

Aureliano Toso, vase, Dino Martens, flaring, white and aventurine wavy atrina glass, unmkd, 11¹/₂ x 7" **400.00**

Aureliano Toso, vase, Dino Martens, ovoid, pulegoso glass, with multicolored floating patches, c1950, 12 x 5" **2,800.00**

Avem, vase, designed by Giorgio Ferro, anse volante, deep green body with 3 pulled holes and iridescent surface, c1952, 11" h. **935.00**

Barovier, bowl, scallop shaped, opalescent glass, with candle holders, unmkd, 6 x 6", price for pair **350.00**

Barovier, candlesticks, pr, applied latimo grapes and gold foil, c1940, 7¹/₂" h, 3" d **575.00**

Barovier, dish, oval, sommerso glass, red and amber, silver leaf, unmkd, 3 x 6³/₄" **70.00**

Barovier, vase, fluted, flaring, gold leaf, turquoise, and clear glass, unmkd, 7 x 5¹/₂" **150.00**

Barovier, Seguso & Ferro, vase, ftd, faceted, red glass with controlled bubbles, iridized overall, gold foil applied handles and base, unmkd, 11¹/₂ x 7" **650.00**

Barovier & Toso, conch shell, iridescent, c1940, 3³/₄" h, 9" w **200.00**

Barovier & Toso, sconces, pr, rigadoso technique, large clear leaves with applied granulation inside, orig standard, 11" h, 6" w **1,500.00**

Barovier & Toso, table lamp, blue, white, and green swirling acanne glass base, Barovier/Milano paper label, 18 x 8" d **350.00**

Barovier & Toso, vase, quilted fazzoletto, opaline glass, applied pink rim, unmkd, 5¹/₂ x 10¹/₂" **200.00**

Barovier & Toso, vase, scalloped, pink cordinato oro glass, with gold foil, unmkd, 8¹/₂ x 7" **275.00**

Cenedese, cane vase, ovoid, pink and blue glass diagonal strata, pulled and corroded surface, foil label, etched "Cenedese," 12 x 8" **750.00**

Cenedese, figurine, bear, Alfred Barbini, vetri scavo, 5³/₄" h **825.00**

Cenedese, figurine, owl, Antonio Da Ros, sommerso glass, clear and black, silver leaf, foil label and etched "Cenedese," 2¹/₂ x 6³/₄" **250.00**

Cenedese, figurine, pear, green and clear sommerso glass, sgd, 8¹/₂ x 4¹/₂" **100.00**

Cenedese, figurine, toucan, Antonio Da Ros, sommerso glass, blue, green, and smoky glass, mkd "Alberto Toso" and dated, 7 x 7¹/₂" **1,400.00**

Cenedese, pitcher, slender, blue and white latticino glass, unmkd, 10 x 3³/₄" **200.00**

Cenedese, urn, blue-green, and gold vetro scavo, unmkd, 18 x 7" **800.00**

Dominic Labino, vase, blown glass, tear shaped, emb with free-form drips and covered in gold mirrored glaze, etched "Labino/1975," 6 x 3" **1,200.00**

Fratelli Toso, attributed to, bottle, blue and white cane glass, unmkd, 18" h **100.00**

Fratelli Toso, attributed to, ewer, blue and white latticino glass with copper ribbons and gold leaf, unmkd, 11¹/₂ x 6¹/₂" **150.00**

Fratelli Toso, bottle, tapered, red and white acanne glass, white flame shaped stopper, foil label, 16¹/₂ x 4¹/₂" **175.00**

Fratelli Toso, bottles, yellow and white latticino glass, spherical stoppers, unmkd, 13 x 5", price for pair **700.00**

Fratelli Toso, carafe, pink and orange acanne glass, unmkd, 8 x 6" **175.00**

Fratelli Toso, vase, classically shaped, green and white spiraling canes, unmkd, 9 x 11¹/₂" **300.00**

Fratelli Toso, vase, corseted, blue and beige acanne glass, unmkd, 11 x 4¹/₂" **150.00**

Loredano Rosin, figurine, kneeling nude female, agatelike effect in yellow, green, blue, and brown glass, sgd "Loredano Rosin," 5³/₄" h, 11" l **925.00**

Murano Studio, bowl, blue-red centered gold on white millefiori fused, against and within colorless disk form, 5¹/₂" d **60.00**

Murano Studio, compote set, 7 pc, swirling clear glass bowls with gold leaf, blue and gold dolphin stems, unmkd, 6" h **450.00**

Murano Studio, figurine, penguin, colorless glass with black and white sommerso glass dec, price for 3, 6½", 10¼", and 16½" h 350.00

Murano Studio, vase, cased glass, coarse pink powder application, flared form cut and curled at rim, enhanced by gold foil to ext, 4" h, price for pair 350.00

Murano Studio, vase, elongated square form, cobalt blue, each side with etched and enameled designs in the manner of Miro, J Arp, Modgliani, and K Appel, red, green, yellow, and white, base inscribed "Aureliano Toso Murano," 19½" h 1,600.00

Murano Studio, vase, flared cylinder, colorless glass enhanced by gold dust, symmetrical trapped bubbles and maroon pulled to create plaid effect, 4¾" h 175.00

Murano Studio, vase, Marc Chagall style, executed by Aldo Bon, free-blown colorless glass with applied ear handles, blue facial features and 3 maroon bands, "Marc Chagall" at lower band, inscribed "Aldo Bon – Aureliano Tose – Murano" at base, 12¾" h 1,500.00

Salir, vase, murrina, clear, gold leaf handles and stem, applied with blue, red, green, and white band of flower murrina, c1930s, 8" h 600.00

Salviati, attributed to, compote, ftd, lemon-yellow, green rim, 6¾" h, 8¾" d 275.00

Salviati, attributed to, urn, double-gourd, red, 7¾" h, 4½" w 200.00

Salviati, attributed to, vase, tear shaped, sommerso glass, yellow and red, 13½ x 3½" 400.00

Salviati, serving dish, pink and white latticino glass, aventurine rim, unmkd, 11¼" d 125.00

Salviati, vase, flame shaped, sommerso glass, white and purple int dec, 7 x 3½" 100.00

Salviati, vase, flame shaped, sommerso glass, white and purple int dec, sgd and dated 1959, 11½ x 4½" 800.00

Salviati, vase, free-form, sommerso glass, clear, amber, and blue glass, 7 x 3½" 100.00

Seguso, attributed to, vase, free-form, sommerso glass, clear, amber, and blue glass, 7 x 1½" 100.00

Seguso, attributed to, vase, ovoid, blue, green, and clear, 6 x 9" 550.00

Seguso, bottle, attributed to Flavio Poli, flash shaped, sommerso glass, purple and clear, unmkd, 10½ x 7" 650.00

Seguso, bowl, Flavio Poli, bowl, flaring eggplant sommerso glass, wavy rim, Tiffany & Co Italy acid-stamp, 5 x 15" 1,000.00

Seguso, candle holders, pr, figural, couple in pink and white dress with gold leaf, foil labels, 9½" h 800.00

Seguso, vase, ovoid, sommerso glass, blue, green, and clear, 6 x 9" 550.00

Simone Cenedese, bottle, clear glass, applied abstract green dec, sgd, 12 x 4½" 125.00

Tagliapietra, vase, flared form, opaque white with black powder application cased to clear glass, gray spiral ribs, black rim, base inscribed "Tagliapietra/Angelin Effetre International Murano 1986 12/100," 450.00

Tagliapietra, vase, flattened ovoid form, extended neck of opaque white with black powder application cased to clear glass, medial red band, transparent cobalt blue base, inscribed "Lino Tagliapietra Effetre International Murano 1986 23/100 Italy," 1986, 11¼" h 925.00

Unknown Maker, figurine, geese, sommerso glass, blue and white, unmkd, 16" h, price for pair 350.00

Unknown Maker, goblet, 2 handled, dolphin support with gold leaf, blue cup and base, clear handles and ruffle sides 225.00

Unknown Maker, vase, fazzoletto in marbled vetro latimo and amethyst glass, blue iridescent int, 13" h, 15" w 200.00

Varma, attributed to, bowl, designed by Alfredo Barbini, clear, internal dec with hot molded fish and green swirls, unmkd, c1935, 4" h, 9½" w 225.00

Venini, attributed to, hanging fixture shades, yellow and white vetri acanne, unmkd, 11 x 7½" 175.00

Venini, dish, green zanfirico caning, etched "Venini/Murano/Italia," 7" d 175.00

Venini, floor lamp, flaring ceramic pedestal base covered in celadon glaze, large Murano prism-glass rod shade, 64 x 18" d 1,700.00

Venini, pilgrim flask, Vittorio Zecchin, clear blue glass, c1925, 12 x 4½" 250.00

Venini, sorbet cups, Vittorio Zecchin, set of 6, green and purple sofiati glass with iridized surface, unmkd, c1920, 4 x 4½" 200.00

Venini, vase, designed by Sergio Asti, flaring, opalescent white glass, Venini label, 12 x 10¼" 400.00

Venini, vase, flaring, opalescent white glass, Venini label, 12 x 10¼" 475.00

Venini, vase, Napoleone Martinuzzi, long flaring neck, bulbous neck, linear dec with 3 applied rings at neck, unsgd, 11½" h 150.00

Vistosi, vase, Enrico Capuzzo, dimpled cylindrical bicalmo, half clear, half latimo, paper label, c1960, 10" h 110.00

Zecchin-Martinuzzi, vase, designed by Napoleone Martinuzzi, opaque body created with white int and light blue ext with looping translucent blue handles and ring foot, diamond acid stamp "Made in Italy," c1930s, 12" h 465.00

Murano, figurines, flamenco dancers, red, black, white, and clear with gold leaf, unmkd, 13" h, price for pair, $110.00. Photo courtesy David Rago Auctions, Inc.

VERNON KILNS

In 1912 George Poxon established Poxon China in Vernon, California. Initially the company made tiles. Following World War I production shifted to earthenware dishes and hotel and restaurant ware. In 1928 George Poxon turned the company over to his wife Judith and her brother James Furlong. The company was renamed Vernon China.

In 1931 Faye G. Bennison bought Vernon China and changed the name to Vernon Kilns. Initially the company produced decal ware utilizing older Vernon China/Paxon shapes. An earthquake in 1933 shattered most of the company's inventory and did extensive damage to the kilns. This proved a blessing in disguise as Vernon Kilns introduced numerous new shapes and pattern lines. Art ware also was introduced, remaining in production until 1937.

In 1940 Vernon Kilns signed a contract with Walt Disney Productions to make figures of the characters from *Dumbo, Fantasia,* and *The Reluctant Dragon.* Specialty transfer print ware was introduced in the 1930s. The late 1940s and early 1950s saw the production of hundreds of commemorative patterns and series such as Moby Dick and Our America.

The Coronada shape line was introduced in 1938, Melinda in 1942, San Marino in the mid-1940s, and Anytime in 1955. Hand-painted Organdie and Brown-Eyed Susan were popular patterns.

In January 1958 a decision was made to close the company. Metlox Potteries, Manhattan Beach, California, bought the molds, modified some, and continued production of Anytime, Barkwood, Brown-Eyed Susan, Organdie, Sherwood, and Tickled Pink for a year. Although the Vernon Kilns plant closed, the corporation remained alive until it was legally dissolved in 1969.

References: Susan and Al Bagdade, *Warman's American Pottery and Porcelain,* Wallace-Homestead, Krause Publications, 1994; Harvey Duke, *The Official Price Guide to Pottery and Porcelain, Eighth Edition,* House of Collectibles, 1995.

Newsletter: *Vernon Views,* PO Box 945, Scottsdale, AZ 85252.

Gingham, creamer, 1 pt, 6" h, $12.00.

Arcadia, bread and butter plate	$6.00
Arcadia, cup and saucer	10.00
Arcadia, dinner plate	12.00
Arcadia, gravy	22.00
Arcadia, lug chowder	12.00
Arcadia, luncheon plate	12.00
Arcadia, vegetable bowl, round	15.00
Autumn Leaf, dinner plate	5.00
Autumn Leaf, soup bowl	7.00
Bel Air, creamer	12.00
Bel Air, cup and saucer	12.00
Bel Air, dinner plate	12.00
Bel Air, gravy boat, blue and green plaid	25.00
Bel Air, platter	15.00
Bel Air, salt and pepper shakers, pr	20.00
Bel Air, sugar, cov	14.00
Bel Air, tumbler	20.00
Brown Eyed Susan, bread and butter plate	2.50
Brown Eyed Susan, creamer, ice lip	6.00
Brown Eyed Susan, cup and saucer	6.00
Brown Eyed Susan, dinner plate, 9³/₄"	6.00
Brown Eyed Susan, salad plate	4.00
Brown Eyed Susan, salt and pepper shakers, pr	10.00
Gingham, bread and butter plate	2.50
Gingham, bulb jug, 1 pt	25.00

Gingham, bulb jug, 1 qt	35.00
Gingham, butter, cov	45.00
Gingham, casserole, cov	45.00
Gingham, chicken pot pie, cov	30.00
Gingham, chop plate, 12"	12.50
Gingham, chowder	12.00
Gingham, coaster	30.00
Gingham, coffee carafe	40.00
Gingham, cup	5.00
Gingham, dinner plate, 9³/₄" d	8.00
Gingham, eggcup	25.00
Gingham, gravy, round	12.00
Gingham, pitcher, streamline, 2 qt	35.00
Gingham, platter, oval, 14¹/₄" l	15.00
Gingham, salad bowl, individual	20.00
Gingham, salad plate, 7¹/₂"	4.00
Gingham, salt and pepper shakers, pr	10.00
Gingham, soup, flat	13.00
Gingham, teapot	55.00
Gingham, tumbler	28.00
Hawaiian Flowers, chop plate, blue, 12"	165.00
Hawaiian Flowers, salt and pepper shakers, pr, maroon	65.00
Heavenly Days, butter, cov	15.00
Heavenly Days, cup	2.50
Heavenly Days, dinner plate, 10" d	4.00
Heavenly Days, tumbler	28.00
Heavenly Days, vegetable, 7¹/₂"	6.00
Homespun, bread and butter plate	4.00
Homespun, colossal cup and saucer	125.00
Homespun, dinner plate	12.00
Homespun, dinner service, including one each 11" pitcher, 9" bowl, 5" and 7" mixing bowls, 12" divided bowl, creamer and sugar with tray, cov butter, gravy, and salt and pepper shakers, two skillet spoon rests, five cups and 6" soup bowls, nine saucers, ten dinner plates, eleven fruit bowls, and twelve salad plates, price for 65 pcs	150.00
Homespun, salt and pepper shakers, pr	16.00
Homespun, water set, 3 qt pitcher and six 14 oz tumblers	100.00
May Flower, baker, 9¹/₄"	25.00
May Flower, bread and butter plate	8.00
May Flower, chowder	15.00

May Flower, creamer.................................15.00
May Flower, cup and saucer 25.00
May Flower, dinner plate, 10" 18.00
May Flower, fruit..................................12.00
May Flower, gravy boat.............................35.00
May Flower, nappy, 9"..............................38.00
May Flower, platter, 13½"...........................40.00
May Flower, salad plate, 7½".........................12.00
May Flower, salt and pepper shakers, pr.................24.00
May Flower, sugar, cov..............................25.00
Michigan Coast Line, cup and saucer...................25.00
Michigan Coast Line, plate, 9½" 25.00
Moby Dick, tumbler, brown........................195.00
Organdie, bulb jug, 1 pt 25.00
Organdie, bulb jug, 1 qt 35.00
Organdie, butter, cov 45.00
Organdie, casserole, cov 45.00
Organdie, chicken pot pie, cov 30.00
Organdie, coffee carafe.............................40.00
Organdie, eggcup 25.00
Organdie, pitcher, streamline, 2 qt....................35.00
Organdie, soup, flat 13.00
Organdie, tumbler.................................28.00
Salamina, salad plate, 7"............................65.00
Souvenir Ashtray, Indiana, red 20.00
Souvenir Plate, Evergreen State 15.00
Souvenir Plate, New York 15.00
Souvenir Plate, North Carolina 15.00
Souvenir Plate, San Diego, brown 20.00
Tam O'Shanter, butter pat 30.00
Tam O'Shanter, casserole, cov 45.00
Tam O'Shanter, chicken pot pie, cov 30.00
Tam O'Shanter, coaster 30.00
Tam O'Shanter, coffee carafe.........................40.00
Tam O'Shanter, flowerpot, 4½" 35.00
Tam O'Shanter, pitcher, 3 qt 45.00
Tam O'Shanter, salad bowl, individual 20.00
Tam O'Shanter, soup, flat 13.00
Tam O'Shanter, teapot..............................55.00
Tam O'Shanter, tumbler.............................28.00

VIETNAM WAR

The Vietnam War divided America. As a result, there are two distinct groups of collectibles: anti-war demonstration and military.

Destabilization followed the withdrawal of the French from Indo-China. In the early 1960s American military advisors were in South Vietnam assisting the country's military. In May 1962 President Kennedy sent 1,800 U.S. Marines to Thailand to protect it from a possible invasion by communist forces from Laos. On June 16, 1962 two U.S. Army officers were killed north of Saigon. On November 1, 1963, the government of President Diem was overthrown by South Vietnamese armed forces. America recognized the new government on November 7, 1963.

America increased its military and economic aide to South Vietnam in 1964. Mounting casualties during 1965 spurred protests. By the end of 1966, the United States had 400,000 troops in South Vietnam. The casualty count was over 6,600 killed and 37,500 wounded. Nguyen Van Thieu was elected president in 1967 amid charges of election fraud. Dissent continued to mount, reaching a fever pitch in the late 1960s and 70s. North Vietnam launched the Tet offensive on January 30, 1968.

Although Nixon reduced the U.S. troop commitment in 1969, major anti-war demonstrations took place in October and November. America continued to disengage from Vietnam. By December 1971 American troop strength dropped to 184,000. On March 30, 1972, North Vietnam crossed the DMZ and entered South Vietnam from Cambodia.

A peace agreement was signed on January 22, 1973. It proved ineffective. The South Vietnamese government fell to the North in 1975. America's presence in Vietnam ended. President Ford offered amnesty to deserters and draft evaders in September 1974. A general pardon was issued in 1977.

References: Richard J. Austin, *The Official Price Guide to Military Collectibles, Sixth Edition,* House of Collectibles, 1998; Jim Fiorella, *The Viet Nam Zippo: 1933–1975,* Schiffer Publishing, 1998; Ron Manion, *American Military Collectibles,* Antique Trader Books, 1995.

Newsletter: *Vietnam Insignia Collectors Newsletter,* 501 West 5th Ave, Covington, LA 07433.

Ashtray, souvenir, black, mother-of-pearl inlay in form of
  flowers, brass inner tray, 6" d $25.00
Beret, wool, green, black leather sweatband, black cot-
  ton lining, tie in rear, dated 1971...................85.00
Book, *Offerings at the Wall—Artifacts From the Vietnam
  Memorial Collection* 25.00
Book, *Vietnam 3rd Brigade, 82nd Airborne Division, Jan.
  to Dec. 1969,* hardcover, large format, 140 pp 40.00
Bracelet, POW, names..............................25.00
Cigarette Lighter, "CO A 1st," engraved "CO A 1st,
  ENGR BN, QUANLOI, VIETNAM, 66-67-68" 40.00
Duffel Bag, canvas, olive drab, web straps, mkd "US,"
  dated 1972 ....25.00
Grenade, olive drab, iron body, plug, handle, and safety
  ring, dated 1968 ....20.00
Helmet, helicopter aviator's, blue ext with gold and
  white pattern, dark blue star over each ear, center pull
  visor with cov, boom mike, and earpiece 235.00

Recruiting Sign, 2-sided, litho metal, dated "Jan. 1969," 38" h, 25" w, $132.00. Photo courtesy Collectors Auction Services.

Jacket Patch, "1st Cav/15th Transportation" 25.00
Jacket Patch, "362 Tropospheric Scatter Communications" 60.00
Manual, *Blue Book of Coastal Vessels South Vietnam,*
    Navy, hadcover, illus, 556 pp, 1967 . . . . 85.00
Medal, Air Force Commendation, parade ribbon and
    lapel bar, orig case 20.00
Medal, Vietnam Service, Japanese-made. 20.00
Metal Insignia, Airborne Para Wing, 1½" l 35.00
MP Belt, with magazine pocket, night stick with holster 35.00
Newspaper, "Vietnam Peace Pacts Signed," 1973 . . . . 12.00
Patch, green B-52 in center, "Peace Hell, Bomb Hanoi"
    border, 4" d. 20.00
Pinback Button, "March on Washington, San Francisco
    April 24, Out Now, NPAC," 1971, 1⅝" d 20.00
Plaque, commemorative Navy NC-4, rect, wood and
    brass, May 10, 1969 . . . . 25.00
Poster, "Know Your Enemy," color, illus of 4 soldiers and
    flags including Viet Cong officer and soldier, NVA sol-
    dier, and medic, MACV Command, 1967, 16 x 25". 225.00
Record, *Dick Gregory at Kent State,* 2-record set, Poppy,
    1970, May 4, 1970 Kent State shooting account 50.00
Rucksack, tropical, US Army 135.00
Trench Art, Cobra chopper model, brass, moving rotor
    and tail rotor. 100.00
Trench Art, urn made from 105mm shell, brass, fluted
    top, inscribed "Da Nang Vietnam, Nov 66/Nov 67" 40.00
Unit Patch, "ADS-605th Trans Co Pace Setter". 45.00
Wristwatch, souvenir, 1st Infantry Division 55.00
Yearbook, "Big Red One" 45.00

VIEW-MASTER

William Gruber, a Portland, Oregon, piano tuner, and Harold Graves, president of Sawyer's, a Portland photo-finishing and post-card company, were the two principals behind View-Master. On January 20, 1939, a patent was filed for a special stereoscope utilizing a card with seven pairs of views. Sawyer, Inc., manufactured and sold View-Master products.

The Model A viewer, with its flip front opening and straight viewing barrels, was introduced in 1939. It was replaced by an improved Model B viewer in 1943. The more familiar Model C square viewer arrived in 1946 and remained in production for eleven years.

By 1941 there were more than 1,000 View-Master sales outlets. During World War II, View-Master made special training reels for the United States Navy and Army Air Corps. View-Master's golden years were 1945 to 1960. Hundreds of new reels appeared. The three-pack set was introduced.

In 1966 General Aniline and Film Corporation (GAF) purchased Sawyer's. GAF introduced new projects and the 3-D talking View-Master. Arnold Thaler purchased View-Master in 1980, only to sell it to Ideal. When Tyco acquired Ideal, View-Master was part of the purchase. Today, the View-Master brand name is owned by Mattel, the result of its purchase of Tyco in 1997.

References: Sharon Korbeck (ed.), *Toys & Prices,* Krause Publications, 1999; John Waldsmith, *Stereo Views: An Illustrated History and Price Guide,* Wallace-Homestead, Krause Publications, 1991.

Collectors' Club: National Stereoscopic Assoc, PO Box 14801, Columbus, OH 43214.

View-Master Reels. Left: Cisco Kid and Pancho, #960, $5.00. Right: Picture Tour of Scenic Wonders, DR-49, $1.00.

ACCESSORIES

Camera, Personal 3-D, with custom film cutter $175.00
Projector, Sawyer's or FAF, plastic single lens 10.00
Viewer, Model A, flip front opening, straight barrels 25.00
Viewer, Model B, black Bakelite, streamlined design, flip
    front, 1944–48 . . . . 25.00
Viewer, Model H, GAF 10.00

REEL SETS

Aesop's Fables, B309 . . . . $10.00
Annie Oakley in Indian Waterhole, B470 . . . . 25.00
Arlington National Cemetery, A818, Edition A 6.00
Automobile Racing, B671 . . . . 20.00
Banana Splits, B502 . . . . 8.00
Barbie's Great American Photo Race, B576 . . . . 10.00
Batman, B492. . . . . 15.00
Bedknobs and Broomsticks, B366 . . . . 10.00
Buffalo Bill, Jr, B464 . . . . 25.00
Busch Gardens, A233 . . . . 12.00
Daniel Boone, B479 . . . . 15.00
Dark Shadows, B503. . . . . 20.00
Denver Museum of Natural History, A338 . . . . 8.00
Fat Albert and the Cosby Kids, B554 . . . . 4.00
Grand Tour of Asia, B215 . . . . 15.00
Green Hornet, B488 . . . . 50.00
King Kong, B392. . . . . 8.00
Knott's Berry Farm and Ghost Town, A235 . . . . 12.00
Land of the Giants, B494. . . . . 30.00
Lassie, Look Homeward, B480. . . . . 10.00
Love Bug, B501 . . . . 3.00
Man on the Moon—Nasa's Apollo Project, B658 . . . . 8.00
Mark Twain's Huckleberry Finn, B343 . . . . 30.00
New Zoo Revue, B566 . . . . 10.00
Partridge Family #2, B592 . . . . 40.00
Planet of the Apes, B507 . . . . 18.00
Rin-Tin-Tin, B467 . . . . 10.00
San Diego Wild Animal Park, A207 . . . . 10.00
Shipstads and Johnson's Ice Follies, B776 . . . . 25.00
Statue of Liberty, A648 . . . . 6.00
The Flying Nun, B495 . . . . 50.00
The Littlest Angel, B381. . . . . 3.00
The Monkees, B493 . . . . 25.00
The Three Musketeers, B426 . . . . 15.00
Treasure Island, B432 . . . . 6.00

SINGLE REELS

A Day at the Circus, Ringling Bros and Barnum & Bailey, #702	**$2.00**
Carnival, Rio de Janiero, Brazil, #675	**4.00**
Carriage Cavalcade, #362	**15.00**
Dover, Kent, England, #1015	**1.00**
Garden Flowers of Spring, #980	**1.00**
Gene Autry in "The Kidnapping," #951	**5.00**
Gettysburg National Military Park, PA, #9047	**3.00**
Hawaiian Hula Dancers, Hawaii, #61	**4.00**
Historic Philadelphia and Valley Forge, PA, #349	**1.00**
Home of Santa's Workshop, North Pole, NY, #9058	**4.00**
Jamestown, #262, 1955	**10.00**
Kew Gardens, London, England, #1009	**15.00**
Mexican Bullfight, #523	**3.00**
Mobile, Alabama, #358, 1955	**10.00**
Mormon Temple, Tabernacle and Grounds, #122	**7.00**
Mount Vernon, #76	**6.00**
Niagara Falls, Ontario, Canada, #375	**1.00**
Oklahoma, The Sooner State, #370	**2.00**
Old Covered Bridges, New England, SP-9020	**5.00**
Oregon Caves National Monument III, #93	**4.00**
Performing Elephants, St Louis Zoo, #925	**1.00**
Race Horses of the Bluegrass Country, KY, #342	**3.00**
Rocky Mountain National Park, Colorado, #101	**2.00**
Roy Rogers, King of the Cowboys and Trigger, #945	**5.00**
San Jose and Vicinity, Costa Rica, #541	**8.00**
Scenes of Ecuador, #613	**3.00**
Scenes of Lookout Mountain, Chattanooga, #327	**4.00**
Sitka, Alaska, 1950, #305	**2.00**
Skiing in the Laurentians, Quebec, #391	**10.00**
The Florida Keys, #368	**8.00**
Wild Animals in Natural Habitats, Africa, #901	**1.00**

WADE CERAMICS

In 1958 A. J. Wade, George Wade and Son, Wade Heath & Co., and Wade (Ulster) combined, formed The Wade Group of Potteries, and went public.

George Wade and Son, located at the Manchester Pottery in Burslem, is the best known of the group. Prior to World War I, the company made industrial ceramics, concentrating heavily on the needs of the textile industry. After the war, the company made insulators for the electrical industry.

A. J. Wade, George's brother, established a firm to market glazed tiles and faience fireplace surrounds. A. J. Wade became a partner in Wade, Heath & Co., a manufacturer of Rockingham jugs, teapots, etc. In 1935 Colonel G. A. Wade, a son of George Wade, gained control of A. J. Wade's two companies. Previously, in 1926/28, Col. Wade assumed control of George Wade and Son.

In the late 1920s, George Wade and Son introduced a line of moderately priced figurines. They did so well the company added a line of animals. Production of these figurines ceased during World War II when the company shifted to wartime production.

In 1938 Wade, Heath & Co. acquired the Royal Victoria Pottery. A line of tableware was introduced. A license was acquired from Disney to produce character figurines. Although heavily devoted to wartime production in the early 1940s, the company did manufacture a line of utilitarian dinnerware and tea ware.

In 1950 Wade (Ulster) was established. Located in Portadown, Northern Ireland, the company produced industrial ceramics.

The ceramic giftware industry went into decline in the 1960s. The Wade Group focused on industrial production. When the giftware industry revived in the 1970s, The Wade Group returned to the market. Wade Heath & Co. devotes its efforts to commission and special contract orders, serving a large number of clients ranging from breweries to tobacco companies. In 1969 Wade (PDM) was established within The Wade Group to deal with promotional items, working with glass, plastic, and tin, in addition to ceramics.

Wade is best known in the United States through its Red Rose Tea premiums. These are made by George Wade & Son. Different sets are made for the American and Canadian market. Some figures are based on figures in the "Whimsies" line. Do not confuse the two. Whimsies are slightly larger.

References: Pat Murray, *The Charlton Standard Catalogue of Wade, Vol. One: General Issues, Third Edition* (1999), *Vol. Two: Decorative Ware, Second Edition* (1996), *Vol. Three: Tableware, Second Edition* (1998), Charlton Press; Pat Murray, *The Charlton Standard Catalogue of Wade Whimsical Collectables, Fourth Edition*, Charlton Press, 1998; Ian Warner and Mike Posgay, *The World of Wade, Collectable Porcelain and Pottery* (1988, 1993 value update), *Book 2* (1995) Antique Publications.

Collectors' Clubs: The Official International Wade Collectors Club (company-sponsored), 3330 Cobb Pkwy, Ste 17-333, Acworth, GA 30101; Wade Watch, 8199 Pierson Ct, Arvada, CO 80005.

Basket, Flaxman Ware, purple flowers and green leaves on cream ground, mkd "Flaxman Wade Heath England"	**$70.00**
Biscuit Barrel, Garden Wall shape, brown tree on tan archway, maroon and yellow flowers with green leaves, cream ground, brown squirrel finial, ink stamp "Wade Heath England," 1935–37	**135.00**
Jug, Harmony Ware, yellow, red, and green flower on white ground, 1957–62	**50.00**
Milk Jug, maroon and yellow flower with green and brown leaves on white ground, copper trim, green ink stamp "Harvest Ware Wade England," c1948–52	**35.00**
Money Box, Bengo, beige, white on face and feet, sitting in yellow basket, unmkd, 1965	**325.00**
Posy Bowl, 3 ftd, light brown, imp shamrocks band, mkd "Irish Porcelain" over shamrock with "Made in Ireland"	**10.00**
Red Rose Tea Premium, beaver, light brown, emb "Wade England," 1985–90	**6.00**
Red Rose Tea Premium, elephant, sitting, light blue, emb "Wade England," 1993–present	**5.00**
Red Rose Tea Premium, kitten, gray, emb "Wade England," 1990–95	**6.00**
Red Rose Tea Premium, polar bear, white, emb "Wade England," 1992	**10.00**
Red Rose Tea Premium, ringmaster, light gray, emb "Wade England," 1996–present	**5.00**
Red Rose Tea Premium, turtle, light gray, emb "Wade England," 1983–95	**10.00**
Souvenir, tortoise, "Devile's Hole, Bermuda" on brown shell, emb "Wade Porcelain Made in England," c1976	**30.00**
Sweet Tray, Lady and the Tramp scene on white ground, yellow rim, mkd "Scenes from Walt Disney's 'Lady & the Tramp' Sweet Tray by Wade England," and "Copyright Walt Disney Productions. Made in England," 1955	**20.00**

Teapot, cov, decagonal, Canton shape, multicolored cottage and garden motif on cream ground, acorn shaped finial, black inkstamp "Wadeheath England" with lion, 1933–37, 4 cup.................... **55.00**

Vase, Zamba series, black rhythmic dancers silhouette on white ground **200.00**

Whimsie, barn owl, light brown, green base, emb "Wade England," 1977 .... **20.00**

Whimsie, fawn, brown, blue ears, emb "Wade England," 1971........................... **7.00**

Whimsie, pipe stand, Corgi, honey brown, green stand, emb "Wade England," 1973–81 .... **35.00**

Whimsie, puppy, standing, honey brown, brown ears and nose, black and gold label "Genuine Wade Porcelain Made in England," 1969–82 .... **15.00**

Whimsie, squirrel, gray, light brown head and legs, yellow acorn, emb "Wade England" **7.00**

WAGNER WARE

In 1891 Milton M. and Bernard P. Wagner established the Wagner Manufacturing Company in Sidney, Ohio. William, a third brother, soon joined the company. In order to add a line of skillets, Milton and Bernard purchased the Sidney Hollow Ware Foundry in 1903, placing William in charge. Finding the two companies in direct competition, Sidney Hollow Ware was sold and William bought into the main company as a partner. Louis, a fourth brother, joined the company a short time later.

Wagner Manufacturing made brass casting and cast-iron hollow ware, some of which was nickel plated. Wagner was one of the first companies to make aluminum cookware. The line included cake and ice cream molds, coffeepots, percolators, pitchers, scoops, spoons, and teapots. The company won numerous awards for its aluminum products between 1900 and 1940.

Several generations of Wagners were involved in the company management as individuals died and passed stock interests to their sons. In 1953 Philip Wagner, one of Milton Wagner's sons, was serving as president. He made it known he wanted to sell the company. Cable Wagner, William Wagner's son, purchased the Wagner Hotel Company. Randall Company of Cincinnati, Ohio, purchased the balance.

In 1957 Randall's Wagner Division purchased the Griswold Cookware line from McGraw Edison. Textron of Providence, Rhode Island, acquired the Randall Company in 1959. Textron's Wagner Division acquired the Durham Manufacturing Company of Muncie, Indiana, a manufacturer of casual leisure furniture for household use. In 1969, Textron sold its household line to General Housewares Corporation, a holding company. The sale included all patent and trademark rights for Griswold and Wagner.

Reference: David G. Smith and Charles Wafford, *The Book of Griswold & Wagner: Favorite Piqua, Sidney Hollow Ware, Wapak,* Schiffer Publishing, 1995.

Newsletter: *Kettles 'n Cookware,* PO Box 247, Perrysburg, NY 14129.

Angus Broiler Skillet, double mark................... **$35.00**
Chicken Pan Lid, #1400 .... **75.00**
Deep Skillet, #8, 5-ring cov.................... **65.00**
Drip Drop Roaster, #7, round, raised letter cover **85.00**
Fat Free Fryer **35.00**

Five Star Griddle Set **65.00**
Flop Griddle, #2 .... **370.00**
Gem Pan, D **60.00**
Griddle, #9, wood handle, stylized logo............... **65.00**
Griddle, #14, bail handle **95.00**
Krusty Korn Kobs, early variation, tab handles, "Pat Pending"........................... **90.00**
Popover, #1323........................... **30.00**
Roaster, #3, oval, mkd "Wagner, Sidney O," nickel bottom, black iron top with gate mark.............. **250.00**
Roaster, #4, with trivet, oval, cast iron **295.00**
Roaster, #7, with trivet, oval, 5 ring cov **325.00**
Roaster, oval, raised letter cov, nickel............... **225.00**
Roaster Lid, #7, oval, mkd "Wagner Drip Drop Baster" **200.00**
Scotch Bowl, #11, Sidney Holloware, chrome **95.00**
Sizzle Server **60.00**
Skillet, #2 .... **120.00**
Skillet, #7, raised letter cov with knob handle, mkd "Wagner, Sidney O" **125.00**
Skillet, #9, 4 digit number, black iron............... **65.00**
Skillet, #9, heat ring, raised letter cov.............. **75.00**
Skillet, #11, heat ring, Sidney center mark **135.00**
Skillet, #11, stylized logo, nickel................. **75.00**
Skillet, #12, raised letter cov, nickel................ **165.00**
Skillet Roaster, #9, nickel..................... **225.00**
Toy Griddle, bail handle, plated.................. **70.00**
Toy Waffle Iron Paddles, aluminum **100.00**
Waffle Iron, miniature, cast iron.................. **225.00**

WALLACE CHINA

The Wallace China Company, Vernon, California, was founded around 1931. The company made vitrified, plain and transfer printed wares for the hotel, institution, and restaurant markets. Willow ware in blue, brown, green, and red transfers was produced during the 1930s and 1940s.

Wallace China is best known for its Westward Ho houseware line, the result of a 1943 commission from the M. C. Wentz Company of Pasadena. Wentz wanted restaurant barbecue ware. Till Goodan, a well-known western artist, created three patterns: Boots and Saddles, Pioneer Trails, and Rodeo. His name is incorporated in most designs. A three-piece Little Buckaroo Chuck set for children and the El Rancho and Longhorn dinnerware patterns also were designed by Goodan.

In 1959 Shenango China Company acquired Wallace China. Wallace China operated as a wholly owned subsidiary until 1964 when all production ceased.

References: Jack Chipman, *Collector's Encyclopedia of California Pottery, Second Edition,* Collector Books, 1998; Harvey Duke, *The Official Price Guide to Pottery and Porcelain, Eighth Edition,* House of Collectibles, 1995.

Chuck Wagon, bowl, 6¾" d........................ **$35.00**
Desert Ware, bowl, Blue Willow pattern. **20.00**
Hibiscus, bread and butter plate **3.00**
Hibiscus, cup and saucer **7.50**
Hibiscus, platter **10.00**
Pioneer Trails, chop plate, 13" d. **200.00**
Rancho, dinner plate, 10½" d **40.00**
Restaurant Ware, creamer, Shadowleaf pattern, 3½" h....... **15.00**
Restaurant Ware, salt and pepper shakers, pr, Shadowleaf pattern **45.00**

Hibiscus, dinner plate, $8.00.

Restaurant Ware, soup bowl, gray and white, 5³/₄" d **20.00**
Restaurant Ware, water pitcher, Bird of Paradise pattern **100.00**
Rodeo, ashtray, 5¹/₂" d **100.00**
Rodeo, bread and butter plate, 7¹/₄" d. **45.00**
Rodeo, cup and saucer, 7¹/₂ oz **65.00**
Surfer Girl, dinner plate, 10¹/₂" d **40.00**
Westward Ho, ashtray, Boots and Saddle, 5¹/₂" d. **45.00**
Westward Ho, ashtray, Will Rogers. **45.00**
Westward Ho, chop plate, 13" d **175.00**
Westward Ho, creamer, ftd **75.00**
Westward Ho, dish, 6¹/₂" d. **35.00**
Westward Ho, napkin ring. **50.00**
Westward Ho, platter, oval, 15¹/₂" l. **175.00**
Westward Ho, salad bowl, 13 x 5". **400.00**
Westward Ho, soup bowl, 5³/₄" d **55.00**
Westward Ho, sugar, open, small. **55.00**
Westward Ho, vegetable bowl, oval, 12" l **175.00**

WALL HANGINGS

This is a catchall category for the myriad of objects that hung on living room, dining room, bedroom, and kitchen walls since 1945. Looking at 1960 Sperry and Hutchinson S & H Green Stamps Distinguished Merchandise Ideabook, one finds oval framed hand-colored fruit prints, Syrocco Baroque-style scones, fruitwood cutout wall plaques featuring Early American scenes, a brush-stroked reproduction print of Romney's Miss Willoughby, and a Mirro five-piece coppertone mold set.

Whether a pair of 1950s' plaster Balinese dancers in pink costumes or a late 1960s' abstract bird made from teakwood and copper, period defining wall hangings are attracting strong collector and decorator interest.

Hanger, yarn wrapped over wood stick frame creating
God's Eye design, 19" **12.00**
Plaque, abstract bottles, chrome, 1950s **$30.00**
Plaque, fruit, painted chalkware, 1950s **8.00**
Plaque, Hagen-Renaker, ceramic, prancing horses, 15 x
22". **65.00**

Plaque, Higgins, bird, brown and green on ochre
ground, etched "Higgins". **120.00**
Plaque, University of North Dakota, ceramic, oxen
pulling covered wagon, 5" d **225.00**
Plaque, Yan Torno, Art Deco, bronze circular plaque of
Statue of Liberty, mounted on lucite square, incised
signature, 17" d **125.00**
Sconce, Valenti, for Tetrarch, "Pistillo," bright silver plas-
tic fixture and chromed light bulb surrounded by radiating tubular stalks topped with spheres, stamped
mark, 13 x 24" **450.00**
Sculpture, Scheier, mixed media, abstract outline of
baby and parents made from nails, mounted inside
guanacastle wood frame in the shape of a yawning
cat's mouth with crushed marble teeth, incised
"Scheier '63," 29" d **3,500.00**
Sculpture, tin, pair of pheasants in flight, individual
feathers soldered to frame, c1960, 32" l **35.00**
Tapestry, Robert Motherwell, wool, blue and green,
woven initials "RM" in lower right, c1965, 113¹/₂ x
98". **1,000.00**
Tapestry, Scheier, "Man in Fish," dark brown and gray,
1964, 77 x 25" **1,500.00**

WALL POCKETS

The earliest American wall pockets were made by folk potters in Virginia's Shenandoah Valley. The flower wall pocket became a standard household form in the 1920s and remained popular through the end of the 1940s.

When the post-war Modern design styles became popular, wall pockets were out. The wall pocket regained some of its former popularity in the 1960s and 1970s. Import companies, such as ENESCO, included wall pockets in their catalogs. These new examples stimulated interest in collecting older ones.

References: Marvin and Joy Gibson, *Collectors Guide to Wall Pockets: Affordable & Others*, L-W Book Sales, 1994; Joy and Marvin Gibson, *Collector's Guide to Wall Pockets: Book II*, L-W Book Sales, 1997; Betty and Bill Newbound, *Collector's Encyclopedia of Wall Pockets*, Collector Books, 1996, 1998 value update.

Collectors' Club: Wall Pocket Collectors Club, 1356 Tahiti, St Louis, MO 63128.

CERAMIC

Abingdon, figural, acanthus leaves, white, 8³/₄" h **$35.00**
Block Pottery, emb morning glories on white disks, mkd
"Block Pottery #2, California," 5³/₄" h **20.00**
California Pottery, figural, mallard, 6" h **20.00**
Camark, figural, cup and saucer, 7¹/₂" h **18.00**
Camark, figural, flour scoop with emb flowers, green, 8" h . . . **12.00**
Czechoslovakia, bird on branch, mkd "Made in
Czechoslovakia," 6" h **50.00**
Czechoslovakia, pocket, orange and black, 5¹/₂" h **20.00**
Frankoma, figural, cowboy boot, prairie green, 6¹/₂" h. **18.00**
Germany, heart-shaped, hp scene, souvenir of Hamburg **35.00**
Gilner, figural, elf perched on bunch of bananas, mkd
"Gilner, California," 7¹/₂" h. **30.00**
Goebel, figural, inverted umbrella, 1930s, 7" h. **55.00**
Hull, figural, violin, white, #85, 7" h **50.00**

Morton Pottery, figural, cockatiel, pastel colors, 8" h, $25.00.

Italy, pocket, emb flowers, bark-textured ground, 8" h **20.00**
Japan, figural, basket of fruit, cobalt basket, mkd "Made in Japan," 8" h **25.00**
Japan, figural, parrot on branch, mkd "Made in Japan," 7½" h **35.00**
Japan, figural, peony, mkd "Made in Japan," 8" h **30.00**
Japan, figural, Scottie dog and blue picket fence, mkd "Made in Japan," 1920s, 5½" h **25.00**
Japan, figural, Spanish galleon, pink and blue luster, mkd "Made in Japan," 7" h **45.00**
Japan, pocket, Art Deco stylized flowers, gold luster, mkd "Made in Japan," 8½" h **40.00**
Japan, pocket, black dragon on textured ground, 7" h **15.00**
Japan, pocket, moriage-type floral dec on blue ground, mkd "Made in Japan," 8½" h **40.00**
McCoy, figural, mailbox, green, 7¾" h **25.00**
Red Wing, figural, violin, pink speckled glaze, 13½" h **25.00**
Roseville, basket, La Rosa, emb floral swag, 7½" h **135.00**
Royal Copley, figural, apple, 6" h **20.00**
Shawnee, white pocket with emb red feather, 5" h **30.00**
Weller, figural, flowering tree, Woodcraft, 8" h **125.00**

GLASS

Dugan/Diamond, vase shape with emb bird and grapes dec, marigold carnival glass, 7¾" h **$40.00**
Fostoria, vase with vertical ribs, clear, 8¼" h **80.00**
Imperial, inverted whisk broom, white milk glass, Daisy and Button pattern, 7½" h **30.00**
Jeannette, Anniversary line, clear, 6½" h **15.00**
Tiffin, trumpet vase, blue satin, 9½" h **60.00**
Unknown Maker, basket formed from seashell and coral branches, blue opalescent, 7" h **100.00**
Unknown Maker, rect with black silhouette of tree-lined pond with swans, gold ground, 5¼" h **25.00**
Unknown Maker, violin, aqua, 10" h **18.00**
US Glass, pocket shape with emb flowers, blue, 6" h **45.00**

PLASTIC

Ardee Products, red vase with emb flowers, 5¾" h **$4.00**
Plas-Tex, cup and saucer, blue, floral dec, #PT 833, 6" h **6.00**
Unknown Maker, coffeepot, black and white, 9¼" h **5.00**

WARNER BROTHERS

The Warner Brothers Animation Studio, located initially in a bungalow dubbed Termite Terrace, produced over 1,000 six- and seven-minute theatrical cartoons between 1930 and 1969. Cartoon Hall of Fame characters who appeared in these shorts included Bugs Bunny, Daffy Duck, Elmer Fudd, Porky Pig, the Road Runner, Sylvester, the Tasmanian Devil, Tweety, Wile E. Coyote, and Yosemite Sam. Creative artists include Tex Avery, Bob Clampett, Friz Freleng, Chuck Jones, and Bob McKimson. The voice of Mel Blanc gave a distinct personality to each character.

During the 1940s and 50s Warner Bros. characters appeared on movie screens and in comic books and newspapers. The launching of The Bugs Bunny Show on ABC in 1960 introduced them to a new audience. In the 1970s and 80s the Warner cartoons were shown at film festivals and made available on video cassette and laser disc.

Warner found it owned a licensing goldmine. Warner Bros. stores appeared in shopping malls in the early 1990s. Warner Bros. continues to pursue a vigorous licensing program.

Although third in popularity behind Disney and Hanna-Barbera in cartoon collectibles, Warner Bros. collectibles have established a strong collecting niche. Collectors are advised to look beyond the superstars at characters such as Bosco, Foghorn Leghorn, Pepé Le Pew, and Speedy Gonzales.

Reference: Bill Bruegman, *Cartoon Friends of the Baby Boom Era*, Cap'n Penny Productions, 1993.

Alarm Clock, Bugs Bunny, metal, reclining Bugs smiling on front with left arm holding carrot, arm moves back and forth as clock ticks to simulate Bugs eating, Richie Premium Corp, ©Warner Bros Cartoon Inc, late 1940s, 1½ x 4 x 4⅜" **$175.00**
Bank, Beaky Buzzard, figural, cast metal, colorful Beaky holding hand to mouth standing next to brown barrel bank, on green accent metal base with name in relief on front, ©WBC in relief on left side, c1940s, 3 x 5¾ x 4¼" **100.00**
Bank, Bugs Bunny, figural, vinyl, smiling Bugs in basket full of carrots, "What's Up Doc?" incised on front in black, ©Homecraft Productions, 1972 Warner Bros Inc, 13" h, 5½" d **50.00**
Bank, Porky Pig, figural, bisque, smiling full figure Porky with hands behind back, name incised on reverse of head, c1930s, 5" h **50.00**
Bank, Sniffles, figural, metal, wearing gray outfit with red tie, brown shoes, standing next to brown barrel bank, on green accent base with name on front, ©WBC, late 1940s, 4¾" h **100.00**
Bobbing Head, Bugs Bunny, composition, holding carrot, ©Warner Bros Pictures Inc, Japan, c1960, 7" h **100.00**
Bobbing Head, Elmer Fudd, composition, holding rifle, ©Warner Bros, c1960, 6¼" h **100.00**
Cake Decoration, Tweety and Sylvester, plastic image of Sylvester licking his lips and raising paws overhead to grab Tweety who is holding hammer, in orig clear plastic bag attached to 4¾ x 8½" diecut hanger card, card reverse has color photo of cake top on cake, Wilton, ©1979 Warner Bros Inc **15.00**
Christmas Card, Bugs Bunny, "What's Cookin'?/Recipe For Holiday Cheer," inside art depicts artist Bob Clampett boiled in kettle stirred by Bugs, c1942 . . . . **200.00**

Drinking Glass, Bugs Bunny, Welch's Looney Tunes Collector Series #1, 1994, 4" h, $.50.

Coloring Book, Bugs Bunny taking photo of Elmer, #1147, Whitman, ©1966 Warner Bros Pictures Inc, unused, 8 x 10¾" 25.00

Comic Book, Porky Pig March of Comics Book, #71, 24 pp, full color, shoe store giveaway, Lobel's imprint on back cov, ©1951 . . . . 15.00

Cookie Jar, Yosemite Sam, ceramic, white, with cookies text in red, colorful image of Yosemite Sam facing viewer with both pistols drawn against desert western ground, Warner Bros-Seven Arts Inc, McCoy, 1950s, 10½" h, 6¼" d 175.00

Diecut, cardboard, Bugs Bunny playing mandolin, wearing blue and red cape, green curtain backdrop roses in foreground, "Looney Tunes & Merrie Melodies" comic books premium, late 1940s, 7¾ x 10" 25.00

Disc Pitcher, Bugs Bunny, blue, Fiesta 75.00

Doll, Bugs Bunny, stuffed cloth and vinyl, smiling vinyl face and yellow vinyl shirt front and ears trimmed in red cloth, red and white polka-dot stuffed cloth body and ear backs, pink nose, early 1950s, 21" h 50.00

Drinking Glass, Slow Poke Rodriguez, Warner Brothers Collector Series, Pepsi, 1973, 16 oz 35.00

Drinking Glass, Yosemite Sam and Tweety, Welch's Jelly, 1976 . . . . 8.00

Figure, Bugs Bunny, 6¾" h figure in 2 x 5½ x 8" h diecut box designed as theatre stage, ©Warner Bros Inc, 1976 Dakin & Co, San Francisco 50.00

Figure, Foghorn Leghorn, vinyl, ©Warner Bros Inc, 1970, R Dakin & Co, 8½" h 25.00

Figurine, Bugs Bunny, ceramic, Shaw, 1940s, 3¾" h 75.00

Figurine, Sniffles, ceramic, seated, with hands behind back, wearing yellow tie and hat, blue pants, brown shoes, Shaw, late 1940s, 4½" h 100.00

Game, Looney Tunes, Milton Bradley, 1968 . . . . 35.00

Magazine, *Coronet*, Dec 1945, 7-pp Bugs Bunny autobiography, color and black and white photos, includes color painting by Norman Rockwell, 5⅜ x 7½" 25.00

Mug, Tom & Jerry, white, Christmas scene, Fiesta 15.00

Napkins and Coaster Set, "Bugs Bunny Good Cheer," 36 Bugs Bunny cocktail napkins and 24 Porky Pig diecut cardboard cocktail coasters, Christmas themes, Goodmark Hollywood, ©WB, late 1940s 100.00

Paint Book, Bugs Bunny Magic Paint Book, Kool-Aid premium, 1961 . . . . 25.00

Paint Book, Bugs Bunny Porky Pig Big Paint Book, Whitman, #1152, 96 pp, 8¼ x 11¼" 50.00

Pencil Holder, Elmer Fudd, metal, smiling and waving Elmer holding shotgun, standing next to bucket pencil holder, green base with name on front, ©WBC, 4¾" h . . . 100.00

Pie Baker, Sylvester, yellow, Fiesta 65.00

Pinback Button, Bugs Bunny, "What's Up Doc?," 1959 . . . . . . 50.00

Planter, Elmer Fudd, ceramic, wearing blue hat, holding black hunting rifle, kneeling grass in front of white picket fence, Shaw, 4 x 4¼ x 5¼" 100.00

Pull Toy, Elmer Fudd Fire Chief, applied paper image of smiling Elmer as fire chief on 2 sides, right arm operating metal bell on front which rings as toy is pulled, Brice Toy Novelty Inc, ©Warner Bros Cartoons Inc, 1940s, 3½ x 9 x 6¼" 175.00

Pull Toy, Tweety, Fisher-Price, #777, diecut wood, revolving Tweety on wagon, ©Warner Bros Cartoons Inc, early 1950s, 1¼ x 6¼ x 4¼" h 100.00

Salt and Pepper Shakers, pr, Bugs Bunny, smiling full figure Bugs with carrot in right hand and yellow glove on left hand waving, ©Warner Bros Inc stamped on underside, 4⅛" h 75.00

Sauce Boat, Bugs Bunny, blue, Fiesta 45.00

Serving Tray, Daffy, turquoise, Fiesta 60.00

Teapot, Porky Pig, pink, Fiesta 85.00

Teapot, Tweetie, white, Fiesta 85.00

Vase, Bugs Bunny, ceramic, figural Bugs standing beside tree, ©Warner Bros Cartoon Inc, late 1940s, 2¼ x 5¼ x 7¼" 75.00

Wall Hanging, Speedy Gonzalez, figural, ceramic, gold foil stickers for ©Warner Bros, 1986 and Bai-Dotta, Sacramento, CA, 3 x 8½ x 11¾" 50.00

WATCHES

Watches divide into three main collecting categories: (1) character licensed, (2) pocket, and (3) wrist. Character licensed watches arrived on the scene in the late 1930s. Although some character pocket watches are known, the vast majority are wristwatches. Collectors divide character watches into two types: (a) stem wound and (b) battery operated. Because they are relatively inexpensive to make, battery-operated licensed watches are frequently used as premiums by fast-food companies.

Pocket watches are collected by size (18/0 to 20), number of jewels in the movement, open or closed (hunter) face, case decoration, and case composition. Railroad watches generally are 16 to 18 in size, have a minimum of 17 jewels, and adjust to at least five positions. Double-check to make certain the movement is period and has not been switched, a common practice.

The wristwatch achieved mass popularity in the 1920s. Hundreds of American, German, and Swiss companies entered the market. Quality ranged from Rolex to Timex. Again, collectors divide the category into two groups: (a) stem wound and (b) battery operated.

In the early 1990s a speculative Swatch watch collecting craze occurred. The bubble burst in the late 1990s. Prices have fallen sharply. The craze had a strong international flavor.

Watch collecting as a whole enjoys one of the strongest international markets. On this level, brand name is the name of the game. Watches are bought primarily as investments, not for use.

References: Hy Brown, *Comic Character Timepieces,* Schiffer Publishing, 1992; Gisbert L. Brunner and Christian Pfeiffer-Belli, *Wristwatches,* Schiffer Publishing, 1993, 1997 value update; Edward Faber and Stewart Unger, *American Wristwatches, Revised,* Schiffer Publishing, 1997; Heinz Hample, *Automatic Wristwatches from Germany, England, France, Japan, Russia and the USA,* Schiffer Publishing, 1997; Robert Heide and John Gilman, *The Mickey Mouse Watch,* Hyperion, 1997; Helmut Kahlert, Richard Mühe, and Gisbert L. Brunner, *Wristwatches: History of a Century's Development, 3rd Edition,* Schiffer Publishing, 1994; Cooksey Shugart, Richard E. Gilbert, and Tom Engle, *Complete Price Guide to Watches, 19th Edition,* Collector Books, 1999; *W.B.S. Collector's Guide for Swatch Watches,* W.B.S. Marketing, n.d.

Periodical: *International Wrist Watch,* PO Box 110204, Stamford, CT 06911.

Newsletter: *The Premium Watch Watch,* 24 San Rafael Dr, Rochester NY 14618.

Collectors' Clubs: National Assoc of Watch & Clock Collectors, 514 Poplar St, Columbia, PA 17512; The Swatch Collectors Club, PO Box 7400, Melville, NY 11747.

Character Watch, Hopalong Cassidy, US Time, saddle box stand, 1950, $400.00.

Character, Aladdin, 1³/₈" d gold metal case with hinged lid, top of lid has raised image of Genie coming out of magic lamp, when side button is pressed lid pops open and watch dial pops up, full color dial illus of Genie with gold dots for numerals, inside case lid mkd "To Commemorate The Release Of Disney's Aladdin," case reverse has image of Mickey and "Made Exclusively For the Disney Store," comes in black velvet pouch which is contained in heavy cast metal magic lamp with removable top, orig 3 x 8¹/₄ x 4¹/₂", MIB **$100.00**

Character, Batman, Dabs, 1³/₈" d goldtone metal case, dial illus of Batman against red circle ground, black numerals on white rim, cardboard insert with Superman, Captain Marvel, and Aquaman in 2¹/₄ x 6 x ³/₄" in blue plastic box, ©1977 DC Comics Inc **100.00**

Character, Bionic Woman, MZ Berger & Co, Inc, 1" d goldtone case, Bionic Woman in blue jumpsuit breaking through watch face, orig box, ©1976 Universal City Studios Inc **45.00**

Character, Dale Evans, Ingraham, chrome luster metal bezel, Dale in red and brown outfit and black boots, name in tiny black lettering, silvered hue with red numerals, c1949 . . . . **100.00**

Character, Gene Autry, Wilane, Swiss movement, underside of case engraved "Always Your Pal Gene Autry," silvered brass bezel, Autry on rearing Champion, silvered metal link chain band with bottom center identification band, 1948 . . . . **100.00**

Character, Jimmy Carter, Goober Time Co, 1¹/₄" d dial, brown, red, gray, and blue Carter caricature with large toothy smile, smaller peanut body, "Original Jimmy Carter From Peanuts To President" on dial, red, white, and blue fabric wristband, 1976 . . . . **50.00**

Character, John F Kennedy/Martin Luther King, red and white face with white ground, black outline illus of JFK and Martin Luther King and "United In Time," red, white, and blue fabric band, Swiss, 1971 . . . . **50.00**

Character, Li'l Abner, chrome cased metal, silver accent face and numbers, black and white smiling Abner face with name in black letters, 7¹/₄" l black leather band, mid-1950s **200.00**

Character, Little Pig, US Time, 1¹/₈ x 1¹/₂" silvered metal case, Fiddler Pig on silver ground, red numerals and hands, 1947 . . . . **100.00**

Character, Lucy Van Pelt, United Features Syndicate, Inc, Lucy wearing yellow dress, white straps, ©1952, c1970 . . . . **40.00**

Character, Mickey Mouse, Bradley, 1¹/₈" sq silvered metal case, Mickey on silver ground, hands point at black numerals, 1-pc metal bracelet, 1970s **75.00**

Character, Mighty Mouse, chrome accent case, white face, black numbers, smiling Mighty Mouse with arms as hands of watch, 8¹/₂" l black leather strap, c1980s **75.00**

Character, Orphan Annie, New Haven Clock Co, orig box, 1935 . . . . **180.00**

Character, Popeye & Olive Oyl, gold luster metal bezel, Popeye and Olive Oyl at boat's tiller wheel, chrome luster underside with silver image of Popeye, Olive, Wimpy, Swee'pea, Jeep, and possibly Brutus, black laced leather straps, gold luster buckle, ©1944, MIB **25.00**

Character, Smokey Bear, Hawthorne, Smokey with spade and shovel for hands, "Smokey Bear Prevent Forest Fires," 7¹/₄" l white vinyl band with gold accent clasp, 1¹/₂ x 2³/₈ x 9" yellow diecut box with clear plastic holder, orig price tag, 1970s **100.00**

Character, Snoopy, Timex, tennis player Snoopy with right hand for hour and tennis racquet for minutes, tennis ball goes around edge for second hand, orange numbers, blue denim cloth ground, blue denim band, with tags, instruction manual, and orig 2¹/₂ x 3¹/₂ x 4" molded clear plastic case with green base, red plastic insert designed like doghouse roof holding watch, c1970 . . . . **75.00**

Character, Snow White, Snow White on white ground, no straps, 1¹/₂" l bright yellow case, 1950s **75.00**

Character, Space Explorer, Bradley Time, 1/8" d chrome luster bezel, star-studded night sky with white numerals, conventional hands overlaid by miniature diecut astronaut joined by tether to space capsule, rotates full cycle every 60 seconds, chrome metal link expansion band, orig plastic hinged display case, Swiss, c1960s **100.00**

Character, Spiro Agnew, caricature, waving flag with 1 hand, "V" sign with other, orig red sued straps, c1972 . . . . . **75.00**

Character, The Lion King, employee watch, 1¾" gold-tone metal case, adult Simba, Timmone and Pumbaa gazing up at sky, mkd "Limited To 1750" with text describing scene on dial, orig 2¾ x 2¾ x 3" wood box . . . **100.00**

Character, Tony the Tiger, Kellogg's, gold luster metal case, Tony the Tiger above 1989 Kellogg copyright, brown leather straps with gold finish buckle, orig brown plastic display case inscribed "Kellogg's Frosted Flakes Cereal," brown velveteen lining, ©1989 . . . . **50.00**

Commemorative, "First Disneyana Convention," Mickey portrait on yellow and orange sunburst ground, purple rim, red and blue text "1st Disneyana Convention 1992/Walt Disney World Resort," crystal faceted-like diamond gives off prismatic effect, green slipcase with large Mickey portrait silhouette, in case with emb "Limited Edition" and Mickey portrait on lid, reverse has Mickey silhouette with "Made Exclusively For the Walt Disney Theme Parks and Resorts" **100.00**

Pocket Watch, Buck Rogers, Ingraham, diecut copper lightning bolt hands over color dial, Comet Man image imp in metal back, orig silvering on case, 2" d, 1935 . . . . **1,000.00**

Pocket Watch, Mickey Mouse, Ingersoll, 2" d silvered metal case, dial illus of Mickey with hands pointing at numerals, second hand disk with 3 Mickey images, English version, 1934 . . . . **1,000.00**

Pocket Watch, Popeye, plain dial, New Haven, c1936 . . . . . **375.00**

Pocket Watch, Roy Rogers, Ingraham, c1960 . . . . **85.00**

Pocket Watch, Uncle Sam, silvered metal case, bottom center sweep second hand over illus of tiny aircraft, second hand movement. **200.00**

Swatch, High Beam/Night Vision, SE1752-GM, 8-hole band, 1991 . . . . **65.00**

Swatch, Lady Limelight/Limelight Special, SE4074-LB, Limelight Special, 8-hole black band, 1985 . . . . **200.00**

Swatch, Polka Dot/Dancing Steps, SE1686-LP, 8-hole leather band, 1991 . . . . **50.00**

Swatch, Stalefish/Cold Fever, SE1766-GG, Jay Vignon artist, 8-hole band, 1991 . . . . **60.00**

Swatch, Strawberry Fields/Bright Flags, SE1692-LK, 8-hole band, 1991. . . . . **50.00**

Swatch, Stream/Sport Code, SE1922-GK. **50.00**

Swatch, Tennis Grid, SE8380-GW, red case and hands, 1983. . . . . **550.00**

Wristwatch, Alpha, 17j, chronograph, stainless steel, c1950. . . . . **140.00**

Wristwatch, Bulova, Accutron, "Spaceview," gold filled, c1960. . . . . **200.00**

Wristwatch, Elgin, 17j, stepped case, gold filled, c1935 . . . . . **80.00**

Wristwatch, Hamilton, "Bailey," 19j, gold filled, 1951 . . . . . . **80.00**

Wristwatch, Longines, 17j, 14k, fancy lugs, diamond dial. **700.00**

Wristwatch, New Haven, 7j, engraved bezel **35.00**

Wristwatch, Rolex, Air King, 25j, stainless steel, c1962 . . . . . **400.00**

Wristwatch, Timecraft, Tiffany, 17j, chronograph, stainless steel, c1950 . . . . **175.00**

Wristwatch, Timex, bright luster gold metal bezel, blue denim dial face with matching denim wrist strap, dial face has small gold dot for each hour, orig $24.95 price card plus string warranty card, warranty folder inserted in back of display case, orig 2½ x 3 x 4" styrene plastic display case, c1970s **75.00**

WATERFORD CRYSTAL

Waterford Crystal, Waterford, County Waterford, Ireland, traces its lineage to a crystal manufacturing business established by George and William Penrose in 1783. Although this initial effort to manufacture crystal and other glassware in Waterford only lasted sixty-eight years, the items produced enjoyed an unequaled reputation.

The end of flint glass production in Dublin around 1893 marked the demise of almost three centuries of glassmaking in Ireland. In 1902 sand from Muckish in Donegal was brought to the Cork Exhibition where London glass blowers used a small furnace and made drinking glasses cut in an "early Waterford style." This attempt to create an interest in reviving glassmaking in Ireland failed.

In 1947, almost fifty years later, a small glass factory was established in Ballytuckle, a suburb of Waterford, located approximately one-and-one-half miles from the site of the Penrose glasshouse on the western edge of the city. Apprentices were trained by immigrant European craftsmen displaced by World War II.

The management of Waterford Crystal dedicated its efforts to matching the purity of color, inspired design, and the highest quality levels of 18th- and 19th-century Waterford glass. Capturing the brilliance of the traditional, deeply incised cutting patterns of earlier Waterford pieces provided an additional challenge.

Waterford Crystal continued to grow and prosper, eventually moving to a forty-acre site in Johnstown, near the center of Waterford. In the early 1980s computer technology improved the accuracy of the raw materials mix, known in the crystal industry as the batch. Improvements in furnace design and diamond cutting wheels enabled Waterford craftsmen to create exciting new intricate glass patterns. Two additional plants in County Waterford helped the company meet its manufacturing requirements.

Waterford Crystal stemware consists of essentially twelve stem shapes with a variety of cutting patterns which expand the range to over thirty suites. Many popular patterns have been adapted for giftware, providing an opportunity to acquire matching bowls, vases, and other accessories. In addition to producing stemware, giftware, and lighting, Waterford Crystal also executes hundreds of commissioned pieces. All Waterford Crystal can be identified by the distinctive "Waterford" signature on the base.

References: Bob Page and Dale Frederiksen, *Crystal Stemware Identification Guide,* Collector Books, 1998; Harry L. Rinker, *Stemware of the 20th Century: The Top 200 Patterns,* House of Collectibles, 1997.

Avoca, champagne, fluted, 7⅜" **$30.00**

Avoca, cocktail **30.00**

Avoca, iced tea **35.00**

Avoca, juice **32.00**

Avoca, old fashioned. **28.00**

Avoca, sherry, 5¼" **25.00**

Avoca, water goblet, 7" **30.00**

Ballyshannon, champagne, fluted 24.00
Ballyshannon, cordial 20.00
Ballyshannon, iced tea, ftd 30.00
Ballyshannon, water goblet 22.00
Carina, brandy 22.00
Carina, cordial, 4⁵/₈" 18.00
Carina, iced tea, ftd. 30.00
Carina, sherry, 5¹/₄" 22.00
Claria, champagne, fluted, 9". 12.50
Claria, iced tea, 8" 14.00
Claria, wine, 8" 12.00
Comeragh, champagne, 5¹/₄" 40.00
Comeragh, finger bowl, 3⁷/₈". 50.00
Comeragh, port, 4¹/₂". 35.00
Comeragh, shot glass, 2³/₈". 30.00
Comeragh, tumbler 35.00
Comeragh, water goblet 45.00
Hanover, brandy, 5¹/₄" 18.00
Hanover, bud vase 20.00
Hanover, champagne, fluted, 8³/₄" 15.00
Hanover, decanter, 12¹/₄". 70.00
Hanover, highball, 5⁷/₈". 14.00
Hanover, old fashioned, double, 4" 15.00
Hanover, water goblet, 8¹/₂". 16.00
Hanover, wine, 7⁵/₈". 16.00
Hanover, wine, balloon, 8⁵/₈". 20.00
Kylemore, brandy, 5¹/₄" 40.00
Kylemore, champagne, fluted, 7⁷/₈". 40.00
Kylemore, cocktail, 4³/₄". 32.00
Kylemore, highball 30.00
Kylemore, jug 85.00
Kylemore, juice, flat, 3⁵/₈". 35.00
Kylemore, tumbler, flat, 5". 30.00
Laurent, champagne, fluted, 8¹/₄". 15.00
Laurent, iced tea, 7⁵/₈". 17.50
Laurent, water goblet, 7⁵/₈". 15.00
Wynnewood, champagne, fluted 24.00
Wynnewood, iced tea 28.00
Wynnewood, water goblet. 22.00
Wynnewood, wine 20.00

Hanover Pattern. Photo courtesy BC Design Inc.

WATT POTTERY

In 1886 W. J. Watt founded the Brilliant Stoneware Company in Rose Farm, Ohio. The company made salt-glazed utilitarian stoneware. Watt sold his business in 1897. Between 1903 and 1921 Watt worked for the Ransbottom Brothers Pottery in Ironspot, Ohio. The Ransbottoms were Watt's brothers-in-law.

In 1921 Watt purchased the Globe Stoneware Company in Crooksville, Ohio, renaming it the Watt Pottery Company. Watt made stoneware containers between 1922 and 1935.

In the 1930s Watt introduced a line of kitchenware designed to withstand high oven temperatures. Pieces were rather plain with decoration limited to a white and/or blue band. The mid-1940s' Kla-Ham'rd series featured pieces dipped in a brown glaze.

Watt's Wild Rose pattern, known to collectors as Raised Pansy, was introduced in 1950. Production difficulties resulted in a second pattern design, marketed as Rio Rose but called Cut Leaf Pansy by collectors.

Watt introduced new patterns each year during the 1950s. Although Watt sold patterns under specific pattern names, collectors group them in a single category, e.g., Starflower covers Moonflower and Silhouette. Watt introduced its Apple series in 1952, producing pieces for approximately ten years. Several variations were produced. The Tulip and Cherry series appeared in the mid-1950s. Rooster was introduced in 1955. The Morning Glory series arrived in the late 1950s followed by the Autumn Foliage in 1959. Lines introduced in the 1960s met with limited success.

Watt also made advertising and special commission ware. Pieces marked Esmond, Heirloom, Orchard Ware, Peedeeco, and R-F Spaghetti may have Watt backstamps. Watt was not evenly distributed—50% of the company's products were sold in New York and New England, 25% in the greater Chicago area, a small amount distributed by Safeway in the southern and western states, and the balance throughout the midwest and northeast.

On October 4, 1965, fire destroyed the Watt Pottery Company factory and warehouse. Production never resumed.

References: Sue and Dave Morris, *Watt Pottery,* Collector Books, 1993, 1996 value update; Dennis Thompson and W. Bryce Watt, *Watt Pottery,* Schiffer Publishing, 1994.

Collectors' Clubs: Watt Collectors Assoc, PO Box 1995, Iowa City, IA 52244; Watt Pottery Collectors USA, Box 26067, Fairview Park, OH 44126.

Apple, baker, cov, #67, 2 leaf $120.00
Apple, baker, cov, #84, square 2,100.00
Apple, baker, cov, #96. . . . . 110.00
Apple, baker, cov, #96, with stand and box 155.00
Apple, baker, cov, #601. . . . . 150.00
Apple, bean pot, #502, oversized 2,000.00
Apple, canister, #72, 2 leaf 850.00
Apple, chip bowl, #119. . . . . 110.00
Apple, dinner plate, divided 1,600.00
Apple, ice bucket, #59 . . . . 175.00
Apple, ice lip pitcher, #17, salesman sample 500.00
Apple, mug, #501. . . . . 350.00
Apple, pitcher, #15 . . . . 110.00
Apple, pitcher, #15, 2 leaf. 105.00
Apple, pitcher, #16, 2 leaf 150.00
Apple, pitcher, #17, plain lip 250.00
Apple, platter, #49 . . . . 200.00

Apple, salt and pepper shakers, pr, barrel 525.00
Apple, spaghetti bowl, #39 . . . . 150.00
Butterfly, baker, cov, #67 . . . . 400.00
Butterfly, mixing bowl, #6 . . . . 150.00
Butterfly, refrigerator pitcher, #69, restored 675.00
Campbell Kids Bean Pot, #76 . . . . 80.00
Chinese Bowls, price for 3 . . . . 75.00
Coffee Server, #115, aqua 160.00
Coffee Server, #115, autumn foliage 160.00
Coffee Server, #115, Par-T-Que 160.00
Confetti, bean cups, #75, price for pair 280.00
Cross Hatch, cookie jar, #21 . . . . 160.00
Cross Hatch, mixing bowl, #5 . . . . 75.00
Cross Hatch, pie plate, #33 . . . . 200.00
Cross Hatch, pitcher, #16 . . . . 375.00
Daisy, mixing bowls, 5, 6, 7, and 8 . . . . 150.00
Daisy, pitcher, old style 385.00
Dogwood, plate, 8½" d 200.00
Double Apple, creamer, #62 . . . . 250.00
Dutch Tulip, canister, #72 . . . . 375.00
Dutch Tulip, cheese crock, #80 . . . . 500.00
Dutch Tulip, dinner plate, divided 575.00
Dutch Tulip, mixing bowl, #5 . . . . 105.00
Dutch Tulip, salad bowl, #73 . . . . 205.00
Goodies Jar, #59 . . . . 180.00
Goodies Jar, #72 . . . . 195.00
Goodies Jar, #76 . . . . 135.00
Kitty Dish, yellow, 5" d 160.00
Morning Glory, cookie jar, cov, cream, dome top 425.00
Morning Glory, mixing bowl, #5, with adv 25.00
Morning Glory, mixing bowl, #6, yellow 75.00
Mug, #61, with "Kevin" 450.00
Mug, #501, Trapnell's Café 150.00
Mug, #701, "Marilyn" 200.00
Oval Baker Rack 95.00
Pansy, spaghetti bowl, #39 . . . . 125.00
Pie Plate, chicken decal 250.00
Rooster, bowl, #66 . . . . 100.00

Rooster, casserole, cov, #87, lug, blade lid 225.00
Rooster, cheese crock, #80 . . . . 1,000.00
Rooster, coffee canister 875.00
Rooster, pie plate, #33, with adv 700.00
Rooster, pitcher, #15, red adv 125.00
Rooster, pitcher, #17 . . . . 2,400.00
Rooster, tea canister 1,050.00
Starflower, baker, open, #96, 4 petal 40.00
Starflower, bowl, #120, 4 petal 130.00
Starflower, cheese crock, #80, 4 petal 500.00
Starflower, mug, #61, 5 petal 220.00
Starflower, pitcher, 5 petal 200.00
Starflower, pitcher, 5 petal, with adv 250.00
Starflower, sugar, open, #98 . . . . 350.00
Starflower, tumbler, #56, rounded 175.00
Starflower, tumbler, #56, slant sided 160.00
Tear Drop, baker, cov, #84, sq 350.00
Tear Drop, baker, cov, #86, oval 600.00
Tear Drop, cheese crock, #80 . . . . 475.00
Tear Drop, spaghetti bowl, #39 . . . . 175.00
Tulip, bean pot, #76 . . . . 300.00
Tulip, bowl, #96 . . . . 100.00
Tulip, spaghetti bowl, #39 . . . . 300.00

WEDGWOOD

In 1759 Josiah Wedgwood established a pottery near Stoke-on-Trent at the former Ivy House works in Burslem, England. By 1761, Wedgwood had perfected a superior quality inexpensive clear-glazed creamware which proved to be very successful.

Wedgwood moved his pottery from the Ivy House to the larger Brick House works in Burslem in 1764. In 1766, upon being appointed "Potter to Her Majesty" by Queen Charlotte, Wedgwood named his creamware "Queen's ware." The Brick House works remained in production until 1772.

Wedgwood built a new factory in Etruria in 1769, the same year he formed a partnership with Thomas Bentley. Wedgwood's most famous set of Queen's ware, the 1,000-piece "Frog" Service created for Catherine the Great, Empress of Russia, was produced at the Etruria factory in 1774.

By the late 1700s, the Wedgwood product line included black basalt, creamware, jasper, pearlware, and redware. Moonlight luster was made from 1805 to 1815. Bone China was produced from 1812 to 1822, and revived in 1878. Fairyland luster was introduced in 1915. The last luster pieces were made in 1932.

In 1906 Wedgwood established a museum at its Etruria pottery. A new factory was built at nearby Barlaston in 1940. The museum was moved to Barlaston and expanded. The Etruria works was closed in 1950.

During the 1960s and 1970s Wedgwood acquired many English potteries, including William Adams & Sons, Coalport, Susie Cooper, Crown Staffordshire, Johnson Brothers, Mason's Ironstone, J. & G. Meakin, Midwinter Companies, Precision Studios and Royal Tuscan. In 1969 Wedgwood acquired King's Lynn Glass, renaming it Wedgwood Glass. The acquisition of Galway Crystal Company of Galway, Erie, followed in 1974.

In 1986 Waterford and Wedgwood merged. The Wedgwood Group, now a division of Waterford Wedgwood, consists of six major divisions: Wedgwood, Coalport, Johnson Brothers, Mason's Ironstone, Wedgwood Hotelware, and Wedgwood Jewellery. The Wedgwood Group is one of the largest tabletop manufacturers in

Apple, cookie jar, #503, $330.00. Photo courtesy Gene Harris Antique Auction Center, Inc.

the world. It is a public company comprising eight factories and employing 5,500 people in the United Kingdom and overseas.

References: Susan and Al Bagdade, *Warman's English & Continental Pottery & Porcelain, 3rd Edition,* Krause Publications, 1998; Robin Reilly, *Wedgwood: The New Illustrated Dictionary, Revised,* Antique Collectors' Club, 1995; Harry L. Rinker, *Dinnerware of the 20th Century: The Top 500 Patterns,* House of Collectibles, 1997; Harry L. Rinker, *Stemware of the 20th Century: The Top 200 Patterns,* House of Collectibles, 1997.

Collectors' Club: The Wedgwood Society, The Roman Villa, Rockbourne, Fordingbridge, Hants, SP6 3PG, U.K.

Bough Pot, cov, light blue jasper, applied white foliate and classical relief, limited edition of 200, printed and imp marks, c1985, 6" h **$500.00**

Bowl, "Dancing Hours," black jasper, applied white relief, imp mark, 1964, 10" d **350.00**

Bowl, lustre, octagonal, fish patter Z4920, mottled blue ext, mother-of-pearl int, printed mark, c1920, 6" d **375.00**

Bust, Shakespeare, black basalt, raised title, imp mark, 1964, 10" h **375.00**

Candlesticks, pr, black basalt, modeled as dolphins, mounted to rect bases with shell-molded borders, imp marks, 1971, 9" h **1,500.00**

Crocus Pot and Tray, terra-cotta jasper, figural hedgehog, imp mark, 1971, 11" l tray **700.00**

Daventry Bowl, lustre, fairyland Nizami pattern int with border of wolves and stags, ext with floral designs in shaped panels, printed mark, c1920, 7⁷⁄₈" d **5,500.00**

Figure, fallow deer, Skeaping, cream glaze, imp artist and factory mark, 20th C, 7" h **115.00**

Figure, Peregrine Falcon, porcelain, freeform base, dec in color, Raptors Collection, limited edition of 100, modern, 15" h **575.00**

Figure, Taurus the Bull, modeled by Arnold Machin, black glazed with gold printed signs of the zodiac, imp mark, c1968, 14" l **350.00**

Figure, tiger and buck, Skeaping, moonstone glaze, imp artist and factory mark, 20th C, 8" h **200.00**

Flower Holder, black basalt, Aphrodite on crested wave, pierced freeform rocky base, early 20th C, 12" h **1,375.00**

Humidor, cov, light blue jasper, white applied classical subjects and urns between arched panels, limited edition of 200, printed and imp marks, c1985, 9" h **800.00**

Plaque, Goddess Thetis, black jasper, applied white relief of female figure modeled seated on rock, imp mark, mid 20th C, 7" d **115.00**

Plate, 3-color jasper diceware, green dip with lilac quatrefoils on white ground, surrounding central portrait of Josiah Wedgwood, limited edition of 250, printed and imp marks, 1979, 9" d **550.00**

Plates, "Claire Leighton," Queen's ware, black transfer printed, New England Industries series, imp and printed marks, surface scratches, c1952, 10" d, set of 6 . . . . . . **315.00**

Plates, "Georgia," Queen's ware, blue transfer printed, printed marks, mid 20th C, 10³⁄₈" d, set of 12 . . . . **175.00**

Portrait Medallions, boxed set of 14, blue jasper, applied white relief, limited edition of 200, fitted case, imp and printed marks, 1973 . . . . **750.00**

Salad Bowl and Servers, yellow jasper dip, applied black fruiting grape vines and acanthus leaves, silver-plated tools and bowl rim, imp mark, c1930, 8⁵⁄₈" d **1,150.00**

Canopic Vase, cov, primrose jasper, applied bands of terracotta hieroglyphs in relief, imp mark, 1978, 9" h, $920.00. Photo courtesy Skinner, Inc., Boston, MA.

Vase, cov, 3-color jasper, light blue dip with yellow quatrefoils to white ground, pierced cov with white applied quatrefoils, limited edition of 200, imp mark, 1974, 5" h **635.00**

Vase, cov, light blue jasper, applied white classical relief, imp mark, 1969, 11" h **375.00**

Vase, designed by Keith Murray, black basalt, spherical body on pedestal base, engine-turned banding, imp and printed mark, footrim chip restored, c1940, 7" h **525.00**

Vase, yellow jasper dip, applied black classical and foliate relief, imp marks, c1930, 6" h **975.00**

Water Ewer, black jasper, applied white figure and foliate relief, limited edition of 50, printed and imp marks, 1986, 16" h **2,000.00**

AUCTION PRICES – WEDGWOOD

Skinner, Inc., Fine Ceramics Auction, December 12, 1998. Prices include a 15% buyer's premium.

Bust, Mercury, black basalt, waisted circular socle, imp marks, wing restored, 20th C, 9" h **$977.50**

Chess Set, designed by Arnold Machin, solid black and white jasper, consisting of 24 pcs (8 additional pcs "as is"), imp marks, fitted wood case, c1971, 19 x 19" case **1,035.00**

Girandoles, pr, mounted brass and crystal, black jasper dip drum bases with white classical relief, imp marks, modern, 11" h **1,955.00**

Portland Vase, green jasper, white classical relief, base with half-length figure wearing Phrygian cap, imp mark and AW, 1962, 10" h **1,610.00**

Vase, cov, 3-color jasper diceware, dark blue jasper dip with green quatrefoils and rim bands and white classical and foliate relief, limited edition, imp marks, finial reglued, 1977, 9" h **546.25**

Vase, cov, Canopic, gilt-dec black basalt, applied bands of hieroglyphs in relief, limited edition of 50, imp mark, 1978, 9" h **3,105.00**

Wine and Water Ewers, pr, black jasperware, applied white figures and relief, limited edition of 50, printed and imp marks, 1986, 16" h **4,312.50**

WELLER

Samuel Augutus Weller established the Weller Pottery Company in Fultonham, Ohio, in 1872. In 1888, Weller moved operations to Zanesville. By 1890 a new plant was built.

During a visit to the 1893 Columbian Exposition in Chicago, Weller saw Lonhuda ware. He bought the Lonhuda Pottery and brought William Long, its owner, to Zanesville to supervise production at Weller. When Long resigned in 1896, Weller introduced Louwelsa Weller, based on Long's glaze formula.

Weller purchased the American Encaustic Tiling Company plant in 1899. By 1900 Weller enjoyed a virtual monopoly on mass-produced art pottery. Soon Weller was exporting large amounts of pottery to England, Germany, and Russia.

In the 1910s Japanese potteries made almost exact copies of Weller products that sold in the American market for half the cost. Weller increased its production of ware for the floral and garden industries to offset the financial losses.

Weller purchased the Zanesville Art Pottery in 1920 and incorporated. Several new lines were introduced in the late 1920s. Weller's son-in-law became president in 1932. Divorce from his wife forced him to leave the company. The divorce settlement entitled him to reproduced Zona dinnerware, which he took to Gladding, McBean.

In 1945 Essex Wire Corporation leased space in the Weller factory. By 1947 Essex Wire bought the controlling stock of the company. The factory closed in 1948.

References: Sharon and Bob Huxford, *The Collectors Encyclopedia of Weller Pottery,* Collector Books, 1979, 1998 value update; Ralph and Terry Kovel, *Kovels' American Art Pottery,* Crown Publishers, 1993.

Collectors' Club: American Art Pottery Assoc, PO Box 1226, Westport, MA 02790.

Basket, Woodcraft, green and brown, unmkd, 9¾" h **$225.00**
Bowl, Claywood, emb floral dec, 6¼" d **50.00**
Bowl, Cloud Burst, green, 7" d **30.00**
Bowl, Ivory, tan highlights, 4½" d **35.00**
Bowl, Woodcraft, squirrel pattern, green and brown,
   mkd "Weller Ware," 4" h, 8" d **250.00**
Bud Vase, Woodcraft, green, red, brown, and ivory, imp
   "Weller," 10" h, 4½" d **80.00**
Center Bowl, Lavonia, lavender and blue, 11" d **60.00**
Centerpiece, Roma, applied rose design, red and green
   on ivory ground, imp "Weller," 4¼" h, 10¼" w **75.00**
Console Bowl and Flower Holder, Glendale, yellow,
   blue, green, and brown, mkd "Weller," 2¾" h, 15½" d . . . **700.00**
Console Set, Glendale, bowl, flower holder, and pr can-
   dlesticks, blue, yellow, green, red, and brown, mkd
   "Weller Ware," 15" d bowl, 2¼" h candlesticks **635.00**
Figure, Coppertone, frog, incised "Weller Potter 12," 4 x
   4" **600.00**
Figure, Coppertone, frog, Weller Pottery ink half-kiln
   stamp and "12," 6¼" h **925.00**
Flower Bowl and Flower Frog, Claywood, emb stylized
   flowers, 5" d **115.00**
Flower Frog, Brighton, flamingo, imp "Weller," 6" h **285.00**
Flower Frog, Brighton, king fisher, blue, 7" h **175.00**
Flower Frog, Muskota, fish, unmkd, 2½ x 4½" **300.00**
Flower Frog, Woodcraft, frog and water lily, imp
   "Weller," 5 x 5" **400.00**

Flower Holder, Muskota, swan, paper label, 2½" h, 5¾" w . . . **225.00**
Hanging Basket, Woodcraft, fox heads and apples,
   unmkd, 4½" h **715.00**
Jardiniere, Bouquet, lilys of the valley, green, script
   "Weller," 8½" h **150.00**
Jardiniere, Ivory, panels of emb open roses, 11" d **100.00**
Jardiniere and Pedestal, Baldin, raised apple design, red,
   green, and brown, 31¾" h, 13" d **800.00**
Pitcher, Woodcraft, brown, green, and ivory, imp
   "Weller," 12½" h, 7¼" w **925.00**
Umbrella Stand, Flemish, raised apple design, green,
   red, and brown, 22½" h, 11" d **700.00**
Umbrella Stand, raised floral design, Bedford, unmkd,
   20½" h, 10¼" d **375.00**
Vase, Ardsley, emb cattails, green, 11" h **125.00**
Vase, Bonito, 2-handled, floral dec, script "Weller," 5½" h . . . **150.00**
Vase, Burnt Wood, stylized flowers, imp "Weller," 10½" h **175.00**
Vase, Chase, 3-part, emb hunt scene in white on matte
   blue ground, incised script "Weller," 9" h **285.00**
Vase, Claywood, emb grape dec, 10" h **100.00**
Vase, Cloud Burst, mottled purple, 6" h **60.00**
Vase, Coppertone, 2-handled, bulbous, incised "Z," 6½" h . . . **475.00**
Vase, cylindrical, emb stylized poppy pods, matte green
   glaze, unmkd, 10½" h **775.00**
Vase, Flemish, raised foliate design, brown and green,
   unmkd, 15¾" h **300.00**
Vase, Florenzo, flower holder lid, green, ivory, and
   brown, mkd "Weller Pottery," 7½" h, 6¾" d **225.00**
Vase, Forest, raised design, green and brown, mkd "54,"
   12" h **650.00**
Vase, Glendale, 2 parrots, stamped "Weller," 9" h **775.00**
Vase, Hudson Light, hexagonal, white and purple wiste-
   ria on shaded green and white ground, diestamped
   "Weller," 11¼" h" **300.00**
Vase, La Sa, ovoid, landscape and trees, mkd "La Sa,"
   7½" h **550.00**

Vase, Patra, red, blue, and brown fan dec, green rim and handles, brown textured body, incised "Weller Pottery," 3¼" h, $100.00.
Photo courtesy Ray Morykan Auctions.

Vase, Manhattan, light green and yellow, script "Weller,"
6½" h **70.00**

Vase, Marvo, green, stamped "Weller Ware," 8½" h **80.00**

Vase, Marvo, raised leaf design, butterscotch and green,
Weller Pottery mark, 9" h, 7" d **225.00**

Vase, Patricia, 2-handled, mottled tan and green, script
"Weller," 8" h **175.00**

Vase, Pumila, matte green and butterscotch, mkd
"Weller Ware," 10¼" h **225.00**

Vase, Roba, emb flowers, white to green matte glaze,
11" h **65.00**

Vase, Silvertone, purple, green, and red, mkd "Weller
Pottery," 7½" h **350.00**

Vase, Silvertone, raised floral dec, green, white, and lavender, mkd "Weller Ware," paper label, 10½" h, 7" d **700.00**

Vase, Sydonia, mottled blue matte glaze with green
base, incised "Weller Pottery," 5" h **150.00**

Vase, tree-form, brown and green, incised "Weller
Pottery," 6¾" h, 3½" d **150.00**

Vase, Woodcraft, applied squirrel and owl, 18½" h **1,100.00**

Wall Pocket, Glendale, emb polychrome birds, unmkd,
12" **650.00**

Wall Pocket, Woodcraft, owl, green, brown, and ivory,
unmkd, 11" h **500.00**

WESTERN COLLECTIBLES

This category divides into three parts: (1) items associated with working cowboys and cowgirls such as horse tack, wagon trail memorabilia, everyday work clothes, dress duds, and rodeo memorabilia; (2) material related to the western dude ranch, and (3) objects shaped like or portraying images associated with the American West. It does not include items associated with literary, movie, and television characters.

Americans went western crazy in the 1950s, partially the result of the TV western. Western maple furniture was found in living rooms, dens, and children's bedrooms. Western motifs from riders on bucking horses to Mexicans taking siestas beneath cactus decorated everything from dinnerware to linens. The western revival of the early 1990s reawakened collector interest in this western motif material from the 1950s. As the decade ends, the craze seems to be abating, largely the result of high prices asked by dealers for commonly found items.

References: Judy Crandall, *Cowgirls: Early Images and Collectibles*, Schiffer Publishing, 1994; Michael Friedman, *Cowboy Culture, 2nd Edition*, Schiffer Publishing, 1999; Dan and Sebie Hutchins, *Old Cowboy Saddles & Spurs: Identifying the Craftsmen Who Made Them, Sixth Annual*, Horse Feathers Publishing, 1996; William Manns and Elizabeth Clair Flood, *Cowboys: The Trappings of the Old West*, Zon International, 1997; Joice Overton, *Cowboy Equipment*, Schiffer Publishing, 1998; Jeffrey B. Snyder, *Stetson Hats and the John B. Stetson Company, 1865–1970*, Schiffer Publishing, 1997.

Periodical: *American Cowboy*, PO Box 6630, Sheridan, WY 82801.

Newsletter: *Cowboy Guide*, PO Box 6459, Santa Fe, NM 87502.

Collectors' Club: Zane Grey's West Society, 708 Warwick Ave, Fort Wayne, IN 46825.

Apron, white cotton, bib style, colorful printed scene of
cowboys at chuck wagon dishing up grub, "Come &
Get It!," 37 x 19" **$20.00**

Ashtray, 2 cow hooves painted black applied to wooden
rect base, metal ashtray on top, brown and white fur
accents, 9 x 7 x 3½" **30.00**

Badge, Sheriff, Lancaster County, NE, eagle top, photo
accompanies with Sheriff Mile Halloway, 1942 . . . . **175.00**

Badge, white metal, star shaped, "Wells Fargo Agent,"
"Tales of Wells Fargo/Overland Prod" and copyright
1958 on reverse, 2¼" h **25.00**

Belt Buckle, brass, oval, 50th Houston Livestock Show &
Rodeo, 1982, 3¾" l **20.00**

Book, *Boots & Saddles*, or *Life in Dakota With General
Custer*, Elizabeth Custer, Norman, 280 pp, University
of Oklahoma Press, map and illus, part of Western
Frontier Library series, 1961, dj **15.00**

Book, *Cowboy Spurs & Their Makers*, Pattie, Jane, 172
pp, hardback, color and black and white photos, dj **20.00**

Book, *Picture Maker of the Old West, William H Jackson*,
Jackson, Clarence S, 308 pp, black and white photos
and illus, ©1947, dj. **20.00**

Book, *Time Life Series, "The Old West,"* series of 13, 200
pp, black and white photos and color illus, includes
"Alaskans," "The Loggers," "Canadians," "Gamblers,"
"Expressmen," "Townsmen," "Chroniclers," "Forty-
Niners," and "Trailblazers" **50.00**

Bottle Opener, cast iron, Mexican sleeping under cactus **50.00**

Catalog, Leroy Shane Novelties, Authentic Western
Merchandise, Indian Craft Hit Toys, 1949, 48 pp **12.00**

Chaps, rodeo cowboy's, red leather body, brown leather
waist belt with small strap and buckle on front, 3
brown leather 4-leaf clovers riveted to each leg near
hip, 3 adjustable straps around each thigh, 1940–50s **125.00**

Cigar Label, Sam Houston Cigars, Houston wearing flat
Texas hat, holding walking stick **8.00**

Coasters, set of 6, Wrangler adv, bucking bronco and
rider illus, 3½" d **125.00**

Comic Book, "Western True Crime," #16, Oct 1948, Fox
Feature Syndicate **25.00**

Poster, cardboard, Cherokee Ranch Rodeo of Oklahoma, appearing in Nazareth, PA, red, yellow, and black on white ground, 14 x 24", $15.00.

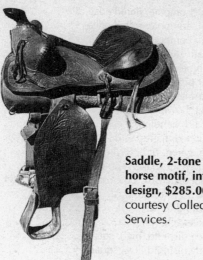

Saddle, 2-tone leather, horse motif, intricate tooled design, $285.00. Photo courtesy Collectors Auction Services.

Figure, cowboy, celluloid, holding gun, yellow shirt, blue pants, red on hat, neckerchief, and chaps, black and silver accents on gun, Japan, 1930s, 6¼" h 50.00

Handkerchief, white cotton, red and brown embroidered scene of cowboy on horse with lasso 15.00

Lamp, ceramic, brown, cowboy on bucking bronco 45.00

Lighter, table, silver plated, figural horse, detailed western-style saddle, lighter insert on horse back, Occupied Japan, 4½" 25.00

Magazine, *Western Stars,* Vol 1, #6, Jul–Sep 1950, western features attributed to writers Rocky Lane, Roy Rogers, Bill Elliott, Smiley Burnette, etc, special sections include John Wayne, Gene Autry, and Roy Rogers, 12 new cowboy movies reviews. 45.00

Mantel Clock, brown toned metal, horse in western saddle standing next to metal clock with raised depiction of cowboy gear at bottom, gray face, black and white numerals, mkd "Lincoln" on front of face, wooden base, 17 x 5 x 11¼" 35.00

Photograph, cowboys roping and branding cattle on prairie, c1920, 6 x 4". 22.00

Photograph, group on horseback descending canyon trail, guide wearing 10-gallon hat and kerchief, black and white, dated 1925, 7 x 5" 10.00

Pinback Button, brass, "Lasso 'Em Bill/California Gold," center picture of young cowboy in hat and chaps holding rope, 1930s, 1¼" d 15.00

Pinback Button, "Jimmy Dean 23rd Annual Tri-State Rodeo," Fort Madison, IA, black lettering on light pink ground, 1970, 2¼" d 20.00

Pinback Button, "Sitting Bull/Old West Trail," aluminum, front portrait, reverse with title printed over head of buffalo, 1960s, 1" d. 15.00

Playing Cards, cowboy riding bucking bronco, red and white ground, Rodeo Awards, Winston Cigarettes adv 20.00

Postcard, scenes from desert Southwest 4.00

Postcard, Texas Centennial Expo 1936, 9 panel fold-out, various Texas landmarks, stamp cancelled 20.00

Postcard Folder, Bronco Busters, Wild West Cowboys Souvenir Folder, full color, 20 panels, unused 18.00

Print, Northern Pacific North Coast, "Montana Roundup," orig shipping tube. 100.00

Program, Tuscon, AZ Rodeo, Feb 1939, illus, folding map, large format, 36 pp 20.00

Program, World Championship Rodeo, Gene Autry photo, 1941 . . . . 10.00

Restaurant China, chili bowl, Tepco Western Traveller, Wells Fargo, 5" d 18.00

Restaurant China, cup and saucer, Wellsville Cowboys 12.00

Restaurant China, fruit bowl, Tepco Western Traveler, Wells Fargo, 4¾" d 15.00

Restaurant China, platter, Tepco Western Traveler, saddle pattern, 13¼" l 150.00

Salt and Pepper Shakers, pr, plastic, horseshoes 10.00

Scrapbook, Southwestern postcards, snapshots, and other travel ephemera, 1940–50s 50.00

Sheet Music, *Home on the Range,* Fuller, Andrew, 1932 . . . . . . 5.00

Sheet Music, *The Utah Trail,* Bob Palmer and Tex Ritter, 1928. . . . . 6.00

Spurs, pr, Tex-Mex style, leather straps stamped in western motif 75.00

Timetable, Nevada Pony Express, 1960 Centennial Re-Run, offset litho, framed, 22 x 14" 75.00

Whip, leather, braided russet color, 9 ft 20.00

WESTMORELAND

Westmoreland, Jeannette, Pennsylvania, traces its history to the East Liverpool Specialty Glass Company and the influence of Major George Irwin. Irwin was instrumental in moving the company from East Liverpool, Ohio, to Jeannette, Pennsylvania, to take advantage of the large natural gas reserves in the area. Specialty Glass, a new Pennsylvania Company, was established in 1888. When the company ran out of money in 1889, Charles H. and George R. West put up $40,000 for 53% of the company's stock. The name was changed to Westmoreland Specialty Company.

Initially Westmoreland made candy containers and a number of other glass containers. In 1910 the company introduced its Keystone line of tableware. Charles West had opposed the move into tableware production, and the brothers split in 1920. George West continued with the Westmoreland Specialty Company, changing its name in 1924 to the Westmoreland Glass Company.

Westmoreland made decorative wares and Colonial-era reproductions, e.g., dolphin pedestal forms, in the 1920s. Color, introduced to the tableware lines in the early 1930s, was virtually gone by the mid-1930s. Amber, black, and ruby were introduced in the 1950s in an attempt to bolster the line.

In 1937 Charles West retired and J. H. Brainard assumed the company's helm. Phillip and Walter Brainard, J. H.'s two sons, joined the firm in 1940. In an effort to cut costs, all cutting and engraving work was eliminated in the 1940s. Grinding and polishing of glass ceased in 1957. No new molds were made until the milk glass surge in the early and mid-1950s.

The milk glass boom was over by 1958. While continuing to produce large quantities of milk glass in the 1960s, Westmoreland expanded its product line to include crystal tableware and colored items. The effort was unsuccessful. Attempts to introduce color into the milk glass line also proved disappointing. The company kept its doors open, albeit barely, by appealing to the bridal trade.

In the search for capital, an on-site gift shop was opened on April 12, 1962. The shop produced a steady cash flow. Shortly after the shop opened, Westmoreland began selling seconds. Another valuable source of cash was found.

By 1980 J. H. Brainard was searching for a buyer for the company. After turning down a proposal from a group of company employees, Brainard sold Westmoreland to David Grossman, a St. Louis–based distributor and importer, best known for his Norman Rockwell Collectibles series. Operations ceased on January 8, 1984. Most of the molds, glass, historic information, catalogs, and furniture were sold at auction.

References: Lorraine Kovar, *Westmoreland Glass, 1950–1984* (1991), *Vol. II* (1991), *Vol. III: 1888–1940* (1998), Antique Publications; Chas West Wilson, *Westmoreland Glass,* Collector Books, 1996, 1998 value update.

Collectors' Clubs: National Westmoreland Glass Collectors Club, PO Box 100, Grapeville, PA 15634; Westmoreland Glass Society, PO Box 2883, Iowa City, IA 52244.

Note: All items are white milk glass unless noted otherwise.

Beaded Edge, plate, blackberry dec, 7" d	$9.00
Beaded Edge, plate, blackberry dec, 10" d	45.00
Beaded Edge, plate, peach dec, 7" d	9.00
Beaded Edge, plate, plain dec, 7" d	30.00
Beaded Edge, plate, plum dec, 7" d	9.00
Beaded Edge, plate, strawberry dec, 7" d	9.00
Beaded Edge, tumbler, ftd, apple dec	15.00
Beaded Edge, tumbler, ftd, peach dec	15.00
Beaded Edge, tumbler, ftd, plain dec	11.00
Beaded Edge, Grape, cup and saucer	10.00
Bud Vase, flowers dec	12.00
Colonial, creamer, flat, laurel green	25.00
Colonial, vase, ftd, green mist	30.00
Della Robbia, bowl, flared, 12" d	47.00
Della Robbia, chocolate box, cov, round	145.00
Della Robbia, compote, ftd, 5"	55.00
Della Robbia, iced tea, ftd	45.00
Della Robbia, sherbet	28.00
Della Robbia, water goblet	35.00
Dolphin, candlesticks, pr, hexagonal base, almond, 9" h	100.00
Dolphin, serving tray, center handle, crystal mist	40.00
Doric, bowl, cupped, ftd, golden sunset, 10" d	28.00
Doric, cake salver, ftd, dark blue mist, 11" l	35.00
English Hobnail, bowl, rolled edge, green, 10¾" d	45.00

English Hobnail, compote, flared edge, 5½"	38.00
English Hobnail, compote, rolled edge, 5"	38.00
English Hobnail, compote, straight edge, 5½"	38.00
English Hobnail, tidbit tray, 2-tier, center handle, brandywine blue	60.00
Figurine, pouter pigeon, apricot mist, 2½" h	25.00
Figurine, pouter pigeon, crystal, 2½" h	25.00
Fruits, punch set, bowl, base, 12 cups, and ladle	275.00
Hobnail, bowl, ftd, handled	20.00
Lotus, bowl, cupped, flame, 9" d	45.00
Lotus, compote, green, 6" h, 8¼" d	40.00
Lotus, salt and pepper shakers, pr, pink	35.00
Maple Leaf, chocolate box, cov, round, flat blue pastel, 3¾" h, 6½" d	30.00
Old Quilt, bowl, ftd, 6" d	18.00
Old Quilt, candlesticks, pr, 4" h	20.00
Old Quilt, candy dish, ftd, high, square	27.00
Old Quilt, candy dish, ftd, low, square	22.00
Old Quilt, cheese dish, cov, round	45.00
Old Quilt, cigarette box, cov, 5 x 4"	35.00
Old Quilt, cruet with stopper	25.00
Old Quilt, iced tea, 5¼" h	16.00
Old Quilt, pitcher, flat, 8" h	32.00
Old Quilt, sugar, cov, 6½" h	25.00
Old Quilt, tumbler, ftd, 4¼" h	10.00
Paneled Grape, ashtray, large	18.00
Paneled Grape, banana bowl, ftd	235.00
Paneled Grape, basket, handled, oval, 6" l	20.00
Paneled Grape, bowl, lipped, 10" d	77.00
Paneled Grape, bowl, ruffled	24.00
Paneled Grape, butter, cov, ¼ lb	30.00
Paneled Grape, cake plate, pedestal	85.00
Paneled Grape, cake salver, brandywine blue	100.00
Paneled Grape, candlesticks, pr, 4" h	22.00
Paneled Grape, chocolate box, round	50.00
Paneled Grape, compote	60.00
Paneled Grape, cup	8.00
Paneled Grape, cup and saucer	30.00
Paneled Grape, goblet	14.00
Paneled Grape, gravy boat with liner	70.00
Paneled Grape, iced tea, flat, 6" h	25.00
Paneled Grape, jug, 1 qt	19.00
Paneled Grape, mayonnaise, 3 pc, crystal	35.00
Paneled Grape, pitcher, 1 pt	42.00
Paneled Grape, pitcher, 1 qt	40.00
Paneled Grape, pitcher, 7¾" h	32.00
Paneled Grape, pitcher, 8½" h	35.00
Paneled Grape, planter, 3 x 9"	60.00
Paneled Grape, planter, 5 x 9"	19.00
Paneled Grape, rose bud vase, 18" h	50.00
Paneled Grape, salt and pepper shakers, pr	25.00
Paneled Grape, shakers, pr, ftd	25.00
Paneled Grape, sugar, cov, ftd, spoon holder	40.00
Paneled Grape, toothpick holder	30.00
Paneled Grape, vase, pulled, 14" h	55.00
Paneled Grape, wine goblet	20.00
Princess Feather, salt, amber	25.00
Waterford, bonbon, heart shaped, 8"	58.00
Waterford, bowl, flat, 10" d	75.00
Waterford, cake plate, 2 handles, pink	17.00
Waterford, cake salver, low	85.00
Waterford, compote, 5½"	60.00
Waterford, relish set, forest green	35.00
Waterford, saucer, pink	6.00

Paneled Grape, creamer and open sugar, $20.00.

WHEATON

Wheaton Glass, a division of Wheaton Industries, Millville, New Jersey, manufactured commemorative bottles, decanters, and flasks between 1967 and 1974. Series included American Military Leaders (1974), Christmas, Great Americans (1969), Movie Stars, Patriots (1972), Presidential (1969), and Space. Wheaton bottles were sold by franchised dealers, at Grandma Wheaton's Shop (Millville), and through mail order (Collectors Guild and Bathsheba's Bottle Book).

Wheaton Industries assigned production to the Wheaton Historical Association in 1974. Series production continued from 1975 to 1982. Editions were limited, approximately 5,000 bottles, and made on a semi-automatic bottle making machine rather than the fully automated equipment employed by Wheaton Industries. The Millville Art Glass Co. obtained a licensing agreement from the Wheaton Historical Association and added a few new bottles to the Christmas and Presidential series.

In 1996 Wheaton Glass was sold and renamed Lawson-Mardon-Wheaton.

Wheaton Glass also manufactured copycats (stylistic copies) of 19th-century bottles and flasks between 1971 and 1974. Most were marked "Nuline," "W," or "Wheaton, NJ" on the base. Amber, amethyst, blue, green, milk, and ruby were the colors used.

Reference: Lois Clark, *Wheaton's,* published by author, 1998.

Collectors' Club: Classic Wheaton Club, PO Box 59, Downingtown, PA 19335.

Special Commemoratives, Spirit of 76, iridescent topaz, $30.00.

Americana Antique Bottles, Franklin Glass House, pink..... **$20.00**
Americana Antique Bottles, Liberty Bell, amber **25.00**
Americana Inkwells, Daniel Webster's Recorder Ink, ruby **50.00**
Americana Inkwells, Tuckahoe Country 1891 School, avocado **25.00**
Americana Miniatures, Liberty Bell, aqua **20.00**
Americana Miniatures, RIP Casket, poison bottle, green **16.00**
Americana Mugs, The Mayflower/Plymouth Rock, topaz **10.00**
Astronauts Decanter, Apollo 12, iridescent ruby **35.00**
Astronauts Decanter, Apollo 14, iridescent blue **8.00**
Astronauts Decanter, Skylab II, clear frosted **20.00**
Astronauts Plate, Apollo 15, clear **25.00**
Astronauts Plate, Skylab I, amber **16.00**
Bank, Coal Stove, ruby **45.00**
Bank, Uncle Sam, blue **40.00**
Campaign Decanter, Democrat 1968, Humphrey/ Muskie, donkey, green........................... **16.00**
Campaign Decanter, Democrat 1972, McGovern/ Shriver, donkey, topaz **16.00**
Campaign Decanter, Democrat 1972, McGovern/ Shriver, reversed portraits, donkey, topaz **80.00**
Campaign Decanter, Republican 1972, Nixon/Agnew, elephant, amethyst **14.00**
Christmas Decanter, Christmas Holly, 1973, ruby **20.00**
Christmas Decanter, Christmas Tree Balls, 1983, light blue **30.00**
Christmas Decanter, Snow Flake, 1980, ice blue.......... **25.00**
Colonial Antique Series, Dr Fisher's Bitters Bottle, green **25.00**
Colonial Antique Series, Eight-Sided Elixir Tonic Bottle, cobalt.. **40.00**
Colonial Antique Series, Skull Poison Bottle, amethyst **40.00**

Colonial Jars, Army Drum/Finley's Volunteer, pink.......... **30.00**
Colonial Jars, Cape May Bitters/Lighthouse, blue **20.00**
Commemorative Plate, Betsy Ross, blue................. **16.00**
Commemorative Plate, Frank H Wheaton Sr. Centennial Birthday, blue **20.00**
Custom Flask, Cornucopia/Wheaton Village, green **30.00**
Custom Flask, General Lafayette/Liberty and Union Anchor, topaz **16.00**
Custom Flask, Wheat/Paddleboat, blue.................. **16.00**
Custom Flask, Wm H Harrison/Log Cabin, green **14.00**
Evangelist Decanter, St John, iridescent amethyst **25.00**
Great Americans Decanter, Charles Hughes, iridescent blue **16.00**
Great Americans Decanter, George Patton, iridescent blue **14.00**
Great Americans Decanter, Martin Luther King, irides- cent topaz **12.00**
Great Americans Decanter, Reverend Billy Graham, iri- descent green **10.00**
Great Americans Decanter, Thomas Edison, cobalt **14.00**
Hollywood Star Decanter, WC Fields, aqua **35.00**
Presidential Decanter, George Washington, clear **25.00**
Presidential Decanter, James Monroe, iridescent topaz **75.00**
Presidential Decanter, Jimmy Carter, iridescent blue **20.00**
Presidential Decanter, John Tyler, light amber **60.00**
Presidential Decanter, Thomas Jefferson, ruby **25.00**
Presidential Mini Decanter, Herbert Hoover, iridescent aqua.. **12.00**
Presidential Mini Decanter, James Garfield, iridescent amethyst **12.00**
Presidential Mini Decanter, Martin Van Buren, iridescent green **4.00**
Presidential Mini Decanter, Theodore Roosevelt, irides- cent green... **20.00**
Presidential Mini Decanter, William Taft, iridescent amethyst **7.00**
Presidential Plate, Abraham Lincoln, black............... **20.00**
Presidential Plate, Abraham Lincoln, blue................ **16.00**
Presidential Plate, John Kennedy, black................. **60.00**
Presidential Plate, John Kennedy, blue **25.00**
Special Commemoratives, Mother's Day decanter, frosted..... **16.00**
Special Commemoratives, Violin bottle, scroll stopper, clear.. **20.00**

WHISKEY BOTTLES, COLLECTIBLE

This market has fallen on hard times. The speculative bubble burst in the mid-1980s. Prices did not stabilize, they totally collapsed for most examples. Most manufacturers, distributors, and collectors' clubs have disappeared. Today more bottles are purchased for their crossover theme than they are for their importance as collectors' special editions whiskey bottles. Although often priced higher by sellers, the vast majority of bottles sell for less than $10, if a buyer can be found at all.

The Jim Beam Distillery offered its first set of novelty (collectors' special edition) bottles during the 1953 Christmas season. Over a hundred other distillers followed suit.

The early 1970s was the golden age of collectors' special edition whiskey bottles. Several distillers offered miniature series. By the late 1970s the market was saturated. Most distillers returned to the basic bottle package.

The argument still rages as to whether or not a bottle is worth more with its seal unbroken. Check the liquor laws in your state. Most states strictly prohibit selling liquor without a license. Value has always centered on the theme of the bottle. The liquor inside has never affected value. As a result, an empty bottle has the same value as a full one.

References: Ralph and Terry Kovel, *The Kovels' Bottle Price List, Eleventh Edition,* Crown Publishers, 1999; Jim Megura, *The Official Price Guide to Bottles, Twelfth Edition,* House of Collectibles, 1997; Michael Polak, *Bottles: Identification and Price Guide, Second Edition,* Avon Books, 1997.

Collectors' Clubs: International Assoc of Jim Beam Bottle & Specialties Club, 2015 Burlington Ave, Kewanee, IL 61443; National Ski Country Bottle Club, 1224 Washington Ave, Golden, CO 80401.

Ballantine, Golf Bag	**$5.00**
Ballantine, Old Crow Chessman	5.00
Ballantine, Seated Fisherman	8.00
Ballantine, Zebra	10.00
Ezra Brooks, Bighorn Ram, 1973	15.00
Ezra Brooks, Bowler, 1973	8.00
Ezra Brooks, Clown with Balloon, 1973	20.00
Ezra Brooks, Elk, 1973	25.00
Ezra Brooks, Florida Gators, 1973	10.00
Ezra Brooks, Hereford, 1971	12.00
Ezra Brooks, North Carolina Bicentennial, 1975	10.00
Ezra Brooks, Queen of Hearts, 1969	5.00
Ezra Brooks, Western Rodeos, 1973	15.00
Garnier, Baltimore Oriole, 1970, 11" h	10.00
Garnier, Christmas Tree, 1956, 11½" h	50.00
Garnier, Rooster, 1952, 12" h	15.00
Jim Beam, Alaska, star shaped, Regal China, 1928, 9½" h	40.00
Jim Beam, Antique Telephone	45.00
Jim Beam, Baseball, 1969	20.00
Jim Beam, Blue Cherub Executive, Regal China, 1960, 12½" h	50.00
Jim Beam, Bohemian Girl, 1974, Regal China, 14½" h	10.00
Jim Beam, Charlie McCarthy, 1976	18.00
Jim Beam, Delco Freedom Battery, 1978, plastic top	20.00
Jim Beam, Grant Locomotive, 1979, 9" h	45.00
Jim Beam, Harolds Club—Nevada, 1964, silver	100.00
Jim Beam, Kentucky Black Head, Regal China, 1967, 11½" h	10.00

Jim Beam, Corvette Stingray, 1963, 12½" l, $28.00. Photo courtesy Collectors Auction Services.

Jim Beam, Nebraska, 1967, 12¼" h	**5.00**
Jim Beam, Preakness, Regal China, 1970, 11" h	5.00
JW Dant, California Quail	5.00
JW Dant, Eagle	4.00
JW Dant, Mountain Quail	4.00
JW Dant, Prairie Chicken	3.00
JW Dant, San Diego	4.00
Luxardo, Alabaster Goose, 1960–68	15.00
Luxardo, Cherry Basket, 1960	10.00
Luxardo, Dragon Pitcher, 1958	8.00
Luxardo, Sudan, 1960, 13½" h	8.00
McCormick, Barrel, Barrel series, 1968	15.00
McCormick, Pony Express, Car series	40.00
McCormick, Tom T Hall, Country and Western series, 1980	30.00
Old Fitzgerald, Hillbilly, 1954, pt, 9⅛" h	10.00
Old Fitzgerald, Man O' War Decanter, 1969	4.00
Old Fitzgerald, Ohio State Centennial, 1970	10.00
Ski Country, Blackbird, Bird series	35.00
Ski Country, Scrooge, Christmas series	30.00
Ski Country, Skunk Family, Animal series	25.00

WHITMAN TV BOOKS

The Whitman Publishing Company is a subsidiary of the Western Printing & Lithographing Company. Organized initially to bail out a failed business customer, the Whitman Publishing Company produced 200 items by 1929 in quantities consisting of 14 million books and 1.5 million games. By 1957 sales had reached $80 million. The company had plants in Hannibal (Missouri), Mount Morris (Illinois), Poughkeepsie (New York), Racine (Wisconsin), and St. Louis (Missouri).

This category is devoted to 8" books designated as 50¢ juveniles and specifically those authorized versions associated with television shows from the 1950s to the 1970s. Although laminated photographic covers became the norm in the mid-1950s, it is possible to find some titles with a plain cover. Be alert to later printings with different cover artwork.

Peeling lamination, split spines, darkened paper, and faded cover colors are common condition problems. Finding examples in excellent condition or better is difficult.

Whitman's success spawned imitators. A. L. Burt Company, M. A. Donahue & Company, Goldsmith Publishing, Grosset & Dunlap, Saalfied Publishing, and Triangle Books are just a few.

Reference: David and Virginia Brown, *Whitman Juvenile Books,* Collector Books, 1997.

Annie Oakley in Danger at Diablo, #1540:49, 282 pp,
1955. . . . . $35.00
Bat Masterson, #1550, 282 pp, 1960 . . . . 25.00
Beverly Hillbillies, The Saga of Wildcat Creek, #1572,
212 pp, 1963 . . . . 15.00
Bewitched, The Opposite Uncle, #1572, 212 pp, 1970. . . . . . 30.00
Big Valley, #1569, 214 pp, 1966 . . . . 32.00
Bonanza, Killer Lion, #1568, 212 pp, 1966. . . . . 25.00
Circus Boy Under the Big Top, #1549, 282 pp, 1957 . . . . . . 40.00
Combat, The Counterattack, #1520, 210 pp, 1964 . . . . 25.00
Dr Kildare, The Magic Key, #1519, 210 pp, 1964 . . . . 20.00
Family Affair, Buffy Finds a Star, #1567, 140 pp, 1970. . . . . 25.00
Flipper, The Mystery of the Black Schooner, #2324,
190 pp, 1966 . . . . 12.00
Fury and the Mystery at Trapper's Hole, #1557, 282 pp,
1959. . . . . 28.00
Garrison's Gorillas and the Fear Formula, #1548, 210 pp,
1968. . . . . 25.00
Gilligan's Island, #1566, 212 pp, 1966 . . . . 28.00
Hawaii Five-O, The Octopus Caper, #1553, 212 pp,
1971. . . . . 20.00
Ironside, The Picture Frame Frame-Up, #1521, 212 pp,
1969. . . . . 18.00
I Spy, Message From Moscow, #1542, 210 pp, 1966. . . . . . 35.00
Janet Lennon at Camp Calamity, #1539, 212 pp, 1962 . . . . 25.00
Land of the Giants, Flight of Fear, #1516, 212 pp, 1969. . . . 30.00
Lassie, Forbidden Valley, #1508, 282 pp, 1959 . . . . 12.00
Lennon Sisters, The ?Secret of Holiday Island, #1544,
282 pp, 1960 . . . . 10.00
Lucy and the Madcap Mystery, #1505, 210 pp, 1963 . . . . . 45.00
Man From U.N.C.L.E., The Affair of the Gunrunner"s
Gold, #1543, 212 pp, 1967 . . . . 20.00
Maverick, #1566, 282 pp, 1959. . . . . 30.00
Mission: Impossible, The Priceless Particle, #1515,
212 pp, 1969 . . . . 15.00
Mod Squad, Assignment: The Arranger, #1538, 210 pp,
1969. . . . . 20.00
Munsters, The Last Resort, #1567, 214 pp, 1966. . . . . 35.00
Patty Duke and Mystery Mansion, #1514, 212 pp, 1964 . . . . 30.00

Real McCoys and Danger at the Ranch, #1577, 212 pp,
1961. . . . . 25.00
Rebel, #1548, 212 pp, ©1961 . . . . 30.00
Restless Gun, #1559, 282 pp, 1959 . . . . 35.00
Rifleman, #1569, 282 pp, 1959 . . . . 40.00
Rin Tin Tin and Call to Danger, #1539, 282 pp, 1957 . . . . . 28.00
Sea Hunt, #1541, 210 pp, 1960. . . . . 35.00
Star Trek Mission to Horatius, #1549, 210 pp, 1968 . . . . . . 65.00
Voyage to the Bottom of the Sea, #1517, 212 pp, 1965. . . . . 38.00
Wagon Train, #1567, 282 pp, 1959 . . . . 25.00

WICKER

Wicker is a generic term used to describe woven objects made from cane, fiber, dried grasses, rattan, reed, rush, or willow. Wicker as a term was not used until the early 20th century. While most individuals think of wicker primarily in terms of furniture, it was used for a wide range of materials from baskets to window boxes.

Wakefield and Heywood were fierce competitors in the wicker furniture market through the 1870s, 80s, and 90s. In 1897 the two firms merged, creating the Heywood Brothers and Wakefield Company. The company had a virtual monopoly on the wicker furniture market until the 1920s.

In 1917 Marshall B. Lloyd of Menominee, Michigan, invented a machine that twisted chemically treated paper that in turn could be woven by his Lloyd loom. Lloyd's art fiber furniture featuring a closely woven style gained rapid acceptance. In 1921 Heywood Brothers and Wakefield Company, now officially Heywood-Wakefield, purchased Lloyd Manufacturing.

Collectors have little interest in post-1930 wicker. Its only value is as secondhand furniture. Use form (coffee tables and end tables) and weave (loosely woven) to identify post-1930 wicker.

Reference: Tim Scott, *Fine Wicker Furniture: 1870–1930*, Schiffer Publishing, 1990.

Arm Chair, plain tight weave, barrel shaped, rounded
back continuing to sides, braided edges, upholstered
slip seat cushion, slightly arched apron, wrapped feet,
unpainted, 31" h, 23" w $150.00
Bench, white, hoop back, rolled crest rail continuing to
down-curving armrests, very ornate open work
curlicue heart design in back, sides, and apron, tight
weave oblong seat, cabriole legs, X-form stretcher,
1950s, 33" h, 57" w. 350.00
Birdcage Stand, white, tight weave, quarter moon
shaped cage holder raised on wrapped pole standard,
conical base, 74" h 175.00
Cabana Chair, white, int floral upholstery 600.00
Candlestick Holders, natural, 5" h 75.00
Chair, natural, rolled arms, multicolored diamond pat-
tern on back 360.00
Changing Table, white, 3-tiers of wooden shelves, gal-
leried edges, loss to leg wrappings, repainted,
1910–30, 38" h, 36" w, 19½" d 300.00
Child's Rocking Chair, white, tight weave, barrel shaped,
rolled arms, upholstered slip cushion, long skirt,
1910–25, 22" h, 20" w. 175.00
Coat Rack, child's, white, tight weave base, gessoed
roses on base and pole, wooden hooks, 28" h 250.00
Cradle, white, open weave design, cushioned bottom,
crescent lattice work under cradle, ball feet 800.00

*Have Gun, Will
Travel, #1568,
282 pp, 1959,
$35.00.*

Carriage, painted beige, c1930, $150.00.

Crib, white, open weave, fancywork on headboard and
footboard, wrapped legs **650.00**
Desk, white, 2 woven shelves on each side **455.00**
Desk and Chair, white, wooden top, woven seat. **300.00**
Fernery, white, 2 tight weave handles. **240.00**
Floor Lamp, natural, dark stained circular design on
base, brass finial **325.00**
Footstool, white, tight weave sides, upholstered cushion
in recessed rect top with braided edge, out wrapped
curving legs with curlicue brackets, 8" h, 14½" w **125.00**
Hanging Planter, white, figural swan **50.00**
Hanging Planter, white, low center well, sides rising up
and over, 67" h, 31" w, 11" d **250.00**
Inkwell Holder, green, scalloped reed trim, wooden base . . . **175.00**
Lounge Chair, Bar Harbor, white, close weave seat, flat
woven arms, footrest, and ball feet **600.00**
Lounge Chair, natural, tight weave, flat woven arms with
spaces for drinks and magazines, adjustable ottoman
with footrest, blue cushions **500.00**
Loveseat, white, open weave, green floral cushions and
backrest, ball feet **450.00**
Night Stand, white, lift-off shelf reveals bottom hamper,
machine made **200.00**
Planter, natural, tightly woven design, wrapped legs **185.00**
Rocking Chair, white, closely woven seat, braided open
work. **350.00**
Rocking Chair, white, manmade, tight weave back, cen-
tral diamond over X-shape design, demi arms, trapezoidal seat with upholstered seat cushion, straight
skirt front and sides, X-form stretcher with brackets,
31" h, 17" w **150.00**
Rocking Chair, white, orig tie-on back pad and seat
cushion, hand-woven reed seat **350.00**
Sewing Basket, orange, close weave, diamond pattern
on front, wooden shelf, scrollwork on wrapped legs,
hinged lid **200.00**
Sewing Basket, white, close weave, pink fabric on
hinged lid **200.00**
Sewing Basket, white, wrapped circular handles, ball
feet. **175.00**
Smoking Stand, white, 2-tier, cane wrapped supports **200.00**
Sofa, natural rattan, floral cushions **500.00**

Sofa, white, close weave, blue patterned cushions, ball
feet, inner springs in seat **500.00**
Table, white, round, woven bottom shelf, circular woven
top, wrapped legs **300.00**
Table Lamp, natural, orig silk fringe **200.00**
Tea Cart, light blue, tight weave design, leaf pattern on
sides, woven shelf, wrapped legs, lift-out tray **600.00**
Telephone Chair, white, tight weave design, oak side
shelf, storage shelf below **675.00**

WILLOW WARE

Willow ware is a pattern based upon a Chinese legend. A wealthy
father wished his daughter to marry a man he had chosen. Instead,
she ran off with a young lover. The couple was pursued by a group
of assassins (or the father or jilted bridegroom-to-be, depending on
who you believe). They escaped to a pagoda on an island. The
gods took pity and turned them into a pair of turtle doves so they
could be together forever. This story provides the key decorative
elements of the Willow pattern—a willow tree, two pagodas (one
for the father, the other on the island for the lovers), a fence, three
individuals crossing a bridge to the island, and two birds.

As early as the 1830s, over 200 British pottery manufacturers
made pieces featuring a variation of the Willow pattern. By 1900
American, Dutch, French, German, Irish, and Swedish ceramic
manufacturers had copied the pattern. The Japanese also copied
the Willow pattern. It was one of the most popular patterns made
during the "Occupied Japan" period.

Although found primarily in blue, Willow ware also was produced in black, brown, green, mulberry, pink, red, and polychrome. Collectors prefer blue. As a result, harder-to-find colors
often sell for less. Manufacturer is the key to value. Collectors
place a premium on ware made by manufacturers with a reputation for quality.

References: Leslie Bockol, *Willow Ware,* Schiffer Publishing, 1995;
Mary Frank Gaston, *Blue Willow, Revised Second Edition,*
Collector Books, 1990, 1998 value update.

Collectors' Club: International Willow Collectors, PO Box 13382,
Arlington, TX 76094.

REPRODUCTION ALERT: The Scio Pottery, located in Scio, Ohio,
is currently producing a Willow pattern. These poor-quality pieces
are unmarked. A wall plaque (plate) made in China is also being
produced. It is marked "BLUE WILLOW" and impressed "Made in
China."

Note: Pieces listed are blue unless noted otherwise. See Children's
Dishes for additional listings.

Churchill China, bread and butter plate **$3.00**
Churchill China, butter, cov, ¼ lb **15.00**
Churchill China, cereal bowl, 6" d. **4.00**
Churchill China, coffeepot, cov **25.00**
Churchill China, cup and saucer, flat, 2½" **5.00**
Churchill China, dinner plate, 10⅜" d **4.00**
Churchill China, gravy boat. **15.00**
Churchill China, mug, 4¼" h **4.00**
Churchill China, platter, oval, 14½" l **25.00**
Churchill China, salad plate, 8⅛" d **4.00**
Churchill China, salt and pepper shakers, pr. **10.00**

Churchill China, soup bowl, 8" d 5.00
Churchill China, vegetable bowl, round, 8⅞" d 8.00
England, bread and butter plate, 6¼" d 5.00
England, flat soup 18.00
England, platter, 12 x 15" 75.00
England, platter, rect, 9½ x 11½" 60.00
England, salad plate 13.00
England, saucer 1.50
England, vegetable bowl, sq 25.00
Homer Laughlin, platter, oval, 10 x 13" 35.00
Japan, ashtray, 7½" sq 30.00
Japan, bank, stacked pig, 7" h 40.00
Japan, bowl, stacked set of 3 . . . . 175.00
Japan, bread and butter plate, 6" d 5.00
Japan, chop plate 40.00
Japan, condiment set insert 40.00
Japan, creamer 15.00
Japan, cup, 5½" h, 8½" d 70.00
Japan, demitasse cup and saucer 15.00
Japan, double eggcup, 3¾" h 25.00
Japan, plate, pink, 9¾" d 20.00
Japan, reamer, 6" h, 7" w 200.00
Japan, sugar shaker, 5" h 70.00
Japan, syrup, 6" h 100.00
Japan, teacup and saucer, red 15.00
Johnson Brothers, augratin, 8⅞" d 15.00
Johnson Brothers, baker, 10¾" d 30.00
Johnson Brothers, bread and butter plate, 6½" d 4.00
Johnson Brothers, cake plate and server 25.00
Johnson Brothers, cereal bowl 6.00
Johnson Brothers, coffeepot, cov 35.00
Johnson Brothers, creamer 12.00
Johnson Brothers, cup and saucer 10.00
Johnson Brothers, dinner plate, 10" d 9.00
Johnson Brothers, pie server, stainless steel blade 10.00
Johnson Brothers, platter, 12" l 20.00
Johnson Brothers, soup bowl, flat, 8⅛" d 5.00
Johnson Brothers, sugar, cov 15.00
Johnson Brothers, teapot, cov 30.00
Johnson Brothers, vegetable bowl, oval 30.00
Johnson Brothers, vegetable bowl, round 20.00
Meakin, dinner plate, variant pattern, green 25.00
Meakin, salad plate, variant pattern, green 15.00
Morley-Fox, pitcher, multicolored, 10" h 100.00
Occupied Japan, cup and saucer, polychrome variant
   pattern 30.00
Ridgway, platter, sq, 10 x 13" 70.00
Royal China, chop plate 30.00
Royal China, plate, 10½" d 15.00
Royal China, soup bowl, 4 pcs 15.00
Royal Doulton, Real Old Willow, Majestic, bread and
   butter plate, 7" d 10.00
Royal Doulton, Real Old Willow, Majestic, cup and
   saucer, flat, 2⅝" 20.00
Royal Doulton, Real Old Willow, Majestic, dinner plate,
   10½" d 20.00
Royal Doulton, Real Old Willow, Majestic, gravy boat
   and underplate 90.00
Royal Doulton, Real Old Willow, Majestic, platter, oval,
   13⅜" l 80.00
Royal Doulton, Real Old Willow, Majestic, salad plate,
   8½" d 15.00
Royal Doulton, Real Old Willow, Majestic, sugar, cov 70.00

Grimwades, platter, mkd "Ye Olde Willow" above circle with "UHP" (Upper Hanley Pottery) within 6-pointed star surrounded by "Grimwades, Staffordshire, England," 10¼" l, $25.00.

Royal Doulton, Real Old Willow, Majestic, tureen 135.00
Royal Doulton, Real Old Willow, Majestic, vegetable
   bowl, oval, 10⅜" l 60.00
Shenango China, cereal bowl 15.00
Shenango China, dessert bowl 15.00
Shenango China, gravy boat, 6" l 45.00
Shenango China, plate, Canton pattern, 10½" d 50.00
Unmarked, handleless cup and saucer, pink 65.00
Unmarked, ladle, pattern in bowl 120.00
Unmarked, mustard pot, barrel shaped, 2½" h 65.00
Unmarked, pie plate 40.00
Unmarked, salad fork and spoon, 11¼" l 150.00
Unmarked, spice set, wood rack 150.00
Unmarked, tureen 100.00
Unmarked, vegetable bowl 20.00
USA, mug, 3¾" h 10.00
USA, stack cups 3.00

WORLD'S FAIRS & EXPOSITIONS

The 1851 London Crystal Palace Exhibition is considered the first modern World's Fair. America's first was the 1853 New York Crystal Palace Exhibition featuring 4,685 exhibitions, approximately half of which were from the United States. Several World's Fairs were held each decade during the 19th century. In 1928 an international convention was called to regulate the scheduling and method of conducting World's Fairs. Thirty-nine nations signed a Paris agreement creating the Bureau of International Expositions to limit the frequency of World's Fairs and define the rights and obligations of organizers and participants. The Bureau meets biannually.

World's Fairs divide into two basic types: (1) universal and (2) special category. The 1939/40 New York World's Fair and the 1967 Montreal Expo are examples of universal World's Fairs. Spokane's 1974 Expo and Transpo '86 in Vancouver were special category World's Fairs. BIF rules stipulate that one universal fair can be held every ten years, special category fairs can be held every two years but in different countries.

References: Joyce Grant, *NY World's Fair Collectibles: 1964–1965,* Schiffer Publishing, 1999; Howard M. Rossen, *World's Fair Collectibles: Chicago, 1933 and New York, 1939,* Schiffer Publishing, 1998.

Periodical: *World's Fair,* PO Box 339, Corte Madera, CA 94976.

Collectors' Club: World's Fair Collectors' Society, PO Box 20806, Sarasota, FL 34276.

1926, Sesquicentennial, pennant, felt, Independence Hall, Liberty Bell, and flags, "Sesquicentennial International Exposition 1776–1926," © I Rudolph, 11 x 34" **$25.00**

1926, Sesquicentennial, postcard, "Greetings to you from Philadelphia, The Sesqui Centennial," Liberty Bell, garland, and shields, divided back with blue Sesqui Centennial seal, unused **18.00**

1926, Sesquicentennial, poster, Miss Liberty embracing nationality flags above distant view of Philadelphia, "America Welcomes The World," Dan Smith, ©Elliott Brewer, 17½ x 26½" **50.00**

1926, Sesquicentennial, tape measure, celluloid, Independence Hall and Liberty Bell flanked by flags, "The Sesqui-Centennial International Exposition Philadelphia 1776–1926 One Hundred And Fifty Years Of American Independence" **50.00**

1933, Chicago, newspaper, Sinclair Refining Co, "Chicago's World's Fair Edition/Big News, Second Edition," 8 pp, green and white print, 14 greentone photos from dinosaur exhibit, 8¼ x 11" folded size **25.00**

1933, Chicago, parasol, rice paper and wood, bamboo struts, wooden rod handle mkd "Chicago 1933," Japan, 21" d open size **50.00**

1933, Chicago, pennant, red felt, yellow-gold design, "A Century of Progress" in white lettering, Fluted Towers, Adler Planetarium, and Sky Ride scenes, 11 x 28" **25.00**

1933, Chicago, pocket watch and fob, silvered brass, inscribed "Chicago World's Fair 1833–1933," Fort Dearborn building on face, engraved Fort Dearborn against cloud and Chicago skyline ground on back, brass fob with Expo tower and searchlight inscribed "Century of Progress 1833–1933" **200.00**

1933, Chicago, record brush, celluloid, black, white, and silver, "1933/A Century of Progress/Chicago" symbol, Hall of Science, Travel and Transport Building, Administration Building, and Electrical Building, 3½" d **45.00**

1933, Chicago, salt and pepper shakers, pr, silver luster over white metal, "Travel and Transport Building Chicago World's Fair 1933–1934," Federal Building, Hall of Science, and Illinois Host House relief images, mkd "N. Shure Co. Chicago Made In Japan," cork stoppers, 3¼" h **50.00**

1933, Chicago, salt shaker, clear glass, figural beer stein, foil sticker, cork stopper, 2½" h, 1¾" d **25.00**

1936, Great Lakes Expo, lighter, silvered metal, black and white paper wrapper with "Terminal Tower" picture under clear celluloid, 4" h, 1¼" d **75.00**

1936, Texas Centennial, drinking glass, clear, dark blue official seal, reverse with dark blue cowboy on rearing horse, 3½" h **28.00**

1936, Texas Centennial, pinback button, red, white, and blue, longhorn steer symbol on red star inscribed "Texas Centennial 1836–1936" **8.00**

1936, Texas Centennial, postcard, Ford Exposition Building, brief description on reverse, 3½ x 5½" **5.00**

1939, California, comb, plastic, amber, emb goldtone metal case with center brass medallion, pocket size **35.00**

1939, New York, book, *A Guide to Medical and Public Health Exhibits at the New York World's Fair 1939, Together with Information on the Conservation of Health and the Preservation of Life,"* 96 pp, black and white photos, hardcover, 6¾ x 10" **50.00**

1939, New York, bud vase, china, hp scene and "New York World's Fair," solid blue back, Japan, 4¾" h, 2½" d **75.00**

1939, New York, employee cap, dark blue felt garrison cap, inked in orange on both sides, orange fabric piping around bottom, 5 x 11½" **75.00**

1939, New York, newspaper, *Today at the Fair,* Wed, Aug 9, 1939, #99, 8 pp, "Official Daily Program and World's Fair News," 8½ x 12" folded size **50.00**

1939, New York, paperweight, metal, figural Trylon and Perisphere, inscribed "New York, Trylon-Perisphere, World's Fair," 4½" h **50.00**

1939, New York, plate, white china, shades of maroon border design include portrait of George Washington at top center leading both ways to images of 6 exhibit buildings, J&G Meakin, England, 10½" d **100.00**

1939, New York, pocket mirror, glass panels with black and white insert photo of 2 embracing gentlemen, stylized image of Federal Building in blue and silver on orange ground, 2¼ x 3¼" **50.00**

1939, New York, poster, "New York World's Fair," art by Atherton, published by Grinnell Litho Co, 7 x 10½" **100.00**

1939, New York, program, "Billy Rose's Aquacade," 32 pp, Eleanor Holm and Johnny Weissmuller centerfold, 8½ x 12" **25.00**

1939, New York, salt and pepper shakers, pr, silver luster finish, 4" h Trylon pepper, 2" h Perisphere salt, cork stoppers, mkd "J.B." with NYWF copyright symbol **75.00**

1939, New York, scarf, blue fabric, yellow border, 10 exhibit buildings plus Trylon and Perisphere, 19 x 20½" **50.00**

1939, New York, tape measure, enameled metal, orange egg topped by miniature metal insect fly pull, fabric tape, 2½" h, 1¾" d **100.00**

1964–65, New York World's Fair, tray, litho metal, 7⅞" l, $25.00.

1939, New York, timetable, Greyhound NYC transit, "Around the Grounds" **10.00**

1939, New York, tray, tin, silver flashing on floral border, Constitutional Mall, Trylon and Perisphere, and surrounding landscaping, "New York World's Fair 1939" with copyright, made in Japan, 3½ x 5" **25.00**

1940, New York, bank, white metal, replica typewriter, black and gray, white lettering "Underwood New York World's Fair 1940" and Trylon and Perisphere images, National Products Corp, Chicago, 2½ x 2¾ x 1¼" **100.00**

1940, New York, School Admission Ticket Booklet, 5 of orig 10 perforated admission tickets to fair authorized for school student use, 2¼ x 3¾" **25.00**

1940, New York, wallet, dark blue fabric over cardboard, identification card panel, admission ticket tablet, typewritten user's name above "Schaefer Center" and "4/24," 3¼ x 5" closed size **25.00**

1962, Seattle, snow dome, "Space Needle," plastic, Mt Rainier background, 3¼" h **50.00**

1964–65, New York, ashtray, figural Unisphere, painted bisque, 4½" h, 3½" d pedestal base **50.00**

1964–65, New York, brochure, "Progressland," 12-pp GE's Walt Disney Presentation demonstrating role of electricity in progress of man, full color illus, 9 x 12" **25.00**

1964–65, New York, card game, "Official 1964–65 New York World's Fair Children's Card Game," complete with 36 cards, illus of various exhibits, orig box with instructions, Ed-U-Cards **25.00**

1964–65, New York, drinking glass, clear, black and gold art and inscriptions, "New York Central System" above "Route To The World's Fair," streamline engine and passenger car around lower perimeter, 4½" h, 2¾" d **25.00**

1964–65, New York, oversized pencil, wooden, orange with blue and silver Electric Power and Light Building, Solar Fountain, Unisphere, Swiss Sky Ride, and General Motors Building, Japan, 10½" l, ½" d **25.00**

1964–65, New York, paper doll book, "Dress Up for the New York World's Fair," Peter and Wendy punch-out dolls, ethnic costumes, punch-out standup Unisphere and NYWF Twins, Spertus Pub Co, 10 x 14" **25.00**

1964–65, New York, record album, *Musical Memories*, 33⅓ rpm, Belgium Village exhibit, Unisphere and fountain on cov, Belgium Village on back, inner panels with black and white photo spread of Belgium Village ext, in 12¼ x 12½" cardboard folder **25.00**

1967, Montreal Expo, lapel pin, brass **12.00**

WORLD WAR II

World War II collectibles are divided into two basic groups, Allied versus Axis and military versus home front. During the recent 50th World War II anniversary celebrations, home front material received as much attention as military material.

By the late 1930s the European nations were engaged in a massive arms race. Using the Depression as a spring board, Adolph Hitler and the National Socialists gained political power in Germany in the mid-1930s. Bitter over the peace terms of World War I, Hitler developed a concept of a Third Reich and began an aggressive unification and expansion program.

The roots of the Second World War are found in the Far East, not Europe. Japan's invasions of China and Korea and the world's failure to react encouraged Hitler. In 1939 Germany launched a blitzkrieg invasion of Poland. Although technically remaining neutral, America provided as much support as it could to the Allies.

America entered the war on December 7, 1941, following the Japanese attack on Pearl Harbor. There were four main theaters—Western, Eastern, Mediterranean, and Pacific.

The tide of battle turned in the Pacific with the Battle of Midway and the invasion of Guadalcanal in 1942. In 1943 the surrender of General von Arnim in Tunisia and the invasion of Italy put Allied forces in command in the Mediterranean theater. The year 1943 also marked the end of the siege of Stalingrad and the recapture of Kiev. Allied forces regained the offensive in the Western theater on June 6, 1944, D-Day. Germany surrendered on May 7, 1945. After atomic bombs were dropped on Hiroshima (August 6) and Nagasaki (August 9), Japan surrendered on August 14, 1945.

Many armed forces fighting in 1939, 1940, and 1941 used equipment left over from World War I. During the Korean Conflict, many military units used large quantities of World War II equipment. This is why provenance (ownership) plays a critical role in determining the value of a military collectible. Further, beware of the large quantity of Russian material that is flooding the collecting market now that the Iron Curtain has fallen. Much of this material is of recent production and hastily made.

References: Richard J. Austin, *The Official Price Guide to Military Collectibles, Sixth Edition,* House of Collectibles, 1998; Stan Cohen, *V For Victory: America's Home Front During World War II,* Pictorial Histories Publishing, 1991; Stanley Cohen, *To Win the War: Home Front Memorabilia of World War II,* Motorbooks International, 1995; Robert Heide and John Gilman, *Home Front America: Popular Culture of the World War II Era,* Chronicle Books, 1995; Jon A. Maguire, *Silver Wings, Pinks & Greens: Uniforms, Wings, & Insignia of USAAF Airmen in World War II,* Schiffer Publishing, 1994; Ron Manion, *American Military Collectibles Price Guide,* Antique Trader Books, 1995; Jack Matthews, *Toys Go to War: World War II Military Toys, Games, Puzzles & Books,* Pictorial Histories Publishing, 1994; Sydney B. Vernon, *Vernon's Collector's Guide to Orders, Medals, and Decorations, 3rd Revised Edition,* published by author, 1995, out of print.

Periodicals: *GI Journal,* PO Box 2925, Framingham, MA 01703; *Militaria International,* Box 43400, Minneapolis, MN 55443; *Military Trader,* PO Box 1050, Dubuque, IA 52004; *WWII Military Journal,* PO Box 28906, San Diego, CA 92198.

Collectors' Clubs: American Society of Military Insignia Collectors, 526 Lafayette Ave, Palmerton, PA 18071; Orders and Medals Society of America, PO Box 484, Glassboro, NJ 08028.

Note: For additional listings see Nazi Items.

Anti-Axis, ashtray, terra cotta, Hitler head, underside sticker "They're mostly mouth we all agree, The men we call the Axis three, Here's a likeness of the face, Dump your refuse in the proper place," 4½ x7¼" **$175.00**

Anti-Axis, Jap Hunting License, for hunting "Yellow Belly Japs," inscriptions "Season Opened: Dec 7th," and "Ammunition Furnished By Uncle Sam," sponsor text at bottom, 2¾ x 3¾" **50.00**

Anti-Axis, matchbox holder, celluloid over tin, Hitler on front, "In The Allies Grip" on spine, "Mussolini's Note To Adolf" on rear panel, made in Britain, 1 x 1½ x 2¼" .. **100.00**

Anti-Axis, pinback button, "Italy, Germany, and Japan, Can We Lick Them All? You Bet We Can!," blue lettering on white ground, red rim **25.00**

Anti-Axis, pincushion, painted plaster, dual image of Hitler and Tojo head emerging from shared rat body, hip of 1 side has insert tufted purple fabric pincushion, opposite hip has small 1942 patent pending with "A.B.," 2¹/₂ x 2¹/₂ x 5¹/₄" **175.00**

Anti-Axis, postcard, "No Pork Until These Pigs Are Killed," 3¹/₂ x 5¹/₂" **10.00**

Anti-Axis, stamp, gummed back paper depicting bayonet piercing swastika sign, Japanese sun symbols causing blood drops above 1943 date, red, white, and blue, with green border, unused **15.00**

Bank, Tank hollow plaster, olive drab, mkd "U.S.A.," and "B. 1748" from side to side, coin slot at bottom rear of turret, 3 x 5" h, 7¹/₂" l **100.00**

Book, *World War II in Headlines and Pictures*, Philadelphia, *Evening Bulletin*, soft cover, 1956, 10¹/₂ x 14" **35.00**

Bowl, "We Will Remember Pearl Harbor," white, maroon lettering, upper perimeter interspersed by stars, mkd "Made In USA" on underside, 3" h, 5" d **25.00**

Certificate, "Certificate of Appreciation" for 5 years of local directorship, typewritten recipient name, facsimile signature of US Director Lewis B Hershey, orig 9¹/₂ x 12" brown paper mailing envelope from PA Selective Service Headquarters, Harrisburg to Local Board #3, Montgomery County, March 15, 1946 postmark, 8¹/₂ x 11" **25.00**

Doll, Gen MacArthur, composition, fabric uniform, oilcloth shoes with ribbon lacings, molded composition hat to head, jointed arms and legs, paper shield tag pinned to chest inscribed "Gen. MacArthur/The Man of the Hour" with name of maker Freundlich Novelty Corp, NY, early 1940s, 18" h **200.00**

Figurine, plastic, pregnant girl, "Kilroy Was Here" slogan on base, Hartland Plastics, 3³/₄" h **75.00**

Fly Swatter, braided twine, stitched fabric border holding overlay title paper, painted red wooden rod, inscription "The Victory Swatter can't be used to battle the Japs, but the steel saved int he wire handle can" **75.00**

Calendar, salesman's sample, No. J-4401, picture sgd "J. Rosen," 1944, 44" h, 30" w, $55.00. Photo courtesy Collectors Auction Services.

Handkerchief, linen-weave sheer white fabric, red and blue inked "Remember Pearl Harbor" repeated at each corner, design of warships and fighter planes centered by "Island of Oahu" map, 13 x 14" **75.00**

Home Front Service Pins, set of 8, diecut plastic, for wartime war bond campaigns, factory production, plus "Indoor Qualification Rifle Sharpshooter" award pin, bar pin fastener on reverse **50.00**

Juice Tumbler, clear glass, applied paint illus, "Kilroy Was Here," 3" h, 2" d **25.00**

Key Fob, diecut khaki plastic victory symbol, white code symbols on side, reverse names maker "Pharis Accessories" **20.00**

License Plate Attachment, "We Serve," litho tin, emb, red, white, and blue, gold eagle, 4¹/₂ x 10" **45.00**

Lighter, Zippo, black crinkle finish, likeness of USN officer's device applied to side **200.00**

Magazine, *Life*, Dec 22, 1941, 90 pp, photos and articles about Pearl Harbor, 10¹/₂ x 14" **100.00**

Map, Battle Maps Covering All War Fronts, HB Ives Co, New Haven, CT, cartography by CS Hammond, includes 90 cut-out flags **20.00**

Map, Lowell Thomas' War Map of the World, Sunoco, cartography by Randy McNally **12.00**

Map, US Defense Map, Richfield Oil, cartography by Rand McNally **20.00**

Matchbook Case, black plastic case with hinged clear styrene plastic over black and white paper photo of Gen MacArthur **50.00**

Milk Bottle, clear glass, red inscriptions, Infantry soldiers in action, "Buy More War Bonds," "Back Their Attack/Buy More War Bonds/Drink Milk For Health," upper neck has inscription "Use Sealtest Dairy Products," 8¹/₂" h, 4" d **100.00**

Paint Books, boxed set of 3, "I Like To Play," books for soldier, sailor, and aviator, cover art front and back, 12 pp, Saalfield, ©1943, 1 x 7¹/₂ x 9¹/₂" box **75.00**

Pencil Holder, tubular plastic, blue insert cap holding red and white striped short lead pencil, white outer tube with red and blue victory markings plus name of local funeral home sponsor in blue, 3³/₄" l **25.00**

Periodical, *The Forward Observer*, published by the 492 Armored Field Artillery Battalion at Camp Cooke, CA, dated Aug 5, 1944, and Jul 29, 1944 . . . . **12.00**

Photograph, Gen Bradley, black and white, sgd "To Major James M. Stout with highest personal regards Omar N Bradley," reverse mkd "U.S. Army Photograph," 8 x 10" **75.00**

Pinback Button, "Final V-J Day Victory," celluloid, red, white, and blue **25.00**

Pinback Button, "Food For Freedom," red, white and blue, plump pig stepping through letter "V" for victory symbol, Los Angeles maker on rim curl **75.00**

Pinback Button, "General Douglas MacArthur/Fighter For Freedom," bluetone photo, white lettering, red rim **50.00**

Pinback Button, "Launching USS Borie, July 4, 1944," red lettering on white ground **25.00**

Pinback Button, "Sealed Lips Save Ships," red, white, and blue, center dive bomber above warship **50.00**

Poster, "Air Raid Protection Plan," paper, black and white, illus of chain of operations for "When The Bombs Drop!," sponsored by New Hampshire State Council of Defense, 22 x 28" **25.00**

Poster, "Buy War Bonds," U.S. Government Office, 1942, 5½" h, 33" l, $35.00. Photo courtesy Collectors Auction Services.

Poster, "Back the Attack!/Buy War Bonds/3rd War Loan," paper, paratrooper and machine gunner invasion scene, black and white lettering on gray band, Government Printing Office 542562, 1943, 10 x 14"...... **50.00**

Poster, "Bomber Distances," Japanese dive bombers descending on northern hemisphere of world globe, depiction of Pearl Harbor bomb blast and text comparing distance from Japan to Pearl Harbor in relationship to shorter distance from Occupied France to US, red, white, and blue slogan, 18 x 24".......... **100.00**

Poster, "Volunteer For Victory," photo image of young woman emerging from pin-up background held by tack, "now You Be Careful...what you say or write!," US Government issue 633734, 14 x 19½"............ **75.00**

Puzzle, "Fighters For Freedom," Whitman, 250 pcs, from series of 8 picturing Army, Navy or Air Force action scenes, "Double Puzzle" format, orig box, 10 x 16" completed size.................. **25.00**

Record, *The Voice of Your Man in Service*, Pepsi premium, 78 rpm, waxed cardboard, early 1940s........... **50.00**

Ring, Loved One in Service, celluloid, white band with replica of white banner, blue star, and red border........ **25.00**

Sheet Music, *Anchors Away*, 1942.................... **5.00**

Sweetheart Bracelet, brass and enamel, Army emblem center, scissors latch........................ **35.00**

Sweetheart Locket, heart shaped, gold finish, Eagle, globe, and anchor on front................ **18.00**

Sweetheart Pin, Navy, mother-of-pearl, miniature anchor appliqué................................ **30.00**

Whistle, "Regulation/US Army," bright silver luster brass, on silvered metal link keychain terminated by metal hook.................................. **15.00**

WRIGHT, RUSSEL

Russel Wright (1904–1976) is one of the most important industrial designers of the 20th century. In 1931 Wright began selling aluminum and pewter objects from a small studio on East 53rd Street in New York City. It was also during this period that he introduced his Circus Animals series. Suffering financially in 1933 and 1934, Wright's life changed for the better when Americans fell in love with aluminum.

In 1936 Wright, his wife Mary, and Irving Richards formed the Raymor Company. Wright designed exclusively for Raymor for five years, after which time he sold his interests to Richards and formed Russel Wright Associates. In 1951 Wright spelled out his design philosophy in his book, *Guide to Easier Living*.

Wright designs appeared in a wide range of mediums from wood to metal. Acme Lamps Company, American Cyanide (plastic dinnerware), Chase Brass and Copper, Conant Ball (furniture), General Electric, Heywood-Wakefield (a sixty-piece furniture line), Hull Cutlery (flatware), Imperial Glass, Klise Woodworking Company, National Silver (flatware), Mutual Sunset Lamp Company, Old Hickory Furniture, Old Morgantown, and the Stratton Furniture Company are some of the companies that made products based upon Wright's designs.

Russel Wright designed several major dinnerware lines: American Modern for Steubenville (1939–1959), Iroquois Casual for Iroquois China (1946–1960s), Highlight for Paden City (1948), a solid color institutional line for Sterling China (1949), White Clover for Harker (1951), and the oriental-inspired Esquire shape for Knowles (1955). He also designed an art pottery line for Bauer.

Reference: Ann Kerr, *The Collector's Encyclopedia of Russel Wright Designs, Second Edition,* Collector Books, 1998.

Note: See Edwin Knowles (Esquire) and Paden City Pottery (Highlight) for additional listings.

ALUMINUM

Bowl	$75.00
Cheeseboard	75.00
Flower Ring	125.00
Ice Fork	75.00
Sherry Pitcher	250.00
Tidbit Tray, single	85.00
Wastebasket	125.00

CHINA

American Modern, bread and butter plate, gray, 6" d	$3.00
American Modern, butter, cov, glacier blue	200.00
American Modern, carafe, chutney	165.00
American Modern, casserole, cantaloupe	135.00
American Modern, celery, chutney	30.00
American Modern, child's plate	50.00
American Modern, child's tumbler	60.00
American Modern, chop plate, coral	8.00
American Modern, chop plate, gray	25.00
American Modern, cup and saucer, cantaloupe, white, glacier blue	25.00
American Modern, demitasse cup, chartreuse	8.50
American Modern, demitasse cup and saucer, chartreuse	14.50
American Modern, plate, chutney, 10" d	6.00

American Modern, dinner service and serving pcs, seafoam green, bean brown, and granite gray, approximately 180 pcs, some chips, 1939–59, $1,610.00. Photo courtesy Skinner, Inc., Boston, MA.

American Modern, plate, gray, 10" d 6.00
American Modern, salad bowl, chutney 75.00
American Modern, salt and pepper shakers, pr, white,
    glacier blue 35.00
American Modern, teapot, glacier blue 100.00
American Modern, vegetable bowl, chutney 60.00
American Modern, water pitcher, coral 85.00
Highlight, bread and butter plate 8.00
Highlight, dinner plate 25.00
Highlight, salad bowl 65.00
Highlight, sugar, cov 35.00
Iroquois Casual, bread and butter plate, nutmeg 5.00
Iroquois Casual, carafe, charcoal 125.00
Iroquois Casual, casserole, 2 qt, avocado 30.00
Iroquois Casual, cereal bowl, avocado, 5" d 10.00
Iroquois Casual, creamer and sugar, stacking, ice blue 35.00
Iroquois Casual, cup and saucer, gray 15.00
Iroquois Casual, dinner plate, avocado 10.00
Iroquois Casual, fruit bowl, ice blue 5.00
Iroquois Casual, platter, oval, ice blue, 14½" l 30.00
Iroquois Casual, salad bowl, avocado, 10" d 25.00
Iroquois Casual, vegetable bowl, divided, apricot 40.00
Iroquois Casual Redesigned, cereal bowl, white 8.00
Iroquois Casual Redesigned, cup and saucer, pink 10.00
Iroquois Casual Redesigned, fruit bowl, white 12.00
Iroquois Casual Redesigned, gravy boat 150.00
Iroquois Casual Redesigned, pitcher 150.00
Iroquois Casual Redesigned, soup bowl 20.00
White Clover, dinner plate, 10" d 18.00
White Clover, salt and pepper shakers, pr, meadow
    green 40.00

GLASS

Appleman, warming tray, oblong $85.00
Appleman, warming tray, round 100.00
Bartlett Collins, Eclipse, cocktail, 3" 10.00
Bartlett Collins, Eclipse, highball, 5" 15.00
Bartlett Collins, Eclipse, ice tub 40.00
Bartlett Collins, Eclipse, zombie, 7" 20.00
Imperial, Flair, juice, 6 oz 45.00
Imperial, Flair, water, 11 oz 50.00
Imperial, Pinch, iced tea, seafoam, 14 oz 35.00
Imperial, Pinch, water, ruby, 11 oz 32.00
Imperial, Twist, iced tea 35.00
Imperial, Twist, juice 35.00
Old Morgantown, American Modern, double old fash-
    ioned 30.00
Old Morgantown, American Modern, goblet, 11 oz 35.00
Old Morgantown, American Modern, wine, 4 oz 25.00

PLASTIC DINNERWARE

Flair, cup and saucer $12.00
Flair, dinner plate 10.00
Flair, onion soup, cov 18.00
Flair, vegetable bowl, divided 30.00
Meladur, cereal bowl 8.00
Meladur, fruit bowl 8.00
Meladur, salad plate 10.00
Meladur, soup bowl 10.00
Residential, bread and butter plate 6.00
Residential, fruit bowl 15.00
Residential, sugar, cov 15.00

YARD-LONGS

Yard-long is a generic term used to refer to photographs and prints that measure approximately 36 inches in length. The format can be horizontal or vertical.

The yard-long print arrived on the scene in the first quarter of the 20th century, experiencing a period of popularity in the late 1910s and early 1920s. Most were premiums, issued by such diverse companies as Pompeian Beauty and Pabst Brewing's Malt Extract. Some came with calendars and were distributed by a wide range of merchants. Some had titles such as "A Yard of Kittens" or "A Yard of Roses." Always check the back. Many yard-long prints have elaborately printed advertisements on their back.

Yard-long prints are one of the many forms that show the amazing capabilities of American lithographers. Brett Litho, Jos. Hoover & Sons, J. Ottmann, and The Osborne Company are a few of the American lithographers who produced yard-long prints.

Yard-long photographs also were popular in the 1910s and 20s. The form survived until the early 1950s. Graduation pictures, especially military units, banquet photographs, and touring groups are the most commonly found. Many have faded from their original black and white to a sepia tone. Unless stopped, this fading will continue until the picture is lost.

Reference: Keagy and Rhoden, *Yard-Long Prints, Book III,* published by authors, 1995.

Calendar, 1921, woman wearing red coat with umbrel-
    la, sitting on rail, John Clay and Company Live Stock
    Commission **$375.00**
Calendar, 1922, Harvest Moon, sgd "Frank H. Desch,"
    John Clay and Company Live Stock Commission 375.00
Calendar, 1928, woman holding bouquet of roses, left
    corner sgd "Earl Christy," George Peterman, Bell
    Plaine, IA 375.00
Photograph, choral society 35.00
Photograph, civic organization banquet 35.00
Photograph, family reunion 30.00
Photograph, military company grouping 60.00
Photograph, military graduation 35.00

Left: 1923 Pompeian "Honeymooning in the Alps," sgd "Gene Pressler," 27" h, $138.00.

Right: 1925 Pompeian "Beauty Gained Is Love Retained," 28" h, $193.00.

Photos courtesy Gene Harris Antique Auction Center, Inc.

Photograph, scenic, panoramic, Grand Canyon **35.00**
Photograph, school graduation class **20.00**
Photograph, theater group **45.00**
Photograph, tourist group **30.00**
Print, Butterick, "Butterick Pattern Lady," 1930 . . . . **425.00**
Print, Pompeian, "Absence Cannot Hearts Divide," sgd
  "Marguerite Clark," 1921, 7 x 28" **165.00**
Print, Pompeian, "Alluring," sgd "Bradshaw Crandell,"
  1928, 7 x 26" **155.00**
Print, Pompeian, "Honeymooning in Venice," sgd "Gene
  Pressler," verse by William Wetmore Story, 1922, 7 x
  26" **175.00**
Print, Pompeian, "Irrestible," sgd "Clement Donshea,"
  1930. . . . . **275.00**
Print, Pompeian, "Sweetest Story Every Told," sgd
  "Haskell Coffin," 1920, 8 x 27" **275.00**
Print, Pompeian, "The Bride," sgd "Rolf Armstrong," 7 x
  26" **250.00**
Print, Selz Good Shoes, lady holding walking stick,
  1925, 10 x 30" **325.00**

YELLOW WARE

Because it was made from a finer clay, yellow ware is sturdier than redware and less dense than stoneware. Most pieces are fired twice, the second firing necessary to harden the alkaline-based glaze of flint, kaolin, and white lead.

The greatest period of yellow ware production occurred in the last half of the 19th century. By 1900 Americans favored white bodied ware over yellow ware. Although no longer playing a major role in the utilitarian household ceramic market, some yellow ware forms, such as mixing bowls and cake molds, were made into the 1950s by firms such as J. A. Bauer, Brush Pottery, Morton Pottery, Pfaltzgraff Pottery, Red Wing, and Weller.

Reference: Lisa S. McAllister, *Collecting Yellow Ware, Book II,* Collector Books, 1997.

Baking Dish, Hull, blue bands, vertical ribbing **$100.00**
Beater Jug, Brush-McCoy, plain, 5½" h **15.00**
Bowl, slightly flared sides, flared rim, gold accents,
  2³⁄₈" h, 6³⁄₈" d **30.00**
Butter Crock, brown and white stripes, ribbed base,
  7¼" d **150.00**
Candlestick, Jugtown, plain, 7¼" d **125.00**
Canning Jar, cov, tan and white bands, 6" h, 8" d **35.00**
Child's Dish, Weller, shallow, brown bands, 7" d **150.00**
Coffeepot, stacking, plain, grainy texture **150.00**
Colander, Midwestern, white lined, 6-point star, 4½" h,
  10" d **125.00**
Cruet, Ohio, Rockingham glaze, orig stopper, 10" h **400.00**
Custard Cup, blue sponging, slightly flared sides, round-
  ed rim, 1³⁄₄" h, 3⁷⁄₈" d **30.00**
Custard Cup, Rockingham glaze **15.00**
Custard Cup, thin white stripes **40.00**
Dish, cov, blue slip bands on lid and body, 3¹⁄₈" h **100.00**
Food Mold, corn, plain, oval **90.00**
Hanging Salt, Hull, blue bands, vertical ribbing **150.00**
Jug, miniature, plain, "Souvenir from Pearl China and
  Pottery Co" paper label **150.00**
Jug, stepped shoulder, mustard yellow glaze with cobalt
  sponging **110.00**
Lid, plain, 9" d, 7³⁄₄" inner rim **40.00**

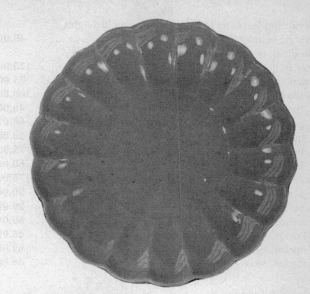

Dish, fluted edges, 4 small rim chips, $30.00. Photo courtesy Collectors Auction Services

Matchsafe, Brush-McCoy, light yellow, ribbed surface,
  Kolor-Kraft Line, 6¼" h **550.00**
Mixing Bowls, nesting set of 3, brown and white bands **110.00**
Mug, brown and white bands, ribbed handle **35.00**
Mug, white center band, 2 brown bands, 3³⁄₄" h **115.00**
Pitcher, Midwestern, emb "Avenue of Trees" design,
  orange highlighting, green and black slip bands, 7" h **150.00**
Planter, Robinson-Ransbottom Pottery, Roseville, OH,
  bowl shape, blue green mottled glaze, 3½" h **20.00**
Pudding Dish, Midwestern, slip-dot flower dec. **60.00**
Reamer, plain **200.00**
Soap Dish, plain, 5½" d **175.00**
Spice Shakers, pr, Morton Pottery, plain, Amish Pottery
  Line **400.00**
Tankard, Morton Pottery, emb dec, 5" h **150.00**
Utilitarian Pitcher, thin black and white center bands,
  6½" h **150.00**

ZANE POTTERY

Adam Reed and Harry McClelland purchased Peters and Reed Pottery in January 1921 and renamed it Zane Pottery. Reed died in 1922. McClelland became president and sole owner.

Reed added new art pottery designs to the established Peters and Reed line. Utilitarian garden wares (bird baths, flowerpots, vases) were an important supplement to the firm's art pottery line. The company used a red clay body until 1926 when it introduced a white clay body.

McClelland died in 1931. His wife continued the business until 1941 when the plant was sold to Lawton Gonder.

Reference: Ralph and Terry Kovel, *Kovels' American Art Pottery,* Crown Publishers, 1993.

Bowl, brown with green accents, 5" d, 2" h **$25.00**
Bowl, Laurel pattern, green matte glaze, c1925, 3½" h,
  8³⁄₄" w **115.00**
Bud Vase, ear handles, blue, mkd "ZPCo," 8½" h **85.00**

Bud Vase, imp leaves and berries design, gold highlights, ivory glaze, mkd "Zane Ware," 6" h 40.00
Candlesticks, pr, speckled blue glaze, mkd "Zane Ware," 10¼" h 125.00
Jardiniere, Moss Aztec, emb flowers, 10" w 75.00
Umbrella Stand, marbleized finish, 17" h 300.00
Vase, brown drip glaze, mkd "Zane Ware," 5" h 40.00
Vase, green and black drip glaze, mkd "Zane Ware," 8" h 60.00
Vase, hp, mkd "Zane Ware," 1921–41, 5" h 30.00
Vase, hexagonal, marbleized finish, 9¼" h 75.00
Vase, Landsun, brown and black, 6" h 60.00
Vase, Peasant Pottery line, ring handles, 6" h, 4" w 175.00
Vase, Sheen ware, 3½" h 50.00
Vase, yellow and blue speckled glaze, 3" h 20.00
Vase, yellow drip glaze, 12" h 60.00
Wall Pocket, Aztec, moth design, 9" h 85.00
Wall Pocket, Egyptian motif, 9" h 65.00
Wall Pocket, Moss Aztec, emb grapes 60.00

ZSOLNAY

Miklós Zsolnay founded the Zsolnay Porcelain Factory, Pecs, Hungary, in 1853. Production divides into three chronological periods: (1) 1868–1897, Victorian eclecticism, historicism, and folklorism; (2) 1897–1920, Art Nouveau, and (3) 1920 to the present, Modernism. Over 11,000 different forms of Zsolnay art pottery have been documented.

In 1925 the company introduced its five churches within a triangle mark. András Sinkó introduced a line of folk art animal and bird designs in the 1930s. Miklós Izso designed a series of figures based on life on the Hungarian Plains and Béla Markup added to the animal figurine line.

Production stopped between 1948 and 1953 as the Socialist government nationalized much of Hungary's industry. In 1953 the company reintroduced eosin glazed porcelain faience pieces. András Sinkó developed more animals and children figurines including his Bison (1956) and Fishing Crane (1959). Antal Gazder created tabletop wares, figurines, and vases featuring abstract modernism designs between 1953 and 1990. Other key post–World War II designers include János Török, János Fekete, György Fürtös, and Judit Nádor.

Reference: Fredrico Santi and John Gacher, *Zsolnay Ceramics*, Schiffer Publishing, 1998.

Figure, elephant, green $60.00
Figure, Elvis Presley, holding guitar, green eosin glaze, 15" h 60.00
Figure, "Repose," designed by János Török, red eosin glaze, unmkd, c1962, 5½" w, 5" h 250.00
Figure, "The Cello Player," designed by Gygory Furtos, factory mark, 8½" h 350.00
Figure, "The Flute Player," designed by János Török, red eosin glaze, unmkd, c1962 . . . . 325.00
Figure, "The Harp Player," streaked green eosin glaze, c1962, 12¾" h 375.00
Mug, iridescent blue glaze, 4½" h 85.00
Ring Holder, iridescent gold glaze, 3¾" h 90.00
Vase, Art Deco, metallic eosin glaze with green turning to copper and back to green, folklore theme with flowers and roosters, form #9340, factory mark, and "B.V.," 1938–39, 9½" h 1,500.00
Vase, organ-shaped, unmkd, 1960s, 4" h 275.00
Vase, stylized birds in black on yellow and white ground, factory mark, 9¼" h 225.00

Dish, figural dove and snail on shallow bowl, iridescent gold glaze, raised red mark, 5" h, 11" w, $633.00. Photo courtesy Skinner, Inc., Boston, MA.

STAR WARS – EXCLUSIVE REPORT

The Force expanded significantly on May 19, 1999, when *Star Wars:* Episode 1 *The Phantom Menace* opened in movie theaters around the world. Lucas has proven himself the most menacing director of the last quarter of the 20th century. No phantom he, Lucas is omnipresent.

I was convinced that *Star Trek* rather than *Star Wars* collectibles would "live long and prosper" until the re-release of the middle *Star Wars* trilogy in 1997. I am now convinced this phrase applies more to the latter. The Force is *Star Wars* and it is definitely with us.

This *"Star Wars* – Exclusive Report" focuses on movie related and paper *Star Wars* memorabilia. Many listings are for one-of-a-kind objects. These obviously command the highest prices. While limited edition items are currently selling well on the secondary market, they have not yet stood the test of time. Beware of a potential disturbance within The Force.

Book, *Star Wars,* Alan Dean Foster, from screenplay by George Lucas, Ballantine, #26061-9, 220 pp, Ralph McQuarrie cov, Dec 1976 .... **$25.00**

Book, *The Empire Strikes Back,* Donald F Glut, from story by George Lucas and screenplay by Lawrence Kasdan and Leigh Brackett, Ballantine-Del Rey, #28392-2, 214 pp, Roger Kastel cov, May 1980 .... **15.00**

Bust, Boba Fett, by Greg Aronowitz, box art by Drew Strutzman, limited edition to 3,000, Legends in Three Dimensions, 1998 .... **200.00**

Cassette, *The Empire Strikes Back:* The Original Radio Drama, National Public Radio, Highbridge, #000-5, Sep 1993, set of 5 .... **30.00**

CD, *Star Wars Triology,* Highbridge, #169-2, set of 9 .... **75.00**

Comic Book, "*Star Wars,*" last issue, Marvel, #107, 1985 .... **65.00**

Comic Book, "*Star Wars* Dark Empire," Dark Horse Comics, #1 .... **25.00**

Figure, pewter, Franklin Mint, Millennium Falcon **200.00**

Figure, pewter, Rawcliffe, Imperial Star Destroyer **80.00**

Greeting Card Proof and Layout Board, *Star Wars,* The Drawing Board Inc, ©1977 20th Century Fox Film Corp, 8³/₄ x 11" proof of card, full color illus serves as card front and pictures R2-D2 and C-3PO, "Peace and Good Will Toward All Mankind," back text "And To Their Faithful Androids," printing information along right edge, with 9¹/₂ x 11¹/₂" orig black and white lay-out board, includes tissue paper overlay sheet with inked printing notations **35.00**

Hologram, Darth Vader, AH Prismatic, #1021/99, 1994, 5 x 3" in 8 x 10" matte. **30.00**

Hologram, Millennium Falcon, AH Prismatic, #1020/33, 1994, 3 x 2" in 5 x 7" matte. **15.00**

Limited Edition Plate, Luke Skywalker and Darth Vader, *Star Wars* series, Hamilton Collection, T Blackshear, 1987. .... **65.00**

Limited Edition Plate, *Return of the Jedi, Star Wars* Trilogy series, Hamilton Collection, M Weisting, 1993 .... **40.00**

Limited Edition Plate, *Star Wars* 10th Anniversary Commemorative, Hamilton Collection, T Blackshear, 1990. .... **95.00**

Limited Edition Plate, *The Empire Strikes Back, Star Wars* Trilogy series, Hamilton Collection, M Weisting, 1993 .... **40.00**

Lobby Cards, set of 8, *Return of the Jedi,* 8 x 10" **75.00**

Lobby Cards, set of 8, *The Empire Strikes Back,* 8 x 10" **100.00**

Magazine, *American Cinematographer,* Jul 1977, "The Filming of *Star Wars*" **100.00**

Magazine, *New Yorker,* Jan 6, 1997, "Why the Force is still with us," George Lucas interview. **5.00**

Magazine, *Star Force,* Oct 1980, Vol 1, #2, featuring *Star Wars,* and *The Empire Strikes Back* **8.00**

Magazine, *Star Wars, The Making of the World's Greatest Movie,* Paradise Press, Inc, 1977. .... **15.00**

Magazine, *Time,* May 19, 1980, Vol 115, #20, *The Empire Strikes Back,* movie profiles, behind the scenes productions, George Lucas **10.00**

Movie Prop, Deluxe Boba Fett Helmet, #82101, fiber-glass, 15" d **750.00**

Movie Prop, Deluxe Darth Vader Helmet, #82116, fiber-glass helmet with lining, limited edition of 500, 15" d.... **750.00**

Movie Prop, pc of Death Star model from *Return of the Jedi,* intricate detail of ship constructed of gray paint-ed foam core, with letter of provenance on Lucasfilm stationery, 18 x 25", framed and matted, 1987 .... **1,600.00**

Movie Prop, test mask, made for aliens in cantina scene, molded foam form mask with gray paint overlay **2,000.00**

Movie Still, *Return of the Jedi,* 11 x 14" **50.00**

Movie Still, *The Empire Strikes Back,* 11 x 14" **100.00**

Lobby Cards, *Star Wars,* 20th Century Fox, 1977, set of 8, $345.00. Photo courtesy Skinner, Inc., Boston, MA.

Poster, *Star Wars* Concert, 20th Century Fox, art by John Alvin, 1978, 24¹/₄ x 37", framed, $3,738.00. Photo courtesy Skinner, Inc., Boston, MA.

Newspaper, *New York Times,* Dec 20, 1980, "The saga beyond *Star Wars".* 5.00
Photograph, Carrie Fisher, sgd 40.00
Photograph, George Lucas, sgd 95.00
Photograph, Mark Hamill, sgd 50.00
Press Book, *Star Wars* 45.00
Press Kit, *Caravan of Courage,* orange logo on blue cov, with set of eight 8 x 10" color lobby cards 25.00
Press Kit, *Star Wars,* silver "SW" on blue cov, "Press Kit" at top with silver Fox logo, brown bag with 17 photos, 1977 . . . . 200.00
Print, Boba Fett: Bounty Hunter, Dave Dorman, sgd and numbered, limited to 1,500 copies, Rolling Thunder Graphics, 1995, 15 x 20" on 19 x 24" paper 45.00
Print, Obi-Wan Kenobi, Dave Dorman, sgd and numbered, limited to 1,500 copies, Rolling Thunder Graphics, 1996, 12 x 15¹/₂" 45.00
Print, Shadows of the Empire, Dave Dorman, sgd, 1996, 24 x 36" 30.00
Program Book, *Star Wars,* 1st printing, slick cov 75.00
Promotional Book, *Star Wars,* black cov with *Star Wars* logo, color photos, orig white box 300.00
Record, *Droid World—The Further Adventures of Star Wars,* Buena Vista, 45 rpm, adapted from Marvel Comics, story by Archie Goodwin, illus by Dick Foes, 24 pp full color illus booklet 10.00
Record, *The Empire Strikes Back,* Chalfont Digital Records, LP, orig motion picture soundtrack, performed by The National Philharmonic Orchestra, conducted by Charles Gerhardt, 1980 . . . . 25.00
Record, *The Story of The Empire Strikes Back,* Buena Vista Records, LP, dialogue, music, and sound effects from orig motion picture soundtrack, 16 pp full color photo booklet, features voices of Mark Hamill, Harrison Ford, Carrie Fisher, Billy Dee Williams, Anthony Daniels, James Earl Jones, Alec Guinness, and Frank Oz, narration by Malachi Throne, 1983 . . . . 25.00
Sketch, Han Solo, Luke Skywalker, Chewbacca, C-3PO, and R2-D2, graphite on pencil on tracing tissue, sgd "R. McQuarrie" lower right, with handwritten description by artist, 1977, 9¹/₄ x 11³/₄" 2,100.00

Sketch, *The Empire Strikes Back,* rebel snowspeeder, ink and felt-nib pen on vellum, blue and red accents, sgd "R. McQuarrie," with handwritten description by artist, c1979, 10 x 16¹/₂" 3,200.00
Sketch, *Return of the Jedi,* Luke Skywalker and Darth Vader dueling in Emperor's Throne Room aboard Death Star, graphite pencil on bond paper, sgd "R. McQ" lower right, c1981, 11 x 11" 500.00
Sketches, C-3PO, entitled "Threepio," graphite pencil on tissue, head and torso, sgd "R. McQ." lower right, together with drawing detailing C-3PO's body from neck to knee, sgd "R. McQuarrie" lower right, with handwritten descriptions from artist, 1977, 13¹/₂ x 11" and 14 x 8¹/₂" 6,325.00
Sketches, Darth Vader, graphite pencil on tissue, ³/₄ profile showing helmet and shoulders, above similar sketch, charcoal pencil on tissue, sgd "R. McQ," together with sketch for production illus for "Tie Fighter Pilot," graphite pencil on tissue, sgd "R. McQuarrie," each with handwritten description from artist, 1977, 9¹/₂ x 6" and 11 x 14" 5,750.00
Statue, Stormtrooper, Don Post Studios, #82022, fiberglass, cast from orig props, limited edition to 500, 6' h 4,500.00
Ticket Stub, *Star Wars,* press preview 5.00

AUCTION PRICES – *STAR WARS* POSTERS

Skinner, Inc., Important Motion Picture Posters, May 1, 1999. Prices include a 15% buyer's premium.

Star Wars, "A long time ago in a galaxy far, far away...," 1977, 20th Century Fox, US half-sheet, style A, framed, art by Tom Jung, variation on style A campaign that created a more "space opera" image for the film. **$2,300.00**
Star Wars, "A long time ago in a galaxy far, far away...," 1978, 20th Century Fox, US 1-sheet, style D, framed, art by Drew Struzan and Charles White III, also known as the "Circus" poster. 1,265.00
Star Wars, "Coming To Your Galaxy This Summer," 1976, 20th Century Fox, US 1-sheet, style A, framed, first American release poster, printed on mylar, sent only to theaters which booked the film far in advance of release 2,530.00
Star Wars, R82, 20th Century Fox, US 1-sheet, framed, art by Tom Jung, third re-release, banner at lower right announces "Revenge of the Jedi" 345.00
Star Wars Birthday, "May the Force be with you. One year old today," 1978, 20th Century Fox, US 1-sheet, framed, photo by Weldon Anderson, sent only to theaters still showing the film on its first anniversary 2,185.00
Star Wars: Return of the Jedi, Revenge of the Jedi, 1982, 20th Century Fox, US advance 1-sheet, framed, art by Drew Struzan, undated version, Star Wars Fan Club was given permission to sell a dated variation of this poster 2,070.00
Star Wars: The Empire Strikes Back, "The Star Wars Saga Continues," 1980, 20th Century Fox, US 1-sheet, style B, framed, art by Tom Jung 373.75
Star Wars: The Empire Strikes Back Radio Drama, 1982, National Public Radio, framed, art by Ralph McQuarrie, distributed to stations airing the Empire Strikes Back drama, budget cutback at NPR prevented widespread release of this poster, 17 x 28" 2,530.00

INDEX